Anders Cullhed
The Shadow of Creusa

Beiträge zur Altertumskunde

—

Herausgegeben von Michael Erler, Dorothee Gall,
Ludwig Koenen und Clemens Zintzen

Band 339

Anders Cullhed

The Shadow of Creusa

Negotiating Fictionality
in Late Antique Latin Literature

Translated by
Michael Knight

DE GRUYTER

For Kerstin

ISBN 978-3-11-055924-8
e-ISBN (PDF) 978-3-11-031094-8
e-ISBN (EPUB) 978-3-11-038836-7
ISSN 1616-0452

Library of Congress Cataloging-in-Publication Data
A CIP catalog record for this book has been applied for at the Library of Congress.

Bibliografische Information der Deutschen Nationalbibliothek
Die Deutsche Nationalbibliothek verzeichnet diese Publikation in der Deutschen Nationalbibliografie; detaillierte bibliografische Daten sind im Internet über http://dnb.dnb.de abrufbar.

© 2017 Walter de Gruyter GmbH, Berlin/Boston
Dieser Band ist text- und seitenidentisch mit der 2015 erschienenen gebundenen Ausgabe.
Druck und Bindung: Hubert & Co. GmbH & Co. KG, Göttingen
∞ Gedruckt auf säurefreiem Papier
Printed in Germany

www.degruyter.com

"And death shall be no more, neither shall there be mourning, nor crying, nor pain anymore, for the former things have passed away." And he who was seated on the throne said, "Behold, I am making all things new." Also he said, "Write this down, for these words are trustworthy and true."

Revelation 21.4–5

For "what communion hath light with darkness? And what concord hath Christ with Belial?" How can Horace go with the psalter, Virgil with the gospels, Cicero with the apostle?

Jerome, *Epistulae* 22.29

Once I was fluent in the fictitious literature of men, but now I stutter in the proclamation of the truth.

Paulinus of Nola, *Epistulae* 40.6

We pray therefore for a respite for the gods of our fathers and our native gods. That which all venerate should in fairness be accounted as one. We look on the same stars, the heaven is common to us all, the same world surrounds us. What matters it by what arts each of us seeks for truth? We cannot arrive by one and the same path at so great a secret.

Symmachus, *Relationes* 3.10

Preface

"Still, they do not belong to the Muse". Those were the words of someone I knew, aimed at certain other people that I happened to know. They could, in fact, be applied to the majority of the learned men (but hardly to the lady) that will be under scrutiny in the present study. The Muses were a constant source of trouble for early Christian intellectuals. The three greatest of the Latin Church Fathers, more or less contemporary with each other, are crucial to my theme. Foremost among them is Saint Augustine, followed by his seniors, Ambrose and Jerome. Around them emerges a host of pious witnesses, missionaries, preachers and learned men, accompanied by one or two profane writers. One of them, the encyclopaedic Martianus Capella, entered into a competitive dialogue with his Muse. So did his successor and North African compatriot Fulgentius, at least until he agreed to be literally seduced by the flirtatious Pierian goddesses. Finally, the last Roman and the first Scholastic, the ingenious Boethius, was forced (or forced himself) to expel them from his elegiac complaints – but only in order to prepare for their reappearance and their new songs, now in a decidedly different key, in the service of Lady Philosophy.

This relationship to the Muses, enthusiastic or antagonistic, will be the uniting bond between the main figures of this book. In addition, they have their Latin language in common, reproduced in the original as well as translated into English. The quotations from Latin will hopefully not make my exposition seem inaccessible or difficult to assimilate for non-specialist readers. They are necessary, because they stem from a culture two thousand years old; every attempt to convert them into modern English implies an adaptation which, however, I am convinced we can live with as long as the original words are close at hand. Among the critical editions and scholarly series that have been at my disposal, the majority of which are based on a philological expertise far superior to my own, I would like to emphasize the Italian Nuova Biblioteca Agostiniana (NBA), created and issued by the editorial house Città Nuova in Rome. During the last four decades, Città Nuova has published all of Augustine's writings, and even if its efforts have some international equivalents – like the Parisian Desclée de Brouwer's series Bibliothèque Augustinienne or the more recent "Translation for the 21st Century" of Augustine's work, printed with the late John E. Rotelle as its founding director by New City Press in the U.S. – I know of no other editorial firm or learned society which to such an extent has made its Augustinian material available on the Web. The greatest of the Western Church Fathers is thus accessible in a good edition to all interested readers worldwide, in Latin as well as in a modern Italian translation.

Whenever I have found satisfying English versions of the Late Antique texts under examination here, I have consistently made use of them. I would especially like to mention James J. O'Donnell's 1992 edition and Maria Boulding's translation (based on O'Donnell) of Augustine's *Confessiones* (*Confessions*), as it is probably the single most frequently quoted work in my book. In some cases I have felt obliged to suggest alternative translations (mostly to emphasize the literal sense of a word or sentence where the translator, for perfectly understandable reasons, has preferred more general or normalized equivalences), marked by single quotes instead of the customary double ones. As for the Latin texts I have had to grapple with on my own, I have tried to convert them into modern English prose, without bothering much about stylistic considerations, hoping to achieve at least a minimum of legibility. Greek texts are generally presented in English, but as soon as individual terms and concepts from the works of writers such as Plutarch, Origen or Proclus acquire special significance for my argument, they are rendered in the (transliterated) original. My ambition has simply been to satisfy both the general reader, interested in these Late Antique negotiations of fictionality which, incidentally, herald a good deal of modern literary criticism, and the initiated specialist.

In order to facilitate a fluent reading, block quotations in prose are rendered in English, while their wordings in the original language – mostly Latin – are presented in the notes or, when extensive, in an appendix to the book. Poetic texts, on the other hand, where rhythm, line breaks and the order of words acquire a particular significance, are first presented in the original language and immediately afterwards in English verse (or sometimes prose, depending on extant translations). If this arrangement sounds somewhat complicated, I am confident that it will be perceived as transparent and natural after a few pages of reading.

Finally, my secondary sources in languages other than English are generally *not* given in the original. There are quite a few of them, due to the comprehensive subject of my book. Sadly, however, it has been impossible for me to cover all my wise and learned predecessors in a field as vast as this: the mapping of Late Antique fiction theory in the West. I can only hope that my selection of sources reflects as truly as possible the main lines of research carried out in this area.

*

Whether the Late Antique Christian intellectuals set out to eradicate the world of classical myth or iconography, or whether they recommended some sort of rescue action or recycling, commonly by means of allegorical representation, it was in the verbal arts that ideas of fictionality were most thoroughly tried and tested. Consequently, textual and contextual analysis of literary works will occupy the main part of this study, supplemented with glances at the period's rich commentary activities, its polemics, and its rhetorical or poetical ideas. I will not enter deeply into stylistic matters, but problems of style will be discussed for the simple reason that *res* and *verba* or, as we would say today, content and form, were inseparable from each other in Late Antique poetry and poetics. To give a short example: in Latin literature, the high style was generally associated with pathetic matters, and the middle style with sheer pleasure. In the former case, the readers or listeners of a poetic work were supposed to be moved through its majestic tone, its eloquent *pompa* or *cothurnus*; in the latter case, the audience expected to be entertained by means of various ornaments and embellishments. Both styles would easily, by means of hyperbole, catachresis and other stylistic devices, lend themselves to fictional matters. Accordingly, a style that differed from everyday speech – what Michael Roberts in adherence to the period's own terminology has labelled "the jeweled style" – was frequently assumed to indicate a subject that deflected from familiar reality.[1] On the other hand, the third, low and satirical or didactic style could in some sense – we shall try to see how – be experienced as expressive of real things and circumstances. Rhetorical and stylistic matters will therefore be treated whenever they trigger issues of fictionality.

Which they do, incidentally, quite often. As a matter of fact, premodern concepts of fiction were frequently linked to figurative language, which throughout Late Antiquity was analysed and categorized in the grammarians' or other educators' learned catalogues. My presentation will respect this general pattern. In addition, it will draw attention to the period's constructions of the human imagination, *phantasia sive imaginatio*, as far as they are connected to fictional matters. In short, a series of concepts from literary theory or the history of ideas, such as 'tropes', 'allegory' or 'imagination', will be essential to my account. Precisely for that reason it should be noted that this is *not* an attempt to formulate even a rough outline of the Late Antique history of the doctrine of tropes or of the concept of imagination. Such studies have already been published by other scholars, and they would surely require quite another arrangement and other limitations than the present work. I will only refer to those learned matters – figurative language, imagination, the liberal arts etc. – as far as they might elucidate the main concern of my investigation. Even with that restriction my subject may seem awkwardly vast, and I obviously cannot claim to have delineated any

---

1 Apart from the jewels, *gemmae*, Roberts registers flowers, *flores*, lights and stars, *lumina* and *stellae*, as particularly frequent metaphors in the ancient rhetorical manuals' treatment of the extravagant style, 1989, pp. 47–65.

exhaustive picture of the period's attitudes to *ficta* and *fabulae*, especially since the character of my material is quite heterogeneous: I will deal with genres and text types such as rhetorical and grammatical tracts, philosophical meditations, biography, letters and sermons, exegetic and hermeneutic theory, Menippean satire, commentaries on profane or sacred literature, allegorical narrative and, finally, didactic, epic and lyric poetry. Throughout this diversity, nevertheless, I have wanted to depict a more or less continuous development, to tell a coherent story, to sketch an overall picture which, in addition, is meant to highlight some of the principal Latin sources of medieval literary culture.

To that purpose I was forced to restrict my investigation to the innovators rather than the traditionalists. Among those former are not only some of the uncompromising proponents of the new faith, setting out to question or even deny the value of pagan literature, but also open-minded Christian intellectuals who would recycle the old tales and tenets to new ends, constituting, as it were, the era's poetical or critical avant-garde: a Lactantius with his advanced theory of 'oblique speech' during the first years of Emperor Constantine's *Roma christiana*, or a Boethius with his difficult balancing act between philosophy and poetry in the death cell in Pavia two centuries later. I have not been able, however, to devote separate chapters to each and everyone of these liminal figures, for instance Tertullian or Jerome, just to mention two crucial names for the early Christian construction of cultural identity (and inevitably recurrent in this book). Still, I hope to have drawn a fairly representative map of the Late Antique era's complex attitudes to the problem of fiction in the Latin language area.

This approach has, as far as I know, few earlier counterparts. The names and texts at the centre of my attention are for the most part well-known, but their overall juxtaposition under the aspect of fictionality is, to all appearances, rare or even untried. Many scholars have certainly highlighted the early Christian writers' relationship to classical literature, and it would be pointless – well, impossible – to enumerate them all in this short preface. Among them, I particularly want to single out Paule Demats, whose first fifty pages of *Fabula. Trois études de mythographie antique et médiévale* (1973) deal with Macrobius, Servius, Arnobius, Lactantius, Augustine and Fulgentius, and Harald Hagendahl, a Swedish Latin professor, renowned for his investigations into the Church Fathers and the classics. To be sure, Hagendahl's specific field of studies is highly pertinent to me – as is Late Antique semiotics, hermeneutics, allegorical interpretation practices or doctrines of styles – but only to the extent that it can be subjected to arguments of fiction theory.

I got an early impulse for this project from an article published in 1964 by the English specialist in Augustine's semiotics Robert A. Markus, a twenty-page-long snapshot of the subject "Paganism, Christianity and the Latin Classics in the Fourth Century", composed, however, without any particular care for the idea of fiction. This concept's early vicissitudes as *plasma*, *fabula* or *figmentum* in Athens and Rome has primarily attracted classical philologists. Now that I wished to suggest the continuation of its history in Late Antique culture, I was able to take advantage of the appendix sections of Ernst Robert Curtius' scholarly classic *European Literature and the Latin Middle Ages*.[1] A great deal of research has, of course, been carried out since 1948, when Curtius published his magnum opus. Some fifteen years later Klaus Thraede was to polemicize against Curtius' allegedly one-sided focus on the medieval reception and transmission of motifs and themes. At this stage (the early sixties of Structuralism) the time had come to supply such research interests with studies in the changes of function of literary language. Thraede refused, however, to take corresponding changes of signification into account: "We are not dealing with semasiology"![2] This is a formalistic point of view that no longer seems tenable. When, for example, a Christian poet described his poem as a 'gift' to God, the topos of the *munus* (gift) – common among pagan ancient poets – was not only endowed with a new function (to ensure the poet eternal salvation) but also with a new meaning (as a testimony of Christian faith).

Furthermore, I could draw support from the Swiss medieval scholar Alexandre Leupin's work *Fiction and Incarnation: Rhetoric, Theology, and Literature in the Middle Ages* (in the French original 1993), where, however, the overall time frame and the central issues look different. My story begins with the Late Antique repudiations of poetry among the Church Fathers, primarily in Augustine, according to whom the human heart's frank speech to God should condemn all secular fiction to shame and silence. I will continue with the inclination for philosophical allegory among the period's grammarians, mythographers and commentators, and I will finally pay attention to some examples of early Christian poetry, still within the Latin Late Antique cultural framework, with a special view to themes such as the Muses, the Sirens, the lyre, the figure of the *vates* and metamorphosis. For his part, Leupin concentrates on medieval fiction theory and its relationship to the Christian idea of Incarnation. He devotes one chapter each to Tertullian and to Isidore of Seville, both of whom are of interest to my study in which, however, they are only treated incidentally as one of the starting points and one of the final witnesses, respectively. In addition, we share Augustine and Martianus Capella as common interests, and I have certain-

---

[1] The fifth and sixth of these excursuses, "Late Antique Literary Studies" and "Early Christian and Medieval Literary Studies", have been especially useful to me, Curtius 1990, pp. 436–67.
[2] Thraede 1963, p. 101.

ly benefitted from Leupin's presentation of the Church Father, with its emphasis on ideas of language and discourse in the *Confessions*.[1] Finally, I would like to mention Paul-Augustin Deproost's article on "Ficta et facta" (1998), which takes an integrated approach to the main theme of this book, Haijo Westra's paper on "Augustine and Poetic Exegesis" (2007, a revised version of an article originally published 1990), which does the same with respect to Augustine, and Karla Pollmann's short but particularly rewarding paper on two notions of fictionality in Hellenistic and Late Antique culture (1999), due to its useful conceptual distinctions on this complex field.

The Shadow of Creusa was originally published in Swedish in 2006. For this thoroughly revised and updated version I have been able to profit from several recent works centred on the ever expanding field of Late Antique studies (and, for that matter, on fiction theory). Among them – just to mention a few – is Peter Gemeinhardt's impressive survey of Christian approaches to ancient pagan learning, *Das lateinische Christentum und die antike pagane Bildung* (2007), a good reminder of the innumerable associations and common grounds which actually linked rather than separated Christianity and antique culture, the former being an integral constituent of the latter in its final phases. Gemeinhardt's *Habilitationsschrift* thus provides a broad background to the Late Antique negotiations of fictionality outlined in my study. And so does, from a different perspective, Alan Cameron's *The Last Pagans of Rome* (2011), based on a wealth of textual evidence, radically questioning the notion of a Late Antique pagan revival in the West. Furthermore, Torsten Krämer's ambitious endeavour to determine Augustine's "cultural identity" between truth and lying, *Augustinus zwischen Wahrheit und Lüge* (2007), and Mark Vessey's anthology *A Companion to Augustine* (2012) provide fresh perspectives on a number of works by the most important author treated in this book.[2] In addition, I have thankfully been able to make use of several recent editions of Late Antique literary works, for instance Robert A. Kaster's bilingual version of Macrobius' *Saturnalia* in three Loeb volumes (2011).

For now I will not tire my readers with further enumerations of my sources of information or inspiration; they will all appear in due time. As for my primary sources they have involved some tricky problems of selection. It was not until a late stage, when my work had come to an end, that I was struck by how closely they reflect the international character of Late Antique literature, due to the Mediterranean world's rich Hellenistic-Roman crossover culture and the prevalence

---

[1] Leupin 2003, pp. 46–76.
[2] Krämer 2007, p. 17.

of the Latin language throughout the region. Among the authors examined in my study are two Iberians, one Aquitanian, one Burgundian, one Dalmatian Church Father (from today's Croatia) and at least five North Africans, possibly six (Macrobius' ancestry is disputed). In the long run, I would like to believe that these influential writers, who sometimes corresponded with each other over a distance of hundreds of miles across the Mediterranean, the Romans' *mare nostrum*, represent an early draft of the cultural construct of 'Europe', a concept which had its first notable success, at the very earliest, with the Carolingians a few centuries later.

Be that as it may, it should be emphasized that it is the constructions, ideas, dismissals or appropriations of fictionality that are at stake here. Even if I have been unable to draw any sharp line between what today would be labelled 'theory' (such as commentaries or treatises) and poetry – all in all 'literature', as far as this study is concerned – I have felt obliged to restrict my research to a number of salient authors, the majority of whom are orthodox Christians or, more precisely, Christians being busy narrowing down orthodox faith. Among the poetic works I have completely ignored are such impressive landmarks as Claudian's mythological epic *De raptu Proserpinae* (*The Rape of Proserpine*, end of the fourth century) or Dracontius' Bible epic *De laudibus Dei* (*The Praise of God*, end of the fifth century), not to speak of Ambrose's hymns, along with Augustine's *Confessions* probably representing the most remarkable stylistic innovation of the period (whereas certain theoretical or ideological declarations of the mighty Milan bishop will be of interest to my argument).

I am naturally well aware of the losses all such omissions might imply for my study, but the important thing for me has been the consistency of focus, the elucidation of the main trends and antagonisms within my overall theme: the negotiations of fictionality in Late Antique Latin literature. To all appearances they testify to a huge cultural process of transformation that might best be illustrated by the emblem of the Phoenix, the legendary bird – perhaps of Egyptian origin, fittingly appropriated by Latin poetry and Christian symbolism – that rises from its own ashes to be born anew. From the early Christian rejection of classical mythology emanate some of Late Antiquity's truly pioneering attempts not only to criticize or domesticate but to remodel and transform the old art of make-believe.

Acknowledgements

I thankfully acknowledge the permissions granted by the following authors and publishing firms to reproduce material that originally appeared in their publications:

Arizona Center for Medieval and Renaissance Studies, Tempe, AZ: Avitus, *The Poems of Alcimius Ecdicius Avitus*, transl. G.W. Shea, Medieval and Renaissance Texts and Studies (172), 1997, pp. 81, 134.

Brepols, Turnhout:
- Arator, *Aratoris Subdiaconi Historia apostolica*, I, ed. A.P. Orbán, Corpus christianorum, Series latina (130), 2006, pp. 214–15, 259, 339–40, 349, 362–63, 388–89, 405.
- Isidore of Seville, *Isidorus Hispalensis Sententiae*, ed. P. Cazier, Corpus christianorum, Series latina (111), 1998, pp. 237–38.
- Maximus of Turin, *Maximi episcopi Taurinensis. Collectionem sermonum antiquam nonnullis sermonibus extravagantibus adiectis*, ed. Almut Mutzenbecher, Corpus christianorum, Series latina (23), 1962, pp. 145–46.

Cambridge University Press, Cambridge: William Shakespeare, *The Tragedy of Hamlet, Prince of Denmark*, ed. J.D. Wilson, The Works of Shakespeare/The New Shakespeare, 1969, p. 56.

The Catholic University of America Press, Washington, DC: Caesarius of Arles, *Sermons*, I, transl. M.M. Mueller, The Fathers of the Church (31), 1956, p. 10.

Cerf, Paris: Avitus, *Histoire spirituelle*, I, ed. and transl. N. Hecquet-Noti, Sources chrétiennes (444), 1999, pp. 194, 196.

Columbia University Press, New York:
- Macrobius, *Commentary on the Dream of Scipio*, transl. W.H. Stahl, Records of Western Civilization (48), 1990, pp. 85, 86, 218.
- Martianus Capella, *Martianus Capella and the Seven Liberal Arts. II. The Marriage of Philology and Mercury*, transl. W.H. Stahl, R. Johnson & E.L. Burge, Records of Civilization (84), 1977, pp. 3, 4, 45, 63, 64, 381.

Gallimard, Paris: Jean-Jacques Rousseau, *Œuvres complètes. I. Les confessions. Autres textes autobiographiques*, eds. B. Gagnebin & M. Raymond, Bibliothèque de la Pléiade, 1959, p. 41.

Hackett, Indianapolis, IN: Boethius, *Consolation of Philosophy*, transl. J.C. Relihan, 2001, pp. 3, 15, 72, 83–84, 90, 92–93, 121–22, 143, 144.

Harvard University Press, The Publishers and the Trustees of the Loeb Classical Library:
- *Ausonius*: Vol. I, Loeb Classical Library 96, transl. Hugh G. Evelyn White, pp. 242, 243, Cambridge, MA: Harvard U.P., 1919.

- Boethius: *The Theological Tractates*, transl. H.F. Stewart, E.K. Rand, & E.J. Tester; *The Consolation of Philosophy*, transl. E.J. Tester, Loeb Classical Library 74, pp. 134, 260, 274, 296, 310, 314, 316, 374, 420, Cambridge, MA: Harvard U.P., Copyright © 1973.
- Macrobius: Vol. II, *Saturnalia*, Books 3–5, Loeb Classical Library 511, ed. and transl. Robert A. Kaster, pp. 222, 223, 224, 225, Cambridge, MA: Harvard U.P., Copyright © 2011.
- Ovid: Vol. I, *Heroides. Amores*, Loeb Classical Library 41, transl. Grant Showerman, 1914, rev. G.P. Goold, 1977, pp. 502, 503, Cambridge, MA: Harvard U.P., Copyright © 1977.
- Ovid: Vol. II, *The Art of Love and Other Poems*, Loeb Classical Library 232, transl. J.H. Mozley, 1929, rev. G.P. Goold, 1939, pp. 13–15, Cambridge, MA: Harvard U.P., Copyright © 1979.
- Ovid: Vol. III, *Metamorphoses*, Books 1–8, Loeb Classical Library 42, transl. F.J. Miller, 1916, rev. G.P. Goold, 1977, pp. 448, 449, Cambridge, MA: Harvard U.P., 1916, 1921, 1977.
- *Prudentius:* Vol. I, Loeb Classical Library 387, transl. H.J. Thomson, pp. 10, 11, 20, 21, 50, 51, 76, 77, 190, 191, 192, 193, 194, 195, 210, 211, Cambridge, MA: Harvard U.P., Copyright © 1949.
- *Prudentius:* Vol. II, Loeb Classical Library 398, transl. H.J. Thomson, pp. 8, 9, 10, 11, 142, 143, 230, 231, 328, 329, 372, 373, Cambridge, MA: Harvard U.P., Copyright © 1953.
- Quintilian: Vol. III, *The Orator's Education*, Books 6–8, Loeb Classical Library 126, ed. and transl. Donald A. Russell, pp. 58, 59, 60, 61, 62, 63, Cambridge, MA: Harvard U.P., Copyright © 2001.
- Virgil: Vol. I, *Eclogues, Georgics, Aeneid I–VI*, Loeb Classical Library 63, transl. H. Rushton Fairclough, 1916, rev. G.P. Goold, 1935; revised with a new introduction 1999, pp. 48, 368, 370, 550, Cambridge, MA: Harvard U.P., Copyright © 1999.

All the above Harvard U.P. copyrights are held by the President and Fellows of Harvard College. Loeb Classical Library ® is a registered trademark of the President and Fellows of Harvard College.

John Hopkins University Press, Baltimore, MD: Joel C. Relihan, *Ancient Menippean Satire*, 1993, pp. 209–10. © 1993 The Johns Hopkins University Press.

Liverpool University Press, Liverpool:
- Avitus of Vienne, *Letters and Selected Prose*, transl. D. Shanzer & I. Wood, Translated Texts for Historians (38), 2002, p. 261.
- Lactantius, *Divine Institutes*, transl. A. Bowen & P. Garnsey, Translated Texts for Historians (40), 2003, pp. 82, 151, 435–36.

New City Press, New York:
- Augustine, *The Confessions*, transl. M. Boulding, The Works of Saint Augustine, a Translation for the 21st Century (1.1), 1997, pp. 53–54, 82–83, 227–28, 228–29.
- Augustine, *Letters*, I–IV, eds. J.E. Rotelle & B. Ramsey, transl. R.J. Teske, The Works of Saint Augustine, a Translation for the 21st Century (2.1–4), 2001–05, vol. I, pp. 28, 174, 222–23, vol. II, p. 18.

Norton, New York: Lucretius, *The Nature of Things*, transl. F.O. Copley, 1977, p. 23.

Ohio State University Press, Columbus, OH: Fulgentius, *Fulgentius the Mythographer*, transl. L.G. Whitbread, 1971, pp. 72–73.

Oxford University Press, Oxford:
- Augustine, *De doctrina Christiana*, ed. and transl. R.P.H. Green, Oxford Early Christian Texts, 1996, p. 125.
- Virgil, *Aeneid*, transl. Frederick Ahl, 2007, pp. 53, 136.

Paulist Press, Mahwah, NJ:
- Augustine, *Against the Academics*, transl. J.J. O'Meara, Ancient Christian Writers (12), 1950, p. 112.
- Augustine, *The Greatness of the Soul. The Teacher*, transl. J.M. Colleran, Ancient Christian Writers (9), 1950, pp. 100–01.
- Maximus of Turin, *The Sermons of St. Maximus of Turin*, transl. B. Ramsey, Ancient Christian Writers (50), 1989, pp. 90–91.
- Paulinus of Nola, *Letters of St. Paulinus of Nola*, I–II, transl. P.G. Walsh, Ancient Christian Writers (35), 1966–67, vol. I, pp. 157–59, 162, vol. II, pp. 33, 267.
- Paulinus of Nola, *The Poems of St. Paulinus of Nola*, transl. P.G. Walsh, Ancient Christian Writers (40), 1975, pp. 58–59, 61, 83, 158–59, 202–03.

Penguin, London: Augustine, *Concerning the City of God against the Pagans*, transl. H. Bettenson, Penguin Classics, 1984, pp. 386, 868.

Pontifical Institute of Mediaeval Studies, Toronto: Avitus, *The Fall of Man. De spiritalis historiae gestis libri I–III*, ed. D.J. Nodes, Toronto Medieval Latin Texts (16), 1985, p. 16.

Random House, New York: Dante Alighieri, *Paradiso*, transl. R. & J. Hollander, 2008, pp. 3, 239.

Scholars Press, Atlanta, GA:
- Arator, *Arator's On the Acts of the Apostles (De actibus apostolorum)*, transl. R.J. Schrader, with J.L. Roberts III & J.F. Makowski, Classics in Religious Studies (6), 1987, pp. 22, 38, 72–73, 76, 80–81, 89–90, 102.
- Augustine, *Augustine on Romans. Propositions from the Epistle to the Romans. Unfinished Commentary on the Epistle to the Romans*, ed. and transl.

P. Fredriksen Landes, Society of Biblical Literature: Texts and Translations (23), Early Christian Literature Series (6), 1982, pp. 54–55.

Society of Biblical Literature, Atlanta, GA: Sedulius, *The Paschal Song and Hymns*, transl. C.P.E. Springer, Writings from the Greco-Roman World (35), 2013, pp. 3, 5, 7, 149, 213, 215.

St. Augustine's Press, South Bend, IN: Augustine, *On Order [De Ordine]*, transl. S. Borruso, 2007, pp. 13, 15, 29, 33, 103, 105.

University of North Carolina Press, Chapel Hill: Virgil, *The Eclogues*, transl. B.H. Fowler, 1997, p. 11.

Westminster John Knox Press, Louisville, KY: Augustine, *Earlier Writings*, transl. J.S. Burleigh, 2006 (1953), pp. 50–51, 62, 275, 276–77.

Patrick McBrine, Southern Connecticut State University: Juvencus, *Libri evangeliorum IIII*, Preface, transl. P. McBrine, 2012, at: http://www.pmcbrine.com/juvencus_praef.pdf.

James J. O'Donnell, Augustine, *Confessions*. I, ed. J.J. O'Donnell, Oxford: Clarendon, 1992, pp. 11, 27, 113, 113–14.

Sigrid Schottenius Cullhed, University of Gothenburg: *Proba the Prophet. Studies in the Christian Virgilian Cento*, diss., 2012, p. 185.

I would also like to thank my translator, Michael Knight, for his efforts with my lengthy exposition, the Swedish Foundation for Humanities and Social Sciences for their generous support, and last but not least my mother, Kerstin Cullhed, who submitted my manuscript to arduous scrutiny as well as relevant queries and comments. This book is for her.

Anders Cullhed

Contents

I   In the World of Make-Believe

Preliminary Remarks —— 3

1   **Fictionality: Theoretical Considerations —— 6**
    And All for Nothing! For Hecuba! —— 6
    Avatars of Fiction, Then and Now —— 10

2   **Fictionality: Historical Circumstances —— 21**
    The Ancient Quarrel (Greece) —— 21
    The Fictional Contract (Rome) —— 31
    The Cobweb and the Rainbow (Plutarch) —— 45

3   **Late Antiquity —— 55**
    Periodization —— 55
    The Issue of Truth —— 60
    The Shadow of Creusa —— 73

II   Augustine: A Restless Farewell. Renouncing *Ficta* in Late Antiquity

Preliminary Remarks —— 83

1   **At the Window in Ostia —— 86**
    Plotinian/Pauline *Raptus* —— 86
    The Speech of the Heart —— 93
    Ineffability —— 110

2   **Recycling the Classics —— 123**
    Weeping for Dido —— 123
    The Liberal Arts —— 158
    The Wounds of Imagination —— 194

3   **The Figures of the Spirit —— 207**
    The Speech of Creation —— 207

The Bible: Tropes and Mysteries —— 215
The Fact of Allegory —— 240

4 In the Heat of the Battle —— 263
Orthodoxy and Heresy —— 266
The Illusions of Culture —— 278

5 "Set me free, O God, from that multitude of speech" —— 292

III Oblique Speech: Implementations of Allegory in Late Roman Learned Culture

Preliminary Remarks —— 303

1 Lactantius: Christian Eloquence —— 313
Pious infiltration —— 313
Veiled Figuration —— 320

2 Servius: The Grammarian's Gaze —— 328
Allegorical Sense —— 330
Poetic Licence —— 335

3 Macrobius: *Narratio fabulosa* —— 346
The Saturnalia —— 346
The Commentary on the Dream of Scipio —— 354

4 Martianus Capella: A Hopeless Mess —— 369
Fabulous Festivities —— 370
Showy Fiction, Naked Learning —— 384

5 Fulgentius: Mythographer and Mythoclast —— 402
A Surprise Visit —— 403
The Flirtatious Muse —— 414
Adorning Greece —— 425

6 Boethius: The Maieutics of Consolation —— 433
Philosophy Sets the Tone —— 434
The Wings of Imagination —— 451
The Limits of Imagination —— 459

IV *Poeta Christianus*: From *Ficta* to *Facta* in Early Christian Poetry

Preliminary Remarks —— 471

1 The Foam of Style —— 477

2 Paulinus and Proba: "A Greater Order" —— 487
   The Lyre of Nola —— 487
   The Female *Vates* —— 503

3 Prudentius: Dreams and Demons —— 518

4 Biblical Epic Poetry: The Orthodoxy of Paraphrase —— 544
   Juvencus: The Pioneer —— 548
   Sedulius: The Food of Poetry —— 555
   Avitus: Non-Fiction —— 570
   Arator: *Documenta* —— 584

V Epilogue: *Ecclesia Triumphans*. Fiction and Figuration on the Threshold of the Middle Ages

Preliminary Remarks —— 605

1 The Old Dreams —— 608

2 The New Library —— 615

3 The Glory of the Mirror —— 629

Appendix: Original Quotations —— 633

Bibliography —— 658
Primary Sources —— 658
Secondary Sources —— 666

Index —— 691

I In the World of Make-Believe

Preliminary Remarks

> Go, go, go, said the bird: human kind
> cannot bear very much reality.
>
> T.S. Eliot, "Burnt Norton"[1]

Most epochs have not felt the readiness of T.S. Eliot's poetical bird to accept people's need to ease their burden of reality in general or, to be more specific, to promote the implementation of alternative realities in literature or in art, for the sake of adventure, escape or exploration. A writer from the early days of the Church who would have claimed with force that, on the contrary, we should be able to endure an unlimited amount of reality was the theologian Tertullian, a stern North African who lived in Carthage during the decades before and after the year 200, the first great Christian thinker who wrote in Latin, "the one great Latin author of the third century" according to a recent scholar in Patristics.[2] Tertullian's outlook might in fact seem just as modern as Eliot's lines from *Four Quartets*, but he meant something altogether different with "reality" than the modern poet. To be precise, Tertullian's reality involved the divine drama of salvation, understood as a history that knows of only one beginning and only one course of events that for many men – among them, to be sure, the writer's own antagonists – will come to a disastrous end in the near future. All other versions of reality were literally nonsense, most conspicuously the ones that could be found in the classical culture that had dominated the Mediterranean world for fifteen hundred years or more. They had created an imaginary universe replete with gods, nymphs, animated natural creatures, marvellous metamorphoses and other strange things: nothing but rubbish in the eyes of the severe apologist Tertullian.[3]

---

[1] Eliot 1963, p. 190.
[2] Edwards 2004, p. 189.
[3] By the term "apologists" I refer, here and henceforth, not only to the writers who during the second century CE composed documents in Greek in defence of the Christian faith (for a convenient overview, see Norris 2004), but also to the later Minucius Felix, Tertullian and Arnobius, who wrote in Latin, in short: to the intellectual advocates of Christianity down to Lactantius in the early fourth century. Much as some of them, such as Justin Martyr, tried to reconcile New Testament Christology with classical Greek *logos* philosophy, I would like to emphasize the

Nevertheless, his exclusive strictness was not the only and not even the dominant attitude to pagan myth in the Christian civilization that began to crystallize, and was soon to achieve hegemony, in the huge Roman Empire. Some hundred years after Tertullian's lifetime, the Emperors Constantine and Licinius were to allow the Christians of the Empire to freely exercise their religion, an act of tolerance that shortly, during the course of the fourth century, turned into monolithic dictates. The orthodox Emperor Theodosius, who reigned towards the end of that century, did not have to bother about allowing the Catholic cult and belief; he prescribed them. Therefore, the doctrine of what the Romans originally had considered a strange Jewish sect turned from subversive preaching into the authorized norm. Consequently, the heat of apocalyptic commitment and of apologetic polemics began to cool off. After having acted as stubborn enemies for three centuries, imperial Rome and Christianity were slowly but steadily beginning to identify with each other.

They actually managed to establish a *modus vivendi* in the eastern part of the Empire, but in the West, not least in the province of Africa, this mutual approach led to a serious crisis during the last few decades of the fourth century. There followed an ultimate and certainly uneven trial of strength before the age-old pagan Empire succumbed and the new religion took over. The schools had always continued to transmit the classical heritage to new generations of Romans, and even at the end of the fourth century the diminishing pagan Senate aristocracy entertained high hopes of a Rome where the Mithras of the Mystery cults, the Emperor and Christ might be worshipped side by side. At the same time, however, the Christian arguments against the pagan world of fiction flared up with renewed force, particularly where the myths and literature of old presented a still vivid temptation. All three great Late Antique Latin Fathers, Ambrose (ca. 340–97), Jerome (ca. 347–420) and Augustine (354–430), were engaged in this campaign. An ascetic cultural radicalism spread over the Roman Empire, an early premonition of medieval monastic fervour centuries later. These increasing tensions came to an early discharge in the famous battle during the 380s over the altar of Victoria, the goddess of Victory. Should she or should she not be restored to her ancient abode in the Senate of Rome? This was a cultural and religious dispute whose actual importance has perhaps been overstated but whose symbolic significance is irrefutable. During the following century, the great majority of Romans realized that the world had changed once and for all. It was impossible to return to the old order of things. Christian religion was to infiltrate

---

strong polemical fire against pagan religiosity and culture that blazes through the writings of, among others, the Assyrian Tatian (Justin's pupil), Irenaeus, Tertullian and Arnobius.

the Empire on all levels, official and private, and eventually establish a cultural network – from the sixth century with important nodes in the monasteries – which took over the responsibility for education in the new Europe emerging from the disturbances of the Germanic migrations across the continent.

Accordingly, the early Christian attacks on poetry and theatre plays were being mitigated (though intermittently relaunched and never forgotten) in the *ecclesia triumphans* of the dawning Middle Ages. In the present book, I have chosen to study the turbulent historical period of Western literature when the issue of fictionality was still felt to be unresolved, hence highly controversial and of vital importance to a range of hermeneutic, educational and existential concerns. It mainly took place during the fourth and fifth centuries, when classical culture had lost its initiative but before the new era of Christianity had defined, legitimized and established a literary institution of its own. In order to draw a sharp line between orthodox Christian faith and pagan mythological lies, the Church Fathers and their allies returned time and again to concepts such as *ficta, figmenta* or *fabulae.* First of all, we have to ask ourselves what these terms really mean – or once meant.

1 Fictionality: Theoretical Considerations

And All for Nothing! For Hecuba!

In Shakespeare's *Hamlet* from around 1600 the young prince needs some proof of his suspicion that something is rotten in the state of Denmark. To be precise, he needs to know if his newly deceased father, the late King Hamlet, was in fact killed by his brother Claudius. To this end, he commands a travelling theatre group to perform some tableaux composed by himself recalling the scene of the king's death. In this famous *play within the play*, illusion turns out to be of foremost importance. If the actors do their job sufficiently well – according to Hamlet's plan – his uncle will surely betray his guilt. As a matter of precaution, they have to rehearse in the presence of the prince, on which occasion they are asked to recite from a drama on the fall of Troy, possibly written by Shakespeare himself, or by one of his rivals among the Elizabethan dramatists. The first actor in the group performs young Pyrrhus' murder of the old King Priam in front of the horrified Queen Hecuba. He exercises his art so skilfully and with such realism that Hamlet soon falls into a melancholy mood, ashamed of his own passivity (2.2):

```
553  O, what a rogue and peasant slave am I!
     Is it not monstrous that this player here,
555  but in a fiction, in a dream of passion,
     could force his soul so to his own conceit
     that from her working all his visage wanned,
     tears in his eyes, distraction in his aspect,
     a broken voice, and his whole function suiting
560  with forms to his conceit; And all for nothing!
     For Hecuba!
     What's Hecuba to him, or he to Hecuba,
     that he should weep for her?
```

Hamlet strikes a chord that vibrates throughout the works of Shakespeare and permeates Early Modern culture. His outpourings are concerned with the power of fiction over the actors and, in a wider perspective, with the power of language or of artistic representation over the human soul. His whole epoch, the Late Renaissance, was more or less obsessed by the problem of representation, by the fact that "a fiction, [...] a dream of passion" could seem more real than reality itself. Such an intuition is sententiously confirmed by the clown Touchstone in another of Shakespeare's plays from around 1600, *As You Like It*. In the third act of this comedy, the peasant girl Audrey does not understand the clown's eloquent effusions. What does the word "poetical" mean, she asks him, with the characteristic ensuing (moral and epistemological) questions: "Is it honest in deed and word? Is it a true thing?" Touchstone answers her in the negative but also, just as characteristically, in an ambiguous way: "No, truly; for the truest poetry is the most faining" (3.3.15–17). It is surely no coincidence that it is precisely he, the court jester, who is responsible for articulating the great paradox of fiction in *As You Like It*. By "faining" – reminiscent of the Latin language's *fingere*, whose supine form, *fictum*, is the origin of our modern 'fiction' – poetry speaks the truth in its own manner. It cannot be done away with as empty figments of the imagination. If the play within the play of *Hamlet* was not meant to be taken seriously, the actor would not shed any tears. It is true that Hecuba might be devoid of any actual reality in Hamlet's kingdom of Denmark or, for that matter, in Elizabethan England: she is admittedly compared to a "nothing". Yet she means something, even something of vital importance, to the spectators of her tragic destiny.

The cogitations of Hamlet, like most passages in Shakespeare bearing on literary or fiction theory, are derived from ancient criticism. Horace (65–8 BCE) knew perfectly well that the poet, according to a familiar sentence from the verse letter known as *Ars poetica* (*On the Art of Poetry*), had to feign suffering in order to make his readers or listeners suffer: "If you want to move me to tears, you must first feel grief yourself" (102–03), *si vis me flere, dolendum est / primum ipsi tibi*.[1] Both Shakespeare's and Horace's words recall the old connections of imaginative literature, particularly of drama and of oral poetry, to rhetoric. Just like the actor or the poet, the Roman legal orator had to put on a show in order to convince his audience, first and foremost the judge, of his case. The *locus classicus* of this theme is to be found in the sixth book of Quintilian's magisterial *Institutio oratoria* (*The Orator's Education*) from the end of the first century CE.[2] There, the great Hispanic pedagogue (ca. 35–100) tells us that if we aim at "arousing emotions", *movendos adfectus*, we must first let ourselves be moved, *moveamur ipsi*. Likewise, if we want to make our words sound likely, *veri similia*, we must try to identify with those who are really affected by the feelings referred to, and "let our speech spring from the very attitude that we want to produce in the judge", *a tali animo proficiscatur oratio qualem facere iudici volet* (6.2.26–27). Quintilian continues, in the translation by Donald A. Russell (6.2.28–30, 34–35):

---

[1] I quote the *Ars poetica* ("Epistle to the Pisones") according to the edition of N. Rudd 1989 and, in English, from T.S. Dorsch 1974.
[2] *The Orator's Education* is rendered, both in the original and in English translation, according to D.A. Russell's Loeb edition in five volumes, 2001.

But how can we come to be moved? Emotions, after all, are not in our own power. Well, I will try to explain this too. The person who will show the greatest power in the expression of emotions will be the person who has properly formed what the Greeks call *phantasiai* (let us call them "visions"), by which the images of absent things are presented to the mind in such a way that we seem actually to see them with our eyes and have them physically present to us. Some use the word *euphantasiōtos* of one who is exceptionally good at realistically imagining to himself things, words, and actions. We can indeed easily make this happen at will. When the mind is idle or occupied with wishful thinking or a sort of daydreaming, the images of which I am speaking haunt us, and we think we are travelling or sailing or fighting a battle or addressing a crowd or disposing of wealth which we do not possess, and not just imagining but actually doing these things! Can we not turn this mental vice to a useful purpose? Surely we can. [...]

Again, when pity is needed, let us believe that the ills of which we are to complain have happened to us, and persuade our hearts of this. Let us identify with the persons of whose grievous, undeserved, and lamentable misfortunes we complain; let us not plead the case as though it were someone else's, but take the pain of it on ourselves for the moment. We shall thus say what we would have said in similar circumstances of our own. I have frequently seen tragic and comic actors, having taken off their masks at the end of some emotional scene, leave the stage still in tears. And if the mere delivery of the written words of another can so kindle them with imagined emotions, what shall *we* be capable of doing, we who have to imagine the facts in such a way that we can feel vicariously the emotions of our endangered clients? (I)

Quintilian establishes some important connections between verbal and mental phenomena which will reappear in the following survey. The capacity of feigning is linked to a special class of *visiones*, known by the Greeks as *phantasiai*, a set of mental "images", *imagines*, of reality. More than four hundred years earlier, Aristotle had put forward a rudimentary analysis of human imagination, but it was not until Hellenistic and Late Antique culture that this faculty of the soul would be assigned a key function in the mind's formation of fictions. The concept of *imago* transferred to language would, in its turn, be considered a crucial technical instrument in the service of fictional representation based on suggestive evidence. According to ancient critics, the linguistic image enjoyed a certain clearness or *evidentia* (in Greek: *enargeia*), a quality which – in the words of Quintilian – makes us seem to be "exhibiting" the events rather than just "be talking about" them (6.2.32). This contrast between *ostendere* and *dicere* vaguely anticipates modern narratology's distinction between 'showing' and 'telling'. It is due to *evidentia* that we actually seem to observe absent things "and have them physically present to us".

It is essential to note that this sort of fiction, operative by means of persuasive pretence and illusions of presence, was not considered the exclusive privilege of poetry or of imaginative literature. On the contrary, it already figures in Aristotle, as the North American literary scholar Kathy Eden observes, in close relation to legal speech.¹ This connection is quite manifest in Quintilian, where it is presented by means of an argument that – in the ancient art of dialectic (or logic) – used to be classified as *a fortiori*. If even the actors of a theatrical performance could be deeply affected by a role which perhaps meant nothing to them, apart from the necessity of scenic illusion, how much greater reason had not the legal orator to get involved in the case of his client! This is, *mutatis mutandis*, a quite similar line of argument that will reappear in *Hamlet*. If any actor on the stage weeps "for nothing! For Hecuba", then surely he, the prince himself, was expected to respond to the murder of his own father: to a world order, as it were, that had been shaken to its foundations.

Perhaps the theme of fiction exercised a special influence on Shakespeare's Elizabethan culture, replete with stage performances, courtly ceremonies and aristocratic self-fashioning. Nevertheless, the contemporaneous mad knight of Cervantes embodied the same theme in another country, in another genre and in another theoretical perspective, where both imitation and imagination regulate the hero's interpretation of reality. On closer inspection, it becomes evident that the question of fiction causes theoretical uneasiness and stirs curiosity, wavering between harsh bans and downright delight, throughout Western literature during the Middle Ages and the Renaissance.

One of the early Christian writers who had most thoroughly got to the bottom of this complex problem was Augustine. Consequently, he is assigned the longest chapter in this book. He dedicated years of his youth to the love of those fictions that he would severely censure later in life, as an influential preacher and leader of the Church. In his *Confessions* (probably composed between 397 and 401) the forty-year-old bishop recalls the theatre-loving young man he once was, constantly attracted to the tragic adventures of the stage: "When the theme of a play dealt with other people's tragedies – false and theatrical tragedies – it would please and attract me more powerfully the more it moved me to tears."² It should not be difficult for the modern reader of these *Confessions* to detect something of Prince Hamlet's wonder at the suggestive power emanating from the stage plays' "fiction" and "dream of passion". In fact, Augustine describes this power as a "foul mange", *turpis scabies*, that he could not get rid of as a young man. He felt an irresistible need to "scrape away at my itching self" upon listening "to such doleful tales being told" (3.2.4), *quibus auditis et fictis*

---

1 This is the main hypothesis of Eden 1986.
2 "Quando mihi in aerumna aliena et falsa et saltatoria ea magis placebat actio histrionis meque alliciebat vehementius qua mihi lacrimae excutiebantur." I quote the *Confessions* from J.J. O'Donnell's edition 1992 and, in English, from M. Boulding's translation (based on O'Donnell's work), 1997a.

tamquam in superficie raderer. This itch is, in short, the subject of the present book.

Avatars of Fiction, Then and Now

So what is fiction, really? To give an answer to this tricky question, one easily feels tempted to paraphrase Augustine's famous comment on the issue of time from *Confessions* (11.14.17): as long as no one confronts you with the problem of fiction, you seem to know what it is, but as soon as you are asked about it, you are at a loss for an answer. It depends partly on the fact that many people take this phenomenon for granted, as if it were a matter of course, a natural product of imagination, given once and for all. That is not the case. Just to quote one modern philosopher, Gregory Currie, who perhaps already paraphrased Augustine in his study *The Nature of Fiction* (1990): "Fiction is one of those concepts like goodness, colour, number, and cause that we have little difficulty in applying but great difficulty in explaining."[1] Currie belongs to the increasing number of scholars who, during the past fifty years, have established fiction theory as a crucial interdisciplinary issue within the Humanities. It is concerned with, among other things, the intricate relationships between truth, fiction and lying. The explicit definitions of these concepts usually vary between cultures, epochs and languages. They actually fluctuate to such an extent that one might feel tempted to identify with a certain – fictional – character of the Swedish writer Hjalmar Söderberg, the newspaper editor Markel in the novel *The Serious Game* (1912), who rather irreverently rephrases 'the old question of Pilate: What the hell is truth?'[2]

During the epoch that will keep us busy in the following presentation, many intellectuals understood perfectly well the difficulties of defining truth. On the whole, Roman Late Antiquity was an epoch in which at least two concepts of cognitive accuracy blatantly came into conflict. There was, in the first place, the classical idea of truth, a concept which Plato had associated to the abstract forms or ideas of unchanging reality and which Aristotle had subjected to an authoritative qualification in his so-called correspondence theory, requiring a basic agreement between the structure of the mind, linguistic propositions and the order of things. The *loci classici* of this Aristotelian definition can be found in the *Metaphysics* (1011b) and the short treatise *Peri hermēneias*, known in Boe-

---

[1] Currie 1990, p. 1.
[2] "Pilati gamla fråga: hvad fan är sanning?" Söderberg 1912, p. 124.

thius' Latin version as *De interpretatione* (*On Interpretation*, 16a, cf. below, p. 100, note 1, and p. 413).¹ And there was, on the other hand, the Christian principle of truth which referred to the authority of the Bible. The former was inclusive: the broad Aristotelian homology between words and things seemed to permit a certain scope for various interpretations of reality. The latter was, in contrast, exclusive: the message of the Spirit did not tolerate ambiguities or human guesswork.

While the old Greek language had registered a rich gamut of terms that reflected the fluctuations of the concept of 'truth' – such as the Homeric *alētheia*, a key term in modern philosophy due to Martin Heidegger's interpretive efforts, or Hesiod's *etētyma* in *Works and Days* (10) – the Romans had as a rule to content themselves with *veritas*, even if this word could be complemented with constructs such as '[the order of] things', *res*, or 'history', *historia*.² Depending on the attitude adopted to *veritas*, fiction among the Romans either came to be understood (more or less in the Aristotelian vein) as an imaginary or discursive mode in its own right, or it could be identified with the insidious activity of lying. The Golden Age poets assiduously explored the former notion, while the Christian intellectuals would adhere to the latter, more exclusive way of thinking.

The modern Western concept of fiction is, to a certain extent, a heritage from the Aristotelian philosophy and (as we shall soon see) poetics. Usually it falls, from an epistemological point of view, somewhere between truth and lying. Normally, it does not claim to convey factual knowledge on the same level as a historical account or a scientific report. On the other hand, modern fiction is seldom (again, in the West) condemned as nefarious fake. It commonly uses a language that does not have to be predicative, and it does not necessarily pretend to register any other reality than its own, sometimes – chiefly in the domains of art, poetry and prose – in accordance with Kantian notions of the aesthetic as something irreducible, impossible to entirely trace back to other experiences such as the satisfaction of desire or the acquisition of knowledge.³ Furthermore, modern fiction can readily be connected to a range of rhetorical or poetical concepts such as invention, fabrication or (with a slight limitation of our perspective) narrative,

---

1 I have used the Loeb editions of *The Metaphysics*, trans. H. Tredennick, Aristotle 1977–80, and *On Interpretation*, trans. H.P. Cook, Aristotle 1962.
2 As for *alētheia* and *etētyma*, see Louise H. Pratt 1993, pp. 95–113. In his 2004 article on "*Aletheia* in Greek Thought Until Aristotle", Jan Woleński registers fourteen words in "the Greek 'truth-family'", of which he cites adjectives such as *atrekes*, *nemertes*, *adolos*, *ortos*, *apseudos*, *etymos* and *etetymos*, p. 341. I quote Hesiod from the new Loeb edition of G.W. Most, 2006.
3 Cf. Janaway 1995, p. 192.

the last of which in its turn can comprise a number of literary genres, all the way from science fiction to the documentary novel.

These two kinds of narrative, probably indicating two extremes along a broad range of modern literary fiction's reality claims, are not chosen at random. Certain theories in this field have lately emphasized the remarkable stability of fiction through the centuries, during which mimetic or, to use a term of our own days, 'realistic' types of narrative are time and again confronted by wonderful, fabulous or magical stories. Such a tension, which is often articulated in the English-speaking countries as a dichotomy of *novel* and *romance*, is an important topic in one of the pioneering Anglo-Saxon books on fiction theory, Thomas G. Pavel's *Fictional Worlds* (1986). This work calls attention to various aspects or characteristics of fiction: its creation of "distance" from ourselves, its tricks to produce recognition ("relevance") in its audience and, finally, its bewildering or confusing effects upon us ("dizziness"). These three "fictional components" are to be observed, according to Pavel, throughout Western literary history. The proportions between them differ considerably, to be sure, but they are discernible everywhere: a set of "familiar elements" joined together in structural units, in constant and glaring contrast to the world of primitive myth.[1] The details of Pavel's analysis might be debatable, but I believe he is right in stipulating certain transhistorical qualities of fiction (right through its breath-taking fluctuations over time).[2] It is thanks to those qualities that, in at least a minimal sense, a metrical rhapsody from, say, archaic Greece makes use of the same kind of authorial voice, deploys the same class of linguistic utterances and presupposes the same type of readerly expectations or reception (to the extent, of course, that reading was involved at all) as, say, a postmodern Manhattan-based novel. Those common characteristics, in short, make a discipline such as literary history possible and make a work such as this feasible to write.

Perhaps the primary distinctive feature of fiction is formed by the two small words *as if*, as important to twentieth-century *als ob* philosophy as they were – albeit in an altogether different sense – to ancient criticism. Fictional literary works like to operate *as if* the persons or the events referred to actually existed. To speak with Virginia Woolf in her frequently quoted essay *A Room of One's Own* (1931), where she recycles a metaphor which we shall trace back to Plutarch, but which is probably as old as Western literature itself:[3]

---

1 Pavel 1986, pp. 147f.
2 For an ingenious and detailed vindication of this argument, see Currie 2014.
3 Woolf 1931, pp. 62f. For the antique conception of poetry as a web, see Scheid and Svenbro 2003.

> Fiction is like a spider's web, attached ever so lightly perhaps, but still attached to life at all four corners. Often the attachment is scarcely perceptible; Shakespeare's plays, for instance, seem to hang there complete by themselves. But when the web is pulled askew, hooked up at the edge, torn in the middle, one remembers that these webs are not spun in mid-air by incorporeal creatures but are the work of suffering human beings, and are attached to grossly material things, like health and money and the houses we live in.

Fiction is sometimes labelled, not without good reason, a serious game, a practice of *serio ludere*. It likes to feign its own truth or to establish its own reality by connecting to well-known historical circumstances, to authentic persons or documented events. Modern theories of fiction tend to transform the conjunction of "damned romancing and lies", known from Henrik Ibsen's drama *Peer Gynt* (2.4), into a disjunction, whereupon it suppresses the word "damned" in favour of other, generally more positive attributes, and finally conceptualizes both of these operations.[1]

One of the keenest literary theorists of later times, Umberto Eco, claims that not only fiction but reality as well must be considered a cultural construction.[2] I cannot but borrow his own exemplification: "The so-called actual world is the world to which we refer – rightly or wrongly – as the world described by the *Encyclopedia Britannica* or *Time* magazine (a world in which Napoleon died on St. Helena, two plus two equals four, it is impossible to be the father of oneself, and Sherlock Holmes never existed – if not as a fictional character)." As an alternative to this encyclopaedic reality, Eco puts forward the "possible" or, as he prefers to call them, the "small" worlds, that is to say, the worlds of fiction, which to a great extent are subject to their own laws and characterized by their proper ontology.[3] He refutes emphatically the modern idealization of art as some marvellous, fundamentally endless field of possibilities, supposedly forming a contrast to the vile necessity we have to cope with in our daily life. Even in their most defiant or negative configurations, the "small worlds" of fiction take advantage of the big one; in this sense they are (in Eco's stronger term) "parasitical", whether we describe them as possible, credible, probable or conceivable. They can ful-

---

1 R.F. Sharp's translation, Ibsen 1936, in the original: "løgn og forbannet dikt", Ibsen 1966.
2 For a good survey of the "changing concept of reality" or "the relativity of the experience of reality" in Western European culture, cf. Assmann 1980, pp. 8, 18–53. An ambitious as well as influential endeavour to detect the (Western) "rise of fictionality" in the development of the Early Modern English novel, Gallagher 2006, fails precisely because it overlooks this instance of generic *Begriffsgeschichte*.
3 See Eco's essay "Small Worlds", 1994, pp. 67, 72.

fil or repudiate, respect or manipulate the reader's expectations, but they always depend upon them and upon the characteristics of the world around us.[1]

If Eco is right, the much-talked-of autonomy of fiction is highly relative, and it seems all the more urgent to focus on the modern fascination with the imaginary – to use a term introduced as a key concept in fiction theory by Wolfgang Iser.[2] Why are we so willingly drawn to fiction? What exactly does its attraction over us consist in? As we have already noted, the answer to such questions certainly differs from culture to culture or even from one writer to another. There is no doubt, however, that Western modernity has to a high degree defined fictionality as a symptom of want and a tool for compensation. Whether parasitical or not, it is supposed to expose an imaginary world that helps us to put up with mundane reality, or even with a restrictive and authoritarian environment. Few writers have established the modern agenda for these excursions into the imaginary as efficiently as Jean-Jacques Rousseau (who, to be sure, despised culture and cherished sincerity at the expense of all pretence). His most eloquent statement in this respect is probably to be found in the first part of the story of his life, which – bearing my leading character in mind – he called *Les Confessions* (*The Confessions*, 1778). In this autobiographical work, Rousseau tells us how, as a restless young man with sharpened senses, he felt an urgent desire for "imaginary objects" or for pleasures he could not even conceive of. At an insurmountable distance from his immediate surroundings, *du véritable*, he slid into the world of fiction:[3]

> At this time my imagination took a turn which helped to calm my increasing emotions; it was, to contemplate those situations in the books I had read, which produced the most striking effect on my mind; to recall, combine, and apply them to myself in such a manner, as to become one of the personages my recollection presented, and be continually in those fancied circumstances which were most agreeable to my inclinations; in a word, by contriving to place myself in these fictitious situations, the idea of my real one was in a great measure obliterated.
>
> This fondness for imaginary objects, and the facility with which I could gain possession of them, completed my disgust for everything around me, and fixed that inclination for solitude which has ever since been predominant. We shall have more than once occasion to

---

[1] Ibid., p. 75.
[2] Iser tries to elude the simple dichotomy of fiction versus reality by introducing this third term: *the imaginary*. "If the fictional text contains real things without being exhausted by the description of these things, then again its fictional component lacks any end in itself. Rather, by virtue of its fictionality, it prepares for something imaginary [sondern ist als fingierte die Zurüstung eines Imaginären]", 1983, p. 121.
[3] I follow the Pléiade edition, Rousseau 1959, p. 41. The English text is from S.W. Orson's translation 1903, p. 35.

remark the effects of a disposition, misanthropic and melancholy in appearance, but which proceed, in fact, from a heart too affectionate, too ardent, which, for want of similar dispositions, is constrained to content itself with nonentities, and be satisfied with fiction. It is sufficient, at present, to have traced the origin of a propensity which has modified my passions, set bounds to each, and by giving too much ardour to my wishes, has ever rendered me too indolent to obtain them. (II)

To Rousseau, fiction appears from the very beginning as a compensation for all the inhibitions that his feelings and instincts had to suffer. In his *Confessions*, fiction provides an outlet for the speaker's desire, but his relief is only temporary and remains incomplete; it does not give him any real satisfaction. Rather it generates uneasiness, irritation and melancholy in his soul. In this manner, Rousseau brilliantly demonstrates a modern version of the mechanisms of literary fiction, while he still – albeit at a great distance – recalls Augustine's *Confessions*, the very prototype of Western autobiography. The crucial difference between these two great confessors, one of Late Antiquity and the other of the Age of Enlightenment, is probably to be found in their respective treatments of the self. Rousseau gets to the bottom of his own sensibility, trying to uncover the origin of his present disposition or state of mind, which once and for all made him an outsider, a restless *promeneur solitaire* among human beings. Augustine, for his part, split himself up into two *personae*; the present writer, who once and for all has beheld truth, appears as a person quite different from the lost and inquiring young man he writes about. Rousseau ties fiction to subjectivity and the narrator's tender heart, in stark opposition to human society. Augustine, on the other hand, sketches a self which at long last is released from fiction, and a heart which is released from all vain dream images, in eager adherence to divine reality.

Both Rousseau and Augustine portray themselves as readers. As a consequence, they bring up the question of the addressees or recipients of fiction: in what manner does the audience of poetry – the readers or listeners – come to be manipulated or seduced by its evocative power? What is it that makes readers take an interest in, or occasionally even believe in, something they actually know or at least suspect is made up? As far as the modern era is concerned, it seems that in order to make the great game of literature come into force, not only the writers but also the readers have to acquire that "negative capability" which John Keats defined in a famous and often quoted letter from 1817: "I mean *Negative Capability*, that is, when man is capable of being in uncertainties, Mysteries, doubts, without any irritable reaching after fact & reason".[1] It is a similar state of

---

1 Keats 1977, pp. 40f.

mind – an inclination to expose oneself, of one's own accord and clear-sightedly, to the suggestive power of literature – which Keats's precursor among the English Romantics, Samuel Taylor Coleridge, identified as the reader's willingness to temporarily withhold the sceptical inquiries of reason. In the fourteenth chapter of that unruly mixture of philosophical, critical and autobiographical reflexions entitled *Biographia Literaria* (1817), Coleridge tells us about his contribution to the epoch-making *Lyrical Ballads* he had composed with William Wordsworth twenty years earlier: "My endeavours should be directed to persons and characters supernatural, or at least romantic; yet so as to transfer from our inward nature a human interest and a semblance of truth sufficient to procure for these shadows of imagination that willing suspension of disbelief for the moment, which constitutes poetic faith".[1]

In Coleridge's declaration appear three key terms, all of which are present in the critical deliberations from fifteen hundred years earlier that make up the bulk of this book:

- In Late Antiquity, it was not uncommon to think of figurative representation as a series of shadows (in Latin: *umbrae*), much dependent on the source of light provided by – not necessarily human – reality.
- These "shadows" were sometimes related to the image-making faculty of the mind that Classical Antiquity knew as imagination (in Latin: *phantasia* or *imaginatio*).
- According to established Aristotelian tradition, but contrary to expanding Christian thinking, such fabulous formations would be able to radiate "a semblance of truth", in other words, appear probable (*verisimiles*).

To my mind, this verbal and conceptual continuity confirms the idea of a transhistorical dimension characteristic of fictionality, highlighted by scholars such as Pavel or Currie. We must beware, however, of granting an air of timelessness to fiction theory, as if it always dealt with the same phenomenon. That is not the case, however stable certain aspects of fictional works (a narrative scheme, figurative elements, illusions of presence) may seem to be. Coleridge's declaration is in fact peculiar to Romantic poetics, and it was precisely the Romantic revolution at the end of the eighteenth century which positively transferred terms like imagination, invention or narration from rhetoric to literary theory proper. Partly for that reason, Coleridge stands out as one of the first great heralds of modern criticism. In the nineteenth and twentieth centuries, the shadow-play analysed in his *Biographia literaria* has time and again been hailed as an end in itself. Mod-

---

[1] Coleridge 1983, p. 6.

ernity has frequently promoted imagination as the hallmark of human creativity whereby the old poetics of probability has been upgraded to the new and, to a great extent, self-sufficient aesthetics of illusion.

On an academic level, the instruments of fiction theory have been considerably refined since 1817, sometimes as a result of an interplay between disciplines such as narratology, semiotics and philosophy. An impressing number of recent symposia and anthologies testify to this development. Equally important contributions to our knowledge of the nature and function(s) of fiction have lately been made by prominent literary figures such as Carlos Fuentes, Italo Calvino and Mario Vargas Llosa, to mention just a few (apart from the already quoted Eco). They are all dependent on an Argentine prose writer and poet who rose to fame in the post-war period owing to a work called precisely *Ficciones* (*Fictions*, 1944). Moreover, irrespective of their individual characteristics, they all cherish an essentially optimistic view on artistic fiction as the privileged expression of subjective imagination in a society dominated by the rational Enlightenment project and by its positivist offspring during the last century. Fictional representation is frequently regarded as a bold outline of alternative realities. Accordingly, this modern tradition marks the opposite pole to the Platonic dialogues' deprecating exposition of the social and epistemological status of poetry. As Eric A. Havelock points out in his seminal work *Preface to Plato* (1963): Plato, surely influenced by his teacher Socrates, objected to an age-long educational tradition in ancient Greece whereby children were imbued with Homer and with the fables of gods, nymphs and satyrs from their earliest days. In a society where *The Iliad* and *The Odyssey* were supposed to offer a set of valid interpretations of reality, what Havelock calls "a sort of tribal encyclopedia", Socrates – with his alternative plea for a concept of truth based on *theōria*, on solid philosophical arguments – must necessarily be accused of atheism and of seduction of the young.[1] In Plato's dialogues concerning these measures against Socrates, *Apology, Crito* and *Phaedo* (certainly coloured by the pupil's admiration for his former master), it is the philosopher who, in the name of truth, bravely remains upright against, and falls prey to, a state ideology based on damned romancing and lies.

Socrates was executed two thousand four hundred years ago. Yet I have often asked myself if the energetic theoretical thrusts in literature and the Humanities of later times, some of which are cursorily outlined above, really have advanced much beyond the sophisticated critical ideas conceived by Plato, Gorgias and the other philosophers or orators of ancient Athens. However

---

[1] Havelock 1982, pp. 12f., 66.

that may be, it would not be difficult to locate the origin of the 'as if' perspective to classical Hellas, even if antique culture lacked any obvious counterpart to our word fiction, a term that appears in modern European literatures at the end of the Middle Ages.[1] In the subsequent chapters, we will, on the other hand, repeatedly come across the Greek *plasma*, *mimēsis* and *mythos* ('formation', 'imitation' and 'myth' respectively) and the Latin *fabula* ('myth' or 'fable'), *ficta* and *figmenta* ('feigned' things, sometimes with special emphasis on figurative representation). Of course we must be careful, as Christopher Gill has remarked in an essay on Plato, not to let any modern, post-Kantian or Flaubertian concept of fiction – disinterested, dispassionate, self-sufficient – infiltrate our understanding of classical Greek poetics. Ancient critics such as Plato had to make up their minds about altogether different types of artistic representation typical of oral culture: ceremonial or dramatic performances originally prompted by a sympotic environment, aiming at strictly delimited audiences, producing effects on its listeners which could be described in terms of persuasion, seduction or relief.[2]

To sum up, while Western literary fiction demonstrates some remarkably stable characteristics, we should be careful not to mistake our modern concepts of make-believe for the *figmenta* of Late Antiquity. The former are, essentially, based on assumptions that probably antedate the hitherto mentioned Kant or Romanticism, going back to the Early Modern era, a Cartesian belief in our capability of separating (subjective) imagination from (objective) reality or, to put it in more analytic terms, on the notion – postmodern philosophers would say the illusion – of a neutral subject having access to sovereign reason as an ultimate ground for its actions and considerations. This radical distinction between the human mind (*res cogitans*) and nature (*res extensa*), typical of the Gutenberg era, would eventually make it feasible to construe fictionality as potential (or non-actual) states of affairs, for example in Lubomír Doležel's "possible-worlds semantics" launched in reaction to various strands of "mimetic semantics", a theory ultimately based on Leibnizian metaphysics and clearly reminiscent of Coleridge's observation on our "willing suspension of disbelief for the moment".[3] It is true that even premodern criticism could accept certain unique privileges on behalf of poetry versus the 'actual world' or at least others types

---

[1] See Wood 1993, pp. XIII f., and Feeney 1993, p. 231.
[2] Gill 1993; Feeney 1993, pp. 235f.
[3] Doležel 1988, p. 481, and 1998, p. 786. Cf. Marie-Laure Ryan's conclusion to her "semantic typology of fiction" 1991: "We regard a text as fiction when we know its genre, and we know that the genre is governed by the rules of the fictional game. And we enter into this game when our concern for the textual system of reality momentarily displaces our existential concern for the affairs of our own native system", pp. 574f.

of discourse – as is patent from ancient theories of 'poetic licence' or the medieval popularity of courtly romances – but they were exceptions to the general rule, hard to conceptualize and constantly under attack.

The culture of the Middle Ages exhibits quite a few examples of this hardcore attitude. In the Thomism which dominated High Medieval philosophy, for instance, all scientific rationality was subordinate to the Church and to theology. Ultimately, it was this institution and this discipline which decided what was real and what was permitted to say or think, sometimes in the light of Biblical sentences such as in John 18.36: "My kingdom is not of this world."[1] Nature was certainly considered both real and dynamic, according to the newly discovered Aristotelian metaphysics, but in the end it was dependent on an ultimate reality located somewhere else. From this perspective, human knowledge was, basically, a matter of logic (which in turn involved disciplines such as physics, ethics, metaphysics or politics), with a conspicuously restricted space for imaginative literature or fiction, theoretically squeezed, as it were, between dialectic (logic) and revelation, frequently associated with dangerous temptations, false doctrines or the play of demons.

In the second book, *De tempore et aevo*, 'On Time and the Eternal', from *Liber decem capitulorum* (*Book of Ten Chapters*), the French schoolmaster and poet Marbode (or Marbodius), elected Bishop of Rennes in 1096, would prefer to have the immoral works of poets banished from men's souls. In an attack on contemporary education, he speaks of the schoolmaster who 'teaches what the poets have feigned and which should be forgotten', *dediscenda docens quae confinxere poetae:* the fornication of Jove, the adventures of Mars and the like.[2] Contemporary students were indoctrinated for no acceptable reason at all by stupid fictions; now they should be deprogrammed as soon as possible. We should perhaps be wary of ascribing this stern rejection of imaginative poetry to Marbode himself, since he was one of the first Western European writers who took advantage of fictional devices in their work.[3] All the same, it seems beyond doubt that in the view of this High Medieval archdeacon and schoolmaster, fiction is something completely different from the sovereign and liberating, creative games of Kant or Coleridge.

As a matter of fact, in Marbode, as in many other medieval condemnations of 'what the poets have feigned', it is difficult not to discern an echo from the

---

[1] The Holy Bible is rendered in the new English Standard Version, 2001.
[2] *PL* 171.1695c. Here and throughout this book I refer to J.P. Migne's famous series 1844–55, *Patrologiae cursus completus. Series latina*, using the short form *PL* followed by volume and column numbers.
[3] Cf. Verbaal 2014, p. 194.

fierce attacks on fiction of the early Christian apologists or of the Late Antique ascetics. Ultimately, of course, their reaction can be derived from Plato's stern rejections of contemporary Athenian habits of teaching literature in that great dialogue called *The Republic*. Consequently, we had better start our survey in ancient Greece.

2 Fictionality: Historical Circumstances

The Ancient Quarrel (Greece)

Any approach to ancient literary criticism, even if it restricts itself to the late Roman Empire, must – if only *en passant* – take notice of its beginnings in archaic and classical Hellas. Almost all innovative efforts in ancient poetics stem from Greek and Hellenistic culture. It was left to the Romans to Latinize and accommodate them to the best of their ability, as if the famous distinction between artful Greece and down-to-earth Rome made by the dead Anchises in Virgil's (70–19 BCE) *Aeneid* would also apply to the field of fiction theory: "Others", that is the Greeks, may handle the "bronzes that breathe in more lifelike and gentler / ways", and bring out living faces from the marble, *excudent alii spirantia mollius aera, / (credo equidem), vivos ducent de marmore voltus*, while the task of the future Romans was to make laws and rule the nations on earth (6.847–53).[1]

In fact, these splendid lines are exaggeratedly modest. The speaker's mighty descendants from the Tiber river banks were after all not *that* insensible to the enticements of the Muses. We might still, twenty centuries later, imagine that we feel the pulse or watch the faces of Anchises and his son, heroes of that supreme fiction called the *Aeneid*. Another work from the Roman Golden Age, Ovid's *Metamorphoses*, became for centuries to come the very epitome of fiction. Not even such a Roman specialty as legal speech escaped elements of fiction (as we have seen in Quintilian), and it was precisely here, in classical Latin literature and rhetoric, that the Late Antique writers of the West would find their immediate points of departure. But then again, taking the long view, Western fiction theory is as old as Western literature and stems from archaic Hellas.

A place of honour in this context is held by the Greek didactic poet Hesiod, supposedly active around 700 BCE. In a suggestive and influential study, the German classical philologist Wolfgang Rösler discerns four phases of the emergence of the concept of fiction in ancient Greece. His scheme is approximate, and in the following presentation I simplify it even further:[2]

- In archaic Greek culture, poetry was fundamentally considered on a par with any historical exposition. The oral poet, or rather the 'singer', *aoidos*, was inspired by the Muses, and the tradition of genealogical tables, legends

---

[1] The *Aeneid* is given in Latin according to H.R. Fairclough's Loeb edition, Virgil 1998 and 2000, while I use F. Ahl's volume 2007 for the English translations.
[2] Rösler 1980, pp. 307f.

and myths, firmly identified with the Homeric epics, was basically true. In this early phase, it was impossible to make any distinction between poetry, history or philosophy. Practically all sources that we know of are framed in verse. We are dealing with a type of oral poetry responsible for a culture's knowledge of its own past. Another German scholar in Greek literature, Richard Kannicht, speaks of "the original primacy of poetry" in this context and emphasizes – following Eric A. Havelock – its public, social and oral character.[1] Margalit Finkelberg, who has published a fine monograph on the birth of literary fiction in ancient Greece, applies the concept of "poetics of truth" to this archaic understanding of a poetry in the service of collective memory. The poet was an inspired seer, singing at the request of the Muses who, in their turn, were considered completely reliable eye-witnesses of events from the distant past, such as the Trojan war.[2] It was on the basis of such notions that Homer could invoke the Muses at the beginning of the so-called catalogue of ships from the second song of *The Iliad:* "for ye are goddesses and / are at hand and know all things, whereas we hear but a / rumour and know not anything" (2.485–87).[3] The Muses are called upon because the poet needs factual information about the Greek host's resources on the eve of the decisive battle of Troy. They are daughters of Mnemosyne, the goddess of Memory; accordingly, they embody the different possibilities of song or speech to register truth, *alētheia*, a word which possibly (its etymology is disputed) is derived from the negative prefix *a* together with *lēthē*, translatable into rather ungainly but straightforward English as "unforgetfulness".[4] Within this cultural framework, the earliest archaic poets would sing, remember and communicate authentic truth – cancel oblivion – in the same breath.

If poetry nevertheless could deviate from the truth, it was because the Muses sometimes withheld information, as Hesiod intimates at the beginning of his *Theogony*. This passage contains the earliest (as far as is known) and – if we are to believe Denis Feeney – in many ways the most

---

[1] Kannicht 1988, pp. 2f., a translation into English and an update of the author's important paper "'Der alte Streit zwischen Philosophie und Dichtung'. Grundzüge der griechischen Literaturauffassung" from 1980 (reprinted 1996).
[2] Finkelberg 1998, pp. 18–33.
[3] I follow A.T. Murray's Loeb translation of *The Iliad* I–II, Homer 1924–25.
[4] Pratt 1993, pp. 13, 17–22. The most famous but also the most disputed contributions to the debate on the significance of *alētheia* are surely Martin Heidegger's bold efforts with concepts such as "Unverborgenheit", "Entbergung" or "Entborgenheit" in *Sein und Zeit* (*Being and Time*, 1927) and later writings. For a summary, see Inwood 1999, pp. 13f.

powerful presentation of fictional discourse in Western literature: "We know how to say many false things / similar to genuine ones; but we know, when we wish, / how to proclaim true things." (26–28)¹ These famous statements have, of course, been the cause of much critical controversy. The first of them tells us that even lies, *pseudea*, can look like reality or truth, *etymoisin homoia*. It describes, according to Kannicht, the specifically poetic characteristics of the epic *aoidē* (song or myth): the fact that its truth is established poetically, or, in modern terms, "the fictionality of its truth".² The second assertion emphasizes, as an alternative, truth straight out, *alētheia*. In this way, Hesiod presents the first suggestion of what Plato, much later, in *The Republic*, would call "a quarrel between philosophy and poetry", which had been going on "from of old" (607b).³

- Finkelberg, for her part, calls attention to the closeness of Hesiod's lines to the passage in *The Odyssey* where the homecoming hero speaks to his wife without having yet revealed his true identity. He pretends that his name is Aethon and that he has received Odysseus in his house, in A.T. Murray's translation (19.203): "He spoke, and made the many falsehoods of his tale seem like the truth".⁴ In the original Greek, the passages from *The Odyssey* and *The Theogony* are next to identical in wording, a conformity which makes Finkelberg suspect a critical allusion to the former in the latter. Thus when the traditionalist Hesiod spoke of "many false things as / though they were true", he conceivably made a covert attack on the new poetics which recently had begun to crystallize in the Homeric epics. There, the "possible" – the plausible and functional lie – had appeared as a new discursive category in addition to true speech.⁵ To Hesiod's dismay, then, the age-old poetics of truth, linked to the Muses, based on catalogues and parataxis in ceremonial contexts, was already being challenged by the circumstantial but none the less ingeniously coherent and cleverly composed *Iliad* and *Odyssey*, possibly in connection with the encoding of these epics

---

1 Feeney 1991, pp. 12f.
2 Kannicht 1988, p. 16.
3 All my quotations from *The Republic* are taken from P. Shorey's Loeb edition, Plato 1937–42. This "quarrel" has attracted a good deal of attention in recent literary research. For a survey centred on Plato and Aristotle, se Barfield 2011, Chapters 1 and 2.
4 For all quotations from *The Odyssey*, I use A.T. Murray's Loeb edition, Homer 1919.
5 Finkelberg 1998, p. 149. Cf. *The Theogony*, 27: *idmen pseudea polla legein etymoisin homoia*, with *The Odyssey*, 19.302: *ske pseudea polla legōn etymoisin homoia*. For her reading of these crucial passages, Finkelberg relies to a great extent on the remarks of Bowie concerning Homer and Hesiod, 1993, pp. 8–23.

in the new medium of writing, which was slowly to supersede the monopoly of the voice in ancient Greek culture after the eighth century.

Both of these early phases in the history of Greek literature belong to the archaic era. As a matter of fact, they should probably be understood as complementary and entangled in each other, engaged in a common shift of emphasis, rather than two strictly separate periods.[1] It could even be argued that the conception of poetry as an inspired version of *alētheia*, pure and untainted truth, should be taken as a regulative principle, activated as required in, for example, the Homeric epics, rather than a general characteristic of some original phase in literary history. Such a pragmatic view, in any case, does justice to the scholars of recent years who have expressed doubts about archaic Greece allegedly clinging to literature's task as a mouthpiece of truth. These critics have, for their part, observed an ancient susceptibility to fiction or fictionality, to verbal display or rhetoric, already noticeable in the earliest Greek poets and critical reactions known to us. In a study of lying and poetry from Homer to Pindar, Louise H. Pratt even asks if at this early stage fiction could not be experienced as an efficient and entertaining way of recording precisely past events. Perhaps untruth could fulfil the task of truth?[2] Pratt's questions seem to outline a suggestive interpretation of Hesiod's sententious *Theogony* 26–28, just as her book registers an impressive range of fictional strategies in archaic culture – of poetry as an artistic activity, *technē*, rather than inspired speech – ever since the appearance of the adaptable storyteller Odysseus and the divine jester of the Homeric Hymn to Hermes.

The two final phases of the emergence of the concept of fiction are easier to define and delimit. They occur (according to Rösler's scheme) in the sixth and fifth centuries BCE, which saw the breakthrough of drama, prose and rhetoric in Greek culture, that is, the Golden Age of classical Athens:

- The poets may make mistakes or be guilty of lying, since they fail in responsibility. In the introduction to his *Metaphysics*, Aristotle quotes some words from the well-known statesman (and poet) Solon from Athens, active around and after 600 BCE: "poets tell many a lie" (983a), *polla pseudontai aoidoi*. This simple proverbial saying was to turn into a formula, repeated again and again in Western literary criticism. In its Latin version, *mendacia poeta-*

---

[1] Glenn Most reminds us that, firstly, the chronology of both Homer and Hesiod is highly uncertain, and, secondly, we are dealing with "Homeric and Hesiodic" long-lived oral poetic traditions which "must have co-existed and influenced one another for many generations before culminating in the written poems we possess", Hesiod 2006, pp. XXIV f.

[2] Pratt 1993, p. 4.

rum, it would regularly infect debates on fiction well into the Early Modern Age.
– The poets sometimes *prefer* the stronger effect to the less spectacular truth.

That brings us to the critical debate on Homer in sixth and fifth-century Greece. It was initiated by Xenophanes of Colophon (d. ca. 475 BCE), who found fault with the poet's anthropomorphic interpretation of the gods, or at least with the propagation and strong influence of this vision of the gods in Greek culture. According to his first elegiac fragment, good banquets should not be disturbed by songs about the quarrels of giants or of centaurs: nothing but fictions, *plasmata*, an unnecessary legacy from an age long past.[1]

In compliance with Xenophanes' remarks, the Ionian natural philosophers established their allegorical interpretation of Homer's works. Theagenes of Rhegium (of whom nothing has been preserved) and his followers deciphered the belligerent gods of *The Iliad* and *The Odyssey* as antagonistic natural elements.[2] It is not until now, during the classic era in the history of Hellas, when the Greeks were slowly changing into readers and texts began to be reproduced on a large scale, that the vocal and sympotic performance of poetry was supplemented and finally superseded by writing, studies, and systematic judgment. As Andrew Ford recently observed in his great work on the origin of Western literary criticism: the singers became makers of texts. Their performance was split into writing (*per se*) and reading (*per se*). Their context-bound songs were changed into self-contained verbal artefacts, more or less solid textual constructions, subjected to grammatical and technical analysis. Consequently, fictional representation gained in significance, an overall development which also embraced the rhetoric that flourished in the new Greek city states, by later writers sometimes labelled the First Sophistic. In this classical culture, Ford remarks, the composition or "making" of songs, *poiēsis*, was better valued than sympotic or public performance, and the verbal skills of their "maker" – the poet – eclipsed other qualities such as wisdom, veracity or tactfulness, all traditionally expected from the *aoidos* of old.[3]

The sophist Gorgias from Sicily (d. ca. 380 BCE) still represented an essentially oral culture, but he laid heavy stress on the unreliability of language

---

1 Andrew Ford cites Xenophanes' first fragment, placing it in the context of archaic sympotic culture, 2002, pp. 46–66.
2 Theagenes was probably active as a grammarian during the late sixth century BCE. Much later, it was an (admittedly vague) reference by Porphyry that would secure his position as the front figure of Homeric allegoresis. See Lamberton 1986, p. 32, and Ford 2002, pp. 68–80.
3 Ford 2002, pp. 1–22, 131f.

and on literature's illusive devices. He liberated the spoken word or *logos* from its metaphysical correspondence with a higher "reality", observes Charles P. Segal, so that it could henceforth be treated as an "art" in its own right, *technē*, and be exploited in the interest of persuasion, *peithō*, without any necessary connection to Being.[1] Finkelberg has attached great importance to the challenging theses of this sophist: "With Gorgias, for the first time fiction is legitimized as an autonomous sphere which cannot be evaluated by using ordinary standards of 'truth' and 'falsehood'."[2] Such a bold concept of fiction was, however, doomed to remain controversial. Accordingly, the old quarrel between philosophy and poetry burst forth with hitherto unknown force. Both Plato's and Aristotle's cognitive theses can, to some extent, be understood as philosophy's efforts to come to grips with a Gorgian, performative concept of discourse. They both struggled to re-establish, each in his own way, a safe connection between *logos* or *nomos* (human speech and thinking, laws and customs) on the one hand, and *physis* or natural reality on the other, in which the latter ought to regulate the former. They succeeded so well, and they were so overwhelmingly effective in their arguments, remarks the French philosopher Barbara Cassin, that we still have difficulty in thinking beyond or against them.[3]

Throughout his dialogues, above all in *The Republic* (as we shall soon see), Plato adopted a sceptical attitude to the lies of the poets. His preferred term in this context, *pseudos*, also occurs in Gorgias' rhetorical work *Encomium of Helen*, where the author registers different makers or producers of false speech, *pseudēs logos* (11). In the *Encomium*, however, this concept does not denote anything insincere or mendacious but rather what we would call a performative act, the outcome of a 'plastic' activity: fiction or *plasma* (in Kathleen Freeman's translation: "persuasions by means of fictions").[4] That is how Gorgias articulates the sophistic conviction about language's capacity for controlling or manipulating the human mind, known as *psychagōgia*, a philosophical project which both Plato and Aristotle would successfully refute, each in his own way. Plato demolished Gorgias' sophistry by means of a restoration, as ingenious as it was conservative, of the Eleatic early fifth-century philosopher Parmenides' distinction between appearance and reality: between *doxa* (people's shifting and unstable 'opinions') and *alētheia*, immutable truth. This powerful dualism paved the way for Plato's (or for his fictional spokesman Socrates') reflections on the lies of the poets in *The Republic* as well as in his other dialogues. Aristotle, too, took up the chal-

---

1 Segal 1962, p. 110.
2 Finkelberg 1998, p. 177.
3 Cassin 1986, pp. 8f.
4 Gorgias' *Encomium of Helen* is included in H. Diels and W. Kranz 1956, trans. K. Freeman 1948.

lenge from Gorgias. Setting out from the new cultural conditions of the fourth century, he followed his teacher and – most conspicuously, perhaps, in his treatise *On Interpretation* – opposed the sophists' radical version of the unstable relationship between words and things. More specifically, but also more importantly in this context, he established a new concept of fiction for poetry's account, based on the principle of *mimēsis*, that is, imitation.

Plato had adopted, developed and sharpened the rationalistic arguments against Homer. His formidable attack on the fictions of poetry sometimes recalls Aristophanes' jest at the indecent behaviour of the gods in comedies such as *The Clouds*, although the philosopher seldom yielded to jokes in this context. On the contrary, art was a very serious business in the eyes of Plato. He did not allow himself to underestimate its psychological and social effects, hence his persistently sceptical attitude. According to the author of *The Republic*, the poet still had, at least in principle, an incontrovertible civic responsibility, which also implied a basic measure of fidelity to "truth", *alētheia*, a concept which Socrates frequently advances as a norm for poetry at the end of the dialogue (607c–608a). The same interlocutor, however, realizes that this norm was seldom respected by the poets, who rather aimed at arousing delight and pain, *hēdonē kai lypē*, in their audience (607a). Commonly, they did not even know what they were talking about. As a consequence, if the poets did not exclusively devote themselves to divine hymns or tributes to good men, they had to be banished from Plato's ideal state.

Notwithstanding this notorious expulsion of the poets, the debate for or against their art's *raison d'être* goes on throughout the dialogue in a truly Socratic manner. The Athenian education of the guardians of the state ought to include histories or "tales", sometimes of a true nature, *alēthes*, and at other times lies, *pseudos*, Socrates observes at the end of Book II. This seems to be a remarkable concession to the use of poetry in the city schools. Socrates sounds surprisingly permissive: quite early in the life of the future guardians, when they are still small children, they should be allowed to enjoy fables or *mythoi*, mostly invented but nevertheless containing a grain of truth (376e–377a). Such passages from *The Republic* stand out as a memento for all scholars wanting to deprive Plato of a genuine engagement in the matter of poetics. Immediately afterwards, however, Socrates advances serious cautions against these fables, not because they convey a lie (which they do only partially) but because "the lie is not a pretty one", *mē kalōs pseudētai* (377d). Thus fiction, the special domain of Homer, Hesiod and the poets, appeared as a hazardous item on the curriculum of the schools: a strange set of improper and incredible stories of the passionate gods, dangerously fraught with quarrel and conflict. Socrates is aware of the fact that lately such tales have been interpreted as "allegories", *hyponoiai*, but subtleties like these tend to elude young people's comprehension (378d). And it is precisely the young boys of Athens, the future guardians of the state, that represent the chief target group of his educational zealotry.

Furthermore, Socrates outlines a rudimentary theory of fiction when he separates actual lies, residing within ourselves and depending upon our ignorance, from their verbal reproduction, "the falsehood in *words*", *logois pseudos* (382b–c). The latter seems harmless at first sight and, in principle at least, it should be able to serve a useful purpose (for the state). Socrates gives an example. When we are ignorant about certain matters of Antiquity, are we not licensed to reconstruct them on our own authority, which amounts to "likening the false to the true as far as we may and so make it edifying"? Here, Socrates surely has the fictions of the poets in mind, frequently employed by the schoolmasters, to all appearances a valid pedagogy. Once again, he seems to make a space for fictional discourse within his educational programme. Well-founded didactic considerations are one thing, however, the Homeric type of tales – false stories of deceitful gods – quite another; the latter sadly lack any divine (or social) legitimacy. "Then there is no lying poet in God", concludes Socrates with epigrammatic authority, *poiētēs men ara pseudēs en theōi ouk eni* (382d). Accordingly, Homer seems inexorably useless for all instructive or edifying purposes in contemporary Athens. The philosopher's God neither needs nor wants him.

These passages from *The Republic* elucidate the difference between Socrates' new philosophical religiosity and the nature of the archaic pantheon. The Homeric gods – human-like, albeit larger than life – certainly had many reasons, in matters of love and war, to indulge in trickery and feigning. From the Attic philosopher's point of view, on the other hand, lying gods represent not only a serious moral flaw but, in the end, a logical self-contradiction. The young boys and future guardians of the state must be infused with respect for religion in order to be "god-fearing men and god-like in so far as that is possible for humanity" (383c), and for this purpose they should not be fed with tales of wondrous metamorphoses or led to suspect Zeus, Apollo and their fellow Olympians of fraudulent proceedings. Eight centuries later, the young Augustine, in the service of another god, would take the Athenian street reformer at his word and represent Divine Being in the sharpest possible contrast to all kinds of fictionality.

In *The Republic*, aesthetics generally, as Robert Lamberton remarks, was subordinated to morals.[1] Nevertheless, Plato would, somewhat paradoxically, play a key role in the development of our Western concept of fiction, not only by virtue of the superb mythic tales with which he interspersed his own dia-

---

[1] Lamberton 1986, p. 21.

logues. His notion of "lies" which sometimes may conceal "truth", his identification of poetry with *mimēsis* and his sharp distinction between this suspect activity, sadly cut off from truth, and crystal clear dialectic analysis, resulted, *malgré lui* or as an extension of his arguments, in a new sense of autonomy conferred on imaginative literature. To recall Rösler's survey, only one last step had to be taken in this process before the archaic view of poetry's essential subservience to truth was to collapse. "When poetry comes to serve other ends than historiography or physics, then poetic 'untruth' is no longer a lie but gains legitimacy."[1]

This insight was first articulated on a theoretical level in Aristotle's *Poetics*. With that, the initiative in the entangled issue of fiction had passed from the archaic poets' and philosophers' frame of reference through Plato's theocratic and metaphysical criticism to the Stagyrite's formalized and genre-oriented poetics. The crucial prerequisite of this epoch-making step in the "ancient quarrel" was probably a more flexible criterion of truth in Aristotle. The revered master Plato's metaphysical *alētheia*, always one and the same, was qualified by a continuing hermeneutic activity in the philosophy of his pupil, involving empirical observation and even rhetorical persuasion. Not until now, with Aristotle, do we encounter a concept of fiction which, however distantly, prefigures our own.

The philosopher develops this concept in at least four crucial chapters of his *Poetics*, all reliant on his conviction of the natural character of imitation. In the fourth chapter, he emphasizes the literary work's interest for its own sake, independent of its model in reality (1448b). Secondly, in Chapter IX, he makes a distinction between historical writing, which sticks to facts, and poetry, which outlines not a factual but a possible reality, "the *kinds* of things that might occur", *hoia an genoito*, yet in view of what was "possible in terms of probability or necessity".[2] For that reason, poetry is "more philosophical and more elevated" than history. The former tends to express "the universal", *ta katholou*, rather than the "particulars" of the latter (1451a–b).

Thirdly, Aristotle returns to this distinction between historiography and poetry from the ninth chapter of *The Poetics* at the end of his work, in Chapter XXV, where he explains that the poet's task is not reduced to the imitation of "the kind of things which were or are the case"; he could also represent "the kind of things that people say and think" or, last but not least, "the kind of things that ought to be the case". All these categories of possible subjects for the art of poetry are

---

1 Rösler 1980, p. 308.
2 I quote the *Poetics* – the Greek original as well as S. Halliwell's translation – from volume 199 in the Loeb Classical Library, Aristotle 1995.

said to be "conveyed in a diction which includes loan words, metaphors, and many stylistic abnormalities: we allow poets these" (1460b).

Such generous concessions to the poets entitle them to start from an event which is known to us (e.g. the Trojan War) in order to make us, the readers or listeners, proceed to something unknown, something that never happened. Aristotle finds, finally, his supreme example of this procedure, recalled in Chapter XXIV, in Homer. The author of *The Iliad* and *The Odyssey* "has taught other poets the right way to purvey falsehoods: that is, by false inference [*paralogismos*]. When the existence or occurrence of *b* follows from that of *a*, people suppose that, if *b* is the case, *a* too must exist or be occurrent; but this is false. So, if the antecedent is false, but were it true some further fact would necessarily exist or occur, the poet should supply the latter: because it knows the truth of the consequent, our mind falsely infers the truth of the antecedent too." (1460a)

This excerpt shows what Aristotle had learnt from Gorgias and Sophistic rhetoric, but the *pseudē* which he is referring to should always proceed from something already known, from real life or history. Furthermore, they are based on *mimēsis*, and, consequently, they should seem probable. This implies that the literary work can easily conflict with reality, as long as it is credible. The poet is entitled to deviate from his model if he knows "the right way to purvey falsehoods", *pseudē legein hōs dei*, for example in order to achieve a certain effect, for the sake of common opinion or inner logic, or in the interest of artistic totality, context or language; that is, in view of everything that Latin tradition would later associate with the poets' privileged 'freedom', the *licentia poetica* vital to Ovid and others. In this manner, the concept of fiction in Aristotelian poetics, observes the North American scholar Wesley Trimpi, came to hold an intermediary position between, on the one hand, the universal claims of philosophical syllogisms and, on the other, historiography's facts as well as rhetoric's hypothetical legal cases and probable deductions, *enthymēmata*, in short, between general purport and actual or invented account.[1]

For Plato, poetry had still been obliged to convey truth, a vocation which, as a rule, it betrayed. For Aristotle, poetry implied a special kind of verbal representation, another type of discourse than the philosophical or the historical, dependent neither on the syllogisms of the former nor on the matter-of-fact accounts of the latter but relying on imitation and internal structure, or more exactly, in Finkelberg's words, a "privileging of the illusionist representation".[2]

---

[1] For an exhaustive survey, with special regard to the roots of ancient fiction theory in classical philosophy and rhetoric, see Trimpi 1971, pp. 1–78 (on *The Poetics*, pp. 43–55).
[2] Finkelberg 2014, p. 162. Finkelberg is anxious to highlight both Plato's and Aristotle's understanding of poetry, "first and foremost tragedy and Homer", as "the art of mimesis, or represen-

It was exempt from the duty to provide impartial information, and it was established for emotional and therapeutic as well as cognitive purposes. Its particular art, *technē*, required a particular type of judgment, based on a particular (what Hellenistic culture would soon call a critical) expertise. To recall an observation made by Ford, the Greek word corresponding to our "fiction" is not after all the old *plasma*, which for Xenophanes had been so difficult to tell from lying, nor is it (I would like to add) Platonic *pseudos*, but quite simply Aristotle's *mimēsis*.[1]

To sum up this concluding phase of the debate on fiction in classical Greece, the fruitful concept of *mimēsis* had in fact been established by Plato himself, in his polemic against poetry's claims to veracity. One generation later, nevertheless, Aristotle treated it in a positive key. To the author of *The Republic*, poetry was a religiously minded celebration at best, but morally corrupt sensation-mongering at worst, only occasionally in touch with true reality. To his follower, poetry was capable of moulding an alternative reality, a particular kind of truth, irreducible to common experience. The *mimēsis* of the former scanned the surfaces of things at random, while the same activity, in the view of the latter, generalized or transformed life's circumstances to a universal level. With that, the old quarrel could finally be settled – only for the time being, to be sure, but with long-lasting consequences for Western culture. A considerable place for poetry had been secured within the confines of philosophy.

The Fictional Contract (Rome)

The old Greek advancements in fiction theory during archaic and classical times were followed by interesting critical achievements in Hellenistic culture, characterized by a mixture of Platonic and Peripatetic traditions as well as a wide range of new philosophical schools, first and foremost the Stoics. This development would colour the Roman reception of Greek culture. An orator such as Cicero or a didactic poet such as Lucretius, who were deeply influenced by Stoic and Epicurean philosophy respectively, are good examples. I shall come back to each of them, but for illustrative purposes I would like to dwell on a somewhat later poet, Ovid (43 BCE – 17/18 CE). That is because his work so brilliantly invalidates a still rather common view of the premodern Western history of the concept of fiction, according to which it lay fallow between Greek Antiquity and the

---

tation (by no means imitation), of reality, whose final product is a plausible illusion, a reality *sui generis*", p. 158.
1 Ford 2002, p. 231.

Italian Renaissance, an extended period of sixteen hundred years dominated by realistically minded Romans, illiterate Germanic tribes and pious institutions such as the Church and the monasteries.¹

Roman culture drew its legitimacy from a set of legendary stories, first and foremost the tale of Aeneas and the Trojan origins of the Roman Empire, encoded in both historical and literary works, most famously the *Aeneid*. The ancient Romans certainly did not conceive of these legends in terms of fiction but as a sequence of reliable tales about their own unique history, shaped and supervised by the gods. Nevertheless, quite a few sophisticated Roman readers were undoubtedly aware of the widely divergent treatment of things long past by different authors or, more importantly, in different genres; moreover, the strong emphasis in Roman rhetoric on the concept of *enargeia* or *evidentia*, a sense of presence induced by eloquent or poetic discourse, resulted in a rich plethora of imaginary scenarios and games of evocative make-believe.² Poets had their specific manner of telling the old stories, and their habitual ways of dealing with the gods (more or less in Homer's mode) were not taken for granted. This is apparent both from critical spirits such as Lucretius, the author of *De rerum natura* (*The Nature of Things*), for whom the gods represented supreme and complete alterity, with nothing whatsoever in common with human beings (5.146–49), and from Ovid, the author of the *Metamorphoses*.

This work in fifteen books from the years around the birth of Christ reflects Ovid's and his countrymen's untiring interest in origins – in the provenance of themselves, of animals and of natural phenomena. A considerable part of Roman literature is dedicated to etiology, inquiries into the causes of things, but no one treated this matter with such epic and imaginative grandeur as Ovid. He framed his narrative scenes in a pathetic mode, with a vibrant sensual force, in order to confer a semblance of credibility on these old tales of fabulous changes. Ancient art and literature, Philip Hardie remarks, had long investigated the problems of visual illusion and verbal fictionality, but Ovid excels by means of his persistent treatment of these questions in his narrative art. The German Ro-

---

1 Cf. Iser 1990, p. 939.
2 For a survey of the strong illusionism in Roman rhetoric and literary theory, involving imagination and centred on devices such as *demonstratio* and *illustratio*, see Vogt-Spira's article 2011, particularly its concluding section on Roman literature's "fictional licence", pp. 30–33. Even if Philip Hardie, for his part, makes a distinction between presence/illusion and fictionality (or between the "ontological moment" and the "epistemological moment" of Ovidian poetics), he immediately concedes that "these two are inextricably connected", 2002, p. 6. On *enargeia* and *evidentia*, see Manieri 1998, pp. 97–154, 173–92.

manist Karlheinz Stierle even goes so far as to label him "the true originator of the European concept of fiction".[1]

The storytellers to whom Ovid lends his voice in the *Metamorphoses* explicitly stress the marvellous nature of the work's sequence of changes. He can even make them argue for or against the truth-value of these strange events. When the river god Achelous has finished entertaining his audience with the story of the drowned Perimele's change into an island, he is immediately corrected by the King of the Lapiths, Ixion's son Pirithoüs (8.611–19):[2]

> 611 Amnis ab his tacuit. factum mirabile cunctos
> moverat: inridet credentes, utque deorum
> spretor erat mentisque ferox, Ixione natus
> "ficta refers nimiumque putas, Acheloe, potentes
> 615 esse deos," dixit, "si dant adimuntque figuras."
> obstipuere omnes nec talia dicta probarunt,
> ante omnesque Lelex animo maturus et aevo,
> sic ait: "inmensa est finemque potentia caeli
> non habet, et quicquid superi voluere, peractum est,
> […]"

> With these words the river was silent. The story of the miracle had moved the hearts of all. But one mocked at their credulity, a scoffer at the gods, one reckless in spirit, Ixion's son, Pirithoüs. "These are but fairy-tales [*ficta*] you tell, Acheloüs," he said, "and you concede too much power to the gods, if they give and take away the forms of things." All the rest were shocked and disapproved such words, and especially Lelex, ripe both in mind and years, who replied: "The power of heaven is indeed immeasurable and has no bounds; and whatever the gods decree is done. […]"

Ovid not only creates storytellers in the *Metamorphoses* but also provides them with fictional audiences, at this point represented by Theseus in the company of friends and nymphs. They are overwhelmed by the technical brilliance of Achelous' story and are "moved" by the transformation of Perimele. Perhaps as a consequence of this empathy, they indignantly reject Pirithoüs' reference to *ficta* (8.614) in this context; what might seem a miracle to human beings, their spokesman Lelex explains, is no match for the gods. The marvellous metamorphoses are due to the gods' supernatural power. Lelex' argument must be understood in the light of Roman religion with its manifestations in contemporary imperial cults (the whole work ends, to be sure, with Caesar's transformation into a god,

---

[1] Hardie 2001, p. 147; Stierle 2001, p. 424.
[2] Unless otherwise noted, I quote both the Latin original and the English translation of Ovid's *Metamorphoses* from F.J. Miller's Loeb edition 1971.

15.745–870), and it was certainly meant to be taken seriously. We cannot know the personal attitude of Ovid to Lelex' god-fearing speech, but in poetry's own language it certainly invalidates Plato's overall condemnation of the lies of the poets; the story of Perimele's metamorphosis – told by a river god! – seems perfectly legitimate. In a more specific sense, Lelex' plea refutes Socrates' philosophical denunciation of the widespread tales about the changes and "shape-shifting" of the gods, known to us from the second book of *The Republic* (383a).

Our uncertainty about Ovid's own opinion on the matter hardly needs to embarrass us. After all, the Ovid to which we have access is the sum of his poetic works, and in the major part of this oeuvre it is possible to discern a distinct voice, a fictional role or *persona*, which constantly plays hide-and-seek with his listeners or readers. For this reason, not even the following declaration permits us to draw any far-reaching conclusions about the poet's position in the "ancient quarrel" between philosophy and poetry. I am referring to the opening of *Ars amandi*, written at the time of the birth of Christ, translated into English by J.H. Mozley under the title *The Art of Love* (1.25–30):[1]

25   Non ego, Phoebe, datas a te mihi mentiar artes,
       nec nos aëriae voce monemur avis,
     nec mihi sunt visae Clio Cliusque sorores
       servanti pecudes vallibus, Ascra, tuis:
     usus opus movet hoc: vati parete perito;
30   vera canam: coeptis, mater Amoris, ades!

> I will not falsely claim that my art is thy gift, O Phoebus, nor am I prompted by the voice of a bird of the air, neither did Clio and Clio's sisters appear to me while I kept flocks in thy vale, O Ascra: experience inspires this work: give ear to an experienced bard; true will be my song: favour my enterprise, O mother of Love.

These lines reject, in turn, poetic inspiration (with Apollo as its origin), the prevailing Roman auspices (the ancient custom of detecting signs by observations of the birds in the sky) and the specifically epic creativity which during Antiquity was considered to spring from the Muses (in Hellenistic times it was commonly assigned to Clio, the protectress of historiography). In other words, *The Art of Love* shall exhibit neither any lyrics, nor any oracular gnomes or epic poetry, but it will give us didactic verse, a genre which was thought to have originated with Hesiod from the town of Ascra. Consequently, the listeners or readers are to expect a work based on *usus*, real life. The speaker is no raving singer but a poet

---

[1] All quotes from *Ars amandi* are from J.H. Mozley's Loeb edition, revised by G.P. Goold, *The Art of Love, and Other Poems* 1985.

who knows what he is talking about by virtue of practical experience, *peritia*. This kind of criticism directed against fiction in the name of initiated knowledge or truth would in due time be exploited by the Christian Biblical epic poets, but in their work – as we shall see – the distance between authorial voice and poetical *persona* will be diminished or even obliterated.[1] Ovid still acted within the boundaries of classical culture, where the very criticism of fiction might, in a work of poetry, be completely fictional. In this excerpt from *The Art of Love*, for example, the poet seems to inculcate the veracity of his words, but he might just as well present us with a parody on the widespread exordial topic of *vera canam* (by which authors used to assure their audiences about the truth-value of the work they were about to read or listen to). We must, as a rule, be cautious about taking this Augustan poet at face value. Precisely his assurances of being honest or veracious might very well be fictional.

That is why it is so difficult to assess Ovid's frequent exercises in the criticism of myths and tales. Is it serious, or is it meant as a joke, or is it both: an instance of a metafictional *serio ludere* mode? When his alter ego of *Amores*, in the shape of an excited lover, dreams of the winged sandals of Perseus, which would permit him to reach his girl-friend as quickly as possible, he suddenly comes to a halt (in his discourse and on his way), realizing that "the wonders whereof I speak are false tales of olden bards; no day e'er brought them forth, and no day will" (3.6.17–18), *prodigiosa loquor veterum mendacia vatum; / nec tulit haec umquam nec feret ulla dies.*[2] The wording of the original is slightly stronger than "false tales"; it focuses on the 'prodigious lies' of the poets or prophets of old. If the blatant contrast between the lover's somewhat trifling predicament and his conjuring up of a host of mythological figures easily leads us to suspect parodical intentions here, it might be more difficult to assess a similar passage in Ovid's versified religious festive calendar *Fasti*. There, in a rather exalted invocation of Vesta, the poet confesses that – in spite of his ecstatic veneration of the goddess at the altar, all wrapped up in prayers – he actually never saw her with his own eyes, and "far from me be the lies of poets" (6.253), *valeant mendacia vatum!*[3]

---

[1] Catherine Conybeare sketches the development of the concept of *persona* from its classical signification of a human agent "without entailing any comment on interior processes" to its Christian emphasis on interiority and "the mixture of spiritual and corporeal in everyone", 2000, p. 133.
[2] For both the Latin and the English text of *Amores*, I have used the Loeb edition of Grant Showerman, revised by G.P. Goold, 1996.
[3] I quote from J.G. Frazer's Loeb edition of *Fasti* 1967.

By means of such exclamations, Ovid actively contributed to the latinization of the old cliché of the lies of the poets, known at least from the days of Solon and Xenophanes some five hundred years earlier, destined to habitual reuse in medieval culture. This is ironic, since his own *Metamorphoses* would frequently be considered the very epitome of *mendacia vatum*. In at least one of his poems, as a matter of fact, Ovid himself joins explicitly, albeit in a comic mode, the old team of laureate liars. I am thinking of *Amores* 3.12, in all likelihood one of the most complex treatments of the theme of fiction in ancient literature. In this elegy, the poet regrets (or feigns to regret) his passionate outpourings over his beloved Corinna in verse. The reason for his distress is simple: his love poems have met with such enthusiastic response that Corinna nowadays seems to be the desirable property of everybody, not only on paper (papyrus) but in real life!

Involuntarily, then, the poet has acted as a pimp, *leno*, and now he complains – admittedly too late – that the Muses and Apollo did not dissuade him from publishing his excited outbursts. For his own part, he had not suspected any harm resulting from his writing, since his readers in any case seldom took poets for truthful "witnesses", *testes*. It would have been better, Ovid notes bitterly, if they had followed existing customs and not attached any great importance to his words. To illustrate this point – the poets' proverbial bent for feigning – the remaining part of the elegy enumerates a selection of their fabulous inventions, several of which were later incorporated in the *Metamorphoses*. Here, Ovid emphasizes, as Godo Lieberg has observed in his study of the *poeta creator*-character in ancient literature, how all these mythical figures and their amazing adventures spring forth from the imagination of the poets. They are nothing but artefacts, fictions, something that he – Ovid himself – and his predecessors had "made up" (accentuated by the repeated verb *fecimus*).[1] The elegy ends, in Showerman's and Goold's interpretation (3.12.41–44):

> Exit in inmensum fecunda licentia vatum,
> obligat historica nec sua verba fide.
> et mea debuerat falso laudata videri
> femina; credulitas nunc mihi vestra nocet.
>
> Measureless pours forth the creative wantonness of bards, nor trammels its utterance with history's truth. My praising of my lady, too, you should have taken for false; now your easy trust is my undoing.

---

[1] Lieberg 1982, pp. 105f. The author returns to the fictionality topic of *Amores* 3.12 in an article 1986.

The "creative" or fertile freedom of the poets, their *licentia poetica* (or as Ovid labels it here, *licentia vatum*), was frequently associated with fictionality and had ever since Aristotle been contrasted with historical accuracy or faithfulness, *historica fides*. For many Late Antique authors, it would represent an abomination, a source of false doctrines and idolatry. For others, it was if not a blessing, at least a useful critical catchword or a plea for the kind of reading which eludes categorical oppositions between true and false. To be sure, the ingenious Ovid carried this freedom unusually far, both in the metafictional statements of his amorous elegies and in the practice of his *Metamorphoses*, where it was certainly extended *in inmensum*. And behind the cunningly parodical or ironic grievances of *Amores* 3.12 – here we have a poet who complains about being believed in! – we might probably detect a subtle defence of the *licentia vatum*, of the poets' right to freely exercise their invention without having to confirm what they are saying.

These lines reveal an essential feature of the Roman literary institution in its classical phase. Right through the Empire's time-honoured religiosity (comprehending a remarkably great number of deities), during the Augustan Age carefully reinforced by decrees from the Emperor himself, there existed – at least on the level of the educated elite – an agreement between author and audience. It conceded the poet great freedom to excel in myths, fables and legends; his readers or listeners, for their part, did not need to take him more seriously than was required by convention.[1] The background of this (generally unvoiced) agreement, or – as I would like to call it, in adherence to modern fiction theory – "contract", is complex.[2] The official propaganda insisted on the presence of the old gods in art and literature. Since the days of Catullus and the *neoterici*, however, Roman writers (and consequently, audiences) had been accustomed to a lighter treatment of the mythological material, with a certain predilection for erotic themes, as a main ingredient of poetry's elegance or *venustas*. Behind this development were also currents of philosophical rationalism or scepticism: five centuries of myth criticism, from Xenophanes to Lucretius, had not passed unnoticed. Ovid could thus rely on (or he thought he could rely on) the classical Roman version of the fictional contract, a historical compromise which was remarkably generous in granting literary imagination a far-reaching exemption in religious as well as moral matters.

---

[1] Fritz Graf observes that myths and *fabulae* were everywhere perceived as poetic fictions rather than religious messages in the Rome of the Late Republic and early Augustan Age, 2002, p. 108.
[2] For a discussion of the fictional "contract between author and reader", with some applications to medieval literature, see Warning 1983, pp. 191–98, in particular p. 194.

This contract allowed the poets to enjoy an authority derived from the Muses, frequently exploited by Horace in his (likewise revived) role as an inspired *vates*, without having to claim a sacerdotal distinction or competence in any literal sense. It kept the old tales of the heroes and deities alive but treated them to a great extent either as a matter of clever erudition, in the neoteric vein, or as a reservoir of *exempla* which were granted a special place in didactic poetry. In the *Metamorphoses*, the myths could be rendered with a host of illusionistic details, while the author repeatedly raised the question of their dubious basis in reality.[1] Now, in the context which Ovid himself creates around *Amores* 3.12, to be sure in the easy-going style of erotic elegy rather than the solemn tone of imperial epic poetry, the listeners or readers had broken the contract, what Denis Feeney calls "this necessary knowing complicity between poet and audience".[2] They had taken his poetical fiction literally: Corinna is considered available, art is considered truthful – and the first to make objections is the artist himself! The contrast with the later Christian authors, who would make the criterion of truth the crucial point for all discourse, including poetry, could hardly be greater.

It is important to remember that Ovid made his objections in a lyrical text where he was entitled to employ fictional devices by virtue of the implied speaker or narrator, not necessarily identical with the poet himself. Here, consequently, there is ample space for a range of parodical or ironic intimations, directed against both the proverbial talk of the lies of the poets and the writers' readiness to seek protection behind this same cliché. That problem, however, does not need to occupy us here. Neither do we have to deal with the fact that what I have called the exemption from immediate reality granted by the fictional contract was a rather fragile privilege. It could be cancelled whenever the divinely legitimatized imperial Power, *Imperator Caesar Divi filius Augustus*, found it necessary. Ovid's own destiny is an obvious case in point, with a bitter and solitary anticlimax on the shores of the Black Sea. The essential thing here is that he, more frequently – and elegantly – than anyone else among the classical Roman poets, made the problem of fiction explicit in his writings. A great part of his poetry is not only a product of invention; it also deals with invention and its power over the human soul.

---

1 Cf. the pertinent remarks of Gian Biagio Conte 1999, p. 354: "For Ovid myth does not have the religious value or the profundity that it has for Virgil; [...] For the highly literary Ovid, the world of myth is above all the world of poetic fictions, [...] The poet who so often joked at the *fecunda licentia vatum* (*Amores* 3.12.41) occasionally smiles at the credibility of what he is recounting, at the poets' innate lack of fidelity to the truth."
2 Feeney 1991, p. 231.

Ovid, then, operated according to a twofold strategy. On the one hand, he assumed the role of the storyteller and entertainer *par excellence*, who could easily disappear behind his fabulous sceneries, who liked to deprive his myths of historicity and literal veracity in order to set up a world of illusions. "I seemed to feel the change", the mythological hero Cephalus remembers in the *Metamorphoses* (7.722) when the goddess Aurora alters his appearance: *inmutatque meam (videor sensisse) figuram*, as if he could not even be sure of what he really felt at the moment of transformation. The aim of his metamorphose is to court his own wife, Procris, in disguise. He had been away from her for a long time, so now he wants to test her fidelity. When she finally starts to yield to his seductive entreaties, he exclaims (in a disputed line): "The poor pretender is here. A poor pretending adulterer I was, but in reality your very husband!" (7.741–42), *Male fictor adest; male fictus adulter, / verus eram coniunx*.[1] In this world of deceit nothing is what it seems to be. On the other hand, Ovid implements, scattered among his wonderful or horrifying myths of nature, recurrent reminders of what really happens in what seems to happen: the marvellous events follow certain patterns and should be ascribed a divine, moral, or natural (etiologic) significance.

Such is "the equivocation between absence and presence" which Philip Hardie traces throughout the Ovidian corpus.[2] Accordingly, this poet's imaginary tales of transformation and change provided an attractive alternative to the severe Platonic pedagogy which, however, would gain new supporters among Christian intellectuals. It was the frequent allusions to mythology and imperial cults in the poetry of the Roman Golden and Silver Ages which gave rise to Tertullian's fierce attacks on pagan literature and which would trigger Augustine's polemical vein in the mighty climax of the whole apologetic tradition: the extended inimical analysis of profane culture in the twenty-two books of *De civitate Dei* (*On the City of God*, 413–26/27).

When Ovid produced his magnificent versions of the ancient game of make-believe, a good deal of the innovative literary power of the Mediterranean region had been transferred to the Latin-speaking area. There, most of the contributions to fiction theory would take place within the field of rhetoric and the school disciplines rather than in philosophy. This development is already on the way in the incompletely preserved tract which during the major part of the Middle Ages would be known simply as "The Rhetoric": the work of Cicero's early years, *De inventione* (*On Invention*, ca. 85 BCE). In its first book, the young orator

---

1 In the notes to his critical edition of *Metamorphoses* VI–X, W.S. Anderson discusses line 7.741 in detail and proposes the translation I am giving here, 1972, pp. 319f.
2 Hardie 2002, p. 3. For a convenient survey, see Graf 2002.

(106–43 BCE) divides a legal speech into six parts, of which the second, *narratio*, treats "events that have occurred or are supposed to have occurred" (1.19.27): *narratio est rerum gestarum aut ut gestarum expositio*.[1] Here, interestingly, the conditional 'such as' we know from Greek fiction theory, the *hoios* of Aristotelian poetics, has been granted a follow-up in the Latin *ut*. Now, the *narratio* was in turn divided into three different kinds of storytelling (the young Cicero loved such technical and hierarchic distinctions, which was a main reason for his popularity during the Middle Ages):
- the account of the case,
- a number of digressions for polemical, comparative, amusing or, on the whole, amplifying purposes, and finally
- pure entertainment, without any public ambition, mostly for the sake of practice.

The third genre can be concerned either with persons or with events (*in negotiis*). These events, finally, are of three different kinds: *fabula*, *historia* and *argumentum*, a conceptual triad which was to exercise a powerful influence on medieval fiction theory.[2]

Fabula depicts events which are neither true nor probable, *fabula est in qua nec verae nec veri similes res continentur*, as in fantastic stories of winged serpents (mythology). *Historia* tells us what actually happened, normally a long time ago, *historia est gesta res, ab aetatis nostrae memoria remota*, as when Ennius deals with the Punic wars in his *Annals*. *Argumentum*, finally, "is a fictitious narrative [event] which nevertheless could have occurred", *est ficta res, quae tamen fieri potuit*, as in the comedies of Terence. Cicero's scheme would from the very start be characteristic of eloquent Roman narratology. We recognize it more or less verbatim in the contemporary but anonymous *Rhetorica ad Herennium*, during the Middle Ages sometimes known as "The New Rhetoric", *Rhetorica nova*, commonly attributed to Cicero down to the Renaissance and well into modern times. There, however, tragedy has replaced the mythological tale as an instance of *fabula* (1.8.13), possibly due to recognition of the fact that Medea and her monsters embodied not only an epic but also a tragic theme, exploited by Euripides.[3] In the Roman Silver Age, Quintilian, true to his habit, would take over his precursor's classification, but in his programme for the accomplished orator, *fabula* is ascribed to both tragedies and poems, *carmina*, with the addi-

---

[1] For *On Invention*, I use H.M. Hubbell's Loeb edition 1993.
[2] See Mehtonen 1996.
[3] I follow H. Caplan's Loeb edition 1964.

tion that the author will leave these genres out of consideration: "We have given poetical Narratives to the *grammatici*" (2.4.2), *grammaticis autem poeticas dedimus*. This demarcation against imaginative literature is typical of the great Hispanic pedagogue.

For our purposes, we can pass over the Ciceronian triad's background in Hellenistic philology. Its most well-known version in Greek was in fact articulated by a later writer, the Sceptic Sextus Empiricus, of whom we know very little; he was probably active in Athens and Alexandria during the second half of the second century CE. In his polemic *Adversus mathematicos* (*Against the Mathematicians*) the term *historia* indicates what has actually happened, for example that Alexander died in Babylon, poisoned by intriguers. *Plasma*, on the other hand, refers to something which never happened yet is similar to reality (and therefore might have happened, according to the Aristotelian conception of the domains of poetry), such as events in comedy or mimes. *Mythos*, finally, represents something that never happened and is definitely false, for example that Pegasus sprang forth from the Gorgon's head when her throat was cut, that Odysseus was changed into a horse or Hecuba into a dog (252, 263–64).[1] Sextus' division seems indicative of what happened to Aristotelian poetics, permeated by philosophical speculation, when it was adapted to the grammatical-rhetorical manuals of Late Greek and Roman culture. The sphere of the probable could just as well be ascribed to everyday comedy as to lofty tragedy, while the fantastic and fabulous was associated with epic poetry.

On the whole, rhetoricians and grammarians were to adopt a more result-oriented attitude to literature than Aristotle who, in his *Poetics*, had not only summarized current practice but also examined the possible work of art: a theoretical model. The *oratores* or *grammatici* of Hellenism and Late Antiquity were rather interested in what was already written, literature *in actum*, not seldom with reduced pretentions. Where Aristotle had wanted to uncover poetry's philosophic potential, marking it off from historiography with reference to its universality, the Romans would emphasize its pragmatic aspects, primarily its capacity to capture and entertain its audience. This version of the fictional contract comes conspicuously to the fore at the beginning of Cicero's dialogue *De legibus* (*On the Laws*) from the middle of the first century BCE (1.1.1–5).

---

1 I have used D.L. Blank's translation 1998. Sextus Empiricus traces this triad back to the Hellenistic grammarian Asclepiades (of Myrleia, first century BCE), 252. The Romans adopted the Greek term *plasma* in the sense of fiction, imaginative creation. In the final book of Martianus Capella's *De nuptiis Philologiæ et Mercurii*, treated further on in the present work, Harmony promises to sing of the divine assembly 'in a shattered fiction', *disgregato plasmate*, 9.913 (below, p. 392).

There, Atticus – Titus Pomponius, Cicero's life-long confidant – wonders if an old oak tree that he had read about in his friend's poem *Marius* still exists. He gets an answer from the writer's brother, Quintus, which already in itself is suggestive of Ciceronian fiction theory: "That oak lives indeed, my dear Atticus, and will live forever; for it was planted by the imagination. No tree nourished by a farmer's care can be so long-lived as one planted by a poet's verses."[1] In this text, then, *poeta* is established both as a parallel case and as a contrast to *agricola*, farmer. His *ingenium* reigns supreme and "plants" its theme rather than imitates it after a model. The tree of fiction survives that of nature.

Atticus, however, appears dissatisfied with Quintus' answer. Looking for a more straightforward explanation, he turns to the author himself, Marcus (Tullius Cicero), with his question: "Was it really your verses that planted this oak tree, or were you following a tradition that this incident happened to Marius as you describe it", *tuine versus hanc quercum severint, an ita factum de Mario, ut scribis, acceperis?* Atticus wants to distinguish 'fiction' from 'fact' in Cicero's poem, *fictane an vera*, especially as many readers rightly expect truth from a work which takes place in Arpinum, east of Rome, the author's own birthplace, and which refers to recent events, *in recenti memoria*. To Atticus, topicality and presence would obviously indicate (as still seems to be the case in much literary criticism) authenticity.

It immediately becomes apparent that Cicero considers the whole issue somewhat naïve, as far as fiction theory is concerned. He certainly does not want to appear to be a liar, *mendax*, but on the other hand, he claims that those readers who expect plain truth from this type of texts, as "of a witness in court rather than of a poet", *non ut a poëta, sed ut a teste*, act inexperiencedly or ignorantly: *faciunt imperite*. Quintus gives him a nod of assent: "As I understand it, then, my dear brother, you believe that different principles are to be followed in history and in poetry", *intellego te, frater, alias in historia leges observandas putare, alias in poëmate*. Marcus confirms this conclusion: Yes, you are right, because the former type of discourse aims at truth, while the latter generally gives priority to entertainment or pleasure, *quippe, cum in illa omnia ad veritatem, Quinte, referantur, in hoc ad delectationem pleraque*.

This is perhaps the most far-reaching attempt of classical Roman literature to narrow down poetry's fictional space between truth and lying.[2] Fiction is res-

---

1 "Manet vero, Attice noster, et semper manebit; sata est enim ingenio. nullius autem agricolae cultu stirps tam diuturna quam poëtae versu seminari potest." I quote *On the Laws* from C.W. Keyes's Loeb edition 1943.
2 For an analysis of the introduction to *On the Laws*, see Lieberg 1986, pp. 23–25. The passage is marred by certain philological obscurities, elucidated by Kenter 1971, pp. 16–36.

olutely separated from fraud and humbug, while its account of lifelike events, on the other hand, in no way appears restricted to documentary evidence. We clearly recognize its demarcation against historiography from *The Poetics*, but the orator Cicero has substituted the audience-oriented pleasure, *delectatio*, typical of Roman attitudes to poetry, for Aristotle's philosophical criterion of *poiēsis*, universality. The problem of fiction is analysed with considerable energy in *On the Laws*, ultimately controlled, however, by a conspicuously pragmatic outlook.

This mixture of an Aristotelian interest in fictional composition with pronounced rhetorical or pragmatic approaches to poetry is just as salient in another Roman author of the Golden Age, Horace. To begin with, his widely spread *Art of Poetry* analyses invention with a special emphasis on composition; false things should be combined with true ones, so that the beginning, middle and end of the literary work are coherent (151–52), *ita mentitur, sic veris falsa remiscet, / primo ne medium, medio ne discrepet imum*. Secondly, Horace argues in favour of probable fiction for the sake of the readers' delight (338): *ficta voluptatis causa sint proxima veris*. His focus on *voluptas* seems at least reminiscent of Cicero's *delectatio*; while aiming at the audience's pleasure, both authors establish a sphere for poetry between fortuitous invention (Horace: *fabula*, 339) and matter-of-fact representation.

Last but not least, such notions of fictional discourse made themselves felt in Late Greek and Roman school teaching. The perhaps most successful of the pedagogues of Late Antiquity (apart from Aelius Donatus), Aphthonius of Antioch, active during the second part of the fourth century, registered a number of text types as a basis for his preliminary rhetorical exercises, *progymnasmata*, various of which satisfy the Aristotelian criteria of credibility and probability. This holds especially good for the fable ("a fictive statement, imaging truth") and the narrative ("an exposition of an action that has happened or as though it had happened").[1] If we add to these instances of *progymnasmata* other items of the Roman school curricula, such as the paraphrases of grammar, the topical doctrine of the images in memory's *loci*, together with the rhetorical-legal doctrine of *inventio* and its analysis of "paradigms", "hypotheses" and other fictitious proofs, we get a fair picture of the breadth of types of fictional discourse known to the intellectuals of Late Antiquity – Church Fathers, grammarians and commentators – when confronted with the problem of the cognitive value of literature.[2]

---

[1] Kennedy 2003, p. 96.
[2] See the final part, "The Quality of Fiction: The Rhetorical Transmission of Literary Theory", in Trimpi 1983, pp. 243–361.

By that time, the knowledge of Aristotelian poetics and of fiction theory in its classical Greek versions had grown weaker, but Roman education proved a remarkably stable institution and, at least in some areas of the former Empire, even survived the first turbulent era of the Germanic invasions. Augustine most likely knew the Ciceronian triad *historia, argumentum* and *fabula*, not only because he was eminently trained in rhetoric, with a solid knowledge of Cicero, but because in his *Soliloquia* (*Soliloquies*), as we shall see (p. 182f.), he resorted to exactly the same example of fabulous invention as the orator from Arpinum: a verse about Medea's winged serpents. Even more important for the medieval knowledge of this narrative taxonomy were the unsurpassed chronicler of the school disciplines, Martianus Capella (below, p. 392), and the prodigious polymath Isidore of Seville (ca. 560–636) who concluded the exposition of grammar in his *Etymologiae* (*Etymologies*) with the assertion that "histories are true deeds that have happened, plausible narrations [*argumenta*] are things that, even if they have not happened, nevertheless could happen, and fables are things that have not happened and cannot happen, because they are contrary to nature." (1.44.5)[1]

In conclusion, the Christian attitudes to literary fiction from the third, fourth and fifth centuries did not arise *ex nihilo* but should be studied and understood in the context of the Roman educational system, based on grammar and rhetoric. Quintilian had firmly submitted poetry to grammar (the middle ground of the curriculum, studied after the elementary training under a *magister ludi* but before the superior discipline of rhetoric). The Romans certainly inherited an essentially Aristotelian concept of fictionality, based om *mimēsis*, but the tacit contract regulating the production, reception and notions of fictional representation in the Empire tended to convert it into clever illusionism, wondrous games of simulation, detached from its Peripatetic claim to universality and firm roots in philosophy. Such a development is already perceptible in Cicero. Even though this versatile orator and philosopher was well read in Greek literature and undeniably sensitive (as we have seen above) to the cognitive potential of invention, it is difficult to avoid the overall impression that to him, after all, poetry primarily served the purpose of light entertainment or of useful oratorical exercise.

In his philosophical dialogues on prophecies and belief in the gods, Cicero reiterated, as Paule Demats notes, the importance of sticking to reality, to *res*

---

[1] "Nam historiae sunt res verae quae factae sunt; argumenta sunt quae etsi facta non sunt, fieri tamen possunt; fabulae vero sunt quae nec factae sunt nec fieri possunt, quia contra naturam sunt." For Isidore's *Etymologies*, I have used W.M. Lindsay's Oxford edition 1911 and the English translation by S.A. Barney *et alii* 2006.

facta or *propiora*, and to keep mythology at a due distance.¹ We must not, of course, mistake his attitude for any modern materialism. Cicero was simply of the opinion that the old gods, inasmuch as they existed, were not granted any worthy treatment in the fantastic myths which philosophers or historians could hardly take seriously. These tales might, at best, be fit for poets. *Poetarum ista sunt*, as the sceptical Cotta observes in Cicero's treatise *De natura deorum* (*On the Nature of the Gods*), with this characteristic addition: "whereas we aim at being philosophers, who set down facts, not fictions" (3.31.77), *nos autem philosophi esse volumus, rerum auctores, non fabularum*.² In theory, these words might just as well, albeit based on an altogether different 'philosophy', serve the Christian apologists and ascetics of the third and fourth centuries.

The Cobweb and the Rainbow (Plutarch)

In Hellenistic philosophical culture, on the other hand, an alternative theoretical and hermeneutical approach to the poets' tales of gods and fabulous events was developed, which would prove seminal to Late Antique negotiations of fictionality: allegorical interpretation. For a telling juxtaposition of this kind of reading (ultimately derived from the Presocratic philosophers' critical deliberations on Homer) with the Aristotelian-mimetic view of fictional representation (qualified by Roman illusionism, as outlined above), we shall take a brief look at the Late Greek writer Plutarch (ca. 46–120 CE) and the essay from his *Moralia* which is generally known under its Latin title *De audiendis poetis* (*How to Study Poetry*), an educational instruction for teachers of young grammar students, designed as a letter from a father to his child, approximately of the same age as the author's own son.

In this short treatise, the students are expected to read poetry as a necessary but temporary exercise, in order to prepare themselves for the higher study of philosophy. Supposedly, they are not able to endure philosophy's relentless sunlight untrained, so they have to get accustomed to its dazzling rays by familiarizing themselves with the gentler gleam of poetry, where truth is only conveyed indirectly, in fictions and fables. Plutarch's take on this issue is of an entirely pedagogic character, closely connected to a school curriculum which, on the whole, assigned literary studies to the preparatory discipline of grammar. Provided that the reading of poetry is accompanied by correct supervision, Plutarch

---

1 Demats 1973, p. 5.
2 I quote from H. Rackham's translation in the Loeb Classical Library 1967.

observes, it is able to afford a joy which does not end in corruption but, on the contrary, paves the way for the elevated truths of philosophy. The young boys must learn to "discern" or uncover the true kernel of a literary work, which ideally should lie hidden behind the text's fair, albeit distracting and sometimes misleading superficial effects. The word Plutarch uses to indicate this commendable discernment is *krisis*, the origin of our "criticism". The students, reminiscent of Odysseus firmly tied to the mast of his ship, would not be allowed to enjoy the Sirens' song with confidence until they had been endowed with sufficient critical judgment. If they lack such *krisis*, Plutarch adds, they will be dangerously exposed to the alluring music. In that case all they can do is plug their ears and rapidly continue their journey towards illumination on Epicurus' – philosophy's – ship (15d–16a).[1]

Plutarch might seem remarkably severe in his warning against the calls of the Sirens, but in fact he follows Aristotle in his understanding of poetry as based on imitation and fiction rather than on metre and diction. Poetry, he observes, makes use of "falsehood combined with plausibility", *memigmenon pithanotēti pseudos*.[2] His wording still gives a faint echo of the archaic qualifications of fictional discourse from *The Theogony* and *The Odyssey*, but the adjective *pithanos*, 'probable', 'convincing' or 'credible', has an unmistakably Aristotelian ring. Literature is, in other words, the art of the possible rather than the actual. Such poetry, subject to the criterion of probability, is far more attractive to us, Plutarch continues, than a formally impeccable account lacking any myths or fiction, *amythos* or *aplastos* (16c). The young boys, however, should learn to see through these fabulous fabrications in order to discover the wholesome truths – of an ethic as well as a philosophic-ideological nature – that hopefully lie hidden among their fascinating though precarious tales. In short, Plutarch recommended a critical interpretation of the poets, with a sound and safe distance to their imaginary worlds. To praise literary imitation did not necessarily imply a correspondingly high estimation of what is imitated, typically immoral stories or characters (18b–d).

---

[1] For *How to Study Poetry*, I follow F.C. Babbitt's Loeb edition 1927. A concise presentation can be found in Schenkeveld 1982.

[2] Luc van der Stockt claims that *mimēsis* in *How to Study Poetry* should most likely be understood as an "adequate reference to reality", and that Plutarch consequently, strongly influenced by Plato, associated *mythos* rather than *mimēsis* with fiction, 1992, pp. 47, 55, 93f. However, the fact that Van der Stockt wants to exclude the concept of *mimēsis* from Plutarch's fiction theory does not invalidate the idea of an Aristotelian impact on *How to Study Poetry*; it only redirects the tract's interest in fiction to another term, that of *mythos*.

On the basis of this "hermeneutics of suspicion" – to borrow David Konstan's application of Paul Ricoeur's parlance on How to Study Poetry – Plutarch evinces an unmistakable tendency to associate literary fiction with figuration.[1] Robert Lamberton even characterizes his treatise as "one of the most precious pieces of evidence we possess" on the hermeneutic dilemma which arises when tropes such as irony or allegory open a breach between reference and referent, possibly resulting in obscurity or insufficient suggestive power.[2] As is usually the case, it is the indecent Homeric passages which elicit this dilemma for Plutarch, as when Hera seduces Zeus in *The Iliad* (14.153–353), or when Demodocus, the court poet of King Alcinous, sings of Ares' and Aphrodite's love-making in *The Odyssey* (8.266–366). Homer's characteristic restraint – he avoids explicit judgments on his gods or heroes, letting the epic action speak for itself – makes it possible for his interpreters, Plutarch remarks, to 'use force against and distort', *parabiazesthai kai diastrephein*, these myths by means of what used to be called *hyponoiai* but nowadays are known as *allēgoriai* (19e–f). The poet's account of Aphrodite's love affair, for example, has been believed to imply that illegitimate children are often born when the positions of the planets Mars and Venus coincide in the firmament.

Instead of such a far-fetched cosmic scenario, Plutarch prefers a moral lesson: the archaic *vates* teaches us that obscene songs and pornographic stories result in a vicious and dissolute way of life. Plutarch, then, seems to exploit Stoic allegoresis for his own purposes. He reacts against the common astrological 'distortions' of the old myths, and he emphasizes that while philosophers are in the habit of adducing examples (*paradeigmata*) in order to impress their lessons, poets are free to either feign the circumstances, *plassein pragmata*, or make use of myths (20b–c). So, within certain carefully prescribed limits, Plutarch obviously considers fiction to be a very useful didactic tool; it certainly deserves to be taken seriously.

Throughout his essentially grammatical-pedagogic and moralizing attitude to his subject, Plutarch, as it were, puts forward a strikingly advanced literary theory, with a keen eye for both poetry's distinctive character as a mimetic activity (a good imitation makes itself independent of its model) – corresponding to rhetoric's *inventio* – and for its figurative language (cf. rhetorical *elocutio*). Poetry issues from truth, at best, but in order to reach full effect and convey its message efficiently, it has to proceed in roundabout ways or step aside, *parachōrei* (16b), and make use of "variety", *poikilos*, and ingenious "diversity", *polytropos* (25d).

---

[1] Konstan 2004, p. 6.
[2] Lamberton 2001, p. 48.

The last of these terms can also, characteristically, indicate someone who has wandered far and wide, someone 'much-travelled', hence 'versatile'.

Still, it seems indisputable that the subordination of poetry to philosophy's more elevated art remains valid throughout Plutarch's tract. Poetry represents, in the eyes of this prudent magistrate and pedagogue, a potentially instructive but hazardous phase in the education of schoolboys, and it is incumbent upon the teacher of grammar not to let it lead them astray. His task consists ultimately in providing his students with adequate judgment, *krisis*, which would make them capable of separating literature's gaudy show from its true kernel – the capability, in short, to extract or bring out, *exagein*, poetry's message from "the realm of myth and impersonation" (36d), *tou mythou kai tou prosōpeiou*. By means of this exegesis, the message should become conveniently accessible to philosophical analysis. Poetry's scope of fiction, then, is both acknowledged and circumscribed in this treatise. Its roundabout ways are declared necessary so that its fundamental meaning, under due pedagogical supervision, will be efficiently impressed on the young readers' minds. Plutarch's final point in *How to Study Poetry* is probably meant to be encouraging, although it might not sound unambiguously attractive to modern ears; after having been accustomed to poetry's mythic obscurity, it is time for the reader to start looking for philosophy's bright sunlight. As a matter of fact, these concluding words seem to anticipate Plutarch's more circumspect concept of fictionality in his later essay *Isis and Osiris*, where myth is reduced to a thin external foil for a higher truth.

To sum up, in *How to Study Poetry*, Plutarch is looking in two opposite directions. Georg von Reutern brilliantly detected this crucial ambivalence in his doctoral thesis on Plutarch's view on poetry as early as 1933. There, von Reutern discerns, on the one hand, the Peripatetic concept of fiction known to us from *The Poetics*, in close connection with the notion of *mimēsis*, characterized by the narrative structure of *mythos*, for the purpose of the audience's delight, *hēdonē*; it offers us, according to the perhaps most suggestive passage of the whole tract, "a mythical fabrication [poem and fiction] which has been created to please or astound the hearer" (17a), *mythopoiēma kai plasma pros hēdonēn ē ekplēxin akroatou gegone*. On the other hand, there is the Stoic tendency, which after all gains ground through *How to Study Poetry*, to convert fiction into an allegorical raiment for, preferably, moral insights. Both of these attitudes to fictional discourse are thus present in Plutarch's treatise. As a matter of fact, they regularly confront each other in ancient literature but are probably nowhere so closely juxtaposed as in *How to Study Poetry*, and it is hard to refrain from wondering how the author could avoid feeling the tension between them. Von Reutern summarizes Plutarch's ambivalent attitude succinctly: he tended to stick with Aristotle in theory but slipped into Stoic allegoresis as soon as he went on to exemplification.¹

*

At the outset of Late Antiquity, we are thus left with at least two models of fictional representation, one (roughly) Aristotelian, the other (roughly) Stoic, both of them vital to our following exposition. In an even broader perspective, against the panorama of antique poetics outlined above, these models seem to presuppose or stipulate two key concepts of fictionality, to a great extent characteristic of classical Greek and Roman literary culture, constituting a mighty heritance to later Western narrative poetry, prose and criticism down to the present day.

– Aristotle's location of poetry's field of responsibility to "the *kinds* of things that might occur" represents what I will understand as a mimetic aspect of ancient versions of fictionality. It sketches a possibility for literature to transgress the local and temporal limitations of its original environment, to articulate statements that have a cognitive value without needing to be true or false, conveying a kind of information irreducible to historical or literal facts. This is what Augustine – in what is, perhaps, the most visionary moment of his long struggle with classical fiction – would call a double-faced truth (below, pp. 179f.): an instance of conditional truth, to be sure, bound to the laws of probability or necessity (a rather severe restriction, as Kurt von Fritz reminds us), but removed from actual reality.² It is commonly based on *narration* and *impersonation*, creating an illusion of presence, suggestive of a reality which it nevertheless refuses to asseverate or vouch for. It normally presupposes a recognition of the ambiguous, negotiable or at least elusive character of truth.

– Ever since Theagenes and the early Homerists and sophists of the sixth and fifth centuries BCE had tried to detect philosophical-mystical wisdom in the mythological extravagances of the poets of old, however, ancient culture knew another type of fictionality, chiefly to be looked upon as a cover for secret insights into the nature of the soul or cosmos. According to this hermeneutic tradition, the works of Homer epitomize on the level of myth or fabulation certain valid intuitions, the veracity of which was confirmed by the initiated philosopher by means of observation and speculation. This type of fictionality is commonly based on *substitution*, on the alleged configuration of something authentic by means of something invented. It normally

---

1 Von Reutern 1933, p. 72.
2 Fritz 1962, p. 451.

presupposes a recognition of the necessarily unequivocal and unconditional nature of truth.

Such a clear-cut distinction between two concepts of fictionality represents unavoidably a generalization and simplification of the remarkably rich gamut of attitudes towards *ficta* or *figmenta* in ancient literary criticism. It corresponds roughly, however, to Karla Pollmann's detection of precisely "two concepts of fictionality" in Hellenistic and Late Antique philosophy: a Platonic-Aristotelian mimetic model, based on the criterion of truth, and a "sign-model", emphasizing the text's referential character.[1] In actual fact they would frequently overlap or get entangled in each other, but for the sake of clarity it might be useful to keep their peculiar characteristics apart at a theoretic level.

We have already traced some avatars of the former concept through Roman literature. As far as rhetoric is concerned, Quintilian particularly emphasizes the legal speaker's method of drawing his arguments *a fictione*, from fictions and hypotheses which resemble the case in question (5.10.95–96), and he knows that the speaker can reinforce his submission of evidence *ex poeticis fabulis* (5.11.17). In this tradition, certain linguistic statements were believed to rely on a third epistemological category apart from true and false. Such a perception of fictionality might also be discerned in the famous depiction of Fame, *Fama*, from the fourth book of the *Aeneid*, not only a supreme instance of *prosopopoeia* in Roman epic poetry but a metafictional masterpiece as well. In the daytime, writes Virgil, *Fama* sits on high roofs or towers, terrifying big cities, "clinging to fiction and falsehood as often as telling the plain truth" (4.188), *tam ficti pravique tenax quam nuntia veri*. "Fiction" and "falsehood" can of course be understood as synonyms here, both signifying plain lies, but such a simple coupling might not do justice to *Fama's* insidious ways. Apart from the true, *verum*, and the erroneous or perverted, *pravum*, she is in the habit of conveying something third, which is neither true nor false but uncertain, something made up but still possible: *fictum*.[2] If that is the case, our four informants – Cicero and Quintilian in rhetoric, Ovid and Virgil in lyric and epic poetry – elaborate, each in his own way, a concept of fiction which ultimately is a heritage from Aristotelian poetics.

---

[1] Pollmann 1999, p. 268.
[2] Feeney stresses that this representation of *Fama* "is the most self-referential moment in the poem [the *Aeneid*]", 1991, p. 187. Hardie, for his part, tends to conflate *fictum* with *pravum* (translating *Aeneid* 4.188 as "clinging to distorted fiction as much as she reports the truth"), but, on the other hand, he certainly projects a classical, or even Hesiodic, concept of fictionality on Virgil's *Fama* when he comments on "her mixture of truth and lies", 2012, p. 107.

An illuminating instance of the latter concept, substantiating a didactic orientation according to the lemma *fabula docet* ('myths teach us'), is to be found in Plutarch's late tract *Isis and Osiris*. There, the writer set his mind on interpreting the Egyptian legends of strange divinities such as Horus, Isis and Osiris, replete with disjointed bodies and other ghastly things. He soon felt the necessity to clarify that he was not dealing with any barbarian oddities, with anything irrational, *alogos*, or fabulous, *mythōdes* (353e).[1] On the contrary, these were serious myths that could and should be interpreted in compliance with established piety and philosophy (355c). Their stories, Plutarch explains in the hermeneutic key passage of the tract, cannot be reduced to "loose fictions and frivolous fabrications", *mytheumasin araiois kai diakenois plasmasin*, of the kind that poets weave and unfold like spiders (358f.). He refutes emphatically such "unestablished first thoughts" (or, more literally, 'first fruits without foundation'), an expression which confirms a thesis that has struck my mind during the work on this book: some of the strongest definitions of literary fiction stem from its distrustful commentators or even opponents.

In Plutarch's syntagm 'first fruits without foundation', *aparchai anypothetoi*, it is possible to recognize the Greek words for 'origin', *archē*, and for 'foundation', 'principle', or 'plan', *hypothesis*. Both terms have a strong Platonic resonance. In Book VI of *The Republic*, they jointly serve Plato's theory of the first and utmost principles or ideas, which constitute their own foundation and cannot be derived from something else (510b–511a). As Wolfgang Bernard has shown, Plutarch alludes by contrast to this terminology and to these concepts of *The Republic*.[2] In *Isis and Osiris*, then, the author rejects the poets' unfounded first fruits of fiction, singled out as the poor opposite to Plato's notion of stable primordial ideas. The old Egyptian myths, Plutarch assures us, are no such empty imaginations; if anything, they provide us with essential information about misery and suffering. Just as the rainbow reflects the light from the sun when it hits the clouds, myths represent a certain way of thinking, *logos*, so as to turn our attention towards higher things (359a). That is to say, these sacred stories embody a kind of fictional discourse other than the hollow cobwebs of the poets. They reflect in motley colours a supreme *logos* beyond their own discursive horizon.[3]

---

[1] Like *How to Study Poetry*, this tract is included in Plutarch's *Moralia*. I follow F.C. Babbitt's Loeb edition 1999.
[2] Bernard 1990, p. 212.
[3] Van der Stockt usefully emphasizes how Plutarch's treatment of the *mythos* concept in *Isis and Osiris*, where it appears as a medium or vessel for a higher truth, stands in stark contrast to Aristotelian poetics, 1992, p. 97.

In comparison with his earlier *How to Study Poetry*, Plutarch has obviously shifted the emphasis from mimetic to substitutive fictionality. Plato might have been the first writer who, still tentatively, expressed this dichotomy in Greek culture. The second and third books of *The Republic* slowly but steadily, guided by a truly Socratic logic, suggest a discrepancy between the verbal devices of poets, irreverent and mendacious alike (though sometimes useful), and on the other hand, true, good and wholesome narratives about the gods. Therefore, it seems only logical that it was the last great upholder of the Platonic Academy, Proclus from Athens (ca. 410–85), who – precisely in a commentary on his predecessor's *The Republic*, within the scope of a detailed speculative system – established a pronounced hierarchy of literary genres, with the inspired symbolic myth at the top and imagination's mimetic figures at the very bottom. We shall have occasion to return to Proclus later in my survey.

Proclus was a sharp literary theorist, irrespective of whether modern readers would feel tempted to subvert his and Plutarch's criticial priorities, both belittling the cobweb (the poets' narrative illusions of presence) in favour of the rainbow (the tricks of indirect or transferred speech, significantly emblematized as colourful discourse). The former represents a kind of poetry which does not confine itself to codifications of the philosophers' *logos* or the pantheon of the priests. It relies upon a mimetic rather than a substitutive or semiotic category of fiction.[1] It simulates as well as enhances the existing state of things. The cobweb, to put it simply, not only duplicates but seem to add something to reality, hence exposed to the accusations of being 'unfounded' which we have noted in the late Plutarch and which were to proliferate in Late Antiquity. This type of fiction is summarized with unsurpassed concision in the second option of the choice which Horace offers the poet, or *scriptor*, in his *Art of Poetry*: "Either follow the beaten track, or invent something that is consistent within itself" (119), *aut famam sequere aut sibi convenientia finge*. That is to say: either you could exploit existing tradition or you could, according to the bolder option, invent or 'feign' a coherent work on its own terms. It is true that this disjunctive either-or choice already implies a distortion of the Aristotelian theory, which in fact relied upon what Horace calls *fama* (rumour, legend, tradition) to make fiction seem probable or even necessary. But on the other hand, Horace's *sibi convenientia* stresses in true Aristotelian spirit the desirable coherence of the fictional

---

1 Cf. Manieri 1998, according to whom the Late Greek sophist Philostratus' concept of *mimēsis* entails "not only the reproduction of natural facts, but also the capability to depart from that pursuit, surpassing it by creating new regular figures, a kind of creative activity which does not ignore imitation but is born precisely from the mimetic disposition naturally inherent in man", p. 62.

work, its consistent formation and, consequently, its aesthetic distinctiveness.¹ This is an important structural aspect of fictionality, which incidentally has come to the fore in the past two centuries, quite conspicuous in the works of Umberto Eco, who insists on the capability of myth and fiction in helping us "to find a shape, a form, in the turmoil of human experience".²

The mimetic or self-supporting fiction was often associated with the poets and their elusive tales. It remains under suspicion through the greater part of my survey. By contrast, the substitutive type of fiction was to have a huge impact on Hellenistic and Late Antique Roman culture. It was frequently linked to the philosophers (or to poets known as philosophers, sometimes even as 'theologians'), and it derived much of its strength from Plato's dialogue *Timæus*, from Stoic speculation and from the prevailing religious mysteries. It was often identified with literary allegory, and was later to become a dominant feature of medieval culture. Its most powerful stronghold during the Hellenistic era was probably the Stoic school in Pergamon, Asia Minor, where pretty well every line of *The Iliad* or *The Odyssey* could be analysed as a container of a transferred sense (as seems to have been the case in the monographs on Homer composed by the grammarian or *kritikos* Crates of Mallus from the early second century BCE, who favoured the detection of physical-cosmological learning in the poet's mythical tales).³ Later Hellenistic criticism in the wake of Crates' – extravagant – allegoresis took for granted that truth was constantly one and the same, indivisible, revealed to the great poets, philosophers or seers of long ago, and recorded in their writings: in Homer, the infallible moral teacher of the Stoics, in Plato, the philosophical authority for all Neo-Platonists, or in Moses, the law-maker of the Jews (and subsequently of the Christians). If different authorities seemed to disagree with each other, the common strategy was to explain their contradictory statements as divergent rivulets from the same source. In this sense, much Hellenistic philology was of an apologetic character.

Crucial to such speculative hermeneutics was that Homer, as well as Plato and Moses, in the eyes of their interpreters of later days, had thought fit to encode truth in symbols and riddles, for one thing because they tried to protect it from unauthorized admirers. Now it was up to Hellenistic exegesis, for exam-

---

1 Horace's *fama* could perhaps best be rendered as 'tradition', without any essential difference between myth and history. His *sibi convenientia*, 'consistency', could, for its part, have both plot and delineation of character in view while also covering Aristotelian "probability". See Brink 1971, pp. 197f.
2 Eco 1994, p. 87.
3 For an excellent exposition of Hellenistic allegory, see Most 2010. For a short survey of Crates and his followers, see Pépin 1976, pp. 152–67.

ple the author of the *Quaestiones Homericae* (*Homeric Questions*), generally known as Pseudo-Heraclitus, probably active during the first century CE, to uncover the actual significance of the old texts, not least where they seemed offensive, as when the Homeric myths embroiled the gods in erotic adventures. To these interpreters, a literary work typically seemed split between the words on the one hand – frequently improper, cryptic or even absurd – and the author's irreproachable albeit concealed intent on the other. As a consequence, it should be handed over to philological or mystagogical expertise for due decoding. For the purpose of our inquiry, it is of vital importance that Christian readers – as Heinrich Dörrie has pointed out in a fine essay on the methods of ancient exegesis – took over these tools for interpretation from the Hellenistic schools.[1] Their version of allegory was commonly considered superior to mimetic narration and impersonation, inasmuch as its referent was held to be unequivocally valid. As we shall see, however, Augustine's cutting-edge hermeneutics came to challenge them both, the cobweb as well as the rainbow, in favour of typological explanation, where both the referent and the reference were deemed historical, hence true.

---

[1] Dörrie 1974.

3 Late Antiquity

Periodization

For the concept of "Late Antiquity", I have made use of Manfred Fuhrmann's ground-breaking 1967 article on the Latin literature of this period; it has been my ambition to treat the age between the third and the seventh centuries CE in the West as a fairly coherent epoch *sui generis* (rather than some loose label on a heterogeneous set of works, writers and genres during the transition from Antiquity to the Middle Ages, "a no-man's-land of literary history"). Nevertheless, the dividing lines between Late Antiquity and the preceding as well as the following era have necessarily been drawn rather sketchily. As for the former, of course, the very term "Late Antique" indicates the continuity with antique culture. France's leading specialist in this field of literary history, Jacques Fontaine, speaks of an "aesthetic continuity" which situates the epoch "within Hellenistic-Roman Antiquity, where it appears as the last creative phase, from the third to the sixth century", with the fourth century as its productive culmination.[1] At the other end of the period, Pope Gregory the Great (ca. 540–604) or the polymath Isidore of Seville are usually adduced as more or less symbolic figures of transition.

Late Antiquity is characterized by the breakthrough of Christianity as a leading religious, historical and cultural force. Within the Latin-speaking sphere, Fuhrmann ascertains, this epoch is pervaded by intense literary activity, above all during the flourishing years 350–400 with their "immense delight in experiments", nevertheless marked off both backward and forward in time by periods relatively scanty of imaginative literature, the third and the late seventh centuries. The great cultural carriers of this age were the aristocracy of the Roman Senate and the schools, which indefatigably taught ever new generations grammar and rhetoric. Furthermore (in compliance with Wolfgang Kirsch), the Church should be added as a third initiator and inspiring force in the cultural life of Late Antiquity, just as it is helpful to recall the expansion of the Empire's literary activities from the centre towards the provinces, particularly Gaul, Spain and Northern Africa, which took place during the whole period.[2]

In addition, I will exploit trends in recent research which emphasize the intertextual play or interference (even during the polemics) between pagan and Christian literature, rather than regarding them as two separate discursive or ge-

---

[1] Fuhrmann 1967, pp. 62, 65; Fontaine 1988, p. 56.
[2] Fuhrmann 1967, p. 75; Kirsch 1988, p. 16.

neric systems, or associating them with classical 'form' and new 'content' respectively.[1] Finally, I will steer away from the conception of the epoch, common among earlier historians of literature, as an era of cultural decadence. A great number of later investigators of *Late Antiquity, die Spätantike* or *l'Antiquité tardive* have, on the contrary, accentuated the absurdity of reading the literature from this period through lenses adapted to a poetics which stems from an earlier age. It is true that religious persecutions, civil wars, periods of hunger and foreign invasions succeeded each other during the final phase of the old Empire. Nevertheless, Peter Brown, in his survey of the cultural and religious history of these years of seeming crisis, *The World of Late Antiquity* (1971), a book which heralded a new interest in the period in several disciplines of the humanities, remarks that to all appearances fourth-century Rome was not on the eve of disaster; it could, in fact, be described as a rather rich and well-balanced society.[2]

We might actually ask ourselves, following Brown, Fontaine and Siegmar Döpp, if the crucial decades during the fourth and fifth centuries, roughly coinciding with the career of Augustine, did not in fact signify one of the most productive periods – or even, to quote Mark Edwards, "a second Golden Age" – in the history of Latin literature.[3] To my mind, these years herald the splendid beginning of a new cultural era rather than epitomizing the sad eclipse of classical tradition, an outlook I will try to substantiate in the following chapters. In addition, as we have already seen established by Fuhrmann, this tradition had been exposed to a serious disruption during the preceding century, which is why Alan Cameron considers the resurgence of poetry in the post-Constantine era as "one of the most intriguing features of the literary culture of Late Antiquity".[4]

Research in this field has thus advanced conspicuously during the last forty years. As late as 1976, the North American professor of English, Macklin Smith, in

---

[1] A thorough plea for this intertextual (or intercultural) approach can be found in Fontaine 1977, pp. 463–72.

[2] Brown 1971, p. 34. The theory of decadence stems from a venerable line of primarily English and German historians, long influenced by Edward Gibbons's classic *The History of the Decline and Fall of the Roman Empire* (1776–88). One of the scholars who has done most to invalidate this association of Late Antiquity with decadence and barbarity is precisely Brown; for a personal retrospect of his efforts and a discussion of later trends in this field of research, see Brown 1997.

[3] Brown 1971, pp. 116f.; Fontaine 1980, p. 268; Döpp 1988, p. 22; Edwards 2004, p. 209.

[4] Cameron 2004, p. 328. In opposition to Cameron, Marc Mastrangelo discerns a "decline of poetry" in the fourth-century West due to its loss of "cultural authority" to patristic prose, 2009, p. 312. Even with due consideration of the Church Fathers' frequent attacks on pagan poetry, this hypothesis seems hard to defend in view of masters such as Ausonius, Prudentius or Claudian.

his monograph on Prudentius' allegorical verse tale *Psychomachia* (*The Fight for Mansoul*, ca. 400), could still complain that "few literary historians specialize in late antiquity, and thus classicists, medievalists, and general readers tend to neglect this period".[1] This resigned attitude is hardly justifiable only a few decades later, quite the reverse: Late Antique studies have proliferated as never before at faculties of Theology and Humanities all over the Western world, sometimes inspired by analogies with certain twentieth-century developments, a trend which has made scholars such as Andrea Giardina worried about an "explosion of Late Antiquity".[2] Nevertheless, I would assume that to many readers this period is still relatively unknown in regard to its main features or characteristics. Here are some of its historical and cultural landmarks in a very concise chronology:

- The year 313, when the Emperors Constantine and Licinius issued the Edict of Toleration in Milan, in which Christianity was declared a legitimate religion all over the Roman Empire.
- 325, the year of the first council of Nicaea in Minor Asia, a huge step towards a united Church throughout the Empire, with the approval of a creed which, to a large extent due to its anti-Arian affirmations (in short, declaring Christ as true God, co-eternal with the Father and begotten from His same substance), would gradually be associated with Christian orthodoxy.
- 330, when Constantine relocated the capital of the Roman Empire to the newly founded Constantinople, for which reason the old city on the Tiber remained the metropolis of the Senate aristocracy – and of a diocese, the importance of which was on the rise – rather than of imperial power.
- The years 362–63, when Rome's last pagan Emperor, Julian the Apostate, initiated into the Mithraic cult and the Eleusinian Mysteries, for some eighteen months took various measures to restore Hellenistic polytheism as the official religion of the Empire, e. g. by preventing Christians from teaching grammar and rhetoric. For Julian, venerable traditional education, *paideia*, was inconsistent with what he called the faith of the atheists or the Galilean superstition. Consequently, he considered it hypocritical to teach Homer's,

---

[1] Smith 1976, p. 6. As for the title of Prudentius' best-known work, I will stick to the Latin *Psychomachia*, since it is more or less universally known and used.

[2] Giardina 1999 ("Esplosione di tardoantico"). This "explosion" due to a series of nineteenth- and twentieth-century identifications with Late Antiquity is, indeed, a fascinating cultural phenomenon in its own right, apart from the fact that it has generated much research on early Christianity, Patristics and Biblical epic poetry; for a comprehensive study, see Reinhart Herzog's essay "'Wir leben in der Spätantike'. Eine Zeiterfahrung und ihre Impulse für die Forschung", 2002, pp. 321–48.

Hesiod's and the classical rhetoricians' works without believing in their words.
- The year 380, when the Emperors Gratian and Theodosius cancelled the Milanese Edict of Toleration in order to promulgate a new edict, in Thessalonica, charging all subjects of the Empire to profess the faith – adopting the Nicene creed – of the bishops in Rome (Pope Damasus) and Alexandria.
- 384, when the magnanimous senator and city prefect Quintus Aurelius Symmachus asked the Emperor Valentinian II to return the old altar of the goddess of Victory to the Senate in Rome.
- The following year, 385, when Jerome, after having revised the extant Latin versions of the Gospels, took up residence as a monk in the Holy Land in order to proceed with the gigantic task of translating the Old Testament from the Greek Septuagint, and later from the original Hebrew, into Latin. This work was completed two decades later with the edition of the Bible which the Romans would call *editio nostra* or *codices nostri*, ever since the High Middle Ages commonly known as *Versio vulgata* or just *Vulgata*.[1]
- The year 387, when Augustine and his mother Monnica reached God from the seaport of Rome, Ostia (probably the single most important episode of this book).
- 395: The orthodox and powerful Theodosius the Great passed away after having minimized what was left of Rome's pagan culture, whereupon his huge realm once and for all was divided into two halves, the Eastern and Western Roman Empire.
- The year 402, when one of Theodosius' two heirs, Honorius, abandoned the unsafe Milan, the administrative and strategic centre of the Empire during the better part of the fourth century, in order to establish the forbidding Ravenna on the Adriatic coast of Italy, protected by swamps and marshes, as the new capital of the West.
- The disastrous 410, when Rome, the *urbs aeterna*, proved to be anything but Eternal. The city was conquered and plundered for three days in August by a host of Visigoths, a Germanic people from Dacia (present-day Romania), under the command of King Alaric.

---

1 The end of the year 404 is frequently put forward as the probable *terminus ante quem* for the completion of the Vulgate, e.g. in Sparks 1970, p. 516. For the sake of simplicity I will henceforth treat the Vulgate as Jerome's personal work, even though he hosted a workshop for his great project, cf. Sutcliffe 1969, pp. 99f., and Loewe 1969, p. 108. During Late Antiquity, the label *editio vulgata* was reserved for the set of Greek Bible books which Jerome took as his source (his Vulgate was not used widely until the eighth century).

- 476, when the Germanic chief Odoacer dethroned Romulus Augustus, Rome's last Emperor, proclaiming himself the new King of Italy. This installation of the first barbarian ruler of Italy signalled the fall of the once mighty Roman Empire in the West.
- 524, or perhaps the following year, at the very latest 526, when Boethius, "the last Roman and the first Scholastic", was put to death in Pavia at the order of Theoderic the Great, Arian king of the new Ostrogoth kingdom in northern and eastern Italy.
- The year 529, when the East Roman Emperor Justinian closed the last school of philosophy in Athens, the Platonic Academy, nearly a thousand years old, and when, according to tradition, Benedict of Nursia founded the monastery of Monte Cassino between Rome and Naples.
- The year 636, which saw the death of Bishop Isidore of Seville, for the next five hundred years the most important source on ancient culture and knowledge available to the West.

During the three centuries between the first and the last of these dates, the unceasing efforts among synods, congregations and the early Fathers to establish Christian faith and determine Christian doctrine caused a cultural shock which was to send vibrations through the next thousand years of European civilization. As we have seen, this period was characterized by the new religion's victory and expansion all over the Mediterranean area but also, during the decisive years 350–400, from the pagan Emperor Julian to the publication of works such as the *Confessions* and the Vulgate, by long drawn-out intellectual controversies. In addition, there were not only vexed disputes but huge cultural differences within triumphant Christianity as well, for instance between – just to exemplify with two extremes – a converted aristocracy in Gaul, trying to reconcile old tradition with new faith, *romanitas* with *christianitas*, and, on the other hand, the Egyptian Desert Fathers who wished to escape from mundane concerns altogether, and whose adages and anecdotes, collected during the late fifth century in *Apophthegmata patrum* (*Sayings of the Fathers*), would prove a steady lecture in both Eastern and Western monasteries for centuries to come.[1]

---

[1] Cf. the contributions of Garth Fowden, Christopher Kelly and Richard Lim to the anthology *Late Antiquity. A Guide to the Postclassical World*, edited by G.W. Bowersock *et alii* 1999.

The Issue of Truth

The early ecclesiastic distrust of pagan imagination might seem to be a side issue in the history of theology, but an important aim of the present work is to emphasize its exemplary status. It corresponded to an essential need for distinctions and delimitations on the part of the Church Fathers during their struggle to establish orthodoxy in dogmatic matters. Their tense relation to the world of classical mythology should be understood against a wide institutional, religious and hermeneutical background. Christianity had started to expand in a culture not only characterized by imperial and mystery cults but also, in scholarly circles, by Hellenistic Scepticism and Alexandrian philology. For centuries, wise philosophers, commonly with Stoic affiliations or sympathies, had spent much energy in dissecting Homeric mythology in the light of learned disciplines such as etymology and natural or moral philosophy. Furthermore, the old gods inherited from Greek religion had to cope with the typically Roman proliferation of new local deities from all over the Empire, many of which were worshipped in esoteric contexts, as in the mystery cults imported from Egypt or Persia. Some of them survived to a great extent as philosophical principles, elementary spirits or demonic forces. They did not appear any more, as in archaic times long ago, "in living myths, steaming with belief", to quote the Italian specialist on Plotinus, Vincenzo Cilento.[1]

In a rough outline, I would like to follow Paule Demats's distinction between two kinds of myth criticism in ancient culture, the historical-euhemeristic and the philosophical-allegorical:[2]

- The former has its name from the Greek writer Euhemerus, who around 300 BCE pursued a rationalistic and genealogical analysis of the Olympian pantheon, probably – his work has not survived – in the form of a romance, *Hiera anagraphe* (*The Sacred Inscription*), according to which the old gods were originally earthly heroes and conquerors. Zeus, for example, had once been celebrated as the king of the whole world on the distant island of Panchaea in the Indian Ocean, where he was deified by his contemporaries while he was still alive. In another version of Euhemerus' lost romance, Zeus had been a Cretan prince who established his own cult, subdued various peoples, had temples erected to himself and was buried in Knossos. Posterity started to worship him as a true god.[3] This way of explaining the

---

1 Cilento 1960, p. 247.
2 Demats 1973, pp. 11–16.
3 For a recent overview of the different versions of *Hiera anagraphe*, and particularly of the later Greek and Roman writers' possible misrepresentation of its original sense, see Roubekas 2012.

myths, which would soon take firm root in Rome through the agency of Euhemerus' translator, Ennius (239–169 BCE), did not admit any hidden meanings or doctrine under the cover of the divine tales, but rather a historical course of events that had been distorted for various reasons, such as popular superstitions or the extravagancies of the poets. Ancient thinkers influenced by this rationalistic outlook were interested in reconstructing these events. Augustine would exploit their results in the *City of God* as a part of his polemic against mythology. For him, euhemerism was a proof of many pagans' scepticism of their own religion (6.7, 7.27). This ambitious exposition, later recycled by Isidore of Seville (*Etymologies* 8.11), forwarded Euhemerus' myth criticism to generations of medieval scholars and clergymen.

– The advocates of the philosophical-allegorical interpretation of myths, on the other hand, assumed – as we have already been able to establish – a covert meaning of the old tales. The fabulous (though frequently contradictory or preposterous) episodes known from Homer and the Greeks were explained as a veil for secret and profound insights into the order of the universe, the nature of the soul or moral discrimination. When philosophers set out to uncover this true, albeit concealed significance of the mythological stories, they could not proceed as the euhemerists did, claiming to expose historical facts. Instead, they had to draw support from some doctrine or school, commonly associated with Stoicism or Neo-Platonism.

Of these two strategies characteristic of pagan myth criticism, the early Christian apologists, Demats observes, frequently resorted to euhemerism (Lactantius, a principal witness of the present work, is one of them). They were interested in showing how the myths derived their origin from historical individuals or episodes. The old tales of the gods had come into existence due to the superstitions of ancient times or, at best, because of certain wise pagans' efforts to find excuses for their countrymen's infamous polytheism. If euhemerism could thus be recycled in apologetic contexts, various early proponents of the new faith felt dubious about the value of moralizing myth interpretations (we shall soon listen to Arnobius expressing such doubts), and the philosophical allegoresis which claimed to reveal a mystical wisdom in the pagan legends was altogether rejected; as a matter of fact, it came under suspicion of contributing to the survival of the old gods.[1] These misgivings later turned out to be justified. When Christianity had been declared the authorized religion of the Roman Empire, the last intellec-

---

[1] Demats, p. 45.

tuals of fading pagan culture such as Macrobius, Proclus and other Neo-Platonists took a new interest in allegorical myth interpretation.

At that time, however, the Western Church had to some extent left the early sectarianism's aggressive phase behind, and Neo-Platonic or Stoic speculation commonly infiltrated the Christians' own ranks. In the North African Fulgentius, probably active during the early or middle sixth century, we shall see how both systems of belief, the pagan-mythological world of legends and Christian faith, were smoothly juxtaposed, yet without any mutual intercourse. Eventually, the High Middle Ages would witness them in a perfect blend within the overall Catholic framework of Dante's *Comedy*. On the other hand, medieval authors never ceased to recycle the old cliché of the lies of the poets and their general unreliability. Were they not even associated with insidious demons or with the Evil One himself? Quite a few of these declarations of distrust stemmed from the early apologists.

In their eyes, the ancient gods remained controversial, whether they appeared as secret cult objects, faded cultural memories or schoolbook examples. Tertullian and those who shared his opinions reinstated and radically sharpened classical myth criticism in their polemics against pagan superstitions and heresies, but they were also forced to confront a new problem: how was it possible to gain credibility for the extraordinary circumstances, things or actions, especially the miracles of Christ, that are mentioned in the Bible? From a traditional and widespread Roman point of view, it was the new Christian tenets that seemed fictitious. Thus Caecilius, a pagan in the Latin apologist Minucius Felix' exquisite dialogue *Octavius,* possibly written in the late second or early third century, criticizes his Christian interlocutor's belief in the resurrection of the dead: "Your figments of diseased imagination and the futile fairy-tales invented by poets' fancy to give sweetness to their song have been rehashed by your credulity into the service of your God" (11.9).[1]

In the following survey, we will frequently come across this kind of accusation, for the most part, however, directed against the pagans. This is already evident in Minucius Felix. As soon as the eponymous Christian protagonist of his *Octavius* is called upon to speak, he announces his decision to present the truth with this characteristic specification, *una:* the truth is one and one only. Thus, all through *Octavius*, in which we for once have the rare opportunity to share the perspective of both antagonistic camps, it becomes obvious what an

---

1 "Omnia ista figmenta male sanae opinionis et inepta solacia a poetis fallacibus in dulcedinem carminis lusa a vobis nimirum credulis in deum vestrum turpiter reformata sunt". Trans. W.C.A. Kerr and G.H. Rendall in the Tertullian and Minucius Felix Loeb edition of 1977 (1931).

important part Late Antique attitudes to fiction played in the period's overarching cultural and religious dispute. *Both* sides, each referring to the gibberish of the poets, could accuse their opponents of making use of deceitful fictions. Henceforth, however, with one or two exceptions such as the Late Roman senator Symmachus, I will have to restrict myself to the victorious Christian arguments in this field, not only because of their amazing critical and innovative energy but also due to the simple fact that they are much better documented than those of the diminishing pagan wing.

*

A relatively common Christian strategy was to reject fictional tales and fables on the basis of what might be considered patriarchal arguments. Several of the apologists liked to adopt a supposedly responsible, reality-minded and male attitude in their polemics, whereby *ficta* came to be associated not only with the poets but also with irresponsible games in general, indecent mischief and female fancies. One of the best examples of this approach is to be found in the rhetorician Arnobius, active in North Africa around the turn of the fourth century. In his main work, a seven-book long petition against pagan culture, *Adversus nationes* (*Against the Heathen*, written in response to Diocletian's persecutions, in fact one of our main sources on the Late Antique world of myths), Arnobius gives an account of the legend of Attis, highly topical as a cult object in contemporary Rome, frequently associated with homosexuality and even cases of self-castration among its worshippers. The pagans should be ashamed, according to the author, for coming up with such old wives' tales (5.14):[1]

> Pray, when you read such tales, do you not seem to yourselves to hear either girls at the loom wiling away their tedious working hours, or old women seeking diversions for credulous children, and to be declaring manifold fictions under the guise of truth?

Arnobius repudiates indignantly his hypothetical adversaries' accusations against the Christians for superstition and impiety. It is you, he points out, once again regarding the bloodstained cult of Attis, that "either listen to or believe, or yourselves invent about them [the gods], stories so degrading", *qui tam*

---

[1] "Cum historias, quaeso, perlegitis tales, nonne vobis videmini aut textriculas puellas audire taediosi operis circumscribentes moras: aut infantibus credulis avocamenta quaeritantes anus longaevas, et varias fictiones sub imagine veritatis expromere?" *PL* 5.1110a–b. I follow the English translation by H. Bryce and H. Campbell in the series *The Ante-Nicene Fathers. Translations of the Writings of the Fathers down to A.D. 325*, edited by A. Roberts *et alii*, 6, 1957. The translators entitle Arnobius' work *Adversus gentes* in accordance with Jerome's short biography of the author – one sentence! – in *De viris illustribus* (*On Famous Men*), 79, *PL* 23.687a.

foedas de illis vel auditis, vel creditis, vel ignominiosas ipsi compingitis fabulas. The true cult, on the other hand, and the dignified attitude towards these gods – in whom the apologist anyhow has lost his faith – is to be found in the human heart (4.30): *cultus verus in pectore est, atque opinatio de diis digna.*

Admittedly, Arnobius proceeds, the pagans themselves, embarrassingly conscious of the erotic elements in their myths, try to explain these indecencies away as "fictions of poets, and games arranged for pleasure": *sed poetarum, inquiunt, figmenta sunt haec omnia, et ad voluptatem compositae lusiones.* That is of no help from the severe perspective of this apologist, who refuses to draw any sharp distinctions between religious, philosophical and poetical discourse. The poets – he proceeds – would either have exploited traditional matter as a source of *fabulae* for their songs (that is, they restrict themselves to recycling existing tales and beliefs), or "they would have assumed to themselves so great licence as to foolishly feign what was almost sheer madness" (4.32).[1] The juxtaposition of these two alternatives seems to reflect the choice which we have seen Horace offer the poets in search of a subject for their work (above, p. 52): they could either stick to the reservoir of tradition or they could plunge into fiction, "invent something that is consistent within itself", *aut famam sequere aut sibi convenientia finge.* Arnobius, however, impatiently rejects both ways. As for the later purpose, he is not in the least prepared to allow the poets to take refuge behind the famous poetic licence. It definitely did not provide them with any alibi in this religious context, where the reputation and the dignity of the gods were at stake.

Ultimately, as if he had set out to block all escapes for his addressees, Arnobius imagines them to resort to the technique of allegory. The piquant Homeric story of how Vulcan surprised his wife Venus with her lover Mars *in flagranti* would in that perspective, that of allegorical interpretation, demonstrate how desire and anger in comfortable association must be controlled by reason. Even so, Arnobius objects, why should we tackle the problem in such a roundabout way and with such lascivious anecdotes? What prevented you from "expressing each thing by the words and terms proper to it", *suis unamquamque rem verbis, et suis significationibus promere?* In this way, the apologist provocatively calls into doubt a hermeneutic tradition that permeated Hellenistic and Late Antique culture; he refuses to understand the point of hiding the gods under a "veil of allegorical obscurity", *allegoricae coecitatis obumbratio*, or of describing them "with allegorical ambiguity", *ambagibus allegoricis* (5.41–42).[2] Such methods could

---

[1] "aut ipsos sibi tantum licentiosi voluisse juris asciscere, ut confingerent per stultitiam res eas quae nec ab insania procul essent remotae". *PL* 5.1063b–67a.
[2] *PL* 5.1156b–57a.

only drag them into the dirt and furthermore make people confused, perhaps even – inappropriately – excited. With that, it is time for Arnobius to sum up his arguments (5.43):[1]

> But what the meaning of this is, is already clear to all. For because you are ashamed of such writers and histories, and do not see that these things can be got rid of which have once been committed to writing in filthy language, you strive to make base things honourable, and by every kind of subtlety you pervert and corrupt the real senses of words for the sake of spurious interpretations; and, as oft times happens to the sick, whose senses and understanding have been put to flight by the distempered force of disease, you toss about confused and uncertain conjectures, and rave in empty fictions [*et inanium per rerum figmenta bacchamini*].

Arnobius' final point demonstrates his clever polemical style, a rhetorical *tour de force* as such, based on climax, a simile and a hint at the Bacchantic mysteries (*bacchamini*, you 'revel', 'rave like Bacchae'), precisely the kind of cult which comes under fire in *Against the Heathen*. I have made use of Arnobius at this preliminary stage of my enquiry, since at the very beginning of the century which is the centre of attention for my survey, the 300s, he outlines some general trends in Late Antique criticism of fiction:
- The frequent allusions to pagan rites, particularly orgiastic ones, such as the cult of Attis or the Bacchantic mysteries. As a consequence, fiction is associated with moral dissolution.
- The references to children, girls and old women. Fiction is more than once presented as gendered: an outcome of female fantasies in contrast to a male, sound and solid principle of reality.
- The stress on Christian man's meditative "heart", *pectus*, in opposition to the rites and the cult of images located in the pagan temples. Fiction is accused of relying on external means, all sorts of narratives, spectacles and sceneries, as opposed to pious meditation.
- The association of fictional exposition to linguistic manipulation, in *Against the Heathen* represented by 'subtleties', *argutiarum modi*, but also – as is suggested by the verb *invertire* ('turn upside down') – by tropes (literally 'turns'). This amounts to what rhetorical doctrine of style, *elocutio*, common-

---

[1] "Sed quid sit istud, iam promptum est omnibus: nam quia talium scriptorum, historiarumque vos pudet, nec abolere videtis posse ea, quae sunt foede semel in commentarios relata, nitimini cohonestare res turpes, atque omnibus argutiarum modis pro rebus subditis, verborum invertitis corrumpitisque naturas; atque ut olim accidere male sanis assolet, quorum turbida vis morbi sensum atque intelligentiam depulit, confusa atque incerta iactatis, et inanium per rerum figmenta bacchamini." *PL* 5.1158a–b.

ly labels the figures of thought and the figures of diction respectively (both of which, as we have seen, were exploited by Arnobius himself).
- The presentation of allegory as the erudite alibi of fictionality, sometimes as one of the tropes mentioned under the previous item, but most frequently as a special type of text or exposition, a narrative mode which Arnobius brands with three common attributes: obscurity, *coecitas*, the veil, *obumbratio*, and roundabout ways or ambiguities, *ambages*.
- Last but not least, the anchoring of fictionality in *literary* exposition, in "poetry", a discursive space reserved for a whole gamut of wilful visions, fantasies and representations, traditionally defended by means of the key concept of 'poetic licence', *licentia poetica*, recently under frequent attacks from the apologetic camp, in Arnobius aggressively connected to the idea of mental dissolution, *insania*.

On this last point, Arnobius' immediate follower (according to Jerome), Lactantius, would adopt another, more conciliatory attitude.[1] *Against the Heathen* was not to have its true successors until the turn of the next century. In virtue of his both detailed and relentless struggle against the old cults and rituals, Arnobius in fact anticipates one of Late Antiquity's strongest and most brilliant pleas against classical culture and mythology, Augustine's *On the City of God*.

The Church Fathers actually returned so frequently to *figmenta poetarum* in contrast to Biblical (and their own) *sinceritas*, that it is easy to be tempted to mistake their statements in these matters for routine-like clichés.[2] Even so, the commitment and urgency of their arguments indicate the delicacy of the problem. The debate had been brought to an early culminating moment at the end of the second century, when the Greek-speaking Platonist Celsus (Kelsos), probably of Roman origin, exposed the new Christian religion to devastating philosophical criticism. The Bible's tales of the Virgin Birth, the miracles and the Last Judgment were in Celsus' eyes of the same fictional character as the old myths or the Dionysian mysteries, impossible for any reasonable man to believe or partake in.[3] More than fifty years later, he was to be refuted by another Platonizing thinker, Origen (ca. 185–254), a brilliant theologian of extensive reading, the foremost representative of early Christian allegoresis in third-century Alexandria, who repeatedly made it clear to his opponents that the Bible was inspired by the Spirit and consequently rescued from human – wilful, subjective, arbitrary – fiction.

---

[1] Jerome speaks of Lactantius as *Arnobii discipulus* in *On Famous Men*, 80, PL 23.687b.
[2] Robert A. Markus goes so far (perhaps too far) as to discern "shadow-boxing" on both sides during the ideological polarization of the late fourth century in the West, 1974, p. 8.
[3] For a good presentation of Celsus' polemics, see Chadwick 1966, pp. 22–30.

This argument was put to the test when it was applied to those books of the Old Testament which for many exegetes, particularly in the sophisticated Alexandrine setting, appeared primitive or incompatible with Christian piety. Confronted with this difficult issue, the purported occurrence of fabulous elements in the Holy Writ, Origen found himself obliged to resort to precisely the same method of interpretation that half a century later Arnobius would criticize in his attacks on pagan culture: allegoresis. As Karla Pollmann has observed, he tended to adapt his line of argument to that of his pagan adversaries, declaring the Bible books liable to the same kind of interpretation as the Greek myths, hence de facto treating them as *plasma*, based on an alleged "essential compatibility between the Biblical and the Greek 'myths'".[1] From this point on, the Song of Songs became the touchstone in this context. It might (understandably) be tempting to read these old Jewish wedding songs as a tale of profane love. Consequently, they would be the main object of a powerful tradition of allegorical reinterpretation among saintly Christian exegetes throughout Late Antiquity and the Middle Ages, starting with Origen himself and later to be continued, among others, by the holy Bernard of Clairvaux in High Medieval France and the devout Carmelite friar Saint John of the Cross in Renaissance Spain.

The fundamental principle for this on-going exegesis through the centuries is already to be found at its source: Origen's commentary and his two sermons on the Song of Songs, *in Canticum Canticorum*, translated into Latin around the turn of the fifth century by the mutual rivals Rufinus of Aquileia and Saint Jerome respectively.[2] These works are based on the conviction that the old Jewish nuptial poem, replete with ritual games and sensual imagery, must in fact refer to a holy truth not explicitly stated in the text: the union between Christ and the Church, alternatively between God and the Christian soul. "If these words are not to be spiritually understood, are they not mere tales? If they conceal no hidden mystery, are they not unworthy of God?" (1.2), *haec si spiritualiter non intelligantur, nonne fabulae sunt? Nisi aliquid habeant secreti, nonne indigna sunt Deo?*[3] These questions are nothing but rhetorical, of course, as Origen knows from the very start that the Holy Writ will not condescend to simple tales.

This early need to separate the Bible's spiritual meaning from the *fabulae* of mythology and folklore was even more intensely felt when Christianity began to

---

[1] Pollmann 1999, pp. 272f.
[2] Origen's crucial importance for the medieval exegesis of the Song of Songs has been confirmed by much modern research and is stressed in two recent inquiries, Astell 1990, pp. 1–24, and – especially – Matter 1990, pp. 20–48.
[3] I quote Origen's first sermon *in Canticum Canticorum* (which has only survived in Jerome's translation) after *PL* 23.1121b and, in English, after R.P. Lawson's edition 1957.

dominate the Roman Empire as its new authorized religion, with a climax in the decades around the turn of the fifth century. The polemic heat characteristic of these years is evident from the fact that Origen himself came under suspicion, not for his allegorical exegesis of the Bible but for his general interest in certain Pythagorean and Platonist ideas typical of his Hellenistic education, such as the pre-existence (and ensuing incarnation) of the soul. The Patriarch of Alexandria, Theophilus (d. 412), attacked him fiercely. In a paschal letter for the year 401, rendered in Latin by Jerome (once a great admirer of Origen's work), Theophilus fulminated against the *error* and *insania* to be found in the outrageous works of 'this Origen who invented so many things, following his own error rather than the authority of the Scriptures', *Origenes tanta confingens, et non scripturarum Auctoritatem sed suum errorem sequens* (96.5 – 6).[1] The time had come, then, for the ascetic Origen himself – continually on his guard against the intrusion of what he considered *fabulae* in exegetical matters – to be accused of wanton inventions in explaining the Christian doctrine.

According to Theophilus, Origen's worst sin appears precisely to have been the propensity to blur the distinction between dogma and fiction: 'he interspersed the philosophers' subtleties through his own treatises; from an unfortunate commencement he proceeded to myths and other follies [*in fabulas quasdam et deliramenta*], in order to turn the Christian dogma into a game and a joke [*ludum et iocum*]; instead of divine doctrine's truth, he made use of the human intellect's arbitrariness' (96.6).[2] For Theophilus and Jerome (as for the bulk of Late Antique Christian intellectuals), orthodox *dogma* or *doctrina* was decidedly non-negotiable. They espoused a categorical claim for truth, which did not admit any pluralist or idiosyncratic perspective whatsoever. They certainly did not care for *humanae mentis arbitrium* and even less, of course, for any detection of fictional discourse, however permeated by Greek philosophy, in the Holy Writ.

*

It should be sufficient with one more example to elucidate this exacerbated as well as triumphant patristic attitude to pagan culture. Ambrose, Bishop of Milan, spiritual mentor of Augustine, is certainly one of the key figures in Western theology during this period. In his commentary on the Gospel of Luke, explaining the story of how Jesus transforms five loaves of bread and two fishes

---

1 *PL* 22.777–78.
2 "Philosophorum argutias propriis tractatibus miscuisset, et a malo exordio in fabulas quasdam et deliramenta procedens, Christianum dogma ludum et iocum faceret, nequaquam divinae doctrinae veritate utens, sed humanae mentis arbitrio". *PL* 22.778.

into a meal sufficient for five thousand people, he makes the following reflection (6.88, cf. Luke 9.10 – 17):[1]

> The pagans sometimes amuse themselves with comparisons between their own gods' fictional rather than factual works [*non facta, sed ficta*] and the benefactions of Christ. Their myths certainly tell about a king that all he touched upon was transformed into gold. But his very banquet became his funeral; even the napkins he clasped with his fingers stiffened, the food rattled in his mouth and gave him wounds rather than alimentation, the beverages choked up in his throat and were not easier to swallow than to throw up. This was a prosperity worthy of such prayers, gifts worthy of such a supplicant, a generosity worthy of such a collector! Such are the benefactions of the idols: when they appear useful, they cause even worse harm. On the contrary, the gifts of Christ seem small though they are immense, and they do not concern any particular individual but the whole people; for the food just kept increasing in the mouth of those who ate, and even if they considered it a bodily sustenance, they were in fact consuming the nourishment of their eternal salvation. (III)

This passage demands our interest for at least three reasons:
- First, there is Ambrose's ingenious juxtaposition of Christ with the mythological Midas. If we think of it as blasphemous, our reaction would surely have pleased the cunning bishop: so overwhelming is the bounty of the former, generous with secular as well as celestial nourishment, and so immense is the greediness of the latter. This is not only a religious but also a moral contrast, which inevitably affects the quality of their miracles; where Christ manages to achieve the inconceivable, to alleviate hunger by means of pretty well nothing, Midas fails to nourish even himself with all his fabulous riches.
- Secondly, we note the antagonistic constellation of the *facta* of Christology and the *ficta* of mythology.
- Thirdly, Ambrose's eloquence strikes us as brilliant, based upon antitheses (*convivia* versus *feralia*, *alimenta* versus *vulnera* etc.), reiteration (*digna* repeated three times) and intensification or climax (with an exalted culmination in the last two words).

This kind of rhetoric is characteristic, as it clearly demonstrates a tension among the majority of the Christian writers. In theory, they excelled in disconnecting themselves from the elegant style of the Golden Age masters, commonly associated with pagan deceitfulness and vanity, but in practice it proved difficult to do

---

1 Ambrose's *Expositio evangelii secundum Lucam* is quoted according to *PL* 15.1692a–b (translation mine).

without it, even during their attacks on ancient mythology. Thus, Late Antique Christian apologists, theologians and poets would readily heckle or scorn the traditional repertoire of fabulous tales but found it hard to get rid of its discursive framework, because they made use of a language which had long been tried and tested in classical rhetoric and poetry, where precisely these *ficta* were a matter of utmost concern.

Furthermore, in order to verify and perhaps even to mark off and explain their true faith, early Christian intellectuals typically *needed* a clear-cut negative, a common counter-image, as it were, that could serve to highlight the superiority and veracity of their own message, and they found it in the age-old pagan mythology: a set of flippant *ficta* or *fabulae* which time and again were contrasted with Christian *veritas*. The model for this whole strategy had already been outlined in the New Testament: "For we did not follow cleverly devised myths when we made known to you the power and coming of our Lord Jesus Christ, but we were eyewitnesses of his majesty" (2 Peter 1.16), *non enim doctas fabulas secuti notam fecimus vobis Domini nostri Iesu Christi virtutem et praesentiam sed speculatores facti illius magnitudinis.*[1] Here, the author's reference to himself as an eyewitness is paramount. He (probably a later writer than the apostle Simon Peter) has been made a 'spectator', *speculator*, of the greatness of Christ, to which he subsequently can testify from his own experience, in stark contrast to the myths which – by virtue of the attribute "cleverly devised", *doctae* – are depicted as artificial, most likely with an allusion to vain learning and, perhaps, to poetry and the widespread *poeta doctus* complex. The Greek original reads *sesophismenoi mythoi*, where we recognize 'sophisms' as well as 'myths', both habitually adduced as contraries to straightforward Christian truth.[2]

This line of argument would recur in Augustine, who sometimes had to deal with popular comparisons between Christ (or other Biblical figures) and alleged 'magicians' such as Apuleius or Apollonius of Tyana. Nowadays, after Hugo Rahner's and other scholars' research, we have a rather good picture of these conciliatory revisions of the old Greek, Near Eastern and Egyptian myths concerning the planets, miraculous plants, Orpheus, Odysseus fettered to the mast of his ship and the like, frequently favoured in Alexandrian allegoresis from the second and third centuries, particularly in Origen's master Clement (ca. 150 – 215).[3] Con-

---

[1] I quote Saint Jerome's Latin Vulgate from the fourth edition of The German Bible Society's *Biblia sacra iuxta vulgatam versionem*, eds. B. Fischer *et alii*, 1994.
[2] For the original version of the New Testament I rely on the Nestle-Aland edition, *Novum Testamentum Graece*, 1979.
[3] Rahner 1971, pp. 69 – 88, 181 – 222, 328 – 86. Lamberton modifies Rahner's somewhat enthusiastic exposition: Clement actually objected firmly to the Homeric divinities while trying to en-

fronted with this kind of syncretic reinterpretation, or just popular legend-making, of pagan figures or conceptions within a Christian context, Augustine and other ecclesiastical teachers or preachers from the crucial period around the turn of the fifth century felt obliged to implement a process of separation, whereby reprehensible fictions would come out on one side and orthodox preaching, the *kerygma*, on the other.

Ambrose's short comparison between Christ and Midas might seem insignificant or even trivial; nonetheless it reminds us of the rivalry between faiths or *Weltanschauungen* typical of Greek and Roman Late Antiquity. To many traditionally educated Romans, the concept of truth actually seemed negotiable, at least as far as it concerned the divine. This comparably relaxed attitude, conspicuous in Cicero, was inherited from ancestral custom, *mos maiorum*, a long tradition of philosophical and religious tolerance, prescribed as a part of the Empire's policies as it expanded over the huge Mediterranean region, characterized by its plethora of local cults and beliefs. As long as the citizens observed officially imposed rituals (usually some kind of nominal sacrifices to the gods), and as long as they acknowledged the absolute authority or even holiness of the Emperor (in particular during the Dominate), they indubitably enjoyed a remarkable degree of freedom in their individual faith.

In a volume entitled *Kultur und Conversion*, the German philologist Christian Gnilka quotes that 'old question of Pilate', which we have already adduced as crucial to all matters of fictionality (above, p. 10). When the Roman governor was confronted with Christ's claim of having "come into the world – to bear witness to the truth", he closed his interrogation with this lapidary question: "What is truth?" (John 18.37–38). To elucidate this famous scene, Gnilka cites some *auctores* from the first century BCE, all of whom had expressed opinions in the fields of religious psychology or sociology: the statesman and scientist Marcus Terentius Varro (116–27), and Cicero, who had reflected on the nature of the gods in his philosophical dialogues. Gnilka reaches the conclusion that Roman intellectuals, ever since their first deliberations on the subject (such as Cicero's *On the Nature of the Gods*) right down to the urban prefect of Rome, Symmachus, and his famous *relatio* in defence of traditional Roman polytheism (384 CE), as a rule insisted on the liberal opinion – rooted in Hellenistic philosophy – that as long as we do not have any exact knowledge or any reliable eyewitness accounts of the gods, it is up to anyone to bring about his own way to salvation.[1]

---

hance the prestige of Christian tradition by showing how the one and only Revelation had penetrated, however dimly, to the foremost pagan writers, 1986, pp. 78f.
1 Gnilka 1993, pp. 9–18.

In this both traditionalistic and relatively permissive Roman religious atmosphere, characterized by the worship of the Emperor and all sorts of popular beliefs as well as by philosophical pluralism, Christ's and his apostles' unconditioned claim for truth had to appear scandalous. It forced their followers to death and martyrdom for some ten generations, until their holy conviction was transformed into the imperial state religion during the fourth century. In the year 384, the internal Roman balance of power was, accordingly, completely altered. The conservative Symmachus represented a small (albeit still influential) pagan minority, mainly belonging to the Senate aristocracy, and he fought for a cause which in fact was already lost, while his Christian adversaries, led by Ambrose, the powerful Bishop of Milan, enjoyed public support for their refusal to compartmentalize truth.

At present, I shall not dwell on this highly interesting debate between Symmachus and Ambrose, well covered by scholars from different fields of Late Antique studies (see below, pp. 532ff.). The aristocratic senator's dispatch might serve, however, as a reminder of the constructivist character of Hellenistic-Roman culture's philosophical and religious attitudes. In such a multicultural setting, the concept of truth, as a rule, did not rest on any overall epistemological basis but could be disputed on the basis of sometimes widely different, mutually competing beliefs or interpretations of reality. These disagreements, which concerned the very foundations of human knowledge, the *epistēmē*, as it were, of Late Antique Mediterranean civilization, were certainly aggravated during the late fourth century, when they frequently involved concepts of fiction or fictionality.

The following survey concentrates on those Christian writers, the cultural radicals of Late Antiquity, who (surprisingly quickly) got the better of their pagan opponents, contributing to the religious, philosophical and even literary agenda for centuries to come. From our later perspective, their cause might seem an easy one, because they undeniably knew where truth was to be found: in the Bible. The Holy Writ was true, and everything which was considered incompatible with it was false. If Symmachus had maintained that different roads led to the same God, his opponent Ambrose replied sternly that only one road was true, or indeed Truth itself, while all other paths led astray, hopelessly lost in obscure fictional woods.

However, just to add one last specification to this highly complex field of studies, such an uncompromising and self-confident attitude was not possible for all Christians. It was characteristic of the period's polemics and proselytism, of its preaching and triumphant declarations of principle, but in real life – as we can learn from Augustine's *Confessions* – matters of faith did not always seem so unambiguous and clear-cut. Since even Augustine, Jerome and their generation had been imbued with pagan poetry from early childhood, and since Roman education was exclusively dedicated to classical learning, to grammar (including literary studies) and to rhetoric, many early Christians could hardly avoid questions like the following: How did their true faith relate to the powerful, immensely rich philosophical tradition inherited from Pericles' Athens? Were Virgil, Ovid and the canonized pagan poets to be considered unconditionally incompatible with the Bible? Or did they in fact expose themes sometimes consonant and sometimes discordant with the Gospel? Such issues triggered in turn linguistic and hermeneutical questions, which the Latin Fathers to a great extent inherited from Hellenistic philology, Stoic allegoresis and the theologians of Alexandria. In Ambrose's Luke commentary 6.88, it is characteristically Midas' miraculous powers that are considered 'fictional' in contrast to Christ's 'factual' works. But would not precisely this comparison indicate that the *tale* of Midas, the myth, was likely to communicate some useful or even true knowledge? And as soon as the pagan myths, by definition false from a categorical Christian perspective, were believed to conceal some valuable meaning, the issue of fictionality emerged inevitably.

That is why even a combative spirit like Jerome from time to time might demonstrate a certain ambivalence about pagan culture. Even if quite a few of the Late Antique Christian intellectuals maintained the declared non-existence of Midas and the other well-known protagonists of the old myths (an airy nothing, after all), they devoted considerable energy to clarify the possible significance of precisely those figures. From the very start, the Biblical writers had drawn a sharp dividing line between what Saint Paul, in a phrase frequently quoted by later apologists, had called "truth" on the one hand and "myths" on the other, *alētheia* and *mythos*.[1] But even Paul, as we shall see, could reuse pagan beliefs for his own purposes. The great Christian process of separation – the *kerygma* here, *fabulae* there – was, in fact, seldom simple.

The Shadow of Creusa

If there is one main thread running through the following presentation of Late Antique ideas and theories of fiction, it would be the oscillation between the young Christian advocates' bold radicalism – manifest in the words of Revela-

---

[1] "For the time is coming when people will not endure sound teaching, but having itching ears they will accumulate for themselves teachers to suit their own passions, and will turn away from listening to the truth and wander off into myths." 2 Timothy 4.3–4.

tion (21.5), "Behold, I am making all things new" – and their lingering attachment to the old order of things. Even if this tension is particularly characteristic of Augustine, it is perceivable in a number of his contemporaries as well. One of the like-minded brothers in faith that the North African Church Father corresponded with was the Gallo-Roman monk and Bishop Paulinus of Nola (ca. 355–431), naturalized in Campania. He belonged to one of Aquitania's wealthiest landowning families, emerged early as a literary and administrative talent, and as a young man professed rather dutifully the Empire's newly authorized religion. The real turnabout in Paulinus' life took place around the year 390, due to the influence of his wife Therasia, to his meeting with the aged monastery founder and missionary Martin of Tours and furthermore to private tragedies: the murder of his brother and the death of his eight-day-old son. Paulinus was converted to a life based on prayer and asceticism, first in Therasia's Spanish homeland and then in Nola, Campania, east of Naples, where he had worked as a provincial governor in his youth. He was to pass the remainder of his days in Nola, piously adhering to the cult devoted to the local patron, Saint Felix. He spent eight years around the turn of the century to the construction of a new sanctuary dedicated to this Campanian man of God, long believed to have died a martyr's death as a consequence of the persecutions during the third century.

Not even the austere Paulinus was able to provide a final or unambiguous solution to the problem of fictional discourse, but his deprecating gestures are numerous and illustrative.[1] In a letter from the early fifth century (49.8–9) he rails, with characteristic eloquence, against

> those empty minds, which by the false worship of their own imaginings consecrated in fiction the construction of the ship of the ill-fated Argonauts, and which even today believe that they see the ship in heaven and count it amongst the companies of stars [...]. Let us, however, take no thought for what is false and foreign; let us not mingle the lies and poison of those who perish with the light of our truth. We have our own ships, so that we can more worthily cite examples which are true and our own. We have the ark of Noe, the ship to Tharsis, the ship of the man of Tarsus.

---

[1] "Eorum vanitas, qui errore eo quo colunt omne quod fingunt factam Argonautarum infelicium puppem fabulosis litteris sacraverunt atque etiam nunc in caelo videre se credunt et inter astrorum choros numerant [...]. Sed fugiamus a fictis et alienis neque mendacia et venena pereuntium nostrae veritatis lumini misceamus. sunt nobis nostrae naves, ut dignius veris et domesticis utamur exemplis. habemus et arcam Noe. habemus et navem Tharsi navemque Tharsensis." Paulinus' letters are quoted from the edition of W. von Hartel and M. Kamptner 1999, and, in English, from P.G. Walsh's translation volumes 1966–67.

Labels such as *vanitas* and *error* will time and again be applied to classical literary fiction by Late Antique Christian intellectuals. *Vanitas* not only implies futility but also raises the concept of 'emptiness', just as *error* might denote a labyrinthine wandering in addition to its obvious meaning of a mistake. In this apologetic perspective, pagan fiction is precisely "empty", devoid of substance, unlike the new faith's own, unconditional and substantial Gospel; and fictionality's muddle of roundabout ways is put in sharp contrast to Him who, according to John 14.6, is the way (the only one), and the truth (the only one), and the life (the only one worth living). The disparaging allusions to astrology observable in Paulinus' letter are likewise typical of the late fourth-century Christian polemics, reminiscent of the early apologists, yet typically striking a triumphant note. Its recent spokesmen felt that they were doing away with the lies of a dying culture, *mendacia pereuntium*, and they recurrently brought out the contrast between the testimony of the Bible and the overall ancient learning known as the 'liberal arts', *artes liberales*, 'education' or simply 'culture', in Greek: *paideia*.

Nevertheless, even as late as during Paulinus' lifetime it would have been difficult to separate and weed out this ancient heritage from any specifically Christian education. The Church would not take on the responsibility for teaching until later, after the fall of the Empire; the schools' grammar and rhetoric pedagogues provided instruction in Cicero, Virgil and the Roman poets as a matter of course. This conservative curriculum assured an astonishing continuity throughout Roman Antiquity, not least in Gaul, and programmed practically all schoolboys in accordance with the same cultural code.[1] Several of the writers under scrutiny in this book reacted later in life against their traditional upbringing and education – vexedly, aggressively or ironically – but their very polemic is frequently permeated by the old code's discursive and conceptual framework.

An outstanding example of a classically educated Christian intellectual is Paulinus himself. His teacher in the Bordeaux of his childhood had been none other than Ausonius, the fourth century's most brilliant poet of the Roman Empire. Paulinus' cultural militancy bears every trace of a revolt against his intellectual and literary father. In polemical contrast to his mentor's allegedly halfhearted Christianity, he rarely neglected to inculcate an uncompromising polarity between *us* and *them*, as in the emphatic opposition between "foreign" and "our own", *domestici* and *alieni*, above. In this fashion, Paulinus and his fellow believers were quick to establish a tradition of their own, an alternative to the

---

[1] Cf. Theodore Haarhoff: "For behind the shifting scenes of Roman and Barbarian, Pagan and Christian, there is a continuity which reaches to the present day", namely "the immense fabric of Roman Education", 1920, p. 1.

great classical mythology. *They* – the "foreign" – get excited about Argo, well-known from ancient epic and tragedy, the first ship ever built (on account of which it still figures in the final lines of Dante's *Comedy*, Paradiso 33.96).¹ *We*, for our part, have our own ships, literal or metonymical, known from the Bible: Noah's ark as well as, respectively, the Old Testament prophet Jonah (sailing to the city of Tarshish) and the Apostle Paul, a native of Tarsus, capital of the Roman province of Cilicia. What is particularly interesting in this context is Paulinus' pun, possibly inspired by typological readings of the Bible, on Jonah's Tarshish and Paul's Tarsus. Precisely such constellations revealed the rhetorically schooled Roman descendant beneath the unforgiving professions of Catholic faith.

To all appearances, classical fiction, transmitted to new generations of Romans by the teaching of grammar and rhetoric in the schools, seldom released its hold on the Christian writers' souls, not even in their most aggressive and ascetic moments. Perhaps even the arrogance of their pronouncements might testify to this continuous attachment. I started this introductory survey by quoting Hamlet's remarks on the theatre group he sent for with the aim of untangling the machinations at the Danish court after his father's death. It is perhaps no coincidence that the actors in the group, when they are supposed to prove their ability to capture the audience's minds with "a passionate speech" (2.2.437), are asked by Hamlet to present a tableau from burning Troy. It is, in fact, in that place of disaster that one of Western literature's emblematic scenes of the enchanting power of fiction originates. I am thinking of Aeneas' departure from the devastated city at the end of the second song in Virgil's *Aeneid*. The Trojan hero has just put his father, his son and his household gods in safety outside the city walls. Now he returns into the fury and the flames in search of Creusa, his wife. His own home is already destroyed, and King Priam's once mighty citadel is occupied by the Greek invaders. Troy is burning everywhere around him. Finally, Aeneas hurries through the streets in the dark, calling for Creusa but, as it turns out, in vain (2.771–94):

771 Quaerenti et tectis urbis sine fine furenti
 infelix simulacrum atque ipsius umbra Creusae
 visa mihi ante oculos et nota maior imago.
 obstipui, steteruntque comae et vox faucibus haesit.

---

1 I use Dante's *Comedy* in G. Petrocchi's edition, 1966–67. All quotations in English are from the recent translation by J. and R. Hollander, 2002–08.

775 tum sic adfari et curas his demere dictis:
"quid tantum insano iuvat indulgere dolori,
o dulcis coniunx? non haec sine numine divum
eveniunt; nec te comitem hinc portare Creusam
fas aut ille sinit superi regnator Olympi. [...]"
790 haec ubi dicta dedit, lacrimantem et multa volentem
dicere deseruit, tenuisque recessit in auras.
ter conatus ibi collo dare bracchia circum;
ter frustra comprensa manus effugit imago,
par levibus ventis volucrique simillima somno.

Then my eyes saw, while I dashed in an endless search through the city's
buildings, a vision, my fear's worst fulfilment: the ghost of Creusa,
looming before me: her image was as I remembered, but grander.
Stunned, hair standing erect, voice choked in my throat, I stood stock-still.
Uttering words to allay my concerns, she addressed me in this way:
"Why, sweet husband and partner, are you indulging your frantic
grief so intensely? For these events haven't evolved without heaven's
guidance. You can't take Creusa from here as companion. That isn't
God's will. The ruler of lofty Olympus expressly forbids it. [...]"
When she'd said this, though I wept and so wanted to utter so many
words, she deserted me, fading away on the winds without substance.
Three times I tried to encircle her neck with my arms as I stood there,
three times, alas, all in vain. For the image eluded my grasping
hands, like a slight puff of air, as a dream flutters off from a dreamer.

Creusa no longer exists but appears to Aeneas as a shadow or a phantasm, an *imago* which in his eyes seems larger than her figure was in life. She has already become a fiction, as it were, a dreamlike *simulacrum*, unsubstantial and yet urgent, evincing an inexplicable integrity. At that moment, Creusa becomes more real to her spouse than anything else: the devastated Troy, the broken dynasty, the task ahead – to found Rome – which she suggests with her words. Still, inevitably, she is reduced by the wind, doomed to dissolve and melt into air.

This scene, one of the most powerful in classical literature, would capture readers' imagination for centuries to come. Telling evidence of its attraction can be found in Augustine's great contemporary, Jerome. At least two passages in his voluminous oeuvre testify to his memories of *Aeneid* II. In a letter written in 412 from Bethlehem, where he had moved in 388 to work on his translation of the Bible, he tells of his horrified reaction to the news of the fall of Rome under the Visigoth barbarian invasion two years earlier (127.12). This letter gives ample evidence of the saint's identification with the Latin culture which he frequently, in polemical contexts, could reject as inflated pomp. As he ponders on "the dreadful rumour" (about the fall of Rome) that has reached him from the

West, his voice sticks in his throat. His sobs make him unable to dictate the letter he is in the process of drafting: "The City which had taken the whole world was itself taken".[1] This was red-hot contemporary history even in 412, two years *post eventum*, but Jerome resorts to classical literature in order to recreate within himself the horrors of the siege and plundering. At first, his thoughts go to the Hebrew tradition he knew so well from his work with the Old Testament. He alludes to Isaiah's lament over the fall of the kingdom of Moab – "Because Ar of Moab is laid waste in a night, / Moab is undone" (Isaiah 15.1) – and to the Psalmist's mourning over the destruction of Jerusalem: "O God, the nations have come into your inheritance; / they have defiled your holy temple; / they have laid Jerusalem in ruins." (Psalms 78/79.1) Whereupon Jerome immediately, and without any explicit mentioning of his source, passes on to Aeneas' memories of burning Troy from the second song of Virgil's epic (2.361–63): "Who could translate into words that night's disaster and killings? / Who could shed tears that express those oceans of pain that engulfed us? / That day an old city died after so many years of dominion."[2]

The Biblical and epic voices both mourn the fallen city in a kind of alternating song. In this way, Jerome's letter clarifies in a flash the main reason why the early Christian radicals, despite all their accusations or gibes against myth and poetry, ran into so many difficulties when struggling to disavow their own cultural memory, that is, to dismantle the temple of beliefs, images and echoes that Virgil and other classical authors had erected. Most of them lived in a historical period of violent and brutal change, from the fourth to the sixth century, in the Western parts of what once had been the magnificent Roman Empire, where the internal tensions of the realm as well as the pressure from the Germanic tribes were felt more and more painfully. For all his Christian apologetic fervour, Jerome was also a Roman, and the issue of fictionality thus became inextricably linked to that of his cultural identity: who he really was.

This ultimate dependence on the classical heritage becomes even more evident in Jerome's commentary on the Old Testament prophet Ezekiel. There he remembers the Sundays of his boyhood in Rome, when he used to descend into the

---

[1] "Terribilis de Occidente rumor affertur, [...].Haeret vox, et singultus intercipiunt verba dictantis. Capitur Urbs, quae totum cepit orbem", *PL* 22.1094. If not otherwise stated, for all English versions of Jerome's letters I have used the translation by W.H. Fremantle, G. Lewis and W.G. Martley in P. Schaff's and H. Wace's series *Select Library of the Nicene and Post-Nicene Fathers of the Christian Church* 2.6, 1979, the spelling of which I have slightly modernized.

[2] In Jerome's quotation (literally echoing Virgil's original): "Quis cladem illius noctis, quis funera fando / explicet, aut possit lacrymis aequare dolorem? / Urbs antiqua ruit, multos dominata per annos".

catacombs in the company of friends to contemplate – and shudder at – the tombs of the apostles and the martyrs. The atmosphere in the opaque darkness of the crypts was terrifying, he remembers, 'and when we were surrounded by the pitch-black night, that line of Virgil occurred to us: "Horror beleaguered my mind; even silence itself brought me terror"' (12.40, cf. *Aeneid* 2.755), *et caeca nocte circumdatis illud Virgilianum proponitur: Horror ubique animos, simul ipsa silentia terrent.*[1] The subterranean darkness made the boy recall Aeneas' quest for his dead wife in crumbling Troy. The shadow of Creusa made its presence felt all the way into the night of the catacombs.[2]

Her affinity with dreaming (*volucrique simillima somno*) will reappear in different versions throughout this book. It seems quite natural that to Augustine, as we shall see shortly, this final scene from *Aeneid* II would seem paradigmatic of the cognitive status of literary fiction. It is true, of course, that the author of the *Confessions*, permeated by a more reliable refulgence from elsewhere, recoiled from the image of Creusa. But he could not forget its irresistible attraction to the young reader he once was. I would like to think that such a reader is reincarnated time and again in the following presentation. He or she knows that Hecuba is something more than mere "nothing", and that it is the shadow of Creusa that shows the way to the future, far away from the burning city.

---

1 *PL* 25.375b.
2 Possibly Jerome's *caeca nocte circumdatis* also alludes to another of Virgil's sacrified female figures, Eurydice, who in the final book of the *Georgics* is obliged to return to the underworld, "wrapped in uttermost night" (4.497), *ingenti circumdata nocte*, since her husband had turned around to look at her. I quote the *Georgics* from H.R. Fairclough's Loeb edition of *Eclogues. Georgics. Aeneid I–VI* 1998.

II **Augustine: A Restless Farewell**
Renouncing *Ficta* in Late Antiquity

Preliminary Remarks

> There, in the company of Angels, all are righteous and holy, who enjoy the word of God without reading, without letters: for what is written to us through pages, they perceive there through the Face of God.
>
> Augustine, *Expositions on the Book of Psalms* (119.6)[1]

Saint Augustine is without doubt the most important of the writers discussed in this book. His influence reaches far beyond the realm of literature; it permeates not only central disciplines like theology or philosophy but also Christian rhetoric and concepts of history, not to speak of hermeneutics and semiotics through the centuries, down to our modern day. Thanks to his being "the most profound and prolific" of the Latin Church Fathers, he became, as Marcia L. Colish points out, an authority throughout the whole of the Middle Ages, second only to the Bible.[2] The two adjectives she uses to describe him, profound and prolific, which are usually hard to reconcile, also explain why the longest chapter in this book is devoted to him. His productivity is almost incredible; it comprises fourteen heavy, double-columned volumes, 32–45, in Migne's *Patrologia latina*, and can only be explained by Antiquity's advanced system of stenography from dictation. Yet another troublesome (but exciting) circumstance in this connection is that Augustine's works are extremely dependent on their shifting contexts. Both his life and his works are the opposite of desk philosophy untouched by the hurly-burly of life. Most of what he wrote was specifically *directed* and came about in special situations for special purposes, not least polemic or didactic, often addressed to particular persons and not easily packed in neat and tidy parcels. Augustine was never a systematic thinker like Porphyry, as his biographer Peter Brown explains: "His life will be littered with lines of thought that are not worked through to their conclusion, and with abandoned literary enter-

---

[1] "Ibi omnes iusti et sancti, qui fruuntur Verbo Dei sine lectione, sine litteris: quod enim nobis per paginas scriptum est, per faciem Dei illi cernunt." If not otherwise stated, I quote Augustine in his original Latin according to the Italian Nuova Biblioteca Agostiniana (NBA) series, *Opera omnia di Sant'Agostino*, in course of publication since 1965, 1–45, based on Migne's *Patrologia latina*, and in English from the series *Select Library of the Nicene and Post-Nicene Fathers of the Christian Church*, edited by P. Schaff *et alii*, 1.1–8, 1978–79.
[2] Colish 1968, p. 8.

prises."[1] This, of course, makes great demands on anyone who hopes to analyse his work.

Quite simply, it is my intention to show how Augustine closed the door on literary fiction. This door had stood open, or at least ajar, in Greek and Roman traditions for almost a thousand years, ever since the time of Homer and Hesiod. But I would also like to emphasize the continuity, or rather the inseparable coexistence of antique and Christian culture that has been pointed out by so many contemporary scholars like Brown, Alan Cameron or the French Latinist Jacques Fontaine.[2] Pagan writers had not only produced magnificent examples of fiction for posterity, they had also provided sharp tools for a consistent criticism of fictionality. In addition, I shall touch on a number of other aspects of Augustine's writing such as epistemology, linguistic theory, hermeneutics, semiotics, aesthetics or rhetoric, only, however, in order to throw light on his advances and retreats in matters of fictionality.

Right from the very start of his writing career, from what has been called his "conversion to philosophy" in the mid-380s, Augustine began to question the value and uses of fictional representation.[3] He abandoned the rhetorical-aesthetic culture he had grown up with in favour of a theology that in the end turned out not to allow any room for literature. This development in his intellectual career had considerable – some would say fateful – consequences for medieval literary criticism, which was sometimes inclined to reject poets as liars. If individual statements in Augustine's writings are taken out of their context, they may indeed, at least for an art or literary scholar, give a depressingly pessimistic and utilitarian impression. Paintings, statues and other mimetic works, *huiusmodi simulata opera* as they are called in the key treatise *De doctrina christiana* (*On Christian Doctrine*), in the main composed shortly before 400, are normally seen as part of mankind's superfluous inventions: "Finally, the thousands of fictional stories and romances, which through their falsehoods give people great pleasure, are human institutions. Indeed, nothing should be thought more peculiar to mankind than lies and falsehoods, which derive exclusively from mankind itself." (2.25.39)[4]

---

[1] Brown 2000, p. 116. John J. O'Meara makes a similar point: "In spite of the picture of him [Augustine] as the great definer of doctrines in the West, he was also profoundly questioning, profoundly aporetic", 1992, p. 91.
[2] Cf. Cameron 2004, pp. 342f. For a convenient survey, see Fontaine 1982.
[3] Cf. the chapter "La conversion à la philosophie" in Marrou 1938, pp. 161–86.
[4] "Milia denique fictarum fabularum et falsitatum, quarum mendaciis homines delectantur, humana instituta sunt. Et nulla magis hominum propria, quae a se ipsis habent, existimanda sunt

But in actual fact, Augustine was ambivalent about the truth value of fiction, and it was only after a long process, a long drawn-out farewell, that he decided to doubt the possibilities of literature – and by that he meant classical poetry and drama – to play a meaningful role for his Christian belief or preaching. His continuous tendency to rely on rhetorical devices, his interest in the theatre and his life-long reuse of Virgil indicate that his doubt was not categorical. There remained scattered through his writings a possibility within the overall programme, on the road to salvation *per corporalia ad incorporalia*, to uphold both the school disciplines ('the liberal arts') and poetry.[1] But in the long run, Augustine set his sights on the end of the road at the expense of all secular means of getting there, that is, he focused on the difficult truth of the Incarnation at the sacrifice of all rhetorical magnificence, on the purity of the divine vision at the cost of the ambiguity of human art.

In the following, I shall sketch a few critical stages on this Augustinian way to a devotion beyond speech and, indeed, beyond (linguistic) signification. My starting point will be what I perceive to be the most critical of them all, as witnessed by the writer in superbly, albeit paradoxically eloquent words. This was a blessed moment in Augustine's life, but also an early culmination of the semantic and semiotic criticism that stretched over five decades of his epoch-making intellectual career. It was to be directed not only against fictionality, but against the basis of fictionality in human imagination, against its foremost manifestation in ancient culture, poetical language, and against its prime instance in Roman literature, the *Aeneid*, in short: against the shadow of Creusa.

---

quam quaeque falsa atque mendacia." For *On Christian Doctrine* I follow both the Latin text and the English translation provided by R.P.H. Green 1996.
1 See *Revisions* in R.J. Teske's edition: "I wanted [...] to arrive myself at incorporeal things by way of corporeal ones" (1.6), *per corporalia cupiens ad incorporalia*, trans. B. Ramsey, Augustine 2010.

1 At the Window in Ostia

Plotinian/Pauline *Raptus*

In the ninth book of his *Confessions*, Augustine had come far on his way to the true faith. He had described his childhood and teenage errors in his hometown of Thagaste (now Souk Ahras in the northeast corner of Algeria) and in Carthage, city of students and of theatres. He had accounted for his decisive journey to Rome and Milan, the old and the new capital city respectively of the Roman Empire, his meeting with Archbishop Ambrose, his career as a teacher of rhetoric, his long-standing relationship with a concubine and his mother's arrival in Milan; the deeply religious Monnica had become uneasy about her son's unchristian lifestyle. Augustine had also told his readers about his philosophical journey via Manichaeism to Neo-Platonism, his increasing spiritual discontent and need of faith, and his conversion in the Milanese garden in August 386. Finally, he had described his meditative retreat with his mother, his son Adeodatus, his brother Navigius and a couple of friends or pupils, to Cassiciacum, the peaceful farm north of Milan, close to Lake Como at the foot of the Alps, where he wrote his philosophical dialogues during the autumn and winter of 386–87. More briefly, he had told about his baptism by Ambrose on the eve of Easter, 24–25 April 387.

By that time, Augustine had decided to withdraw to the town he came from, Thagaste, to live a quiet, meditative and secluded Christian life, occupying himself with prayer and reading – as a presage of medieval monastery life – together with his mother and a few brothers in faith. He is at the great dividing line in his life. What happened to him after his return to Africa is not revealed in his *Confessions*, but with hindsight we know how capitally he failed to live up to his contemplative intentions. Yes, he came to Thagaste in 388, but on a journey to the seaport of Hippo Regius (now Annaba) a few years later he was ordained – quite involuntarily – by the town's congregation, and after that there was no turning back. For the rest of his life he worked to spread the Christian faith in North Africa. His daily tasks included not only exegesis and commentary but also missionary work, polemics and practical parish activities. In 396 he was made Bishop of Hippo. He would die in the same town thirty-four years later, precisely when the Vandals had begun to besiege it, the beginning of their hundred years' rule of the African provinces.

But now it was the summer of 387. On the way home to Africa, Augustine was forced to make a stop at Ostia, the old port of Rome, because the usurper Maximus had blocked the way for all sea traffic. A century and a half earlier, Ostia had been the scene for Minucius Felix's apologetic little dialogue *Octavius*, and now it was a popular resort for Senator Symmachus and his urban circle of statesmen and intellectuals, the last pagan enclave with power and influence in the West. During these summer days at the mouth of the Tiber, Monnica passed away. This sad event turned out to be a decisive episode in the Augustinian salvation drama. The writer lingers at length over his mother's background, her marriage and the last days of her life. One day at Ostia, shortly before the end, the two of them stood at the window of their lodgings (an archetypal place for gazing out or longing for far-away lands), looking over the garden. They were "far from the crowds", *remoti a turbis*, Augustine remarks, entering deeply into a conversation which was to lead them out of this world. The addressee of the text is God the Father Himself (9.10.23–24):

> We were alone, conferring very intimately. Forgetting what lay in the past, and stretching out to what was ahead, we inquired between ourselves in the light of present truth, the Truth which is yourself, what the eternal life of the saints would be like. Eye has not seen nor ear heard nor human heart conceived it, yet with the mouth of our hearts wide open we panted thirstily for the celestial streams of your fountain, the fount of life which is with you, that bedewed from it according to our present capacity we might in our little measure think upon a thing so great.
>
> Our colloquy led us to the point where the pleasures of the body's senses, however intense and in however brilliant a material light enjoyed, seemed unworthy not merely of comparison but even of remembrance beside the joy of that life, and we lifted ourselves in longing yet more ardent toward *That Which Is*, and step by step traversed all bodily creatures and heaven itself, whence sun and moon and stars shed their light upon the earth. Higher still we mounted by inward thought and wondering discourse on your works, and we arrived at the summit of our own minds; and this too we transcended, to touch that land of never-failing plenty where you pasture Israel for ever with the food of truth. Life there is the Wisdom through whom all these things are made, and all others that have been or ever will be; but Wisdom herself is not made: she is as she always has been and will be for ever. Rather should we say that in her there is no "has been" or "will be," but only being, for she is eternal, but past and future do not belong to eternity. And as we talked and panted for it, we just touched the edge of it by the utmost leap of our hearts; then, sighing and unsatisfied, we left the first-fruits of our spirit captive there, and returned to the noise of articulate speech, where a word has beginning and end. How different from your Word, our Lord, who abides in himself, and grows not old, but renews all things. (I)

This episode is rightly well-known, "famous, too famous", to quote James J. O'Donnell, responsible for the edition of the *Confessions* used throughout this book.[1] An eminent scholar of medieval literature and poetry like Eugene

---

[1] Augustine 1992 (III), p. 122.

Vance has described it as "one of the great moments in the metalanguage of the West".¹ It is not possible here, not even cursorily, to go into such theologically loaded questions as to whether or not the intermezzo at Ostia represents a genuine mystic experience, a matter which is energetically debated in Augustinian research. For our purpose, it is first and foremost the author's treatment of imagery, imagination and fictionality that seems to be important. The following analysis aims at demonstrating how these phenomena are bound up with his attitude to language. The issue of verbal communication is actually crucial to the experience of Augustine and Monnica at the window in Ostia, rendered possible by means of a language not only hitherto unheard of but, in fact, unheard.

*

The Ostia passage condenses and rephrases in inventive ways the two great traditions of ideas that are discussed and analysed throughout the *Confessions:* the Hellenistic Neo-Platonic and the Jewish-Christian. By looking more closely at one single little word, it is easy to illustrate its twin roots in Plotinian philosophy and Pauline soteriology.

The word is *ante*. Augustine and Monnica reach out to what lies "ahead", *in ea quae ante sunt*. This expression bears an unmistakeable trace of the Platonizing thinker Plotinus' great work *The Enneads*, in which the philosopher's mystical goal, the One, is repeatedly described in terms of what lies *ahead* or *before*, in space, time or importance: "And Intellect is competent to see its own things and the things before it. The things in it also are pure, but those before it are purer and simpler – or rather that which is before it. It is not therefore Intellect, but before Intellect." (6.9.3)² The repeated references to the position of the One before (*pro*) the Intellect make a distinct impression. The corresponding Latin term in the Augustinian text, *ante*, like its Greek original, probably signals spatial and chronological as well as hierarchical priority, but nonetheless it points to an altogether different supremacy than the Plotinian transcendence. It carries an equally strong echo of Paul's Epistle to the Philippians in which the author is metaphorically on the running track, hoping to win the race in view of a divine reward: "But one thing I do: forgetting what lies behind and straining forward to what lies ahead" (3.13), in Jerome's version *in priora*.³ In comparison with the

---

1 Vance 1982, p. 34.
2 I quote Plotinus' *Enneads* from A.H. Armstrong's Loeb edition 1966–88.
3 Philippians 3.13 is regularly indicated in the margin of 9.10.23 in the editions of *Confessions*. I give Jerome's translation of Paul's likewise ambiguous *emprosthen*, in spite of his Vulgate not being accessible – at least not in its final shape – to Augustine at the time of his completing the *Confessions*.

Egyptian philosopher's veritable "rush" towards the One in the *Enneads* 5.5.4, Augustine's essentially Pauline way to God is not only directed towards a different goal but laid out for a different community (the writer and his mother), marked by a different intimacy and, last but not least, by a different kind of writing, which will be closely examined here.

Scholars have diligently noted and debated the influence of Plotinus (ca. 205–70), born in Egypt and active in Rome, on the works of the Church Father. The first to point out the ethereal philosopher's role in this context was Augustine himself, in some of the dialogues from Cassiciacum composed in the autumn 386, *Contra academicos* (*Against the Academics*) and *De beata vita* (*The Happy Life*). In the former document, to a large extent a dispute with Hellenistic Scepticism in the Ciceronian vein, the author speaks of how "Plato's doctrine, which in philosophy is the purest and most clear, the clouds of error having been removed, shone forth especially in Plotinus. This Platonic philosopher is regarded as being so like Plato that one would think that they had lived at the same time. The interval of time between them is, however, so great that one should rather think that Plato had come to life again in Plotinus." (3.18.41)[1]

In *The Happy Life* Augustine reports briefly on his intellectual development, including his contact with 'a few of Plotinus' books' (1.4).[2] This information was to be confirmed in the *Confessions* some ten years later, when the author acknowledges his debt to "some books by the Platonists, translated from the Greek into Latin" (7.9.13), *quosdam platonicorum libros ex graeca lingua in latinam versos*. Everything indicates that these references are first and foremost to the *Enneads* in a translation by another North African scholar, the rhetorician and grammarian Marius Victorinus, born about the year 300, commonly called Victorinus Afer because of his origin. His sensational conversion to the true faith, described in detail by the presbyter Simplicianus in the introduction to the eighth book of the *Confessions*, seems to be a direct presage of Augustine's own spiritual rebirth in the same book (8.12.28).

The first modern scholar to emphasize Plotinus' importance for Augustine was the Belgian Jesuit Paul Henry. According to him, both the convert in Cassi-

---

[1] "Os illud Platonis quod in philosophia purgatissimum est et lucidissimum, dimotis nubibus erroris emicuit, maxime in Plotino, qui platonicus philosophus ita eius similis iudicatus est, ut simul eos vixisse, tantum autem interest temporis ut in hoc ille revixisse putandus sit." English translation by J.J. O'Meara in Augustine 1950a.

[2] "Lectis autem Plotini paucissimis libris". For the reading *Plotini* rather than *Platonis*, see Henry 1934, pp. 82–89. There have been divergent opinions of Augustine's knowledge of Greek. He probably had a basic command of the *koinē*, but it seems fair to assume that he only consulted works in Greek if no Latin translations were available to him.

ciacum in 386 and the confessor in Hippo around 400 would have regarded the Egyptian philosopher as "a kind of profane messenger of the Word of God".[1] Henry pursues his thesis of a Plotinian Augustine energetically, in an obvious polemic against those of his Catholic adversaries who wanted to keep the Church Father free of infection from pagan temptations. Henry was surely right about this, and he has understandably had energetic successors like Pierre Courcelle and Robert J. O'Connell.[2] Still, some scholars insist on an absolute distinction between the two mystic experiences, among them Thomas Williams, who claims in an interesting but forced essay that "Augustine regards the vision at Ostia as utterly different from anything he could have got from the Platonists".[3]

Martha Nussbaum seems more balanced in her assumption that Augustine was both fascinated by and critical of the Platonic type of ascent towards transcendent reality. Its overall scheme provided him with a model for philosophical contemplation, a paradigm whose incentive – the striving for self-sufficient impassivity when finally within reach of the absolute One – had, however, in the *Confessions*, to be replaced by a restless, unquenched thirst. The confessor's biographical self never finds any rest, never manages to free himself from his contingent existence, from his memories, feelings and personal responsibility. He is driven by a passionate tension and longing, the object of which, God, is always its ultimate agent.[4] We may well ask whether Nussbaum does not underestimate the impassioned pulse and dramatic rhythm that permeate even the *Enneads*, but her argument makes an important point. The relationship of the Augustinian

---

[1] Henry 1934, p. 90. In addition, see Henry 1981, his groundbreaking work in this field (French original version 1938, *La vision d'Ostie*), which stresses the correspondences between the Ostia episode and its "sources", the *Enneads* 1.6 and 5.1, pp. 15–23.

[2] Henry's most diligent follower in detecting Neo-Platonic traces in the *Confessions* is probably Courcelle, who dedicates seventy pages to the influence of the "Platonic books" on this work, 1963, pp. 17–88. The monograph of O'Connell 1968 focuses throughout on the Neo-Platonic influence on Augustine's view of man during the years following his conversion.

[3] Williams 2005, p. 150f. Brian Dobell, for his part, acknowledges the fundamental difference between the solitary, provisional Platonic ascent and the shared Ostia experience, mediated by Christ, considering the latter to be "described in terms of the Incarnational theology that Augustine began developing in the mid-390s", 2009, p. 222, whereas in 387 "Augustine would not have seen this difference between the Christian and Platonic ascents", p. 223.

[4] Nussbaum 1999. In addition, useful reminders about the tension between the old philosophy and the new faith (frequently inimical to philosophical culture) but also observations of their "common ground", with great relevance to the study of Augustine, are to be found in De Vogel 1985, pp. 27–37. Similarly, John Peter Kenney admits the significance of Platonist "foundationalist epistemology and hierarchical metaphysics" to Augustine, while Platonic (Plotinian) theology ultimately proves incompatible with the *Confessions:* "In Augustine there is no solitary flight of the alone to the alone", 2005, p. 145.

ascension theme to its Plotinian counterpart could with good reason be described in terms of imitation as well as correction.

The Church Father's adherence to the *Enneads*' matrix is undoubtedly there, especially in his earlier writings. The rise of the soul is portrayed in his Cassiciacum dialogue *De ordine* (*On Order*), in 386, and is thereafter a sedulously varied theme throughout his works.[1] In the seventh book of the *Confessions*, repeatedly cited by Henry, Augustine describes how in Milan, inspired by his readings of the Neo-Platonists, he learnt to practise deeper introspection and attain a purer vision: "I entered under your guidance the innermost places of my being; [...] and with the vision of my spirit, such as it was, I saw the incommutable light far above my spiritual ken, transcending my mind", *intravi in intima mea duce te,... et vidi qualicumque oculo animae meae supra eundem oculum animae meae, supra mentem meam, lucem incommutabilem*. This new discipline, philosophy's inner way upwards, began from an existential bottom point, what Augustine calls "a region of unlikeness", far from God: *regio dissimilitudinis*, his own version of Plotinus' *tēs anomoiotētos topos* (7.10.16, cf. the *Enneads*, 1.8.13).

A similar mental journey is depicted later on in the same book of the *Confessions*, with an evident adherence to the Egyptian philosopher, as an ascension towards ever clearer views and insights. With a starting point in the beauty of things and bodies, the author's alter ego rises from the sensory level of perception "to that inner power of the soul", *inde ad eius interiorem vim*, in all probability an indication of our lower mental faculties, such as imagination. He proceeds to calculating reason, *ad ratiocinantem potentiam*, which has to free itself from its muddled tangle of shadowy images, *contradicentes turbae phantasmatum*, in order to raise itself to the heights of intelligence, *ad intellegentiam suam*. It is on this intellectual level that Augustine's seeker after truth receives an authentic vision "in the flash of one tremulous glance", not of the Godhead in any personal sense but of its invisible qualities, "that which is", as if his earlier journey had been troubled by unreal sights and phantasms, now finally dispelled (a truly Plotinian experience): *et pervenit ad id quod est in ictu trepidantis aspectus* (7.17.23).

The term *ictus* is, admittedly, not easily translated. It can mean blow, stroke, attack or thrust, and it can – like the *ante* from the Ostia chapter, as we have already seen – ring with both a Plotinian and a Pauline resonance. As for Plotinus, Pierre Courcelle speaks in this context of a "shock" or violent collision, citing one of the last *Enneads*' expressions for the ultimate vision of the soul: "It

---

[1] For a short but helpful survey, see Van Fleteren 1993.

saw, as if in utter amazement" (or literally 'as if struck', 6.7.31).[1] To this could be added Plotinus' intriguing sensation, expressed elsewhere in his work, of 'rushing' or 'leaping' towards the One (5.5.4). In both these *Enneads*, the key words in question, *plēgeisa* ('struck') and *aixai* ('rush') respectively, are connected with verbs denoting vision.

The same bewildering insight is central to the famous apocalyptic phrasing in 1 Corinthians 15.51–52, where Paul looks forward to the resurrection "in a moment, in the twinkling of an eye". The Greek text *en atomōi, en rhipēi ophthalmou* is translated by Jerome in the Vulgate as *in momento in ictu oculi*, a wording that Augustine was to echo in the *Confessions* 7.1.1, *in ictu oculi*, as well as in his major treatise *De trinitate* (*On the Trinity*), completed after more than twenty years' work in about 420: *in ipso namque ictu oculi* (14.19.25).[2] To sum up, at the climax of the Milanese ascension, Augustine is shaken by what he sees, according to the highest possible example in both philosophical (Plotinian) and apostolic (Pauline) tradition, linked to each other by the seminal term *ictus*, but he is not able to retain such an overwhelming vision and has to return to everyday life, albeit with the wistful memory of the experience in his mind, likened to a lingering fragrance.

This event undoubtedly points forward to the miracle at Ostia, as has been amply demonstrated by several scholars after Henry, such as Courcelle, André Mandouze, Frederick van Fleteren and Colin Starnes.[3] Such a pattern of anticipation and fulfilment makes the Plotinian ascent functional within the narrative design of the *Confessions*, in which a number of episodes from Books I–VIII look forward to the convert's revealed insight. But in the light from Ostia – that is, from the faith the writer has at last found – all contemplation restricted to philosophy is at the same time discredited, debunked as a delusion that could

---

1 Courcelle 1950, p. 166.

2 I would hesitate to conclude, though, that Augustine alludes specifically to the wording of Jerome; he might just as well be recycling one of the older Bible versions, *Veteres Latinae*, which he seems to have preferred to the Vulgate (apart from the Gospels). For Augustine and the Vulgate, see Sparks 1970, p. 519, Bonner 1970, pp. 544–46, O'Donnell 2005, pp. 126–28, and Houghton 2008, pp. 5–21.

3 The verbal and structural parallels between these Augustinian *ascensiones* were established by Courcelle 1950, pp. 222–26, and arranged in two neat tables by Mandouze 1968, pp. 686–97. Van Fleteren has dedicated several works to the ascent described in the seventh book of the *Confessions*, conveniently summarized in 1994. In a keen article 1992, Starnes, for his part, explains the peculiar nature of the Ostia experience by referring to Monnica's presence. Williams, on the other hand, in his article 2005 (originally published 2002), draws a sharp line between the two ecstasies, the former – Platonic – of an intellectual or contemplative nature, the latter affective, auditive and Christological.

prove to be as precarious as Manichaeism. With Augustine's own wording: "after reading the books of the Platonists", *lectis platonicorum illis libris,* he kept talking as if he were already "skilled" or experienced, *peritus,* but since he did not seek the way to God in Christ, he "would more probably have been killed than skilled", *non peritus sed periturus,* if he had pursued their path (7.20.26).

Here, the rhetorical play on words – *paronomasia* – brings out the secluded self's mortally dangerous trust in Plotinian contemplation: it lacks support in the experience of Christ. That is why it will soon be eclipsed by the journey of the united souls of mother and son from Ostia, where the decisive "shock" is no longer situated in the eyes but in the heart. This transition from the philosophical gaze to the *ictus* of the pious breast in the *Confessions* seems indicative of a paradigmatic shift in the sensibility or the literature of the epoch, increasingly preoccupied by the inner dialogue with God. In short, the Ostia experience should be understood against this general background: it signalled the relocation of both the philosopher's and the apostle's moment of transfiguration to the human heart.

The Speech of the Heart

The convert is not alone in this momentous event; his mother is there too, and as an unvoiced condition for the whole scene, there is the presence of Christ. The difference compared to the *Enneads'* closing words (6.9.11) about the "escape in solitude to the solitary" is evident. Thus the Ostia passage reflects Augustine the confessor's scepticism of the pagan philosophers who believed they could arrange their lives at their discretion. Admittedly, they deserved esteem for their way towards ever higher levels of contemplation, where – according to *On the Trinity* (13.19.24) – they "have been able to understand and discern the invisible things of God by those things which are made". But at the same time, they appeared to be self-sufficient, and without the intermediary Christ their insights were doomed to be both accidental and imperfect.[1] Above all, the discursive gap between the confessor and the philosophers seems to be as great as the ideological distance. That is the theme of this section. The convert's

---

1 "Illi autem praecipui gentium philosophi, qui invisibilia Dei, per ea quae facta sunt, intellecta conspicere potuerunt, tamen quia sine Mediatore, id est, sine homine Christo philosophati sunt" (cf. *On the Trinity* 13.7.10). The main difference between Augustine and the Platonists, observes Robert A. Herrera, consists in the Church Father's repeated emphasis on Christ as the sole Mediator. Crucial Christological concepts or beliefs, such as the bodily resurrection, appeared habitually barbarian and vulgar to the refined Neo-Platonist philosophers, 1994, p. 171.

ascension is staged within the framework of a *narrative*, or even a personal life story, the first of its kind in Western literature. It stands in sharp contrast to, for example, Plotinus' conceptual exposé and complete lack of interest in his own person, as well as to Augustine's Greek predecessors' theoretical tracts in general.

Plotinus' pupil and later editor, Porphyry of Tyre (ca. 235–305), wrote a short biography of his master, known as *Vita Plotini*, commonly included in editions of the *Enneads*, where he recalls that his master "seemed ashamed of being in the body". Moreover, the philosopher never spoke of his race, his parents or his homeland, and did not allow himself to be portrayed (1).[1] In contrast, the *Confessions* make use of classical narrative techniques, such as episodic composition (up until the Ostia chapter, just before the work's transition to philosophy and Biblical exegesis in the concluding Books X–XIII), carefully reproduced dialogues and scarce but evenly distributed accounts of the narrator's whereabouts. First and foremost, the *Confessions* rely on the structure and power of rhetoric. The language of the Ostia chapter quoted above, for example, is characterized by syntactic figures such as the typical enumerations by means of triads usually labelled *tricola*, registered in the pseudo-Ciceronian *Ad Herennium* (4.19.26): "eye has not seen nor ear heard nor human heart conceived it", "sun and moon and stars shed their light upon the earth", "we mounted by inward thought and wondering discourse on your works" (*ascendebamus interius cogitando et loquendo et mirando opera tua*).

There is also, in the following paragraph, chiasmus – *non ipsa nos fecimus, sed fecit nos* (9.10.25) – and the figure of speech labelled *gradatio* in *Ad Herennium* (4.25.34): intensification by degrees, or climax. Last but not least, the Ostia account, like the whole of the *Confessions*, is consistently directed at an interlocutor, God. It is He who is addressed as *tu* ("you") throughout the work, it is He who is the imagined recipient of the writer's questions, appeals and meditations. Thus, the classical narrative and rhetorical techniques are complemented with those of Biblical prayers or psalms. Indeed, Augustine has transposed the three lyric modes of the Old Testament Book of Psalms – the hymns, the laments, and the thanksgivings – into refined Latin prose, using them to suggest a coherent life history.

Among all other interlocutors of the *Confessions*, Monnica stands out, and now she is about to leave her son for ever. Precisely when he plans to embark on his journey to Africa and the province of his birth, where he will work as a

---

[1] I use Armstrong's translation of *Vita Plotini*, prefixed to the first of the *Enneads* in his Loeb edition 1969.

Christian philosopher, preacher and bishop for the rest of his life, this great intellectual and kerygmatic project is anticipated by an intense though transitory and, most importantly, *shared* experience of his heavenly homeland. This is an *ascensio* that, still in sharp contrast to Plotinus' solitary *anabasis*, should be understood as a dialogue between mother and son, or more exactly a *conloquium dulce*, a "sweet" or intimate conversation inaugurating a new phase in the history of Western discursiveness. Charles Taylor calls it "the language of inwardness" or "the inwardness of radical reflexivity", a crucial step between Plato and Descartes in the making of the modern identity in the West, a turn to the self which is also a turn to God "within".[1] I would like to call it the speech of the heart, with important points of departure in the Gospels, according to Matthew's well-known words: "For out of the abundance of the heart the mouth speaks" (12.34), *ex abundantia enim cordis os loquitur*. Oral performance is (or should be) a manifestation of an interior discourse which is, in the last instance, dictated by faith.

*

In the Pauline Epistles, the picture becomes even clearer than in Matthew or the other Gospels. The speech of the heart is a recurrent theme in Paul's letters, which place great weight on the inner conviction of the Christian individual, to a certain extent in contrast to the many legal prescriptions and instructions for cult practices of the Old Testament. "They show that the work of the law is written on their hearts", asserts Paul, in an ecumenical spirit, about the Gentiles in his Epistle to the Romans, 2.15, *qui ostendunt opus legis scriptum in cordibus suis*. Later in the same epistle, he clarifies this message by explaining that Christ is the end of the law. The new righteousness which comes from faith rather than the law claims that "'The word is near you, in your mouth and in your heart' (that is, the word of faith that we proclaim)", 10.8, *prope est verbum in ore tuo et in corde tuo hoc est verbum fidei quod praedicamus*.

In short, there is no doubt about the early Christian need to break away from the Mosaic Law and the old dispensation. The legitimacy for a new discourse was established by referring to the (internal, individual) message of the heart rather than to the (external, ritual) rules of the law book. Furthermore, the Church Fathers would develop their doctrine of "the word of the heart", *verbum cordis*, in polemical contrast to pagan culture which they were quick to depict as all too rhetorical or philosophical-cerebral. In a letter precisely from the time of the composition of the *Confessions*, Jerome states that "sense is in the heart, the dwelling of the heart is in the breast. People ask where the principal place of

---

[1] Taylor 1989, pp. 130–32.

the soul is. Plato says it is in the brain, Christ shows it in the heart" (64.1), *sensus in corde est, habitaculum cordis in pectore. Quaeritur ubi sit animae principale. Plato in cerebro: Christus monstrat in corde.*[1] In his letters, Paulinus of Nola is repeatedly arguing along the same lines. Thus he opens his *Epistula* XXXVIII with an expression of delight in his addressee's faith "which, as your lips have attested, is born in your heart", *quam corde conceptam ore testatus es*, whereupon he proceeds to praise Paul for his refusal to glory in lofty speech or in knowledge of the Law (38.1).[2]

Thus Augustine, Jerome and Paulinus all articulate a new Christian view of language and communication, whereby optimal speech is understood to be a fundamentally transparent medium for the Spirit or the divine message, in the sharpest possible contrast to the florid language of rhetoric. This idea could find some support in earlier Roman authors, above all perhaps in Seneca and certain austere philosophers of the Stoic tradition. Now, however, it gained hegemony among the leading theologians of Late Antique culture, usually with a critical eye towards the *flosculi* or *genus floridum* of pagan eloquence and poetry.[3]

Such flowery language was commonly associated with fictionality. The showy *flores*, *colores* or *lumina* of eloquent style indicated the presence of *ficta*. When, some hundred years later, the incipient monastery culture of the Middle Ages tried to explain and encourage *lectio divina* (the kind of devout and joint Bible reading that should result in prayer and the meditation of the heart), it frequently sounded a note of warning precisely against reading habits weaned on works of fiction, aimed at pure entertainment. Let us listen to the French theologian, monk and later Bishop, Caesarius of Arles (ca. 470–542), one of Augustine's most ardent successors, who pointed out in his first sermon the responsibility of priests for diligently spreading *verbum cordis* (1.10):[4]

---

1 *PL* 22.608 (my translation). This letter by Jerome serves to illustrate the doctrine of *verbum cordis* in Quacquarelli 1972, p. 197.
2 For a thorough examination of the status of the concept of *homo interior* in Paulinus, see Conybeare 2000, pp. 131–60.
3 Cf. Fontaine 1988, p. 62.
4 "Non solum maioribus festivitatibus, sed etiam reliquis temporibus omni die dominico verbum dei praedicemus, nec in ecclesia tantum, sed, sicut supra suggessi, et ad convivium lectionem divinam relegi faciamus, et in conloquio, in consessu, in itinere, et ubicumque fuerimus, repudiatis ociosis fabulis et mordacibus iocis verbum domini fidelium cordibus referre festinemus". Caesarius' sermon is quoted after the edition of G. Morin 1953, and, in English, according to M.M. Mueller's translation 1956.

Let us preach the word of God as much as we can, every Sunday at all times, as well as on the major feasts. Not only in church, but, as I mentioned above, even at a banquet we should have the sacred text read over again; in conversation, at an assembly, on the road, or wherever we are, let us hasten to reject idle gossip [*ociosae fabulae*] and biting jokes and to speak the word of the Lord to the hearts of the faithful.

A proper *lectio divina*, then, presumes that all *fabulae* are set aside. Augustine's *Confessions* actually contain several drafts for this kind of *lectio* – passages that slip into prayer – and are governed by the same anti-law and anti-pagan mechanisms in their pleadings for the speech of the heart. In his early years, the work's narrator suffers from the pedantic, compulsive methods of his pedagogues, and his way to conversion goes first and foremost via reading, discussion, prayer and meditation. Despite his success as a teacher of rhetoric and his philosophical orientation along marked tracks, at first of the Manichees and later of the Platonists, he remained dissatisfied with his life, as is evident from the familiar assertion on the first page of the *Confessions*: "and our heart is unquiet until it rests in you" (1.1.1), *inquietum est cor nostrum donec requiescat in te*.

Moreover, the *Confessions* are largely built up as a story of temptation, in which the protagonist's heart has to confront various kinds of fictions and fantasies. Nowhere does he find peace of mind or satisfaction. In the clear light of retrospection, Augustine realizes that during these years up to his rebirth in 386, he was tried by the Lord, who speaks with him or even cries to him throughout his intellectual and moral blindness, whereupon he finally learned to pay attention "as one hears a word in the heart" (7.10.16), *sicut auditur in corde*.

When, in the eighth book, the narrator has reached the most famous episode of the work, his conversion, the decisive drama takes place as much in his heart as in the Milanese garden. Augustine describes his struggle for faith as "all this argument in my heart" (8.11.27), *ista controversia in corde meo*, and before he flings himself down beneath the fig tree, this inner scene dominates the entire process: "But as this deep meditation dredged all my wretchedness up from the secret profundity of my being and heaped it all together before the eyes of my heart, a huge storm blew up within me and brought on a heavy rain of tears." (8.12.28)[1] The narrator's profound self-reflection, then, literally brings his own despair in the sight of his heart, *in conspectu cordis mei*, whereupon the actual conversion takes place. Augustine hears a child's voice from the neighbouring house, repeatedly urging him to pick up his Bible and read, *tolle lege, tolle lege*, and when he subsequently hits upon Paul's Epistle to the Romans

---

1 "Ubi vero a fundo arcano alta consideratio traxit et congessit totam miseriam meam in conspectu cordis mei, oborta est procella ingens ferens ingentem imbrem lacrimarum."

13.13–14, he feels an immediate relief, as if "the light of certainty flooded my heart" (8.12.29), *quasi luce securitatis infusa cordi meo.*

With this all-transforming experience, Augustine's way to Ostia, Africa and his vocation is marked out. As soon as the Lord has pierced his heart with the arrow of His love, the convert gives up his teaching of rhetoric, ironically with a pronouncedly ornate phrase: he decided to "withdraw the service of my tongue from the market of speechifying" (9.2.2), *subtrahere ministerium linguae meae nundinis loquacitatis.* Consequently, when the tenth book is begun, in which the author comments on his own writing project, he lets his first interlocutor, God Himself, understand that he now wishes to act according to the truth "in my heart by confession in your presence, and with my pen before many witnesses" (10.1.1), *in corde meo coram te in confessione, in stilo autem meo coram multis testibus.*

Here, the primacy of inner speech is unequivocal. The confession of the heart is aimed at God, while that of the pen is directed to the author's fellow beings. So now – to round off this selective review of the presence of the heart in the *Confessions* immediately before and after the conversion – we are faced with a new question: the identity of the present confessor rather than the past sinner, of the writer holding the pen rather than the seeker shedding tears. That is the issue the writer wishes to elucidate in the closing books of his work, for the benefit of those who have only heard of him but never got to know him, since "none of these have laid their ears to my heart, though it is only there that I am whoever I am" (10.3.4), *auris eorum non est ad cor meum, ubi ego sum quicumque sum.* Augustine's metaphorical language could evidently associate the heart with both the mouth and the eyes, with speech as well as sight, and along similar lines, as Ulrich Duchrow has pointed out, he would sometimes connect it to man's lower and sometimes to his higher (rational) soul. In a broader cultural-historical perspective, the Church Father's mature writings are dominated by the Hebrew-Biblical tradition, where the heart was treated as a general sign for man's inner life, combined with the Stoic association – visible in, for example, *On the Trinity* (15.15.25) – of the heart with our "inner and true word", *verbum verum nostrum intimum*, the immediate intuition or intention that precedes all linguistic articulation.[1]

From the small collection of examples above, we can draw at least three conclusions:
- The speech of the heart is, firstly, something other than that of the professional teacher of rhetoric, an inner voice in defiance of that "market of speech-

---

[1] Duchrow 1965, pp. 19f., 122–48 (the chapter "Das innere Wort"), 188.

ifying" – Ciceronian eloquence – which set the tone for classical Roman culture.
- Secondly, the speech of the heart seems both Biblically orientated and orally conceived – echoing prophetically inspired as well as everyday spoken discourse – in marked contrast to the literary language taught, analysed and paraphrased in grammar schools, the learned world's *lecta verba*.[1] The Christian speaker, Augustine says in the last book of *On Christian Doctrine*, prefers to please by matter rather than by words. The more truthful his speech is, the better it will be since "the words must serve the teacher, not the other way round" (4.28.61), *nec doctor verbis serviat sed verba doctori*. This is Augustine's contribution to the early Christian argument for a simple style, *sermo humilis*, but in his *Confessions* this problem is in more than one sense a matter of the heart for him.
- Thirdly, this is a kind of speech that reveals the speaker's real identity, "whoever I am", right through the emotionally charged discourse of the *Confessions*, explicitly targeting two kinds of audience. On the one hand, Augustine delivers an orally conceived account aimed at the only recipient who has access to his heart's voice without the mediation of vocal cords or words, namely God; on the other hand, this speech has been encoded in a text flowing from "my pen" to comfort and guide the confessor's fellow beings, his "many witnesses". As a spiritual guide in Hippo, Augustine tells us in *On the Trinity*, he was aided "by my tongue and by my pen, of which two yoked together in me, Love is the charioteer" (3.PR.), *lingua ac stilo meo quas bigas in me caritas agitat*. Even though, in more than one respect, he inaugurates or at least presages a new Christian culture of writing – as when he adds, in *On the Trinity*, that he has learnt many things by writing which he did not know before – his works are typically dominated by several types of discourse that are, basically, of an oral nature, such as prayers, sermons, confessions or polemics.

"While I write or speak of these themes", *haec dum scribo vel eloquor:* that is how Prudentius introduces his collected poems (*Praefatio*, 43) a few years after the *Confessions*.[2] Hovering between speech and writing is typical of a culture that is based on both grammatical schooling and rhetorical drill, just as it characterizes a great number of the period's Christian writers, who felt as much at home in the genres of intimate prayer or liturgical psalms as in those

---

1 For this contrast, see Smolak 1985.
2 All quotations from Prudentius are from H.J. Thomson's Loeb edition (I–II) 1993–95.

of Biblical exegesis or early canon law (*ius antiquum*). In addition, we have reason to remind ourselves of the epoch's common method for the production of letters and even books: prolific Church Fathers like Augustine and Jerome ordinarily dictated their works to a team of employed scribes. Finally, Augustine returned regularly to speech as the guiding principle for his language. Naturally, the author of the *Confessions* does not overlook the fact that he is writing a book, that he is recording his experiences for the benefit of present-day and future readers, but on several occasions he juxtaposes the evidence of his pen with that of his mouth or voice: "if I am to confess to you with tongue and pen", *si totum confitear tibi ore meo et calamo meo*, alternatively by "my voice and my pen", *vox et stilus meus* (12.6.6). A bold metaphor like the pen's tongue, 11.2.2, *lingua calami*, is significant (notwithstanding its Biblical precedent in Psalms 44.2/45.1). The pen speaks, that is to say, according to Aristotelian hermeneutics, it translates the inner speech, or the divine speech the confessor thinks he hears in his inner being, into squiggles on papyrus or parchment.[1]

*

Augustine's colloquy with his dying mother aims to give an idea of this inner speech, the distinctive feature of the miracle at Ostia. His commentator James J. O'Donnell notices that the standard verb in recollections of visions, 'to see', *videre*, so typical of Plotinus (*blepein, theōrein*), and for the so-called Plotinian vision in the seventh book of the *Confessions*, is conspicuously absent here. This is an apt observation. It is not only a "spiritual era" that differentiates the seventh and ninth books of the *Confessions*, but also a paradigmatic shift from the initiative of the solitary vision to that of words and dialogue.[2] If the episode at Ostia thus introduces, as it were, a new kind of mystery in Latin literature, that of communication and orality, it should be added that it presents an extraordinary communication and a paradoxical orality, characterized by its vibrating silence. This is surely the supreme instance of the speech of the heart in Augustine's work: an intuitive exchange of thoughts that takes place right up to the

---

1 In *On Christian Doctrine*, Augustine explains that people once had to start designating words by means of letters, *instituta sunt per litteras signa verborum*, since their spoken sound passes away in the air (2.4.5). As for written words, B. Darrell Jackson detects "two stages of signifying: (1) written 'words' signify spoken words, and (2) spoken words signify things", 1972, p. 113. This approach, widely diffused in Hellenistic culture, had a solid basis in Peripatetic philosophy. In the opening paragraphs of *On Interpretation* (16a), Aristotle maintains that "written words are the signs of words spoken"; these spoken words are in turn "symbols or signs of affections or impressions of the soul", which, finally, are representations of "objects". Cf. Eco 1986, pp. 27f.
2 Augustine 1992 (III), p. 128. Cf. Quinn 1994, p. 268.

point when the two interlocutors, after having their common longing fulfilled for a breathless moment, are obliged to return to the usual clatter of their (and other people's) physical voices.

The account of their experience begins as a flashback to an ordinary conversation in pleasant isolation, *conloquebamur ergo soli valde dulciter*, normally a favourable condition for a philosophical dialogue, but it soon becomes clear to the reader that the writer's pen is registering inaudible words. The communication between mother and son effectively takes place in their inner being. Their hearts are in accord (or, more precisely, coalesce into one sole heart): "yet with the mouth of our hearts [*ore cordis*] wide open we panted thirstily for the celestial streams of your fountain" (9.10.23), *sed inhiabamus ore cordis in superna fluenta fontis tui*. This Christian mini-congregation now has to try to imagine – Augustine's verb is *cogitare* – heavenly glory. This task, too, like the whole of the Augustinian confession pattern, is adjusted in accordance with both Platonic and Pauline models.

First, the two people conversing have to discover, in the footsteps of Plato's erotic philosophers and Plotinus' priestly thinker, that physical pleasure, *carnalium sensuum delectatio*, is not enough. This is certainly not a particularly ascetic attitude but only a recognition of the inadequacy of the senses. Thereafter the ascension itself commences "in longing yet more ardent" (9.10.24), initially through the elementary world of the bodies and then onwards and upwards, through the heavens that, according to Ptolemy's ancient astronomical system, surrounded Earth. But just as clearly as in the *Symposium* or the *Enneads*, this cosmic adventure is an expression of, or runs parallel to, an inner journey: "Higher still we mounted by inward thought and wondering discourse on your works, and we arrived at the summit of our own minds; and this too we transcended".

The other condition for this psychosomatic enterprise emerges from Paul's Second Epistle to the Corinthians, in which the writer, with a strategic glance at the ecstatic rituals of his Hellenic addressees, says he knows a Christian man – possibly himself – who was carried away to the third heaven fourteen years ago, "whether in the body or out of the body I do not know, God knows." Subsequently, this heaven is identified with Paradise, where the newly arrived "heard things that cannot be told, which man may not utter" (12.2–4). The question of corporeal or spiritual ascension remains hanging in the air, barely answered with a characteristic 'I cannot tell', *ouk oida*, in the Vulgate: *nescio*, which eloquently subordinates the doctrinaire message to the reality of faith. It is equally interesting that Paul's vision culminates in the impression of being addressed: the enraptured man "heard things", albeit in the form of a hidden message that may not be revealed. The ambiguous state between corporeal and spiritual rapture, as well as the reference to an esoteric message at the end of the journey, are in telling contrast to the speechless spiritual experience that characterizes the meeting with the One at the end of the *Enneads*. Here, Paul probably based his account on the Psalms and the prophets, a recycling of Jewish tradition that – as we shall shortly see – would later be of use to Augustine.

We find the arguably most conscientious remarks that the Church Father ever made on this passage from Paul in his detailed commentary on the Book of Genesis, *De Genesi ad litteram* (*The Literal Meaning of Genesis*, 401–15), namely in the twelfth book of that work, devoted to our concepts of Paradise. Here, the author distinguishes three kinds of visions: the corporeal-sensory or "bodily", *corporale*, the "spiritual" or *spiritale*, which corresponds to our disposition to transform sense impressions into mental images or recollections – garments, as it were, for the mind's emerging concepts – and finally the "intellectual", *intellectuale*, which is restricted to pure ideas (12.7.16). As Robert A. Markus points out, this brief list gives us a key to Augustine's understanding of the knowledge provided by the senses and imagination, of dreams, prophesies and inspiration, in short: a series of issues concerning the faculties of the mind.[1]

The Church Father's classification presumes a hierarchy among man's spiritual powers, typical of Late Antiquity (and soon, also, of the Middle Ages), in rising order: 1) the senses, *sensus* (perceptual, dealing with sense impressions), 2) the faculty of representation, *spiritus* (semiotic, dealing with images or signs in need of interpretation), and 3) the intellect, *intellectus* or *mens* (conceptual, bent on dissolving images, signs and portents into clear notions). Of these powers of vision or recognition it is not, as one might think, the third – intellect, normally considered as superior – but *spiritale* that Augustine dwells upon, partly because it does not merely observe real images, whether present or absent, but also creates "fictitious ones the imagination may have constructed" (12.6.15), *fictas, sicut cogitatio formare potuerit*.[2] In order to clarify this argument, Augustine gives us an example that is also found in *On the Trinity* (8.6.9): we imagine the Carthage we have known and remember in a certain way, as an *imago vera* (whether we are there or not), but the Alexandria that we do not know in another way, as an *imago ficta* (since we have never been there). Both cities are represented within us as images, pertaining to our spiritual vision.

---

[1] "The Eclipse of a Neo-Platonic Theme: Augustine and Gregory the Great on Visions and Prophecies" (1981), reprinted in Markus 1994, pp. 204–11. All quotations from *The Literal Meaning of Genesis* are from E. Hill's translation 2002b.
[2] For Hill's (perfectly adequate) translation of *cogitatio* into "imagination", see below, p. 195, note 1.

It is evident that this significance of cogitation or imagination both fascinated and worried Augustine. *Spiritalis visio*, he states, processes memory's enormous reservoir of images; it is thus capable of forming "likenesses" of absent bodies, *absentium corporum similitudines*, but quite a few of these images "are fabricated in it as it chooses, or shown to it quite apart from its choice" (12.24.51), *finguntur multae pro arbitrio, vel praeter arbitrium demonstrantur*, as in dreams or ecstasy. Obviously, we have to understand this spiritual vision, inherently inclined to both mnemonic and fictional representations, as Augustine's version of the human imagination, a fascinating problem that will be analysed in our next section (below, pp. 194ff.).

Apart from these assets in our psychic economy, the three types of vision will give prominence to as many hermeneutic strategies – three ways of understanding a text or, more specifically, the challenging Biblical texts. The commentator resorts to a simple example from the Gospel according to St. Matthew: the exhortation "You shall love your neighbour as yourself", spoken by Christ (22.39). In the first place, this commandment occupies our eyes: we quite simply read the letters. In the second place, our spirit or *spiritus* allows us to imagine our neighbour even when he or she is absent. In the third place, our intellect leaves the individual person out of account in order to concentrate on the general notion: the concept of love.

This theory of text interpretation (12.6.15, 12.11.22) can be schematized as follows:
- The first type of understanding or "vision", the physical, focuses on the letters.
- The second, the "spiritual", goes beyond the letters on the lookout for "obscurely significant signs" (12.18.39), *obscurae significationes*, typically indicated by figurative language – all kinds of tantalizing imagery – while awaiting
- the third, the conceptual analysis of the intellect.

Here, we shall especially examine the possibilities for interpretation that Augustine associates with the first two types of seeing. *Visio corporalis* can either focus on the actual meaning of words, *proprie*, or operate with typological exegesis, based on a specific kind of "transferred sense", *translatum vocabulum*, permitting events or characters of the Old Testament to be translated into terms of Christological truth. It is characteristic of Augustine that he should regard this sort of reading, according to which, for example, Adam prefigures Christ, as a "bodily" method of interpretation, secure from the arbitrariness of imagination. He cites the Pauline reference to the signs of the Old Covenant – *sacramenta* – as "shadows of what is to come", *umbrae futuri*, taken from the Epistle to the Colossians 2.17; there, the commandments of the law are described as "a shadow of the things to come, but the substance belongs to Christ". The enigmatic portents of the Old Testament are thus incarnated, consummated and elucidated in (the body of) Christ. This type of exegesis, which likewise will be subject to scrutiny in a later section of this chapter (below, pp. 240ff.), can never neglect a term's literal meaning (12.7.17).

As for the *visio spiritualis*, it is illustrated by the passages that deal with speaking in tongues in 1 Corinthians 14, a form of expression in which imagination is hyper-active, rich in *obscurae et mysticae significationes*, which remain suggestive but incomprehensible until the intellect, *mens*, steps in. These obscure figurations are, suitably, construed as imagination's counterpart to the tropes of rhetoric, demonstrating the type of utterance "whose significance is wrapped up in images and likenesses of things", *significationes velut imagines rerum ac similitudines* (12.8.19). If the "bodily vision" is bound to matter, history and letters, this "spiritual vision" is keenly alive to signs and miracles, both in real life and in the Biblical text. If Augustine's examples of spiritual vision sometimes seem a bit outlandish, drawn from paranormal experiences such as ecstasies, speaking in tongues or dealing with prophecies, we should remember that they are in fact consistent with his overall method of demonstration: to delineate perfectly normal functions or faculties of the human mind by referring to extreme cases.

All three types of vision analysed in *The Literal Meaning of Genesis* are closely interconnected. On the hermeneutic level, the "bodily" typology respects the Biblical text's historical-horizontal dimension, whereas the "spiritual" vision favours, as it were, a vertical interpretation of the Holy Writ, aiming at mystic significations that only intellectual analysis can finally secure. On the cognitive level, the eyes perceive things, *res*, imagination produces an image or representation of these things, *rerum imaginatio*, whereas the intellect provides an interpretation of these images, *imaginationum interpretatio* (12.9.20). All three ways of seeing thus form a coherent hierarchic order that, ideally, allows human reason to "climb" from lower to higher levels: *ab inferioribus ratio ad superiora conscendat*. Such prospects clearly reveal the Neo-Platonic basis of Augustine's scheme of visions (12.11.22, 12.24.51).

It is particularly the distinction between the second and the third types of vision that is important for Augustine. *Visio spiritualis*, he observes, often appears in dreams and does not always need to be true. It might operate with meaningless images, and it might leave a certain room for demonic fancies in our mind. Under normal circumstances, it surely provides us with indispensable recreations or recordings of our sense experience, but it might just as well play tricks on us. The soul can 'feign' or form something out of mere suspicion or false assumptions, whereupon it mistakes such projections for real bodies, the existence of which it assumes without having ever seen them (12.25.52): *quod sibi suspicione falsaque coniectura finxerit, hoc etiam in corporibus putat, quae non visa coniectat.* In such passages, this commentary on Genesis, somewhat unexpectedly, presents a masterly analysis of the human mind's propensity to spawn fictional configurations: masterly, but also critical, for this game of make-believe has actually no value in the Augustinian epistemology. The images the soul produces or projects by itself, sadly lacking any basis in reality, lead nowhere. By contrast, the intellectual vision which ultimately detaches the soul from the region of bodies, images and resemblances, is always true and appears in the genuine prophets, those visionaries who, like Daniel of the Old Testament, are gifted with the ability not only to experience but to interpret dreams and revelations (12.9.20).

This brings us to the main point of Augustine's analysis of the paradisiacal experience in the Second Epistle to the Corinthians 12.2–4 ("I know a man in Christ who fourteen years ago was caught up to the third heaven"…). Eventually, it is classified as an intellectual vision of eternal life, reminiscent of Paul's more famous premonition of bliss "face to face" in 1 Corinthians 13.12, possible to recall but actually impossible to recreate in human words. Even against a Biblical background it appears with an exceptional aura, different from both Moses' corporeal meeting with the Lord on Mount Sinai (Exodus 19.18) and from the "spiritual" visions of Isaiah or the Book of Revelation. The Augustinian understanding of Paul's rapture in *The Literal Meaning of Genesis* suggests an ascension towards God contemplated "in his very substance as God" (12.27.55), *in ea substantia qua Deus est*, at long last beyond bodily perception and, in turn, beyond memories, beyond the indications of signs and beyond the fictions of imagination. The Church Father's favouring of the intellect bears the hallmark of Neo-Platonism, except for the fact that the rapture under consideration culminates in speech, even in conversation. In Augustine's interpretation of this Pauline experience, the radiance of the Lord is accessible "not in code but clearly, to the extent that the human mind can grasp it, depending on God's grace as he takes it up, so that God may speak mouth to mouth [*os ad os*] with any whom he has made worthy of such conversation [*colloquium*] – the mouth of the mind not the body" (12.26.54).[1]

*

---

[1] "Per speciem, non per aenigmata, quantum eam capere mens humana potest, secundum assumentis Dei gratiam, ut os ad os loquatur ei quem dignum tali Deus colloquio fecerit; non os corporis, sed mentis".

There we must leave *The Literal Meaning of Genesis*. We have learnt that God can be seen, firstly, in a corporeal form, secondly, in a metaphorical or imaginary form and thirdly, in a purely substantial form, all within a coherent hierarchy of visions. Moreover, we have learnt that the third and optimal intellectual vision is inseparable from a dialogue or *colloquium*, an oral exchange *os ad os*, beyond the words or signs of human language and impossible to reconstruct afterwards. Now, these lessons might well help to elucidate Augustine's and Monnica's sublime experience at Ostia. Not that I dare to pronounce an opinion on the vexed question as to whether Augustine in person, like Paul and some of the apostles, was granted a truly intellectual vision.[1] But his description of the event at Ostia is structured according to the same hierarchy of visions that was to provide the framework for the final book of *The Literal Meaning of Genesis*.

The Ostia narrative has as its starting point "the pleasures of the body's senses", activated by *visio corporalis*, which immediately has to yield to the other two types of visionary experience, accomplished by imagination (*cogitatio*) and intellect (*mens*) respectively: "Higher still we mounted by inward thought and wondering discourse [*interius cogitando et loquendo*] on your works, and we arrived at the summit of our own minds [*mentes*]; and this too we transcended". Thus God's works become the subjects of Augustine's and Monnica's gazes, reflection and discourse, in proper order: at first, that is, of the perception and imagination that belonged to the lower faculties of the soul in premodern tradition, and, eventually, of the mental dialogue between mother and son. At this final point, the internalization of their experience has already set in, so we have to imagine a kind of speech within, *interius*, which no longer needs to be expressed by a physical voice – with a cogent formulation from Augustine's late text *De continentia* (*On Continence*): "For many things we say not with the mouth of the body, and cry aloud with the heart" (1.2), *multa enim corporis ore non dicimus et corde clamamus*.[2]

The Church Father had already paid attention to this form of speech in his work *De magistro* (*The Teacher*) from 389, a dialogue between himself and his son Adeodatus. God has to be sought, he says there, in the innermost and secret corners of the rational soul, in the "inner man", *interior homo*, an expression Augustine borrows from Paul (Ephesians 3.16) and which, leaning on further Biblical sources, he locates "in the temple of the mind and on the bed of the heart", *in templo mentis, et in cubilibus cordis*. There, in the intimate chamber of the heart,

---

[1] Such a possibility is at least left open in Teske 1994, p. 298.
[2] For a long time this short treatise was thought to have been written around the mid-390s, due to its arguments directed against the Manichees. Recently, however, a number of scholars have proposed a much later date for the composition of *On Continence*, cf. Hunter 1995.

one can pray in silence with no need for resounding words, *sonantia verba*. This is to be understood as an immediate and inaudible discourse that is created in the soul when we "use words in thinking", *ipsa verba cogitamus* (1.2).[1] Accordingly, the speech of the vocal cords, of the tongue and the lips, is only an incomplete and unreliable expression of a discourse that has already taken place within us, for a single second or for many years, and that has been stored in our memory for future use such as prayer, teaching or any type of urgent communication.[2] It is at this internal level – enlightened by a divine *illuminatio*, beyond the human dependence on signs and words to which Augustine, the great theorist of interpretation, devoted such analytical skills – that the two travellers communicated with each other at the window in Ostia.[3]

It is in the nature of things that their silent speech involves the extinction of desire. The pious Monnica, who had always worried about her son's debauchery, appears ever more insistently throughout the *Confessions* as a counter-force to the widespread commerce with bodies as well as words. In his autobiography, Augustine repeatedly links language to desire, as Eugene Vance has shown in a thought-provoking study.[4] There is a tendency in the *Confessions* to connect the Law – and, consequently, the Old Testament's literalism – to carnal matters and sexuality, hence the whole work may be described as a liberation (or as the

---

1 All quotations from *The Teacher* are from J.S. Burleigh's translation, Augustine 2006.
2 For further discussions of the *interior homo*, of the inaudible and the verbal communication, cf. the final part of *The Teacher*, 12.40 – 14.46, and the treatise *De fide et symbolo* (*Faith and the Creed*, composed 393), according to which "there is a vast difference between our minds and the words with which we try to show what is in our minds" (trans. J.S. Burleigh, Augustine 2006): *inter animum autem nostrum et verba nostra, quibus eumdem animum ostendere conamur, plurimum distat*. This is because we do not "beget" spoken words, we "make" them, and there is a world of difference here between immediate *gignere* and contrived *facere*. To Augustine, in fact, human souls seem conspicuously closed within themselves (cf. Louth 1989, p. 153). Nevertheless, they need to cooperate, hence their dependence on linguistic communication, however inadequate. They attempt to divulge themselves by issuing *indicia* such as words, expressions or gestures, "so many devices that serve our purpose to make known what is within our minds. But we cannot produce anything exactly like our minds, and so the mind of the speaker cannot make itself known with complete inwardness. Hence also there is room for lying", *tot scilicet machinamentis id quod intus est demonstrare cupientes: quia tale aliquid proferre non possumus, et ideo non potest loquentis animus penitus innotescere; unde etiam mendaciis locus patet* (3.4). From this Augustinian perspective, articulate discourse or *sonantia verba* cannot but appear as second-degree speech.
3 Duchrow emphasizes the intuitive *illuminatio* which Augustine associates with the speech of the heart, 1965, pp. 146f., 176. For concise but suggestive comments on Augustine's concepts of the inner man, illumination and God's presence in the human soul, see Harrison 1992, 144 – 52.
4 Vance 1989, the section "Confession, Love, and the Law", pp. 6 – 11.

documentation of a liberation) from the text of the Law, carved in the Tablets of Stone, to Christ's redemptive words in the confessor's heart. The Law engenders prohibitions, and prohibitions engender desire. The first nine books of the *Confessions* register the author's captivity under this mechanism of desire, not only as a brothel visitor but also as a teacher of eloquence, both of which are in the end related activities. Both are dependent on regulations of economy – we remember the convert's dismissal of "the market of speechifying" – and on a dialectic between coercion and desire.

But when Augustine in Milan begins to understand the Bible's text differently, as in a well-known episode from *Confessions* VI, where he observes Bishop Ambrose engaged in silent reading (6.3.3), he realizes the full meaning of the Pauline formula: "For the letter kills, but the Spirit gives life" (2 Corinthians 3.6), *littera enim occidit Spiritus autem vivificat*. Joseph Anthony Mazzeo reminds us that Augustine himself soon followed Ambrose's example. At the exhortation of a child's voice in the conversion scene, shortly after he had witnessed the bishop's silent reading, he was to open the Bible at the Epistle to the Romans and start reading *in silentio* (8.12.29). By means of this new type of reading, he learnt to listen to the teacher within him, *in interiore homine*, whom he soon – in *The Teacher* (11.38) – would identify with Christ.[1] The whole of Augustine's autobiography is, on closer inspection, designed as a dialogue with Christ, even though we only hear the author's own lines. It is a text constantly composed with this Teacher in mind, an intimate record of the penitent sinner's memories, prayers and thanksgivings, a written examination, as it were, from the school of the heart. Immediately before the event in Ostia, the pupil had explained his mother's conciliatory nature with a characteristic reference to their common divine master: "You, her intimate teacher, instructed her in the school of her heart" (9.9.21), *docente te magistro intimo in schola pectoris*.

Only the Inner Teacher, Robert A. Markus observes, could simultaneously teach us about reality and about the language that makes it comprehensible.[2] It is as if the silent intimacy with the Biblical text finally released Augustine from the literal content of the Law – from the dialectic between coercion and desire driven by the linguistic significants – to inaugurate a new redeeming way of reading that this Teacher (the Word Incarnate) had made possible. That experience changed everything. Therefore it is completely understandable that Augustine abruptly breaks off the biographical presentation in the *Confessions* after the vision at Ostia, in order to devote the remaining four books to a philosophical

---

1 See Mazzeo 1962, p. 191, and Duchrow 1965, pp. 66–69, 174–78.
2 Markus 1972, p. 71.

analysis of time and memory followed by a rudimentary commentary on Genesis. The Ostia episode, "the turning and pivotal point" of the author's life story (Eugen Dönt), marks the work's transition from narration to meditation, its reorientation of the convert's search for truth from the spectacle of the world to the microcosm of memory.[1] The *Confessions*, then, progress from struggle with the written Law, whose literal terms appeared to teach all kinds of absurdities or aberrant ideas (6.4.6), *perversitas*, to the redemptive reading of the Lord's countenance, beyond speech, text and language, beyond the syllables of time, *sine syllabis temporum*, an experience which seems reserved for the angels but which the Biblical witnesses – Genesis, the Psalms, Isaiah, the Evangelists, Paul – hold in prospect for us (13.15.18). In this angelic reading, desire is eventually vanquished along with the instances of fictionality it tends to engender: dreams, projections, narratives. The mirror can be put aside for the face-to-face encounter.

We have followed Augustine and Monnica through the domains of the eyes and signs, subjected to the first two types of vision (implemented by bodily sight and imagination respectively) delineated in *The Literal Meaning of Genesis*. But their experience does not end there. Their final goal is already indicated at the outset of the Ostia episode, where they had opened the mouths of their hearts to the heavenly "streams" from God, "your fountain, the fount of life which is with you", *superna fluenta fontis tui, fontis vitae, qui est apud te*. In the intellectual vision as described in *The Literal Meaning of Genesis*, "the blessed life is to be drunk from its own fountain" (12.26.54), *beata vita in fonte suo bibitur*. Thus with an eminent example in the Platonic tradition's *anabasis*, modified by the Pauline scheme for the soul's *raptus* as Augustine would later expound it in his commentary on the Genesis, the two wanderers ascend towards the world of the intellect, *mens*, the Latin equivalent of the Greek *nous*, to finally reach beyond even that enlightened stage. At this extreme point, they certainly anticipate the enraptured being in *The Literal Meaning of Genesis*, who is allowed to behold "above itself" (12.31.59), *supra se*.

At this point, the couple in Ostia seem to stand at the gates of their goal, the blessed life that will soon be Monnica's for good, identified here with the help of an Old Testament prophecy that relies on the ancient Jewish idea of God as the Good Shepherd with his flock: "I will feed them with good pasture, and on the mountain heights of Israel shall be their grazing land. There they shall lie down in good grazing land, and on rich pasture they shall feed on the mountains of Israel." (Ezekiel 34.14) In the retrospective light from *The Literal Meaning of Gen-*

---

[1] Dönt 1971, p. 359.

esis, the explanation of these kinds of vision, the prophetic ones, should be ascribed to the illuminated intellect, *mens*, rather than the restless power of imagination or cogitation, *spiritus* (12.9.20). In the Ostia episode, then, the eternal present of "Wisdom" seems to be held out as the ultimate prospect for mother and son: the *sapienta* "through whom all these things are made", past and future.

This *sapientia* is Augustine's version of the *logos* – the creative Word – of the Prologue to St. John, where it is explicitly identified with the only-begotten Son (John 1.14). The same Christological *Verbum* would later, correspondingly, be made the subject of the intellect's vision in *The Literal Meaning of Genesis* (12.34.67). In both cases, in his autobiography as well as in his exegetical work, Augustine adapts almost word for word the Biblical qualification of this Word: "All things were made through him" (Joh. 1.3), *omnia per ipsum facta sunt*.

It is time to reach a conclusion. The parallels between Augustine's autobiography and the Genesis commentary are subtle but striking. All three types of vision detailed by the exegete in the twelfth book of *The Literal Meaning of Genesis* – those of the senses, the imagination and the intellect – have, at this stage of the Ostia episode, been activated in due order. Consequently, the scene is set for the incomparable wonder, where even the interior dialogue between mother and son must come to a halt. The author's reference to the good pasture and the mountains of Israel, that is, eternal bliss, works primarily as a prolepsis – anticipatorily – in the text (as it was used prophetically by Ezekiel). The *sapienta* of intellectual rapture is so far not an existing reality but remains the ultimate goal for the two characters at the window, or, to be more precise, the subject of the colloquy in their hearts: "And as we talked and panted for it"...

Ineffability

At this stage, one of the few true mysteries occurs that can be registered in this lengthy survey. The travellers reach their goal. The world of representation and speech fades away, the forebodings of cogitation and its images are fulfilled when supreme *sapientia* suddenly seems within Augustine's and Monnica's reach: "we just touched the edge of it by the utmost leap of our hearts; then, sighing and unsatisfied, we left the first-fruits of our spirit captive there, and returned to the noise of articulate speech, where a word has beginning and end." The remarkable aspects of this passage are best presented in bullet points:
- The experience is momentary. The adverb in the original text is *modice*, which in this context means something like 'barely'.

- The experience is not visual. It cannot, at this stage, be described as a vision any more. Perception and imagination have certainly carried Augustine and Monnica along the way, but no further, for no man is granted the privilege to see God in life, as Augustine assures us in several of his works, for example *On the Trinity* (2.16.27).
- The scene of the invisible miracle is the heart. Augustine even writes *toto ictu cordis:* in a single heartbeat or, perhaps more literally, in one single stroke or blow from our heart.
- This ultimate experience is, as in the Plotinian system, beyond language, ineffable, but it does allow a sigh or exhalation (*suspiravimus*), an expression without words, possibly – as Pierre Courcelle assumed – a symptom of deficiency even at the climax of the ecstasy, perhaps in a premonition of its transitory nature.[1]
- In principle, the scene should be repeatable, for the dying mother as well as the newly-converted son. The spiritual *primitiae* ("first-fruits") that the travellers surrender at the place of their revelation (of *sapientia*, *logos* or Christ), carry the hope of a return.[2]
- These *primitiae* are a reminiscence of Romans 8.23: "And not only the creation, but we ourselves, who have the firstfruits of the Spirit, groan inwardly as we wait eagerly for adoption as sons, the redemption of our bodies." Augustine reused this Pauline formula several times, for instance in his doctrinaire short treatise *Faith and the Creed*, where the first fruits become a proof of faith, as it were, offered by moaning Creation's spiritual part: "This whole creature 'groaneth and travaileth until now', but has put forth the first-fruits of the spirit because it has believed God and has already a good will." (10.23)[3] Although the Ostia account centres on or moves towards a wordless experience, it is, like Augustine's other writings, even at the very climax of mystic exaltation, brimming with Biblical echoes and text fragments, principally from the Book of Psalms and Paul.
- In the aftermath of the mystic experience, Augustine and his mother are once again left with plain ordinary language, now described as sheer din, *strepitus*, and, in its capacity of verbal discourse, necessarily linked to the fluctuations of time: "the noise of articulate speech, where a word has begin-

---

[1] Courcelle 1950, pp. 223f.
[2] For an ambitious account of these *primitiae spiritus*, understood as contemplation's "foretaste" or "pledge" of eternal bliss, see Pépin 1951, pp. 198f. Cf. Chapter 7, "The Ostia Ascent", in Dobell 2009, pp. 213–27.
[3] "Haec autem omnis creatura ingemiscit et parturit usque nunc; dedit tamen primitias spiritus, quia credidit Deo, et bonae iam voluntatis est."

ning and end". It is the comparison with the instantaneous and intuitive idiom of the heart that now makes this all too human speech, that of the lips, appear strident, subject to an erratic, never-ceasing exchange of fortuitous thoughts and opinions.

*

After this climax, sadly restored to secular reality and its language, it remains for Augustine and Monnica to try to reconstruct or express their experience in analytical terms, that is, to sum up their adventure in conceptual language (9.10.25):

> Then we said, "If the tumult of the flesh fell silent for someone, and silent too were the phantasms of earth, sea and air, silent the heavens, and the very soul silent to itself, that it might pass beyond itself by not thinking of its own being; if dreams and revelations known through its imagination were silent, if every tongue, and every sign, and whatever is subject to transience were wholly stilled for him – for if anyone listens, all these things will tell him, 'We did not make ourselves; he made us who abides for ever,' – and having said this they held their peace for they had pricked the listening ear to him who made them; and then he alone were to speak, not through things that are made, but of himself, that we might hear his Word, not through fleshly tongue nor angel's voice, nor thundercloud, nor any riddling parable, hear him unmediated, whom we love in all these things, hear him without them, as now we stretch out and in a flash of thought touch that eternal Wisdom who abides above all things; if this could last, and all other visions, so far inferior, be taken away, and this sight alone ravish him who saw it, and engulf him and hide him away, kept for inward joys, so that this moment of knowledge – this passing moment that left us aching for more – should there be life eternal, would not *Enter into the joy of your Lord* be this, and this alone? And when, when will this be? When we all rise again, but not all are changed?" (II)

"Then we said"... By their conditional wording in this conversation (if...if...if...), mother and son hypothetically extend the contact of their innermost hearts with the divine *logos* or *sapientia* into timelessness. They evoke, announce and gaze into eternity. The promise of the "first-fruits" is imagined to come true. The transient contact with God is taken to be lasting: *si continuetur hoc*, literally: "if this will continue"... The requirement for this blessed state is that everything worldly and human subsides. It might well be described as the result of what later Western tradition has been accustomed to label negative theology. Its key word is *silere* (to be silent), repeated in a suggestive sequence that probably – one of Henry's most beautiful discoveries – imitates a corresponding passage in the *Enneads* (5.1.2), where the body, the elements and heaven itself will come to rest and be "still", *hēsychos*, for the benefit of the soul's free vision.[1]

---

[1] Henry 1981, pp. 16f.

However, Augustine expands this brief sequence of the philosopher into a long, winding phrase of 183 words, arranged in conditional form, with the subjunctive as the dominant mode of the verbs, a monological reconstruction of his and his mother's joint talk. Here "the tumult of flesh" is supposed to have receded into silence, together with the elements' *phantasiae*; this term seems to be of both a semiotic and a mental nature, connected to the world of signs as well as the faculty of perception, more or less as in Plotinus. The stations of the journey return in rapid summary: the heavens, too, are deemed to have fallen silent, the revelations of dreams and the imagination have been silenced, and the soul is assumed to transcend its usual state of self-reflection, *transeat se non se cogitando*. Thus Augustine is careful to tick off the introductory phases of his and his mother's way upwards, both those of outer, elementary, and those of inner, mental reality.

During this experiment of conditional thought, neither the Creation nor the human soul are treated as analogies suggestive of their divine origin but rather as clamours to be silenced, as obstacles to be overcome on the road of negation. The resources of mental economy that Augustine had learnt to distinguish in the classical Peripatetic tradition (perception, imagination, reflection) are shut down one by one. That is not all, however: in a correspondingly hypothetical way, "every tongue, and every sign", *omnis lingua et omne signum*, will be reduced to silence. Such wording may remind the modern reader of what Ernst Robert Curtius has labelled the "inexpressibility topoi" of antique (and, later, medieval) literature, or of what his successor Klaus Thraede – with a starting point in the Book of Proverbs, 10.19 – has called "the identification of talkativeness with sin" in the Christian accommodations of the same topos.[1] Augustine, however, stages a semiotic clean riddance, voicing a deep mistrust of the resources of human expression when faced with divine mystery, which may be related to but far exceeds the usual topic. Hence, even the world of linguistic signs has to give way when representing the miracle at Ostia. Readers of the *Confessions* may remember how the author initially contrasts the rules of grammar and rhetoric, *pacta litterarum et syllabarum*, with the gift of salvation (1.18.29). The ascension towards God, in Augustine's version, is ultimately of an apophatic nature or, to be more precise, a project aiming at complete understanding of the Inner Teacher's wordless speech.[2]

This is perhaps most evident in the Church Father's commentary on John, *In evangelium Ioannis tractatus* (*Lectures or Tractates on the Gospel According to St.*

---

[1] Curtius 1990, pp. 159–62; Thraede 1963, p. 110.
[2] Cf. Breyfogle 1999, p. 149.

John), probably dating from the mid-410s, where the readers are warned against getting entangled in their own web of representations and images. Being able to understand the mystery of the Holy Trinity evidently requires an *ascensio* of the same kind as the commentator himself had experienced at Ostia. In his wondrous soul (*animus*) or in his intellect (*mens*), man can rise above everything corporeal, even beyond the heavenly bodies themselves. In the end, the mind, too, has to be abandoned on the journey towards divine reality, since it is liable to change and variation (20.12):[1]

> Pass therefore beyond all changeableness; not only beyond all that is seen, but also beyond all that changes. For thou hast passed beyond the flesh which is seen; beyond heaven, the sun, moon, and stars, which are seen. Pass, too, beyond all that changes. For when thou had done with those things that are seen, and had come to thy mind, there thou didst find the changeableness of thy mind. Is God at all changeable? Pass then, beyond even thy mind.

That is the remarkable journey the evangelist John had made. He drew away from all perceptible reality, away from the flesh, from the earth beneath his feet, the waters he could see, the air where the birds fly, from the sun, the moon and the stars. Moreover, he left all spirits – *spiritus*, which cannot be seen – behind, and finally he even went beyond his intellect, *mens*. Thus did he get to know divine speech, *logos*, in Johannite speculation connected with the pre-existence of the Son: "See God, see His Word inhering to the Word speaking, that the speaker speaks not by syllables, but this his speaking is a shining out in the brightness of wisdom" (20.13), *Vide Deum, vide Verbum eius inhaerere Verbo dicenti: quia ipse dicens non syllabis dicit; sed splendore sapientiae fulgere, hoc est dicere*. The structural parallel between the experience outlined in the commentary on the Gospel and that of the *Confessions* is considerable. One by one, St. John "passes beyond" earthly life, the elements, the cosmos, imagination and intellect, in accordance with the three-part pattern *extra se – intra se – supra se*, in order to get acquainted with another kind of speech than discursive language, not dependent on the syllables of human grammar, a Word shining with God's Wisdom.

Augustine would in turn, when expounding Jesus as "the light of the world" in the same commentary on St. John, project the evangelist's experience onto his audience, the congregation at Hippo, to which he offered the prospect of a col-

---

[1] "Transi ergo omnem mutabilitatem; non solum omne quod videtur, sed et omne quod mutatur. Transisti enim carnem quae videtur, transisti coelum, solem, lunam, et stellas quae videntur; transi et omne quod mutatur. Iam enim istis transactis veneras ad animum tuum, sed et ibi invenisti mutabilitatem animi tui. Numquid mutabilis est Deus? Transi ergo et animum tuum."

lective *ascensio* on the return of Christ. In conformity with the Ostia ascension, this heavenly journey shall be made without any reading, priests or texts, including the Holy Writ (35.9): "Then, in presence of such a day, lamps will not be needed: no prophet shall then be read to us, no book of an apostle shall be opened; we shall not require the witness of John, we shall not need the Gospel itself. Accordingly all Scriptures shall be taken out of the way"...[1]

When the commentator looks forward to the time at which he and his congregation will behold this true light, he proceeds to use a more affected style, packed with questions and exhortations, as if to move his audience. What shall we see? "Wherewith shall our mind be fed?", *unde pascetur mens nostra?* Where will the joy come from, that "neither eye hath seen, nor ear heard, nor hath gone up into the heart of man?" (cf. 1 Corinthians 2.9) Let us yearn for, or, even more strongly, "let us pant for our home above", *supernae patriae suspiremus!* This is an eloquent instance of the Church Father's ecstatic mode, certainly reminiscent of his Ostia account, both in its soaring flight, its literal panting – *suspiravimus/suspiremus* – and in its gloomy cadence (coloured by Solomon's wisdom): "I feel that your affections are being lifted up with me to the things that are above: but the body, which is corrupt, weighs down the soul; and, the earthly habitation depresses the mind while meditating many things. I am about to lay aside this book, and you too are going to depart, every man to his own house." (35.9)[2]

The whole of this commentary paragraph is, as Antonio Quacquarelli points out, an excellent example of Christian rhetoric or, more precisely, of the "humble" homiletic level of style, *genus dicendi simplex*, a kind of mental dialogue with God, intended to immerse the audience in moments of a highly charged silence.[3] The longing of the heart is directed upwards, towards God, it is shared by a community, and it looks forward to setting aside "this book", *codex iste*: the text from St. John's Gospel that is being commented on, and, in a transferred sense, all the coding in signs that characterizes our existence on earth. From the *Confessions* we recognize the ascension (the repeated *in superna*), the holy pasture, the recycling of 1 Corinthians 2.9, the blessed sigh, the farewell to scripture and codex... In conclusion, perhaps the renowned Bishop of Hippo, while

---

1 "Tunc praesente tali die lucernae non erunt necessariae: non legetur nobis Propheta, non aperietur codex Apostoli, non requiremus testimonium Ioannis, non ipso indigebimus Evangelio. Ergo omnes Scripturae tollentur de medio".
2 "Sentio vestros affectus attolli mecum in superna: *sed corpus quod corrumpitur, aggravat animam; et deprimit terrena inhabitatio sensum multa cogitantem.* Depositurus sum et ego codicem istum, discessuri estis et vos quisque ad sua." Cf. the Vulgate's *Sapientia*, 9.15.
3 Quacquarelli 1972, p. 201.

preaching the Gospel to his North-African countrymen, was able to reuse, consciously or unconsciously, his remarkable experience from long ago, the summer of 387, when the Heaven momentarily stood open for the congregation *in nuce* that consisted of Monnica and himself.

*

After the hypothetical vanishing into silence of the analogous systems of the Creation and language, the two interlocutors in Ostia stand wide open for the divine message. They are evidently expecting some sort of immediately poignant announcement, in explicit contrast to the communication by figures or signs of the natural elements and human words. Augustine and Monnica may, if the conditions of their negative stance are met, listen to the Godhead Himself, "not through fleshly tongue nor angel's voice, nor thundercloud, nor any riddling parable, hear him unmediated, whom we love in all these things, hear him without them, as now we stretch out and in a flash of thought touch that eternal Wisdom who abides above all things".

The pattern is the same as earlier in this section. An essentially Neo-Platonic matrix, the theme (or scheme) of an ascension towards divine reality, carefully staged in hierarchical phases but in the long run of an ecstatic nature, takes on a New Testament colouring that emphasizes the distance or gap rather than the steps or stairway between God and the Creation. In his and Monnica's longing to finally "hear him unmediated", Augustine seems to recall the probably most influential of all Pauline pericopes: the contrasting in the first Epistle to the Corinthians of our current horizon, an enigmatic mirror, with the imminent vision face to face, that is, of the cognitive patchwork of the present with the radiant revelation of the future (13.12). It should be noted, however, that the Plotinian priest too had to leave the world of images behind in order to face transcendent reality, and that the enthusiastic souls of the *Enneads* too seemed "to be disposed towards" or, literally, "to reach out towards", *echein pros*, the One (6.9.11, 5.3.14). In short, all three of these inspired writers – Paul, Plotinus and Augustine – turn their backs on the world of images, most effectively evoked by the Church Father in his locution *per aenigma similitudinis*, when the longed-for meeting with the Godhead seems close at hand.

At that blessed moment when the mother and son stand at the window and reach out, they resemble angels, or more exactly: they gain an immediate receptivity for God's message which is normally reserved for the angels. For comparison's sake, O'Donnell has adduced the eighth book of *The Literal Meaning of Genesis*, in which God communicates with the spiritual part of His Creation, first and foremost the angels, in a way that no language can represent (8.25.47): "Inwardly, that is to say, God speaks to it in a wonderful and inexpressible way: neither through writing imposed on bodily materials, nor through words sounding in bodily ears, nor through the likenesses of bodies such as are formed in the imagination [*in spiritu imaginaliter*], as happens in dreams or in a kind of ecstatic state".[1] Similarly, "all dreams and imaginary revelations", *somnia et imaginariae revelationes,* and likewise "every tongue, and every sign" had to be silenced in order to make God's speech audible in Ostia.

This is a language without a medium. Neither pen nor mouth nor imagination can do it justice. The God that speaks thus to Monnica and Augustine is the high *artifex* of Creation, normally revealing Himself in His works, "whom we love in all these things". At present, however, His speech ignores Creation's huge index of signs and signals; it does not emerge from the great sounding board of the universe. Augustine and Monnica believe that they "hear him without them", *ipsum sine his audiamus,* that is, without the elements, nature or the stars. At this climactic point, the mystic experience in Ostia differs from its Milanese premonition from the seventh book of the *Confessions.* There, at the decisive moment's *ictus,* the Platonically inspired Augustine, supported by the Epistle to the Romans 1.20, had seen God's invisible qualities as they are perceived in his work, *per ea quae facta sunt intellecta* (7.17.23). Here, in the ninth book, by contrast, the semiotic or figurative *per ea* is no longer valid. We are left with the negative *sine his,* that is, radical alterity.

This is the speech of negative theology rather than that of universal analogy, and it fills its listeners with anticipation. Even though they immediately have to return to the everyday order of discursive language, they retain a reminiscence of it, a memory of this rapid insight, *rapida cogitatio,* a recollection of this moment of understanding, *hoc momentum intellegentiae,* that presages the resurrection to eternal life at the end of time. Once again, in the terms of *The Literal Meaning of Genesis,* we seem entitled to classify Augustine's and Monnica's jubilant experience as a genuinely prophetic *visio intellectualis.*

*

Thus Augustine has finished his (and his mother's) report on what happened at the window in Ostia. The fact that it was so dependent on conditional and negative phrases is bound up with his overall scepticism of the ability of words to represent reality in general and divinity in particular. Augustine's linguistic criticism is based on Greek speculation, primarily on the semantic scheme prevalent

---

[1] "Intus ei quippe loquitur Deus miro et ineffabili modo, neque per scripturam corporalibus instrumentis affixam, neque per voces corporalibus auribus insonantes, neque per corporum similitudines, quales in spiritu imaginaliter fiunt, sicut in somnis, vel in aliquo excessu spiritus, quod graece dicitur *ekstasis*". For O'Donnell's comment, see Augustine 1992 (III), p. 134.

in Stoic philosophy which he had adjusted for his own purposes in his early work *De dialectica* (*On Dialectic*) from 387. There he had distinguished four aspects of human words:
- *verbum* (the word, as it were, in its own right, the linguistic unit called "word"),
- *dicibile* (the pronounced word's conceptual meaning, the thought or content of an expression),
- *dictio* (the word's referential qualities along with its pronounciation, that is, the entire expression, subsuming *verbum* and *dicibile*: the actual utterance),
- and finally *res* (the word's extra-linguistic referent).[1]

In *On Dialectic*, it was first and foremost the *dicibile* category – "that of the word which is not sensed by the ears but by the mind and is held enclosed in the mind itself" (5), *quidquid autem ex verbo non aures sed animus sentit et ipso animo tenetur inclusum* – that formed the basis of Augustine's idea of a mental language that precedes vocal expression. We have already come across this "inner word" in *On the Trinity*, where the author observes that "the word that sounds outwardly is the sign of the word that gives light inwardly" (15.11.20), *verbum quod foris sonat, signum est verbi quod intus lucet*. In phrases such as these, Augustine tried to convey the idea of an original intention or intellective meaning within human beings that had to be converted into external speech – and, consequently, jeopardized – for the purpose of communication and intersubjectivity.[2] There is no doubt that this process was a persistent source of concern in all his mature writings.

Augustine's serious doubts about the tongue's and the voice's capability to trustworthily reproduce the inner word is evident from his instruction to Deogra-

---

[1] All quotations in English from *On Dialectic* are from J. Marchand's translation, available on the Web, 1994. Among those who have thoroughly investigated Augustine's ideas and notions of language are Duchrow, 1965 (for *On Dialectic*, see pp. 42–62), and Mayer, 1974. The Church Father's theory of signs – conspicuous in a writer who has frequently been considered the first semiotician of the West – changed over time and cannot be treated in any detail here. Succinct presentations, not necessarily in mutual accordance, can be found in Markus 1972, Jackson 1972, Todorov 1992, pp. 36–56, and Dawson 1995 (for the "inner word", se pp. 126f.). Markus, who provided us with the classical investigation of Augustine's semiotic ideas in his article from 1957 (reprinted 1972), has probably also written the best overview of this field, including important bibliographic references, 1966. A penetrating analysis of the semantic key concepts in *On Dialectic* is available in Stock 1998, pp. 138–45. For more concise presentations, see Ruef 1995 and Kirwan 2001.
[2] Kirwan convincingly demonstrates the continuity between Augustine's concept of *dicibilia* in *On Dialectic* and his later (Christianized) notion of "inner words", 2001, pp. 199–201.

tias, deacon of Carthage, on teaching the faith to uneducated catechumens, *De catechizandis rudibus* (*On the Catechising of the Uninstructed*, ca. 400). The author begins this short treatise by admitting that he often distrusts his own speech (2.3, translation slightly modified):

> Indeed with me, too, it is almost always the fact that my speech displeases myself. For I am covetous of something better, the possession of which I frequently enjoy within me before I commence to body it forth in ringing words: and then when my capacities of expression prove inferior to my inner apprehensions, I grieve over the inability which my tongue has betrayed in answering to my heart. For it is my wish that he who hears me should have the same complete understanding of the subject which I have myself; and I perceive that I fail to speak in a manner calculated to effect that, and that this arises mainly from the circumstance that the intellectual apprehension diffuses itself through the mind with something like a rapid flash, whereas the utterance is slow, and occupies time, and is of a vastly different nature, so that, while this latter is moving on, the intellectual apprehension has already withdrawn itself within its secret abodes. (III)

The inner speech proceeds as fast as our thought, whereas our "ringing words" inevitably lag behind. The abundance of the heart is obviously – despite the sentence already quoted from the evangelist Matthew (12.34) – awkward to express. Here it is treated as an "intellectual apprehension", *intellectus*, to which the words on the tongue cannot do justice. Characteristically, Augustine resorts to a simile in order to give an idea of this inner speech: it pierces the soul "with something like a rapid flash", *quasi rapida coruscatione*. The possibility for such an intimate discourse to be converted into an audible message and, hence, be made subject to communication, proves ultimately dependent on divine intervention. If the sound of the human voice does not merely die like empty noise in the ears of its listeners, Augustine assures us in his commentary on the Gospel of St. John, it is because it penetrates their souls to "reveal" its meaning as the result of supreme illumination: "what they understand is given them within, flashes within, is revealed within" (26.7), *quod intellegunt, intus datur, intus coruscat, intus revelatur.*[1]

The contrast between this understanding at lightning speed and the emptiness of ordinary speech certainly recalls the Ostia episode from the *Confessions*, where the moment of supreme intellection, *momentum intellegentiae*, is linked to an equally rapid thought, *rapida cogitatio*, or thrust of the heart, *ictus cordis*, before the "noise" of the lips and the sluggish sequences of discursive language regain predominance. The same pattern appears in *On the Catechising of the Uninstructed*, almost like an echo from the roughly contemporary *Confessions*:

---

[1] Ulrich Wienbruch thoroughly analyses this act of understanding in his study 1971, pp. 87–89.

"Wherefore we have to surmise how far the sound of our mouth must be from representing that stroke of the intelligence" (2.3), *quapropter coniiciendum est, quantum distet sonus oris nostri ab illo ictu intellegentiae.* This sceptical attitude to human expression, according to which the sound of the voice necessarily diverges from memory's inner discourse, which in turn cannot do justice to the original conception or "stroke" of the intellect, will survive into the Middle Ages, to be repeated point by point in Dante's *Comedy* (Inferno 28.4–6, Paradiso 33.55–57, 121–23).

Few or none of the apologists and the early Christian Fathers felt as intensely as Augustine the enticement of "the inner master's" silent teaching, exempt from the disturbances and misunderstandings of all human communication, in short: the enticement of devotion and silence. Later on in *On the Catechising of the Uninstructed*, the author emphasizes "the fact that our intelligence is better pleased and more thoroughly arrested by that which we perceive in silence in the mind, and that we have no inclination to have our attention called off from it to a noise of words coming far short of representing it" (10.14), *magis nos delectat et tenet quod in silentio mente cernimus, nec inde volumus avocari ad verborum longe disparem strepitum.* Once again this treatise echoes the Ostia passage, where Augustine and Monnica had to return "to vocal expressions [*strepitus*] from our mouth". Discursive language cannot possibly do justice to mystery. It can only lead away from it, *longe dispar.* The revelation is ineffable. Nonetheless, the author of the *Confessions* knows of course that, when he is to represent the religious experience for his audience or readers, he only has this imperfect language to rely on.

In *On the Catechising of the Uninstructed*, the Bishop of Hippo makes it perfectly clear to the anxious addressee of his treatise, who is in doubt about his teaching methods, that as long as we have to wait for the final revelation – for the day, he explains, that no eye has seen, no ear has heard and no heart has felt – we should not underestimate the provisional value of our speech for the purpose of instructing the uneducated (2.4). These words allude to 1 Corinthians 2.9, precisely the Pauline clause that marks the starting point of the dialogue in Ostia, where Augustine and Monnica question each other about the eternal life of the saints, which "eye has not seen nor ear heard nor human heart conceived". And – one is tempted to add – which no tongue or pen has represented. This beatified existence, then, is ineffable, but the three paragraphs 23–25 from the ninth book of the *Confessions* will nevertheless have to do. This is made clear by Augustine when, immediately after his account for the blessed experience, he adds: "So did I speak, though not in this wise exactly, nor in these same words" (9.10.26), *dicebam talia, etsi non isto modo et his verbis.*

What you are reading here, he reminds his readers, may at least give you a hint of the *ictus* that shook our hearts.

This small addition in the first person singular is remarkable. It seems to contradict the presentation of the whole of the preceding paragraph as a dialogue between Monnica and Augustine, or more exactly as their joint "inner" speech: *Dicebamus ergo...* So was it only Augustine who spoke? Yes and no. No, because the Ostia account describes the communication between two persons by virtue of a mystic experience (in which Monnica, who had been a pious Christian for decades – and who was moreover uneducated, hence saintly inspired – probably assumed the role of the initiated rather than that of the initiand).[1] Yes, because when the writer looks back on this episode a decade post factum, he is obliged to use his own memory and his own words, both indispensable and yet inadequate resources for the record of his and Monnica's shared contact with divine reality.[2]

The difference between past experience and present recollection/recording is a prime theme in Augustine's work. He returns continually to his necessary but frustratingly inadequate attempts to translate the inner and intuitive speech into discursive *verba*.[3] He frequently and anxiously dwells upon the lapse of time that is inherent in every expression of language (particularly in writing), with the possible exception of the holy texts inspired by the Spirit. Human words are always a reconstruction and can never be simultaneous with the experience itself. This insight is vital for the author of the *Confessions*. Precisely for that reason, the Ostia account is such a representative but at the same time unique passage in his work. It is a brave attempt based on the only means available to the author, the sounds of the vocal cords or the squiggles of the pen, however inadequate and provisional, to reproduce the speech of the heart. He does not content himself with recalling, rehashing or paraphrasing this speech; he aims rather at an immediate representation, permeated with the illusion of presence. As far as humanly possible, he attempts to push the inner word towards the foreground of discursive language, in short: to say the ineffable.

---

1 It is significant, Alexandre Leupin observes, that the "language of truth" characteristic of the ecstasy in Ostia "comes forward in an exchange with the mother, and thus places her in contrast with the sophistic discourse of the rhetors and of the father", 2003, p. 59. Cf. Stock 1998, pp. 116f.
2 Courcelle understands the transition from "we said" to "I said" as an acknowledgement on the part of the writer that he alone assumes the responsibility for the text's Platonic discourse. "In reality" both speakers would probably have expressed themselves in the manner of Monnica, in a more distinctly Christian language, 1950, p. 226. Unfortunately, the words employed by Augustine and his mother *dans la réalité* must remain anybody's guess.
3 Cf. Matthews 1972, pp. 181–90; Harrison 1992, pp. 54–59.

This is of course an unachievable project, and no one knew it better than Augustine himself. He now disavows his own text, or, to be more precise, he admits that it is dependent on a certain mode and choice of words or, as we would say, a certain style: *isto modo et his verbis*. The speech of the heart lacks style, or rather transpires beyond style, whereas our discursive language has a tendency to continually relapse into rhetorical and narrative patterns. Brian Stock, one of the surprisingly few scholars who has analysed the Ostia account from a literary point of view, has noted that, despite its overt suspension of perception, it is punctuated by verbs of movement, "thereby creating the impression of a narrative sequence".[1]

Correspondingly, the first nine books of the work Augustine called *Confessions*, unique among his otherwise philosophical, theological and hermeneutical writings, are reminiscent of a narrative, with a narrative's figurative and fictional devices. But it is a narrative that unfolds like a thin veil, close to being torn apart or swept away, barely concealing the irrepressible need to tell the truth that drives the confessor's inner speech, whether it entails a dialogue with his dying mother or turns to the everlasting God. Thus his personal biography becomes a sort of makeshift, a discursive web that paradoxically struggles to unravel itself in order to uncover another Script, non-figurative, non-narrative and emphatically non-fictional, dictated by *Deus artifex*.[2]

---

[1] Stock 1998, p. 119.
[2] Cf. Flores 1975, p. 7; Kenney 2005, p. 147.

2 Recycling the Classics

Weeping for Dido

The Plotinian and the Augustinian transcendental ventures, taken together, constitute a powerful paradigm for the ambivalent attitude towards images (*eidōla, imagines*) that characterizes Christian premodern culture. This field of study is difficult to survey, but it is of great interest in a number of disciplines such as theology, with its subdivisions of exegesis and dogmatics, philosophy, history of art, semiotics, hermeneutics and rhetoric. Here, we shall restrict ourselves to examining its relevance to Late Antique approaches and responses to fictional representation.

The issue of fiction was hardly of any importance for Plotinus. In his system, all representation was in principle – and in good Platonic tradition – judged to be inferior goods. Transcendence was best sought along philosophy's *via negativa*, by means of abstraction and reduction. In as far as images, imagination or words could actually give us some idea or premonition of the One (on this point Plotinus, in contrast to a number of iconoclasts in Western tradition, did at least leave room for hope), they have nothing to do with fiction or narrative fabrication; on the contrary, they epitomize a power of vision that penetrates so deeply into the nature of things that it might grant us an intimation of their archetypal origin.

For Augustine, however, fiction was a problem that could not be ignored. It was inevitably tied up with the question of language, the theory of signs and hermeneutics in general. On this point too he is detailed in his *Confessions*, relying on this work's all-pervading distinction between the author's illuminated present and the protagonist's precarious past. Already as a child in Thagaste, he had imbibed fictitious stories through both eyes and ears, that is, he had listened to tales and watched plays. As he remorsefully confesses, "I hankered to win myself glory in our contests, and to have my ears tickled by tall stories which only made them itch more hotly; and all the while that same curiosity more and more inflamed my eyes with lust for the public shows which are the games of grown-ups." (1.10.16)[1] The memory of his itching ears and shining eyes tells us something of the boy's early excitement, however rueful, about the world of literature and the theatre. It is significant that later in his *Confessions*, Augustine was to

---

[1] "Amans in certaminibus superbas victorias et scalpi aures meas falsis fabellis, quo prurirent ardentius, eadem curiositate magis magisque per oculos emicante in spectacula, ludos maiorum".

use exactly the same metaphor, itching, about his equally guilt-ridden erotic desires (9.1.1), *scalpendi scabiem libidinum*. The confessor is even more condemning when he recalls his strong childhood enchantment with the *Aeneid* (1.13.21–22):

> What indeed is more pitiful than a piteous person who has no pity for himself? I could weep over the death Dido brought upon herself out of love for Aeneas, yet I shed no tears over the death I brought upon myself by not loving you. O God, you are the light of my heart, bread for the inward mouth of my soul, the virtue wedded to my mind and the innermost recesses of my thought; [...]
>
> But now let my God cry more loudly in my soul, so that your truth may tell me, "No, that is not the case; it is not true. The primary teaching is better in every respect." I am undoubtedly more ready today to forget the wanderings of Aeneas and so forth than how to write or read. Curtains may well hang at the entrance to schools of literature, but they serve less to signal the prestige of elite instruction than to conceal error. [...] If I then go further and ask which would be a graver handicap in this life, to forget how to read and write, or to forget those poetic fantasies, can one doubt what answer would be given by anyone in his right mind? Sin I did, then, in boyhood, by preferring those frivolous tales to much more useful attainments, or rather by loving the one and loathing the other. Already the jingle, "One and one make two, two and two make four," was hateful to me, whereas a wooden horse full of armed men, Troy afire, and the shade of Creusa – these were a spectacle on which I delighted to gaze, and as empty as they were entertaining. (IV)

Here again we come across the paradox we have already met in the ninth book of the *Confessions*, where the author reports his decision to withdraw the service of his tongue from the market of speechifying. Precisely in his diatribes against rhetoric, here literature, Augustine is at his most eloquent. The oft-quoted introduction to the extract above is an elucidating example.

There we find a rhetorical question, *rogatio*, framed antithetically, initially governed by the figure called *polyptōton schēma* in Greek and which Quintilian defines as a change of case (9.3.37): the Latin word for the adjective "piteous", *miser*, is repeated in the comparative, in the ablative of the positive and in the present participle of the corresponding verb, also in the ablative.[1] Immediately thereafter, the diction is intensified by means of three powerful metaphors, the last of which has a strong note of personification. From beginning to end in the *Confessions* we are reminded in this manner – by exclamations, questions, straightforward addresses to God, corrections of what has just been said, rhyth-

---

1 Quintilian takes as his closest starting point Cicero's *On the Orator* (3.54.207): *quod in multis casibus ponitur*. In his *Confessions*, Augustine repeatedly applies this figure to the verb forms, mostly for the sake of pathetic effect: "I was not yet in love, but I was enamored with the idea of love, [...]. In love with loving, I was casting about for something to love" (3.1.1), *nondum amabam, et amare amabam,... quaerebam quid amarem, amans amare*.

mic cadences – of the author's skill in creating the appearance of speech jotted down for recitation. It was intended to be read aloud, to be heard, as scholars have observed.[1] In fact, Augustine exploits his superior rhetorical talent and education to deliver a deathblow at literary fiction.

Like his predecessors in classical philosophy, the Church Father refers to his unadulterated inner being, to the soul that has held out through the tumult of life, forming a reliable link to the divine. His strategy is evident from the metaphors of the introductory clauses quoted above. God is addressed as the light of the speaker's heart, as bread for the inward mouth of his soul, and even – if I try to translate word for word – as 'the virtue that weds my intellect with the bosom of my imagination', *virtus maritans mentem meam et sinum cogitationis meae*. This is a bold configuration of the author's mental scenario, where God acts as a priest officiating at the wedding of his intellect with his intuitive thinking, but it also underlines the unique significance Augustine was to place on the Pauline "inner man", *homo interior*, throughout all his writings (above, p. 106).

The fact that it is the *Aeneid* that comes under fire is quite natural. When Augustine thought of fiction, he thought of the *Aeneid*, irrespective of the historicity he might have ascribed to Aeneas and his foundational journey from Troy to Italy. In the essay on burial customs written in his old age in the 420s, *De cura pro mortuis gerenda* (*On Care to Be Had for the Dead*), he warns against popular superstitions such as that the unburied deceased cannot cross the river of death, whereupon he cites *Aeneid* 6.327–28 with the attendant rhetorical question: "Who can incline a Christian heart to these poetical and fabulous figments" (2.3), *quis cor christianum inclinet his poeticis fabulosisque figmentis*, since Christ taught us that our enemies have no power over us after death? Later in the same treatise, Augustine even sharpens his tone, fulminating against the Virgilian *poetica falsitas* (10.12). The bite of his rebuke is indicative of the *Aeneid*'s position as the centre of the Roman canon. Virgil's work would indeed appear as the foremost instance of classical poetry – imitated, commented on and allegorized – throughout the Middle Ages and well into the seventeenth century. To the intellectuals of Late Antiquity, Virgil would practically embody the very concept of *poetria* and of model Latin usage in general. This is to a high degree due to the Roman school system, carefully mapped in modern research ever since Henri-Irénée Marrou's masterly work on the history of antique education.[2]

---

[1] O'Connell 1978, p. 91; Ferrari 1992, p. 102.
[2] Cf. Marrou's chapter on "Rome et l'éducation classique", 1948, especially pp. 359–89. For an updated presentation, see Gemeinhardt 2007, pp. 27–51.

The pupils began by learning to read and write in primary school with a *litterator* or *magister* (in wealthy families they could start to learn earlier at home under the supervision of a *paedagogus*, often a Greek-speaking and sometimes freed slave).[1] Then ensued instruction, frequently inculcated by means of slaps and blows, in the two fundamental subjects of grammar and rhetoric, in that order.[2] The Late Antique education with a *grammaticus* generally followed a basic textbook, *Ars grammatica* or *Ars maior*, if necessary studied in the concise compendium *Ars minor*, written by the Roman Aelius Donatus, Jerome's teacher. To the Middle Ages Donatus would appear to be more or less synonymous with grammar, included by Dante in the solar sphere of Paradise for his teaching in "the first art" (Paradiso 12.137–38): "quel Donato / ch'a la prim' arte degnò porre mano". From the sixth century onwards, his *Ars maior* would frequently be complemented by the voluminous *Institutiones grammaticae* composed by the North African Priscian, who taught in Constantinople (fl. ca. 500).

Normally, grammar occupied the pupils throughout their early teens. It included orientation in correct Latin – at the level of letters, syllables and word classes – as well as in classical literature, *enarratio poetarum*, and it often involved working through the great poets' works, line by line, studying prosody and metre but also mythology, life and institutions. Literary studies were, on the whole, considered to be of the utmost importance. As a matter of course, it was the first activity mentioned in Cicero's oft-quoted definition of grammar's domain in *De oratore* (*On the Orator*): "the study of poets, the learning of histories, the explanation of words and proper intonation in speaking them" (1.42.187), *in grammaticis, poetarum pertractatio, historiarum cognitio, verborum interpretatio, pronuntiandi quidam sonus*.[3]

After such grammar drills, it was time for the pupils – those pupils, that is, whose families could afford it – to move on to rhetoric under a *rhetor* or *orator*, with Cicero and Quintilian on the schedule. Ever since the fourth century, the lessons of this eloquent couple were passed on and popularized by the so-called *rhetores latini minores*, whereby their (especially Cicero's) original idealistic visions of an eloquence impregnated by philosophy or by civil responsibility had to surrender to the dictates of the textbooks. Fundamental to this education were the famous five parts of rhetoric: the subject of the speech, its disposition, its ornamentation, its memorization and its performance. During their studies in finding the subject matter of the speech, *inventio*, the pupils frequently practised

---

[1] See the chapter "Inside the School" in Haarhoff 1920, pp. 52–118.
[2] For the following exposé I have made special use of the introductory survey "Prestige de l'éducation romaine au Ve siècle" in Riché 1962, pp. 41–51.
[3] For Cicero's *On the Orator*, I follow E.W. Sutton's and H. Rackham's Loeb volumes I–II 1942.

their skills in *declamationes* or in the form of simulated trials, *controversiae*, where they had to retell a given theme in their own words, divided into a number of fixed components. As a rule, they had already been able to practise elementary paraphrasing within grammar's programme for imitation of canonical texts; in addition, either a *grammaticus* or a *rhetor* would sometimes have exposed their students to certain introductory rhetorical exercises, *progymnasmata*, that included items such as narrative, description and impersonation. Throughout all the years of education, Virgil provided most of the literary material for these exercises. Learning to vary and adorn a *locus Virgilianus* was often the first step in the rhetorical training which succeeded grammar studies.

It is no wonder that among these generations of boys and, at least in some wealthy families, girls, the Augustan writer would seem to embody the very concept of poetry, literature or *artes* in general. In addition, several of his distinctive features were to make the Christians favourably disposed towards him, despite growls from Tertullian, Jerome and others. His Late Antique success was based not only on the *Aeneid*, with its transformation of Homeric heroism into Roman *pietas*, but also on the touches of mysticism in the *Georgics* and on the pastoral themes in the *Eclogues*. Jacques Fontaine has shown how easily the young shepherd boys of the *Eclogues'* idyllic settings merged with the one and only Good Shepherd in both Christian poetry and Christian art, in Prudentius as well as in the apse of San Apollinare in Classe outside Ravenna.[1] The recurrent Late Antique challenges to traditional Roman culture seem only to have escalated this phenomenon. The more ancient education and philosophy decayed, as pointed out by Karl Hermann Schelkle, who has carefully mapped Augustine's reuse of Virgil (the basis of all later studies on the subject), the stronger the poet's reputation grew as the greatest witness of its disappearing glory.[2]

Our modern world knows no counterpart to this massive impact of one single writer on a whole literature. There were few or no ways to escape from Virgil or what has been labelled the cult of Virgil. Those Romans who devoted themselves to poetry even as adults did not need to worry much about anxieties of influence, since the authority of the *Aeneid*, the *Georgics* and the *Eclogues* pervaded their whole culture. Composing verse on an ambitious scale about serious subjects quite simply meant speaking, more or less properly, Virgilian. Consequently, all poets (or for that matter, all writers) could count on a mere fleeting allusion to the *summus poeta* being identified by their educated listeners or readers, immediately activating early memories of grammar studies in their audien-

---

[1] Fontaine 1980, pp. 214–39.
[2] Schelkle 1939, p. 2.

ces. Among those ex-schoolboys were also the Church Fathers, who found it difficult – not to say impossible – to relieve themselves of their boyhood reminiscences of the poets' poet. In the words of Alun Hudson-Williams: "To Tertullian, Jerome, Augustine, and others Virgil was a vivid presence all their lives."[1]

To all appearances, this presence was felt just as strongly even by such a high dignitary as Archbishop Ambrose, the mightiest representative of Western Christendom during the reign of the Emperors Gratian and Theodosius at the end of the fourth century. David S. Wiesen cites a passage from his tract on the Holy Spirit, *De spiritu sancto*, which expressly refers to the pagan writers (2.5.36):[2]

> Gentile writers, following ours as it were through shadows, because they could not imbibe the truth of the Spirit, have pointed out in their verses that the Spirit within nourishes heaven and earth, and the glittering orbs of moon and stars. So they deny not that the strength of creatures exists through the Spirit, are we who read this to deny it? But you think that they refer to a Spirit produced of the air. If they declared a Spirit of the air to be the Author of all things, do we doubt that the Spirit of God is the Creator of all things?

The argument is cleverly structured according to the dialectic principle of *a fortiori*. Ambrose reuses one of the best-known passages from the *Aeneid* (6.724– 26): Anchises' Stoic/Neo-Platonic explanation to his son – on the latter's visit to the realm of the dead – that a great Spirit gives life from within, *spiritus intus alit*, to heaven and earth, the moon and the stars. Now, Ambrose proceeds, if pagans already expressed this rudimentary insight, how much more powerfully should not we (illumined by true faith) believe in the Creation by the Holy Spirit as depicted in Genesis? Through the metaphor of the shadow, constitutive in this context, the Archbishop contrasts Virgil's dim intuition with the enlightened assurance of the Christians. In this way, he manages to reverse the established power relationship between the two cultures: *gentiles homines* "follow" our own writers but still fumble in the dark. Ambrose's recycling, *chrēsis*, of the poets' poet was characteristically two-edged, both an acknowledgement of Vir-

---

[1] Hudson-Williams 1966–67, p. 12.
[2] "Gentiles homines per umbram quamdam nostros secuti, quia veritatem Spiritus haurire non poterant; quod coelum ac terras, lunae quoque stellarumque micantium globos Spiritus intus alat, suis versibus indiderunt. Ergo illi per Spiritum non negant virtutem subsistere creaturae: nos qui legimus, denegamus? Sed flatilem putatis ab illis spiritum designatum. Si illi auctorem omnium flatilem Spiritum declararunt, nos dubitamus Spiritum Dei esse omnium creatorem?" I quote Ambrose from *PL* 16.750b–c, trans. H. de Romestin in P. Schaff's and H. Wace's *A Select Library of the Nicene and Post-Nicene Fathers of the Christian Church* 2.10, 1979. Cf. Wiesen 1971, p. 84.

gil's intriguing (albeit mistaken) intuitions and a firm indication of a new cultural hierarchy with the Christian authors at the top.

*

In the first book of his *Confessions*, Augustine tells us how in school he was required "to produce a speech made by Juno expressing her anger and grief at being unable to repulse the Trojan king from Italy", *ut dicerem verba Iunonis irascentis et dolentis quod non posset Italia Teucrorum avertere regem.* Faced with this task he was "obliged to follow the errant footsteps of poetic fantasies", *figmentorum poeticorum vestigia errantes sequi cogebamur.* The model of the exercise was of course the *Aeneid*, and the young Augustine evidently had the ability to enter into the feelings of the invented figure, *adumbrata persona*, which had been allotted to him. He seems, indeed, to have been among those pupils who best clothed the thoughts of the fictional heroes or deities "in apt words", *verbis sententias congruenter vestientibus* (1.17.27). It was along these paths, in his grammar and rhetoric classes, that Augustine the boy came into contact with the national epic of the Romans and learnt to love it. Judging from the slightly earlier extract quoted above (p. 124), he was particularly fascinated by the events which permitted the poet to excel in rhetorical pathos, like the tragic episodes with Creusa, the wife of the hero, and with Dido, his mistress, even if the converted confessor sniffs at such fancies (mere "smoke and wind", *fumus et ventus*), preferring the teaching of elementary reading and writing.

The key sentence in the extract is the following: "Curtains may well hang at the entrance to schools of literature, but they serve less to signal the prestige of elite instruction than to conceal error." That is how Augustine – again, under the pale cast of retrospective thought – sums up his literary studies. The syntagm *tegimentum erroris* recalls both the cognitive argument (we cannot rely on the erroneous poets) as well as the moral (they are a threat to manners and customs) from Plato's *The Republic*. The writer of the *Confessions* found no sources of mystic wisdom in Virgil and the other pagan poets, no esoteric insights of the kind that later periods learnt to expect of classical literature (or of classical *artes* in general, from astrology to philosophy). All he saw was this *tegimentum erroris*, a concept whose two terms are equally important.

With regard to the second term: literature deceives, it is fake, an outcome of *error*, a Latin word meaning both 'straying about' and 'mistake' or 'fault', an ambiguity that Petrarch, certainly a writer haunted by Augustine throughout his life, was to take great advantage of. Thus literature is not for real but it pretends to be, concealing its circumventions and delusions behind a 'covering' (the first term) or veil of authenticity. The confessor held no hopes about the pagan Virgil. His bitter words about *dementia, poetica illa figmenta* and *illa inania* inevitably express a condemnation of the dead Creusa's ghost or 'shadow'. Augustine's phrasing *ipsius umbra Creusae* is taken directly from the *Aeneid*, 2.772. One should perhaps add that his disapproval is remarkably severe. Harald Hagendahl feels obliged to return to stern Tertullian's onslaughts from the early third century to find a hostility to traditional Roman culture comparable to that of the *Confessions*, "this manifesto of fanatical religiosity".[1]

Precisely the shadow would be another appropriate metaphor for profane poetry in Augustine's – as in Ambrose's – eyes. *The Shadows of Poetry* is actually the title of a study devoted to "Vergil in the Mind of Augustine". There, however, the picture of the relationship between poet and theologian is, interestingly, made much more ambiguous. The author, Sabine MacCormack, goes so far as to present Augustine as "Vergil's most intelligent and searching ancient reader".[2] Her opinion is not, of course, formed *ex nihilo*. Domenico Comparetti, in his classical study from 1872 on the medieval reception of Virgil, reminds us that the Church Father, despite the condemnation in his *Confessions*, had a high esteem for the poet and quoted him extensively, even in his late magnum opus, *On the City of God*.[3] Furthermore, in his major study of 1967, Hagendahl presented convincing evidence of Virgil's presence throughout Augustine's writings, with two equally strong but altogether different peaks in the novice's dialogues or treatises (386–91) and the bishop's *City of God* thirty years later. In Augustine's early writings, Virgil emerges as the apogee of all liberal education, while in the works of his old age, the poet is mainly treated as a representative of the pagan civilization that is the target of his polemic.

To put it simply, 'our poet' from the Cassiciacum dialogues, *noster poeta*, later became 'their poet', *eorum poeta*.[4] This is an observation that holds good even if the overall picture could be nuanced in both cases. As long as Augustine could embrace the possibility of some sort of classical and Christian cultural synthesis, well into the 390s, Virgil certainly contributed to shaping his language, style, ethos and world view, even though a sceptical or at any rate ambiguous attitude to the *summus poeta* is perceptible quite early in his writings. On the other hand, as is clear from Gerhard Müller's learned thesis on the forms and functions of the Virgilian quotations throughout Augustine's writings, the Church Father kept appreciating Virgil to the end of his life, even if he did so – to borrow the phrasing of Danuta Shanzer – "only at subconscious level".[5]

---

[1] Hagendahl 1967, p. 715.
[2] MacCormack 1998, p. xv.
[3] Comparetti 1997, pp. 90f.
[4] Hagendahl 1967, p. 456.
[5] Müller 2003; Shanzer 2012, p. 173.

The advocate of the City of God, amidst his strenuous attacks on the *Aeneid*'s pantheon, could not conceal his admiration for the epic poem's artistic qualities. Even in his *Confessions*, the Aeneidian subtext is unmistakable, *pace* Hagendahl, as in the scene from the fifth book, often commented on, where the narrator departs from Carthage for Rome, leaving the abandoned Monnica crying like another Dido on the shore (5.8.15). Moreover, some scholars, among them Camille Bennett, have pointed out that Augustine's restless search for divine response and peace in his *Confessions*, his vacillation between a number of philosophical world views and doctrines of faith, together with his final enlightenment and intention to found a new congregation for the purpose of contributing to the realization of the Kingdom of God on earth, would imitate the travels of the Trojan hero around the Mediterranean, aiming for the new city and the new Empire. Bennett even thinks it is likely that Augustine's and Monnica's dialogue in Ostia "is virtually an allegorized version of the last meeting of Aeneas and his father in *Aeneid* VI".[1]

This is a bold hypothesis that possibly overstates the case. But it is true that Virgil – the unsurpassed *auctoritas* of Latin culture in the grammar teaching of the schools, venerated for his almost encyclopaedic wisdom – had been interpreted allegorically ever since the second century. This type of reading was to be reinforced during the fourth century and continued throughout the whole of the Middle Ages.[2] It was to a certain extent shared by Augustine, though he never, at least not in his preserved writings, came even close to the excesses in Virgilian allegoresis which we will examine in the course of the next chapter, in Fulgentius, and which would still survive in a famous High Medieval commentator such as Bernardus Silvestris (*fl.* ca. 1150). Yet the Church Father could ascribe prophetic status to Virgil as late as in the tenth book of the *City of God*. There, Augustine addresses an eloquent speech to Porphyry, Plotinus' disciple and editor as well as a renowned opponent of Christianity, demonstrating that even pagan oracles recognize Christ: the greatest of poets, *poeta nobilissimus*, had actually portrayed Him "in a poetical manner certainly", *poetice quidem*, since he had represented Him "by an imaginary portrait of another person" (10.27), *in alterius adumbrata persona*.[3]

---

1 Bennett 1988, p. 65.
2 For this cult of Virgil and its roots in Hellenistic allegoresis, see Wiesen 1971 and Bažil 2009, pp. 101–05. The Christian poets' new and more profound "assimilation of Virgil" during the fourth century is concisely examined in Fontaine 1980, pp. 156f.
3 All English translations of passages from the *City of God* are from Henry Bettenson's volume in the Penguin Classics series 1984.

To strengthen this argument for Virgil as a proto-Christian seer, Augustine quotes the introduction to one of the poet's most famous texts, the Fourth Eclogue, in which the dream of a new Golden Age on earth is presented in lines 4–10:[1]

4   Ultima Cumaei venit iam carminis aetas;
5   magnus ab integro saeclorum nascitur ordo.
    iam redit et Virgo, redeunt Saturnia regna;
    iam nova progenies caelo demittitur alto.
    tu modo nascenti puero, quo ferrea primum
    desinet ac toto surget gens aurea mundo,
10 casta fave Lucina: tuus iam regnat Apollo.

The last age of the Cumaean Sybil's song has come.
The mighty sequence of ages is born and begins anew.
Now the Maiden returns. The reign of Saturn returns.
Now a new generation descends from heaven on high.
At the birth of the child in whose time the iron race
shall cease and a golden race inherit the whole earth,
smile, O chaste Lucina: now your Apollo reigns.

These verses have become known as the Messianic Eclogue, as Christians, ever since the early fourth century and the reign of Constantine the Great, were prone to identify the poem's *puer*, who will inaugurate a new era of peace and prosperity on earth, with the forthcoming Christ (born by a Maiden, cf. the *Virgo* in line 6). Augustine adheres to such an understanding of *Eclogues* IV. It was in the figure of this boy, the author of the *City of God* claims, that the pagan poet had made a draft of Christ. We shall return to this reading; here, it is of interest for us that the words Augustine uses, *in alterius adumbrata persona*, virtually echo the passage in the first book of his *Confessions*, where he remembers his skill in assuming the part of Juno – an invented figure, *adumbrata persona* – during his paraphrasing exercise at school (1.17.27). Thus, while the confessor still feels guilty when he recalls his empathy with an empty fiction, the author of the *City of God* imagines he sees Christ Himself behind the pagan draft! Even if Virgil had applied his usual "poetical manner" to his subject, the foretold child of *Eclogues* IV is no gratuitous fabrication, such as the Olympian deities;

---

[1] The *Eclogues* are rendered as in H.R. Fairclough's Loeb edition 1998. For the English translation I have used B.H. Fowler's version from 1997.

in this case, after all, the poet proceeded veraciously, *veraciter tamen*.¹ In Augustine's interpretation of the Messianic Eclogue, then, the adjective *adumbratus* no longer primarily means freely or wilfully sketched – invented – but rather depends on its literal meaning: *adumbro* = to cast a shadow on something or someone. In the last instance, the poem's shadow-like child refers to the imminent light of the world. If the poetical *persona* remembered in the *Confessions*, Juno, was suggestive but entirely fabulous, lacking all substance, the Virgilian *puer* cited in the *City of God* 10.27 stands out as a dim presage of the Saviour.

Evidently, the Church Father continues, referring to line 4 of *Eclogues* IV, the poet could not say this on his own, as "it is immediately apparent that this passage was derived from the Sibyl of Cumae", *hoc a Cumaea Sybilla dictum esse incunctanter apparet*. The noblest of poets will thus resemble an inspired seer, *vates*. He has to gain authority for his words from above. When his fiction is to be reinterpreted as a Christological draft and presage, he is no longer supposed to speak *a se ipso*, but his voice becomes sibylline, a pagan counterpart to the Old Testament prophets. It is in Late Antique comments like these that we find the cultural-historical embryo of Michelangelo's composition in the ceiling of the Sistine chapel, where Jeremiah, Isaiah and their likes are lined up facing the Sibyls of Antiquity, including the one from Cumæ. In spite of his recurrent anti-classical diatribes, Augustine was among the foremost representatives of this Christian appropriation of pagan oracles and divination, but he was far from the only one and definitely not the first.

He rather belonged to a growing group of Christian intellectuals, identified by Pierre Courcelle, that incorporated segments of antique culture, primarily the heritage from Rome's *summus poeta*, in their new religion. It is possible that the Emperor Constantine himself, judging from his *Oratio Constantini* addressed to the Saints, had understood the Fourth Eclogue as a Christological presage written in allegorical code.² The pioneer of this type of reading was, at any rate, the Church Father Lactantius (ca. 240 – 320), another topic for my next chapter. In the last book of his *Divinae institutiones* (*The Divine Institutes*), concerned with the life of the blessed, Lactantius reproduces several sibylline confirmations of

---

1 Cf. Hagendahl 1967, pp. 443f., and Augustine's *Epistolae* (*Letters*) 137.3.12, where the Church Father quotes two lines from the prophecy of the Fourth Eclogue (13–14) as a portent of Christ's salvation work.
2 This oration, the authorship of which was long contested, has come down to us appended to manuscripts of Eusebius of Caesarea's *Life of Constantine*. Cf. Courcelle 1957; Drake 1985, p. 335; Kirsch 1989a, p. 69.

the prophet Isaiah's vision of the Millennium, to which he supplies the following comment (7.24):[1]

> This will be the time for all those things to happen that the poets claimed for the golden age when Saturn was king. The mistake about them arises from the fact that prophets foretelling the future keep putting plenty forward like that, delivering it as if it has taken place. Visions were put before their eyes by the divine spirit, and they saw things in their sight as if in process and completion. Their words of prophecy were slowly spread by rumour, but those outside God's mystery did not know their scope; they thought it was all stuff over and done with long before, because it simply could not take place in the reign of a man. (V)

The prophets, then, are informed about future things in such sharp visions that they express them as if they had already taken place. However, this ingenious capacity entails a side-effect: the poets who later recycle the messages of the prophets for their own purpose but are "outside God's mystery", *profani a sacramento*, make the mistake of confusing their predictions with completed facts. Lactantius rounds off his argument with a brilliant exception to the rule, thirteen lines of verse from *Eclogues* IV (slightly transposed: 38–41, 28–30, 42–45, 21–22) that describe the Golden Age in its appropriate future tense, whereupon he states: "Vergil follows the Sibyl of Cumae in saying this", *quae poeta secundum Cumeae Sibyllae carmina prolocutus est.*[2]

Thus Virgil is supposed to have prophesied about the Millennium. A number of Christian poets would try their hands at similar types of reading of the Fourth Eclogue, but mostly (as Courcelle points out) not in Lactantius' chiliastic but in Constantine's Christological key. In Proba, Prudentius, Sedulius and Fulgentius, to mention just a few names that will come to the fore in this survey, the Eclogue's *puer* is taken to refer to the child Jesus. This thought was as bold as it was controversial, and it certainly provoked a number of protests. Towards the end of the fourth century, for instance, Jerome critically examines such Christians who (like himself!) had taken up Bible studies after a past in the company of the pagan classics, *saeculares litterae*.

They do not deign to find out, he complains in a letter to Paulinus of Nola in 394, what the prophets and apostles really "intended", *senserint*; instead, they "adapt conflicting passages to suit their own meaning, as if it were a grand way of teaching – and not rather the faultiest of all – to misrepresent a writer's views and to force the scriptures reluctantly to do their will." The prime example

---

[1] *PL* 6.810a. All quotations from Lactantius are from Migne's *Patrologia*, English translations (of *The Divine Institutes*) by A. Bowen and P. Garnsey 2003.
[2] *PL* 6.810b.

of this bad hermeneutics given by Jerome is precisely the many indulgent readings of the Fourth Eclogue's prophecy of a newborn child, nothing but childish whims, *puerilia*, which do not impress him at all: Virgil remains as he always was, "the Christless Maro", *Maro sine Christo* (53.7).[1] Here, Jerome voices the radically hostile attitude towards the classics, which possibly enjoyed stronger popular support than the concessions and compromises of the frequently Neo-Platonically inclined highbrows. Notwithstanding such stern assertions, even the monk in Bethlehem had appreciated Virgil ever since his school days, of all poets the one who – in Hagendahl's words – came closest to his heart.[2]

The two greatest of the Latin Church Fathers were evidently able to adopt variable attitudes to the greatest of the Latin poets. It is not easy to systematize their complex relation to him, even though various attempts have been made. Thus Arthur Stanley Pease has arranged the stages of Jerome's intellectual career in a classic threefold sequence: the talented youngster drilled in grammar is in turn succeeded by the uncompromising cultural fundamentalist and the late, tolerant pragmatist. The question, however, is whether this scheme really does justice to the abrupt alterations typical of the temperamental saint's exercises in hermeneutics and literary criticism, as a rule dependent on the shifting contexts and addressees of his writings.[3] We shall return to them in a moment.

As for Augustine, there is no doubt that he was recurrently tempted by the possibilities of reading Rome's *summus poeta* allegorically. In a few well-known passages of Virgil's work, such as the Fourth Eclogue's sibylline vision, the pagan poet would have voiced Christian premonitions. This is a type of interpretation that proves crucial to the *Epistolae ad Romanos inchoata expositio* (*Unfinished Commentary on the Epistle to the Romans*) that occupied the Church Father around the middle of the 390s. The text under scrutiny in this commentary, Paul's letter to the Christians of Rome, begins with the writer presenting himself as "a servant of Christ Jesus, called to be an apostle, set apart for the Gospel of God, which he promised beforehand through his prophets in the holy Scriptures" (1.1–2). Augustine observes that these prophets had belonged to the Jewish people – but not only to them (3):[4]

---

1 "Taceo de mei similibus, qui [...] nec scire dignantur, quid Prophetae, quid Apostoli senserint; sed ad sensum suum incongrua aptant testimonia; quasi grande sit, et non vitiosissimum docendi genus, depravare sententias, et ad voluntatem suam Scripturam trahere repugnantem." *PL* 22.544.
2 Hagendahl 1958, pp. 101, 276.
3 Pease 1919, p. 167. Hagendahl expresses his doubts, 1958, p. 98.
4 Both the Latin text and the English translation are from P. Fredriksen Landes's edition 1982.

> For there are alien prophets as well, in whom also are found some things which they heard of Christ and prophesied. This sort of thing is said even about the Sibyl, which I would not readily credit were it not for one of the poets, the greatest in the Roman language. This poet, before describing the renewal of the world in a way which seems to harmonize and accord well with the kingdom of our lord Jesus Christ, prefaced a verse by saying:
> *The last age prophesied by the Cumaean song has now come.*
> And everyone knows that the "Cumaean song" is the Sybil's. Therefore the Apostle, knowing that the books of the Gentiles contain these witnesses to the truth (as he also most clearly showed in the *Acts of the Apostles* when speaking to the Athenians), not only said "through God's own prophets," (lest anyone be seduced into some impiety by the witness to the truth found in false prophets), but he also added "in the Holy Scriptures," wishing undoubtedly to show that the writings of the Gentiles, so very full of superstitious idolatry, ought not be considered holy just because they say something about Christ. (VI)

Thus, judging by the commentator, there were two kinds of seers: primarily the Jewish and genuine prophets and, in the second place, the pagan and literary *vates*. This is after all a comparatively broad-minded declaration. The Sibyl is granted a place alongside the Old Testament visionaries, by virtue of the great Virgil's authority. Augustine's source is once again the notorious prophecy in the *Eclogues* (4.4), whose description of a new Golden Age is applied directly to the forthcoming reign of Christ. With this syncretic interpretation, the dividing line between orthodox and pagan traditions in the Church Father seems to be more blurred than ever. Accordingly, immediately after the quotation from the *Eclogues*, he alludes to Paul's speech to the Areopagus in Athens (Acts 17.28): "for 'In him we live and move and have our being'; as even some of your own poets have said, 'For we are indeed his offspring.'" With these words, remarks E.K. Rand, Paul laid the foundation of Christian humanism.[1] Even the Holy Writ could refer to pagan poets. The question was only how and to what extent they should be decontextualized, reinterpreted and cleansed before they could be 'put to use' for the purposes of the new faith.[2]

---

[1] Rand 1929, p. 35.

[2] This concept of 'use' rests on a solid basis of the theology of the Fathers themselves (see *On Christian Doctrine*, 2.40.60–61) and has, in modern times, been especially investigated by Christian Gnilka in various studies on the early Christian recycling – *chrēsis* or *usus* – of pagan culture, 1979, p. 142; 1984, pp. 18–22, 44–91. The term has proved handy, as a corrective to certain modern tendencies to either simply attach the incipient Christian literature to ancient poetics or to understand it as a "substitute" for the classical heritage; see Gnilka 1979, p. 148. Nevertheless, the concept of *chrēsis* certainly requires further specifications. Juvencus' reuse of the classics is not identical to that of Prudentius, which in turn differs from that of Arator, just to mention a few of the names treated in this study. In addition, the Christian reinterpretation of ancient mythol-

Augustine comes up with the expected reservations at exactly this point. It was important to be on one's guard against pseudo-prophets, a constant threat throughout the Church Father's writing, fraught with anxiety about improper manipulations of the truth. Even if the Sibyl and a certain number of pagan seers had been able to detect Christological presages, they were brimming with "superstitious idolatry" and for that reason can only be counted as second-hand witnesses. This argument is further developed in the polemic address to the Manichaean Bishop Faustus from the years 397–98, *Contra Faustum Manichaeum* (*Reply to Faustus the Manichaean*). There, the author admits that the Sibyls, Orpheus, "Hermes, if there ever was such a person", *nescio quis Hermes*, and other pagan poets or philosophers may have stumbled across some truth about God or the Son of God. However, such findings do not make any great difference, he notes, since strictly speaking they are nothing but involuntary and isolated strokes of luck in speeches or texts that in their entirety legitimate the worship of demons and idols (13.15).[1]

This argument is typical of Augustine. He was constantly hypersensitive to the dilemma of both the split soul and the split discourse, to the instable relationship between human reference and divine referent which the more robust Jerome, not particularly keen on philosophical inquiries, could disregard. It is perhaps in this ambivalent attitude, fascinated and detached at the same time, that we come closest to Augustine's feelings about Virgil. It might also be described as a tension between on the one hand a Neo-Platonic (inclusive) type of reading, in search of mystic signs of divine wisdom through antique poetry ever since Homer, Orpheus and other seers from time immemorial, and on the other hand the orthodox (exclusive) view of literature and the Bible that became increasingly important for the Church Father as the years passed.

The same ambivalence can be detected much later in Augustine's writing, for instance in a letter dated 411 or 412 in which he dwells on Christ's supreme lesson to mankind: "He came, of course, as a source of teaching in order that, once his authority became present also in the flesh, it might confirm those truths that were usefully uttered here before, not only by the holy prophets who spoke only the truth but also by the philosophers and the poets and authors of such litera-

---

ogy obviously transcends the domains of poetry. The standard – though now somewhat dated – work on this vast field is Rahner 1971 (German original, 1945).

1 Courcelle observes that in most cases Augustine's reuse of the Fourth Eclogue is to be found in his correspondence with cultivated and distinguished pagans, for instance the Roman senator Volusianus, in the clever hope of being able to convert them to the true faith by referring to the venerated Virgil, 1957, p. 315. Cf. Chaffin 1972, pp. 523f.

ture who mingled many truths with errors, as no one can doubt." (137.3.12)[1] Thus, even when Augustine seems to hit a more tolerant note, as in this letter where Christ's wisdom essentially confirms certain premonitions embedded in ancient literature, he cannot refrain from airing his suspicions of the poets' lies. As witnesses to the truth, they cannot match the Biblical prophets, nor really the ancient philosophers, but nonetheless there is some useful knowledge, and even certain glimpses of the history of salvation, to be rescued from their works. They fulfilled the purpose of dressing truth in words, albeit imperfect and partly misleading, while awaiting the Incarnation of Christ.

A decade into the new century, then, Augustine could still pay his respects to Virgil, but his esteem is reserved, and all things considered, it seems likely that his relationship to the Augustan poet describes a falling curve over time.[2] It is difficult to give a specific turning point, even though the return to Thagaste and the newly appointed presbyter's increasingly polemic commitment in the early 390s played a large and perhaps decisive role in this context. The self-examination that emerges from the first book of his *Confessions*, like the hermeneutics that characterizes several of his later writings, has in any event a tendency to distinguish true from false in literature and to reject all figments of imagination as superfluous and dangerous illusions.

It therefore seems logical that in his last great work, *On the City of God*, Augustine not only quoted *Eclogues* IV but made room for a full-scale assault on the pagan poets. Moreover, his attack was not restricted to the notoriously scandalous ones; it was just as strongly directed against those "poets who were also called 'theologians'", *poetae, qui etiam theologi dicerentur*. They had admittedly sung the praises of gods, but their work actually referred to remarkable people, *magni homines*, to elements in God's Creation or angelic powers. It may well be, Augustine continues, that, among so many vain and false things, these poets sometimes – as if at random – happened to sing the praises of the one and only true God, but it makes no difference: due to their polytheism they denied God the cult that rightfully belonged only to Him. Not even the well-known "theologians" of times immemorial, poets like Orpheus, Musæus or Linus, had been

---

1 "Magisterium quidem ut ea quae hic ante dicta sunt utiliter vera, non solum a Prophetis sanctis, qui omnia vera dixerunt, verum etiam a philosophis atque ipsis poetis, et cujuscemodi auctoribus litterarum (quos multa vera falsis miscuisse quis ambigat?), illius etiam in carne praesentata confirmaret auctoritas". All Augustine's letters are quoted in English from the four volumes in R. Teske's New City Press edition 2001–05.
2 Cf. Westra 2007, pp. 16f. Not everyone would agree with this assumption. Gerhard Müller, for instance, reaches the conclusion that Augustine's relation to Virgil through the years does not show any real development, 2003, p. 426.

able to refrain from disgracing their gods with wanton myths (18.14), *nec a fabuloso deorum suorum dedecore etiam ipsi se abstinere potuerunt*.

Here we observe the Bishop of Hippo in the midst of the cultural separation process characteristic of Late Antique apologists. It was typically directed against the integrative endeavours of the fourth and fifth centuries, represented by authors such as Proba, appropriating classical epic poetry for Christian purposes, reduplicating, as it were, certain parallels in contemporary art between the Gospels and the myths. But it meant little to the ageing Augustine if Orpheus and his fellow singers from the pagan past, either legendary pristine theologians or recorded poets, had now and then intuitively caught some glimpse of God among all the gods. In the eyes of the ascetics, the one and only *Deus* would have nothing whatsoever to do with invented idols. Along with the liberal interpretive strategy being its opposite – the allegorical type of reading adopted by Lactantius and his successors – this caution against the 'disgrace' of everything fictional or mythical, *fabulosum dedecus*, would run all through Western European culture right up to the Early Modern Age.

*

The Augustinian distrust of *ficta* should be understood in the context of the general transition in the fourth and fifth centuries from what Marrou, in his great study of *Saint Augustin et la fin de la culture antique*, called the old "literary" to the new "Christian" culture. The classical world of myths, oracles and ritual observance was at the very heart of pagan art and literature, setting up a mighty obstacle to the Christians' missionary work among Gentile intellectuals. It was right there, in the legacy from Virgil and Ovid, that the rivalry of the old culture with the new religion's *doctrina* was most intense; and it was consequently there that Christian campaigners found occasion to raise a warning flag.

Augustine's reaction to the literature he grew up with must be described as violent, but he shared it with many of his pious predecessors. They felt obliged to condemn classical poetry, Marrou points out, for the following three reasons: it was permeated with the old pagan gods, it was wantonly erotic and altogether replete with sensual attractions, hence morally unacceptable, and – in a formulation from *On the Trinity* – it was more concerned with "exactness of words", *verborum integritas*, than with the "truth of things", *veritas rerum* (14.11.14). Against the latter fault, illustrated with Virgil, Augustine launched forcefully the principle of *res non verba*, that is, a mainly instrumental view of language.[1] Marrou's argument appears to be fully applicable to the overall development of

---

[1] Marrou 1938, pp. 345–50.

Augustine's work. To be convinced, one has only to glance at the *Retractationes* (*Revisions*) from the 420s, the Church Father's retrospective and strikingly critical examination of his life and works, or, to quote the brilliant Rand: "a list of *errata* submitted to the Divine Reader, who would scan the whole book of his life".[1]

In the Cassiciacum dialogue *Against the Academics*, one of the works Augustine had written – according to the rueful judgment of his old age – when he was still a catechumen, "involved in and puffed up with worldly literature" (PR.3), *saecularium litterarum inflatus consuetudine*, he had personified love of beauty and love of wisdom as two sisters or actually birds, *philocalia* and *philosophia* respectively (1.1.3).[2] In his *Revisions* he condemns the whole of this fantasy as improper and stupid, *inepta et insulsa*. This is because *philocalia* is either to be seen as an instance of poetic trifles, *nugae*, or else she represents the only beauty worthy of its name, identified in true Platonic spirit with wisdom, for which reason she will be merged with philosophy "when it comes to incorporeal and lofty matters", *in rebus incorporalibus atque summis*. In neither case is it befitting to speak of two sisters. The whole argument makes a rather gloomy impression. Spiritual enlightenment is evidently, at this late stage of the Church Father's career, the only goal worth striving for.

The gap between *Against the Academics* and the *Revisions* is certainly wide. But even if the shift from *fictum* to *factum* dominates the overall picture of Augustine's writings, poetry never lost its attraction for him. The Bishop of Hippo remained a great rhetorician, with an artistic peak in his *Confessions* and their verbal somersaults, like the *Quid enim miserius misero non miserante se ipsum* quoted above. Such a skillfully applied figure, the *polyptōton schēma* of 1.13.21, hardly lives up to his *res non verba* strategy. The young rhetorician, for his part, had showed continual interest in the classical poets, above all of course Virgil, right up to his conversion. As late as the summer of 386, Augustine's culture remained essentially literary, observes Marrou.[3] Unfortunately, none of the texts from the days of his youth has survived, but the farther back we go in his oeuvre, the greater the chance we have of being able to detect a sensibility for or even an appreciation of the mode of literary fiction.

---

1 Rand 1929, p. 253.
2 For the *Revisions* I have used B. Ramsey's translation in the New City Press edition 2010. The juxtaposition of *philocalia* with *philosophia* in *Against the Academics*, 2.3.7, is probably derived from Plato himself: cf. the mythical representation of metempsychosis in *Phaedrus* (H.N. Fowler's Loeb edition 2005), where the soul "that has seen the most" will be reborn as "a seeker after wisdom or beauty", a *philosophos* or *philokalos* respectively, 248d.
3 Marrou 1938, p. 164.

It is important to bear in mind, though, that not even the young Augustine, the brilliant rhetorician in search of a tenable world view, betrays any unreserved enthusiasm for the Muses. The unmistakable interest in poetry that is apparent in the Cassiciacum dialogues is subdued and controlled by the writer's demand for logical consistency and philosophical urgency. After having presented his little fable about the birds called *philocalia* and *philosophia* in *Against the Academics*, the thirty-two-year-old Augustine adds, rather ironically, that he has suddenly become an Aesop and that his gifted pupil, Licentius, will reproduce the story more beautifully in a poem, "for indeed, he is almost an accomplished poet" (2.3.7), *poeta est enim pene perfectus*. The author's irony is soon aggravated into reproach. The overriding concern for himself and for his pupils at the philosophical retreat at Cassiciacum, he stresses at the beginning of Book III, has to be the search for truth. In view of this obligation, another of his adepts, Trygetius, has diverted himself unnecessarily with Virgil, while Licentius has wasted his time on "poetic composition", *fingendis versibus vacavit*. However, Augustine does not give up the hope that *philosophia* will get the upper hand over *poetica* as well as any other discipline in his pupil's mind (3.1.1).

It seems clear that the newly-converted philosopher can still understand and half-heartedly accept literary activity, but that he is growing increasingly impatient with poetry and its poor cognitive value. Soon he once again catches Licentius, "whose thirst for Helicon could never be quenched, eagerly trying to think out verses" (3.4.7), *cui nunquam sitienti Helicon subvenisset, excogitandis versibus inhiantem*. Here, the 'gaping' (*inhians*) would-be *vates* evidently becomes the target of caricature, though sketched with a light hand. The teacher allows Licentius to keep on with those breathless poetical exercises, not because he is especially enchanted by such an art, *non quod me nimis delectet ista perfectio*, but because he hopes his pupil will get tired of it once he has learnt to master it. Poetry, then, appears to be theoretically dead in *Against the Academics*. At best it might be acknowledged as a preliminary exercise for philosophical reflection, a didactic strategy deeply rooted in Hellenistic and Late Antique culture, paradigmatically outlined by Plutarch in his *How to Study Poetry*.

This scheme emerges everywhere in the writings from Cassiciacum. Various therapeutic, pedagogic and pragmatic functions may be ascribed to poetry, but as soon as the question of truth arises, it has to give way to the superior discipline of philosophy. Nonetheless, the young Augustine proves unable to resist the aesthetic allure and expository capability of fictional discourse. Precisely when he is about to refute it on a critical-conceptual level, he makes use of it in his figurative language. The story of the two birds is a case in point. The sisterly as well as hierarchic relationship between the *pulchritudo* of aesthetic enjoyment and the *sapientia* of philosophical contemplation, where the latter is given precedence, is illustrated with an allegorical fable. The defamed fictionality inevitably colours the author's metaphors and examples.

This pattern becomes even clearer towards the end of *Against the Academics*, when the writer's friend and fellow student Alypius compares the Sceptics to the Proteus of pagan myth, the sea god who had the power of prophecy but could change his form as he pleased to escape inquisitive visitors. Augustine may well have met him in, for instance, Virgil's *Georgics*, where the keeper of bees Aristaeus, with supernatural help from his mother, gets control of the slippery seer and quick-change artist whose many shapes alter and confuse (4.406): *variae eludent species*. In Alypius' wording, Proteus becomes an image and a mirror, so to speak, *imago et quasi speculum*, of the leery Academics who doubt everything, including our possibilities to get any trustworthy knowledge whatsoever.

Let us hope, exclaims Alypius, that some deity, *numen*, can help us to catch this god (as in Virgil), that is, to subdue these doubters, so that we might be shown the truth we so dearly long for (3.5.11)! The first-person speaker of the dialogue – Augustine – immediately expresses his delight at his friend's comparison, which, in his eyes, proves to be the highlight of the whole discussion (3.6.13):

> With what profound understanding and sensitiveness to what is best in philosophy did you direct our attention to Proteus! Proteus, of whom you all know, is introduced as a symbol of truth. You will see, young men, from this that the poets are not entirely despised by philosophy. Proteus, as I say, plays in poetry the role of truth which no one can hold if, deceived by false representations, he slackens or lets loose the bonds of understanding. It is these representations which, because of our association with corporeal things, do their best to fool and deceive us through the senses which we use for the necessities of this life, even when we have already grasped truth and hold it, so to speak, within our hands. (VII)

Here the writer demonstrates a remarkably subtle treatment of the Proteus figure. He steers Alypius' metaphorical use of the sea god away from the application to the wriggling Academics in order to direct it towards the elusive truth itself. Thus the figure does no longer primarily signal aporetic undecidability but appears as a congenial metaphor for truth. This interpretation is subsequently further developed and refined. Proteus, Alypius' terse *imago veritatis*, is expanded into an outright allegory in the form of personification. The god is made to perform the "role" of truth, *veritatis persona:* in all his shifting forms he is there to be seized, held fast and seen through. Thus he even epitomizes Augustine's early readiness to instrumentalize fictionality. The slippery divinity from Virgil's (and Homer's) tales emerges as a metaliterary key figure, an icon of artistic figuration, a congenial representative of poetry's propensity to dissimulate and fabricate, but also of its ability – right through its flickering metamorphoses – to indicate truth.

Few passages in the Church Father's voluminous oeuvre bear such clear witness to the huge difference between the writings from his youth and from his old age. In the *City of God*, Proteus would emerge in the same metaliterary light, but in that late work he is solely treated as an incarnation of all the fictionality that lies and leads astray, as false as he is malicious, a pagan version of Satan. This anathema should be understood in its context: the ageing Augustine's violent polemic against the religious whims and ceremonies of pagan – classical – culture. They are (often sneeringly or sarcastically) waved aside as poor illusions, "the invention of lying demons", *fallacium daemonum commenta*. Augustine cites 2 Corinthians in his argument: "even Satan disguises himself as an angel of light" (11.14), *satanas transfigurat se velut angelum lucis,* where the Latin *transfigurare* (like *metaschēmatizetai* in the original text) might precisely refer to quick-change artistry. Alongside Paul he adduces Virgil and the *Georgics*, where Proteus is empowered with the ability to take on all kinds of shapes (4.411), *formas se vertet in omnis*. Augustine now transfers this same talent to the prince of demons (10.10):[1]

> For it is from the Devil that these phantoms [*phantasmata*] come. The Devil longs to ensnare men's wretched souls in the fraudulent ceremonies of all those false gods, and to seduce them from the true worship of the true God, by whom alone they are purified and healed. And so, as is said of Proteus,
> *he turns himself into all shapes,*
> sometimes appearing as a ruthless persecutor, sometimes as a fraudulent helper; in either case he seeks man's hurt.

In the pious heat of battle of Augustine's old age, the mythological quick-change artist is inevitably deprived of the exemplary figurative function he was entrusted with in *Against the Academics*. His shifting images no longer conceal any truth but only deceive and ensnare. This denunciation is driven home with the Church Father's usual rhetorical efficiency: on God's side a polyptoton (*a vero veri Dei cultu*), on Satan's side three symmetrical participles in an asyndeton: *hostiliter insequens, fallaciter subveniens, utrobique nocens*. Proteus' tricks merge into magic ceremonies and diabolic pursuits. This is symptomatic of the Late Antique

---

[1] "Eius enim sunt illa phantasmata, qui miseras animas multorum falsorumque deorum fallacibus sacris cupiens irretire et a vero veri Dei cultu, quo solo mundantur et sanantur, avertere, sicut de Proteo dictum est, *formas se vertit in omnes*, hostiliter insequens, fallaciter subveniens, utrobique nocens."

culture that tended to degrade the old pagan gods to demons.¹ Later on, we shall see how the Christian poets of this epoch expressed similar ideas, how a Prudentius or an Avitus staged the demons' or precisely the Devil's Protean metamorphoses in their verse.

Back in Cassiciacum, however, Augustine could present Proteus as a paradoxical *imago veritatis*. This is, in its own way, a premonition of the inventive Proclus' spectacular interpretation of the Homeric seagod as an angelic intellect with the eternal and rational souls (the seals!) in his wake, a multifarious being, impossible to apprehend for a mind subject to time, which can only grasp his numerous appearances sequentially, in their flickering series of transformations. In both cases, in the young Augustine's *Against the Academics* as well as Proclus' commentary on Plato's *The Republic* (1.112–13), we recognize the Neo-Platonic project to secure a place for classical literature, time-honoured and ingenious but frequently impious or unreliable, on the safe ground of philosophical speculation, preferably by means of allegory or symbolism.² Their reuse of the classics did not imply an acceptance of fabulousness in itself (on the contrary), but it did mean a readiness to seek truth – the truth of philosophy – through fiction.

Such allegorizing interpretation presupposes a fairly sophisticated kind of critical reflection, typical of the early Augustine, allowing for a factor of uncertainty in all reading, an inevitable gap between the author's intention and the reader's understanding. This is evident from the early short treatise *De utilitate credendi* (*The Usefulness of Belief*) from 391, in which the author reckons with three kinds of reading error:
- when the reader takes something false as true, whereas the author himself did not believe in it (the reader is misled),
- when the reader again takes something false as true, and the author has done the same (both are misled),
- when the reader perceives something true in the work, even though the author himself has not realized it (the former eclipses the latter).

In the last case, Augustine adds, the reading can be useful and might, on closer inspection, bear plenty of fruit.

The first error occurs if the student, after having read the sixth book of the *Aeneid*, 566–69, really assumes that King Rhadamanthus of Crete was a judge in the underworld, which not even Virgil himself believed. The second error occurs

---
1 Schelkle 1939, p. 56.
2 For Proclus' commentary on *The Republic*, I have used W. Kroll's edition 1899–1901 and A.J. Festugière's translation 1970. Cf. Lamberton 1986, p. 227.

if the reader relies on a writer like Lucretius, whose atomic theory was plainly false. The third and most interesting error, which in fact may be profitable, is exemplified with the reader who embraces Epicurus' altogether commendable exposition on the art of self-control, *continentia*, without caring or knowing about the philosopher's morally offensive ideas, according to which bodily pleasure is man's supreme good (4.10).[1]

As far as is known, Epicurus did not engage in fictional representation, but it is obvious that this last type of reading would be in accordance with Augustine's allegorical approach to the pagan poets, primarily Virgil, repeatedly implemented in his early post-conversion writings, reminiscent of Neo-Platonic hermeneutics. The majority of those poets had lived too early to be blessed with the Christian grace, but even so they had unquestionably provided the world with invaluable insights, regardless or in spite of their own intentions. Augustine develops this argument further in *The Usefulness of Belief*, but we do not need to follow it through. Its perspicuous awareness of the reader's difficulty to ascertain the writer's intentions was of long standing in the rhetorical handbooks' treatment of *inventio*. In their investigations of *stasis* (or, in Latin, *status*, the theory of conflict in a legal case), Cicero and his successors had thoroughly analysed the gap or asymmetry between writing, *scriptum* (the written law), and intention, *voluntas* or *sententia* (the aim of the lawgiver), that an orator had to take into consideration.[2]

Thus if it was possible, on the basis of rhetorical *stasis* theory, to ignore (or feign to ignore) an author's intention, his text seemed all of a sudden available for new interpretations. This Ciceronian support for the novice's hermeneutics should be complemented with the paradigm of Paul's paramount reading strategy. Throughout his missionary work, the Apostle to the Gentiles had understood how to skilfully proclaim and argue in favour of the new faith in terms of the old religion, to reinterpret pagan conceptions of the divine in a Christian context. His method is perhaps most evident in the well-known passage from the Acts of the Apostles, where he is asked to explain the meaning of his newfangled message to the puzzled citizens of Athens: "So Paul, standing in the midst of the Areopagus, said: 'Men of Athens, I perceive that in every way you are very religious. For as I passed along and observed the objects of your worship, I found also an altar with this inscription, 'To the unknown god.' What therefore you worship as unknown, this I proclaim to you.'" (Acts 17.22–23) With these words, the apostle

---

[1] I follow J.S. Burleigh's translation, Augustine 2006.
[2] See Eden 1997, p. 8, and, in general, Kennedy 1999, pp. 99–122, according to whom "stasis theory remained the heart of rhetorical invention until the end of the Renaissance", p. 100.

gave an example of Christian recycling rather than dismissal of pagan religiosity. The cult of the Athenians is not rejected out of hand but scrutinized in search of elements liable to reinterpretation in the light of the true faith.

Augustine never wholly abandoned this Pauline readiness to reread the dubious Gentile 'letter' illuminated by the unerring Christian 'spirit'. Canonized pagan works such as Virgil's *Eclogues* could be understood as expressing something else than what the author had intended. They contained numerous obscure ideas, messages or premonitions that awaited their true explanation. This is a type of hermeneutics that presupposes a cultural split vision, as it were, along with a sophisticated understanding of the complex cognitive value of fiction, and it is still active (as we have seen) in the *City of God*. However, in the bishop's profuse production, above all from the time of his *Confessions* onwards, it was to meet increasingly keen competition from a more literal exegesis that would not easily disregard authorial intent, and from a more rigid type of theology based on an exclusive criterion of truth.

For our purposes, we must content ourselves with an explanatory example. In a sermon from about 410, Augustine contrasts the Archangel Gabriel's annunciation in Luke 1.33: "and he will reign over the house of Jacob forever, and of his kingdom there will be no end", with Jupiter's reassuring words about the coming Roman Empire to the hero's worried mother in the *Aeneid*: "I am imposing no bounds on his realm, no temporal limits. / Empire that has no end is my gift" (1.278–79), *his ego nec metas rerum nec tempora pono; / imperium sine fine dedi*. All those who have thus promised eternal life here on earth were not guided by truth but "have lied through flattery", *adulatione mentiti sunt*, observes Augustine in his sermon, with a telling, somewhat condescending reference to Virgil as "a certain poet of theirs", *poeta illorum quidam*, not even mentioning his name.

Virgil lied, since nothing secular will endure. All shall pass away, Augustine emphasizes, not only Rome but heaven and earth too. At this stage of the exposition, the former Carthaginian teacher of rhetoric presents himself with a clever trick known from both the school exercises, where the pupils were made to perform dialogues with mythological or historical figures, and from the Roman courtrooms. He gives the floor to his opponent (*Sermones* 105.7.10):

> Perhaps if we had a mind to press Virgil on this point, and tauntingly to ask him why he said it; he would take us aside privately, and say to us, "I know this as well as you, but what could I do who was selling words to the Romans, if by this kind of flattery I did not promise something which was false? And yet even in this very instance I have been cautious, when I said, 'I assigned to them an empire without term of years,' I introduced their Jupiter to say it. I did not utter this falsehood in my own person, but put upon Jupiter the character of untruthfulness: as the god was false, the poet was false [*mendax vates erat*]. For would

ye know that I well knew the truth of it? In another place, when I did not introduce this stone, called Jupiter, but spoke in my own person, I said,
  'Th' impending ruin of the Roman state.'
See how I spoke of the impending ruin of the state. I spoke of its impending ruin. I did not suppress it." When he spoke in truth he was not silent as to its ruin; when in flattery, he promised that it should abide for ever. (VIII)

That is how the encounter with Rome's foremost poet – *the* poet – could have taken place in the Church Father's imagination. The passage is certainly constructed with superior rhetorical cunning. It pretends to make an effort to do justice to Virgil, here not merely "a certain poet of theirs" but identified by name. The poet is permitted to prove that he is actually well aware of the principle that says that all worldly – Roman – authority is doomed to die, and he is allowed to confirm his insight with reference to a line from his *Georgics* (2.498), as a countermove against the preacher who has accused him on account of Jupiter's prophecy of Rome's future greatness in *Aeneid* I. Thus "Virgil" is cleverly made to defend himself against an adversary who has not managed to distinguish between when the poet is speaking in his own person and when he lends his voice to fictional beings.

The argument is so consummately and convincingly constructed that readers of today might understandably regret the dramatist whose skills were lost to the world in Milan in 386. At the same time it conveys its chilly message right through the rhetorical *prosopopoeia:* Virgil admits that he had paid his fellow Romans rash compliments. He had flattered them with Jupiter's words against his better judgment, and since this Jupiter is nothing but a false god, he had acted as a mendacious poet, *mendax vates.* In this way, Augustine splits the writer into the teacher of wisdom who spoke frankly in his *Georgics* and the epic poet who resorted to devious fictions in his *Aeneid.* In the end, the authority of the truth-teller Virgil could only be saved at the cost of the fiction maker.

*

The hesitancy between synthesizing incorporation and exclusive disqualification of pagan culture, with an increasing trend towards the latter, characterizes Augustine's intellectual career and is yet another way of describing the subject of this chapter. In fact, these strategies struggled continually for the initiative among the early Church Fathers. We have seen the former demonstrated as early as in Paul. For an example of the latter, the doctrine of Christian exclusivity, it seems convenient to take a glance at one of the best-known documents of patristic literature: Jerome's twenty-second epistle, from 384, in which the author, after a long tirade pervaded by horror of sex, warns not only against marital infidelity but also against "adultery of the tongue", *adulterium linguae,* the besetting sin of rhetoricians and poets. For, he asks rhetorically, what has Horace to do with the Book of Psalms, Virgil with the Gospels or Cicero with Paul? (22.29) Here, the tension in the Church Fathers and the early Christian poets between literary *romanitas* and pious *christianitas* – temporarily mitigated about half a century earlier by the Bible poet Juvencus, who tried precisely to reconcile Virgil with the evangelists – deepened into a gaping chasm.

To clarify his strong dichotomies, Jerome moves on to tell the story of what he calls his own misfortune. Early on in his career, he says, he had broken up from his home and family for the kingdom of heaven. But not even when he had left Rome for Jerusalem could he bring himself to get rid of his beloved library. He fasted, but only to recover with the help of Cicero. He spent the nights in tears over his sinful past, but only to return to Plautus. If, on the other hand, he read the prophets, their language seemed terrible and uneducated to him: *sermo horrebat incultus.*

This cultural split led to a crisis which almost killed Jerome. His attacks of fever went so far that people began to prepare for his funeral. Then he fell into a hallucinatory vision before God the Father Himself, a judge whose radiance forced the accused onto the floor. There he was interrogated about "who and what I was" – his circumstances or condition – whereupon he swears that he is a Christian. The judge accuses him without further ado of deceit: "Thou liest, thou art a follower of Cicero and not of Christ. For 'where thy treasure is, there will thy heart be also.'" These words, echoing the Gospel of St. Matthew (6.21), are among the best known that Jerome left to posterity – *mentiris, ait, Ciceronianus es, non Christianus: ubi enim thesaurus tuus, ibi et cor tuum.*

After being duly whipped and when the listeners at the trial had burst into prayer for him, the feverous dreamer is granted mercy. However, his release seems conditional: the bystanders had reminded the judge of the possibility to subject the sinner to torture if he would ever relapse into reading books by pagan authors. "Lord", the accused cries out, "if ever again I possess worldly books, or if ever again I read such, I have denied Thee", *Domine, si unquam habuero codices saeculares, si legero, te negavi*, whereupon he finally opens his eyes. The writer of the letter assures his addressee that this was no vain dream, since he actually found himself beaten black and blue. He immediately regained his health and thereafter kept to the holy scriptures, *divina*, steering away from the mortal ones, *mortalia* (22.30).[1]

"This is a true story, and it may well put to shame the lying marvels described by Greek and Roman pens", exclaims Jerome when speaking of an ascetic

---

[1] *PL* 22.416–17.

brother in faith in a letter of 374: *cedant huic veritati, tam Graeco quam Romano stylo, mendaciis ficta miracula* (3.4).¹ In such statements it is easy to feel the writer's readiness to issue a categorical ban on profane literature, a temptation that should not be underestimated among the apologists, stylites and other ascetics who wanted to cleanse Christian culture of all classical ingredients. We shall soon see it in full force in Tertullian, but as for Jerome – in his youth as fascinated by Roman literature as Augustine, educated by none less than Donatus, the great grammarian, and later well versed in Greek – he hardly managed to observe his austere reading programme. At least he cited the *Eclogues* as well as the *Georgics* and the *Aeneid*, not to speak of Cicero and other ancient authors, in later letters.² As Hagendahl remarks, this constant reuse of classical literature can hardly be explained away as the outcome of scattered or vague reminiscences from Jerome's youthful reading.³

In another of his best-known and often quoted letters addressed to the rhetorician Magnus, written in 397 or 398, listed by Rand as a *locus classicus* for the relation of the young Church to pagan culture, Jerome pleaded for more or less the same hermeneutic exploitation (or to use a milder term, accommodation) that we shall soon see Augustine recommend in the contemporary *On Christian Doctrine*.⁴ Just as Moses, Solomon and Paul had assumed the right to quote from pagan writers, Jerome maintains, the Church's intellectuals can and should appropriate the treasures of secular culture and, after due revision and retouching, put them at the service of the Christian message.

Here, Jerome, more or less as obsessed as he was embarrassed with sex, resorted to an allegorical reading of the old Jewish family and criminal law as it was recorded in Deuteronomy 21.10 – 13. If a man should take prisoners in battle and happen to fall in love with a beautiful woman among them, he should – according to the Deuteronomist – bring her to his home, and there "she shall shave her head and pare her nails. And she shall take off the clothes in which she was captured", whereupon she shall remain in the house of her captor for a full month before he can take her as his wife. "Is it surprising", Jerome cuts in, "that I too, admiring the fairness of her form and the grace of her eloquence, desire to make that secular wisdom which is my captive and my handmaid, a matron of the true Israel? Or that shaving off and cutting away all in her that is dead

---

1 *PL* 22.333.
2 See for instance Jerome's letters 52.1 written in 394; 125.11 from 411 (quoting the "most beautiful lines", *pulcherrimi versus*, of *Georgics* 1.108 – 10, *PL* 22.1078); and – for the *Aeneid* – 127.12 from the following year.
3 Hagendahl 1983, pp. 88 – 91. Cf. Eiswirth 1955, pp. 9 – 29, and Pease 1919.
4 Rand 1929, p. 64.

whether this be idolatry, pleasure, error, or lust, I take her to myself clean and pure and beget by her servants for the Lord of Sabaoth?" (70.2)[1]

In a later chapter devoted to the "Poeta christianus", I shall give several examples of how this kind of Christian annexation of the domains of classical literature, primarily in epic poetry, could take place in practice. A key concept that will be used in the examination of this recycling of antique literature is 'counter-imitation': the adoption of a motif, a metaphor or a topos whose content will be radically altered in its new context and whose source, accordingly, will appear in an ambiguous light – as a model, yes, but even as such, outdone, amended and improved upon.[2] Jerome already practised counter-imitation when he pointed out, in his commentary on Isaiah (following Origen), that *physici* and astronomers usually claim that the moon borrows its light from the sun. Their hypothesis is taken to be confirmed by "what the poet showed in his little line of verse: 'the moon rises under no debt to her brother's rays'", *quod et poeta uno versiculo demonstravit: Nec fratris radiis obnoxia surgere luna*. This quotation is from *Georgics* 1.396, where Virgil portrays a scene in the countryside after rain when the moon for once seems to shine with her own light (in contrast, that is, to her usual debt of gratitude to the sun). Jerome immediately proceeds to insert the pagan line of verse into an allegorical argument, *tropologice*. The moon represents the Church: it grows in times of peace and shrinks under persecution. After having been exposed to trials and tribulations in the dark, it regains its former radiance, illuminated by the sun of righteousness (18.826–27).[3] The Church Father decontextualizes, adapts and distorts his model, which actually refers to the moon's seeming independence of her usual source of light after rain. But as we have seen (judging by the well-known declaration in the letter quoted above), he felt himself free to shave and trim his servant, "that secular wisdom", as he thought fit.

Weeding out or annexation, this was evidently the question for Jerome. His ambivalence may have been expressed in extreme terms – Hagendahl observes that his violent swings between yes and no to the classics never evened out into

---

[1] "Quid ergo mirum, si et ego sapientiam saecularem propter eloquii venustatem, et membrorum pulchritudinem, de ancilla atque captiva Israelitidem facere cupio? et si quidquid in ea mortuum est, idololatriae, voluptatis, erroris, libidinum, vel praecidio, vel rado: et mixtus purissimo corpori vernaculos ex ea genero Domino Sabaoth?" *PL* 22.666. Cf. Godel 1964.
[2] The useful term 'counter-imitation' (or 'imitation by contrast', *Kontrastimitation*) proceeds from Klaus Thraede's dictionary article "Epos" 1962, cols. 1039–41, though my definition comes closer to Van der Laan's "imitation contrastante", 1993, p. 151.
[3] *PL* 24.6774d. Cf. Messina 2002, pp. 132–39.

any stable balance – but it was in no way unique or idiosyncratic.¹ The German Latin scholar Ulrich Eigler actually considers the monk of Bethlehem to be typical of a paradoxical age, the late fourth century in the Western Roman Empire, characterized by a rich cultural diversity as well as deepening religious and ideological clefts.² There were small or no possibilities for peaceful integration here. Still, thanks to his proficiency in languages and his solid education, and despite his outsider position among his contemporaries, Jerome appears as a key figure in the highly charged field between classical literature and the new faith.³ His very attacks on Virgil, Cicero and other literary celebrities reveal in fact a deep fascination, something quite different from any ascetic indifference, a cultural bond that seems all the stronger precisely because it frequently appears to be involuntary.⁴

This attachment is just as noticeable in Augustine or in Paulinus of Nola, and it must be understood not only with reference to their common education but also against the background of the specific period of transition that was theirs. Exactly during this stage of late Roman history, when the new religion had established itself right up to the level of the Empire's political, financial and cultural elite, the channels between the classical heritage and the Christian doctrine appeared to be more open than ever before. The older apologists had as a rule adopted a more implacable attitude. The austere Tertullian had harshly censured stage performances, the work of the Devil among men, in his *De spectaculis* (*The Shows*): "And then all this business of masks, I ask if God can be pleased with it, who forbids the likeness of anything to be made, how much more of His own image? The Author of truth loves no falsehood; all that is feigned is adultery in His sight. The man who counterfeits voice, sex or age, who makes a show of false love and hate, false sighs and tears, He will not approve, for He condemns all hypocrisy." (23.5–6)⁵ In diatribes such as these,

---

1 Hagendahl 1958, p. 92.
2 Eigler 2001, pp. 187–91.
3 Cf. Andrew Cain's observation that "in the final tally, then, the historical Jerome was an extremely marginalized figure in his own time and therefore a far cry from the 'Saint Jerome' construct of medieval hagiography that heavily influenced most scholarly traditions down to the twentieth century and some even down to the present day", 2009, p. 3.
4 Cf. Ludwig 1977, p. 357.
5 "Iam vero ipsum opus personarum quaero an Deo placeat, qui omnem similitudinem vetat fieri, quanto magis imaginis suae? Non amat falsum auctor veritatis; adulterium est apud illum omne quod fingitur. Proinde vocem sexus, aetates mentientem, amores, iras, gemitus, lacrimas asseverantem non probabit: omnem enim hypocrisin damnat." Tertullian's works are throughout rendered in their original Latin versions according to E. Dekkers's Corpus christianorum edition of the author's *Opera* I–II 1954. If not otherwise stated, English versions are from A.

based on simple equations such as pretence = sin, *mimēsis* = cheating, Tertullian effectively ruled out all negotiations of fictionality.

The Carthaginian Father thus rarely betrays the ambivalence which would sometimes characterize Late Antique Christian attitudes to fiction and classical literature or drama. He preferred to fulminate against all secular literature, philosophical or poetical, epic or dramatic, repeatedly referring to a clean-cut, all-pervading cultural dichotomy between truth and lying, piety and crime. This opposition would certainly make itself felt all through the Middle Ages, but the question is whether it was ever so implacable as when it was first articulated in Latin (*The Shows*, 17.6–7):[1]

> If we spurn the teaching of the world's literature, as convicted of folly before God, we have a clear enough rule as to those classes of public spectacles where the world's literature is drawn upon for the comic or tragic stage. If these tragedies and comedies, bloody and lustful, impious and prodigal, teach outrage and lust, the study of what is cruel or vile is no better than itself. What in action is rejected, is not in word to be accepted.

Here Tertullian may be basing his diatribe on Paul's admonition in 1 Corinthians 3.19: "For the wisdom of this world is folly with God." However, he expands the strategic argument of the Apostle to the Gentiles to a general attack on classical literature, not only as it could still be embodied on the stage, *in spectaculis*, but also as it was canonized and taught in the rhetoric and grammar classes of the schools. During this onslaught, all margins for fictionality disappear, all possible suggestions of aesthetic distance or *licentia poetica* are simply cancelled. What was not possible in real life was equally impossible in fiction, or even in language itself, according to the extract's final sentence: *quod in facto reicitur, etiam in dicto non est recipiendum*. Words are denied all rights to act for themselves. They are brought back to existing things – to reality, which is homogeneous and unequivocal – according to the well-known tenet 'grasp the subject, the words will follow', *rem tene, verba sequentur,* which was frequently adduced in classical rhetoric but probably originated with Cato the Elder (234–149 BCE), who as a matter of principle was suspicious of ornate language. This old

---

Menzies's edition in *The Ante-Nicene Fathers* series by A. Roberts *et alii*, 3, 1957. *The Shows* is rendered according to T.R. Glover's translation 1977 (1931).
1 "Si et doctrinam saecularis litteraturae ut stultitiae apud Deum deputatam aspernamur, satis praescribitur nobis et de illis speciebus spectaculorum, quae saeculari litteratura lusoriam vel agonisticam scaenam dispungunt. Quodsi sunt tragoediae et comoediae scelerum et libidinum auctrices cruentae et lascivae, impiae et prodigae, nullius rei aut atrocis aut vilis commemoratio melior est: quod in facto reicitur, etiam in dicto non est recipiendum."

Roman was by all accounts as austere and inimical to the Muses as Tertullian four centuries later.

It is from such starting points that this son of a Carthaginian officer, as the first of the Church Fathers (and among the first in Late Roman culture), replants the age-old accusation against the poets for being liars in Christian soil. This manoeuvre was to have incalculable consequences for future Western debates on the cognitive status of poetry. The key text in this context is Tertullian's contribution to classical psychology, *De anima* (*A Treatise on the Soul*), a Christian sequel to Aristotle's text with the same title. There, the author argues energetically and often contemptuously or ironically against the old belief in metempsychosis (or *metensomatosis*), which condemns certain people to be reborn as animals in the next life. He points out that Ennius, the first successor to Homer on Roman soil, dreamt that his famous literary ancestor had remembered his previous existence as a peacock: "However", Tertullian adds, "I cannot for my part believe poets, even when wide awake", *sed poetis nec vigilantibus credam*. At this point, he changes into a teasing mode: peacocks sing so badly that Homer himself would probably have been ashamed of his winged pre-existence. On the other hand, the ancient Greek would certainly have appreciated his reputation in posterity as the father of the liberal arts, *pater liberalium disciplinarum*. Be that as it may, the Church Father concludes, as far as poets are concerned, they are welcome to transform into peacocks or swans; the latter at least have a beautiful voice (33.8–9).

The principle of reality that Tertullian pleads for in his *Treatise on the Soul* is of an exclusively Christian kind. Admittedly, it allows for holy miracles – a kind of metempsychosis, as it were, ordained and controlled by God – but it certainly rejects all kinds of poetic frenzy (57.12):[1]

> The power of God has, no doubt, sometimes recalled men's souls to their bodies, as a proof of His own transcendent rights; but there must never be, because of this fact, any agreement supposed to be possible between the divine faith and the arrogant pretensions of sorcerers, and the imposture of dreams, and the licence of poets. But yet in all cases of a true resurrection, when the power of God recalls souls to their bodies, either by the agency of prophets, or of Christ, or of apostles, a complete presumption is afforded us, by the solid, palpable, and ascertained reality (of the revived body), that its true form must be

---

[1] "Sed etsi quasdam revocavit in corpora dei virtus in documenta iuris sui, non idcirco communicabitur fidei et audaciae magorum et fallaciae somniorum et licentiae poetarum. Atquin in resurrectionis exemplis, cum dei virtus sive per prophetas sive per Christum sive per apostolos in corpora animas repraesentat, solida et contrectabili et satiata veritate praeiudicatum est hanc esse formam veritatis, ut omnem mortuorum exhibitionem incorporalem praestrigias iudices."

such as to compel one's belief of the fraudulence of every incorporeal apparition of dead persons.

The space for "licence" – inventions, make-believe, bold fantasies – that classical criticism could grant literature was of no value to Tertullian. Some of his austere sentences might, if disconnected from their context, sound like bold nineteenth-century positivist assertions: "Now things are not true because they appear to be so, but because they are fully proved to be so" (57.10): *non enim quia videntur vera sunt, sed quia adimplentur.* In fact, it would be fair to say that Tertullian was a 'realist' in the only reasonable meaning that could be given to such an anachronistic label in a Late Antiquity apologetic context. Strongly influenced by the Jewish-Christian emphasis on the body, on literal meaning and history, he tried to ascertain a "solid" and "palpable" reality in the midst of all the superstitions, thaumaturgy and beliefs in demons among his contemporaries. During this guard duty, the traditional *licentia poetica* of the pagan writers had to go.

Tertullian's cannonades have to be understood against the background of the persecuted Early Church. In the first place, it was, of course, literally under attack in Tertullian's own life time, under the reign of Emperor Septimus Severus, with serious repercussions in North Africa, but it also risked being confused with other Oriental religions gaining ground across the Empire, all focused on the death and resurrection of a god. Consequently, for the young Church's pious champions it was important to draw the dividing line between true faith and false superstition as sharply as possible. The tone of their writings frequently changed into an apocalyptic mode, as when Tertullian ends *The Shows* by looking forward to the Judgment Day. He appears happy with the thought of what he will see. There will be kings who wail in the dark with Jupiter himself, philosophers who have denied or belittled the existence of the soul (probably the Epicureans) and who are now being destroyed by fire, actors who finally find a use for the full force of their voices: "And, then, the poets trembling before the judgement-seat, not of Rhadamanthus, not of Minos, but of Christ whom they never looked to see" (30.4), *etiam poetas non ad Rhadamanthi nec ad Minonis, sed ad inopinati Christi tribunal palpitantes!* Among the condemned in this last-mentioned group, the Church Father might in all probability include Virgil, considering that Minos as well as Rhadamanthus, both Kings of Crete, act as judges in the *Aeneid*'s underworld (6.432, 566).

The Judgment Day did not arrive, as many early Christians thought it would, but within a hundred years or so their religion rose to triumph in the Roman Empire. Tertullian's categorical rejection of anything that could possibly be suspected of idolatry was gradually supplemented, at least in certain learned contexts, by bold attempts at appropriation – several of them the subject of analysis in later chapters of this book – or by the type of compromise that seems to have characterized the highly sophisticated Ausonius of Bordeaux (ca. 310–94): classicizing in his erudition and poetry, Christian in his faith. During the fourth century, it was not unusual in scholarly and/or aristocratic circles that religion, as with Ausonius, became a predominantly formal or nominal matter. Understandably, however, a number of influential authors soon reacted against this double bookkeeping. Jerome's tormented convulsions in the Holy Land are a case in point. Ausonius' own disciple, Paulinus of Nola, who exchanged his literary career in his home country for an ascetic life in Campania, was equally sensitive. When the Aquitanian master tried to re-establish contact with his favourite pupil, Paulinus retaliated with a verse polemic which to a high degree was aimed at the traditional poetic licence or fictionality (10.19–42). It was probably written a few years before the Augustinian *Confessions:*[1]

19 Quid abdicatas in meam curam, pater,
20   redire Musas praecipis?
    negant Camenis nec patent Apollini
       dicata Christo pectora.
    fuit ista quondam non ope, sed studio pari
       tecum mihi concordia
25 ciere surdum Delphica Phoebum specu,
       vocare Musas numina
    fandique munus munere indultum dei
       petere e nemoribus aut iugis.
    nunc alia mentem vis agit, maior deus,
30   aliosque mores postulat,
    sibi reposcens ab homine munus suum,
       vivamus ut vitae patri.
    vacare vanis, otio aut negotio,
       et fabulosis litteris
35 vetat, suis ut pareamus legibus
       lucemque cernamus suam,
    quam vis sophorum callida arsque rhetorum et
       figmenta vatum nubilant,
    qui corda falsis atque vanis imbuunt
40   tantumque linguas instruunt,
    nihil ferentes, ut salutem conferant
       aut veritate nos tegant.

---

[1] Paulinus' poetry is quoted from the edition of W. von Hartel and M. Kamptner 1999, and, in English, from P.G. Walsh's translation volume 1975.

> Why, father, do you bid the deposed Muses return to my charge? Hearts dedicated to Christ reject the Latin Muses and exclude Apollo. Of old you and I shared common cause (our zeal was equal if our poetic resources were not) in summoning deaf Apollo from his cave at Delphi, invoking the Muses as deities, seeking from groves or mountain ridges that gift of utterance bestowed by divine gift. But now another power, a greater God, inspires my mind and demands another way of life. He asks back from man His own gift, so that we may live for the Father of life. He bids us not spend our days on the emptiness of leisure and business, or on the fictions of literature, so that we may obey His laws and behold His light which is clouded by the clever powers of philosophers, the skill of rhetoricians, and the inventions of poets. These men steep our hearts in what is false and empty. They form only men's tongues, and bring nothing to bestow salvation or to clothe us in the truth.

The *pater* who is addressed in the first line above, the intellectual father of the letter-writer, his former master, has to give way to the author of life itself, *vitae pater*. His old heritage of learning, with special emphasis on literature and poetry, is dramatically divorced from the ethos of the Christian cultural revolution: *fabulosae litterae* and *figmenta vatum* bring nothing but lies and emptiness, so they have to be discarded from the new doctrine of salvation. The urbane reconciliation between the ancient rhetorical-literary tradition and Christian allegiance, which seems to have attracted Ausonius, became inconceivable – as Charles Witke has shown in a painstaking analysis – in the *Either-Or* choice that the zealous Paulinus set up. If we invoke Apollo, we shall be deaf to Christ and vice versa.[1]

This is a consequence of the radical transformation of the Pauline subject: the old self has not only been reformed, it has been replaced by a new one. The verse letter alludes to that process in its later hexameter part (131–35): "For I shall freely admit, if you are thinking of the old me whom you knew, that I am now no longer the man I was when I was not considered wayward. (Yet I *was* wayward, my eyes enveloped in falsehood's darkness, wise in what God brands as foolishness, living on death's sustenance.)"[2] In lines such as these, a cultural gap opens up. Harald Hagendahl has remarked that Christian poetry does not contain any documents in which the spiritual contrasts of this transitional period appear as sharply as in Ausonius' and Paulinus' poetical correspondence: "on the one hand, the lukewarm Christian, the man of the world and the poet who remained in his inner being a man of Antiquity, on the other hand, the monk-like zealot for whom religion meant everything and who

---

1 Witke 1971, p. 47.
2 "Nam mea si reputes quae pristina, quae tibi nota, / sponte fatebor eum modo me non esse sub illo / tempore qui fuerim, quo non perversus habebar / et perversus eram, falsi caligine cernens, / stulta deo sapiens et mortis pabula vivens."

considered that philosophers, rhetoricians and poets only obscured God's light."[1]

It should be clear by now that this process of separation was complex, sometimes painful and frequently – as in Jerome, Paulinus or Augustine – contradictory. Paulinus' modern biographer, Dennis E. Trout, observes that the saint's poetic technique was indistinguishable from the stylistic devices that his verse letter condemns.[2] The poet's technical excellence, evident in his rhetorical questions, his use of sharp contrasts, his many classical allusions and his pun on the word *munus* (task, gift), reveals his dependence on classical culture in the midst of his rupture with it.[3] When defending the choice of his first place of refuge after breaking up from Bordeaux – Hispania, in Ausonius' eyes a half-barbarian province – Paulinus could actually endorse comic as well as fictional modes of writing: 'may it even be permitted to play with things made up' (10.260), *liceat quoque ludere fictis*, to ward off his master's biting satire of his new residence. To cite another foremost scholar of early Christianity: after his conversion, Paulinus often claimed that the Muses had been silenced in his ears, but he continued to make diligent use of the skills he had learnt from them.[4]

We have already touched upon the fundamental cause of the ambivalence in Paulinus' farewell to the Muses: the Late Antique educational system where the two disciplines of grammar and rhetoric based much of its teaching on fictional writing, not least Virgil's. With such a schooling from early years on, it was not easy to simply disinherit oneself of canonized literary culture. According to his own report, the young Augustine was shocked by the simple language that he met in some of the Biblical clusters of texts that preceded Jerome's Vulgate, usually referred to by the generic term *Vetus Latina* (or, better, in the plural, *Veteres Latinae*). Their style seemed "unworthy" to him, *indigna*, in comparison with Cicero's noble diction, he recalls in his *Confessions* (3.5.9), a reaction that runs strikingly parallel to that of his contemporary Jerome. Neither Augustine, nor Jerome, nor Paulinus, then, managed very successfully to repress their experiences of the two trivial disciplines, virtually interwoven with fictional literature. In his *Confessions*, we remind ourselves, Augustine would signal his break with the rhetoric of the schools in sophisticated rhetorical figures. In this respect, he was typical of

---

1 Hagendahl 1983, p. 73.
2 Trout 1999, p. 82.
3 For an investigation into Paulinus' profuse employment of figurative language, especially metaphors and paradoxes, repeatedly evoking typological and Christological issues, see Conybeare 2000, pp. 111–30.
4 Frend 1974, p. 122.

the fourth and fifth century Christian intellectuals.[1] The Virgil who, in the view of the older apologists, or at least to Tertullian, had stood out as the very epitome of the old pagan culture, and whom they accordingly referred to as 'your' or 'their' poet, had for quite a few Christian writers of the fourth century, when the beliefs of the once remote Jewish sect were being redefined as the authorized religion of the Roman Empire, become 'our poet'.[2]

But for the ageing Augustine, as we have seen, Virgil tended once again to be 'theirs'. Even though the Church Father's attitudes to *ficta* could vacillate considerably, they tended to get more critical and sometimes downright repulsive as time went on. The herald of the City of God found it difficult to shed any tears for Dido. Classical culture's literary and philosophical heritage remained a stumbling block throughout his career. There, Virgil is a constant presence, but it inevitably involved Late Antique education in general, usually summed up under the heading of the seven liberal arts, the *artes* or *disciplinae liberales*.

The Liberal Arts

The second book of *On Christian Doctrine*, Augustine's programme for a Biblically-based rhetoric and hermeneutics, but also his main exposition on cultural and semiotic theory in general, composed in the late 390s, is a key document for our understanding of the Church Father's relationship to the pagan cultural heritage. Among the ancients, he observes, we will find plenty of mendacious fables and astrological superstitions, *simulata et superstitiosa figmenta*, that we nowadays have no reason to concern ourselves with, but, on the other hand, the established *liberales disciplinae* – along with history, natural science and numerology – are accepted (2.40.60). In this context Augustine is especially inclined to acknowledge, with due reservations, the Pythagorean and Platonic philosophical traditions.[3]

Among those intellectual currents, Christians could to a great extent recognize parallels to their own faith (as we have seen in connection with the Ostia episode from the *Confessions*), and now – in *On Christian Doctrine* – this affinity is provided with a genetic explanation. It turns out that Augustine's teacher in Milan, Saint Ambrose, had recently discovered that Plato made his legendary

---

[1] Cf. Evenepoel 1993, pp. 36f.
[2] See Heck 1990.
[3] Frederick van Fleteren gives a good description of the fusion of *artes* with Platonic tradition, possibly stemming from Porphyry, in the young Augustine, 1995, p. 19. Krämer offers a comprehensive overview of research on Augustine's relation to the liberal arts, 2007, pp. 23–35.

journey to Egypt during the time of the prophet Jeremiah. This means that the Greek philosopher had been in contact with Jewish culture in the Egyptian Diaspora and, on that account, was able to borrow from "our literature" (2.28.43), *nostrae litterae*, rather than the other way round. Accordingly, towards the end of the book, Augustine pursues the teachings of his venerated mentor. The philosophers, "especially the Platonists", *maxime Platonici*, seem really – as if by chance – to have established ideas that are true and agree with our faith, so now it is time for us to take them back (2.40.60):[1]

> These treasures – like the silver and gold, which they did not create but dug, as it were, from the mines of providence, which is everywhere – which were used wickedly and harmfully in the service of demons must be removed by Christians, as they separate themselves in spirit from the wretched company of pagans, and applied to their true function, that of preaching the gospel.

As so often in his linguistic and rhetorical deliberations, Augustine uses a figure of speech to illustrate what he means, in this case a simile with typological implications based on Exodus, borrowed from his Alexandrian predecessor among the Church Fathers, Origen: at present, we Christians are, in a spiritual sense, in the same situation as the children of Israel when they left Egypt. They took with them the riches they needed for their journey, and in a corresponding way we should now exploit rather than reject the cultural heritage of Antiquity on our way into the new age of the Church.[2]

On the one hand, during the rest of his career Augustine continued to condemn classical mythology, in particular the indecent tales of the gods, and to call epic literature in question, with the *Aeneid* as the great stumbling block. From this perspective, the roughly contemporaneous *On Christian Doctrine* I–III and the *Confessions* form important negative turning points for his (seldom uncritical) interest in the fictional world of pagan culture, a curiosity which – as we shall soon see – had coloured his works from Cassiciacum, in particular *On Order* and the *Soliloquies*.[3] On the other hand, the Church Father never ceased to borrow pedagogical examples from the *poeta nobilissimus*, and he always left the door ajar to the treasury of classical philosophy, especially to its Platonic sections. There, to his mind, a good reader – both analytically skilled and firm in

---

[1] "Quod eorum tamquam aurum et argentum, quod non ipsi instituerunt sed de quibusdam quasi metallis divinae providentiae, quae ubique infusa est, eruerunt, et quo perverse atque iniuriose ad obsequia daemonum abutuntur, cum ab eorum misera societate sese animo separat debet ab eis auferre Christianus ad usum iustum praedicandi evangelii."
[2] See Gnilka 1984, pp. 88–91; Schäublin 1995, p. 54; Griffiths 2000, pp. 10f.
[3] Schäublin 1995, pp. 53f. Cf. MacCormack 1998, p. 64.

faith – would surely be able to find grains of gold in the obscure recesses of the ancient texts. Augustine applied exactly the same metaphor to his use of "some books by the Platonists" in the *Confessions:* they became, as it were, his own Egyptian gold (7.9.15).

The relevant passage from Exodus reads: "The people of Israel had also done as Moses told them, for they had asked the Egyptians for silver and gold jewellery and for clothing. And the Lord had given the people favour in the sight of the Egyptians, so that they let them have what they asked. Thus they plundered the Egyptians." (Exodus 12.35–36) A little more than a century and a half after Augustine's composition of his great works, the retired Roman statesman Cassiodorus would base his monastic study programme *Institutiones divinarum et sæcularium litterarum* (*An Introduction to Divine and Human Readings*) on this quotation, with an explicit reference to *On Christian Doctrine* in 1.28, whereby the metaphor of the Egyptian gold was destined for rich repercussions in the history of Western education. But Jerome too had declared in a letter, as we saw above, that he wished to make use of classical culture for the sake of its elegant speech and beautiful words; thus he took a worthy prisoner into the service of Israel (70.2). Paulinus of Nola joined forces with the great Church Fathers in his letters to both of them and to his other correspondents. In an epistle dated 400–01, highlighted by Christian Gnilka as a spectacular example of the early Christian authors' 'use' or *chrēsis* of pagan culture, he imagines the possibility of putting the vain myths of the Gentiles, *inanes fabulae*, at the service of "truthful and serious discussion" (16.7), *in usum veri ac serii sermonis*.[1] May it be sufficient for you, Paulinus undauntedly urges his Aquitanian addressee and friend Jovius (16.11),

> to have taken from them your fluency of speech and verbal adornment, like spoils taken from enemy arms, so that stripped of their errors and clothed in their eloquence you may adapt to the fullness of reality the sheen of eloquence used by empty wisdom to deceive. Thus you may adorn not the empty body of unreality but the full body of truth, and ponder thoughts which are not merely pleasing to human ears, but also of benefit to human minds.[2]

Here, Paulinus seems to assume a basic distinction between linguistic signs and their meaning, or, more precisely, between speech's ornamentation and its con-

---

[1] Gnilka 1979, p. 145.
[2] "Tibi satis sit ab illis linguae copiam et oris ornatum quasi quaedam de hostilibus armis spolia cepisse, ut eorum nudus erroribus et vestitus eloquiis fucum illum facundiae, quo decipit vana sapientia, plenis rebus accommodes, ne vacuum figmentorum sed medullatum veritatis corpus exornans, non solis placitura auribus sed et mentibus hominum profutura mediteris."

tent.¹ The former has no value of its own but is completely dependent on the latter. On the other hand, embellishment is fully justified if the subject is legitimate, that is to say Christian and, hence, true. The metaphor of *medulla*, marrow, in contrast to the "sheen" or literally 'make-up' of language, *fucus*, is characteristic of this concept of truth and returns with exactly the same function – as Paulinus' commentator Werner Erdt has shown – in both Jerome and the fifth-century poet Sidonius Apollinaris.² To this couple might be added Prudentius and Sedulius (below, pp. 496, 562). In short, figuration is perfectly legitimate as long as it enhances real – in contrast to fictional – circumstances.

Likewise in his twentieth ode, the subject of a closer analysis later in this study, Paulinus rejects all "invented" songs, *adficta*. He aims at writing as trustworthily as a historian, discarding the deceits of poetry, *sine fraude poetae*, since it is not worthy of a servant of Christ to tell lies: *absit enim famulo Christi mentita profari*. Nevertheless, he confesses in the same ode, he does not hesitate to take advantage of the techniques or "art" of poetry, *licet arte poematis utar* (20.28–30). Paulinus can evidently reject the fictionality of classical literature but accept its artistic devices and linguistic graces. It is these he wants to steal from the (now minimized) enemy in order to apply them to his new and perfect Christian understanding of reality.³

This holy troika from the turn of the fifth century is enlightening with respect to the status of classical literature, as taught and used in grammar and rhetoric, among the period's Christian intellectuals. They can all plead, on a general level, for a *translatio studii* in the wake of Origen, but they differ among themselves concerning its implementation. Jerome and Paulinus argue for reactivating the old artistic devices in the service of the new faith, a procedure that presumes

---

1 In an article on Paulinus and pictorial art Helena Junod-Ammerbauer registers a corresponding "rift between truth and its imitation" in the poet's work, which is in certain contrast to classical aesthetics of illusion, 1978, p. 46.
2 Erdt 1976, p. 260. Cf. Jerome's comment on Isaiah 55.1 regarding the kind of knowledge 'which is not to be found among the leaves and flowers of words but in the marrows and fruits of sense' (15.645), *sapientiam, quae non est in foliis ac flore verborum, sed in medullis ac fructibus sensuum*, PL 24.530b, and Sidonius Apollinaris' praise, in one of his letters, of a young priest: "He cares much for literature, but chiefly for religious literature, in which he is more concerned with the pith of the sense than with the froth of the words" (7.13.2), *summa homini cura de litteris, sed maxime religiosis, in quibus eum magis occupat medulla sensuum quam spuma verborum* (for Sidonius' letters, I follow W.B. Anderson's Loeb edition 1936-65). In his remarks on Isaiah 11.6 Jerome distinguishes, with the same pedagogical zeal, between the Biblical text's chaff, the plain words, and its wheat, 'its inner marrow, the sense which can be found in the letter' (4.160), *interiorem medullam, sensum qui invenitur in littera*, PL 24.148b.
3 Cf. Green 1971, pp. 17f., and Costanza 1972, p. 612.

the traditional distinction in antique rhetoric between *res* and *eloquium*, while Augustine seems to find it more difficult to separate the pagans' fictional constructions of reality from their rhetorical skills.

Admittedly, he can, at earlier stages of his career, remind us of his two colleagues, as when in his polemic against the Manichee Adimantus from 394, *Contra Adimantum Manichaei discipulum liber unus*, he states that the Biblical writers have energetically examined the matter of their subject, the contents or 'things', *res*, whereas their profane colleagues mostly concern themselves with words, *verba*. In this treatise, the classical writers, in particular dazzling orators like Cicero, are granted linguistic and stylistic expertise; in contrast, 'our authors', *nostri auctores*, the prophets and evangelists of the Bible, profit from a superior contact with reality (11). But in his later writings, starting from *On Christian Doctrine* and the *Confessions*, it is classical education in a broad sense, including philosophy – particularly of Platonic extraction – rather than the splendour of words that Augustine seems willing to exploit for the benefit of the new faith. In the end, however, notwithstanding such shifts of emphasis, the learned priests Augustine, Jerome and Paulinus are in complete agreement on one point: the condemnation of classical culture's delight in fictions, or in what – from their perspective – could be considered as fictions.

In this critical stance originates the medieval version of the old accusations against the poets for being liars. In his poem XXXI Paulinus expressly rejects the deceptive fictions, *commenta*, that are promulgated with the purpose to scare small children: the stories of Cerberus, Charon, Ixion and their likes (475–82). The Neo-Platonically influenced novice Augustine might still be in two minds about his attitude towards the world of classical fiction, but there is no doubt that cultural conflict rather than conciliation became an increasingly important theme in his thinking. In 394, his former student Licentius, who was so fond of poetry, had asked him for a copy of his treatise on the art of music, *De musica*. In his letter of reply, Augustine declines, warning his ex-pupil of becoming obsessed with music or grammar and recommending him to start thinking about his way of life instead: Licentius ought to go to Campania to learn from Paulinus' example. The Aquitanian servant of God had without hesitation cast off the arrogance or pride of this world, *grandis fastus seculi huius*, to meekly submit himself to Christ's yoke (26.5).

Augustine could just as well have adduced the example of Jerome, who in his commentary on Paul's Epistle to Titus 1.2–4 explains that the liberal arts may give us knowledge but that they lack piety, *pietas:* 'If anyone knows the art of Grammar or dialectic, it is to be able to express himself correctly and distinguish between true and false. Geometry, arithmetic and music too offer us true knowledge. But their knowledge is not that of piety. The knowledge of piety is a matter of knowing the Law, understanding the prophets, believing in the Gospel, and not neglecting the apostles.' (690)[1]

Jerome could benefit from a more thorough education than most of his learned contemporaries, including Augustine. He was "without doubt the greatest scholar among the Latin fathers" (E.K. Rand), but the *artes* seem to occupy a rather modest place among his declared intellectual priorities. This impression is confirmed by Rudolf Eiswirth's dissertation, which investigates the Bible translator's attitude to art and literature.[2] On several occasions, as in the above-mentioned commentary on the Epistle to Titus, Jerome juxtaposes the 'pious' and the secular sciences, Bible exegesis and scholarly learning, with the positive accent on the former. One is frequently struck by the force of his attacks, the linguistic pungency demonstrated by Donatus' erstwhile student, usually more vehement than the corresponding reservations by the Bishop of Hippo.

In this respect Jerome emerges as a Western prototype, an intellectual who distances himself from his own education in the service of a revolution with peasants and fishermen in the front line. He often inclines to the opinion that all one needs to know about both *artes* and poetry is in the Bible. In short, wherever Homer and his successors were not harmful, they were at least superfluous![3] In one of his choleric letters written in 373 or 374, slightly reminiscent of Tertullian, Jerome even looked forward to the Judgment Day which would not only have a Jupiter burning "amid real fires", obviously in implicit contrast to the metaphorical flames that normally indicate the god's desire in classical literature, but would also exhibit Plato as "a fool", *stultus*, and a pointlessly arguing Aristotle (14.11).[4] In their mythological or philosophical Egypt – such is the conclusion one could reasonably draw from Jerome's caustic diatribe – we all look for gold in vain.

*

---

1 "Si quis Grammaticam artem noverit, vel dialecticam, ut rationem recte loquendi habeat, et inter falsa et vera diiudicet. Geometria quoque et arithmetica et musica habent in sua scientia veritatem; sed non est scientia illa pietatis. Scientia pietatis est nosse Legem, intelligere prophetas, Evangelio credere, apostolos non ignorare." *Commentariorum in Epistolam ad Titum liber unus, PL* 26.558c–d.
2 Rand 1929, p. 131; Eiswirth 1955, p. 33.
3 The Book of Numbers contains, according to a letter from Jerome to Paulinus of Nola written in 394, all the mysteries of arithmetics, Job offers us "all the laws of logic", *omnes leges dialecticae*, and David alone is tantamount to the great poets of ancient Greece and Rome (53.8, *PL* 22.545–47, see below, p. 485). Cf. Curtius 1990, pp. 446f., and Eiswirth 1955, pp. 47f.
4 "Exhibebitur cum prole sua vere tunc ignitus Iuppiter; adducetur et cum suis stultus Plato discipulis; Aristoteli argumenta non proderunt." Jerome's Letter XIV is given according to the Loeb edition by F.A. Wright 1933.

The Late Antique and medieval *artes* were, as a rule, classified in two major groups:[1]

- *Trivium* comprised dialectic (logic) as well as the two arts that the young Augustine was drilled in: grammar and rhetoric. These three subjects were all connected to language and were considered elementary, the basis for all further knowledge, which is why they were placed first in the Late Antique and medieval education system.
- *Quadrivium* dealt with *res* rather than *verba* and included music, arithmetic, geometry and astronomy. These four disciplines were thought to be closely related. All four, including the first, which referred to music theory rather than musical performance, actually investigated the mathematical structures, commonly described in terms of numbers and proportions, which permeated the created world.

At an early (pre-Christian) stage, this system looked rather different. There, for example, the Roman polymath Marcus Terentius Varro, active during the late Republic, had included in his pioneering *Disciplinae*, the nine books of which were later lost, the more practically oriented arts of architecture and medicine. But at least after the success of Martianus Capella's *De nuptiis Philologiae et Mercurii* (*The Marriage of Philology and Mercury*), published in the fifth century, the 'seven liberal arts' became a concept all but self-evident for the learned Cassiodorus and Isidore in the sixth and seventh centuries respectively.[2] It is also relevant to note that the Romans, with their constant cultural inferiority complex towards the Greeks, sometimes felt a particular pride of their skills in grammar and rhetoric, while dialectic and the remaining, theoretically full-fledged disciplines could willingly be ascribed to the superior Greek learning. Finally, even if the division of the arts into the two main categories outlined above is evident in the works of Augustine and Martianus Capella, the terms *trivium* and *quadrivium*, popular during the High Middle Ages, are of a later (Carolingian) date.

Gemeinhardt makes clear that apart from grammar and rhetoric, which constituted the bulk of regular Roman education, the liberal arts – the *enkyklios paideia* – were learnt within the framework of philosophical schools or, as in the case of Augustine, by independent studies.[3] For a long time Augustine nursed a giant plan to devote a systematic study to all of the arts (as is clear from *Revisions*, 1.6), a project doomed to be abandoned when ecclesiastical, dogmatic

---
[1] One of the best and certainly most well-written studies in this field is still Rand's "The new Education", 1929, pp. 218–50. Gemeinhardt gives an excellent updated survey, 2007, pp. 46–51.
[2] See Shanzer 1986, pp. 14–17.
[3] Gemeinhardt 2007, p. 50.

and exegetic questions took possession of his agenda. But throughout his career he would profit from his solid knowledge of the core liberal arts in particular, and during his early years as a convert he could still envision a philosophical blending of the new religion with classical culture. Admittedly, it was not long before this inveterate seeker became aware of the cracks that were to split up this synthesizing project, but it fascinated him for years and coloured his writings from the period immediately following his conversion. Moreover, the theoretical tracts and dialogues on the arts written in Cassiciacum disclose the magnetic power that literary fiction kept exerting on Augustine's mind during this critical phase of his life. Just as interestingly, they point to the reasons why he would feel obliged to exclude it from matters concerning "true religion".[1]

One of Augustine's earliest preserved texts is the philosophical dialogue *On Order*, written about six months before his Ostia experience, in the autumn of 386 in Cassiciacum. This work shows that the convert, in contrast to what the flashback in his autobiography leads us to believe, was still attached to his Virgil. On one occasion, he was sitting at a meal, he reveals, listening to "half a book by Virgil", *dimidium volumen Virgilii*, as he used to do every day (1.8.26).[2] However, in spite of this completely natural presence of the Roman poet in his everyday life, the author soon launches a severe censure of his interlocutor Licentius' indulgence in the Muses and, particularly, in poetry as a privileged form of self-examination.

Licentius was the son of Augustine's friend Romanianus and also one of his students in the liberal arts (perhaps, specifically, in rhetoric). Consequently, it was appropriate for the convert, still in his teacher role, to reprimand and exhort him, especially as the young man had "suddenly [and remarkably] discovered poetry" (1.2.5), *repente admirabiliter poeticae deditus*. Now, Augustine and Licentius are sitting up one night, discussing the order of the universe, the main topic of the whole dialogue. When the latter, possibly in a Stoic spirit, suggests that nothing takes place outside the given pattern, the teacher is moved by his pupil's philosophical insight and praises him for having already come a good way beyond Helicon, the mountain traditionally associated with the inspiration of the

---

[1] *De vera religione* is the title of one of Augustine's philosophical works composed after the conversion (in 390–91). Bennett devotes some interesting pages to the attitudes towards fiction in the dialogues *On Order* and *Soliloquies*, 1988, pp. 50–54. The anthology edited by Karla Pollmann and Mark Vessey 2005 on Augustine and "the disciplines" is likewise vital to this research field, particularly – as for the Cassiciacum writings – the essays of Catherine Conybeare, pp. 49–65, and Shanzer, pp. 69–112. Cf. Krämer 2007, pp. 70–94.
[2] All quotations in English from *On Order* are from S. Borruso's translation.

Muses in ancient Greece, whose peak the student until now had striven for as if towards heaven.

But when Augustine exhorts his pupil to develop his thoughts, Licentius is forced to ask for time to think, since his mind happens to be somewhere else. The teacher – "A." – becomes noticeably annoyed (1.3.8):[1]

> Here I somewhat feared that he might wholly stray from philosophy by his poetry.
> **A.** – I feel sorry for your singing and howling these verses of yours in all kinds of rhythms. They are erecting a wall, between you and the truth of things, thicker and more impenetrable than the one that divided the lovers Pyramus and Thisbe you are crooning about. At least they could whisper to each other through a crack.

It would be fully understandable if Licentius was upset by his teacher's stern tone; he recites – or perhaps paraphrases – his Ovid, more precisely the masterly melodrama of Pyramus and Thisbe from the *Metamorphoses* (4.55–166), and gets a good telling-off for his pains. But Augustine seems to have reacted as he regularly did throughout the better part of his life whenever the question of truth was raised. Here, in this early episode of *On Order*, he converses with his protégé about one of the main subjects of philosophy and of the *quadrivium* disciplines: the structure of the universe. Still, not even then can poor Licentius stop himself from being distracted by the frivolous Roman poet's songs. The master feels frustrated.

The young man sinks into silence but soon recovers, avers his commitment to philosophy and declares himself ready to defend the principle of the rational order of the universe. For it is not poetry, *poetica*, he reassures his master, that makes him shun the arduous search for truth; it is rather his obstinate despair about finding it, *inveniendi veri diffidentia*, that holds him back. If only he could, he would be happy to tear down that wall his teacher just mentioned, before it had grown too high, barring all access to philosophical insight. Once again, Augustine reacts with enthusiasm (1.4.10):

> Here, seeing that I was getting happier than I could have possibly desired or dared, I blurted out this verse:
> **A.** – "*May sovereign and fatherly Apollo fashion a god.*" Start with this, and He who now gives but hints to our minds will lead us to where we are meant to fix our abode. Aren't there two sovereign Apollos? One dwells in caves, on mountains, in forests, in the smell of incense and of cattle, violently causing madness. The other, no less true and no less sov-

---

1 "Hic ego non nihil metuens ne studio poeticae penitus provolutus a philosophia longe raperetur: Irritor, inquam, abs te versus istos tuos omni metrorum genere cantando et ululando insectari, qui inter te atque veritatem immaniorem murum quam inter amantes tuos conantur erigere; nam in se illi vel inolita rimula respirabant."

ereign is, not to mince words, Truth itself, whose prophets are those who can be wise. Therefore, Licentius, let us rely on piety and be on our way. We shall extinguish the dangerous fire of stifling desires under our stomping feet. (IX)

There are at least two reasons for looking so attentively at *On Order* in this context: the dialogue's important chronological position, after Augustine's conversion but before his baptism and Ostia, and its ambivalent attitude as soon as poetry is mentioned. In this respect, *On Order* is typical of the Cassiciacum dialogues in general, with their pronounced Neo-Platonic inspiration. So far, it is not theology but philosophy that is Augustine's guide in his search for truth and his corrective of those frivolous poets who only too willingly run away from *ipsa Veritas*.

As we have seen, Greek and Roman culture had lived with that tension ever since the Ionic philosophers had attacked Homeric mythology in the sixth century BCE. Moreover, it became a notable feature of the Platonic tradition, and we shall later attend to Boethius' famous version of the conflict in the introduction to *De Consolatione Philosophiae* (*The Consolation of Philosophy*). In *On Order*, however, superficially at least, Augustine demonstrates great loyalty to the literary culture he grew up with. It was not only that he listened to half a book of Virgil each day in Cassiciacum, but the "fatherly Apollo" of the Roman poet (the line is from *Aeneid* 10.875) is taken as a starting point for an interesting case of counter-imitation, a device which would prove successful in Late Antique poetry. The god is expressly disconnected from pagan religiosity – primarily as we know it from the sixth book of the *Aeneid*, where the Cumæan Sibyl is filled with *altus Apollo* in her cave (6.9) – to be identified with the philosophical Truth that the New Testament identified with Christ.

Few passages among Augustine's writings reveal so tellingly how intimate Augustine was with the *Aeneid*. Hagendahl has shown how this paragraph calls attention to two further episodes in Virgil's epic.[1] The first occurs in the eleventh book, where the Etruscan warrior Arruns calls on Apollo, "greatest of gods", *summe deum*, and the deity of the mountain Soracte, with a prayer for help to trap the Amazon Camilla: "We are your chief devotees and heap up, for rites in your honour, / Bonfires of pine-wood. We walk, for we trust in our righteous devotion, / Straight through the blaze, press the soles of our feet on the / deep-layered embers" (11.785–88).[2] When Augustine exhorts Licentius to

---

[1] Hagendahl 1967, pp. 437f. Cf. Gunermann 1973, pp. 190–92, and MacCormack 1998, pp. 137f.
[2] "Quem primi colimus, cui pineus ardor acervo / pascitur et medium freti pietate per ignem / cultores multa premimus vestigia pruna".

mobilize an equivalent piety in order to trample the fires of lust beneath his feet, he thus transforms Virgil's ritual formula into a moralizing appeal.

The second relevant *Aeneid* passage evoked by "A." in *On Order* is from Book III, where Aeneas tells Dido and her Carthaginian court of his arrival at Delos, Apollo's island. The hero had immediately asked the god for advice and help for himself and his exhausted men: "Who do we follow? Or where do you tell us to go or to settle? / Give us a sign to interpret, slip into our minds and inspire us!" (3.88–89), *quem sequimur? quove ire iubes, ubi ponere sedes? / da, pater, augurium atque animis inlabere nostris*, to be compared with Augustine's promise, quoted above, that fatherly Apollo "who now gives but hints to our minds will lead us to where we are meant to fix our abode", *si sequimur quo nos ire iubet atque ubi ponere sedem, qui dat modo augurium nostrisque illabitur animis*. With such refined tricks of allusion, Augustine recalls not only classical literature's Phoebus in general but precisely the oracular god who revealed to Aeneas and his men – in his typically obscure Pythian language – their final destiny. Here, in *On Order*, this vatic Apollo is paralleled by 'another one', Truth itself, commonly identified with Christ, the new spiritual leader who will likewise show his faithful followers the true course and goal for their daring (philosophical) enterprise.

In Cassiciacum, then, Augustine could not but reject Ovid, the supreme fiction maker of the *Metamorphoses*, since he had erected a wall between truth and poetry. In contrast, it was possible for the convert to accept Virgil, the epic poet of the *Aeneid*, because he had indicated or heralded the Truth, albeit in veiled terms. Much later, in his *Revisions* (1.3.2), Augustine would regret both that he had "attributed a great deal to the liberal disciplines", *multum tribui liberalibus disciplinis*, and that he had cited the Muses as if they were gods, "albeit jokingly", *quamvis iocando*, in *On Order*. As a matter of fact, there is every reason to doubt the humour in this not very cheerful dialogue. In substantial parts, it rather suggests the young rhetoric teacher's and novice's continuing close bond to Virgil, the Muses and poetry.

In the autumn of 386 Augustine was on the verge of breaking up from them, but in *On Order* he could still use Apollo, present in all the underlying *Aeneid* passages, as a prototype for the new god he had found, or was on the way to finding. The oracular deity is decontextualized and cleansed of the ecstatic pagan rites so as to be re-usable as a thin, almost transparent version of Christ. Conversely, when Augustine composed his *Confessions* ten years later, the Apollo of Virgil lay dead and inoperative. After all, according to the confessor's flashback, the *Aeneid* could only offer "curtains" serving to "conceal error", "frivolous tales" and, in short, an empty "spectacle". The faithful confessor believed himself to have seen a Truth that no longer allowed any manoeuvring under the cloak of fictional figures or devices.

In *On Order*, such undermining of the legitimacy of poetic discourse is first and foremost, albeit not exclusively, restricted to the *Metamorphoses*. When young Licentius soon returns to the dialogue's actual topic, the order of being, he realizes that his sought-after philosophical vision must, of Platonic necessity, exclude verse (and, implicitly, the fictional licence that verse would entail): "let me tell you: I have suddenly lost interest in all this poetry", *non vobis dubitem dicere: pigrior sum ad illa metra subito effectus*. The old quarrel between philosophy and poetry seems once again to have ended in the former's favour, to Augustine's great relief. Here, we first listen to the newly enlightened pupil's praise of rational thinking and then the reassured teacher's comment (1.8.21):[1]

> An indescribable light now shines within me. I swear that philosophy is much more attractive than Pyramus, Thisbe, Venus, and Cupid, and such like amorous stories.
> Then he sighed and gave thanks to Christ. I was delighted to hear all that; why deny it? I don't care about whatever anyone may say, except perhaps that I may have exceeded due measure in my rejoicing.

Augustine's undisguised satisfaction at Licentius' dismissal of Ovidian "amorous stories" of all kinds, *omnimodi amores*, seems characteristic. At this stage of his career, he seems to have experienced the fictions of poetry as a source of worry, doubt and pangs of conscience, to some extent probably because of their frequent recourse to erotic themes that would remind him of his own lifestyle as unmarried, with a concubine and a son, Monnica's constant concern. This is at any rate what might be deduced from his (or his Licentius') metonymic figures for the art of poetry above: Pyramus and Thisbe, Venus and Cupid. Moreover, Augustine would later in his career typically associate both fiction and figuration with tormented desire.

Poetry seems surprisingly early in his life to have generated a kind of ache in his soul, which now at length, in Cassiciacum, began to fade. Hence his contentment in Licentius' discovery of rational philosophy's supremacy over fabling poetry. At the same time, we have every reason to take Augustine's hesitation at the end of the extract quoted above seriously. Perhaps the newly converted Christian philosopher really did go too far in his sense of relief at Licentius' decision?

---

1 "Alia, longe alia nescio quid mihi nunc luce resplenduit. Pulchrior est philosophia, fateor, quam Thysbe, quam Pyramus, quam illa Venus et Cupido talesque omnimodi amores. Et cum suspirio gratias Christo agebat. Accepi ego haec, quid dicam, libenter; aut quid non dicam? Accipiat quisque ut volet, nihil curo, nisi quod forte immodice gaudebam."

Could or should the venerable *vates* such as Ovid, not to speak of Virgil, really be suspended so easily and so speedily?

*

In *On Order* Augustine answers such questions by granting poetry a place within the system of the *artes*, this work's royal road to truth. That move is characteristic of his theory of art all along the line. Karel Svoboda and Robert O'Connell have both reminded us of its affiliations to ancient and especially Platonic practice in the way it connects poetry or painting to the methods and aims of rational thinking. The Church Father's aesthetics, O'Connell emphasizes, converts the poet, the painter or the musician into a kind of mathematical theoretician. It betrays a tendency, in sharp contrast to broad currents of modern criticism, to rationalize art: to transfer it from the experience of the senses to the judgment of reason or the intellect, all within the framework of the liberal arts.[1]

So Licentius' toil with his verses might in fact prove compatible with his care for "order". As it turns out, sober and concentrated studies of the liberal arts, *eruditio disciplinarum liberalium*, of which at least grammar, rhetoric and music might call attention to poetry, awaken and tease our desire for truth. "Return to the Muses", at least provisionally, Augustine thus exhorts Licentius: *vade ergo interim ad illas Musas!* In plain words: finish that paraphrase or commentary over which you are pondering! Poetry does not necessarily entail distraction or pernicious daydreaming; it might just as well suggest genuine insights into the order of things. It may happen, for instance, that when Licentius has described how Pyramus and Thisbe kill themselves, he will be able to make their fictional suffering productive, that is, turn it into a moral story (1.8.24):[2]

> At that point, the emotional climax of the story, you have your opportunity. Consider the curse of that unclean lust and poisoned passion as the basis for that miserable end. Then turn to praising that clean and sincere love by which disciplined characters made beautiful by virtue are raised up by a philosophical mind. In so doing they not only escape death, but enjoy the happiest of lives.
>
> Licentius became silent, reflected a while, nodded, and then retired.

---

[1] Svoboda 1933, pp. 5, 20–48; O'Connell 1978, pp. 15–27.

[2] "In dolore ipso quo tuum carmen vehementius inflammari decet, habes commodissimam opportunitatem. Arripe illius foedae libidinis et incendiorum venenatorum exsecrationem, quibus miseranda illa contingunt, deinde totus attollere in laudem puri et sinceri amoris, quo animae doctae disciplinis et virtute formosae copulantur intellectui per philosophiam et non solum mortem fugiunt, verum etiam vita beatissima perfruuntur. Hic ille tacitus ac diu consideratione nutans, motato capite abscessit."

Here, Augustine demonstrates a successful method for recycling the controversial classics, frequently considered immoral, on a Christian basis. They can actually be read and interpreted as a resounding rejection of vice and an equally eloquent plea for virtue. The fictional narrative, focused on desire, is corrected by moral admonition and outshone by philosophical contemplation. It is by such means, moralizing periphrase and hymnic devotion to philosophy, not by fantastic inventions or passionate stories about another kind of love than the Christian, that poetry will be worthy of its place in the scheme of the *disciplinae liberales*, the main subject of *On Order*.

This is not the place for any detailed analysis of that scheme, laid out in the second book of the dialogue. Man's reason, *ratio*, can attain proper illumination by means of suitable schooling in the three language disciplines and the four higher, mathematically based arts. If poetry has a place in this context, it is certainly not because of its melodious sounds, colours or other sensual qualities. Augustine makes this clear when he articulates another crucial distinction, namely between the senses in themselves and, on the other hand, what the senses convey or transmit: *aliud ergo sensus, aliud per sensum*. A beautiful gesture, for example, might please the senses, but it takes a mind endowed with reason to understand the beautiful meaning of such a movement, that is, to interpret it as a signal. Augustine quotes some lines from Virgil's *Georgics*, about the dark winter and the bright summer (2.480–81), with a similar conclusion: the verse itself is one thing, its meaning another. The fact that a verse "sounds reasonable", *rationabiliter sonat*, does not actually amount to saying that "it makes sense", *rationabiliter dictum est* (2.11.34).

In passages such as these, the focus on the inaudible inner word of the soul or the heart emerges at the expense of the euphony of the lips, a prioritization that interested us in our previous section. As a matter of fact, in *On Order*, it is only from this rationalistic viewpoint, with the emphasis on meaning rather than speech, that poetry can be considered a legitimate subject for grammar studies. It was primarily there, in the first of the trivial disciplines, that the examination and evaluation of poetry belonged, in full accordance with the curriculum Augustine grew up with. In an article on Licentius' and his teacher's relationship to poetry, Domenico Romano describes the latter's attitude towards classical literature in *On Order* as "conciliatory". Christian poets had the right to use myths as material for their poetry. The older Augustine, on the other hand, would repudiate that attitude, "abandon the compromise", and in general turn his back on the culture of the pagan world.[1]

---

[1] Romano 1961, pp. 7, 10.

This is a correct and apt observation, but even the young (or almost middle-aged) Augustine, the newly converted and Neo-Platonically inclined author of the Cassiciacum dialogues, had obvious problems with irruptions of fictional discourse into didactic or philosophical verse. He repeatedly returns to the myths' fabulous inventions as he knew them from ancient literature, as though the grammarians – being responsible for the elementary study of written texts – had got a cuckoo in their nest with this troublesome poetry. Who can accept, the author of *On Order* asks in an attack on the aristocratic pride in classical education, that anyone who has never heard of Daedalus' flight is accused of ignorance? With the same or greater right, he insinuates, should the person who 'invented' the story of the winged journey from Crete be considered a liar, *mendax ille qui finxerit*, those who believe in it fools, and those who ask about it shameless (2.12.37)! Poetry, and knowledge of poetry, in brief *poetica*, seemed after all to be a somewhat uncomfortable ingredient within the cycle of the liberal arts.

After grammar, Augustine proceeds to the other disciplines. It soon becomes clear that his short review of the liberal arts in *On Order* forms a rising curve: an early *ascensio*, as it were, in the Church Father's work. After having been granted an insight into grammar, logic and rhetoric, human Reason (*ratio*) is ready to continue upwards (2.14.39):

> From here, reason wanted to take off into the heights of contemplation of divine things. Not to fall off those heights, though, it sought to climb in steps along a path hewn by its own devices. It sought that beauty which can exclusively be attained in simplicity without bodily eyes, but the senses stood in the way. Therefore it slowly turned its attention towards those same senses. These, staking a claim for the possession of truth, distracted it from its pursuit of higher things with their oppressive clatter. The ears were first, claiming as their possession the very words which had served as the basis for grammar, logic, and rhetoric. By its immense powers of analysis, however, reason saw at once the difference between a sound [*sonus*] and the reality it symbolized [*id cuius signum esset*]. It understood that the only thing the ears can do is to sort out sounds into three kinds: the human voice, wind, and percussion instruments. Tragedians, comedians, choirs, and all those who in one way or another sing, produce the first. Trumpets and similar things, the second. Guitars, harps, drums, and anything else that on being hit produces a sound, the third. (X)

Using as their starting point the traditional classification of the *artes*, readers of or listeners to the dialogue could expect that after the language arts had been dealt with, the writer would proceed to music, the first of the mathematical disciplines. Now, that is certainly the case, as we understand from the extract quoted above, but Augustine gives his own, strikingly independent version of the standard pattern.

Firstly, the traveller, the increasingly personified Reason, is not satisfied: she is in a hurry to proceed upwards, but the sound of music, like all stimuli of the senses, slows her down. Secondly, the classification is complicated by the references to tragedy and comedy in this musical context. Thus, Augustine is probably calling attention to the elements of song in Roman drama, but it is also evident that he has in mind all kinds of oral performance, not only those of the theatre. His mention of "all those who in one way or another sing" may very well include recitations of poetry in general, a common medium for literary communication throughout antique culture. Accordingly, if written literature, commentaries and poetics were subject to grammar, poetry practised as an oral art could be considered a subdivision of music.

This will soon become clear when Reason in *On Order* realizes that the art she has now taken into consideration – music – is of the simplest kind, *vilissima*, unless its sounds are configurated according to special measures in time and to even proportions between acute and grave syllables. And so it came about, Augustine reports, that Reason recognizes the same basic patterns (*semina*) in language that she had already, in terms of metrical feet and accents, studied in grammar. By attending to the sense of hearing, she is now able to polish this metrical system, learn to apply caesuras or rhythmic units and divide the flow of discourse into evenly distributed lines (2.14.40):[1]

> This is how reason begat *poetry*; and seeing in poets' work the combined strength of words and rhyme, gave them a special place of honor, together with the license to compose any fiction they wished, but within reason. And since poets drew their matter primarily from grammar, the first of the disciplines in time, reason gave grammarians the power to judge poets.

Here, we seem to be witnessing a veritable recognition of poetic fictionality, or rather, in a wording that is characteristic of the young Augustine, the 'reasonable' or 'rational lie', *mendacium rationabile*, commonly implemented by the poets. They are granted the right to lie, then, provided they do so sensibly, knowledgeably and methodically.

That is a strong pronouncement, and quite a few scholars have, accordingly, drawn far-reaching conclusions from this passage in *On Order*. Helene Homeyer notes that it acknowledges imaginative literature's special status among human activities and links up with classical poetics when it grants poetry the power to "let the imagination reign free". None of the Christian writers from the following centuries would venture to follow Augustine in this direction, she points out. The

---

[1] "Sic ab ea poetae geniti sunt: in quibus cum videret non solum sonorum, sed etiam verborum rerumque magna momenta, plurimum eos honoravit eisque tribuit quorum vellent rationabilium mendaciorum potestatem. Et quoniam de prima illa disciplina stirpem ducebant, iudices in eos grammaticos esse permisit."

Venerable Bede, Alcuin, Rabanus Maurus and their early medieval colleagues all resorted to the Late Roman subjection to the textbooks, replete with prescriptions and practical examples: "They differ from their pagan predecessors only in including examples of the work of Christian poets (from Juvencus, Sedulius, Venantius Fortunatus, Arator and others). Not once do they utter the thought that it would require special talent or that imagination would play a role when writing poetry; everything is thus narrow-mindedly aimed at mere drilling, at mastering the purely technical work."[1]

Homeyer's observation is striking, but if we look at *On Order* as a whole, this emancipatory passion for poetic imagination unfortunately becomes weaker. As a matter of fact, Augustine had other reasons than purely technical ones for classifying poetry under music. They are both art forms that have to arrange their material by "regular timing" (2.14.40), *certa dimensione temporum*. And as soon as Augustine confronts the question of time, he deals with a problematical matter, since he is operating on the level of the human senses, more precisely of speech and the voice. What he could verify regarding poetry in his survey of grammar – its vocal sounds should be distinguished from its conceptual meaning – applies *a fortiori* to music. Both poetry and music hold their places in the cycle of the arts thanks to their rational or logical consistency. Against the backdrop of this theoretical system, their specific sound patterns are in the long run ruled out as imperfect or flawed semiotic configurations, as unreliable agents for mental, cosmic and, eventually, divine structures.

In *On Order*, then, music – subsuming poetic diction – constitutes the fourth stage on Reason's journey towards the heights. All through its sensuous rhythms and modulations it is (or should be) controlled by a conceptual pattern that Augustine, in a Pythagorean way, captures in the term *numeri:* numbers and their proportions. This interest in numbers will return later in his dialogue *De musica* (*On Music*), composed in the 390s as a part of the project he had already sketched out in Milan – to devote one treatise to each of the liberal arts – but which was never completed, in some measure because his confidence in the system decreased with the years.[2]

In the sixth and concluding part of Augustine's dialogue on music, one of the interlocutors, *Magister,* looks back on the previous five books' long-drawn-out analysis of various metrical and rhythmical phenomena. All this work – *Magister* explains – has been spent by him and his pupil, *Discipulus,* so as to

---

[1] Homeyer 1970, pp. 143f.
[2] As for the dating of the work, see Martin Jacobsson's edition of *De musica liber VI*, Augustine 2002a. My quotations from *On Music* VI are all from Jacobsson's thesis.

be able, if possible, with reason as their guiding star, to persuade gifted (and preferably young) persons to steer away "from the carnal senses and carnal literature" (6.1.1), *a sensibus carnis atque a carnalibus litteris*, and win them over for God. It is only for this reason that they have endured the company of grammarians and poets for such a long time. *Magister*'s contrast between divine contemplation and poetic recreation could hardly be sharper. On the one hand, there are the blessed beings that have been permeated with the mysteries of Christian purity and "have flown past everything childish", *cuncta puerilia transvolaverunt*, on their way towards the one and only true God. It is not for them that the teacher and his pupil had entered into this dialogue, since they have probably already lost interest in the quirks of poetry. On the other hand, however, there are "those who, devoted to secular literature, are entangled in great errors and wear out their good minds with trifles, without any idea of what they enjoy in them."[1] It is for their guidance that *On Music* has been composed.

If these misled souls could only learn the correct way to enjoy poetry or music – to subject their fascination with rhythm to the benefit of the soul – they would avoid all distress caused by literature and have their eyes opened to "the place of the most blessed security", *beatissimae securitatis locus*. Thereby we are able to infer one of the most important results of *Magister*'s analysis in *On Music*. Literature in itself can be saved by virtue of its technical resources, provided they are placed at the service of the true faith. But there is not much that can be done about poetry's fictional core. It has only trifles to offer, *nugae*. This is a term we have already met in the earlier Cassiciacum dialogue *Against the Academics*. We shall come across it again in a number of Augustine's works: *The Usefulness of Belief*, *De vera religione* (*Of True Religion*) and the *City of God*, each time with the purpose of depriving fictional representation of the status it had enjoyed in ancient Greece and Rome. "The truth of poetry is in its form, not its content", as Eugene Vance has incisively put it.[2]

Magister's fundamental viewpoint – the sensual and fictional substrata of music or poetry should be subjected to the formal principles of these arts – was already expressed in *On Order*. Even though the 'reasonable lie', *rationabile mendacium*, can be glimpsed as a theoretical possibility in this tract, the author expresses some doubt about its actual applications, since he is under such strong influence from the Platonic suspicion of the evidence of the senses (2.14.41):

---

[1] "His enim haec scripta sunt, qui litteris saecularibus dediti magnis inplicantur erroribus et bona ingenia in nugis conterunt, nescientes, quid ibi delectet."
[2] Vance 1982, p. 29.

> When Reason realized that with the help of number it had organized all the foregoing, it called number divine and almost eternal. And so it grievously tolerated that the splendor and purity of number should be somewhat clouded by the material sound of voices. Now number is a mental construct and, as such, ever present in the mind and understood as immortal. Sound, on the other hand, is temporary and fleeting, but can be memorized. As a result poets, with the leave of reason, created the fiction that Jupiter fathered the Muses from Mnemosyne (Memory). Good luck to their progeny, if any, but this hybrid of senses and mind came to be called *music*. (XI)

In such passages from *On Order*, already redolent with the speculations on time typical of the *Confessions* ten years later, music seems highly interesting to Augustine as an *ars*, that is, as a theoretical discipline, but considerably more problematic in practice. In this respect, it calls to mind his Cassiciacum representations of the human soul, theoretically capable of apprehending God but in practice subject to the jurisdiction of the senses, memory and imagination. Thus music is portrayed as a kind of liminal art, participating in the divine order of numbers thanks to intellect, yet not capable of matching geometry and astronomy, the next disciplines to be treated in *On Order*, since it cannot escape the sensual imprints of sound in the memory.

So far this discipline has not been given a name in *On Order*. Because some of its practitioners, the poets, had already been granted the privilege of crafting reasonable lies, Augustine recapitulates, they invented the story of the nine Muses, gifted with the splendid origin of Jupiter and Memory. This is clearly a – rather sophisticated – reference to the tale told by Hesiod in the *Theogony* (53–62). The Greek poet's mythological version of the divine source of music was an attempt, according to Augustine, to do justice to the rational content of this art, but at the same time this myth is explicitly presented as a fiction: *confictum est*. Consequently, Hesiod's age-old story becomes in itself a perfect metaphorical example of the hybrid art of music (and, by way of association, of poetry as well), joining sense to sound, reason to memory, and – in the final instance – universal order to wayward fictionality. The outcome of Augustine's enquiry is that a shadow is cast on the legitimacy of this art, as if it was unable to live up to its divine ancestry, burdened with its doubtful sensual ingredients. There is a good deal of scepticism in the author's concluding parenthetical clause "Good luck to their progeny, if any", literally: 'it may be questioned whether their progeny has any similarity [with its origin]', *quaerendumne quid propagini similiter inesset?* The Muses' resemblance to their divine (rational) parentage evidently remains uncertain. The rationality of their art seems inseparable from the quirks and whims of human perception.

In the immediate aftermath of his conversion, then, Augustine appears to have adopted an almost compulsive ambivalence towards fictional representation or, more precisely, the licence of the poets. He was attracted by it, he even took advantage of it in his dialogues, while he seldom managed to get rid of his doubts about its cognitive value and theoretical legitimacy. A few paragraphs later in *On Order*, when he deals with geometry and astronomy, he seems once again to have left the resources of fictionality behind for good. At this advanced stage, Reason is operating in the region of pure numbers. She is granted the privilege to observe them in their true proportions, Augustine tells us, 'by imagining and reflecting on them inside herself' (2.15.43): *quas in seipsa cogitando atque volvendo intuebatur verissimas*. With this visionary method she actually anticipates the couple in Ostia, who in a similar way would imagine (and talk about and marvel at) God's work in their inner being, *interius cogitando et loquendo et mirando opera tua*. Admittedly, Augustine's and Monnica's experience is characterized by its togetherness (they both share it), and in the autobiography the rational order of numbers would be exchanged for God's Creation, but the ascending movement in combination with introspection is the same. Moreover, in analogy with the later Ostia episode, Reason's purified gaze in *On Order* struggles successfully to escape from gross matter. When, dwelling in the lofty regions of geometry and astronomy, she tries to recall sensory things, all she can distinguish are the fuzzy 'shadows and traces' of numbers. It is these *umbrae atque vestigia* that downgrade music's cognitive potential and fill poetry with their faltering fantasies.

Finally, after having established the disciplines of numbers, Reason – in *On Order* strongly Platonically coloured – becomes aware of her extraordinary power. She is seized with a magnificent idea: perhaps she herself constitutes the number by which everything shall be measured, or, alternatively, perhaps it is towards that absolute number – the key to the secrets of the universe – that she is on her way. Encouraged by this prospect, she grasps with all her strength at this number which soon, hopefully, will reveal eternal truth for her, *qui iam universae veritatis index futurus*. Yet she cannot completely lay hold of it. Augustine compares this coveted truth with the ever-changing Proteus that we have already seen his student Alypius introduce for exactly the same purpose in *Against the Academics* (above, pp. 142f.): as an elusive *imago veritatis*, slipping out of our fingers.

Thus once again, for the last time, the author of *On Order* draws on poetry in his dialogue's Platonically inquisitive discourse. Virgil provides him with a mythical figure on which he bestows an epistemological significance: "The false images of things countable, however, distract us from that most hidden principle and attract our mind [*cogitatio*] to themselves, often obliterating previous knowledge from it" (2.15.43).¹ That is to say: precisely when we thought we had the 'index' of universal truth within our reach, it escaped us, just as the mythical Proteus had escaped from Homer's Menelaus or Virgil's Aristaeus. In the end, the images that kindle our imagination block our access to conceptual truth, an unfortunate cognitive barrier that Augustine suggests by virtue of – a poetic image: the elusive Protean quick-change artistry, known from *The Odyssey* and the *Georgics*. This paradox is typical of Augustine the convert. Fables, myths, and metaphors permeate a discourse that actually aims to save both the intradiegetic listener and the extradiegetic reader from fables, myths, and metaphors, in short: from the precarious fabrications of fictional discourse.

*

In the winter of 386–87, while Augustine and Monnica were still staying in Cassiciacum, shortly before she passed away at Ostia, the convert composed another work in two books which he called *Soliloquies* (literally "Discourses in solitude" or "Talking to one's self"), a neologism that was to prove productive in the history of European languages. Actually, despite the title of the tract, it introduces two interlocutors, Augustine and his Reason, *Ratio*. One of their topics is the concept of falseness. Both in the *Soliloquies*, "the most advanced and weighty piece among the Cassiciacum dialogues" according to Henry Chadwick, and in the somewhat later *Of True Religion*, one of his first writings aimed at the Manichees, the Church Father ponders on the problems of untruth, and in both cases he draws a fundamental distinction between fraud and a type of "lying" or dissimulation whose aim is not deceitful.² Here, we shall focus on the latter type of falsehood which, by and large, merges into the concept of fiction.

In these works, Augustine's argument sometimes gets rather intricate, and his nomenclature betrays some inconsistencies, but this is of less importance for us. We can well ignore the subtle oscillations of the taxonomy in the *Soliloquies* as well as *Of True Religion*.³ The crucial and, for the convert, totally characteristic distinctions are made in the dialogue from Cassiciacum, where intentional or pragmatic falseness is divided into two simple categories: the

---

1 "Imagines enim falsae rerum earum quas numeramus, ab illo occultissimo quo numeramus defluentes, in sese rapiunt cogitationem et saepe illum cum iam tenetur elabi faciunt."
2 Chadwick 2009, p. 37.
3 The terms and concepts in *Of True Religion* 33.61 are examined in Horn 1979. A short but excellent survey of the Church Father's definitions of falseness and lying (influenced by Stoicism), where, however, the issue of fictionality is left out of consideration, is to be found in Colish 1983, pp. 25–38.

fallacious, *fallax*, and the mendacious, *mendax*. By the former, Augustine signals the urge to deceive and to dupe, shared by both humans and animals. As for the latter, he observes that mimes, comedies and many poems, *multa poemata*, are admittedly full of lies, but their aim is to amuse rather than deceive us, *delectandi potius quam fallendi voluntate* (2.9.16).

"Lies" can evidently be acceptable or at least excused when they are designed to entertain an audience. This conclusion seems, basically, Horatian. But it soon becomes apparent that the author, or rather the dialogue's Reason, does not content himself with such pragmatic arguments. True to his habit, he demands a philosophical investigation into the concept of fiction, an inquiry which must focus on mimetic issues, accounting for the extensive class of phenomena in life that "pretends it is and is not", *esse tendit et non est*. It includes natural occurrences like reflections, refractions of light in water and shadows of bodies as well as various kinds of hallucinations or dreams. Finally, it also embraces art, or in Reason's more precise wording: "And every picture, statue, or similar work of art tries to be that on which it is modelled", pretending to be what they cannot be (2.9.17).[1] "Augustine" – the interlocutor, not the writer – is immediately curious about the stance of fiction in this context. How is it possible, he wonders, to distinguish "poems and jests", *poemata et ioca*, and other types of artistic performance or dissimulation, from this broad mimetic category?

The answer to this question in the *Soliloquies* is perhaps the closest Augustine – the writer, not the interlocutor – ever came to a coherent theory of fiction. It demonstrates how fascinated he was by the nature of fictional representation, and theatrical illusion in particular, as late as the year of his experience in Ostia in 387, but also how he quietly but firmly excludes such instances of mimetic art from the vision of truth he now had to aim for. That is why a quotation *in extenso* is required here (2.10.18):

> R.—It is one thing to will to be false and another not to be able to be true. We can classify comedies, tragedies, mimes and the like with the works of painters and sculptors. The picture of a man, though it tries to be like him, cannot be a true man any more than a character in the books of the comedians. These things are false not from any will or desire of their own, but from the necessity of following the will of their authors. On the stage, Roscius wants to be a false Hecuba, but by nature he is a true man. By so wanting, he is also a true tragedian, so far as he fulfils the part. But he would be a false Priam if he gave himself out as Priam and was not. But here emerges a strange fact which nobody doubts.

---

[1] "Quid omnis pictura vel cuiuscemodi simulacrum, et id genus omnia opificum? nonne illud esse contendunt, ad cuius quidque similitudinem factum est?" All quotations from *The Soliloquies* are from J.S. Burleigh's translation 2006.

> *A.*—What is that?
>
> *R.*—In all such matters truth and falsehood are inevitably intertwined; indeed, if there is to be truth in one respect there must be falsehood in another. How could Roscius be truly a tragic actor if he refused to be a false Hector, Andromache, Hercules or the like? How could a picture of a horse be truly a picture if the horse were not false? How could there be a man's face in a glass, true as such, though not truly a man? So if a certain kind of falsity is necessary in order that there should be truth, why do we dread falsity and seek truth as a great boon?
>
> *A.*—I don't know, unless it is because there is in these examples nothing worthy of our imitation. After all, unlike actors, reflections in mirrors, or Myron's brass cow, we ought not to be both true and false: true in our proper garb but false as dressed up to represent something else. We ought to seek the absolute truth, not that double-faced thing that is partly true and partly false.
>
> *R.*—You are asking something great, nay divine. (XII)

The fictionality of the mimetic arts forms a special category of falsehood in this discussion, since it betrays a strange ambivalence or contradiction. Here, the author of the *Soliloquies* takes the analysis considerably further than his predecessors in the Platonic tradition, who were generally obedient to the sharp distinction between true concepts and second-rate imitations, based on the Greek philosopher's own works. If Augustine in *On Order* focused on epic poetry, and if he would analyse the art of verse in *On Music*, he now takes his main examples from the stage. The theatre was another of his great, early passions from which he felt increasingly obliged to refrain, and which he eventually subjected to strong moral and religious reservations.[1]

But in the *Soliloquies* his interest in the art of theatrical performance, probably stemming from his Carthage days, is still alive even if his main outlook is exclusively philosophical. "Augustine" and Reason enter into a discussion on acting as a supreme instance of fictional representation. Here, it is accepted as a cognitive category in its own right, faithful to itself and its peculiar nature precisely while it deviates from its models in real life. Reason refers to the famous Roman actor Roscius (d. 62 BCE, one of the young Cicero's closest friends) and the conclusion he draws from his observations is paradoxical, hence the judgment *mirabile*. To be as "true" an actor as possible, Roscius has to produce as "false" Trojans – a Hecuba, a Priam, a Hector, an Andromache – or as "false" a Hercules as possible. The falser the role, that is, the more illusorily Roscius acts on the stage, the better and truer he will be as an actor. Reason's argument might just as well be presented in the reverse: fictions have to deviate from real

---

[1] For Augustine and the theatre, see Weismann 1972, pp. 123–95.

life as far as they follow their author's sovereign mastery or free-will, *fingentis arbitrium*.

This is one of the truly splendid moments in the on-going examination of fictionality that recurs in Augustine's work. It even seems reminiscent of Aristotle's investigations into the essence of mimetic art.[1] Legitimate fictions are not altogether true, but they are not altogether false either. Their very essence consists of imitation, hence the paradox which says that the stronger the illusion they suggest, the truer they are to themselves. This is, it might be claimed, a remarkably modern argument, looking far forward into the history of literature and aesthetics. Both in its leading idea and with its specific example it anticipates Hamlet's disturbing insight: "And all for nothing! / For Hecuba!"

In the *Soliloquies*, however, this argument's triumph is short-lived. With an impeccable feeling for the dialogue genre, Augustine has let Reason analyse fiction and saved his namesake's judgment for last. In his eyes, neither actors, nor natural reflections nor the *simulacra* of sculptors, as true to their mimetic character as they are false to their original models, appear to be attractive examples. That is because truth is one and indivisible. Changing guise and allowing oneself to be assimilated into a foreign form of existence or condition, *habitus*, is considered as destructive as in the third book of Plato's *The Republic*. With his well-formulated reservation about what he calls "that double-faced thing" in contradiction with itself, *bifrons ratio sibique adversans*, partly true and partly false, "Augustine" lodges his protest against Reason's Aristotelian case. This disapproval was to become increasingly audible throughout the Church Father's writings in the 390s and during the following century.

Both his fascination and his reservations soon generate new manifestations in the *Soliloquies*. Here too, the liberal arts are discussed, as in *On Order*, and a shadow seems to fall over grammar, since, as Reason points out, it deals with all those "fables and obvious falsehoods", *omnia illa fabulosa et aperte falsa*, which "Augustine" had declared he dislikes (2.11.19). The latter specifies his judgment by offering a Horatian definition of *fabula:* it is a "falsehood" composed for use or pleasure, *compositum ad utilitatem delectationemve mendacium*, and it comes under grammar of necessity, since that discipline is responsible for all the prod-

---

1 This is not to say that Augustine would have ticked off the arguments of the *Poetics*, either in the *Soliloquies* or anywhere else. Among Aristotle's writings, Augustine – strongly dependent on translations – knew the *Categories* in Marius Victorinus' Latin version. Moreover, the Neo-Platonic authors and Cicero had probably provided the Church Father with at least elementary insights into some basic tenets of Aristotelian philosophy. Nothing, however, indicates that he had any direct knowledge of the *Poetics*, the main ideas of which, on the other hand, colour many strands of Hellenistic and Roman literary theory. Cf. Weismann 1972, pp. 137f.

ucts of human language that are entrusted to memory and letters, that is, tradition "whether transmitted orally or in writing", *memoriae litterisque*. Fictional stories are granted a prominent place in this tradition. It is the grammarian's task not to invent such *figmenta* but to analyse them, accounting for their 'method' or 'theory', *ratio*. In other words, the discipline of grammar adopts as a matter of principle a neutral attitude to its material. Its *enarratio poetarum* is of a purely technical nature and seems in no way responsible for poetry's lack of truth.

This argument seems to prepare the way for a positive judgment of grammar, but "Augustine" soon challenges and corrects his own reasoning, perhaps owing to the author's mixed memories of his experiences from school. As we have to learn and memorize the old myths in grammar classes, backed up by the authority of masters and the long-standing Roman education system, it seems after all likely that the pupils think they are true. Surely the grammar teachers cannot be drilling their pupils with lies? Faced with this accusation, Reason once again takes it upon himself to defend both grammar and poetry. He puts forward the example of Daedalus, already adduced as a typical example of the fictional material grammar deals with in *On Order* (2.12.37). Has your teacher ever tried to get you to believe that Daedalus really flew? he asks his interlocutor. No, "Augustine" is forced to admit, acknowledging that the Cretan artificer's fame does not result from an actual flight but depends on the indisputable existence of the myth, *fabula*: "certainly that is true", *hoc non nego verum esse*. Well, in that case, Reason retorts with a note of triumph, you learned something true from the myth of Daedalus. He reminds "Augustine" of his previous argument: precisely because the story is false – it does not agree with reality – it is an authentic fable, that is a true fiction, *vera fabula!* The grammar student "Augustine" had, in other words, learnt to identify a truly mythical, non-historical narrative (2.11.20).

Thus Reason refuses to give up his analysis of *figmenta* in neutral or even positive terms, vaguely reminiscent of Aristotelian poetics, granting fictional discourse a certain amount of autonomy, and on top of that he rescues grammar as a respectable *ars* in this verbal duel with the author's namesake. In fact, both grammar and dialectic are central to his argument throughout the *Soliloquies*. He soon proceeds to identify fiction's peculiar nature by means of a linguistic and logical analysis of the concepts of true and false. His efforts in this direction are put to test when the two interlocutors, for the last time in the dialogue, return to the problem of falsehood (2.15.29). Here, "Augustine" seizes the opportunity to challenge Reason's Aristotelian framing of fictionality, based on the concept of *mimēsis*, according to which *falsum* in the sense of a copy always implies "some imitation of the true", *ad verum nonnullam imitationem*. "Augustine" dissents by citing Medea, skilled in magic, known from classical myths, epic poetry and drama, a recurrent figure (as we shall see) both in the author's *Confessions* and in his letters. When this witch is described as flying through the air with a team of winged snakes, nobody would surely claim that her story reflects something true? Surely it is completely preposterous from beginning to end, 'absolutely nothing', so it does not, in fact, imitate anything at all: *quippe quae nulla sit, nec imitari aliquid possit ea res quae omnino non sit.*

Reason is (of course) ready with an answer, whereby he gives proof of his eminent dialectic powers. He retorts quite simply that since Medea's team of winged snakes does not exist, her story can be neither true nor false. If Reason's arguments at this point begin to exhibit disquieting similarities to mere quibbling, his logic, nevertheless, seems formally irreproachable: "If it is false it exists. If it does not exist it is not false", *si enim falsum est, est: si non est, non est falsum.* The writer's alter ego can hardly believe his ears; such an obviously superstitious line of poetry as "huge winged serpents joined together by a yoke", *angues ingentes alites iunctos iugo* – isn't that false? The example shows how crucial this argument is for the early Augustine's theory of fiction. For, as Karel Svoboda assumes in his monograph on the Church Father's aesthetics, it is almost certainly taken from Cicero's *On Invention* (1.19.27), where the young rhetorician cites precisely this line as an example of the mythical tale, *fabula*, that is neither true, like *historia*, nor probable, like *argumentum* (cf. above p. 40).[1]

"Augustine's" question leads Reason to the final justification of literary fiction in the Cassiciacum dialogues. Evidently, this defence of poetry summarizes the *Soliloquies*' preceding arguments in favour of fictional discourse, while exploiting Stoic notions of the difference between external (physical or vocal) signs and mental content, that is, between the assertion and what is asserted, equally important for the confessor a few years later. It is correct, Reason admits, that what is affirmed here (Medea's snakes) does not exist; it imitates nothing and cannot therefore be labelled in terms of true or false. But the affirmation or statement itself, the *sententia* or *enuntiatio*, exists – thus does Reason end his plea – and even if it is false, it imitates true statements. For it would have been formulated in exactly the same way if Medea had in fact fastened the snakes to her chariot. Whether one believes it or not, its particular mode of expression, *quod ita dicitur*, is based on imitation. Consequently, even if the statement is false it is not fraudulent, *falsa, non etiam fallens*, whereby it meets the formal requirements for a fictional utterance.

---

1 Svoboda 1933, pp. 52f.

"A witty and interesting exposé" – that is how Svoboda characterizes Reason's subtleties.[1] The wittiness is perhaps a matter for discussion. To me, Reason's argument seems rather convoluted and faltering, as if the author had stumbled on unexpected difficulties in trying to sort out the concepts and was struggling to find a solution to their aporias. It is precisely this struggle with the problem of fictionality, which is not only presented by the dialogue but actually enacted in its text, that gives the account in the *Soliloquies* its special interest. It shows how "Augustine" learns to discriminate between reference and referent, a distinction that would prove decisive for the pioneering semiotic theses in, for example, *On Christian Doctrine*. "Now I understand," he exclaims, "that there is a great difference between mere statements and the objects about which statements are made" (2.15.29), *iam intellego multum interesse inter illa quae dicimus, et illa de quibus dicimus aliquid*. At the level of the reference – that is, of signs, words or sentences – it seems possible, then, to imitate the truth by means of formally false statements, a peculiar kind of discourse that is simulated but not fraudulent, hence fictional. To sum up, in the *Soliloquies* from 386–87, both dialectic and grammar are employed to narrow down the "double-faced" – ambiguous or self-contradictory – source of knowledge provided by the mimetic arts, for instance poetry and drama. This is the convert's somewhat tortuous attempt to understand and do justice to fictional representation, a discourse or performance in its own right, within a consistent philosophical or logical scheme.

As a matter of fact, Augustine would return to grammar's *enarratio poetarum* throughout his writings, but his Aristotelian curiosity in the mimetically ambiguous nature of poetry cooled as time passed. The Bishop of Hippo Regius became increasingly inclined to label profane literature as *nugae*, trifles, and he never ceased to wonder at the fact that such an irresponsible activity, based on free invention, could be the subject of such a serious (or at least acknowledged) discipline as grammar. Similar thoughts even appear in contexts where one would not expect to find them, in works of a dogmatic or exegetic nature. It is as if Augustine found it easier to understand and define some of the cornerstones of theology such as Creation, the sacraments or the Holy Writ by marking them off from their persistent contrast: idiosyncratic fancies, enchanting storytelling, pagan myth, in short, fiction. This is the mechanism that is triggered when,

---

[1] Ibid., p. 51.

around the turn of the fifth century, he ponders on the correct interpretation of texts in *On the Catechising of the Uninstructed* (6.10):[1]

> For if, even in handling the fables of the poets, which are but fictitious creations and things devised for the pleasure of minds whose food is found in trifles, those grammarians who have the reputation and the name of being good do nevertheless endeavour to bring them to bear upon some kind of (assumed) use, although that use itself may be only something vain and grossly bent upon the coarse nutriment of this world: how much more careful does it become us to be, not to let those genuine verities which we narrate, in consequence of any want of a well-considered account [*redditio digesta*] of their causes, be accepted either with a gratification which issues in no practical good, or, still less, with a cupidity which may prove hurtful!

The argument follows the dialectic structure known as *a fortiori*. The bishop claims that secular grammar teaching, treated here with considerably less respect than in the convert's philosophical dialogues, tries to take advantage of the poets' fictions, which have been made only to amuse people while hardly containing anything of value. How much more important, the author completes his argument, must it not be for us – Christian teachers – to supplement our entirely true instruction with real explanations of cause and effect, that is, to trace back all marvellous things we "narrate" to the solid basis of the history of salvation and to divine love, so that they are not misunderstood, distorted or used wrongly. The whole passage is permeated by metaphors of digestion, already employed in classical Roman rhetoric.[2] Fictions give little or no nourishment, *cibus*, and even in grammar teaching there is a risk that they only satisfy plain secular gluttony, *sagina saecularis*. Presuming that the participle *digesta* retains something of its literal meaning, Augustine's argument finally emphasizes the importance of the truths of faith being properly 'digested'. Be that as it may, we recognize the basic strategy of his exposition: to define the correct linguistic or discursive usage, here in a didactic context, by erasing all traces of sweet but sly fictionality.

*

When the slightly more than thirty-year-old Augustine made up his mind to seek God by means of philosophical or logical (dialectic) inquiries, he was particular-

---

1 "Si enim fictas poetarum fabulas et ad voluptatem excogitatas animorum, quorum cibus nugae sunt, tamen boni qui habentur atque appellantur grammatici, ad aliquam utilitatem referre conantur, quamquam et ipsam vanam et avidam saginae saecularis: quanto nos decet esse cautiores, ne illa quae vera narramus, sine suarum causarum redditione digesta, aut inani suavitate aut etiam perniciosa cupiditate credantur."
2 See Quintilian 2001 (vol. IV), 10.1.19.

ly well equipped for the task. Had he not found what he was looking for, he would certainly have made himself a name in one or more of the scholarly careers typical of his epoch. Pedagogical theory in the Roman Empire of Late Antiquity prescribed, as Max Laistner observes, an all-round educational ideal, the *paideia* inherited from Hellenistic culture, but in practice, rhetoric was patently predominant.[1] In this field, Augustine's competence was truly superb: he had conducted a school of rhetoric in Carthage for many years, and he had successfully pursued his activities as a rhetor in Italy. Moreover, apart from his skills in eloquence, his curiosity and knowledge about grammar, poetry and music, philosophy and dialectic, hermeneutics and semiotics, history and pedagogy, were remarkable. With such a sterling education at his disposal, it is understandable how Augustine in his Cassiciacum dialogues, as well as here and there in his later writings, came close to crediting the arts with a capacity to point towards the divine and interpret the sacred truths of faith.

Another piece of evidence concerning the young Augustine, the liberal arts and poetry can be found in the dialogue *De quantitate animae* (*The Greatness of the Soul*), written a year or so after the *Soliloquies*, at the end of 387 or the beginning of 388, when the convert was still in Rome, just before his departure for Africa. This dialogue takes place between Augustine and his lifelong friend Evodius, and, for the moment, it is of interest to us in one respect only. Towards the end, it depicts an ascension towards God in rough accordance with Platonic tradition. Such an account is obviously pertinent to an examination of the *ascensio* that Augustine had experienced with Monnica just about six months earlier, at Ostia, and which he would recall so tenderly in his *Confessions* from the late 390s.

In *The Greatness of the Soul*, Augustine is about to explain both the magnitude and the eminence of the soul to Evodius, and for this purpose he chooses, along Platonic lines, to divide the human mind into seven different levels, on closer inspection seven stages on the way to illumination, from the life-giving principle – the first, vegetative level – right up to the final ecstasy of contemplation. At the second level, he finds the five senses, dreams, instincts, the ability to procreate and the material memory, all those faculties or qualities we have in common with animals.

At the third level, that of discursive reason, the specifically human activities appear. This is the abode of our cultural memory with all its crafts, industries, sciences and arts (33.72):[2]

---

[1] Laistner 1951, p. 10.
[2] J.M. Colleran's translation, Augustine 1950b.

The invention of so many symbols in letters, in words, in gesture, in sound of various kinds, in paintings and statues [*figmenta*]; the languages of so many peoples, their many institutions, some new and some revived; the great number of books and records of every sort for the preservation of memory and the great concern shown for posterity; [...] the power of reason and thought, the floods of eloquence, the varieties of poetry, the thousand forms of mimicries for the purpose of entertainment and jest, the art of music, the accuracy of surveying, the science of arithmetic, the interpretation of the past and future from the present. (XIII)

The list is exhaustive and includes, additionally, handicraft and mechanical disciplines such as agriculture and town or city planning, cult ceremonies, politics and the art of war. Throughout this prolific exposition, however, the liberal arts stand out: grammar with its supervision of language and signs – here, Augustine's semiotic interests are particularly evident – together with the flow of rhetoric, the *vis ratiocinandi et excogitandi* of dialectic, music, geometry, arithmetic, and, finally, astronomy (here more or less identical with astrology). Literature, paintings and *figmenta*, in this context probably with special reference to sculpture, are given a relatively prominent place in this enumeration of legitimate cultural phenomena, all subjected to the enquiries of the rational soul. Moreover, "thousand forms of mimicries for the purpose of entertainment and jest", *ludendi ac iocandi causa milleformes simulationes*, most certainly including theatrical performances, are registered between the references to poetry and music. All such interests, activities or skills contribute to the enlightenment and the ennobling of the soul.

This ambitious curriculum is a remarkable outcome of the young Augustine's didactic or educational philosophy – with his own concluding words: "These things bear the mark of greatness and they are characteristically human", *magna haec et omnino humana*. However, there are at least two reasons for being wary of interpreting such pronouncements as jubilant expressions of approval. We should remember that we are still only at the third level of the soul's ascent – the best is yet to come – and, the author remarks on a critical note, both educated and uneducated people, both good and evil persons, participate indiscriminately in all these activities. Augustine proves unable to come up with any guarantees whatsoever that the liberal (or mechanical) arts will be exercised properly, and he seems sceptical about their possibilities to form, as it were, a springboard towards the truly intellectual heights for the soul willing to learn.

The later and higher stages on the way of this soul through the treatise are summed up as follows. The fourth stage has "goodness" and purification as its main theme. Such *bonitas* more or less corresponds to what Diotima in Plato's *Symposium* had treated as moral beauty, by which the soul turns inwards, towards its own nature, and becomes aware of its precedence over physical Creation (210). It is here that the Augustinian introspection sets in. This level involves a process of purification: a heightened awareness of the gap between the soul's final destination, pure being, and the soiled existence it is leaving behind. Its enterprise begins to take on an ascetic turn. As the soul rejoices in its own superiority, it begins to "withdraw from sordid things", *sese abstrahere a sordibus*, washing away all earthly stains, making itself clean and well-ordered. In a fifth step, this purification process is completed: the soul is already resting within itself, whereby it can turn towards God with a new confidence and prepare for the contemplation of truth (33.73–74).

Subsequently, at the sixth stage of the soul's journey, there remain the efforts to get accustomed to the radiant vision of the Godhead. Since its light is blinding, this acclimatization turns out to be difficult, for which reason many beings fall back into the darkness of the old, secular life. That is what happens when our faculty of thought or imagination, *cogitatio*, is too hasty, not having completely freed itself from the mire of passions and mortal things (33.75). At long last, the soul reaches the enduring vision of truth, the end of the whole process, a joy that the author has some difficulties in expressing, even if others – some "great and peerless souls", *magnae quaedam et incomparabiles animae* – have dressed it in words as far as is humanly possible. Augustine adds that he looks forward to this blessed state for his own part, when he will attain the uttermost cause, the Creator or highest principle of everything, "or whatever other more appropriate appellative there may be for so great a reality", *ad summam illam causam, vel summum auctorem, vel summum principium rerum omnium, vel si quo alio modo res tanta congruentius appellari potest* (33.76). These words apply to God, of course, but the author's terminology is strikingly philosophic or, more specifically, Platonic/Plotinian.

Now that we have come so far, Augustine continues, alluding to Ecclesiastes (1.2), we shall actually realize how everything under the sun is nothing but "vanity of vanities", *vanitas vanitantium*. Solomon's crucial term in this famous syntagm, *vanitas*, vanity or emptiness, denotes everything that is false, *fallacia*, Augustine explains, while the "vanities" or, to be more precise, the substantiated adjective in the genitive plural, 'of vain people', refers to those who allow themselves to be deceived, or who deceive, or both: *vel falsi, vel fallentes, vel utrique intelleguntur*. Such an outcome of the mind's journey in *The Greatness of the Soul* from 387–88 seems hardly promising as far as poetry is concerned (even if Dante, as Rand claims, was to use this account as a pattern for his vision of Paradise).¹ The gap between our illusions here on earth and the purified soul's blessed contemplation seems huge, and the liberal arts – including their examinations of ratiocination, eloquence and poetry – are, at best, temporarily instrumental to the latter's state of illumination. Their usefulness to the whole process is evidently, to express it mildly, propaedeutic and limited.

Augustine's weakened hopes about poetry as a means of instruction is exemplarily manifest in his treatise *De mendacio* (*On Lying*), immediately before the *Confessions*, where he distinguishes between *mendaces*, deliberate liars who enjoy deceiving people, and *mentientes*, those who lie against their will (11.18). The former category of liars is as a matter of principle unforgivable, as we have already learnt from the *Soliloquies*. But should it not be possible to exempt *mentientes*, people who happen to lie unwillingly, perhaps for a good cause or at least with unharmful intentions, from the general denunciation of all falsehood?

That seems to be the case at the beginning of the relevant passage from *On Lying*. Augustine dwells with a certain understanding on those "who by a lie wish to please men, not that they may do wrong or bring reproach upon any man; for we have already before put away that kind; but that they may be pleasant in conversation." They differ from plain "liars" in the strict sense of the word by not feeling comfortable with their falsifications, beeing prepared "to please by agreeable talk, and yet would rather please by saying things that were true, but when they do not easily find true things to say that are pleasant to the hearers, they choose rather to tell lies than to hold their tongues. Yet it is difficult for these sometimes to undertake a story which is the whole of it false; but most commonly they interweave falsehood with truth, where they are at a loss for something sweet."² Here, Augustine had all kinds of storytellers and fiction-makers in mind, among them most certainly those fabricators of comedies or *multa poemata* whom we have already met in his *Soliloquies*, people who lie for the sake of entertainment rather than to deceive us, *delectandi potius quam fallendi voluntate* (cf. above, p. 179). We note, however, that the instructive purpose of fictional tales – the didactic function that Horace famously had attributed to poetry and that repeatedly crossed Augustine's mind in Cassiciacum, where he had out-

---

1 Rand 1929, pp. 259–66.
2 "Qui de mendacio volunt placere hominibus, non ut alicui faciant iniuriam vel inferant contumeliam; iam enim supra hoc genus removimus; sed ut suaves sint in sermonibus suis. [...] istis autem placere libet de suaviloquio, qui tamen veris mallent placere; sed quando non facile inveniunt vera quae grata sint audientibus, mentiri eligunt potius quam tacere. Difficile est tamen ut isti totam narrationem falsam aliquando suscipiant; sed plerumque veris falsa contexunt, ubi suavitas eos deserit."

lined the concept of "the rational lie", *mendacium rationabile* – is conspicuously absent when we reach *On Lying* in 394–95.

That is why the author of the tract eventually disapproves of this seemingly harmless storytelling too. Its hedonistic elements – in Horace's account of the aim of poetry in *Ars poetica:* delight (333), *delectatio*, or charm (343), *dulce* – are to be distrusted, as they exclude all rationality. Consequently, even the *mentientes* of the tract must be rejected; in the end, they cause great damage, since they prefer to please rather than tell the truth: *valde obsunt... quia se malunt placere, quam verum*. This criticism recalls yet another moralizing aspect of Augustine's reservations against literature. To the Christian doubt about the frivolity and enticing appeals of poetry he adds his suspicions of the poets' vanity, in glaring contrast to the modesty of the evangelical writers. The author of *On Lying* was already captivated by the message as well as the humility of the Holy Writ, preparing the ground for the condemnation of poetry that he would soon deliver in the *Confessions* and in his later writings concerning the liberal arts.

Here, we shall only pay attention to one key document in this context, namely the Church Father's epistle to his fellow Bishop Memor (Memorius) in Apulia from 408 (or the following year), forwarded by another brother of the Church, Possidius. In this letter, which was written because he was not able to send Memorius a checked and corrected version of *On Music*, Augustine explains that Possidius had been a student of his, and that he had nourished him "with the bread of the Lord" rather than with "that literature that those enslaved to various desires call liberal" (101.1): *est enim per nostrum ministerium non litteris illis, quas variarum servi libidinum liberales vocant, sed dominico pane nutritus*.

Now, against the evil and ungodly persons who boast that they have been schooled in the liberal arts, Augustine wishes to cite "the writings that are truly liberal", *litterae vere liberales*, which say: "So if the Son sets you free, you will be free indeed." (John 8.36) At this late stage in the bishop's career, obviously, the arts and their textbooks have been once and for all surpassed by the Holy Writ. His downgrading of their prestige is evident from what perhaps turned out to be the most powerful attack on the language disciplines that he ever wrote (101.2):

> For he allows us to know what liberal content those disciplines have that are called liberal by those who have not been called to freedom. After all, they have consonant with freedom only what they have consonant with the truth. For this reason that Son himself says, *The truth will set you free*. Those countless and impious stories, therefore, with which the poems of pagan poets are filled, are in no way consonant with our freedom, nor are the proud and polished lies of the orators, nor, finally, are the wordy sophistries of those philosophers who either have not known God at all or, *though they knew God, did not glorify*

> him as God or thank him. Rather they became vain in their thoughts, and their foolish heart was darkened. And though they said that they were wise, they became fools, and they exchanged the glory of the incorruptible God for the likeness of an image of a corruptible man and of birds, animals, and reptiles. And those who did not worship these images or worshiped them only to a certain point did, nonetheless, *worship and serve a creature rather than the creator.* Heaven by all means forbid that anyone should rightly call liberal arts the frivolities, the deceitful insanity, the windy nonsense, and the proud error of these unhappy men. For they did not know the grace of God through Jesus Christ our Lord, by which alone we are set free from the body of this death, and they did not perceive in those studies what is true. (XIV)

In these Pauline periods, it is the core subjects of the school system that are under fire from the Church Father. One by one, he repudiates the fictions or *fabulae* of poetry (the domain of grammar), the pomp of rhetoric and the subtleties of dialectic. Admittedly, later in the letter, he deals in more positive terms with history which at best can result in accurate accounts of things past, and with the art of numbers or harmonies which might indicate a way to the higher secrets of truth. However, Augustine explains, it was only a temporary break from "greater and more important cares" (101.3), *curae maiores magisque necessariae*, that allowed him to write *On Music*, whose first five books he characterizes as full of technicalities, incomprehensible to anyone who is not a specialist in this field. The letter sets two human ideals and concepts of education directly against each other, each with a corpus of its own: on the one hand, classical culture's *urbanitas* and *paideia*, based on the encyclopaedic culture of the liberal arts, and, on the other hand, rightful religion's *pietas* and *doctrina*, based on the Bible's infallible authority, discernible in the very title of the text that would first of all formulate a programmatic Christian alternative to the old educational system's language arts, namely Augustine's own *On Christian Doctrine*.

The dividing line between the two cultures was the question of truth. Evidently, the liberal arts were disparaged not because they necessarily would be used to teach outright lies but because they lacked clear distinctions between true and false. This criticism may seem astounding, since such subdivisions were generally entrusted to the competence of dialectic, but in the letter to Memorius it was precisely the philosophers' "wordy sophistries", *garrulae argutiae*, that were hardest hit by Augustine's fulminations. His disapproval is in turn based on his increasing conviction that the only secure instrument for distinguishing truth from lying is the teaching of the Holy Spirit as we find it in the Bible. Without this guidance, even devout brothers and sisters in faith constantly run the risk of having empty fictions expelling God from their hearts.

Whereas some of the early Christian writers from the fourth and fifth centuries attempted to establish connections between the David of the Psalms and the

Orpheus of pagan myth, both of whom were supposed to herald Christ, the writer of the letter to Memorius decidedly preferred immediate prevention to later cure. He was not even inclined – as in some of his other writings – to grant certain decent pagan intellectuals (who as if by chance had come across some legitimate truth) any premonitions of Christ. Here, all such conciliatory attitudes are gone. The liberal arts knew of no protective barriers against wilful fabrication, so they could easily end up in idolatrous cults. The effective medicine against such fancies was the Bible, where the problem of truth, by virtue of verbal inspiration, was solved *a priori*. In the Holy Writ there were no passing whims or lies, just spiritual nourishment in abundance, the sole learning that leads to the only salvation that counts in the long run, ascertained with an allusion to another letter, Paul's Epistle to the Romans: "Wretched man that I am! Who will deliver me from this body of death?" (7.24)

Some of the wordings in the letter to Memorius are typical of the more specific objections that Augustine could now make to the liberal arts. There is, firstly, his reference to rhetoric's "proud and polished lies", *inflata et expolita mendacia*.[1] This criticism should be understood in connection with the Church Fathers' frequent pleas for a radical change of style in Christian sermons, prayers or psalms, from the ornate diction which was often taught and admired in the grammar or rhetoric classes of the schools to a lower and simpler style, *sermo humilis*, adapted to spoken (rather than Ciceronian) Latin and to the language of the Christian congregations. In a letter written in 381 to the Bishop of Lyons, Ambrose begins by reminding his addressee how "very many deny that the Sacred writers wrote according to the rules of art. Nor do we contend for the contrary; for they wrote not according to art, but according to grace, which is above all art; for they wrote that which the Spirit gave them to speak." (55.1)[2]

Later on, we shall devote a special section to this landslide in language and literary history (pp. 477ff.), in which Augustine was one of the prime movers. He drew his conclusions from the comparisons he was able to make between the sophisticated audiences he knew from Rome or Milan and the uneducated crowds he was faced with as Bishop of Hippo. In his magisterial work on the develop-

---

[1] Kevin L. Hughes emphasizes this scepticism about self-indulgent or "narcissistic" rhetoric as a main incentive to the mature Augustine's dismissal of the liberal arts, 2000, p. 100.

[2] "Negant plerique nostros secundum artem scripsisse. Nec nos obnitimur; non enim secundum artem scripserunt, sed secundum gratiam quae super omnem artem est. Scripserunt enim quae spiritus his loqui dabat." I quote the letter, number 8 in most editions of Ambrose, after the author's *Epistulae* 1968–96; for English translations of Ambrose's letters, I use the Oxford edition from 1881.

ment of oral and written Latin from the fourth to the ninth century, Michel Banniard stresses the importance of *On Christian Doctrine* in particular for the "revolution" that the simple style meant for the rhetorical hierarchies of classical education.¹

Equally significant is, secondly, the accusation in Augustine's letter to Memorius directed against the philosophers for having become "vain" (or for having vanished) "in their thoughts" or imaginations, *evanuerunt in cogitationibus suis*, a critical remark based on the Epistle to the Romans 1.21–25. The mature Augustine was sceptical about what he understood to be the appeal of the liberal arts to the seductive imagination rather than to the enlightened intellect. This is a sore point that appears as early as in the final pages of (the far more arts-friendly) *Soliloquies*. There, the novice had suggested a similar cognitive ascension as in *The Greatness of the Soul* a year or so later: those who had been acquainted with the school disciplines are not content, Reason asserts, until they have seen the face of truth "whose splendour glimmers even now in these liberal arts", *cuius quidam in illis artibus splendor iam subrutilat*. However, the same protagonist warns, these arts also radiate another kind of light, "some false colours and shapes", *falsi colores atque formae*, across the mirror of thought (2.20.35),

> and often deceive inquirers into thinking that that is all they can know or look for. These imaginations are to be avoided with the greatest care. They are proved fallacious because they vary as the mirror of the mind varies. The face of Truth remains one and immutable.²

It is obvious that Augustine's scepticism about the arts is connected with his distrust of the *imaginationes* that play as enticingly as deceivingly across "the mirror of the mind", much as this mirror may be directed towards the face of truth. It is as if they put a blush on this face when it is reflected in the human mind. Jean Doignon, who has devoted a short study to this passage in the *Soliloquies*, compares them with the figures that stand in the way of geometry's pure forms in the same dialogue (2.18.32), or with the "false images of things countable" that obscure the one and only true number in *On Order*; and, last but not least, he reminds us of the allegory that forms the prologue of *The Happy Life*, where the inquiring souls who have crossed the world's stormy seas have to face the fear

---

1 Banniard 1992, p. 75.
2 "Falluntque inquirentes saepe, ac decipiunt putantes illud totum esse quod norunt vel quod inquirunt. Ipsae sunt illae imaginationes magna cautione vitandae; quae deprehenduntur fallaces, cum cogitationis variato quasi speculo varientur, cum illa facies veritatis una et immutabilis maneat."

of an enormous rock at the entrance to philosophy's safe haven (1.3). This rock attracts sailors with its false brilliance but is both dangerous and empty, "a symbol of glittering rhetoric", as Doignon puts it.[1]

In all these cases, in *Soliloquies*, *On Order* and *The Happy Life*, truth is obscured by the fictitious and deceitful images that interfere with the process of philosophical pursuit. Accordingly, the Augustinian reservations about the faculty of unreliable imagination proceed from the early Cassiciacum dialogues but, as I shall try to demonstrate, permeate all his writings.

The Wounds of Imagination

When Augustine and Monnica seek God at the window in Ostia, they yearn for the silencing of the elements' *phantasiae* and, furthermore, the silencing of all "revelations known through its [the soul's] imagination", *imaginariae revelationes*. A phantom-like or imaginary reality of both an external and an internal nature, of Creation as well as the human soul, must obviously subside so that the journey's longed-for goal will be accessible.

This kind of phrasing should be assessed against the backdrop of Augustine's undeniable interest in images and imagery in general. It was rooted both in the Jewish-Christian doctrine of the Creation, where God had made man in His image, after His likeness, *faciamus hominem ad imaginem et similitudinem nostram* (Genesis 1.26), and in Plotinian cosmology, where each level of the universe reproduces the closest level above in descending order, from the One to lifeless things, but where at the same time these emanations, by upward and inward contemplation, struggle to refine their likeness to the paramount model: the potential return of all images to the archetype.

In both Hebrew and classical tradition, then, figurativeness could be ascribed to Creation itself, a more or less broken reflection of its divine origin. However, Augustine also adopted the widespread conviction of Greek philosophy – of the Peripatetics, the Platonists, and the Stoics – that for better or worse man had access to a special image-making ability in his soul: imagination. This is yet another stumbling block throughout the Church Father's writings, highly relevant to his attitude towards the issue of fictionality, frequently associated with the false creeds that were circulating among contemporary heretical sects as well as the literary heritage of pagan culture.

---

[1] Doignon 1984–85, p. 122.

The doctrine of images is a central theme in one of Augustine's most important works, *On the Trinity*, both a powerful investigation into the nature of the Trinity and an ambitious analysis of the human mind. That is because if the Godhead can be defined in terms of Father, Son and Holy Spirit, and if man was created in God's image and likeness, then he too, or more precisely the human soul, will be threefold, possible to describe as a series of triads at various levels. *On the Trinity* is largely devoted to these mental triptychs, the imprint of the Trinity on our psychic organization, the best-known of which is probably the triad consisting of "inner" or spiritual man's memory, reason and will, *memoria, intelligentia* and *voluntas*.

When our soul wants to gain knowledge of God, it is thus well advised to observe and analyse itself, in accordance with the introspective pattern we recognize from the *Enneads* or Augustine's own *Confessions*. But when it tries to orient itself in its inner being, it is forced to start from the evidence of physical and external indications, "examples of likenesses from outward things pertaining to the body" (11.1.1), *de corporalibus exterioribus similitudinum documenta*. Our dependence on the images provided by our senses might be unfortunate in theory, but it is nonetheless inseparable from man's lot. It is with a kind of rugged resignation that Augustine notes that in our natural state we unfailingly give in to physical and spatial categories. Even if man, whom Augustine in a Pauline spirit labels *animalis homo*, is created in God's image and likeness, human beings find it difficult to understand the Trinity, since they are so dependent on their sense impressions, reflected or reproduced in the imagination, a kind of intuitive thinking in images, in short, *cogitatio:* "For he cannot think [*cogitare*] except under the conditions of bulk and space, either small or great, since phantasms or as it were images of bodies flit about in his mind." (7.6.11)[1]

---

1 "Non enim potest cogitare nisi moles et spatia, vel minuta vel grandia volitantibus in animo eius phantasmatis, tamquam imaginibus corporum." The term *cogitatio* is not easy to grasp, but it seems clear that Augustine frequently associates it with the mind's power of imagination, *phantasia* or *imaginatio*, although he tends to describe it as a mental activity rather than a faculty of the soul. In the eleventh book of *On the Trinity*, the Church Father locates this *cogitatio* to the second of man's cognitive triads (11.3.6): it consists of memory, "internal vision", *interna visio*, and will, all consolidated into one sole activity, *coactus*, hence Augustine's designation *cogitatio*. It should be understood as a kind of reflexion of the lowest grade in our soul, close to intuition, a systematization or synthetization of the store of images in memory, which still lacks the authority of rational thinking (cf. 11.7.12, 11.8.13 and 11.9.16). When we read the evangelist John 1.6–7 ("there was a man sent from God, whose name was John" etc.), Augustine remarks later in *On the Trinity*, "we think of the man John under that phantasy which is impressed on our memory from the notion of human nature" (13.1.2), *hominem autem Ioannem in phantasia cogitamus, quae de humanae naturae notitia impressa est nostrae memoriae*. Moreover, the *Solilo-*

As a matter of principle there is, admittedly, a hierarchical and perfect balance in man's soul that was originally created in God's image and likeness, but reason, *ratio*, or the inner man, *homo interior*, constantly runs the risk of slipping too far "into outward things", *nimis in exteriora prolabitur*. This process amounts to a sliding away from the generic and the universal into the private and personal, *a communi universo ad privatam partem*. The human soul thus loses its sovereign generalizing view of Creation, to be drawn towards changing forms and corporeal motions, and since it does not always have them accessible – they come and go – "it is wrapped up in their images, which it has fixed in the memory, and is foully polluted by fornication of the phantasy", *cum eorum imaginibus, quas memoriae fixit, involvitur, et phantastica fornicatione turpiter inquinatur* (12.8.13 – 9.14). Along these lines, Augustine links imagination not only to imagery, but to memory and desire as well, on the whole with a negative outcome.

Thus a discontinuous series of passages in *On the Trinity*, primarily in Books XI and XII, makes up what is perhaps the sharpest analysis in Late Antiquity of the activities of the imagination. Augustine's overall emphasis is on its readiness to diminish, enlarge or regroup things known, as well as on its ability to imagine absent or non-existent phenomena. His account is, in several respects, epoch-making. In her ambitious panorama over the history of the concept of imagination, Eva Brann remarks that Augustine's coupling of this faculty to will – his stress on the affective nature of imagination – was pioneering, just as his introduction of the term *imaginatio* (based on *imago*, image) as an alternative to the Greek *phantasia* would prove decisive for later medieval language usage.[1] In *On the Trinity* these terms could shift throughout the work, mostly between *imaginatio*, *visio interna* and *cogitatio*. Against the background of Augustine's lifelong oeuvre, it seems clear that this relentlessly operative imagination, with its ability to portray, simulate or distort reality, is close to what the Church Father – as we have seen – classified as *visio spiritualis* in *The Literal Meaning of Genesis* and to

---

quies 2.20.34 contains an outright translation of the Greek *phantasia* or *phantasma* into the Latin *cogitatio*. In fact, this term recurs frequently throughout Augustine's writings. Todd Breyfogle observes that it is used as a synonym of *imaginatio* in the twelfth book of *The Literal Meaning of Genesis*, 1999, pp. 146f., while Gerard Watson relates the dictionary entry *cogitatio* to "imagination" as well as "thought-processes" in *Augustinus-Lexikon* 1986. Augustine's contemporary Jerome relied more than once on the term *cogitatio* to indicate imagination under the aspect of desire (burdened with guilt), as in a letter from 411, where he looks back on his youthful indulgence in sin and vices; he was not even helped by his fasts, since his mind was burning with – tempting – fantasies (125.12), *mens tamen cogitationibus aestuabat*, PL 22.1079.
1 Brann 1990, pp. 53f. Cf. Bundy 1927, pp. 157–64, and chapter 6, "The Transition to *Imaginatio*", in Watson 1988, pp. 134–61, especially p. 138.

what, in hermeneutical or literary contexts, he used to apprehend and/or condemn as fictional representation.

Thus Augustine, as Karel Svoboda has observed, gradually came to understand literary works as products of the imagination, a completely natural attitude for a modern reader but one of the few exceptions to the rule in antique poetic theory, dominated by the doctrine of imitation (as in Plato and Aristotle).[1] We have to consult Cicero's notion of the matrix of the imagination, *cogitata species*, for all figures and forms of art, introduced in his treatise on the *Orator* (3.9), his successor Quintilian, whom we met in the introduction to this book (pp. 7f.), an inventive critic such as Longinus and his tract *On the Sublime*, perhaps from the first century CE, some Neo-Platonic thinkers and, finally, the Late Greek sophist and orator Flavius Philostratus and his biography of the sage Apollonius from Tyana (see below, p. 361), in order to find similar ideas on this topic, developed to a greater or lesser degree.[2]

Even if Svoboda's observation is striking, all these documents, especially Cicero's and Quintilian's portrayals of the perfect orator, indicate that the exploitation of imagination in the service of illusion was in fact implicit in the Aristotelian tradition that was systematized in Roman and Late Greek rhetoric. It was particularly visible in the theory of *inventio* of legal speech, where imagination could be invoked as a source of suggestive images intended to provoke a strong feeling of presence, *evidentia*, in order to convince the audience (the judge, the jury, the listeners – cf. above, p. 32). However, the most far-reaching attempts in Late Antiquity to account for the role of the imagination in poetic contexts are probably to be found in Neo-Platonic philosophical tradition, which had fascinated the young Augustine and which could still impinge *On the Trinity*. These innovative efforts in Late Antique poetics would eventually find their most systematic expression in Proclus by the middle of the fifth century.

In the fifth and sixth books of his commentary on Plato's *The Republic*, the last pagan philosopher would distinguish three or (to be precise) four types of poems, each with its own content and its own formal characteristics. At the top of the list is inspired poetry, which represents divine things – the life of the immortals – in dense and suggestive *symbola*. Secondly, Proclus registers a didactic type of literature that provides its readers with rational and moral insights. At the bottom he places mimetic poetry, which depicts sensuous things, at best correctly, but in the sub-category *phantastikon* only as they appear to us in elusive images, *eidōla*. As far as we are concerned, it is relevant that in-

---

1 Svoboda 1933, pp. 101f.
2 For the *Orator*, I use H.M. Hubbell's Loeb edition, Cicero 1988.

spired poetry is by definition always true, for the undisputable benefit of the initiated, whereas 'phantastical' poetry – the explanation of which Proclus draws from Plato's negative treatment of the deceptive art of appearances in *The Sophist* (235–36) – presents perceptual illusions, in other words, fictional images or representations, designed to manipulate the readers' or listeners' emotions, their soul's *pathētikon*, subjecting them to (potentially dangerous) suggestive impact, *psychagōgia*.[1]

Thus we do not need to wait for Dante and the Renaissance authors of poetics to study the connection between the craft of poetry and imagination in full swing. However, we will look in vain in Late Antique culture for the considerable weight that the great Florentine writer, not to speak of the enthusiastic addicts to the Muses of later (Early Modern or Romantic) times, placed on this constellation. The Platonic theory of art, which left its mark on Augustine's *On the Trinity* in the early fifth century and was magnificently modulated as well as summarized by Proclus, generally speaks against it. In company with the notoriously suspected *phantasia sive imaginatio*, literary fiction – judging by the admirers of both the Trinity and the goddess Athena – could only be downgraded by what in modern English is called guilt by association.

*

Both *On the Trinity* and *The Literal Meaning of Genesis* belong to the new century, but the close connection between discursive imagery and imagination can be traced far back in Augustine's writings. We already find it in the anti-Manichaean address *Of True Religion*, one of the first treatises the convert composed after his return to Africa and Thagaste around 390. This work presents yet another clever definition of imagination, perhaps the most complete among the Church Father's writings alongside the analyses in *On the Trinity*. The apparitions and figures of imagination, *phantasmata*, it turns out, "are nothing but figments [*figmenta*] of corporeal shapes appearing to bodily sense. It is the easiest thing in the world to commit them to memory as they appear or, by thinking about them, to divide or multiply, contract or expand, set in order or disturb, or give them any kind of shape [*figurare cogitando*]. But when truth is being sought, it is difficult to be on one's guard against them and to avoid them." (10.18)[2]

---

[1] Proclus summarizes this scheme in his commentary 6.2, W. Kroll's edition 1899, 1.178.6–179.32. Cf. Sheppard 1980, pp. 162–201, Lamberton 1986, pp. 188–97, Kuisma 1996, pp. 122–30, and below, pp. 362ff.

[2] "Phantasmata porro nihil sunt aliud quam de specie corporis corporeo sensu attracta figmenta: quae memoriae mandare ut accepta sunt, vel partiri, vel multiplicare, vel contrahere, vel distendere, vel ordinare, vel perturbare, vel quolibet modo figurare cogitando facillimum est, sed

This closing observation, or warning, has an immediate relevance for the interpretation of the spiritual adventure in Ostia. In our efforts to reach God or to gain some idea of God's glory, it seems essential to check our propensity to think in images, the *figurare cogitando* that continuously occupies our imagination, what the confessor would call *imaginariae revelationes* (9.10.25). At best, such occasional visualizations can help us a bit on the way, acting as a kind of stimulus for the soul's interpretive activities. In that case, they arouse our curiosity, revealing themselves as signs of a higher order, whereupon they should withdraw to allow the soul's journey upwards to continue without hindrance. On the other hand, they might block the soul of ungodly man, ensnaring it by their physical power of attraction, "so that, when he thinks, he believes he understands, being deluded by shadowy phantasms" (20.40), *cum aliquid cogitat, intellegere se credat, umbris illusus phantasmatum*. Precisely this dependence on physical (bodily) perception makes imagination a frequent target, as Roland J. Teske has observed, for Augustine's anti-Arian polemic.[1] To sum up, if things turn out all right, dreams and subliminal representations can prepare the way for true insight, *intellegentia*, but mostly they confine the soul in a labyrinth of spectral images and deceptive phantasmagorias.

The further Augustine pursues his analysis of the mechanisms of imagination in *Of True Religion*, the more clearly he will associate it with fiction, and the more strongly he will mark his distance or his direct repudiation. The conclusion of this treatise is categorical: no legitimate faith can draw support from the mirages of imagination, *phantasmata*. Any truth is preferable to whatever we might choose to feign: *melius est enim qualecumque verum, quam omne quidquid pro arbitrio fingi potest*. Anything real, be it feeble or seemingly useless things like straw or stubble, is better than the light fabricated by some vain fantasy, *inanis cogitatio*, produced by the guesswork of our will (55.108). O'Connell has rightly observed that Augustine's aesthetic was of an extremely rational nature, becoming increasingly sceptical about all sensuous expressions of beauty, *pulchrum*. As a rule, the Church Father's analyses of written texts, oral discourse and visual art distanced themselves, sooner or later, from what he labelled *curiositas*, fallen man's dependence on signs and images, so as to be able to stretch out towards the lucid *sapientia* of the intellect.[2]

This Platonically tinged view of the quest for knowledge which, on the whole, understood the concept of art differently from the way we do today,

---

cum verum quaeritur, cavere et vitare difficile." All translations into English from *Of True Religion* are from J.S. Burleigh's edition 2006.
1 "Augustine, Maximinus, and Imagination", in Teske 2009, pp. 235–51.
2 O'Connell 1978, pp. 40f.

was to a certain degree that of the entire epoch. Nevertheless, there is undoubtedly a strong sense of personal commitment in Augustine's scepticism of all imaginative extravagances in poetry, painting or philosophy. Imagination was so troublesome – and of such fundamental importance – for him, since it had taken such a strong hold on him in his youth and had for such a long time blocked his own way towards true knowledge of God. This is repeatedly apparent from his *Confessions*, where the author complains about his protracted inability to think of God without a body. My heart cried out, he remembers, "in vehement protest against all the phantom shapes that thronged my imagination", *adversus omnia phantasmata mea*, and with this single defence – the cry, 'blow' or 'thrust' of his heart – he tried to chase away "the cloud of filth" that hovered across the gaze of his mind, *et hoc uno ictu conabar abigere circumvolantem turbam immunditiae ab acie mentis meae* (7.1.1). This wording directly anticipates Augustine's observation of the human soul's fluttering *phantasmata* that we have registered in *On the Trinity*.

Thus Augustine the confessor describes his former self as being caught up in a net of fantasies. Even though he knew better, his heart continually followed such misleading *imagines* (7.1.2). His first Neo-Platonically inspired *raptus*, remembered in the seventh book of his *Confessions*, was made possible, as we have noted, precisely because he left these swarms of illusions behind him to attain 'that which is', *id quod est*, "in the flash of one tremulous glance", *in ictu trepidantis aspectus* (7.17.23). Such a configuration, loaded with mystical resonances, seems, at this stage of our inquiry, easily recognizable:
- the dogged images or shapes of imagination gather in a hazy crowd, *turba*, in the speaker's soul, whereupon
- they are scattered by virtue of the instantaneous *ictus* of the (mental or physical) enraptured gaze, after which inevitably follows
- the relapse into the usual state of things, *solita*. The euphoric self is compelled, in a later wording from the same work, to shoulder anew "the burden of habit" (10.40.65), *consuetudinis sarcina*.

This thematic arrangement is just as easy to detect in the author's account of the experience at Ostia, which presupposes a safe distance from the *turbae* – here the "crowds" of people – and which surpasses everything corporeal, *cuncta corporalia*, to culminate in the heart's *ictus* with a subsequent recoil to the usual "noise" of the lips.

A similar mystical as well as iconoclastic pattern reappears in the remarkable passage from the eighth book of *On the Trinity*, which attempts to grasp the Godhead coinciding with Truth itself, *Deus Veritas*. Here, the author stresses that He should not be thought of (the verb is *cogitare*) in corporeal terms. Our conception of the Trinity must not mislead us into beginning to fantasize about some complex assemblage or combination of parts, *compago iuncturae*, such as the three-bodied Geryon we know from classical mythology, *fabulae*. Again, Augustine approaches God by means of an adverse comparison with fictional creatures. The Godhead is what they are not, hence the definition of Him presumes their exclusion. We have already come quite far along the way, the author states a little further on, if we have understood what God is not before we realize what He is. Such formulas tend to convert this whole passage from *On the Trinity* into an eloquent draft of negative theology. God does not resemble either anything secular or anything observable in heaven, Augustine addresses his readers, neither the light of the sun – not even if you magnify it in "the imagination of your thought", *imaginatio cogitationis* – nor any hosts of angels (8.2.3):

> Behold and see, if thou canst, O soul pressed down by the corruptible body, and weighed down by earthly thoughts, many and various; behold and see, if thou canst, that God is truth. For it is written that "God is light;" not in such way as these eyes see, but in such way as the heart sees, when it is said, He is truth. Ask not what is truth for immediately the darkness of corporeal images and the clouds of phantasms will put themselves in the way, and will disturb that calm which at the first twinkling shone forth to thee, when I said truth. See that thou remainest, if thou canst, in that first twinkling with which thou art dazzled, as it were, by a flash, when it is said to thee, Truth. But thou canst not; thou wilt glide back into those usual and earthly things. And what weight, pray, is it that will cause thee so to glide back, unless it be the bird-lime of the stains of appetite thou hast contracted, and the errors of thy wandering from the right path? (XV)

Here, the language of *On the Trinity* reminds us, as Andrew Louth observes in his enquiry into the origin of Christian mysticism, of the reflections on ecstasy in the *Confessions*.[1] Moreover, commentaries on the treatise generally detect allusions to pilgrimage in this paragraph, replete with both Biblical and Plotinian resonances (cf. the *Enneads* 1.6.8), similarly reminiscent of the author's autobiography.

Thus it seems that when Augustine set out to (re)construct his blessed moments in writing, he consistently used a limited number of building blocks in order to communicate his spiritual experience. In this passage from *On the Trinity*, he configures them as follows, sure enough in accordance with the *Confessions* as outlined above:
- Imagination's sensory world of images, *terrenae cogitationes*, is linked to clouds and mist in a strongly metaphorical expression, *caligines imaginum corporalium et nubila phantasmatum*.

---

[1] Louth 2007, pp. 144.

- Now these shadowy phantasms have to be expelled since they obscure our vision of God coalescent with Truth, a constellation that is both classically philosophical and Jewish-Christian. "Ask not what is truth", Augustine exclaims, since Pilate's old question only generates new vapours in the soul. As for the clear and unimpeded view that is to be opened up, it is of an inner rather than an outer nature, located in the world of the heart. As a matter of fact, it dazzles – somewhat paradoxically – the inquiring protagonist, since it is realized in a stunning "twinkling" or literally 'blow', *ictus*, an overpowering experience which both here and in *On the Catechising of the Uninstructed* is manifested by a flash of lightning, *coruscatio* (see above, p. 119).
- This merciful moment is finally followed by a relapse into an all too well-known normality, constantly associated with sinful appetite or lust.

The idea of our precarious dependence on the flocks of fantasies is typical of Augustine. In the concluding Book VI of *On Music*, he remarks that people find it difficult to concentrate on God's superior order in the universe and all too easily apprehend the movements of the Creation as disorganized and confused, *inordinata et perturbata* (6.11.30). He takes various kinds of rhythm as examples. At first, we perceive them (quite naturally) with our senses, whereupon they are stored as movements in our memory and images in our mind. All the resulting "crowds" of fantasies, *phantasmatum turbae*, will potentially distract us from the higher and true reality, from the vision of God face to face (6.16.51). This overarching pattern – entailing a contrast between theoretically reliable *phantasiai*, based on perception, and irresponsible *phantasmata*, an imaginary world, as it were, of second degree, "images of images" (6.11.32), *imaginum imagines* – may, of course, be varied and adapted according to the needs of different contexts, but it remains fairly constant throughout Augustine's writings. In the end, the Church Father felt obliged to expel the flickering shapes of imagination from his theological vision, partly because they arouse sensual desires that are negative inasmuch as they aim at pleasure, *frui*, for its own sake, and partly because they threaten to slip into irresponsible fictionality. These alarming prospects are closely linked to each other. Here, I can only deal with the relevance of imagination to the problem of cognition or, more precisely, of fictionality. Its long pedigree in the history of ideas, its functions in Augustinian psychology and its relationship to other faculties of the mind (such as memory) will have to be left out of our discussion.[1]

---

[1] For a good enquiry into Augustine's concept of imagination, its mental position and func-

In the prologue to the fourth book of *On the Trinity*, Augustine feels pity for those of his fellow men who have been satisfied with their idiosyncratic world of representations or fantasy, *phantasma*, rather than God's truth. But he also recognizes the beam in his own eye: "I certainly know how many figments the human heart gives birth to. And what is my own heart but a human heart? But I pray the God of my heart, that I may not vomit forth into these writings any of these figments for solid truths" (4.1.1).[1] It is easy to detect a personal note in these expressions. The word *eructuare*, 'belch', 'vomit', is quite strong. On behalf of his present work, then, Augustine declines such eructations – his ingrained aptitude for all kinds of fancies, desires, projections, in short: *figmenta* – in favour of divine truth. Here, it is theology's holy order that is expected to put imagination's phantoms to flight.

Man's dependence on *phantasmata* and *figmenta* evidently applies both to individuals like the author himself (especially when young) and to various groups or interpretive communities, for instance those Manichees who, judging by the *Confessions*, want to "find their joy in externals", in carnal or physical things, and "lick even the images of these things with their famished imagination" (9.4.10), *volentes enim gaudere forinsecus ... imagines eorum famelica cogitatione lambiunt*. This seems indeed to be mankind's lot. Show me one single person, Augustine exclaims in perhaps the most frequently quoted passage from *Of True Religion*, "a single man who can see without being influenced by imaginations derived from things seen in the flesh": *date mihi qui videat sine ulla imaginatione visorum carnalium*. The Rome that I can imagine is always another city than the one that actually stands on the Tiber and is therefore a false Rome. The same is true of the sun in the sky and of our friends: in addition to the one real sun, for instance, we might at any time conjure up imaginary ones in our thought. Augustine's suspicion of these latter is repeated like a mantra: 'false is the one I feign by imagination', *falsus est iste quem cogitans fingo*. Even the author himself might – regrettably – be reduplicated in this manner, going where he likes and speaking to whom he likes by virtue of his imagination and its games of make-believe, *figmento cogitationis*, always in sharp contrast to the moments of his intellectual contemplation of truth (34.64).

---

tions, see the chapter "Imagination" in O'Daly 1987, pp. 106–30. Mary Carruthers rightly observes that Augustinian psychology has to be understood in the context of trinitarian theology rather than Aristotelian faculty psychology, 2000, p. 34.

[1] "Ego certe sentio quam multa figmenta pariat cor humanum. Et quid est cor meum nisi cor humanum? Sed hoc oro Deum cordis mei ut nihil ex eis figmentis pro solido vero eructuem in has litteras".

Let us chastise our *phantasmata* and ban these trifling and deceitful games – *tam nugatorii et deceptorii ludi* – from the theatre of our souls, Augustine preaches a little later in *Of True Religion* (50.98). The association with drama in terms like *ludi* or *spectaculum mentis* is significant. All through his voluminous production, Augustine links, in this critical manner, the problem of iconic imagination to that of histrionic and literary fiction. Such deprecating gestures were not unusual among contemporary Christian writers. In a letter dated 396, Paulinus of Nola assures his addressee that his certainty about the posthumous blessings of the faithful did not originate in "human opinions, the fictitious dreams of poets, or the images of philosophers", *ab humanis opinionibus nec a fabulosis poetarum somniis aut philosophorum phantasmatis*, but in God himself, the source of all truth. Those who know His message, laid down in the testimony of the prophets or the apostles, have no need for the lies of the poets, *mendacia poetarum*, or for the erring opinions of philosophers (13.25).[1] If we are to believe the pious ascetic from Campania, human imagination had without good reason permeated the works of poets and philosophers alike. In classical times, the latter had often accused the former of contriving irresponsible inventions. Now both groups appeared in the Christian writers' eyes as evenly matched, that is to say, equally reprehensible fiction makers.

However, none of the apologists or Church Fathers devoted as much analytical energy to imagination as Augustine. For our purposes, it will be enough to examine yet another of his critical remarks, which is of special interest as it occurs so early among his writings: a letter he wrote to his Carthaginian friend Nebridius shortly after his return to Africa in 388. There, the convert discusses in detail the inevitable attachment of the imagination to our senses. His analysis is reminiscent of a regular Peripatetic or Stoic tract. Our imagination, he writes – following Aristotle's definition in *On the Soul* (428b) – is dependent on external impressions that stick in our memory.[2] But the figure Augustine uses to describe this state of things is hardly Aristotelian, quite the reverse: imagination is defined as a "wound" in the soul, "inflicted by the senses" (7.2.3), *nihil est aliud illa imaginatio, mi Nebridi, quam plaga inflicta per sensus*.

This letter is actually occasioned by a question from Nebridius as to how we can visualize faces and forms we have never seen with our own eyes. In his answer, Augustine divides our fantasies into three categories: those we perceive through our senses, those we believe in unaided by any sense impressions

---

[1] For the pejorative treatment of the concept of *phantasma* (detrimental perception, detrimental philosophy, detrimental art) in Paulinus, see Erdt 1976, pp. 244f.
[2] I have read *On the Soul*, frequently referred to with its Latin title, *De anima*, in W.S. Hett's Loeb edition 1957.

and those we consider with our reason, *unum sensis rebus impressum, alterum putatis, tertium ratis*. The first type of fantasy is quite simply based on the reality that we observe, have observed or have learnt to identify in some other way from our senses. Augustine exemplifies his argument with places where we are not physically present (Carthage), absent faces (Nebridius' own face) or dead friends (the recently deceased Verecundus, the writer's host in Cassiciacum). We immediately recognize the Aristotelian linking of imagination to perception. The third type of *imagines* consists mainly of numbers, rhythms and proportions, all subject to reason, in particular among people schooled in the logic and mathematical arts. Even if we understand them correctly, they are liable to bring forth "false imaginings", *falsae imaginationes*, due to our ingrained processing of all such figures by means of divisions and conclusions. If that seems bothersome, the tone of the letter darkens considerably when Augustine takes on the second type of fantasies (7.2.4):

> Those fall under another kind that we suppose to have been or to be in a certain way, for example, when for the sake of argument we imagine certain things that in no sense are an obstacle to the truth, the sort of things we picture when we read histories and when we hear or compose or invent myths. For I picture for myself the face of Aeneas, as I want and as it comes to my mind, the face of Medea with her winged serpents bound to the yoke, the faces of Chremes and a certain Parmenon. In this kind there are also included those that were substituted for the truth either by the wise who disguise a truth in such figures or by the foolish who found various superstitions, such as Phlegethon of the underworld, the five caves of the nation of darkness, the North Pole that holds up the heaven, and a thousand other portents of the poets and heretics. We say even in the midst of an argument: Suppose that there are three worlds, one on top of the other, such as this one world is; suppose that a square shape encloses the earth, and the like. We frame and think of all these as the mood of our thought would have them. (XVI)

In connection with this analysis of imagination, Sabine MacCormack has cited *Aeneid* 6.264–67, where the poet asks the gods and the silent shadows for help to depict Chaos, Phlegethon and the secret things of the underworld.[1] It is the world of poetry, superstition and fiction that Augustine focuses on in his letter to Nebridius, and even if he still appears as an impartial philosopher, we cannot mistake his reservations.

This subtle investigator of the soul and language realizes very well our natural desire to drive an argument with the help of suppositions and hypotheses. He is fully aware of the ways in which reading generates fictional representations, and he can equally well understand the habit of intellectual pagans,

---

1 MacCormack 1998, pp. 141f.

"the wise", to resort to tropes in their (true) speech when necessary, *aliquid veri talibus involventes figuris*. So far we have no difficulty in recognizing the probing philosopher from Cassiciacum. But when passing fancies intrude upon matters of religion, the convert is no longer prepared to make any concessions to classical culture. Even though Virgil still probably qualifies as one of the *sapientes* who enjoy his respect, the poet ends up in dangerous company with heretics due to his mythological scenarios, especially those in *Aeneid* VI. When indulgent allegorical interpretation is laid aside or ignored, the conflict between (true) knowledge and (false) fiction proves to be implacable: "For those things that we suppose and believe or invent [*fingimus*] are in every respect absolutely false, and those things that we see and sense are certainly far more true, as you recognize." (7.2.5)[1]

Augustine's analysis of the combinatory brilliance and associative-analogical mechanisms of imagination triumphs again in this epistle, but its main argument is nonetheless presented as a warning. For the very reason that imagination acts so freely and figures its representations so easily, we – the faithful – have every reason to beware! The gloomy closing words of the letter allude once again to *Aeneid* VI: "I earnestly warn you, my very dear and most delightful friend, not to enter into friendship with these shadows of the lower world and not to hesitate to break off that friendship you have begun. For in no way do we resist the senses of the body, which is for us a most sacred duty, if we show fondness for the blows and wounds they inflict." (7.3.7)[2] Augustine's letter concludes, then, with the ascetic metaphor of the wound, a few paragraphs earlier associated to the faculty of imagination, in this case stirred by Roman literature's supreme instance of epic poetry. The convert is firmly resolved to let his scars heal in peace.

---

[1] "Nam illa quae putamus et credimus, sive fingimus, et ex omni parte omnino falsa sunt, et certe longe, ut cernis, veriora sunt quae videmus atque sentimus."
[2] "Monuerim [...] nullam cum istis infernis umbris copules amicitiam, neve illam quae copulata est, cunctere divellere. Nullo enim modo resistitur corporis sensibus, quae nobis sacratissima disciplina est, si per eos inflictis plagis vulneribusque blandimur."

3 The Figures of the Spirit

Augustine's recurrent scepticism or repudiations of the world of imagination depend to some extent on his semiotics, which was to be one of his most important contributions to Western philosophy. In *Of True Religion*, as we shall soon see, he assumes two parallel systems of signs, both capable of producing complex figurations, those of nature and of language. In this section, after a brief presentation of the Church Father's theory of Nature's script – its more or less cryptic message encoded on earth or in the skies, the analogical network of Creation – we shall focus on his view of language and its particular way of representing or figuring meaning. It is probably in this field, abundant with hermeneutical, rhetorical and exegetical issues, that research on Augustine has been most active in recent years. Our following presentation is exclusively focused on the way the two sign structures relate to, determine or even frame the issue of fictionality.

The Speech of Creation

One of Augustine's most concentrated and revealing inquiries into God's ways of communicating with mankind is to be found in *Of True Religion* (50.98, Burleigh's translation slightly altered):

> Let us use the steps which divine providence has deigned to make for us. When we delighted over much in silly figments, and grew vain in our thoughts, and turned our whole life into vain dreams, the ineffable mercy of God did not disdain to use rational creation subject to his law [*rationali creatura serviente legibus suis*] to teach us by means of sounds and letters, by fire and smoke and cloudy pillar, as by visible words. So with parables and similitudes in a fashion he played with us when we were children, and sought to heal our inward eyes by smearing them with clay. (XVII)

On closer inspection, the whole of this extract rests on a Biblical foundation. In the early days of mankind, Moses heard the Lord, received the tablets of stone and saw the cloud alternate with fire in the sky. Likewise, it is still our duty to interpret the signals God once laid down – and continually lays down – in Creation. That is how the dust of vain fantasies will be lifted from our eyes, and we shall see as clearly as the blind man when Christ, according to John (9.6), had anointed his eyes with mud.

That this longed-for clarity of vision interacts with Augustine's characteristic ascension theme seems clear from the text's reference to "the steps which divine providence has deigned to make for us". God leads us to blessedness, to use a phrase from *The Teacher*, "by steps suited to our poor abilities" (8.21), *gradibus quibusdam infirmo gressui nostro accommodatis*.[1] The extract from *Of True Religion* demonstrates that at least the early steps on our way towards elucidation face us with certain semiotic challenges: a series of exercises, as it were, in a divinely prescribed interpretation of signs. Augustine sets up the codes we have to break in two broad categories:

- The sounds of speech and the letters of writing, that is, oral and written language.
- The things themselves: yet another language (in a transferred sense), a rich and varied amount of "visible words", *quaedam verba visibilia*, embedded in Creation.

This interest in signs, and in words as the privileged type of signs, will soon be one of the central themes in Augustine's writings. God has established two immense and fine-meshed systems of signs or figures available to our interpretive abilities, the meaning of which is warranted by His eternal law: language and the hierarchical order of things, organized as a series of *gradus* for the benefit of our defective intellectual powers. We recognize this consideration for our frail humanity from *On the Trinity*. Here is the origin, or at least one early suggestion, of a literary topos that would find its unsurpassable expression a thousand years later with Beatrice's divine tutorial in Dante's Paradise (4.40 – 48). In *Of True Religion*, where God turns to us "when we were children", *infantia nostra*, the Latin term functions not only as a historical reminder of the ancient vicissitudes of the Jews but just as much as an etymological pointer to the small child in want of speech, *infans*. In our present infantile state, then, we need "parables and similitudes" to be able to understand reality, for which reason God is benevolent enough to put his Creation's huge network of analogies at our service.

This phenomenon was already known in Alexandrian allegoresis, where Origen had been prone to characterize God's simplified language to mankind – sometimes likened to a father's words to his children, a teacher's to his students or a doctor's to his patients – with the term *symperiphora* ('accomodation', 'adjustment').[2] Admittedly, it is only a matter of temporary aid, relevant to the preliminary stages of true vision, Augustine points out, but nonetheless this holy scheme of signs would guide the faithful on their first steps towards God. Imagination's "silly figments", on the other hand, *figmenta ludicra*, tend to block true insight and should if possible be eliminated. They were denied any natural place

---

[1] Cf. *On Order*, 2.9.27.
[2] Hanson 1959, pp. 225 – 28. Cf. Wiles 1970, pp. 464f.

in the semiotics of Creation which here, with inexorable logic, is called rational: *rationalis creatura*.

This ancient concept of the eloquent speech or text of Creation permeates Augustine's writings, frequently – as in *Of True Religion* – in contrast to the unsubstantial fictions of human arbitrariness. In the *Confessions*, the cosmos is penned in accordance with the matrix of the Old Testament: "Moreover you alone, our God, have made for us a vault overhead in giving us your divine scripture. The sky will one day be rolled up like a book, but for the present it is stretched out above us like the skin of a tent" (13.15.16).[1] The ancient concept of a heavenly script is specified here, on the pattern of the prophet Isaiah, as a bookroll, one of the earliest presages of the concept of the world as a book, *liber mundi*, which would gain such popularity in the High Middle Ages, turned into didactic poetry by Alan of Lille and into paradisiacal *terza rima* by Dante.[2] This is Augustine's way of metaphorically expressing the insight into the double nature of signs which he simultaneously formulated with such theoretical discernment and pregnancy in *On Christian Doctrine:* "Some signs are natural, others given" (2.1.2), *signorum igitur alia sunt naturalia, alia data*.

By far the most important category of "given" or conventional, that is, intentional signs are the *verba* of human language, which will be the main subject of our next sections. *Signa naturalia*, for their part, are exemplified, precisely as in *Of True Religion*, with the smoke that indicates fire. This is a kind of sign that is not controlled by any human intention. It amounts to the figurations of the elements, the stars in the sky, in sum, all the natural phenomena that in a transferred sense could be described as letters in a cosmic or divine alphabet. There, in the sign system of Creation itself, *analogia entis*, we can read about and acquire knowledge of God and his all-embracing reality.

In the same semiotic and rhetorical treatise, Augustine makes a crucial distinction between the things that are there to be used, *uti*, and those that are there to be enjoyed, *frui*. This difference agrees with a Platonic contrast between material and invisible (divine) reality. It is the latter that is to be enjoyed to the full.

---

[1] "Aut quis nisi tu, deus noster, fecisti nobis firmamentum auctoritatis super nos in scriptura tua divina? caelum enim plicabitur ut liber et nunc sicut pellis extenditur super nos." Cf. Isaiah 34.4 and Psalms 103/104.2.

[2] Cf. the frequently quoted lines from a *rhythmus* by Alan on all things created, likened to a book, a picture and a mirror of ourselves: *Omnis mundi creatura, / quasi liber, et pictura / nobis est, et speculum*, PL 210.579a, and Dante's even better-known lines, from the last canto of the *Comedy*, on all scattered leaves of the universe which are finally bound, with love, into one single volume: "Nel suo profondo vidi che s'interna, / legato con amore in un volume, / ciò che per l'universo si squaderna", Paradiso 33.85–87.

The world of the senses can only be explored or 'used' as a preparation for this ultimate pleasure and repose. Mankind's decisive problem in this connection is its lack of patience: rather than aiming at eternal bliss it would like to enjoy the fruits of this transitory world right now, which, accordingly, tend to become an end in themselves. Instead, these fruits should be considered as signs, and nothing else, for God's immaterial reality. Thus Creation constantly shows the way or refers to its Creator, a Pauline thought to which Augustine gives a Neo-Platonic emphasis: "in other words, to ascertain what is eternal and spiritual from corporeal and temporal things" (1.4.4), *hoc est ut de corporalibus temporalibusque rebus aeterna et spiritalia capiamus.*

One of the Church Father's most suggestive expressions of this phenomenal web of signs – to be used rather than enjoyed – is to be found in his long fifty-fifth letter, written in 400 and addressed to his layman brother Januarius, who had asked him about various liturgical and ceremonial issues connected with the ecclesiastical year and the sacraments. The obvious and simple fact that the Holy Writ occasionally relies on the heavenly bodies as similitudes for the representation of divine mysteries (55.6.11), *ducitur ex eis aliquando similitudo ad divina mysteria figuranda*, does not necessarily mean that they are to be worshipped, Augustine emphasizes. The Bible actually draws materials for such figurative purposes from the whole of Creation. Not only the heavenly bodies but doves and serpents, as in Matthew 10.16, or the harp, in the Book of Psalms, might provide "signs to represent the mysteries of the word of God" (55.7.12), *ad mysteria verbi Dei, similitudinum signa.*

Correspondingly, Augustine continues, with his usual suspicion of the theatre, the Holy Writ's occasional reliance on such figures does not in any way entitle us to act as bird-watchers or snake-charmers, or to long for the depraved pleasures of the playhouse (where harp music was commonly performed). This cautionary exemplification is soon followed by a virtual catalogue of Creation's legitimate signs and signals (55.7.13):

> Thus with the freedom of Christians we use the rest of creation, the winds, the sea, the earth, birds, fishes, animals, trees, and human beings in many ways for speaking, but for the celebration of the sacraments we use only a very few, such as water, wheat, wine, and oil. [...] But if any symbolic likenesses are taken not only from the heavens and the stars, but also from the lower creation for the presentation of the mysteries, the result is a certain eloquence of a teaching conducive to salvation that is suited to turn the affections of the learners from visible things to invisible ones, from bodily things to nonbodily ones, and from temporal things to eternal ones. (XVIII)

In this letter to Januarius, Augustine accepted the difficult challenge of distinguishing the Biblical interpretation of the world both from Manichaean astrological conceptions and from the backbiters of Christianity who accused it of worshipping material things. He solved the problem brilliantly. On the one hand, he emphasizes that the whole of Creation is there to be used by the Holy Writ and its expositors; on the other hand, he underlines the role of figuration in this context. If Creation at all levels is interpreted as a storehouse of figures "for the presentation of the mysteries", *ad dispensationem sacramentorum*, as in the Bible, its encoded message can arguably be ascribed an eloquence of its own, *eloquentia quaedam*.

The language of Creation is evidently of a rhetorical nature and can therefore just as well be qualified as the speech of Creation. Augustine does not, however, content himself with such a general label but moves on to specify this all-pervading eloquence of Being for Januarius. He refers to the crucial purpose of rhetoricians to arouse strong "affections" in order to move their audiences, as defined by Quintilian in more or less the same terms (8.PR.7), *ad movendum adfectus*. In his treatise on the *Orator*, Cicero had especially emphasized the role of figuration or, more exactly, of metaphors for this emotional effect (39.134), "because these figures by virtue of the comparison involved transport the mind and bring it back, and move it hither and thither; and this rapid stimulation of thought in itself produced pleasure."[1] Augustine takes over Cicero's wording but adapts it in accordance with his Christian needs and purposes. For him too, the *similitudines* of speech seem pivotal, but here they are, in the first place, applied to God's Creation; secondly, they do not arouse any pleasure in themselves, and thirdly, their rapid swinging to and fro in the imagination has been replaced by an irreversible one-way movement. Their function in Augustine's Christian eloquence is to "turn" (literally, move or transfer) the audience's or the readers' feelings from the *signa* of physical Creation to *sacramenta*, the holy mysteries of a spiritual order, and finally – by implication – to the divine referent or *res*.

A few years earlier, in the *Confessions*, Augustine had set out to put our provisional dependence on signs into perspective by imagining, for the sake of contrast, a cognitive state altogether different from that of the human mind. The angels, who dwell above the skies, the author declares on the final pages of his autobiography addressed to God, "have no need to look up at the vault and learn by reading your word in it", *non opus habent suspicere firmamentum hoc et legendo cognoscere verbum tuum*. They do not need to take any detours through created things to get to know the origin of Creation itself. The angels be-

---

[1] "Eae propter similitudinem transferunt animos et referunt ac movent huc et illuc, qui motus cogitationis celeriter agitatus per se ipse delectat."

hold God face to face, a vision that circumvents the syllables of time, *sine syllabis temporum*. In that blessed state they are able to read, follow and love the unalterable divine will (13.15.18). Once again, Augustine the rhetorician applies his figurative devices – here: the symmetrical triad of verbs – as if to give an indication of the heavenly eloquence he can only imitate in temporal and sequential discourse: *legunt eligunt et diligunt*.

The codex of the angels, then, is never closed; their *liber* is never rolled up. Poor humans, on the other hand, are constrained to trying to grasp the divine Word in the enigma of the clouds or in the mirror of the skies: here, the subtext from the First Epistle to the Corinthians 13.12 is easily perceptible. The angels' *sapientia* is unmediated, intuitive and instantaneous; our *scientia* is semiotically conditioned, discursive and changing over time. As an example, Augustine takes the "sacred signs" of the moon and the stars, *sacramenta quae variantur temporibus*. In His goodness, God has taught us to perceive everything in the light from the book of the firmament, but, as yet, it is only accessible to us in the categories of time, "through signs, and transient phases, and passing days and years", *in signis et in temporibus et in diebus et in annis*. This final twist of the *Confessions* 13.18.23, construed as a polysyndetic coordination, impresses the predicament of time on the readers, the chronological patchwork to which Augustine devotes the eleventh book of his autobiography.

The great code of Creation includes the crown of Creation: mankind, according to the Bible made by God in His image, after His likeness. No writer before Augustine, and none between him and Montaigne, drew such far-reaching psychological conclusions from this analogy. In *homo sapiens*, or more precisely in his soul, the work of Creation appears in its full potential. That is why the Church Father made psychology a central theme, possibly *the* central theme, in his philosophy as well as in his theology. It is the structural parallelism between the Trinity and the human soul that forms the basis of what has frequently been called his main work in these two disciplines, *On the Trinity*. By self-examination, our inquiring mind might provide us with important clues about the nature of the Godhead. With good reason, introspection could be called the very nerve in Augustine's writing, and nowhere is it practised with such vibrant sensitivity and such piercing persistence as in his *Confessions*. His framing of the miracle at Ostia testifies to this effect. Here, the writer and his mother begin by traversing the world of things, *cuncta corporalia*, then move on to the cosmos – the sun, the moon and the stars – and then further on, into themselves: "Higher still we mounted by inward thought"…

But even though this analogical construction of Creation, including the human mind, bears witness to its divine origin, even though the gaze *extra se* and *intra se* prepares for the move *supra se*, the system has its natural limitations. Despite the experience at Ostia, Augustine remained as convinced as Paul – and Plotinus – that we inevitably see dimly, as in a mirror. For all its suggestive hints and indications, the speech of Creation finally leaves its listeners unsatisfied. This is a pessimistic admission that finds an outlet in the unexpected closing lines of On the Trinity (15.27.50), where those mental triads that had been framed and lined up throughout the work as an abundant series of analogies with the Trinity are suddenly collapsed, as if to demonstrate once and for all the inadequacy of all semiotic codes before God: "But among these many things which I have now said, there is nothing that I dare to profess myself to have said worthy of the ineffableness of that highest Trinity; I would rather confess that the wonderful knowledge of Him is too great for me, and that I cannot attain to it".[1]

We recognize the last words of this resigned declaration from the psalmist in the Bible (138/139.6). They tell us that the imagery of both Nature and language is, after all, deficient: temporary compensations, or, at best, pledges for a purer and clearer understanding of divine things. Such scepticism, however, does not imply any radical rejection of those ultimately flawed semiotic networks. What use is it for the human race, Augustine asks in the same text that we started out from above, Of True Religion, if divine Providence speaks to us in this way, 'by rational, generative and corporeal Creation' (50.99), per rationalem, et genitalem, et corporalem creaturam? His own answer to this question takes the form of what might be called a minimalistic programme for the knowledge of God; such speech alone, however insufficient, proves at least helpful in our efforts toward illumination. Even if Nature has only succeeded in awakening our curiosity about its Creator, it has fulfilled its task and can retire out of our focus. Once we have learnt how to interpret the text of Creation, we are able to decode its figurations and may begin to read between the lines.

But whether this programme outlines knowledge's ideal progress from Nature to the Creator or from the human soul to the Trinity, it definitely brackets our fictions or fantasies. They simply fulfil no purpose among the indications about the Creator that Creation makes available to us. This is a characteristic dismissal we recognize by now. In Of True Religion the 'jests' or 'trifles', nugae, of poetry and the stage add up to the sacrifice that has to be made on the way towards enlightenment (51.100 – 52.101):

> Putting aside, therefore, all theatrical and poetic trifling, let us by the diligent study of the divine Scriptures, find food and drink for our minds; for they are weary and parched with

---

[1] "Verum inter haec quae multa iam dixi, et nihil illius summae Trinitatis ineffabilitate dignum me dixisse audeo profiteri, sed confiteri potius mirificatam scientiam eius ex me invaluisse, nec posse me ad illam". Translation slightly modified.

the hunger and thirst of vain curiosity, and desire in vain to be refreshed and satisfied with silly phantasms, as unreal as painted banquets. Let us be wholesomely educated by this truly liberal and noble game. If wonderful and beautiful spectacles afford us delight, let us desire to see wisdom "which teaches from one end to the other with might, and pleasantly disposes of all things." What is more wonderful than incorporeal might making and ruling the corporeal world? What more beautiful than its ordering and adorning the material world?

All admit that these things are perceived by the body, and that the mind is better than the body. Will not the mind by itself have some object that it can perceive which must be far more excellent and far nobler? We are put in mind by the things of which we are judges to look to that standard by which we judge. We turn from artistic works to the law of the arts, and we shall behold with the mind the form by comparison with which all the things are tarnished which its very goodness has made beautiful. "For the invisible things of God from the creation of the world are clearly seen, being understood by the things that are made, even his eternal power and Godhead." (XIX)

The final quotation is taken from the Epistle to the Romans 1.20. The whole passage presupposes a clear distinction between the invisible Creator and the visible objects of Creation: things and bodies. This distinction is framed in aesthetic categories. Augustine is fully aware of women's and men's attraction to poetry and the theatre, in other words, to the fictional worlds of art. He wants to show that in the long run they deceive us. They hold out the promise of nothing but painted and hence meaningless banquets. The alternative of the didactic novice is, suitably, an altogether different "game", *ludus*, from which we can learn something sensible. This game is not only more noble than theatrical tricks but also "truly liberal", *vere liberalis*, possibly in contrast to the seemingly free or liberal arts. Here, Augustine's guiding argument is construed *a fortiori*: if we are already so enchanted by plays and poetry which tempt us with their beauty, but on closer inspection prove to be mere trifles, how wonderful will not God's own art appear to us?

This way of thinking presupposes a conception of *ars*, aesthetic as well as linguistic or mathematical, that was fairly widespread in antique culture: true art is of a theoretical nature. It consists of a set of axioms, definitions and discernments that can be variously materialized or demonstrated in each individual work. This ideal, a theory of art that *a priori* surpasses each individual manifestation of art, is actually a logical consequence of Platonic aesthetics. "Some perverse persons prefer a verse to the art of versifying", Augustine complains in *Of True Religion*, "because they set more store by their ears than by their intelligence. So many love temporal things and do not look for divine providence which is the maker and governor of time." (22.43)[1] It is such an emphasis on theory that lies behind the term *ars* for disciplines such as astronomy or geometry. In this perspective, God can appear as the superior artist (39.72), *summus artifex*, the unseen and creative but also the "ordering and adorning" principle, *ordinans et ornans*, that governs the visible universe.

Accordingly, God can be praised as a consummate rhetorician or even a poet, whereupon Creation emerges as His copiously figured speech or poem. This idea, which along with the world-as-a-book theme will frequently appear throughout Western literature, has its *locus classicus* in Augustine, in the eleventh book of the *City of God*, where God deals with the world order as with a beautiful poem, and adorns it, as it were, with antitheses, *ordinem saeculorum tamquam pulcherrimum carmen etiam ex quibusdam quasi antithetis honestaret*. Just as such antitheses – in Latin commonly known as *opposita* or, in Quintilian (9.3.81), *contraposita* – embellish speech, Augustine underlines, so does God present the beauty of the world or of history: its tensions eventually fade into an overall harmony. That is how He implements "a kind of eloquence in events, instead of in words", *quaedam non verborum, sed rerum eloquentia* (11.18). This superior form of figuration, that of reality itself, is necessarily both more instructive and more beautiful than actual poetry's or the living theatre's structurally analogous but vain and deceptive fictional diversions.

The Bible: Tropes and Mysteries

One of several conceivable ways of describing Augustine's career would be to highlight a shift from the inquisitive young man's philosophical intellectuality, with strong Platonic overtones, to the bishop's hard-won experience of the intellect's shortcomings caused by original sin. His increasing concern for cognitively enfeebled man, erring among divergent doctrines of faith and a plethora of superstitious beliefs, led him to an intense study of the unique medium of knowledge that God had provided for the human race, the inexhaustible cure for its damaged powers of reason: the Bible.

Over the years, Augustine became inclined to make a distinction between three kinds of writing:

---

[1] "Itaque, ut nonnulli perversi magis amant versum, quam artem ipsam qua conficitur versus, quia plus se auribus quam intellegentiae dediderunt: ita multi temporalia diligunt, conditricem vero ac moderatricem temporum divinam providentiam non requirunt".

- the Biblical, which is true,
- and the classical pagan, which sometimes may be true (for example, in historiography or in the strictly theoretical expositions of the liberal arts),
- but is frequently false (as in much epic poetry or drama).

Thus the Bible is unique. Much more effectively than the obscure speech of Creation, it grants us access to the truth. Nonetheless, it was composed by human beings, characterized by certain techniques of configuring and communicating meaning typical of all human writing. Accordingly, it makes use of the same kind of tropes that are registered in the arts of grammar or rhetoric and which permeate the suspect pagan fictions. That is why the Bible requires an interpretive theory of its own that takes into account its status both as a sacred document and as a linguistic artefact. Such is the background of the Church Father's pioneering achievement in the fields of exegesis and hermeneutics.

At the beginning of *On the Trinity*, Augustine marked out the middle course between negative theology and Bible studies, a path that was to prove crucial to medieval religiosity. In theory, God appears ineffable, impossible to capture in human and sensory categories such as colour or sound, memory or oblivion, time or space. Consequently, we must purge our souls of all that is worldly before we can contemplate His true being or, as Augustine puts it, before we are able "to see ineffably that which is ineffable" (1.1.3), *illud ineffabile ineffabiliter videri*. Again, we can perceive the Church Father's double obligations to the *Enneads* (the purgation of the soul) and to Paul (the vision face to face). It seems equally clear that even in our actual godforsaken state there is room for hope, since the Bible grants us a provisional and at least approximate knowledge of God. It resorts to all kinds of things – however low or apparently insignificant – in order to speak about Him (1.1.2):

> In order, therefore, that the human mind might be purged from falsities of this kind, Holy Scripture, which suits itself to babes has not avoided words drawn from any class of things really existing, through which, as by nourishment, our understanding might rise gradually to things divine and transcendent. For, in speaking of God, it has both used words taken from things corporeal, as when it says, "Hide me under the shadow of Thy wings;" and it has borrowed many things from the spiritual creature, whereby to signify that which indeed is not so, but must needs so be said: as, for instance, "I the Lord thy God am a jealous God;" and, "It repenteth me that I have made man." But it has drawn no words whatever, whereby to frame either figures of speech or enigmatic sayings, from things which do not exist at all. And hence it is that they who are shut out from the truth by that third kind of error are more mischievously and emptily vain than their fellows; in that they surmise respecting God, what can neither be found in Himself nor in any creature. (XX)

Like quite a few of Augustine's writings, *On the Trinity* insists on the ability of the intellect to "rise" (*assurgere*) towards God, but here text interpretation – exegesis – is highlighted as a critical step of this process. The Church Father thus proposes an important departure from the Plotinian pattern, probably due to the fact that, not least during the late phase of his career when *On the Trinity* was written, Augustine had the Christian community and congregation rather than the enlightened elite in mind. In general, he emphasized more strongly than Plotinus the precarious dependence of frail mankind on the body and the senses. Ragnar Holte has observed how, as early as in his first commentary on Genesis, *De Genesi contra Manichaeos* (*On Genesis. A Refutation of the Manichees*) from 388–89, Augustine takes as his starting point the Fall of Man, which had destroyed mankind's direct communication with God. As a consequence, the human race turned outward, obsessed by the material world, neglecting or repressing God's presence in the soul. Notwithstanding, thanks to the Incarnation and the books of the Bible, humanity was given an opportunity to provisionally "recover its original state".[1] In the New Covenant, the Bible could be read as a replica of the Word Incarnate, of Christ's own *sacramentum*. There, in the Holy Writ, God had made His intention with Creation uniquely manifest, even when it was expressed in figures – such as similes or metaphors – so as to fit in with fallen man's inadequate powers of understanding.

In *On Genesis. A Refutation of the Manichees*, Augustine remarks that the story of the Creation of man in the second chapter of Genesis "is to be analyzed in figurative, not literal terms, to put the minds of those who seek the truth through their paces, and lure them away from the business of the world and the flesh to the business of the spirit" (2.1.1).[2] Along these lines, several years before his intensified studies of Paul in the middle of the 390s, Augustine, profoundly engaged in polemics with the Manichees, warned against the danger of getting stuck at the sensory level of the text. Such an immersion in the literal sense represented basically a hedonistic way of reading that the Church Father, at this stage of his career, would condemn in the strongest terms. He refused to give priority to *verba* before *res*, to images before things, to signs before their significance, essentially in accord with the Neo-Platonic primacy of "enjoyment" (of the transcendent signified) at the expense of "use" (of transitory signifiers) that

---

1 Holte 1958, pp. 331f. Cf. Dawson 1995, pp. 128–31.
2 E. Hill's translation, Augustine 2002b ("non aperte, sed figurate explicatur, ut exerceat mentes quaerentium veritatem, et spiritali negotio a negotiis carnalibus avocet"). For a comparison between the ideas of figuration in *On Genesis. A Refutation of the Manichees* and *On Christian Doctrine*, see Teske 1995.

we have seen him sketch out in the pious semiotics that permeates the first book of *On Christian Doctrine*.

On the basis of such a spiritualizing text theory, Augustine stressed the key function of the Holy Writ for salvation, in principle available to each and every one of us. He could draw support for this viewpoint from his own crucial experience of Bible reading, thoroughly documented in his *Confessions*.[1] There, it is surely his use of Paul at his conversion in the garden that is the best-known episode (8.12.29), but his ensuing Bible studies, accompanied by song and prayer, are perhaps even more significant. In Cassiciacum, Augustine read the Book of Psalms, he recalls in his *Confessions*, uttering cries: *voces dedi*. He would like to show the Manichees what the fourth psalm "did to me", *quid de me fecerit*, and, moreover, between the words of the psalm he added his own (9.4.8). This is an early example of the oral as well as "meditative" reading of the Bible that would prove instrumental in the development of medieval monastic culture.[2]

It might be characterized, in short, as a profound personal engagement with the text, a spiritual exercise, an interpretive process aiming at intuitive recognition: "As I read these words outwardly and experienced their truth inwardly I shouted with joy" (9.4.10), *et exclamabam legens haec foris et agnoscens intus*. This new way of reading, by and large unknown in Antiquity, was probably gaining ground among pious Christians precisely in the fourth century. To all appearances it was embraced by Plotinus' translator, Marius Victorinus, who, if we are to believe the churchman Simplicianus in the *Confessions*, untiringly researched all Christian writings: "he drank in courage from his avid reading" (8.2.4), *legendo et inhiando hausit firmitatem*. But like no other ecclesiastical teacher of the fourth and fifth centuries, Augustine would saturate his soteriology with rhetoric and hermeneutics. To him, salvation was to a high degree a matter of reading comprehension, of the art of correctly understanding and explaining the holy message that had been preserved in the words of the Scripture.

The key to this deciphering process can be specified in one simple phrase: the study of signs and figures. Augustine, the trained teacher of rhetoric, had of course a sharp eye for the figurative language of the Bible, but it was not simply a matter of analysing the prophets and the evangelists according to some tem-

---

[1] In his autobiography, Augustine recalls affectionately the bishop who had once comforted Monnica when she worried over her young son's Manichaean inclinations: "He will find out for himself through his reading how wrong these beliefs are, and how profoundly irreverent" (3.12.21), *ipse legendo reperiet quis ille sit error et quanta impietas*.
[2] Brian Stock has meticulously elucidated Augustine's importance for this kind of contemplative Bible reading in his two works published in 1996 and 2001.

plate in Cicero's or Quintilian's manuals. As we may remember, the convert had taken leave of "the market of speechifying". On that market, speakers normally wanted to move, teach or amuse their audiences. The Bible, for its part, was certainly not intended for amusement, but its authors had understood the importance of capturing their readers, and above all their ambition had been to communicate an irreproachable truth about sacred things. Consequently, the Holy Writ demanded a keen analytical and stylistic competence of its expositors that, reinforced with an updated set of semiotic tools, could do justice to the Spirit's own figures.

Augustine developed this new discipline, a revolutionary achievement in the field of cultural theory, in *On Christian Doctrine*, the bulk of which (1–3.35.51) was completed at about the same time as, or just before, his *Confessions*, while the remainder of Book III and the whole of Book IV were written – after a remarkable lapse in time – during the last years of his life. But he returned to the study of figures of speech, as we shall see, in a series of different contexts, and we shall give it our attention since it frequently raises issues concerning fiction or fictionality. It should be pointed out, however, that in this particular field, Augustine's terminology could shift over time. The following survey will focus on his basic attitudes to figuration and text interpretation as they appear from a strikingly mobile set of critical concepts. In the briefest possible of summaries, with reservation for the fluctuations of the Church Father's vocabulary, we might characterize his innovative contribution to the Late Antique ideas of discursive imagery as follows. With important starting points in Pauline hermeneutics, he established *allegoria* as the central figure of the Bible, its main trope, released from its dependence on the metaphor. To that purpose he actually expanded his concept of allegory far beyond the traditional scope of a rhetorical trope. It became a whole new way of writing or a special system for generating meaning, typical of the Bible's mystical method of communicating its divine message. In Augustine's eyes, it became first and foremost a technique for short-circuiting the network of fictional tensions that tended to infiltrate all language, including that of the Bible.

*

In the Roman Empire that had recently become (officially) Christian after more than a thousand years of ancestral worship, emperor cults and all sorts of mystery religions, one source of dogmatic conflict after another flared up. That is why it was so essential for the Church Fathers in general, and the North African Augustine in particular, to recognize, define and delimit true faith on the basis of the Bible. During the early years of his career, in the light of his Neo-Platonic and Pauline hermeneutics, Augustine often had occasion to highlight the spiritualizing imagery of the Bible. This was one of the recurring themes in the long-lasting polemic he carried on against the Manichees shortly before and after the turn of the fifth century. The stumbling block in this context was the Old Testament, which many Manichees read literally and thus, with reference to all its supposed absurdities and contradictions, tried to disqualify as a Christian document. This was an intricate problem, since Augustine's line of defence – suggesting that the language of the Old Testament was actually figurative – might in turn provoke suspicions of fictional strands in the verbally inspired text. If the Bible shared fundamental structures of meaning and interpretive issues with all kinds of figurative language, the task remained to identify its particular or indeed unique way of representing divine truth.

One of Augustine's first clashes with the Manichees is reported in *De moribus Ecclesiae catholicae et De moribus Manichaeorum libri duo* (*On the Morals of the Catholic Church, and On the Morals of the Manichaeans*, henceforth *On the Morals*) from the late 380s. There, he went on the offensive against his opponents' materialism, demonstrating the intimate connection between the Testaments while emphasizing the edifying power of the Bible's style (1.17.30):

> What more do you wish? Why do you resist ignorantly and obstinately? Why do you pervert untutored minds by your mischievous teaching? The God of both Testaments is one. For as there is an agreement in the passages quoted from both, so is there in all the rest, if you are willing to consider them carefully and impartially. But because many expressions are undignified, and so far adapted to minds creeping on the earth, that they may rise by human things to divine, while many are figurative, that the inquiring mind may have the more profit from the exertion of finding their meaning, and the more delight when it is found, you pervert this admirable arrangement of the Holy Spirit for the purpose of deceiving and ensnaring your followers. As to the reason why divine Providence permits you to do this, and as to the truth of the apostle's saying, "There must needs be many heresies, that they which are approved may be made manifest among you," it would take long to discuss these things, and you, with whom we have now to do, are not capable of understanding them. I know you well. To the consideration of divine things, which are far higher than you suppose, you bring minds quite gross and sickly, from being fed with material images. (XXI)

For Augustine, the Christian preacher and teacher, the Bible was an exemplary document since it spoke to common and educated people alike. It satisfied both his burgeoning egalitarian and his lingering esoteric concept of the text. This is evident in his polemical treatise against the Manichees, where he eloquently argues, just as we have seen him do at the beginning of *On the Trinity*, for the Bible's eminent ability to address widely different interpretive communities. On the one hand, Biblical discourse could resort to low levels of style in order to adapt to simple minds bent down to earth. It speaks humbly or modestly, *submisse*, a Ciceronian term that Augustine would use in *On Christian Doctrine* to indicate the low, didactic style (4.17.34). The writers of the Bible had exploited it for pedagogical purposes, we understand from *On the Morals*, so as not to discourage the uneducated readers or listeners but to direct their gaze, little by little, towards the heights.

On the other hand, there are passages in the Holy Writ replete with figures of speech associated with a different level of style and aimed at a different category of readers, those familiar with literature. Thus Augustine launched his own variant of the resilient Horatian formula appealing to profit as well as delight, which he applied to this initiated understanding of the Bible. The profit consists in the intellectual and exegetical training, *exercitatio*, advanced readers get while trying to decode and understand the sometimes difficult imagery of the Holy Writ. The delight comes from the wonderful findings, *inventa*, which result from their arduous tasks of interpretation. This double reward in store for assiduous Bible students is formulated most succinctly by Augustine in *On Christian Doctrine* IV, where the obscure passages of the Holy Writ are declared useful for the reader's faculties of understanding, "not just by making discoveries but also by undergoing exertion" (4.6.9), *non solum inventione verum etiam exercitatione*. Admittedly, the fourth book of *On Christian Doctrine* was conceived long after *On the Morals*, in the last years of the author's life, but it is not unlikely that this Augustinian emphasis on *exercitatio*, audible throughout his works, originates from his early anti-heretical controversies. The literally minded Manichees had to be convinced of the benefit of the intellectual exercise that the Bible's figurative language demanded of its interpreters.[1]

The Manichees were actually just one of the problematic groups that Augustine had to confront in schismatic circumstances, and during the last two decades of his life he no longer needed to refute them in writing, partly because his earlier polemical efforts had been so efficacious. This success, however, made his reputation grow across the whole of the Mediterranean region. He was frequently consulted in dogmatic or exegetical matters from various provinces, and in this correspondence he often seized the opportunity to describe the Biblical type of figuration in greater detail. One of the fellow believers who turned to the increasingly famous Bishop of Hippo to ask for advice was Consentius of Hispania Balearica (the Balearic Islands). He had difficulties with a group of heretics, the Priscillianists, who used to preach their allegedly false – ascetic –

---

[1] Marrou presents and discusses at length the technique for *exercitatio animi* in Augustine, 1938, pp. 299–327, while O'Connell highlights its important place in his anti-Manichaean polemics, as in his *Confessions* on the whole, 1969, pp. 15f.

doctrines under the cloak of orthodoxy. Consentius sought to combat them with their own weapon: infiltration. But was this legitimate? Was it permissible to dissimulate or even lie for a good cause? To get answers to such questions, Consentius wrote to Augustine, who answered with a whole treatise in 420, *Contra mendacium* (*Against Lying*), to be read alongside the tract *On Lying* that he had already devoted to this subject twenty-five years earlier, in 394–95. Both works, in particular *Against Lying*, take the problem very seriously, studying it from various angles, but it is not difficult to sum up Augustine's fundamental attitude: lies are never defensible, not even as a means to a good end, for in the long run they will always compromise the true faith, despite any short-term benefits.

Against Lying indicates that Consentius had pondered a great deal on the question himself. He seems to have found it particularly difficult to deal with the critics of Christianity who pointed out the obvious absurdities and errors that could be found in both Testaments. However, the master in Hippo took great pains to untie the knot. Yes, Jacob may seem to lie in Genesis 27, Augustine admits, when he deceives his dim-sighted father into mistaking him for his older twin brother Esau, and this is potentially a serious problem, since it concerns a patriarch, one of the Bible's authoritative figures; still, this Biblical passage does not represent a lie but a *mysterium*. To explain this term, the Church Father provides a long section that seems so fundamental for his understanding of tropes and figures that I feel obliged to reproduce it virtually *in extenso*, although I have divided it into four paragraphs to facilitate the reading. It starts from the discussion of Jacob's stratagem (10.24):

> The which if we shall call lies, all parables also, and figures designed for the signifying of any things soever, which are not to be taken according to their proper meaning, but in them is one thing to be understood from another, shall be said to be lies: which be far from us altogether. For he who thinks this, may also in regard of tropical expressions of which there are so many, bring in upon all of them this calumny; so that even metaphor, as it is called, that is, the usurped transferring of any word from its proper object to an object not proper, may at this rate be called a lie. For when he speaks of waving corn-fields, of vines putting forth gems, of the bloom of youth, of snowy hairs; without doubt the waves, the gems, the bloom, the snow, for that we find them not in those objects to which we have from other transferred these words, shall by these persons be accounted lies. And Christ a Rock, and the stony heart of the Jews; also, Christ a Lion, and the devil a lion, and innumerable such like, shall be said to be lies.
>
> Nay, this tropical expression reaches even to what is called antiphrasis, as when a thing is said to abound which does not exist, a thing said to be sweet which is sour; "*lucus quod non luceat, Parcæ quod non parcant.*" Of which kind is that in holy Scripture, "If he will not bless Thee to Thy face;" which the devil saith to the Lord concerning holy Job, and the meaning is "curse." [...] All these modes of speaking shall be accounted

lies, if figurative speech or action shall be set down as lying. But if it be no lie, when things which signify one thing by another are referred to the understanding of a truth, assuredly not only that which Jacob did or said to his father that he might be blessed, but that too which Joseph spoke as if in mockery of his brothers, and David's feigning of madness, must be judged to be no lies, but prophetical speeches and actions, to be referred to the understanding of those things which are true; which are covered as it were with a garb of figure on purpose to exercise the sense of the pious inquirer, and that they may not become cheap by lying bare and on the surface. Though even the things which we have learned from other places, where they are spoken openly and manifestly, these, when they are brought out from their hidden retreats, do, by our (in some sort) discovering of them, become renewed, and by renewal sweet. Nor is it that they are begrudged to the learners, in that they are in these ways obscured; but are presented in a more winning manner, that being as it were withdrawn, they may be desired more ardently, and being desired may with more pleasure be found.

Yet true things, not false, are spoken; because true things, not false, are signified, whether by word or by deed; the things that are signified namely, those are the things spoken. They are accounted lies only because people do not understand that the true things which are signified are the things said, but believe that false things are the things said. To make this plainer by examples, attend to this very thing that Jacob did. With skins of the kids, no doubt, he did cover his limbs; if we seek the immediate cause, we shall account him to have lied; for he did this, that he might be thought to be the man he was not: but if this deed be referred to that for the signifying of which it was really done, by skins of the kids are signified sins; by him who covered himself therewith, He who bare not His own, but others' sins. The truthful signification, therefore, can in no wise be rightly called a lie. And as in deed, so also in word. Namely, when his father said to him, "Who art thou my son?" he answered, "I am Esau, thy firstborn." This, if it be referred to those two twins, will seem a lie; but if to that for the signifying of which those deeds and words are written, He is here to be understood, in His body, which is His Church, Who, speaking of this thing, saith, "When ye shall see Abraham, and Isaac, and Jacob, and all the prophets in the kingdom of God, and yourselves cast out. And they shall come from the east and from the west and from the north and from the south, and shall sit down in the kingdom of God; and, behold, there are last which shall be first, and there are first which shall be last." For so in a certain sort the younger brother did bear off the primacy of the elder brother, and transfer it to himself.

Since then things so true, and so truthfully, be signified, what is there here that ought to be accounted to have been done or said lyingly? For when the things which are signified are not in truth things which are not, but which are, whether past or present or future, without doubt it is a true signification, and no lie. But it takes too long in the matter of this prophetical signification by stripping off the shell to search out all, wherein truth hath the palm, because as by being signified they were fore-announced, so by ensuing have they become clear. (XXII)

This is the voice not only of the Church Father and theologian Augustine but also of an intellectual who for fifteen years or so had been teaching rhetoric full time. When, for edifying, polemic or exegetic reasons, he entered deeply into studies of the Old Testament, he could not but recognize the plethora of rhetorical figures in the text. In the above-quoted example, he starts out by adducing a series of samples from the manuals. Here, of course, is the master trope, that is, the metaphor, *translatio*, "transferring", as it were, a term from its proper object to an "improper" or non-literal one, registered as a matter of course in rhetorical – or grammatical – treatises since the days of Aristotle. It was frequently illustrated, both in Cicero's *On the Orator* (3.38.155) as in Quintilian (8.6.6), with precisely the vines studded with gems.

Similarly, Augustine deals with the paradox or oxymoron, classified in *The Orator's Education* under the same Greek name as here, *antiphrasis*, mainly as a subdivision of allegory (8.6.57) or irony (9.2.47). In *Against Lying*, it is even adduced as two instances of *paranomasia* or punning (notoriously difficult to reproduce in translation): *lucus quod non luceat, Parcae quod non parcant.*[1] Augustine's Biblical example of paradox, on the other hand, probably comes closest to irony, the figure which makes a word express the opposite of what it actually stands for: the verb "bless" in Satan's challenge to God in Job 2.5, rendered in the Vulgate as *tunc videbis quod in facie benedicat tibi* (literally: 'then you shall see how he will bless you to your face'), is to be understood as "curse". Finally, the bishop dwells at length on allegory, primarily as it appears in the story of Isaac's two sons, Jacob and Esau, in Genesis 27.

However, in this paragraph it is not the technical analysis that is the main concern but, as the context and the title of the treatise indicate, the problem of lying. Augustine is painfully aware how intricate a question it is. The crux of the matter is, firstly, that the Bible does not establish any system of its own for *elocutio* but employs the same figurative language as poets and orators, and, secondly, that all tropes constantly manipulate the meaning of words. Their distinguishing mark is ambiguity, or as Augustine himself neatly remarks in his *Confessions:* the Biblical authors' *dicta figurata* are tricky since they can express one thing in several ways, and, conversely, since one expression can be understood in several ways: *ut una res multis modis enuntietur et una enuntiatio multis modis intellegatur* (13.24.36–37).

The Church Father's decisive question in this context turns out to be the following: since the Biblical signifiers are displaced, exchanged or, in short, manipulated according to the rules of this advanced figurative language, how can we know that their signifieds are not altered too, by virtue of the same clever manoeuvrings? If that is the case, surely the text is laid wide open for all sorts of

---

[1] The Latin noun *lucus* signifies 'grove', while the verb *lucere* means 'clear up' or 'shine'. The *parcae* are the Roman equivalence to the Greeks' *moirai*, the Fates, while *parcere* signifies 'spare' or 'pardon'.

lies. Furthermore, since the usual catalogues of tropes do not concern themselves with the issue of truth, either in grammar or in rhetoric, readers might understandably feel a lack of firm ground for judging the cognitive value of any figurative text. It was this shortcoming that the Priscillian heretics exploited for their cunningly double-tongued preaching, which had led Consentius to ask for advice on the problem.

Augustine's ingenious solution was to a great extent to be adopted by medieval Europe. He was too experienced in rhetoric to try to avoid the question of the displacements and condensations of tropes. On the contrary, he emphasized the degree of figuration in the Bible and, likewise, its puzzling consequences for the readers or listeners: occasional obscurity and, in theory, a potentially uncontrollable dispersion of meanings. Nevertheless, to cite again the last book of the *Confessions*, we need never doubt the veracity of this figurative language: *verum est enim* (13.24.36). The same certainty governs Augustine's analysis in *Against Lying*. He is demonstratively anxious to highlight *vera*, the Biblical truth.

His argument is cleverly organized. First, he shows that the tropes of rhetoric only share their formal structure, which is based on a gap between overt statement and underlying reality, with the act of lying. As for their actual purpose or function, however, they are cognitively neutral (they might convey true as well as false information) and thus cannot in any way be reduced to deceit. Hence, the fact that the style of the Bible is richly ornamented does not at all mean, as Consentius' Spanish adversaries seem to have intimated, that it lies. To elucidate this argument, Augustine cites the story of how Jacob, on apparently false grounds, had gained his father's blessing and Esau's birthright. After a thorough analysis, there remains not a shadow of doubt: the Biblical allegory tells the truth. It is only at first glance that Jacob appears to act falsely when he puts on the skins of the young goats. He actually anticipates or represents the Christ of the New Testament, who would take upon Himself the sins of the world. What appeared to be a lie emerges as a prophecy. And since Jacob was part of Jewish history, listed as one of the patriarchs, we can be sure that he had real existence – that he was a literally true creature – as well.

Such a junction of literal truth with historical (or soteriological) anticipation implies that the linguistic figuration's signifier and signified are firmly linked to each other in accordance with a pattern that we shall return to in the next section, devoted to Augustine's typological allegory. This device allowed no room whatsoever for lies, since it was trustworthy throughout, in words or in deeds, *seu verbo seu facto*. That the Bible was altogether true was a conviction that grew increasingly strong in Augustine over the years. Even the seemingly preposterous or absurd episodes recounted by the Jewish authors were to be held confirmed once and for all since Christ, the Word Incarnate, had fulfilled the Old

Testament's obscure prophesies. In contrast to the figures of the poets and the rhetoricians, the Biblical equivalents were never there for their own sake, that is, merely (or mainly) for ornamentation. Their chief function was to inculcate their factual content, the sacred *res* that the Holy Spirit wanted to communicate to mankind through their agency.

"Since then things so true, and so truthfully, be signified", *tam vera tamque significentur veraciter*... With this exegetic procedure, which admittedly allowed a tension or an asymmetry between image and sense in the Holy Writ but nonetheless included them in one and the same Christological truth, Augustine made a pioneering contribution to the medieval interpretation of the Bible. But at the same time, he closed the door on fictionality in his text theory. He resolutely tied Christian figurative language to Christian faith at every step. Consequently, he chose the way of hermeneutic exclusivity rather than that of openness and dialogue. This is clear from *Against Lying*, where he used a traditional image to illustrate the difficulty of interpreting Old Testament texts: perplexing configurations like Jacob's disguise, Joseph's apparently mocking talk to his brothers and David's feigning of madness serve as a kind of covering, *amictus*, with the task of – at least provisionally – hiding or shrouding, *obtegere*, the truth from the readers.

It should not surprise us that Augustine found a justification for the Biblical exegetes' painstaking efforts which in itself is metaphorical: the need to dress the body in order to conceal it, as well as the ensuing desire to strip it of its clothes. This is actually a phenomenon that recurs with remarkable regularity in the history of Western stylistics: the analysis of tropes is seldom able to dispense with tropes. In this case, the metaphor has slightly erotic overtones: the message of the text appears as a body, covered by the clothing of intriguing figures so as to arouse the interpreter's desire more strongly. Accordingly, the act of interpretation is described as a matter of unclothing. The obscurity of the text serves not to confuse or repel the readers but to stimulate their curiosity and to exercise their exegetic sensibility (*ut sensum... exerceant*). Once they have succeeded in revealing the message in its naked lustre, their joy of discovery will be all the stronger. An author who contents himself with a straightforward presentation of his case, on the other hand, runs the risk of looking lacklustre and unworthy of interpretive efforts.

At this point in Augustine's argument, there reappears, despite his readiness to acknowledge the richness of the Bible's shifting styles, a tension between his popular revivalist Christianity – everyone should understand what is said – and an eloquent elitism rooted in classical culture. The latter agreed with the conviction of Alexandrian allegoresis that esoteric messages require an obscure style, an idea that in turn stems from ancient cults, Pythagorean speculation and Orphic or sibylline mysteries, all governed by what Hugo Rahner calls the tendency to make a secret of matters of religion, a proclivity that to some extent amounts to "a sociological law".[1] However, we have no reason to dwell in detail on this religious and philosophical background to Augustine's hermeneutic exclusivity. He probably articulated it most succinctly in Book IV of *On Christian Doctrine:* "So I realize that I must say something also about the eloquence of the prophets, in which much is obscure because of their figurative language. Indeed, the more opaque they seem, because of their use of metaphor, the greater the reader's pleasure when the meaning becomes clear" (4.7.15), *dicendum ergo mihi aliquid esse video et de eloquentia prophetarum, ubi per tropologiam multa obteguntur. Quae quanto magis translatis verbis videntur operiri tanto magis cum fuerint aperta dulcescunt.*

As Marrou has pointed out, that is how a literary substratum or even a rudimentary aesthetics lived on in Augustine's later writings, which would be exploited by conceited poets from the Early Middle Ages down to the Late Baroque period.[2] This is surely one of the great paradoxes of the African bishop's groundbreaking theory of interpretation. On the basis of his own experiences, he was as concerned about the power of desire over our lives as about the abysses of misunderstanding or disinformation that appeared to disturb linguistic intercourse; in addition, as the years passed, he expressed increasingly strong reservations about profane poetry. Nevertheless, he must be considered one of the first great advocates of literary obscurity in the West, and perhaps the most subtle of them all, based on a hermeneutics articulated in erotic terms. Its chief transmitter to the Middle Ages would be Isidore of Seville, who in the small section on tropes from his *Etymologies* recycles (and vulgarizes) the main argument of *Against Lying*. Metaphorical expressions and other tropes are, according to Isidore, "veiled in figural garb", *figuratis amictibus obteguntur*, to exercise the reader's understanding "lest the subjects grow common from being stripped bare and obvious", *ut sensus legentis exerceant, et ne nuda atque in promptu vilescant* (1.37.2).

This take on figurative discourse could provide the subject for an investigation of its own. It would conceivably show how both the erotic and rhetorical mechanisms of desire from which the Church Father had liberated himself in the name of theology returned with renewed strength in his hermeneutics. As far as our perspective of fictionality is concerned, we will have to content ourselves with the observation that they probably elicited his watchful attitude to-

---

[1] Rahner 1971, p. 38.
[2] Marrou 1938, p. 489. Cf. Mehtonen 2003, pp. 95f.

wards deceit in *Against Lying*. The term that triggered the crucial paragraph of this treatise that we have subjected to analysis, *mysterium*, served, like the recurrent veil metaphor, to distinguish the Biblical figures from those of profane rhetoric or grammar. For this purpose, Augustine linked up with Paul. The Apostle to the Gentiles had resorted to both the mystery and the veil in order to reinterpret pagan and Jewish ritual customs in a new Christian context.

His epistle to the congregation at Ephesus is particularly rich in references to the *mystērion* that was revealed in Christ. This "mystery", the Bible's set of sacred signs, was frequently highlighted by Augustine in his exegetical writings, for example in his *Lectures or Tractates on the Gospel According to St. John*, where it is usually termed *sacramentum*. The changing of water into wine at the wedding at Cana in the second chapter of the Gospel is an example of this kind of sacred sign which, *mystice*, is granted a divine significance (9.1).[1] Moreover, in the third chapter of the second Epistle to the Corinthians, Paul reminded his readers how Moses was obliged to put a cloth or veil over his face after he had seen God's glory at Mount Sinai. Subsequently, the narrow-minded Jews had left the veil hanging in the temple, and "that same veil remains unlifted, because only through Christ is it taken away" (2 Corinthians 3.14). One of Augustine's richest applications of the veil metaphor is based on this Pauline Christology. In *The Usefulness of Belief*, he appointed Christ the superior *paedagogus* who had helped us to remove the Old Testament's veil, *velamen*, to reveal what lies "obscure and hidden", *obscurum atque adopertum*, in the text (3.9). This image originates in Greek speculation, where *parapetasma* ('curtain') or *kalymma* ('veil') were standard terms for the kind of myth that required allegorical exposition.[2] It seems to be particularly common in Origen, who, when addressing the story of Creation in *Peri archōn*, in Latin known as *De principiis* (*On First Principles*), emphasized that the Bible "comprehends matters of profounder significance than the mere historical narrative appears to indicate, and contains very many things that are to be spiritually understood, and employs the letter, as a kind of veil, in treating of profound and mystical subjects" (3.5.1).[3]

---

[1] Cf. a little later in the same commentary: "For now let us begin to uncover the hidden meanings of the mysteries", 9.3, *iam enim incipiamus ipsa sacramentorum operta detegere*. The Vulgate translates Paul's recurring term *mystērion* with *sacramentum* as well as *mysterium*; this alternating usage is particularly evident in Ephesians 3.3–4.

[2] Sheppard 1980, p. 16.

[3] "Maiora quaedam intra se contineat, quam historiae narratio videtur ostendere, et spiritalem in quam maximis contineat intellectum atque in rebus mysticis et profundis velamine quodam litterae utatur". All quotations from *On First Principles* in Latin are from the French edition of H. Crouzel and M. Simonetti 1978–84, and, in English, from F. Crombie's translation in *The Ante-*

Sacramenta were there to be deciphered and the veil to be lifted by the initiated interpreter. The great challenge that occupied the leading Christian intellectuals of this period, namely the establishment of an orthodox set of dogmas sharply marked off from pagan ideas and heretical doctrines of all kinds, proceeded from and returned to the text of the Holy Writ. The Biblical script had to be set off in various ways from the surrounding text environment, subjected to correct methods of interpretation and protected from profanations and misreadings. The task of securing the cognitive status of the Bible's figurative discourse was part of this arduous work. Few or none did more than Augustine to this end. For him, the instability of meaning that characterized tropes normally allowed certain possibilities for fictionality to infiltrate human language, a set of hermeneutic idiosyncrasies which, however, the Bible's "mystical" figures theoretically ruled out. Behind *their* veil lurked nothing but divine truth.

*

One matter of concern for many pious exegetes and Church potentates was for a long time the Bible's so-called absurdities. Jean Pépin devotes a chapter to this subject in his great book on ancient and medieval allegory, where he pays due attention to Augustine. It turns out that the Bishop of Hippo, compared with predecessors like Origen or Gregory of Nyssa, upheld as strongly as he possibly could the letter of the Bible, a strategy that is evident in the title of his commentary on Genesis, *The Literal Meaning of Genesis*. Only when the Old Testament prophets or God's own words appear "absurd" if taken literally, may we assume that they should be understood *figurate* (11.1.2). The same attitude to interpreting ostensibly preposterous passages characterizes *On Christian Doctrine:* when the proper meaning of words appears incomprehensible or unreasonable, *cum sensus, ad proprietatem verborum si accipiatur, absurdus est*, we have to ask ourselves whether the statement is not to be taken "by means of one or other of the tropes", *illo vel illo tropo* (3.29.41).[1]

On closer inspection, this strategy goes far back in Augustine's writing, at least as far as to *Of True Religion* from 390–91: "Every language has its own special modes of expression which seem absurd when translated into another language" – such is his comment on the low style, *loquendi humilitas*, that he recognized, indubitably with some anguish, in the Bible.[2] His examples are

---

Nicene Fathers edited by A. Roberts *et alii*, 4, 1956. For Origen's use of the veil metaphor, see Crouzel's helpful note to this passage, 1980, pp. 102f.
1 Pépin 1987, pp. 167–86.
2 "Habet enim omnis lingua sua quaedam propria genera locutionum, quae cum in aliam linguam transferuntur, videntur absurda."

descriptions of God's anger, sorrow and other emotional qualities, but he also cites Biblical references to His hands, feet and other limbs. Are they to be understood in accordance with the human body's visible shape or at an intellectual and spiritual level (50.99)? The author leaves this question open, but the context indicates that he preferred the latter alternative.

Detecting and decoding figurative passages became Augustine's principal method of straightening out the absurdities or contradictions to be found in the Holy Writ, typically in the Old Testament, the riddles of which were thus converted into doctrinal messages. This is perhaps most apparent in the sixth book of the *Confessions* (6.4.6), where the probing author, eagerly involved in his philosophical inquiries, worries about the *absurda* he has come across in "the ancient writings of the law and the prophets", *vetera scripta legis et prophetarum*. The problem is solved as soon as Ambrose has taught him the meaning of 2 Corinthians 3.6: "For the letter kills, but the Spirit gives life." Evidently, God had to be disassociated from all kinds of visualization or bodily presence in order to be understood properly. This was a far more difficult undertaking for a Late Antique intellectual than it would turn out to be for his modern successors, who have become used to confronting – I borrow the Austrian writer Hermann Broch's wording – a god who can no longer be named or portrayed, "arisen and immersed in the endless neutrality of the absolute".[1]

Augustine and Broch looked at God from diametrically opposite angles. The twentieth-century novelist shrinks back from the blank world of modern abstraction, stripped of all ornamentation and all imagery, whereas the young Augustine experienced a great liberation at being able to disengage his Lord from fantasies, figures and fictions, typical of pagan cults and divinities. Nowhere, neither in his autobiography nor in *Of True Religion*, *On Christian Doctrine* or *The Literal Meaning of Genesis*, would the Church Father accept any absurdities about or by God *ad litteram*. He immediately treated such utterances as a kind of intentionally bewildering language which the exegete, by means of his expertise in figuration, had to identify and decode to fit comprehensible patterns. We find this way of treating obscure passages from the Holy Writ on the first pages of *On the Trinity*, which were quoted at the beginning of this section (above p. 216). Here, Augustine distinguishes three ways of speaking about God in a transferred sense, depending on the sources of the figurative terms. His technical vocabulary, including terms such as *transtulit* and *traxit*, indicates the main type of figuration he had in mind: the metaphor, *translatio*.

---

1 "Aufgestiegen und versunken in die unendliche Neutralität des Absoluten", Broch 1932, p. 185 (my translation).

The first two metaphorical techniques for speaking about God are treated by the Church Father with a generosity he could not always muster. References to divine properties taken "from things corporeal", *ex rebus corporalibus* (e.g. the protecting wings in Psalms 16/17.8, "hide me in the shadow of your wings"), were considered acceptable. Likewise, God could stand being metaphorically equipped with abstract qualities from spiritual Creation, *de spiritali creatura* (e.g. "I the Lord your God am a jealous God", Exodus 20.5). With such a broad framework conceded to Biblical figuration, the whole of Creation could serve as a reservoir of formulas and figures ultimately referring to the Godhead. Both visible and invisible, both natural and human reality were recognized as legitimate sources for the Biblical writers' analogical talk about God. However, it was not deemed acceptable to attribute to Him phenomena that did not exist at all, *quae omnino non sunt* (1.1.2). Augustine's example of such vain and, implicitly, fictional strategies, characteristically absent from the Bible, is symptomatic: the scandalous ideas of a God who generates himself. All similar notions are firmly condemned as heretical, since "there is nothing whatever that generates its own existence" (1.1.1), *nulla enim omnino res est quae se ipsam gignat ut sit*. Most likely, it is possible to detect a specific address for these fulminations on the first pages of *On the Trinity*: the ancient and widespread story of the Phoenix, the fabulous bird which is reborn from its own ashes in ancient Egyptian or Oriental mythology, as Ovid puts it in his *Metamorphoses:* "which itself renews and reproduces its own being" (15.392), *quae reparet seque ipsa reseminet*.

In this context, it is certainly relevant that the Phoenix had been associated with Christ ever since the earliest days of the Church, a connection that (as we shall see in the next chapter) had been exploited by Lactantius as well as – perhaps more surprisingly – Tertullian, in his treatise *De resurrectione carnis liber* (*On the Resurrection of the Flesh*). For this dogged apologist, the wonderful Phoenix had seemed to be "a most complete and unassailable symbol of our hope" (13.1), *plenissimum atque firmissimum huius spei specimen*, that is, the hope of resurrection. On this point, the author of *On the Trinity* adopted a more rigorous attitude: the self-generating creatures of poetry and mythology do not belong among the figures of the Spirit. It was all right to speak of God in metaphors, according to Biblical patterns, with terms (or, in modern parlance, vehicles) taken from Creation, from the entire system of correspondences of existing reality, physical or spiritual. Nevertheless, He was not to be dressed up in fictional discourse, based on non-entities, that is, things or creatures *quae omnino non sunt*, since such imagery was considered fraudulent (and, typically, derived from pagan tradition). That was the single, albeit unconditional, limitation that Augustine imposed on his rhetorically coloured Biblical hermeneutics in

On the Trinity. However, in a few of his writings, as we shall now see, he proved indeed able to detect instances of fictionality in the Holy Writ, provided that such make-believe could, ultimately, be rationalized as the strategic outcome of pious intentions or divinatory knowledge.

*

We have studied some examples of how Augustine dealt with figurative language in the Bible. His arguments might vary over time and be expressed in fluctuating vocabulary, but, as a rule, they elaborate the fundamental viewpoint put forward to Consentius in *Against Lying*. There the Church Father explains that, even if at first sight it may seem possible to mistake the Old Testament's prophetic utterances for lies, they are actually instances of figurative language which, correctly interpreted, will be found to be true: *in figuris autem quod velut mendacium dicitur, bene intellectum verum invenitur*. Augustine tests a similar assumption on certain expressions in the New Testament, above all those pronounced by the apostles, who sometimes demonstrate a startling relationship to truth. They should be understood as "figures prenunciative", *figurae praenuntiativae*, he emphasizes, which can admittedly be reminiscent of lies but actually relate to the destiny of the Christian Church or the dramatic course of events at the end of time. This argument results in a crucial definition: "A lie, namely, is a false signification with will of deceiving. But that is no false signification, where, although one thing is signified by another, yet the thing signified is a true thing, if it be rightly understood." (12.26)[1] Technically speaking, the apostles' signifieds are true, hence their speech is prophetic. They make use of veracious figures rather than intentional lies.

Thus Augustine was extremely sensitive to the issue of possible cases of pretence in the Bible. A well-known example is his reaction to Jerome's interpretation of Galatians 2.11–14, in which Paul confronts Peter for hypocritically withdrawing from the company of the Gentiles in Antioch as soon as his fellowmen among the Jews arrived. In the Vulgate, Paul labels this sudden retreat on the part of Peter a false show or feigning, and in his commentary on Galatians 2.13 (written in 387) Jerome extends this kind of *simulatio* to Paul as well; the conflict between the two venerable apostles was supposedly not for real, but staged in order to – diplomatically – satisfy both the Jews' and the Gentiles' claims to the right faith: 'How can we imagine the task of such mighty pillars of the Church, Peter and Paul, these formidable vessels of wisdom, among the

---

[1] "Mendacium est quippe falsa significatio cum voluntate fallendi. Non est autem falsa significatio, ubi etsi aliud ex alio significatur, verum est tamen quod significatur, si recte intellegatur."

mutually opposed Jews and Gentiles? If not as a feigned conflict for the sake of peace among the believers, strengthening the Church's faith by their holy altercation'.[1]

In a letter to Jerome from 394–95, Augustine first made clear that he did not acknowledge any righteous or defensible feigning on the part of these great apostles; what Jerome had understood as strategic *simulatio*, he blatantly identifies as lying, *mendacium*, and any recognition of such falseness in men like Peter and Paul would certainly open the floodgates to suspicions of deceit and false pretence in the Holy Writ. "For lies can be seen as useful even in the praises of God in order that the sluggish might be set afire with love for him, and in that way the authority of holy and pure truth will nowhere be certain in the holy books" (28.3.4), *possunt enim videri etiam de laudibus Dei esse officiosa mendacia, ut apud homines pigriores dilectio eius ardescat; atque ita nusquam certa erit in Libris sanctis castae veritatis auctoritas.* In short, Augustine is anxious to exculpate Paul from all clever, short-term stratagems. The Apostle to the Gentiles is entirely serious in his rebuttal, and he is fully entitled to criticize Peter for his calculated move (as is also evident from Augustine's *Epistola* 82.2.8, composed in 404–05).

Here, we recognize the typical Augustinian anguish for any utterance liable to make use of make-believe, particularly in the Holy Writ. If the Biblical writers just for once, *semel*, could be suspected of pretence, in this context placed on a par with downright deceit, no matter for whatever dutiful reason (*aliqua officiose*), hermeneutic anarchy seems close at hand "so that each person believes in them what he wants and does not believe what he does not want" (28.3.5), *ut in eis quod vult quisque credat, quod non vult non credat.* To Augustine, Jerome's exegesis completely entrusts the burden of interpretation to the reader, stripping the Biblical text (dictated by the Spirit) of its inherent authority. This approach to the issue of possible make-believe in the Holy Writ is even more pronounced in another letter (written in 397), where Augustine airs his concerns over Galatians 2.11–14: "Will he [Paul] be thought to have spoken the truth where he says what the reader holds, but when something turns up contrary to the view of the reader, it will be ascribed to a useful lie?" (40.3.3), *an ibi verum dixisse videbitur, ubi hoc dixerit, quod lector sapit; cum vero contra sensum lectoris aliquid occurrerit, officioso mendacio deputabitur?*[2]

---

1 "Quid putamus tantas Ecclesiae columnas, Petrum et Paulum, tanta vasa sapientiae inter dissidentes Judaeos atque gentiles facere debuisse? nisi ut eorum simulata contentio, pax credentium fieret, et Ecclesiae fides sancto inter eos jurgio concordaret." *PL* 26.340c.
2 Cf. Krämer 2007, pp. 98–100.

Still, the most troublesome issue of all remains: Christ's veiled speech, discussed in *Against Lying* 13.27–28. When, in the Gospel according to St. Luke, Jesus is on His way to see the synagogue patron's daughter, the crowd gathers round Him. A woman brushes against the fringe of His garment from behind, and He asks: "Who was it that touched me?" (8.45) This seems confusing to Augustine, since the omniscient Christ should know! In the same puzzling way, the Saviour in the Gospel according to St. John wonders where the Jews have laid the dead Lazarus (11.34). An Augustine scholar easily feels how questions such as these send vibrations all through the Church Father's work. They raise the complex issues of make-believe and dissimulation in respect of the Saviour Himself. They are no longer restricted to grammar teachers, to Virgil, Moses or the prophets. Here, they involve the Son of God, the very fulfilment of all truly inspired prophecies. His "Who" and "Where" are strange: naturally He need not be in any doubt at all. How, then, are we to understand the Christological words and deeds that simulate ignorance?

There is a simple answer: in essentially the same way as we assess other pronouncements known from the Holy Writ. What is remarkable in this part of Augustine's argument is not so much his theory as his terminology: his bold association of fictionality with the One who was the way, and the truth, and the life. Christ did "feign that He knew not", *nescire se finxit*, and thereby actually expressed, in both cases (the "Who" and "Where" questions), a truthful signification, *significatio verax*. His simulated ignorance turns out to be, in the eyes of Augustine, a figure for a quite real lack of information. That is because the sick woman and the dead Lazarus refer to those "whom even He Who knew all things did in a certain sort know not", *quos etiam qui cuncta sciebat quodam modo nesciebat*, namely the Gentiles and the Jews of the Old Covenant respectively. Christ's puzzling questions must evidently be understood as substitutive figures, as signs of that partial ignorance about the old pagan and Jewish cultures, which belonged to His humanity.

However, Augustine took his ultimate touchstone for this crucial exegetic issue from the last chapter of the Gospel according to St. Luke, where a few verses are dedicated to Christ's journey to the village of Emmaus after His resurrection. To all appearances, this episode had been put forward by the heretical Priscillianists as an alibi for telling lies. Here, it is the Bible text itself that expressly associates Jesus with dissimulation. He seems to want to continue His journey, but the disciples persuade Him to stay with them in the village over night. Luke's words are: "So they drew near to the village to which they were going. He acted as if he were going farther" (24.28). In the translations available, including the Vulgate that Augustine by now (around 420) surely used for his study of the Gospels, the last words of the sentence are: *ipse se finxit longius ire*, where *finxit* is a quite reasonable translation of the Greek *prosepoiēsato* (from the verb *prospoiein* = 'pretend', 'lay claim to'; 'feign', 'allege'). Consequently, the question must be asked once again: could Jesus actually pretend? Feign?

Augustine commented on this problem in a paragraph of *Against Lying* that is one of the most ingenious, as far as fiction theory is concerned, in his entire Christian work. Here, he demonstrated a remarkable susceptibility to the kind of poetical diction or discourse that, in other contexts, he used to wave aside, increasingly impatiently as the years passed. He took his starting point in precisely the Latin word for 'pretend', *fingere* (13.28):

> The Evangelist, saying, "But He Himself feigned [*finxit*] that He would go further," hath put that very word in which liars too greatly delight, that they may with impunity lie: as if every thing that is feigned is a lie, whereas in a truthful way, for the sake of signifying one thing by another, so many things use to be feigned. If then there had been no other thing that Jesus signified, in that He feigned to be going further, with reason might it be judged to be a lie: but then if it be rightly understood and referred to that which He willed to signify, it is a mystery [*sacramentum*]. Else will all things be lies which, on account of a certain similitude of things to be signified, although they never were done, are related to have been done. Of which sort is that concerning the two sons of one man, the elder who tarried with his father, and the younger who went into a far country, which is narrated so much at length. In which sort of fiction [*genus fingendi*], men have put even human deeds or words to irrational animals and things without sense, that by this sort of feigned narrations but true significations, they might in more winning manner intimate the things which they wished. Nor is it only in authors of secular letters, as in Horace, that mouse speaks to mouse, and weasel to fox, that through a fictitious narration a true signification may be referred to the matter in hand [*ut per narrationem fictam ad id quod agitur, vera significatio referatur*]; whence the like fables of Æsop being referred to the same end, there is no man so untaught as to think they ought to be called lies: but in Holy Writ also, as in the book of Judges, the trees seek them a king, and speak to the olive, to the fig and to the vine and to the bramble. Which, in any wise, is all feigned, with intent that one may get to the thing which is intended, by a feigned narration indeed, yet not a lying one, but with a truthful signification. This I have said on account of that which is written concerning Jesus, "And Himself feigned to be going further:" lest any from this word, like the Priscillianists, wishing to have license of lying, should contend that beside others even Christ did lie. But whoso would understand what He by feigning that did prefigure, let him attend to that which He by acting did effect. For when afterwards He did go further, above all heavens, yet deserted He not His disciples. In order to signify this which in the future He did as God, at the present He feigned to do that as Man. And therefore was a veritable signification caused in that feigning to go before, because in this departure the verity of that signification did follow after. Let him therefore contend that Christ did lie by feigning, who denieth that He fulfilled by doing that which He signified. (XXIII)

Perhaps the remarkable arguments of this paragraph could be arranged in three logical steps:

- Firstly, Augustine shows that both of the Bible's Testaments could take advantage of the same fictional mode as profane literature or, concretely, the moralizing animal fables found in Aesop's work or in Horace's satires (2.6) and epistles (1.7).
- Secondly, he comes to the conclusion (or sets out from the thesis) that this kind of fiction is legitimate; even though it may seem to be false at first sight, it proves to be fundamentally truthful. In conjunction with his *Two Books of Questions on the Gospels*, to be dealt with on the next few pages, this must be the Church Father's most eloquent sanction of fiction ever, not only in the hands of secular writers but in the Bible itself, in both the Old and the New Testament. His examples are taken from the Book of Judges 9.8–15 (the fable of the king of the trees) and the Gospel according to St. Luke 15.11–32 (the parable of the prodigal son).
- Thirdly, as the finishing touch, Augustine traces elements of fiction in Christ Himself, who, with His feigned gesture at Emmaus – "he acted as if he were going farther" – was actually, in a concealed manner, foreshadowing His imminent ascension to Heaven for His disciples.

There is a suggestive terminology in this Augustinian analysis that seems reminiscent of classical theories of fiction. Step by step, the Church Father tries to narrow down the kind of narrative constructions, *fictae narrationes*, "which, on account of a certain similitude of things to be signified, although they never were done, are related to have been done", *quae propter quamdam rerum significandarum similitudinem, cum gesta non sint, tamquam gesta narrantur*. In this definition, we recognize the emphasis on the resemblance with – rather than the direct enunciation of – the referent: the mimetic element which is so crucial to the Aristotelian *Poetics*. We might even perceive the conditional subordinate clause, literally 'as if they had taken place', *tamquam gesta*, as an echo of the famous kinds of things "that might occur", *hoia an genoito*, from the same treatise. Although we are at a late stage of Augustine's career in this text from the year 420, these turns of phrase might remind us of the young, philosophically advanced investigator of theatrical discourse, who a little more than thirty years earlier had analysed "double-faced" fictionality in his *Soliloquies*, "true in our proper garb but false as dressed up to represent something else" (above, pp. 179f.).

At the same time, it seems obvious that, to Augustine, this legitimate fiction must now be identical with figuration, first and foremost as it is implemented in Christ's parables. As a matter of fact, the Aristotelian probability method is ruled out from the *fictae narrationes* discernible in the Biblical text. Ultimately, Augustine's reference to the evangelists' conditional way of telling stories 'as if they had taken place' proves to be nothing but a relic from his philosophical past. The mimetic mode of poetics has to yield to, or merge into, the figurative mode of rhetoric. The distinction between (Biblical) imagery and lying is firmly drawn: neither the prophets, nor Christ nor His disciples lie. Since their speech is dictated by the Holy Spirit, they give voice to truth, albeit indirectly. To feign (*fingere*) truthfully (*veraciter*) amounts to indication – particularly of forthcoming events – by figuration, that is, "signifying one thing by another", *aliud ex alio*, a key formula that Augustine reuses five times in *Against Lying* and which he had already employed in order to explain allegory in *On the Trinity* (15.9.15).

The Church Father was fully aware how the indirect or concealed speech of Christ and other Biblical characters to a certain extent shares its semiotic structure, that of dual signification, with lying. Accordingly, he always considered it insufficient to defend the devices of this particular kind of scriptural diction – its parables, metaphors and personifications – by referring to their formal construction. They rather derive their legitimacy from the infallible writer who is behind the text, the Holy Spirit, and from the kerygmatic (never deceitful) intention of those that participate in their dissemination among human beings: Christ, the apostles and their successors. On such a basis, of course, the truthfulness of the imagery of Biblical figuration is guaranteed right from the start. The "something else", that is, the referent (the *aliud*), of an expression or a gesture recorded in the Holy Writ has always already come to pass, *gestum*, or will take place, *futurum factum*.

This Biblical type of fictionality can hardly be considered the art of the possible. It might be described, at its simplest, as a kind of figurative language based on a real or even surreal (divine) tenor, whether it consists of metaphors, exemplificative characters or *prosopopoeiae*. We are facing a unique set of *mysteria* or *sacramenta*, the Pauline term we have already seen reserved for Biblical tropes in *Against Lying*. Consequently, in Augustine's doctrine of figurative speech, the "mystery" became the sacred equivalent to the profane fable or myth. In the long term, this manoeuvre was to have significant consequences for the medieval theory of literature. If Augustine mobilized the innovative energy in this domain, the Catholic doctrine of figurative discourse, it was again Isidore of Seville who took care of its dissemination, albeit in a somewhat flattened form. About two centuries later, he would use the above-quoted passage from *Against Lying* to legitimate morally useful and edifying fictions, what he called *fabulae ad mores*, in the introductory chapter of *Etymologies* that he devoted to grammar (1.40.6).

It is doubtful whether Isidore realized that this passage is a telling example of internal Augustinian recycling. As a matter of fact, the Church Father had already dealt with Jesus' make-believe gesture on His arrival in Emmaus, namely in his *Quaestionum evangeliorum libri duo* (*Two Books of Questions on the Gospels*) from the years immediately before the turn of the fifth century. However, in that document he had not yet started to narrow down the particular nature of sacred figuration under the aspect of mystery. At this comparatively early stage, he was still able to content himself with freeing the Biblical examples of simulation from the suspicion of lying by referring to their figurative nature. They were fundamentally to be considered like any other tropes, regardless of context (2.51.1, my translation):

> Not everything that we feign, then, is a lie; it is only by feigning something which signifies nothing that we indulge in lying. So whenever our invention [*fictio*] is derived from some signification, it is no lie but a figure of truth. If it were not so, everything which has been said in a figurative manner by wise and holy men, or by the Lord Himself, must be considered lies, since our habitual understanding tells us that there can be no truth in such talk. Take for example the man who had two sons, of whom the minor took his share of the paternal heritance and left for distant shores, and other circumstances intertwined in this narrative: they are not reported as if there ever was anyone who had experienced this with his two sons, or who had inflicted this upon them. They should, accordingly, be considered inventions [*ficta*], and the reality they refer to is so much greater and incomparably different, that surely the true God should be inferred from this fictitious man. As a matter of fact, not only words but things too might be feigned without lying in order to denote something real. That is the case with what has been told us of the Lord Himself: He was looking for fruits in the fig tree during the season when it still bore no fruit. There can be no doubt that He was looking there, though everybody knew that this tree bore no fruit, whether due to infertility or the season. Hence, a fiction that can be derived from some truth is a figure, while the fiction that lacks such reference is a lie. (XXIV)

This argument, drawn from Augustine's commentary on the parable of the prodigal son (Luke 15.11–32) and Jesus' curse on the fig tree (Mark 11.12–14), is basically identical with the discussion in his tract against lying twenty years later. The Bible never lies, not even in the passages where remarkable and to all appearances invented or feigned things are narrated. It always stands on firm, real (divinely real) ground. But the commentary deserves special interest since it is more unguarded in its wording. Firstly, it links up with Augustine's ideas on the allegorical colouring of all Biblical absurdities or incongruities. The sublime reality that is referred to in the story of the prodigal son differs so flagrantly, *tam longe alteque*, from the narrative itself that the father in question must be none other than God the Father. To put it in technical terms, the referent's radical distance or difference, its otherness or dissimilarity compared to its reference, indicates an allegorical meaning, more or less as in modern literary theory.

Thus the remarkable events in the Bible can, in this commentary from the turn of the fifth century, be identified as figures of speech. And, secondly, the former teacher of rhetoric knows very well that as long as such figures relate to – visible or invisible – reality, pointing at an authentic referent, they do not lie but implement the fictional mode. The abundant reliance on terms like *fictio* and *fingere* in this exegetic context is even more striking than in *Against Lying*, undoubtedly because the commentator does not yet seriously confront the thorny problem of the possible misrepresentations or deceits of scriptural language. In the later treatise, intentionality is paramount, for which reason the author appeals to the infallible authority of the Spirit behind the Biblical texts; in the earlier commentary, by contrast, referentiality is paramount, for which reason the author thinks and argues pragmatically. There, in *Two Books of Questions on the Gospels*, he quite simply needs a legitimate strategy for dealing with the Bible's strange or seemingly irrational tales, and he finds it in the discipline he once had abandoned: rhetoric. His main argument is based on a simple syllogism. Premise 1: the stylistics of rhetoric (*elocutio*) had long identified figures of speech as an advanced form of fictional, not mendacious language. Premise 2: the Bible sometimes uses figures of speech. Conclusion: in those cases, the Bible does not lie but relies on the fictional mode.

To sum up, at a relatively early stage, at least at the time of his *Questions* (ca. 400), Augustine appears to have taken an interest in the profuse occurrences of eloquence in the Holy Writ. With his thorough literary and rhetorical schooling, he had no difficulty in accepting and analysing the Bible's tropes; on the contrary, he found himself at home among them. But eventually, in his capacity as a renowned bishop and a polemical teacher of the Church, he was forced to confront the suspicion of mendacity in all imagery, presumably as a consequence of the kind of exegetic and dogmatic conflicts that lay behind Consentius' letter of 420. By now he distinguished a particular type of Biblical figuration, which we have seen him present in terms such as *mysterium* or *sacramentum*. It differed from the usual tropes of grammar and rhetoric by virtue of its verbal inspiration and divine origin. Last but not least, this sacred eloquence excluded the hypothetical mode of fiction in favour of its substitutive mode, which Augustine associated with the representation of *aliud ex alio*, in short: veiled speech. Eventually, *Against Lying* demonstrates how the Cassiciacum dialogues' tentative Aristotelian efforts to come to grips with fictionality as a unique narrative mode based on mimesis, a cognitive instrument in its own right, succumbed to tropological concerns in the Church Father's exegetic writings.

This promotion of substitutive at the expense of hypothetical fictionality in a Biblical context became even stronger when Augustine focused on the trope that he considered the most important. As a matter of fact, it was so important that he tended to describe it as if it were something more than a trope, a semiotic procedure operating on its own terms: allegory. We have already glimpsed it in the previous discussion. Now we shall present it, if the expression be allowed, in full figure. Allegory proved to be Augustine's decisive answer to the question of what constituted the special language of the patriarchs, the prophets and the apostles. He was not able, after all, in his constant endeavours to narrow down the unique character of the Biblical texts, to put his mind to rest by referring to verbal inspiration. It is as if, in the long run, he experienced that solution to the main problem of interpreting the Bible – the problem of truth – as too unreliable or perhaps too convenient. Instead, Augustine continued to ponder on the possibility that the Bible's "mysteries", right through their formal agreement with the tropes of rhetoric, were characterized by a special structure of signification. These deliberations led him to concentrate on the typological allegory, a discursive figure which he came to expand into an entire semiotic category.

The Fact of Allegory

Allegory, or *hyponoia*, as it was often called in pre-Christian times, and allegoresis, the interpretation of texts in terms of allegory, already had a long history. They originate to a large extent in what Robert Lamberton, in the preface to his monograph on the Neo-Platonic readings of Homer, calls one of the great ironies of Greek intellectual history: "at the source of the tradition and at the dawn of Greek literacy, we find in full bloom a tradition of oral poetry apparently so utterly secularized, irreverent, and disillusioned that the gods could be used for comic relief."[1] Homer remained a stumbling block for the ancient literary critics and philosophers, as admired for his art and for his presence at the very source of Greek culture as he was considered troublesome because of his morals and his way of treating the gods. Throughout antique culture, ever since Xenophanes of Colophon up to Proclus of Athens, as Werner Jaeger observes, there was a demand for the gods' grandeur and dignity, which presupposed that they should speak and behave 'as befits a god', *theoprepēs*.[2] Since Homer's epics hardly meet that requirement, they were frequently considered to have a deeper, concealed and sacred meaning.

As early as the sixth century BCE, the Pythagoreans might have converted Homer into a "theologian".[3] The Presocratic philosophers gained deep ethical

---

1 Lamberton 1986, p. VII.
2 Jaeger 1961, pp. 48f.
3 Lamberton 1986, pp. 31–43.

and scientific illumination from his great epic works. Their successors during Hellenism, including the grammarian Heraclitus (or Pseudo-Heraclitus, often associated with the Stoic school), reacted against Plato's condemnation of Homer's educational value while looking for veiled wisdom in *The Iliad* and *The Odyssey*. On the whole, the Stoics took a remarkable interest in allegorical interpretation, forming – to quote George R. Boys-Stones – "the only major philosophical school of the Hellenistic period with an interest in allegory at all".[1] They sometimes resorted to etymological methods in their efforts to expose the true meaning of the ancient myths, purportedly some aspect of the one and only, all-pervading universal *logos*. Specifically, an analysis of the words' roots and syllables was expected to uncover a text's true, usually moral, physical or euhemeristic sense.[2]

Alongside the Stoics' materialistic understanding of texts, a mystical type of hermeneutics was gaining ground during the Hellenistic period in close association with the widespread religious mysteries. This development is evident around the turn of the first century CE in Plutarch, who could also use the word 'allegory' even if he preferred to speak in terms of a symbolic, enigmatic or mysterious sense.[3] By then it had already reached one of its peaks in the Jewish philosopher Philo of Alexandria (ca. 20 BCE – 40 CE), a formidable crossover phenomenon in Late Greek culture, constantly on the lookout for a hidden sense in the Pentateuch, 'the five scrolls', that is, the first five books of the Old Testament. Philo liked to compare the exegete's continuing penetration of the Bible, as Jean Pépin notices, to the initiation into the sacred mysteries.[4] For his spectacular readings of the Pentateuch, he still preferred the term *hyponoia* but could also make use of *symbolon*, complemented by the adjective *tropikos* or, more seldom, *typos*. In Philo's life time, the allegorical interpretation of the Bible was an established tradition in Alexandria, remarks Richard Hanson, and it tended to translate the Old Testament's laboriously assembled, divergent, and genre-dependent texts into Hellenistic philosophy or physics.[5] As a result, there arose the well-known tension in the Eastern Mediterranean between, on the one hand, Alexandrian allegoresis and, on the other hand, a more literal interpreta-

---

1 Boys-Stones 2003, p. 189.
2 For Pseudo-Heraclitus' applications of "substitutive" allegoresis, based on etymological word-by-word analysis, see Bernard 1990, pp. 15–21.
3 Plutarch's crucial tract in this respect is *Isis and Osiris*, though it focuses on myth explanation rather than text interpretation (in contrast to the work of his youth, *How to Study Poetry*). For examples of *allēgoria* in *Isis and Osiris*, see Plutarch 1999, 363d (cf. above, p. 51).
4 Pépin 1987, p. 10.
5 Hanson 1959, pp. 40, 45.

tion of the Bible which during Late Antiquity would be associated with Syrian Antioch.

The heritage of Philo's speculative, etymologically oriented method remained a dominant force in the exegetical circles of the Egyptian metropolis. Its Christian breakthrough took place with the stunning achievements of Clement of Alexandria and his disciple Origen in the decades round the year 200. Later, in the powerful Neo-Platonic speculation of the fourth and fifth centuries, principally in Proclus' commentaries on Plato's dialogues, allegorical interpretation became an instrument for uncovering mystical (aporetic) senses in the ancient Greek texts.[1] By then, classical rhetoric had long since appropriated allegory, registering it as a main attraction in its set of tropes, in Latin at the very earliest in the *Rhetorica ad Herennium*, where it was listed under the name *permutatio:* "Allegory is a manner of speech denoting one thing by the letter of the words, but another by their meaning" (4.34.46), *permutatio est oratio aliud verbis aliud sententia demonstrans.*

The definition in Cicero's seminal dialogue *On the Orator* is both linked up with and in contrast to that of the metaphor: "for from this class of expression comes a development not consisting in the metaphorical use of a single word but in a chain of words linked together, so that something other than what is said has to be understood" (3.41.166), *nam illud quod ex hoc genere profluit non est in uno verbo translato sed ex pluribus continuatis connectitur, ut aliud dicatur, aliud intellegendum sit.* The speaker, Crassus, notes that this figure "is a valuable stylistic ornament; but care must be taken to avoid obscurity" (3.42.167), *est hoc magnum ornamentum orationis. In quo obscuritas fugienda est*, a reminder that would be habitually ignored by many speculative enthusiasts up to the present day. In *The Orator's Education* a century and a half later, Quintilian was to provide the classical definition of allegory, to which we shall soon return: "Allegory, which people translate *inversio*, presents one thing by its words and either a different or sometimes even a contrary thing by its sense" (8.6.44), *allegoria, quam inversionem interpretantur, aut aliud verbis, aliud sensu ostendit, aut etiam interim contrarium*. In the first and milder version, where the words and their meaning merely follow divergent paths, allegory could probably be understood as a continuous series of metaphors, what Quintilian elsewhere calls *continua metaphora* (9.2.46). In the later version, where allegory's sense actually clashes with its words, it approaches irony.

---

[1] See the chapters "Mimesis: Eicon and Symbol" in Coulter 1976, pp. 32–72, and – the slightly deviating – "Allegory, Symbols and Mysteries" in Sheppard 1980, pp. 145–61.

The same rhetorical tradition frequently associated another figure of speech, *aenigma* (from the Greek *ainos:* 'clever saying', 'riddle', 'story'), with allegory. To keep them apart, Crassus, in *On the Orator*, had used a quantitative classification: allegory extended metaphor to several words, and enigma in its turn extended allegory to an entire phrase (3.42.167), *in oratione, id est in continuatione verborum*. The sober Quintilian, for his part, had made a qualitative distinction, complaining about the kind of allegory that had gone astray in obscurity, *aenigma*, a defect in speech, nevertheless exploited among the poets (8.6.52).

Notwithstanding especially Cicero's great importance, it was the Late Antique grammarians' profuse inventories of tropes that did most to communicate the classical repertoire of figures to medieval culture. This grammatical tradition took a particular interest in the enigma, perhaps a natural development in view of the discipline's responsibility for *enarratio poetarum*, regularly dealing with texts considered covert and obscure. In the section *De tropis* of his widespread school grammar *Ars maior*, Donatus explained: 'Allegory is the trope by which something else is signified than what is said' (3.6), *Allegoria est tropus, quo aliud significatur quam dicitur*. This figure is provided with no fewer than seven subdivisions, of which *aenigma* 'is an assertion which is obscure because of some concealed likeness of things, such as 'my mother gave birth to me, and soon she will be born out of me', which means that water thickens to ice and will flow away from it again.'[1] Donatus' example may seem trivial, but his emphasis on the esoteric nature of the allegorical enigma in terms such as *obscurus* and *occultus* is characteristic.

The twentieth century's reawakened research interest in allegory, thanks to learned scholars like Pépin, his predecessor Henri de Lubac and others, has covered this field well, and nowadays there are plenty of surveys and symposium volumes on the subject.[2] Augustine returned to it throughout his exegetic

---

[1] "Aenigma est obscura sententia per occultam similitudinem rerum, ut *mater me genuit, eadem mox gignitur ex me*, cum significet aquam in glaciem concrescere et ex eadem rursus effluere." I quote from H. Keil's and T. Mommsen's edition 1864 (translation mine).

[2] As far as allegory's pre-Christian history is concerned, Pépin 1976 is probably still the most exhaustive study. For Late Antiquity and the Middle Ages, see Pépin 1987, in particular the first four chapters which deal with the allegorical tradition from Philo to Porphyry. De Lubac's magisterial investigation in four volumes 1959–63 concentrates on the conception of the fourfold meaning of the Bible in medieval exegesis. Cf. the chapters "Ancient Configurations" and "Rites of Passage: Transitions between Antiquity and the Middle Ages" in Whitman 1987, and, in addition, the same Whitman's conference volume 2000, pp. 33–45. Finally, Pompeo Giannantonio presents a thoroughly substantiated exposé on medieval allegory in the second chapter of his *Dante e l'allegorismo* 1969, pp. 91–185 (for Augustine, see pp. 110–18). A dense summary of Augustine's theory of allegory is available in Harrison 1992, pp. 89–95.

work. The following will have as its main objective an explanation of how he came to mark off a particular Biblical kind of allegory from the rhetorical trope that passed under the same name. This so-called "mystery" became a central issue for him, as we shall see, since it *a priori* guaranteed an authentic or veracious type of linguistic figuration, safely immune to the discursive fictionality prone to infiltrate all ornaments of rhetoric.

To put it shortly, in order to narrow down this particular method of establishing reliable meaning, Augustine felt obliged to resort to a hermeneutic separation process, which I will have to simplify for brevity's sake. His fascination with eloquent display had to submit to his preoccupation with allegorical gravity. This, however, was a slow and arduous development. Augustine never forgot the rhetorical tradition based on Cicero in which he had been brought up. It still colours significant sections of *On Christian Doctrine* where, as David Dawson observes, the author would conform to the language disciplines and register allegory as one of the tropes of figurative discourse (3.29.40). He could even use the term "allegory" as a synonym for figurative language in general, the *tropica locutio* which in turn became a special case of his overall sign theory. Thus, Dawson concludes, "figurative speech and allegory are essentially the same in *De doctrina christiana*, and they share the linguistic structure of the sign".[1] Notwithstanding all such traces of the Church Father's rhetorical training, he took an increasing interest in Christianized Hellenistic methods of interpretation, focused on allegorical deciphering of canonized pagan or sacred texts. His persistent attention to the eloquent trope finally had to yield to a mystical method of signification: a semiotic strategy or technique, reserved for the Bible, which could appear under different names in his works. The one he preferred was *allegoria*, sometimes qualified as *aenigma*.

*

The most important incentive for Augustine's theory of the truthful allegory can be found in the Holy Writ itself. We learn from the author of the *Confessions* that even in his early years he had studied the Bible, but his refined rhetorical and classical schooling had caused him to turn away from it. He was simply not prepared for this type of unpolished barbarian literature, so different from the elegant and urban Roman poetry he had grown up with. To him, the Bible with its many strange tales in the low style had simply seemed "unworthy", *indigna*, compared to "Cicero's dignified prose", *tulliana dignitas*: "My swollen pride recoiled from its style and my intelligence failed to penetrate to its inner meaning"

---

[1] Dawson 1995, pp. 139f.

(3.5.9), *tumor enim meus refugiebat modum eius et acies mea non penetrabat interiora eius.*

At the time of writing, the confessor fortunately knows better. He has learnt to adapt his interpretive intelligence to the Biblical letter's humble or low level in order to be able to penetrate its inner secrets. In both his *Confessions* and a number of his later writings, Augustine teaches us exegetics. The fifteenth and last book of *On the Trinity* is an ingenious commentary on the crucial sentence in Paul which we have already glimpsed in this chapter: "For now we see in a mirror dimly" (1 Corinthians 13.12). The term "dimly" or 'enigmatically', *in aenigmate*, is in fact incomprehensible, Augustine remarks, to anyone who has not familiarized himself with the doctrine of tropes. In particular, he refers to the trope which the apostle himself had exploited in another famous passage: his comment in the Epistle to the Galatians on the story known from Genesis of Abraham's two sons, one by his female servant (Hagar) and one by his "free" wife (Sarah). "Now this may be interpreted allegorically", Paul had emphasized (Galatians 4.24), in the Vulgate: *quae sunt per allegoriam dicta.* In the retrospective light of the new faith, Ishmael and Isaac stand for two covenants, the old one of the Jews and the new one of the Christian Church. To be able to classify this kind of transferred sense, Paul had tried a participle of the verb *allēgorein*, 'to speak differently', a concept that by now had superseded the old *hyponoia* in Greek tradition. In the wake of Jerome, Augustine translated the term literally as *allegoria* in *On the Trinity* (15.9.15).

The Church Father continued his commentary with a definition of allegory – quite in line with contemporary rhetorical and grammatical practice – as the trope by which we get to understand something through something else, *tropus ubi ex alio aliud intellegitur.* On this point his exegesis agrees with that of Jerome, who, in his comment on the same key verse from the Epistle to the Galatians, assigned the *figura* or *tropus* of allegory to the domains of poetry and rhetoric: it was common to both profane and Biblical literature, and it 'presents a message whose meaning differs from the words themselves', *aliud praetendit in verbis, aliud significat in sensu.*[1] Still, Augustine pushes his analysis even further. He adds that the proper sense of allegory is self-evident to most people: "here the meaning is patent to all but the very dull", *nisi multum tardis iste sensus in promptu est.* On an overall level, then, allegory might be transparent, but it has various subdivisions, one of which is *aenigma*, defined as "an obscure allegory", *obscura allegoria.*

---

[1] *PL* 26.389c.

We seem to recognize the classification we have met in Donatus: the enigma as an obscure, special case of the general concept of allegory. In *On the Trinity*, however, Augustine stresses more strongly than anyone before him that this *aenigma* is fundamentally situated outside language (15.9.15):[1]

> But when the apostle spoke of an allegory, he does not find it in the words, but in the fact [*in facto*]; since he has shown that the two Testaments are to be understood by the two sons of Abraham, one by a bondmaid, and the other by a free woman, which was a thing not said, but also done [*factum*]. And before this was explained, it was obscure; and accordingly such an allegory, which is the generic name, could be specifically called an enigma.

In contrast to the standard allegory trope, the enigma presupposes a method of signification that Augustine locates beyond words. More precisely, it operates with a twofold constitution of meaning. The Old Testament (linguistic) statement refers to a certain kind of reality, Abraham's two sons, a carnal *factum* that in turn becomes a (non-verbal) sign for the utmost sense of the whole construction: the two covenants. In this case, then, it is not only words but just as much things, persons and events – a kind of "visible words", *quaedam verba visibilia*, as we remember from *Of True Religion* (50.98) – that carry meaning. This is a figure that transgresses the limits of language. It extends into the circumstances, *in factis*, or, alternatively, into reality, *in facto*. And this reality is fundamentally of a divine nature. In the Church Father's eyes, there is no doubt about who the final referent of this kind of allegory is. The ultimate goal for all our interpretive activities must be the comprehension of the triune God and his work of salvation, that is, to proceed *ad intellegendum Deum* (15.9.16).

It seems, accordingly, clear that what Augustine called "enigma" in *On the Trinity* interacts or blends with what we have already learnt to identify as his typological or Biblical-mystical method of interpretation. His designations for it altered considerably during his writing career. They did not necessarily involve the concept of allegory. When, in various contexts, Augustine sketched out different levels of interpretation of the Old Testament – a set of early drafts of the so-called *quadriga*, the theory of the Bible's four meanings, which was to have a noticeable theoretical influence on medieval exegesis – he might for instance, in *The Usefulness of Belief*, experiment with the term *analogia* (3.5–7).[2] In addition,

---

1 "Sed ubi allegoriam nominavit Apostolus, non in verbis eam reperit, sed in facto, cum e duobus filiis Abrahae, uno de ancilla, altero de libera, quod non dictum, sed etiam factum fuit, duo Testamenta intellegenda monstravit; quod antequam exponeret, obscurum fuit: proinde allegoria talis, quod est generale nomen, posset specialiter aenigma nominari."
2 Besides *The Usefulness of Belief*, which distinguishes between the Biblical text's *historia, aetiologia, analogia,* and *allegoria*, see *Of True Religion*, 50.99, which directly anticipates the medi-

as pointed out by Cornelius Mayer, the author of two extensive monographs on the Church Father's theory of signs, although he could vary between *umbra*, *mysterium* and *typus*, it was the term *figura*, one among the Vulgate's renderings of the Greek *typos*, that he came to prefer.[1] The way this particular type of figuration is structured and how it differs from the standard rhetorical set of tropes becomes even clearer in *On Christian Doctrine*. There, Augustine uses the term 'transferred signs', *signa translata*, for the allegory *in factis*, typically implemented in the Holy Writ. It occurs, he explains, "when the actual things which we signify by the particular words are used to signify something else: when, for example, we say *bovem* and not only interpret these two syllables to mean the animal normally referred to by that name but also understand, by that animal, 'worker in the gospel'", that is to say, Luke (2.10.15).[2]

The actual coupling of the ox to Luke was customary. From the earliest days of the Church it had been common to depict or configure the four evangelists as, in turn, an angel (or winged man), a lion, an ox and an eagle. The Biblical starting point for this type of symbolism was, as a rule, the vision of the four winged creatures in Ezekiel 1.4–14, reused in the Book of Revelation 4.7. As for the ox, Augustine refers to the Pentateuch and to Paul, but for the moment we need not worry about particular Bible passages. What is essential in this context is that

---

eval historical-literal, allegorical (typological), moral-tropological, and anagogical *quadriga*. The theory of the four senses of the Bible originates from Alexandrian theology and would perhaps receive its most famous articulations in Thomas Aquinas and Dante; nonetheless, in a 1958 article, Morton W. Bloomfield has demonstrated that the scheme was never implemented in any systematical manner in medieval culture. The same could be said of Augustine: his readers would look in vain for any applications on a large scale of the *quadriga*, and this model is of no importance to such crucial exegetical works as *The Literal Meaning of Genesis* or *On Christian Doctrine*. Not even in the *De Genesi ad litteram imperfectus liber* (*Unfinished Literal Commentary on Genesis*), where the author initially, 2.5, registers the same fourfold scheme as in *The Usefulness of Belief*, do we find any actual application of it.

1 Mayer 1974, pp. 458–63.

2 "Translata sunt, cum et ipsae res quas propriis verbis significamus, ad aliquid aliud significandum usurpantur, sicut dicimus bovem et per has duas syllabas intellegimus pecus quod isto nomine appellari solet, sed rursus per illud pecus intellegimus evangelistam". These *signa translata* have been examined from different angles in recent research, but their Biblical-mystical field of application seems incontrovertible. The editors of the latest edition of *On Christian Doctrine* in the French Bibliothèque Augustinienne, Isabelle Bochet and Goulven Madec, make a relevant observation in pointing out that, in the first book of the treatise (1.2.2), all examples of things which in addition turn out to be signs – the ram that Abraham sacrificed, the stone Jacob used as a pillow, the piece of wood which Moses threw into the waters – might help us to understand Augustine's concept of *signa translata*: it is designed to "include the figures in the Biblical sense of the term, where they become something else than metaphors", 1997b, p. 492.

both of the Augustinian examples of Biblical allegory we have been looking at, the sons of Abraham and the ox, are taken from the old Hebrew scriptures but are explained with reference to the New Testament. In short, they presume the typological relationship between the Testaments. Consequently, we might schematize the two-stage allegory of the enigma as follows:
- A word or concept in the Old Testament, for example 'ox', refers to a being, an event or a thing in substantial reality, in this case the animal ox. So far the meaning of the text is literal.
- The text's literal referent, the 'type' (in our example the ox), points in turn to a person, an event or a thing in the New Testament, the 'antitype' (here: Luke the Evangelist). In the course of this semiotic procedure, which turns the first tenor of the figure into a new vehicle, the sign is 'transferred', *translatum*, to its final meaning.

Even if Augustine in *On the Trinity* could consider the "enigma" to be a special case of allegory, it seems as if the Biblical-typological kind of figuration, an entire semiotic strategy requiring a corresponding hermeneutic competence, ought to be distinguished from the other figures listed in the handbooks of rhetoric and grammar, from Aristotle to Donatus. One of these is, of course, the allegory understood as a trope which, for the sake of clarity and contrast, we might call the eloquent allegory. Typological interpretation always takes the literal sense into account, as Robert A. Markus has pointed out, whereas the eloquent allegory can ignore it.[1] It seems only natural that Augustine – who devoted his analytical energy to the problem of time more subtly than any other philosopher of Antiquity or the Middle Ages, most intensely in Books X and XI of his *Confessions* – should thus subject Biblical imagery to a temporal optic, charging it with historical and soteriological significance. He made exegesis dependent on man's historicity. The Old Testament's veracity appeared indisputable since its enigmatic prophecies had been fulfilled as a result of the Incarnation.

*

In order to establish and delimit the allegory *in facto* (or, as it were, *in tempore*), Augustine thus distinguished between the trope that is based on speculative analogy and the 'type' that presupposes an extant historical substratum. His pioneering predecessor, Origen of Alexandria, had detected a great many allegories of the former kind in the Bible, amounting to a figurative language that suggested a higher, mystical and timeless significance. The background to Origen's alle-

---

[1] Markus 1996, p. 11.

goresis is complex, with elements of Platonic dualism, Hellenistic commentaries on Homer and Philo's speculative exegesis, but there is no doubt about its immediate cause: his heated battles with the intellectual pagans who, in their criticism of the new faith, had set out to recycle the classical arguments against the Homeric depiction of the gods. Foremost among them was Celsus (see above, p. 66), who – one or two generations earlier – had aggressively highlighted the Old Testament God's scanty or even lack of mightiness and dignity, *theoprepeia*.

Origen's answer was undoubtedly inspired by Platonist notions of the inferiority of matter compared with spiritual reality. He accused Celsus (and some of his own Christian brothers) of excessive attention to the letter of the Bible. His early key treatise in the field of hermeneutics, *On First Principles* from the 210s or 220s, is preserved in a few extracts and in Rufinus' Latin translation from about 400. There, the author criticizes the Gnostics, his indefatigable adversaries, for abandoning the true faith and letting themselves be led astray by "various inventions and fables", *figmenta varia ac fabulae*. This is because they have not read the Bible in search of its spiritual sense but only "according to its literal meaning", *secundum litterae sonum* (4.2.1–2). For his own part, he distinguished – in *On First Principles* – three senses of the Holy Writ: one corporeal (literal), one psychic and one spiritual, identified in terms such as *sarx* (or *sōma*), *psychē* and *pneuma* respectively, with a heavy emphasis on the last.[1] In this way, the Church Father from Alexandria tried to extract and subsequently isolate the transcendental contents of the Holy Writ from its letter which, read or listened to in its own right, threatened to lure the audience away from its firm signification into the dangerous waters of unreliable fiction. This was Origen's way – Werner Jaeger observes – of safeguarding a Christian culture or *paideia*, based on the Bible, more or less as the Stoics' school had launched its theories of allegorical interpretation to justify the Homeric world of erratic divinities against philosophical rationalism.[2] In Origen's eyes, the books of the Bible were not primarily (or merely) an expression of what Hellenistic Greek-speaking writers would call *pistis*, 'faith' in the sense of conviction or belief, but of the 'knowledge' or 'wisdom' with mystical colouring known as *gnōsis*.

Such an attitude to figurative discourse is characteristic of the Hellenistic and Late Antique Platonizing tradition – detectable in the Christian Clement of Alexandria one generation earlier as well as in the pagan Proclus of fifth-century Athens – that discerned a fictive layer in the ancient poets, a curtain or a

---

[1] On the Scripture's threefold *intellegentia*, in Latin related to *corpus* (that is *communis iste et historialis intellectus*), *anima* and *spiritus*, see 4.2.4.
[2] Jaeger 1961, p. 49.

'screen', *parapetasma*, beautiful and seductive albeit potentially misleading and false.[1] Origen felt the presence of such a screen in the Bible, and he yearned to look behind it. Accordingly, even if he was not as open-minded about pagan literature as his predecessor Clement, and even if he did not overlook the literal and typological senses of the Old Testament, he was inclined, as Richard Hanson has shown in his monograph, to expand his allegorical exegesis into a more unrestricted, philosophical interpretation of the Holy Writ. This approach depended to a certain extent on the dehistoricization, typical of much Hellenistic hermeneutics, that colours Origen's dealing with the Bible texts in general and his understanding of the Jewish law, the Christian sacraments, the Incarnation and eschatology in particular. If such exegetical attitudes were taken to their extreme, every single detail in the Holy Writ would be granted a spiritual equivalent in invisible reality.[2]

In his confutation of Celsus, Origen spoke repeatedly about the importance of reading the Biblical writers figuratively, *tropologein*, in order to deduce their 'purpose', *boulēma*. This is exactly the same procedure, he stresses, as Celsus and other pagan authors had legitimately applied to literary works, and it inevitably entails 'reshaping', 'reconstructing' or 'restoring' them, *anaplassein*, in Henry Chadwick's translation: "interpret allegorically" (1.42).[3] Origen himself had already implemented such reading strategies in *On First Principles*. According to this earlier treatise, anyone who cared for truth need not be concerned about "words and language", *nomina et sermones*, which in any case vary between nations; he should rather direct his attention to the content of the message than to the words that convey it (4.3.15), *et hoc magis, quod significatur, quam qualibus verbis significetur*. Moreover, in his exegetic practice, as numerous scholars have pointed out, Origen occasionally reduced his three meanings to two: he could read some (purportedly weird or absurd) Biblical passages as if they were devoid of bodily sense altogether, while he consistently considered both Testaments in complete possession of a psychic as well as spiritual meaning.[4] He argued as if it were possible for the exegete to isolate the sacred referent from the linguistic reference, to make the substantial signified completely supersede the accidental signifiers.

As time passed, Augustine, for his part, became unsure about this, or, to be more precise, in this particular kind of interpretation he sensed the danger of pagan habits of reading, attuned to fictional texts, infiltrating the exegesis of

---

[1] Lamberton 1986, p. 80.
[2] Hanson 1959, pp. 235–88. Cf. Chadwick 1966, p. 112, and Wiles 1970, pp. 478f.
[3] I quote from M. Marcovich's edition, 2001, and H. Chadwick's translation, 1980.
[4] Wiles 1970, pp. 467–70, Trigg 1998, pp. 33f., and Vogt 1999, pp. 183f.

the Holy Writ. If Origen had warned his gnostic opponents that focusing on the letter of notably the Old Testament would only promote the deplorable culture of *figmenta* and *fabulae*, Augustine feared, by contrast, the allurement of fictionality at the other pole of Biblical allegoresis, in the unrestrained or idiosyncratic determination of the text's spiritual meaning potentially resulting from Alexandrian exegesis. Whereas Origen felt the need or even necessity to open up the Scripture, making its possible sense(s) "multiply diffusely", Augustine, as it were, increasingly came to aim at hermeneutic closure in his expositions of both Testaments.[1]

Origen's spiritualizing Biblical exposition usually dealt with allegory in terms of words and their mystical or eternal meaning, while Augustine's understanding of *signa translata* depended much more heavily on the letter and on historical time, more exactly the history of salvation, and on the exegetic guidance offered to us by the Biblical writers themselves, first and foremost Paul. When we call this kind of reading 'typological', the terminology is based on the ancient Greek word *typos*, originally 'mark' or 'impression', later also 'mould', 'matrix' and similar things. This is a manner of interpreting the Bible which, supported by the Pauline epistles, searches the Old Testament for 'types' (cf. Romans 5.14, where Adam is explained as "a type of the one who was to come") that anticipate and are eventually fulfilled in the New Testament's corresponding 'anti-types' (cf. 1 Peter 3.21, where Baptism is explained as an *antitypos* of the Flood), throughout with links or pointers to Christ.[2]

Thus Origen and Augustine adopted different attitudes to the Old Testament. The former had no difficulty in detecting misunderstandings and misinterpretations in the Jewish texts. A typical case: after having listed a number of the trials and tribulations that had struck the children of Israel during the exodus from Egypt, Paul comes to the conclusion that "these things happened to them as an example, but they were written down for our instruction, on whom the end of the ages has come" (1 Corinthians 10.11). The English translation "example" echoes the Greek *typikōs* (in the Vulgate translated as *figura*). When Origen ex-

---

[1] Cf. the very first sentence of Origen's sermon on the Exodus: "I think each word of divine scripture is like a seed whose nature is to multiply diffusely, reborn into an ear of corn or whatever its species be, when it has been cast into the earth" (1.1), *videtur mihi unusquisque sermo Scripturae divinae similis esse alicui seminum, cuius natura haec est, ut, cum iactum fuerit in terram, regeneratum in spicam vel quamcumque aliam sui generis speciem multipliciter diffundatur.* I follow W. Baehrens's edition of Rufinus' Latin version of Origen's sermons 1920; English translation by R.E. Heine 1982.

[2] In both these cases the Vulgate translates *typos* with *forma*: Adam is, according to Romans 5.14, a *forma futuri*, and Baptism in 1 Peter 3.21 is understood as the New Covenant's equivalence, *similis formae*, of the Flood.

pounded Exodus in his *Homilia in Exodum* he certainly drew support from Paul but tended to ignore the historical authenticity and exemplary power of the Old Testament episodes.

"Do you see," he rhetorically asks his readers, "how much Paul's teaching differs from the literal meaning [*historica lectio*]? What the Jews supposed to be a crossing of the sea, Paul calls a baptism; what they supposed to be a cloud, Paul asserts is the Holy Spirit." Evidently Paul was in a position not only to explain but to rectify the assumptions of the Jews. Origen argues almost as if these latter had misinterpreted their own history rather than anticipated the Christian drama of salvation: "Does it not seem right that we apply this kind of rule which was delivered to us in a similar way in other passages? Or as some wish, forsaking these things which such a great Apostle taught, should we turn again to 'Jewish fables?'" (5.1)[1] The author borrows his last polemically charged expression from Paul himself (cf. 1 Titus 1.14, the Vulgate's *iudaicae fabulae*), but judging from this whole passage, it seems fair to conclude that he was liable to detect unreliable fictional ingredients in the literal layer of meaning of the Old Testament.

His countermove was the spiritualizing allegory, capable of dissolving the old patriarchs' and the prophets' literal messages – sometimes contradictory, inappropriate or unbelievable – in irrefutable conceptual meaning. The example from Origen's homilies on Exodus indicates Paul's and the New Testament's decisive importance for this decoding process, but, in a larger perspective, it was based on Greek philosophy and the richly ramified system of correspondences and analogies that formed Late Antiquity's and the early Middle Ages' "cultural encyclopedia", to borrow Umberto Eco's expression.[2] This kind of high-flying allegoresis has triggered a good deal of scholarly attention lately, perhaps due to its impressing imaginative range, but it certainly became a target for some trenchant criticism among ascetically minded intellectuals at the end of the fourth century in the Latin West. Geoffrey Lampe has observed that it did not

---

[1] "Videtis, quanto differat ab historica lectione Pauli traditio: quod Iudaei transitum maris putant, Paulus baptismus vocat; quam illi aestimant nubem, Paulus Spiritum sanctum ponit; [...]. Nonne iustum videtur, ut traditam nobis huiusmodi regulam simili in ceteris servemus exemplo? An, ut quidam volunt, haec, quae tantus ac talis Apostolus tradidit, relinquentes rursum ad 'Iudaicas fabulas' convertamur?"

[2] Eco's implementation of this concept – recycled by Martin Irvine in his major survey of the period's "textual culture" 1994, pp. 246, 260–71 – seems inspired by the famous "Porphyrian tree", a hierarchical scheme ordering and classifying the universe according to Aristotelian universals or substances, the basis for all later medieval versions of the principle of the *analogia entis*. See Eco 1986, pp. 57–68, 103–05.

rely on any consistent internal criteria for its interpretive procedures.¹ Consequently, it was commonly perceived as somewhat arbitrary in its conclusions, potentially blurring the line between Alexandrian philology's way of dealing with ancient myths and Christian exegesis of the Bible.

For his part, Augustine learnt to recognize a material continuity between the two covenants. In *On the Catechising of the Uninstructed* he dwelled on Genesis 25.26, where the birth of the twins Esau and Jacob is described: the former came first, followed by Jacob "with his hand holding Esau's heel". In the same way, Augustine explains, Christ made part of His body manifest in advance, in the words of the patriarchs and the prophets. The Church Father concludes his brief interpretation by reusing the Epistles to the Romans and to the Corinthians: "Wherefore all things which were written aforetime were written in order that we might be taught thereby, and were our figures, and happened in a figure in the case of these men. Moreover they were written for our sakes, upon whom the end of the ages has come." (3.6)² Thus the Pauline basis for Augustine's hermeneutics is exactly the same as Origen could refer to, but the shift in emphasis compared to his predecessor's spiritualizing allegory is unmistakable. His typological method of interpretation is established on firm historical ground and depends primarily on the Biblical text's own indications.

*

How Augustine worked out this exegetic strategy, consummately detailed in *On the Trinity* and *On Christian Doctrine*, deserves its own investigation and need not be examined more closely here. To a certain extent it was already outlined *in nuce* by the first generations of Christians, most notoriously (and cleverly) by Paul. It was of interest to Jerome, who in a letter to Paulinus of Nola from the mid-390s could distinguish the historical narrative of the Books of Kings, *historia*, characterized by its straightforward vocabulary, *verba simplicia*, from the hidden meaning beneath the surface of the letters, *in litteris sensus latens*, corresponding to the future trials of the Christian Church. Furthermore, the Church Father in Bethlehem noted that the Old Testament prophets "have typical meanings far different from their literal ones", *multo aliud quam sonant in littera praefigurant*. In this spirit he read Jonah's shipwreck as a presage of Christ's suffering, *passionem Domini praefigurans* (53.8).³

---

1 Lampe 1969, pp. 165f.
2 "Quapropter omnia quae ante scripta sunt, ut nos doceremur scripta sunt, et figurae nostrae fuerunt; et *in figura contingebant in eis: scripta sunt autem propter nos, in quos finis saeculorum obvenit*." Cf. in turn Romans 15.4, 1 Corinthians 10.6 and 10.11.
3 *PL* 22.546.

The same typological principle controls Prudentius' preface to his poem *Hamartigenia* (*The Origin of Sin*), triggered by the story of Cain and Abel, the latter of whom is considered a type of Christ: "So the tale of olden times took its beginning from things that were to be, and the last deed was indicated by the first" (PR.25–26), *ergo ex futuris prisca coepit fabula / factoque primo res notata est ultima*. Ever since the sixth century BCE and the days of Theagenes of Rhegium, allegory had been implemented along three main lines according to the category of its referents: physical (the gods or heroes representing elements of nature; Agamemnon = the ether), psychological (these same figures representing human qualities; Aphrodite = desire) and moral (Hercules at the crossroads = virtue). Now, however, Augustine, Jerome and Prudentius, all three belonging to the same generation, present us with a different class of transference of meaning. Typological interpretation, as the Clement specialist Willem den Boer underlines, makes the decisive difference between Jewish-Christian and pagan allegory.[1]

How the former was detached from the latter during the first few centuries of our era is a complicated matter. To all appearances, neither Clement nor Origen made any clear-cut distinction between these two interpretive strategies but let them quite simply be termed allegory. Both theologians from Alexandria were still dependent on Hellenistic allegoresis as it had been practised by Philo. In that tradition, for example, the bronze serpent in Numbers 21.9 represents a call for self-discipline, while Sarah and Hagar in Genesis 16–17 simply stood for sacred wisdom and secular education, *paideia*, respectively.[2] This is in striking contrast to the Pauline understanding of Abraham's wife and her maidservant as "two covenants" in Galatians 4.24, the *locus classicus* of typological interpretation in the Bible. But the line of demarcation between what the Hellenistic schools had classified as allegory, symbol or paradigm and what we – nowadays – call Biblical typology was by no means as clear as it may seem with our hindsight. We are well advised to infer that classical pagan modes or models of exposition regularly infiltrated Jewish-Christian hermeneutics.[3] The temptation to overlook the historical circumstances and the literal meaning of the Old Testament texts was latent all through the exegetic culture of Late Antiquity and could at any time come to the fore, as when Prudentius dared to apply the term *fabula*, charged with associations of myth and fictionality, to the story of Cain and Abel in *The Origin of Sin*.

---

1 Boer 1973, p. 18.
2 Lampe 1969, pp. 171f.
3 For examples, see Reinhart Herzog's article "Metapher – Exegese – Mythos. Interpretationen zur Entstehung eines biblischen Mythos in der Literatur der Spätantike", 2002, pp. 115–53.

That is why the Latin Fathers of the fourth century, particularly Jerome and Augustine, felt so intensely the need to create and maintain certain fundamental distinctions in this rough and turbulent field. Origen had founded such an influential and powerful paradigm that it was inevitable to assess and challenge it in order to establish one's own exegetic authority. We are reminded of Beryl Smalley's statement in her pioneering work *The Study of the Bible in the Middle Ages:* "To write a history of Origenist influence on the west would be tantamount to writing a history of western exegesis."[1] As early as the third century, the theologians of Antioch had entered into a controversy with their Alexandrian colleagues for the purpose of emphasizing the literal and historical meaning of the Bible. If they accepted typological interpretation, they restricted its range of applications considerably; to Theodore of Mopsuestia, an Antiochene contemporary of Augustine, the bronze serpent was a type of Christ – one of three available (along with the blood of the lamb and Jonah in the belly of the whale) in the whole of the Old Testament.[2] The Antiochenes, however, exercised little influence on the Latin West, and no one, at any rate, devoted such painstaking theoretical attention to this tension in Late Antique exegesis as Augustine.

It is relevant to this context that at an early stage of his career, as a convert, he had indubitably been impressed by Origen's spiritualizing interpretation of the Bible, as it was crucial to his venerated teacher Ambrose. The Milanese Archbishop was the Western Church's most authoritative spokesman for the spiritual meaning of the Bible, partly by virtue of a series of comments on the Song of Songs, deeply influenced by Origenist exegesis.[3] And he had most decisively helped Augustine, as we have seen in the latter's *Confessions* (6.4.6), to experience the liberating force of Paul's famous words to the congregation in Corinth: "For the letter kills, but the Spirit gives life" (2 Corinthians 3.6), thereby drawing aside the "veil of mystery" that used to conceal the Scripture's message to his catechumen's enquiring mind. The very metaphor, *mysticum velamentum*, points at least indirectly to Origen as well as to Paul. Nonetheless, once established in Hippo Regius, Augustine felt obliged to restrain this hermeneutic joy of discovery in favour of an increasing need to regulate the conditions for a more austere, typologically oriented exegesis.

---

[1] Smalley 1984, p. 14.
[2] Akiyama 2001, p. 49.
[3] Cf. Matter 1990, p. 25. In addition, there are some scholars embracing the hypothesis of an early direct Origenist influence on Augustine; in his study of 2009, György Heidl goes so far (perhaps too far) as to postulate a decisive experience of the Alexandrian Father's *Homilies on the Song of Songs* on the part of Augustine in 386–87, the years of his conversion and baptism.

The turn of the tide in this respect probably came about as early as the 390s, when Augustine was busy studying Paul and issuing his anti-Manichaean treatises, where it certainly was vital to demonstrate the close relation between both Testaments.[1] In his later work, he returned to the fundamental assumptions of typology. The Hebrew prophets, he noted in his polemic against Faustus the Manichee, are crammed with portents, *praeconia*, about Christ: "Often the reference is allegorical or enigmatical, perhaps in a verbal allusion, or in a historical narrative" (12.7), *per allegorias et aenigmata, partim verbis solis insinuantur, partim etiam facta narrantur.* Augustine primarily applied this typological scheme in his readings of the Pentateuch, the Psalms, the prophets and the Gospels. I have already quoted his references to the sons of Abraham in *On the Trinity*, to the evangelical ox in *On Christian Doctrine* and to Jacob/Esau in *On the Catechising of the Uninstructed* as examples of the allegory *in facto*. An equally telling illustration, dependent on the Pauline metaphors of shadows that we have seen Augustine exploit in *The Literal Meaning of Genesis* (above, pp. 103f.), is to be found in his commentary on the Gospel according to St. John 11.55, when speaking of the Jewish Passover (50.2):[2]

> But that celebration was a shadow of the future. And why a shadow? It was a prophetic intimation of the Christ to come, a prophecy of Him who on that day was to suffer for us: that so the shadow might vanish and the light come; that the sign might pass away, and the truth be retained. The Jews therefore held the passover in a shadowy form, but we in the light.

For Augustine, the typological allegory was a way of checking the diffusion of meaning in language that he knew so well and felt so uneasy about. It forced him to read both literally – in this case to reflect on the Jewish Passover, on the slaughter of the lamb and the marking of the doorposts with its blood (cf. Exodus 12.7) – and to solve the shadow-like *significatio* of the Old Testament letter in the light of the truth where all the portents of the Old Covenant were fulfilled, in Christ.[3]

---

[1] See Mayer 1974, pp. 194–97.
[2] "Sed illa celebratio umbra erat futuri. Quia est, umbra futuri? Prophetia Christi venturi, prophetia pro nobis illo die passuri: ut transiret umbra, et lux veniret; ut transiret significatio, et veritas teneretur. Habebant ergo Iudaei Pascha in umbra, nos in luce."
[3] The themes of the shadow and the truth had precedences in the Bible (cf. Colossians 2.17: "These are a shadow of the things to come", *quae sunt umbra futurorum*), but it was Clement of Alexandria and, above all, Origen who combined them into the standard antithesis which – as Neil Adkin has demonstrated in a short article – became "extremely frequent" among the Fathers, 1984, p. 245.

This might, to a certain extent, be a question of a hermeneutics whose constant aim was – to quote Simon Brittan – "finding new ways of saying the same thing".[1] But thanks to Augustine, it developed into a decisive argument for the unity of the Testaments, a central issue in the exegetical controversies of the fourth and fifth centuries, not least in his own polemic against the Manichees. In his *Reply to Faustus the Manichaean*, for example, the Bishop of Hippo looked upon the Old Testament in its entirety as a "figure" for the New (16.19). In the long term, this kind of *figura* evolved into the basis of the Western Church's historical-dynamic perspective on the Bible and the Revelation, as a powerful corrective to the spiritualizing and metaphysical speculation of the Alexandrian theologians. This process is evident throughout the Middle Ages, whose secular and ecclesiastical leaders at an early stage – admittedly at an official-dogmatic rather than at a practical-exegetic level – repudiated Hellenizing Origen (and even condemned him as a heretic) to the advantage of Augustine. The Latin Father's elegant account of the close connection between the two Testaments was frequently quoted or paraphrased: 'The New lies concealed in the Old, and the Old is revealed in the New', *et in Vetere Novum lateat, et in Novo Vetus pateat*.[2]

Just as Origen's paradigm was at the root of practically all mystical interpretations of the Bible which flourished during the Early and High Middle Ages, it is difficult – as Gerald Bonner has remarked – to overestimate the importance of this Augustinian version of typology for later Western exegesis.[3] It can still be detected in Dante's congenial imagery: Beatrice explains the river of light, the living sparks and the flowery meadows in the Empyrean as signs or portents, "shadowy prefaces of their truth" (Paradiso 30.78), "di lor vero umbriferi prefazi". Beginning with Adam and the Garden of Eden, the key types of the Old Testament might indeed be considered a set of shadowy prefaces to Christological or apocalyptic truth, though Beatrice's bold implementation of such allegories *de facto* in a work of fiction, a *commedia* or *poema*, would undoubtedly have met with the African bishop's strong disapproval. In his eyes, the exclusive domain reserved for this privileged kind of signifiers was the Holy Writ.

Such restraint did not prevent Augustine from being able to identify allegories of the traditional rhetorical type – more or less as we have seen him distinguish other well-known tropes – in the Bible. A beautiful example of this sensi-

---

[1] Brittan 2003, p. 2.
[2] I quote from *Questiones in Heptateuchum* (*Questions Concerning the Heptateuch*), 2.73, written in 419–20. Augustine had already sketched out this sentence in *De spiritu et littera* (*A Treatise on the Spirit and the Letter*), 15.27, a few years earlier, possibly inspired by the typologically minded second-century apologist Irenaeus.
[3] Bonner 1970, p. 554.

tivity to eloquent figuration is to be found in the *Enarrationes in Psalmos* (*Expositions on the Book of Psalms*) which occupied him for some twenty years, partly in parallel with *On the Trinity*, culminating around 415. The comment in question deals with the invocation of the Creator of the world in Psalms 104.3: "he makes the clouds his chariot; he rides on the wings of the wind", in the Vulgate 103.3: *qui ponis nubem ascensum tuum qui ambulas super pinnas ventorum.* Augustine notes in his first exposition on this psalm that "the wings of the wind" should refer to its swiftness, hence the verse tells us that God's words are faster than all winds. This, he adds, seems at least to be the meaning of the text at first glance, 'but let us seek something that lies deeper inside, so that these words might indicate some figurative sense to us' (103.1.12), *pulsemus ad aliquid interius, et figurate aliquid nobis indicent istae litterae.*[1]

This deeper or 'inner' meaning of 'the wings of the wind' is elucidated by Augustine in a passage that is the most consummate description of the eloquent allegory – allegory as a trope – that I have found in his works. The winds, he explains, refer *in figura* or, more specifically, *in allegoria* to our souls, since they are invisible yet physically perceptible (103.1.13):

> But you must not think that I, by mentioning allegory, have said something pertinent to the theatre. There are actually some words that we have in common with plays and games, even ill-reputed ones, precisely since they are nothing but words, engendered by our tongue. Still, these words have their place in Church as well as on stage. After all, I have not said anything that the Apostle himself did not assert, when he claimed on account of Abraham's two sons: *Now this may be interpreted allegorically.* An allegory is at hand when something seems to be announced in words while it signifies something else to the mind. It is in this sense that Christ may be called a lamb – or is he an animal? Christ is likewise called a lion – is he, do you think, a beast? Christ is called a rock – is he something stiff? Christ is called a mountain – is he protruding from the earth? In this way, then, there seem to be many sayings which announce something while they signify something else; and this is called allegory. Accordingly, anyone believing that my use of the term allegory has anything to do with the stage might just as well believe that our Lord was referring to the amphitheatre by the word parable. You can see for yourselves what happens in a city with lots of spectacles being performed. I would feel more confident delivering a speech in the country, since people living there have probably never heard of allegories, if not from the Bible. Thus, just as we qualify allegory as a figure, we claim that a sacred mystery conveyed by figurative speech is an allegory. How, then, shall we understand this: *he rides on the wings of the wind?* We just said that the wings should be understood as a figure for the souls. So what are the wings of the winds, that is, the wings of the souls, if not the power which makes them soar upwards? Hence, the wings of the souls are virtues, good deeds and righteous actions. They are all neatly paired, which means that all commandments are of

---

[1] All translations from Augustine's first exposition of Psalms 103 are mine.

two kinds. Anyone who loves God and his neighbour, then, has a winged soul and is able to fly freely, borne by this holy love, all the way to the Lord. (XXV)

In this paragraph, Augustine applies his overall theory of figurative language – as we have tried to explain it in the light of tracts such as *On Christian Doctrine* or *Against Lying* – specifically to allegory. His definition of allegory as a trope is in perfect accordance with the standard rhetorical manuals: in this figure 'something seems to be announced in words while it signifies something else to the mind'. Now, allegory in this general and technical sense can sometimes be put to frivolous use, while on other occasions it might serve unimpeachable purposes. As an eloquent device it is, *per se*, neutral. Consequently, its legitimacy is completely dependent on situation, context, and genre. In the exposition of Psalm 103, Augustine does not seem to make any principal distinction between typological interpretation (as in Galatians 4.24) and other – legitimate – kinds of Biblical allegory; as far as can be judged, they are all subsumed under the definition 'sacred mystery conveyed by figurative speech', *sacramentum figuratum*. Here, then, Augustine contents himself with a nod in passing to the Pauline typology, while he concentrates on the Psalmist's reference to the wings of the wind, which he exposes to a clever mystical-Origenist kind of explanation, translating it, point by point, into abstract concepts. On the one hand, this figure seems to 'announce' (*sonare*) wind and wings in plain words; on the other hand, it is to be grasped *in intellectu* as signifying something else: human souls (the winds) and a series of moral qualities or deeds (the wings), which in turn can be reduced to the two main commandments of the love of God and of our neighbour.

Notwithstanding the speculative elegance of such interpretative exercises, allegory as a trope depended on cultural assumptions, settings and circumstances. Consequently, it was a hazardous device to use, in particular as it shared its bifurcated structure of meaning, the art of dissimulation, with theatrical acting. That is why the exegete recognizes that it would be safer to apply the figurations of the Psalms in some sermon or public talk delivered in the countryside, *in agro*, knowing full well that he would be understood correctly, since the rural inhabitants had not grown accustomed to ambiguous or covert speech. He would presumably find it more difficult to operate in an urban environment, where people flocked to the theatres, the public setting for mimicry, masques and fiction. Here, Augustine probably argued with a special eye to the notorious theatre fans of Carthage. We also recall from the *Soliloquies* how well he had personally captured the allure of theatrical illusion. For that very reason, the bishop was anxious to distinguish his pious implementations of allegory from the double-tongued speech of the stage. *His* allegory is a *sacramentum figuratum*, situated in a Biblical context, the direct opposite of the dubious theatrical performances.

This commentary on the Psalms might give us a clue to the reason behind Augustine's increasing focus on the allegory *in facto*. Even though he was keen on stressing the mysterious – sacred – foundation of the two Testaments, guaranteed by the Holy Spirit, he could not secure it theoretically as long as he treated the Biblical figures as customary rhetorical tropes, exposed to the readers' or listeners' arbitrary hermeneutic competence, ultimately depending on the "cultural encyclopedia" of the epoch. From a technical point of view it was not easy, especially in environments still heavily influenced by pagan culture, to explain the difference between the mysterious figurations of the Holy Writ on the one hand, and theatrical tricks of impersonation or deliberate lies on the other. This is apparent from Augustine's definition of exactly that, mendacity, in his short treatise *On Lying*: "Wherefore, that man lies, who has one thing in his mind and utters another in words, or by signs of whatever kind. Whence also the heart of him who lies is said to be double; that is, there is a double thought" (3.3).[1] His definition undeniably comes close to those that Cicero and Quintilian used to determine allegory (to quote the latter once again, 8.6.44: *aut aliud verbis, aliud sensu ostendit, aut etiam interim contrarium*). In its function or capacity as a trope, allegory obviously risked being mistaken for lying or acting, both characterized by this *duplex cor*, the former to deceive, the latter to entertain. Dissimulation was certainly common practice in the theatres, but the message of the Spirit refused to acknowledge any 'double heart' whatsoever.

To sum up, Augustine seems to have insisted on his theoretical distinction between the figures of eloquence and the false language of lying. In that sense, he remained faithful to his advanced education in rhetoric. His long-standing experience of the world of tropes might even have been useful to him when Ambrose drew his attention to the necessity of reading the Bible figuratively, of extracting the divine meaning from the "letter" of the text: the liberating experience he reports in his *Confessions*. But in his exegetical practice he did not always find it easy to maintain or explain the clear-cut distinction between figurative discourse and the double-tongued speech of deceit or pretence. The strenuous efforts he made to distinguish the Scripture's *sacramenta* from the tropes of poetry, the theatre or the marketplace testify to his persistent problem

---

1 "Quapropter ille mentitur, qui aliud habet in animo, et aliud verbis vel quibuslibet significationibus enuntiat. Unde etiam duplex cor dicitur esse mentientis, id est, duplex cogitatio".

with the semblance of fiction, the *licentia vatum* which classical culture had accustomed its readers to suspect in figurative language.

Augustine's Pauline assurance that "the spirit gives life", as Robert A. Markus stresses, seemed to result in a multiplicity of interpretive possibilities that risked weakening the absolute authority of the Biblical text.[1] If the exegete *in verbis* had difficulty in securing his interpretation among the plethora of readings made possible by Late Antique hermeneutic culture, the allegory *in facto* could, on the other hand, draw support from the Bible text at the level of both the reference and the (final) referent. By virtue of its focus on the imperative force of the Biblical letter, it could offer Augustine a hermeneutic equivalent to the salvation work of the Incarnation, dependent on Christ's bodily nature, ever since the second century a crucial tenet in the early Church's anti-Gnostic polemics. To all appearances, it provided him with a welcome possibility to ward off the shadow of Creusa from his deliberations on figurative discourse.

Thus Augustine increasingly came to emphasize the special exegesis that the Bible required, the type of "enigma" that in the end had to be read and interpreted differently from the tropes of rhetoric and grammar. As we have intimated, a great number of medieval masters would learn from this hermeneutic and semiotic pioneering achievement, schematized (and simplified) in the neat dichotomy of two kinds of allegory that the Venerable Bede would launch three centuries later, in *De schematibus et tropis* from about 700, as *allegoria in factis* and *allegoria in verbis* (2.12), of which the former was illustrated with precisely Augustine's example: Paul's interpretation of Abraham's two sons in the Epistle to the Galatians 4.24.[2] In modern times, this dichotomy still survives among many scholars, most notably in the work of Erich Auerbach, who has demonstrated the consequences of typological interpretation for poetry with both solid erudition and exceptional sensitivity. He traces its focus on the historical

---

[1] Markus 1996, pp. 12–22. Augustine's Pauline studies in the early 390s could only reinforce his polemical attitude to the exclusive Jewish literalism. This does not mean, however, that he regarded the Law as invalidated. On the contrary, he exerted all his energy in defending, on the one hand, the Old Testament against the Manichaean charges of primitive carnality, and, on the other hand, in correcting Origen and other predecessors who had reinterpreted crucial preceptions of the Law – for instance concerning circumcision – in a spiritualizing manner. As Paula Fredriksen has shown, Augustine consistently read the Old Testament typologically as well as *ad litteram*, 2000, pp. 139–49.

[2] Bede's *De schematibus et tropis* is best studied in C.B. Kendall's edition 1991. In his article on "'Allegoria in factis' et 'Allegoria in verbis'" 1975, Armand Strubel, for his part, prefers to distinguish between Augustine's semiotic, Bede's rhetorical and Thomas Aquinas' hermeneutic treatment of both allegory types.

moment, the pivotal event and the individual being deep down in Dante's infernal circles.[1]

---

[1] See first and foremost the ambitious article "Figura" in Auerbach 1984 (on Augustine, pp. 37–43), and the chapter on Dante in the even more famous *Mimesis* 1968, pp. 174–202.

4 In the Heat of the Battle

Throughout the previous section we have seen Augustine argue for the truth of the Bible at all steps in the interpretation process, in both words and things: "Since then things so true, and so truthfully, be signified", *cum igitur tam vera tamque significentur veraciter...* If at times he could resort to terms like *fictio* or *fingere* in his commentaries on the Holy Scripture, he normally had in mind a kind of sacred eloquence, implemented to bolster the impact of the Christian message.

Perhaps the Bishop of Hippo would have arrived at another understanding of the use and legitimacy of fictional devices if he had not been obliged to stand in the polemical frontline of the expanding African Church. The young Augustine, the philosophical seeker, had shown a marked curiosity about both ancient epic and theatre, an interest that actually – at least judging by his *Confessions* – could evolve into deep fascination. This attention to the poets and the stage was by and large abandoned by the convert, but it nevertheless continued to make itself felt in the bishop's exegetic and apologetic writings. In the years before his conversion in 386, he had undoubtedly taken an interest in classical concepts of fiction. His philosophical reflections from Cassiciacum, dealt with above in the section on the liberal arts, certainly testify to this attentiveness, in particular his deliberations in the *Soliloquies* – however reserved – on the "double-faced" half-truth of theatrical or pictorial representation.

Concerning Augustine's later writings, Karla Pollmann has cited some evidence based on classical logic in *On Christian Doctrine*, as when the author tries to identify various kinds of falsehood: "We may also subdivide it, saying that there are two kinds of falsehood, one consisting of things which cannot possibly be true, another of things which are not true, but could be." (2.35.53)[1] Augustine exemplified this argument with the propositions that seven plus three make eleven (never true under any circumstances) and it rained on January 1st (which, even if it happened to be false, asserts "something which could have been true", *quod fieri potuerit*). It is obvious that the second kind of falseness, of a contingent rather than a necessary kind, is related to both the Aristotelian probability's *mimēsis*, dependent on "the *kinds* of things that might occur", *hoia an genoito*, and the plausible fiction Cicero called *argumentum*, that is, *ficta res, quae tamen fieri potuit* (cf. above, p. 40).

---

1 "Possumus etiam dividere, dicentes duo esse genera falsi, unum eorum quae omnino esse non possunt, alterum eorum quae non sunt, quamvis esse possint." See Pollmann 1996, p. 185.

With hindsight, an observer of later times might take Augustine's ultimate no to fictionality as necessary or at least predictable. As time passed, the domains of probability were curtailed and, finally, wiped out in a hermeneutics that had learnt to identify truth with orthodoxy.[1] The great heritage of classical literature was reduced to, at best, harmless *nugae*, pure trifles, and in the worst case to morally detrimental seduction. Nonetheless, the philosopher in Cassiciacum had once adopted a more open attitude to the conditional, split or ambiguous discursive mode of poetry and drama. The advanced analysis of fictionality in the *Soliloquies* had been followed up by the somewhat later *Of True Religion*, where the author devoted a few pages to the satisfaction we feel when we figure out or decipher *spectacula*, games and shows of all kinds. They arouse a *curiositas* in us that seeks "the joy of knowing things", *de rerum cognitione laetitia*. What can be more attractive, asks Augustine, than the truth that every spectator wants to arrive at? "Hence he takes great care not to be deceived, and vaunts himself if he shows more acuteness and vivacity than others in watching and learning and judging."[2] The audience does its best, he continues, to see through the juggler and his arts, to discover his tricks and catch him out, precisely because everybody ultimately aims at "the comprehension of truth", *comprehensio veritatis* (49.94).

In other words, lies, simulation, jugglery itself spur us on to discover the truth behind the spectacle. This is an idea that at least approaches certain ancient assessments of fictionality (in which imaginative or figurative representation is appreciated due to its didactic potential), but which Augustine, exactly as in the *Soliloquies*, began to abandon as soon as it was formulated, because – pessimistically – he feared the possibility of double-dealing among the audience he is describing. They profess themselves to be lovers of truth, he remarks in *Of True Religion*, but they are actually so sunk "in trifles and baseness", *nugae et turpitudines*, so addicted "to jests and games", *ioci et ludi*, that they inevitably get stuck in the game of make-believe, that is, in the spectacle's elusive *ficta*. In short, when we rejoice in these performances we inadvertently part company with truth, losing the ability to "discover what they imitate, and so we pant for them as if they were the prime objects of beauty. Getting further away from

---

[1] Brian Stock gives a concise summary of Augustine's development from the *Soliloquies*, where Reason supposes literary works to be "true in one sense and false in another: in fact, they establish their truths by means of their falsehoods", to the *Confessions*' Pauline and "progressive view of self-representation based on realistic principles and operating within the master narrative of the Bible", 2010, p. 194.

[2] "Cum vehementer ne fallatur invigilat, et inde se iactat si aliquid acutius ceteris, et vivacius in spectando cognoscat et iudicet?"

these primal objects we embrace our phantasms" (49.95).[1] By now it should be easy to detect the mechanism that controls such arguments. Phantasms take command of our souls, blocking our access to truth. This paragraph from *Of True Religion* gives us an early glimpse of the pious exegete and the polemical apologist whom we shall meet in this section, where *spectacula* are a controversial issue.

Thus did the Church Father mark out his path towards God at the expense of literary fiction. This choice was certainly a very likely one for a theologian who based his ideas on Platonic premises, at least to the extent that their classical dualism was allowed to decide his attitude towards art and poetry. Moreover, such misgivings about fictional discourse and stage performances were a presumable consequence of his mystical renunciation requiring, in the words of the Ostia episode from the *Confessions*, that "every tongue, and every sign, and whatever is subject to transience were wholly stilled" in order to establish contact with divine reality. Finally, Augustine's moral anxiety weighed increasingly heavily in the scales. Where Aristotle, in some famous passages from Chapters VI, XIII and XIV of his *Poetics*, could appreciate tragedy for its *katharsis*, its purging effect on the audience, the Bishop of Hippo Regius saw – as Alexandre Leupin has observed – the exact opposite: its readers/spectators/listeners were captured and soiled in the idolatry of imagined passions.[2]

In this context, Augustine adopted and adapted for his own purposes the advanced criticism of myth and fiction that pagan culture itself had directed against the world of fables. As we saw in the short introductory overview above, it had all begun when, in the archaic *Magna Graeca*, Xenophanes rejected Homer's and Hesiod's unrestrained anthropomorphism, followed by Plato, who in the second chapter of *The Republic* criticized the same poets for their irresponsible lies about the band of criminal, disputing, weeping or camouflaged Olympians (377d–383c). Thus Augustine was by no means the first to use this combative strategy, but few if any of his intellectual Christian brothers in faith proved able to apply it with such superior conceptual skills, and with such success. In his two capacities of militant Church teacher and polemical cultural historian, he benefited first and foremost from Plato's edifying pedagogy, Varro's philosophical theology and the theories of logic and natural science of the Stoics. He exploited these paradigms for a broad attack directed against the very core of classical culture: the old gods and the cult ceremonies celebrated by their wor-

---

[1] "Non iam invenimus quarum rerum imitamenta sint, quibus tamquam primis pulchris inhiamus, et ab eis recedentes amplexamur nostra phantasmata".
[2] Leupin 2003, p. 64.

shippers, the Mediterranean civilization of the great Pan whose decease he did everything to hasten.

Orthodoxy and Heresy

The main explanation of this cultural euthanasia on the part of Augustine is to be found in the dogmatic context of the patristic period which we have glimpsed here and there in the previous presentation, a virtual minefield for many champions of the new faith. His life coincided with a period of transition between Antiquity and the Middle Ages, when the battle of authority in grasping, defining and divulgating a valid concept of truth was heated between various schools of philosophy and spiritual movements, both within and outside the young Christian Church.

Certainly, the Christian majority had good reason to feel confident of victory, especially since the Emperor Theodosius (347–95), a strong proponent of Nicene orthodoxy, took on the mission to terminate once and for all any lingering pagan customs in the Roman Empire. Classical culture and religiosity were definitely hard pressed; the 380s and 390s were undoubtedly, as Alan Cameron has shown in his recent magisterial re-examination of these years' cultural tensions in the Roman Empire, "a period when the pace of conversion to Christianity was accelerating".[1] But at the same time, the precise definition of the fundamental tenets of the faith were occupying the minds of bishops, priests and theologians as never before. From the very beginning, Christian groups everywhere in the huge and culturally diversified Mediterranean region had been engaged in the formation of the Biblical canon while interpreting the Scripture in different ways. Nonetheless, they had been able to coexist and to encourage each other under the pressure of the Roman persecutors. But as the Church became institutionalized, and from the early fourth century even enjoyed the Emperors' support, there arose a Christian need for a theoretically underpinned common creed, that is, an orthodoxy, that required various decades and a number of synods – among which Nicaea (325) and Chalcedon (451) were the most important – to establish the right faith and to condemn rival factions as heretics, *haeretici*, a term borrowed from the Greek *hairesis*, which originally meant 'option' or 'choice'. The historian Averil Cameron remarks that, basically, every group in this Late Antique turbulence considered the others' alternatives to be heretical,

---

[1] Cameron 2011, p. 4.

but with the help of clever theologians and strong rulers, the orthodox Catholic faith slowly but surely gained ground to become dominant in the West.[1]

Foremost among these theologians were the Church Fathers, fully occupied with securing methods for inferring the truth about God, the world and humankind, constantly involved in dogmatic quarrels with or battles against heretics. In *On the Trinity* Augustine testifies to "the zeal with which I burn that our faith may be fortified against the error of carnal and natural men" (3.Pr.): *pro studio quo fidem nostram adversus errorem carnalium et animalium hominum muniri inardesco*. This was a militant attitude that served him well as a presbyter and a bishop, persistently engaged in disputes with Donatists, Manichees and Pelagians, and, moreover, stationed in a region – the province of Africa – where both the apologetic and the apocalyptic temperature was higher than in many other parts of the Roman Empire.

Augustine took the danger of schism, the threat of the disintegration of the Church, very seriously. In stark opposition to the ritual purism and separatism of the Donatists, he adopted a dynamic view of the Church that aimed at a general ('Catholic') *ecclesia triumphans* in the Roman Empire.[2] Accordingly, he came to battle against the Donatists – a minority in the Empire but remarkably strong in Africa – in a series of doctrinal treatises. He was just as categorically opposed to the British (or perhaps Breton) monk Pelagius, active in Rome and Africa around the turn of the fifth century, who emphasized the significance of the individual initiative in the salvation drama. Augustine refuted, energetically and successfully, the Pelagians by launching the austere doctrines of original sin and predestination. On the whole, as a consequence of his engagement in all these schismatic matters, contemporary theology's and Church politic's ongoing polarization and acute demands for clear distinctions tended to repress the dialectic or dialogue-oriented way of writing, not to mention the interest in poetry's or drama's narrative and performative versions of truth respectively, which had once engaged the novice in Italy.

The Christian fractions that Augustine struggled to pinpoint as heretics did not exhaust his polemical energy. Even though the Roman Empire around 400 was by and large Christianized, a classicist pagan culture still survived, its supporters not tiring of questioning the Bible's monopoly of the truth. Augustine succinctly expressed their predicament in his *Expositions on the Book of Psalms*: "The idols remained rather in the hearts of the pagans, than in the niches of the temples" (98/99.2), *magis remanserunt idola in cordibus Paganorum, quam in*

---

[1] Cameron 1993, p. 22.
[2] Brown 2000, pp. 207–21.

locis templorum. Though Alan Cameron has done a great deal to demolish the concept of a "pagan revival" in late fourth-century Rome, the long-drawn-out struggle over the restoration of the altar of Victoria to that city seems indicative of the hopes the tradition-loving senators could invest in their faith and their cult – and in their cultural heritage – as late as in the 380s and 390s (see below, pp. 532f.). Moreover, ever since the beginning of the fourth century, the Christian elite had to some extent adapted its reading habits and literary taste to the venerable classical culture, principally in the Greek-speaking East, where Constantine's counsellor and biographer Eusebius (ca. 260–340), Church historian and Bishop of Caesarea in Palestine, had adopted the integrative legacy from Origen, particularly the fusion of pagan (Platonist) philosophy and Christian faith. Supported by Eusebius' and Constantine's example, leading representatives of the Church Triumphant revealed themselves increasingly as adherents to both Greek education and Roman imperial ideology.

Many conservatives and intellectuals were attracted from this time onwards by Arianism, a philosophical rationalization of the mystery of Incarnation, named after the presbyter Arius (Areios) of Alexandria (d. 336). Arianism refuted the Catholic dogma of the Holy Trinity: the Son was denied the divine essence of the Father in order to be revered as the most eminent of created beings, a mediator between God and mankind. After 313, on the other hand, many pagans – even if for no other reason than for the sake of their careers, contacts and good reputation – would try to appear outwardly as Christians without putting much weight behind their words. The boundaries between orthodox doctrine and pagan culture, which to a present-day observer might seem obvious, were in fact, particularly in the late fourth century, in a fluid state. Peter Brown has rightly called attention to the frescoes that were discovered in a catacomb in Via Latina south-east of Rome in 1956, where scenes from the Bible and classical mythology stand side by side, as an indication of the lure of syncretism.[1] Even if this example would be an exception to the general rule, it is not isolated, and its mere existence is striking.

This intimacy between old culture and new religiosity in the mid-fourth century was perceived as a problem by a convinced pagan like Julian the Apostate, while a great number of the period's intellectual Christians – as Robert A. Markus claims – saw no difficulty in combining the classics with the Gospels.[2] But it was from the Christian side that the century's attempts to reach a *modus vivendi* over issues concerning cult and faith came under attack in the 380s and 390s. As

---

[1] Brown 1961, p. 9.
[2] Markus 1974, p. 3.

so often in the history of Catholicism, the Church's dealings with the political power generated a radical counter-movement. This reaction was strong, so strong that some scholars have tried to identify "a second conversion" among members of the upper Christian classes, this time to a life of self-discipline and abstinence. Jerome, John Cassian and Paulinus of Nola all testify to this movement.[1] Brown emphasizes that such an ascetic breakthrough in Rome, associated with habits of the Eastern Mediterranean world and to some extent inspired by the Desert Fathers in Egypt, marked a major departure from the Christian traditions of the city and, on the whole, of the Western Empire.[2] At a time when the concept of *orbis christianus* was beginning to be identified with *orbis romanus*, extreme steps to preserve the particular Christian identity and faith evidently seemed attractive to a number of clerics and theologians.

Julian's repressive decrees had certainly contributed to this polarization. They should have dispersed the ideas of a coexistence based on compromise and consensus that broad-minded groups in both camps had embraced. The Christians' new separatism, on the other hand, would entail terrible consequences for the period's cultural climate and imperial politics, with well-known examples from Alexandria, the African capital of Hellenism. There, perhaps in 391, the fanaticism of the monks and the holy men of the desert contributed actively to the destruction of the famous Serapis temple (the Serapeum), and in 415 a Christian mob lynched the Neo-Platonic philosopher Hypatia, one of the few female intellectuals we know from Late Antiquity. This shock-wave of ascetic "terrorism" (I borrow the term from Brown), cleverly exploited by the orthodox as well as tactical Theodosius, sent reverberations throughout the whole Empire and could hardly avoid influencing even moderate Christian groups.[3]

The Donatists' re-awakening of the memories of the Diocletian persecutions and Prudentius' hymns on Spanish and Roman martyrs, composed in the early fifth century (when the Roman Empire had long ceased creating martyrs) were other indications of the period's increasing unrest. The persistent threat from the barbarians in the north and east might also have contributed to the retreat from the turmoil of worldly life which attracted quite a few intellectuals of the late fourth and early fifth centuries. Now, Augustine was certainly no pillar saint; he took a great responsibility for the salvation work in his North African congregations, but he realized that compromises with the pagans or heretics were out of the question if he were to succeed in his mission. The apologetic po-

---

[1] Kirsch 1983, p. 331.
[2] Brown 1961, p. 5.
[3] Brown 1971, p. 104.

sition gained renewed momentum, now with the support of the mighty monastic movement of the late fourth century, and, as Karla Pollmann observes, it continuously forced Christian intellectuals to narrow down the particular, not to say unique nature (non-mythical, non-fictional, non-negotiable) of the Bible texts.[1] They saw it as their main duty, on the basis of the Holy Writ, to establish, preach and defend the true faith, *vera fides*, a concept that could only be written in the singular. Even to hint at pluralism or syncretism in this context would be to play into the hands of the enemy.

Thus I believe our general picture of the period extending over the crucial years around the turn of the fifth century must remain ambiguous. On the one hand, the wave of asceticism spreading over the Roman Empire indubitably exacerbated the tensions between the dwindling pagan conclaves and triumphant Catholicism. On the other hand, as we learn from Robert A. Markus, "the dividing line between 'pagan' and 'Christian', always liable to shift, was especially unstable at the end of the fourth century and early in the fifth", or from Carol Harrison: "Christianity was inextricably, unavoidably, linked with, formed by and understood within the parameters of classical culture."[2] That is one of the reasons why the classically educated Augustine took the opportunity to reuse arguments from his literary-rhetorical background when it suited his purposes, above all in his recurrent debates with the Manichees, the representatives of a strictly dualistic religion of a Gnostic type founded by the Persian prophet Mani, dead in prison (or perhaps crucified) around 275 CE. Here, the Church Father had dangerous opponents to deal with. Firstly, at this time they were remarkably strong: their cosmology and world view, which depended on the idea of a universal struggle between the principle of light and the darkness of matter, gained acceptance around the year 400 in a network of (officially illegal) cells all over large parts of the Mediterranean region, not least among intellectuals and scribes. Secondly, their strategy was to incorporate the Christian articles of faith into their own syncretic belief, thereby neutralizing them. According to Peter Brown's apt characteristic, the sectarian Manichees were "the 'Bolsheviks' of the fourth century: a 'fifth-column' of foreign origin bent on infiltrating the Christian Church, the bearers of a uniquely radical solution to the religious problems of their age".[3]

The fact that Catholic Christianity would emerge victorious from the battles between these doctrines of faith was to a certain extent precisely due to Augus-

---

[1] Pollmann 1996, p. 186.
[2] Markus 2000, p. 199; Harrison 2000, p. 214.
[3] Brown 2000, p. 35.

tine's shrewd thinking and efficient eloquence. By recycling arguments from the sophisticated classical understanding of fictional representation, turning them against the Manichees' literal interpretation – and ensuing disapproval – of the Old Testament, he made his opponents appear both coarse and naïve. That is why we, somewhat paradoxically, discover some of the Church Father's most advanced and initiated characteristics of fictionality in his voluminous refutation of the Manichaean Bishop Faustus, composed at the same time as his *Confessions*, shortly before the year 400. His autobiography describes how the spectacular Faustus had arrived in Carthage when the author was twenty-nine years old, that is, in 383. This renowned teacher and preacher was certainly sharp-tongued, a polished speaker, and evidently an agreeable person too; but his inadequate education had so disappointed the expectant young Augustine that it contributed to his rupture with the sect (5.3.3 – 5.7.13). Now, fifteen years later, Faustus had delivered a frontal assault against the – according to Manichaean belief, carnally pernicious – Old Testament. Consequently, Augustine stepped in to act in defence and counterattack.[1]

In the fifteenth book of his diatribe, Augustine compares the lies of the poets, *poetica mendacia*, with the figures and notions of Manichaean cosmogony, *figmenta cogitationum tuarum*, to the former's advantage; they appear to be more serious and more suitable, since they deceive no one (15.5). We recognize this argument – which is certainly not altogether flattering to poetry – from the Cassiciacum dialogues. It will soon be expanded in the work's twentieth book, in which the two bishops argue about the nature of the Godhead. Augustine has nothing good to say about the Manichees' astrologically tinged polytheism, which identified God with a mystical light while locating the Spirit in the atmosphere, deriving the Son's power and wisdom from the sun and the moon respectively. Precisely this blatant materialization of the Trinity should have worried and upset him. It was self-evident to the Christian apologist that his monotheistic religion expressed the truth, whereas the beliefs of Faustus and his likes were completely outrageous; more so, in fact, than the beliefs of the old pagans (20.9):

> For this reason we say that you are worse than Pagans, while you resemble them in worshipping many gods. You are worse, because, while they worship things which exist though they are not gods, you worship things which are neither gods nor anything else, for they have no existence. The Pagans, too, have fables [*fabulosa figmenta*], but they know them to be fables [*fabulae*]; and either look upon them as amusing poetical fancies, or try to ex-

---

1 The fundamental study in this field, Augustine's anti-Manichaean polemics, is probably still Mayer 1974, where the relevant documents are presented on pp. 79 – 86. For a convenient overview, see Roland J. Teske's article "St. Augustine, the Manichees, and the Bible", 2009, pp. 111 – 25.

plain them as representing the nature of things, or the life of man. Thus they say that Vulcan is lame, because flame in common fire has an irregular motion: that Fortune is blind, because of the uncertainty of what are called fortuitous occurrences: [...] and so with many other fables. The great absurdity is in their continuing to worship these beings, after giving such explanations; for the worship without the explanations, though criminal, would be a less heinous crime. The very explanations prove that they do not worship that God, the enjoyment of whom can alone give happiness, but things which He has created. And even in the creature they worship not only the virtues, as in Minerva, who sprang from the head of Jupiter, and who represents prudence, – a quality of reason which, according to Plato, has its seat in the head, – but their vices, too, as in Cupid. Thus one of their dramatic poets says, "Sinful passion, in favour of vice, made Love a god." Even bodily evils had temples in Rome, as in the case of pallor and fever. Not to dwell on the sin of the worshippers of these idols, who are in a way affected by the bodily forms, so that they pay homage to them as deities, when they see them set up in some lofty place, and treated with great honor and reverence, there is greater sin in the very explanations which are intended as apologies for these dumb, and deaf, and blind, and lifeless objects. Still, though, as I have said, these things are nothing in the way of salvation or of usefulness, both they and the things they are said to represent are real existences. (XXVI)

But you Manichees, Augustine concludes his caustic argument, you are worse than the pagans, who nowadays blush at what remains of their old culture! You believe in and worship things that you have no images of, *nec pingendo aut sculpendo*, and which do not even exist, vain and false things, nothing but emptiness: *illa igitur omnia vana sunt, falsa sunt, nulla sunt*. Here, the discussion focuses on the Manichaean (and ancient Roman) polytheism, but a concept such as *fabulosa figmenta* indicates its relevance for Augustine's approach to fictionality in general. His argument seems to have two starting points in antique tradition: first, the triadic *narratio* taxonomy that we have seen exemplified in Roman rhetoric or in Sextus Empiricus, and, secondly, Aristotle's notion of poetry – famously articulated in his *Metaphysics* – as the expression of an original and intuitive knowledge.

In Augustine's eyes, the Manichees foster what in rhetoric's narrative theory was known as *fabula* and what Sextus Empiricus had called *mythos:* pure inventions with no basis in reality, represented here as futile illusions with no other function than to mislead people's hearts. In contrast to such castles in the air, the Church Father puts forward the pagan fictions (not including the Manichaean fabrications, since Faustus and his supporters could look upon themselves as Christians, even though Christianity was only one of several ingredients in their universal religion). The myths and legends of classical culture are, in this perspective, reminiscent of rhetoric's *argumenta* or Sextus Empiricus' *plasma*. They are not in strict accordance with truth but they have a foundation in reality. Augustine seizes the opportunity to remind his opponent of another distinction made by the pagans, that between poetic fantasies aimed at amusement (rather than fraud, the logical outcome of the Manichaean figments of imagination) and figurative paraphrases of real circumstances, whether of a physical or moral nature. It is this latter understanding of fiction – in particular, the tales of the gods – that arouses Augustine's interest. We have good reason to identify it with the speculative-allegorical explanation of myths that enjoyed wide popularity in Hellenistic and Late Antique culture, particularly in Stoic philosophical contexts.[1]

Interest certainly does not mean acceptance. Augustine emphasizes that the pagans themselves had eventually realized that inventions of this kind, making Vulcan represent fire or Venus love, are tales without substance ("they know them to be fables", *esse illas fabulas norunt*), but they portray and worship their divine protagonists all the same, against – as it were – their better judgment. This is reprehensible and entails distressing moral consequences, not least when pure concepts like Pallor or Fever are personified for the sake of the cult. Such criticism seems characteristic of the Church Father's Platonically negative attitude towards the demoralizing poets. Even so, he could feel sympathy for the (presumably enlightened) infidels who were ashamed of their own culture. In his eyes, these pagans would escape the error of confusing signs with their underlying reality, precisely that besetting sin (typical of Manichaean hermeneutics) which he concurrently censured in *On Christian Doctrine*: the widespread treatment of figurative ways of speaking, *figurate dicta*, as if they were proper – literal – expressions, *proprie dicta*, a mistake indicative of carnal, hence reprehensible modes of thinking (3.5.9 – 3.9.13). The pagans, then, come out remarkably better than the Manichees in these Augustinian ruminations. Even though they do not worship the only true God, they are at least no slaves to literalism. They do not take signs for things. Their eyes are opened to the great illusions of their own culture, that is, to their fictional, hence imaginary and contingent representations of the gods.

Here, finally, Augustine applies a historicist aspect to Greek and Roman culture. Unlike the outrageous notions of insidious Manichaeism, the pagans' main tenets are supposed to be known to everyone, based on ancient traditions of which only certain fragments, *reliquiae*, remain. The structure of this argument recalls the famous opening to Aristotle's *Metaphysics*: philosophy began as a re-

---

1 O'Connell observes that the Stoic philosophers tried to reconcile "belief" in the gods with a "philosophic" knowledge of the universe. Accordingly, they favoured a pantheistic interpretation of the civic gods as personifications of the elements or of natural forces, 1968, p. 97. Additionally, in consequence, these Stoics would diligently embrace the rationalistic allegoresis of Homer, as when Pseudo-Heraclitus read Zeus' embraces of Hera in *The Iliad* 14.346 as an expression of the atmospheric ether enclosing the air, cf. De Lacy 1948, pp. 259 – 63.

sult of people's amazement and wonder at the world they lived in. Initially, it expressed itself in mythical notions of an eternal original element (such as water). These ideas, Aristotle continues, were gracefully treated by Homer and other poets, soon to be systematized by Thales of Miletus and the natural philosophers, though only tentatively and intuitively (982–85). Later on, however, this primordial knowledge was inevitably replaced by a rational discourse in the spirit of Socrates, based on general concepts, analogies and inductive explanations of causes, culminating in Aristotle's own syllogistic art of ratiocination (992b). Correspondingly, the enlightened pagans in the contemporary Roman Empire, Augustine seems to argue, had left their most primitive superstitions and cult ceremonies behind them; they even blush at the traces of them. Although they still cling to the worship of their age-old gods, they have lost their actual faith in them, being prone to reduce them to *fabulosa figmenta*, contrived circumlocutions for existing events or settings.

While examining the pagan world of fiction as an alternative to Manichaean sham, Augustine seems to detect the kind of split or covert discourse he had perceived in the figurations of rhetoric: an existing reality is assumed to be cloaked in metaphorical images or allegorical tales. However, based on his progressive construction of cultural history, later developed on a grand scale in the *City of God*, he considered the classical era's *figmenta*, along with their speculative explanations, as having been largely superseded by the Bible's *sacramenta* or *allegoriae*. And he spotted the decisive difference between these types of semiotic representation in their referents or basis in reality. Where the pagan philosophers' fabrications had been restricted to the world of Creation, the Biblical writers' veiled allegories referred to the Creator, or more precisely to the Holy Trinity and its effects throughout history from the Creation of the world to the Incarnation, the destiny of the Church and the Last Judgment.

Thus the extract from *Reply to Faustus the Manichaean* documents a broad historicist outlook on the Hellenistic period's naturalizing or moralizing allegories of a Stoic brand. Here, Augustine detected a philosophical elucidation of the nature of signs, which he recognized from his own work in the fields of hermeneutics and exegetics: letters and images were there to provide a deeper meaning. Nevertheless, his enthusiasm was moderate. Even though the pagan philosophers had demonstrated their eminent interpretive skills, they remained tied to Creation. Their speculative criticism of myths regularly ended up in assumptions about the cosmos and the elements, all the visible world that for Augustine, in turn, constituted a web of signs referring to divine reality. Consequently, they had only got halfway with their semiotic analysis, incapable of expanding their field of vision beyond matter. This pattern of argument returns, with an extended range of application, in the third book of *On Christian Doctrine*, composed at about the same time as the polemic against Faustus.

There, Augustine extended his exegetical criticism to the type of Jewish religiosity which, closely linked to matter and the body, took figurative signs literally. On the basis of the Pauline words about the letter that kills and the Spirit that gives life, he complains about the "miserable kind of spiritual slavery", *miserabilis animae servitus*, to which the Jews surrendered themselves when they conceived of the Sabbath as a day in the week or when they associated a sacrifice with a slaughtered animal or the fruits of the earth, sadly incapable of raising their soul's range of vision beyond the bodily Creation so as to be able to drink of the eternal light (3.5.9). Yet the Jews did in fact worship the only true God, despite their primitive, literal faith. In other words, they had access to the right signs and worshipped the right God but did not worship Him rightly.

The pagans, for their part, made use of the wrong signs, Augustine continues; they resorted to images made by the hand of man, *simulacra*, which they took for – likewise erroneous – gods. It is true that some of their enlightened spokesmen such as, perhaps, Stoic philosophers (that is how, on an analogy with *Reply to Faustus the Manichaean*, I understand "any of them", *aliqui eorum*), interpreted these images as signs and nothing else. Here, Augustine, exactly as in his anti-Manichaean tract, identifies an accurate semiotic strategy in pagan culture, while he is just as anxious to immediately add his reservations. The class of signs he is referring to point, after all, only to Creation; and was it really so much better, he asks, to take a statue of Neptune for the sea or for all the water on earth rather than for the god himself? "Inside its attractive shell this husk is a jangle of fine-sounding stones; but it is the food of pigs, not men": *haec siliqua intra dulce tectorium sonantes lapillos quatit; non est autem hominum sed porcorum cibus* (cf. Luke 15.16). When all is said and done, the intellectual heathen elite had scant use for its semiotic competence. Its philosophers were still encumbered with "the oppression and the delusion of this servile and carnal condition", *servili carnalique onere atque velamine* (3.7.11).

To put it succinctly: even though Augustine rejected the ideas of the pagan philosophers, he accepted and even took advantage, when necessary, of their hermeneutic method. Accordingly, he proved able, in the heat of the battle, to skilfully play off a conceptual allegoresis of a Stoic type against the deplorably literal Manichees. Elsewhere in *Reply to Faustus the Manichaean*, he resorted to classical poetry as an equally effective corrective to his adversaries. They had frequently accused the Old Testament of all kinds of crimes, ignominy and immorality. A considerable part of Augustine's treatise is devoted to contesting these allegations. In the twenty-second book, he attacks those Manichees who had blamed the patriarchs and prophets for their supposed baseness and vices, *flagitia* (22.25, translation slightly modified):

> Such critics are incapable of understanding that certain virtues in great minds resemble closely the vices of little minds, not in reality, but in appearance. Such criticism of the great is like that of boys at school, whose learning consists in the important rule, that if the nominative is in the singular, the verb must also be in the singular; and so they find fault with the best Latin author, because he says, *Pars in frusta secant*. He should have written, say they, *secat*. And again, knowing that *religio* is spelt with one *l*, they blame him for writing *relligio*, when he says, *Relligione patrum*. Hence it may with reason be said, that as the poetical usage of words differs from the solecisms and barbarisms of the unlearned, so, in their own way, the figurative actions of the prophets differ from the impure actions of the vicious. Accordingly, as a boy guilty of a barbarism would be whipped if he pled the usage of Virgil; so any one quoting the example of Abraham begetting a son from Hagar, in defence of his own sinful passion for his wife's handmaid, ought to be corrected not by caning only, but by severe scourging, that he may not suffer the doom of adulterers in eternal punishment. This indeed is a comparison of great and important subjects with trifles; and it is not intended that a peculiar usage in speech should be put on a level with a sacrament, or a solecism with adultery. Still, allowing for the difference in the character of the subjects, what is called learning or ignorance in the proprieties and improprieties of speech, resembles – on a very different level – wisdom or the want of it in reference to the grand moral distinction between virtue and vice. (XXVII)

This complex argument is remarkable or even sensational, since Augustine normally cited the Bible to legitimate his rejection of the fictions of poetry. Here, he proceeds in the opposite direction: he resorts to Virgil in order to elucidate the Bible's figurative style and hence, indirectly, to justify its impeccable moral content. This was the Church Father's clever way of disarming Faustus' and his supporters' misgivings about the Old Testament and more specifically about Abraham, who lay with his wife Sarah's maidservant. At the basis of his apologetic argument is certainly the Biblical typology that Paul had established with his interpretation of Hagar as the Old Covenant in Galatians 4.24. The Manichees had not understood this deeper meaning of the Biblical text, Augustine maintained. In this respect, they are like schoolboys claiming to have discovered grammatical weaknesses in Virgil, for example in *Aeneid* 1.212, where the poet lets *pars*, 'a number of', be followed by a verb in the plural, *secant*, or in the next book of the epic poem, where he spells the Latin word for religion with a double l (2.715).

There is no mistaking the respect for Virgil that Augustine could express when it suited his purposes. Judging from his *Reply to Faustus the Manichaean*, the Roman poet, *latinae linguae doctissimus auctor*, was not only a sage but also a clever stylist. He had deliberately worked with figures, *schemata*, as well as neologisms or changes in the orthography of words, *metaplasmi*. For this description, Augustine probably used Donatus' grammar, where *barbarismus* and *solo-*

ecismus were cited as linguistic "vices", *vitia*, closely followed by paragraphs on their permitted equivalents in poetry, *metaplasmi* and *schemata* (3.1–5).[1] He could have drawn further support for his legitimization of Virgil's technical idiosyncrasies from Quintilian. In the first book of *The Orator's Education*, which is devoted to grammar, the Roman rhetorician had emphasized that a *grammaticus* should not reproach the poets for their linguistic peculiarities in front of his class, since they were inevitably subject to metrical demands. That is why linguistic errors, *vitia*, are given special labels when they appear in poetry: *metaplasmus enim et schematismus seu schemata* (1.8.14).

Such artistic devices, Augustine stresses, have nothing to do with simple linguistic errors, just as little as the prophets' *figurata facta* can be termed sins or vices. The principal idea behind his argument is clear. Precisely as in the case of Virgil, the books of the Bible spoke figuratively, even if that term in their case should be given a stricter or, indeed, a typological or mysterious signification. A number of actions described in the Old Testament which at first sight seem to be blatantly immoral or sinful, can be understood in a different way, actually the only valid way, when they are read in the historical context of Christian salvation. Cornelius Mayer has cited a later passage from the same book in *Reply to Faustus the Manichaean*, where Augustine correspondingly saw himself obliged to defend the story in Genesis of the patriarch Judah who lay with his daughter-in-law Tamar (in the belief that she was a prostitute, 38.13–19). The Church Father comments: "so in the prophetic Scriptures, where both good and evil actions are recorded, the narrative being itself prophetic, foretells something good even by the record of what is evil, the credit being due not to the evil-doer, but to the writer." (22.83)[2]

As we have already seen, for Augustine, the Bible's way of storytelling is prophetic. Thus in the figurative perspective of the history of salvation, something evil can signify something good in the future. The exegete's attention should therefore be transferred from the protagonists in the text, who admittedly may behave reprehensibly, to the representation itself, which is never reprehensible. In polemical contrast to the Manichaean gross fixation on the literal content of the Holy Writ, the Church Father launched a sophisticated form of analysis focused on the typological pattern of the Old Testament narrative and the Biblical writers' intention, ultimately inspired and controlled by the Holy Spirit. This her-

---

[1] For two good presentations of Donatus' system, cf. the concise Purcell 1996, pp. 23–28, and the almost exhaustive Holtz 1981.
[2] "Ita in Scripturis propheticis, non tantum bona hominum, verum etiam et mala facta narrantibus, quoniam prophetica est ipsa narratio, significetur aliquid de malis operibus hominum etiam futurorum bonorum, non peccantis opere, sed scribentis." Cf. Mayer 1974, pp. 376f.

meneutic strategy shows, in fact, traces of the advanced theory of fiction that Augustine had envisioned in Cassiciacum ten years earlier, when the actor Roscius was declared to be faithful to the characters he performed on the stage in so far as he was unfaithful to their historical or mythical models (cf. above, pp. 179f.): the more suggestive (illusory, that is, "false") his impersonation, the better his performance (true to his art)! There is no doubt of the benefit the anti-Manichaean polemicist could draw from his knowledge of classical literature, not least drama, and its fictional mode, detached from historical reality, so as to be able to disclose the prophetic meaning of the Bible, detached from the patriarchs' and the prophets' apparently dubious morals.

Now, as we might remember, Augustine had already contested Roscius' clever art in the *Soliloquies*, and by the turn of the century he could certainly not afford any cognitive double dealing of the kind he had scrutinized in his early dialogue. He obviously felt obliged to mobilize the critical reservations that regularly appeared in his writings as soon as he referred to fiction or fictionality in exegetic and dogmatic affairs. Right at the beginning of his argument, Augustine makes it clear that the comparison between Genesis and the *Aeneid* that he is about to implement is restricted to external appearances, *nonnulla specie:* the two texts are actually incommensurable. Even though their juxtaposition is permissible, he adds a little later, the books of the Bible rely "in their own way", *in genere suo*, on figuration, a syntagm reinforced in the argument's climax: *longe in diverso genere*. Finally, then, it is a question of a comparison between the great issues of the Bible concerning salvation and the ultimate destiny of man on the one hand, and the "trifles" of literature and grammar teaching, *minimae res*, on the other. This is a typical and, of course, strategic downgrading of that fictional mode on which Augustine could, simultaneously, capitalize in his anti-Manichaean polemics.

The Illusions of Culture

Perhaps the best-known of Augustine's attacks on the *fabulae* or *figmenta* of antique mythology and literature are to be found in his long-term project *On the City of God*, completed a few years before his death, for instance in the second book's criticism of pagan civilization in general and its pantheon in particular. Here, too, as Peter Brown observes in his biography of Augustine, we should presuppose a specific addressee for his polemic, namely the Roman aristocracy, who defended their superior culture, hailing Virgil's work as its unsurpassed artistic expression, and whose main philosophical frame of reference was provided by Platonists such as Plotinus and Porphyry. This was the refined Roman elite that Macrobius was to portray in his dialogue *Saturnalia*, to be discussed in our next chapter; Augustine had learnt something of its taste and customs during his stay in Italy, and after the fall of Rome in 410 it would to some extent re-emerge in Carthage. It may seem an insignificant, anachronistic relic in his brave new Christian world, but Brown emphasizes the threat that the Bishop of Hippo might have felt from this pagan stronghold: "Seen in this light, the *City of God* is the last round in a long drama: written by a former protégé of Symmachus, it was to be a definitive rejection of the paganism of an aristocracy that had claimed to dominate the intellectual life of their age."[1]

However, Augustine's relationship to classical literature was certainly ambivalent even at this late stage of his life.[2] His sources of knowledge about the Roman culture and history that the *City of God* deals with were often the poets, and he could acknowledge them, especially Virgil, who is profusely quoted in the work's first and fifth books, characterized as "a great poet" or indeed "the best and most renowned of all poets" (1.3), *poeta magnus omniumque praeclarissimus atque optimus*, alternatively "their outstanding poet" (5.12.2), *poeta insignis illorum*. Admittedly, when Virgil and his colleagues "wrote and sang" about the conquered gods of Troy and, by implication, of Rome, their message seems outrageous, as if the destiny of Rome were to depend on vanquished deities from the very start. Yet the poets did not lie; on the contrary, "they were men of sense, and truth compelled them to admit the facts" (1.3).[3] In lamenting fallen Troy, Virgil seems to imply that even the Roman Empire was to collapse one day, with no reliable guardian deities to defend it, a prediction which had come fatally true with the sack of Rome in 410, repeatedly recalled on the first pages of the *City of God*. In fact, Augustine even traces a faint reflection of Christian salvation history in Virgil's great epic, when he quotes Jupiter's famous words to his troubled daughter Venus from Book I – her son shall found an empire "that has no end" (1.279) – as a presage of the heavenly kingdom subject to "the one true God" (2.29.1), *Deus unus et verus*.

These appreciative judgments are, however, far from whole-hearted throughout the work. Virgil's account of Aeneas and his destiny was constantly open to question; the *Aeneid*'s description of the Greek ravages in burning Troy might not be entirely reliable, since its author was prone to exploit the usual "manner of poets" (1.4), *poetarum mos*. Further on in the treatise even this canonical writer

---

1 Brown 2000, p. 300.
2 I take this ambivalence, not only to classical literature but to the "aesthetic experience" in general, to be the main point of Westra's seminal article 2007, cf. p. 21.
3 "Non itaque, cum de diis victis illa conscriberentur atque canerentur, poetas libebat mentiri, sed cordatos homines cogebat veritas confiteri."

can be waved aside as just another erratic fiction maker (18.15, 19.12.2). On the whole, the author of the *City of God* maintains an unfavourable and sometimes mocking attitude to the Virgilian or Ovidian "baseless poetic fantasy" (18.16), *fabulosum poeticumque mendacium*, that he doggedly scrutinizes throughout the work. After his introductory tributes to Virgil, Augustine regularly associated the poetry of classical culture with its false gods.

Above all, he attacked theatre performances, *ludi scaenici*, the festivals and the public spectacles, a demonic *pestilentia* that allegedly had infected the whole of Rome at the time of its fall (1.32). Augustine had often censured the theatre, as Karel Svoboda reminds us, but never so harshly as in the *City of God*. The citizens of Carthage, like the Romans, loved the theatre, while Augustine considered it a disgraceful stronghold for remnants of the old pagan religion, to a significant extent responsible for the contemporary decline in morals.[1] The gods had made extensive use of histrionic *figmenta* or *fabulae* for their cult. Among these divertissements, the bishop found it easiest to accept tragedy and comedy.[2] Undoubtedly, they too could be indecent through their plots, he admits in the second book, but in contrast to other spectacles they avoided the obscenity of words, *verborum obscenitas*, and they were presented to the younger generation as an integral part of the time-honoured studies in the liberal arts (2.8), *studia, quae honesta ac liberalia vocantur*. This recognition anticipates the remarkable acknowledgement of human culture's varied manifestations to be found at the end of the work (22.24.3), including "the marvels in theatrical spectacles, in which man's contrivances in design and production have excited wonder in the spectators and incredulity in the minds of those who heard of them".[3]

Specifically, it was the poets' notoriously disrespectful treatment of the gods that was the main target of Augustine's critical remarks in the *City of God*. At first sight, this frontal attack on the poetical versions of the Greek and Roman pantheon may seem strange, as if the author really should have respected the old Olympians. And, in fact, the Church Father went as far in his empathy with pagan customs and beliefs as he possibly could. On repeated occasions, he ex-

---

1 Svoboda 1933, p. 173.
2 During Late Antiquity, the term *spectacula* referred to tragedy and comedy as well as to mimes, pantomimes, gladiatorial combats, horse-races and other public contests or shows. Cf. Weismann 1972, p. 25.
3 "In theatris mirabilia spectantibus, audientibus incredibilia facienda et exhibenda molita sit". We should certainly be on our guard not to mistake these eloquent effusions at the end of the *City of God* for any radical change of attitude to secular culture on Augustine's part. Weismann remarks that it is after all only a matter of – with the author's own words a few lines further down, 22.24.5 – "the consolations of mankind under condemnation, not the rewards of the blessed", *miserorum sunt damnatorumque solacia, non praemia beatorum*, 1972, p. 177.

erted himself to consider Jupiter and his circle as legitimate manifestations of the primitive Romans' religiosity, only to express his horror at the treatment they had to put up with in literature. He had no understanding for the argument of defence that, after all, the stories told of the gods are nothing but "lying inventions" (2.10), *falsa atque conficta*. If that is the case, so much the worse! This was, in the stern bishop's eyes, nothing but a sad lack of respect for the deities, undoubtedly inspired by fraudulent and cunning demons. The great Plato had refused "to let the gods be slandered by false accusations of crime at the impious caprice of poets" (8.21.2), *noluit deos per impiam licentiam poetarum falsis criminibus infamari*, and certainly did right when he expelled the ungodly and immoral bards from his ideal republic (2.14).

A similar onslaught is made in the fourth book's survey of the inconsistencies and contradictions of the old Roman religion, perceived as a tangled skein of poetic fables, the one more bizarre than the other. Even though, here too, the author's fulmination is particularly aimed at poetry, it cracks down on traditional Roman society at large. As a cultural critic, the Church Father exploits and develops a solid apologetic heritage, reinforced with a remarkably sarcastic bite. While the pagan grammarian Servius, whom we shall meet in the next chapter, had made a crucial distinction between the literary and philosophical sense in Virgil's works, the former linked to a series of *fabulae* and the latter to *veritas*, the elderly Augustine would in his most belligerent moments consider both types of signification equally preposterous. The fact that Virgil did not follow *figmenta poetica* but *philosophorum libri* when (in the *Georgics*, 2.325–27) he had described how Heaven, the Almighty Father, had descended in showers of live-giving rain into the lap of his delighted spouse, did not make the story any better or any more credible. Augustine amuses himself with precisely the Stoic allegorical myth interpretation from which he had once drawn support for his anti-Manichaean polemics. In this late work, he ironically highlights its inherent absurdities: Juno's lap must signify the earth that received the rain, so she impersonates the fertile earth, but on the other hand the Earth, *Terra* or *Tellus*, was known as the mother of the gods, hence the mother of Jupiter!

What a strange people – the writer sums up his observations – who honoured their gods by making them commit such (incestuous) crimes at the theatre! The cult of the Vestal virgins, and similar futilities, all *vanitas*, only got what it deserved when it was extinguished once and for all "by him who was born of a virgin" (4.10), *qui est natus ex virgine*.[1] In this context, too, Augustine hypo-

---

[1] MacCormack remarks that Augustine might have drawn some of his arguments concerning the supposed contradictions and absurdities in Roman (and Virgilian) mythology from the *Divine*

thetically predicts the objections that intellectual Romans could make in their defence: that these myths were only laughable "poetical fictions, not to be attributed to the true divinities" (4.17), *ridenda figmenta poetarum, non veris attribuenda numinibus*. But this time he condescendingly waves aside such arguments. They only confirmed what he already knew: that the poets dealt with mere trifles and lies that no one should take seriously. If the pagans themselves saw things in this way (and, it is worth adding, many of them had in fact done so, from Xenophanes and Heraclitus of Ephesus, with their attacks on Homer's anthropomorphic pantheon almost a thousand years earlier, right up to the Stoics and Neo-Platonists of later times), could not he, the faithful Bishop of Hippo, with even greater right reject these indecent old wives' tales?

The fourth and sixth books of the *City of God* seek support for this kind of criticism in named old Roman writers. In the fourth book, Augustine dwells upon the tripartite listing of their divinities supposedly dating from the pontiff and lawyer Quintus Mucius Scaevola, elected consul in 95 BCE: one tradition concerning the gods was derived from the poets, one from the philosophers, and yet another one was attributed to the statesmen. For our purposes, we need only take note of the first category, the ancient poets' understanding of the deities, which, according to the pontiff himself – if we are to believe Augustine – was simply trifling: "The first tradition was trivial nonsense, a collection of discreditable fictions about the gods", *primum genus nugatorium dicit esse, quod multa de diis fingantur indigna*. Roman literature, Augustine continues, makes it mercilessly clear why Scaevola so violently rejected this tradition. The poets had, as it were, deformed the gods, made them into thieves and adulterers, allowed three goddesses to enter a beauty contest so as to get the losers to overthrow Troy, and turned Jupiter into a bull or a swan to let him have intercourse with women on earth. They had permitted a goddess to marry a man, Saturn to eat his own children... The bishop does not mince his words: there are no weird or vicious inventions in the world that cannot be found in these myths, *nihil denique posse confingi miraculorum atque vitiorum, quod non ibi reperiatur* (4.27).

In the sixth book, he brings Scaevola's system into agreement with Varro's similar classification of the gods in *Antiquitates* (ca. 40 BCE), a huge history of Roman culture in forty-one volumes, only fragments of which have survived. This work was actually an important as well as challenging model for the *City of God:* an inexhaustible source of information for the Church Father and, at

---

Institutes of Lactantius, active less than a century earlier (the starting figure of my next chapter), 1998, pp. 33f. Tertullian could probably have provided him with an even greater part of this anti-pagan artillery.

the same time, a pagan record to be revised and corrected. Now, Scaevola's poetic tradition was made to correspond to his later countryman's mythical (*mythicon*) or fanciful (*fabulosum*) version of the gods, replete with *ficta* that in fact – according to Varro himself – blatantly offended the dignity and nature of the immortals. Augustine could thus find support for his criticism of fiction in the old Roman predilection for gravity and rigorous morals (embraced by Varro's mighty protector Octavian, the future Emperor Augustus). He admired, characteristically, Varro for his honest efforts to evade the mist of ambiguity, *caligo ambiguitatis*, surrounding these mendacious myths, *mendacissimae fabulae*, and he lamented over the Romans' blunder not to have listened to such a wise and clear-sighted writer. They had, on the contrary, ignored Varro's philosophical interpretation of the gods, his *genus physicon*, based on Heraclitean cosmology, Pythagorean numerology and Epicurean atomism, in order to heedlessly continue enjoying the poets' and actors' heretical fictions (6.5.1–2).

Nevertheless, as Gerard O'Daly has observed, Augustine criticized the Roman polymath for having himself authorized polytheistic genealogies and practices.[1] In the opinion of the Church Father, not even Varro realized that actually the poets and the priests, to the delight of demons, had formed a "fellowship of deception", *consortio falsitatis*. Basically, they had their gods in common: the idols of poetry and the theatre, or of the festivals and spectacles, one great abomination for the true God. According to this Augustinian conspiracy theory, those two corporations had complemented each other, in the sense that the latter provided the former's fancies with an official stamp of authority. The poets' fabulous theology had voiced "unspeakable fictions of human imagination about the gods", *de diis nefanda figmenta*, whereupon the priests had blessed them in their cult. Inasmuch as poetry "reveals, or else invents", *prodit aut fingit*, the shameful deeds of the gods, it remains for the officiating ministers to either (deviously) certify their veracity or to simply delight in their false gibberish (6.6.1–2). In short, the scandalous fictions of the pagan myths are a delusion, framed by the poets and authorized by the priests, albeit – in the last instance – the result of demons' destructive activities among human beings. And to Augustine, it is perhaps best to add, these demons were anything but fictional.

*

Such condemnations of the poets and their works were delivered late in the Church Father's life and, moreover, in a polemic context. The whole of the *City*

---

[1] "Augustine's Critique of Varro on Roman Religion" (1994), reprinted in O'Daly 2001, pp. 65–75.

of God was written as a reaction to the ungodly but widespread rumours that the sensational sack of Rome in 410 was due to the new influence of the Christians on the city. The previous presentation, however, has hopefully demonstrated that Augustine's scepticism of the Muses goes far back in his career. The main key to its remarkable significance for his life achievement is surely to be found in his *Confessions*. In all the first nine books – that is, the work's autobiographical part – fictional representations are more or less emphatically experienced as a problem, sometimes treated in detail, sometimes mentioned casually. The remorseful memories of the author's childhood attraction to the *Aeneid* and of his youthful interest in the theatre have already been discussed. If on other occasions Augustine seems to express greater understanding for fictional devices, it is only to be able to play them off against his adversaries' narrow-minded literalism. In the third book, for example, he begins to reveal his early Manichaean delusions: mere phantoms, as it were, glimmering fancies, *phantasmata splendida*, empty games of make-believe, *figmenta inania* (3.6.10). In comparison with these philosophical phantasmagorias, literary fiction might after all turn out to be a better alternative (3.6.11):

> Where were you at that time? How far from me? I was certainly roving far away from you, and debarred even from the pods I was feeding to pigs. The fables of schoolmasters and poets are far better than the snares then being set for me; yes, verses, songs and tales of Medea in flight are undeniably more wholesome than myths about the five elements being metamorphosed to defeat the five caverns of darkness. These latter have no truth in them at all and are lethal to anyone who believes them, whereas I can turn verse and song into a means of earning real food. When I sang of Medea in her flying chariot I was not vouching for any of it as fact, nor, when I listened to someone else singing of it, did I believe the story; but I did believe the Manichean lies. All the worse for me! By these stages I was led deeper into hell, labouring and chafing under the scarcity of truth, because I was seeking you, my God, not through that power of the mind by which you have chosen to rank me above the beasts, but only through carnal inclination. To you do I confess this, for you showed mercy to me before ever I could confess it. You were more intimately present to me than my innermost being, and higher than the highest peak of my spirit. (XXVIII)

The logic of the comparison is reminiscent of Augustine's contemporary *Reply to Faustus the Manichaean* where, as we remember, the scenarios of the philosophers as well as Virgil seemed preferable to the Manichaean absurdities. The author's benevolent declaration provides a personal background to several of the subtle analyses of fictionality we have examined in the previous presentation, in particular from the period immediately following his conversion. Augustine resolutely rejects the Manichaean philosophical-physical heresies as "snares", *decipula*, a term which seems closely related to the *fallaciae* that he had disapproved of in his *Soliloquies*. A notably better judgment is passed on the fictions of grammarians and poets, *fabellae*, since they at least do not require people to believe in them. If this declaration from the *Confessions* is really based on Augustine's own childhood experience, it is possible that the advanced notions of fictionality we have seen him scrutinize in Cassiciacum – where the dramatic actors' and the sculptors' method of imitation was registered as "double-faced", *bifrons*, and 'self-contradictory', *sibique adversans* – were anchored in his own past, in an early fascination with poetry's exceptionally evocative power: the greater the disloyalty to the incidents, characters or circumstances in real life, the better the art. Such displays of skill, the Church Father now seems to suggest, might even lead to something better than art. Anyone who can take fictional representations for what they are and not mistake them for reality might turn them into "real food", *vera pulmenta*. There should be no doubt about what sort of food Augustine refers to, since his *Confessions* repeatedly return to the self's hunger and thirst for the Godhead he seeks – a yearning that he would at least provisionally be able to quench in "the fables of schoolmasters and poets".

Here, the accent is placed firmly on the readers (or spectators) and their needs. Even if the worlds of fiction are unreliable, or for the very reason that they do not claim to be true, they may find a certain resonance within us. Admittedly, they cannot be compared to the typological kind of figuration controlling the Biblical texts – the truth of which is guaranteed at every stage of the process of interpretation, from the letter through the immediate referent down to the final meaning – but they may even so be of use for inquiring souls constantly engaged in acts of interpretation. The prerequisite for such an existential hermeneutics is that the text is detached from the author's intention so as to relate to the reader's response. We might remind ourselves of the wise old doctor who, according to the *Confessions*, taught the young Augustine that a person who resorts to the pages of poets, *paginae poetae*, will frequently find some verse "which is wonderfully apposite to the question in hand", *mirabiliter consonus negotio*, even if the poet himself "was singing of an unrelated matter and had something quite different in mind", *longe aliud canens atque intendens* (4.3.5).

Terms and phrases such as these give us a good glimpse of the *Confessions*' and, on the whole, Augustine's complex relationship to poetry and literature, characterized by a strange mix of personal dependence, theoretical interest and apologetic aggression. These elements in his criticism of fiction are inevitably entangled in one another but, as the years pass, the last one – his apologetic zeal – seems to get the upper hand. God exists within the self right from the beginning of life, as the confessor explains many times in his autobiography, frequently recalling what he learnt from Monnica, who had tried to implant the true faith in her child from the very first moment. But then, in the long years leading up to his conversion, sensory excitations in general, erotic desires in particular and all kinds of heated phantasmagorias, philosophical delusions or phantoms intervened, blocking the way between the author and his God. The *Confessions* were written to dismiss them, perhaps not only programmatically but in a performative sense as well, hence the work's recurrent ingredients of prayer and expressions of invocation or liberation. Still, the *Confessions* also testify to the willpower that this sacrifice required of its author, due to his ingrained love of poetry. In this autobiography, we are struck time and again – as in the *Soliloquies* and several other works of Augustine's, not only the early ones – by the author's susceptibility to figuration and ambiguity (unique in my material), his interest in the *velamen* of poetic discourse, in fiction's particular cognitive status, in Virgil, and in the subjective or existential hermeneutics liable to interpret the literary work as an answer to the reader's questions or concern, *negotium*, all of which provide clear evidence of his own overwhelming experiences from reading.

This sensibility is still apparent, albeit dimmed or patchy, in the *City of God*. Thus the shift in Augustine's attitude towards fiction cannot be schematized into any neat and evenly falling curve. Throughout the great work of his old age, we often seem to hear two voices intermingling: a younger man of letters, with poetry and rhetoric as his very breath of life, and an older, strikingly stern cultural critic. The former speaker – the literary scholar – regularly breaks in on the sixty-year-old bishop, especially to provide him with historical, poetical or mythological examples from the pagan repertoire, with Virgil as the unfailing well to draw from.

This interaction results in a strange kind of split discourse permeating the cultural criticism of the *City of God*. The examples and quotations taken from the poets were there, of course, to serve as evidence for the author's arguments. Whether they are supposed to provoke disapproval (of the moral decline in the Roman world) or arouse admiration (for God's finger in history), they have to be illustrative, and they will only be that if they can be taken seriously, as instances of real courses of events, characters, or attitudes. At the same time, however, a good deal of the bishop's efforts are put into rejecting the pagan tradition in general as inauthentic, dissolving it into vain delusions and old wives' tales. It is as though Augustine now and again makes room for a humanistic version of himself, coming up with mythical *exempla* and attractive poetry, whereupon he cannot help but notice that his polemic tone begins to weaken and grow lax, for which reason he immediately rectifies his presentation.

A simple case in point: in the *City of God* 19.12, the author discusses the innermost longing of all living beings for peace. To find the ultimate example, he follows his habitual practice: he goes to Virgil. In the eighth book of the *Aeneid*, the poet describes the giant Cacus, the son of Vulcan, a man-eating cave monster who was killed by Hercules in a violent struggle (8.184–267). Augustine presents Cacus in some detail, dwelling on his name and origin, just to prove how even such a horrible beast was only trying to find harmony between body and soul, in short: peace and quiet. That is how this double discourse works in the *City of God* (as it frequently does in Paulinus of Nola or Prudentius as well). The author discusses and analyses mythical fantasies and pagan fictions – in this case virtually monstrous ones – in all seriousness, conceivably tempting his readers to mistake them for real beings or historical events. But then, at times quite abruptly, this potential kind of misunderstanding is corrected (19.12.2):[1]

> Perhaps, after all, he never existed or, more probably, he was not like the description given by poetic fantasy; for if Cacus had not been excessively blamed, Hercules would have received inadequate praise. And therefore the existence of such a man, or rather semi-human, is discredited, as are many similar poetical fictions.

Here, Augustine juxtaposes both of his most common critical attitudes to fictional matters. Cacus may have been all made up, an idiosyncratic outcome of mythical imagination, or he may be understood as a legendary version of some existing man, as in Hellenistic and Early Christian euhemeristic interpretation. Be that as it may, Augustine continues, in Virgil's presentation he is functional. He has to be there to provide substance to the stories of Hercules' heroic deeds. This observation certainly seems congenial to much Greek and Roman epic poetry, closely demonstrating a seminal function of the ancients' *licentia poetica*: the fabulous inventions served to endow the literary work with structure and consistency. But as an argument in a treatise whose main purpose was to kill off pagan culture, Augustine's interest in Cacus might undoubtedly seem curious – hence the author's deprecating attitude towards his own example.

It is not easy, then, to condense Augustine's complex relationship to literary fiction, as it appears from the *City of God*, in any neat formula. But right through what I have called the work's split discourse, he was driven, by virtue of his mystical as well as his polemic vein, to assign all inventions after the "manner of poets" to the pagan lies, *mendacia*, which unnecessarily block that vision of God's precious truth which had been granted him and which, at least in theory, should appeal to each and everyone. In practice, *figmenta* continued to lure peo-

---

[1] "Verum iste non fuerit vel, quod magis credendum est, non talis fuerit, qualis poetica vanitate describitur; nisi enim nimis accusaretur Cacus, parum Hercules laudaretur. Talis ergo homo sive semihomo melius, ut dixi, creditur non fuisse, sicut multa figmenta poetarum."

ple away from Him. "Is not a soul that sighs for such make-believe gods wantonly forsaking you, trusting in illusions and feeding the winds", *talibus enim figmentis suspirans anima nonne fornicatur abs te et fidit in falsis et pascit ventos?* This question had already been asked by Augustine in his *Confessions* (4.2.3) on account of his taking part in a theatre competition some time in his twenties. The term *fornicatur* colours the reprehensible *figmenta* with nuances of immorality and lack of faith. In such wordings, Augustine voiced his categorical and hence negative attitude to the nature of fiction, leaving no space for any alternative interpretations, imitations or recreations of reality between divine truth and demonic deceit. Tertullian had already expressed this unconditional antagonism with unsurpassable concision two centuries earlier, in his *Ad nationes* (*To the Nations*): 'there is simply no room for fiction, where there is reality' (2.12.24), *vacat fingendi locus, ubi veritas est.* Similar misgivings about the world of make-believe threw a long shadow over the last phase of Augustine's career. In such a bleak version, fictionality certainly offers no nourishment for the soul, no possibility of elucidation or transformation, only illusions and fallacies which, at best, are different in degree but not in kind from the blasphemous deceits the Manichees had come up with.

*

Finally, in a broader perspective, this Augustinian scepticism should be understood against the background of ancient culture's respect for, as well as fear of, the power of the spoken and the written word. The introductory chapter of this work suggested a connection between, on the one hand, the breakthrough of writing in Greek literature, philosophy and science some nine hundred years before Augustine's lifetime, and, on the other hand, the pioneering contributions to Greek fiction theory soon made by philosophers such as Gorgias (in rhetoric) or Aristotle (in poetics). In his ground-breaking work *A Preface to Plato*, Eric A. Havelock emphasized the importance of this new culture of writing for the development of myth criticism and a rational way of thinking in classical Hellas, articulated by Plato as a strong reaction against the traditional oral "Homeric encyclopedia".[1] Several later scholars, however, have approached this issue from a different perspective.

Literacy brought not only new possibilities of analysis and criticism but also new methods of verbal suggestion and persuasion. In a series of investigations into reading practices in ancient Greece, Havelock's pupil Jesper Svenbro has demonstrated the highly controversial nature of writing in the eyes of Plato

---

[1] Havelock 1982, pp. 61–86.

and, in several respects, in archaic and classical Greek culture at large. At an early stage, it seems, the activities of reading and writing were associated with power and the exercise of power. Once an author had committed his words to writing, he could no longer control their ways of signification. Accordingly, the reading and interpretation of written documents should ideally be subject to strict supervision within the framework of a well-defined, congenial and philosophical environment such as the Platonic Academy. On the other hand, the laboriously struggling readers, in particular the young and inexperienced ones, faced with unspaced texts without punctuation marks, ran the risk of being deprived of their integrity and ending up in the power of the author (or his work), so the task of reading aloud was commonly entrusted to literate slaves.[1] There is no room here to do full justice to Svenbro's research in this field – according to which the Greeks configured the act of reading as a kind of pederastic power game – or to the discussion his theses have aroused. They certainly cast an intriguing light on the archaic and classical culture where the written word became a dominant medium, demonstrably associated with ideas of manipulation, influence and subjection.

To cut this long story short – perhaps embarrassingly short: ever since its establishment in archaic Greece, the culture of writing in the West was accompanied not only by outstanding literary activities but also by priests' reprimands, philosopher's suspicions and teachers' instructions, a series of practices for the purpose of control or authority. The correct interpretation of documents was of the utmost importance, precisely because texts appeared to force their way into their readers, making claims on them and doing everything to ensnare them in their toils. The reading and writing culture of Late Antiquity was, of course, different from that of archaic Lesbos or classical Athens, but as Peter Brown has shown in a stimulating essay, the Christian Church in the fourth and fifth centuries was permeated with what might be called a metaphysics of presence. Neither texts nor images were met at a distance but were expected to disclose glimpses of Paradise, of the dead saints or of the deeds of the martyrs, to the believers here and now. In this respect, the Christians did not differ greatly from the pagans: their sacred places – primarily the church interiors – were characterized by reverence, the presence of the Godhead and the need to internalize signs and images. Not until the late sixth century, with Pope Gregory the Great as the paradigmatic leader, was the attention of the faithful turned from "participation" to "vision". The members of the congregation became to a lesser degree *adoratores* and to a greater degree *lectores*; the sacred images

---

[1] See Svenbro 1993, pp. 142, 166–68 and 187–216 (the final chapter).

lost their character of living presence and became quite simply *picturae* to be read and interpreted. Both texts and images came to be understood as messages about divine reality rather than as holy cult objects.[1]

These notions about participation and presence in Late Antique culture pertain primarily to the liturgy. Brown applies them first and foremost to the use of images, and even so his claims should probably be further qualified (as Ian Wood pointed out in a rejoinder), but I believe they might contribute to our understanding of Augustine's suspicions about fictional discourse.[2] The Church Father was active within the framework of a culture in which not only spectators at theatrical performances and audiences at orations, recitations or homilies acted as participants in unique events, but readers of books as well. There was actually a constant risk of the reader being not only influenced but, as it were, 'bewitched' by a text. In a fascinating essay on fictionality and enchantment in Apuleius' novel *Metamorphoses*, better known as *The Golden Ass* (ca. 160–70 CE), Andrew Laird notes that the Greek word *psychagōgia* ('to lead souls') was often understood as a kind of bewitchment in antique culture. In his short work *Encomium of Helen*, a seminal text for all discussions of ancient theories of fiction, dating from the end of the fifth century BCE (cf. above, p. 26), Gorgias had already presented drugs, *pharmaka*, visions, *opseis*, sorcery, *goēteiai*, and last but not least speech, *logos*, as sources of enchantment or even deceit, *apatē*, of human consciousness: a series of manipulations considered a recurrent ingredient of the ancient Mediterranean civilization (8–18).[3] For the orator Gorgias they offered interesting possibilities. As Charles P. Segal emphasizes, he presented the human soul as hypersensitive to the virtually physical force, *dynamis*, that emanated from *logos* and from the art of rhetorical persuasion, the Greek *peithō*.[4]

For Augustine, far later, these strategic possibilities changed into sheer apprehension. His sceptical watchfulness could obviously derive from his own wide experience of the clever art of rhetoric, but above all he realized the difficulties fictional discourse would present for Christians in a culture such as that of Late Antiquity, permeated with myth and magic. The great majority of these Christians, not to speak of the pagans who ought to be won over to the true faith as soon as possible, had little chance of distinguishing sacred truth from all sorts of superstitions and idolatry. In Augustine's (elderly) eyes, the *Aeneid* – to exemplify with the foremost literary work of pagan civilization – was certainly not a story to be enjoyed in the first place for excitement or for its masterly

---

[1] Brown 1999, pp. 26, 33.
[2] Wood 1999.
[3] Laird 1993, pp. 170–73.
[4] Segal 1962, p. 106.

language; it contained a whole repertoire of attitudes, practices and ideas, many of which were still respected and taken quite seriously, that were simply incompatible with Christian belief. The philosopher Apollonius (of Tyana, surrounded by rumours of various miracles and notorious for his supernatural capacities), the Church Father noted in a letter written in 411–12, was admittedly a better character than Jupiter and the other pagan gods, but was it not simply ridiculous "to compare or even to prefer Apollonius and Apuleius and the other experts in the arts of magic to Christ?" (138.4.18), *quis autem vel risu dignum non putet, quod Apollonium et Apuleium, caeterosque magicarum artium peritissimos conferre Christo, vel etiam praeferre conantur?*

That is in itself a highly rhetorical question. First, the fiction-maker and novelist Apuleius is associated with one of his main topics, magical customs and witchcraft, a biographical reading already widespread during this Berber writer's own lifetime, and, subsequently, those who had tried to promote him as a rival to Christ Himself are rejected. Such comparisons were probably quite common. Augustine's letter is in reply to Flavius Marcellinus, a high official at the court of Honorius and an imperial envoy in Africa, who had complained about the non-believers who "falsely claim that the Lord did nothing more than other human beings were able to do. In fact, they set before us their Apollonius and Apuleius and other practitioners of the arts of magic, and they claim that their miracles are greater." (136.1)[1] Augustine certainly took Marcellinus' complaints seriously. In several letters, he expresses his distress about the preposterous comparisons of Apuleius with Christ (102.32, 137.4.13). This strange juxtaposition actually tells us a good deal about the status of fictional literature in the Late Antique Roman Empire, inevitably entangled in controversies about superstition, heresy and idolatry, probably one of the strongest cultural-historical contrasts to Kant's and modernity's notion of a detached, autonomous art. In this environment, marked by a formidable cultural struggle that concerned souls as well as ideas, concepts and words, Augustine could not afford to give in to the weaknesses of his youth. It would not do to weep for Dido.

---

[1] "In quibus nihil amplius Dominum, quam alii homines facere potuerunt, gessisse mentiuntur. Apollonium siquidem suum nobis et Apuleium, aliosque magicae artis homines in medium proferunt, quorum maiora contendunt extitisse miracula."

5 "Set me free, O God, from that multitude of speech"

In a letter written at the same time as he composed his *Confessions*, perhaps at the turn of the year 397–98, Augustine reports on his arrival in the town of Tubursicum, south of Hippo Regius. There he visited his Donatist colleague, Bishop Fortunius, obviously hoping for some interesting exchange of opinions. Rumours of his arrival spread rapidly over the town, and a considerable number of people gathered in or around Fortunius' house. However, Augustine notes disappointedly, not many of them came for the sake of his and Fortunius' main topics, that is, the question of salvation and the notion of the true Church that had aroused the Donatist controversy (44.1.1):

> We, however, saw that there were very few in that whole crowd who desired that the issue be treated in a useful and salutary manner and that so important a question on so important an issue be discussed with wisdom and piety. But the rest had assembled for the spectacle of our quarrel, as it were, almost in manner of the theater rather than for instruction toward salvation with Christian devotion. Hence, they could neither offer us silence nor hold a discussion with us attentively or at least in modest and orderly fashion, except, as I said, for those few whose intention was seen to be religious and undivided. Therefore, everything was thrown into confusion by the noise of those speaking freely and without control in accord with the impulse of the mind of each person, and neither he nor we were able to obtain, either by asking or even at times by threatening, that they offer us a polite silence. (XXIX)

This kind of experience is undoubtedly reflected in the *Confessions*. Augustine knew better than most people what power of suggestion the spoken word had over people. The crowd in Tubursicum had flocked to Fortunius' house as if to attend a verbal duel between the two bishops, a virtual gladiatorial combat.[1] Even a seriously dogmatic dispute, *altercatio*, in this case admittedly inflamed by the schismatic circumstances, threatened at any moment, as soon as the opportunity arose, to turn into entertainment, theatre, performance, drowned in unchecked noise at the expense of the calm and silence that the cause required.

It is high time to sum up and draw conclusions. Despite all that was said and done, fictionality remained an unsolved problem for Augustine; unsolved because the theologian that he became had to disqualify all kinds of mimetic artifice as tools of faith, that faith which unceasingly hungered for (divine) reality, whereas the eloquent speaker he had always been knew that such *figmenta*

---

[1] Cf. Westra 2007, p. 21.

often attract people far more strongly than the naked truth. Augustine himself did not stop feeling that attraction. At an early stage of his career, as a Christian philosopher in Cassiciacum, he had outlined a rudimentary theory about the cognitive duplicity of fictional representation, which certainly presupposed an intense acquaintance with at least epic poetry and drama. As a priest and later a bishop in Africa, he returned continually to the great reading experience of his youth, Virgil; as a gifted preacher, he sketched out a Christian rhetoric in which tropes played a decisive role; as an exegete, he pondered deeply on the relationship between eloquent and Biblical figurative stratagems; and as a cultural philosopher, he continued to draw support and examples from the pagan fictions that he had long since theoretically disqualified.

It is equally true that, from early on in his career, Augustine felt a distrust of fictional discourse that grew stronger as time passed. We have noted that it was not only the African bishop's evangelical and polemical passion but likewise the Christian philosopher's Platonic premises that fuelled this scepticism. If man's soul, or more precisely the human intellect, reigned supreme at a higher level of being than material reality – including the projections of that reality in fantasy or poetry – and if this intellect ultimately aimed at apprehending a divine truth that was not of this world, it could hardly be satisfied with *figmenta*, least of all when they were of a morally dubious nature.

The human conclusions about God based on analogies drawn from the liberal arts, introspection or imagination were on the whole of limited value. At best, they met the propaedeutic function that Augustine could attribute to our attempts to grasp God's eternity and transcendence by means of mutable and sensory signs. Apart from the words of the Holy Writ, resulting from the verbal inspiration bestowed by the Spirit on the Biblical writers, all representations, linguistic or not, were contingent, dependent on context, liable to misinterpretation, insufficient to suggest (the ultimately divine) truth. As a matter of fact, few ancient writers adopted as seriously as Augustine the linguistic scepticism that Plato had expressed through the philosopher Hermogenes, one of the interlocutors in his dialogue *Cratylus:* "no name belongs to any particular thing by nature, but only by the habit and custom of those who employ it and who established the usage" (384d), possibly because the Church Father's rhetorical past had left him with such eminent insights into the readiness of words to constantly slip into idiosyncratic, indeterminate or multivocal patterns of meaning.[1]

Another way to understand this distrust in human language would be in terms of semiotics. The kind of insight Hermogenes had voiced in Plato's dia-

---

1 I quote *Cratylus* from H.N. Fowler's Loeb edition 1926.

logue gave rise to a perception in Augustine of what some modern scholars, primarily Umberto Eco (based on Charles S. Peirce), have labelled as "unlimited semiosis" in language: a sign refers to an object, which in turn points to another object in a (theoretically) endless chain of representations.[1] The Church Father's typology and his recurrent references to "the inner teacher's" wordless instruction were two different ways of trying to check this bewildering dissemination of meaning. The former both calls attention to and revises the figurative techniques of rhetoric; the latter is based on Stoic sign theory and retraces Plotinus' philosophical way of negation. Accordingly, on the last page of *On the Trinity*, Augustine begs his God to set him free "from that multitude of speech which I suffer inwardly in my soul" (15.28.51): *libera me, Deus meus, a multiloquio quod patior intus in anima mea*.

The concept of *multiloquium*, "multitude of speech", has a Biblical starting point in the Book of Proverbs, where Solomon pleads in favour of restraint and control in the use of language: "When words are many, transgression is not lacking, but whoever restrains his lips is prudent" (10.19), *in multiloquio peccatum non deerit qui autem moderatur labia sua prudentissimus est*. Most importantly, the term is typical of the pious polemics with apologetic colouring of Late Antiquity. It occurs several times in Augustine as well as in Paulinus of Nola, and it is closely linked to the Christian theory of the Bible's exemplary humble style. In his letters, Paulinus frequently pushed this idea to its limit, so that his version of sacred speech approached sheer stammering (modelled on the Whitsuntide speaking in tongues): "Once I was fluent in the fictitious literature of men, but now I stutter in the proclamation of the truth" (40.6), *quondam in litteris humanarum fabularum loquaces, nunc in veritatis balbutimus eloquiis*.

Yet another aspect of this problem was brought up by Ambrose in his voluminous discussion of Psalm 118 in which he counted *multiloquium* among the deadly vanities that darken the human soul. The bishop actually compares such multitude of speech to the gaze of a harlot, delivering mortal wounds through her window (5.30).[2] In his *Confessions*, as we have seen, Augustine had already assigned high-sounding eloquence to the sphere of economics, undoubtedly well supported by contemporary reality in streets and marketplaces, where words could regularly be bought and sold as required. In his commentary

---

[1] Augustine's problem with "unlimited semiosis" has been touched upon in Irvine 1994, p. 175. Eco returns regularly to Peirce's ideas on this topic throughout his semiotic works, first (I believe) in *A Theory of Semiotics* 1976, pp. 71f., later especially in his articles "Unlimited Semiosis and Drift: Pragmaticism vs. 'Pragmatism'" from 1983 (1990, pp. 23–43), and "Peirce and the Semiotic Foundations of Openness: Signs as Texts and Texts as Signs", 1984, pp. 175–99.
[2] Ambrose 1999.

on the Psalms, Ambrose sharpened this criticism of contemporary public life, branding verbosity as a special case of the period's (notoriously widespread) prostitution.

The closing pages of *On the Trinity* (written, we should perhaps remember, by one of Antiquity's most productive and prolix authors) take the form of a prayer that the author should be allowed to escape from words, thoughts and concepts, expressing a desire to merge into the blessed collective that ignores all difference – the very hallmark of human life on earth – in favour of one shared identity and one unanimous Word or *Logos*. It is significant that at this final stage of his great work, Augustine abandons exegetic analysis in order to address God in the second person: the devout type of discourse that initiated, interspersed and ended his *Confessions*. The abilities of the Christian orator, he noted later in the fourth book of *On Christian Doctrine*, will derive "more from his devotion to prayer than his dedication to oratory" (4.15.32), *pietate magis orationum quam oratorum facultate.* When neither Platonic conceptual discourse nor the poets' figurative language sufficed for his purposes, he settled whole-heartedly on that appeal to the Godhead which was modelled on the Word Incarnate. To determine his position in philosophical terms: the gap between expression and being seemed as insurmountable as it ever was in the Platonic tradition, principally in Plotinus' system, "the philosophy of silence" (Cilento).[1] But whereas the Egyptian thinker had defied this gap by the prophetic voice of an isolated visionary, Augustine opted for that inner and silent speech that ideally would characterize the Christian community, once tried and tested with paramount consequences together with Monnica in the summer of 387: prayer.[2]

This meditative vein of Augustine's intellectual and hermeneutic project boded well for the mystically permeated theology of the High Middle Ages, of the Cistercians, the Victorines and their likes, but hardly for the survival of the Muses. Harald Hagendahl concludes his major study of the Church Father and the Latin classics with a well-founded protest against the tendency among earlier scholars to assume a conciliation between Christianity and Antiquity in the former's works. Notwithstanding his life-long interest in Virgil, Cicero and other ancient writers, Augustine contributed substantially to the great divide between the two cultures that persisted (albeit occasionally transgressed) all through the Mid-

---

[1] Cilento 1960, p. 308.
[2] In the *Confessions*, observes James J. O'Donnell, Augustine "devised an idiom by which it is possible to pray in a literary medium", 1985, p. 83.

dle Ages.¹ The relentless bishop's categorical schemes of exclusion came to completely overshadow the inquiring novice's integrative attempts.

It seems logical, then, that the *Confessions* move on from story to commentary, or from narration to reflection – with the Ostia miracle at the transitional stage; and, moreover, that Augustine stopped writing dialogues, a polyphonic genre with fictional elements, after being ordained in 391. In his own cognitive terms from *Of True Religion* (51.100): only when we acquire insight into God do we have the possibility of gaining a permanent *sapientia*, leaving all our erring behind, extinguishing all our *curiositas*, sensual as well as intellectual, within. The most conspicuous stage on this way to abnegation and renunciation in Augustine's writing is probably epitomized by his *Confessions*, both in the work's thematic constellations and in its overall structure. The first nine books are guided by the self's unquenched *curiositas*, which entails a style characterized by subjectivity, impassioned rhetoric and narrative stratagems. After his conversion, his baptism and the experience of God at Ostia, however, the confessor's intellectual life was dominated by *sapienta*, so the last four books are written in a spirit of philosophy and exegesis. The soul's pilgrimage was over. All fictional devices could be set aside at the very moment when the pilgrim reached his goal.

Here, we are undoubtedly faced with a contradiction. O'Connell even points to "a gigantic paradox" in Augustine's works, the same contradiction that he detects "on virtually every page" in the *Enneads*. Both the Egyptian philosopher and the Numidian bishop unceasingly warned their readers against thinking in images. Both proclaimed the ability of the human soul to make contact with an intelligible and ineffable world beyond all sensory imagery. Yet "both lead us up to and depict their overworld in images so evocative as to rank them among the greatest philosophic artists Western thought has known".²

It is a similar kind of paradox that I have wanted to outline in the pages above, emblematically concentrated to the episode at the window in Ostia. This marks the peripeteia in the *Confessions:* the critical juncture of the work. Throughout the first nine books the author recalls and reports a great number of dialogues: his way to conversion is largely marked by a series of conversations. The most important of these is the last one: Augustine's and Monnica's sublime intercourse at Ostia, characterized by complete consensus, actually presented as if the two speakers were communicating with one tongue – or rather

---

1 Hagendahl 1967, p. 729.
2 O'Connell 1978, pp. 119f. Cf. Krämer's observation that "even when Augustine takes pains to distance himself from the traditional literary system, he remains deeply rooted in it", 2007, p. 146.

one heart. In this perspective, the Ostia episode appears as a brilliant product of the cultural instability of early Christianity: it vacillates not only between rhetoric and asceticism but also between the oral now and the parchment's remembrance. It is a bold attempt to inaugurate the kingdom of God in discursive images, to register a moment of unison and inaudible speech in faint and lonely writing. Even if the actual Ostia dialogue did not proceed "in this wise exactly, nor in these same words", its record in the *Confessions* gives a utopian version of the spiritual community of the Christian congregation.

Such was Augustine's answer to the question he puts so persistently throughout his writings: how should the living speak with the living? This is the main problem for *On the Catechising of the Uninstructed* from about 400, a work that focuses from beginning to end on the difficulties, delays and obstacles apparently inherent in human communication. Teachers have to adjust to their catechumens, the author observes, in fraternal, paternal or maternal love; ideally, he or she should be at one with them at heart, *copulati cordi eorum*. Such a "sympathetic disposition of mind", *animi compatientis affectus*, in both parties actually makes them "dwell" in each other's souls: *habitemus in invicem* (12.17). It is a communion of this type, two hearts in harmonious interaction – a kind of paradisiacal communication, beyond the contingency of signs – that Augustine recalls from Ostia. Then, in the tenth chapter, when Monnica is gone and her son is at last restored to the true faith, the autobiography enters into the mode of – as one commentator put it – "existential reflection".[1] In Ostia, the biography, the dialogue and the storytelling still control the account, although the novice wants to free himself from precisely these narrative modes or devices – and, indeed, from the self, from discursive speech and time. After all, his and Monnica's great moment of insight, *hoc momentum intellegentiae*, demanded that "all other visions, so far inferior, be taken away". The mode of narration was soon to give way to contemplation, just as – in the two following books of the *Confessions*, devoted to the issues of memory and temporality – the categories of past and future time were to be dissolved, as it were, in a subjective present.

The rapture at Ostia, then, marks a liminal point in the narratological context of the *Confessions:* a climax of the previous chapters' repeated attempts – Manichaean, Platonic and, finally, Pauline – to approach the Godhead as well as a presage of the new life in Christ that awaits Augustine. It stands out as the critical juncture of the whole work, after the biographical and before the philosophical/exegetical chapters. Moreover, if we limit our range of vision to

---

[1] Bright 2003, p. 155.

the ninth book of the *Confessions*, we can, with Brian Stock, distinguish at least an implicit contrast between the author's activities in Cassiciacum, where conversation, reading and writing were still paramount, "a Christianized version of classical *otium*", and the extraordinary communion at Ostia, prefiguring the Paradise of the elect, where such means of communication will be superfluous.[1]

If we broaden our perspective on the Church Father's writings to the period between Cassiciacum and his bishopric of Hippo Regius, that is, between his philosophical dialogues and the *Confessions*, we will arrive at a similar result. Those ten years sealed the fate of fiction in Augustine's overall theory of knowledge. This process had already begun in the fairly open-minded *Soliloquies*, where Reason, *Ratio*, put forward a suggestive theory of fictional representation based on the – vaguely Aristotelian – idea that a true role performance presupposed a departure from the personal or historical circumstances in reality. The other speaker of the dialogue, however, "Augustine", refused to be impressed by such clever arguments: he demonstratively sets his mind on seeking "the absolute truth, not that double-faced thing that is partly true and partly false". Reason cannot but reply approvingly: "You are asking something great, nay divine."

Those great and divine things were what Augustine found, one might add, at the expense of the feats of imagination and all kinds of beguiling or "double-faced" representation, at the window in Ostia. In what are perhaps his foremost contributions to the theory of literary fiction, the Charles Eliot Norton lectures in 1993 published under the title *Six Walks in the Fictional Woods*, Umberto Eco assumes that reading fiction means playing a game that allows us to give sense to the immensity of things that happened, are happening or will happen in our real life: "By reading narrative, we escape the anxiety that attacks us when we try to say something true about the world."[2] As for Augustine, the opposite might be claimed: that the (divine) truth he had sought after so long and painstakingly at last granted him relief, while fiction – associated with enslaving desire as well as vain pretence – caused him an anguish that became increasingly severe as the years passed.

If the above discussion at any point has hinted at some disappointment with this turn of events in Augustine's oeuvre, let me add in conclusion that from the Church Father's own point of view, his development certainly seemed both logical and necessary. In sharp contrast to modern assumptions about the value of literary studies, the later Augustine could understand the entire cycle of *paideia* in terms of obligation and coercion. Those disciplines "that are called liberal",

---

[1] Stock 1998, p. 113.
[2] Eco 1994, p. 87.

we have seen him insist in a letter dated 408 or 409, "have consonant [*habent congruum*] with freedom only what they have consonant with the truth". This stern verdict is directed against liberal education at large, but, as we remember, Augustine immediately specifies his main target, namely the language arts, primarily the "countless and impious stories […] with which the poems of pagan poets are filled" (above, p. 190).

Antique literary culture, as it appears in famous records such as Aristotle's *Poetics* or Horace's *Ars poetica*, had been able to distinguish between historical or philosophical truth and the type of narrative representation which made use of *licentia poetica*, normally composed in verse, commonly relying on figurative discourse. This exception of *licentia vatum* from *historica fides* (to reuse Ovid's terms) was cancelled in Augustine's later works. He interpreted Christ's words in John 8.32, "the truth will set you free", to mean that *all* freedom derives from the truth and that this truth is *one*, identical with the Saviour and His work. That was his way of establishing a 'congruity' between the concepts of truth and freedom, a concord, as it were, which excluded the venerable fictions of pagan culture, construed as fruits of a misguided and false imagination. In the years 408–09, the Bishop of Hippo, regularly faced with manifestations of unbelief and idolatrous cults, could no longer accept any compromises with classical tradition. The only freedom worthy of the name was the one that released the body from death.

In the light of the epoch's religious schisms, it becomes clear how Augustine, under pressure from circumstances, turned away from literary culture in general, and from its incipient tendencies to unite *romanitas* with *christianitas* in particular, in search of the uncompromising devotion and practice of inner prayer that attracted the contemporary Desert Fathers, albeit without ever being granted their retreat from the world. We may perhaps regret that he proved unable to accommodate the old songs, Virgil and the shadow of Creusa in his devotional agenda. We may regret, too, that he abandoned his youthful attempts to arrive at a broad, synthesizing philosophical outlook. There are various ways of approach to Wisdom, *sapientia*, Reason had decreed in his *Soliloquies* shortly after his conversion, as if he were echoing, in the name of tolerance, Senator Symmachus' famous dispatch to Emperor Valentinian II a few years earlier (cf. below pp. 532ff.). "Each man according to his soundness and firmness", the thirty-two-year-old Augustine maintained in a conciliatory mode, "takes hold of that unique and truest Good" (1.13.23).[1] But in the *Revisions*, written in his old age,

---

1 "Sed non ad eam [sapientiam] una via pervenitur. Quippe pro sua quisque sanitate ac firmitate comprehendit illud singulare ac verissimum bonum."

came the rebound: "Again, what I said, 'There is not one way to a union with wisdom,' does not sound right. It is as though there were another way apart from Christ, who said, I am the way. This offence to pious ears should have been avoided" (1.4.3).[1]

The holy man who wrote these words had once and for all ceased to thirst for the allurements of poetry. For his own part, as the first nine books of his *Confessions* had eloquently and frequently explained, he felt that the worlds of imagination and fiction ensnared him. Ostia became his main emblem, as it were, not only for the moment of ultimate understanding or communion but also for liberation. The fact, in the end, that this vibrant momentum can never be recalled as it really was, but only by the erratic means of human words, of writing and narrative, was something the confessor himself was the first to admit. Well aware of the fictionality which in this broad sense is inherent in language itself, the reality distortion field inevitably suffusing all words heard in the air or seen on parchment, he seems to insist on telling us: we were there. We really experienced it. It happened.

---

[1] "Item quod dixi: *Ad sapientiae coniunctionem non una via perveniri*, non bene sonat, quasi alia via sit praeter Christum qui dixit: *Ego sum via*. Vitanda ergo erat haec offensio aurium religiosarum".

III **Oblique Speech**
Implementations of Allegory in Late Roman
Learned Culture

Preliminary Remarks

> Sic ego nunc, quoniam haec ratio plerumque videtur
> tristior esse quibus non est tractata, retroque
> volgus abhorret ab hac, volui tibi suaviloquenti
> carmine Pierio rationem exponere nostram
> et quasi musaeo dulci contingere melle,
> si tibi forte animum tali ratione tenere
> versibus in nostris possem, dum perspicis omnem
> naturam rerum, qua constet compta figura.
>
> So now, since my philosophy often seems
> a little grim to beginners, and most men
> shrink back from it in fear, I wished to tell
> my tale in sweet Pierian song for you,
> to paint it with the honey of the Muses,
> hoping that thus I might fix your attention
> upon my verse until you clearly saw
> how all of nature is arranged and shaped.
>
> Lucretius, *The Nature of Things* (1.943–50)[1]

Christianity's amazing metamorphosis from an apocalyptic-revolutionary sect to the authorized religion of the Roman Empire in the early fourth century had important and obvious consequences for its intellectuals' attitudes to the antique literary heritage. In the first few centuries of our era, as the classical philologist Siegmar Döpp has pointed out, most Christians thought they were living close to the end of the world: the return of the Lord (the *parousia*) and Judgment Day were considered to be imminent. Moreover, one Dutch expert on the lyric poetry of this epoch, Pieter G. van der Nat, notes that the new faith initially spread (mainly) among Jewish and Greek-speaking communities with low levels of literacy in the Eastern Mediterranean region. It had only slowly penetrated the West, where it reached the intellectuals at a comparatively late stage.[2] That is why it is

---

[1] I quote Lucretius from Josef Martin's Berlin edition 1972 and, in English, from Frank O. Copley's translation 1977.
[2] Döpp 1988, p. 32; Van der Nat 1977, pp. 191–97.

only logical that, from the point of view of the earliest congregations, life on earth seemed to be a provisional and rather desolate affair, a *peregrinatio* which left neither time nor energy for immersions in games of make-believe, least of all if they joined up with the classical world of gods, assuming intercourse with the Muses. Somewhat later, around the year 200, when Tertullian and other apologists began to face up to pagan rites and customs, the old issues of literature and truth, inherent in ancient culture since the days of Hesiod, began to gain new importance. Christian habits or genres of discourse, imbued with the Bible, were determinedly put to the service of proclamation and preaching, the *kerygma*, and were strategically identified with a low or "humble" style in contrast to the ostentatious *eloquentia* of Roman tradition.

But during the fourth century, the Church's relations with both the Roman state and the pagan world came to be radically modified; this religious-political process was soon to influence the period's cultural and literary theory as well as its epic and lyric poetry. The victorious Church, on the brink of a universal undertaking of salvation and missionary work, could no longer conceive of itself as a persecuted minority movement, hostile or at best indifferent to cultural life. When the intellectuals began to fill its own ranks, it could no longer content itself with ignoring the classical system of education, *paideia*, the very foundation of the institution of literature in the West. This is what Peter Brown, in his study of the Late Antique world, called "the conversion of Christianity" to antique culture.[1] In the contemporary Christians' own terms, the same process could be described as a compromise between the religion founded by simple fishermen, *piscatores*, and the culture borne up by learned speakers, *oratores*. If our previous chapter dwelled on the dissonances in this process, closely monitored through the works of the most important Church Father in the West, we shall now focus on the attempts to build bridges, or, more precisely, on the progressive endeavours to legitimize literary fiction on the new conditions dictated, directly or indirectly, by the *ecclesia triumphans*.

For the first time it seemed possible to put poetry, as it was taught and read in Roman schools, at the systematic service of the Christian message. In their search for predecessors in the art of framing complex doctrine in Latin verse, pious authors found Lucretius, Döpp observes, the poet who had turned the demanding Epicurean philosophy into sonorous hexameters.[2] But soon the presence of other Roman writers made itself felt, first and foremost the matchless paradigm of Virgil. Should not the principal drama of humanity, the story of In-

---

[1] See the seventh chapter in Brown 1971, "The Conversion of Christianity, 300–363", pp. 82–95.
[2] Döpp 1988, p. 32.

carnation and Salvation, be presented in as reverent Latin as possible, linked to the greatest of Roman writers? The Church Father Lactantius and the Biblical poet Juvencus were in the forefront of this development of Christian culture from separatism to synthesis. Thanks to their efforts, a new 'use', *chrēsis*, of the old poets was established during the early fourth century, a kind of literary recycling that created new possibilities – and, incidentally, new problems as well – for the intellectuals of the Church.

We have already seen Augustine articulate his passionate and penetrating, yet in the long run sceptical viewpoints on the cognitive value and benefit of profane poetry. However, his scepticism was intersected by another approach that developed as the result of an interchange between scholarly writers (both pagan and Christian) and classical tradition from the fourth to the sixth centuries. It is a selection of their works which will claim our attention in the following presentation. They would all engage in the time-honoured issue of the allegoric mode of literature, with respect to the production as well as the interpretation of poetry, and they were all intrigued by the canonized Roman authors, in the first place, obviously, Virgil.

The writer who prepared the way for the Augustan poet in this Christian context, in accordance with the principle of one common god for the unbaptized and the faithful, *unum esse deum*, was the African apologist Minucius Felix. A few decades into the third century, he wrote a dialogue in Ciceronian style that we have already come across in passing, *Octavius*, set in Ostia. It contains references to the *Georgics* (4.221–23), the *Aeneid* (6.724–29) and several philosophical classics, foremost among them Plato's dialogue *Timaeus*, as witnesses of the one and only God, in classical manner labelled the great Artificer (17.11), *deus artifex*, or "the constructor of all things in heaven and earth" (19.14), *caelestium terrenorumque fabricator*.[1] On closer inspection, it appears that Minucius distinguishes between two antique cultures, one superstitious and objectionable, the other based on a number of enlightened philosophers and poets, hence a disavowal of the former.

Apart from his conspicuous interest in classical writers such as Plato and Virgil, it is Minucius' description of "an ignorant tradition, charmed or captivated by its pet fables" (20.2), *antiquitas inperitorum fabellis suis delectata vel capta*, that deserves our attention. This is because it tries to depict a culture enchanted

---

[1] The key role of Minucius Felix in this context is emphasized in Heck 1990, pp. 110f. It was already brought out by Gerard L. Ellspermann who, in his thesis on the early Christian attitude to pagan culture, distinguishes two "streams of thought" in the epoch's intellectual life, one integrative, originating with Minucius Felix, and one exclusive with its main starting point in Tertullian, 1949, p. 255.

by tales of imaginary beings, all kinds of monstrous marvels and miracles, "or any other fiction of folk-lore fell upon willing ears", *quicquid famae licet fingere*, here firmly discarded as lies, *mendacia*. Among them are mythical creatures like Scylla, the Chimaera, a beast of many forms, the Hydra or the Centaurs (notorious punchbags in this context) as well as human beings changed into birds, beasts, trees or flowers, the subject of old wives' tales, *aniles fabulae*. It is evident that such Ovidian stories, dealing with the dispersion of human identity as a consequence of some all-pervading metamorphosis, was a particularly sensitive matter in this context, a prototype for the fictional scenarios that had to be rejected. If such oddities had actually occurred, remarks Octavius, the dialogue's Christian interlocutor, they would still be occurring, but obviously nothing like this does happen, hence it never happened (20.3–4). As for the gods, he explains them away with an explicit reference to Euhemerus (21.1).

Octavius emphatically deprecates the poets for their role in propagating such *fabulae et errores*. He locates the source of infection of all these myths and delusions in the teaching of the schools, *studia et disciplinae*, and "especially in the works of poets, who have had such a fatal influence in injuring the cause of truth" (24.1), *carminibus praecipue poetarum, qui plurimum quantum veritati ipsi sua auctoritate nocuerunt*. Worst of all was Homer, who had outrageously involved the gods in the Trojan war, so Plato was right to expel him from his ideal republic. From the author's monistic viewpoint, Octavius' argument is perfectly understandable. Spicy mythological details such as Mars caught in bed with Venus were hardly compatible with his noble vision of one divine principle permeating the universe. "Figments and falsehoods of this kind" – the juxtaposition is significant: *huiusmodi figmenta et mendacia* – only serve to corrupt the minds of young people for life, while the truth is in fact obvious to everyone, at least to those who look for it (24.8). In such belligerent phrases, Minucius appears as a genuine apologist, and sure enough it is the vigorous polemic that dominates his dialogue. Still, in sharp contrast to Tertullian, his great contemporary, he exploited the enlightened pagan tradition for the benefit of his eponymous protagonist's spiritualizing interpretation of the created world.

From Lactantius and the fourth century onwards, this process of annexation would accelerate to the point that virtually every *poeta christianus* – to begin with a contradiction in terms, later a honorary title – referred to the author of the *Aeneid*. In both pagan and Christian circles of the dying Roman Empire there grew up a controversial tendency to understand Virgil allegorically, a way of interpreting him that we have already seen accepted by Augustine, albeit with reservations, and refuted by Jerome (above, pp. 133ff.). Such modified reading habits are in turn bound up with the widening gap between cultivated written language and everyday spoken Latin in the late Empire, a development that

Erich Auerbach has described in a well-known essay.¹ These are the centuries when the production, reception and interpretation of literature were to an ever increasing extent merging into scholarly culture, becoming a matter for pedagogues, highbrows and a fairly restricted learned elite. In Seth Lerer's words: "As the arena of literary studies moved from public declamation to private study, and as the exercise of language moved from forum to classroom, the contexts for the reading and writing of literature narrowed. Broadly speaking, literature began to lose its public, as works such as the *Aeneid* were read not as political poems celebrating a social and historical order, but rather as allegories of education, whose realm of action was not the world but the classroom."²

We shall trace the impact of this type of Virgilian allegoresis on a limited number of encyclopaedists, philosophers, commentators and polymaths in Late Antiquity. Their epoch was marked by a deepening breach between spoken and written language. The canonical names of the cultural tradition, not only Virgil but also writers like Seneca or even Cicero, the foremost orator of classical Rome, became progressively a matter of books, reading and grammatical analysis for the initiated, commonly disconnected from their traditional task of promoting the patriarchal foundations of the ideology of the Empire. This is what Wolfgang Kirsch calls "the lexicalization of the poetic word" in Roman schools, or what Catherine M. Chin understands as grammar teaching's removal of single lines of poetry, notably Virgilian poetry, from their original signifying contexts, turning them into "symbols of grammatical knowledgeability".³ The *Aeneid* was subjected to an ongoing dehistoricizing and schematizing process. It ceased to be read as a civic appeal or imperial apology and was increasingly comprehended as a demonstration of erudition, to a certain extent of an esoteric nature. Its hero was being transformed from a Roman prototype into an allegory of the human lot.⁴ The poet himself could be envisaged as a philosopher of the initiated sort that we shall meet in Servius, Macrobius and Fulgentius. All of them, each in his own way, articulated the reverential reception of Virgil in the culture of Late Antiquity. It was this concept of Rome's *summus poeta* that was at the centre of the so-called Virgilian lottery, *sortes Virgilianae*, practised right up to

---

1 "The Western Public and Its Language", Auerbach 1993, pp. 235–338.
2 Lerer 1985, pp. 3f.
3 Kirsch 1989a, p. 68; Chin 2008, p. 17.
4 Cf. Chapter IV, "Vergil and Augustine", in Mazzotta 1979, pp. 147–91.

the level of the Emperor: the *Aeneid* was opened at random in order to get a hint about one's future destiny.¹

Both the reading and the interpretation of literature were characterized by patent professionalization and specialization. Late Antique masters of rhetoric readily appointed their art – since long deprived of its former political or civic function in the Senate and public *fora* – the queen of each and every thing inside the classrooms, *omnium regina rerum oratio*.² The grammarians, for their part, refused to be outdone. Servius' extensive *In Vergilii carmina commentarii* (*Commentaries on Virgil's Poems*) and Tiberius Claudius Donatus' line-by-line commentary on the *Aeneid*, basically read as a display of rhetorical skills on an epic scale, *Interpretationes Vergilianae* (ca. 400), testify to this development. The analysis and exposition of the classics became the privileged discipline of learned men of letters: the grammarians and rhetors, the pedagogues, the commentators, the aristocratic connoisseurs. And it was first and foremost the classics that counted: no post-Augustan poet at all was admitted to the collection of examples in Aelius Donatus' widespread grammar, where Virgil stood out as the dominant name. In the fourth century, a literary-rhetorical education in accordance with the conservative ideals of the Senate and province aristocracy was considered, as Kirsch observes in a bibliographical survey, the best prerequisite for a career in the civil service, not only by the scholars themselves, such as Lactantius or the young Augustine, but also at the highest imperial level.³ This broad cultural reorientation resulted in a rich plethora of what we nowadays call "paraliterature" (below, p. 598). Venerable ancient types of text like the ode, the elegy or the epic poem faced competition from the commentary, the dialogue, the diatribe, the anthology, and hybrid genres like the Menippean satire, cento poetry, and the kind of scholarly 'patchwork' or 'miscellany' of moral philosophy, history, dogmatic theology and scriptural commentary epitomized by Clement of Alexandria's *Strōmateis*.

This overall development was considered deeply regrettable by many leading nineteenth and twentieth-century researchers, influenced by Romantic conceptions of literature – as when F.J.E. Raby, in his voluminous survey of the secular Latin poetry of the Middle Ages, laments over school culture's obsession with rhetorical drills, verse exercises and other "trifles".⁴ Nevertheless, the ele-

---

1 Comparetti 1997, pp. 47f. For a sceptical approach to the practice of these *sortes* as they are traditionally understood (actually calling the existence of antique Virgilian divination into question), see Ekbom 2013.
2 Hagendahl 1983, pp. 49–51.
3 Holtz 1981, p. 117; Kirsch 1989b, p. 135.
4 Raby 1957, pp. 44f.

mentary fact that boys (and to a lesser extent girls) from both Christian and pagan families went to the same schools, shared an established rhetorical culture and plodded through identical classics explains a great deal of the common topics, repertoire and style, right across religious boundaries, which were apparent in fourth and fifth-century Roman literature. Julian the Apostate's ban on Christian pedagogues teaching rhetoric and grammar during the early 360s was of short duration, the occasional exception that proves the rule regarding traditional education's relevance for the great crossover trends of Late Antique culture.[1]

Several solid works, such as Louis Holtz's monograph on Aelius Donatus and his significance from the fourth to the ninth centuries (1981), Martin Irvine's study of *ars grammatica* as a leavening agent for literary theory in Late Antiquity and the Middle Ages (1994), Catherine M. Chin's *Grammar and Christianity in the Late Roman World* (2008), not to mention Rita Copeland's and Ineke Sluiter's magnificent *Medieval Grammar and Rhetoric* (2009), an anthology of almost a thousand pages, have given us better information about the decisive role of grammar for culture in general and for the understanding of poetry in particular during this long period. The first of the liberal arts introduced practically all Western students (including, of course, all prospective writers) for more than a thousand years to what we now call literary studies.[2] In a broad sense, this discipline covered correct language use and literary instruction. In a narrower sense, the latter, entrusted with the task of teaching "the art of interpretation", *scientia interpretandi*, could involve four elements: the principles of reading aloud, involving vocabulary, morphology and prosody (*lectio*), the exposition of the subject and the figures of speech (*enarratio*), textual criticism (*emendatio*) and critical judgment (*iudicium*).[3] It is against this scholarly background, common to Christian and pagan writers alike, that the contributions of Late Antiquity to both poetry and the tradition of commentaries should be considered, frequently comprehended precisely in terms of *grammatica*.

Thus schools imprinted on their students certain reading habits which – duly internalized – came to influence their understanding of literature later in

---

[1] See Duval 1987, pp. 167f.
[2] Although Irvine now and then probably overstates his view of grammar as the foundational matrix of medieval culture, his work of 1994 surely remains an outstanding survey, a kind of miniature encyclopaedia in this inexhaustible field.
[3] Ibid., pp. 4–8, 50–63. This classification is to be found at least as early as in Quintilian, 1.4.3. The definition of the subject could of course be further detailed. In his *Etymologies*, Isidore would divide grammar into twenty-three (!) sections, including *schemata, tropi, prosa, metra, fabulae* and *historiae*, 1.5.4.

life. The techniques for explication of the classics and their myths that dominated Late Antique education were the historical-euhemeristic and the philosophical-speculative. Both these types of reading left their marks on the authors who will be discussed in the following presentation. They became known to Roman culture through Ennius' Latin translation of Euhemerus and through the philosophical currents that explained the myths allegorically, principally the Stoic and Neo-Platonic schools. We shall see how they marked one of the early representatives of Christian theory of culture and interpretation, Lactantius, and the pagan grammarian Servius, both passionate readers of Virgil. After a presentation of the most influential – in the long term – of these key figures in Late Antique poetics, Macrobius, we shall look at a few works that not only analyse but also exploit the fictional mode. Among them is, first, Martianus Capella's allegorical exposition of the liberal arts, framed as a mythical story: *The Marriage of Philology and Mercury*. Secondly, we shall inspect Martianus' North African compatriot, the mischievous Fulgentius, both when he comments on Virgil and when he ponders, critically as well as nostalgically, on the myths and Muses of the ancient Mediterranean civilization, forced to retreat from the newly Germanized Western world. Finally, we shall examine Boethius' famous dialogue *Consolation of Philosophy* as an ingenious test of the possibilities and limits of fictional discourse.

None of these last three authors' works bear any deep traces of the Christian religion that concomitantly was taking over the Roman Empire. All of them, with the exception of Fulgentius' commentary on Virgil, are so-called Menippean satires, a mixed form of verse and prose that originated in Hellenistic times but enjoyed a kind of breakthrough in Late Antique culture. In its polyphonic discourse, to cite Peter Dronke, low and high style, prayer and burlesque, scholarship and fiction tended to influence, relativize or even undermine each other.[1] Most notably, the updated adaptations of this genre in Martianus, Fulgentius and Boethius differed considerably from its earlier carnivalesque and ludicrous standard version, replete with grimaces over human pomposity. Now they rather served various intertextual, narratological or metafictional purposes: a symptom as good as any of the impact of grammar teaching and rhetorical exercises on Late Antique literature.

This genre-specific alteration is also indicative of the distance that separated the period's greatest philosophers in the Latin language, Augustine and Boethius, from a major predecessor such as Plotinus, who was not interested in grammar, rhetoric or logic, who eschewed all kinds of life-writing and who pre-

---

[1] Dronke 1994, p. 5.

ferred the ancient Platonic Academy's oral tradition. The Late Antique authors' remoteness from the Egyptian third-century thinker is, of course, due to context and genre: it is one thing to engage in philosophical teaching but quite another to comment on the Bible or indulge in Menippean satire. Nevertheless, this distance bears witness to a landslide in the cultural activities of the early Christian era. The predominantly oral Roman culture, with its focus on performance in situation-bound contexts, and with public recitations, controversies in the marketplace, civic eulogies or improvised declamations as regular events, was increasingly rivalled by a written and learned culture of Hellenistic origin. In all probability this development favoured the philological expertise and speculative allegories that we shall examine in the following presentation.

The way of dealing with classical literature in Late Antique erudite circles turned out to boost interest in substitutive at the expense of mimetic fictionality, a reorientation of critical attitudes which it will be my task to detect in Lactantius and his successors. They tended to look upon the pre-Christian poets who seemed worthy of their attention as so-called primeval theologians, *prisci theologi*, filled with esoteric wisdom and vague, albeit authentic religious intuitions, commonly dressed up in mythological imagery, the artistic equivalents of the sibylline oracular utterances that were in wide circulation from east to west throughout the Roman Empire. On the one hand, such a concept of ancient poetry sharpened the interpreters' sensitivity to discursive figuration. If, for example, they read the *Aeneid* as an encrypted message concerning the human lot, they would naturally feel the necessity to decipher its master code, as is demonstrated by Fulgentius' moral exposition of the poem. Their concentration would be focused on the literary work's veiled or 'oblique' speech, on tropes in general and allegorical discourse in particular. Accordingly, *figmenta* returned to the centre of hermeneutic attention, now primarily located in the works' figurative layer of signification: its imagery.

However, on the other hand, as David S. Wiesen has pointed out in a pertinent study, this willingness to understand fictional literature as covert messages – encrypted wisdom – entailed a blurring of the classic (Aristotelian) distinction between poetry, philosophy and religion.[1] If epic poems were read as encoded information about, for instance, the ages of man or the hierarchy of being, their mimetic mode ran the risk of being relegated to the periphery of critical concern. Intradiegetic devices such as internal context, character *(dramatis personae)* or irony would seem irrelevant and uninteresting. Canonical works appeared to be virtual strings of moral *exempla* or oracular utterances, independ-

---

[1] Wiesen 1971, p. 74.

ent of narrative structure or focalization, exclusively reliant on the time-honoured authority that was readily ascribed to their authors. In short, when philosophical allegoresis identified an esoteric or even divine message beneath the story's figurative layer, it threatened to neutralize its imaginative power, resolving its illusion of presence into plain conceptual meaning. This pattern actually goes far back in time; as early as in classical Greece, the allegorical interpretations of Homer had been implemented to refute the natural philosophers' ridiculing of the poet's supposedly absurd fantasies (above, p. 25). The Alexandrian Fathers had inherited this focus on allegorical imposition to the detriment of attention to narrative; it is quite evident in Origen who, in his first sermon on the Song of Songs, noted that the evangelists had abstained from presenting us with "tales ands stories", *fabulae et narrationes*, in favour of *mysteria* (1.4), a distinction that Augustine would adopt for his own purposes.[1] In other words, the mode of profane fiction was never to be trusted at its face value; it imparted, at best, some useful premonitions, conjectures or ideas to be extricated from its bewildering scenes and events.

In conclusion, the heritage of Hellenistic hermeneutic culture, especially of Platonic and Stoic provenance, was palpable during the whole of the dying antique era. Pagan or Christianized Neo-Platonism made itself more or less strongly felt in all the writers discussed in this chapter. They were pioneers in their definitions and exploitations of the allegoric mode of discourse, but for none of them did the question of mimetic fictionality have any decisive impact on their bold attempts to reorientate critical attention (as well as human ambition) *per corporalia ad incorporalia*.

---

[1] "Observa, inquam, et invenies in Evangelica lectione non fabulas et narrationes ab Evangelistis, sed mysteria esse conscripta". *PL* 23.1123b.

1 Lactantius: Christian Eloquence

The great inaugural figure of Christian allegorical interpretation is the rhetorician and imperial tutor Lactantius from the province of Africa (ca. 240–320). He was active a little less than a century before Augustine, in the dramatic decades of the early fourth century during the Emperor Diocletian's gory persecutions of the Christians (which probably contributed to his conversion), followed by Constantine the Great's spectacular Church-friendly rule. He made his career as a respected teacher of rhetoric and was summoned to the imperial residence in Nicomedia, just south of Constantinople, by Diocletian himself. To posterity, however, Lactantius is known for his *Divine Institutes*, an apology in seven volumes for the new faith he had converted to, and a polemic against the pagan religion he was born into and grew up with. This ambitious work was the optimal "intellectual monument of the reign of Constantine", in the words of E.K. Rand, and later, incidentally, one of the first books (if not the very first) to be printed in Italy.[1]

In addition, as Reinhart Herzog has remarked, the *Divine Institutes* is the most prominent known example of a Christian interpretation of classical pagan authors on a large scale, an integrative attempt of the kind that Augustine was to condemn in his *On Christian Doctrine* (3.7.11).[2] Lactantius, admired as a Christian Cicero by Jerome and later by Renaissance humanists such as Boccaccio – who quoted him profusely in his *Genealogia deorum gentilium* (*Genealogy of the Pagan Gods*) – and Pico della Mirandola, set himself to unite traditional culture with the new faith, *sapientia* with *religio*. The former included not only ancient philosophy but poetry and rhetoric as well. Significantly, both the ambitious format and the title of his main work link up with Quintilian.[3]

Pious infiltration

The first chapter of the *Divine Institutes*, addressed to Constantine himself, is a declaration of intent that was to win the ears of allegorically minded posterity. To a great extent, Lactantius takes as his point of departure Cicero's late eulogies to philosophy's *otium*, in which eloquence had to step back in favour of a profound search for truth, undisturbed by worldly concerns. In tracts such as *Dispu-*

---

[1] Rand 1929, p. 63.
[2] Herzog 2002, p. 160.
[3] Cf. Alfonso 1966, p. 9, and Heck 1988, pp. 164, 168f.

tationes Tusculanae (*Tusculan Disputations*) and *De officiis* (*On Duties*), the ageing Roman rhetorician had put his superb feeling for language at the service of wisdom and secluded meditation. But Lactantius' *sapientia* was naturally of a different kind than Cicero's and that of other pagan philosophers. When he maintains that "there is no sweeter food for the soul than the knowledge of truth" (1.1), *nullus enim suavior animo cibus est, quam cognitio veritatis*, he refers to Christian illumination (possibly by way of an indirect retort to Pilate).[1] As long as it is *that* truth that is to be expounded, that of the Gospel, Lactantius can to a remarkable extent rely on the procedures of pagan eloquence.

For example, he praises rhetoric's common staging of fictitious lawsuits, *exercitatio illa fictarum litium*, since, thanks to those exercises, "I can now use my plentiful command of rhetoric to plead the cause of truth to its end", *ut nunc maiore copia et facultate dicendi causam veritatis peroremus*. Admittedly, he continues, it is possible to defend the truth without eloquence; that has been proved by many, including the Biblical writers, but when a speaker addresses educated circles, his pleading will always be considerably more effective if it is adorned with the light of polished speech, *lux orationis* (1.PR.).[2] Here, Lactantius appears as a trailblazer of sorts. He was the first writer to take on the difficult task, after the earlier apocalyptists' and apologists' attacks on all pagan blether, of legitimizing a high style for the purpose of the new faith. He put classical rhetoric at the service of Christian instruction. The epic Bible poets would soon follow in his tracks. We shall even see that Lactantius could accept fictional stories as long as they concealed the Bible's *causa veritatis* under their poetic cloak.

So far we must content ourselves with one powerful example of how this Christian Tully proceeded in his eloquent efforts to substantiate his faith. He would readily resort to the *auctores*, he explains, in order to cite them as witnesses of the truth. By these authoritative sources he actually meant the writers who were commonly used against the Christians, namely the poets and the philosophers. With their help, Lactantius sets out to prove that there was only one God. For their own part, indeed, they had not professed this sacred truth, but their works speak for themselves: "Though the poets have devoted odes to the gods and have glorified the deeds of gods in paeans of praise, they are in frequent agreement that everything is held together and guided by a single spirit or mind." (1.5)[3] In this pioneering way, Lactantius treated the pagan poets' mythol-

---

[1] *PL* 6.118a.
[2] *PL* 6.114b–115a.
[3] "Poetae igitur, quamvis deos carminibus ornaverint, et eorum res gestas amplificaverint summis laudibus, saepissime tamen confitentur spiritu vel mente una contineri regique omnia." *PL* 6.129a–130a.

ogy and polytheism in terms of narrative or stylistic devices, belonging to the *inventio* or *elocutio* of their rhetoric, where expansion and adornment, *amplificatio* and *ornatus*, were considered traditional virtues. However, at a more profound and authentic level of their texts, there emerges, for those who read them closely, one single God.

First among these time-honoured poetic authorities in the *Divine Institutes* is Orpheus, most ancient of all poets, guided by nature as well as reason (1.5), *natura igitur et ratione ducente*, towards awareness of the one true Creator.[1] After exhibiting a certain scepticism about the evidence of Homer and Hesiod, Lactantius registers Virgil as foremost among the Roman poets "for closeness to the truth", *non longe afuit a veritate*, whereupon he quotes lines 6.724–27 from the *Aeneid*, already cited by Minucius Felix, where Anchises teaches his son about the great *spiritus* or mind, *mens*, which permeates the enormous body of the universe. Similarly, Ovid is praised for his words in the *Metamorphoses* about God as the Creator of the world (1.57), *mundi fabricator*, or the craftsman of all things (1.79), *opifex rerum*. Lactantius can only conclude that "if only Orpheus or our two Roman poets had persisted in standing by what nature led them to feel, they would have understood the truth and would have grasped the doctrine that we accept" (1.5).[2] Thus he outlines his philosophical-allegorical theory of poetry in a nutshell. A few ancient poets, under the guidance of Nature – almost a formula in this section, *natura ducente* – had actually come across or at least suspected certain insights, which nowadays Christ or the Christian faith reveal to all who want to see them.

The pagan philosophers' authority and judgment are appreciated even more than those of the poets, since "people trust them to have pursued the search for truth rather than fiction", *non rebus commentitiis, sed investigandae veritati studuisse creduntur*. A cloud of witnesses, from Thales through Plato, "considered the wisest of them all", *qui omnium sapientissimus iudicatur*, to Cicero and the Stoics, headed by Seneca, testify to this verdict (1.5).[3] Notwithstanding this gesture of deference to the philosophers, we are allegedly provided with even more reliable evidence by the Sybils and the holy oracles. Whereas the poets are commonly supposed to have occupied themselves with empty fictions, *vana fingentes*, and while the philosophers could be wrong because they are, after all, only human beings, the Sybils were in the position of adducing divine authority

---

[1] *PL* 6.131a.
[2] "Quod si vel Orpheus, vel hi nostri, quae natura ducente senserunt, in perpetuum defendissent, eamdem quam nos sequimur, doctrinam comprehensa veritate tenuissent." *PL* 6.131b–133a.
[3] *PL* 6.133a, 6.135a.

for their words (1.6). Such an observation would interest Augustine in the *City of God* a hundred years later (18.23).[1]

At long last, however, the devout rhetorician would only ascribe an instrumental value to pagan culture. "Philosophy, oratory and poetry are all pernicious", he maintains, "for the ease with which they ensnare incautious souls in beguiling prose and the nice modulations of poetical flow."[2] These words of warning are from the beginning of the fifth book of the *Divine Institutes*, on closer inspection a bitter reminder of the time of Diocletian's persecutions. According to Lactantius, then, the pagans should not be read on their own terms. Notwithstanding all their innate wisdom, readers are well advised to beware of their Siren calls. At the end of the day, their dulcet tones, all sweets or honey, frequently prove toxic: *mella sunt haec venenum tegentia* (5.1).[3]

To Lactantius, this tension between superb art and suspect contents in ancient literature recalled the example of Lucretius (ca. 99–55 BCE), as charming with his verses as he was poisonous with his proverbial atheism. The Christian rhetor was indubitably fascinated by this Epicurean poet-philosopher, the second most frequently quoted author in the *Divine Institutes* after Virgil.[4] Yet he had difficulties, of course, with Lucretius' atomistic materialism. Starting with the *Divine Institutes*, the didactic Roman poet would actually be a notorious stumbling block for pious writers right down to modern times. In his great hexameter poem *The Nature of Things*, he had turned Epicurus' deliberately ungodly philosophy into polished verse. His agenda for this cunningly artistic indoctrination is to be found in the work's first book, quoted in the epigraph to this chapter. There, the poet declares his intention to express his potentially "grim" philosophy "in sweet Pierian song", painting it "with the honey of the Muses, / hoping that thus I might fix your attention / upon my verse". Read in this context, Lactantius' caustic comment on the pagan "honey, hiding poison" can well be taken as an attack on Lucretius.

Or it might be taken as clever case of *chrēsis*, that is, Christian recycling of pagan culture. It was not difficult for the rhetor and his fellow believers to, as it were, turn Lucretius against himself, making use of the atomist poet's violent

---

[1] *PL* 6.140a. See the chapter on the sibylline and hermetic writings in Ogilvie 1978, pp. 28–36. For Lactantius' adherence to Plato and the Stoics, his polemics against the Epicureans, and his recurrent references to Hermes Trismegistus or the Sibyls, see Hagendahl 1983, pp. 38–48.
[2] "Nam et in hoc philosophi, et oratores, et poetae sunt, perniciosi quod incautos animos facile irretire possunt suavitate sermonis, et carminum dulci modulatione currentium."
[3] *PL* 6.549a.
[4] Messmer 1974, p. 118. For Lactantius' ambivalent relationship to Lucretius, see ibid., pp. 81–87, 118–21, in addition to Hagendahl 1958, pp. 48–76.

assaults on polytheistic mythology for their own ends. It only needed a small adjustment of the terms to convert his polemical enlightenment programme into a paradigm for a new kind of Christian poetry, particularly suitable for irresolute and wavering readers. Lactantius exploited this possibility in his *Divine Institutes:* "Simply rim the cup of wisdom with honey from heaven, so that bitter medicine can be drunk unawares with no hostile reaction: the initial sweetness beguiles, and the harshness of the bitter flavour is concealed beneath the covering of sugar." (5.1)[1] This trick, a reuse that presupposed a drastic decontextualization of the pagan poet, was innovative. Admittedly, Lactantius' programme adhered to well-known prescriptions within Roman eloquence that emphasized an orator's obligation to adorn his speech in order to avoid tediousness and bored audiences.[2] Various scholars have noted that Quintilian had already quoted Lucretius for a similar purpose – to endorse the practice of wrapping up dry instruction in pleasant words – in *The Orator's Education* (3.1.4). But it was Lactantius that Christianized this scheming method of teaching (or, depending on perspective, manipulation). One of the first to follow in his tracks was Jerome, in a letter from 415 (133.3).[3]

Lactantius based his ideas on his own experience as a teacher of rhetoric at the court of Diocletian at Nicomedia. He was painfully aware that both the learned and the powerful notabilities of this world, *sapientes, et docti, et principes huius saeculi*, dismissed by Paul in 1 Corinthians 2.6–8, used to a smooth and eloquent style, *expolitum ac disertum*, distrusted the Bible for the very reason that large parts of it were written in an unadorned and unrefined way, in the low style.[4] Thus, Lactantius grants us a fascinating insight into the reading habits of the traditional Roman aristocracy. The style of the text was no empty façade; it was perceived as an index of its truth claims. In these eminent circles, a low style was associated with popular delusions and trifles, whereas graciously adorned language held out expectations of a certain level of seriousness: "Anything rough on the ears they assume is untrue, and nothing is credible unless it provides aesthetic pleasure; they weigh by garb and not by truth." (5.1)[5] Lactan-

---

1 "Circumlinatur modo poculum coelesti melle sapientiae, ut possint ab imprudentibus amara remedia sine offensione potari; dum illiciens prima dulcedo acerbitatem saporis asperi, sub praetextu suavitatis occultat." *PL* 6.550a.
2 This strategy is probably derived from Greek literature. Alan Cameron, referring to Plato, identifies it as "a commonplace of didactic poetry", 2004, p. 333.
3 Cf. Hagendahl 1958, pp. 64, 274f.
4 *PL* 6.550a.
5 "Adeo nihil verum putant, nisi quod auditu suave est; nihil credibile, nisi quod potest incutere voluptatem: nemo rem veritate ponderat, sed ornatu." *PL* 6.550b.

tius himself, of course, regarded this state of affairs in exactly the opposite way: while the discursive humbleness of the Christians wanted to communicate a truth that is not of this world, the higher eloquence of Roman culture hankered after glory and circulated among the wealthy, serving young authors, lawyers and statesmen as a source of income and an aid for their careers, more or less ignoring the concerns of the poor and uneducated, including their religion – up until the Constantine present, as the rhetor pointedly avows.

For Lactantius made up his mind to do no less than convince the Roman cultural elite of the excellence, not to say preeminence of the Christian faith. For that purpose he had to break the established link between stylistic level and subject (*res*) in eloquent discourse. Lactantius looked upon himself as a superior successor to Tertullian – who in his eyes had been too defensive, aiming at apology rather than teaching – and to the orator and martyr Cyprian (d. 258), Bishop of Carthage, who had tried in vain to refute a certain Demetrianus, probably a high-ranking Roman official, by adducing testimony from the Bible. Cyprian's attempts at persuasion were doomed to failure from the start, he remarks, since Demetrianus simply considered the Bible as "silly fiction and lies", *vana, ficta, commentitia*. For his own part, Lactantius decided to rely on pious infiltration, acting, as it were, as a Fifth Columnist in the enemy's ranks. To that end, he set out to exploit "arguments based in logic", *argumenta et ratio*, rather than Biblical language, that is, a type of discourse that a pagan civil servant or rhetorician would recognize, understand and respect.

Accordingly, Lactantius appropriated and updated a didactic method we recognize from Hellenistic and classical Roman literary culture, not only developed by Lucretius but by Plutarch as well. When faced with opponents who are seriously hidebound, he argued, it might be wise to postpone the overt Christian lectures – which would be counterproductive in this context – so as to only let the audience sense the first faint glimmer of faith. After such preliminary hints, it should be possible to increase the intensity of illumination "little by little", *paulatim*. If, on the other hand, the audience were exposed to the overwhelming force of the Spirit from the start, the preacher's efforts might result in nothing but bewilderment. Lactantius makes a telling comparison with infants who cannot endure strong and solid food, but to begin with have to be nurtured on milk (5.4).[1] Along similar lines, we have seen how Plutarch aimed at gradually accustoming young boys to the mythical shadow-play of poetry before they were considered ready to turn their gaze towards the bright sun of philosophy (above, p. 45). Dante's Beatrice would not express the idea very differently a thousand

---

[1] *PL* 6.562b–563b.

years later, when she progressively adjusts her pilgrim's powers of vision and understanding to the initially blinding light of Paradise. The major part of the *Comedy's* last *cantica* can thus be read as Beatrice's gradual *far disposto* (Paradiso 30.54) of her sometimes childlike apprentice on his way towards the highest mysteries. The classical matrix for this heavenly pedagogy is clearly to be found in writers such as Lucretius, Plutarch or Lactantius.

So Cyprian made a mistake, the latter continues in the *Divine Institutes*, when he resorted to the Bible in order to rebuke the obdurate Demetrianus. Instead, what the bishop needed was "men's evidence" rather than God's, *humana testimonia*, provided by philosophers and historians, to convince the Roman official by referring to his own authorities. This is the mighty task that Lactantius takes on at the time of writing, hoping to have followers so that learned and eloquent people from now on will begin to engage their talents "on this battlefield of truth", *in hoc veritatis campo*. If that would be the case, he confidently rounds off these reflections on the stratagem of pious infiltration, all false beliefs and all philosophy would surely fade away as soon as everyone had realized that the Christian alternative actually amounts to the one and only religion and the only true wisdom (5.4).[1]

The optimistic Lactantius' hopes for successors were to be thoroughly granted. He had outlined a Christian strategy for instruction and persuasion which would soon be reinforced by the great Fathers of the Latin Church, Jerome and others. It is difficult to over-estimate the importance of this ingenious programme of conversion for Late Antique negotiations of fictionality. Even if Lactantius had been sceptical about the value of the information that poetry's *ficta* would offer its readers, he evidently realized their strategic potential. Tertullian had inherited and implemented the Old Testament attitude of exclusivity, where the laws of ethnical, cultic and ritual purity were of crucial importance. As soon as he detected ingredients of poetry or theatre in his cultural environment, he typically reacted with a grimace. In contrast, Lactantius saw an opportunity for covert, albeit legitimate, Christian indoctrination. This North African teacher in eloquence, always sensitive to his audience's interests and expectations, studied the old myths and poems as inquisitively and with the same purpose as the Apostle to the Gentiles had once examined the Athenians' altar to an unknown god (above, pp. 145f.). Such materials provided him with an ideal basis for persuasion and display of proof.

In short, the *Divine Institutes* articulated no more than a rudimentary, mainly instrumental or pragmatic theory of fiction; nevertheless, this work proved to be

---

1 *PL* 6.563b–564a.

a rescue operation that would form the basis of an increasingly significant policy of appropriation within Christian hermeneutics. It had as important consequences for the epoch's flourishing Biblical epic poetry as for its tendency to convert the leading pagan stories, fantasies and legends into enlightening paradigms and moral tales. This inclination in Lactantius to channel fictionality into exemplary narrative and figuration, inaugurating the Late Antique and medieval concepts of oblique or integumental speech, certainly deserves an examination of its own.

Veiled Figuration

When the classical poets sang of the gods' indecencies and fornication, Lactantius remarks, we should not take their verses at face value, since they actually had certain human individuals in mind, to whom they gave the rank of divinities. Here, as far as the pagan writers are concerned, he applied a euhemeristic technique for interpretation: their *ficta* deal mainly with human beings whom they had transformed into gods to produce certain effects.[1] Lactantius exemplifies their strategy with the well-known story of Jupiter covering the beautiful Danaë with a golden shower (so as to be able to seduce her), a mythical embellishment of an erotic courtship – or, to put it bluntly, of sex trade or even rape – at a regal level. The poets who had described the excited king as a god had used the golden rain as a suitable figure for his majesty. Correspondingly, they had spoken of an iron rain to describe the multitude of arrows and spears in the air during a battle (1.11).

Lactantius was just as categorical in his analysis of the story of the eagle-like Jupiter carrying off young Ganymede: it is a poetic figure, *poeticus color est!* In actual fact, the youth had been captured by a legion that had an eagle on its standard. Alternatively, the ship that carried him away had an eagle as its figurehead, not unlike the ship that abducted the girl Europa, its bow decorated with a bull.[2] The rhetor's own comment on his euhemeristic interpretations is actually a key passage in Late Antique poetics (1.11):[3]

> People with any sense of their own intelligence realise that a living and earthly body cannot exist in the sky, and so they dismiss the whole tale of Ganymede as false; but they fail to

---

[1] For Lactantius' and the early Christian authors' appropriation of Euhemerus, see Ogilvie 1978, pp. 55–57.
[2] *PL* 6.169b–170b.
[3] *PL* 6.171a–172a.

see that it all happened on earth, matter and lust being earthly things. The poets have thus not created events – if they did they would be impostors – but they have added a certain colour to events. They were not writing in denigration but in a desire to embellish. That is what deceives people, especially because all the while that they think of these things as poetical fictions they are worshipping what they do not recognise. They do not know the limits of poetical licence and how far one may go in a fiction, since a poet's business lies in transposing reality into something else with metaphor and allusion and in covering up the misrepresentation with charm [*cum officium poetae sit in eo, ut ea, quae gesta sunt vere, in alias species obliquis figurationibus cum decore aliquo conversa traducat*]. To misrepresent the whole of one's subject matter is merely inept, however; to do that argues a liar, not a poet. (I)

Even if the poets could hardly lay claim to the philosophers' or the Sibyls' prestige, they were not, at least not in principle, to be regarded as disreputable liars. They took an actual event as their starting point, to which they added "colour" (a term borrowed from the rhetorical doctrine of style). Specifically, according to Lactantius, the poets presented such events under the cloak of figurative discourse; since they adorned nothing but existing reality, they were in fact expected to depart from historical truth and actual circumstances. They converted true occurences into *aliae species*, 'other appearances', by means of *obliquae figurationes*, an indirect or literally 'oblique' kind of speech. Therein consists the notorious "poetical licence" in Lactantius' version. It relies, basically, on a rich and varied set of metaphorical transpositions of 'what really happened', *ea, quae gesta sunt vere*, to a discursive register, as it were, of second degree.

Such is Lactantius' way of marking off the poets' area of responsibility from both historiography's straightforward reporting and wayward imagination's erratic flights. If this allocation of discursive options might recall the main tenet of Aristotelian *Poetics*, it is important to remember that the Greek philosopher's screening instruments had been conditionality and probability, that is, philosophical (epistemological) criteria; Lactantius, for his part, referred to rhetorical figuration. Thus he sowed – or perhaps replanted – a seed that was to bear abundant fruit in medieval culture, at its richest in the *fictio* that Dante would entitle the *Comedy*.[1] It seems perfectly feasible to establish this relationship at a genetic level, since Lactantius' version of the "poet's business", as Ernst Robert Curtius points out, was to be recycled by Isidore of Seville in his great etymological dictionary from the early seventh century, certainly one of the crucial links between the cultures of Late Antiquity, the Carolingian era and the erudition of the High Middle Ages.[2]

---

1 For the term *fictio* in Dante, see *De vulgari eloquentia*, 2.4.2.
2 Curtius 1990, p. 454. Cf. the section on "Poets", *De poetis*, in Isidore's *Etymologies*, 8.7.10.

The formula *obliquae figurationes* was Lactantius' way of pinpointing the idea of figurative language being a cloak or a covering for profound truths in a literary text. This concept probably originates from Hellenistic allegoresis, but now, in the *Divine Institutes*, it became the prime instrument for the interpreter's attempts to capture the characteristics of poetic writing. Nothing is entirely feigned by the poets, Lactantius notes, *nihil igitur a poetis in totum fictum est*, and he continues cautiously: "There is some element perhaps of adaptation and concealment by metaphor so that the truth can be hidden in wraps" (1.11), *aliquid fortasse traductum, et obliqua figuratione obscuratum, quo veritas involuta tegeretur.*[1] A powerful example would be his analysis of the celebrations of the Golden Age executed by Ovid, Virgil and other classical poets, which we find in the fifth book of the *Divine Institutes*. Before the breakthrough of philosophy, Lactantius tells us, the poets had been revered as teachers of wisdom. These sages had been in the habit of calling the state of the world under Saturn's reign the Golden Age, a perfectly adequate label for a god-fearing period when justice was still respected among mankind: "This is not to be treated as poetical fiction but as truth", *quod quidem non pro poetica fictione, sed pro vero habendum est*. Virgil's glorified presentation of the Golden Age's primitive communism in the *Georgics* (1.126–27) must, consequently, be understood as "a poetical image", *more poetico figuratum*, a metaphorical exposition of a society that cared about generosity and relief of the poor (5.5).[2]

It is a fairly advanced poetic theory that appears from these interpretations and examples, but it certainly leaves no room for fiction as a mimetic category, dependent on impersonation and narrative stance. The term *traductum*, which was to form the basis for the concept of 'translation' in all Romance languages, is significant in this context: the poets "transpose" or 'carry over' existing materials into 'other', that is non-literal words and representations, hence they are engaged in a process of appropriation rather than fabrication. This view of poetic activity is illustrated by Lactantius with a plethora of terms for clothing, concealing or veiling. In stark contrast to Augustine's painstaking analysis of the dilemma connected with such infringements of the Christian demands for verity, Lactantius considered it downright legitimate to treat truth as a contraband of sorts, concealing it by means of a lie, since such tricks allow devout authors to secretly

---

[1] *PL* 6.172b. Cf. further on in 1.11: "The poets thus got it right, but obscured it with a sort of veil", *vera sunt ergo quae loquuntur poetae, sed obtentu aliquo specieque velata* (*PL* 6.175a), or in 2.10: "I said, however, that the poets did not usually tell total lies: they wrapped what they were saying in figures of speech, and so kept it obscure", *verum quia poetas dixeram non omnino mentiri solere, sed figuris involvere, et obscurare quae dicant* (*PL* 6.313b).
[2] *PL* 6.564a–565b.

inflict it on their audience without needing to overtly challenge the latter's traditional loyalties. Thus we are in the position to link his argument for 'oblique' or figurative language to his stratagem for righteous infiltration of the pagan elite: the (Christian) message should be edged into the readers or listeners in furtive ways so as not to repel them at first sight. By all accounts, it was the cultivated Romans' frowning when faced with scriptural *sermo humilis*, and, in addition, their ingrained familiarity with classical mythology, that dictated these tactics on behalf of figurative discourse in the *Divine Institutes*.

This impression is reinforced by the *Epitome divinarum institutionum* (*Epitome of the Divine Institutes*), that Lactantius probably completed shortly before his death in 320. After having discussed the Olympian gods along well-known euhemeristic lines, he anticipates the objection that their stories are all a matter of fiction invented by the poets, *ficta haec esse a poetis*, whereupon he immediately counters such hypothetical criticism: "This is not the usage of the poets, to feign in such a manner that you fabricate the whole, but so that you cover the actions themselves with a figure, and, as it were, with a variegated veil. Poetic licence has this limit, not that it may invent the whole, which is the part of one who is false and senseless, but that it may change something consistently with reason." (11.1)[1]

This (characteristically) figurative account of figurative language amounts to one of the most apposite and suggestive expositions of fictionality I have come across in Late Antique culture, starting with *quasi*, the 'as if' typical of the rhetorical simile as well as of fictional modes of speech: "and, as it were, with a variegated veil", *quasi velamine aliquo versicolore*. Even though Lactantius set a clear limit to the freedom of literature for the purpose of restricting the poets' narrative schemes to what Ernst Messmer calls a core of truth, he was anxious to safeguard their proverbial licence as long as it was implemented *cum ratione*.[2] In short, epic or didactic poets had the right to exchange some elements for others, that is, to enfold real circumstances in elaborate imagery, as long as they proceeded "consistently with reason".[3]

---

[1] "Non est hoc poeticum, sic fingere, ut totum mentiare, sed ea, quae gesta sunt, figura, et quasi velamine aliquo versicolore praetexas. Hunc habet poetica licentia modum, non ut totum fingat, quod est mendacis et inepti, sed ut aliquid cum ratione commutet." *PL* 6.1025c–1026a. All quotations from Lactantius' *Epitome* (the authenticity of which has been questioned) are from Migne's *Patrologia*, English translations by W. Fletcher from the *Ante-Nicene Fathers* series edited by A. Roberts *et alii*, 7, 1951.

[2] Messmer 1974, pp. 12, 15.

[3] As is clear from his *Epitome*, Lactantius commonly identified this judicious application of tropes with the use of panegyric devices in epic poetry: "You see, then, that the poets did not

In this way, Lactantius resorted to the traditional euhemeristic-historical and, to a lesser extent, the philosophical-allegorical approaches to pagan poetry, not to criticize but to expose its mythological scenarios as evidence of the Christian faith. That is why he was inclined to detect premonitions of the – one and only – truth in the works of the old *auctores*, in Orpheus, Virgil and Ovid, albeit in a distorted form, refracted through a multifaceted prism. In the second book of his *Divine Institutes*, to offer one last example, the author explains the historical background of the ancient poets' ingenious transposition, commonly embedded in a web of misrepresentations, of the divine message. He recounts the Biblical story of the Creation according to Genesis 2.7: "then the LORD God formed the man of dust from the ground and breathed into his nostrils the breath of life, and the man became a living creature", whereupon he notes certain similarities with the classical myth of Prometheus, who was also believed to have moulded man out of clay (according to the *Metamorphoses* 1.82–88). Thus, first Genesis and then Ovid, in that order. This, says Lactantius, ought to mean that the poets had handed on rather than invented the story of the Creation of man (2.11):[1]

> They are wrong not about the event but about its agent. They had had no contact with literature containing the truth; they had merely absorbed into their own poetry what had been handed down in the predictions of the prophets and kept in a god's shrine, despite its corrupt derivation from fantasies and vague prejudice; truth usually gets diluted like that, and corrupted in popular talk, with everybody adding their bit to the tradition.

In sum, the poets' stories are based either on hearsay or on more or less dubious fruits of reading. They should therefore be considered as second-hand evidence. This insight has decisive consequences for Lactantius' concept of a literary work. If the poets are to be considered latecomers in a predominantly oral context, dependent on myths and all sorts of superstitions, they must, of course, be read critically. Nevertheless, their mythological embroidery and strange flights of

---

invent all things, and that they prefigured some things, that, when they spoke the truth, they might add something like this of divinity to those whom they called gods; as they did also respecting their kingdoms" (12.1), *vides ergo, non omnia poetas confinxisse, et quaedam praefigurasse, ut cum vera dicerent, aliquid tale numinis adderent iis quos deos esse dicebant; sicut etiam de regnis*. See PL 6.1026b.

1 "Res eos non fefellit, sed nomen artificis. Nullas enim litteras veritatis attigerant: sed quae prophetarum vaticinio tradita, in sacrario Dei continebantur, ea de fabulis et obscura opinione collecta et depravata, ut veritas a vulgo solet variis sermonibus dissipata corrumpi, nullo non addente aliquid ad quod audierat, carminibus suis comprehenderunt". PL 6.312a–b (2.10 in Lactantius 2003).

imagination may contain some original and even sacred knowledge, "a core of truth", and it is up to their modern interpreters to extract it.

*

By virtue of his stratagem of rhetoric infiltration and his reliance on oblique speech or poetic figuration, Lactantius is one of the true pioneers in early Christian literary theory. His advanced programme for instructing (or indoctrinating) the pagans by appropriation of their cultural heritage did not, however, prevent him from criticizing their religious beliefs and practices as unforgivingly as Tertullian. Wherever there are imitations (portraits, statues) of the Godhead, *simulacra*, there is no religion, he observes at the end of the second book of the *Divine Institutes:* what is made of earth cannot conceal anything heavenly. The old Platonic dualism, directed against artistic (re)production, comes to the fore: "Anything copied must be false; nothing can ever be called true which fakes the truth by dye and imitation." (2.19)[1] This reference to dye (cosmetics), *fucus*, had ever since Cicero been prevalent in moralizing Roman writers' censure of exaggerated imagery and ostentatious speech. Such criticism is hardly typical of Lactantius, an eager supporter of figurative discourse in poetry, but here he uses it to reject skilful illusion, *mimēsis*, in religious, particularly ceremonial and ritual contexts.

This criticism of idolatry undoubtedly points forwards to Augustine. The Bishop of Hippo Regius would, however, despite his inclination for Virgil and despite his long-standing experience of tropes, condemn the widespread weakness for all kinds of make-believe as unworthy of God's elect. Lactantius, for his part, generously accepted the fictional mode of poetry as long as it was implemented in consistently 'oblique' ways, that is, by means of rhetorical devices such as paraphrase, metaphor and amplification. This is certainly due to the fact that, unlike his North African compatriot and successor, he generally restricted the target audience for his pious infiltration to the educated pagan elite.[2]

For this specific purpose he could hardly come up with any objections in principle to the poets' customary *fucus*. On the contrary, they are fully entitled "to increase the grace and charm of their poetry with a variety of images" (1.11), *ut figuris versicoloribus venustatem ac leporem carminibus suis addant*.[3] Lactantius made his own contribution to Roman literature with a hymn to the

---

[1] "Quidquid enim simulatur, id falsum sit necesse est; nec potest unquam veri nomen accipere, quod veritatem fuco et imitatione mentitur." *PL* 6.344b–345a (2.18 in Lactantius 2003).
[2] Alfonso calls attention to Lactantius' emphasis on the elegance of rhetoric with the aim of making the new religion acceptable for the highbrows of his day, 1966, p. 10.
[3] *PL* 6.175b.

Phoenix (the authorship of which has been contested), a literally multicoloured bird descended from classical tradition, an archetype, as it were, for the many spectacular metamorphoses in Greek and Roman mythology, recently, however, appropriated by proponents of the new religion as an allegory of the death and resurrection of Christ. It was, as could be expected, Ovid who was responsible for its main appearance in Roman literature (at the very end of the *Metamorphoses*, 15.392–407), and the pagan Emperors had already minted it on their coins, to be followed by both Constantine and Theodosius. In his *Carmen de ave Phoenice* (*Song of the Phoenix*), the rhetor presents the bird in a rather vague, hermetic-syncretic version, with unmistakably Christian overtones.[1]

Such recycling of pagan mythology seems to be in complete accordance with Lactantius' own programme for a new Christian literature. In his *Divine Institutes* he analysed the fictions of poetry in terms of transposition, figuration and colouring, all referring to artistic adaptations of real events, circumstances or life stories.[2] Against this background, the problem of lying for a rightful cause, which a hundred years later would beset Augustine, was not viewed as particularly troublesome. Ultimately, Lactantius argued as if the poets' sometimes surprising or even offensive displacements of linguistic signifiers had no impact on the signifieds whatsoever, that is, as if they were only applying an iridescent verbal film to incontrovertible historical facts. As a consequence, he did not hesitate to acknowledge the poets' configurations as perfectly legitimate: 'The lie the poets tell is one of names, not fact' (1.19), *mendacium enim poetarum non in facto est, sed in nomine*, as if lying *in nomine* would be a downright harmless activity.[3]

It is probably from this at least provisional lack of moral condemnation of poetry that Lactantius' work draws its strength. His *Divine Institutes* is indicative of the expectations among quite a few Christians in the early fourth century, on the threshold of the Edict of Milan and Emperor Constantine's conversion, when a new sense of confidence or triumph would temper the early apologists' implacable attacks on pagan culture. When, at the turn of the next century, Augustine was to close several of the doors that Lactantius had appeared to open, his vigilant posture is certainly bound up with the new ascetic currents in the struggling Empire, which made old Tertullian's cannonades seem to reverberate

---

[1] A number of texts giving evidence of the Greek and Latin speculation about the Phoenix, among them Lactantius' *carmen*, are registered and discussed in Hubaux and Leroy 1939. Marialuise Walla dwells on Lactantius in her corresponding survey 1969, pp. 119–96. See also Fontaine 1981, pp. 53–66, and Kirsch 1989a, pp. 72–79.
[2] Cf. Pépin 1976, pp. 440f.
[3] *PL* 6.215b–216a.

anew. But the scepticism we meet in the *Confessions* goes deeper than that, partly due to its author's profound acquaintance with the Bible (in stark contrast to Lactantius' relative neglect of it).

As I have tried to show, Augustine was distrustful of fictional devices precisely because he took them so seriously. With his eminent linguistic genius, he realized how difficult it was to control the dissemination of their meaning and, indeed, to check their "unlimited semiosis" in the multicultural Mediterranean world, a formidable challenge to the Biblical hermeneutics he was trying to establish. Despite his rhetorical training, he could not escape the unpleasant suspicion that the poets' manipulations with *nomina* compromised their *facta* as well. Lactantius escaped this dilemma thanks to his confident distinction between words and things. He thus succeeded in legitimizing poetic discourse for Christian purposes, but at a price. It ran the risk of being reduced to rhetoric's flowery *ornatus*, to a set of standardized tropes, to strategic amplification or mandatory gilding of the only truth that counts.

2 Servius: The Grammarian's Gaze

What Lactantius did for Christian eloquence, the implementation of a rudimentary theory of fiction, was introduced by Servius into the learned tradition of commentary about one hundred years later, albeit in this case dispersed in bits and pieces among a wealth of historical, circumstantial and grammatical information.

The highly learned Maurus Servius Honoratus, sometimes referred to as Servius Grammaticus, composed his impressive *Commentaries on Virgil's Poems*, about two thousand pages long, at approximately the same time as Augustine was writing his *Confessions*, around or shortly after the year 400. This is actually the only complete commentary on Virgil's collected works which has come down to us from ancient times, probably created in competition with a similar but long-lost masterpiece of erudition by the author's great predecessor within the *ars grammatica*, Donatus. If so, the latecomer in this field, that of Virgilian commentaries, evidently outshone his model. Servius' work is, "without question", Martin Irvine claims, "the most important and influential commentary on a classical work known in the Middle Ages".[1] For generations of medieval students it simply turned out to be, in the widespread format of the gloss and marginal notation, inseparable from Virgil's own text. That is, of course, why these *Commentaries* are of special interest, but it is not altogether easy to summarize their author's critical theory or praxis, since his work is rather heterogeneous, adopting a set of mixed approaches to Virgil's work. In addition, precisely due to its popularity, it presents so many philological difficulties in the form of variants and interpolations that some scholars prefer to speak of the *Commentaries* in terms of 'the Servius tradition' rather than as a permanent or established text.[2] Nevertheless, certain general interpretive attitudes or strategies may be traced through the extant materials, which here – for practical reasons – are limited to the author's treatment of the *Aeneid*.

The pagan Servius exhibits an inclination, widespread in the fourth and fifth centuries, to synthesize a range of antique philosophical currents into a mysti-

---

[1] Irvine 1994, p. 126. On the relation between Servius' and Donatus' commentaries on Virgil, see Stok 2012.

[2] I follow the edition of G. Thilo and H. Hagen 1881–1902 (reprinted in the Cambridge Library Collection 2011), still generally regarded as the standard edition of the full commentary, replete with Late Antique interpolations, some of which may be derived from Donatus. In addition there is the ambitious so-called Harvard edition, the first part of which was subjected to severe criticism after its publication in 1946 and which remains incomplete. All translations of Servius into English are mine.

cal-spiritualizing outlook. At the same time, his *Commentaries* mark a decisive step into the scholarly culture of Late Antiquity; he treated Virgil's works both as an encyclopaedia to consult and as a source of information on the characteristics of the Latin language. There are, then, two contrasting voices alternating through his work: that of a curious thinker, susceptible to the purported esoteric evidence in Virgil's poems, and that of a predominantly matter-of-fact-oriented polymath and philologist. Servius thus systematized reading habits that had won ground among the Roman intelligentsia ever since Virgil's death four centuries earlier, which on the one hand (in Seneca's manner) tended to understand the poet as an initiated sage, and on the other hand (like Quintilian) turned his work into an inexhaustible store of *exempla* at the disposal of teachers of grammar and rhetoric.[1]

Still, the latter approach certainly eclipses the former in Servius' *Commentaries*. Robert Kaster highlights the work's "quasi-bureaucratic treatment of Virgil", as foreign to modern taste as it is attentive to the *Aeneid*'s observance of the rules of grammar – so attentive, in fact, that its author tended to perceive Virgil's occasional departures from correct linguistic usage as bothersome, blatantly unconcerned about the four hundred years that separated the poet's Latin from his own.[2] Thus Kaster reinforces the image of Servius as a somewhat pedestrian glossator, safely relying on his grammatical authority and rather too generous with his linguistic remarks, stylistic observations and information on miscellaneous cultural, geographical or historical matters. Various commentators on the commentator have emphasized that, as a rule, he implemented his allegorical interpretations with discrimination. Domenico Comparetti, for instance, explains that Servius preferred to read Virgil's works literally, *simpliciter*, wherever allegory seemed superfluous to him, *non necessaria*.[3]

While Comparetti's and Kaster's accounts elucidate Servius' admittedly detached and sometimes even pedantic attitude to his subject, they do not do full justice to his methods of interpretation. Even though massive circumstantial evidence and linguistic observations dominate his *Commentaries*, he was unquestionably fascinated by the oracular tradition surrounding the *Aeneid*, to the delight of later Christian and more unconstrained exploiters of Virgil's profundity, from Fulgentius to Bernardus Silvestris. In conclusion, Servius seems to hold a middle course between the Scylla of arid matter-of-fact explanation and the Charybdis of hermetic speculation. He took a genuine interest in Virgil's ob-

---

[1] Abundant examples of this early reception of Virgil are to be found in the commented anthology compiled by J.M. Ziolkowski and M.C.J. Putnam 2008.
[2] Kaster 1980b, p. 223.
[3] Comparetti 1997, p. 59.

scure and visionary lines, where he suspected a cloaking of vatic wisdom, but what makes him unique (in the context of this survey) are his discreet interpretations of such passages, his determination to accept ambiguity while trying out a range of diverse explications of the poet's mantic moments, and – last but not least – his professional respect for the narrative fabric and internal consistency of Virgil's work.

In the following presentation, I will give a few examples of how Servius implements his allegorical readings of Virgil, whereupon I will try to highlight this grammarian's unusual susceptibility to the generic integrity of the *Aeneid* and hence of poetic fiction.

Allegorical Sense

Of the four types of allegoresis that Julian Ward Jones Jr. distinguishes in Servius' *Commentaries*, it seems convenient to blend the first into the second.[1] Hence we are left with three classes of allegorical interpretation in the grammarian's work:
- the euhemeristic or historical,
- the scientific or physical,
- the moral or philosophical.

Firstly, the euhemeristic-historical allegory is repeatedly brought to the fore in these *Commentaries*, for instance when Servius rationalizes Jupiter's encouraging prophecy on the foundation of Rome (1.257–96). He demonstrates the common claim that Romulus and Remus were breastfed by a wolf to be nothing but make-believe, *fabulosum figmentum*, fabricated for the purpose of cloaking the Roman race's repellent origin: its first ancestress, Rhea Silvia, would quite simply have taken a lover, supposedly Mars, the god of war. The outcome of their affair were the legendary twin brothers who were put out to drown, but mercifully rescued by a shepherd whose wife, an ex-prostitute, brought them up. However, despite such disreputable ingredients, this fable of the twins and the wolf is no 'inappropriate' invention taken out of the air, *nec incongrue fictum est*, Servius adds, since we actually call prostitutes she-wolves – animals which, by the way, are protected precisely by Mars (1.273). In short, the invention is acceptable, since decorum is respected. The game of make-believe cleans up Rome's barbaric past and, in addition, is in agreement with established language and cult usage.

---

1 Jones 1961, pp. 217f.

Servius thus demonstrates the *Aeneid*'s figurative transpositions of existing events and circumstances as forcefully as Lactantius. When the hero, in the first song of the poem, has arrived at the Libyan coast and tells Venus, disguised as a hunting woman, that his mother – none other than Venus herself – has shown him the way across the Mediterranean (1.382), the commentator notes that Virgil 'at this point, in passing, touches on history, which, by the law of poetic art, he cannot present openly', *hoc loco per transitum tangit historiam, quam per legem artis poeticae aperte non potest ponere*. In historical reality, that is, Aeneas had followed the morning star, *Veneris stella*, across the sea, but since the *Aeneid* is an epic poem and not a chronicle, it relies on circumlocution and personification (substituting the goddess Venus for the eponymous planet).

In this manner, Servius is careful to point out how Virgil normally used 'history' as his starting point, a reality-based material which the poet, however, continuously adapted according to the requirements of his epic work, in keeping with the demands of narration, fiction and figuration, ultimately with the 'law' of the poetic art or the genre, *lex artis poeticae*, in his case observed and demonstrated with supreme finesse. By virtue of the same law, Lucan (39–65 CE) did not 'deserve' to be included among the poets since his epic poem *De bello civili* – about the civil war between Caesar and Pompey – sticks to plain facts and hence should be classified as a historical rather than a poetic work: *Lucanus namque ideo in numero poetarum esse non meruit, quia videtur historiam composuisse, non poema*. According to Servius, poetry outshines historical writing, not only by virtue of its universality (as Aristotle had claimed) but because of its narrative elaboration and veiled, figurative style. His resulting expulsion of Lucan from the domain of poetry would later be passed on to medieval culture by Isidore (*Etymologies* 8.7.10).[1]

Secondly, a similar readiness to rationalize everything in Virgil's work that, *prima facie*, might seem nonsensical, immoral or simply erroneous, characterizes the grammarian's physical allegoresis, a heritage from the Stoic schools of philosophy. In these *Commentaries*, it frequently results in some edifying conclusion, fitting in with a moralizing approach to the text. Natural scientists or *physici*, Servius notes, habitually interpret the gods as elements or planets and are hence able to explain away the scandalous fact that, among the ancients, Juno is usually called both Jupiter's sister and his wife. She is *aer*, the lower layer of air close to the earth, while he is *aether*, situated far above the earth's atmosphere. Consequently, they must be regarded as being related, at the same time as she is subservient to him, so 'by tradition they are termed spouses', *mariti traditum*

---

[1] Von Moos 1976, p. 102.

nomen est (1.47). This must indeed be considered an effective method – a decoding of Virgil's mythology in a detached Stoic and rationalizing spirit, complemented by a typically pragmatic reference to 'tradition' – to neutralize the incestuous fantasies about the gods that Augustine was to deplore, deride and attack in the *City of God*.

Thirdly, and most importantly, Servius outlined a firm philosophical basis for Virgil's mythical universe. Unsurprisingly, this speculative hermeneutics is most patent in his comments on *Aeneid* VI. The story of Aeneas' *katabasis* or visit to the dead appeared to the grammarian as a virtual treasury of arcane wisdom: 'The whole of Virgil is full of knowledge and in that respect this book [*Aeneid* VI] takes pride of place, with most of the material derived from Homer. And while some things are told in a straightforward way, many things concern history, and much is based on the profound knowledge of the philosophers, the theologians, and the Egyptians' (6.Pr.).[1] It was from such an esoteric viewpoint that Servius interpreted Virgil's version of the kingdom of the dead, *inferi*, as a vision of life on earth, that is, an image of our existence 'at the bottom', *infima*, of the universe. Correspondingly, he supposed the river Styx's nine circles to epitomize the nine cosmic spheres.

In this most famous book of the *Aeneid*, then, Servius is liable to explain 'everything that has been invented about the Underworld' (6.127), *omnia quae de inferis finguntur*, by means of learned allegoresis. The punishments in Tartarus actually represent various temptations and vices, and the golden bough is understood as a replica of the letter Y, in turn a Pythagorean figure for man's choice of the right path in life. 'Beneath a mythical image', the commentator adds to this observation, 'Virgil teaches the right way of living, which gives the souls permission to return to the upper world' (6.136), *sub imagine fabularum docet rectissimam vitam, per quam animabus ad superos datur regressus*. Evidently, this comment recalls Anchises' lecture on the elect souls' ascent from subterranean Elysium to life beneath "heaven's / dome" (6.750), *supera convexa*; in Servius' reading of *Aeneid* VI, the significance of 'the upper world', *superi*, is thus relocated from Virgil's 'poetical' or 'fictional' mode, where it amounts to life on earth (as opposed to the realm of the dead), to the grammarian's 'philosophical' or 'rational' mode, where it amounts to heavenly bliss (as opposed to life on earth), a characteristic transfer of meaning which is made explicit in the comment on 6.719.[2]

---

[1] "Totus quidem Vergilius scientia plenus est, in qua hic liber possidet principatum, cuius ex Homero pars maior est. et dicuntur aliqua simpliciter, multa de historia, multa per altam scientiam philosophorum, theologorum, Aegyptiorum".
[2] Cf. Jones 1961, p. 221.

Along these lines, Virgil's kingdom of the dead is turned into an image of human life. Servius treats the *Aeneid*'s sixth book as an allegory of the learned and philosophical type that his contemporary or somewhat later colleague among Roman intellectuals, Macrobius, would call a *narratio fabulosa*. He provides it with a short, theoretical comment when, in the introductory part of the book, the Sibyl is possessed by the god (Apollo) and looks into Aeneas' future. She sees what awaits the hero: new wars, the Tiber filled with blood, a new Achilles born in Latium (6.86–90). Servius remarks that this second Achilles is in fact Turnus, and that the poet presently, or rather his Sibyl, speaks as 'in the pastoral poems', *in bucolicis*, where it is said that another Tiphys will arise and another Argo will carry heroes. This comparison refers to Virgil's Fourth Eclogue and its prophecy of imminent days of glory on earth, similarly rendered in a Pythian key, moreover with an explicit reference to the Cumæan Sibyl. There, in *Eclogues* IV, as we have seen (above p. 132), a new Golden Age is heralded in accordance with antique culture's cyclical conception of history. The Argo will sail again, as at the dawn of time, with Jason and his heroes, including the helmsman Tiphys, towards Colchis and the Golden Fleece. With this reminder of the *Eclogues* (4.34–35), Servius emphasizes the Sibyl's clairvoyance; as a matter of fact, such veiled prophetic announcements could well be registered as a fifth category in Jones's list of Servius' types of allegory.

The transfer of meaning thus exemplified in these *Commentaries* had, ever since the days of Lactantius, made the *Eclogues* and the *Aeneid* freely accessible to the inventiveness of Christian readers, including a few innovative poets (Juvencus and Proba). But the pagan grammarian obviously refrains from all syncretic appropriations of Virgil's work. In his *Commentaries*, the Fourth Eclogue serves merely as an elucidatory complement to *Aeneid* VI, where the Sybil keeps to the internal context of Virgil's epic poem. She does not prophesy the Incarnation or the Millennium at the end of time but Aeneas' future main opponent on the battlefields in Latium, Turnus. Now, Servius adds, this Pythian way of speaking – allusive, cloaked, indirect, figurative (in this case by way of metonymy: another Achilles = Turnus) – is in fact a discursive mode which the *prophetae* have in common with the *poetae*. He is as convinced as Lactantius about the Sibyl's ability to act as a model for the poets. He actually adopted, directly or indirectly, the Christian rhetor's notion of 'veiled figuration', which in turn goes back to classical allegoresis and sacred mysteries.

Servius himself traces the origin of this figurative method to the Delphic oracles. Specifically, commenting upon the Cumæan Sibyl's covert prophecy about Turnus, he remarks that 'she rolls up the truth in obscure turns of phrase', and continues immediately, by way of explanation: 'for even if she tells us the truth, it remains concealed. That is why Apollo is called Loxias, which means oblique'

(6.89), *obscuris vera involvens, nam licet vera sint, latent: unde Apollo loxias dicitur, id est obliquus*. On closer inspection, this comment includes an implicit quotation from Virgil: the clause 'she rolls up the truth in obscure turns of phrase' occurs eleven lines further down in the *Aeneid*, where the poet characterizes the Sibyl's enigmatic introduction to the underworld in precisely those words (6.100): *obscuris vera involvens*. Hence, Servius seems to suggest that Virgil had inherited or appropriated such obscure language – vital to crucial passages of both the *Eclogues* and the *Aeneid* (and probably of the *Georgics* as well) – from the Pythian tradition, which in turn goes far back in ancient Greek culture. This assumption is confirmed by his complementary piece of information: for the same reason as the Sibyl wraps the truth in obscure riddles, the god who possesses her, Apollo, is called *loxias*, derived from the Greek *loxos*, meaning 'sloping', 'oblique'.

This is a by-name rich in implications. Ever since archaic or early classical Greek tradition, Apollo had appeared in a double, not to say paradoxical configuration: the illuminating or enlightening *Phoibos* and the 'oblique' (obscure, ambiguous or veiled) *Loxias*. The latter name was used especially for the deity who delivered his oracular answers from Delphi. This might be Servius' most emphatic linking of covert language to Delphic or sibylline lore. For all his linguistic, cultural-historical and geographical observations, he thereby powerfully rehabilitates the literary Roman Golden Age's idea (particularly salient in Horace) of an affiliation between the poet and the seer or *vates*. The discreet grammarian ascribes a Pythian authority to poetical discourse, characterized by its 'oblique' representation. This association, barely hinted at by Lactantius, was to achieve triumphs in Macrobius' and Proclus' Neo-Platonically coloured poetics and, mostly thanks to the former's agency, gain ground in later Western tradition. It is at least implicit in the influential Isidore of Seville who, in the eighth book of his *Etymologies*, registered the poets and their concealed speech just before the section on the Sybils (8.7).

In conclusion, there is no doubt that Servius took the trouble to demonstrate and, when necessary, reinforce poetry's links to the truth criterion of history, science or philosophy. It was primarily this aspect of his *Commentaries* that would win posterity's approval: a didactic approach that was to have an unmistakable impact on medieval culture, particularly when the author (on rare occasions) applied it to the *Aeneid* on a grand scale: 'We should note that he [Virgil], in the manner of feigned legal cases, provided these first six books with epilogues since he also intended them to bear upon life in general. To each of them he gave a special subject: to the first, omens; to the second, pathos; to the third, errors; to the fourth, ethos; to the fifth, festivities; and to the sixth, knowledge.'

(3.718)¹ With such comments, drawing support from rhetoric's *genus iudiciale*, translating the epic poem's intricate narrative into a set of clear-cut subjects, Servius not only prepared the ground for Fulgentius' mythographic and conceptual decoding of Virgil, dealt with below, but also heralded the medieval technique of allegoresis that was to culminate with the consistent implementation of the notion of *integumentum* in Bernardus Silvestris' commentary on *Aeneid* I–VI.

Poetic Licence

Thus the Virgil who emerges from these *Commentaries* is a complex figure: on the one hand, a man of learning operating in the allegorical or philosophical mode, sometimes even slipping over into sibylline speech, on the other hand, a poet, constrained by his art, operating in the fictional mode; in short, as we have seen, merging *philosophia* with *figmenta poetica*. Even if Servius does not, and perhaps cannot, draw any sharp dividing line between these aspects of the author of the *Aeneid*, they reflect radically different conceptions of him. The polymath communicates profound wisdom, while the poet is free to merge myths, fantasies and creatures of varying veracity into his work, exploiting to the full his *licentia poetica*. Obviously, Servius wants to have it both ways, and a modern reader might easily get the impression that he runs into a contradiction in terms, construing Virgil as an initiated philosophical sage and an inventive fiction maker at one and the same time. Still, such a composite view of the *Aeneid* might just as well be turned into the grammarian's advantage; it certainly runs counter to our common inclination to encapsulate a literary work in an overall genre, mode or style. For Servius, Virgil's epic poem was indeed a fictional piece of writing, in the sense of 'fictional' we have just outlined, but it was a historical and a philosophical work as well.

Let us look at an example of how Servius registers evidence of Virgil's poetic licence even where the *Aeneid*'s allegories reach their peak of dense speculation, that is, in Book VI. In its famous *invocatio*, Virgil had asked the powers of the underworld for strength (and permission) to depict their realm, to which his hero is about to descend in the footsteps of the Sibyl (6.264–67):

---

1 "Notandum sane quia controversiarum more epilogos dedit sex istis prioribus libris, quos et esse bioticos voluit. nam singulis res singulas dedit, ut primo omina, secundo pathos, tertio errores, quarto ethos, quinto festivitatem, sexto scientiam."

264 Di, quibus imperium est animarum, umbraeque silentes
265 et Chaos et Phlegethon, loca nocte tacentia late,
   sit mihi fas audita loqui; sit numine vestro
   pandere res alta terra et caligine mersas.

Gods, under whose command are the breeze-like souls, and you silent
ghost-shadows, Chaos and Phlegethon, speechless spaces, extending
deep into night, say it's right to give voice to the things I have heard of,
grant your assent to disclose what's submerged in the earth's pit of darkness.

The commentator assures us that this is 'a passage full of profound knowledge', *plenus locus alta sapientia*, although philosophers have disagreed about the fate of souls after death. He goes on to specify some of their ideas of the underworld, explaining, for instance, the presence of Chaos and the infernal river Phlegethon in line 6.265 by referring to the natural philosophers' theory of the chaotic origin of being, in particular Heraclitus' notion of fire as the primordial element (Phlegethon = 'fire-flaming'). Here, Servius obviously credited Virgil with an esoteric understanding of the primeval mysteries of Creation. Nevertheless, the poet had wisely preferred to give 'a general idea' rather than line up erudite accounts of the (infernal) realm of the gods, *prudentissime tenuit generalitatem*, and his prayer to the powers of the underworld for the right to reveal his arcane knowledge is explained with the laconic comment that 'when he is now about to disclose his profound wisdom, he blends in poetic licence' (6.266), *de alta dicturus prudentia miscet poeticam licentiam*.

Thus Servius' sensitivity to the poetic (or fictional) mode persists throughout his *Commentaries*, even when he focuses on the most speculative and abstruse of the *Aeneid*'s books. Virgilian passages that seem particularly hard to interpret are not only presumed to refer to insights of a historical, natural, moral or philosophical kind but are understood 'in accordance with the poetic manner' (2.255), *more poetico*. On several occasions, the commentator generously, or perhaps resignedly, leaves the epic poem's meaning indeterminate and open to a range of possible interpretations, as in his recommendation regarding *Aeneid* 1.743 (which concerns the origin of men and beasts). If you consider the *fabula*, Servius tells his readers, the human race might be descended from Prometheus, or from Deucalion and Pyrrha (that is, according to the first book of Ovid's *Metamorphoses*), but if you ask for *veritas*, you had better consult the philosophers (such as, supposedly, Thales of Miletus, Heraclitus, Democritus or Epicurus), according to whom we originate from water, fire, atoms or the four elements conjointly.

This alternation between the *Aeneid*'s poetic and philosophical modes as a basis for explanation of the work is particularly conspicuous in Servius' comments on another famous passage from the sixth book, lines 127–29, where the Sibyl shows Aeneas the way down into the underworld: "All nights, all days too, dark Dis's portals lie open. / But to recall those steps, to escape to the fresh air above you, / there lies the challenge, the labour!", *noctes atque dies patet atri ianua Ditis; / sed revocare gradum superasque evadere ad auras, / hoc opus, hic labor est*. The commentator remarks: 'This is said either in a poetic fashion or in accordance with the profound knowledge of the philosophers', *aut poetice dictum est aut secundum philosophorum altam scientiam*. Once again, this either/or sentence, *aut... aut*, leaves the field of interpretation remarkably open. Virgil might be following either of two ways:

- he has invented or feigned the gate of Dis – like the underworld scenario in its entirety – according to his own genius and the licence of the poets, admittedly on the basis of tradition and popular belief but mainly with an eye on the context and the rhetorical effects of these lines,
- or he is reproducing philosophical insight into the righteous souls' return to their heavenly origin after death.

In sum, Servius implicitly allocates the figurative passages of the *Aeneid* to different positions along a referential scale ranging from pronounced fiction to allegorical paraphrasing. This means that in practice he repeatedly leaves the question of the Virgilian poetry's truth-value unanswered. The sceptical commentator's distance to the ancient legends surrounding the gods is evident, but he consistently avoids accusing Virgil of espousing frivolous lies or primitive superstitions. On the contrary, he adopts the professional grammarian's approach to the text, being fully aware that the poetic mode, *mos poeticus*, or *ars poetica* (specifically the Homeric nonlinear narrative, cf. *Commentaries* 1.Pr.), with its demand for invention, arrangement and effect, requires certain manipulations of the subject matter. To be sure, we look in vain for any specific notion of fictional autonomy in Servius (or in any of the writers examined in this survey), but he does signal a susceptibility to the text's shifting levels of cognitive claims that is certainly striking in the cultural climate of Late Antiquity.

If the poet, then, is entitled to exploit a plethora of mythical fantasies and fictional configurations, whereas the philosopher communicates profound truths under the cloak of allegory, a good deal of the commentator's task would be to find out who is in charge in any given passage of the literary work. It may be the poet, the philosopher or on some occasions both, as in Servius' comment on the meaning of 'heaven', *caelum*, in *Aeneid* 6.719: 'He mixes poetic figments with philosophy and presents popular opinions as well as the signification of truth and natural reason', *miscet philosophiae figmenta poetica et ostendit tam quod est vulgare, quam quod continet veritas et ratio naturalis*. The fact that it was not easy to distinguish the ingredients of this subtle synthesis, to know whether Virgil used *figmenta poetica* or practised philosophical teaching, is even more evident from his comment on *Aeneid* 6.893–96, surely one of the most complex versions of the problem of poetry and truth left to us by Late Antiquity.

This passage of Virgil's epic poem, based on *The Odyssey* 19.559–69, describes Aeneas' return from the underworld. "Sleep opens twin double portals", it states. "The first, made of horns, grants an easy / exit, it's said, for real ghosts. On the second, one sees a rich lustre, / crafted with dentils of elephant tusk in fantastic perfection. / Dead souls, though, send deceptive dreams up above to the heavens."[1] It is through this last portal, the ivory gate, that Aeneas and the Sibyl return to Cumæ. Servius provides these suggestive lines, frequently annotated and discussed in the commentaries on the *Aeneid*, with an extensive explanation:

> He says that the true shadows slip out through the *gate of horn*, and by these *shadows* he means true dreams. The poetic sense is obvious: he wants us to understand that everything he has said is false. From a physiological standpoint, indeed, the gate of horn signifies our eyes which, moreover, bear the colour of horn and are more robust than our other bodily organs, since they are not affected by the cold, as Cicero observed in his treatise on the nature of the gods. On the other hand, the gate of ivory, referring to our teeth, represents our mouth. Now, as everybody knows, all things we say can be false, whereas the things we see are undoubtedly true. That is why Aeneas is sent out through the ivory gate.
>
> The passage has yet another meaning: we know that Sleep is depicted with a horn, and learned men tell us that dreams which seem to agree with a person's circumstances and prospects come true. This kind of dream is adjacent to horn. That is why the gate of horn is feigned as true. But dreams that rise above circumstances and are overloaded with ornaments and empty boasting are said to be false. That is why the ivory gate, being profusely decorated, is feigned as *false*. (II)

To all intents and purposes, Servius reads the Virgilian scenario with the two gates as the poet's own comment on his multi-layered scheme of signification. He seems to distinguish two senses of the passage, which subtly blend into each other:

– The first sense, the 'poetic', is reinforced by a 'physiological' explanation of the two gates. This is based on an established assumption, widespread in the Greek *scholia* to *The Odyssey*, associating the gate of horn, *cornu*, to the transparent cornea of the eye, that is, clear vision (supposedly reliable),

---

[1] "Sunt geminae Somni portae; quarum altera fertur / cornea, qua veris facilis datur exitus umbris, / altera candenti perfecta nitens elephanto, / sed falsa ad caelum mittunt insomnia Manes".

while the ivory gate, by virtue of an analogy with tooth enamel, is taken to represent our mouth, that is, our organ of speech (notoriously unreliable).¹ Consequently, the fact that Aeneas leaves the underworld through the latter exit would indicate that his passage through the realm of the dead was nothing but invention, characterized by the trickery of the mouth rather than the truth of the eyes! Such is the 'poetic' sense of this passage: Virgil 'wants us to understand that everything he has said is false', *vult autem intellegi falsa esse omnia quae dixit*. The entire argument is certainly presented in a sophisticated manner – the poet's words are turned against the veracity of his own story – but it is also characteristic of Servius' relaxed attitude to this *locus classicus* of Roman literature, *Aeneid* VI.

- Secondly, Servius suggests an alternative reading, *alter sensus*, based on esoteric symbolism and Late Antique dream interpretation, which as a rule, by means of a sometimes detailed taxonomy, distinguished prophetic from deceptive dreams.² His remark that Sleep is depicted with a horn probably alludes to contemporary iconography surrounding the god of sleep, Hypnos, frequently portrayed with a drinking horn, *cornu*, from which sleep-inducing liquid dripped onto tired human beings. Against this background, the grammarian links the gate of horn to genuinely prophetic dreams, accurately reflecting the dreaming person's *fortuna* and *possibilitas*; they obviously represent plausible (or, even better, forthcoming) versions of reality, hence the poet's trick to 'feign the gate of horn as true', *cornea vera fingitur porta*. Vain dreams of wealth and grandeur, on the other hand, are associated with the ivory gate. This second explanation of the two gates is of a speculative (philosophical) and didactic nature: the poet attempts to teach us something about the nature of dreams.

Like no other author in the present material, the grammarian's stance in cognitive matters is characterized by this open-minded approach: the frequent possibility of 'yet another meaning'. Such hermeneutic openness or indecision is typical of Servius' position in a cultural-historical perspective, half-way between time-honoured but remote Antiquity and the new Christian world. He was sel-

---

1 For the *scholia* to *The Odyssey* 19.559–69, cf. Haller 2009.
2 In his commentary on Cicero's account for Scipio's dream in *On the Republic*, subject to analysis in the next section of this volume, Macrobius lists five categories of dreams, each one provided with a Greek and a Latin designation: the enigmatic *oneiros/somnium*, the prophetic *horama/visio*, the pythic *chrēmatismos/oraculum*, the nightmare or *enypnion/insomnium*, and finally the hallucinatory *phantasma/visum*. This classification was to have a great significance for medieval oneiric speculation. See Macrobius 1994, 1.3.1–3.

dom able to muster any real faith in the mythological tales Virgil had made use of in his works; nonetheless, he kept uncompromisingly within the boundaries of classical culture, registering dreamlike marvels as well as common figures of style and thought with the same curious but detached care. To the Christian propagandist Augustine, his contemporary colleague in the field of rhetoric, fictional discourse represented both a dangerous temptation and a challenging provocation. To the pagan grammarian Servius, such discourse was simply integral to the poetic work, a cognitively instable type of text, reliant on narratological and rhetorical considerations.

According to these *Commentaries*, then, Virgil made consistent use of his poetic licence, whether to invent freely (exploiting the possibilities of *fabulae*) or to present his readers with convincing stories, likely scenarios and thought-provoking examples. Consequently, Aristotle's formula for probable representation, "the *kinds* of things that might occur", *hoia an genoito*, was still conducive – as the Italian Latinist Caterina Lazzarini has pointed out – to Servius' work.[1] This is apparent from the grammarian's remark on *Aeneid* 1.235, where Venus reminds Jupiter that he had promised a brilliant future for the Romans, descendants from Troy, that is, "from restored blood of Teucer", *revocato a sanguine Teucri*. Here, Servius notes, Virgil has replaced the real ancestor of the Trojans, Dardanus, with the Cretan Teucer, 'since poets are in the habit of employing names from neighbouring provinces or persons', *quia solent poetae nomina de vicinis provinciis vel personis usurpare*.

This might seem a trifling point, but the issue of the origin of Troy was certainly important to Servius, since it had bearing on Rome's ancestry as well. Dardanus, born in Italy (according to legend), was for obvious reasons a popular candidate for all Romans trying to identify a progenitor for the Trojan, and hence their own, race. Since Servius takes this opinion for granted, he naturally registers Virgil's reference to Teucer as a trope (to all appearances the kind of metonymy which enforces an exchange of names). Such a figure, he explains, seems reasonable in this context, since Crete is not far from Troy. His observation leads to the following pivotal reflection (quoted by Lazzarini), in the translation of which I give the relevant terms in their original Latin:[2]

> And one should understand that *fabula* and *argumentum*, that is, *historia*, differ from each other, since *fabula* is a story that deviates from nature, whether or not it takes place, as in

---

[1] Lazzarini 1984, pp. 117–24.
[2] "Et sciendum est, inter fabulam et argumentum, hoc est historiam, hoc interesse, quod fabula est dicta res contra naturam, sive facta sive non facta, ut de Pasiphae, historia est quicquid secundum naturam dicitur, sive factum sive non factum, ut de Phaedra."

the case of Pasiphaë, whereas history is something told in accordance with nature, whether or not it takes place, as in the case of Phaedra.

In this remark, Servius explicitly bases his argument on the narratological triad that we recognize from classical rhetorical taxonomy (cf. above, p. 40), seminal to Late Antique and medieval literary theory: *historia* (true accounts), *fabula* or myth (false inventions, running contrary to nature) and *argumentum* (plausible fiction). Nevertheless, he accommodates and reorders these traditional Ciceronian terms in a highly interesting manner. In the first place, he seems to subsume *argumentum* under *historia*, which now, accordingly, has to cover both what might happen and what has truly happened, so that the triple system is simplified into a neat contrast between unnatural mythology and valid history. Secondly, as Lazzarini observes, the grammarian operates solely on the level of discursive or literary evidence in order to drive home his distinction. Thus it is only the credibility of a narrative event, its naturalness, that vouchsafes its historicity; whether or not it ever took place is of less importance.[1] That is why a bizarre myth, *fabula*, in theory, can represent real events, *facta* (strange things might happen), whereas a credible chronicle, *historia*, conversely, does not necessarily present us with accurate facts.

Servius' intriguing conflation of *historia* with *argumentum* seems to be completely in agreement with his remarks, quoted above, on *Aeneid* 6.893–96. It seems clear that the vain dreams passing through the ivory gate would translate into *fabulae*: pure inventions. As for the dreams slipping through the gate of horn, they might be understood either as downright true, perhaps – in view of the commentator's reference to our eyes, *oculi* – comparable to eye-witness evidence, pertaining to the sphere of *historia*, or as probable versions of reality, attributed to Sleep with his horn, that is, shadowy premonitions or drafts of truth, pertaining to the sphere of *argumenta*. Basically, just as in his comment on *Aeneid* 1.235, Servius leaves us with two fictional options, *fabulae*, dispatched from the ivory gate, or *historia/argumenta*, escaping through the gate of horn.

What consequences does this updating of the Ciceronian narratological triad entail for Servius' interpretive practice? The answer can be made brief: a remarkable sensitivity to the manifestations of Virgil's *licentia poetica*. By way of conclusion, let us test his simple scheme on the *Aeneid* as a whole by recalling some of the observations I have picked out from his *Commentaries*. The poem's *historia* is, as could be expected, altogether acceptable, whether it refers to real events, like the Trojan war (considered authentic throughout Antiquity),

---

[1] Lazzarini 1984, pp. 123, 134. Cf. Vogt-Spira 2011, p. 32.

or to possible though contrived circumstances (in accordance with nature), as when Cretan Teucer, by virtue of metonymy, is appointed the ancestor of the nearby Trojans. Even the fantastic or unnatural *fabula* seems adequate as long as it reflects real matters, in however roundabout ways; Servius actually exerted himself to legitimize even ostensibly weird episodes or settings in Virgil's works by implementing a truth criterion as broad as possible. Thus, for instance, both etymologies and literary evidence would serve as a valid basis for the poet's inventions. At all these levels of fictional discourse, Virgil's poetic licence or 'mode', *mos poeticus*, is at work.[1]

This way of reading the *Aeneid* presupposes a strikingly generous hermeneutics, open to a plethora of approaches to the text, keenly aware of what we today would label polysemy in a literary work, with a remarkable understanding of poetry's demand for a certain distance from reality. Servius' comment on *Aeneid* 3.46 is indicative of his interpretive broad-mindedness: it concerns one of the enthralling as well as uncanny passages of the poem, in which Aeneas tells Dido and her retinue of his arrival in Thrace. He had climbed a mound to get some sprigs of myrtle for his sacrificial altar, but the twigs immediately began to ooze blood because King Priam's son, Polydorus, murdered by the King of Thrace, lay buried there. The dead prince's voice reaches the terrified Aeneas from inside the mound: "spiked into me was a seeding of iron / weapons which sprouted and yielded a harvest of sharp-pointed spear-shafts" (3.45–46), *hic confixum ferrea texit / telorum seges et iaculis increvit acutis*.

It is hardly likely, Servius remarks drily, that it was this shower of spears that ended the boy's life, since he was assassinated, not killed on the battlefield. Moreover, the claim that the spears should have produced green shoots is downright weird, not to say monstrous: *mirum est, nisi monstruosum sit*. Still, the episode seems appropriate since Virgil took it from Roman history, *traxit autem hoc de historia Romana*. Romulus had once thrown a spear from the Aventine to the Palatine, where it stuck in the ground, began to blossom and turned into a tree. To all appearances, then, legendary or literary precedents were enough to satisfy Servius' requirements of valid fiction:[2]

> It is reprehensible, indeed, for the poet to feign something which entirely deviates from truth. Virgil is after all blamed for having turned ships into nymphs, and for his story of

---

[1] Cf. Demats 1973, pp. 28f.

[2] "Vituperabile enim est, poetam aliquid fingere, quod penitus a veritate discedat. denique obicitur Vergilio de mutatione navium in nymphas; et quod dicit per aureum ramum ad inferos esse descensum; tertium, cur Iris Didoni comam secuerit. sed hoc purgatur Euripidis exemplo, qui de Alcesti hoc dixit, cum subiret fatum mariti."

the descent into the underworld by virtue of a golden bough, and thirdly, for letting Iris cut off the hair of Dido. But this last occurrence is excused by the example of Euripides, who says the same of Alcestis when she met the fate of her husband.

In this paragraph, Servius refers to three well-known episodes from the *Aeneid* (10.230–31, 6.136–636 and 4.693–705), all of them exposed to earlier interpreters' disapproving remarks about lack of credibility. Evidently, Servius would, in theory, be prepared to agree with their criticism. It is reprehensible, he says, to make up something that completely, *penitus*, deviates from truth. This standpoint is probably the result of influences from both traditional Roman poetics and rhetoric, as exemplified by Horace and Quintilian respectively, and from the pedagogical care for young boys' upbringing that we have seen exemplified in Plutarch and Lactantius.[1] In addition, Servius should have found it difficult to ignore the massive contemporary Christian criticism of the fabulous flights of fancy in pagan epic poetry.[2] Nevertheless, Virgil's linking of the Dido episode's sad ending to a Greek model (Euripides' tragedy *Alcestis*) vouched for a legitimate piece of fiction based on classical learning.

In like manner, when necessary, Servius could resort to etymology in order to elucidate apparent idiosyncrasies in Virgil's work. This is clear from his comment on *Aeneid* 1.159–60, which depicts Aeneas' arrival at the sheltered harbour outside Carthage: "Deep in an inlet there's somewhere to beach, where the flanks of an island / jutting across force breakers to crash and to channel their fury / into its various coves", *est in secessu longo locus: insula portum / efficit obiectu laterum, quibus omnis ab alto / frangitur inque sinus scindit sese unda reductos*. This is a case of *topothesia*, the commentator remarks, a description of an imagined place, 'that is, a place invented in compliance with the poet's licence. So as not to appear to diverge entirely from truth, Virgil described the harbour of Carthage in Spain. Incidentally, it is clear that this place exists nowhere in Africa, but he placed it there for good reasons by virtue of its similar name.'[3]

Cartagena on the south-east coast of Spain, known to the Romans as *Carthago nova*, was indeed famous for its natural harbour. Hence, Servius seems to

---

[1] Robert A. Kaster remarks that, basically, Servius framed his *Commentaries* as the instrument of a teacher; the work remains at a level suitable for schoolboys, making its way word by word and line by line through Virgil's text, 1997, p. 170.
[2] Cf. Stok's apposite portrait of Servius, anxious to depict the old gods as *ficti:* in this respect, the pagan grammarian's position appears to be "totally compatible with the sensibilities of Christian readers", 2012, p. 482.
[3] "Id est fictus secundum poeticam licentiam locus, ne autem videatur penitus a veritate discedere, Hispaniensis Carthaginis portum descripsit. ceterum hunc locum in Africa nusquam esse constat, nec incongrue propter nominis similitudinem posuit."

think, Virgil had preferred to take advantage of his *poetica licentia* and project the Spanish port onto the African Carthage. The similarity (or identity) of both cities' names could authorize such a clever device. By now we recognize the recurrent dual structure of the grammarian's argument: on the one hand, an erudite care for the documentary basis of Virgil's work, on the other hand, a professional respect for the poet's licence to manipulate his subject matter as required, normally only constrained by the fidelity to nature and logical consistency – this *secundum naturam* and *nec incongrue* – of his metonymic adjustments or relocations.

The time has come to sum up. Servius repeatedly took the trouble to distinguish Virgil's idiosyncratic additions and imaginative embroideries from the *Aeneid*'s supposedly authentic basis in Roman tradition. For this purpose, he defines the work as a heroic poem, which is evident from 'the divine as well as human characters, and from the fact that it contains both true and feigned things; for it is clear that Aeneas had reached Italy, but that Venus had spoken to Jupiter, or that Mercury had acted as a messenger, is made up' (1.PR.).[1] Thus in the *Aeneid*, historical truth alternates with fiction, erudition with invention. Aeneas is an authentic person, whereas the gods are imaginary figures, though fully acceptable within the high style. Such observations are characteristic of Servius' pragmatic hermenutics. He typically abstains from polemics, rectifications or monopolistic claims of interpretation. He is the only exegete in my present investigation who, as it were, habitually seems to take a step behind his object, pointing out its peculiarities as if it were located in a showcase, reporting on alternative possibilities of reading or on divergencies among earlier commentators, sometimes expressing astonishment or distress, but not necessarily needing to attach the text to one single meaning.

This conspicuously dispassionate or discreet approach indicates Servius' strength as a literary critic, resulting from an unusual sensitivity to the complexity and ambivalence of the poetic text, reinforced by a scholarly curiosity in Virgils' fictional reconfigurations of circumstantial *res gesta*. Against the backdrop of Late Antiquity's increasing dogmatic and kerygmatic pressures on poetry, however, the drawback of precisely such critical virtues becomes evident. Servius' analytical detachment could sometimes slip into sheer reluctance to interpretation when faced with the problems of explaining the *Aeneid*, a resigned attitude which brings the cultural vulnerability of the lingering Roman pagan

---

[1] "Est autem heroicum quod constat ex divinis humanisque personis, continens vera cum fictis; nam Aeneam ad Italiam venisse manifestum est, Venerem vero locutam cum Iove missumve Mercurium constat esse conpositum."

enclaves into immediate focus. They were as sure about literary decorum as they were uncertain about their gods. When we are to account for the *Aeneid*'s deities, Servius remarks in his *Commentaries* (1.297), we simply have to stick to the old myths since truth is ignored, *in deorum ratione fabulae sequendae sunt, nam veritas ignoratur*. The contrast to the mature Augustine's passionate ongoing dispute with Virgil, as if it were a matter of life and death, could hardly be greater.

For our purpose, however, Servius stands out due to his frank acknowledgement of the *Aeneid*'s numerous exploitations of poetic licence. His occasional temptations to spot allegorical profundity in Virgil's work were consistently checked by the grammarian's disinterested gaze on his material, particularly sensitive to the requirements and integrity of the poetic narrative. Servius thus established the convincing image of classical Rome's *summus poeta*, a teacher of wisdom as well as an inventive master of the Latin language, whom we meet at the beginning of Dante's *Comedy*. There, significantly, the Florentine wanderer praises the greatest of all poets (Inferno 4.80), *l'altissimo poeta*, both for his profound knowledge, as when he is saluted in terms of "the famous sage" (1.89), "famoso saggio", and for his rhetorical flow, "the fountainhead / that pours so full a stream of speech" (1.79–80), "quella fonte / che spandi di parlar sì largo fiume".

3 Macrobius: *Narratio fabulosa*

When, in his great double monograph on the Late Platonic philosophy's impact on Latin tradition, Stephen Gersh is to account for the Roman author Macrobius, who flourished shortly after 400, he ascertains that "we finally come to a Neo-Platonist in the fullest sense of the word".[1] He bases his observation on two works by Macrobius: the dialogue *Saturnalia* and the commentary on the last part of Cicero's treatise on the republican form of government, *De re publica* (*On the Republic*), a dream narrative attributed to the famous Roman general Scipio Aemilianus (185–129 BCE), the conqueror of Carthage. The latter work in particular was to be copied, read, admired and quoted throughout the Middle Ages.

The Saturnalia

The very real grammarian Servius, examined in the previous section of this study, was actually granted a fictional existence as well. He is one of the interlocutors, portrayed as "by far the greatest of all teachers" (1.24.20), *litteratorum omnium longe maximus*, in Macrobius' *Saturnalia*, a voluminous dialogue from about 430, seven books of which have been preserved for posterity. It is set among Rome's highest aristocracy, the last stronghold of ancient pagan culture in the Empire, at a three-day-long gathering organized to celebrate the Saturnalia festival on 16–19 December, probably within the time span of 382–384.[2] A range of subjects are discussed by the noble guests, such as the digestion in human beings, their nervous system, the old pagan carnival that gave the work its name, several myths and rites of the Mediterranean world, various ideas about the seasons, the identification of all sub-celestial deities with the Sun, etymologies applied to the names of months or gods: a seemingly endless series of more or less peculiar *antiquitates*, all kinds of *arcana* from the religions and customs of ancient times. Vettius Agorius Praetextatus, for example, the host of the meeting on the first day, explains that Apollo is sometimes called *Loxias* since he, the sun god, moves along an oblique orbit across the heavens or slants his rays

---

[1] Gersh 1986, p. 493.
[2] I quote the *Saturnalia* (in Latin and English) from R.A. Kaster's Loeb volumes I–III 2011. Earlier scholars were prone to date the work to the years immediately following the early 380s, when the dialogue takes place; for the readjusted dating, see Cameron 1966. As for the exact year of the fictional dialogue, Cameron has recently revised his original assumption of 384 in favour of 382, 2011, pp. 243–47.

down on us (1.17.31). This suggestive etymology would obviously have been of interest to the authentic Servius who, as we have seen, detected 'oblique' or equivocal speech in the Sibyl of Cumæ, the priestess of Apollo, the god whose oracular ambiguities had, in turn, earned him the name of Loxias (cf. above, pp. 333f.).

Those taking part in the symposium could not be more prominent in contemporary Roman society. There was the nobleman, senator, high priest and governor Praetextatus (d. 384), the natural *primus inter pares* of the assembly, fluent in Greek and interested in philosophy, an expert on Roman, Hellenic and Eastern cults. There was Symmachus (ca. 340–402), whom we recognize as the urban prefect of Rome and the official spokesman of pagan culture in the famous conflict over the goddess of Victory's altar at the Forum in Rome in 384. And there was Nicomachus Flavianus, who in his capacity as praetorian prefect of Italy reopened the pagan temples before he committed suicide, faithful to his Roman ancestors, after losing the battle against the Emperor Theodosius at the river Frigidus in the Julian Alps in early September 394; not to mention other distinguished members of the Roman elite.

Among such prominent *nobiles*, the school teacher Servius, as Robert Kaster remarks in a penetrating article, must have adopted a rather modest attitude.[1] Macrobius portrays him in his youth, shy and reserved in the company of these celebrated governors and senators. If Alan Cameron's dating of *Saturnalia* to the year 430 is correct, Praetextatus and his interlocutors were all dead, and their senatorial class was already largely Christianized, when the work was composed. In that case, Macrobius gives us a glimpse of the sophisticated, upper-class Roman culture which was just about to sing its swan song during the final phase of the past century. The early 380s was also, significantly, the period which saw the conflict over the Victoria altar (not mentioned at all in the *Saturnalia*). The whole work is a sovereign demonstration, as it were, of the way the Roman aristocracy administered its cultural capital under the threat of extreme devaluation. Macrobius meticulously retraces the polished jargon and topics of that upper-class community, frequently associated with concepts such as *urbanitas* or *romanitas:* an elitist traditionalism for which classical culture in general and literature in particular constituted a unifying element, and where everything new or only oldish – for instance, Galilean monotheism – could be waved aside as vulgar or bizarre inventions.[2] Peter Brown has, congenially, perceived "a whole culture running hard to stand still" in the *Saturnalia:* "Like men who

---

[1] Kaster 1980a, p. 224.
[2] For an extensive presentation of the participants in Macrobius' dialogue, and of the author's work as a whole, with the emphasis on its background in Late Antique erudition, particularly in Neo-Platonic philosophy, see Flamant 1977, pp. 25–87, 192–205.

put their money in a safe foreign bank, these last pagans were anxious to invest their beliefs in a distant, golden past, untroubled by the rise of Christianity."[1]

Consequently, it is hardly worth while searching for melancholic or defeatist feelings in Macrobius' dialogue. The symposium guests had other, more important matters than the ascendancy of the Christians to talk about, namely Virgil, dead four centuries earlier but nevertheless their main link to Rome's glorious past. Moreover, in view of Servius' presence among them, we should not be surprised at the recurrent issue of the *Saturnalia* 3–7: Virgil criticism. Just as in Roman grammar teaching and in Servius' slightly later *Commentaries*, it is the poet's erudition and craftsmanship that are in focus. On the whole, the lettered interlocutors present us with a Virgil "devoted to scholarship where matters of fact are concerned, and to elegance in choosing his words" (3.11.9), *poeta enim aeque in rebus doctrinae et in verbis sectator elegantiae*. Macrobius' dialogue is not less than Servius' work loaded with pedantic and schoolmasterly verbiage, a tendency that has sometimes been considered characteristic of Roman literary theory (or even Roman literature) at this late stage. Lengthy passages from the fifth and sixth books of the *Saturnalia* are devoted to extensive demonstrations of erudition for the purpose of establishing Virgil's numerous debts to his Greek and Roman predecessors. Even though the protagonists of the dialogue well-nigh unanimously praise the Empire's *summus poeta* as the indisputable climax of the Roman literary canon, they treat him as a voice from a distant past, an old dictionary to be taken out and browsed through, an archaeological remnant from a culture that has seen its heyday, albeit still glowing with reflections of its former glory.

At this point, we would be wise to remember the fictional character of the *Saturnalia* dialogue. We cannot, of course, deduce Macrobius' own attitude to Virgil from the discussion of his fictional characters, where, furthermore, it is important to note who says what. When, for example, Virgil is censured for his indecencies or "embarrassing flaws", *pudenda*, and for his words or phrases borrowed from barbaric languages (1.24.6), it is one of the three uninvited guests at the symposium, Evangelus, who raises the criticism. Now, if his name is indicative of his faith, he is certainly not (in his capacity as a Christian) a reliable source in the eyes of the other interlocutors. Be that as it may – both Cameron and Kaster have serious doubts about Evangelus' identity as a Christian, – while Praetextatus and practically all the others at the symposium protest loudly, it is not Virgil's masterly stylistic skills or narratological finesse that they adduce

---

[1] Brown 2000, p. 299.

against the dissident.[1] Instead, they praise the infallible Roman poet for his expertise in religious legislation, sacrificial customs, premonition, astronomy – for everything, a modern reader might be tempted to think, except his aesthetic qualities.

These are certainly fulsome words of praise. Yet it is difficult to agree with the North-American historian Herbert Bloch that the main purpose of such effusions would be to present the *Aeneid* as a "pagan Bible".[2] On the whole, the distinguished symposium guests steer away from the construction of Virgil as an inspired *vates*, the oracular fountain of wisdom that appears now and then in Servius' *Commentaries* and which we will soon see fully developed in Fulgentius. Instead, they stroll about among his works as in an antiquarian library. Even their excursions into allegory usually end up in some eccentric cultural-historical rather than sibylline piece of information. The kind of expertise that is attributed to the poet the first time he is mentioned in the dialogue seems characteristic. Caecina, ex-governor of Numidia, praises Virgil for his way of describing daybreak in *Aeneid* 5.738–39, "Damp Night is rounding her course at its midpoint, / Sunrise comes cruelly upon me with panting horses and hot breath", laudably in accordance with the old Roman way of counting the hours. The poet had thus visualized the official Roman division of day and night "with a subtle and veiled allusion to the ancient custom, as befits a person dealing with poetic material" (1.3.10), *ut hominem decuit poeticas res agentem, recondita atque operta veteris ritus significatione*.

In view of the overwhelming cultural shift that was accelerating in the Empire during the early fifth century, the *Saturnalia* might for good reasons be classified as a serious case of cultural belatedness. It seems strange to think that the dialogue was probably written when Augustine was completing (or had completed) his lifework; and, perhaps even more strange, that it was written as if the Church Father or the new culture he embodied did not exist. While the world had changed around him, Macrobius went on examining several hundred years of old pagan rituals and beliefs. Perhaps it was important for him to establish Virgil as the quintessence of *romanitas*, an encyclopaedia of specifically Roman customs, religion and history, at a time when this concept was seriously challenged or renegotiated. On the other hand, we do not have access to any information concerning Macrobius' own faith. The great majority of earlier scholars supposed he was a pagan, but for all we know he might very well have been a

---

[1] Cameron argues for the view that Macrobius first and foremost would have introduced Evangelus as an uninvited guest at the party, somewhat bad-tempered, lacking in *urbanitas*, a stock character in antique dialogues ever since Plato's *Symposium*, 2011, pp. 253f., 595–97.
[2] Bloch 1963, p. 210.

Christian author, targeting a Christian audience (virtually the only audience that was left in the 430s), calling attention to the dying – or at least radically transformed – Empire's venerable past.[1] If so, Macrobius would rather foreshadow another pagan dialogue, in this case definitely created by a Christian writer in a Christianized culture, Boethius' *Consolation of Philosophy* composed one hundred years later, than embody any cultural belatedness. In short, the world of pagan concepts and beliefs was coming to an end during the fifth and sixth centuries, hence it was gradually losing its power as a shaping religious and moral force in Roman citizens' lives. Thus, to Macrobius and Boethius, it seemed possible to treat traditional myths and legends with respect rather than scorn, as a quarry of antiquities or as allegories of prudence respectively. This policy certainly does not apply to ascetics or struggling preachers, to devout believers like Paulinus of Nola or Augustine, both of whom knew the overwhelmingly seductive power of Virgilian fiction, but it holds true for well-educated officials and patricians such as Macrobius (Christian or not) and Boethius.

That is why Macrobius does not in the least feel the need to resort to Virgil's Fourth Eclogue for the purpose of turning the poet into a Christian before Christianity, or to read Aeneas' Roman *pietas* as a presage of Catholic *caritas*. He does not devote a single word to any such updated versions of the *summus poeta*, nor does he reveal any interest in the popular *sortes Virgilianae*, since his Virgil simply appears as a vigorously expanded metonym for long-standing, venerable *romanitas*. When the sibylline prophecy in *Eclogues* IV is brought up among the party guests, it is treated without any Christological allusions whatsoever (3.7.1). The dialogue's emphasis is elsewhere: its circle of noble Romans show an apparently endless interest in Dido's libation, the custom of decorating oneself with laurel wreaths close to the altar of Hercules near Circus Maximus in Rome, and a number of other customs or ceremonies, many of which are registered in the *Aeneid*. In addition, Virgil's embodiment of Roman cultural know-how is extended to the domains of grammar and rhetoric. The fourth book of the *Saturnalia* inspects the various arguments that the poet – now hailed as an orator – would have found among the "places", *loci*, listed in the antique assessments of *inventio*. The emphasis here, as befits a rhetorical analysis, is on the ability of the arguments to move the listeners' or readers' emotions, but the

---

[1] Cf. Cameron 2011, pp. 265–72, 567–626. The traditional theory of a pagan Macrobius is still evident in Irvine's detection, based on a juxtaposition of Augustine's *City of God* and the *Saturnalia*, of "two competing discourses, Christian and pagan, in early fifth-century educated Roman society". In his dialogue, Macrobius would have preferred eloquent silence to explicit attack: "Christianity is missing because it is everywhere implicitly presupposed but systematically excluded", 1994, p. 144.

speaker (whose identity is doubtful due to lacunae in the extant manuscripts) also touches on their mimetic aspects. Among the most efficient of these *loci* are the ones based on likeness, *a simili*, for example the image (*eikōn* or *imago*): "It is produced either when an absent person's physical form is described or when a non-existent form is imagined" (4.5.9), *ea fit aut forma corporis absentis describitur aut omnino quae nulla est fingitur.*

The speaker's illustrations of the latter type of imagery, pure invention, seem fairly trivial: monsters like Scylla or startling personifications like *Discordia, Bellona, Fama* or *Furor*, all present in Virgil's works, designed to create fear. Furthermore, his definition of the *imago* was fairly standard at the time; thus we have seen Augustine distinguish between two ways of treating God in figurative discourse, on the one hand through imagery based on "things corporeal", *ex rebus corporalibus* (of which he approved), and, on the other hand, by means of analogies drawn from non-existing things, *quae omnino non sunt* (which he rejected, cf. above, p. 231). Macrobius simply registers these rhetorical techniques as two instances (among quite a few) of Virgil's rhetorical and formal mastery, without even noting the cognitive challenges that issued from the activity of feigning something non-existent (a constant headache for Augustine).

As a matter of fact, the author of these *Saturnalia* does not seem to care much for the fictional aspect of Virgil's works. He treats them as (admittedly outstanding) antiquarian evidence rather than imaginative constructs. It is important to note, however, that his interest in Virgil's ancient material includes the poet's literary sources. In the dialogue's fifth book, the Greek philosopher Eustathius presents a lengthy exposition of the literary models for the *Aeneid*, first and foremost the inevitable Homer, whose *poetica disciplina* – the much admired *in medias res* technique – would constitute a powerful pattern for his Roman follower (5.2.9).[1] Moreover, in the famous Dido episode, Virgil had adapted the love story of Medea and Jason from Apollonius' epic poem *The Argonautica* for his own purposes. Everyone knows, Eustathius continues, that the Carthaginian queen actually remained chaste and virtuous, but now, so many centuries later, time has bestowed an "appearance of truth", *species veritatis*, on Virgil's rendering of her destiny. The poet's readers have slowly but steadily come to accept his version of the love-sick queen, whereupon it has been exploited by painters, sculptors and weavers as well as actors. They have all learnt to ignore or suppress the fabulous nature of the poet's narrative, preferring "to celebrate as true the sweetness that the artist instilled in human hearts", *pro vero celebrari quod pectoribus humanis dulcedo fingentis infudit* (5.17.5 – 6).

---

1 Cf. Horace's *Ars poetica*, 147–50, and Servius' *Commentaries*, 1.Pr.

This is an interesting take on the *Aeneid*'s fictionality, vaguely reminiscent of Ovid's ironic complaint about his audience's "easy trust" in his poetic impersonation of Corinna (above, p. 36), offering, as it were, a curious twist of euhemerism. While Lactantius as well as Servius had thought of certain fabulous or mythological figures as imaginative recreations of persons living long ago, Eustathius detects an original *fabula* in the *Aeneid*, a purely intertextual construct without any basis in reality, which years, authority and habit had made probable or credible. Dennis H. Green has highlighted this passage from the *Saturnalia* as a striking version of the fictional contract in Late Antiquity: "Macrobius describes here how Virgil's audience, fully aware of the historical truth, nonetheless accept his fiction as if it were true by a process of make-believe of which they are conscious."[1] Green's observation seems valid, although it should be added that Macrobius' erudite interlocutors do not evince any enthusiasm about this long-term reception of the *Aeneid*, and even less for the poet's muddling with (supposedly) historical facts. In those places of his dialogue where Virgil's unsurpassed qualities as a recorder of age-old Roman *historia*, *mores* or *fama* are in any way felt to be in conflict with his poetic licence, it is the latter that gets the worst of it. In this work cultural nostalgia definitely outshines inventive *fabula*. Eustathius goes so far as to say that he blames Virgil for sometimes having followed his own wit rather than Homer in the *Aeneid*. The Dido episode makes him burst out: "I only wish that for this part, too, Maro had found material to follow in his mentor – or some other Greek author" (5.17.4), *maluissem Maronem et in hac parte apud auctorem suum vel apud quemlibet Graecorum alium quod sequeretur habuisse*.

Robert Kaster remarks that Eustathius' criticism recalls the choice that Horace had presented to poets in *Ars poetica* (119): to follow paradigmatic *fama*, in this case Greek literary tradition, or to feign. The precise terms might vary in the *Saturnalia*, where Virgil just as well could be projected as wavering between his learned *diligentia* or *doctrina* and his personal *ingenium*, but the speakers in the dialogue never hesitate about their preference for the first option.[2] Thus, in their reserved attitude towards 'the charms of the feigning poet', *dulcedo fingentis*, these conservative senators and scholars could somewhat paradoxically fall in with the radical Christian ascetics. The latter had articulated a powerful spiritual alternative to the pagan culture which they found permeated by *figmenta*. Eustathius, for his part, reinstated a concept of classical tradition in the light of *fama* or *doctrina*, ideally cleansed of all passing fancies of fictionality.

---

[1] Green 2002, p. 14.
[2] Kaster 1980a, p. 236.

Another scholar, Sabine MacCormack, has drawn a telling comparison with Augustine. In the *Saturnalia*, Macrobius neatly evaded the Church Father's continuous concern in all matters of interpretation – his uneasiness about the arbitrariness of signs (potentially resulting in a dissemination of meaning raised to "unlimited semiosis") – by referring to the overall correspondence of Virgil's verbal art with the created world.[1] This approach is actually reminiscent of the grammatical commentary tradition, culminating in Servius' work, which had devoted attention to all sorts of things, big and small, in Virgil's poems: to odd curiosities as well as divine mysteries. Macrobius, however, focused on the poet's diction rather than his topics. Virgil had quite naturally been proficient in a plethora of styles, Eusebius remarks, since his eloquent art epitomizes all of creation (5.1.18–19):

> He followed no guide but nature, the very mother of all things, and he wove her into the fabric of his verse, like the harmony produced by different tones in music. Indeed, if you carefully examine the world itself, you will see a great similarity between that divine creation and this poetic one: just as Maro's eloquence is a complete whole that responds to the characters of all people – now brief, now abundant, now dry, now colorful, now all at once, sometimes gentle, sometimes turbulent – so the earth itself has fertile fields and meadows in one place, shaggy woods and rugged crags in another, dry desert sands here, places soaked by springs there, and part opened up to the desolate expanse of the sea. (III)

This is a remarkable piece of Virgil criticism. The poet's variety of styles is supposed to reproduce the variety of nature. To Macrobius, they manifest a *discordia concors* analogous with divine creation. Thus if the poetic work, in the eyes of this pagan Neo-Platonist, was comparable with the cosmos, its author would logically – as probably Ernst Robert Curtius was the first to point out – appear as a colleague to the very architect of the universe.[2] Such spectacular assumptions in fifth-century literary theory were to bear fruit a thousand years later, with the Renaissance humanists, some of whom would conceive of the poet as an *alter deus*; but for the time being they did not generate any corresponding exaltation of his fictional mode, least of all in Macrobius.[3] On the contrary, this author's

---

[1] MacCormack 1998, p. 88.
[2] Curtius 1990, p. 444. Kaster, too, underlines the singular character of this passage, Macrobius 2011 (vol. II), p. 224.
[3] On the notion of the poet as a "second god", see Tigerstedt 1968. Lieberg summarizes the discussion, 1982, pp. 159–73, albeit with the questionable conclusion that "only the modern spirit has expressed what the ancient poets would have liked to say" concerning poetry's innovative potential, p. 172. Lieberg believes that the creative (as opposed to imitative) poet occurred as a – rhetorical – figure in ancient tradition, in Virgil, Horace, Ovid and others, but was not established on a theoretical level before the groundbreaking Early Modern treatises by authors such as

praise of the *rota Vergilii* – the poet's implementation of multifarious styles, resulting in a work of great variety – linked as firmly as Servius the *Aeneid* to history, tradition and nature. Both commentators, however, recognized, each in his own way, the integrity of fictional discourse. To Servius, the proverbial poetic licence was recurrently operative in Virgil's works, and Macrobius, as we shall see now, even claimed to identify a new discursive category in ancient literature: the philosophical narrative, drawing on imaginary matter, specifically mythological events and settings.

The Commentary on the Dream of Scipio

The *Saturnalia* presents a rather mixed symposium, from lengthy catalogues of Virgil's sources in ancient literature to quite relaxed exchanges of views, sometimes cheerful and sometimes polemic, on Roman religion and *mores*. A much more coherent and systematic theory of the nature of fiction, highly influential in later medieval literature, is to be found in Macrobius' *Commentarii in Somnium Scipionis* (*Commentary on the Dream of Scipio*). "Central to this project is an exploration of fiction itself, its kinds, its qualities, its uses", observes Suzanne Reynolds.[1] Specifically, Macrobius' *Commentary* concerns the remarkable final passage of Cicero's *On the Republic*, a partly preserved philosophical dialogue written shortly before 50 BCE, dealing with a range of attitudes to the Roman constitution and to the ideal form of government, projected onto the general and statesman Scipio Aemilianus, active about a hundred years earlier, and some of his friends.

Cicero's dialogue ends with the story of a dream, known as *Somnium Scipionis*, "perhaps the most beautiful piece of Latin prose ever written", if we are to believe Karl Büchner.[2] The general, who is visiting Africa in 149 BCE, calls on an old family friend and, after a generous welcoming dinner, falls fast asleep. In a dream he sees his dead adoptive grandfather, the legendary Scipio Africanus,

---

Scaliger, Tasso or Shaftesbury. Since Lieberg, however, relies on Curtius's thesis that the notion of *poeta creator* is derived from the *creator ex nihilo* in Jewish-Christian tradition, he should have difficulties in explaining its success with the Latin Golden Age poets. The simple solution to this problem would be to make the main tenets of Aristotelian poetics and rhetorical invention operative within the framework of Ovidian illusionism and Virgilian fictionality. Thus the *mimēsis* which once granted poets a certain amount of fictional space in the *Poetics* would already anticipate the configurations of the *poeta creator* in the Roman Golden Age.

1 Reynolds 1996, p. 140.
2 Büchner 1976, p. 18.

who once led the Roman forces in the decisive and victorious battle against Hannibal's army during the second Punic war. "From a lofty place which was bathed in clear starlight" (6.11.11), *de excelso et pleno stellarum illustri et claro quodam loco*, Africanus shows him Carthage – which, incidentally, he is shortly about to destroy.[1] The dream soon expands into an exposition of the origin of the souls, and of their final destination along the Milky Way, among the stars, where the vision takes place. There Scipio meets his father, Paulus, one of the spirits that have shuffled off their mortal coil, or rather escaped "from the bondage of the body as from a prison" (6.14.14), *e corporum vinculis tamquam e carcere*, to live the true life above the stars, in contrast to the gloomy existence down on earth, which, according to Africanus, is a state of death.

Scipio bursts into tears at the sight of his father and begs that he too be parted from life at the earliest opportunity. His wish causes Paulus to deliver a long speech about the necessity of human beings to complete their temporary duty as guardians of "that sphere called Earth, which you see in the centre of this temple" (6.15.15), *illum globum, quem in hoc templo medium vides, quae terra dicitur.* On this point, Paulus is of course echoing the author himself, the republican, lawyer and statesman Marcus Tullius Cicero, with his strong emphasis on *pietas*, on responsibility and civic spirit, the *patria* that is Rome. There is also, however, a poet sporadically emerging from Cicero's discourses, letters and philosophical works, and in this final part of *On the Republic* he excels in imaginative flights and visionary language, as in Paulus' account of the cosmic temple, the music of the spheres and universal harmony: the whole geocentric picture of the world, contemplated from the Milky Way. Despite this dazzling panorama, with immense starry spheres in all directions, Scipio repeatedly turns his eyes towards the earth, which "seemed to me so small that I was scornful of our empire, which covers only a single point, as it were, upon its surface" (6.16.16), *iam ipsa terra ita mihi parva visa est, ut me imperii nostril, quo quasi punctum eius attingimus, paeniteret.*

Africanus reproaches Scipio for this unceasing interest in the universe's insignificant midpoint. To bolster his criticism, he exploits arguments from well-known *loci* in classical tradition such as the barren regions of the earth, or the limited spread and short duration of fame, all expressions of philosophical contempt for the world in marked contrast to Paulus' previous speech about the importance of duty and responsibility. Scipio is taught the Platonic lesson that only the body is mortal: "For that man whom your outward form reveals is not yourself; the spirit is the true self, not that physical figure which can be

---

[1] All quotations from *On The Republic* are from C.W. Keyes's Loeb edition 1943.

pointed out by the finger" (6.24.26), *nec enim tu is es, quem forma ista declarat, sed mens cuiusque is est quisque, non ea figura, quae digito demonstrari potest.* Thus at this stage, when the dream dialogue is drawing to a close, Cicero skilfully intertwines the message of the dutiful statesman with the sagacity of the Platonic philosopher. Africanus explains that the soul or *mens*, the eminent part of man, should be used for noble activities, and the noblest of them all are "those undertaken in defence of your native land". In short, those who both care about *curae de salute patriae* and look beyond earthly pleasures, towards "what lies outside" the world of matter, *ea quae extra erunt*, will hasten their return to the abode of the souls among the stars, that is, to the place of the two generals' current conversation (6.26.29). On these demanding as well as encouraging words from his grandfather, Scipio suddenly awakens from his dream.

C.S. Lewis has highlighted those components in the story that are incompatible with Christian faith: the idea of a special heaven for righteous statesmen, of the body as our occasional and wretched shell, of the soul becoming a god upon its arrival at the stars.[1] All these imaginary configurations are based on Platonic models, and it was precisely this Platonic connection – the Ciceronian dialogue's reuse of Plato's *The Republic* – that Macrobius took as the starting point for his *Commentary on the Dream of Scipio*, perhaps composed around 430. Thus he dealt with two works, one Greek and one Latin, devoted to the ideal form of government and the noble civic spirit, both of which ended with a vision of the life hereafter: one was a "fiction", *commentum*, the myth about Er's cosmic transmigration in Plato's dialogue (614–21), and the other was a dream, *somnium*, likewise located among the heavenly bodies (1.1.3).[2]

How, then, Macrobius wondered, are we to explain this structural and thematic similarity? Such a question immediately draws attention to mythological discourse, the ingredient in *The Republic* that had long caused complaints against the Greek philosopher, in particular from those Epicureans who loudly claimed that "philosophers should refrain from using fiction since no kind of fiction has a place with those who profess to tell the truth", *a philosopho fabulam non oportuisse confingi, quoniam nullum figmenti genus veri professoribus conveniret.* If such elevated subjects as the fate of the souls in the heavens should be treated, these detractors had maintained, it would be better to use simple language of one's own, *simplex et absoluta insinuatio*, rather than tarnish the gateway to truth with a lie, *mendacium:* a piece of theatre from the world of fiction,

---

[1] Lewis 1983, pp. 27f.
[2] All quotations from Macrobius' *Commentary* are from J.A. Willis's edition 1994 (1970) and, in English, from W.H. Stahl's translation 1990 (1952).

composita advocati scaena figmenti (1.2.4). Macrobius actually did not care much for Epicurean rationalism, but he certainly took such anti-mythological arguments seriously, since he realized that their censure of Plato struck at Cicero's dream narrative as well. This recognition resulted in what is for us the seminal part of the whole commentary: an examination of the relationship between philosophical and fictional discourse.

There is no doubt that in this *Commentary*, philosophy is shown as prior or superior to fiction, but on certain conditions the latter might serve the former, hence distinctions – several, as we shall see – have to be made. Essentially, Macrobius relied on arguments that had been put forward in earlier Neo-Platonic speculation, mainly in Porphyry and his well-known allegorical explanation of Homer's description of the cave of the nymphs on Ithaca (*Odyssey* 13.102–12), partly based on such etymologies that were to interest the interlocutors of the *Saturnalia*. Robert Lamberton has called Porphyry's text "the earliest surviving interpretive critical essay in the European tradition", contrasting it with Aristotle's, Horace's and Longinus' more totalizing or categorical pieces of criticism.[1] It would be just as legitimate to label *De antro nympharum* (*On the Cave of the Nymphs*) as one of the main sources of philosophical allegorism in Western literature. Inspired by ancient Greek, Eastern and Egyptian mysteries, Porphyry, in short, explains the cave of the nymphs as an image of the universe. In his introduction, he emphasizes that Homer's account of the cave is neither a straightforward geographical description nor "fabricated merely by poetical license", *kata poiētikēn exoysian plassōn*; instead, Homer is practising the art of speaking in allegories and riddles, *allēgorein kai ainittesthai* (2–3).[2]

At an early stage, Porphyry introduces the key term of the interpretive strategy governing *On the Cave of the Nymphs*, namely *symbolon*. It immediately becomes clear that this device allows for ambiguity. For some people, Porphyry explains, a cave might symbolize invisible or intelligible reality, but in *The Odyssey* or in Plato it rather epitomizes the material cosmos, that is, the world of the senses (7–9). Its northern entrance (corresponding to the Sign of Cancer) was open for those souls who were to be incarnated in a human body, while its southern exit, in Homer reserved for the gods, identified by Porphyry as the Sign of Capricorn, was intended for the released souls that would leave life for immortality. All the details in Homer's description – the nymphs and their purple

---

[1] Lamberton 1985, p. 120.
[2] I use L. Simonini's 1986 edition of *L'antro delle ninfe* for Porphyry's Greek text, and T. Taylor's translation, reprinted 1991, for all quotations in English.

webs, the bees and their honey, the bowls and the urns – are, accordingly, granted the status of "image and symbol" (21), *eikōn kai symbolon*.

It is deeply fascinating to follow Porphyry through this short exposition, in which he repeatedly refuses to expound the famous cave as simply the result of poetic licence (2), a wilful fiction, *plasma*, or a pleasant story, *diēgēma* (21); to be sure, he is quite prepared to characterize Homer's discursive mode in terms of *mythos* or *plasma*, but this fictional mode is held to be derived from truth, from a reality of an ultimately divine nature. Thus Porphyry implements the critical conversion of narrative or poetic *ficta* into philosophic *allegoria*, which would prove remarkably successful among a number of writers in the Latin-speaking world of Late Antiquity, for instance Macrobius and Boethius.[1]

It was precisely Macrobius' presentation of the issue, that, in turn, would form the basis of practically all Neo-Platonic literary criticism in the medieval West. Philosophy, he notes in his *Commentary* (1.2.6–21), can make use of certain myths, but not all. Macrobius' general attitude to myth is, at the outset, characterized by suspicion: the very term, *fabula*, signals something false. On closer inspection, myths, or stories based on myths, can have two purposes: to caress the ear or to call for moral improvement, *in bonam frugem*. Those authors who merely accomplish the former aim, providing pure reading pleasure, like the comedy writer Menander or the novelists Petronius and Apuleius, can immediately be disqualified for all serious philosophical purposes. They are better suited to the children's nursery, *in nutricum cunas*.

In other words, literature's moral usefulness is of the highest priority for Macrobius. The type of story that lives up to this criterion can in turn be divided into two classes. In the first and less important one, the subject is fictitious and the plot interwoven with lies: *in quibusdam enim et argumentum ex ficto locatur et per mendacia ipse relationis ordo contexitur*, for example, Aesop's animal fables. Even this kind of story must be ruled out from philosophical use. The second type of moral story, on the other hand, is crucial to Macrobius. There, it is only the plot or the characters, not the subject, that are invented (1.2.9):[2]

> The second rests on a solid foundation of truth, which is treated in a fictitious style [*per quaedam composita et ficta*]. This is called the fabulous narrative to distinguish it from the ordinary fable [*narratio fabulosa, non fabula*]; examples of it are the performances of

---

[1] For the close relationship between Macrobius' *Commentary* and *On the Cave of the Nymphs*, see Pépin 1987, pp. 81–84.

[2] "In aliis argumentum quidem fundatur veri soliditate sed haec ipsa veritas per quaedam composita et ficta profertur, et hoc iam vocatur narratio fabulosa, non fabula, ut sunt ceremoniarum sacra, ut Hesiodi et Orphei quae de deorum progenie actuve narrantur, ut mystica Pythagoreorum sensa referuntur."

sacred rites, the stories of Hesiod and Orpheus that treat of the ancestry and deeds of the gods, and the mystic conceptions of the Pythagoreans.

Now we are at least beginning to glimpse the kind of story that Macrobius is looking for, to all appearances a philosophically underpinned update of the myth interpretations we have registered in Hellenistic allegoresis and in Porphyry, Lactantius and Servius. In the *narratio fabulosa*, the truth is presented under a fictional cloak. The author's examples (Orpheus, the Pythagoreans) suggest that it is a matter of a fairly esoteric genre. His "truth" explicitly refers to holy or mysterious secrets.

Even at this point, however, Macrobius is anxious to distinguish between different subtypes of philosophical fictions. For example, he seems embarrassed about narratives in which "the presentation of the plot involves matters that are base and unworthy of divinities and are monstrosities of some sort", *contextio narrationis per turpia et indigna numinibus ac monstro similia componitur*, as when the gods commit adultery or Saturn castrates his heavenly father. Again, the philosophers decline and withdraw. Thus we have finally reached the only kind of fiction they can accept and which, in Macrobius' readings, rounds off both Plato's *The Republic* and Cicero's *On the Republic*. In this category of *narratio fabulosa*, "a decent and dignified conception of holy truths, with respectable events and characters, is presented beneath a modest veil of allegory", *sacrarum rerum notio sub pio figmentorum velamine honestis et tecta rebus et vestita nominibus enuntiatur* (1.2.11). This definition is essential. Mythical fiction becomes a seemly cloak for evidence of sacred truth.

To judge by Macrobius' prime examples, Plato's and Cicero's texts, the holy things dealt with in a *narratio fabulosa* concern first and foremost the fate of man after death, transmigration and divine or cosmic matters. They are further specified when the author a little later recommends using mythical stories "when speaking about the Soul, or about spirits having dominion in the lower and upper air, or about gods in general" (1.2.13), *cum vel de anima vel de aeriis aetheriisve potestatibus vel de ceteris dis loquuntur*. These references to the "spirits" and "the upper air" (the ether) probably include the planets, which had long been associated with the Olympian gods, from Mercury to Saturn. Accordingly, guided by these clues in Macrobius' commentary, we can narrow down the subject matter of his *narratio fabulosa* to the Neo-Platonic concept of the world soul, *psychē* or *anima:* the whole of the material universe, its structure and history.

This, in sum, was Macrobius' contribution to the almost one-thousand-year-long tradition of classical myth criticism. Based on Neo-Platonic theories of the image and on Stoic *interpretatio physica*, he presented an up-to-date version of *fabula* or *figmenta*, depicted as veils or clouds (the semi-transparency of the metaphors is symptomatic) of decorous figurative language covering the cosmos and its mysteries, nature and the elements. With this elaborate definition, Macrobius probably delivered the most influential Late Antique theory of literary fiction. Its material was drawn from mythology, its subject was derived from natural philosophy in the widest possible sense (including astrological speculation), and its function was inferred from established grammatical or rhetorical doctrines of figuration.

*

The world soul, however, was only the third of the hypostases forming the order of the universe, according to the common Neo-Platonic scheme:
- The One (*to hen*), sometimes called the Good (*tagathon*) and sometimes God (*theos*), in Latin commonly known as *summum bonum*,
- Intellect or Mind (*nous*), in Latin: *mens*,
- and the World Soul (*psychē*), in Latin: *anima mundi*.

Now, for the writer who aspired to deal with the higher, spiritual levels of reality – Intellect (Mind), or the very first cause: the Good itself, – not even a *narratio fabulosa* would be up to the task. Accordingly, philosophers who dared to look beyond the universe of material Nature or the Soul in order to take truly transcendent things into consideration had to abandon mythological discourse altogether (1.2.14 – 16):

> When, I repeat, philosophers speak about these, the Supreme God and Mind, they shun the use of fabulous narratives. When they wish to assign attributes to these divinities that not only pass the bounds of speech but those of human comprehension as well, they resort to similes and analogies [*similitudines et exempla*]. That is why Plato, when he was moved to speak about the Good, did not dare to tell what it was, knowing only this about it, that it was impossible for the human mind to grasp what it was. In truth, of visible objects he found the sun most like it, and by using this as an illustration opened a way for his discourse to approach what was otherwise incomprehensible. On this account men of old fashioned no likeness of the Good when they were carving statues of other deities, for the Supreme God and Mind sprung from it are above the Soul and therefore beyond nature. It is a sacrilege for fables to approach this sphere. (IV)

Jean Pépin ends his great panorama of the history of Greek allegorism from the Presocratics up to Late Antiquity with precisely this paragraph.[1] It might be described as an adamant dismissal of ancient mythology at the highest divine level of philosophical discourse, conceivably a strategic defensive measure from the

---

1 Pépin 1976, p. 213.

pagan outposts of Late Antique culture, faced with the aggressive criticism of myths and fiction by Christian intellectuals of the fourth and early fifth centuries, orchestrated by Ambrose, Augustine and Jerome. Thus Macrobius highlighted an alternative to mythical stories when speaking of holy things, a discursive and semiotic praxis that (despite the somewhat misleading term "simile") refused all imitation or replication in favour of a non-mimetic type of signs. By all accounts, this method was derived from hermetic Neo-Platonism with its starting points in Plotinus and Porphyry.

Wesley Trimpi has broadly distinguished two ways of evaluating human knowledge in classical and Late Antique culture, both based on Aristotelian tradition. The first alternative assesses knowledge according to its correctness or "accuracy", *akribeia*, while the second considers the extent to which it deals with "higher" and "more wonderful" things, *beltiona* and *thaumasiōtera*.[1] Trimpi exemplifies the two alternatives' relevance to figurative presentation with an anecdote related by Flavius Philostratus (ca. 170–245) in his biography of the Neo-Pythagorean philosopher and wonderworker Apollonius of Tyana. On a visit to Egypt, Apollonius ventures into a discussion with the so-called gymnosophist or 'naked philosopher' Thespesion on the possible manners and, in the first place, the suitability of rendering a god in pictorial representation.

The Greek complains – somewhat impolitely – that the Egyptian gods are unworthily represented in ridiculous or absurd animal figures; by contrast, his own countrymen's divinities are on most pious and honourable display in Olympia and other shrines. Thespesion replies with a tricky counter question: did your great Phidias go to Heaven in order to study the gods' forms for his work? He thereby implies that the Greeks are not in a position to claim any better authenticity for their sacred images, since their artists never saw the gods with their own eyes anyway. Apollonius retorts that Phidias did not rely on imitation; he was rather guided by "something supremely philosophical", namely his *phantasia*. The Greek goes on to explain that imitation, *mimēsis*, can only render what has actually been observed, while man's *phantasia* is capable of producing something far more remarkable, something never seen by human eyes. Specifically, this faculty of our soul can "conceive" (or 'suggest'), *hypotithēmi*, the unseen by referring to existing things. The gymnosophist, to all appearances unimpressed, replies: for our part, we revere our gods by representing them as "symbols", *xymbolika*, with no presumptions of credibility (since all deities are beyond human frames of reference). Thus, by rejecting imitation as well as sug-

---

[1] Trimpi 1983, pp. 97–106. The terms are from the very first clauses of *On the Soul* (1.1), Aristotle 1957, 402a.

gestion in favour of symbolic portrayal in their religious art, the Egyptians would quietly accept the insurmountable distance between the divine and the human, thereby emphasizing their gods' elevated and majestic stature (6.19).[1]

Apollonius does not buy this argument, but we hardly need to follow his and Thespesion's discussion any further. Trimpi concludes that the problem that is at the focus of their attention reflects the momentous tension between mimetic and symbolic procedures of representation which became increasingly strong during the first five centuries of our era.[2] The former were based on a relationship of similarity or continuity between the image and its object, including those analogies that trigger metonymical and metaphorical discourse, as stressed by Augustine in *On Christian Doctrine:* the words of a transferred expression, *figurata locutio*, "will be found to be taken either from things that are similar or things that are in some way connected" (3.25.34), *aut a similibus rebus ducta invenientur aut ab aliqua vicinitate attingentibus*. Symbolic representation, on the other hand, presupposed a gap between the pictorial or linguistic reference and its referent; it reinforced the kind of figuration where "the sign is not the thing", to use the words of the Swedish scholar Inge Jonsson in an excellent introduction to the theory of imagery in Western tradition.[3] In antique critical praxis, this type of symbolism was probably best expressed in the fifth-century Athenian philosopher Proclus' commentary on Plato's *The Republic*.

Proclus embraced an idealistic passion for the idea of the consistency and homogenous nature of the Greek cultural heritage. In his eyes it had continuously evolved around the same spiritual mysteries. Although he shared this belief with several Late Antique Neo-Platonic philosophers, he was probably unique in articulating it on the basis of an equally high estimation of poetry as of philosophy. Both of these disciplines would substantiate his project to establish a pagan canon in competition with the Christians' demonstrably successful Bible. Two names testify to this remarkably synthesizing enterprise: Plato was undeniably the *primus inter pares* of Proclus' Pan-Hellenic canon, while Homer – incidentally the major target of precisely Plato's *The Republic* – appears as its second great representative.

Since this canon had to be constructed as a homogenous tradition, the need arose to harmonize the infallible thinker with the brilliant poet. This was a tricky task which Proclus solved – as Anne Sheppard has shown – by distinguishing

---

1 I follow C.P. Jones's Loeb edition, vol. II, Philostratus 2005. This famous passage is thoroughly analysed, juxtaposed with e.g. Cicero's equally well-known deliberations on Phidias' vision of the gods by means of his imagination (*Orator*, 2.8–9), in Männlein-Robert 2003.
2 Trimpi 1983, p. 105.
3 Jonsson 1983, p. 13. Cf. Ladner 1979.

between analogical and symbolic representation, both of which he detects throughout *The Iliad* and *The Odyssey*, and both of which he deems typical of inspired poetry, the highest category of art, sanctioned by Plato himself (cf. above, p. 197).[1] It is in the sixth part of Proclus' commentary on *The Republic* that the main concepts of this original poetic theory are developed, at the very last hour of Greek pagan culture, highly dependent on a notion of absolute truth, eternally and universally valid, common to a philosopher like Plato and a poet like Homer. In this bold harmonizing system, logical and mythical discourse ought to express identical things, only in different ways.

Proclus was an indefatigable optimist about the potential of human language to designate true reality through either of the two figurative forms of expression that he reckoned with: the analogical and the symbolic. His analogical method is based on the concepts of model, *paradeigma* and copy, *eikōn*. The copy is relegated to low levels of reality in the Neo-Platonic cosmos; nevertheless, it is reminiscent of, and can thus convey at least a hint of, its higher model. By contrast, Proclus continues, the inspired *symbola*, or *synthēmata*, need not exhibit any similarity to their objects at all. On the contrary, they can be designed as their opposites, as when the frequently indecent Olympian gods of Homer in a 'mystical' or 'enigmatic' manner embody insights into the ultimate secrets of being, only revealed to the initiated exegetes.[2] As Robert Lamberton puts it, referring to Proclus' comment on *The Republic* 1.198.15–16: "Perhaps the most striking and original point in Proclus's poetics is this: 'Symbols are not imitations of that which they symbolize.'"[3]

Proclus' system may be reminiscent of Macrobius', but even a brief sketch like the present one reveals that he did not turn his back on the low-comedy anecdotes that the North African author had considered unworthy of a philosophical *narratio fabulosa*. Quite the reverse, it was precisely the offensive Homeric passages that Proclus tended to read symbolically: the anecdotes about how Hera tricks and seduces Zeus (*Iliad*, 14.153–351) or about Ares and Aphrodite (*Odyssey*, 8.266–366). In such stories, the symbolic language, as it were, weaves

---

1 Sheppard 1980, p. 197.
2 Proclus' exact terms for these procedures of figurative designation could shift, as the Finnish graecist Oiva Kuisma has observed, 1996, pp. 54f., but the fundamental distinction between emulating and symbolic signs would essentially remain intact throughout his commentary on *The Republic*. The former, the tools of analogy, could sometimes refer to a 'model' of heavenly or divine nature. Consequently, even if they presuppose a relationship of similarity, they should not be mistaken for any instances of mimetic poetry, which is the lowest of the three or four types of poetry registered in Proclus' system, limited to factual and sensory – or, in the worst case, illusory – information. Cf. the chapter "Mimesis: Eicon and Symbol" in Coulter 1976, pp. 32–72.
3 Lamberton 1986, p. 190.

a curtain, *parapetasma*, that readers have to penetrate, typically by analysing the words' etymologies, in order to make the text meaningful. If, for instance, the episode with Hera and Zeus is read 'according to secret doctrine' (1.140.11), *kata tēn aporrēton theōrian*, it deals with the origin of cosmos from two complementary principles at the level of the divine intellect.

Proclus might sometimes colour this esoteric symbolism with magic and theurgic elements, but as a rule he did not distinguish it in any conclusive way from allegory.[1] He frequently treated it as a common characteristic of the primeval poets or seers, *prisci theologi*, and first and foremost of Homer. It could also be described as 'demoniac', *daimonios*, since, paradoxically, the lowest band of supernatural beings, the demons, were able to infiltrate the visions or dreams of human beings in order to communicate knowledge of the highest things in the cosmic chain: of the angels or the gods, of the future or the past (1.85.26 – 86.23). This symbolic type of representation in literature or art, based on the ancient mysteries of the Eastern Mediterranean world and on Late Greek esoteric speculation, had been roughly sketched on a theoretical level by Macrobius and was now established within a broad philosophical framework by Proclus. It was destined to become seminal to the negative or apophatic theology which, through the agency of Dionysius the Areopagite and his Carolingian translator (and commentator) John Scotus Eriugena, would constitute a challenge to the manifold applications of "the universal resemblance of things" – to quote Michel Foucault – that permeated the culture of the High Middle Ages.[2]

*

The decisive difference between Proclus and Macrobius is to be found in their assessment of Homeric (or mythological) poetry's claims to philosophical gravity. While the Athenian Neo-Platonist would register symbolic operations on the highest possible cognitive level in Homer's stories of the gods, Macrobius had chosen to isolate non-mimetic (symbolic) structures of signification from mythology. The former were reserved for invisible, noetic or conceptual reality, the latter – purged of all indecencies – was exclusively applied to the concerns of the material universe: the world soul. His resistance to licentious *fabulae* in both these kinds of representation served not only the purpose of warding off Christian attacks on promiscuous pagan fancies but was also, in sharp contrast to Proclus, loyal to Roman rhetoric's traditional doctrines of style and decorum, according to which low comedy could not possibly signal sublime things. After having thus

---

1 Kuisma 1996, p. 62.
2 Foucault 1973, p. 49.

clarified the contrast between those "similes and analogies" that might indicate the ineffable, and the *narratio fabulosa* that would apply to matters concerning the soul and the cosmos, Macrobius did not examine the former any further. Evidently they did not require any particular defence, whereas the mythical narrative could still need to be justified in order to convince potentially mistrustful readers.

For this purpose, Macrobius lined up arguments inspired by the same spirit of esoteric or hermetic religiosity, characteristic of Late Antiquity, that we have seen Augustine exploit in his Bible hermeneutics. A "frank, open exposition", *aperta nudaque expositio*, would be unacceptable, he points out, to that Nature which takes shelter under a coat or covering so as to avoid people's rude attempts to comprehend her through their senses. Conversely, she would certainly like to have her secrets treated *per fabulosa* by wise and sensible people (1.2.17). Accordingly, her sacred rites are traditionally hidden, as it were, underground, 'in the rabbit burrows of figuration', *figurarum cuniculis*. In this context, Macrobius refers, as could be expected, to the Eleusinian mysteries as well as to the ancient Presocratic and Pythagorean philosophers' covert ways of talking about the gods, recycled by the eponymous speaker of Plato's *Timaeus*, their spiritual heir in direct line of succession, by all accounts considered to be a fully authentic author (1.2.18–21). Thus the figures of narrative discourse served as "Nature's" means of protecting herself from improper profanation.

It is time to summarize and look forward. Macrobius classified the subject of his commentary as a *narratio fabulosa*, that is: he reads the Ciceronian *Dream of Scipio* as a philosophical exposition of the soul's cosmic adventures, framed as a fictional narrative. His definition of the genre seems exemplary. In addition, it closely corresponds with Cicero's actual text: a dream tale with metaphysical as well as ethical (moral) implications. In Macrobius' eyes, it not only dealt with lofty things but was composed with due respect for its theme, in a style worthy of its subject. The influence of his commentary on the Middle Ages proved crucial. Together with the Late Antique philosopher Chalcidius' Latin translation and exposition of *Timaeus* (fourth century CE), it remained for eight centuries the foremost source of knowledge of Platonic and Neo-Platonic philosophy in the West. Alongside Martianus Capella's mythological allegory of the liberal arts, my subject of the next section in this study, it also provided the early Middle Ages with a good deal of the astronomical and geographical information the period sorely needed. Macrobius' *Commentary* is typical of the Late Antique (and many medieval) attempts to appropriate classical culture, helplessly in love with compilations, catalogues, glosses, compendia and encyclopaedic listings. It is sixteen or seventeen times as long as its subject, which it mostly utilizes as a "framework" – I borrow the term from the North American translator of the commentary, William Harris Stahl – for the display of the author's own Neo-Platonic doctrines.[1]

Thus the Latin Middle Ages would readily take up the concept of *narratio fabulosa* launched in Macrobius' *Commentary*. To begin with, this category of storytelling enjoyed the great advantage of being elaborated in the only classical language that was generally known from the fifth to the fifteenth century in Western Europe. In addition, it provided medieval scholars and literati with a well-needed compromise solution to the interpretation issues that profane literature kept raising, a viable alternative or countermeasure to the apologists' and the Church Fathers' onslaughts on the pagan Muses. Not only the materialistic Epicureans but, for instance, quite a few Christian bishops and ascetics among Macrobius' contemporaries had treated ancient mythology harshly, to say the least, wondering at how even Plato had been unable to resist its allurements. In a letter from the year 400–01, already cited above (p. 160), Paulinus of Nola ironically remarks that not only common people had embraced such "crazed ideas", *deliramenta*, as the old Greek notion of the spinning Fates; raving Plato himself, *Plato delirans*, had depicted universal Necessity as an old woman with her distaff, manoeuvred by the Moirai (the Fates), her three daughters, all singing in harmony (cf. *The Republic* 616–17). "He so abused the ears of men with pride in his empty eloquence," Paulinus thunders, "that he did not blush to insert such comic prattling of an old wives' tale in his writings in which he was bold enough to discuss the nature of God as if he were knowledgeable about it."[2] We must take such inventions for what they are, the bishop rounds off his polemic: quite simply outbursts of Attic eloquence. They are made to soothe our ears but should certainly not be allowed to upset the foundations of our judgment, *non debent sensuum fundamenta convellere* (16.4).

Macrobius' hermeneutic programme was diametrically opposed to Paulinus'. The mythical tale contains a hidden truth, a philosophical message, and as a rule it is most forcefully configured by the poets, at its best by the main subject of *Saturnalia*, namely Virgil, who in the dream commentary is praised for being "well trained in all of the arts" (1.15.12), *disciplinarum omnium peritissimus*. Later in his *Commentary*, the author deals with the tendency in ancient culture to elevate certain founders of cities and prominent statesmen to the status of gods in heaven. The Roman poet, for his part, Macrobius notes, recalling Anchises' posthumous speech to his son in the *Aeneid* (6.722–51), sent his heroes to the

---

[1] Macrobius 1990, pp. 12, 26, 43f.
[2] "Tantum abusus est humanis auribus adrogantia inanis facundiae, ut ridiculam anilis fabulae cantilenam non erubesceret scriptis suis, quibus de divina etiam natura quasi conscius disputare audebat, inserere."

mythological underworld – but only to designate the lofty ether, beyond the skies, as their ultimate abode, in agreement with ancient speculation. In this way Virgil made allowance for both "the poet's imagination and the philosopher's accuracy", thereby demonstrating his "twofold training" (1.9.8), *ut geminae doctrinae observatione praestiterit et poeticae figmentum et philosophiae veritatem*.

Here, too, in *Aeneid* VI, we are obviously faced with a *narratio fabulosa* in the sense already established by the commentator. The poet's Elysian Fields, infernal rivers and lofty ether serve to embody the esoteric intuitions of the philosopher. This instance of a "twofold training" or, as it were, 'twin method', *gemina doctrina*, was derived from Hellenistic exegesis, probably – as Antonie Wlosok has observed – of importance to Virgil himself, and at all events exploited by Servius.[1] No one, however, articulated it within such a cogent and concise theoretical framework as Macrobius. The North African author thus powerfully contributed to the transmission of this seminal version of fictionality from Late Antique to medieval culture. Édouard Jeauneau, Peter Dronke and Frank Bezner have convincingly demonstrated the significance of his concept of *narratio fabulosa* for the notion of *integumentum* in the grammatical and rhetorical traditions of the High Middle Ages, particularly in the so-called School of Chartres, one of whose foremost masters, William of Conches, would comment on the commentator in his *Glosae super Macrobium*. Joel C. Relihan has even singled out Macrobius' presentation as "the fullest consideration of the varieties and proprieties of fictional discourse extant from antiquity".[2]

Ultimately, of course, this key treatise of Neo-Platonic hermeneutics presupposes the Ionic natural philosophers and their rationalizations of Homer. Incidentally, Macrobius was able to accommodate their theory of the four elements, already frequently adduced in the Stoic explanations of *The Iliad* and *The Odyssey*. Quite a few *physici*, he remarked in his *Commentary*, have taught us that ethereal fire is due to moisture. They had come to this conclusion from the observation that Nature has located the ocean directly under the celestial spheres' hot zone, that is, round the equator (2.10.11):

> They claim that Homer, the originator of all conceits about the gods, hid this subtle truth beneath the cloak of poetic imagery when he said that Zeus, invited to feast with the Ethiopians, went off to Ocean with the other gods, that is with the planets. They say that by this allegory Homer meant that the planets drew their nourishment from the water and that he

---

[1] Wlosok 1987.
[2] Relihan 1993, p. 182. Cf. Jeauneau 1973, pp. 265–308; Dronke 1974, pp. 13–78; Bezner 2005, pp. 263–98.

called the Ethiopians "kings of the celestial tables" because only Ethiopians inhabit the bank of Ocean, a race whose skin has been burned black because of the sun's nearness. (V)

Throughout this commentary, Homer is constructed as a didactic – rather than mystical – storyteller, deliberately imparting a wealth of philosophical, cosmological or geographical information "beneath the cloak of poetic imagery", *sub poetici nube figmenti*, that is, essentially, mythology (Macrobius makes good use of the term *figmentum* for the ancient myths but dispenses with all forms of *allegoria*). The explanation given above seems characteristic. When, at the beginning of *The Iliad*, Thetis tells her angry son that "Zeus went yesterday to Oceanus, to the blameless Ethiopians for a feast, and all the gods followed with him" (1.423–24), she is actually presenting, the commentator claims, oceanographical and astronomical evidence: the goddess's words refer to the way Jupiter and the other planets draw their nourishment from the ocean round the equator.

Such is the design and procedure of an exemplary *narratio fabulosa*, Macrobius' own contribution to the ancient tradition of allegorical interpretation, updated in the light of Roman rhetorical theory of decorum and hierarchization of styles. It arrived as a rescue operation in favour of the badly strained concept of *fabula*, carried out at the very moment when antique culture was fading out (or at least in a process of radical change). This contribution was to echo down the centuries and be of invaluable importance for the medieval writers who ventured to legitimize art and literature theoretically, a demanding task during an epoch which, precisely in theory, would readily turn away from fiction.

4 Martianus Capella: A Hopeless Mess

To get an idea of what unites medieval literary taste with modern sensibility, we would be well advised to examine multifaceted and passionate works like Dante's *Comedy* or the lyrics of the troubadours. To get an idea of what distinguishes medieval literary taste from modern sensibility, we cannot possibly do better than go to the North African polymath Martianus Capella, born in Madaura (not far from Augustine's Hippo Regius), and his allegorical story in nine books, *The Marriage of Philology and Mercury*, completed – it has been suggested in recent years – after the middle of the fifth century.[1]

The only thing that actually happens in Martianus' work is precisely what its title promises, but the marriage in question gives rise to hundreds of pages of learned elucidations centred on the seven liberal arts, of which both the wealth of evidence and the intricate Latin can put any modern reader's patience to the test. This did not prevent the work from becoming the foremost source of information on the *artes* for the Middle Ages. It enjoyed widespread popularity and was circulated in a large number of manuscripts. The *Marriage*, as I shall call it henceforth, satisfied the period's taste for hierarchically systematized erudition, and the author's way of imparting encyclopaedic knowledge within a narrative framework met with response in Carolingian as well as High Medieval Europe, despite his pagan vein. Post-Renaissance culture has not shown Martianus the same generosity. C.S. Lewis's biting description in *The Allegory of Love* testifies to modernity's lukewarm attitude to the *Marriage:* "this universe, which has produced the bee-orchid and the giraffe, has produced nothing stranger than Martianus Capella."[2]

Until the 1960s, most people agreed with Lewis. There was something monstrous about this super-allegorical and florid textbook in epic format. But there is no doubt that the *Marriage* has regained at least scholarly interest in the past fifty years or so. The Martianus who struck Lewis as bizarre in 1936 can surprise

---

[1] Danuta Shanzer discusses the difficult problem of dating Martianus' work, hypothetically suggesting the 470s or 480s as the most probable date for its composition, 1986, pp. 5–28. This is still, however, a matter of discussion. Lucio Cristante – the editor of the ninth and final book of the *Marriage* – prefers (as most earlier commentators) the year 429, when the Roman proconsularship in Carthage was probably over, as a *terminus ante quem*, but goes so far as a hundred years back for a corresponding *post quem*, Martianus Capella 1987, p. 30. A good English introduction to the *Marriage* is provided by its translator William Harris Stahl (where the date for its composition, however, is assumed to have been some time between the second and the fourth decades of the fifth century, reflecting common opinion before Shanzer's work), 1971, pp. 12–16.
[2] Lewis 1979, p. 78.

us, by virtue of his experiments in irony and his ingenious manipulations of myths, in 2015. Several commentators, like Joel C. Relihan, have preferred to care less about the author's erudite extravagance and more about his playful manoeuvrings of a number of generic and stylistic devices: "Martianus writes not an encyclopedia but a Menippean satire that parodies encyclopedic knowledge."[1]

As early as 1972, Fanny LeMoine, the pioneer of this renewed scholarly attention to Martianus, attempted to "re-evaluate" the *Marriage* within the context of an ancient tradition of works that aimed to present their readers with a synthesis of the overall cosmic pattern.[2] Even more importantly, she highlighted the interaction between the various levels of narration in the *Marriage*, a rewarding field of research highly relevant for my own approach to the work. It turns out that Martianus operates with alternate authorial voices, staging a clever game both with his own presentation and with his readers, presumably the strongest investment of Late Antique literary culture in what recently has been branded metafiction, "a borderline discourse, a kind of writing which places itself on the border between fiction and criticism, and which takes that border as its subject", to quote a modern anthology on the subject.[3]

Fabulous Festivities

Martianus begins his work with a hymn devoted to the god of marriage, celebrated in classical Roman culture as Hymen (1.1):[4]

1   Tu quem psallentem thalamis, quem matre Camena
       progenitum perhibent, copula sacra deum,
    semina qui arcanis stringens pugnantia vinclis
       complexuque sacro dissona nexa foves,
5   namque elementa ligas vicibus mundumque maritas
       atque auram mentis corporibus socias,
    foedere complacito sub quo natura iugatur,
       sexus concilians et sub amore fidem;
    o Hymenaee decens, Cypridis quae maxima cura es […].

---

[1] Relihan 1993, pp. 137f.
[2] LeMoine 1972, p. 229.
[3] Currie 1995 ("Introduction"), p. 2.
[4] All Latin quotations from the *Marriage* are from J. Willis's edition 1983, while all translations into English are from W.H. Stahl's, R. Johnson's and E.L. Burge's version 1977. My line numbers reflect the position of verses in each piece of poetry (rather than, as in Willis, on the printed page).

> Sacred principle of unity amongst the gods, on you I call; you are said to grace weddings with your song; it is said that a Muse was your mother. You bind the warring seeds of the world with secret bonds and encourage the union of opposites by your sacred embrace. You cause the elements to interact reciprocally, you make the world fertile; through you, Mind is breathed into bodies by a union of concord which rules over Nature, as you bring harmony between the sexes and foster loyalty by love. Fair Hymen, you are the main object of the Cyprian's care; [...].

Martianus' Latin is often difficult, apart from the fact that the manuscripts of his work offer quite a few challenges (partly due to their great number) and that he has a predilection for obscure or esoteric topics. Even if we nowadays avoid labels such as *barbarus scriptor* (applied to Martianus by Joseph Scaliger, the great Renaissance philologist in Leiden), doggedly accompanied by prejudiced mumble about "African turgidity", *tumor Africus*, the *Marriage* is undeniably a hard read, lining up rare words in convoluted periods.[1] Martianus' chief principle of style is that of accumulation and variation, in complete accordance with the contemporary taste for eloquent amplification, *copia*, already manifest in the introductory invocation quoted above, where the Latin syntax barely manages to cope with the poet's load of ornaments and supplements.

At the same time, this short *exordium* to the *Marriage* reveals how concepts – more or less dressed up in human apparels – had gained ground as main players in Latin literary discourse. Admittedly, the technique is not new. It can be detected in the *Aeneid*, where Sorrows, Senility, Terror, Poverty and a host of other potentates haunt the entrance to the underworld (6.273–81), or in Ovid's *Metamorphoses*, where icy Scythia is depicted as the home of Pallor, Fear and "gaunt Famine", *ieiuna Fames*, the last of whom is given a detailed, full-length portrait (8.788–808). This device can further be studied in Apuleius' novel with the same name, *Metamorphoses* (otherwise known as *The Golden Ass*), in all probability one of the texts that inspired Martianus, as well as in several works of Late Antiquity, most famously Prudentius' hexameters on the battle between vices and virtues, *Psychomachia*, exclusively populated by belligerent *prosopopoeiae*.

Not unlike Prudentius, Martianus piles up his personified concepts throughout the *Marriage*. It is to a large extent these incarnate notions that form the plot of his work, in animated interaction with each other and with the Olympian gods. Here, in the introductory hymn, the chief topic is universal harmony, pro-

---

1 On Scaliger, see Robinson 1918, p. 160. Cf. Stahl's comments on the style of the *Marriage* in W. H. Stahl *et alii*, 1971, pp. 28–40. Lucio Cristante complains that none of the three modern critical editions of the work in its entirety (from 1866, 1925 and 1983) is satisfying, 1987, p. 1. In addition to the last of these I have profited from the impressive bilingual edition (the Latin text of which is based on Willis) by Ilaria Ramelli 2001.

vided by Hymen, hailed as the representative of love or desire but also of music or poetry: he plays the harp or sings, and was born of the Muse. Hymen embodies the fundamental concord through Creation that both Macrobius and Boethius, and indeed the whole of Late Antiquity, in many respects a world where everything fell apart, loved to celebrate. Martianus was to eulogize it in his most eloquent manner in the final book of the *Marriage*, devoted to the art of music, where Harmony praises the cosmic unity of opposites in a pyrotechnical showpiece charged with sparks from Plato's *Timaeus* and Pythagorean philosophy of numbers. The writer makes no attempt, however, to Christianize this world order in the *Marriage*, which remains a profoundly pagan work from beginning to end.

After the authorial I has recited the introductory chant, a "Martianus" intrudes into the story, to all appearances the narrator's eponymous son, expressing his annoyance that such a white-haired old man should "chatter silly trifles" (1.2), *nugulas ineptas aggarrire*. The young man rebukes his father for acting like a blear-eyed priest who absent-mindedly starts singing a hymn before he has even opened up his shrine: may he now reveal what he just said and explain the significance of his obscure words! The storyteller is surprised at this accusation of being cryptic or incomprehensible; after all, a celebration of Hymen should obviously signal the theme of marriage. Nonetheless, he readily meets his son's wishes:[1]

> I shall unfold to you a story which Satire invented in the long winter nights and taught me by the dimming lamplight – that is, unless its length discourages you.

Whereupon the story immediately begins. It is symptomatic that young Martianus is prevented from declining or even commenting on this proposal, since the author needs to install him as an audience – a readerly presence – in his tale. All he gets is a short excuse for "the length", *prolixitas*, of the tale which is to follow.

Thus the first person to present criticism (framed, to be sure, as an exordial topos) of the *Marriage* for being long-winded was in fact the author himself! He was fully aware of the demands of classical rhetoric for effective presentation, and he flouted them as undauntedly as consistently. The story should be clear, seem probable and be kept short, his Rhetoric teaches us in true classical spirit within the framework of a story that on all three points blatantly contradicts her rules (5.551). Together with Fulgentius, Martianus is the only writer among my

---

[1] "Fabellam tibi, quam Satura comminiscens hiemali pervigilio marcescentes mecum lucernas edocuit, ni prolixitas perculerit, explicabo."

sources for the issue of Late Antique fictionality who proceeds ironically, employing the device which we nowadays know as 'the unreliable narrator'. The rebellious son's comment about his father's stupid trifles clashes palpably with the high-flown tone of the introductory hymn, inevitably casting a parodic light on the blear-eyed, chattering authorial I.

This need not mean that we should not take this speaker seriously, as Fanny LeMoine points out. Martianus simply exploits the topic of modesty required by tradition, albeit taken to extremes. His prefatory staging of the hymn, the priest and the temple as well as his (fictional) son's call for him to "reveal" and disclose the hidden secrets of his solemn chant (using the verbs *vulgare, reserare, revelare*), may well serve as reading instructions: have patience with me, even though I might sound prolix and unconcentrated, for I speak of learned and divine matters (in a disguise which my son does not seem to understand)![1] In this case, we might expect a *narratio fabulosa* in Macrobius' sense of the term, specifically, perhaps, in view of the speaker's purported drowsiness, an inspired dream tale.

Thus the narrator of the *Marriage* begins to recount the story that he has promised his son (and readers) to tell. It will continue all through the work, driven by a curious polyphonic mechanism; a sublime subject (the wedding) and a didactic exposition (on the arts) is time and again infiltrated by what Mikhail Bakhtin, in an essay on the pre-history of the novel, calls a "parodic-travestying, indirect, conditional discourse".[2] The whole account is, as we have already been told, a *fabella* that the author is supposed to have picked up from – personified – Satire by the flickering light of a lamp or lantern at night in wintertime. His reference to *Satura* gives us an early hint of the work's form, precisely the mixture of verse and prose, of styles and themes (ranging from pedestrian grammar lessons to sublime cosmic apotheosis), which had probably characterized the Roman Menippean satire ever since Varro's *Saturae Menippeae*, incidentally composed by the author who wrote the standard work in Latin on the arts, *disciplinae*, of classical education.

Moreover, lamplight was a traditional figure for night studies. In his listing of common devices and formulas in Latin prose prefaces, Tore Janson shows how ancient writers from Callimachus (third century BCE) onwards were careful to emphasize the nightly diligence, associated with scholarly studies, that they de-

---

[1] LeMoine 1972, pp. 36f. Alexandre Leupin emphasizes the strong elements of irony and "duplicity" throughout Martianus' work, turning the *Marriage* into an ingenious "cryptogram" for pagan propaganda or hermetic mysteries, 2003, p. 79.
[2] Bakhtin 1994, p. 138.

voted to their works.[1] Since Martianus emphatically returns to the faint or flickering lanterns and his vigil in the final lines of two of the books in the *Marriage* (2.219, 9.998), we have reason to suspect a parody of this topic, even if these *lucernae* may be read as a further indication of the learned nature of his narrative. In the world of Menippean satire, ironical stratagems did not necessarily rule out serious or didactic aims. The fact that the lanterns grow dim may underline this parodic aspects of Martianus' exordial paragraphs. In addition, if we read the text's *mecum* with *marcescentes*, not only the lanterns but the speaker himself start to droop, due to his old age or simply his drawn-out vigil. Such a reading would certainly confirm his status as an unreliable narrator.[2] Finally, the verb *explicabo* indicates his imminent narrative activity. It is reasonable to understand this term in its transferred and long-established conventional sense of expounding, representing or explaining something, but the literal meaning of the word ('unroll', 'unfold') suggests the possibility that the authorial I – or some other writer – has written down the whole story on one or probably several scrolls, which he will now unroll while reading them aloud for his suspicious son.[3]

The story told by Satire is about how Mercury, messenger of the gods, decides to get married. The only question is to whom. After having to discard a number of attractive alternatives such as Sophia (Wisdom), Mantis (Prophecy) or Psyche (the Soul), Mercury realizes that he needs to consult Apollo. He searches for his fellow god in a world that the Sibyls and oracles seem to have abandoned. It is tempting to read it as a Late Antique cultural waste land, at any rate a typical contrast to the prosperity the earth can expect when Mercury has found his spouse. Eventually, he locates Apollo near Delphi. The god of prophecy makes him an offer he cannot refuse: Philology, supremely educated, omniscient, all-seeing, and, as if those qualities were not sufficient, perfectly at home on the Mount of Parnassus (1.22).

From the Carolingian epoch onwards, the Middle Ages would interpret this couple, Philology and Mercury, as a Ciceronian union of wisdom and eloquence, *sapientia* and *eloquentia*, sometimes translated into parallel constellations such

---

[1] Janson 1964, pp. 97f., 147f.
[2] Interestingly, Shanzer proposes a figural interpretation of these *lucernae* as the speaker's eyes, in analogy with the dead metaphor *lumina*, 1986, p. 56, a suggestion which seems to disagree, however, with the flickering *lucernae* (to all appearances literal) in 2.219.
[3] Cristante assumes, referring to the *volumina* mentioned in the *Marriage*, that Martianus actually appears to have used the old scroll, since each of the nine books in the oldest manuscripts was headlined with the complete title of the work, along with the author's name in the genitive, a type of information which inevitably would have seemed redundant to a reader of one single codex, 1987, pp. 383f.

as intellect and letters. However, the myth of this holy marriage, Danuta Shanzer supposes, was rather of an eschatological nature: a story about the fallen human soul's divine redemption. The same esoteric theme permeates a famous intermezzo in one of Martianus' probable models, Apuleius' novel *Metamorphoses*, namely the story of tormented love between Cupid (Amor), the god of love, and Psyche, daughter of a king. It ends with the girl being snatched up to heaven to be wedded to her beloved, accompanied by the gods and the Muses (6.23– 24).[1] Luciano Lenaz, who has edited the second book of the *Marriage*, remarks that Mercury too possesses a considerable amount of arcane wisdom, while presenting convincing evidence that the apotheosis of Philology is based on or alludes to mysterious initiation rites in Late Antique Rome.[2]

Mercury is delighted with Apollo's proposal, appoints several *disciplinae* (the Liberal Arts) to his household and begins to educate himself so as to be able to live up to his intended bride. First of all, however, the arrangement requires the assent of a divine council. There Jupiter, the king of the gods, pleads for Mercury to be granted his wish. He extols his son as "my trust, my speech, my beneficence, and my true genius, the loyal messenger and spokesman of my mind, my sacred honour" (1.92), *nostra ille fides, sermo, benignitas / ac verus genius, fida recursio / interpresque meae mentis, honos sacer*. His words of praise are indicative of the eclecticism of this work, where the gods can be identified with the planets and the natural elements as well as with a range of virtues, skills, psychological qualities or Neo-Platonic principles. Here, we see how Jupiter expects Mercury, addressed as *sermo* (speech or eloquence), to be his spokesman before humans or other gods, that is, to translate the messages of his lofty intellect, *mens* (the normal Latin equivalent of the Greek *nous*), into words.[3] This enthusiastic announcement of the seamless union between contemplation and discourse suggests yet another alliance of wisdom with eloquence, forming an unspoken argument in favour of the marriage in question. Not surprisingly, the

---

1 I follow J.A. Hanson's Loeb edition of *Metamorphoses* 1989. Cf. Shanzer 1986, pp. 65f. Gabriel Nuchelmans, 1957, has demonstrated how Cicero's juxtaposition of *sapientia* with *eloquentia* in the opening of *On Invention* (1.1.1–1.4.5) was to be recycled throughout the Middle Ages, from the Carolingian era onwards regularly associated with the *Marriage*.
2 Martianus Capella 1975, pp. 6–26, 101–20.
3 Franz Eyssenhardt presents another interesting variant in his 1866 edition of the *Marriage*, where Jupiter's praise of Mercury ends with the words *interpresque meae mentis ho nous acer*, characteristically linking the Latin *mens* to the Greek *nous*. Stahl, Johnson and Burge translate in agreement with this wording: "spokesman of my mind, the sacred Nous", though they substitute "sacred", *sacer*, for Eyssenhardt's 'sharp' or 'swift', *acer*; since I prefer Willis's *interpresque meae mentis, honos sacer*, I have revised their translation accordingly.

proposal is accepted by acclamation, after which preparations can be started for the wedding.

In the second book of his work, Martianus emphasizes even more the hermetic implications of his main topic, the marriage, exposing it to symbolic interpretation based on esoteric knowledge (2.101–05). Philology is told what awaits her among the Olympians. In order to test her proposed husband's suitability, she arranges a clever maths test: she sets her mind on finding out the numerical value of Mercury's name. Rather than relying on designations that can vary among different peoples and rituals (say Hermes among the Greeks, Mercury among the Romans), she focuses on the name Jupiter gave his son at his birth, known only through "the ingenuities of the Egyptians" (2.102), *Aegyptiorum commenta*, that is – as the reader is expected to understand – Thot. Philology thus links Mercury to the god of writing and arithmetic in ancient Egypt, spelt *thōuth* by the Greeks who sure enough had associated him with Hermes. Now, from each end of this name, Philologia extracts the letter θ (*thēta*), which translates into the most perfect of all numbers among the Greeks, that is 9, as perfect a figure for Martianus as later for Dante. To this double *thēta* she adds the letter that is worshipped in all temples for its "cubic solidity", ω (*ō mega*) or 800, where 8 = 2 raised to the power of three, just as 100 = 10 raised to the second power, hence (as Martianus' readers ought to understand) its *soliditas cybica*.

Finally, Philology concentrates on the letter that the wise man of Samos (Pythagoras) interpreted as a sign of "the dual ambiguity of mortal fate", *bivium mortalitatis*, referring to the Greek capital letter Y (numerical value: 400), which was supposed to graphically depict a crossroads, in turn symbolizing the parting of ways in life. No sooner said than done: 2 x 9 + 800 + 400 = 1218, a number that, after being duly divided by 9 (according to the venerable rule of nine), leaves Philology with a remainder of 3. After a corresponding mathematical operation, her own name results in a remainder of 4. She reaches the conclusion that she and Mercury, judging from the divine number of seven, are made for each other. The complex mathematical calculation required to reach such a simple conclusion and to arrive at such simple numerals, which probably also suggest the seven liberal arts, is most likely intended to be a parody of the learned Pythagoreans' unconstrained excesses in the field of numerology.[1]

---

[1] For the description of Philology's arithmetic operations, originally clarified by the sixteen-year-old (!) Hugo Grotius 1599, I rely on Ramelli's commentary, Martianus Capella 2001, pp. 779f.

As if by chance, Philology's dear mother, Phronesis (Wisdom), rushes into her daughter's bedroom to dress her for the wedding, whereupon the Muses join the party for collective celebration. The last of them, Thalia, directs a hymn to the bridal couple, hinting at the universal significance of this marriage whereby the eloquent god will be united with the learned girl (2.126):

```
31  Nunc, nunc beantur artes,
    quas sic sacratis ambo,
    ut dent meare caelo,
    reserent caducis astra
35  ac lucidam usque ad aethram
    pia subvolare vota.
    per vos vigil decensque
    nus mentis ima complet;
    per vos probata lingua
40  fert glorias per aevum.
    vos disciplinas omnes
    ac nos sacrate Musas.
```

Now, now the arts are blessed, which you two so sanctify that they allow men to rise to heaven and open to them the stars and allow holy prayers to fly up to the clear sky. Through you the mind's intelligence, alert and noble, fills the uttermost depth, through you proven eloquence brings everlasting glory. You bless all subjects, and you bless us, the Muses.

Thalia's outpourings form the climax of the Muses' congratulations to Philology and her (still absent) bridegroom, a lyrical piece in startling contrast to the girl's recent pedestrian exhibition of Pythagorean learning, a song of praise permeated by a utopian mood – which makes for somewhat melancholy reading in view of the state of European culture for centuries to come. The hymn expects the divine *nous* to permeate the human intellect, yet another Platonized version of the imminent wedding. By virtue of this blessed marriage, the arts, *disciplinae* – including the Muses' fields of responsibility – will flourish, Thalia hopes, to such an extent that mortal beings, *caduci*, will be able to reach the ether with their prayers. She thus envisions an apotheosis in the sign of both Neo-Platonic philosophy and the time-honoured ideal of *paideia*.

Thalia's hymn is characteristic of the philosophical or even religious dimension of Martianus' work, notwithstanding its close ties to Menippean satire. Seven of the nine books of the *Marriage* are devoted to the arts that the marriage is about to bless (*beantur artes*). The author wants to present their accumulated learning to his readers, thereby indicating the conditions for the eagerly awaited flourishing of culture in the brave new world of the fifth century. In that sense, Martianus' intention is didactic. And precisely for that very reason he is anxious to make his exposition as attractive as possible. Thus he relies on a set of deities, concepts and stock legends borrowed from classical tradition, with the aim of preparing for pleasant as well as instructive reading. Martianus exploits well-known personifications and standardized attributes. Accordingly, his story of Philology's and Mercury's marriage seems to meet the criteria for the kind of *narratio fabulosa* that Macrobius recently had launched, where "a decent and dignified conception of holy truths, with respectable events and characters, is presented beneath a modest veil of allegory". Still, Martianus gives his own twist to this didactic-mythological genre, partly because his Menippean satire challenges any strict distinction between jest and dignity, and partly because he does not withhold the true "philosophical" sense of his work 'in the rabbit burrows of figuration', as Macrobius would have it (above, pp. 359, 365). Quite the reverse: he brings out its meaning under a very thin layer of figuration, expressly commented upon and even called into question within the frame story of his work.

For the purpose of establishing further affinities with Macrobius *Commentary*, Martianus' *Marriage* might well be characterized as yet another case of a cultural rescue operation. It would have seemed important to muster the remains of classical education in times of crisis, for this is how most intellectuals experienced the aftermath of the fall of Rome into barbarian hands in 410.[1] This urgent need to conduct an inspection of the survivals of ancient learning is intriguingly reflected when the priestess Athanasia (Immortality) examines Philology's body before the wedding ceremony; she finds it swollen and advises the girl to throw up what is filling her. In a hallucinatory scene, perhaps inspired by some rite of purgation from the ancient mysteries, the girl's vomiting "turned into a stream of writings of all kinds" (2.136): *in omnigenum copias convertitur litterarum*. A series of scrolls and volumes in every possible language stream forth from the maiden's mouth, some of papyrus, others bound in linen or skin, a few inscribed on linden bark. Some were written in holy ink, the letters of which were thought to depict living beings: evidently a reference to the legendary learning and hieroglyphics of Egypt, which even in ancient Greece was considered the origin of all civilization.

Athanasia now has these sacred messages carved into stone, to be hidden in a cave at the site of Egypt's venerable shrines. Meanwhile, a number of girls, the Muses as well as the Arts, save what they can from Philology's vomit, including instructions for geometry and music. This scenario seems open to various inter-

---

[1] Danuta Shanzer even allows herself an allusion to T.S. Eliot's desolate vision of European postwar civilization, when she describes the *Marriage* "as a *summa* of pagan knowledge, religious and secular, handed down by Martianus to his son, or perhaps even as fragments shored against his ruin. Martianus may have fancied himself as the last of a line of learned men", 1986, p. 28.

pretations. On the one hand, its drastic or low-styled concreteness within the framework of such a high (divine) context might well make the reader suspicious, especially in view of the *Marriage*'s Menippean impetus. Perhaps the flow of books is meant to offer an ironic foretaste of the information the Arts will impart in the following books? In that case, Philology will, as it were, get her own vomit (the accumulated knowledge and skills of the liberal arts) back as a wedding present. On the other hand, it would be quite possible, in line with the work's pedagogical or pseudo-utopian purposes, to interpret the vomiting as an allegory for the admittedly precious but undigested and heterogenous mass of erudition that Philology now has to rid herself of before entering the way towards the stars: an allegory, that is, for the somewhat abstruse or disconnected pieces of classical learning that the girl will soon be able to enjoy anew, refined and systematized within the cycle of the liberal arts.[1]

When the virgin has thrown up this virtual library, duly blessed by Athanasia's mother Apotheosis, the time has come for her to enter the carriage, watched over by the acoustically yoked Work and Love, *Labor* and *Amor*, which will take her up to heaven. It is a stately procession that sets out, with the Muses at the head, towards "the summit of the citadel of the sky" (2.146), *ad culmina arcis aeriae*. There, Philology is met by Juno, who shows her the world of the ether with all the planets, alternately called "gods" or "inhabitants of heaven", which mysteriously constitute the hidden causes of everything (2.150), *ipsi dicuntur dii, et caelites alias perhibentur causarumque latentium arcana componunt*. The goddess refers of course to the celestial bodies' influences on earthly matters, not merely a tenet of fortune-telling soothsayers but a crucial theme in Western philosophical speculation and literature from *Timaeus* to Dante's *Comedy* (and later). It is indeed a profusely populated space that is presented to the wide-eyed Philology before she continues her journey. She quickly puts the seven planets and the fixed stars behind her, giving herself time to sing the praises of the sun in a syncretic hymn, and finally leaves our cosmos, "the whole mass and fabric of heaven" (2.201), *totam caeli molem machinamque*, to arrive at the frontier of the intelligible world of the Empyrean.

There she kneels and offers up a silent prayer, "concentrating the whole attention of her mind", *tota mentis acie coartata*, modelled on ancient ritual, while she "uttered certain words with her inner voice", that is, the voice of her mind:

---

[1] Luciano Lenaz discusses at length the vomiting of Philosophy as a version of the Late Antique theme 'purge of learning': human or worldly knowledge must be forgone when the virgin is about to behold the true light in heaven, Martianus Capella 1975, pp. 23–25. His assumption would be hard to reconcile, however, with the fact that the Arts recycle this established learning throughout the remainder of the work (Books III–IX).

vocabula quaedam voce mentis inclamans. Martianus' focus is obviously on *mens* here, indicating the increasingly Neo-Platonic character of the vocabulary in the second book of his work. The future bride pays reverence to "the presiding deities of the world of pure understanding, and to their ministers, to whom the powers of the sensible world owe veneration, and to the entire universe contained by the depth of the infinite Father; then she invoked those certain three gods" (2.202–04).[1] Her invocation is probably directed at the Neo-Platonic triad we have met as the One, followed by its two foremost hypostases, Intellect and Soul. Philology's journey to heaven is undeniably depicted with a certain pathos, and she actually reaches her goal, the uttermost edge of the universe, moreover with an explicit reference to "the mysteries of Plato" (2.205), *Platonis mysteria*. Relihan rightly observes that the remaining books' exposition of the Homeric assembly of gods and their prolix lectures by and about the seven Arts, seem a long drawn-out anti-climax after this fervent adoration at the ultimate fringe of the universe.[2] Yet I cannot help but think that Martianus' text, even in this sublime episode, poises on the verge of irony with its *quodam, quaedam, quosdam* and *quandam* ('in a certain Empyrean', 2.202, *empyrio quodam!*), indicative of the satirical – and ambiguous – mode that intermittently surfaces throughout the *Marriage*.

Thus at the end of the second book, Philology has reached her journey's end. A white-hot flood of milk runs up: the Milky Way, possibly an allusion to the Ciceronian *Dream of Scipio* that we have seen Macrobius analyse as an instance of a mythical tale.[3] This is the place for the wedding which will now be celebrated, a matchless feast with syncretic ingredients. The Muses strike up a song, and the Olympians come together along with renowned half-gods such as Hercules, Castor and Pollux as well as a magnificent host of angelic beings, *angelicique populi pulcherrima multitudo*. Another group of wedding guests turns out to be "the souls of the ancients who had attained celestial bliss", *animaeque praeterea beatorum veterum:* divinely gifted Greek and Roman poets like the legendary Linus, Homer or the seer from Mantua, *Mantuanus vates*, that is, Virgil. Their joint presence certainly vouches for a splendid party, but Martianus' characteristic mixture of styles and ambiguous mode surfaces once again. The tableau soon becomes parodic, or at least slightly comic, with all its astonishingly mixed and unconnected activities, suggested by means of predictable or over-

---

[1] "Intellectualis mundi praesules deos eorumque ministros sensibilis sphaerae potestatibus venerandos, universumque totum infinibilis patris profunditate coercitum, poscitque quosdam tres deos".
[2] Relihan 1993, pp. 147f.
[3] It should be added, though, that the association of the Milky Way to the Olympian gods is much older than Macrobius. Cf. the overture to the *Metamorphoses*, Ovid 1971, 1.168–71.

explicit attributes: in the crowd appear Orpheus playing his lyre, Plato and Archimedes rolling golden spheres, a fluorescent Heraclitus, a dripping wet Thales, a Democritus surrounded with atoms, a Pythagoras pondering on celestial numbers, an Aristotle on the lookout for his *Entelechia* – the philosopher's term for, roughly, actuality or realization (in contrast to potentiality) – among the heavenly regions, and, to round off with a stylish instance of rhetorical *zeugma*, an Epicurus carrying roses, violets and "all the allurements of pleasure", *totae illecebrae voluptatum*, in his arms. A crowd of Greeks are singing discordantly, perhaps another hint at the bewildering cultural heritage from Hellas (cf. our remarks on Philology's vomiting above), soon to be overcome by the "harmonious songs of the Muses", *Musarum carmina concinentum*, which had initiated and will now conclude Martianus' presentation of the blessed wedding congregation (2.207–13).

Here, at the climax of the work, when Mercury steps forward to show his gifts to his bride, foremost among them the learned servant maids he has engaged, Martianus interrupts his narrative by directly addressing his readers. A great part of the fable has now been told, he declares, *transcursa, lector, parte magna fabulae*, laudably – but hardly credibly – implying that he does not intend to be long-winded. Dawn breaks, so he reverts to the frame story, which on closer inspection is executed on three levels corresponding to as many narrative situations, the first two oral and the last sustained by writing, all (probably) set at night time:[1]

- In the first place, as we have seen, the whole of the story is related by Satire to Martianus on a winter's night.
- Secondly, this story is in turn retold by the narrator to his recalcitrant son, as is evident from the beginning and the end of the work (1.2, 9.997).
- Thirdly, at this point of the *Marriage* – the final lines of the second book – the narrator addresses the reader while representing himself as composing his work in the early hours of the dawn.

We shall soon see that the narrator and his Muse, Satire, may have quite different opinions about their story and how it should be told. On repeated occasions, they embark on more or less heated discussions on this topic, a skirmish that in fact colours all three levels of the frame story.

When Martianus now turns to his reader, he emphasizes his actual toil with pen and paper or, more correctly, quill and papyrus. If, at the second story level,

---

[1] Sabine Grebe comments on the frame story's different levels (or stages) in her voluminous habilitation thesis 1999, pp. 24, 848–57.

he reads aloud from one or more scrolls that he is "unfolding" (in accordance with the literal understanding of *explicabo* suggested above), at this third level he rather appears as a writer, filling column after column, *pagina*, of a scroll, emphatically aware of the importance of finishing his work in time.[1] Thus the author enacts the writing of his work – its expansion across his scroll(s) – within the work itself (2.219 – 20):

> 5   Ac ni rosetis purpuraret culmina
>   Aurora primo <et> convenustans halitu
>   surgens fenestras dissecaret lumine,
>   adhuc iugata compararet pagina
>   quocumque ducta largiorem circulum.
> 10 nunc ergo mythos terminatur; infiunt
>   artes libelli qui sequentes asserent.
>   nam fruge vera omne fictum dimovent
>   et disciplinas annotabunt sobrias
>   pro parte multa nec vetabunt ludicra.
> 15 habes quid instet, si potestas caelitum
>   faveantque Musae et chelys Latoia.

> If the dawn were not touching the rooftops with purple, making them beautiful with its first breath as it rises and cleaves the windows with light, page after page would make my story longer to cover every aspect. So now the mythical part [*mythos*] is ended; the books which follow set forth the arts. With true intellectual nourishment they put aside all fable [*omne fictum*] and for the most part explain serious studies, without however avoiding entertainment. Now you know what will follow, given the goodwill of the heavenly powers and the Muses and the lyre of Latona's son.

And in fact, the next seven books of the work are devoted one to each of the Liberal Arts. Mercury's seven servant maids will now have Philology as their mistress: first, Grammar, Dialectic and Rhetoric, then Geometry, Arithmetic, Astronomy and Music, in that order. As if to deliberately shatter the *Marriage's* thin layer of fictionality, the author informs us that his story of the divine wedding, the *mythos*, is completed. In that "mythical part" of his work, he has devoted a considerable amount of attention to the Muses, and he still hopes for their assistance, but now he announces a sharp break in his narrative. Fiction reaches as far as this, up to the author's extravagant account of the galactic feast, but no

---

1 "The expression *iugata pagina* indicates that Martianus still uses the classical book scroll, where the single sheets are fastened to each other, resulting in a *rotulus* various meters long", ibid., p. 850. In fact, the scrolls consisting of sheets attached to each other would under extreme circumstances reach a length of thirty metres, in which case their circumference increased dramatically. Cf. Lenaz' comment in Martianus Capella 1975, p. 233.

further. A plethora of fictional devices – such as the age-old Olympian pantheon, the practice of impersonation and the fable of the wedding, reminiscent of Apuleius – are employed throughout Books I and II, characteristically beginning and ending with the Muses, operative all the way through this first part of the *Marriage*. That is why this work was to have such a powerful impact on twelfth-century writers such as Bernardus Silvestris and Alan of Lille, both of whom composed philosophical fables focused on the liberal arts, in Latin prose mixed with verse. By virtue of works such as Bernardus' *Cosmographia* and Alan's *Anticlaudianus*, allegorical (or integumental) fictionality made its comeback on a grand scale in Western European literature. The final lines in the second book of the *Marriage*, on the other hand, seem to signal its demise. The time for *mythos* is over, and all *fictum* will have to recede in favour of 'true nourishment', *frux vera*. The very wording might remind us of another North African countryman of Martianus, the most influential of them all, Augustine, who repeatedly had complained about the malnutrition caused by unwary immersion in the world of make-believe.

To sum up, in Books I and II of the *Marriage*, Martianus had converted the main approach of ancient allegorical explanation, to interpret legendary heroes or gods as virtues, vices or natural forces, into a creative allegorical method (as Prudentius had already done in his slightly earlier *Psychomachia*). All the principal actors of his work are epitomes of ideas or notions, the majority of which are of a Neo-Platonic extraction. They embody certain natural, cosmic, psychological or cognitive qualities, sometimes in combination with each other, framed as either antique deities or personified concepts. They form the allegorical *dramatis personae* we have encountered in the first two books of the *Marriage*, all of whom now, however, according to the author, must give way to *frux vera*. As was the case with Macrobius' *narratio fabulosa*, this curious display of allegorism could perhaps be interpreted as an answer to the triumphant Christians' criticism of pagan religiosity. In the *Marriage*, classical mythology was turned into a staged revel or masque, the illusion of which was readily scattered by the author himself: the old *fabulae* thrown up – to use Martianus' own metaphor – as volume upon volume.

In this respect, too, the final lines of the second book are significant. If the light of dawn did not break, the author declares, he would keep scribbling all over the sheets fastened together, *iugata pagina*. Judging from this concession, Martianus might be the first author in European literature who explicitly stems his flow of writing. Perhaps he even emerges as the first (fictional, to be sure) graphomaniac. He knows or feels it himself: a *mythos* of the elaborate, ornamented and speculative kind that he had implemented may, in theory, be varied and embellished for as long as he likes. Hence it should be brought to an end. It is time for the Arts to take the stage.

Showy Fiction, Naked Learning

To follow the polymath's personified Arts in detail through the *Marriage* would involve a deep immersion into the library thrown up by Philology, an examination that would burst the seams of this presentation. However, something should be said about Grammar and Rhetoric, the two ladies who seem most pertinent to the issue of fictionality. At the very beginning of the third book, devoted to Grammar, the author cheerfully departs from his proud declaration on the previous page. The "mythical part" of the *Marriage*, it turns out, is only finalized in the sense that the story referred to by the work's title is brought to an end. Thus Martianus leaves the mode of action for that of instruction. Nevertheless, his consistent impersonation and profuse ornamentation must go on, thereby ensuring the unbroken presence of fictionality – theatricality – in his work (3.221–22):[1]

```
1    Rursum Camena parvo
     phaleras parat libello
     et vult amicta fictis
     commenta ferre primum,
5    memorans frigente vero
     nil posse comere usum,
     vitioque dat poetae
     infracta ferre certa,
     lasciva dans lepori
10   et paginam venustans,
     multo illitam colore.
     "atquin prioris ille
     titulus monet libelli
     mythos ab ore pulsos
15   Artesque vera fantes
     voluminum sequentum
     praecepta comparare."
     at haec iocante rictu
     "nil mentiamur" inquit
```

---

[1] The final line of 2.222 is defective. Here it is given in the conjecture from Eyssenhardt's edition 1866, in accordance with the topic of getting dressed/undressed, or appearing ornate/unadorned, that permeates this exordium of the *Marriage's* third book. Willis prefers *fugis iugabo ludum*, read as a dialogue, in Stahl *et alii:* "'Are you running away?' 'I am joining in the game'".

```
20    "et vestiantur Artes.
      an tu gregem sororum
      nudum dabis iugandis,
      et sic petent Tonantis
      et caelitum senatum?
25    aut si tacere cultum
      placet, ordo quis probatur?"
      "certe loquentur illae
      quicquid fuat docendum,
      habitusque consequentur
30    asomato in profatu."
      "haec nempe ficta vox est,
      et devius promissi es;
      cur ergo non fateris
      ni figminis figura
35    nil posse comparari?"
      his me Camena vicit.
      nudis iugabo ludum.
```

Once again in this little book the Muse prepares her ornaments and wants to tell fabricated stories at first, remembering that utility cannot clothe the naked truth; she regards it as a weakness of the poet to make straightforward and undisguised statements, and she brings a light touch to literary style and adds beauty to a page that is already heavily colored.

"But," I cried, "in the previous book notice is given that the myths have been put away and that the precepts in the volumes which follow are a work of those Arts which tell that which is the truth."

But with a laugh she joked at this and said: "Let us tell no lies, and yet let the Arts be clothed. Surely you will not give the band of sisters naked to the bridal couple? Surely they will not go like that before the senate of the Thunderer and the heavenly gods? To say no more about embellishment, what is to be the program?"

"Surely let them speak on their own teachings, and let them be clothed in incorporeal utterance."

"Now you are deceiving me and are not consistent with your promise; why do you not admit that your work cannot be composed except by the use of imagery?" With these words the Muse got the better of me. I will join a show to my naked subject.

Here, an intense dialogue takes place between the author and his Muse, the *Camena*, probably Satire (who has told the fable of the divine marriage to him). She bickers with the author, who in the previous *metrum* – as we remember – had promised the reader, from now on, to impart plain instruction in the seven arts, cancelling all *mythos* in his work ("So now the mythical part is ended"). The Muse refuses to give up her sway over his text, disapproving of a dry and boring presentation in which utility, *usus*, and straightforward statements, *infracta certa*, would predominate at the expense of ornamentation. Her main argument is that lies are one thing (which we should do without), but dressing up the Arts is quite another (which we cannot do without). While the author sets out to devote the subsequent exposition to forthright teaching, she is anxious to safeguard the good old combination of *docere* with *delectare*.

Martianus' Muse illustrates in exemplary fashion the Late Antique tendency, vital to this chapter, to correlate fictionality with embellishment and figuration. The reference to the ornaments for her breast in line 2 above, *phalerae*, a term frequently associated with the adornments of language, seems characteristic. This whole passage is virtually studded with pointers to the elegance, brilliance and colour of literary style.[1] The Camena basically maintains the right to unrestrained *elocutio* or, strictly speaking, *cultus* (garb, attire, ornament), in the books to come. She even links fiction to figuration in one and the same genitive metaphor: *figminis figura*. When she wishes to continue letting "the Arts be clothed", her strategy has less to do with the world of imagination than with eloquent *festivitas*. The implication of her argument is that we should expect to meet the liberal Arts embellished by means of imagery or, on a more concrete level, as instances of "personification" (in Greek: *prosōpopoiia*), in the pseudo-Ciceronian *Ad Herennium* registered as a figure of thought, *conformatio* (4.66.53), and in the truly Ciceronian *On the Orator*, recycled by Quintilian, as *personarum ficta inductio* (3.53.205).[2] Since this device as a rule implies a series of adjuncts such as speeches, escorts, clothes, ornaments and attributes, it is liable to expand into a full-scale allegory.

The narrator makes a last attempt to prove his point, putting forward the barely translatable proposal *habitusque consequentur / asomato in profatu* (lines 29–30): he insists that his Arts will be dressed up in "incorporeal utterance". They are to appear as disembodied conceptual creatures, devoid of the cloaks of figuration, perhaps as a result – as Leupin would have it – of the logic of "a modern, Christianized science", without the need for rhetorical embroidery.[3] In short, Martianus would prefer to go straight to the point. But the clever Muse immediately observes that he expresses his purist opposition to figures by means of a figure: *habitus*, 'costume' or 'dress'. Admittedly, this term is ambiguous. In this particular context, it should be noted that classical Roman

---

[1] As for the *phalerae*, see Janson 1964, pp. 140f.
[2] The Danish Latinist Brian Møller Jensen has brought to my attention that it is precisely Cicero who is responsible for one of the most efficient and well-known applications of the figure of *prosopopoeia* in Latin literature, namely in his speech for the defence of Caelius, *Pro Caelio*, Cicero 1960, where it is labelled *persona introducta*, 35.
[3] Leupin 2003, p. 82.

rhetoric commonly employed it to designate the style or tone of language.[1] However, since the present dispute of the *Marriage* concerns the possible clothing of the Arts (*et vestiantur Artes*), the concrete or physical meaning of *habitus* seems more important in this argument. As a consequence, Martianus seems to be guilty of a double paradox: a) he proposes, literally, to "clothe" his subject, the Arts, in disembodied (clear, transparent) speech, and b) he argues for unadorned discourse by means of rhetorical adornment (a trope). His Muse thus catches him with a flagrant contradiction, as if she were distantly foreboding the schemes of late twentieth-century deconstruction, wishing to detect traces of rhetorical stratagems in authors who in the name of authenticity believe they can do without rhetoric. Be that as it may, she emerges as the winner of this debate: the Arts should not need to walk naked through the work.

If the Muse's victory signals a triumph for the fictional manner in the *Marriage*, it is on one specific condition: that it is freed from every suspicion of lying, *nil mentiamur*. The Arts' costume should only serve to provide a certain lustre to the school disciplines of Late Antiquity. Supposedly, this purely decorative application of *figmenta* was intended to neutralize the suspicion of unreliability in literary texts that troubled many contemporary readers, particularly Christians. Thus Martianus links up with the poetics characteristic of the period, very much determined by rhetorical considerations. With hindsight, this development seems logical. As poets and grammarians increasingly concentrated on the third branch of rhetoric, matters of style and verbal adornment, fictional presentation was potentially released from the issue of alternative or competing realities – from its "double-faced" project, as the early Augustine would have it – in order to merge with figuration: *figminis figura*. This seems to be the significance of the key passages we have examined in the transition from the second to the third book of Martianus' work. *Mythos*, the fable of the holy wedding and its Olympian management, had done its job in the *Marriage*, but that does not imply a plain rejection of the fictional manner in favour of factual ("naked") exposition. Instead, Martianus will stick to impersonation throughout his work. It is this kind of allegorical "show" (*ludus*) – static, accumulative, arranged in serial tableaux – which from now on will characterize the *Marriage*.

In the introduction to this chapter I have, in broad terms, tried to sketch the cultural-historical background of this development: the scholarly and aristocratic literary culture of Late Antiquity, where the old mythology was as diligently

---

[1] Cicero thus makes his Crassus introduce the three styles of speech in *On the orator*: "If you also want to hear about general character and tone of diction", 3.52.199, *si habitum orationis etiam et quasi colorem aliquem requiritis*.

explored as ever before, not only among pagan writers, without necessarily being believed in.[1] This process runs parallel to, or presupposes, a similar development in rhetoric, which had once enjoyed such triumphs in the *agora* of Pericles' democratic Athens or in the Forum of Cicero's republican Rome. As the real power in the Roman Empire had been transferred to the Emperor's person, and the Senate had lost its former political integrity, the civic importance of classical eloquence had diminished. Even though it remained the cornerstone in a public administrator's career, it was subjected to a "literaturization" (I borrow the term from George A. Kennedy) centred on written composition, imitation of models and an increasing interest in style; of rhetoric's five main parts, the third, *elocutio*, became progressively dominant, so that the whole discipline sometimes gravitated towards a doctrine of figuration.[2]

Late Antique rhetoric is in many respects a far cry from Cicero's paradigm, both from his early work *On Invention*, where *inventio* or schemes and 'places' of argumentation are the *prima ac maxima pars rhetoricae* (2.59.178), and from his mature dialogue *On the Orator*, where eloquence is associated with Roman civic spirit and philosophical interests. A little less than 150 years later, Quintilian – a faithful Ciceronian indeed – already reflects the changing conditions for Roman eloquence, precisely in his (conservative) reaction to them. He turned passionately against what he perceived as an ongoing feminization of rhetoric. Contemporary practitioners of the art neglected the traditional masculine substance of argumentation; conversely, they cared too much for exquisite feminine elegance in their speech. Orations were nowadays merely composed with the aim to amuse and to provide sensual pleasure, *voluptas*, Quintilian complained. He yearned for the good old verbal duels in the Forum, and he even compared the present upholders of the discipline with slave dealers who had their young male goods castrated, so that these would look and sound like women: an unnatural and reprehensible custom (5.12.17–22)!

Now, several hundred years later, the Visigoths had sacked Rome, a new religion had taken over the former Empire, and the literaturization of eloquence had been completed. This development should also be seen in the light of slow coming changes in the Roman media landscape. The reading of literature was normally still done aloud, since textual culture was dependent on *scriptura continua*, script without punctuation or spacing between words, which was the rule in continental Latin until the Carolingian era.[3] But the material conditions

---

[1] Cf. Cameron 2004, pp. 342f.
[2] Kennedy 1999, pp. 129f.
[3] See Saenger 1997, p. 4.

for literacy were indubitably subject to momentous modifications. During the last centuries before our era, a new writing material had begun to replace papyrus and wax: parchment, which was made by treating animal hide and was invented – according to Pliny the Elder – in the city of Pergamon in Asia Minor (present-day Turkey). By and by, thanks to increasingly advanced technological developments, it was possible to use both sides of calfskin, goatskin or sheepskin for writing, whereupon the first bound 'books' in our sense of the word, *codici*, saw the light of day, probably on Roman territory in the first century BCE. It is true that the established scroll continued to dominate book production for another two or three centuries, but during Martianus' lifetime the new era's *codex* had begun to eclipse it, not least thanks to Christianity's early and persistent investment in the medium, first on papyrus and from the fourth century onwards on parchment. Even if the new material was not necessarily cheaper or more convenient (as earlier research liked to claim), it would certainly do as an innovative and religious-politically powerful alternative to the Jews' venerable Torah scroll and the pagans' ancient *volumina*.[1]

The *Marriage* introduces Grammar, with an implicit reference to the Greek word for 'letter', *gramma*, as an old woman, born in Memphis (in Egypt, the cradle of the art of writing), equipped with a writing case, a penknife, ink, wax tablets and 'glued pieces of Nilotic shrub', *Niloticae fruticis collemata*, a metonym for the papyrus sheets made of rushes glued together to make scrolls (3.225). The fact that Grammar is furnished with, as it were, an out-of-date medium, the papyrus scroll, only helps to strengthen the impression of her Egyptian aura and ancient wisdom. Practically all references to writing technology in the *Marriage* allude in fact, more or less indirectly, to the medium of the scroll. There is the introduction's literal 'unrolling', *explicabo*, of the story, there is the *iugata pagina* that threatens to form an unwieldy roll at the end of the second book (2.219), there is the paraphernalia of Grammar, there is "the scroll's red staff, almost hidden by its many folds", *voluminis / vix umbilicum multa opertum fascea*, wrapped up by Rhetoric's swollen eloquence at the end of Book V (5.566), and, finally, the work's concluding mention of nine *volumina* (9.997). Thus, Martianus' *Marriage* alludes to the expanding writing culture of Late Antiquity, borrowing prestige from ancient – originally Egyptian – media technology.

Grammar launches on a long exposition of her art until Minerva interrupts her, since all the gods have got bored with her tirades on the word classes.

---

[1] One of the best introductions to ancient (and particularly early Christian) book production is still Skeat 1969. For updated overviews, see Gamble 1995, pp. 42–81, and (considering Augustine's writings) Stroumsa 2012.

The wedding risks ending in one big yawn. Martianus' self-irony never lets him down. Minerva tells Grammar to spare the celestial senate from her all too elementary information about solecisms, barbarisms, tropes, *metaplasmi* and figures of speech (3.326). Some of the topics she is forced to leave out are soon taken up by Dialectic in her discussion of *aliena verba*, metaphors, elucidated with standard examples from Cicero's or Quintilian's works (4.359). Dialectic goes on skilfully explaining the logical works of Aristotle but finally, setting out on an account of the fallacies, becomes too convoluted and obscure for the wedding party. Boredom threatens once again; the Olympian bridegroom (who probably has other things on his mind) becomes impatient and signals to Minerva to put a stop to Dialectic's exposition.

Now it is time for Rhetoric to enter the stage, attired in a splendid robe that "was adorned with the light of all kinds of devices and showed the figures of them all, while she had a belt under her breast adorned with the rarest colors of jewels" (5.426), *quod omnium figurarum lumine variatum cunctorum schemata praeferebat; pectus autem exquisitissimis gemmarum coloribus balteatum*. Stahl and Johnson remark in a note that Martianus is punning here, recycling a range of terms that all may be applied to rhetorical ornamentation: the light, *lumen*, stylistic devices and figures of various kinds, *figurae* and *schemata*, colours, *colores*, and jewels, *gemmae*.[1] Evidently, *elocutio* and the doctrine of figuration characterize Rhetoric's appearance from the very start.

Martianus does not miss the chance to demonstrate scholarly learning in this field too; he lets Rhetoric make an extensive examination of all her five traditional parts. From our perspective, what is particularly striking is surely her short exposition on the "direction" of the subject or the case, *ductus causae* (5.470–71). This is a term the author has borrowed from Consultus Fortunatianus, one of the Late Antique *rhetores latini menores*, probably a contemporary of Augustine and, by and large, an important source for the rhetorical section of the *Marriage*. Some possible modern translations of the term might be: course, orientation, conduct or flow.[2] Martianus attempts a definition of *ductus:* 'a pro-

---

[1] Martianus Capella 1977, p. 156.
[2] George A. Kennedy describes the theory of *ductus* as the "most unusual feature" of Fortunatianus' Ars rhetorica and defines it concisely as the "treatment of the orator's intent", 1999, p. 123. Françoise Desbordes derives the concept of *ductus* from the *controversiae figuratae* of rhetorical tradition: it covers "the overall conduct of the speech" with special reference to figuration, veiled discourse, the transference of meaning throughout the text. Thus *ductus*, on the level of discourse, would be the equivalent of tropes on the level of words and of figures on the level of sentences, 1993, pp. 74f. Mary Carruthers devotes a short section to *ductus* in The Craft of Thought, which, citing Martianus, defines the concept as the "flow" of a text: "Indeed, ductus

gressive movement throughout the case, retained under a figure', *agendi per totam causam tenor sub aliqua figura servatus*. In the wake of Fortunatianus, he distinguishes five variants of this overall discursive method: simple, subtle, figurative, oblique and mixed.

In *ductus simplex*, the words reflect the speaker's thoughts. *Subtilis* occurs when the speaker's mind intends A but his words say B, as when someone lies with good intentions. We come across *figuratus* "when modesty forbids us to say something openly because of its obscenity and it is expressed under some other representation, dressed in clothing, as it were", *cum aperte quid dicere prohibet verecundia propter obscena, et significatione alia atque integumentis vestita monstratur*. The fourth type of *ductus*, the "oblique", *oblicus*, is equally interesting: it is implemented when fear prevents us from speaking openly, hence "we show that it must be presented in an underground manner of speaking", *per quosdam fandi cuniculos obicienda monstramus*. Lastly, *mixtus* is defined as a combination of the previous two types, occasioned by shame as well as fear.

Martianus' definition is meant to cover the progressive movement, *tenor agendi*, from beginning to end of a speech or composition. That is why his Rhetoric assigns the five types of *ductus* to *inventio*, the first branch of her discipline, whereas her *colores* apply to single parts of the speech and, accordingly, are treated as devices of style, *elocutio*. Nevertheless, Martianus' *ductus* obviously gravitates towards the doctrine of figuration. His reference to the cover or "clothing" – *integumentum* – of "the figurative" stratagem is particularly striking, as it both recalls Satire's exhortation from the beginning of Book III, "let the Arts be clothed", and forebodes the manifold Chartrian and, in general, High Medieval implementations of this crucial concept in allegorical interpretation. At the same time, of course, Martianus' motivation for this type of *ductus*, modesty or shame due to obscenity, outlines a common cause for metaphors, circumlocutions and euphemisms in Western literature down to the nineteenth century. Even more far-sighted is his indication of the "underground manner of speaking", characteristic of oblique discourse. These *fandi cuniculi*, literally 'rabbit burrows of speech', seem intriguingly reminiscent of Macrobius' *figurarum cuniculi*, 'rabbit burrows of figuration', from the introduction to his *Commentary on the Dream of Scipio* (above, p. 365). However, the two authors' arguments for making truth go underground in oral or written composition differ. Whereas the com-

---

insists upon movement, the con*duct* of a thinking mind on its *way* through a composition", 2000, p. 77. Finally, Fortunatianus' latest editor, Lucia Calboli Montefusco, examines both authors' use of this idea in an article from 2003, where she also detects it – in the simplified sense of "figurative speech" – in Servius, pp. 118–23.

mentator wished to steer clear of the possible profanation of a sacred message, basing his argument on ancient philosophical speculation and mysteries, the polymath envisages a kind of covert speech driven by fear, a conspicuous reminder of the significance of encoded literary language in totalitarian regimes, regional or imperial, well before our modern times.

After having dealt with the figures of speech and tropes crucial to the doctrine of style – a list that medieval writers, who were frequently exposed to the *Marriage* from their early school years onwards, would consult as studiously as Cicero's or Donatus' corresponding inventories – Rhetoric completes her exposition with a brief survey of the various parts of a speech from beginning to end. She divides the second part, *narratio*, into four types: the first three consist of the triad known from Cicero and Quintilian that we have come across several times in this study, *historia*, *fabula* and *argumentum*, to which she adds a kind of statement typical of business or law (5.550). History is to be found in Livy. Mythology, *fabula*, is neither true nor probable, as when Daphne is transformed into a tree. The argument registers not what happened but what might have happened, *quod non facta, sed quae fieri potuerunt*, for example, when a young man in a comedy is afraid of his father and falls in love with a prostitute. Lastly, the commercial or legal type of statement combines history and argument.

The main triad belongs to rhetoric's conventional apparatus – the illustration of *argumentum* with reference to comedy was already used by Cicero – while the particular type of discourse pertinent to law and affairs, *negotialis vel iudicialis assertio*, seems to be Martianus' particular contribution to this taxonomy, perhaps one of the "new things" he refers to in the final paragraph of Book V, where he assures his reader that Rhetoric offers certain *novella* "which former ages overlooked" (5.566), *quae vetustas praeterit*. More importantly, the notions of *fabula* and *argumentum* both seem to describe the author's own narrative procedures in the *Marriage*, though with a peculiar shift towards the new type of allegorical arrangement characteristic of Late Antiquity, reflected on a theoretic level in the doctrine of *ductus* which he could pick up from the period's *rhetores minores*.

On closer inspection, we find that *argumentum*, under the name of its Greek equivalence, *plasma*, appears on two occasions in the *Marriage*, both of them in the ninth and last book devoted to the art of music. The first time is when Harmony promises to account for the planetary hierarchy of gods 'in a shattered fiction' (9.913), *disgregato plasmate*, and the second time – in the work's final lines – when the whole scenario with the seven Arts is presented, somewhat ironically, as if it was enacted 'in a rustic fiction' (9.998), *agresti plasmate*. The variance between the two passages is considerable, but they share their focus on didactic impersonation, hence linking the fictional manner of the *plasma/argumentum* to allegorical exposition. *Fabula*, for its part, in theory neither true nor probable, seems first and foremost to be applied to the *fabella* of the pre-nuptial arrangements in the first two books of the *Marriage*. However, even if this mythological story, from the perspective of Late Antique literary theory, would seem more fantastic and improbable than the work's long drawn-out *argumentum* in Books III–IX, it too is controlled (as we have been able to establish) by the author's allegorical technique.

It turns out, then, that the theory of the *ductus* of an oral or written composition – a continuous account 'retained under a figure' – proves to be a surprisingly adequate instrument for the analysis of Martianus' art. As far as I know, no rhetoric manuals of Late Antiquity ever came any closer to the idea, common in modern literary theory, of allegory's 'different' or alternative way of signifying (cf. the Greek *allēgorein*, to speak differently) as an overall expository practice rather than as eloquent ornamentation, a trope. To be precise, the *Marriage*, like many epithalamia, implements the third type of *ductus*, where figures and periphrases continually cover the material of the work with a (rather transparent) "clothing". But it also relies on the fourth and more arduous variant of *ductus*, the "oblique" or indirect presentation, as when Martianus describes his story of the divine wedding as 'entangled in fastidious conducts' (2.219), *morosis implicata ductibus*, perhaps against the backdrop of the idiosyncratic business of elaborating a blatantly pagan myth about the ennobling of the human soul in a cultural milieu controlled by Vandals.[1] If so, the rhetorical orientation characteristic of the *Marriage* could best be labelled as *mixtus*, a description that goes well, as we shall see, with the 'mixed' inspiration of the work.

Thus the theory of *ductus* is crucial to our understanding of Martianus' achievement. Since it deals with the work as a whole, it does better justice to the particular allegorical character of the *Marriage* than the inventories of tropes which abound in contemporary textbooks of grammar or eloquence. It is, quite simply, better updated. It reminds us of the fact that Martianus was writing in a period of transition. If Shanzer's dating of his work to the later part of the 400s is correct, brilliant poets such as Claudian or Ausonius had been dead for at least fifty years, and Rome's great pagan literature, however admired, however studiously commented on by learned grammarians or quoted by well-read aristocrats, belonged to the past. Its project of interpreting contemporary culture's fundamental ideas, visions or fears had to a large extent been appropriated by Chris-

---

1 Lenaz, however, maintains that *morosi ductus* is not to be taken as a rhetorical term but as a reference to the "roundabouts of the narrative", *ambages narrationis*, Martianus Capella 1975, p. 232. The difference seems, to say the least, subtle.

tian Fathers, poets and preachers. In short, fictional Latin literature found itself in a somewhat awkward situation, squeezed as it were between a glorious past and a precarious present. Against this background, it tended to be framed as a thin foil for encyclopaedic information, cultural theory and linguistic comments. This trend characterizes Macrobius' *Saturnalia*, and we shall soon examine its effects in Fulgentius, but no work mirrors it as closely as Martianus' *Marriage*, whose Muse after the first two books wants to safeguard the fictional staging, while the author himself envisages a plain, matter-of-fact exposition, "incorporeal utterance", *asomato in profatu*. The Muse came off victorious from this debate, as we have seen, but on condition that her fictionality was restricted to figuration, *figminis figura*, in actual fact purely scholarly or didactic allegory. Consequently, as Jon Whitman observes, Martianus aspired, in his peculiar ambiguous and "disordered" manner, to a theory of philosophical fiction that would not be systematically articulated until the *integumentum* theorists of the twelfth century.[1]

*

The battle over the status of fictionality in the text continues throughout the whole of the *Marriage*, and it is typical of Martianus' whimsical style of writing – right through his heavy didacticism – that the polarized positions of the narrator and his Muse prove instable: they might in fact be completely reversed. The author who pleads for a plain and straightforward account against the Muse's artificial devices at the transition between Books II and III will later speak in defence of fiction when Satire seems to have changed course and accuses him of dressing up her *fabella* with various diversions. At this point, the opening of Book VIII, Satire's doubts about where the exposition is heading are, from a classicizing point of view, understandable. After all, her story stages a celestial event on a magnificent scale, mostly set in the Milky Way, the scene of the wedding (and of the ensuing performance of the Arts). Nevertheless, it is presented in widely varying styles. Certain proclamations and descriptions, most of which are connected with the Olympian pantheon, are delivered in the same high-flown tone as we met in the work's introductory invocation of Hymen. Now, in contrast, at the beginning of the eighth book devoted to Astronomy, Martianus ventures on a burlesque digression concerning the bald satyr Silenus who lies snoring, whereupon he is woken up from his drunken stupor, staggers around and is carried off amid peals of laughter from the assembled gods (8.804–05).

This whole scene links up with the antique tradition of low-comedy descriptions of the deities, originating in Homer, which Augustine had criticized so em-

---

[1] Whitman 1987, p. 104.

phatically or even sarcastically in the *City of God*. Confronted with this scenario, Satire – responsible for the *fabella* in the *Marriage*, as we remember from the introduction to the work – finds herself obliged to intervene by scolding the narrator, whom she tirelessly tries to get to behave properly: "You," she says, "Felix, or Capella, or whoever you are, with a sense to match the beast's whose name you bear, are you going out of your mind with the intrusion of this unseemly jesting?" (8.806)[1] Felix was yet another of Martianus' names, and *capella* is the diminutive form of *capra*, the Latin word for 'goat'.

Just as in the introduction to the *Marriage*, then, the narrator is depicted as a babbling fool, this time by the originator of the fable herself, Satire. If she has previously accepted Martianus' habit of insinuating an addition (*adiectio*) or two to her learned story, she now sharply reproaches him for having gone too far with the burlesque Silenus intermezzo. "Enough of that", she tells him, "and hereafter do not try to defend your nonsense or justify your conduct as licence appropriate to a wedding ceremony" (8.807): *apage sis nec postidhac nugales ausus lege hymeneia et culpae velamine licentis obnuberis*. Her rather tortuously worded rebuke probably refers to the particular immoderation associated with the epithalamium genre (cf. Martianus' mention of *nuptialis licentia* in 8.804) but might have a wider bearing too, indicating the "licence" that poets – as we have repeatedly observed – were traditionally granted in Roman literature. By now, it was no longer an attractive option in the eyes of this stern supervisor. As emphatically as Macrobius, she demands moderation and dignity of the mythical story. In the best (or from a modern point of view, possibly the worst) spirit of Late Antiquity, she condemns the *licentia poetica* as a cowardly smoke screen concealing the author's flagrant violation of mandatory decorum.

After this scolding, poor Martianus seems at a loss for an answer; crestfallen, he asks Satire who is going to continue the story next. In answer, she inaugurates Astronomy's book with a splendid lyrical view of the cosmic spectacle, a celestial vision in the grand style, and concludes with an explicit dig at the author, who has proven incapable of managing such distinguished matters appropriately: wouldn't you "rather fashion cheap and silly fictions", she asks him caustically, "than listen to a girl discoursing on the stars" (8.808), *tu fingere ludicra perstas / viliaque astriloquae praefers commenta puellae?* Again, we are reminded of the fact that it is she who tells the work's *fabella* to the diligently scribbling (though unreliable) Martianus, and one of the requirements for a *narratio fabulosa*, as we

---

[1] "Satura illa, quae meos semper curae habuit informare sensus, 'ne tu' ait, 'Felix, vel Capella vel quisquis es, non minus sensus quam nominis pecudalis, huius incongrui risus adiectione desipere vel dementire coepisti. [...]'"

recall from Macrobius' *Commentary*, was the absence of anything that might seem shameful and unworthy of the gods, *turpia et indigna numinibus*. On the basis of such exacting criteria, she has to reject the kind of fiction that appears incompatible, *incongruus*, with her celestial subject.

In the face of this dead serious reprimand from Satire, the narrator cannot help laughing, even though it might be considered unseemly. Apparently he has cheered up, so he refuses to be ashamed of his flippant use of poetic licence, this time by referring to his great predecessors from the Golden and Silver Ages of Latin literature: "Am I to dispense with all imaginary creatures [*figmenta*] and introduce no pleasantry or mirth to relieve the boredom of my readers? Come to your senses, Satire; leave off your tragic ranting, and take a hint from the young Pelignian poet: 'Young lady, take my advice and smile.'" (8.809)[1] Here, the question of genre enters Satire's and Martianus' discussion, raised by the intertextual references. The author's plea for *figmenta* derives supports from an epigram by Martial (2.41), beginning with the line "Laugh if you have any sense, girl, laugh" followed by a reference to "the Paelignian poet" – an allusion to Ovid, born at Sulmona, the ancient Paelignian Sulmo, in Abruzzo.[2] Thus the grand old man of Roman fiction, the author of the marvellous tales of metamorphoses, Ovid, and the notoriously witty epigrammatist Martial are adduced to substantiate the "pleasantry or mirth", that is, 'the union of elegance and fun' that Martianus relishes, *leporis iocique permixtus*, in his rebuttal of Satire's prudish accusations.

With this cunning argument, the narrator makes an ironic point: his Muse, Satire, has let her real nature down. The ancient Menippean satire was in fact *permixta*, a genre that was not only "mixed" as to its form (prose interfoliated with verse) but also in content. It offered plenty of room, Martianus stresses, for "scornful and elegant subtlety", *irrisoria lepidaque versutia*, directed at the poets' customary inflatedness, *vatum tumores*, and it readily abandoned the high style of orators, *cothurnus*, along with other inspired follies, *lymphatica*.[3] As for now, however (this is the narrator's point), when Satire gets upset about staggering Silenus and wants to get rid of "unseemly" inventions, so as to safeguard the unity and decorum of style, she literally appears to be highbrow,

---

[1] "Ergone figmenta dimoveam, et nihil leporis iocique permixti taedium auscultantium recreabit? Paeligni de cetero iuvenis versiculo resipisce, et ni tragicum corrugaris, ride, si sapis, o puella, ride."
[2] "*Ride, si sapis, o puella, ride*" / *Paelignus, puto, dixerat poeta*. Martial probably alludes to some lost poem by Ovid. I quote from D.R. Shackleton Bailey's Loeb edition 1993.
[3] For the dislocation of the meaning of the word *cothurnus* from tragic actors' footwear to bombastic style in general, see Janson 1964, p. 140.

superciliosa, unabashedly oblivious of her Menippean roots. Martianus, for his part, stubbornly defends the mixed form of the work against his Muse's classicizing separation of styles.

Their controversy obviously raises the issue of the work's genre, a question still under debate. In an article from 1981, Haijo Westra analyses the *Marriage's* difficult junction between two discursive "modes", which he identifies as allegory on the one hand, "a sublime mode, anti-ironic in character", and satire on the other hand, ironic and "fundamentally anti-sublime".[1] The elevated tone repeatedly clashes with the mockery throughout the work. Now, Satire has every right to scold the author, in Westra's opinion, since the humour or irony she advocates is, after all, of the elegant and graceful kind, fully in accord with decorum, in contrast to the burlesque tomfoolery of the Silenus episode. This persistent tension between serious content and entertaining presentation eventually became, according to Westra, an "insoluble" problem for Martianus; the dilemma was later to be solved by Boethius in the *Consolation of Philosophy*, where all comic elements in the Menippean vein are suppressed after the first book in favour of a consistently high and serious style throughout the remainder of the dialogue.[2]

Westra cleverly uncovers the conflicting forces in Martianus' narratological framework. However, it remains to be seen if his treatment of the *Marriage* as a *projet raté* really does justice to the work's particular purpose and characteristics, in many respects different from those of the *Consolation*. As far as can be judged, Martianus strikes me as being in full control of his means of expression. He explicitly resorts to the elements of burlesque fiction in Menippean satire, playing them off against the Olympian-cosmic allegory. Furthermore, his implementation of such mockery does not seem limited to softening up the didactic presentation, so as to make it appetizing or easily digested (such metabolic metaphors do seem appropriate in this context). He rather challenges its monopoly in an ambitious, literary experiment. On closer inspection, the only thing that Martianus' voluminous didactic work has in common with Boethius' concise *Consolation* is the Menippean satire's formal mix of verse and prose. Martianus recurrently puts his pedagogical zeal to test, turning his work's sometimes bombastic teaching into a parody of itself, relieving the seriousness of the myth with disarming comments while highlighting its representation as a written artefact. Between the extensive didactic sections of the *Marriage*, he even lets the narrator and his Muse exchange positions in the frame story's ongoing debate on the

---

[1] Westra 1981, p. 199.
[2] Ibid., p. 211.

work's genre, figuration and style, as if to further emphasize the arbitrariness of its literary construction. These intricate twists of composition do not seem to be a problem to Martianus. On the contrary, I would describe them as vital to a good-humoured and clearly intentional destabilization of the main genres that are exploited in the text, namely the mythological *fabella*, starting from the introductory epithalamium, and the didactic exposition.

In a later article, Westra wisely downplayed the notion of the *Marriage*'s mixture of styles as precarious to its author. Here, however, he emphasized all the more strongly his view of the work as a school textbook, spiced with entertaining features in accordance with Horace's recommendations. Consequently, he polemized against Relihan, raising doubts about the latter's interpretation of Martianus' unusual blend of allegory, burlesque and encyclopaedia as "evidence of a deliberate (or unconscious) deconstruction of antique learning".[1] Westra has an obvious distaste for recent attempts to make Martianus a post-modernist *avant la lettre*, and the undeniable success of the *Marriage* in medieval school teaching, based on the work's educational usability, may perhaps strengthen his case. It could be objected, though, that a more curious implementation of Horace's *prodesse/delectare* prescription than this hotchpotch of verbose erudition and mythical festivities within a satirical as well as metafictional frame story is hard to imagine. And, furthermore, that every literary epoch, including the Carolingian or the High Medieval periods, tends to appropriate the work according to its own taste as inexorably as the late twentieth century did. The medieval commentators on the *Marriage* clearly cared little for precisely those metafictional qualities which seem to have elicited the present-day interest in the work, substantiated by scholars such as LeMoine, Relihan and Siegmar Döpp, the last of whom has analysed Martianus' management of the diegetic and extra- or metadiegetic levels of the text in terms of narrative metalepses.[2]

*

The last book of the *Marriage* is devoted to Harmony's monistic and numerological outpourings, a Neo-Platonic preliminary on a galactic scale, as it were, to the pleasures of the bridal bed. Finally, the author once again addresses his son (who has been left out of the work ever since its introductory scene): 'So here you have the old wives' tale, Martianus, that Satire told with mixed inspiration in the lamp light' (9.997), *habes anilem, Martiane, fabulam, / miscillo lusit*

---

[1] Westra 1998, pp. 120f.
[2] Döpp 2009. The commentaries on the *Marriage* by Eriugena, Remigius of Auxerre, Bernardus Silvestris (?) and an anonymous (post-Carolingian) author have recently been edited and translated in a volume of 2500 pages by Ilaria Ramelli 2006.

quam lucernis flamine / Satura. Whether one reads, like Willis and Cristante, *miscillo* (with *flamine*) or, like the earlier editor of the work, Franz Eyssenhardt, *miscilla* (with *Satura*), there clearly surfaces yet another reference to the 'mixed' nature of the antique satire genre, a last vindication of the Menippean mixture of styles and subjects characteristic of the *Marriage*.

This work might well be described as one of Latin literature's most uninhibited experiments, an encyclopaedic inventory of Late Antique erudition embedded in partially contradictory layers of fiction, an impure work that insists on problematizing its own hybrid character, even in its concluding portrait of the narrator's Muse (9.998):[1]

6   Haec quippe loquax, docta indoctis aggerans
    fandis tacenda farcinat, immiscuit
    Musas deosque, disciplinas cyclicas
    garrire agresti cruda finxit plasmate.

   Our garrulous Satire has heaped learned doctrines upon unlearned, and crammed ineffable matters into utterable; she has commingled gods and the Muses, and, suffering from bad digestion, she has invented the entire cycle of the arts, prating in a rustic fiction.

Judging from the – literal – negotiations of fictionality between the narrator and Satire, it is evident that Martianus Capella, in contrast to Augustine, dropped all suspicions about poetry's "imaginary creatures", and that, in contrast to Macrobius, he was prepared to liven up his mythical story with the "unlearned" and "rustic" appeal of Menippean wit. In these final verses of his work, he presents its main subject, the instruction of the liberal arts, as nothing but a fruit, undigested (*cruda*), of Satire's invention. Thus Martianus' *Marriage* shows, paradoxically or at least unexpectedly, a certain affinity with the apophatic currents of contemporary mysticism, notably flourishing in the eastern part of the Empire. All worldly knowledge, which towards the end of the fifth century could still be summed up in the "cycle of the arts", is eventually exposed as the outcome of a loquacious Muse, entrapped in fictional discourse, the result of a number of interpretations or stories that are mutually contradictory. Divine reality, for its part, if it exists, is both unknowable and ineffable, *tacenda*, to borrow the au-

---

1 Here, the translation of Stahl *et alii* is thoroughly modified; moreover, in the first line of this quotation I follow Cristante rather than Willis (whose *docta doctis* disagrees with the overall logic of the passage, according to which Satire brings opposite elements together). The reading of *cruda* as an apposition to *Satura* – rather than the object of *garrire* – occurs in both Cristante and Relihan. The latter refers in this context to the original culinary sense of "satire", 1993, pp. 14f., 224.

thor's term. As far as I can see, this truly mixed or even heterogeneous combination of mysticism, pedantry and humour makes Martianus Capella unique in Late Antique culture or at least, as C.S. Lewis would have it, a counterpart to the bee-orchid and the giraffe in the realm of literature, and that might not necessarily be a bad thing.

It is time to sum up and draw conclusions. Even if Satire, appearing in the frame story of the *Marriage*, hardly subverts the seriousness of the Arts' prolix demonstration of learning, with their climax in Astronomy's and Harmony's magnificent visions of the cosmos, her ironic mode certainly deflates the allegorical *mythos* (I–II) and didactic *artes libelli* (III–IX) at strategic points throughout the work. Nobody, not even Lewis, has described this extraordinary literary crossbreed as succinctly and brilliantly as the author did himself. As if he realized the idiosyncratic nature of the *Marriage*, he reapplied the reversal of roles between himself and Satire at the end of his work, making the latter complain about the whole project. She had envisaged a stately cloak for herself, *chlamys*, worthy of a Greek priestess in the service of Mars, and she had expected "to be admired for my learning and refinement" (9.999), *doctis approbanda cultibus*.[1] Instead, she had to make do with the crazy, garrulous, ageing, not very well-off and – again – blinking Carthaginian Felix Capella. For his part, Martianus – or, strictly speaking, the work's narrator – is not at all upset by this description of himself. The last two lines of the *Marriage* (admittedly open to slightly divergent interpretations) seem construed as the narrator's apology to his son for the trivialities he has lined up, pleading his advanced age as an excuse: "And so, my son, in accordance with the testimony of an old man, show indulgence, as you read, for the trifles which he has produced" (9.1000): *testem ergo nostrum quae veternum prodidit / secute nugis, nate, ignosce lectitans*. Ultimately, thus, nobody – neither the blinking poet nor his frustrated Muse – wants to take responsibility for the hopeless mishmash (the literal meaning of the word *satura*) that Martianus Jr. and subsequent readers have had to share.

Here, we are surely facing the most disconcerting ending and the least flattering self-portrait that Latin literature has handed down to us. Everything was just an old man's rambling thoughts, mere trifles! Nonetheless, this pseudo-acknowledgement works remarkably well as a description, ironic or not, of the long-winded fantasy that the author had laboriously jotted down, as quaint as it was learned: a mixed literary composition controlled by the allegorical *ductus*, whose lack of thematic, stylistic or discursive purity was the whole point. The

---

[1] Cristante registers the slightly different meaning "worthy of the approval of the learned", preferred by Maïeul Cappuyns and a few other commentators, Martianus Capella 1987, p. 385.

last page of the *Marriage* (9.997–1000) throws a particular metafictional light on the work's title and mythical topic, the indissoluble union between Philology and Mercury. To whom in fact does she, the very epitome of human learning, give her hand? The groom, Mercury or Hermes, embodies not only eloquence, the gift of the gab. Apart from that, the Greeks had associated him with the Egyptians' Thot, the god of writing, but had also worshipped him as the god of merchants and thieves, of dissemblance and disguise. He was not merely responsible for carrying Zeus' messages to his fellow deities or to mankind but likewise appeared as the Olympian pantheon's trickster, the quicksilver (mercury!) in the ancient system of divinities, the rascal who, in the famous Homeric hymn, invented the lyre whose strings were made of gut from the cows he had stolen from Apollo.[1]

Hermes was in one and the same person "an interpreter [*hērmēneus*] and a messenger", "wily and deceptive in speech", "oratorical", to quote Socrates in Plato's dialogue *Cratylus* (407e–408a). Various ancient sources thus represent him as a curiously unreliable figure, but without him, not even Zeus would be able to assert his authority. Martianus presents his special twist to this paradoxical state of things in the *Marriage*, which surely abounds with useful erudition, transmitted, however, by means of Satire's "rustic fiction" and, in addition, transcribed by himself, an unreliable narrator of sorts. Still, without their interference, human learning would remain a series of spectral figures, "clothed in incorporeal utterance". This is, as far as can be judged, an essentially bold and subversive message from the fifth century, an original claim for fictional discourse in a period when the Western world was preparing for the absence of the Muses. Nonetheless, they would make a last spectacular appearance in the work of my next source for Late Antique negotiations of fictionality.

---

[1] For an exhaustive presentation of the precocious (newborn!) musician, cattle thief and trickster Hermes, see the editors' commentary on his hymn in T.W. Allen, W.R. Halliday and E.E. Sikes 1963, pp. 267–74.

5 Fulgentius: Mythographer and Mythoclast

The Late Antique taste for philosophical allegory reached its climax in the interpreter of myths Fabius Planciades Fulgentius, frequently labelled 'the mythographer', probably active during the first part or (as Gregory Hays has suggested) around the middle of the sixth century. Like Augustine and Martianus Capella, the latter of whom he refers to, Fulgentius was a North African. Since Carolingian times, he has repeatedly been associated with his contemporary namesake Saint Fulgentius, Bishop of Ruspe (in present-day Tunisia, d. 533), but nowadays this identification is highly disputed.¹ He is primarily known for two original works: his moralizing explanations of myths in *Mitologiarum libri tres* (*The Mythologies*), a Menippean satire in the wake of Martianus' *Marriage*, and his analysis of the sense of the *Aeneid* in a small tract with the telling title *Expositio Virgilianae continentiae* (*The Exposition of the Content of Virgil*), the first consistently allegorical commentary on the Roman poet's *magnum opus*.² It has for a long time had such a bad reputation among scholars for its systematic allegoresis that it has probably not been feasible to re-evaluate it until recently.³ These are the only texts by Fulgentius that will be examined in the following presentation.

However, it should be added that other works of his have been preserved, such as the remarkable *De aetatibus mundi et hominis* (*On the Ages of the World and of Man*), a history of the world that begins with the Creation and ends in 363 CE. It relates the Biblical story, Alexander's triumphs, the history of the Roman Republic, and the lives of Christ, the apostles, and lastly, the Emperors down to the reign of Julian the Apostate. On closer inspection, this probably uncompleted work proves to be a so-called lipogram, a manieristic literary form based on the consistent exclusion of one letter of the alphabet. For modern readers, the lipogram is first and foremost known through the French prose-writer Georges Perec, a member of the experimental Oulipo group and author of the novel *La Disparation* (1969), which avoids the letter 'e', the most frequent vowel in the French language, all through its 300 pages. For his part, Fulgentius intend-

---

1 For a meticulously documented discussion of the date and identity of Fulgentius, see Hays 2003.
2 For the meaning of *continentiae* as 'sense', 'explanation' or 'signification' (rather than merely 'content'), common in the period's Biblical and Neo-Platonic exegesis, see Tullio Agozzino's preface to the edition I use for the Latin text of the *Exposition*, Fulgentius 1972a, p. 22. Cf. the title of the latest translation of the work (into French, with a good introduction and an updated bibliography), *Virgile dévoilé*, Fulgentius 2009.
3 Rand's concise remark on Fulgentius in his *Founders of the Middle Ages* is symtomatic: "he too, unhappily, is one of the Founders", 1929, p. 278.

ed to leave out a new letter for each one of the twenty-three volumes he planned for his work (for which reason he could not mention Adam and Eve – 'Eva' – by name in Book I). This peculiar strategy of *On the Ages* indicates the experimental and ironic spirit (reminiscent of Martianus), the irreverent or even mischievous attitude to his cultural heritage and the ambition to recycle classical erudition for purposes which are anything but classical that are characteristic of all Fulgentius' works.

A Surprise Visit

Fulgentius' efforts in *On the Ages* to apply various technical methods for control or constraint in his writing originate in the same understanding of language and signs that forms the basis of his allegoresis. It might be summarized as an approach to the relation between words and things which differs as greatly as possible from that of Augustine. Fulgentius left no room at all for any arbitrariness or possible gaps in linguistic signification. On the contrary, the meaning of words was supposed to reside in their etymologies.

The old conviction that the origins of words are indicative of their sense was crucial to Fulgentius' *Exposition*, where he initially hesitates about whether he should begin to speak at all. It is late on earth, and if the author were to confine himself to considering what the miserable present demanded, *nostri temporis qualitas* (137) or *mediocritas* (139), he had better remain silent. This poor 'quality' or 'mediocrity' of the age probably refers to the cultural climate in the province of Africa, where the long-standing Vandalic indulgence with classical poetry might have been perceived as threatened by a rising suspicion of pagan traditions or simply, as Hays suggests, by an emerging anti-intellectualism.[1] However, since Fulgentius' mind feels strengthened by "the basis of a new rule", that of love or charity – *novo caritatis dominatui fulcitur*, maybe some sort of friendly encouragement – he sets out on his project to explain Virgil (137).[2] He signals straight away that he is about to decipher the poet's works for cognitive purposes; at this initial stage, at least, he is on the lookout for their "physical secrets", *Virgilianae continentiae secreta physica*. To begin with, the *Eclogues* and *Georgics*

---

1 Hays 1998, p. 134. Cf. Rauner-Hafner 1978, p. 11. For an interesting survey of Vandalic Africa as "a society secure enough in its Christianity that it has nothing to fear from poetic fictions", see Hays 2004, p. 130.
2 All quotations in English from the *Exposition* are from Stokes's translation (a few times slightly modified), Fulgentius 1972b. For the interpretation of *novo caritatis dominatui*, see Hays 1998, pp. 134–36.

are dealt with at express speed. They prove to provide plenty of useful instruction in cosmology, botany, music, medicine and fortune-telling, but the author hints at such teaching's controversial nature – it might bring "danger rather than praise", *plus periculi quam laudis* – perhaps due do its patently pagan nature (138).

In order to cope with his ambitious project, Fulgentius directs a few verses to the Muses, the *Eliconiades* or *Pierides*, followed by a request to be granted an encounter with "the Mantuan seer" in person, *persona Mantuani vatis*, so as to be initiated into "the obscure circumlocutions", *fugitivi amfractus*, which run through the poet's works. And – *mirabile dictu* – suddenly he is standing there, Virgil, five centuries dead, with an appearance that befits inspired poets, known since the days of Plato, with staring eyes, mumbling their secrets, "holding raging discussions with themselves" (140), *latranti intrinsecus tractatu*. The frightened author asks the poet to soften his features, since he is not in search of any abstruse things in the *Aeneid:* no Pythagorean mystical numbers, no Platonic ideas or Aristotelian entelechies (as registered in Martianus' *Marriage*, cf. above, p. 381). As far as can be judged it is, once again, the risk of heresies and other controversial doctrines that holds Fulgentius' curiosity at bay. He strategically assures his high interlocutor that all he wants from him is the kind of elementary knowledge that a grammar teacher, in view of his monthly salary, habitually passes on to his pupils.

The Italian editor of the work, Tullio Agozzino, has devoted a painstaking article to the ideas and the culture that form the background to this Pythian Virgil. Naturally, the view of the poet as an inspired instrument and an "insane" bard (to quote from *Mythologies*, 1.25), *insanus vates*, has deep roots in classical culture, in the notion of poetry being "a divine dispensation", famously articulated in Plato's dialogue *Ion* (534c).[1] This idea is in turn derived from older beliefs or assumptions of archaic Greece, updated as needed in early Christian culture on account of the Old Testament's rich evidence of prophetic frenzy. It may well be asked, however, if in his learned essay Agozzino does not turn a blind eye to the elements of caricature in Fulgentius. There is a striking difference, as Julian Ward Jones Jr. has pointed out, between the mythographer's meeting with the *summus poeta* and his predecessors' reception of Virgil.[2] In the *Exposition*, Virgil does not appear merely in the guise of the wise seer but as the proverbial schoolmaster,

---

[1] Agozzino 1972. *Ion* is given in W.R.M. Lamb's translation, Plato 1925b. I quote Fulgentius' *Mythologies* from R. Helm's 1898 edition; when possible, English translations are from L. Whitbread's volume 1971, except for the prologue where I have used Relihan's version 1993, pp. 203–10.

[2] Jones 1964, pp. 274f.

who cross-examines his adept with a stern face. Before he agrees to begin to explain the *Aeneid*, he demands that Fulgentius, suddenly reduced to a grammar schoolboy, should recount the epic poem's first book so as to be sure that he does not speak to "deaf" ears – actually 'old-fashioned', *arcaici*, perhaps in the sense of primitive or even, as Agozzino tentatively suggests, pagan ears (148).[1] In other words, this is a lesson that requires well-prepared homework (and, perhaps, true faith).

Seth Lerer, too, has stressed Fulgentius' idiosyncratic profile in this didactic context.[2] The mythographer does not seem interested in extracting any "Egyptian gold" from pagan eloquence for the benefit of Christianity, the great task that Augustine had sketched out in *On Christian Doctrine*. Moreover, we are just as far from the sophisticated cultural memory, replete with classical quotations and antiquarian retrospection, that Macrobius had projected on his distinguished guests at the Roman symposium in *Saturnalia*. In this *Exposition*, we are rather invited to overhear a dialogue between the schoolmaster and his pupil in a private study, and probably also – we can never leave out this possibility in Fulgentius – a parody of the pedantic features that would mar much grammar teaching, including the *enarratio poetarum*. The work's Late Antique dialogue form generates powerful satirical and metafictional overtones, as it had already done – albeit for other purposes, and on a much larger scale – in Martianus' *Marriage*.

Both Jones and Lerer are justified in their claims, but I would like to emphasize that Fulgentius' critical or parodic treatment of the *vates* motif not only challenges but in fact links up with long-standing Roman tradition. Lucretius had already attacked "hierophantic threats" and priests' "endless fantasies" in *The Nature of Things* (1.102–05), followed by the satirists Persius and Juvenal during the first century CE. They form a mighty counterpoise to the Augustan poets, to a Virgil's or a Horace's conception of themselves as pontiffs of the Muses, to cite the words of the latter: *Musarum sacerdos*.[3] In later years, the Greek Church Father and Patriarch of Constantinople, John Chrysostom (ca. 347–407), and several other Christian writers had adopted this demeaning portrayal of a *vates* for their own polemic use, now depicted as a bearded pagan philosopher with

---

1 Fulgentius 1972a, p. 79.
2 Lerer 1985, p. 57.
3 Lucretius conceives of his interlocutor Memmius as overpowered by *vatum / terriloquis dictis* and thus warns him: *multa tibi iam fingere possunt / somnia*. Horace proclaims himself *Musarum sacerdos* in *Odes* 3.1.3, edited by K. Quinn 1997. Irvine aptly observes that "Vergil thus becomes the *grammaticus* who interprets his own poem, supplying a philosophical *enarratio* of the epic *narratio*", 1994, p. 158, missing, however, the point of Fulgentius' parodical scenario.

a long cloak and staff.[1] The tension in Fulgentius between the Virgilian phantom's Delphic apparition and the "tablets" he holds ready in his hands 'to compose his work', *ad opus conficiendum tabulae,* is anyhow conspicuous. Indicative of the author's tongue-in-cheek approach, it prepares the reader for the work's oracular-allegorical take on the *Aeneid* in terms of a blatantly humdrum classroom type of dialogue.

Virgil frowns, since for a moment he mistakes his listener for a crude reader, blocked by "the coarse thickness of your mind", *adipata grassedo ingenii,* probably considered typical of pedestrian grammar studies, intent on the letter of the text, incapable of understanding its hidden sense.[2] Nevertheless, the poet changes his mind when he realizes that poor Fulgentius is rather suffering from "the fearful terror of the times", *temporis formido periculosa,* so he urges him to open his ears. The venerable master agrees to let his inquisitive pupil sip his genius's overwhelming torrent from a small urn: *de nostro torrentis ingenii impetu breviorem urnulam praelibabo* (143). Here, the initiation theme is struck, which also implies the necessity of adapting the occult message to the neophyte's imperfect understanding, hinted at by the term of address that Virgil systematically uses with him: *homuncule.* Thus, in the poet's small urn – an appropriate figure for the imminent explanation of his work, as compact as it is initiated – the apprentice and "little man" Fulgentius will discover something different and more valuable than the usual (year-long) classroom instruction.

This humble approach to the poets' poet was to characterize Western literature for well over a thousand years; it would, for partly different reasons, prove as unmistakable in Dante in the early fourteenth century as in the bulk of Italian *cinquecento* poetics. It did not, however, as we have already been able to ascertain, prevail unequivocally in Fulgentius. After a detailed analysis of the famous first line of the *Aeneid*, Virgil himself acknowledges his precarious position as a pre-Christian poet. Despite his matchless literary status, he never managed to catch sight of the truth about the blessed (Christian) life, which only by generous chance had scattered a few sparks "on our stupid minds", *stultis mentibus,* that is, over himself and a few other pagans (146). Fulgentius would return to the poet's flimsiness towards the end of the dialogue, where he expresses surprise at his master's readiness to blur his brilliant genius with such crazy fumes as the idea of metempsychosis in *Aeneid* VI. How indeed could he, Virgil, who had expressed himself so "mystically", *mystice,* in his pastoral poems (here, of course, the author has the sibylline prophecy from the poet's Fourth Eclogue

---

[1] Laistner 1951, p. 54.
[2] Cf. Agozzino's comment in Fulgentius 1972a, pp. 75f.

in view, ever since the days of Constantine the Great and Lactantius interpreted as a portent of Christ), come up with such nonsense? How could this unparalleled authority suddenly "wheeze out something Academic" (that is, Platonic), *Academicum quippiam stertens?* Had he perhaps deliberately mixed these dark and wild berries among his sweet apples, as if to darken the tapers of his wisdom, *sapientiae funalia caligare?* (161–62)

In such turns of phrase Fulgentius displays a noteworthy lack of respect for the old seer. The repeated attribute *stultus* (foolish, stupid) is remarkably strong, in stark contrast to Dante's portrait of "the courteous, all-discerning sage" (Inferno 7.3, "quel savio gentil, che tutto seppe"). The authors of the High Middle Ages would habitually recycle the imagery that Fulgentius (like others before him) had relied on in his explanation of Virgil – a cloak of fiction or a smokescreen, *caligo*, conceals the real message of the *Aeneid*, hence demanding to be removed – but with them the tone would become considerably more reverent.[1] In spite of Fulgentius' scolding, however, the Virgil of his *Exposition* does not seem offended. On the contrary, he makes it clear (with a smile, *subridens*) that he is not trying to make his epic poem conform to correct – Christian – norms and notions of later times: "If I did not foolishly state an Epicurean idea amidst so many Stoic truths", he explains, "I would not be a pagan. The complete truth is known only by those of you on whom the light of truth has shined. When I took the job as a speaker in your books, I did not agree to discuss what I ought to have thought, but rather what I actually thought." (162)[2] While this admission is indicative of Late Antique Christianity's common demonization of Epicureanism, it provides us with an important clue to our understanding of the *Exposition*. Its author does not purport to reinterpret the *Aeneid* anachronistically, in the light of Christian faith. Fulgentius' Virgil would rather read his own epic poem as a philosophical manual, perhaps – considering his reference to *tantae Stoicae veritates* – with special attention to the Stoic ideas of virtue, freedom from passions and adjustment to the necessities of fate or providence.

It is in this moral spirit, as we shall now see, that Virgil comments on his writing. In his minor works, he tells his eager listener, he had presented doctrines about the order of Nature, *physici ordinis argumenta*, so as to give a more complete picture of human life in the twelve scrolls that form the *Aeneid*

---

[1] For this type of medieval text theory, see first and foremost Frank Bezner's magisterial survey 2005, which, significantly, opens with a chapter on Fulgentius, pp. 1–14.
[2] "Si, inquit, inter tantas Stoicas veritates aliquid etiam Epicureum non desipissem, paganus non essem: nullo enim omnia vera nosse contingit nisi vobis, quibus sol veritatis inluxit. Neque enim hoc pacto in tuis libris conductus narrator accessi ut id quod sentire me oportuerat disputarem, et non ea potius quae senseram lucidarem." Translation slightly modified.

(143). There, in his epic poem, mankind's complete condition – its original nature, its improvement by knowledge and its final state of happiness – will emerge "under the figurativeness of history" (147), *sub figuralitatem historiae*. After this declaration of intent, the Roman poet begins to explain his *Aeneid* as an allegorical representation of the stages of human life. This is Fulgentius' innovative contribution to the art of reading Virgil. His method is based on consistent decontextualization. Individual episodes are dislodged from their epic context to be serially added to each other in a compact allegorical exposition mirroring human life, ultimately concerning nothing less than the destiny of mankind (148), *humanum genus*.

The *Aeneid* opens with a shipwreck, which signifies both our troublesome entry into life and our mother's birth pains; it is not by chance that it is precisely Juno, the goddess of childbirth, who causes the wreckage. When Aeneas steps ashore near Carthage, he meets his own mother, the goddess Venus, without recognizing her, just as new-born babies more or less immediately get to see their mother without realizing what she will mean to them (149). In the second and third books, Aeneas is drawn into the magic world of myths, *fabulae*, just as "childish prattle", *puerilis garrulitas*, habitually goes there. This supposedly immature fascination with fabulous tales is reflected in the poem's episode with the Cyclopes, recounted to Aeneas by the frightened Greek Achemenides (3.613–54), whose name – according to the expositor – includes the word *acos*, sorrow. Thus, when a boy has recently freed himself from fear of those who have brought him up, and while he is still too young to feel the sorrows of (rational) thinking, he is liable to behave inconstantly and arrogantly like the Cyclopes, whose one-eyedness must be understood to signify reckless pride. Nonetheless, things will get better; the fact that it was Odysseus who blinded Polyphemus with a red-hot pole indicates that foolish pride is blinded by the fire of genius. It is equally logical that the poem's third book leads up to Aeneas' burial of Anchises, testifying to the son's liberation from the weight of his father's all too strong authority, *paterni vigoris pondera* (151–52).

Having come so far, the reader who knows his/her *Aeneid* is hardly surprised that the hero now, in Book IV, has reached the age of desire for hunting and erotic adventures. The storm that forces Aeneas into the fateful cave is supposed to represent youth's mental confusion, from which only Mercury – the god of intelligence, *deus ingenii* – can save him (152). Upon the young man's yearnings follows the sagacity of adulthood. Love has to be buried in the ashes of oblivion, like poor Dido on the funeral pyre. After the fifth book, where mature Aeneas has restored the memory of his father, the time has come for his real initiation into the mysteries of life as well as death. For this purpose, to begin with, the hero has to rid himself of his 'erring vision' (in Greek, *planonorus*); consequently,

Aeneas' drowsy helmsman Palinurus falls overboard. Thus the hero is ready to visit the temple of Apollo, the abode of studies and learning. From now on his zeal is directed towards "the deep, secret mysteries of wisdom", *sapientiae obscura secretaque mysteria* (153).

At this point, Fulgentius' etymological inventiveness reaches a climax. Aeneas' fellow Trojan and companion on his travels, Misenus, had dared to challenge the gods to a musical contest. On that account, he was drowned by the indignant Triton and shortly afterwards washed ashore. Now he has to be buried. The Greek word *misio* corresponds to the Latin *obruo* ('cover', 'conceal' or 'bury'), Virgil tells us, while *enos* translates into *laus* ('praise'), and *tetrimmenon* (cf. Triton) into *contritum* ('downtrodden' or 'crushed', that is 'contrite'). The Misenus episode, then, amounts to saying that "unless you bury the trappings of false pride [praise], you will never enter into the secrets of wisdom", *nisi vanae laudis pompam obrueris, numquam secreta sapientiae penetrabis*, that is, sound contrition should extinguish all vainglory. The impressed narrator of the dialogue readily seizes the opportunity to confirm the compatibility of this Virgilian insight with Christian standards. Our divine doctrine, he remarks, preaches that God does not despise a contrite and humiliated heart. His vatic interlocutor further emphasizes this agreement by pointing out that he had assigned the task of burning Misenus' body to Coryneus. Since the Greek word *carin* means 'grace' and *eon* 'time' or 'age', *saeculum*, the burial of Misenus signals that the age of grace must necessarily bury the ashes of false pride (153–54).

It is time for Aeneas to grasp the Golden Bough. Hardly surprisingly, it represents *scientia*, while its golden colour stands for "the splendour of eloquence", *claritas facundiae:* yet another example of the synthesis between *sapientia* and *eloquentia* that Cicero had recommended in his introduction to On Invention (1.1.1) and which Martianus had clothed in mythical attire. Having completed his education in the liberal arts, literature and philosophy, Virgil's hero is ready to descend into the underworld. Unfortunately, the first things he sees on his subterranean journey are Diseases, War, Discord, Old Age and other miseries. However, this is logical (like everything else in Fulgentius' version of the *Aeneid*), since Aeneas by now, armed with wisdom, can see through the smokescreens of the visible world. The names Charon and Acheron both contain one of the Greek words for time, *ceron:* the ferryman sagaciously takes the hero across the swirls and eddies of Acheron, the river of Death, brimming with temporal filth and moral ordure (155–56). Aeneas' ensuing meeting with Cerberus provides him with a useful exercise in such legal and forensic confrontations that an adult man needs to be able to deal with. Thereupon he beholds Dido, "now an empty shadow of her former love and passion". Virgil immediately explains the signification of her appearance: "In the consideration of wisdom and in tearful repentance, lust, long dead of neglect, is recalled." (157)[1]

Little remains here of the silently furious figure that turns her back on the hero in the *Aeneid*'s Grieving Meadows; nor do we see much of the tragic queen who made the young Augustine weep. Both the Roman poet and the Church Father had treated Dido, the main female character of the *Aeneid*, with utmost seriousness, even if the former made her fall victim to the political project that drives the epic poem, the foundation of the City of the future, and even if the latter, on mature consideration, came to deplore the tears of his past self, caused by the Carthaginian queen's sad fate. In Fulgentius, however, proud Dido is completely deprived of her epic identity, fading into an aspect of the hero himself. She is reduced to a shadow of Aeneas' desire, badly flattened out in the allegorical discourse of the Virgilian ghost.

The sight of the tortured potentates in Tartarus is a reminder of other temptations that should be avoided in life, reviewed by means of further etymologies. Once Aeneas has arrived in Elysium, he fastens the Golden Bough to the holy doorpost: "This shows that when one has finished his schooling, the completed knowledge should be etched in his memory, which is in the brain, just as the branch is affixed to the door."[2] And as Proserpina is Queen of the underworld, memory is the queen of knowledge. It is "gliding along", *proserpens*, in Elysium to reign "in freed minds", *elisis mentibus*, for ever: a Neo-Platonic climax in spectral Virgil's exposition. The first figure that Aeneas sees in Elysium, Musaeus, surpassing everybody else, stands for "the gift of the Muses", *quasi Musarum donum:* a tribute to poetry. The hero gets to see his newly dead father, Anchises; in other words, he learns to observe moral dignity. And he contemplates Lethe, the river of oblivion, so as to forget his "youthful follies", *pueritiae levitas* (160).

The second half of the *Aeneid* is dealt with more swiftly. The beginning of Book VII addresses Caieta, Aeneas' wet-nurse, whom the hero buries on his arrival in Italy (in present-day Gaeta, north of Naples). By means of an adventurous etymology, Fulgentius' bard derives her name from *coactrix aetatis*, "the slave driver of youth", adding that the old word *caiatio* denotes the "thrashing of a child", *puerilis caedes*. With Caieta dead and buried, then, the hero's – that is, man's – reverence or even fear of his severe master(s) is gone (162–63). Having come so far in Fulgentius' dialogue, the reader might be forgiven for worrying whether mankind in this pseudo-Virgilian version will ever grow up. Aeneas

---

[1] "Quasi amoris atque antiquae libidinis umbra iam vacua. Contemplando enim sapientiam libido, iam contemptu emortua, lacrimabiliter paenitendo ad memoriam revocatur."
[2] "Quo clareat, dum perfectionem, omisso iam labore discendi, memoriae, quae in cerebro est, sicut in postibus perpetue infigenda".

seems to remain an irresolute apprentice, grappling with some overwhelming authority, for most of the *Exposition*. After having arrived safely at his final destination, Latium, he at least excels in good deeds by eliminating Turnus (frenzy), Mezentius (contempt of God) and Messapus (hatred of words or speech), all of whom are commented on etymologically. The narrator ends by urging the imagined reader of the dialogue to carefully pluck these 'thorns', *tribuli*, out of his breast (166). This exhortation might seem somewhat abrupt but probably serves as a covert incentive to allegorical reading, especially as the verb for 'pluck' is the same as for 'read': *legere*. The importance of reading, and of reading correctly or "carefully", *cautius*, is thereby established at three levels in Fulgentius' *Exposition*, roughly corresponding to modern narratology's metadiegetic, diagetic and extradiagetic levels:

- Aeneas is recreated as an everlasting apprentice in the fictional Virgil's self-commentary, continually forced to decipher his shifting environments and to free himself from fear or exaggerated esteem for his masters, *paedagogantis suspectio* (163).
- The narrator of the dialogue, the authorial I, is turned into an student in Aeneas' footsteps, as it were, taught by the same authoritative commentator, the oracular grammarian Virgil, in the art of reading his epic poem.
- The unknown recipient of the dialogue, who (in its first line, 37) is addressed as "holiest of the Levites", *Levitarum sanctissime*, and now as a "master" (166), *domine*, is finally summoned to read the present work, the *Exposition*, and to read it well.[1]

To conclude, this is how the very master narrative of Roman culture is converted into a series of pedagogical exercises, whether parodically intended or not, in Late Antique scholarly culture.

In his standard work on Virgil's significance for medieval literature (1872), Domenico Comparetti is merciless in his criticism of the *Exposition*. The Italian scholar's dependence on Burckhardtian historicism and, in all, nineteenth-century liberalism is unmistakable. Fulgentius disregarded "every law of common sense", Comparetti argues; it is difficult to understand how any sane person could have undertaken a work such as the *Exposition*, and even more difficult to understand how other sane persons should have accepted it as an object for serious attention. Comparetti seems to react particularly strongly against the *Exposition's* anachronistic features. Its impersonation of Virgil quite uninhi-

---

1 This address of Fulgentius' *Exposition* might be an officer of the Church, e.g. a deacon. Be that as it may, he is probably fictional, cf. Rauner-Hafner 1978, pp. 9f.

bitedly quotes Petronius, born a century later than himself, and he is even made to speak as if he were the author of the present work, referring to the *Mythologies* (cf. 156–57)! In Comparetti's eyes, the North African writer appears "as a caricature of all who went before or followed after him in the field of allegorical interpretation". Interestingly, this last remark, however negative, implies both a link between Fulgentius and Martianus and, perhaps even more importantly, an indirect confirmation of the mythographer's significance for the medieval commentary tradition. Comparetti refers with good reason to Bernardus Silvestris (whom he mistook for Bernard of Chartres, as did most scholars of the nineteenth century) and to John of Salisbury.[1]

It is mainly for this reason that the *Exposition* has been given fairly extensive attention above. Like no one else, Fulgentius exhibits the esoteric nature of Late Antiquity's understanding of Virgil. In contrast to the author of *Saturnalia*, he made Virgil's epic poem in its entirety the subject of a coherent explanation, and in contrast to the far more prolix Servius, he considered the work to be an exclusively allegorical project. The shade of Virgil comments on himself in the role of *grammaticus* as well as *rhetor*, and in point after point his epic poem is made to reflect the phases of (male) life from birth to maturity in accordance with a threefold structure that the German researcher Gabriele Rauner-Hafner, perhaps somewhat schematically, has described in terms of *natura* (the experiences of childhood), *doctrina* (education or theory), and finally *felicitas* (practical-ethical maturity).[2] Accordingly, the fictionality of the work is throughout restricted to its figurative way of speaking, *figuralitas*, which has to be penetrated to grasp the text's true message. This is a procedure that includes translating the inverted chronology of the epic narrative into the continuous order of an allegorical exposition. Bernardus Silvestris would essentially implement the same method in twelfth-century France, albeit with a stronger emphasis on Platonic metaphysics, in his *Commentum super sex libros Eneidos Virgilii*, the Middle Ages' most spectacular commentary on (the first half of) the *Aeneid*.[3]

This method of treating Virgil's text as a consistently encoded discourse, one long oracular message, was to great extent, as we have seen, based on etymology. On this point too, Fulgentius' *Exposition* contributed to the agenda of a great number of medieval commentaries on classical texts. The etymological ap-

---

[1] Comparetti 1997, pp. 112, 116f.
[2] Rauner-Hafner 1978, p. 32.
[3] Cf. the translators' preface to Bernardus Silvestris 1979, p. xix, and moreover Baswell 1985, who, however, evinces a surprisingly negative attitude to Fulgentius, emphasizing the High Medieval author's "far more energetic, imaginative, graceful, and nuanced" commentary, pp. 183, 189.

proach presupposed the idea that words taken for themselves – including their smallest details, sounds and syllables – communicate knowledge of reality. The name of a person or a thing says something about the nature of that person or thing, in accordance with the old Latin formula *nomen/omen*. Correspondingly, Servius had made use of etymologies in his *Commentaries*, probably inspired by Stoic philosophers who, in their various examinations of poetry, frequently conceived of fixed connections between names, *onomata*, and things.[1]

Of course, the more or less systematic application of this etymological method goes much farther back in time. As a principle for literary interpretation it had already been used in Homeric criticism by Democritus in the fifth century BCE. Plato had exhaustively investigated the same strategy in his discussion of the names of gods, elements, concepts and things. In *Cratylus*, Socrates summarizes the realist position of the dialogue's eponymous interlocutor thus: "I suppose, Cratylus, you mean that when anyone knows the nature of the name – and its nature is that of the thing – he will know the thing also, since it is like the name, and the science of all things which are like each other is one and the same. It is, I fancy, on this ground that you say whoever knows names will know things also." (435d–e) The method did not go undisputed – Cratylus is famously rebutted by the nominalist Hermogenes in the same dialogue (above, p. 293) – but it would later be embraced by Plotinus and his Neo-Platonic followers, not least Proclus (apart from the Stoics). In addition, Jan Pinborg has stressed that the starting point for all medieval semantic analysis was the introductory declaration of Aristotle's small treatise *On Interpretation:* "Words spoken are symbols or signs of affections or impressions of the soul" (16a), *sunt ergo ea quae sunt in voce earum quae sunt in anima passionum notae.*[2] This by no means crystal-clear sentence would frequently be taken as a pretext for the kind of etymological speculation that had attracted Fulgentius and which was to achieve its early medieval breakthrough on an encyclopaedic scale in Isidore's *Etymologies* about a hundred years later.

In Fulgentius, then, the allegorical type of interpretation that had characterized much natural-philosophical and Stoic speculation in ancient Greece and Rome, and whose application in Late Antique commentaries we have glanced at in this chapter, reached new heights. In his *Exposition*, sounds, letters, sylla-

---

1 See De Lacy 1948, pp. 256–59.
2 Pinborg 1967, p. 36. I quote the famous 16a sentence from Aristotle 1962 and, in Latin, from G. Verbeke's and L. Minio-Palluelo's *Aristoteles Latinus* (Aristotle 1965). For a few concise surveys of this vast research field, see the articles of Klaus Grubmüller, Wolfgang Haubrichs and Willy Sanders in *Verbum et signum* (vol. I), edited by H. Fromm *et alii* 1975, pp. 209–30, 231–66 and 331–40.

bles and words were continually transformed into coded signs for "the secrets of wisdom". Fulgentius thereby presented an extreme schematic version of the allegorical hermeneutics which, to a great extent, was Late Antiquity's answer to the mimetic type of fictionality that had interested, worried and finally repelled Augustine. It circumvented or suppressed the Church Father's insight into language's capability of make-believe, of suggesting alternative – rather than translating actual – versions of reality.

Thus the problem of narrative literature's cognitive undecidability (as far as it was perceived as a problem) simply disappeared in the eyes of Fulgentius' gesticulating poet and his likes, since words in themselves were ascribed an original, ontological and timeless signification. It was only to the uninitiated reader, ignorant of the Greek language or of classical culture, that poetry appeared obscure. Fundamental linguistic and philosophical competence seemed sufficient to get rid of potential obstacles to deciphering the text, without any need to introduce conditional assumptions into the interpretation process. This overall approach in Late Antique critical thinking would spawn a good deal of medieval literary commentaries' obsession with details that often seem peripheral to modern readers, such as the history or morphology of individual words. It is indisputable that Fulgentius was deeply fascinated by such exercises; whether or not he really took them seriously remains an open question.

The Flirtatious Muse

The Virgil figure in Fulgentius' *Exposition* can only legitimize the plot of his epic poem as a disguised account of the progress of human life. A similar allegorical approach, consistently conceptualizing the old tales, comes to the fore in the North African writer's explanation of myths in three books, although it is undermined by a prologue even more ironical than that of the *Exposition*. Here, too, in the very difficult, sometimes jumbled and corrupt text of the *Mythologies*, the author begins by presenting a gloomy picture of "the lamentable misery of our time" (1.1), *nostri temporis erumnosa miseria*. What seems important to him now is to save his skin and put his house in order. The men in power have plenty of time for oppression, the rich for plundering, the citizens for losses and the poor for tears. It is the turbulent era of the sixth century in the province of Africa that is mirrored in such lines (whether before or after the surrender of the Vandals to the Byzantine Emperor in 534), a time – the narrator continues – when there is no demand for rhetorical competence or poetic fame any longer; people are just too busy worrying about impending famine. However, the seriousness of these tirades does not prevent the author from gleefully displaying his eloquence. He plays with the words for fame, *fama*, and for hunger, *fames:* "nor does it [our time] defend the reputation of poetry, but it must look out for the hunger at its doorstep" (1.2), *nec famae adsistendum poeticae, sed fami sit consulendum domesticae.*

Despite these miserable circumstances, Fulgentius urges his listener or reader, once again addressed as *domine*, probably some superior, perhaps a patron, to prick up his ears: "Hear me then awhile as I begin to weave for you a tale wrinkled with an old woman's furrows, which recently I concocted from pungent Attic wit and the midnight guiding lamp, a tale tricked out in the fantasies of dreams in such a way that you will see in me no mad poet, but rather observe an interpreter of dreams divining drowsy trifles." (1.3–4)[1] The references to the old woman and the night lamp link up with the *Marriage of Philology and Mercury*, indicating the genre Fulgentius is about to exploit: the garrulous Menippean satire with its mixture of verse and prose, dating far back in Roman literature but lately renewed by Martianus. There, in the *Marriage*, the woman referred to had been associated with the genre itself, an "old wives' tale", *anilis fabula*, whose tall stories would go in all directions. The night lamp, as we have seen, was a convention in this satirical context but fits in well with the content of Fulgentius' presentation: the make-believe of dreams, *somniale figmentum*. In addition, it serves to highlight the author's distance to poetic activities. His role is not that of the frenzied poet, he says, but to account for dreams, a time-honoured occupation that was certainly disputed within the Church but which attracted supporters even among Christians, first and foremost perhaps the Neo-Platonic Synesius of Cyrene, Bishop of Libya (active around the turn of the fifth century).

We recognize the distrust of crazy poets and their stories from the *Exposition's* initial impressions of Virgil. But how seriously should we take Fulgentius' new role as an interpreter of dreams, *onirocreta?* This too seems rather questionable, to say the least. The narrator's information that his story is "tricked out", *delusa*, from the make-believe of dreams might already raise doubts. Moreover, the Latin *ariolor* can, in addition to its meaning of 'predict' or 'tell fortunes' be translated more disparagingly as 'talk nonsense', and, last but not least, the outcome of the narrator's interpretation of dreams will be "drowsy trifles", *soporis nugae*. Thus in the very first lines of the *Mythologies*, the author gives a hint of his ironic distance to the fabulous material that he is going to deal with. I have not, he stresses, been guided by the lanterns of Ovid's *Heroides*, that is, the lamps

---

1 "Parumper ergo ausculta dum tibi rugosam sulcis anilibus ordior fabulam, quam nuper Attica saporante salsura, nocturna praesule lucerna commentus sum, ita somniali figmento delusam, quo non poetam furentem aspicias, sed onirocretam soporis nugas ariolantem advertas." Translation slightly modified.

which occur in that work's recounting of the tragic love story of Hero and Leander. This is a clever declaration that not only recalls the night-working author's sources of light but likewise those that frequently shine in erotic myths, in Ovid as well as Apuleius. As a matter of fact, the author tells us, he has profited from a quite different *lucerna*, namely "that which drew our academic rhetorician so close to the empyrean that it nearly made the sleeping Scipio a citizen of heaven" (1.5).[1] This affirmation presumably refers to the stars that illuminate the celestial traveller's adventure in Cicero's *Dream of Scipio*, expounded by Macrobius as a *narratio fabulosa*. Like his North African countryman and predecessor, Fulgentius refuses to understand the myths literally. He too is (or seems) willing to expose them to philosophy's cooler light, but at the same time his somewhat disrespectful style indicates a certain reserve towards the Macrobian paradigm, chiefly, as we shall see, towards its demands for decorum and decency, which his *Mythologies* will ostentatiously neglect.

The narrator (or, as we might call him for the sake of convenience, Fulgentius) evidently finds himself in some sort of rural retreat, and before he takes on his explanations of myths, he sets out for a walk on his estate, sadly ravaged by the barbarian invaders. The enemy soldiers have left behind fear and poverty, memories of massacres and plundering, a waste land in both a cultural and a material sense. In this landscape, Fulgentius sits down in the shade of a tree and launches into "some sort of song and poem", *melos quoddam carminis*, directed at the Muses. This resembles, of course, an invocation, the usual prayer for inspiration at the beginning of a poem: "Open up your baskets of words, full of flowers" (1.11), *verborum canistra plenis / reserate flosculis*. More precisely, the author pleas for access to the themes that the shepherd from Ascra had executed on his ancient rock, that Maro once praised in Mantua's wooded pastures or that the Maeonian laughed at in his poem about the battle of the frogs (1.12).

The pattern repeats itself. The invocation, the location and the topics habitually related to the Muses and their gift of inspiration are recycled or imitated in an ambiguous light, as if to emphasize the scenario's conventional or hackneyed character. Fulgentius' disrespectful words about the Muses' sacred fountain, Hippocrene's "garrulous spray" (1.11), *loquax nimbus*, may already make the reader suspicious. The following gestures of reverence to the didactic poet Hesiod (from Ascra) and the Mantuan Virgil (Maro) certainly recall ancient mythology in bucolic settings, but the obeisance to the short epic parody *Batrachomyomachia* (*The Battle of Frogs and Mice*), in ancient times ascribed to Homer, who ac-

---

[1] "Quae nostrum achademicum rethorem ita usque ad vitalem circulum tulit, quo pene dormientem Scipionem caeli civem effecerit".

cording to legend was born in Maeonia (Lydia), raises the question of the type of inspiration Fulgentius actually asks for. Along these lines, an ironic authorial role is established in the *Mythologies*. It pretends to present serious and didactic stories in the Macrobian style, while undermining such philosophical claims through signals of satire or parody. The technique of foregrounding the unreliable narrator, typical of Menippean satire, is reminiscent of Martianus' self-projection as a chattering priest at the beginning of the *Marriage*. In the *Mythologies*, interestingly, it is implemented by an assumably Christian writer.

Exactly as in the *Exposition*, the invocation results in immediate supernatural presence. At least three of the Muses quickly materialize before Fulgentius. Only one of them is introduced to us in detail: Calliope, the patroness of epic poetry, evidently already known to the writer since she is characterized as *familiaris*. With a playful stroke of the palm of her hand she warms his breast and "infused it with the sweetness of the poetic itch" (1.13), *poeticae proriginis dulcidinem sparsit*. Their reunion is certainly agreeable to the narrator, literally inspired by Calliope's intimate advances. Still, he repeatedly alludes to her loquaciousness, honouring "the garrulous maiden", *verbosa virago*, asserting that ever since the harsh lashes of his school years – in grammar classes – he is familiar with her *verbosae fabulae* (1.14). This talkative Muse proceeds to tell her story. Once she was in the service of none other than Jupiter, being a citizen of great Athens; later she was honoured by Rome but driven into exile as a result of war, finding refuge in Alexandria, now with satire, comedy, tragedy and epigrams in her repertoire (a possible reference to contemporary Alexandrian literature). In recent years, however, she has been obliged to leave the Egyptian metropolis as well, since it is virtually invaded by the followers of Galen, *Galeni curia*, a host of literally dangerous surgeons. Thus Calliope sketches an early version of the *translatio studii* topos and, additionally, indulges in satire against physicians, virtually foreboding the argument against medicine on behalf of literary culture enacted in Petrarch's famous *Invective contra medicum* (*Invectives against a Physician*).

Fulgentius is evidently impressed by unfortunate Calliope's story, indicative of poetry's recent exile into the wilderness, and seems prepared to receive the Muse into his home. Yet she wonders: does he really dare to do that? After all, the barbaric invaders are said to be so averse to any scholarly or literary exchange, *litterarii mercati*, that they send literate people straight to the torture chamber and executioner's room (1.17)! Fulgentius encourages her: it is not as bad as that. He quotes Virgil's *Eclogues* (in a corrupt and obscure passage) to show her the power and influence of literary tradition, even in these extreme times, provided it is well managed. After these assurances, intimacy increases between the author and his Muse. Calliope strokes his hair, and having put her hand round his neck "more enticingly than was fitting", *mollius quam decuit*, she affirms that from now on he is accepted as a novice in the "Anacreontic mysteries", *Anacreontica sacra*, ostensibly a rather odd distinction, considering Anacreon's reputation as the proverbially raving (drunken) bard. However, this Greek lyric poet from the sixth century BCE was commonly associated with erotic themes as well. Hence, judging from the present context – the flirtatious Calliope's appearance in an introduction to a commentary on frequently erotic myths – these mysteries should most likely serve to prepare the narrator for his imminent explanation of the passionate love stories and frivolous deities from archaic Greece.

Calliope begins the initiation process by offering the novice fair "grace of instruction", *dogmatis gratia*, an ambiguous syntagm with possible Christian overtones. She jokingly calls him her young recruit or soldier, *tirunculus*, advising him to "take into the seats of your ears, free from business, what can be scratched out on Egyptian papyrus" (1.19): *quidquid libet Niliacis exarare papiris, feriatis aurium sedibus percipe!* This is a clear allusion to the well-known prologue to Apuleius' *Metamorphoses*, in which the author, implementing a peculiar *captatio benevolentiae*, declares his intention to caress the readers' benevolent ears with a pleasant whisper, replete with various *fabulae*, if only they would "look upon this Egyptian paper written with a ready pen of Nile reeds" (1.1), *modo si papyrum Aegyptiam argutia Nilotici calami inscriptam non spreveris inspicere*. Both of these prologues, along with the frame story in Martianus Capella's *Marriage*, imply a literary communication at an oral as well as written level, with explicit references to ancient Egypt and its venerable papyrus medium. Joel C. Relihan suggests that this link to Egypt in Apuleius (and, I gather, in Fulgentius) signals fantastic fiction rather than – as in Martianus – hermetic wisdom.[1] In that case, it would be feasible to infer that Calliope proposes to recount the old mythological (fantastical, fictional) tales, written down from time immemorial, such as the story of Cupid and Psyche, crucial to Apuleius' novel. In these roundabout ways, then, making his Muse allude to Anacreontic mysteries as well as Egyptian papyrus, Fulgentius seems to signal the main topic of his work: the erotic myths from ancient Greece.

For our purposes, at any rate, it is neither necessary nor possible to follow the narrator's negotiations with his high-born guest in full detail. All through their twists and turns and shifting positions in Martianus' style, they develop a fascinating discussion about the necessity of poetry or myth at a time that has proclaimed the death of Great Pan. The outcome of their exchange could

---

[1] Relihan 1993, p. 279. Here, too, the text is corrupt. I follow Relihan's reading, p. 207.

be summarized as an acceptance on the part of the narrator to take on the task imposed on him, on a condition that proves decisive for his work: since he is not able to take the old mythological material at its face value, or even treat it altogether seriously, he will deconstruct rather than reconstruct it. In short, he pictures himself as intrigued by the myths as well as by their Pierian protectress – but at a distance. Fulgentius' way of greeting Calliope as "your noble garrulousness", *generosa loquacitas*, is only one of several ironic devices in his argument. We have already seen him adopting an unresponsive attitude towards the lanterns that occur in the stories of Ovid's and Apuleius' mythical lovers, and now, considering Calliope's enticing behaviour and "Anacreontic" preferences, he sharpens his tone against erotic fiction. For instance, he takes pains to dismiss Jupiter in circumlocutions such as the "horned adulterer", *cornutus adulter* (turned into a bull to conquer Europa), or 'a false bird', *falsa ales* (the eagle abducting Ganymede towards the sky). Hero and Psyche, for their part, gabble poetic gibberish, *poeticas garrulantes ineptias* (1.20), a phrase that faintly echoes Martianus' white-haired storyteller, accused by his son of gabbling silly trifles, *nugulas ineptas aggarrire*.

With these piercing remarks Fulgentius probably takes a particular gibe at Ovid, the Roman poet who more than any other was associated with the titillating legends of the gods. The *Metamorphoses*' opening sentence reads: "My mind is bent to tell of bodies changed into new forms" (1.1–2), *in nova fert animus mutatas dicere formas / corpora*. Fulgentius' twist of his predecessor's explanation of intent has a critical ring to it: 'My wish is to make manifest how vain things have been transformed, not to obscure manifest things by transforming them' (1.21), *mutatas itaque vanitates manifestare cupimus, non manifesta mutando fuscamus*. That is, he will lay bare the mythical stories, as trifling as they are abstruse, rather than inventing new ones. Ovid is clearly Fulgentius' target here: the latter's examples of reprehensible myth treatment – making an elderly god neigh or letting the Sun prefer an old woman's wrinkles to his own rays – are directed at precisely the episodes of the *Metamorphoses* in which Saturn is transformed into a horse (6.126) and Apollo into his beloved Leucothoe's mother (4.219). It is obvious that the Late Antique mythographer wants to present the Golden Age poet as an unnecessarily mystifying or, alternatively, a too candid fiction maker. His own task will be to unravel the magic threads of the ancient transformation tales, to explain rather than to extend them. He is neither an inventor nor a recreator but a critic of myths, or, to borrow a label recently applied to Fulgentius by Emily Albu, a mythoclast: "And so I aim for the real effects of things, so that once the lie [*fabulosum commentum*] of deceitful Greece has been laid to rest we can recognize what the mystic medulla in them ought to mean." (1.21)[1]

Calliope realizes appreciatively that her new protégé is on the lookout for something great and important – the actual meaning of the old myths – though scarcely accessible, since these tales, or at least their significance, have been left "untouched", *intacta*, for centuries. Accordingly, she urges him to seek help from Philosophy and Urania (the Muse of Astronomy). Moreover, when their "mystical arts", *misticae artes*, give him some breathing space, she promises, he will get a wanton lady to relax with: playful Satire. The narrator feels obliged to reject her generous offer, since his temperamental wife would attack this new guest in their house with her bare nails and kick her back to the Mount of Helicon! Oh no, Calliope assures him, there is no need to worry: all wives fear Satire (1.22–23). At this humorous stage of the conversation, Fulgentius includes a poem in hexameter, parodically packed with mythical periphrases for the fall of night, immediately recapitulated in laconic prose: "and, to conclude in as few words as possible, it was night" (1.25), *et, ut in verba paucissima conferam, nox erat*. This implicit gibe at the wordy poets is sharper than ever, hitting the authorial I as well: since he had forgotten the simple name of night, he "was going mad in verses like an insane poet", *ut insanus vates versibus delirabam*, a confession that was to arrest Curtius's attention in his appendix on the topos of "the poet's divine frenzy" in medieval literature.[2] As if to confirm the inspired narrator's self-mockery, Calliope breaks into his bedroom, only to find him lying there "unawares", *necopinanter*, with his eyes drooping in a gentle sleep, *marcentia languore somni lepido lumina* (1.25).

In this way, Fulgentius exposes his alter ego as a caricature of the obsessed poet, despite its initial restraint. This drowsy bard will now be restored to a sober state (and to sober discourse) by Calliope and her friends, in the first place Satire, who finally – after being announced several times – enters his room, not mentioned by her name but fully recognizable: *lasciviens*, wrapped in ivy, with a shameless face and her mouth full of abuse. She immediately evinces the necessary competence for her task of unravelling and conceptualizing myths: "Her ironic eye darted about with such a penetrating native wit that she could have described even the meanings deeply hidden in drunken writings." (1.25)[3] Her figure, inevitably reminiscent of Martianus' *Marriage*, is congenial to the whole pre-

---

[1] "Certos itaque nos rerum praestolamur effectus, quo sepulto mendacis Greciae fabuloso commento quid misticum in his sapere debeat cerebrum agnoscamus." Cf. Albu 2011.
[2] Curtius 1990, p. 474.
[3] "Cuius ironicum lumen tam rimabunda vernulitate currebat quo mentes etiam penitus abstrusas temulentis inscriptionibus depinxisset".

sentation, a Menippean satire in which her role is to bring out the actual content of the ancient myths, by means of a transferred epithet (hypallage) labelled "drunken writings", *temulentae inscriptiones*. It would be difficult to come up with a more brutal description of classical mythology: the deranged doodling of frantic poets, hardly worth taking seriously if it were not for the "mystic medulla" that they might conceal.

Thus it will be the ironical and analytical Satire, assisted by her Pierian sisters Urania and Philosophy, both introduced gleefully tongue-in-cheek, who will guide the author during his excursions into mythology. If you follow them, Calliope assures him, they will make you heavenly, at which point she explicitly has in mind another kind of *raptus* than the one bestowed on Nero. This Emperor had only been able to count on "poetic praise", *poeticae laudes*, for his celestial promotion. As for the mythographer, on the other hand, Calliope hints at an apotheosis in the Platonic style, implemented as a result of mystical arguments, *misticae rationes*. Hence, Fulgentius' prologue reflects as powerfully as Boethius' more famous scenario at the beginning of the *Consolation*, albeit in an ironic key, philosophy's virtual dethronement of poetry in the learned culture of Late Antiquity.[1]

It is characteristic of this development that the mythographer reports so carefully, and in all likelihood parodically, on his distinguished guides' appearances. Curtius has remarked that the Muses of classical culture were not ascribed any particular personalities, like the Olympian gods, but embodied "a purely intellectual principle", potentially dissociated from the Greco-Roman pantheon. Luciano Lenaz adds that Martianus Capella still respected this tradition.[2] The same could be said of Boethius. Fulgentius, for his part, disregards it completely. With his intimate presentation of the flirtatious Calliope and his comic arrangement of her notorious sisters, he catalyzes, as it were, the transformation of the Muses into clichés in Late Antique literature. Their aura has dimmed, and their proverbial poetic enthusiasm is – for the time being – inoperative. Thus Calliope is blatantly clear about the type of inspiration that the mythographer can await from his eminent guests (1.27):[3]

---

[1] Cf. the apt observation by the Italian philologist Silvia Mattiacci on "the rejection of poetic fictions, considered together as a bit of a joke confronted with the seriousness of philosophical-allegorical interpretation" in the prologue to the *Mythologies*, 2002, p. 265

[2] Curtius 1990, p. 229; Martianus Capella 1975, p. 13.

[3] "Neque enim illos de his expectas effectus, quos aut poema ornat aut deflet tragoedia aut spumat oratio aut cachinnat satyra aut ludit comedia, sed in quibus et Carneadis resudat elleborum et Platonis auratum eloquium et Aristotelis sillogismaticum breviloquium. Nunc itaque pande mentis cubiculum et aurium fistulis audito nuntio mentibus intromitte quod excipis; sed enerva

For you ought not expect of them the effects that a poem tricks out or a tragedy laments or a speech spews forth or a satire cackles or a comedy plays, but those in which Carneades' hellebore sweats, and Plato's golden language and Aristotle's syllogistic pithiness. So now open up the chamber of your mind and take into your mind what you receive from the message heard in the pipes of your ears; but unstring all that is mortal within you, lest the succession of such holy instruction sit uncomfortably in recalcitrant recesses.

The soon-to-be dispatched exposition of the old myths will evidently not respect the traditional literary genres: poetry, tragedy and the like. On the contrary, Fulgentius is told that he will feel the effects of *helleborus*, the (toxic) Christmas rose, which in Antiquity was popularly thought to be a cure for madness. In this case, Calliope might be referring specifically to poetic madness, perhaps coupled with melancholy, frequently associated with creative talent. In addition, she presents hellebore as an attribute of Carneades, the Sceptic philosopher who led the Academy of Athens in the second century BCE, widely renowned for his skills in argumentation and reasoning, cleverly refuting all traditional opinions or inherited truths. For the purpose of uncovering the core of the ancient myths, then, Fulgentius is supposed to make use of Carneades' aporetic arguments, Plato's superior eloquence and Aristotle's concise syllogisms. One thing seems beyond doubt: his mythography will rely on penetrating philosophy rather than unruly poetry.

Thus the prologue to the *Mythologies* launches one attack after another on the literary, purportedly mystifying framing of the old mythological stories. For this purpose, Fulgentius also resorts to self-irony inasmuch as he appears as a raving poet, in blatant contrast to his critical intentions and to Calliope's admonitions. His prologue establishes an even more wavering and unreliable narrator than the one we met in Martianus' *Marriage*. Against his better judgment, the author seems to be at the mercy of the magnetic power of the myths, a poet incorrigibly dedicated to his dreams and their *somniale figmentum*, as in the final lines of the night poem (1.25.1–2):

Iam simulacra modis mentes fallentia plastis
mollia falsidicis replebant stramina signis;
[...]

Now phantasms, deceiving the mind with fictitious images, were filling soft beds with treacherous signs...

---

totum mortale quod tibi est, ne tam sacrati series dogmatis scrupulosis rite non residat penetralibus."

As a mythoclast, Fulgentius is obviously besetting a version of himself as a bemused poet. Consequently, the narrator's authority seems seriously undermined in this remarkable text which, against the backdrop of the ravaged Mediterranean world after the Germanic invasions, grants us a glimpse of antique culture's on-going farewell to the fictions that had once ensured its continuity and legitimacy. In the prologue to the *Mythologies*, the tales of the gods and their escapades are associated with, in turn, garrulity, frivolity and drunken frenzy. Not even Augustine could have dreamt of a more effective disablement of the classical world of myths, in the hands of a jester who has made up his mind to unravel these "drowsy trifles".

The time has come, then, for Satire, Urania and Philosophy to begin their inspection of the timeworn fabulous material. They will carry to extremes – possibly parodic extremes – the conversion of narrative threads of fiction into a philosophical web of conceptual terms, which seems to be the dominant trend in Late Antique literary criticism. Judging by Calliope's closing words in the prologue, they intend to squeeze all the juice out of the myths until only the old, dry skin is left (1.27–28):[1]

> So now we will speak first of the nature of the gods, and whence so great a pollution of foul credulity has fixed itself in stupid minds. For although there are some who reject the innate nobility of their heads and in their rustic and antique sensibilities are as wise as acorns, and their numbed wits are hidden in an all-too-thick cloud of stupidity, nevertheless, errors never arise in the human senses unless driven in by random impulses, as Chrysippus says in his work *On Fate:* "Impulses roll on by unpredictable forces."

The mischievous Muse considers mythology's miracles and adventures from the greatest possible distance. When Fulgentius wrote his work, to all appearances in the sixth century, their original significance and relevance lay, naturally, buried in the distant past. During the preceding millennium they had been exposed to criticism or sheer refutation from Ionic natural philosophers, Plato, Euhemerus, Epicureans, Stoics and, last but not least, Christians. Calliope associates them with folly, uncontrolled impetuosity and rural coarseness, the proverbial acorns of a Golden Age which she envisages as anything but golden. The adjective *aricinus* refers to the ancient city of Aricia in Latium, known for its sacred grove

---

[1] "Ergo nunc de deorum primum natura, unde tanta malae credulitatis lues stultis mentibus inoleverit, edicamus. Quamvis enim sint quidam qui spreta capitis generositate aricinis atque arcaicis sensibus glandium quippiam sapiant atque eorum altiori stultitiae nubilo soporata caligentur ingenia, tamen nequaquam aput humanos sensus nisi fortuitis conpulsationibus moti nascuntur errores, ut etiam Crysippus de fato scribens ait: Conpulsationibus lubricis volvuntur incursus."

with a temple dedicated to Diana. Against this age-old and purportedly superstitious cult, the Muse launches the Stoic philosopher Chrysippus (third century BCE) and his analysis of the fleeting or false whims and fancies that might influence – or, preferably, be controlled by – human beings. Now when Calliope and her sisters take on the presentation in *Mythologies*, it is to a large extent this type of accidental impulsivity, primarily aroused by desire and lust, that is considered the driving force of the myths. In bluntly anachronistic terms, Fulgentius could be said, *mutatis mutandis*, to be testing a psychoanalytic approach to his material, especially in view of his tentative equation of myths with dreams. His ambition is, where possible, to lay bare the true (conceptual, historical or subliminal) significance of these fanciful, not to say weird or bizarre, inventions from the early days of Greece.

During the subsequent examination of the myths, it is not easy to guess which of the Muses is speaking. Shortly after the prologue, in the section concerning the myth of Saturn, it seems clear that we are listening to Philosophy's opinions (1.33), but thereafter nothing is said about the specific speaker of each explanation, as if the author had forgotten or quite simply did not care about his frame story. Furthermore, the question remains open as to how seriously we are supposed to take the philosophically minded Muses who are conducting this investigation. What kind of authority does Fulgentius attach to their critical analyses? They certainly invest a great deal of energy, probably inspired by both Stoic and Christian ideas, in finding fault with the obsessed poets and denouncing the primitive myths: nothing but nonsense, they claim. But the irony of the prologue is surely directed at their outlandish looks and behaviour as well: at seductive Calliope and shameless Satire, at sanctimonious Urania, stubbing her big toe, and white-haired Philosophy, smelling something rotten (in the mythological material, presumably). Thus, in the metafictional prelude to the *Mythologies*, vaguely reminiscent of the frame story in Martianus' *Marriage*, Fulgentius subjects the authorial voices of his work, the narrator's as well as his Muses', to a critical or even satirical examination. To him, as to Martianus, fiction remained an unsolved problem, and his attempt at a solution, too, is reminiscent of his North African predecessor: exposing the *figmenta* to energetic disclaimers that tend to undermine themselves. The result of this tortuous process was – and still is – known from arithmetic: a double negative gives a positive outcome. This would surely be the ultimate paradox of Fulgentius' *Mythologies*: perhaps, after all, right through the author's parodic exposure of the ancient myths, the work reveals an incurable nostalgia for the colourful tales of long ago?

The medieval reception of Fulgentius indicates at least that the sceptical Muses' hellebore, their anti-poetic antidote, had only a short-lived effect, if any. The author's self-conflicting strategy – to recall and deny the world of gods and legends in the same breath, to line up the ancient tales for easy reference only to undermine their authority by implementing devastating euhemeristic or philosophical myth criticism, to register the poets' material while ironically degrading the poets themselves – assured his work success even among strict medieval examiners. They did not have to 'moralize' him, as they did with the seductive but notoriously offensive Ovid, because he had already taken care of that process himself. Fulgentius might in fact well appear as "an anti-Ovid", to borrow Relihan's designation, in the sense that his Muses' remarkably concise and uncommitted reports on the myths, frequently resorting to fanciful etymology, amount to the stylistic opposite of the Golden Age poet's captivating and illusionistic quick-change turns.[1] Due to this terse mythography, Fulgentius eventually contributed to the integration of the ancient deities and their tales into the medieval literary canon, crucial to the works of the anonymous so-called Vatican mythographers (of whom the first might date from the ninth century), and later, of course, to paramount writers such as Dante or Boccaccio.[2] Caught in the transition from Late Antiquity to the early Middle Ages, he confronted the accelerating decline of the art of poetry, as if he were already perceiving something of the anguish which permeates Friedrich Hölderlin's famous question from another epoch when the gods would seem irretrievably gone: "What is the use of poets at a time of dearth?"[3] His solution to this problem was a stroke of genius: he handed over the Olympians, emblematic of poetry's lost power, to their pungent adversaries, Calliope and the critical Muses of philosophy. Fulgentius betrayed their time-honoured integrity, be it numinous or fictional, only to assure their survival for centuries to come.

Adorning Greece

We cannot be sure, then, of the Muses' actual presence in Books I–III of the *Mythologies*, since, with one or two exceptions, they do not explicitly reappear in the work. In the following section I will, however, judging from the clues in the prologue, consider them as Fulgentius' vicarious narrators. Their high-speed review of classical Greek myths follows roughly the same principles of in-

---

1 Relihan 1993, p. 154. For a further elucidation, see Relihan 1984, aptly concluding that "the narrator cannot maintain his stance as an anti-Ovid", p. 90, and Venuti 2011.
2 The standard work here is Chance 1994 (on Fulgentius, see pp. 95–128).
3 "wozu Dichter in dürftiger Zeit?", from the poem "Brot und Wein", Hölderlin 1986 (trans. M. Hamburger), p. 111.

terpretation as the *Exposition*. The tales of the gods are explained throughout with references to etymologies and allegorical significations of a metaphysical, natural (elementary), astronomical or moral type.[1] Mercury killed the giant Argus with one blow from his scythe, in accordance with the meaning of the Greek word *argos:* idle, useless. What does 'such a fantastic fiction of the Greeks', *tam fabulosum Greciae commentum,* tell us if not that even one hundred guards or spies (Argus' one hundred eyes) are useless without astute bargaining or trading? A sly thief and merchant – such as Mercury – outwits them all with his cunning foresight. Such imagery is consistently exploited by "Greece and its poetic gossiping, always decked in falsehood and yet lying with good intent", *et honeste mendax Grecia et poetica garrulitas semper de falsitate ornata* (1.56–57). Danaë was seduced by a golden shower made of coins rather than water; thus her story informs us about the power of money. It was not a real eagle that abducted Ganymede; during a battle, Jupiter simply snatched the youth under war standards carrying a picture of an eagle. Europa was not taken by a bull; the same god carried her away on a ship with a bull as its figurehead (1.58). And so on and so forth.

All these examples are to be found in Lactantius. The euhemeristic strategy could evidently be implemented along roughly the same lines in sixth-century North Africa as in fourth-century Asia Minor. Notwithstanding, Fulgentius' Muses consistently rely on etymology, as if to underpin their speculations with a grammatical or, from the author's own perspective, scientific foundation. Etymological clues occur with the same frequency, and generally seem just as far-fetched, when the Muses employ philosophical allegoresis (rather than euhemeristic speculation) in their argument. Paris' proverbial judgment is said to be between contemplative, active and sensual life (2.65–66). Venus' name, in the accusative *Venerem,* potentially results from the Stoics' understanding of a life given to vice as a vain matter, *vanam rem.* The goddess is also called Aphrodite, we are told, with a reference to the Greek word *afros,* meaning foam. Her name originates either from the idea that desire is aroused intensely but finally comes to nothing, like foam, or from the fact that ejaculated sperm actually does foam (2.70).

This kind of argument is indicative of the *Mythologies'* wary and disengaged attitude to the fictional heritage from ancient Greece. More brutally, perhaps, than any Late Antique writer, Fulgentius' Muses disenchanted the world of classical myths, not by means of polemic and denunciation (in the Christian apologetic style) but by draining it of life, stifling its imaginative power and inspecting

---

[1] Cf. the excursus on Fulgentius in Gersh 1986, pp. 757–65.

it from a detached distance, as if they were investigating a puppet show obeying a curious set of rules. In Latin literature, Greece had long enjoyed a respectable reputation for its myths and legends, sometimes in contrast to the juridical, oratorical and martial arts of Rome, and at a later date to Christianity's claims to non-negotiable truth. This magnificent Greek world of fiction could now, in Late Antique culture, be perceived as obsolete, at worst a crazy spectacle of vain superstitions, at best equipped with a nostalgic aura or credited with a mystical meaning under its flamboyant exterior. Martianus' Art of Astronomy explained that while the Greeks had filled the skies with mythological fictions, *fabulosisque commentis Grai complevere caelum*, she for her part was content to submit her scientific observations: *ego praecepta potius edisseram disciplinae* (8.817). In a similar spirit, we have seen the narrator of the prologue to *Mythologies* wave aside the literal meaning of the myths as vain trifles, *nugae* and *vanitates*. It was their mystical sense or substance, literally "medulla", that he wanted to access (1.21), *misticum cerebrum*.

This term, *cerebrum*, reappears in the Muses' explanation of Leda and the swan, a story of the ill-fated union between power (Jupiter) and injury or abuse (Leda): the result of their intimacy was the twin brothers Castor and Pollux, tragically separated by the former's death, and the all too tempting Helen, the cause of the Trojan war. This is yet another myth 'tasting of some mystical medulla' or substance (2.93): *haec fabula mistici saporem cerebri consipit*. Thus, the idiosyncratic Muses' ironic distance to the ancient *fabulae* does not keep them from taking interest in their esoteric sense. The tales of the gods are lined up as if they were the outcome of mass (re)production, followed by brief comments concerning their supposed conceptual meaning. A third example involving the Muses' quest for the myths' *cerebrum* is found in the last book's report on the satyr Marsyas' musical contest with Apollo. Like the Orpheus legend, this episode is presented as an illustration of the art of music, in perfect accordance with the Muses' expository hermeneutics: 'Now, then, we may seek the inner medulla of this mysterious story' (3.126), *nunc ergo huius misticae fabulae interiorem cerebrum inquiramus*.

It is obvious that "Greece" in these Late Antique rationalizations of myths serves as a code word for fiction or fictionality, and fiction proves in turn to be synonymous with figuration: eloquent embroidering or ingenious paraphrasing of erudite or 'mystical' themes. Greece itself is presented as a figure, to be exact a *prosopopoeia*. Once upon a time, she (*Grecia* is feminine) had ornamented geographical, astronomical, moral and other scholarly matters so as to change them beyond recognition. The mythographer now pretends to take upon himself the arduous and unrewarding task of scraping away these embellishments in order to restore her original discernment. When discussing Perseus and the Gorgons, his Muses set out to 'declare what adorning Greece wanted to signify under such subtle imagery' (1.61): *quid hac sibi tam subtili sub imagine ornatrix Grecia sentire voluerit, edicamus*. Greece is labelled *ornatrix*, 'adorning', an epithet which, specifically, would suggest a lady's maid or hairdresser, whose tasks were normally, in ancient culture, performed by a slave.

Even though ingenious Greece had produced remarkable inventions, Fulgentius' Muses have difficulty in taking her frills and fancies seriously. In their search for the substance of the old myths, they embody a self-reliance which might be deemed modern, in the sense of the Latin *modernus*, indicating a major breach between past and present time. This modernity comes to the fore in the work's account of the Ixion myth. Juno had adorned a cloud in her image, Ixion made love to the cloud, and as a result of this union the Centaurs were born. The narrator comments drily: "As there is nothing more attractive than Roman truth, so there is nothing more fanciful [*ornatius*] than Greek lies", *sicut nihil Latina gratiosius veritate, ita nihil Greca falsitate ornatius*. The story of the unlucky Ixion, bound to a rotating wheel in Tartarus, is explained as a story about the rise and fall of ambitious people. The wheel in the pagan myth represents, from an enlightened modern perspective, the wheel of Fortune (2.95–97). The Muses' lack of interest in the actual events of the stories is notable, as when they – happily unconcerned about the authorial intention, as stated in the prologue, to ignore the love stories recounted in Ovid's *Heroides* – deal with the myths of Cupid and Psyche or Hero and Leander. After having briefly recapitulated the former tale, the narrator suddenly gives up and leaves it at that "since Apuleius has described such a conglomeration of falsehoods very fully in almost two books", *quia haec saturantius et Apuleius pene duorum continentia librorum tantam falsitatum congeriem enarravit*. This decision not to go on, since the topic is already treated elsewhere, is characteristic. The review of the mythical events (Psyche's descent to the underworld and similar "falsehoods") can be skipped, but the "gist of the interpretation" of the story, its *tenor sentiendi*, is inevitably determined: it refers to desire's (Venus') traps for the human soul (3.113–18).

Thus the secrets of ancient Greece are allegedly laid bare in Fulgentius' (or his Muses') analytical discourse. We will have to make do with one single full-scale example (2.82–84):

> The Sun fairly reveals the adultery of Venus, while the Moon is accustomed to keep it secret. Venus lay with Mars, and the Sun, detecting her, betrayed her to her husband Vulcan, who forged steel-hard fetters and, enchaining both the deities, showed them lying in their shame. She, in her grief, inflamed with love the five daughters of the Sun – that is, Pasiphae, Medea, Phaedra, Circe, and Dirce. Let us look into what the prating of poets [*poetica garrulitas*] may allude to by this. Certainly for our present age there remains full evidence of

this fable, for valor corrupted by lust becomes clear at the witness of the sun, whereby Ovid in the fifth book of his *Metamorphoses* says: "This god was the first to see." And this valor corrupted by lust is shamefully held in the fetterlike grip of its ardor. She thus inflamed with love the five daughters of the Sun, that is, the five human senses devoted to light and truth and as if made dark by this corrupting of the Sun's brood. For this reason also they chose names of this kind for the five daughters of the Sun: first, as was seen, Pasiphae, that is, for *pasinfanon*, which in Latin we call evident to all, for sight looks into the other four senses since it sees the one who gives utterance, notices what can be touched, looks on what has been tasted, and points to what can be smelled; the second, Medea, for what is heard, that is, *medenidean*, which in Latin we call no sight, for the voice is hollow in the body; third, Circe, for touch, that is, as if one said in Greek *cironcrine*, which in Latin we call judgment of the hands; fourth, Phaedra, or odorous, as if one should say *feronedon*, for bearing sweetness; fifth, Dirce, judge of taste, that is, for *drimoncrine*, which in Latin we call judging what is bitter. (VI)

This extract from the *Mythologies* evinces a good deal of Fulgentius' particular type of modernism. It is, on the one hand, permeated by a pronounced moralism: Venus seems rightly castigated, and her story elicits a gloomy picture of the depravity that desire causes in human life. On the other hand, it is characterized by systematic and detailed speculation, based on fanciful etymologies. However, we find hardly any sensitivity to the myths' inner nerve, to their dramatic potential or emotional power, in Fulgentius' Muses. His dismissive words about poetic garrulity are characteristic. The old Olympian pantheon serves merely to satisfy the taste of his Muses – and, as it would turn out, that of centuries to come – for moralizing allegory.

In her study of the mythographers of Antiquity and the Middle Ages, Paule Demats adopts a strikingly lukewarm attitude towards Fulgentius. In her eyes, he already embodies the medieval clerks' feelings of superiority over the pagan myths. To her it seems obvious, for example from the "garrulous [!] and confused" prologue to *Mythologies*, that Fulgentius did not take his subject very seriously: "The only thought that the Middle Ages could discern in Fulgentius could be summed up like this: the myth or fabulous fiction (*fabulosum commentum*) does not oppose truth, nor is it a veil designed to deprive profane people of the secrets of a divine knowledge. It is the lavish and complex embroidery with which *Graecia ornatrix* decorated the ideas that philosophy, fortunately, would explain in clearer language. The mythographer's work consists in transcribing these two versions of one and the same discourse, while all he hears in the former is an echo in advance of the latter."[1]

---

1 Demats 1973, pp. 55, 60 ("en n'écoutant dans la première que l'écho anticipé de la seconde").

As a matter of fact, various modern critics have shared Demats's impression of a "confused" presentation in Fulgentius' *Mythologies*. Be that as it may, we cannot exclude the possibility that the author betrays a certain ambivalence or even ran into some contradictions in his treatment of the ancient myths. The specialist in the history of Western allegory, Jon Whitman, for instance, found it difficult to distinguish any "coherent poetic or philosophic design" in the *Mythologies:* "Fulgentius aims less at conceptual order than impromptu invention." The material is disparate, the author's approach to it is "disjointed, sometimes arbitrary", and his allegorical method is now physical, now ethical, now euhemeristic. Martianus himself would have been dissatisfied at finding his mystical Mercury reduced to the status of trader and thief.[1] Even the sympathetically inclined Relihan seems to have some difficulties with the work's superficially moralizing interpretations, in which "pagan mythological creatures demonstrate their own allegorical bloodlessness".[2]

At this point, however, it should be apparent that I hold this allegorical anaemia to be the whole point of Fulgentius' project. It is also perceptible in Martianus' *Marriage*, even though that work's presentation of the Olympian gods still oscillates between mystical exaltation and satirical pranks. Indeed, scurrilous or fickle Satire appears in both these writers as a Muse, fully exploiting the possibilities of her genre, the Menippean satire, hence we may be in doubt, *pace* Whitman, as to whether Martianus would have shown surprise at Hermes' criminal and mercantile activities in the *Mythologies*. Notwithstanding, Fulgentius demonstrates even more strongly than his predecessor the irretrievable on-going Late Antique transformation of the mythical deities into – ink on papyrus. That is the real gist of his intention to illuminate 'vain things transformed', *mutatae vanitates*, or of Calliope's indirect exhortation to the poet to record what he is about to hear on Egyptian papyrus, *Niliaci papiri*. It was in such black-and-white or "bloodless" configurations, as literary ghosts, that the antique gods would survive the transition into medieval culture.

In a sense, the *Aeneid* seems to have left a much deeper mark on Augustine's soul than on Fulgentius'; the former kept struggling with his childhood impressions of "Troy afire, and the shade of Creusa", whereas the latter unabashedly dismissed Dido as an epitome of the kind of love which the male hero must learn to suppress. For the same reason Fulgentius' *Mythologies* are at a great distance from Augustine's constant worries about signification in general and fiction in particular. At times, the mythographer's Muses might remind us of mod-

---

[1] Whitman 1987, pp. 106f.
[2] Relihan 1993, p. 161.

ern solvers of crossword puzzles, indefatigably searching for the answers to the tricky clues that antique poetry and mythology had left behind. Their apparent unresponsiveness to the tales they explain does not preclude, however, the presence of a certain cultural nostalgia in the author's project. To be sure, his works do not exhibit the sense of continuity in relation to the classical world that still, for all their antiquarian interests, characterizes Servius' or Macrobius' writings.

Fulgentius recorded a pagan world that definitely belonged to the past, that had thrived on unsubstantial inventions, engendering embarrassing poetical effusions – yet had been able to come up with such amazing things! A key phrase in this context is his Muses' conclusion after having reported on how Teiresias was transformed into a woman, later to be blinded by Juno and granted the gift of prophecy by Jupiter: 'Greece is as bewildering for its lies as it is admirable for its fictions' (2.77), *Grecia enim quantum stupenda mendacio, tantum est admiranda commento*. I have chosen to translate *commentum* ('invention', 'fabrication', sometimes applied to poetry in particular) as 'fiction' here, since Fulgentius obviously wanted to express a contrast to lying, analogous to the well-known distinction between *argumentum* and *fabula*. For all its undulating curlicues, even the story of Teiresias has something to tell us (the blinded and queer *vates* representing the shifting seasons of the year). From this perspective, 'adorning Greece', replete with fabulous fictions, shimmers as a solace or refuge beyond the devastated reality of the present. Her peculiar ringlets form a glaring contrast to "the lamentable misery of our time".

For Augustine, the ancient gods were still a potential threat to the Christian faith. Even though their purportedly idiosyncratic behaviour had been challenged and refuted by several generations of apologists, their lingering cultural presence still demanded that he, in the *City of God*, mobilized all his polemic energy and all his critical subtlety to combat their harmful influence. For Fulgentius' Muses, on the other hand, they are already well and truly neutralized. Demats is perfectly right about that. For the mythographer (or, strictly speaking, his Pierian narrators) the stars and the elements were no longer gods, and the gods no longer objects of worship. They had survived as mere names, the etymologies of which revealed facts or ideas that were still, after all, useful to know.[1]

Interestingly, Fulgentius proved incapable of relating his reluctant fascination with antique culture to his Christian faith; indeed, he dispensed completely with any particularly Christian reinterpretations or reuse, *chrēsis*, of the old myths. On the whole, he actually ignored the religion on which his modernity was based, to the effect that his *Mythologies* exhibits, as it were, a kind of dou-

---

[1] Demats 1973, p. 59.

ble-entry bookkeeping system. Cupid (greed) persuades Psyche (spirit) not to look upon his countenance (3.118), "that is, not to learn the pleasure of greed (thus Adam, although possessing sight, does not see himself as naked until he eats of the tree of covetousness)".[1] The pagan tale and the Bible text are arranged side by side, like two parallel tracks running through history, ideally elucidating but never interfering with each other. Augustine himself, as we have seen, could interconnect them with reference to Platonic or Virgilian forebodings of Christian insights. They never met in the mythographer's work.

Correspondingly, the Christian author of the *Mythologies* was anxious to maintain a certain distance to the pushy Muses' presence under his roof, despite Calliope's shameless flirtation. Thus in his idiosyncratic way, he foreshadowed the later Carolingian humanists who, as Curtius has shown, would make room for the Muses in their secular poetry of eulogy and friendship, sometimes even in an erotic or festive mode, while explicitly banning them from their spiritual writings.[2] In a poem dedicated to Charles the Bald, John Scotus Eriugena would tellingly contrast "the songs of the Muses and games of chattering satyrs" on the one hand, *Moysarum cantus, ludos satyrasque loquaces*, with, on the other hand, the words of the Christian prophets which "proceed with harmonious beauty", *modulamine pulchro / Consona procedunt* (1.13–16).[3] It was probably not until the literature of the High Middle Ages that the Muses, with their leader Apollo, would be rehabilitated on a grand scale within the divine scheme of things.[4] Nevertheless, one of the key figures of the turbulent Migration Period, who saw to it that the ancient gods and Muses, however outrageous, garrulous and ultimately non-existent, were accessible for coming generations, was definitely Fulgentius the mythographer and mythoclast.

---

[1] "Id est cupiditatis delectamenta discat – unde et Adam quamvis videat nudum se non videt, donec de concupiscentiae arbore comedat".
[2] Curtius 1990, p. 237.
[3] From the poem *Hellinas Troasque suos cantarat Homerus*, trans. M.W. Herren, John Scotus Eriugena 1993.
[4] For a brief survey of this development, see Kupke 1992.

6 Boethius: The Maieutics of Consolation

Lactantius, Servius and Macrobius were all active in the fourth and fifth centuries. The dating of Martianus Capella's *Marriage* varies, normally to different stages of the 400s, and scholars usually place the composition of Fulgentius' work to the early or mid-sixth century. His *Mythologies* is at all events of a later date than the *Marriage*. This quintet of writers, all of whom, each in his own way, were attracted by the possibilities of allegorical configuration and interpretation, had a magnificent successor in the government official, translator and philosopher Anicius Manlius Severinus Boethius (ca. 480 – 525), who was active precisely in the transitional period between fading Antiquity and the dawn of medieval culture.

Thanks to his intellectual achievements, too, Boethius emerges as a borderland figure in this broad cultural context. A member of the Senate in Rome and Master of the Offices at the royal court in Ravenna under Theoderic the Great, King of the Ostrogoths, he was one of the last intellectuals in the Western half of the Roman Empire who was completely fluent in Greek. He was familiar with classical philosophy, a zealous translator of Aristotle, educated in the traditional *paideia* system, above all in dialectic and the four mathematical arts, but also the author of subtle Christological analyses. In many respects, Boethius was actually the last Roman and the first Scholastic, as the German medievalist Martin Grabmann once famously labelled him.[1] I will try to elucidate the kind of philosophical therapy and allegorical poetry that characterizes his best-known work, *The Consolation of Philosophy*. This dialogue has been the subject of intense research in the past few decades. Joachim Gruber's major commentary from 1978 (revised in 2006) has made it clear that echoes from classical Greek and Latin literature are to be found in virtually every line of the work. Thus the *Consolation* presents an astonishing intertextual assemblage, reworked into a coherent whole, which is all the more remarkable as it was composed under literally mortal circumstances.

---

[1] "Boethius, der letzte Römer – der erste Scholastiker", in Grabmann 1909, pp. 148–77; as a matter of fact, Grabmann is reusing a portrayal of Boethius by the Italian humanist Lorenzo Valla.

Philosophy Sets the Tone

In 523, Boethius is locked up in his death cell, accused by his master, Theoderic of Ravenna, of lese-majesty. After years of more or less stable coexistence between the Eastern and Central Mediterranean's three political focal points, the Emperor in Constantinople, the royal court at Ravenna and the Senate/Pope in Rome, these were unruly times. The new Emperor Justin, uncle of the famous Justinian the Great, had begun to strengthen relations with the Pope and the Senate, probably with the aim of undermining Ostrogothic authority in Italy. Theoderic now suspected that Boethius had withheld information about subversive correspondence between the senator Albinus and Constantinople. Boethius seems to have defended his case – he might even have dared to endorse the integrity of Albinus and the Senate against Ravenna – but to no avail. Even if the accusations against him were false, as he boldly maintained, they were devastating. By all accounts, the charge was never completely investigated. The philosopher fell victim to top-level political manoeuvring and, in addition, to local envy (not least, sadly, on the part of his fellow senators). Moreover, he was probably suspected of practising sorcery (black magic, astrology), a type of accusation sometimes put forward against erudite highbrows. As First Minister, *magister officiorum*, in Ravenna, Boethius had acted as a man of principle, albeit incautiously, and had made powerful enemies at the court of the ageing, increasingly hard-pressed Theoderic.[1]

It is now, during his long period in prison, that Boethius composes his *Consolation* in five books, a complaint over his adverse fate but likewise an impressing display of Stoic resignation and self-discipline. The work is designed as a dialogue written in *prosimetra*, a blend of verse and prose that we recognize from the Menippean satire, practised by both Martianus and Fulgentius, which would attract quite a few medieval followers. In fact, the *Consolation* enjoyed as great a success as Martianus' *Marriage*. Admittedly, the work was not able to save the life of its author who was cruelly tortured and clubbed to death by Theoderic's henchmen in Pavia (in 524 or 525, at the very latest in early 526). On the other hand, in the words of the Dutch mediaevalist Ferdinand Sassen, the *Consolation* became "the most beloved reading-book of the Middle Ages". Apart from the Bible, Sassen continues, no other book has left so strong a

---

[1] For two initiated surveys of the circumstances around Boethius' death, see Chadwick 1981, pp. 46–56, and Matthews 1981.

mark on this epoch's culture as Boethius' last work, preserved in more than 400 manuscripts.[1]

Pierre Courcelle, who has examined the *Consolation*'s sources and its fate in posterity's literary and artistic reception as diligently as he did with Augustine's *Confessions*, provides us with overwhelming documentation in his 1967 study. Among the proof of the Middle Ages' appreciation of Boethius there is Alcuin's discovery of the *Consolation* for the benefit of Carolingian culture and King Alfred the Great's personal translation of the dialogue into Old English at the end of the ninth century, followed by Chaucer's into Middle English five hundred years later. Furthermore, there are the detailed commentaries associated with the school of Chartres, not only on the *Consolation* but likewise on Boethius' *opuscula sacra*, in particular his treatise on the Trinity, predictably entitled (like Augustine's far more voluminous work on the same subject) *De trinitate*. Last but not least, there is Dante's reverence in the Heaven of the Sun, where the Roman nobleman holds a prominent position as the eighth of twelve wise spirits forming a crown of light, presented by Saint Thomas Aquinas (Paradiso 10.124–29):

124 Per vedere ogne ben dentro vi gode
125 l'anima santa che 'l mondo fallace
　　 fa manifesto a chi di lei ben ode.
　　　Lo corpo ond' ella fu cacciata giace
　　 giuso in Cieldauro; ed essa da martiro
　　 e da essilio venne a questa pace.

　　　Within it rejoices, in his vision of all goodness,
　　 the holy soul who makes quite plain
　　 the world's deceit to one who listens well.
　　　The body from which it was driven out
　　 lies down there in Cieldauro, and he has risen
　　 from martyrdom and exile to this peace.

　　　　　　　　　　　　*

The *Consolation* begins with an allegorical scene deeply rooted in antique culture, notably in Plato's dialogue *Crito*, where Socrates imagines he is visited in his death cell by "the laws and the commonwealth" (50a), and in *The Shepherd of Hermas*, the most comprehensive of the Apostolic Fathers' works, written in Greek during the first half of the second century CE (if not earlier), where an authoritative female figure appears from the sky to a shepherd confessing his sins in a dream. Boethius' version of this scenario became in turn the main matrix for

---

[1] Sassen 1984, p. 109.

the High Middle Ages' accounts of visions and divine visitations, for instance in Alan of Lille, Dante or William Langland.[1] In addition, more importantly in this context, it is emblematic of a common distrust or even repudiation of fictionality in Late Antique culture. It epitomizes the "ancient quarrel" between philosophy and poetry known from Plato's dialogues. As we have been able to establish, this dispute had been paradigmatically settled in Aristotle's *Poetics* by virtue of the author's *mimēsis* concept; still, it was certainly alive in Hellenistic learned circles and reopened on a large scale by the Church Fathers, most ambitiously by Augustine, as in his story of the two birds *philocalia* and *philosophia* in *Against the Academics* (above, p. 140). Boethius joins the Platonic tradition when he lets his alter ego, sentenced to death, receive a serious female guest whose "countenance demanded absolute reverence" (1.PR.1), *reverendi admodum vultus*.[2] She appears at the very moment when he sits pondering on his youthful passion for poetry, *carmina*, and on his close intercourse with the Muses, those *camenae* that once were his pride and joy. Now, in his hour of need, they grant him consolation but are described as lacerated, *lacerae* (1.M.1.3). They seem powerless in the face of the tragedy that has befallen him.

This introductory passage is written in elegiac couplets, richly echoing classical Latin literature. The metre itself is revealing. It recalls Ovid, another Roman writer who was brought down by his master. In his detailed commentary on the *Consolation*, Joachim Gruber identifies its many reminiscences of Ovid, not least from *Tristia*, the exiled poet's desperate lamentations in elegiac couplets, and another scholar, Anna Crabbe, emphasizes the significance of these initial verses for the entire work; they prepare the way for the author's rejection of precisely an Ovidian approach to affliction, and, specifically, of the elegiac Muses.[3] Thus, at one and the same time, the greatest illusionist of Roman poetry is recalled as the protagonist's historical companion in misfortune and dismissed as a possible model for dealing with adverse fate. Moreover, the elegiac piece of verse that the prisoner composes in his death cell wets his face 'with true tears' (1.M.1.4), *veris fletibus*, an early hint, perhaps, at the work's refutation of the fictional mode associated with the Golden Age poet's graceful, pathetic and melancholic verse.

Boethius' guest, the serious matron, initially appears as a hallucination. She is both young and old, in accordance with a common topos in Late Antique (and,

---

[1] I quote *Crito* from the Loeb edition, Plato 2005. Cf. Bogdanos 1977, pp. 34, 42–45, and Dronke 1994, pp. 38f.
[2] For the Latin text of Boethius' *Consolation* I follow H.F. Stewart's, E.K. Rand's and S.J. Tester's Loeb edition 1997 (1918), while the English translations are from J.C. Relihan 2001.
[3] Gruber 2006, pp. 54–61; Crabbe 1981, p. 245.

later, medieval) tradition, and sometimes she seems to be of normal stature, sometimes "she would seem to strike at the heavens with the crown of the top of her head", *nunc vero pulsare caelum summi verticis cacumine videbatur*.¹ Her clothes are torn, but there can still be seen the Greek capital letters Π and Θ woven in her robe, *pi* and *thēta*, representing practical and theoretical philosophy respectively. There is no doubt that this awe-inspiring lady is a personification of Philosophy. The meaning of her apparition is, albeit fragmentarily, written on her clothing. Her venerable figure as well as the books and the sceptre in her hands are in direct contrast to the elegiac Muses that dictated the introductory verses to the despairing narrator.

Here, as Relihan observes, Boethius brings in yet another well-tried convention, this time from ancient comedy. There, too, the author might present himself as imperfect or inadequate for his task, sometimes by presenting the very genre embodied on the stage, making her complain about him.² While Fulgentius had parodied this concept in his *Mythologies* with the apparition of critical Calliope, Boethius would rather recycle it for his own purposes. Accordingly, his Philosophy, despite her great dignity, becomes remarkably angry when she catches sight of the prisoner's female company – the elegiac Muses – in his cell (1.PR.1):

> And then, when she saw that the women who were sitting at my bedside were the Muses of poetry, dictating words to my tears, she was upset for a time. Who, she said, her pitiless eyes ablaze, let these little stage whores come visit this invalid? They do not tend to his pains with any sort of a remedy; not only that, but they actually encourage them, adding their own sweet poisons. For these are the women who choke out the rich fields of reason's fruits; theirs are the barren brambles of the passions; they acclimatize the mortal mind to disease, and do not liberate it. Now, if it were some unhallowed man that your sweet nothings were leading astray, as is your all-too-common custom, I'd think that this could be tolerated with less annoyance – after all, my efforts would not be under attack in such a one as that. But him! Raised in the disciplines of the followers of Parmenides and Plato – But no; just you get out of here, you Sirens, sweet unto shipwreck; leave him to *my* Muses for his convalescence and his cure.

---

1 Horace had used the same formula in the final line of his *Ode* 1.1, where the protagonist is about to strike the top of his head against the stars out of pride and joy, *sublimi feriam sidera vertice*, if only Maecenas is prepared to list him 'among the lyric poets', *lyricis vatibus*. This formula obviously signalled euphoria beyond measure in ancient literature, as when Medea in Ovid's *Metamorphoses*, envisioning a future with Jason in Greece, experiences happiness to the effect that she will touch the stars with the top of her head: *et vertice sidera tangam* (7.61). Read against the backdrop of Horace's *Carmen* 1.1, Boethius' adaptation of the topos might be interpreted as a signal of the transference of authority from the classical *vates* to Lady Philosophy.

2 Relihan 1993, p. 188.

> This chorus line, thus scolded, stared down at the ground in sorrow; by their blushing they revealed their disgrace and they went out the door, depressed. (VII)

Philosophy's speech begins strikingly with a rhetorical question, which by means of its strong invective, "these little stage whores", *hae scenicae meretriculae*, charges her argument with strong emotion. After putting forward her indictment, she generalizes the case to apply to the state of illness of all mankind. Her tirade culminates in an implementation of the dialectic *locus* or 'place' *a fortiori*: the problem of the Muses' enticements would normally affect simple people, say an uneducated person, *profanus*, but it becomes all the more serious and intolerable when a man like Boethius, schooled in classical philosophy, yields to them. Finally, the stern matron rounds off her argument by urging these "Sirens" to depart. No sooner said than done: the author's cherished Muses leave at once.

They do not even make an attempt to defend themselves against the accusations Philosophy has thrown at them. She cunningly links them to theatrical as well as epic examples of indecency and fornication: after having scolded them as whores of the stage, she finally addresses them as "Sirens". Thus Boethius applies the *moral* argument against fiction. It originates, as we have seen, in classical Greece and was put to frequent use by the Church Fathers, who had fiercely attacked the theatre for its immorality, as witnessed by Augustine's heated assaults in the *City of God*. Moreover, in Boethius' dialogue, Philosophy depicts the Muses' art as completely ineffective when faced with the depression that her protégé is enduring. And not only that: they actually increase his pain rather than curing it. Here, the *pathological* argument against fiction comes to the fore: it is treacherous and dangerous, tempting us with its allures but exercising a disintegrating effect on our souls. Lastly, Philosophy's outpourings against the Muses mobilize – as would be expected from her – the *philosophical* argument against fiction. The domains of reason, the *ratio* of ancient wisdom, have to be cleansed of the "thorns" of passion in order to bear fruit. The idealistic Greek notion of pure thinking, launched by 'Eleatics' like Parmenides and 'Academics' like Plato almost a thousand years earlier, still attracts Boethius, the last representative of this venerable classical tradition.

Lady Philosophy's dismissal of Boethius' Muses calls attention to an aspect of the Late Antique issue of fictionality that would require a separate investigation: its gendered discourse. All the authors treated in the present work except one are men, but their Muses, like those of the ancient Greeks, are females. Augustine had been attracted by them as a young man but would renounce them in his old age. Martianus had bickered with his *camena*, and Fulgentius was on the verge of being seduced by his Calliope. In eloquence, moreover, there had been a tendency, at least since the days of Cicero, to associate a densely figurative style with curling irons, makeup and finery, frequently linked to the topos of female vanity. This close connection between elaborated style and jewellery or rouge could at times implicate secular erudition and fictionality as well. We have already seen Martianus present all the Arts as women, and we have seen Fulgentius label Greece, the very epitome of classical mythology, as *ornatrix*, a lady's maid or hairdresser. David Chamberlain remarks in a fascinating study that Boethius, in his treatise *De musica* (*On Music*), prefers a "temperate, simple and masculine" kind of music to an "effeminate, violent or fickle" one (1.1), *modesta ac simplex et mascula nec effeminata nec fera nec varia*.[1] Now Philosophy, in a spirit reminiscent of *On Music*, identifies the tearful Muses as seductive and depraved, with an emasculating influence on the condemned author, while she herself represents a male and virtuous type of thinking, immediately prepared to expel the meretricious goddesses.

Thus in Boethius, Philosophy resembles a man disguised as a woman. She is in command of her own Muses, the philosophical ones. *Their* music is controlled by reason and may be described in terms of a carefully dosed antidepressant drug. It is in accord with the harmony of the spheres, it regulates the changes of the element and the seasons, and it tempers the state of human souls. Philosophy and her Muses, too, dwell on the notion of *amor*, though not in the sense of fickle passions coming and going between individuals but as a mighty power permeating the universe. Consequently, Boethius' consolatory treatise appears as a crucial link in the tradition of the idea of cosmic love, exactly halfway between Plato's *Timaeus* and Dante's *Comedy:* "O how happy the mortal race, / were Love king over all your hearts, / Love that heaven accepts as king!" (2. M.8.28–30), *O felix hominum genus, / si vestros animos amor / quo caelum regitur regat*.

It is quite natural for Philosophy, very much aware of the therapeutic resources of poetry and music, to dismiss the prisoner's Muses as "Sirens", referring to the dangerous female creatures who had tempted the returning hero of *The Odyssey* with their beautiful but deadly song (12.165–200). Her usage of the Sirens in a transferred or generalized sense was by no means original. It was already exploited, in a positive key, by Ovid in *The Art of Love:* "The Sirens were wondrous creatures of the sea, who with tuneful voice detained vessels, how swift soe'er they sailed. [...] A persuasive thing is song: let women learn to sing" (3.311–12, 315), and, dismissively, by Plutarch in *How to Study Poetry* from *Moralia* (15d).[2]

---

[1] Chamberlain, pp. 383f. For Boethius' text, I follow G. Friedlein's Teubner edition 1867 and C. Bower's translation 1989.
[2] "Monstra maris Sirenes erant, quae voce canora / quamlibet admissas detinuere rates. / [...] Res est blanda canor: discant cantare puellae".

The Church Fathers would follow the latter, interpreting the Sirens of classical mythology as emblematic figures for the dangerous combination of dissemblance and depravity. This kind of moralizing explanation of myths was surely known to Servius when, in his commentary on the *Aeneid*, he accounted for the nature, origin and function of the seductive nymphs *secundum fabulam*, only to reach the conclusion that *secundum veritatem* they 'were whores who reduced passers-by to destitution, thereby, in fictional terms, causing them shipwreck' (5.864).[1] As Erich Kaiser has shown in a learned essay on topical scenes from *The Odyssey* in ancient literature, the Sirens had for centuries been identified with, or, alternatively, envisioned as competitors to the Muses.[2] Boethius employs both strategies in his own way. In his version, Philosophy immediately recognizes the Sirens as "the Muses of poetry", only to let them compete with her worthier and, in the first place, more proficient counterparts. Consequently, they have to surrender and exit from the *Consolation*.

There, Philosophy becomes an allegorical figure in a new story, whereby she repeats a narrative pattern – the supernatural correction of a hero gone astray – which is based on precisely *The Odyssey*. It is at the beginning of Homer's epic poem that we find the war veteran, longing to return home, on Ogygia, Calypso's island, forced by the beautiful nymph to lead a demoralizing and irresponsible life of idleness (1.11–62). The situation seems even worse for Aeneas when he ends up in Dido's arms, since he blatantly tends to forget his mission, "with no thought or respect for the cities that fate's words / grant him" (4.225), *fatisque datas non respicit urbes*. In both cases, it is Hermes (Mercury) who, at the command of the highest god, contrives and supervises the hero's return to prescribed order. Boethius however, was not an epic poet but a philosopher, so in the *Consolation's* death cell it is allegorical Philosophy that has to release the author's alter ego from his entanglement in the web of fiction so as to restore his reason's unimpeded view of the universe, of the cosmic numbers and the causes of things, beautifully extolled by herself (1.M.2).

Thus we have uncovered the ostensibly paradoxical mechanism that governs Boethius' dialogue: fictionality is censured and rejected, point by point, in favour of philosophy – by means of arguments drawn from ancient mythology and fiction. On closer inspection, the paradox proves easy to solve. The sentimental Muses who are dismissed at the beginning of the *Consolation* epitomize the irrational kind of poetry that relies on fables and fabrications, leaving all in-

---

1 "Secundum veritatem meretrices fuerunt, quae transeuntes quoniam deducebant ad egestatem, his fictae sunt inferre naufragia."
2 Kaiser 1964, pp. 117f.

tellectual or moral responsibility aside. While embodying the elegiac mode that had been implemented – with unsurpassed virtuosity – by Ovid in his works on transformation, love and exile, they force the deeply distressed prisoner, as Thomas Curley has noted, to passively write at their dictation: "Lo! Their cheeks harrowed, the Muses come tell me the words I must take down" (1.M.1.3), *Ecce mihi lacerae dictant scribenda camenae.*[1]

By contrast, the poems that Philosophy keeps reciting throughout the dialogue are inspired by other Muses, her own, who rather encourage the prisoner to pause for thought and to widen his mental horizon far beyond his personal predicament. They promote as well as embody Philosophy's rational music. They explain as well as execute her therapeutic message. Their songs are framed as concise, allegorical scenarios in Macrobius' sense – a set of minimalistic, versified *narrationes fabulosae* – and as the fuel of Philosophy's on-going refutation of the prisoner's depressive mood. Accordingly, lyric poetry is far more important for the work as a whole – regularly switching between verse and prose – than in Martianus' or Fulgentius' Menippean satires, where the *metra* play a comparatively minor role. In conclusion, the far-sighted Lady Philosophy expels the sonorous but dangerous "Sirens", whose mythical prototypes had enchanted the sailors in *The Odyssey* or *The Art of Love*, so as to be able to install her own Muses in Boethius' company. To this end, she might in fact rely on more acceptable predecessors in Roman Golden Age poetry, the *learned* Sirens, "skilled in song", *doctae Sirenes*, that none other than Ovid had summoned in his *Metamorphoses* (5.555), yet another well-known feature of the epic or lyric repertoire: an emblem of the erudite poet, *poeta doctus*.[2] If this is the case, her move is characteristic of both the intertextual ingenuity and the Muses' philosophical domestication in Boethius' *Consolation*.

Philosophy can thus begin her professional treatment of the gloomy prisoner. His spiritual suffering is quickly diagnosed as "lethargy" (1.PR.2), the Greek word for drowsiness or, literally, forgetfulness. Her cure is planned accordingly. By means of teaching, dialogue and lyric poetry, the patient will be helped to remember who he really is and hence access his true being (as a philosopher). Vaguely reminiscent of Fulgentius' analytical approach to ancient mythology, Philosophy's therapeutic method sometimes seems to forebode twentieth-century psychoanalysis, apart from the fact that in Boethius' *Consolation* – as Curley emphasizes – it is the doctor rather than the patient that talks, and that her cure in no way attempts to make the patient aware of any repressed libidinous in-

---

1 Curley 1986, p. 224.
2 Cf. Kaiser 1964, p. 119.

stincts; on the contrary, she tries to endow him with apprehension of and insight into metaphysical reality.[1]

And, as it turns out, the therapy works. In the early parts of the dialogue, Boethius refuses to accept his fate. His beautiful hymn to the creator of the canopy of heaven (1.M.5) aims to clarify the contrast between the cosmic order and Fortune's fickle harrying on earth. It is with pain, grief and anger that the prisoner articulates his resounding protest against the lot of mankind. But his own choice of words in the commentary on the same hymn indicates that his complaints lack solid evidence and are due to a failure to recognize the true nature of his illness. He has howled like a dog in his unceasing pain, *continuato dolore delatravi*, and Philosophy rebukes him for the prayer he has entrusted to his raging Muse, *Musa saeviens* (1.PR.5). Towards the end of the work Boethius knows better. He remains silent, and his Muse no longer rages.

Step by step, the bitter patient's soul will heal and be restored to recognition, not only of himself but of human destiny and the world at large. From a broad perspective, the therapy he is exposed to is based on classical culture, on the Platonic theory of recollection, *anamnēsis*, and on the Socratic emphasis on self-knowledge: "You have ceased to know who you yourself are", Philosophy rebukes Boethius (1.PR.6), *quid ipse sis, nosse desisti*. However, her treatment seems first and foremost to be dependent on closer models. In recent years, Martha Nussbaum has highlighted Hellenistic philosophy's remarkable interest in pragmatic, not to say psychiatric matters. Various Epicurean, Sceptic and Stoic thinkers did not concern themselves primarily with theoretical reflection but struggled to cope with or to overcome human suffering, acknowledging medicine as their paradigm and addressing their readers as patients.[2] Boethius links his work to this tradition, personifying Hellenistic Philosophy (partly Platonizing, partly Stoic) as a therapist and converting his own alter ego into her patient.

Thus her method presupposes classical culture's "followers of Parmenides and Plato" but is mainly based on later philosophical schools, making assiduous use of the liberal arts. Euclidean geometry is adduced (3.PR.10), and the syllogisms of dialectic are applied throughout the dialogue, so as to make the afflicted prisoner admit that the points of Philosophy's case "stand together, woven from the most solid lines of argument" (3.PR.11): *cuncta enim firmissimis nexa rationibus constant*. She, for her part, refers to eloquence, "the persuasive power of the sweetness of rhetoric", which, however, must be dispensed in judicious doses; in addition, she relies just as heavily on music, or rather poetry, "this mu-

---

[1] Curley 1986, p. 219.
[2] Nussbaum 2009, pp. 3–12.

sical handmaiden from our own house", who sees to it that her instruction varies between lighter and graver tones (2.PR.1).[1] Philosophy is a skilful teacher and therapist who, like several of her antique predecessors, for example Lucretius, the author of the motto for this chapter, knows that the bitter medicine has to be sweetened to go down. That is a crucial trick, because her message to the prisoner is rather harsh in its repeated insistence on *ataraxia*, detachment in the face of wayward Fortune's vicissitudes, a virtue based on old Roman tradition, updated on a theoretical basis in the moral doctrine of Late Antique Stoicism.

Even though Philosophy seems eclectic in her repertoire of topics and ideas, increasingly strong and enticing Platonizing tones emerge from her austere doctrine of moderation. The healing of the soul is on several occasions expressed in terms of ascension, for instance in the ninth *metrum* of the third book that was destined to achieve spectacular success in posterity, quoted throughout the Middle Ages. It is the only poem of the work composed in hexameters, a solemn invocation of the Father of things, based on Plato's *Timaeus* as well as Neo-Platonic speculation, ending in a prayer for release from misty earth (3.M.9.22–26):

22   Da pater augustam menti conscendere sedem,
      da fontem lustrare boni, da luce reperta
      in te conspicuos animi defigere visus.
25   Dissice terrenae nebulas et pondera molis
      atque tuo splendore mica!

Grant to the mind, Father, that it may rise to your holy foundations;
grant it may ring round the source of the Good, may discover the true light,
and fix the soul's vision firmly on you, vision keen and clear-sighted.
Scatter these shadows, dissolve the dead weight of this earthly concretion,
shine in the splendor that is yours alone.

Some syntagms or phrases of this poem seem reminiscent of Christianity which overall, to many (later) readers' surprise, is conspicuous by its absence from the *Consolation*.[2] In such passages from the dialogue, a Carolingian commentator

---

[1] "Adsit igitur Rhetoricae suadela dulcedinis quae tum tantum recto calle procedit, cum nostra instituta non deserit cumque hac Musica laris nostri vernacula nunc leviores nunc graviores modos succinat." For the interpretation of *Musica* as poetry, see Mueller-Goldingen 1989, p. 375.
[2] One scholar who refused to be surprised was C.S. Lewis, who remarks that the author of the dialogue quite simply respected the Aristotelian distinction between disciplines, each with its proper method and area of responsibility: "If we had asked Boethius why his book contained philosophical rather than religious consolations, I do not doubt that he would have answered, 'But did you not read my title? I wrote philosophically, not religiously, because I had chosen the consolations of philosophy, not those of religion, as my subject. You might as well ask why a book on arithmetic does not use geometrical methods'", 1983, pp. 77f. In fact, the twelfth cen-

like Remigius of Auxerre or a master of the school of Chartres like William of Conches would, as Courcelle has shown, find support for their characteristic efforts to bring Plato into agreement with John the Evangelist, the Ideas of the Demiurg with the Word of God.[1]

The fourth book of the dialogue begins with a beautiful Platonizing *metrum* devoted to the ascension of the soul towards God – soon to be analysed – only to return to the theodicy problem: the contrast between the flagrant injustices on earth and the great harmony, *concordia*, that prevails in the universe (4. M.6.19). The fifth book, finally, deals with epistemological issues, in explicit opposition to the Stoic theory of our mind as a blank page (5.M.4.7), *aequor paginae*, exposed to sensory impressions. In this context, Boethius lists mankind's cognitive possibilities at four hierarchical levels (5.PR.4):

- our senses, *sensus*, which receive impressions from external things,
- imagination, *imaginatio*, discerning the shape of these things, their *figura*, without taking their actual matter or significance into account,
- our higher reason, *ratio*, subjecting the inner form of things, their *species*, to a generalizing analysis,
- while, finally, divine *intellegentia* is able to observe the original and common form of all things, their *simplex forma*, by virtue of its pure sight, *pura mentis acies*.

This systematic arrangement of the faculties of the soul already heralds scholastic psychology (and epistemology), while its basic concepts are derived from the Aristotelian tradition inaugurated with *On the Soul*, later to be exploited and modified by Plotinus, Augustine and Proclus.[2]

Of special interest for our investigation is Boethius' linking of the concept of *figura*, the external form or shape of things, to the supervision of imagination. In conformity with Augustine, Boethius prefers the term *imaginatio* to *phantasia*, denoting an intermediate faculty of the soul operating in close connection with the senses without being dependent on them: "Even if it has taken from the senses the starting point of seeing and forming shapes, nevertheless it is

---

tury's best readers of Boethius, such as Conrad of Hirsau or John of Salisbury, had essentially said the same thing: see Courcelle 1967, pp. 343f. Boethius' English translator V.E. Watts emphasizes the presence of the *Gloria* of Western liturgy, the Lord's Prayer and St. John's Gospel in the final lines of 3.M.9, Boethius 1986, p. 98. For other observations of Christian overtones in the dialogue, see De Vogel 1973, Mohrmann 1984 and (more reservedly) Shanzer 2009, in particular pp. 240–44.

1 Courcelle 1967, pp. 278–90, 306–13.
2 For Proclus' place in this context, see Kuisma 1996, p. 88.

in the absence of sense that it casts its gaze over each and every thing of the senses by a rationale of judgment that is not of the senses but of the imagination." (5.PR.4)[1] Thus imagination can sometimes proceed on its own, without any direct contact with the outside world, *sine materia*, such as (we may infer) in sleep or in visions. The assumption that it operates with a particular intensity in poets is not expressed verbatim in the *Consolation*, but it is suggested in the author's commentary on Aristotle's *Categories*, where the soul 'makes up' of its own accord, *fingit*, strange hybrid creatures like centaurs and chimeras, traditionally associated with the myths of the poets. These are projections that cannot be turned into objects of our knowledge since they lack substance or models among existing things: they 'subsist only in imagination', *sola imaginatione subsistunt* (229b–c). Here, Boethius bases his argument on the same Aristotelian tradition as Augustine but omits the Church Father's reservations, safeguarding the philosopher's strictly analytical perspective. The sensations and the images of imagination, he notes in his commentary on Aristotle's *On Interpretation*, serve as a kind of raw material for the mind's generation of concepts. They resemble the first sketches, *primae figurae*, that artists make before they start painting (2.28.15).[2]

Higher up on the ladder of knowledge are discursive reason and intuitive intellect. This neat hierarchy is arranged so that each mental faculty covers the competence areas of the lower ones. Accordingly, intellect masters the cognitive activities of the senses, imagination and reason by virtue of its matchless power of vision: "it perceives reason's universal and imagination's shape and sense perception's material, but not by using reason or imagination or the senses but by the characteristic single stroke of mind [*ictu mentis*], formally, if I may use the word, seeing all things in advance." (5.PR.4)[3] Augustine had relied on the same *ictus mentis* to indicate the overwhelming and immediate contact with God. Implicitly, then, Boethius safeguards the transcendent climax of human recognition that had been crucial to both Plotinus and the Church Father. While the lowest and inert animals get by with their senses, all higher creatures

---

[1] "Imaginatio quoque tametsi ex sensibus visendi formandique figuras sumpsit exordium, sensu tamen absente sensibilia quaeque conlustrat non sensibili sed imaginaria ratione iudicandi."
[2] For Boethius' commentaries on Aristotle's *Categories* as well as *On Interpretation*, see Magee 1989, pp. 84f., 97f., 103. Cf. Gerard O'Daly's 1993 article "Sense-Perception and Imagination in Boethius, Philosophiae Consolatio 5 m. 4", reprinted in O'Daly 2001, pp. 338f.
[3] "Nam et rationis universum et imaginationis figuram et materiale sensibile cognoscit nec ratione utens nec imaginatione nec sensibus, sed illo uno ictu mentis formaliter, ut ita dicam, cuncta prospiciens."

along the chain of being need a certain measure of imagination. Reason, however, is reserved for humanity alone, whereas the intellect, properly speaking, is a divine prerogative (albeit within reach – the ultimate goal – of human beings): *ratio vero humani tantum generis est sicut intellegentia sola divini* (5.PR.5).

With that, Boethius has outlined the cognitive scheme underlying the ascension topos which is at the heart of several poems of the *Consolation*. It clearly emerges from the last *metrum* recited by Philosophy, who at such a late stage appears more as a monological lecturer than a dialogue partner. This poem begins with a snapshot of the many forms of life on earth, the majority of which appear looking downward, with dull and heavy senses (5.M.5.10 – 15):

10   Unica gens hominum celsum levat altius cacumen
       atque levis recto stat corpore despicitque terras.
       Haec nisi terrenus male desipis, admonet figura,
       qui recto caelum vultu petis exserisque frontem,
       in sublime feras animum quoque, ne gravata pessum
15   inferior sidat mens corpore celsius levato.

       Not so the race of mortal men, who can lift their upraised heads high,
       stand with body upright and imponderous, look to earth below them.
       Be not a creature of earth! Be not ignorant! The posture thus reminds you:
       You who reach for the heights with your upturned gaze, pointing face to heaven,
       you must lift spirit as well to such altitude – mind must not be weighed down,
       must not sink down below where the body is, raised to higher stature.

In sublime feras animum quoque... The ascent towards celestial heights is a recurrent theme of the book's *metra*, styled in exemplary fashion in the above lines, with reference to the body (11), the shape or "posture", *figura*, apprehended by imagination (12), the lower part of the soul, *animus* (14), and lastly the higher mind: intellect or *mens* (15). This arrangement is presented for the benefit of the listening prisoner. He too would do well to lift himself up above the miserable circumstances surrounding him. With that, as it were, the Muses of Philosophy have completed their task. By virtue of their truly visionary imagery, they have successfully treated the condemned prisoner's depressive state of mind and dispelled his melancholy.

Thus the *prosimetrum* form is crucial to the efficiency of Boethius' philosophical fiction in the *Consolation*. In his particular version, where hymnic or elegiac *metra* are implemented as illustrations of a persuasive philosophical discourse, it was destined for success in medieval culture. Even though many of the poems appear as consummate works of art in their own right, they are conceived as allegories, substantiations or amplifications of Philosophy's message. They translate her conceptual ideas into images, myths and stories, thereby implementing her therapeutic programme for the prisoner in distress. They all serve to sweeten her bitter – yet, in the end, effective – medicine. As soon as the eminent matron in the introduction to the work has purged poetry of its destructive powers, she can start to use it for her own purposes: as allegorical narrative as well as therapeutic *remedium*.[1] An example: when, in Book IV, Philosophy is going to explain the difficult issues of fate and providence, she warns her patient that he has to abstain from all pleasures that come with "the delights of music and song", *musici carminis oblectamenta*; once she has put her argument in order, however, she will return to him with such enchantments (4.PR.6). She keeps her promise. Having completed her arduous Stoic theodicy, she notes that Boethius needs a moment's relaxation, albeit useful and instructive, before he can move on: "But I see that you have been for some time now both burdened by the weight of the question and exhausted by the great length of the explanation, and so you are waiting for some sweetness that comes from song."[2]

The dialogue form, for its part, had been tried and tested in classical literature with a number of well-known results, first and foremost in Plato, of course. In the Late Greek period, it had been employed in the highly allegorical *The Shepherd of Hermas*, cited above as one of the possible sources for Boethius' *Consolation*. But there were also, in Latin literature, Cicero's transcriptions of his philosophical conversations, and – on a large scale – his *On the Orator*, an ambitious discussion and presentation of the art of rhetoric and its appropriate ethical foundation, inspired by the *otium* of an aristocratic country retirement in traditional Roman style. In addition, from the immediately preceding centuries there were Minucius Felix' *Octavius*, Augustine's philosophical dialogues from Cassiciacum and Macrobius' encyclopaedic *Saturnalia*, to name but a few.[3] Specifically, Boethius reused some dramatic works by Seneca, who had been forced by his imperial master, Nero, to commit suicide in 65 CE, thereby probably emerging as a companion in misfortune to the prisoner in Pavia, yet another martyr for philosophy. Seth Lerer, who has devoted a monograph to Boethius and the literary dialogue genre, emphasizes that this reuse allowed the Late Antique writer to measure his imprisoned protagonist against his Hispanic prede-

---

1 See Curley 1987, p. 359. Curley analyses shrewdly and thoroughly the relation between poetry and prose in Boethius' *Consolation*, albeit upholding the questionable hypothesis that poetry's relevance diminishes after the third book. I will argue for the opposite point of view.
2 "Sed video te iam dudum et pondere quaestionis oneratum et rationis prolixitate fatigatum aliquam carminis exspectare dulcedinem."
3 In his examination of the early Christian Latin dialogue, Peter L. Schmidt particularly highlights the parallels between Augustine's *Soliloquies* and Boethius' *Consolation*, 1977, pp. 124–29.

cessor's Stoic models, such as Orpheus or Hercules, and to enhance Philosophy's versified advice with the authority of the tragic chorus.[1]

The most obvious of the Seneca adaptations in the *Consolation* are probably to be found in the last *metrum* of the third book, where Orpheus descends to the underworld. This is presumably one of antique culture's most beautiful recreations of the legendary poet's trauma, rivalling Virgil's and Ovid's better-known versions in the *Georgics* (4.453–527) and the *Metamorphoses* (10.1–85, 11.1–66) respectively. Boethius subjects the theme to a moralizing treatment, which principally focuses on the final phase of Orpheus' story, the two lovers' failed attempt to return to life on earth together (3.M.12.52–58):

52 Vos haec fabula respicit
    quicumque in superum diem
    mentem ducere quaeritis.
55 Nam qui Tartareum in specus
    victus lumina flexerit,
    quidquid praecipuum trahit
    perdit, dum videt inferos.

   Mortal men! This tale points at you,
   you who seek to conduct your minds
   to the light of the day above:
   Let no man give a backward glance
   in defeat, to the caves of Hell –
   what he takes with himself as his
   he will lose when he sees the dead.

Here, too, the allegorical mode is implemented in paradigmatic fashion. The poem begins with a four-line introduction, setting the Stoic theme, after which the tale of Orpheus is told, ending with the seven lines quoted above: the *expositio* illuminating the meaning of the story. The myth is explicitly put at the service of philosophy, whereby no less a person than the emblematic figure of poetry in antique culture is made to act as *exemplum*. The Thracian poet represents 'whosoever', *quicumque*, tries to raise his mind, *mens*, to the skies. He thus heralds the soul that ascends to heavenly heights in the next poem of the work (4. M.1), albeit with the decisive difference that he does not stand the test. Boethius' Orpheus, as O'Daly remarks, is an *Orphée moralisé* of Neo-Platonic extraction, held up as too attached to his worldly love.[2] The poetic mode is thus linked to

---

[1] Lerer 1985, pp. 237f.
[2] O'Daly 1991, p. 191. More importantly, perhaps, Boethius' dejected interpretation of the Orpheus figure is in stark contrast to the scattered attempts in early Christian tradition, manifested

erotic passion, signalling, just like the Sirens at the beginning of the dialogue, a warning to the prisoner in his cell.

This poem recalls, in part verbatim, Seneca's tragedy *Hercules furens* (*The Madness of Hercules*), where the Orpheus episode is presented incidentally, in connection with the hero's own adventures in the underworld. The fact that Boethius' Lady Philosophy recycles *The Madness of Hercules* actually implies, as Lerer observes, that she echoes "the Muses of poetry", those "little stage whores" she had initially expelled from the work.[1] Lerer's observation is pertinent and, moreover, confirmed by Philosophy's slightly earlier reference to Euripides' *Andromache* for the purpose of censuring vainglory (3.PR.6). It is important to note, however, that both these cases of reliance on fictional evidence sound a note of warning. Philosophy exploits tragedy in the interest of admonition; she reuses the literary-mythical material for therapeutic and pedagogical purposes. This is her way of realizing the notorious *fabula docet* formula. Thus the management of poetic fiction in Boethius' dialogue opens with anathema and expulsion but later turns into an amazing alignment of instructive examples in the service of Philosophy.

That is why the myth of Orpheus and Eurydice, on their way up from the realm of the dead towards light on earth, can be recycled as an allegory of the soul's Platonic ascension towards the world of the gods. Apart from his introductions of Aristotelian logic, it was first and foremost thanks to his lyrical presentations of Plato's ideas and Neo-Platonist thought that Boethius would exercise such a huge influence on medieval literature. In him, later generations found not only a brave martyr for a noble cause but also a poet who had successfully imitated the great sage of Greece with his technique of adorning a philosophical dialogue with a series of metaphors and myths. In addition, from a typical medieval perspective, Boethius seemed to have three advantages over Plato himself. First, he could be read in Latin; second, he had framed his myths as verse scenarios; and last but not least, his Christian faith could be relied upon, documented as it was in his theological tracts.

Among the numerous myths that are interspersed throughout Plato's dialogues, the cave simile and Er's story of his journey in the afterlife, from Books VII and X of *The Republic* respectively, are probably the best known. The latter deals with metempsychosis and posthumous recollection (*anamnēsis*). As we recall, Macrobius singled out this visionary tale as the prototype for a *nar-*

---

in the Roman catacombs, to identify him with the Saviour. Such efforts substantiate a syncretic version of the scriptural Good Shepherd (John 10.1–16), presumably derived from older tendencies to equate the two harp players Orpheus and David. See González Delgado 2003, pp. 8f.
1 Lerer 1985, pp. 240f.

ratio fabulosa in his commentary on the *Dream of Scipio*. One of Philosophy's poems in the *Consolation* is devoted precisely to Platonic *anamnēsis*. It ends like this (3.M.11.11–16):

11 Haeret profecto semen introrsum veri
   quod excitatur ventilante doctrina.
   Nam cur rogati sponte recta censetis,
   ni mersus alto viveret fomes corde?
15 Quod si Platonis musa personat verum,
   quod quisque discit immemor recordatur.

   There clings within the seed of truth – make no mistake –
   aroused and fanned by proper teaching into flame.
   How could you mortals freely think the truth when asked
   were there no live coal buried deep in heart's cold ash?
   For if the Muse of Plato cries the truth out loud
   all that forgetful mortals learn, they recollect.

The reference to *Platonis musa* might recall yet another passage from Plato's dialogues, rich with implications for the Greek philosopher's take on fictionality, namely *Phaedrus*, where Socrates explains the tale of the locusts (259a–d).

When the Muses came to the world, the philosopher tells us, some people were so taken by delight in their songs that they forgot to eat or drink and eventually faded away. From their race arose the locusts. These were granted the gift of life-long singing, so as to be able to inform the Muses about their worshippers on earth: "and to Calliope, the eldest of the Muses, and to Urania, who is next to her, they make report of those who pass their lives in philosophy and who worship these Muses who are most concerned with heaven and with thought divine and human and whose music is the sweetest."[1] That is why Socrates and his interlocutor in *Phaedrus* have every reason not to fall asleep in the noonday heat. In that case the locusts would laugh at them, but – this is how the philosopher drives home the point of his tale – "if they see us conversing and sailing past them unmoved by the charm of their Siren voices, perhaps they will be pleased and give us the gift which the gods bestowed on them to give to men", that is, the art of the philosophical Muses.

Plato's story seems to offer a virtual matrix for the Socratic maieutics that permeates the *Consolation*. The locusts are identified with the Sirens. Their untiring scraping has a soporific and hence harmful effect on people. But in fact they are servants of the Muses, indeed of the highest, heavenly and philosophical Muses. It is precisely these Platonic deities who, under Philosophy's supervision,

---

[1] Translation H.N. Fowler, Plato 2005.

are called upon to perform in Boethius' work. Moreover, as Gerard O'Daly has observed, their principal part is accompanied by several other antique contributors to a consistent theory of poetic discourse. Thus, in addition to *Platonis musa*, Philosophy's staging of lyrical *exempla* seems indebted to both Aristotle's notion of a generalizing, mimetic kind of narrative, specified in the ninth chapter of his *Poetics* (1451b), and to Horatian tradition's emphasis on the moral profit and didactic purpose of poetry.[1] In short, the *Consolation* accomplishes a rich synthesis of the ideas on the nature of literary fiction that had been launched throughout antique culture ever since Plato had both rejected it and employed it in his dialogues.

Accordingly, even though Boethius lived and worked a century after Augustine and, like his North African brother in faith, could subject the concept of the Trinity to subtle theological reflexion, his Philosophy is far more rooted in classical tradition, constantly reconciling her epistemological and ethical inquiries with her literary interests. In contrast to the aged Church Father's orthodox denunciation of his own fable about the birds *philocalia* and *philosophia* in *Against the Academics*, she repeatedly makes use of the antique myths about Orpheus, Odysseus (4.M.3) or Hercules (4.M.7) for cognitive and moral purposes. Thus Boethius rehabilitated the Muses under the jurisdiction of philosophy. Among the later medieval authors and commentators, it was particularly the masters associated with the school of Chartres that would highlight (and learn from) his intercourse with Plato's Muse. Both Bernardus Silvestris and Alan of Lille were sensitive to the 'fluttering doctrine', *ventilans doctrina*, that seemed to breathe through the *metra* of his *Consolation*. Based on Platonizing speculation, systematic theology and allegorical techniques, they would successfully calibrate the Boethian tension between philosophy and fiction in their poetry.

The Wings of Imagination

In order to specify the nature of Boethius' philosophical fiction, we shall need to look more closely at one of the lyrical showpieces in his dialogue. When Philosophy and her increasingly compliant patient have reached the fourth book, she feels ready to show him "the way that can carry you back home" (4.PR.1): *viam tibi quae te domum revehat ostendam*. She will give his soul – *mens* – wings to allow it to ascend to the heights and return to its true homeland on her trusty

---

[1] O'Daly 1991, pp. 44–50. Moreover, O'Daly makes some efforts, albeit less convincing, to detect traces of Proclus' Neo-Platonic poetics in Boethius' verse, pp. 62–69.

carriage. Philosophy elucidates this project in a poem that from beginning to end is devoted to the theme of ascension (4.M.1):

```
1    Sunt etenim pennae volucres mihi
         quae celsa conscendant poli.
     Quas sibi cum velox mens induit,
         terras perosa despicit,
5    aeris inmensi superat globum,
         nubesque postergum videt,
     quique agili motu calet aetheris,
         transcendit ignis verticem,
     donec in astriferas surgat domos
10       Phoeboque coniungat vias
     aut comitetur iter gelidi senis
         miles corusci sideris,
     vel quocumque micans nox pingitur,
         recurrat astri circulum
15   atque ubi iam exhausti fuerit satis,
         polum relinquat extimum
     dorsaque velocis premat aetheris
         compos verendi luminis.
     Hic regum sceptrum dominus tenet
20       orbisque habenas temperat
     et volucrem currum stabilis regit
         rerum coruscus arbiter.
     Huc te si reducem referat via,
         quam nunc requiris immemor:
25   "Haec," dices, "memini, patria est mihi,
         hinc ortus, hic sistam gradum."
     Quod si terrarum placeat tibi
         noctem relictam visere,
     quos miseri torvos populi timent
30       cernes tyrannos exules.
```

See what I have: These are swift-beating wings for you,
  alert to rise to heaven's heights;
swift-thinking mind, once these wings are attached to it,
  looks down to earth in vast disgust.
Quickly surpassing the limitless atmosphere
  it sees the clouds behind its back;
soon it transcends fire's tapering element
  that glows in ether's rapid course,
vaults itself into the dwellings that hold the stars,
  and the ways of Phoebus are its own.
Or it may follow the path of the cold old man,
  the fiery planet's satellite;

or on the bright-painted canvas of midnight black
   may retrace the circles of a star.
Then when it has been exhausted in orbiting
   it leaves the polestar far behind,
and as the master of true light's preeminence
   it rides on rapid ether's back.
Here with the scepter and reins of the universe
   in hand, is found the Lord of kings,
and he, unmoving, controls the swift chariot,
   as fiery judge of all the world.
Now if your path takes you back to this place again,
   which now you look for unrecalled,
you will say, "Now I remember my fatherland –
   here was I born, here shall I stand."
Then should it please you to view on the earth below
   the night that you have left behind –
pitiless tyrants, whom desolate peoples fear,
   you will behold as exiles there.

The matrix of this poem's representation of mind as a passenger in a chariot destined for celestial heights is, as practically all Boethius' modern commentators have noted, the famous portrayal of the likewise winged *psychē* as the driver of a two-horse carriage ascending towards the abode of the gods in Plato's *Phaedrus* (246). However, in the Greek philosopher's dialogue, there is heavy traffic of gods and human souls up among the skies, whereas Boethius' Philosophy restricts the scenario to the lonely traveller in her chariot. As Courcelle remarks, Augustine had already reused this Platonic theme in a Christian context. In the eighth book of his *Confessions*, the author is ashamed of his tardiness in following God's ways. His conscience rebukes him for his secular aspirations and, in particular, for his irresolution in renouncing sex, reminding him that "other people are given wings on freer shoulders, people who have not worn themselves out with research, nor spent a decade and more reflecting on these questions" (8.7.18).[1] Inasmuch as the ascent of the soul was a popular theme among Stoic writers too, in Seneca and others, it becomes evident that the allegory in 4.M.1 is firmly anchored in classical as well as Christian tradition. After all, the ascent towards celestial heights, as Helga Scheible notes in her monographic study on the poetry of the *Consolation*, had belonged to the

---

[1] "Umerisque liberioribus pinnas recipiunt qui neque ita in quaerendo attriti sunt nec decennio et amplius ista meditati". Cf. Courcelle 1967, p. 197.

stock themes in Greek and Latin poetry (and prose).[1] Nonetheless, Boethius was prone to systematize his mapping of the heavenly journey's stations in a way that anticipated later developments of this topos.

By his time, the Alexandrian astronomer and geographer Ptolemy had presented a detailed and authoritative picture of the cosmos in the work that became known in the West as the *Almagest* (ca. 150 CE). Martianus Capella and Boethius, the latter of whom put the *Almagest* into Latin in a translation that has not survived, initiated the trend to encode the Ptolemaic world picture into poetic imagery, a tendency that would culminate with Dante's Paradiso eight centuries later. In this tradition, earth is commonly shown as surrounded by three elemental layers, the spheres of air, water and fire in that order, *aeris inmensi globus*, *nubes* and *ignis vertex* in 4.M.1.5–8, which reached up to the first of the planetary orbits, that of the moon. Then came the ether, the supralunar cosmos of the heavenly bodies, "the dwellings that hold the stars", *astriferae domus*. In that region, Boethius' cosmonaut enters "the ways of Phoebus", that is the sun, the middlemost of the planets, traditionally associated with Apollo. After having served as a "satellite" – or literally as a soldier, *miles* – of "the fiery planet", probably Mars, and after having joined the seventh and last planet, Saturn, that "cold old man", the winged mind is close to her final destination. Only the huge sphere of the fixed stars remains, *astri circulus*, the glittering night that surrounds the cosmos with its silence.

Finally, it is time for the traveller to leave even the planet spheres and the ether behind, emerging into a divine region beyond the known universe, all in accordance with the matrix of the *Phaedrus*. Boethius, however, in stark contrast to Plato's celestial procession of divinities, speaks only of one god or, more precisely, "the Lord of kings". This powerful figure too, described as the blazing judge of all things, *rerum coruscus arbiter*, navigates a chariot, albeit a metaphorical one: that of the cosmos. Motionless himself, *stabilis*, he steers his swift carriage, whose astronomical orbit is suggested by his grasp of the "reins of the universe", *orbis habenae*. Having come so far on her journey, the soul seems to have reached her goal. Struck by a déjà vu feeling, she "remembers" her lofty origin and can peacefully end her journey up there, on the back of the ether, in her old homeland, *patria*. This is an unmistakable indication of Platonic anamnesis. Now, if faraway mind turns her gaze downwards, towards the earthly night

---

[1] Scheible 1972, pp. 126–28. Cf. O'Daly 1991, pp. 204–06, who – based on a suggestion from Anna Crabbe – highlights the contrast between the journey of Philosophy's winged mind in 4.M.1, gradually approaching her heavenly *patria*, and that of Daedalus in Ovid's *Metamorphoses*, yet another aeronaut returning home from his exile under a tyrant (8.183–84), ending in disaster (the loss of his son).

she has left behind, she meets a gloomy, yet potentially consoling sight: grim tyrants, once the fear of their peoples, have been thrown into exile. Heaven-born mind has eventually come home, while the tyrants on earth are made homeless.

This final turn of the poem's dominant perspective – backwards, recalling earthly night and terror – may seem surprising, but it is derived from a well-known model: the Ciceronian *Dream of Scipio* that we have seen Macrobius comment on and which Boethius certainly knew. His adoptive father-in-law, the Roman nobleman Symmachus, had revised a manuscript of the commentary. Courcelle has even gone so far as to assume that Boethius had access to it in prison.[1] More importantly, Cicero's dream story seems in full accordance with Philosophy's theme in this fourth book of the *Consolation*, devoted to the theodicy problem. From a philosophical viewpoint, taking into account the unalterable order of things, providence and fate claim their due. In the long run, the evil potentates of this world are always losers. Thus the final couplets justify the work's title. They speak the language of consolation to the chastened prisoner. In addition, they are indicative of the philosophical rather than mystical character of the ascent in 4.M.1. Whereas Boethius' predecessors on the poem's flight towards transcendental heights, Plotinus and Augustine, had registered a vibrating presence of the divine at the end of the journey, Boethius initiates an examination of a theological or philosophical problem, notoriously difficult to solve.

So where does fiction stand in this cosmic adventure, resounding with Platonic overtones? The answer to that question is bound up with the identity of the poem's "Lord of kings". Who is he? Could he be the only one left of the divine triumphal processions celebrated in *Phaedrus?* In that case, perhaps, the leader himself, Zeus, borne on a winged chariot, overlooking the universe (246)? Or is he a personification of some metaphysical principle such as the One, associated here, in Neo-Platonic style, with fiery light? Or does he represent a version of the Christian Godhead, subjected to dialectic analysis in Boethius' theological treatise *On the Trinity?*

To all appearances, this figure spans a wide range of significations in which Aristotelian terminology infiltrates the overall Platonic register. The poem's reference to *rerum arbiter* seems reminiscent of Philosophy's definition of God as the origin of all things (3.PR.10), *rerum omnium princeps*. Such designations recall, in turn, the conceptual apparatus of *On the Trinity*, very much present in 3.PR.10,

---

[1] Courcelle 1967, p. 123. Nevertheless, Boethius complains about the scanty or simply non-existent library in his cell, 1.PR.4. Yet another case of precedence for the final peripeteia in 4.M.1 might be found in *Phaedrus:* Scheible has observed that the Platonic dialogue ends with a cosmic vision, including an enumeration of the fallen soul's incarnations, among which the ninth and lowest corresponds to the tyrant, 1972, p. 132.

where Philosophy, by syllogistic reasoning, reaches the conclusion, accentuated as absolutely true, that "the source of all things is also in its own substance the highest Good", *quod omnium principium sit, id etiam sui substantia summum esse bonum verissima ratione concluserim*; this is exactly the kind of argument that would earn Boethius the reputation of being the first Scholastic. Similarly, the poem's remarkable contrast between the celestial Lord's own immobility and the "swift" chariot he controls reminds us of the Aristotelian insight that the prisoner had voiced in the work's preceding prose section: there is "one who, remaining unchanged himself, arranged these multiplicities of change" (3.PR.12), *unus qui has mutationum varietates manens ipse disponeret*. For all the Platonic colouring of these couplets, then, their references to an ultimate cause and an unmoved mover are undoubtedly based on "my good Aristotle", *Aristoteles meus*, to use Philosophy's own words (5.PR.1), the thinker whose fate in medieval Europe up to the twelfth century would be more or less bound up with Boethius' translations and commentaries. In fact, such concatenations of the two greatest names of classical philosophy were frequently implemented in Late Antique culture. Porphyry, for instance, translated and commented on by Boethius, had already employed Aristotelian conceptual analysis within the framework of Platonic metaphysics.

The king-like Lord surfaces in several places of the *Consolation*, most conspicuously, perhaps, in 4.M.6. There, he appears anew against a splendid astronomical backdrop – the sun, the stars, in short, cosmic harmony:

```
34  Sedet interea conditor altus
35  rerumque regens flectit habenas
    rex et dominus fons et origo
    lex et sapiens arbiter aequi
    et quae motu concitat ire,
    sistit retrahens ac vaga firmat.
```

And the creator sits still through all, above all,
guiding the reins and controlling the whole world,
its king and its lord, its source and beginning,
its law and its judge, its wisdom and justice.
He impels things to move, to changing of state;
he recalls them to halt, makes stand what wanders.

It would not be difficult to establish certain detailed correspondences between the portrait of this "creator" and that of the Lord of kings in 4.M.1. They have the management of the reins – here *flectit habenas*, there *habenas temperat* – and the controlled tension between stillness and movement in common. Yet, in 4.M.6 it is chiefly the sovereign's double nature that claims our interest. On the one hand, he is described as a person: the high founder or creator (34), *conditor altus*, king and lord (36), *rex et dominus*, a wise judge (37), *sapiens arbiter*. On the other hand, he is designated as a principle: the source and origin of the world (36), *fons et origo*, not only the judge but the law itself (37), *lex*. He thus appears paradigmatic of the allegorical type of presentation that characterizes the poems in Boethius' *Consolation*. Nature's inherent conformity to providential law is demonstrated by a series of myths, metaphors and personifications, all introduced for the purpose of steering the hesitant prisoner towards the conceptual discernment that in the end will bring him solace.

This equilibrium between person and principle occurs throughout the dialogue and is certainly intentional. In 1.M.5, the prisoner invokes the "creator of the sphere bearing the fixed stars" (1), *stelliferi conditor orbis*, who controls the heaven's movements from his eternal throne (43–44):

> O iam miseras respice terras
> quisquis rerum foedera nectis.
>
> Now, now have regard for pitiful nations,
> whoever you are who bind the world's concord.

This cosmic ruler or, three lines below, *rector*, later called *bonus rector* (4.PR.5), typically anonymous, is reminiscent of the Platonic demiurge who governs the world by virtue of his eternal reason in the famous hymn 3.M.9, sung by Philosophy. He too is an unmoved mover – "resting unmoved, you put all things in motion" (3), *stabilisque manens das cuncta moveri* – characterized by his blinding light. The hymn culminates in a prayer to be allowed to ascend to this fatherly figure's majestic throne, soon to be realized in 4.M.1, the subject of our analysis. Nonetheless, both the prisoner and Philosophy refuse to fix his identity more definitely, sticking to the former's *quisquis* (1.M.5.43), "whoever you are".

This indefinite pronoun reappears, characteristically in the neuter, in 3.PR.12. There must be someone or something that regulates the being of all created things, admits the prisoner, and "whatever it is", *hoc quidquid est*, he prefers to call it by the name we are all familiar with, God. Philosophy approves of what she hears, adding a simile: this power, identical with the Good, "is as it were the tiller and the rudder by which the world machine is kept fixed, secure, and undecomposed", *hic est veluti quidam clavus atque gubernaculum quo mundana machina stabilis atque incorrupta servatur*. In our poem 4.M.1, the sceptre and the reins have replaced the tiller and the rudder (19–20), but the term for immobility or firmness, *stabilis*, is the same (21). Against this background – the presence of a divine albeit unknown principle regulating all things – the identification of the poem's "Lord of kings" (19) with the same God that Augustine worshipped certainly seems feasible, especially since Philosophy in 3.PR.12 (as many scholars have noted) recycles the Wisdom of Solomon in the Old Testament.[1] Even so, it was obviously vital for Boethius to leave room for indecision on this point. Eventually, we have to comply with his deliberately tentative, groping, ambiguous way of speaking: *quisquis* or *hoc quidquid est*... Hence, it seems hazardous to establish any closer ties to the Christian deity, either in the *Consolation* as a whole or in 4.M.1. To sum up, Boethius invests the recurrent transcendental potentate in his dialogue with qualities, attributes and activities that might recall *The Iliad* 2.204 ("There is one ruler, there is one king", 1.PR.5), the mythical Zeus or the Demiurge from Plato's *Phaedrus* and *Timaeus* respectively, Aristotle's philosophical principle analysed in the twelfth book of his *Metaphysics* ("something which moves without being moved", 1072a), and, finally, the Wisdom of Jewish-Hellenistic extraction, possibly fused with elements from Late Antique Stoic as well as Neo-Platonic speculation.[2] That is why this figure emerges as the very epitome of Boethius' remarkable capacity of synthesizing Late Antique philosophical culture in its last hour.

In conclusion, it seems reasonable to read 4.M.1 as a lyrical *narratio fabulosa*, a speculative myth in verse. It registers in glittering metaphorical code the Pythagorean-Ptolemaic world picture, Platonic anamnesis, the Aristotelian prime mover and the Neo-Platonic theme of the ascension of the soul. It is not least for this reason that the poems of the *Consolation* were to be so admired, and at times debated, in medieval culture. They would constitute widespread reminders of profane poetry's resources to communicate philosophical insight, whether or not it was compatible with Christian faith. For the sake of comparison, Crabbe adduces Augustine's censure of his protégé Licentius' Muses in the Cassiciacum dialogue *On Order* (cf. above, pp. 165f.). There, the pupil was presented with the choice between Pyramus and Thisbe's love on the one hand, and the higher love that leads to *vita beata* on the other. This Augustinian part-

---

[1] In the deuterocanonical Bible book known by that name, the Wisdom of Solomon, written in Greek by a Jewish author, probably in the second or first century BCE, wisdom is celebrated as "fairer than the sun / and surpasses every constellation of the stars. / Compared to light, she is found more radiant" (7.29). In addition to this cosmic stature and intense luminosity, she "spans the world from end to end mightily / and governs all things well" (8.1), in the Vulgate: *adtingit enim a fine usque ad finem fortiter et disponit omnia suaviter*. Cf. Philosophy's description of the highest Good "that governs all things forcefully and arranges all things sweetly" (3.PR.12), *quod regit cuncta fortiter suaviterque disponit*. I quote the Wisdom of Solomon from the revised edition of *The New American Bible* 2010.

[2] Scheible refers to the Zeus figure of *Phaedrus*, adding that "under the mythical surface all those elements are reunited, from which Boethius' philosophically based representation of God is assembled", 1972, p. 131.

ing of ways was unconditional. There was no third, no possible compromise between Ovid, the notorious poet of pagan fiction, and Paul, the Apostle to the Gentiles. Boethius, for his part, seemed to demonstrate that mythical poetry and didactic prose could very well live together, to the benefit of both parties.[1] However, his way of applying Macrobius' allegorical theory also set a limit. He exploited the philosophical narrative to communicate profane erudition and classical wisdom, but he deliberately left the God of Christianity out of its immediate referential range. In this respect, Boethius might remind us of his contemporary Fulgentius. They both relied, as it were, on a kind of double-entry bookkeeping. They both left the project of integrating the highest Catholic *dominus* – God the Father or the Holy Trinity – into a fictional setting untried.

The Limits of Imagination

Ultimately, then, Boethius' dialogue presupposes a gap between poetic imagination and the Godhead, explicitly articulated in *On the Trinity*, where the author, following Aristotle, distinguishes three kinds of speculative knowledge, *naturalis*, *mathematica* and *theologica*.[2] The first of these, physics, proceeds rationally, mathematics systematically (*disciplinaliter*) and theology intellectually (since its object, the divine substance, *dei substantia*, lacks both matter and motion). Now, in theology, dealing with the divine, "we should not be diverted to play with imaginations, but rather apprehend that form which is pure form and no image" (2), *neque diduci ad imaginationes, sed potius ipsam inspicere formam quae vere forma neque imago est*. Imagination and its privileged means of expression, the image (material or rhetorical), is resolutely severed from the realm of the divine.

In *On the Trinity*, this limitation of human beings' cognitive and discursive potential is not exclusive to imagination; Boethius imposes it on reason as well. God is something different from and more than an ordinary substance, so his being cannot, like all other things, be determined with the aid of the ten Aristotelian categories (following the pattern of 'when', 'where', 'how' etc.), that Porphyry had integrated into his Neo-Platonic scheme, certainly relevant to Boethius two centuries later. Consequently, neither the images of imagination nor the concepts of reason, left to themselves, can comprehend or grasp

---

[1] Crabbe 1981, p. 252.
[2] I quote Boethius' theological tractates, in Latin as well as in English translation, after the Loeb edition by H.F. Stewart, E.K. Rand and S.J. Tester 1997.

God. They are both powerless to reach beyond the level of ordinary substances, *ultra substantiam* (4). For theological deliberations, only the highest and noblest of the faculties of our soul, the intellect, is appropriate. Specifically, the Father, the Son and the Holy Spirit relate to each other as identicals, *ut eius quod est idem ad id quod est idem*, whereas "all perishable, transitory objects" are characterized by their "otherness", *alteritas*. In order to comprehend the triune Godhead, then, "we ought not to be led astray by any imagination, but raised up by pure understanding [*simplici intellectu*] and, so far as anything can be understood, thus far also we should approach it with our understanding [*intellectus*]." (6)[1]

These passages from *On the Trinity* are indicative of the breach that separates the author's devotion from the religiosity of Augustine, whom Boethius nevertheless recognizes as his main source for the ideas of the tract (PR.).[2] Whereas the Church Father seldom had been able to suppress his personal and kerygmatic involvement on behalf of the new faith, the Roman aristocrat located his theology in the theoretical sphere of "pure understanding", *simplex intellectus*. The figurations of imagination and the discernments of reason, on the other hand, were reserved for his analysis of contingent existence: the mapping of both the human soul and the sublunary world that he pursued so boldly in his death cell.

Accordingly, Philosophy's Muses, in the *metra* of his *Consolation*, were free to operate with fictional representation, specifically mythical events and settings. Their dominant Stoic and Neo-Platonic outlook allows imagination to stretch its analogies from the miserable life on earth up to "the Lord of kings", whether his name was Jupiter, Wisdom or the Unmoved Mover. This synthesizing vision, their bold attempt to assess the wretched state of mankind in a cosmic or universal context, is no foregone conclusion; being more or less absent from the *Consolation's* early poems, it grows stronger and stronger as the dialogue proceeds. The prisoner's initial indulgence to "the grief-ridden mode" (1.M.1.2), *maesti modi*, is not suitable for philosophical myths, since it is limited to the self's narrow perspective. It is only Philosophy's mature Muses, educated in the spirit of Macrobius' *Commentary*, that are able to transfer the music of the spheres to that

---

1 "Quod si id [a relation of identicals] in cunctis aliis rebus non potest inveniri, facit hoc cognata caducis rebus alteritas. Nos vero nulla imaginatione diduci sed simplici intellectu erigi et ut quidque intellegi potest ita aggredi etiam intellectu oportet."
2 For the contrast between Boethian and Augustinian theology, particularly regarding the doctrine of Trinity, see Chadwick 1981, pp. 220f., 249–51.

of words, mainly in the third, fourth and fifth books of the work, thereby offering efficient *exempla* for the prisoner in his cell.¹

It is in these poetic passages that imagination's visionary activities achieve their triumphs in Boethius' *Consolation*.² Several of them, not only the sublime vision 4.M.1 but also the variation on *Timaeus* 3.M.9 and the Orphean-Senecan mythological narrative 3.M.12, form brilliant allegorical scenarios in Macrobius' style. It is first and foremost these items that provide the "music" that supplements Philosophy in a refined, virtually fugal pattern of composition. Identical or similar themes are repeated in different, at times contrasting keys (as Philosophy herself explains in 2.PR.1). That is why traditional mythology – as Relihan observes – makes its presence felt more and more in the poems, while the work's philosophical material becomes increasingly abstract.³ The more complex the line of thought, the greater the need for mythology's *exempla*, enforced by means of music (poetry). Accordingly, the verse sections gain momentum throughout the *Consolation*, increasingly administered by the work's wise mentor: in Book I, three of them are voiced by the harrowed prisoner, but in the remaining four books only one (5.M.3), symptomatically arranged as a series of questions.

This fundamental strategy does not imply, however, the feasibility of reducing the philosophical Muses' lyrical contributions to a purely illustrative or ornamental function. As Christian Mueller-Goldingen and Peter Dronke have assumed, their imagery might well point to intuitions or insights that lie beyond and defy the powers of expression of Philosophy's prose; and undoubtedly, they create, as O'Daly explains, "a vigorous and sophisticated sequence in their own right, reflecting and elaborating the Latin poetic tradition from Lucretius to Seneca's tragedies". Nevertheless, O'Daly continues, this sequence of poems adapts tradition's imagery, myths, and motifs to the work's overall structure.⁴ Thus Boethius concentrates the fictional ingredients of his dialogue to a number of lyrical voices that effectively reinforce Philosophy's therapeutic method. Broadly following Plutarch, the Stoics and Macrobius, they complement her piercing *logos* with their suggestive *mythos*.⁵

---

1 Cf. Lerer 1985, pp. 166f.
2 This is the standpoint of Elaine Scarry in a compelling essay 1980: "It is the poems, or meters, that represent the imaginative mode of cognition", p. 100.
3 Relihan cites 3.M.12, 4.M.3 and 4.M.7 in this context, Boethius 2001, p. XXI. Cf. the chapter on "The Nature and Function of the Mythical Motifs" in O'Daly 1991, pp. 178–235.
4 Mueller-Goldingen 1989, pp. 377f., Dronke 1994, p. 43, O'Daly 1991, p. VII. In addition, see Curley 1986, pp. 243–53 ("Verse in the *Consolatio* functions as a 'pharmakon'", p. 245).
5 For Plutarch, philosophy and poetry, see particularly *How to Study Poetry*, 15f.

In the dialogue's prose, on the other hand, Philosophy's analytical and moral discourse sets the tone: she epitomizes paramount reason, to the investigation of which the Aristotelian logician Boethius had devoted his scholarly career, and whose "universal point of view" (5.PR.4) *universalis consideratio*, provides us with the conceptual key to the poems' mythical-metaphorical messages. Admittedly, the prose sections are framed as a dialogue, in which there is a tension – initially quite strong, eventually mitigated – between the prisoner's despair or irresolution and Philosophy's harsh cure. Nonetheless, it is her explanations, admonitions and lecturing that test the narrator and push their conversation forward. They direct the condemned Boethius' attention towards the source and foundation of mankind's existence: from an immanent point of view, a *fatum* of Stoic extraction, or, in a wider perspective, a transcendental power, sometimes called God, *deus*, frequently referred to in Neo-Platonic terms.

Philosophy's method is both rhetorical-persuasive and dialectic-syllogistic, based on premises and conclusion, *propositiones* and *consequens* (or *conclusio*), so that all her points "stand together, woven from the most solid lines of argument" (3.PR.11).[1] In rare cases, as Thomas Curley has observed in a penetrating analysis, she might also rely on figurative language in the prose sections, as when she introduces Fortune as a *prosopopoeia* in 2.PR.2, but this is the exception that proves the rule.[2] Any indication of an immediate experience of the Godhead, such as a Neo-Platonic *raptus*, is located in the poems' encoded allegories, commonly construed in the conditional or exhortative mode. Philosophy emphasizes that "the motion of human rational argument cannot set itself next to the simplicity of divine foreknowledge" (5.PR.4), *humanae ratiocinationis motus ad divinae praescientiae simplicitatem non potest admoveri*. She keeps to her field of responsibility, to "human rational argument", throughout the work, even on

---

[1] For the dialectic method in the dialogue, see especially 3.PR.10, 3.PR.11 and 4.PR.4.
[2] Curley 1986, p. 255. Curley is one among a limited group of Boethius scholars who, interestingly, has tried to establish parallels between the *Consolation*'s cognitive scheme, as outlined in 5.PR.4, and its formal structure. For this purpose, however, he basically ignores the *prosimetrum* character of the work, maintaining that Philosophy gradually adjusts to her interlocutor, so that she initially stimulates his *sensus* (Book I), whereupon she activates his *imaginatio* (Book II) and finally appeals to his *intellegentia* (Book V), pp. 217–19, 237–39, perhaps an overstatement of her calculating pedagogy. Scarry prefers to have it both ways; on the one hand, she proposes a dialectic relationship between the *Consolation*'s imaginative poetry and conceptual prose (forestalling my own approach in this section), while, on the other hand, she identifies a "steady upward progression from the realm of sense in book 1 to the realm of Insight in book 5" of Boethius' dialogue, 1980, pp. 105f., 108–24. Even further in this attempt to detect an overall conceptual structure in the *Consolation* goes Robert McMahon 2006, pp. 211–66.

its last page, where she refers to the hopes and prayers, *spes precesque*, that are directed towards God. Medieval commentators would take this wording as proof of Boethius' Christian faith, but it might just as well, or even more probably, voice the Stoic-Platonic providential monism which pervades Philosophy's final lessons.

In conclusion, Boethius' *Consolation* is based on a network of subtle correspondences between imaginative-allegorical poetry on the one hand and didactic as well as persuasive ratiocination on the other hand. Now, Philosophy concedes that there might be something more to it, since, after all, her range of vision is limited to what syllogistic logic would be liable to deduce and establish. She is well aware that intellect surpasses discursive reason: "And the eye of understanding [*intellegentiae oculus*] exists as something higher yet; for it has passed beyond what is encompassed by universality and views the one simple form itself in the pure vision of the mind." (5.PR.4)[1] This visionary gaze seems to transcend the reach of our normal faculties, as if it presupposed angelic or even divine cognitive capacities. Still, as Günter Ralfs has suggested, it is not inaccessible to human beings.[2] Philosophy ends her epistemological exposition in the fifth book accordingly (5.PR.5):[3]

> And for this reason let us raise ourselves up, if we can, into the head of that highest intelligence, for it is in that place that reason will see what it cannot gaze upon within itself, and that is this: in just what way a fixed and definite foreknowledge can still see even those things that do not have definite outcomes, and how this is not mere conjecture but the simplicity of the highest knowledge instead, knowledge bounded by no limits.

It is indeed a remarkable optimism that Philosophy is made to express in this eulogy to intellectual vision. It may turn our thoughts to the Neo-Platonic visionaries of a much later date, to Renaissance writers such as Pico della Mirandola or Giordano Bruno, but it remains articulated as an appeal, characteristically put forward in the hortative and conditional mode: "let us raise ourselves up, if we can...". The intellect's possible vision of God goes beyond the domains of both imagination and reason.

---

[1] "Intellegentiae vero celsior oculus exsistit; supergressa namque universitatis ambitum ipsam illam simplicem formam pura mentis acie contuetur."
[2] Ralfs 1984, p. 372.
[3] "Quare in illius summae intellegentiae cacumen, si possumus, erigamur; illic enim ratio videbit quod in se non potest intueri, id autem est, quonam modo etiam quae certos exitus non habent, certa tamen videat ac definita praenotio neque id sit opinio sed summae potius scientiae nullis terminis inclusa simplicitas."

This deliberate limitation of the *Consolation's* field of vision explains the absence of the triune Godhead in the work. Boethius composed a philosophical work formally designed as a Menippean satire or *prosimetrum* in which the dialogic feature is essential and the lyric poems act as musical illustrations, framed as allegorical myths. However, he conspicuously omits both the activities and concerns of the senses (not worthy of being clothed in Philosophy's words) and their opposite, the intellect's mystical vision of God (transcending the referential domain of Philosophy's words). Boethius thus remained faithful to the classical education, *paideia*, to which he had devoted his life. Regardless of the question of genre, which has already been touched upon, this loyalty, as Victor Watts points out, might well be indicative of the author's belonging to an age "in which the ancient classical culture had become assimilated to Christianity, but not absorbed by it".[1] The Roman schools remained pagan, as we have seen, long into the era of the triumphant Church.

To sum up, fictional devices are certainly allowed to operate across wide domains in Boethius' *Consolation*, communicating Ptolemaic astronomy as well as Platonic metaphysics in a number of lyrical scenarios, repeatedly encoded in the repertoire of classical mythology, faithful to the paradigm that Macrobius had outlined in his *Commentary on the Dream of Scipio*. That is the gist of the re-education or permutation of the old Muses in the service of Philosophy. They are, however, only permitted to exercise their arts on precisely these conditions: they had to stick to their core competence as defined by, broadly speaking, traditional *paideia* and various strands of Hellenistic philosophy. Here too, where fictionality's area of responsibility is marked off from any higher and spiritual realm of being, Boethius is actually only following Macrobius' recommendations in his *Commentary* (1.2.13–16, partly quoted above, p. 360):

> We should not assume, however, that philosophers approve the use of fabulous narratives, even those of the proper sort, in all disputations. It is their custom to employ them when speaking about the Soul, or about spirits having dominion in the lower and upper air, or about gods in general. But when the discussion aspires to treat of the Highest and Supreme of all gods, called by the Greeks the Good (*tagathon*) and the First Cause (*proton aition*), or to treat of Mind or Intellect, which the Greeks call *nous*, born from and originating in the Supreme God and embracing the original concepts of things, which are called Ideas (*ideai*), when, I repeat, philosophers speak about these, the Supreme God and Mind, they shun the use of fabulous narratives. When they wish to assign attributes to these divinities that not only pass the bounds of speech but those of human comprehension as well, they resort to similes and analogies. That is why Plato, when he was moved to speak about the Good, did not dare to tell what it was, knowing only this about it, that

---

[1] Boethius 1986, p. 30.

it was impossible for the human mind to grasp what it was. In truth, of visible objects he found the sun most like it, and by using this as an illustration opened a way for his discourse to approach what was otherwise incomprehensible. On this account men of old fashioned no likeness of the Good when they were carving statues of other deities, for the Supreme God and Mind sprung from it are above the Soul and therefore beyond nature. It is a sacrilege for fables to approach this sphere. (VIII)

With his reference to "similes and analogies" Macrobius probably had in mind, as we have seen, a mystical-symbolic rather than a mimetic category of discourse, as when Plato had represented the incomprehensible Good by the sun. The great philosopher had been obliged to resort to such an astronomical symbol, detached from narrative context, for lack of any valid fictional devices, since *fabulae* were not admitted to the divine dimension of reality: *quo nihil fas est de fabulis pervenire*. Boethius would take Macrobius at his word. His *metra* encode the *figurae* of imagination, Philosophy examines and generalizes the individual *species* that belong under reason, while the intellect's *simplex forma* is left out of the dialogue's explicit presentation.

Menippean satire, Relihan notes, demonstrates a remarkably loyal attitude to this division between fictional processing of the lower orders of reality and reticence about the absolute. Philology prays in silence at the very frontier of Being in Martianus, Fulgentius refers only obliquely to his Christian religion, and, last but not least, Boethius is pointedly discreet about his faith in the *Consolation*.[1] This is a thought-provoking observation, even though I do not believe that the unfortunate senator's dialogue needs to be tied harder than necessary to the conventions of the Menippean genre. Boethius deals with this type of satire in a completely different manner than his predecessors. To him, laughter, parody, or breaches of style were not major issues.[2] All the more important was the consolation provided by poetry as well as philosophy in the face of the apparent injustice or futility of existence.

Then again, why did Boethius go to such great lengths to circumvent intellect's vision of the Christian Godhead in his last work? Was his reticence regarding ultimate reality – as Relihan implies – due to the law of genre, reaching, as it were, right into the death cell in Pavia? Or was it rather due to his conviction, reminiscent of Augustine and Neo-Platonic tradition, of God's fundamental ineffability? A bolder version of Relihan's thesis would be to assume that Boethius actually chose the Menippean satire for his dialogue, deliberately or not, precise-

---

[1] Relihan 1993, p. 183.
[2] For a critical examination of Relihan's rather firm linking of Boethius' *Consolation* to the Menippean genre conventions, see Shanzer 2009, pp. 235f.

ly because of such a conviction. As he framed its mixed form for his own purposes, alternating syllogistic demonstration with poetic examples, he turned it into the perfect medium for both the pedagogy of philosophy and the therapy for melancholy. But it offers no room for divine reality. "Extend your humble prayers into the lofty heights", *humiles preces in excelsa porrigite*, Philosophy urges the prisoner – and all his readers – on the last page of the *Consolation*, but *that* kind of prayer does not admit articulation in words, unlike the two previous ones in the work: the invocation of the creator of the starry sky in 1.M.5 and the hymn to the originator of heaven and earth in 3.M.9. A number of commentators have highlighted the fact that Boethius does not end his work with a lyric poem; he thus dispenses with the concluding counterpart to the introductory lines of verse which the requirements of the genre (respected by Martianus) prescribed and which readers would have expected. Towards the end of the *Consolation*, Philosophy simply becomes increasingly monological, the prisoner increasingly silent – and that is it.

This type of restraint, emulating what in rhetorical tradition would be considered a figure of speech, *reticentia* or *aposiopesis*, is even more noticeable in Boethius' polemic against Eutyches, one of the fifth-century Monophysite theologians in the East (rejected at the Council of Chalcedon in 451), who had maintained that Christ after the Incarnation possessed one single – divine – nature rather than, as Catholic belief would have it, two. In his treatise *Contra Eutychen et Nestorium* Boethius asserts that even if Nature's substantial and accidental qualities can be explored by the intellect, "God and matter cannot be apprehended by the intellect, be it never so whole and perfect, but still they are apprehended in some way through the removal of other things" (1).[1] Here, even *intellectus* seems disqualified as a cognitive instrument for the purpose of grasping divine reality. Nonetheless, the author seems to envisage an alternative way to God, the *via negativa* or, as he puts it, *ceterarum rerum privatio*, inherent in Neo-Platonic tradition and famously elaborated by Dionysius the Areopagite, whose writings were put into circulation at about the same time as Boethius lived and died, in the early sixth century.

We have already detected traces in Augustine of this radical reduction as a means to attain access to the Godhead, for instance in his Ostia vision: "if this could last, and all other visions, so far inferior, be taken away", *si continuetur hoc et subtrahantur aliae visiones...* It would be echoed throughout the apophatic

---

[1] "Et accidentia et substantiae definiuntur; haec enim omnia intellectu capi possunt. [...] deus et materia integro perfectoque intellectu intelligi non possunt, sed aliquo tamen modo ceterarum rerum privatione capiuntur."

theology of the Middle Ages for centuries to come. Eventually, in the innovative culture of the High Middle Ages, it would be intersected by bold efforts to combine the world of holy faith with that of fictional poetry. Boethius had come to a halt where Alan of Lille would devise a *Deus artifex* proceeding like a poet, or where Dante would depict the Godhead in terms of three rotating circles.[1] That his consolatory ruminations from the death cell would nevertheless emerge as the inaugural work of medieval culture seems quite natural. With the poignant discourse that permeates the work's prose, fully exploiting the dramatic potential of Late Antiquity's philosophical *ratio*, and with such compelling *metra* as the poem of the winged soul's flight towards the stars, Boethius had achieved more than enough.

---

[1] I am referring to *Anticlaudianus* 5.124–27, Alan of Lille 1955 (cf. below, p. 595), and to Dante's Paradiso 33.115–20, respectively.

IV *Poeta Christianus*
From *Ficta* to *Facta* in Early Christian Poetry

Preliminary Remarks

> Non conferre Deo velut aequiperabile quidquam
> ausim, nec Domino famulum conponere signum;
> ex minimis sed grande suum voluit Pater ipse
> coniectare homines, quibus ardua visere non est.
> parvorum speculo non intellecta notamus,
> et datur occultum per proxima quaerere verum.
>
> I would not venture to compare anything with God as though it were on a par with Him, nor to match with the Lord a star that is his servant; but the Father himself has willed that men infer his greatness from what is but small, since they cannot see the things on high. In the mirror of the small we mark things we do not understand, and we are permitted to seek the hidden truth by means of what is at hand.
>
> Prudentius, *The Origin of Sin* (79–84)

The major Church teachers were as a rule sceptical of secular poetry. We have followed Augustine on his way from reading Virgil in Cassiciacum to the strikingly critical attitude towards classical culture that characterizes his anti-Manichaean treatises and the *City of God*, written in his old age. Likewise, we have seen the dreamer Jerome establish his well-known dichotomy between true faith on the one hand, old eloquence or "worldly books", *codices saeculares*, on the other. In this chapter we shall examine a few more examples of the difficulties the young Christian culture faced when dealing with fictional representation – and of its difficulties in doing without it. In Roman Late Antiquity, especially in the decades around 400, an impulse to make a clean sweep of the discredited old order, to establish a new human being in a new universal congregation, had to grapple with the powerful tradition that was based on Virgil, Ovid and classical culture. This was not a heritage that could easily be disposed of. Two writers seem to me to bear particularly striking witness of this dependence, since they adopted, as a matter of principle, a pointedly negative or even aggressive attitude towards pagan culture and its Muses.

We have already met the first of them, Tertullian, reputedly one of the sterner critics of poetry and theatre among the Latin apologists. But even in the most austere period of his life, when he professed himself an adherent of the ascetic and chiliastic revivalist movement known as Montanism, he felt obliged – as Laistner points out – to accept at least a minimum of humanistic education, as in this passage from *De Corona* (*The Chaplet*): "Let Mercury have been the first who taught the knowledge of letters; I will own that they are requisite both for the business and commerce of life, and for performing our devotion to God. Nay, if he also first strung the chord to give forth melody, I will not deny, when listening to David, that this invention has been in use with the saints, and has ministered to God." (8.2)[1] Tertullian was quite right, of course. Mercury, in this passage from the *Chaplet* evidently treated as a metonym for classical poetry, had already laid the foundation for a Christian literature. Poetic sensibility and skills had powerfully influenced or, indeed, partially framed Roman education for centuries. Literary culture permeated not only what we nowadays would call aesthetic taste but all oral and written composition, hence all (cultivated) usage of the Latin language. Consequently, much as Tertullian's radical brothers in faith would like to eradicate all traces of Mercury's talents, it became difficult, or actually impossible, to renounce Rome's literary heritage when its old language was to be put in service of the new faith.

Our second writer is John Cassian (ca. 360–435), born in the region of Scythia at the Black Sea or perhaps Gaul (his origin is disputed), a contemporary of Augustine and Jerome, sometimes labelled the founder of Western monasticism, and in any event a major introducer of Eastern asceticism in the West. He entered a cloister in Bethlehem in the 380s, whereafter he spent some fifteen years as an apprentice with Egyptian monks and desert hermits before he went to Constantinople, Rome and finally Marseilles, where he founded a monastery and a nunnery, setting an example for Benedict of Nursia a century later. Cassian's *Collationes patrum* (*Conferences*) is based on his Egyptian experience, in essence an account of his conversations with the Desert Fathers. A passage in the fourteenth book suggests that he had received a scholarly upbringing, typical of the educated upper classes in the Late Antique Roman Empire, which had left its mark on his mind. Now an ardent penitent, Cassian complains to his interlocutor, Abbot Nesteros, about how difficult it was to rid himself of its traces (14.12):[2]

---

1 "Primus litteras Mercurius enarraverit: necessarias confitebor et commerciis rerum et nostris erga deum studiis. Sed et si nervos idem in sonum strinxit, non negabo et hoc ingenium eius sanctis fecisse et deo ministrasse, audiens David." Cf. Laistner 1951, p. 51.
2 Cassian's *Conferences* are rendered in E.C.S. Gibson's translation from P. Schaff's and H. Wace's series *Select Library of the Nicene and Post-Nicene Fathers of the Christian Church* 2.11, 1978, and, in the original, from M. Petschenig's edition of the author's *Opera* II, 1886.

> A special hindrance to salvation is added by that knowledge of literature which I seem already to have in some slight measure attained, in which the efforts of my tutor, or my attention to continual reading have so weakened me that now my mind is filled with those songs of the poets so that even at the hour of prayer it is thinking about those trifling fables, and the stories of battles with which from its earliest infancy it was stored by its childish lessons: and when singing Psalms or asking forgiveness of sins either some wanton recollection of the poems intrudes itself or the image of heroes fighting presents itself before the eyes, and an imagination of such phantoms is always tricking me and does not suffer my soul to aspire to an insight into things above, so that this cannot be got rid of by my daily lamentations. (I)

For dogmatic reasons, Augustine criticized Cassian for his Pelagian inclination to boost the free will of the individual irrespective of the saving grace of God, but the author of the *Confessions* would definitely have recognized himself in *Conferences* 14.12. Judging by this account, the base adventures narrated by the poets, problematic because of their fabulous as well as improper nature, came stealing upon Cassian even in his prayers. Their subjects, love and war, indicate fairly clearly the indoctrination of his soul by classical epic poetry. The author's "imagination of such phantoms", *phantasmatum imaginatio*, moulded during his early school years of literary studies, constantly had new trickeries in store for him, blocking the way upwards for his intellect, *mens*, bent on ascension. The project of cutting off those emotional ties to pagan literary culture became as desirable as difficult, hence a life-long enterprise, for both Augustine and Cassian. Saint Benedict would soon join them in this undertaking, prescribing – in his famous monastic Rule – the latter's *Conferences* as common evening reading for his monks at Monte Cassino (42.3, 73.5).[1]

The apologetic distrust of the fictional worlds of profane literature remained deep, long into the fifth century. Indeed, seldom has Peer Gynt's disparaging remark on "damned romancing and lies", quoted at the beginning of this book (p. 13), been so frantically foretold as during the first few centuries of the triumphant young Church. The Christian struggle against the lingering classical culture was by no means of an academic character; it was a matter of taking the initiative and dictating the terms of the debate in an on-going struggle over the legitimate interpretation of reality. Admittedly, pagan religiosity – basically a series of cults, mysteries and festivals, several of which were of Eastern or Egyptian origin and examined in Macrobius' *Saturnalia* – had been hard pressed in many parts of the Empire ever since the days of Constantine, but it was still around, sometimes even energetically practised, hence a potential threat to

---

[1] I have read Saint Benedict's Rule in B.L. Venarde's bilingual edition 2011.

the Christian faith.[1] On various authoritative ecclesiastical levels, bishops were firmly warned against reading the classics. Those disciplinary canons known as *Statuta ecclesiae antiqua*, which were compiled in late fifth-century Gaul but depended on earlier tradition, declare that 'a bishop should not read pagan books': *episcopus gentilium libros non legat*.[2]

To all appearances, this rule was sometimes overlooked, so the most powerful pope of the ensuing transition era, Gregory the Great, in at least one case, as we shall see, felt obliged to warn his bishops against the temptations of 'secular literature' (below, pp. 574f.). One of the more specific reasons for this Western scepticism of *ficta* and *fabulae* was decreasing intercourse with Byzantine culture and the Greek language. Roman intellectuals' first-hand contacts with the Eastern parts of the Empire had by the time of Gregory deteriorated considerably. The Roman popes and their increasingly powerful bishops, not least in the culturally dominant Gaul of the fifth century, trod in the footsteps of the later Augustine; with some pungency directed against the proverbial Greece of myths and old wives' tales, they could even invoke the *romanitas* of earlier times – the Stoic virtues and the self-sacrificing civic spirit that had once built the Empire – for their consolidation of Christianity. In this alliance between stern *virtus* and triumphant *fides* there was little room for poetic licence to prosper.

Such licence was in fact cancelled, now and again explicitly, by the pious versifiers who will now be the subject of our discussion. They were for a long time treated with a certain scepticism by modern literary historians, but during the past few decades they have become the object of quite intense scholarly interest. For all practical purposes, these poets made common cause with Augustine and Jerome: a sharp line was drawn between the fictional worlds of pagan epic poetry and evangelical truth. In the frequently pointed prologues to their works, this distinction was considered imperative; it did not admit any space for the fictional mode of 'as if'.[3] The stories of Orpheus and Eurydice, of stunning metamorphoses and Olympian or natural deities, were of no use to Christians since they were deemed to be mendacious. The orthodox Catholic interpre-

---

[1] Cf. Smith 1976, pp. 89–108.
[2] *PL* 56.881a. The *Statuta ecclesiae antiqua* were for a long time attributed to the fourth council at Carthage in 398. However, as Jane E. Merdinger observes, the council was cancelled; political turbulence in the region, caused by the Berber potentate Gildo's insurrection, prevented the bishops from convening in Carthage that year, 1999, p. 249.
[3] Cf. Jauß 1983, p. 425, a short but extremely rewarding survey of the problem of fictionality in Western premodern literature (though I do not concur with Jauß in his insistence on an "original lack of distinction between fiction and reality" purportedly characteristic of European literatures from Late Antiquity to the twelfth century, p. 423).

tation of the world, on the other hand, was unconditionally true. God had created the world out of nothing; Adam, woefully assisted by Eve, had permanently damaged human nature in causing the Fall, for which reason the history of the Jews, recounted in the Old Testament, gives evidence of trials and tribulations, external threats and internal strife. God's only-begotten Son, however, had delivered mankind from evil through His Incarnation. The restoration and salvation work He had made possible was at present carried out by the Christian Church and would in due time (quite soon, according to the conviction of many early congregations) culminate in the drama of the Last Judgment.

Jupiter, Venus and the other Olympians had, of course, nothing to do with all this, except for being potential obstacles on the way towards salvation. They were to be considered pure chimeras, idols that could only blur the Christian's field of vision and should be relegated to sempiternal oblivion – or, at best, to the cabinet of religious curiosities that Augustine had scrutinized in his *City of God*. This Christian hostility (or strategic dismissal) of pagan culture, particularly of its cults, myths and theatrical performances, had reached its climax in the first centuries of our era, thriving among belligerent apologists such as Tatian or Tertullian. After the reign of Constantine, when the recently persecuted minority religion rose to authorized dominance, this antagonism lived on as an undercurrent in the Empire, blossoming forth towards the end of the fourth century as an ascetic reaction in Paulinus of Nola and other zealous Christians. These cultural radicals would not stand any compromises, least of all with the classical world of fiction. They would rather identify with the message of the Revelation (21.4–5): "'And death shall be no more, neither shall there be mourning, nor crying, nor pain anymore, for the former things have passed away.' And he who was seated on the throne said, 'Behold, I am making all things new.' Also he said, 'Write this down, for these words are trustworthy and true.'" John's apocalyptic passage has the virtue of linking the original Christian yearning to break away from the old order, *ecce nova facio omnia*, to both the act of writing and the demand for truth. The task of God's scribe was to register and seal His unadulterated message to struggling mankind.

Striving to accomplish this undertaking, however, Christian writers found themselves locked in the general dilemma we have seen exemplified in Tertullian and John Cassian; they were supposed to detach themselves from a culture to which many of them – not to speak of their predecessors – had been accustomed since infancy. Specifically, they were faced with the problem that their new truth, at least in theory, demanded a new kind of writing. And, as a matter of fact, a modern, ground-breaking type of literature was in the process of being developed. Encouraged by the Gospels, prelates, preachers and hagiographers all over the Christian world, as Erich Auerbach has demonstrated in a well-known article, had begun to subvert or at least loosen up the traditional literary culture's system of genres and inveterate sensitivity to decorum. They implemented a style that was based on the Bible, corresponded to the Orthodox Church's main tenet, the Incarnation of Christ – *et verbum caro factum est* (John 1.14), – and, in short, was closer to contemporary colloquial Latin, *sermo humilis*.[1] Nonetheless, for the pious writers of the period who based their work on established literary genres, such as epic poetry composed in hexameter verse, this style remained a theoretical principle rather than living practice. Even in that capacity, however, the ideal of 'ordinary speech' was of great importance, not least for the intellectuals' self-fashioning and positioning in discussions of fictionality. The question of style was in fact crucial for the framing of Christian attitudes towards fictitious presentation. Consequently, when we are about to establish the characteristics of a new type of writer in Late Antiquity, the *poeta christianus*, this issue requires a separate consideration.

---

[1] Auerbach 1993, pp. 25–66.

1 The Foam of Style

The idea of a correspondence between low style and evangelical ethos was vital to the great majority of Christian writers. Minucius Felix had already made his Octavius in the dialogue of that name declare that "the more unskilled the utterance the clearer is the reasoning, for it relies not on tricks of eloquence or graces of style, but is sustained on its own merits by the rule of right" (16.6), *quo imperitior sermo, hoc inlustrior ratio est, quoniam non fucatur pompa facundiae et gratiae, sed, ut est, recti regula sustinetur.* The clarity and, by implication, the rectitude of the message would thus benefit from an unsophisticated style. Octavius' criticism is, of course, aimed at inflated pagan eloquence. It reflects, in fact, a cultural turn of the tide, the new faith's parting of ways from classical rhetoric, which will be of special interest for us insofar as it involved distrust or patent rejection of pagan, purportedly fictional literature.

Such conflations of discursive refinement with cognitive or moral shortcomings were particularly common in the fourth and fifth centuries, as if brilliance of style automatically cast a shadow over the content of words – or over their lack of content. This construction, as it were, of guilt by association is easy to detect in Ambrose's perhaps best-known letter (73.2), addressed to the Emperor Valentinian II in 384, a document that (as we shall shortly see) challenged the very survival of classical culture in Rome. In opposition to the *verborum elegantia* of pagan eloquence, the energetic Archbishop called attention to the actual state of things, or more precisely the "force of facts", *vis rerum:* "For as Holy Scripture teaches us, the tongue of learned and wise men is golden, and endowed with highly-decked words, and glittering with splendid elegance as with the brightness of some rich colour, and so captivates and dazzles the eyes of the mind with a shew of beauty. But this gold, if closely handled, may pass current outwardly, but within is base metal."[1]

Ambrose's contrast between the external splendour of words and their inner emptiness was a topos exploited particularly vigorously by Jerome. The monk in Bethlehem, in fact, returns time and again to this denunciation of polished and urbane speech. On several occasions he pleaded for the low style, characterized by apostolic simplicity and purity of words, *apostolicorum simplicitas et puritas*

---

1 "Aurea enim, sicut scriptura divina docet, est lingua sapientium litteratorum, quae faleratis dotata sermonibus et quodam splendentis eloquii velut coloris pretiosi corusco resultans capit animorum oculos specie formosa visuque perstringit. Sed aurum, si diligentius manu tractes, foris pretium, intus metallum est." (18.2 in earlier editions of Ambrose's letters).

verborum, in stark contrast to the virtuosities of rhetoric.¹ I quote this allegation from the third part of the Church Father's commentary on the Epistle to the Galatians, which repeatedly recycles the early Church's association of the language of the Gospels with that of Jesus' disciples, commonly labelled the speech of fishermen, *sermo piscatorius*. Jerome was even more detailed in a letter to Pope Damasus in 384 (36.14):²

> I know this is awkward for the reader, but whoever penetrates into Hebrew literature should avoid relying on Aristotelian arguments. Likewise, he should neither take advantage of any rill from the wide stream of Tullius' eloquence, nor caress his ears with Quintilian's flowers of speech and school declamations. Our tongue should rather be straightforward, resembling everyday language, and shun any redolence of learned studies. It should explain its subject, put forth its sense and clarify what seems obscure, avoiding all luxuriant constellations of words. Let others be eloquent and receive praise for it, if they want, and let them weigh foaming words in their swollen mouths. To me it is enough to speak so that I will be understood and, since I examine the Scripture, to imitate the simplicity of the Scripture. (II)

This epistolary statement corresponds to several similar announcements in the invocations of the Holy Spirit characteristic of the period's Biblical epic poetry, scattered with dismissive references to the flowery style of pagan eloquence. When Jerome warns against *Aristotelis argumenta*, probably the philosopher's logic works, his famous *Organon*, he also seems to express his distrust of rhetoric's *inventio*, the doctrine of locating and implementing arguments among a number of 'places', *topoi* (in Latin: *loci*), for the composition of a speech or text. To all appearances, however, it is principally Cicero's and Quintilian's emphasis on linguistic ornamentation that he disapproves of: the detailed catalogues of tropes and other figures that fill quite a few pages in their examinations of style, *elocutio*.

In particular, Jerome calls his papal addressee's attention to Quintilian's flowers of speech, *flosculi*, and the 'stream' or 'caress' of eloquent language, three points of attack that would soon constitute stock themes or 'places' in similar Christian assaults on the classics and their Muses. The Church Father continues by dealing with the *verba* of pagan eloquence in terms of foliage and foam, that is, as transient and vain ostentation compared with the laudably low style of the Bible. This latter mode of expression should, conversely, be employed for the purpose of explaining the Holy Scripture, both its literal sense (*rem explicet*) and its deeper, allegorical meaning (*sensum edisserat, obscura manifestet*).

---

1 *PL* 26.399b.
2 *PL* 22.458–59 (translation mine).

Jerome's diatribe should be understood against the background of the extraordinary status that rhetoric enjoyed in the educational system of Late Antiquity. This discipline was no longer taught for public appearances in the Forum and the law courts, but rather in its capacity as an instrument of power in the hands of the imperial court and the Roman elite, as the privileged language of the literate and the learned, and, indeed, as the basis or even epitome of Roman civilization, the Empire's cultural bulwark against the increasingly strong assaults of the barbarians.[1] More than any other of the Latin Fathers, except for Augustine, Jerome was superbly trained in, not to say dependent on, this rhetorical culture, although his studies over several decades of the Bible's original texts induced him to repudiate the convoluted Latin of the orators and the poets.

A complex but illustrative example of the erudite monk's inflamed attitude towards the foaming words of the grand style – what could reasonably be called a love-hate relationship – is to be found in his commentary on Isaiah. In 33.15–16, the prophet, interpreting the Lord's words, had proclaimed that a righteous man will be rewarded for his irreproachability: "his bread will be given him; his water will be sure." The commentator explains that 'the pagan myths understand these things as ambrosia and nectar. We, however, shall interpret them as the bread and ever-flowing water of divine law' (10.438), *quae gentilium fabulae in ambrosia et nectare intelligunt. Nos autem panes et aquas fidelissimas, legem Dei interpretabimur.*[2] To begin with, this remark testifies to Jerome's inclination to single out themes and attitudes of classical culture for rather detailed comparison. His need, even in exegetic contexts, to simultaneously evoke and censure pagan mythology – here the proverbial food and drink of the Olympian gods, always in good supply – is evident, several decades after Constantine's edicts.

If Jerome expresses his preference of divine law to Olympian nectar and ambrosia rather discreetly, he proceeds to a frontal attack when dealing with the subsequent verses from Isaiah, where the prophet predicts the return of the exiled people to Zion, their home country, now freed from its Assyrian oppressors (33.17–19). Then they will see "the king in his beauty", and they will be able to conceive of their hardships as a thing of the past: "Where is he who counted, where is he who weighed the tribute? / Where is he who counted the towers?" In all probability, these rhetorical questions refer to the magistrates of the occupying power. Now, at this much longed-for moment in the near future, they will have departed at last. "You will see no more the insolent people", Isaiah comforts his countrymen, "the people of an obscure speech that you cannot compre-

---

[1] Cf. Haarhoff 1920, p. 153.
[2] *PL* 24.367c (all translations from Jerome's commentary on Isaiah are mine).

hend, / stammering in a tongue that you cannot understand". This is obviously a patriotic and political prophecy put forth for the edification of the burdened Jewish people, but in his commentary, Jerome twists it into a truculent anathema against both Jewish and, in a wider perspective, all (pagan) erudition and eloquence.

This trick already seems prepared in the Vulgate, where "he who counted" in Isaiah, the hated Assyrian official, is rendered as *litteratus*. Moreover, his colleagues are termed 'he who weighs the words of the law', *legis verba ponderans*, and 'the instructor of mere children", *doctor parvulorum*. The translator thus singles out learned men, lawyers and teachers. Who are they, specifically? In his commentary, Jerome identifies them more closely. Here, he substitutes *scriba* for *litteratus*, thus transferring the target of the prophet's accusation from its original referent, the foreign magistrates, to the Jewish *Scribae et Pharisaei*. They are held responsible for deceiving their own people, here described as *imprudens*, where the Vulgate had preferred "shameless" (33.19), *inpudens*. Finally, the commentator intrepidly reinterprets the hard-pressed but soon-to-be liberated addressee of Isaiah's verses – the exiled Jewish people – as the Christians, now happily rescued from precisely this people, the Jews, and their charlatans (10.438–39):[1]

> When the eyes of the believer have seen the king in all his majesty, and his heart remembers the time of terror, he shall no longer have to watch either the imprudent people, the people of the Jews, or the philosophers and orators of this world, who will applaud their own secular erudition and eloquence, and of whom the prophet now says: THE PEOPLE OF AN OBSCURE SPEECH THAT YOU CANNOT COMPREHEND; all their adornment consists in the words, which only have recourse to the foliage and shade of speech but do not possess the fruit of truth. Eventually, Isaiah adds: WHERE THERE IS NO KNOWLEDGE, which is likewise mentioned elsewhere: *I will destroy the wisdom of the wise, and the discernment of the discerning I will thwart.* Why? Since *God made foolish the wisdom of the world*. (III)

Irrespective of the details in Jerome's handling of the original Hebrew text, which I am not competent to discuss, it is clear that the inventiveness of his typological interpretation brutally ignores Isaiah's historical context. The commentator perpetrates astounding hermeneutic violence against the prophet's words. He transforms their persecuted Jewish collective of an age long since past into a portrait of the recently persecuted Christians, a telling misreading that in turn presup-

---

[1] *PL* 24.368a–b. The small capitals indicate the phrase from Isaiah which Jerome annotates, while the text in italics refers to Paul, 1 Corinthians 19–20. It cannot be excluded, of course, that the commentary's switch from the Vulgate's *inpudens* to *imprudens* is due to later copyists' misreadings or emendations.

poses the transmutation of Isaiah's foreign oppressors into Jewish Scribes and Pharisees, here equated with the pagan 'philosophers and orators of this world'.

According to this cleverly calculated reinterpretation of Isaiah, it is they, the *philosophi et oratores mundi*, rather than the Assyrians who express themselves in "obscure speech". To Jerome, their *sermo altus* is nothing but vain grandiloquence, verbal ornaments so elaborated that they end up being incomprehensible. Not unlike Augustine, he seems to mobilize all his rhetorical skills for the purpose of refuting empty rhetoric. Here, he relies on the metaphor: speech = forest (or grove, trees etc.), to the effect that the polished words of eloquence are configured as "the foliage and shade" – subtly evoking a *locus amoenus* – of speech. Their delight is certainly to be found in rich quantities among the representatives of pagan culture, who, however, were cut off from 'the fruit of truth', by implication only accessible to Christians. A reasonable consequence of this idiosyncratic reading of Isaiah could be stated as follows: the wisdom of the world, which God has made foolish, is made to incorporate not only Jewish Pharisaism or classical philosophy and rhetoric but all discourse framed in the high or ornamented style, including poetry, characterized by its billowing yet unreliable brilliance.

Such critical gestures directed against the foam, floridness or charm of style, very common in early Christian culture, were themselves, as Eduard Norden noted in his comprehensive investigation of ancient *Kunstprosa*, carefully styled.[1] Lactantius had already, for strategic reasons (as he set out to convince the pagan cultural elite of the rightfulness of his cause), tried to downplay the notion of Biblical simplicity, and there are certainly plenty of tropes – let alone cases of a forced or affected style – in the writings of Jerome himself, for instance in the famous trial vision of his twenty-second letter (see above, p. 148). The hot-tempered translator and commentator remained to a high degree a *ciceronianus* or a *virgilianus*, whether he liked it or not. The same could be said of the Biblical epic poets of Late Antiquity, shortly to be dealt with in this chapter, and, to varying degrees, of the foremost intellectual figure of the whole period, Saint Augustine. At least one basic reason (already hinted at in the previous presentation) for these Christian advocates' ostensibly paradoxical attachment to the art of rhetoric and, in a wider perspective, to their cultural past, can be established without further ado: the Roman educational system.

---

[1] "To say it succinctly: in theory, Christian authors have from the very start and well into the Middle Ages almost without exception adopted the point of view that writing should be simple, in practice they accomplished quite the reverse." Norden 1909, p. 529. Cf. Roberts 1989, pp. 122–47.

Even though devout intellectuals ever since the early apologists had succeeded in establishing a new religious identity in contrast to the Empire's pagan traditions, the barbarian raids across the Mediterranean area during the fifth and sixth centuries could only reinforce many Christians' feeling of belonging to a civilization based on traditional *paideia*, with grammar and eloquence as its cornerstones. And this feeling – it needs to be repeated – was one they had imbibed, as it were, with their mother's milk. All the Christian authors were products of Roman education. Even if Augustine provided an innovative draft for a learned culture on a religious basis in *On Christian Doctrine*, the Church never produced an educational programme of its own. As Pierre Riché emphasizes, the theological competence of the Church Fathers was completely independent of the established school system. It was not until the first monasteries were founded that alternative teaching methods were established, intended for those who had 'taken leave of the world', castigating traditional rhetoric's ostentatious (or even narcissistic) aspects, focusing on prayer, hymn singing, and meditative scriptural reading (*lectio divina*).[1] Consequently, I will dedicate a minimum of attention to Benedict and his famous Rule at the end of this book, but, inevitably, a more ambitious review of monastic culture's didactic ambitions and methods must fall outside the scope of my discussion.

In short, all antique education was based on grammar and eloquence; rhetoric survived without much difficulty every pious attempt (not seldom rhetorically pointed and profuse) to kill it off. That is why Klaus Thraede distinguishes between, on the one hand, the early Christian poets' theory, insisting on sincerity in the low style, usually propounded as a part of what Curtius labelled the "topics of the exordium" in their works, and, on the other hand, their eloquent practice.[2] This is an important modification of Auerbach's thesis, which, on the whole, tends to subsume actual Christian discourse under the concept of *sermo humilis*.[3] Thraede's (and other scholars') disclosure of a tension between austere theory and magniloquent practice might also be reformulated in terms of a development from the former to the latter; thus Calogero Riggi detects a shift of emphasis from the apologists of the Early Church to the authors of the nascent Middle Ages, when the Bible's *genus dicendi simplex* slowly but steadily had to make room for high-flown modes of discourse.[4] This process of transition would in

---

[1] Riché 1962, pp. 47, 49, 150–63; cf. Marrou 1948, pp. 416–47.
[2] Thraede 1962b, p. 138; Curtius 1990, p. 85.
[3] "The style level of Christian literature, [...], is principally determined by the conception of *sermo humilis*, which may be said to be implicit in it – and though this *sermo humilis* is by no means free from rhetoric, it is nevertheless *simplex* and *apertus*." Auerbach 1993, p. 199.
[4] Riggi 1977, p. 435.

turn be a consequence of the increasingly high social status of Christian authors, frequently recruited from the provincial or even senatorial aristocracy, which, in addition, constituted their prime audience. Juvencus, Proba, Avitus and their colleagues all contribute to this momentous cultural reconstruction. As Rome became Christianized during the fourth and fifth centuries, Christianity was correspondingly, to put it bluntly, Romanized. After the ground-breaking integrative accomplishments of Lactantius and Juvencus, the Early Church's eschatological purging of the classical heritage gave way to a gradual adjustment to the distinguished audiences familiar with Virgil, Horace and Ovid since their childhood.[1]

The institutionalization of the new faith in the Empire was thus crucial to this shift in Christian attitudes towards style. The *ecclesia triumphans* of the fourth and fifth centuries encouraged the ambitions to supplement the Gospels' *sermo humilis* with exultant manifestations of the victory of the faithful and the glory of Christ, treated "in a style both grand and ornate", *et granditer et ornate*, to use Augustine's words from *On Christian Doctrine* (4.20.43). Much has been written about the Church Father's plea for the simple style in this key treatise, a virtual turning point between antique and medieval rhetoric. It would, however, with some justification, be possible to argue that Book IV of *On Christian Doctrine* helped to establish, at a theoretical level, the adorned or "jeweled" style that Christian writers had experimented with ever since Juvencus had paraphrased the Bible in epic fashion a century earlier. This pioneering achievement did not simply revert to traditional Roman eloquence. On the contrary, precisely in the fourth book of *On Christian Doctrine*, Augustine disassociated himself from the Cicero he had grown up with and knew so well, a departure that is not altogether easy to detect since from beginning to end he made use of Ciceronian terminology.

In his treatise on the *Orator*, Cicero had reserved different levels of style or *genera dicendi* for different purposes and subjects: in the main, the low or "plain" style for presenting proof or discussing commonplace matters, the middle style for imparting pleasure, and the high style for persuading and "moving" the audience with reference to lofty subjects (21.69, 29.100–01). This Ciceronian correlation of a hierarchical set of styles with as many subjects did not apply, of

---

[1] Fontaine 1981, p. 69. Wolfgang Kirsch likewise detects a conflict among Christian writers between their mission as pastoral guides, with a particular responsibility for the poor in spirit, and "the Late Antique conceptions of style, which increasingly withdrew from the linguistic reality of everyday life". As an example of this tension, Kirsch adduces the difference between "communicative intention" and "communicative practice" in Paulinus of Nola, 1988, p. 13. In addition, he surveys this development from a Marxist perspective in the second and third chapters of his monographic study 1989a, pp. 55–192.

course, in the Holy Writ. For a number of the pious authors of Late Antiquity it certainly appeared as obsolete. Augustine, for his part, exposed it to important modifications in Book IV of *On Christian Doctrine*, basically because Christian orators, strictly speaking, never had any simple or commonplace matters to communicate: "all matters that we speak of are important" (4.18.35), *omnia sunt magna quae dicimus*. Their vocation concerned mankind's fundamental questions such as the salvation of the soul, and "what is greater than God himself?", Augustine asked rhetorically (4.19.38): *Quid enim deo ipso maius est?*

This reformed view of the doctrine and implementation of styles must, of course, be understood not only against the backdrop of the paradigm of the Scripture but as an outcome of the Church Father's personal experiences. He was, admittedly, at home in the temple of learning, but upon finalizing the fourth book of *On Christian Doctrine* he could look back on many years of field work, countless sermons and great educational efforts in his North-African congregations. He had certainly learnt how to capture and hold the attention of his audiences; to this purpose he laid particular stress on the necessity of variety in style (4.22.51). As Čelica Milovanović-Barham observes in a fine essay, Augustine's dosage of *genera dicendi* was no longer, in the Ciceronian manner, dependent on the speaker's subject but on the effects to which he wanted to expose his audience.[1] That is why he allowed passages in the plain style to intermingle with sublime effusions; moreover, even the middle style, the *temperatum dicendi genus*, relying on the ornamentation of words to please the listeners or readers, could be exploited by Christian preachers, not for ostentation but for their pastoral care (4.25.55). This shift of theoretical emphasis in *On Christian Doctrine* IV is characteristic. The treatise's arguments for the application of *sermo humilis* in serious contexts harked back to early evangelic tradition, while its reliance on the figures of speech and *genus grande* in Christian oratory was in accordance with recent practice.

The flowering of Biblical epic poetry was symptomatic of this stylistic reorientation in the rhetoric and homiletics of the Church Triumphant, as well as of the incipient integration of the Holy Writ in literary contexts. According to strictly apologetic opinion, the verbally inspired Bible books had constituted a unique text which, theoretically, made all poetic and philosophical literature superfluous. This sharp distinction between Christian enlightenment and pagan fancies was not negotiable – as Tertullian underlined in his tract *De praescriptione haereticorum* (*The Prescription Against Heretics*): "What indeed has Athens to do with Jerusalem? What concord is there between the Academy and the Church?

---

[1] Milovanović-Barham 1993, p. 5.

what between heretics and Christians?" (7.9), *Quid ergo Athenis et Hierosolymis? quid academiae et ecclesiae? quid haereticis et christianis?* The apologist's rhetorical questions would later be recycled by Jerome (cf. the second motto to this book), this time against the backdrop of the ascetic movement of the late fourth century that opposed contemporary tendencies to merge Christianity with imperial culture.

Ironically, Jerome's own project of translating the Bible into Latin proved seminal to this integration process. As the fourth century went on, the Holy Writ began to be reconsidered and examined in a literary context. With the Edict of Thessalonica in 380, the time had come for the ancient Hebrew and Greek documents to be promoted as the sacred book of the Roman Empire's authorized religion. Consequently, the demand for exegetic expertise and a reliable standard text was significantly sharpened, which is why, at some time in 382–83, Pope Damasus commissioned Jerome to revise the extant Latin translations of the Gospels: the inception of the Vulgate. In a long letter to Paulinus of Nola in 394, the learned Church Father discussed in some detail the style of the Holy Writ, being fully aware that the justly admired "simplicity of the scripture or the poorness of its vocabulary", *simplicitas, et quasi vilitas verborum*, in the old Latin versions of the New Testament could sometimes be due to "the faults of translators", *vitium interpretum* (53.9).[1] In short, while both Testaments evidently should be considered unique, inspired by the Spirit, it was possible and even useful to analyse them in terms of literature. David was a poet, a Christian Simonides, Pindar, Alcaeus, Horace and Catullus in one person; Job alternated between verse and prose, and the prophets overflowed with rhetorical figures (53.8).

Ancient epic tradition, with its overwhelming flora of myths and legends, known to anyone who had received at least a rudimentary education in grammar, was inevitably in the minds of the Late Antique Christian poets. It was recalled with particular emphasis at the beginning of their works, albeit in distrustful or deprecatory terms, as a series of dream-like visions that it was necessary to abjure or kill off in the name of Biblical truth. Still, more or less manifest allusions to Homer and Virgil were always there, despite all mandatory reservations, constituting a well-known frame of reference, a challenging basis for comparisons and, of course, an efficient indicator of genre: a technique of authorizing the present work by emulating epic loftiness and dignity. These frequent pointers to pagan literature were due, then, not only to overall cultural tradition and education but, as Harald Hagendahl has remarked, to the widespread

---

[1] *PL* 22.549 (in the Schaff and Wace edition 53.10).

conviction of the formal and rhetorical excellence of the classics.[1] Even in those cases – quite a few, in fact – when this assumption was stated in reluctant terms, it seemed inescapable.

Among the great pioneering figures in this context, Lactantius represents the theoretical avant-garde. In the fascinating introduction to the fifth book of his *Divine Institutes*, he had sketched a Christian hermeneutics or pedagogics, according to which ancient eloquence should be put at the disposal of the new faith. We will trace this approach in a number of Christian writers from the fourth to the sixth centuries, moving across the years from the Christianization of the Roman Empire and the Nicaea Church Council (325) through the turbulent era of the Germanic invasions up to the mighty Pope Gregory the Great, whose theological and political activities at a continental level already heralded the Carolingian era. My sample of writers is, of course, limited. This was in fact an innovative, not to say experimental epoch in the fabrication and appreciation of poetry, comparably neglected by most modern authors of literary history. For well over a century they nurtured notions of culture as an organic phenomenon characterized by growth, maturity, peak and decline, and they readily took on the task of (re)constructing national literatures, preferably – wherever possible – inspired by classical Hellas or Rome. Consequently, they tended to belittle the Latin poetry of Late Antiquity, supposedly non-classical, indicative of a declining culture. I shall have to make do with some examples characteristic of the period's ongoing negotiations of fictionality: the Aquitanian Paulinus of Nola, the Hispanic Prudentius and some representatives of the Biblical epic poetry that blossomed from the fourth century onwards, namely, in chronological order, another *hispanicus*, the presbyter Juvencus, the Roman Proba, Sedulius, of whom we know virtually nothing, Avitus from Burgundy and Arator, possibly of Ligurian origin.

---

[1] Hagendahl 1983, p. 50. Cf. Deproost 1998, p. 103.

2 Paulinus and Proba: "A Greater Order"

The Lyre of Nola

Paulinus of Nola, Campania, and his *Carmen* X, addressed to his former teacher Ausonius, have already been cited in the discussion above (p. 155): a "greater God" than Apollo and the Muses condemns "the fictions of literature" and "the inventions of poets" as vain and false. Later in the same verse letter, the author responds to an attempt from his addressee to get him to return, not only to his home district, Bordeaux, but to his earlier reverence for classical culture. Paulinus declines. To him, a zealous convert to Christianity, the ancient Muses seem hopelessly outdated (10.110–18):

110 Revocandum me tibi credam,
    cum steriles fundas non ad divina precatus,
    Castalidis supplex averso numine Musis?
    non his numinibus tibi me patriaeque reducis.
    surda vocas et nulla rogas (levis hoc feret aura
115 quod datur in nihilum) sine numine nomina Musas.
    inrita ventosae rapiunt haec vota procellae,
    quae non missa deo vacuis in nubibus haerent
    nec penetrant superi stellantem regis in aulam.

> I cannot believe that you can obtain my return by addressing your fruitless aim to a non-deity, by supplicating the Castalian Muses whose power is spent. These deities will not help you achieve my return to you and to my native land. Your call, your request, is addressed to deaf nobodies, the Muses; a light breeze will bear it away, by windy gusts. It is not sent to God, so it cleaves to the insubstantial clouds, and does not enter the starry hall of the King above.

Wolfgang Kirsch is probably right in assuming that the whole of Paulinus' work is based on a tension or even contradiction between intention and practice. The future saint emerges as a brilliant rhetorician who, with considerable eloquence, constantly complains about the vanity of rhetoric's *multiloquium*, a clever poet who, in poem after poem, declares his intention not to write poetry, a fervent convert who aspires to enlighten the common herd but normally addresses well-educated intellectuals, whether brothers in faith or not.[1]

Precisely such contradictions, characteristic of several other Late Antique poets, seem rewarding for an investigation into the period's negotiations of fic-

---

[1] Kirsch 1985.

tionality. How were they configured, and how were they mastered? Paulinus' key trick was to deprive the Muses of their status as goddesses. He wrote as if they still existed but had been forced to abdicate their power and authority. The classically educated Church Fathers argued in more or less the same way. This is evident from Augustine's polemics against polytheism in the *City of God* or, on a more unpretentious note, from an aside in a letter written by Jerome to the pious Roman lady Laeta. He congratulates her on her family – an equally pious husband and daughter – flourishing around her ageing father, the heathen pontiff Albinus: "I, for my part, think that even Jove might well have believed in Christ if he had had kinsfolk of this kind" (107.1), *ego puto etiam ipsum Iovem, si habuisset talem cognationem, potuisse in Christum credere*.[1]

In Paulinus' verse letter, Ausonius' prayers are declared to be pointless since they are not addressed to *divina*. The teacher's Muses have lost their authority. Their divine omnipotence, *numen*, has deserted them. In consequence, they do not hear their worshippers at all. They have been reduced to empty signs, to mere 'names' without any basis in reality, elegantly contrasted with their lost divinity by means of the paronomasia *sine numine nomina*. Thus they epitomize Ausonius' sadly sterile appeals, words that serve no purpose, doomed to vanish into thin air: rhetoric as vain verbosity. In Paulinus' new Christian semantics, the content and value of all performative utterances ultimately depends on their addressee. In short, prayers addressed to God are considered authentic (and reach their goal), while all other invocations or supplications are scattered in the wind, as short-lived as the breath that carries their words.

This tension between unconditional Christian truth and empty or futile human discursivity is perhaps most patently expressed in Paulinus' twentieth ode, probably written in the winter of 406. This is one of the panegyric *carmina natalicia* that, every year between 395 and 408, the godly recluse devoted to his patron saint, the martyr St. Felix of Nola, on the day of his death, January 14th, that is, the day of his birth to true life, hence the designation 'birthday songs'. Here, in *Carmen* XX, Paulinus rejoices in a couple of pigs he has been given for the approaching feast, a subject as good as any in the eyes of this pious monk. The poem accounts for various kinds of miracles connected with sacrificial animals. The author assures us that everything he says is for real (20.28–61):

28 Non adficta canam, licet arte poematis utar.
    historica narrabo fide sine fraude poetae;

---

1 Migne's *Patrologia* prefers a more pious wording, *PL* 22.868. I follow F.A. Wright's reading (and translation) from the Loeb edition, Jerome 1933.

30 absit enim famulo Christi mentita profari.
    gentibus hae placeant ut falsa colentibus artes;
    at nobis ars una fides et musica Christus,
    qui docuit miram sibimet concurrere pacem
    disparis harmoniae quondam, [...].
43 ille igitur vere nobis est musicus auctor,
    ille David verus, citharam qui corporis huius
45 restituit putri dudum conpage iacentem,
    et tacitam ruptis antiquo crimine chordis
    adsumendo suum dominus reparavit in usum,
    consertisque deo mortalibus omnia rerum
    in speciem primae fecit revirescere formae,
50 ut nova cuncta forent, cunctis abeunte veterno.
    hanc renovaturus citharam deus ipse magister
    ipse sui positam suspendit in arbore ligni
    et cruce peccatum carnis perimente novavit.
    atque ita mortalem numeris caelestibus aptam
55 conposuit citharam variis ex gentibus unam,
    omnigenas populos conpingens corpus in unum.
    inde lacessitis fidibus de pectine verbi
    vox evangelicae testudinis omnia conplet
    laude dei; toto Christi chelys aurea mundo
60 personat innumeris uno modulamine linguis,
    respondentque deo paribus nova carmina nervis.

Though I use the poet's art, the song I sing will not be invented. I shall tell it with an historian's truthfulness and without the poet's deceit, because a servant of Christ should not utter lies. Such techniques can satisfy non-Christians who cultivate falsehood, but our sole technique is faith, and our art of song is Christ. He has taught us that the wondrous peace of unbalanced harmony was of old achieved in Himself, [...]. So He is truly our poetic inspiration, the true David who has restored the lyre of this body which had long lain idle, its frame crumbling. The Lord has restored it, adopting it for His use when it was silent and its strings broken by that ancient sin. By joining men to God, He has achieved the reinvigoration of all creation to the beauty of its original shape, so that all things might be new, and the dust removed from them. God our Master Himself sought to renew this lyre, and so He hung His own lyre, nailed to the wood of the tree, and gave it fresh life when the cross destroyed the sinning of the flesh. Thus He ordered mortal man from the different nations into a single lyre, and tuned it for heavenly music, drawing peoples of all races into a single body. Then He struck the chords with the plectrum of the Word, and the sound of the Gospel-instrument filled all creation with praise of God. Christ's golden tortoise-shell resounds through the whole world; countless tongues sing a single melody; a new song rings out for God from matching strings.

In ingenious, richly orchestrated texts of this kind, Paulinus launches a successful attack on the pagan world of fiction. In several respects he incarnates the ascetic cultural radicalism of these turbulent years, demanding "that all things might be new, and the dust removed from them". Paulinus bases his main argument on the ambiguous, hence notoriously untranslatable *fides*, the Latin word for both faith and (the strings of) a lyre. When devout conviction, faith, thus coincides with a congenial means of expression, the lyre, there is no room for any *adficta*, literally 'fictional additions'. The poets' inventions are quite simply treacherous, a compilation of lies, *mentita*, characteristic of idolatrous people. The entire argument is structured on the basis of a dichotomy between *us*, the believers, and *them*, the misled pagans. There is no third option. This is made clear by the keyword *ars*, introduced and modulated in the opening lines of the passage above, closely connected to song (oral poetry). *Their* art deals with fiction, hence it is false, typical of people who worship false gods. *Our* art, in contrast, is unconditionally true, dictated by the Saviour of mankind.

The pagan poets' joint fraud is thus effectively counterbalanced by virtue of the poem's crucial configuration, expanded into a complete tableau: humanity epitomized by the Son of God in His capacity as the Father's mouthpiece or, more precisely, musical instrument. Christ, supremely repairing mankind's lost harmony in His person, is a *musicus auctor*. He intones a new music. His body constitutes, as it were, the *corpus* of humanity, damaged due to original sin but by His death potentially restored to its original vigour and beauty, now a single, harmonious tribute to its Creator. Here, Paulinus holds out the prospect of an art in which all Horatian subjectivity or Ovidian equivocation is cancelled, a verbal music announced in the chiasmus of line 29 that sets historical truth against poetical deceit: *historica... fide sine fraude poetae*. It already seems to have become reality in the closing lines of this early draft for a Catholic poetics, where the devout song of praise rises from the mouth of an undivided humanity, completely in line with the "strenuously maintained ideology of unanimity and concord" that, in the wording of Peter Brown, was crucial to Paulinus and "the late-fourth-century *impresarios* of the cult of saints".[1]

This harmonious hymn, executed by a global community following the example of Christ, seems entirely released from the fictional contract traditionally regulating the cognitive status and reception of Roman poetry.[2] Nevertheless, Paulinus presents Christ in artistic terms, as a musical instrument, implementing a typological scheme. The well-known scene from Psalms 136/137, where the children of Israel sat down by the waters of Babylon and remembered Zion, wept

---

[1] Brown 1981, pp. 89f.

[2] Paulinus might even allude to Ovid in 20.29. The Golden Age poet, the classical agent for the fictional contract in Roman poetry, had contrasted *historica fides* with *licentia vatum* in *Amores* 3.12.41–42 (above, p. 36). Paulinus recycles Ovid's antithesis but substitutes, tellingly, the poets' "deceit" for their licence.

and hung up their lyres on the willows, presages the crucifixion. Consequently, the lyre, referred to as *fides*, *cithara*, *testudo* or *chelys*, becomes a *typus* for Christ's sacrificed body, which in turn – in its restored (resurrected) state – heralds the universal Church. Eloquent Paulinus exhibits an impressive synonymic register, including a vague allusion to the Greek lyre, fraudulent Hermes' proverbial tortoise-shell, a prime emblem of the art of poetry, now in the hands of a completely different, altogether reliable God. Helena Junod-Ammerbauer has remarked that a similar metaphoric use of the lyre (or of music instruments in general) had, interestingly, already been tried out by Ambrose.[1]

Junod-Ammerbauer's observation entitles us to generalize our reading of Paulinus' *Carmen* XX. The ode reveals a conceptual pattern that was to control the victorious Christian culture's understanding and use of poetry. Ever since the Golden Age of Roman literature, this art had enjoyed a self-evident status among the aristocratic elite of the Empire. It held a prominent position in grammar teaching, apart from the fact that its images and rhythms could always appeal to the illiterate majority as well. Paulinus and quite a few of his fellow believers continued to appreciate poetry, albeit for different reasons. Firstly, it appeared to be an outstanding propaganda instrument in the service of their faith. Secondly, it was firmly anchored in the Holy Writ: in the Book of Psalms (David's recorded songs), in the prophets and in the Gospels, performed by Christ Himself, the New Covenant's antitype of the Old Testament's David, *ille David verus*, for example in the Sermon on the Mount and in His numerous parables. Last but not least, several Christian writers in the decades around the year 400, as Jean Doignon has shown, felt a Neo-Platonic inclination to look for mystic signs and meanings in the classical poets, mainly in Virgil's works.[2] For all these reasons, theologians, confronted with the task of framing and formalizing a standardized Christian liturgy, relied on a rich assortment of lyrical techniques. In traditional (pagan) culture, however, these techniques would habitually raise expectations of mythological scenarios. That was exactly why it was so important for Paulinus and other early Catholic authors to draw a sharp line between fictional *fraus* and truly inspired praise or *laus* in contemporary poetry.

A similar mechanism can be detected in Paulinus' *Carmen* XV, the birthday song for Felix in the year 398, a recapitulation of the saint's life. An urgent issue in the opening of this ode is the inspiration, rather than the performance or reception, of poetry. Beginning with Juvencus, this would prove a durable topos in

---

[1] Junod-Ammerbauer 1975, p. 50.
[2] For a good example of this penchant in Paulinus, drawn from the edifying story in *Carmen* XX about a heifer, at first rebellious but later laudably devout, see Doignon 1972.

the numerous Late Antique and medieval affirmations of Christian writers' superiority over their pagan predecessors or counterparts. Just as Virgil had drunk at the fountain of the Muses, the Bible was thought to be inspired from above – from much farther above, as it were, than the Muses' Mount Helicon. It was considered to be instilled and written down, word for word, at the dictation of the Holy Spirit. In consequence, Christian poets adapted the invocation of the Muses, common in much classical epic and lyric poetry, for their own purposes, frequently testing its pagan precedents – with a predictable negative outcome – against their prophetic paradigms from the Bible. This is Paulinus' Carmen 15.26–49:[1]

> 26 Surge igitur, cithara, et totis intendere fibris,
>   excita vis animae tacito mea viscera cantu,
>   non tacita cordis testudine dentibus ictis
>   pulset amor, linguae plectro lyra personet oris.
> 30 non ego Castalidas, vatum phantasmata, Musas
>   nec surdum Aonia Phoebum de rupe ciebo;
>   carminis incentor Christus mihi, munere Christi
>   audeo peccator sanctum et caelestia fari.
>   nec tibi difficile, omnipotens, mea solvere doctis
> 35 ora modis, qui muta loqui, fluere arida, solvi
>   dura iubes tu namque asinam reboare loquendo
>   perfectamque tibi lactantes condere laudem
>   fecisti et solidam solvisti in flumina rupem
>   et terram sine aqua subitis manare fluentis
> 40 iussisti, deserta rigans in spem populorum,
>   in quorum arentes animas pia gratia fluxit,
>   quos Christus vivo manans petra fonte refecit.
>   unde ego, pars hominum minima, isto munere fretus
>   roris, Christe, tui vivos precor aridus haustus.
> 45 da verbum de fonte tuo, tua non queo fari
>   te sine; namque tui laus martyris et tua laus est,
>   qui facis omnipotens homines divina valere
>   fortiaque infirmis superas de carne triumphans,
>   aërios proceres vincens in corpore nostro.

So rise, my lute, and strain with every fibre, and you, my soul's strength, arouse my inner self with your silent song, may love pluck the all but silent strings of my heart and strike against my teeth, may the lyre that is my throat resound with the quill that is my tongue. I

---

1 I have removed a semicolon after *vis animae* on line 27 in Hartel's edition of Paulinus' *Carmina* and, hence, slightly modified Walsh's translation of lines 26–29. On ideas of inspiration in Paulinus, see Junod-Ammerbauer 1975, pp. 22–37, and in early Christian poetry overall, Homeyer 1970.

shall not summon Castalian Muses, the ghosts of poets, nor rouse deaf Phoebus from the Aonian rock. Christ will inspire my song, for it is through Christ's gift that I, a sinner, dare to tell of His saint and of heavenly things. For You, Almighty One, it is easy to move my lips in learned rhythms, for You bid the dumb to speak, the dry to flow, the hard to be melted. For it was You who made the ass cry back in speech, and children at the breast to sing Your praises to perfection. You bade the solid rock dissolve into a river, and waterless land to flow with sudden streams, watering the desert to give hope to those peoples. Into their dry souls flowed Your holy grace; it was Christ who refreshed them, the Rock flowing with the living spring. So I, O Christ, who am the least of living men, put reliance on this gift, and in my dryness pray for running draughts of Your water from that spring. Grant me speech from Your fount, for without You I cannot speak Your words. They are Yours because praise of Your martyr is also praise of You, for in Your omnipotence You grant men divine strength. In triumphing over the flesh, You defeat the strong with the weak, and within our bodies conquer the princes of the air.

In the initial lines of this extract from *Carmen* XV, Paulinus identifies his soul and, more importantly, his body as the source of music (song). To begin with, he urges the mental power that Stoic philosophers used to evoke in their treatises, *vis animae*, to transmit silent vibrations through his psychophysical interior: the *viscera*, 'guts', that were a common metonym in Latin tradition for man's innermost being. Subsequently, this movement of his soul is expected to materialize in audible tones, rising from his heart through his throat to finally break into song. More or less as in *Carmen* XX, the poet addresses this living instrument by different names – the *cithara* of his person, the *testudo* of his heart, the *lyra* of his throat or mouth – and here too, the "love" that will strike the notes in his heart is of Christian origin. The Muses and their habitual master, Apollo, are rejected as Pythian aberrations, unreal, the *phantasmata* of poets of old; hence, all attempts to call forth "deaf Phoebus" from the (Delphic) rock seem futile. In stark contrast to this ghost-like pagan scenario appears Christ, who fills Paulinus with His voice as vigorously as He once helped Moses to strike the rock – another rock – to get water in the desert (Exodus 17.1–7, Numbers 20.1–13).

The author cleverly exploits Pauline typology. The Apostle to the Gentiles had interpreted precisely the rock in this episode from the Israelites' wandering in the desert as a type of Christ: "they drank from the spiritual Rock that followed them, and the Rock was Christ" (1 Corinthians 10.4). That is why *Carmen* XV can depict the Saviour as *vivo manans petra fonte*, a rock spouting a living fountain, and, in addition, amplify this configuration in a series of images of drought and irrigation, in the rhetorical tradition from Cicero commonly associated with the arid and inspired style respectively.[1] Such is the sacred liquid that

---

1 Junod-Ammerbauer 1975, pp. 39–44.

now, in the invocation at the outset of *Carmen* XV, supersedes the classical nectar so as to initiate the poets' song of praise in memory of Saint Felix.

The acknowledgement that the poet remains powerless without this inspiration from the one true God is significant. Charles Witke, who has examined a number of these invocations in the literature of the period, stresses the fact that classical culture's construction of the poetic *persona* – its image of the poet – comes to naught in this early Christian poetry.[1] The author was no longer able to put on a mask, to claim a fictional authority or try out different voices in his poetry, but merged into the devout individual behind the poem, the authentic Christian speaker. Another of Paulinus' *Carmina*, the well-known X, is indicative of this completely transformed notion of the poet in nascent Christian literature, where God is said to wholly demand "our hearts, tongues, and heads. He wishes to be the object of our thought and understanding, our belief and reading, our fear and love" (10.64–66), *et corda et ora et tempora; / se cogitari intellegi credi legi, / se vult timeri et diligi.*

"Our hearts, tongues, and heads"… the new Christian poet had to put his whole being, all his oral and mental skills, at the service of God. Yet another specialist in the literature of Late Antiquity, Jacques Fontaine, points out that the poet, as he appears in Paulinus' *Carmen* XV, completely identified his character, including his physical persona, with the lyre. If *Carmen* XX was to present Christ as mankind's particular musical instrument, here – in the eight years earlier *Carmen* XV – it is the poet himself who coalesces with the *cithara*. He is to sing the praise of God by all possible means: with his body, his words and his deeds. Thus Paulinus launches a psychosomatic theory of inspiration based on Stoic physiology, classical poetics and Pythagorean musical theory, filtered through Alexandrian theology and contemporary liturgy, with Christ figuring as *logos* as well as an exemplary musician: a new and universal Orpheus, endowed with the same power over Nature – the earth, the rocks and the animals – as in the ancient myth.[2]

This highly complex invocation ends, interestingly, with the prospect of Christ conquering "the princes of the air", *aërii proceres*, within our bodies. Here too, the ode probably echoes a Pauline passage, namely the Epistle to the Ephesians 2.1–2, where the apostle recapitulates the young congregation's pagan past: "And you were dead in the trespasses and sins in which you once walked, following the course of this world, following the prince of the power

---

[1] "Art becomes a function of the personality of the factual human practitioner, not a learned body of devices inhabited at will by their detachable manipulator." Witke 1971, p. 182, cf. p. 80.
[2] Fontaine 1973.

of the air, the spirit that is now at work in the sons of disobedience". The Vulgate's *princeps potestatis aeris* may allude to evil powers under the leadership of the Devil, supposed to dwell in the atmosphere of air. This windswept element enveloping the earth (according to the Ptolemaic world picture) was widely considered the abode of demons. If similar suggestions were present in Paulinus' text, we would be well advised to recall the common linking of demonology to the fading world of pagan gods established by Augustine in his *City of God* (above, pp. 143, 283). Here, in Augustine and Paulinus, we are certainly a far cry from the "airy nothing" engendered by imagination that Shakespeare would entrust to the poet's shaping power in *A Midsummer Night's Dream* (5.1.16). Their inimical powers of the air, simultaneously (as we shall see) evoked by Prudentius as well, possess a quite real, albeit shadowy, existence, hence an imminent threat to all Christians. That is why, in Paulinus' ode, they must be conquered in our body, that is, in the body of the poet, of his congregation or his Church: in the very "lyre" that Christ has restored and struck for the benefit of mankind by his death on the cross.

It is for the same reason that Prudentius, shortly to be presented here in a full-length portrait, concludes his best-known work, *Psychomachia*, his allegorical story in verse of the battle between vices and virtues, with the hope of a harmonious, Christian human being, cast in one piece. This expectation is appropriately articulated by the personification labelled Concord: "Let our understanding be united by love, our life be in accord in a single aim; where there is separation [*dissociabile*] there is no strength", and further: "let one spirit shape in single structure all that we do by action of soul and body." (762–68)[1] This notion of a coalescence of body and soul determines both Paulinus' and Prudentius' ideas of eloquence. Where the classical authorities in this field, a Cicero or a Quintilian, had excelled in strategic devices, prescribing a range of simulated attitudes, demonstrations of *pathos* or discursive modes, all in accordance with genre and context, Prudentius simply referred to the Biblical writers' inspired speech. The same divine Spirit that once had flowed into the prophets was sent from heaven to wash you in its streams of eloquence, he exclaims in his posthumous greeting to the martyr, teacher of rhetoric and writer Cyprian – Bishop of Carthage, executed in 258 – in his *Peristephanon Liber* (*Crowns of Martyrdom*, 13.9–10). The martyr's diction is praised as a sacred and all-pervading

---

[1] "Quod sapimus coniungat amor; quod vivimus uno / conspiret studio: nil dissociabile firmum est. [...] quidquid gerimus mentisque et corporis actu, / spiritus unimodis texat conpagibus unus."

power, as ambrosia for the heart, a guarantee of absolute truth and moral purity rather than a tool for manipulative persuasion (13.11–14):

> 11 O nive candidius linguae genus! o novum saporem!
> ut liquor ambrosius cor mitigat, inbuit palatum,
> sedem animae penetrat, mentem fovet et pererrat artus,
> sic Deus interius sentitur et inditur medullis.

> What speech is thine! It is purer than snow, and of a new savour! Like an ambrosial liquor which soothes the heart, bathing the palate and penetrating to the seat of the soul, while it sustains the spirit and spreads through the whole frame, it makes us feel God within us entering into our marrows.

The Prudentius expert Klaus Thraede, referring to such effusions, has noted that the poet, within the framework of this metrically flawless hymn, presents faith as a "rhetorical experience".[1] This is a striking observation, but Cyprian's eloquence is in turn presented as pure nourishment, as a Christian equivalent to the Olympian nectar and ambrosia: a wine, a flow or fervour, permeating the recipient's whole organism, his or her soul, limbs and innermost marrow.

Prudentius is even more articulate on this point at the beginning of another hymn in *Crowns of Martyrdom*, namely X, dedicated to Romanus of Antioch, one of the many victims of Diocletian's persecution. His torturers had cut out his tongue, yet, according to the legend, he continued to praise God in a miraculous way. For precisely that reason, the author appeals to him with a prayer for the gift of poetry. After all, this martyr knows better than anyone else that "the voice that bears witness to the truth cannot be annihilated" (10.9), *vox veritatis testis extingui nequit*. By contrast, Prudentius' (alter ego's) voice is weak, stuttering and halting, but – he promises in the hymn's introductory invocation of the martyr – "if thou sprinkle my heart with the dew from on high and flood my breast with the milk of the spirit" (10.13–14), *sed si superno rore respergas iecur / et spiritali lacte pectus inriges*, his hoarse voice will soon grow strong again. Here, it is not so much the style or content of speech that matters but its divine incentive and inception (10.16–22):

> 16 Evangelista scripsit ipsum talia
> praecepta Messian dedisse apostolis:
> "nolite verba, cum sacramentum meum
> erit canendum, providenter quaerere;

---

[1] Thraede 1962b, p. 153.

20 ego inparatis quae loquantur suggeram."
      sum mutus ipse, sed potens facundiae
      mea lingua Christus luculente disseret.

The Evangelist has written that the Messiah himself instructed the apostles in this wise: "Seek not with forethought for words when my mystic doctrine is to be proclaimed. I shall furnish the unready with what they shall say." In myself I am dumb, but Christ is master of eloquence; He will be my tongue and discourse excellently.

The evangelist referred to is Matthew, who in a well-known passage (10.19–20), a *locus classicus* for all Christian ideas of inspiration, tells how Jesus sent out His disciples as sheep among the wolves: "When they deliver you over, do not be anxious how you are to speak or what you are to say, for what you are to say will be given to you in that hour. For it is not you who speak, but the Spirit of your Father speaking through you." The Romanus hymn, however, adds a new colouring to these evangelical words. First, it calls attention to the rhetorical qualities of Christian speech, with Christ as a superior model, *potens facundiae*, emphasizing another kind of eloquence than the Ciceronian or classical, a discourse without any given rules, fully dependent on the incentive powers of the divine master. Secondly, Romanus' anticipated influence will require and occupy the author's whole being. His breast and liver (*iecur*, in ancient medical tradition frequently considered the seat of passions, in a broader sense, like *viscera*, a metonym for the bodily interior) have to be fecundated in order to make the tongue fulfil its task: articulating the divine message, the kerygma. The demand for the believer's psychosomatic unity, crucial to Prudentius as well as Paulinus, precludes – in theory, at least – all calculated impersonation, hence all designs of fictional scenarios, in early Christian poetry.

Such anticlassical postures come to the fore in Paulinus' sixteenth letter and twenty-second ode, both addressed to his learned friend (or relative) Jovius, resident in Aquitania, and both probably written around the year 400.[1] In the letter, already cited above (pp. 160, 366), Paulinus rejects the ancient hypothesis of destiny, *fatum*, or chance, *fortuna*, as responsible for the misfortunes that can strike human beings. Such delusions, he bitingly remarks, have incited certain – perhaps Stoic – *magistri* to isolate a turbulent sphere of life, crammed with all kinds of calamities, from God's direct influence. As a consequence, he continues (based on the Epistle to the Romans 1.21, the same Bible text that we have seen Augustine exploit for his criticism of art and imagination), "they have aban-

---

[1] A detailed commentary on the letter, word for word or sentence for sentence, with various references to *Carmen* XXII, is to be found in Erdt's dissertation 1976.

doned their minds to a great void, and, in the proved words of Scripture, have *become vain in their thoughts*", *missis per inane magnum mentibus evanuerunt, sicut scriptum est et probatur, in cogitationibus suis*. This is because everything comes from Omnipotent God, and everything has a divine meaning. There are no exceptions to this state of things. Just as truly Christian authors were not allowed to adopt a fictitious mask or *persona* in their works, they had no right to exclude any sector of Creation from the Creator's Providence and supervision (16.2).

Still, Paulinus complains, ignorant and erroneous people hypostatize such hollow terms as "fortune", "fate" or "chance" (further examples, evidently, of the complex *nomina sine numine*), endowing them with bodily form for the purpose of worshipping these shamefully fabricated images. His observation is reminiscent of Augustine's polemics against the Manichees, though he soon turns it into a frontal attack on Platonic versions of mythology. The tale of the daughters of Necessity, the Fates, which Plato takes as his starting point for the famous story of Er in the closing pages of *The Republic* (616–17), is quite simply dismissed as eloquent nonsense. Paulinus' conclusion seems devastating for any conciliatory attempt to attach Christian significance to the great Athenian philosopher: "But we must look to Plato only for his pleasant Attic style, not for any relevance in his pointless myth. Such books published only to charm the ear ought not to uproot the basis of our understanding." (16.4)[1] This assault seems not only directed at Plato himself (conspicuously praised for his style) but, in general, at contemporary Neo-Platonic conceptualizations of the old myths, the kind of allegorism that was important to philosophers such as Porphyry and that would form the basis of Macrobius' notion of *narratio fabulosa*. All that is left of Plato's visionary panoramas in this relentlessly polemical letter is empty eloquence, *inanis facundia*, and an old wives' tale, *anilis fabula*, in short, shrivelled husks of the magnificent myths, not only lacking in suggestion or esoteric substance but completely devoid of any serious signification.

After this remarkable exercise in cultural criticism, Paulinus proceeds to personally designed exhortations to his addressee. Jovius had evidently tried to blame his own tardiness in seeking God on his still being fully occupied with worldly matters. To Paulinus, this excuse is merely an instance of eloquence, *facundia*, and slackness: Jovius quite simply lacks the necessary determination to go to the Bible. If he were only to exert himself a little, Paulinus reminds him, he

---

[1] "Sed nobis in illo sermonis tantum Attici comitas, non inanis fabulae spectanda concinnitas; quae demulcendis tantum auribus edita sunt, non debent sensuum fundamenta convellere."

would find it easy to concentrate on spiritual and demanding things, considering his intellectual capacity authenticated by his solid education (16.6 – 7):

> Your breath is fragrant with the bouquets of all poets, your eloquence overflows with the rivers of all orators, and you are watered by the founts of philosophy. You are rich also in foreign letters, filling your Roman mouth from Athenian honeycombs. Tell me, to whom are you paying tribute when you are reading Cicero and Demosthenes from cover to cover? Or when you tire of being steeped in the common run of books, and turn again those pages already read of Xenophon and Plato, Cato and Varro, and many whose books you possess while I perhaps do not know even their names? You have freedom from duties to occupy yourself with these, but you are too busy paying tribute to them to learn of Christ, who is the wisdom of God. You have leisure to be a philosopher, but not to be a Christian.
>
> Change your way of thinking, your style of eloquence! You need not abandon your inner philosophy if only you season it with faith and religion. When it is joined with them, employ it more wisely that you may be God's philosopher and God's poet, wise not in seeking God but in imitating Him, learned in manner of life rather than in tongue, yet with greatness of utterance equalling your deeds.
>
> Be a Peripatetic for God and a Pythagorean as regards the world. Preach the true wisdom that lies in Christ, and be finally silent towards what is vain. Avoid this destructive sweetness of empty literature as you would the Lotus-eaters, who made men forget their fatherland by the sweetness of their berries, or as you would the Sirens' songs, those melodies of baneful seduction. And because we can make use of some features of such empty myths and one or two common clichés for truthful and serious discussion, let me say that not merely literature but all forms of worldly life are Lotus-eaters or Sirens. For the noxious charm of pleasures makes us forgetful of our fatherland, for it blots out God, the common fatherland of all, from man's eyes; and the enticements of desires imitate the myth of the Sirens but bring a calamity that is real. What the Sirens are imagined to have been, enticing desires and alluring vices are in reality – inviting in appearance but poisonous to taste. Enjoyment of them is sinful, and the penalty is death. We must avoid them by being cleverer than Ulysses, blocking not only our ears but also our eyes and our mind, as it sails like a ship swiftly by, so that we may not be seduced by the delight that brings death and drawn on to the rocks of sin, be caught on the crags of death and suffer the shipwreck of our salvation. (IV)

The opening examples of Jovius' skills suggest that he is quite at home with the introductory school disciplines. Above all, he seems to be familiar with rhetoric and poetry, to which are affixed the customary attributes – notoriously suspect in Paulinus' eyes – of linguistic delight: blossoms, torrents and honey. Throughout the whole passage, secular studies are associated with pleasures that would make a modern educationist envious: nothing but sweetness and charms, *dulcedo* and *blandimenta*. By (eloquent) contrast, Jovius does not manage to make himself acquainted with the Bible. Now, it is exactly in such juxtapositions of suspect ancient learning with a deplorable neglect of the Scripture that Paulinus' controversies against pagan culture tend to take a new turn. Indeed, in this letter they literally turn or "change" (in Latin: *vertere*) precisely when the author exhorts his addressee: "Change your way of thinking, your style of eloquence", *verte potius sententiam, verte facundiam!* On closer thought, the old education need not be rejected but should be put to the service of the right faith. Paulinus can even afford to rehabilitate the ancient seer, the inspired *vates*, whose example had been crucial to the Roman Golden Age poets and hence seemed discredited for many Christians. To them it had been associated with idolatry as well as poetical self-sufficiency. Here, in Paulinus' letter to Jovius, the *vates* is projected as a servant of God.

This kind of reasoning was admittedly not unique to Paulinus. We have seen how both Augustine and Jerome could implement a similar Christian recycling, *chrēsis* or *usus*, of pagan myths and concepts. But here the argument is pursued with particular acuity and technical brilliance. It is constructed on the basis of an ingenious paradox. In accordance with his conviction that "we can make use of some features of such empty myths", Paulinus employs ancient mythology's well-known stories of the Lotus-eaters and the Sirens, introduced in the ninth and twelfth books of *The Odyssey* respectively (cf. above, pp. 439f.). However, he indulges in this type of *chrēsis* for one sole purpose, namely to warn his addressee of poetic fictions! The Lotus-eaters and the Sirens are made to embody literature's dangerous temptations for Christian man. In short, Paulinus reuses the allures of pagan myths to illustrate the dangers of pagan myths – strategically having in mind the recipient of his message, to all appearances highly sensitive to the delights of the classics.

Even though Paulinus extends the meaning of the Homeric mythological creatures to include "all forms of worldly life", in particular depraved and sensual pleasures, their proper sense in his argument is determined as the "destructive sweetness of empty literature", *perniciosa inanium dulcedo litterarum*. On this point he is exploiting a particular allegorical manner of treating the classics, characteristic of Late Antique hermeneutics, as we have been able to ascertain in the preceding chapter. Boethius might provide us with the best example. Upon entering the stage in his *Consolation*, Philosophy immediately expels the prisoner's tearful female company, whom she flippantly labels "Sirens", expressly identified with the (elegiac) Muses of classical fiction (1.PR.1). The fact that Boethius was active over a century after Paulinus is of little consequence in this context. Both these authors recycle Hellenistic and Alexandrian allegoresis for their own purposes.

Accordingly, our observations allow us to supplement Hugo Rahner's assumption that the Sirens appear in a twofold form in patristic literature, namely as "symbols both of deadly lust and of deadly knowledge".[1] For the majority of Christian Late Antique writers, liable to convert the Homeric episode of the Sirens into cautionary allegory and morality, they epitomized the attractions and dangers of poetry. When, in a letter dated 405, Jerome warned a girl from Gaul of certain intrepid pleasures, such as excursions and dinners in the company of both sexes, he added that it can be quite difficult to resist the temptations of sweet-sounding singing and music: "Heathen legends tell us that sailors actually ran their ships on the rocks that they might listen to the songs of the Sirens; and that the lyre of Orpheus had power to draw to itself trees and animals and to soften flints." (117.6)[2] The monk in Bethlehem, who actually included the Sirens in the Vulgate, did not hesitate to recycle these two supreme instances of pagan poetry – the songs of the Sirens and the lyre of Orpheus – in order to bring home his moral lesson.[3] On closer inspection, he wished to warn his young addressee against listening to those (male) singers who, presumably, performed their languorous songs with nefarious ulterior motives. Exposed to such moralizing treatment, even the myths emblematic of the charms of poetry and song were deprived of precisely those charms, doomed to survive as concise and clear-cut warning examples.

Similar procedures can easily be detected in Jerome's pen friend Paulinus. In his *Carmen* XV, he launched a categorical No to the "Castalian Muses, the ghosts of poets" (15.30), set in stark contrast to Christ, the poet's true source of inspiration. Still, he relied on the Sirens as well as the Muses to warn against the fictions of old. Moreover, as we can deduce from his letter to Jovius, he expands the terse references to these mythological figures typical of Jerome to entire paragraphs, a set of miniature scenarios, elaborating their dramatic qualities as well as their moral sense: "What the Sirens are imagined to have been, enticing desires and alluring vices are in reality – inviting in appearance but poisonous to taste. Enjoyment of them is sinful, and the penalty is death. We must avoid them by being cleverer than Ulysses, blocking not only our ears but also our eyes and our mind, as it sails like a ship swiftly by, so that we may not be seduced by the delight that brings death and drawn on to the rocks of sin, be caught on the crags of death and suffer the shipwreck of our salvation"... This tendency to amplify

---

[1] Rahner 1971, p. 354.
[2] "Narrant gentilium fabulae, cantibus sirenarum nautas isse in saxa praecipites: et ad Orphei citharam, arbores bestiasque, ac silicum dura mollita." *PL* 22.957.
[3] Rahner remarks that the Alexandrian translators who produced the Septuagint no less than six times mistakenly rendered the Hebrew word for "jackals" or "hen ostriches" as *Seirēnes*. Jerome corrected these passages with the exception of Isaiah 13.22, where *sirenae* are heard in the temples of pleasure, *in delubris voluptatis*, Rahner 1971, pp. 357f.

the pagan myth of the Sirens in captivating allegorical sequences was at the same time, or a little later, developed in full scale by Bishop Maximus of Turin (below, pp. 619f.). Of course, neither Paulinus nor Maximus cared much about the myth's original Homeric context, nor was either of them prepared to grant it any historical or antiquarian value whatsoever. Paulinus simply exploited it as a moralizing proto-Christian fable, his rightful share of "Egyptian gold" (cf. above, p. 160), since he – as well as the bulk of the early Christian poets – refused to conceive of his work in terms of literary tradition but rather as a contribution to the kerygma, a way of preaching, a metrical supplement to the Biblical message.

As a result, the authorial voice rising from these texts is predominantly that of a seer, a successor, as it were, to Isaiah, John and other Biblical prophets. Being a *poeta christianus* at this early stage in the Church's history was by and large equivalent to being a *propheta* or *vates christianus*, granted particular clues to the significance of the Old as well as the New Covenant, from Creation to Judgment Day. After all, prophecy's privileged form of expression was poetry, whose rhythmical and charismatic discourse was considered inspired by the Holy Spirit. In contrast to pagan fiction, this speech permeated by the Spirit could claim to be not only graceful – grammatically correct, rhetorically fluent and metrically accomplished – but, more importantly, veracious. These types of discourse, the epic-mythological and the Biblical-revealed, were habitually played off against each other, as we will see in Bishop Maximus' Good Friday sermon. Fictitious topics could occasionally be introduced in kerygmatic literature and preaching for the sake of eloquence, admonition or instruction, but sooner or later such artifices had to give way to an altogether devout, undisguised as well as unequivocal mode of presentation.

Paulinus paradigmatically implemented this early Christian poetics, which he actually conceived in terms of an anti-poetics, in another of his letters, the twenty-third. Probably written in the year 400, it was addressed to his intimate friend Sulpicius Severus (the author of a famous biography of Saint Martin of Tours, *Vita Sancti Martini*). Our souls, Paulinus declares on an edifying note, are like ships on the waves of the world, armed with the oars of true faith and good deeds on the right and left, and with the word of God as their rudder (23.30):

> They open the sails of their senses to the wind of the Holy Spirit, and they lash the sail of their hearts to the sailyard of the cross, using for ropes the bonds of charity. Their mast is *the rod out of the root of Jesse*, controlling the whole quadrireme of our bodies. If we are fastened to it through the truth of the prophets by voluntary bonds, as in the Homeric story [*cui si iuxta illam poeticam fabulam in prophetica veritate nectamur*], and if the ears of our hearts, not our bodies, are stopped up with faith, not wax, against the enticements

of this world which beguile us variously but harm us equally, then we shall sail safely and harmlessly by the rocks of pleasures, the cliffs of the Sirens, so to speak. (V)

This allegorical configuration of the Christian congregation as a ship, with the cross as its mast, was hardly Paulinus' own invention, but he presents it in a fairly sophisticated version in which his moralizing interpretation is laid over the Homeric model, as it were, piece by piece. The elements of fiction (wax in the ears) are explicitly negated in favour of the real meaning of the story (faith in the heart). The ancient Greek legend was the first to recount the human trial in question, rendered in the form of poetical fiction, *poetica fabula*, constituting a powerful configuration or template singled out by the preposition *iuxta*, 'according to'. Now, however, it is time to fill in the template with "the truth of the prophets", revealed to the faithful as a consequence of the Incarnation. Paulinus' verbatim reuse of Isaiah 11.1, the Vulgate's *virga de radice Iesse*, seems completely consistent with this strategy. In keeping with New Testament typology, for instance in the Revelation, Christ could be suggested in terms of "the root and the descendant of David" (22.16), *radix et genus David*, the long foretold divine offspring of His royal Jewish ancestor. Correspondingly, Paulinus' prophetic discourse not only elucidated but rectified and outshone Homeric fiction. It established a superior and, in all respects, more enlightened form of representation.

The Female *Vates*

This pattern of disclaimers, correction and improvement was evident among the majority of the Late Antique Christian poets. It appears in its most subtle form in the equilibristic *Cento Virgilianus de laudibus Christi* (*Virgilian Cento on the Praises of Christ*), probably composed by the noble Roman lady Faltonia Betitia Proba.[1] Her work is a remarkably condensed Bible paraphrase, consisting of 694 lines taken from Virgil's *Eclogues*, *Georgics* and *Aeneid*, put together shortly after the middle of the fourth century. A few decades later, her copyist at the court of the Emperor Theodosius promised that it would introduce us to a Maro who has undergone a change for the better by being granted divine significance (PR.3–4),

---

[1] The arguments for and against the authorship of Faltonia Betitia Proba, compared to those for and against her granddaughter Anicia Faltonia Proba, are summarized in Schottenius Cullhed 2012, pp. 36f.

Maronem / mutatum in melius divino agnoscere sensu.[1] Thus the greatest of the Latin poets made his most spectacular entry into Christian literature.

In fact he was already there, both in Lactantius' theory of cultural appropriation and in Juvencus' paraphrasing poetic practice. Nonetheless, both the African teacher in rhetoric and the presbyter from Hispania appear relatively modest in their reuse of Virgil compared with the Roman poetess. In her work, the Late Antique reinterpretation of the Golden Age poet was implemented on a large scale, in a strikingly inventive and bold manner. The *Eclogues*, *Georgics* and *Aeneid* were certainly deprived of their historical resonance, pagan ethos and internal drama in this *Cento Virgilianus*, where, in contrast, they were made to emit a new *divinus sensus*. In order to accomplish such audacious (and, as it turned out, controversial) *chrēsis*, Proba relied on the reading and interpretation customs of philosophical and moral allegory, highly characteristic of the period. She deliberately ignored all notions of the historicity, integrity or unity commonly informing a poetical composition when she intertwined Virgil's main works into a single text, selecting a limited number of lines and half-lines, re-ordering and assembling them into a synopsis of the story of salvation, focused on the Creation of the world and on Christ.

Such advanced collage techniques required an amazing memory, a literary *ars memoriae*, which enabled Proba to invest the whole Virgil corpus with new life for her readers. This art of memory allowed her to consistently decontextualize the Virgilian syntagms and phrases, a strategy that seems to have been especially popular in Late Antique learned culture, as cultivated by Hosidius Geta, Ausonius and others.[2] In his treatise *The Prescription Against Heretics*, Tertullian had already complained about the way the arch-heretic Marcion and his supporters had altered and mutilated the Bible, whereupon he pointed out that similar reprehensible arts occurred in profane writers: "You see in our own day, composed out of Virgil, a story of a wholly different character, the subject-matter being arranged according to the verse, and the verse according to the subject-matter" (39.3), *vides hodie ex Virgilio fabulam in totum aliam componi, materia secundum versus et versibus secundum materiam concinnatis*. The question remains, however, whether anyone took this technique so far and applied it so intrepidly as the aristocratic Roman poetess, possibly – according to some of her modern commentators – as a reaction to Julian the Apostate's ban promulgated in 362 on the engagement of Christian instructors in grammar (literature) teach-

---

[1] I follow the edition of K. Schenkl in M. Petschenig's *Poetae christiani minores* (vol. I) 1888, amply annotated with references to the Virgil lines on which Proba's cento was based, and, for my quotations in English, the new translation in Schottenius Cullhed 2012, pp. 185–200.
[2] Bright 1984, p. 81; Kirsch 1989a, pp. 119–23.

ing all over the Empire. In that case, Proba would have made a pedagogic tool available for young people, cleverly demonstrating the compatibility of superior art – Latin poetry at its highest – with true faith.[1]

Proba appropriated not only words and lines but also, like many early Christian poets, structural elements and topics from classical pagan literature, in particular the invocation of the Muses. In her cento, however, God the Father has replaced the Muses or Apollo as the target of the proemial invocation, for which reason the author is converted into His Pythian instrument (9–28):[2]

```
9   Nunc, deus omnipotens, sacrum, precor, accipe carmen
10  aeternique tui septemplicis ora resolve
    spiritus atque mei resera penetralia cordis,
    arcana ut possim vatis Proba cuncta referre.
    non nunc ambrosium cura est mihi quaerere nectar,
    nec libet Aonio de vertice ducere Musas,
15  non mihi saxa loqui vanus persuadeat error
    laurigerosque sequi tripodas et inania vota
    iurgantesque deos procerum victosque penates:
    nullus enim labor est verbis extendere famam
    atque hominum studiis parvam disquirere laudem:
20  Castalio sed fonte madens imitata beatos
    quae sitiens hausi sanctae libamina lucis
    hinc canere incipiam. praesens, deus, erige mentem;
    Vergilium cecinisse loquar pia munera Christi:
    rem nulli obscuram repetens ab origine pergam,
25  si qua fides animo, si vera infusa per artus
    mens agitat molem et toto se corpore miscet
    spiritus et quantum non noxia corpora tardant
    terrenique hebetant artus moribundaque membra.
```

Now, Almighty God, I pray: receive this sacred song
and loosen the mouth of your eternal sevenfolded Spirit,
and open up the inmost of my heart
in order that I, Proba, may disclose all mysteries of the poet.
Now I do not care to seek ambrosian nectar,
neither do I wish to lead the Muses from the Aonian peak.
Vain deception cannot convince me that stones speak
or make me follow tripods decked with laurel and empty vows,
the quarrelling gods of noble princes and defeated Penates.
For it is no concern of mine to increase my reputation through words

---

1 See Elizabeth A. Clark's and Diane F. Hatch's discussion of the date and context of the cento included in their translation volume 1981, pp. 97–121.
2 The English rendering of line 19 has been modified by the translator for the forthcoming Brill edition of her thesis.

and through human endeavor seek a meager glory.
No, soaked in the Castalian source, I, who thirsting
have drunk the drink offering of the holy light and imitated the blessed,
will here begin to sing. God be present and guide my mind:
I will show that Virgil sang about the pious feats of Christ
and tell from the beginning a subject that is known to all,
if there is any faith in my soul, if a true mind flows through my limbs,
shakes my form, and if the spirit mingles completely with my body
as far as it is not checked by unfavorable bodies
or blunted by the earthly joints and mortal limbs.

The tension between "ambrosian nectar" – the inspiration of the pagan Muses – and Biblical prophetic inspiration is at least as evident as in Paulinus. All instances of fictionality are resolutely dismissed as superstition, *vanus error*, illustrated by references to personified natural phenomena such as speaking rocks, and to the ancient polytheism that was still cherished in Roman high society (at the uppermost political level, it flared up for the last time during the reign of the Emperor Julian in the early 360s, perhaps shortly before the composition of the *Cento Virgilianus*). Correspondingly, Proba declares herself completely uninterested in the poetical renown that had been so important for Horace and his likes in Roman Golden Age literature, and which still (as we shall see) had attracted her pious predecessor Juvencus.

Now she sets out to show that the most celebrated of Roman poets in fact wrote about Christ. Proba is obviously not satisfied with merely dismissing the classical world of fiction. In the wake of Lactantius, she brings it to new pastures, most evidently a few lines further on, when it is the turn of the Son to be addressed: "now a new child, in whom every age believed" (34), *iam nova progenies, omnis quem credidit aetas*. This is one of the very earliest Christian reinterpretations of the "new generation", *nova progenies*, and the imminent birth of a child, on which Virgil pins such hopes in his Fourth Eclogue (4.7–8).[1] Even though Proba felt obliged to reject the ambrosia and the nectar, too intimately associated with the Olympian gods of Homer and Virgil, she allows herself to be "soaked in the Castalian source" and drain the libation "of the holy light". The invocation's main terms and gestures are to some extent traditional but can, relocated in Proba's Christian context, be filled with new sacramental sig-

---

1 Cf. *Cento Virgilianus* 377–79, where Proba depicts the flight into Egypt, dwelling on the flowers which surrounded Jesus' cradle: Egyptian liles, "smiling cyclamen" and "soft acanthus", *colocasia, ridens baccar* and *mollis acanthus*, exactly the ones which the earth will pour forth for the new-born child in *Eclogues* 4.19–20 (with their attributes slightly transposed).

nificance: that of Baptism (the spring water) and Holy Communion (the libation), respectively.

Last but not least, Proba emphasizes as strongly as Prudentius would a few years later that the inspiration she yearns for will lay claim to her whole being. She is not the kind of poet who indulges in rhetorical frippery or displays of erudition. Quite the reverse: she is a true *vates*, a prophetess whose heart and limbs have been invaded by the Holy Spirit so as to be enlightened about the mysteries of being, *arcana*.[1] What seems particularly striking in this context is Proba's way of singling herself out by using her own name as well as her physical involvement in the writing process, both indicative of her commitment to the sibylline project. This enterprise demands strong nerves and limbs! The poetic persona emerging from her invocation precludes any kind of make-believe. Like the ancient seeress, a baptized Cassandra, Proba is shaken by a higher power, a "mind" which, this time, is altogether true, *vera mens* (the Holy Spirit).

Naturally, it is of special interest to see which particular Virgil passages Proba reuses for her sophisticated mosaic. Her refusal to lead the Muses from the Aonian peak, that is, from Mount Helicon in Greek Aeonia (Boeotia), positions her in telling contrast to the Roman poet, who proudly, at the beginning of the third book of his *Georgics*, envisions himself to be the first to usher the Greek deities into Latin territory: "I first, if life but remain, will return to my country, bringing the Muses with me in triumph from the Aonian peak" (3.10 – 11): *primus ego in patriam mecum, modo vita supersit, / Aonio rediens deducam vertice Musas*. From her illustrious predecessor Proba thus uninhibitedly borrows language, style, metre (hexameter) and even vocabulary, but her source of inspiration for this patchwork diverges conspicuously from his: "true mind" or Spirit as opposed to his Muses. Her complex relationship to her Golden Age model is particularly apparent in the last lines (25 – 28) of the extract cited above, since they are derived from Anchises' famous teaching on metempsychosis in *Aeneid* VI. The bulk of the world, the dead Trojan tells his son, is nourished by an inner spirit, pervaded by an intellectual power running through its limbs and merging into its great body (6.726 – 27): *spiritus intus alit, totamque infusa per artus / mens agitat molem et magno se corpore miscet*.

This huge bulk or mass, *tota moles*, was an established formula for the material cosmos, here, according to Anchises, wholly permeated with the divine in-

---

[1] Schottenius Cullhed translates the cento's line 12, *arcana ut possim vatis Proba cuncta referre*, as "in order that I, Proba, may disclose all mysteries of the poet [that is, Virgil]". If, however, as Schottenius Cullhed concedes, *vatis* is taken as an attribute to the subject in the nominative case, we would rather be left with "in order that I, Proba, the poet/prophet, may disclose all mysteries", 2012, p. 33, which is the reading underlying my argument here.

tellect. His words would turn into a *locus classicus*, as Courcelle has demonstrated, for the Christian writers who linked up with Stoic and Neo-Platonic speculation, sometimes quoted in connection with another Virgilian *locus*, from the *Eclogues*, where the shepherd Damoetas praises the omnipresent Jupiter: "All is full of Jove" (3.60), *Iovis omnia plena*.[1] Now, in the *Cento Virgilianus*, this universal mind – this all-pervading Jupiter – is supplanted by the Holy Spirit, which, for its part, is expected to permeate every limb of the author's being. In this fashion Proba cleverly converts Anchises' Platonic interpretation of the cosmos into a segment of her sibylline invocation. As a matter of fact, not only the source but the nature, too, of her blessed inspiration differs pointedly from that of classical seers. This Cassandra sets out to reinterpret or, as it were, to revise an earlier set of texts: her purpose is to "show that Virgil sang about the pious feats of Christ". According to this announcement, it is first and foremost the canonized Roman poet's literary achievements that serve as Proba's oracle. Now she will reveal their true meaning, the salvation works of Christ, in blatant conflict with their original sense and cultural context. Thus she makes them yield an oracular answer which in the first place will refute all pagan oracles and in the second place will be transparent to everyone, disclosing "a subject that is known to all", in sharp contrast to the obscurity that had been associated with the caves of Delphi, Cumæ and elsewhere.

Virgil is both recycled and rejected in this literary *Kontrafaktur* (to borrow an apt label from Reinhart Herzog), for all its originality characteristic of the erudite culture of the dying Roman Empire, liable to dissect the ancient poetic works into single lines, sententious phrases or pithy sayings, so as to make them neatly accessible to grammatical analysis, learned commentaries or paraphrases.[2] This scholarly dismantling of the classics prepared the way for the poets, Christian or pagan, to extract passages as needed from their original context to invest them with new meanings in a radically altered setting. Such decontextualization procedures were paramount to Late Antique Biblical epic poetry, and it is precisely in this field that Proba stands out as a pioneer, a few decades before Prudentius' dauntless counter-imitations that will soon claim our attention. I will have to restrict myself to one or two samples from her *Cento Virgilianus*. After having completed the work of His Creation, the Biblical God "saw everything that he had made, and behold, it was very good" (Genesis 1.31), a sense of satisfaction that Proba amplifies thus: "he could not yet fulfill his mind and burned to be-

---

[1] Courcelle traces the reuse of Virgil's famous wording through the works of Lactantius, Proba, Ambrose, Paulinus, Augustine, Prudentius, Macrobius and Fulgentius, 1955b, pp. 37–42.
[2] Herzog 2002, p. 212.

hold / the earth" etc. (110), *expleri mentem nequit ardescitque tuendo / terras...* This particular line is no amalgamation of different sources but taken in its entirety, word for word, from the first book of the *Aeneid*. There, however, it refers to Dido, permeated with ardent desire at the sight of Aeneas (1.713)! Proba's both pious and erudite readers must surely have raised their eyebrows at this scenario: right through the One God's contentment with His Creation vibrates the African queen's desire for the Trojan hero.

Even considering the period's widespread reliance on all kinds of *chrēsis* and counter-imitations, such daring remakes were out of the ordinary in Late Antique literature, and sure enough, Proba – the only woman in this book's male company – has always had her detractors. One of the first was Jerome, who did not mince his words in an already cited letter to Paulinus of Nola written in the middle of the 390s. There he vents his spleen, albeit without mentioning any names, upon the *Vergiliocentonae* who had tried to make a Christian out of Maro: "all this is puerile, and resembles the sleight-of-hand of a mountebank. It is idle to try to teach what you do not know" (53.7), *puerilia sunt haec, et circulatorum ludo similia, docere quod ignores.*[1] This repudiation of the audacious Proba was to continue. In a comprehensive essay on the status of poetry in early Latin Christianity, Willy Evenepoel calls attention to the so-called *Decretum Gelasianum*, a papal decree listing both canonical and objectionable writings, usually ascribed to Pope Gelasius (d. 496), though it was probably drawn up in the early sixth century. Juvencus' and Sedulius' Biblical epics figure among the satisfactory *libri recipiendi*, whereas Proba's cento was rejected among the apocryphal *libri non recipiendi.*[2]

As a spokesman for his faith, Jerome would certainly be prepared to make use of the Latin of the classics to recruit educated proselytes, and in his hermeneutic theory he was not entirely out of sympathy, as we have seen, with the idea of exploiting heathen culture's "fairness of form and grace of eloquence" for his own impeccable purposes (above, pp. 149f.). However, Proba's bold implementation of such a programme went too far for this austere Doctor of the Church. He was inevitably provoked by the kind of synthesizing logic and etymological wilfulness that could link Moses – commonly thought of as the inspired author of the Pentateuch – to legendary Musaeus, one of the primeval Greek prototypes of an oracular bard, addressed as "supreme poet and prophet", *optime vates*, by the Sibyl in the *Aeneid*'s underworld (6.669). This association is implied at the beginning of the cento, in line 36, where Proba remembers Musaeus, foremost

---

[1] *PL* 22.545.
[2] Evenepoel 1993, p. 57.

among mankind's ancestors, *ante omnes*, echoing Virgil's narrative when the Sibyl addresses Musaeus before all other poets and seers among the dead, *ante omnis* (6.667). As a matter of fact, even the Lord Himself is made to emulate Virgilian Musaeus in a key passage of the cento, namely its presentation of the garden of Eden. There, God shows Adam and Eve "bright fields from above" (158–59), *camposque nitentis / desuper ostentat*, in blatant analogy with Musaeus in *Aeneid* VI, who from above, on a hill, points out the Elysian Fields – the abode of Anchises – to Aeneas and the Sibyl: *camposque nitentes / desuper ostentat* (6.677–78). Consequently, educated readers of the cento would recognize the pagan poet's panorama over the Elysian Fields right through God the Father's demonstration of the Garden of Eden.

Notwithstanding Proba's reassurances of her true subject, "the pious feats of Christ", Jerome's reaction seems, from his ascetic point of view, understandable. To quote Reinhart Herzog, one of the scholars who of late have reopened the study of Biblical epic poetry: in her *Cento Virgilianus*, the author attenuated the Christian subject into a "receptive foil" for ancient (Virgilian) ideas and concepts. While she certainly set out to spiritualize the imperial message of Virgil's epic poem, the cento's reminiscences of especially the *Aeneid* in literally each line might easily draw readers' attention from her work's scriptural storyline to its classical model. In addition, Proba knew how to skilfully take advantage of the historical tension that already existed in Virgil's epic – between the destroyed origin (Troy) and the distant goal (Rome) – as a daring parallel to the Bible's typological connection between Paradise lost and regained.[1] Thus her consistently executed experiment emerges as the boldest of the epic Bible paraphrases that flourished during Late Antiquity – perhaps even as an early presage of the astonishing novel entitled *Don Quijote* that Jorge Luis Borges's invented author Pierre Menard set out to (re)write, identical word for word with Cervantes's sixteenth-century text, yet an original creation due to its new context in another century (the early twentieth), another country (France) and another culture (that of modernity).[2]

Unfortunately, Jerome's lack of understanding for Proba's creative project is still evident in modern philologists such as Domenico Comparetti and Harald Hagendahl. Even Charles Witke, author of an important study of Late Antique poetry published as late as 1971, censures the author and her work rather harshly: "Proba cannot see that her poem, *sacrum carmen*, perhaps uniting two great

---

[1] Herzog 1975, p. 31 ("Rezeptionsfolie").
[2] "Pierre Menard, autor del Quijote" was originally published in *Ficciones* 1944, Borges 1980, pp. 47–59.

personal ideals, Vergil and Christianity, is inert because the old words cannot represent the new thing. There is a complete failure of communication. The Vergilian echoes are too loud".[1] Witke's complaint about Proba's lack of words of her own certainly does not do justice either to her particular achievement or to the cento genre in general. Mary Carruthers understood her sampling strategy better when she looked upon it as a cultural rescue operation in Virgil's favour: "And the only way to save him was to re-member him, re-locate and re-pattern him, into a Christian."[2] Last but not least, Martin Bažil's recent thesis on the Late Antique Christian cento demonstrates quite convincingly that Proba's project differs only in degree, not in kind, from the overall practice of "imitative writing" characteristic of Roman grammar education ever since the Hellenistic age.[3]

*

Cento poetry is, from the standpoint of literary history, an extreme variant of what might be called a widespread cut-and-paste technique, an intertextual cannibalization that permeated Late Roman culture. Paulinus resorted to this strategy on a number of occasions, for instance in his twenty-second ode which, like his sixteenth letter, was addressed to the Aquitanian philosopher Jovius. P.G. Walsh explains in a comment on his translation of the poem that it is a *protreptikon*, a work of exhortation or instruction.[4] Here, Paulinus sets out *in medias res*, going straight to the point (22.1–34):

```
1   Iam mihi polliceor sacris tua carmina libris
    condere teque dei flammatum numine Christi
    ora soluturum summo facunda parenti.
    incipe divinis tantum dare pectora rebus
5   subrectosque deo sensus adtollere terra.
    mox oculis caelo nova lux orietur aperto
    intrabitque sacer tacito per operta meatu
    spiritus et laeto quatiet tua viscera flatu.
    heia age tende chelym, fecundum concute pectus,
10  magna movens; abeat solitis inpensa facultas
    carminibus, maior rerum tibi nascitur ordo.
    non modo iudicium Paridis nec bella gigantum
    falsa canis. fuerit puerili ludus in aevo
    iste tuus quondam; decuerunt ludicra parvum.
```

---

[1] Witke 1971, p. 198. Cf. Comparetti 1997, pp. 53f., and Hagendahl 1958, pp. 189, 385.
[2] Carruthers 2000, p. 58.
[3] Bažil 2009, pp. 79–85.
[4] Paulinus of Nola 1975, p. 391.

15   nunc animis gravior, quantum provectior annis,
     aspernare leves maturo corde Camenas,
     et qualem castis iam congrua moribus aetas
     atque tui specimen venerabile postulat oris,
     suscipe materiam, divinos concipe sensus.
20   si decus e falsis aliquod nomenque tulisti
     de vacuis magnum rebus, cum ficta vetustis
     carminibus caneres vel cum terrena referres
     gesta, triumphantum laudans insignia regum:
     non equidem ex illis tu laudem sumere dignus,
25   quos magis ornabas opulenti munere verbi.
     quanto maior ab his cedet tibi gloria coeptis,
     in quibus et linguam exercens mentem quoque sanctam
     erudies laudemque simul vitamque capesses?
     dumque leges catus et scribes miracula summi
30   vera dei, propior disces et carior ipsi
     esse deo, quem dum credens miraris, amare
     incipies et amando deum redamabere Christo.
     hactenus illa tuae vanos tuba vocis in usus
     persona, divinos modo celsius intonet actus.

I promise myself that you are now basing your poems on the sacred books, and that inflamed with the power of Christ God you will loose your eloquent tongue to the highest Father. Start to devote your heart solely to God's affairs. Raise your thoughts from earth and direct them up to God. Then before your eyes the sky will open and a new light will emerge. The Holy Spirit will enter with silent movement your hidden parts, and will rustle in your heart with His glad breath. Come now, wield your lyre, stir your fertile heart to essay a great theme; let that fluency devoted to your customary songs give place, for a greater sequence of topics is now inaugurated for you. Your theme is now not the judgment of Paris or the fictitious wars of the giants. True, this was your sport of old in your childhood days, for games were appropriate to a young child. But now that you are more advanced in years, and accordingly more serious in purpose, you must spurn with adult mind the unsubstantial Muses. You must take up subjects demanded by your age, for which chaste manners are now apposite, and by the venerable appearance of your countenance. You must conceive thoughts of God.

If you have won any glory from fictitious themes or great fame from empty ones by singing of fanciful events in classical lays or by recounting earthly deeds to praise the glory of triumphing kings, you did not deserve to win praise out of those men whom you preferred to adorn with the gift of your rich eloquence. How much greater fame will accrue to you from those themes which will not only exercise your tongue but will also inform your scrupulous mind, and from which you will obtain not only praise but also life! By your sagacious reading and recording of the true wonders of the highest God, your apprenticeship will make you closer and dearer to God Himself. Once you believe in and admire Him, you will begin to love Him, and by loving God you will win reciprocal love from Christ. Let the trumpet of your tongue which has thus far blared for empty purposes now sound forth on a higher note the works of God.

Paulinus' *protreptikon* operates in two phases:
- First, it requires a radical separation between the gentle Muses or battling giants on the one hand, a substantial assortment of pagan untruths, and on the other hand, the song of praise that is axiomatically true since it is based on "the sacred books", that is, the Bible. We remember this distinction from Paulinus' famous verse letter X, but in his *Carmen* XXII he is more specific. With his references to Paris' judgment, the giants and the Muses, he turns his criticism against the old epic and hymnic poetry, which he associates with infantile games. In short, the world of pagan fiction is for children. By contrast, the new Christian poetry befits that wise and moral maturity which Paulinus strategically ascribes to his addressee Jovius, "advanced in years" with "adult mind" and venerable countenance, naturally disposed to chaste manners. Poetic fame is worth as little as the old songs' *ficta*, and panegyric eloquence as well as the gift of inspiration are wasted as long as they serve worldly purposes.
- In a second step, however, typical of these men of both God and letters, this eloquence and this gift are put to Christian use. The idea of inspiration from above, *afflatus*, is retained in Paulinus' ode, as Charles Witke remarks, but it is detached from the Mount Helicon complex and reserved for God or the Holy Spirit, based on the Jewish tradition's own visionary precedents.[1]

A corresponding appropriation of a classical formula can be detected in Paulinus' frequent use of the term *munus* ('gift', 'duty') to describe his poetry, an expression that reappears in Prudentius. In a couple of interesting studies, Salvatore Costanza links it to a new ascetic self-understanding among Christian poets around the year 400. Thus he levels criticism against earlier scholars such as Curtius, who had been content with interpreting these poets' recycling of the *munus* theme as an adoption of a pagan topos: the poet's presentation of a votive offering (a poem) to his master, in agreement with the principle of favour in return for favour, *munera pro muneribus*. Indeed, this conventional pattern of exchange between patron/Maecenas and client/poet seems to be rejected by Paulinus when he uses the term *munus* above (22.25), referring to Jovius' luxurious verbal gift, *opulens munus verbi*, employed for poems of praise. Such commissioned work belongs to the outperformed 'old songs', *vetusta carmina*. By contrast, Paulinus and Prudentius were keen on representing themselves as delivering a truly personal, sincere and sacred tribute to their Lord. It is in this spirit that the former exhorts Jovius to put his verbal talents to different and better

---

[1] Witke 1971, pp. 98f.

(earnest, pious) use, in short: to exchange the cultural economy of old for a new poetics of authentic devotion. Thus Costanza seems perfectly right in assuming that the *munus* theme – like several other classical topoi: false modesty, *affectata modestia*, and so on – gradually became personalized and sacralized in a pious context.[1] Most importantly, in the eyes of the Christian poets, these procedures of accommodation and transformation proved incompatible with their literary ancestors' proverbial *licentia*, since such a 'freedom' would jeopardize their claims to unconditional sincerity and truth.

A two-way strategy thus permeates the relationship of early Christian poetry to pagan literary traditions. A basically sceptical or negative attitude did not exclude a rich gamut of quotations, allusions and counter-imitations. As we have been able to observe, the Christian poets willingly accommodated an extensive set of ready-mades – syntagms, phrases or even entire lines – from the classics, investing them with new meaning and commitment. We have every reason to assume that the educated and well-read Jovius, when reading Paulinus' *Carmen XXII*, would nod in recognition at such expressions as "essay a great theme" (10), *magna movens*, or "a greater sequence of topics is now inaugurated for you" (11), *maior rerum tibi nascitur ordo*. They are drawn from one of the best-known passages from the *Aeneid*, the invocation that introduces Book VII, where the poet addresses the Muse Erato to ask for help in order to accomplish the second part of his work, which is full of battles, heroic exploits and death: "You, goddess, prompt your seer" (7.41), *tu vatem, tu, diva, mone*. The task ahead of him seems arduous, indeed, likened to labour pains in need of a midwife's (Erato's) care: "As the worldview birthing within me is greater, / My labour's greater too" (7.44–45), *maior rerum mihi nascitur ordo, / maius opus moveo*. Greater, that is, in relation to the first six books of the *Aeneid*, which recount the hero's vacillations, escapades and wanderings across the Mediterranean.

For his part, Paulinus refers to the new and greater "sequence of topics", which is inaugurated by the Christian message in contrast to the old pagan fancies: the judgment of Paris, the wars of the giants... He is anxious to demarcate, as unconditionally as possible, evangelical urgency from fictional whims. With his clever usage of *Aeneid* VII he is following Proba, who had already recycled these Virgilian passages in two different places of her *Cento Virgilianus*, on

---

[1] Costanza 1976, pp. 132–49, and 1985, pp. 267–69. Cf. Curtius 1990, p. 86. An exhaustive documentation of this topic is to be found in Thraede 1965, pp. 28–46. Before Costanza, Wolf Steidle had already emphasized Prudentius' Christian *humilitas* at the expense of his conventional reuse of old formulas, 1971, and Helena Junod-Ammerbauer similarly wants to discern a spiritualization in Paulinus of the classical topos of dedication and *causa scibendi*, 1975, pp. 18–22.

both occasions with the same shift of meaning as later in Paulinus. When she is going to sing the praises of God's Creation of the world in the introduction to her work, she exclaims, following Virgil, that a series of great deeds appears before her eyes, *maior rerum mihi nascitur ordo*, whereupon this higher order of things is immediately contrasted with conventional epic themes, *levium spectacula rerum*, such as horses, weapons or battles (45–48). Furthermore, when later in her cento Proba moves from the Old into the New Testament, she feels again the need to draw up a hierarchical distinction, verbatim after Virgil: "I set a greater work in motion" (334), *maius opus moveo*. Thus the Biblical Creation narrative represents a higher order than that of the pagan epic, and Proba's presentation of the New Covenant must in turn be inaugurated as a greater "work" than her account of the old one.

If this reprocessing of classical literature in the service of Christian poetry tended to highlight and reinforce the model texts' moral or devout implications, surely present in the *Aeneid*, it weakened or even abrogated their sense of mimetic contingency. When Proba, Paulinus and their likes invested the old words and phrases with new meaning, attentive readers would be liable to distinguish a certain reverence for Roman tradition in their works, but only on condition that it seemed compatible with Catholic faith, hence deprived of its former integrity, reduced to a preliminary stage – still immature – on humanity's way towards salvation. Games, Paulinus impresses on Jovius, with an echo from 1 Corinthians 13.11, are for children, whereas properly enlightened men, belonging to a mature civilization, should have put them behind for good. Proba had, with the same self-assuredness, relied on the narrative devices of the *Aeneid* such as invocations and prolepses (internal portents) for her typological exercises in the *Cento Virgilianus*. There was simply no place left for any fictional double-dealing, ambiguity or 'as if' hypotheses in these poets' intertextual constructs.

The Christian writers liked to consider their works to be derivative from the original Bible text. They were purportedly (as in Paulinus' *Carmen* 22.1–2) based on "the sacred books", *sacri libri*, dictated by a higher power, which, unlike Hesiod's Muses, did not know of any *pseudea* or make-believe. Time and again, these poets, well aware that they were addressing readers who had begun to doubt the credibility of poetic discourse, asseverated that they only cared about the one truth, *vera*, in contrast to their predecessors who – no matter how beautiful their words sounded – sang of false and vain things, *falsa* or *vana*. As Paulinus puts it further down in his twenty-second ode (33–34): "the trumpet" of Jovius' tongue "has thus far blared for empty purposes". It is surely relevant in this context that the trumpet, *illa tuba*, would easily be associated with battle calls, characteristic of the "empty purposes" of traditional epic poetry. These calls should now recede into silence in favour of higher tones, such as those, perhaps, that sound through the seven trumpets of the Book of Revelation. The Christian poets' numerous references to their "hidden" inner being, their heart or breast, their entrails or limbs, all virtually infused with the inspiration of the Holy Spirit, made it clear that their devotion was total, precluding any possibility of adventurous idiosyncrasies or hypothetical modes of thought. When writing and reading became activities dependent on divine love rather than on rhetoric's *genera dicendi*, on an inner glow of faith rather than on the old doctrine of styles, on the imminent apocalypse rather than on the fanfares of epic battle, the time had come to discard those 'fictions in songs of long ago', *ficta vetustis / carminibus*.

At least (it should probably be added) as long as we can rely on the poets' own self-understanding and declarations of principle. In their poetic practice, on the other hand, they could hardly avoid themes or figures distinctive of fictional discourse, even when trying to ward them off. This is particularly true of Proba's cento. In the transition between its Old and New Testament parts, the author ponders upon her impending project (to retell the story of Christ), by virtue of which she will rise above the ground "and in the fame bear the name during so many years" (337), *et nomen fama tot ferre per annos*. Anyone who knew his Virgil would have recognized the literal presence of the *Georgics* in this line, namely the passage from Book III where the poet girds himself for the purpose of carrying Caesar's (Octavian's) name through the years (3.47): *et nomen fama tot ferre per annos*. On the face of it, this seems to be a marked counter-imitation: in the cento, *Caesar* has had to step back in favour of Christ (who enters the poem a few lines later). Here, however, Proba is walking a virtual tightrope. Apart from the model provided by the Virgilian original, there is nothing to prevent us from reading *nomen* in line 337 as 'my name': a glimpse, in that case, of the poetic fame that the cento's author had emphatically discarded in the introductory part of her work (18–19).

If Proba actually ever cherished such hopes for her own glory, they would not be unjustified. Her *Cento Virgilianus* might be best described as an intrepid grafting of fictional presentation, modelled on the noblest example Roman classicism knew, onto the Holy Scripture. Orthodox readers, at least to judge by Jerome's reaction, could easily feel confused or annoyed by these intersections of Octavian (the future Emperor Augustus), Aeneas or Palinurus with Christ: they inevitably found themselves reading about the latter in words referring to the former. Such dislocations of Virgilian signifiers as well as Biblical signifieds introduced, after all, a certain amount of fictionality's *serio ludere* into a sacred context, notwithstanding the writer's edifying intentions. In short, they encouraged people to read crucial Biblical episodes as if they were epic events.[1] As a result of this clever game, however serious and devout, Proba was rewarded by posterity with blistering criticism, the total opposite of the glorious flight through the years that she had possibly envisioned on behalf of her "name" in the *Cento Virgilianus*.

---

[1] Cf. Kirsch 1989a, p. 139.

3 Prudentius: Dreams and Demons

Based on Proba's powerful example, it might be tempting to deduce a full-blown poetics for the late Empire and the emerging period of the Germanic invasions. The topoi, devices and metres of pagan literature, and even its words or phrases, could be exploited by early Christian writers, particularly in Biblical epic poetry, but only to enhance their orthodox message, which as a matter of principle did not recognize any ambiguity, authorial distance or conjectural discourse. Within the framework of this overarching panorama, various poets were able to draw up their proper strategies, from the early fourth to the late sixth century, that is, from the rule of Constantine to Gregory the Great. Some stressed the incompatibility of Christian truth with pagan lies, others demonstrated a greater willingness, in the wake of Lactantius, to detect traces, however distorted, of divine truth among the ancient poets and philosophers. These contrasting attitudes could appear in different authors more or less contemporary with each other, or sometimes even within the works of one and the same writer. If Proba seems to aim at a crossover construct (with *chrēsis* dictating literally each line of her cento), the lyric poet whom we shall now examine belonged mostly to the belligerent camp, notwithstanding his firm anchorage in Roman imperial ideology, literature and *mores*. Probably none of the Late Antique Christian writers reused classical literature so idiosyncratically and high-handedly as the militant Prudentius (348–ca. 410), a native of the province of Hispania Tarraconensis, for good reasons labelled the Christian Pindar or Horace. Specifically, the bulk of his work seems torn between the old taste for the circus or the amphitheatre, the bloodstained spectacles of the arenas, and the new need for Christian edification.[1] Up to only a century ago, he was widely read in Latin classes all over the Western world, but his frequent gory scenarios, whether detailing the sufferings of historical martyrs or rejoicing in the slaughter of personified vices, have made his poetry more difficult to digest for contemporary taste.

By all accounts, Prudentius became a poet at a rather late age, after he had retired from long and faithful public service. But in the autumn of his life, he was all the more active as a writer in a wide range of genres: hymns, didactic poetry, allegorical epics, versified apologies and legends of martyrs. In the techniques of his lyric poetry as well as the understanding of history that underpins it, he was an untiring mediator between *romanitas* and *christianitas*.[2] In this particular re-

---

[1] For an interpretation of *Psychomachia* as "an ideological reconstruction of the amphitheatre", see James 1999, p. 73.
[2] There is an excellent survey of the research in this field: Bastiaensen 1993.

spect, the verse virtuoso from Hispania Tarraconensis adopted a different approach from that of Augustine. While the North African writer eventually tended to focus on the gap between the two cultures, whereby "Rome" had to make way for the Kingdom of God, Prudentius – who perhaps never lived to experience the disaster that befell the eternal city in 410 – energetically promoted the Empire as the queen of the world, *regina mundi,* and Rome as the capital of the universal Church.

It should be emphasized that this was the mighty realm Theodosius had fought for, ideally permeated by orthodox hegemony, cleansed of all pagan heresies. When, in the first few years of the new century, Prudentius organized his scattered production into an edition of what we today would call his 'Collected Poems', meticulously designed and composed, he contributed his share to this imperial project. He challenged classical poetry on its own ground, wanting to demonstrate, as Walther Ludwig has underlined, that the pagan genres could be transformed and reborn in Christian versions. He aimed to create, as it were, a "literary superstructure" mounted on classical poetry, a counterpart in writing to the martyrs' basilicas that were built on the ancient cult sites of Rome.[1]

This bookish, literary ambition of Prudentius is vital for our understanding of his work, appearing in sharp contrast to Ambrose's liturgical orientation. Whereas the Milanese bishop pioneered the hymnody of the Western Church, the Hispanic poet wrote lyrical texts for private (not necessarily individual) reading and contemplation, principally aimed at the new audience that had emerged from the fourth century's cultural landslide in the West: Christians with a classical education and literary interests, constituting a significant part of the social elite in fourth-century Hispania. To this purpose, he relied on a whole arsenal of ancient themes and metres. In one of his poems from the cycle entitled *Liber Cathemerinon* (*The Daily Round*), a hymn-like grace written in dactylic tetrameters, we find the following telling invocation (3.26–30), frequently quoted by Prudentius scholars:

26   Sperne, Camena, leves hederas,
      cingere tempora quis solita es,
      sertaque mystica dactylico
      texere docta liga strophio,
30   laude Dei redimita comas.

---

[1] Ludwig 1977, pp. 304, 355.

> Put away, my Muse, the paltry ivy-leaves wherewith thou hast been wont to encircle thy brows; learn to weave mystic garlands and tie them with a band of dactyls, and wear thy hair wreathed with the praise of God.

Prudentius has no qualms about addressing his Muse so unreservedly or, later in this hymnic cycle, specifying her main subject, notwithstanding her pagan derivation, as Christ: "He alone shall be my Muse's theme, Him alone my lyre shall praise" (9.3), *hunc Camena nostra solum pangat, hunc laudet lyra*. It was equally unproblematic for this poet, still in the *Daily Round*, to imagine Christ forcing his way into infernal Tartarus (9.71) and returning from Phlegethon or Acheron, two of classical mythology's underworld rivers, to Heaven (3.199–200, 5.128).[1] Similarly, Prudentius could without further ado associate the Antichrist in the Book of Revelation with the monster Charybdis known from seafarers' epics since the days of Homer (6.107), and God the Father with the Olympian Thunderer (6.81).

The latter of these two identifications belongs to the set formulas in Prudentius' poetry. It recurs in his *Apotheosis*, where Christ is labelled the Son of the Thunderer (171). Moreover, it reappears briefly in *The Origin of Sin*, where the author deplores the world's forgetfulness "of the true Thunderer" (376), *veri Tonantis*, and in the *Psychomachia*, with its glimpse of "the face of the Thunderer" (640), *vultus Tonantis*, smiling at His victorious forces. This is how Prudentius implements his programme from the *Daily Round* III. The poet's metres are the old, classical ones, and he keeps invoking his Muse, as during the Golden Age of Roman literature, although he exhorts her to set aside the Dionysian ivy that once adorned the *lyricus vates* in the introductory poem of Horace's *Odes* (1.1.29). The Christian poet's dactyls should tie up other themes and subjects, the "mystic garlands" of true faith.

Technically, then, Prudentius' work was based on a paradox. Time and again he framed his aggressive propaganda on behalf of orthodoxy in terms, to quote Martha A. Malamud, "shaped by the cultural codes that determined the pattern of the classical myths".[2] Malamud's observation probably applies to most of the Late Antique Christian poets, but in the case of Prudentius, this far-reaching recoding of pagan themes and schemes appears almost seamless. He felt no need, as Paulinus did, to reject the old Muse (cf. above p. 155). On the contrary, Prudentius engages her in the service of a new God, includes her in a totally different choir and equips her with other attributes, to the effect that she seems to be par-

---

[1] The subterranean topography inherited from the classics was in fact quite popular among the Christian poets, Latin as well as Greek, and hence hardly controversial in this context, cf. Roberts 1980, p. 405.
[2] Malamud 1989, p. 8.

taking in a sacramental ceremony in which the verse form itself is typically integrated with the theme and the purpose of the poetic work.

The best-known example in Prudentius' writings of such thematic transplantations is the *invocatio* addressed to Christ at the beginning of the *Psychomachia:* "Christ, who hast ever had compassion on the heavy distresses of men" (1), *Christe, graves hominum semper miserate labores*, to be compared to *Aeneid* VI, where the hero prays to Apollo for permission to visit the kingdom of the dead, invoking the god from the bottom of his heart "Phoebus, you've always shown pity for Troy and her burdens of suffering" (6.56), *Phoebe, gravis Troiae semper miserate labores*. Thus the introductory lines to the *Psychomachia* look like a quintessential counter-imitation. Christ replaces Apollo as clearly as mankind replaces the Trojans. While the pagan god was to grant the hero entry to the prophetic mysteries of the underworld, Christ is expected to enlighten Prudentius himself about the struggle within man's soul, that is, the subject of his poem, *psychomachia*. Its setting, finally, is no longer the geographical battle fields of epic poetry but the human breast (6), *pectus*, or heart (10), *praecordia*.

It is difficult to come up with a qualified guess as to contemporary readers' reactions to this complete transference of a Virgilian scenario into Christian terms. It is, of course, reminiscent of Proba's corresponding reprocessing of the *Aeneid*, although it hardly caused its author such dismissive judgments, at least from posterity, as the female poet would occasion. I suspect that this difference in reception is not only due to gender (male vs. female) and genre (Prudentius' hymnic or didactic poetry vs. Proba's full-blown epic paraphrase), but, even more importantly, the fact that – as Macklin Smith has observed – the Hispanic writer parted company with Lactantius' or Juvencus' conciliatory poetics from the early fourth century. His aim was never to bestow cultural authority on Christian poetry or preaching by charging it with epic *gravitas*.[1] He no longer needed such legitimizing underpinning for his poetic exercises, quite the reverse: the outspoken Christology, the universal bearing (for mankind) and the bodily intensity (involving the poet's vitals) of the invocation in the *Psychomachia* implicitly invalidated the prophetic forecasts of its famous model. It might even have exposed Virgil's Pythian masterwork, *Aeneid* VI, as a fantasy from a confused pagan culture, a worn-out fiction that it was now possible to correct in the light of true faith.[2]

---

1 Cf. the final chapter in Smith 1976, "The Assault Upon Vergil", pp. 234–300, and, in addition, Ludwig 1977, pp. 354f.
2 Cf. Mastrangelo 2008: "while Vergil's poetic program in the *Aeneid* is indeed monumental, it is surpassed by the *Psychomachia*'s ambitions to change the individual reader into a 'true' Roman citizen and promote a complete understanding of the universe", p. 170.

None of the Late Antique Christian poets went as far as Prudentius in this kind of reconfiguration and appropriation of the ancestral fictional world. The most flagrant example I have been able to locate in his work is from the *Daily Round* IX, where Christ is celebrated as follows (9.10–15):

> 10 Corde natus ex parentis ante mundi exordium,
>   alfa et Ω cognominatus, ipse fons et clausula
>   omnium quae sunt, fuerunt, quaeque post futura sunt.
>   ipse iussit, et creata, dixit ipse, et facta sunt
>   terra, caelum, fossa ponti, trina rerum machina,
> 15 quaeque in his vigent sub alto solis et lunae globo.

> Born of the Father's love before the world's beginning, called Alpha and Omega, He is both source and end of all things that are or have been or hereafter shall be. He gave the word and they were created, He spoke and they were made – earth, heavens, the deep sea, the threefold fabric of the world, and all that lives in them under the lofty globes of sun and moon.

The echoes from the Psalms in these lines (cf. 32/33.9 or 148.5) should surprise no one. They are part of the normal exegesis of the Bible, modelled on Paul (Colossians 1.15–20): the Psalmist's praise of the Lord as the Creator of all things is transferred to Christ. What is far more remarkable is the echo from *Georgics* IV, where the naiad Cyrene tells her son Aristaeus about the sea god Proteus: "for the seer has knowledge of all things – what is, what hath been, what is in train ere long to happen" (4.392–93), *novit namque omnia vates, / quae sint, quae fuerint, quae mox ventura trahantur.* Thus the Hispanic poet describes Christ in terms that are not only borrowed from a nymph but which initially referred to the mythical Proteus, the proverbial quick-change artist and seer, known throughout ancient culture ever since Menelaus captured him in the fourth book of Homer's *Odyssey* (4.382–570), and, incidentally, crucial to Augustine's analysis of fictional discourse in Cassiciacum (above, p. 142). To sum up: Prudentius, firstly, celebrates the Saviour – He who is the beginning and the end, the truth and the life – in words that Virgil coined within a fictional framework, that of the *Georgics*. On top of that, secondly, these words were originally uttered by a fabulous character, Cyrene, referring, thirdly, to what might be called the very epitome of classical fiction, Proteus, whose manifold forms constantly elude the spectator (4.406), *variae eludent species.*

Even though this multifaceted transposition from Proteus to Christ seems stunning, it is by no means isolated in Prudentius' work. Anton Bastiaensen has identified a similarly ambiguous, intertextually suspect tribute to the Holy Spirit in the opening hymn to the Trinity in *Apotheosis*: "the Holy Spirit is from the everlasting lips" (3), *Sanctus ab aeterno subsistit Spiritus ore*. On closer inspection, this line can bring to mind a completely different adoration than what ascetic piety would admit: the erotic love that Lucretius had observed in his introductory celebration of Venus in *The Nature of Things*, where the poet addresses the goddess with the observation that her reclining lover, the excited Mars, "dangles his life's breath from your lips" (1.37), *eque tuo pendet resupini spiritus ore*.[1] This remarkable recycling technique could make us think of Proba and her equally audacious reuse of Virgil (above, p. 509), but again, the main accent is placed differently in the later poet's work. If Proba had set out to "show that Virgil sang about the pious feats of Christ", Prudentius was bent on substituting spiritual devotion for erotic desire, signalling the retreat of Venus and Mars – metonymically representing Lucretian materialism – in favour of the Spirit, a triumphant transfer of the Latin language from the world of pagan delusions to the truth of faith. To this purpose the Hispanic poet frequently excelled in an accumulative, pathetic and brutal style, so physical in its religious zeal that it is tempting to describe it by resorting to his own words about Peter, crucified upside down in Rome, as celebrated in *Crowns of Martyrdom*: "He knew that heaven is wont to be attained more quickly from a lowly start" (or 'from a low position', 12.19), *noverat ex humili caelum citius solere adiri*.

Accordingly, if we translate this perspective *ex humili* into a low or modest level of style, typically mixed with satirical and bombastic outbursts, reinforced by an aggressive temper, we get a good picture of Prudentius' foremost weapon in his recurrent assaults on what he conceived as pagan superstitions. He could even subject the old pantheon to literally hellish torments. In *Apotheosis*, Apollo, the god of poetry, writhes in pain when he is smitten by the name of Christ, scourged by the lashes of the tongue – *verbera linguae* – that speaks of His miracles. Mercury burns and shrieks correspondingly, and the breath of Jupiter himself "is hot with the fires he knows so well", *notos suspirat Iuppiter ignes* (402–05, 412–13). Delphi's oracles, for their part, have been condemned and silenced ever since the Incarnation. The Sibyls have retired once and for all: "Lying Dodona has lost its maddening vapours. Cumae is dumb and mourns for its dead oracles" (441–42), *perdidit insanos mendax Dodona vapores, / mortua iam mutae lugent oracula Cumae*.

Still, these evocations of Jupiter's pains in Hell and the death of the oracles do not exhaust the range of Prudentius' attitudes towards the old gods. To put it simply, even though Jupiter and his likes seemed defeated or even, in theory, annihilated, the poet did not get rid of them. In practice they retained a shadowy

---

[1] Bastiaensen 1993, p. 121. In addition, it should be noted that Prudentius implements an almost identical reuse of Lucretius 1.37 in *The Origin of Sin*, 932.

existence as phantoms or superstitions, reappearing throughout his work, no matter how denied or derided. In his versified polemic against the great Roman statesman and orator Symmachus, characterized by a euhemeristic as well as Stoic criticism of the pagan deities, Prudentius contemptuously dismisses mistaken beliefs "in shapes of gods that went about in the murky air", *vagae... deum nigrante sub aëre formae*, specifically Jupiter "and the great mob of their gods", *multa et cum plebe deorum* (1.10 – 11, 1.27), nothing but "vain superstition" (1.198), *vana superstitio*. Towards the end of the first part of this ambitious poem, the author calls on Theodosius the Great, known for his orthodox and anti-Arian zeal, to speak. The Emperor sadly notices vapours and smoke darkening the city of Rome: "I see murky shades moving around thee, dark spirits and black idols flitting about thee" (1.423 – 24), *obscuras video tibi circumferrier umbras / caeruleasque animas atque idola nigra volare*. Consequently, he urges the city neither to make gods of natural elements or human virtues any longer, nor to worship any "unsubstantial phantoms that wander at large in the shape of souls or spirits", *animarum / spirituumve vagae tenui sub imagine formae*. And cease to deify – Theodosius continues, addressing Rome – a ghost, a genius or a place, "an apparition that flits through the breezes in the air", *aërias volitans phantasma per auras* (1.445 – 48)! Once again, the location of these unsubstantial figures to the element of air is conspicuous, reminiscent of Paulinus of Nola's *aërii proceres* (above, pp. 494f.). To these poets, the ancient gods tended to become absorbed into the air, turning into 'wandering' (another recurrent attribute, *vagae*) phantoms with a dubious degree of reality.

These phantasms share their airy abode with the demons, ominous elementary beings that in fact could seem quite real to Christian Late Antique or medieval writers, partly because their presence is taken for granted in the Bible, where evil spirits frequently occur in large numbers. They were believed to come flying through the air under the command of the Devil, ever ready to assault weak or sick souls whom they might seize and ruin for good unless they were driven out straightaway, most effectively (in the New Testament) by the agency of the Spirit of God (Matthew 12.28). That is why Paul vigorously condemns them when he preaches against idolatry in Corinth. For the sake of comparison, the apostle refers to the Old Testament description of the infidel Israelites, resorting to worship of false gods during their wandering through the desert. His audience is confronted with a choice. They cannot have it both ways: "I imply that what pagans sacrifice they offer to demons and not to God. I do not want you to be participants with demons." (1 Corinthians 10.20)

Even if the demonic powers Paul denounces lack bodily existence, they certainly seemed able to cause terrifying ravages in human beings. Judging from the Gospels and many other sources, such ingrained beliefs did not lose their grip on the Mediterranean world. There are unclean and wandering spirits, constantly conspiring for the loss of men's souls, explains Octavius in Minucius Felix' eponymous dialogue: they were recognized as *daemonas* by the poets, discussed by philosophers and known to Socrates. In Plato's *Symposium*, Octavius continues, the very concept of Love was derived from their "substance intermediate", *substantia media*, between mortal and immortal beings, that is, between body and spirit (26.8–12). Among the Church teachers, Lactantius and particularly Augustine were anxious about the widespread meddling of demons with the affairs of human life. In his *Divine Institutes*, the former blames these vicious phantoms for having taught men to fabricate images and statues of dead kings (2.17), *imagines, et simulacra fingere*, that is, for turning people away from the service of God in favour of idolatry.[1] Likewise, in the *City of God*, the latter teaches his readers about the harmful and cunning *spiritus* dwelling in the air: Satanic rebellious spirits that have been degraded to this elementary sphere surrounding earth (8.22). By all accounts, as Peter Brown has emphasized, the demons were pivotal to the Late Antique Christian interpretation of the world.[2]

This is certainly not the place for even the briefest sketch of the relationship between the (theoretically) abolished or departed gods of the old Olympian pantheon and Late Antique culture's all the more active and dangerous demons. Still, it seems clear that they were frequently conflated or identified with each other, a correlation that was current not only in Christian tradition from Paul onwards but in Stoic and Neo-Platonic speculation as well, in first-century Apuleius or in fifth-century Proclus.[3] In his *City of God*, Augustine discussed "the malignant devils, which those people [the pagans] regard as gods" (2.10), *maligni spiritus, quos isti deos putant*, and later in the same work, on the basis of spurious etymologies, he spotted Juno's residence among the spirits (of dead heroes) and the demons in the air (10.21). Tertullian, for his part, citing 1 Corinthians 10.20 in *The Shows*, repudiated all theatrical or festival performances, inevitably marred by idolatry: "'Not that an idol is anything', says the apostle, 'but what they [the pagans] do, they do in honour of demons,' who plant themselves in the consecrated images of – whatever they are, dead men or, as *they* think, gods." (13.2)[4] Here, the demons are subjected to the same euhemeristic criticism that the later Church Fathers, including Augustine, were to direct against classi-

---

1 *PL* 6.337a.
2 Brown 1971, p. 54.
3 Van der Laan lists several examples of the period's "metamorphosis of the ancient gods into demons", for the most part drawn from Sedulius' *Paschale carmen*, 1993, pp. 154–57.
4 "Non quod idolum sit aliquid, ut apostolus ait, sed quoniam quae faciunt daemoniis faciunt consistentibus scilicet in consecrationibus idolorum, sive mortuorum sive, ut putant, deorum."

cal mythology: the passage of time would have transformed certain spectacular human destinies into gods, whose cult had in turn degenerated into worship of demons.

When Prudentius introduces demons or any kind of pagan deities in his poems, an entire series of the classical characteristics of literary fiction immediately crystallizes: the hypothetical mode of discourse, the difficulty (or impossibility) of assessing the presentation's claims to reality, the theme of metamorphosis and the interference of imagination. Even if the Hispanic poet – as Gnilka maintains – shared contemporary beliefs in the reality of demons, he certainly endows them with a high degree of fictionality in his poetry.[1] He writes about them *as if* they existed, but merely to emphasize their devious and perfidious nature; the existence they possess is only due to people's erroneous imagination and misled worship. It is the idolatrous cults that make them real, in the eyes of the deceived. In truth, all *daemonas* lack substance, being creatures of air, "ministers of night", *noctis satellites*, according to the *Daily Round*, destined to be scattered by the altogether real Lord at dawn, the "approach of light, salvation, Godhead", *vicinitas / lucis, salutis, numinis* (1.37–44). This demonic volatility is reflected in the very language of one of the vices in the *Psychomachia*, insidious Discord. When she is captured and interrogated about her identity and faith at the end of the poem, she answers that her god is 'variegated', *discolor*, and that he constantly changes shape: "now lesser, now greater, now double, now single; when I please, he is unsubstantial, a mere apparition, or again the soul within us, when I choose to make a mock of his divinity." (709–13)[2]

Discord's allegedly divine Master is thus depicted as a quick-change artist or an illusionist of sorts, actually a rather Ovidian character, though conspicuously lacking the autonomous existence and external plasticity typical of the Golden Age poet's handling of his mythological figures. It may be (the uncertainty is the whole point) a matter of a vision *de phantasmate*, a projection cast by Discord's mind – in as far as imagination or mind can be ascribed to an allegorical personification such as Discord. In any event, her demonic god is obviously subject to her volatile fancies. Moreover, this passage excels in auditory effects and echoing rhythms: *Discordia dicor... deus est mihi discolor*. Such devices need not indicate, as Malamud supposes, "the impossibility of finding stable signs to represent true meanings" in the *Psychomachia* (or in Prudentius' work as a whole), but her observation applies very well to Discord's language, erecting a phantas-

---

[1] Gnilka 1980, p. 433.
[2] "Nunc minor, aut maior, modo duplex et modo simplex, / cum placet, aërius et de phantasmate visus, / aut innata anima est quoties volo ludere numen".

matical god.¹ The fact that she avails herself of a certain kind of rhetoric, rich in puns on words and syllables, reinforces the impression of her mocking, deceitful character. She has cunningly put on "the counterfeit shape of a friend" (684), *sociam mentita figuram*, thereby being able to insinuate herself into the ranks of the virtues. Such a fifth columnist has to be eliminated as promptly as the deity she professes. She identifies him by name as the diabolic Belial (Beliar), one of the idols Paul contrasts with Christ (2 Corinthians 6.15). He was known from Jewish tradition, but his changing shapes also ensure him a classical aspect. This quick-change artist undoubtedly has a past in the ancient world, among the old delusions.

Consequently, Belial stands out against the straightforward allegorical mode characteristic of the *Psychomachia*, in which, as C.S. Lewis observed, "on the one hand, the gods sink into personifications; on the other, a widespread moral revolution forces men to personify their passions."² In both cases, Prudentius exploited the Stoic tradition's substitutive allegoresis, whereby the content and meaning of literary texts were consistently conceptualized, that is, converted into a series of ideas, notions and qualities, commonly of a moral nature.³ He appears, indeed, as the first of Late Antique writers, or possibly the first writer at all, to make these concepts – granting them proper names – the main actors of an entire poetic work. The significance of Prudentius' innovative and trend-setting efforts in the Western development of literary allegory is thus beyond question. In addition, from the perspective of this study, his clearcut conceptual implementation of this mode emerges as a Late Antique alternative or corrective to the narrative open-endedness, thematic ambiguity and hypothetical 'as if' mode characteristic of classical epic fiction. The anthropomorphisms in the *Psychomachia* are so schematically conceived and neatly arranged that they seem completely transparent. The duels between Wrath and Long-Suffering, Pride and Lowliness and their combatants seem settled from the very start. All the main actors of the poem appear as pawns in a black-and-white game whose outcome nobody had to wonder about. They act as perfectly unequivocal exemplary figures, framed as two opposite camps of *prosopopoeiae*, embodying some of the very real forces that were assumed to fight over Christian souls. In contrast, Belial stands out as imagined, vague, Protean, ambiguous, a virtual epitome of disgraceful fictionality in pious Late Antique culture, as unreliable as he is persis-

---

1 Malamud 1989, p. 63.
2 Lewis 1979, p. 63.
3 The distinction between a (Stoic) "substitutive" or atomistic and a (Neo-Platonic) "diairetic" or narrative – normally metaphysical, speculative and esoteric – allegoresis is part of the main argument in Bernard 1990.

tent, as unsubstantial in his nature as he is troublesome in his effects, a bleak residue from the old mythology, last but not least associated with Discord whose other name is Heresy (710), *Heresis*, indicating a series of schismatic views of the Godhead which the author targets elsewhere in his work.

The controversies over questions of faith in which Prudentius engaged did indeed not allow any room for doubt or negotiations. Based on what he conceived to be a solid Christian principle of reality, he denounced all dissident interpretations of the Divine being, pagan and heretical alike, as idiosyncratic "shadows of imagination" (Coleridge's syntagm does not seem out of place here) which should be dismissed from the minds of the righteous, the sooner the better. This unconditional cultural polarization provided the very breath of life for this zealous poet. In his works he repeatedly envisioned a state of bifurcation, where true Christians were expected to free themselves from their bonds to the world of pagan illusions – false gods, false glory, false assuredness – as from a disturbing dream. Now, finally, the hour of awakening had come, a brief, albeit anxious waiting before dawn, as suggested in the *Daily Round* (1.81–92):

```
81    Iesum ciamus vocibus
      flentes, precantes, sobrii;
      intenta supplicatio
      dormire cor mundum vetat.
85        sat convolutis artubus
      sensum profunda oblivio
      pressit, gravavit, obruit
      vanis vagantem somniis.
          sunt nempe falsa et frivola
90    quae mundiali gloria,
      ceu dormientes, egimus:
      vigilemus, hic est veritas.
```

> Let us call on Jesus with our voices, in tears and prayers and soberness; earnest supplication keeps the pure heart from slumbering. Long enough has deep forgetfulness, as we lay curled up, pressed heavily on our sense and buried it while it wandered in baseless dreams. Surely false and worthless are the things we have done because of worldly glory, as though we did them in sleep. Let us awake! Reality is here.

These lines are from the first hymn of the *Daily Round*, introduced by the crowing cock, the herald of dawn, which is immediately juxtaposed with Christ – He who awakens our souls, summoning us to life – in what Reinhart Herzog has called "an allegorical parallelism".[1] This is in perfect agreement with the

---

1 Herzog 1966, p. 58.

poet's interpretation of the loud chirping of birds just before sunrise as a *figura* for our Judge (1.13–16). Such metaphors indicate the ultimately eschatological nature of the subject of this hymn: the awakening from the dream of earthly life to the true reality on Judgment Day.

Prudentius recurrently inculcates this message in his readers, highlighting the urgent necessity for Christians to abandon all erroneous assumptions and delirious ideas about honour or transitory fame, *mundialis gloria*. He envisages the state of sin as an evil dream thwarting men's search for truth, instilling mad desires and vain hopes in their breasts. From this perspective, he sets his mind on calling upon the Saviour in tears and prayers of contrition, all for the purpose of keeping awake, persevering in a state of "soberness". His prayers explicitly prevent the heart from relapsing into (fatal) slumbering. The numerous imperatives in Prudentius' poems, his frequent use of 'Behold!', *ecce*, and his strong Christological concerns invest his poetry – as Jean-Michel Fontanier has shown – with performative accents, as if he wanted to re-enact Christ's sufferings and ultimate triumph in his own words, to impress, indeed, the mystery of Incarnation on his readers, thus arousing them from their threatening state of lethargy.[1] To this purpose, he had to abjure the fictional mode of poetry as yet another trick to allure people into the slumber of earthly life. Prudentius would rather have his readers liberated, as it were, into reality.

For the narrator in this literary universe, it was imperative to distinguish as clearly as possible between truth and deceit – the latter being regularly ascribed to his opponents, usually in terms of something invented, fictitious or fantastic.[2] And the opponents that Prudentius chose as his targets were, not surprisingly, more or less identical with Augustine's habitual adversaries: representatives of the Gnostic and Manichaean currents that spread rapidly through the Mediterranean civilization of the fourth century. It is worth while, Prudentius assures his readers in *Apotheosis*, to expose "the phantom that belongs to a misty doctrine", *nebulosi dogmatis umbra*. It is made up of small particles, *atomi*, united in a minute configuration, "but it fails for lack of body, vanishes away like the wind, and is too fleeting and unsubstantial to maintain itself", *sed cassa cadit ventoque liquescit / adsimilis, fluxu nec se sustentat inani* (952–55).

In view of the reference to *Manichaeus* in this poem (956), the "phantom" exposed to the poet's Lucretian deconstruction is in all probability the Manichees' Gnostic version of Christ as an intermediate being operating across the

---

[1] Fontanier 1986, pp. 131–37.
[2] The most ambitious account of this obsession with unsubstantial creations, counterfeit and airy nothing in Prudentius' work is Gnilka's chapter on "Unechtes in der Apotheosis", 2000, pp. 459–647.

dualistic breach between God and mankind, a spirit equipped with an immaterial (ethereal) body designed to endow people with the insight, *gnosis*, that would lead to their salvation. With his usual polemic energy, Prudentius aggressively attacks such heresies (956–80):

> 956 Aërium Manichaeus ait sine corpore vero
> pervolitasse Deum, mendax phantasma cavamque
> corporis effigiem, nil contrectabile habentem.
> ac primum specta an deceat quidquam simulatum
> 960 adsignare Deo, cuius mera gloria falsi
> nil recipit. membris hic se fallacibus aptans
> fingeret esse hominem ventosa subdolus arte,
> mentitus totiens, [...].
> 974 si natura Dei quae sit, Manichaee, requiris,
> 975 omne quod est, verum est. nam si mendosus agit quid,
> nec Deus est: mendum divinus non capit usus.
> obicis aeterno Domino quod lubricus ad nos
> venerit, adsimulans aliud quam verus habebat.
> obmutesce, furor; linguam, canis inprobe, morde
> 980 ipse tuam, lacero consumens verba palato.

> There moved about, says the Manichean, a phantasmal God without real body, a false appearance, an empty likeness of body, having nothing tangible. Now see first whether it is fitting to ascribe aught that is counterfeit to God, whose pure glory admits of nothing false. Would such a God furnish himself with unreal members, and with cunning make-believe feign himself man, lying [...]. If thou seekest, O Manichean, to know the nature of God, all that He is is real; for if He is false in anything He does, then is He not God; the divine activity admits of nothing false. Thou chargest against the everlasting Lord that He came to us deceitfully counterfeiting something other than He had in his reality. Be silent, thou madman. Bite thine own tongue, thou wicked dog; let thy torn mouth devour thy words.

In these verses, Prudentius lines up a number of themes and topics that Late Antique culture had grown accustomed to associate with the classical world of fiction, in recent years considered chimerical at best, or merely patently mendacious: deities lacking substance (*aërius Deus*), the appearance of ghosts or *phantasmata* associated with people's equally suspect *phantasiae*, a rich gamut of deceitful devices such as simulation, make-believe, trickery, the use of vain art... all in contrast to divine reality which was, by definition, unambiguously true.

Thus Prudentius set out to refute Manichaean dualism in terms of his untiring resistance to all species of *mendax fantasma*. It is symptomatic that the author of *Psychomachia* was prepared to ascribe the same kind of pernicious delusions to classical literature as to contemporary heresies. He tended to decline benevolent speculations on Egyptian gold (as we remember, Augustine's label on proto-Christian strands in pagan culture) or pristine theologians. Prudentius, along with quite a few of his pugnacious fellow-believers, was in the process of painstakingly framing a new, sterling Christian identity on the basis of condemnation and expurgation rather than integration. For this purpose they thought fit to dismiss the Hellenistic mysteries as well as the ideas of Epicureans, Stoics and Manichees as fictitious fabrications from an inferior past, unfortunately still alluring the present world, in short: castles in the air.

Christ, on the other hand, for all His divinity, was definitely of flesh and blood like all human beings, with a genealogy that the evangelist Luke was able to trace some seventy generations back in time, from His father Joseph up to Adam (cf. Luke 3.23–38). For Prudentius, this documentation was without any doubt historically correct. In the face of such convincing proof, the poor Manichee whom the poet deprecates for his rage (*furor*) is obliged to give in. His only way to get out of this dispute unscathed is by recurring to literary imagination, and Prudentius makes it clear that he considers such manoeuvres to be cowardly retreats. In the continuation of *Apotheosis*, the author pictures how the hard-pressed Manichaeus looks for support in poetry, myths and legends in an attempt to transform Christ's authentic genealogy into – fiction (1010–18):

1010   Restat ut aëriam fingas ab origine gentem,
         aërios proceres, Levi, Iudam, Simeonem,
         aërium David, magnorum corpora regum
         aëria, atque ipsam fecundae virginis alvum
         aëre fallaci nebulisque et nube tumentem;
1015   vanescat sanguis perflabilis, ossa liquescant
         mollia, nervorum pereat textura volantum;
         omne quod est gestum notus auferat inritus, aurae
         dispergant tenues, sit fabula quod sumus omnes.

> All that remains for thee is to suppose the whole race from its origin unsubstantial, unsubstantial princes, Levi, Juda, Simeon, unsubstantial David, unsubstantial persons of great kings, the very womb of the pregnant virgin swelling with mere unsubstantial vapour and unreality; that the blood turn thin-bodied and vanish, the bones grow soft and melt away, the structure of quick-moving muscles perish; that the wind carry away our every act in futility, the thin airs scatter it, and the existence of us all be nothing but a tale.

Here, too, we find classical nomenclature of fictionality in full use, from the introductory "suppose" or feign, *fingere*, to the concluding legend or myth, *fabula*. And in this context, too, it should be noted that the term "unsubstantial princes", interestingly enough, is in literal agreement with Paulinus' *aërii proceres* (cf. above, p. 524). In Prudentius' poem, however, it is the Manichees that are blamed for the mistake – and sin – of trying to turn the crucial Jewish-Christian family tree into airy fantasies. The whole extract is dominated by this *aërius*, an adjective that is stressed with anaphoric force and cleverly varied in different declensions and cases (lines 1010–14). This is a scenario that could well have been taken from contemporary reality, where the Manichees (as is clear from Augustine's writings) frequently aimed their polemics in matters of faith at the Old Testament whose stories they considered false and/or immoral. From Prudentius' point of view, they thereby made themselves guilty of heresy since they violated Biblical facts, *omne quod est gestum*, the first of the three or four senses elaborated by the exegesis that was beginning to take shape in Late Antique culture. It was precisely this historical or literal level of meaning that was decisive for the later Augustine. In Prudentius, it was typically associated with physical and bodily matters, as in the quotation above with its emphasis on blood, bones and nerves.

The concluding point of the argument broadens the perspective to comprise human life in general, "nothing but a tale", if we are to believe Prudentius' caricature of a Manichee. To our modern ears, these words probably sound like a distant portent of Macbeth's final soliloquy (5.5), but, more importantly, they seem indicative of the challenge that fictionality presented to the young Church's self-image and claims to legitimacy. The poet aggressively asserted his orthodox monopoly on truth by focusing on the letter of the Holy Writ, on the incontestably historical destinies of Christ and the martyrs, read on their tormented bodies, recalled in the sacraments and in his own poetry. That is how Prudentius articulated his personal, strikingly bloodstained but nevertheless glorious version of the Christian principle of reality. The argument of his spiritualizing opponents, on the other hand, was strategically turned into a clever but in the end deplorable game of make-believe, dissolving not only Biblical history but our very being into air and wind – a *fabula*.

In all of Prudentius' works, this myth criticism, based on a robust sense of our bodily existence, is most conspicuous in the second part of his polemic in verse against Symmachus, the Roman statesman and orator who figures in Macrobius' *Saturnalia* and who in the year 384, in his capacity as *praefectus Urbi*, passionately argued for the importance of restoring the altar erected to the goddess of Victory to the Senate in Rome. The eminence of this monument among Roman citizens was enormous. Except for a few years preceding the reign of Julian (361–63), it had remained in the Curia since the victory of Octavian at Actium in 31 BCE, but the Emperor Gratian had removed it in 382 as part of his campaign against the lingering pagan rituals of the city. In a letter, the third of his so-called *Relationes* (*Memorials*), Symmachus now tried to convince Gratian's younger brother and successor, Valentinian II (thirteen years old), that the altar of Victory should be returned in view of the historically tried-and-true guarantees she and other deities had made that the city would retain its power over the barbarians.

Symmachus, by all accounts a man of compromise and moderation, ostensibly pleaded for a common cause of pagans and Christians, as if they ultimately shared their Godhead. "Every man has his own customs, his own rites. The Divine mind has distributed to cities various guardians and various ceremonies" (72a.8), *suus enim cuique mos, cuique ritus est; varios custodes urbibus cultus mens divina distribuit.*[1] Nonetheless, Valentinian preferred to listen to the even more influential and in this context particularly intransigent Bishop Ambrose of Milan. Here, two of the period's predominant cultural personalities in the West, the nostalgic pluralist Symmachus and the orthodox man of God Ambrose, clashed irreconcilably. Normally, they probably held each other in great respect, apart from the fact that the spiritualizing religiosity of the latter would prove decisive for a protégé of the former: the talented North African Aurelius Augustinus, who precisely in this year, 384, would arrive in Milan (see *Confessions*, 5.13.23). But as is usually the case, their polemic quickly became polarized. In two letters, Ambrose put forward his arguments against the restoration of the Altar of Victory to the Senate with overwhelming rhetorical force. Seldom, if ever, had the Christian claims for a monopoly on truth been formulated so authoritatively as in his second letter. It could only appear exemplary to the eagerly confrontational Prudentius.

In his Memorial, Symmachus had, firstly, referred to Roman tradition (customs and manners, *mos parentum* and *consuetudo*), an institution, as it were, inherited from the ancestors, *instituta maiorum*, that also regulated the citizens' relationship to their gods. Secondly, he had emphasized the fact that the divine may be sought in various ways, all deserving equal respect: "We pray therefore for a respite for the gods of our fathers and our native gods. That which all venerate should in fairness be accounted as one. We look on the same stars, the heaven is common to us all, the same world surrounds us. What matters it by

---

[1] Symmachus' third Memorial is included – as a formal letter, 72a (17a) – in the third part (1982) of the Vienna edition of Ambrose's *Epistolae*, 1968–96, as well as in the Oxford translation of the Church Father's *Letters*, 1881. A powerful plea for the assessment of this celebrated document as a shrewd rhetorical manoeuvre – it would in fact conceal monopolistic claims on account of the old faith, not to be mistaken for any modern principle of tolerance – is to be found in Gnilka 1993, pp. 19–61. Referring to a 1974 paper by John Matthews, Cameron seems to opt for a middle way: Symmachus' report was strategically designed to function across boundaries of religious difference, while "more than eloquence was required" to drive home his argument for the toleration of the state cults, 2011, p. 37.

what arts each of us seeks for truth? We cannot arrive by one and the same path at so great a secret" (72a.2–4, 10).[1]

Ambrose used this generosity in his opponent's line of argument to detect a weak spot. How can I believe you – he asks rhetorically – who admit that you do not even know what you worship? And he continues (73.8):[2]

> By a single path, he says, we cannot arrive at so great a secret. What you are ignorant of, that we have learnt by the voice of God; what you seek after by faint surmises, that we are assured of by the very Wisdom and Truth of God. Our customs therefore and yours do not agree. You ask the Emperors to grant peace to your gods, we pray for peace for the Emperors themselves from Christ. You worship the works of your own hands, we think it sacrilege that any thing which can be made should be called God. God wills not to be worshipped under the form of stones. Nay, your very philosophers have ridiculed this. (VI)

Symmachus and his pagan supporters would thus – according to the Archbishop – be at the mercy of vague hypotheses and pluralistic confusion, whereas the Christians could confidently rely on their faith and rituals, guided by the "Wisdom and Truth of God", *ex ipsa sapientia dei et veritate*. That, Albrecht Dihle remarks, was Ambrose's sophisticated way to express a Christian philosophy of progress which made old Roman beliefs and customs, *mos maiorum*, seem obsolete.[3] For this purpose, the Church Father could even refer to pagan culture's own philosophers (in particular the Stoics), a strategy – attacking the enemy with his own weapons – that Augustine would soon exploit in his *City of God*. But first and foremost, Ambrose drew support from an inner certainty that was impervious to argument. His two letters abound with Pauline references to "the only true God" who is worshipped "by the inmost spirit" (72.1): *ipse enim solus verus est deus qui intima mente veneretur*. They point to a revealed but authoritarian, decidedly non-dialogic knowledge, to that higher truth that can only be written in the singular.

Even if Ambrose did not exercise such influence on Valentinian as many earlier scholars supposed, the young Emperor withstood all further petitions from the senatorial camp in this matter, and even if the altar was temporarily restored by the usurper Eugenius, it was finally removed by Theodosius I – a victor on the

---

[1] "Ergo diis patriis, diis indigetibus pacem rogamus. Aequum est quicquid omnes colunt unum putari. Eadem spectamus astra, commune caelum est, idem nos mundus involvit; quid interest qua quisque prudentia verum requirat? Uno itinere non potest perveniri ad tam grande secretum."
[2] Ambrose's two letters in this controversy, 72 and 73, are in most earlier editions enumerated 17 and 18 respectively.
[3] Dihle 1973, p. 87.

3 Prudentius: Dreams and Demons — 535

battlefield as well as an increasingly implacable opponent of all pagan rites.[1] Theodosius' radical measures accelerated the fall of traditional polytheism in the Empire, particularly among the Roman elite. In recent years, some scholars have tended to dismiss Symmachus and his associates among the senatorial aristocracy as a set of learned dilettantes divorced from present reality, obsessed with antiquarian trivialities, absurdly engaged in customs and ceremonies of old Roman pedigree. This unfavourable judgment hardly stands a confrontation with Symmachus' third *relatio*. Even though the ideological underpinnings of the members of the Roman aristocracy were circumscribed by their narrow social perspective, basically aimed at patronage and client relationships, at the supervision of their country estates and the organization of circuses for the people, the fact remains that with Symmachus and his Virgil-loving circle, portrayed (admittedly in an ideal light) by Macrobius, the last influential bastion of classical culture fell in the West. Within a generation of Symmachus' death, as Alan Cameron points out, there was hardly a pagan left in Rome.[2]

When Prudentius *post festum*, as it were, approached the subject of the Altar of Victory in his *Contra orationem Symmachi* (*A Reply to the Address of Symmachus*), he envisions Theodosius' two Christian sons, the Emperors Honorius and Arcadius, entering into debate with the great orator. In the wake of Ambrose, they present Victory as an idolatrous fiction. Rome's victories – a popular subject for the sworn patriot Prudentius – are a matter of blood, sweat and tears, of soldiers' strength and God's help, rather than of old altars or any imaginary winged maid (2.39–60):

39 Aut vos pictorum docuit manus adsimulatis
40 iure poetarum numen conponere monstris,
    aut lepida ex vestro sumpsit pictura sacello
    quod variis imitata notis ceraque liquenti
    duceret in faciem, sociique poematis arte
    aucta coloratis auderet ludere fucis.
45 sic unum sectantur iter, sic inania rerum
    somnia concipiunt et Homerus et acer Apelles
    et Numa, cognatumque volunt pigmenta, Camenae,
    idola, convaluit fallendi trina potestas.
    haec si non ita sunt, edatur, cur sacra vobis

---

[1] For the scant contacts between Ambrose and the imperial court, see Cameron 2011, pp. 36f.
[2] Cameron 1977, p. 2.

50 ex tabulis cerisque poetica fabula praestat?
    cur Berecyntiacus perdit truncata sacerdos
    inguina, cum pulchrum poesis castraverit Attin?
    cur etiam templo Triviae lucisque sacratis
    cornipedes arcentur equi, cum Musa pudicum
55 raptarit iuvenem volucri per litora curru,
    idque etiam paries tibi versicolorus adumbret?
    desine, si pudor est, gentilis ineptia, tandem
    res incorporeas simulatis fingere membris,
    desine terga hominis plumis obducere: frustra
60 fertur avis mulier magnusque eadem dea vultur.

> Either the handiwork of painters has taught you to make a divinity out of unreal shapes which the poet's licence has feigned, or the painter's pretty art has taken from your shrine something to copy with diverse strokes and melted wax and shape into a figure, making bold to depict it fancifully with coloured paints and aided by the art of her partner poetry. In this way Homer and bold Apelles and Numa follow the same path and conceive baseless visions, and painting, poetry, and idolatry have a kindred aim. The power of deception grew strong in three forms. If it is not so, let it be stated why poets' tales furnish you with objects of worship from pictures and waxen figures. Why does the Berecyntian priest mutilate and destroy his loins, after poetry has castrated the fair Attis? Why also are horny-hoofed horses excluded from the precinct of the goddess of the cross-ways and her consecrated groves, after the Muse has carried away a chaste youth along the shore in a flying chariot, and a wall too gives you a picture of the scene delineated in many colours. Cease, silly pagan, if you have any modesty, cease at last to model incorporeal things in counterfeit bodies; cease to cover a human back with feathers; it is in vain that a woman passes as a bird, a great vulture and a goddess both in one.

Since the subject of the imperial brothers' oration is a statue, the visual arts come into focus. The whole extract depends on the Horatian principle *ut pictura poesis* (cf. *Ars poetica*, 361), even though in Prudentius it is the painters and sculptors that proceed as poets rather than the other way around. In his *Reply*, they either feigned their gods starting from *adsimulata monstra*, portents or any kind of idiosyncratic vision characteristic of the poets, or they imitated sacred images from the pagan sanctuaries, which they had dared to smarten up or recast into gaudily made-up figures, once again inspired by their verbal sister art. In both cases, these painters/sculptors seem to take advantage of the particular distance from reality associated with classical poetry, its long acknowledged *ius poetarum*, and in both cases, the result of their efforts was nonsense, the outcome of games, *ludere*, unbecoming both statesmen and warriors.

Prudentius' *Reply* thus deviates from its Horatian paradigm, where the analogy between poetry and painting rested on the similar type of critical attention these arts expected from their audiences. In Prudentius' poem they rather share

3 Prudentius: Dreams and Demons — 537

the same resources of fictionality: a dubious asset, as it turns out. This is apparent from the author's way of associating both disciplines with idolatry. Homer wrote poetry, Apelles – the famous portrait painter of Alexander the Great – produced pictures, and the legendary second king of Rome, Numa Pompilius (supposed to have established the old kingdom's ministry of cults and pontifical institutions), worshipped idols, all of them conceiving the same "baseless visions" of things, *inania rerum somnia*. In Prudentius' *Reply*, they form a triple alliance for the sole purpose of deception, *fallendi trina potestas*, harshly censured – as Fontanier has remarked – in this Christianized version of Plato's objection to literary or visual arts for only imitating illusions or *phantasmata*.[1]

The rhetorical questions, likewise three in number, that the imperial brothers use as fuel for their argument follow the same pattern. Art and poetry, pagan, that is, are no innocent activities. They give rise to or encourage barbaric customs and habits:

- The myths of the poets provide the people with idols, depicted in "pictures and waxen figures". This general statement is substantiated by two examples:
- On the basis of the poets' representations of mutilated Attis, the ecstatic cult of Cybele – hailed as the Magna Mater in Rome – has been gaining proselytes among the priests in Phrygia.
- The representations in poetry as well as mural paintings of chaste Hippolytus' sad end, dragged to death by his bolting chariot horses, result in superstitious customs: coursers are still not allowed to approach the goddess Diana's precinct in Aricia, close to Rome.

As in some aphorism from the era of late nineteenth-century aestheticism, reality imitates art. In Prudentius' *Reply*, however, this kind of inverted mimesis is subjected to the poet's moralizing criticism, elegantly underpinned by the allusion to the *Aeneid*'s version of poor Hippolytus' fate (7.778–79). Art, poetic as well as pictorial, has certainly "been effective in propagating superstitions", *ars seminandis efficax erroribus*, asserts Prudentius in his *Crown of Martyrdom* (10.271). In sharp contrast to the idealistic notion of the plastic arts launched by theorists such as Cicero or Plotinus, he accused Phidias and other classical sculptors of being "manufacturers of gods, or the fathers of deities" (10.293), *fabri deorum vel parentes numinum*, responsible for the wretched pagan cults.[2] Neither in

---

[1] Fontanier 1986, p. 126. Cf. *The Republic*, 603b.
[2] Cf. Cicero's *Orator*, 2.8–3.10, and Plotinus' *Enneads*, 5.8.1, both resorting precisely to the example of Phidias.

the *Crown of Martyrdom* nor in the *Reply* were poetry and the visual arts confined to quietly interpreting established religious customs or concepts. They were rather supposed to lay the foundations of those customs or exacerbate their manifestations, with frightening results.

For his articulation of this bleak opinion of poetry, painting and sculpture, Prudentius followed time-honoured patristic criticism rooted in Tertullian's *Shows*, where the demons are keen on bestowing artistic gifts, *artium ingenia*, on man in order to promote the idolatry that feeds on festivals and theatrical performances (10.12). Still, in his criticism of Symmachus, the poet took his rhetorical talents to new heights, as if he was spurred on by his self-assumed task of challenging the illustrious senator. After their alternative assumptions (*aut...aut*), conclusions (*sic...*) and rhetorical questions (*cur...*), his arrogant combatants move on to exhortations. Stop simulating limbs on behalf of invented abstractions or putting wings on a woman's back, they urge the city of Rome. The first demand is aimed at the widespread Late Roman cult of concepts figurated as deities, the second at the technique of merging human with animal forms in the pictorial representations of these idols. Specifically, the imperial brothers are, of course, referring to winged Victory. Both procedures generate fictions that all too easily infiltrate Roman citizens' imagination, resulting in harm to the Empire and laxity of customs.

In this poem, Prudentius speaks as an artistic, philosophical and moral supervisor. He felt nothing but contempt for heretical figments of imagination such as the popular idea of a particular Roman genius, a completely fictitious spirit (2.385–86), *fictus genius*, the image of which is simulated for nothing if not for the purpose of deceit (2.444), *cuius frustra simulatur imago*. Such phantoms could have been dismissed long ago – Prudentius assumes – if only they had not been sanctioned or even invented by poetry and painting, two art forms traditionally invested with exceptional cultural status and suggestive power. Such allegations might create an impression of Prudentius as one of the first poets in Western tradition who actually scolds his own writerly craft. The imperial brothers' distaste for modeling "incorporeal things in counterfeit bodies" (2.58), *res incorporeas simulatis fingere membris*, could easily be turned against his own *Psychomachia*. But in that work, of course, the allegorical figures were supposed to fulfill a legitimate purpose. For this lyrical propagandist, one and the same artistic device would be as reprehensible in a pagan context as it was laudable in the service of Christianity.

This is clear from the final part of Prudentius' verse polemic, where he presents his opponent, Symmachus, the universally acclaimed orator, "that very noble senator [...], who is such a master of the art of speech, so skilful in inventing clever arguments", in an ambiguous light. Symmachus is just as clever, it turns out, in the devious art of putting on a serious mask to give a semblance of dignity. The prestigious orator actually proceeds as a simple actor, "just as a player in a tragedy covers his face with a piece of hollow-shaped wood to utter some great wickedness with all his breath through its gaping mouth." (2.644–48)[1] For all the force in this assault on the art of dissembling, the pious poet's own casuistry must be considered yet another shrewd performance. After having duly praised (or pretended to praise) Symmachus for his erudition and eloquence, he immediately resorts to the association of rhetoric with vain ostentation, widespread at the time, particularly in Christian circles. From that point of his argument it is not far to its conclusion, in which the senator's purportedly bombastic speech is in turn associated with the stage. The tragic actor's mask is disparagingly described as a piece of wood, his message is both blackened and belittled by the vague reference to "some great wickedness", and, finally, his countenance is reduced to a gaping mouth.

Thus even in his *Reply* to Symmachus, more or less as in Augustine's roughly contemporary *City of God*, Prudentius calls attention to the theatre, the art of dissembling par excellence, to illustrate the false, criminal and ridiculous nature of fiction.[2] This is how he contributed to the contemporary Christian campaign, initiated by Theodosius, against lingering pagan traditions and customs in the Empire, including the bulk of its literary heritage. Judging by the "Epilogue" to his poetry, he conceived of his work as a votive offering to God the Father. It was there, in his verse, that he had preached the Gospel. By virtue of his pedestrian poems he had paid his due tithe (7–12):

```
7    Nos citos iambicos
     sacramus et rotatiles trochaeos
        sanctitatis indigi
10   nec ad levamen pauperum potentes.
        approbat tamen Deus
     pedestre carmen et benignus audit.
```

For my part I dedicate my swift iambics and quick-running trochees, for I lack holiness and am not rich enough to relieve the poor. Yet God accepts the uninspired song and in kindness listens to it.

---

1 "Praenobilis ille senator / orandi arte potens et callida fingere doctus / mentitumque gravis personae inducere pondus, / ut tragicus cantor ligno tegit ora cavato, / grande aliquod cuius per hiatum crimen anhelet."
2 A third work severely censuring theatrical performances is Prudentius' hymn to Romanus from *The Crown of Martyrdom*, 10.220–30, where the martyr rails at representations of the Olympian gods on stage, frequently entangled in love affairs, all made up or at least exploited by the poets – *dicis licenter haec poetas fingere*, 216 – for the sake of idolatry.

Here – as has frequently been pointed out – the line of verse offering iambics (7) is trochaic, while the line offering trochees (8) is iambic. The alleged simplicity of this poetry thus immediately proves illusory. As a tribute to God, Prudentius' work exhibits advanced craftsmanship indeed, even if the poet himself was nothing but a worn-out kitchen pot, *obsoletum vasculum*, at the occasional service of Christ, hidden away in a corner in his Father's house ("Epilogue", 25–28).

On a general level, this type of self-fashioning is based on a classical paradigm, the idea of the poet or *vates* as a tool or vessel of the god. But in the first place, Prudentius has thoroughly tinged, and thereby transformed, this topos with Pauline imagery (cf. 2 Timothy 2.20–21), substituting Christian *humilitas* for Horatian *fama*; and secondly, he launches a new notion of the poet, with no tangible precedence in ancient culture, a poetic voice inseparable from its message, that cannot be mistaken for any other but is attached to a specified sender with a name, as open-hearted to his sacred addressees (God, Christ, the martyrs) as it claims to be simple or *rusticus* in its style.

In this spirit, Prudentius ends the second of his hymns in the *Crown of Martyrdom*, dedicated to his fellow countryman Lawrence (Laurentius), now thankfully taken up to Heaven but yet, the poet hopes, prepared to watch over his still living "foster-children", *alumni* (2.573–84):

```
573  Hos inter, o Christi decus,
     audi poetam rusticum
575  cordis fatentem crimina
     et facta prodentem sua.
        indignus, agnosco et scio,
     quem Christus ipse exaudiat,
     sed per patronos martyras
580  potest medellam consequi.
        audi benignus supplicem
     Christi reum Prudentium,
     et servientem corpori
     absolve vinclis saeculi.
```

> Among them, thou glory of Christ, listen to a country poet as he acknowledges the sins of his heart and confesses his deeds. He is unworthy, I know and own, that Christ himself should hearken to him; but through the advocacy of the martyrs he may attain to healing. Be thou gracious and hear the prayer of Prudentius who stands arraigned by Christ, and set him free from the fetters of the world where he is in bondage to the body.

It is in this pleading tone that Prudentius emphasizes his 'rustic' role as a poet and establishes his frank poetic voice (no matter how sophisticated it in fact turned out to be), a transparent personality cultivating the classical topos of modesty for new ends. Here, in line 582, it even appears stamped with the author's own name. Admittedly, this is no common device in Prudentius, quite the reverse, while classical Roman literature, on the other hand, exhibits several examples of such open self-referentiality, in particular among Catullus and the elegiac poets. In the *Crown of Martyrdom*, however, it is the individual (and reformed) sinner who is identified by name; he cherishes hopes for absolution through the mediation of Saint Lawrence, keenly aware of the impossibility of cheating God about his identity, of the utter futility of trying to stage games of make-believe in the court of Christ.

Moreover, it would be fair to say, he is a poet who has learnt the lesson Concord blazoned abroad in his *Psychomachia* (760–68, cf. above, p. 495): a true Christian had to be cast in one piece, accomplishing a union of body and soul "in single structure", *unimodis conpagibus*. Any kind of divided will, *fissa voluntas*, was inconceivable to this belligerent poet. He would ignore the guilty conscience Paul associates with life under the law in the seventh chapter of the Epistle to the Romans, and he would belittle the ambivalent authorial intent Augustine had associated with literary fiction in his Cassiciacum tracts. The life of the faithful should, on the contrary, be in complete accord or literally 'breathe together' with its single purpose (*quod vivimus uno / conspiret studio*), that of salvation.

In fact, not only the committed poet behind this work but the very world it discloses ignores any non-divine or any self-contained level of existence whatsoever, anything *dissociabile*. In conclusion, Prudentius' hymns deliver a powerful refutation of the traditional idea of a privileged *licentia poetica*. He rejected all reliance on any poetic exemption from the order of reality, since this reality (correctly interpreted) constitutes a coherent set of *sacramenta*, sacred or mysterious signs, of God's plan for salvation. It is altogether permeated by a God who sees everything, hears everything and knows everything. The source of truth is one and the same everywhere.[1] It is from this perspective that the poet in the *Crown of Martyrdom* "stands arraigned by Christ", a humble supplicant, in telling contrast to Horace's exalted *vates* or to Ovid's accomplished illusionist.

This does not imply that Prudentius lacked interest in his fellow beings' – ultimately demonic – addiction to fictional portents and vistas. On the contrary, he exhibited what Jean-Louis Charlet has called a remarkable taste for marvels, for surprising spectacles and metamorphoses, by some scholars (Charlet among them) described in terms such as "baroque neo-Alexandrianism".[2] Above all,

---

1 For an excellent (and polemically conceived) presentation of Prudentius' "Natursymbolik", his natural or sacramental rather than literary-rhetorical type of figuration, see Gnilka 1980.
2 Charlet 1986, p. 385.

Prudentius appears to be as attentive to the power of dreams as to that of demons over human life. In the sixth hymn of his *Daily Round*, recounting the poet's thoughts before going to sleep, he praises a good night's rest when "healing pleasure " (6.24), *medicabilis voluptas*, flows through the body's tired limbs. At the same time, however, other powers are set free through the night (6.29 – 40):

29   Liber vagat per auras
30   rapido vigore sensus,
      variasque per figuras
      quae sunt operta cernit;
        quia mens soluta curis,
      cui est origo caelum
35   purusque fons ab aethra,
      iners iacere nescit.
        imitata multiformes
      facies sibi ipsa fingit,
      per quas repente currens
40   tenui fruatur actu.

> The spirit roams free through the air, quick and lively, and in diverse figures sees things that are hidden; for the mind, whose source is heaven and whose pure fount is from the skies, cannot lie idle when it is freed from care. By imitation it fashions for itself images of many shapes, to enjoy a ghostly activity while it courses quickly through them.

These lines present us with the paradox that one of Late Antiquity's finest portraits of the human soul irresistibly venturing into fictional realms stems from one of the period's sternest censors of fictionality. In the first place, the dreamer's "spirit", *sensus* – probably an umbrella term for his inner wits, primarily imagination, considered to be particularly active during sleep – is observant of "figures" disclosing secret things. The dreaming mind thus becomes a somnambular interpreter of signs, capable of detecting their true sense, due to its heavenly origin. Secondly, this mind "fashions", *fingit*, new figures or "images" by imitation, on its own account or for its own pleasure. Once it has generated these *facies*, probably in the faculty of imagination, it traverses them quick as air (or, literally, by virtue of an – evidently enjoyable – 'aery performance', *tenuis actus*), as if the poet wants to emphasize the unsubstantial character of the dreamer's nightly activities. The entire scenario demonstrates a good deal of the nature of classical fiction, as it had been articulated by Aristotle in theory and by Ovid in practice, in the very hour, as it were, of its disappearance. Its true come-back on a broad scale would not be accomplished until the Renaissance, so it seems only logical that Prudentius' analysis of mind's both interpretive and creative activities (decoding extant figures as well as fashioning new ones) would be echoed by Andrew Marvell (1621–78), specifically in his lyrical rhapsody on "The Garden", the sunny place to which the author's mind retires in a kind of drowsy complacency (43–46), "The mind, that ocean where each kind / Does straight its own resemblance find; / Yet it creates, transcending these, / Far other worlds, and other seas"...[1]

Marvell's variation on the ancient topos of the *locus amoenus*, however, is set in full daylight, whereas Prudentius locates human mind's fictional activities (imitation, feigning) in nocturnal dreaming. And in the totalizing Christian vision that characterizes his *Daily Round*, dreaming ultimately proves to be a hazardous activity, to say the least. At times, admittedly, it might grant righteous people indications of future things (with John, the author of Revelation, as an outstanding example), but all the more often "reality is scattered and a lying image makes our minds unhappy and afraid and deceives them with a dark obscurity" (6.45–49), *plerumque dissipatis / mendax imago veris / animos pavore maestos / ambage fallit atra*. Here, Prudentius links up with classical Platonic and Stoic speculation: man gets the dreams he deserves.[2] It is enough for the great majority of human beings, he concludes, if sleep's "unsubstantial phantoms", *vanae umbrae*, threaten no ill (6.123–24). Prudentius, however, would not be Prudentius if he allowed himself to be content with such mild resignation. He brings his *Daily Round* VI to a close with a virtual exorcism of night's demonic powers: "Away, away with the monstrosities of rambling dreams! Away with the deceiver and his persistent guile" (137–40), *procul, o procul vagantum / portenta somniorum, / procul esto pervivaci / praestigiator actu!* In the final lines of this hymn, then, there remains little or nothing of its introductory projection of the dreaming spirit's free flight through the air. Ultimately, all fictional activity is demonized by Prudentius, linked to Satanic trickeries, merging into the secular night that will soon give way to the arrival of the Saviour in the world.

---

[1] Marvell 1983, p. 101.
[2] Charlet 1982, p. 97.

4 Biblical Epic Poetry: The Orthodoxy of Paraphrase

It seems as if poetic practice reached the same discouraging conclusion regarding the merits of fictional representation as had been drawn by patristic, and particularly Augustinian theory. I have tried to identify the features of the markedly non- or anti-fictional *poeta christianus* in Paulinus of Nola, Proba and Prudentius; as a matter of fact, they appear in a significant number of Late Antique writers from the fourth to the sixth century. In this section I would like to focus on a few of these authors, all active within the period's leading literary genre alongside hymns and patristic prose, namely Biblical epic poetry.

Their enterprise proved extremely successful. Writers such as Juvencus or Sedulius were to be studied in classrooms, imitated by poets and admired by an amazing number of readers throughout the history of premodern literature, down to the seventeenth century. Their later literary destiny, on the other hand, was to prove precarious. Many scholars characteristic of modernity, shaped by notions of genres as living organisms (they are born, flourish and decline), of poetic originality and of congruence between content and form have treated them condescendingly. The great expert on the medieval reception of Virgil, Domenico Comparetti, sprung from nineteenth-century positivism and evolutionism, is typical of this unsympathetic attitude: "The utter incompatibility that exists between Christianity and paganism could not fail to cause Christian poetry great inconvenience in its classical dress."[1]

Even such an eminent medieval scholar as Ernst Robert Curtius frankly declares about the Biblical epic poets: "To read them is torture."[2] In the appendix to his *European Literature and the Latin Middle Ages* which deals with Early Christian poetry, he praises Prudentius, who created his hymns on the basis of "high gifts and intense experience", supposedly detached from antique genres and antique literary theory. Still, Curtius is all the more distrustful of the majority of Late Antique writers who continued to cultivate the old genres, supplying them with Christian contents. After a brief presentation of the "smooth, clear" Juvencus, and the "rhetorical magniloquence" of Sedulius, he comes to the dismal conclusion that the Biblical epic, right down to Klopstock in the eighteenth century, was a hybrid lacking inner truth, a *genre faux:* "The Christian story of salvation, as the Bible presents it, admits no transformation into pseudo-antique

---

1 Comparetti 1997, p. 163.
2 Curtius, p. 36.

form. Not only does it thereby lose its powerful, unique, authoritative expression, but it is falsified by the genre borrowed from antique Classicism and by the concomitant linguistic and metrical conventions."[1]

Quite a few scholars – including Curtius and in recent years primarily Michael Roberts – have tried to explain the origin of Biblical epic poetry by referring to the grammar exercises of the schools, where a common task allotted to the students was to retell well-known texts in their own words. Such paraphrases could, at advanced stages, be categorized as switch-overs or remakes, *conversiones*, in which verse would be converted into prose or vice versa. In addition, this kind of exercise provided opportunities to condense the original text (*abbreviatio*) or, even better, enrich and expand it (*amplificatio*) by means of an abundant and varied vocabulary, *copia verborum*.[2] The extant evidence of these paraphrastic drills in Roman schools is reasonably good. Cicero levelled critical objections to them in connection with his discussions of translation in *On the Orator* (1.34.154–55), and Quintilian included them as a part of grammar teaching in the first book of *The Orator's Education*. The Hispanic pedagogue highlights the importance of the students' both painstaking and self-confident internalization of the works they had to read: "Verse they should first break up, then interpret in different words, then make a bolder paraphrase, in which they are allowed to abbreviate and embellish some parts, so long as the poet's meaning is preserved" (1.9.2), *versus primo solvere, mox mutatis verbis interpretari, tum paraphrasi audacius vertere, qua et breviare quaedam et exornare salvo modo poetae sensu permittitur*.

These paraphrasing activities were actually practised throughout the Roman school system. After being introduced to them in elementary grammar classes, the students developed their skills in retelling and amplifying stories as an important part of their preliminary rhetorical exercises, *progymnasmata*, as well as of their final instruction in the delivery of full-blown declamations, deliberative or forensic. Along the whole series of courses, from basic grammar to advanced oratory, these paraphrases necessarily involved a certain amount of critical reflection on literature. This is evident when Quintilian, in Book X of *The Orator's Education*, considers various types of rhetorical training with a strong emphasis on accomplished *imitatio* as the aim of the learning process. In this context, rewriting, or *conversio*, is highlighted as especially suitable for poetic exercises. The idiosyncratic use of words permitted by poetic licence does not preclude

---

[1] Ibid., pp. 458, 460–62.
[2] Ibid., pp. 147f. For the technique of paraphrase, see Kartschoke 1975, pp. 78–121, Jaumann 1995, p. 57, and particularly, with a number of specifications and examples, Roberts 1985, pp. 5–36 (the theory), 37–60, 107–60 (the practice).

the possibility of rendering them in ordinary language, *proprie*. From this perspective, Quintilian maintains, paraphrasing should not be restricted to loyal *interpretatio* but rather be thought of as an effort "to rival and vie with the original in expressing the same thoughts" (10.5.4–5), *circa eosdem sensus certamen atque aemulationem.*

The antique curricula could go a long way in systematizing this activity. Aphthonius of Antioch, for example, divided his *Progymnasmata*, written in the latter part of the fourth century CE (at the very earliest), a formidable pedagogical success recycled in Western schools down to Early Modern times, into fourteen different subsections, including Fable and Narrative.[1] The details of his influential listing need not concern us here. More importantly, Arno Reiff and after him Alexandru N. Cizek, both of whom have elucidated the theory of literary imitation during Antiquity and the Middle Ages, distinguish three types of imitative practices registered in classical and Late Antique Roman sources, including the *Progymnasmata* treatises: *interpretatio* (implicating word-for-word transference, more or less as in translation), the more unconstrained *imitatio* and the outright competitive *aemulatio*. At least the last two would enable students to exploit the possibilities of fictional discourse. Admittedly, a good deal of Roman literary imitation aimed merely at reconstructing traditional (Greek) material in new autochthonous forms, but *aemulatio* could involve new subjects as well as fresh inventions, as stated in Cicero as well as Horace.[2]

Reiff has identified all three types of imitation as listed by Cicero in exemplary fashion, and Cizek emphasizes that they were all practised in Roman schools, first with the grammarian and later with the rhetor.[3] A benevolent observer, willing to disregard the ingredients of corporal punishment and stern reprimands in Roman elementary education, might well consider these literary imitations and rhetorical *progymnasmata* as early precedents for our contemporary courses in creative writing. Notwithstanding, such incessant paraphrasing activities trained the Roman students to develop precisely a creative – in the sense of flexible, experimental or challenging – approach to the classical texts. Their unbroken relevance to Late Antique school teaching is evident, not only from Hermogenes' or Aphthonius' textbooks but also, for instance, from young Augustine's efforts to follow in the tracks of Virgil, to enter into Juno's hostile feelings over Aeneas' conquests in Italy and to render her reactions "in apt words" (above, p. 129).

---

[1] Se Kennedy's scheme in tabular form, 2003, p. XIII.
[2] Reiff 1959, pp. 35, 72.
[3] Ibid., pp. 22–51, Cizek 1994, pp. 44–50.

This is a type of paraphrasing that obviously differs from the passive kind of rewording that seems to have triggered the negative judgments by Curtius and other scholars on Juvencus and his successors. Moreover, research in recent years into intertextuality, which tends to detect (frequently ironic, distorted or otherwise idiosyncratic) rephrasing techniques in virtually all writing, makes it possible to adopt a different attitude to Late Antique Biblical epic poetry. In the past three or four decades, literary scholars, partly in reaction to modernity's cult of originality and such New Critical tenets as the autonomy of the work of art, have become aware of the dynamics and complexity of cultural transformations. Genre purism has had to yield to a new emphasis on literary hybrids and all kinds of polyphonic texts. In addition, scholars like Rita Copeland have successfully highlighted the hermeneutic vitality, with ample space for *inventio*, "heuristic appropriation" and "metaphoric substitution", that traditionally characterized the paraphrasing and translation activities of Roman rhetoric.[1]

This healthy development in late twentieth-century theory has, on the whole, generated a new scholarly interest in the vast metaliterary tradition of commentaries, glosses and paraphrases that runs through the Middle Ages. Judson Boyce Allen has succinctly expressed the revised opinion on these matters held by many scholars of later times: "Some twentieth-century poetic theorists have spoken of the heresy of paraphrase – medieval commentary exists as an assertion of the very orthodoxy of paraphrase".[2] The popularity of this type of literature in the Middle Ages can readily be traced back to Late Antiquity, and particularly to its pedagogical practice, well summarized in Quintilian's definition given above. It granted students great liberties, both in amplification and abbreviation, when they converted chunks of poetry into prose, as long as the author's initial purpose (presumably) remained intact. These grammar school activities both presupposed and fostered the old Roman notion of prose and poetry as basically two kinds of 'speech', merely distinguished by the latter's necessary dependence on metrical rules, *oratio soluta* and *oratio ligata* respectively.

The orthodoxy of paraphrase had already been established at advanced cultural levels in classical Rome. In his speech in defence of the poet Archias, who was capable of improvising a large number of verses at any time, Cicero had praised his client's ability to "repeat his performance but with different words and expressions" (8.18), *eandem rem dicere, commutatis verbis atque sententiis*.[3] Almost four hundred years later, at the time of Christianity's breakthrough dur-

---

[1] Copeland 1991, p. 35.
[2] Allen 1982, p. 211.
[3] I quote *Pro Archia* after J.B. Greenough's and G.L. Kittredge's edition 1902, and in D.H. Berry's English translation 2000.

ing the reign of Constantine, when the persecutions had ended and the apologetic fervour had (temporarily) abated, the time seemed ripe to put selected parts of the Holy Writ into Latin verse, completely in line with established Roman pedagogical practice. This project, however, soon ran into some delicate difficulties. Poetic exercises were by tradition associated not only with instructive grammar classes and dashing demonstrations of rhetoric but also with hazardous fiction. How did such activities fit in with Christian purposes? Furthermore, the epic genre was associated more than any other with the old (pagan) gods, who certainly did not fit in with these writers' pious project. Finally, paraphrasing, at least as it was envisaged and explained by Quintilian, allowed amplification and some remodeling of the master text, in short, possibilities "to rival and vie" with the original (10.5.4–5), *certamen atque aemulatio*. What implications would such rivalry have for Biblical epic poetry, based on texts considered not only canonical but sacred?[1]

Against this background, all practitioners of the new genre felt the need to explain their initiative, normally in the introductory part of their works. To this end, they relied on an argumentative pattern modelled on the dialectical locus *a fortiori:* since the classical writers had been able to dress up their vices, strange inventions and false gods in grand style, we – who know so much better and see things so much clearer – should obviously use our language for higher and nobler purposes.

Juvencus: The Pioneer

It was with this aim in mind that the earliest of the Biblical epic poets, Juvencus, framed the introduction to his paraphrase of the Gospels, *Evangeliorum libri IV* (*The Four Books of the Gospels*, ca. 330). By comparison with his successors, Juvencus stayed rather close to the Biblical text, and, in contrast to Proba, he was destined to enjoy a considerable posthumous success. He was mentioned by Jerome, who highlighted his paraphrasing technique in a brief entry in his collection of short biographies *De viris illustribus* (*On Illustrious Men*, completed in 392–93): 'He was a very noble Spanish presbyter who compiled four books in which, almost word for word, he transferred the four Gospels into hexameter

---

[1] Cf. Herzog 1975, pp. 60–68. Admittedly, Herzog is inclined to highlight the differences between Biblical epic poetry and the Roman school exercises, but it seems evident that the latter stimulated a metaliterary sensibility or taste for paraphrases, glosses, commentaries, amplification and translation. For a balanced discussion of this "paraphrase theory", see Springer 1988, pp. 9–16.

verse' (84).¹ Notwithstanding the appreciation 'almost word for word', *pene ad verbum*, the same critic would describe the project as a somewhat hazardous undertaking in a letter to the Roman rhetor Magnus in 397–98, essentially an early history of Christian literature in pocket size (70.5): "In the reign of Constantine the presbyter Juvencus set forth in verse the story of our Lord and Saviour, and did not shrink from forcing into metre the majestic phrases of the Gospel."²

The two verbs Jerome uses, *transferre* and *explicare*, stress translation and exegesis as two aspects of Juvencus' paraphrasing technique. Moreover, the former term evokes figuration; as Jacques Fontaine points out, the noun *translatio*, 'transference', is the main Latin equivalent of the Greek 'metaphor'.³ This is a significant observation with respect to Juvencus' project. Not even for such a cautious poet, who restricted himself to recreating the Gospels (principally Matthew) in the epic mode, with a heroic vocabulary derived from the *Aeneid*, was paraphrasing an innocent or straightforward activity. It involved not only *amplificatio* and *abbreviatio* but also a set of tropes that inevitably transformed the original texts, hence interpreting them. Thus the Hispanic presbyter set the tone for this type of poetry right down to John Milton's *Paradise Lost*. With regard to his own stylistic and narrative paradigms, he was very conscious of his debt to the two outstanding names of classical heroic poetry. We find them at the beginning of the *Four Books of the Gospels*, each one suggested by means of a periphrasis imbued with as much respect as reservation. The reader of this work will immediately encounter "lofty songs flowing from the font of Smyrna", *celsi cantus, Smyrnae de fonte fluentes*, and "the sweetness of Mincian Maro", *Minciadae dulcedo Maronis*, that is, Homer and Virgil respectively (PR.15–27):⁴

15 Quod si tam longam meruerunt carmina famam,
    quae veterum gestis hominum mendacia nectunt,
    nobis certa fides aeternae in saecula laudis
    inmortale decus tribuet meritumque rependet.
    Nam mihi carmen erit Christi vitalia gesta,

---

1 "Nobilissimi generis, Hispanus presbyter, quatuor Evangelia hexametris versibus pene ad verbum transferens, quatuor libros composuit". *PL* 23.691b.
2 "Juvencus Presbyter, sub Constantino historiam Domini Salvatoris versibus explicavit: nec pertimuit Evangelii majestatem sub metri leges mittere." *PL* 22.668.
3 Fontaine 1981, pp. 70f. Cf. Kirsch 1989a, p. 112.
4 Juvencus is rendered according to J. Huemer's standard edition 1891 and, as for the prologue, in P. McBrine's translation 2012 (all other English translations are mine).

20 divinum populis falsi sine crimine donum.
    Nec metus, ut mundi rapiant incendia secum
    hoc opus; hoc etenim forsan me subtrahet igni
    tunc, cum flammivoma discendet nube coruscans
    iudex, altithroni genitoris gloria, Christus.
25 Ergo age! sanctificus adsit mihi carminis auctor
    spiritus, et puro mentem riget amne canentis
    dulcis Jordanis, ut Christo digna loquamur.

> So even if those songs have earned such lasting fame –
> songs that bind lies to the deeds of ancient men –
> my sure faith in an eternity of everlasting praise
> will grant me immortal glory and render me my due reward.
> For my song will be of the life-giving deeds of Christ,
> a divine gift among the people without the sin of falsehood.
> Nor do I fear that the fires of this world will grip
> my work along with them; for perhaps this will spare me
> from the blaze, when He descends, shining in flame-spewing cloud,
> the Judge, the Glory of the high-throned Creator, Christ.
> So come, Holy Spirit, be the author of my song,
> and dip my heart in the pure streams of sweet-singing
> Jordan, that I may speak things worthy of Christ!

Juvencus' line of argument was to prove paradigmatic for Biblical epic poetry: as time relates to eternity, the errant works of pagan writers relate to my righteous poem. The reason for this prerogative of the Christian author was always the same, though (as we shall see) with interesting variations in the details: they – the pagans, however renowned – had been lying, or, as Juvencus spells out his judgment, they had mixed authentic facts with erroneous fables, whereas he relies exclusively on "sure faith", *certa fides*. In addition, the final lines of the prologue to the *Four Books of the Gospels* elegantly exploit a classical topos: even the most noble of human creations, such as eminent literary works, will fall prey to time, for example being destroyed by fire. This was the fate that once hit the famous library in Alexandria after Caesar had pursued Pompey to the city, judging by a number of classical sources. By contrast, according to the Hispanic presbyter, it was precisely his literary work, specifically the present one, *Four Books of the Gospels*, that hopefully would save himself from another fire, that of Hell, at the end of time.

This immediate focus of the poet's own fate on Judgment Day is significant. His writing has to a high degree become a matter of personal salvation: hence the utmost importance of his being filled with the inspiration of the true Spirit (rather than the spur of the Helicon Muses), in other words, being soaked by the streams of the river Jordan (rather than the springs of Castalia).¹ In this respect, Juvencus appears as a typical representative of the young Christian epic and lyric poetry. While he linked up with the major genre of pagan literature, the hexameter epic, he emphatically took sides against its fictional subjects and entertaining ingredients. On the contrary, the new type of poetry that he was in the process of launching ought, at least in theory, to be granted a purely instrumental value.

Still, this is a notably solemn as well as self-confident invocation in the grand epic style, and even if Juvencus followed the wording of the Bible more closely than his successors in the genre, it soon becomes clear to the reader that he was by no means content just to copy the Gospels *pene ad verbum*, to use Jerome's phrase. In particular, his reference to the streams of the river Jordan is striking, not only as a simple substitute for the classical fountain of Hippocrene but also as an allusion to the Baptism of Christ. Van der Nat has shown how this sacramental reference has been cleverly anticipated by the metonymic circumlocutions for Homer and Virgil, each traditionally associated with a river: the Meles (with its mouth at the port of Smyrna, Homer's birthplace according to legend) and the Mincio (which passes through Mantua in northern Italy, Virgil's hometown). Juvencus highlights the former river's flow and the latter's sweetness for the sake of outdoing them both, in a Christian *aemulatio*, with "the pure streams of sweet-singing Jordan".² His relationship to classical epic tradition, itself metonymically represented by its two famous prototypes, is evidently characterized by continuity as well as rivalry.

Juvencus literally breaks into song, a chant springing forth from the mystery of the sacrament. This inspired immediacy allows him to embroider the Biblical text as needed; appropriately, the introduction to the *Four Books of the Gospels* tells us that this paraphrase is no simple school exercise. From the very start, therefore, it has to be detached from conventional epic purposes such as acquiring earthly glory or ascribing legendary deeds to famous men, so as to be legitimized as evangelical evidence, that is to say – in the long run – as a work of personal salvation. Both Paulinus of Nola and Prudentius were to exploit the same stratagem, clearly borrowed from the Hispanic presbyter. Salvatore Costanza has cited the final lines of Paulinus' *Carmen* XIV (129–35) and of Prudentius' *Crown of Martyrs* X (1136–40) as proof of this agency. Both of them looked forward to

---

1 Salvatore Costanza adduces similar examples of what might be labelled an eschatological poetics in Paulinus and Sedulius, 1985, p. 267. Furio Murru emphasizes the symmetric arrangement of the thematic, the lexical and the syntactic contrasts between pagan *mendacia* and Christian *carmina* in Juvencus' prologue, 1980, pp. 139–50.
2 Van der Nat 1973, pp. 252f.

being counted among the lambs on the right hand of the Judge by virtue of their poetry.[1]

Of special interest in this context is the rich, intertextual register characteristic of Juvencus' *invocatio*, which was meticulously examined by Franz Quadlbauer in a learned essay in 1974. In the inventory thus established, it is the verse narrative *Culex* (*The Gnat*) which might claim our particular attention here. This brief pastoral poem in 414 hexameters is nowadays listed in the group of anonymous poems – probably compiled in Late Antiquity – known as *Appendix Vergiliana*, considered by practically all ancient commentators to have been written by Virgil in his youth. Where Juvencus pleads for inspiration from the Holy Spirit, *sanctificus adsit mihi carminis auctor / Spiritus*, the author of the *Culex* had put his hope in Apollo: "even Phoebus, shall be the fount and source of my song" (12), *Phoebus erit nostri princeps et carminis auctor*.[2] In these introductory lines to the *Culex*, however, the author does not ask for support to tell the story at hand (a parodic portrait of a gnat and its posthumous fate in the kingdom of the dead), but to carry out a future and more ambitious project on a grand, epic scale – believed by ancient interpreters, on the basis of the work's early attribution to Virgil, to be the *Aeneid*. Accordingly, when Juvencus substitutes the Holy Spirit for the *Culex's* Phoebus, the result is not only a recontextualization of a time-tested formula, a Christian reworking of the long-standing Apollonian invocation, but also a genre marker. It is in the epic format and in the grand style that the author of *Four Books of the Gospels* intends to compete with the greatest of Roman poets.

In his erudite and systematic presentation of Christian narrative poetry, written for *Reallexikon für Antike und Christentum* (1962), Klaus Thraede distinguished four "types of reception", that is, four ways of adopting and appropriating elements from classical literature (and mythology) within the radically reconfigured Biblical epic genre in the Latin language:[3]

- apologetic-polemic counteracting or "antithesis",
- transfer of concepts, constellations, topoi and scenarios,
- spiritualizing adaptation,
- and, finally, counter-imitation.

---

[1] Costanza 1976, pp. 147f.
[2] Virgil 2000; Quadlbauer 1974. The attribution of *Culex* to Virgil was commonly accepted at least as late as in the Renaissance (Edmund Spenser translated the poem into English) and is still sustained by a few scholars.
[3] Thraede 1962a, cols. 1035–41.

Judging from Thraede's exemplification, the transitions between these techniques were fairly fluid. Apologetic-polemic counteracting was most common in the *praefatio* (preface or prologue) commonly attached to Biblical epic works. In this introductory section, the authors liked to set off their own pious and truthful purpose against the pagan poets' empty attire and vain delusions, sometimes basing their argument on the censure of myths already articulated by several classical Roman poets, most famously Lucretius. Transfers of concepts and topoi along with counter-imitation were particularly employed by Prudentius, who frequently adopted epic formulas, infusing them with a new (Christian) meaning: his Thunderer, for example, *Tonans*, translates into God (cf. above, p. 520).

It would not be difficult to cite instances of all these types of reception in Juvencus' prologue, which is an accomplished example of *aemulatio Virgilii*, moreover counter-imitating Horace, Propertius and Ovid, the very cream of Roman Golden Age writers. Thus the innovative potential of Juvencus' project should not be underestimated. In his monograph on Prudentius, Thraede reminds us of the questions each and every Late Antique *poeta christianus* must have confronted. How could poetry be vindicated in the face of truth? How was it possible for poets to do justice to the historical situation of orthodox Christianity without alienating their art from its ancient origin? How was the on-going reception of classical models possible in spite of all the recent defamation of poetry?[1] Additionally, one could add the following issues: had not everything essential already been said, in verbally inspired and hence unsurpassed ways, by the canonical contributors to the Holy Writ? And even if the idea of Christian poetry was accepted, was it possible or even desirable to incorporate the heritage from the classics into this poetry, thereby fostering such cultural hybridity as had been thoroughly discredited in the apologetic polemic?

Prudentius' hundred-years-older countryman Juvencus would have pondered more intensively than most other writers on these questions. He was virtually the first in the genre and had no given models to fall back on. He gave his firm answer with the *Four Books of the Gospels*, one of the pioneering works of literary history – which is no longer read or even remembered. Jerome was right, after all: it was a hazardous enterprise that Juvencus had ventured upon. After Lactantius' bestowal of theoretical legitimacy on classical rhetoric in the service of Christianity, he was the first to put this project into effect on a large scale, a powerful alternative to *sermo humilis*, the apostles' (supposedly)

---

1 Thraede 1965, p. 21.

simple style.[1] The result was a highly ornamented version of the Gospels in which the author himself, in the final lines of the poem, took the opportunity to authorize his eloquent undertaking with reference to the Grace of God, *gratia Christi*, which had shone so strongly on him 'that the glory of divine law was pleased to accept the worldly ornaments of language in my verses' (4.804–05), *versibus ut nostris divinae gloria legis / ornamenta libens caperet terrestria linguae.*

In his intertextually lavish prologue, Juvencus employed lyric, elegiac and epic genre markers drawn from pagan tradition for the sole purpose of outdoing them, point for point, in the name of his divine *carminis auctor*, the Spirit. This artistic achievement was made possible precisely by – to borrow Thraede's taxonomy – transfer of concepts and topoi, spiritualizing adaptation and counter-imitation. The many junctions in classical epic poetry of history (*veterum gesta hominum*) with fabrication (*mendacia*) had left behind a series of matrixes that the Christian poet was about to fill with "the life-giving deeds of Christ". He immediately carries this programme – articulated in lines 15–20 – into effect, as if it was a performative statement: the Holy Spirit takes over Apollo's task, the river Jordan washes away Hippocrene, the water of Baptism replaces Olympian nectar. As Wolfgang Kirsch has pointed out in his monograph on fourth-century Latin epic poetry, there is an existential rather than a mythical, poetic or even philosophical truth at stake here: "The concept of fictionality, or of mimesis of secular events and being, is from the very start inconceivable in his [Juvencus'] work."[2]

Consequently, Juvencus inaugurated an entirely new type of Christian literature which made ample use of classical poetry's authorial gestures, figurative discourse and epic formulas, renouncing, however, such poetry's fictional/mimetic mode. After Constantine's conversion and the emerging acceptance of Christianity in the Empire, wide circles of cultivated Romans throughout the Mediterranean world resorted to the new faith. Virtually all of them had been drilled in rhetoric and knew their Virgil inside out from their school years. As Jean-Louis Charlet has underlined, it was their need for a Christian poetry as refined and elaborate as the pagan literary legacy that the *Four Books of the Gospels* was destined to satisfy.[3] A new Empire was becoming a fact, a Christian

---

[1] For a recent systematic examination of Juvencus' paraphrastic technique and rhetorical enhancement of his Biblical models, see Thor 2013. For my purposes in this study I disregard Commodian, perhaps the first of all Christian poets, by all accounts active during the third century, author of a *Carmen apologeticum*.
[2] Kirsch 1989a, p. 103.
[3] Charlet 1988, p. 84.

Rome, requiring new artistic expressions drawing on – rather than rejecting – prestigious imperial culture, superimposing itself onto the former apologetic contentiousness.

If Lactantius had provided the theoretic platform for this literature, it was Juvencus who supplied its first specimen, even though he mitigated the rhetor's bold notions of poetic licence and oblique figuration in his deferential paraphrase of the Gospels. This ornate account of the life, death and resurrection of Christ was in any case enough to change Latin epic poetry for good. Where earlier modern scholars showed a tendency to conceive of Biblical epic poetry as a doubtful matter of pouring new wine into old wineskins, it seems more rewarding to study how the classical artistic devices and the evangelical topics inevitably were adjusted to each other in an innovative literary hybrid looking to the future.

The Hispanic poet tinged the Christology of the Gospels – originally an import from the Mediterranean world's opposite, eastern end – with the *gravitas* of age-old epic tradition and, by implication, with the glory of the Empire and the metropolis. Thus he set out to show his contemporaries, in the close wake of the reign of Constantine, what the Gospel according to Matthew would look like in the grand style which, conversely, was finally made to express truly great things, ostensibly freed from its ballast of fabulous myths and fictional tales of all sorts. "After Virgil, it is truer to say that no great development was possible, until the Latin language became something different": with these words, the great classicist of twentieth-century modernism, T.S. Eliot, would grant Rome's *summus poeta* an unparalleled status as a Western "classic".[1] Perhaps now, under the massive influence of the new faith, the Latin language was actually in the process of becoming something different and could look forward to a new poetic spring. Thanks to Juvencus, the concept of a Christian literature was no longer a contradiction of terms.[2]

Sedulius: The Food of Poetry

Among the poets who developed Biblical epic poetry after Juvencus, we can only discuss a few in this study, each offering his own solution to the challenge of proclaiming Christian truth by means of discursive modes and stylistic figures

---

[1] Eliot 1945, p. 22.
[2] The assessment of Juvencus has fluctuated among literary historians. While Franco Stella thinks of him as a "mediocre poet", 2001, p. 18, I would rather concur with Deproost who emphasizes his "audacious" project, 1998, p. 112.

associated with classical literature. Several of the genre's popular devices such as the transfer of warfare themes from pagan epic poetry to Christian eschatology or the spiritualization of military service by virtue of the (slightly personified) Pauline virtues *fides* and *spes* are presented in the following declaration: "Meanwhile, as I duly lighten the way with my words, / and hope and faith accompany my progress to the heights, / I make my way more easily to the topmost citadel at last. / [...] Your glorious arms, / good king, I carry as I bring up the rear of your army."[1]

Here, it is one of Juvencus' most skilful successors, Sedulius, who is speaking. He presents yet another authorial I who puts his personal existence at stake for the sake of the good cause along with the right text, a soldier in God's holy army with words as his weapons. Sedulius gives an account of this – metaphorical – military service in his splendid Easter hymn, *Paschale carmen* (or *Carmen paschale*, *The Paschal Song*), a Bible epic poem in five books, written in hexameters, later complemented with a prose version to make a 'twin work', *opus geminatum*, possibly the first of its kind. After an Old Testament prelude, the poem focuses exclusively on the life of Christ the Redeemer, with great emphasis on His miracles. Soteriology and the Incarnation are at the centre of the whole work, whether the perspective is typological, so that the Christ of the Gospels is heralded by figures and episodes from the Old Covenant, or mystical-anagogic, so that Christ Himself anticipates the victory of the Church, the Resurrection of the Dead and Judgment Day at the end of time.

Sedulius was active in the 400s, probably in the first half or around the middle of the century, possibly in Italy, or perhaps in Greece. We know practically nothing about his life or person.[2] Not even the letters to a certain *presbyter* and *venerabilis pater* Macedonius in which Sedulius explains the intentions underlying his Easter hymn provide any definite biographical evidence.[3] There, nonetheless, the author tells us that he used to apply himself to secular studies, occupied with his "useless career" to the detriment of his soul's good, devoting his skills in literary studies to playing "fruitless games" rather than serving God.

---

[1] "Interea dum rite viam sermone levamus, / spesque fidesque meum comitantur in ardua gressum, / blandius ad summam tandem pervenimus arcem. / [...] Decus armaque porto / militiaeque tuae, bone rex, pars ultima resto." I quote *Paschale carmen* 1.334–36, 343–44, in Latin and in English, from C.P.E. Springer's recent volume *The Paschal Song and Hymns*, Sedulius 2013. Cf. *Aeneid* 8.309.

[2] Paul van der Laan tentatively dates the *Paschal Song* to ca. 430, 1993, p. 134. As for our scant information on Sedulius, see Springer 1988, pp. 23–29 (updated in the author's introduction to Sedulius 2013, pp. xiv–xvii), and especially Green 2006, pp. 135–43.

[3] The two letters to Macedonius affixed to the *Paschal Song* in the manuscript tradition are reproduced by Springer in Sedulius 2013, pp. 210–21.

However, such references to the *inane vitae* and poetry's vain *lusus*, as well as formulas of modesty such as the author's apparent demeanor as "a novice in a little skiff", *parva tiro lintre*, on the immense ocean of his undertaking, were common enough among Christian poets of the period, especially perhaps in Biblical epic poetry.[1] That does not make them any less interesting to us. This first letter to Macedonius takes the form of an intellectual autobiography which, even though it omits all specific personal information, has few counterparts in Late Antique literature.

To begin with, then, Sedulius had followed the ways of the world, aspiring to acquire secular wisdom, but as soon as the inner fog, *interior caligo*, had cleared from the eyes of his heart, *cordis oculi*, he felt he would be committing a sin of omission if he did not put his scholarly competence at the service of Christian truth. So he decided, after certain hesitation and some doubts about his own ability, to begin his poem "inviting others with admonitions of the truth to enjoy the fruits of the good harvest", *alios exhortationibus veritatis ad frugem bonae messis invitans*.[2] This short survey of the experiences and intentions behind the *Paschal Song* activates at least six thematic complexes partly known from the exordial topics of either classical or Christian poetry, namely:

- literary activity configured as a potentially perilous sea voyage,
- the contrast between the narrator's unenlightened youth and his reformed present state,
- the duty to make use of one's talent in order to illumine one's fellow men, introducing them to the true faith (and avoid the guilt of omission known as *culpa silentii*),
- the painful awareness of one's own inadequacy, here aggravated to fear and *trepidatio* at the thought of the arduous task lying ahead,
- the association of writing with personal salvation: the words of the poet's own work were supposed to put him on guard against the Devil's future stratagems,
- and, finally, the moral or virtuous purpose that justifies the whole enterprise, configured by the metaphor of the good harvest, a trope which is further elaborated in the Easter hymn's introductory self-presentation: the poet offers his readers a modest Passover/Easter meal, *paschales dapes*, after having picked "a few greens" or vegetables, *exiguum holus*, from his poor gar-

---

[1] Ibid., pp. 210f. Green observes that the poetological topic of navigation is derived from classical Roman literature (Horace, Virgil, Statius), 2006, p. 155, note 130.
[2] Sedulius 2013, pp. 212f.

den, in stark contrast to the tables loaded with food and drink of the rich (PR.1–16).[1]

On the basis of these starting points, poetic activity is decidedly detached from any kind of carefree indulgence or frivolous pleasure traditionally associated with (secular) literature. On the contrary, the *Paschal Song* is supposed to indicate that its author had fully accepted his civic responsibility and his duty as a Christian learned man, familiar with the liberal arts, to enlighten people. This is a serious enterprise, he emphasizes, in which the elements of pleasure or play only serve to promulgate true faith:[2]

> But I will not put off explaining briefly why I chose to compose this work in metrical form. Best father, as you also know from your tireless experience in reading, only rarely has anyone turned the gifts of divine power into a composition of this type, and there are many for whom instruction in worldly letters is all the more attractive because of the delights of poetry and the pleasures of verse. These readers pay slighter attention to whatever they read in the way of oratorical eloquence, since they take hardly any pleasure in it; but what they see honeyed with the allurement of verse they take up with such eagerness in their hearts that by repeating it again and again they become sure of it and store it up in the depths of their memory. So, I think that these readers' habits should not be disregarded but handled in accordance with their established customs and nature, so that each of them should be won for God of their own will in greater accord with their own disposition. Nor does it matter by what occasion someone is initiated into the faith, as long as once he has set off down the road of liberty he does not seek out again the snares of wicked slavery in which he had been previously trapped. Excellent father, this is the rationale for my work; it is not a frivolous one, as you have learned, but appropriate; if its plan is worthwhile and does not displease you, I hope that it may be given the favor of your kindly approval, so that you may take a tiny break from writings that are loftier and gladly enjoy humbler fare. (VII)

Sedulius' project amounts to putting the Biblical subject, God's or the Holy Spirit's inspired "gifts" to mankind, into verse, *metrica ratione*. The element of paraphrase is retained here, as the term *aptavit* ('fitted', 'adjusted', 'adapted') indicates. However, again, as in Juvencus, paraphrasing is no easy or unambiguous enterprise. It takes advantage of poetry's time-tested acoustic or metrical delights, termed as *deliciae*, *voluptates*, and finally, in a climax, *blandimento mellitum* – what has been sweetened with pleasure, charms or flattery – all for the sake of exhortation and pastoral care.

---

[1] For a general view of these topics, see Donnini 1978. Curtius discusses nautical as well as alimentary metaphors in his chapter on "Metaphorics", 1990, pp. 128–44.
[2] Sedulius 2013, pp. 212–15.

In this address to the venerable Macedonius, Sedulius implies a tension, by no means self-evident, between rhetoric and poetry. Many readers who immerse themselves in written orations are rarely rewarded for their efforts, he remarks, since these declamatory pieces leave them indifferent or even bored, while those who let themselves be taken in by the charms of poetry learn to store its message properly. This is a mnemotechnical stratagem that would not have seemed unfamiliar to Augustine. According to the Church Father's *Revisions* (1.19.1), he had composed a hymn in the form of an acrostic, an *abecedarius*, designed to impress his anti-Donatist case on the minds of ordinary readers. We have previously considered the new authorial role that was established in early Christian literature. Sedulius seems just as anxious to establish a new readerly role, or rather, to emphasize new expectations of the effect of literature on its readers. The primary aim of Biblical epic poetry was not to tickle their fancies with elegant metaphors for the enjoyment of art; nor could it limit itself to the old triad of entertaining, moving or teaching. Its new message was, in fact, to quote the words of a German poet a millennium and a half later (inspired, ironically, by an archaic torso of Apollo): "You must change your life."[1]

Based on such praiseworthy purposes, the delights of poetry presented no problems. On the contrary, they might legitimately be employed for an all-embracing good cause. Accordingly, Sedulius set his mind on exploiting as well as reforming traditional habits of reading poetry. To this end, he could, to a certain extent, rely on the clever rhetorical strategy of Lucretius, adapted for Christian purposes by Lactantius (as we have noted, pp. 316f.): harsh truths must sometimes be conveyed in sweet words in order to exert their long-term beneficial influence on readers.[2] In the *Paschal Song*, however, such techniques of capitalizing on readerly habits were taken even further: they would be adaptable to the "established customs and nature", *insita consuetudo vel natura*, of widely differing readers. In addition, they would hopefully prove more efficient than earlier stratagems for convincing or reforming a literate audience, minimizing the risk of a relapse into "the snares of wicked slavery". Finally, the closing modesty topos of the letter extract above only underlines the pragmatic and strategic character of this draft for an up-to date Christian poetics. The Easter hymn is not the outcome of any "frivolous" intention (in modern parlance, we might perhaps interpret the adjective *supervacuus*, literally 'superfluous' or 'redundant', as aesthetisizing or self-sufficient); it was rather dictated by care for what is conve-

---

1 "Du mußt dein Leben ändern." From Rainer Maria Rilke's poem "Archaischer Torso Apollos" in *Neue Gedichte*, Rilke 1979, p. 83.
2 Cf. Springer 1988, p. 37.

nient or "appropriate", *commodus*. Incidentally, Sedulius was to have huge success with this programme for a persuasive Christian poetry, as it was implemented in his famous poem. Almost as emphatically as Martianus' *Marriage*, the *Paschal Song* testifies to the huge gap between the premodern era's taste and our own. Today, it is by all accounts as rare on academic curricula as Juvencus' *Four Books of the Gospels*, known to few and read by even fewer students, while it featured regularly as a minor classic in European grammar teaching throughout the better part of the Middle Ages.

It begins as follows (1.17–26):

17 Cum sua gentiles studeant figmenta poetae
    grandisonis pompare modis, tragicoque boatu
    ridiculove Geta seu qualibet arte canendi
20 saeva nefandarum renovent contagia rerum
    et scelerum monumenta canant, rituque magistro
    plurima Niliacis tradant mendacia biblis,
    cur ego, Daviticis assuetus cantibus odas
    chordarum resonare decem sanctoque verenter
25 stare choro et placidis caelestia psallere verbis,
    clara salutiferi taceam miracula Christi,
    [...].

Since pagan poets try to trick out their fictions
with pompous phraseology, and use tragic bombast,
or the comic Geta, or any other style of singing
to re-create the cruel contagions of wicked deeds
and memorialize criminals in song, in the traditional way,
passing on multiple lies in books of papyrus from the Nile,
why should I, who am used to sound out in the songs of David
the psalms for the ten-stringed lyre, standing in awe
in the holy choir and singing with gentle words of heavenly things,
keep silent about the famous miracles of Christ the Savior,
[...].

From the very start, the poet makes interesting reservations against specific genres and predecessors within pagan literature. Admittedly, he expresses his criticism at a general level when he waves aside 'any art of singing', but his attack on the grand style, *grandisoni modi*, seems aimed at epic poetry (i.e. Virgil) and tragedy in particular. In addition, the verb *pompare*, possibly a *hapax* in Latin literature, directs the reader's associations to public spectacles. It is derived from the noun *pompa*, which originally meant any kind of 'public procession', for instance at festivals, circus games or triumphs, but it was also associated with qualities such as showing off or ostentation, for instance in rhetoric, above all in the festive speeches of the *genus demonstrativum*, which used to excel in precisely the kind of ornamental language the Christian writers rejected.[1] The bellowing of tragedy may in turn refer to a number of mythical episodes involving oxen, bulls or cows, regularly performed on the theatrical stage of those days; moreover, it possibly alludes to the original meaning of the word tragedy, 'goat song', while *Geta* surely refers to the slave Geta in Terence's plays *Phormio* and *Adelphi* (161–160 BCE), in this context a metonym for the genre of comedy, which often used slaves in the principal parts.[2] Thus Sedulius seems to allude to all three main genres of classical literature in this introduction to his *Paschal Song:* heroic poetry, tragedy and comedy.

These epic and dramatic genres are now presented, as in Augustine's perhaps contemporary or slightly earlier *City of God*, as a threat to both morals and religion. In particular, Sedulius associates them with the book-roll, "in the traditional way" (*ritu magistro*) scribbled all over with lies. In just a few lines he thus neatly links fictionality, *figmenta*, to the classical literary genres as well as to immorality and idolatry, all providing typical characteristics of pagan culture, in turn metonymically represented by the ancient medium for writing, originating in the Nile Delta. The poet makes it perfectly clear that seniority and tradition do not count for much in this context; they are to be rejected in favour of his own, as it were, modernist approach, signalled by his familiarity with "the songs of David". These *Davitici cantus* obviously epitomize the culture of the living voice in the expanding Christian communities, in short, choral hymn singing, centred on heavenly things or circumstances, *caelestia*, in stark contrast to the learned but fictional, hence mendacious chronicles or recitals inscribed on the age-old papyrus rolls.

It is allegedly in this Christian environment that Sedulius was trained as a poet, so it is there he seeks support for his present enterprise: to tell of the miracles of Christ. If pagan fictions had been pompously advertised or even 'bellowed' in the grand style by the epic or tragic poets, all the more reason for him not to keep silent about the Gospels' unequivocal truth (the adjective *clarus*, "famous", is of course associated with light and clarity). This line of argument *a fortiori*, heightened by the rhetorical question "Why should I keep silent?", emphasizes the sincerity and authenticity of the poet's message, whose gentle words, *placida verba*, likewise outperform the pagan poets' *grandisoni modi*. By such argumentative devices, Sedulius, as Salvator Costanza has observed,

---

[1] Salvatore Costanza translates *pompa* as "dire con enfasi", 1985, p. 261. For an examination of the term with examples from Cicero, Jerome (*Ep.* 22.2) and others, see Gualandri 1979, p. 82.
[2] Alternatively, Sedulius might refer to the North African writer Hosidius Geta and his tragedy *Medea* (designed as a cento, ca. 200). Such repeated emphasis on tragedy, however, seems redundant in this context.

turns Juvencus' comparatively respectful dissociation from Homer and Virgil into a sarcastically superior attitude.[1] The earliest Christian poetry's tentative challenges of the great names in classical literature have now developed into the victorious Church's self-confident *aemulatio*.

A few lines later in the *Paschal Song*, pagan culture is specified essentially as Greek civilization, disseminated across the Mediterranean world (1.37–44):

> 37 Haec mihi carmen erit. Mentes huc vertite cuncti.
> Hanc constanter opem laesis adhibete medullis,
> quos letale malum, quos vanis dedita curis
> 40 Attica Cecropii serpit doctrina veneni,
> sectantesque magis vitam spirantis odorem
> legis Athenaei paedorem linquite pagi.
> Quid labyrintheo, Thesidae, erratis in antro
> caecaque Daedalei lustratis limina tecti?
>
> > This will be my song. Everyone, turn your attention here!
> > Apply this remedy continually to your damaged hearts
> > into which a deadly evil, obsessed with idle questions,
> > Attic philosophy, filled with Cecropian venom, has crept,
> > and pursue instead the aroma of the law that breathes life,
> > leaving the filthy stench of the countryside of Athens behind.
> > Why wander around the cavernous labyrinth, you sons of Theseus,
> > and haunt the dark doorways leading into Daedalus's building?

As a virtual successor to Paul, Sedulius turns to each and everyone with the prospect of a general evangelization, and his tools for this purpose will be the *carmen*, the *Paschal Song* he is about to perform and which hopefully will permeate the very marrow of his audience. Thus the poet announces his work as a kind of sacred remedy for the evils of pagan civilization, reminiscent of the *linguae genus* we have seen Prudentius praise in his *Crown of Martyrdom*, an art that aims at something more than instruction or entertainment, a language that will strike the audience in their hearts and kidneys. The listeners to Sedulius' Easter hymn are ostensibly damaged by Greek philosophy's heresies as well as original sin, a miserable plight translated into a scenario drawn from classical mythology. They are addressed as *Thesidae* with reference to the tale of Theseus, according to which King Minos of Crete forced the city of Athens to send its young men to be sacrificed to the taurine monster in the labyrinth of Knossos, the Minotaur: an instance of cultural memory suggesting both lust and death, bestial Eros and blind Thanatos, pagan sacrificial rites and occult learning. To all appearances,

---

[1] Costanza 1985, pp. 259–62.

these "sons of Theseus" are invoked as a metonym for the Athenians trapped in the maze of death, who in turn represent the readers of the Easter hymn, haunted by paganism, erring in the labyrinthine darkness of their dangerous delusions. Thus a prototypical specimen of fiction, the myth of Theseus, is recycled in the *Paschal Song* for the purpose of disowning Greek civilization, that is, the very foundation of classical fiction.

Soon, however, this desolate image of labyrinthine wanderings is countered by the prospect of the unmistakably right way, leading to the Saviour (1.79–87):

79 Pande salutarem paucos quae ducit in urbem
80 angusto mihi calle viam verbique lucernam
   da pedibus lucere meis, ut semita vitae
   ad caulas me ruris agat, qua servat amoenum
   pastor ovile bonus, qua vellere praevius albo
   virginis agnus ovis grexque omnis candidus intrat.
85 Te duce difficilis non est via; subditur omnis
   imperiis natura tuis, rituque soluto
   transit in adversas iussu dominante figuras.

   Show me the way which leads the few to the city of salvation
   by the narrow path and cause the lamp of the word
   to shine before my feet, so that the trail of life
   may lead me to a rustic sheepfold where the good shepherd
   watches over his happy flock, where the lamb with white fleece,
   born of a virgin ewe, leads the way, and all his shining flock enters.
   With you as guide the way is not hard; all nature is subject
   to your rule and, with its usual protocol relaxed,
   everything changes into just the opposite at your lordly command.

The passage's imagery is primarily Biblical, focusing on the Good Shepherd, Christ, who keeps a watchful eye over His flock: the faithful, the congregation (led by Himself, curiously reduplicated as a white 'lamb of a virgin sheep', *virginis agnus ovis*). It offers a striking contrast between "the cavernous labyrinth" (1.43) and the accurate path, between the implied bull monster and the innocent flock of sheep. This abrupt change of scene is typical of Sedulius' technique; immediately before, he has conjured up a vision of the wasteland of delusion, *steriles plagae* (1.50), just to make it fade away in favour of the realm of the blessed, *sedes beatae* (1.54), and now Daedalus' dark abode gives way to the Good Shepherd's pleasant fold. That is how the poet of the *Paschal Song* consistently converts the old order of nature into new and "opposite" figures.

This transformation is just as much of an intertextual nature. "Show me the way which leads the few to the city of salvation"... As Sedulius' publisher Johann Huemer points out in a note to his modern standard edition (1885), this line echoes the Cumæan Sibyl in the *Aeneid*, who in a state of ecstasy foresees Aeneas' fate after landing in Latium: "The first pathway to safety, / One you anticipate least, will emerge from a Greek city's portals" (6.96–97), *via prima salutis, / quod minime reris, Graia pandetur ab urbe.*[1] The Sibyl refers to Pallanteum, the Greek emigrant King Evander's city on the Palatine which was to come to Aeneas' aid in the war against Turnus. Sedulius, for his part, refers to the heavenly Jerusalem. Not only nature, then, but even literature, pagan literature, is displaced and transformed into adverse (Christian, scriptural) figures through the Easter hymn. This is an apposite strategy for a poet who liked to proceed by paradoxes and antitheses.[2] Sedulius appears among the truly advanced counter-imitators in early Christian literature. When pagan culture had been purged of its prevailing philosophical, religious and ceremonial patterns, "with its usual protocol relaxed", *ritu soluto,* in accordance with Jerome's recommendations in one of his letters (70.2, above, pp. 149f.), it was laid open to the poetical-rhetorical process of transformation that the *Paschal Song* both refers to and implements: *transit in adversas figuras.*

This transition seemed feasible since Sedulius discerned in every epoch a semiotic substratum – certain rudiments of art or poetry, philosophy or religion, that bear witness to God (1.93–102):

```
93   Indicio est antiqua fides, et cana priorum
     testis origo patrum, nullisque abolenda per aevum
95   temporibus constant virtutum signa tuarum.
     Ex quibus audaci perstringere pauca relatu
     vix animis committo meis, silvamque patentem
     ingrediens aliquos nitor contingere ramos.
     Nam centum licet ora movens vox ferrea clamet,
100  centenosque sonos humanum pectus anhelet,
     cuncta quis expediet, quorum nec lucida caeli
     sidera nec bibulae numeris aequantur harenae?
```

To this the faith of the ancients is witness, the hoary antiquity
of the earlier fathers is testimony, and, never to be eclipsed
by time, the signs of your powers endure forever.
To touch on a few of these in the course of my presumptuous retelling
is a task I can barely undertake to do. It is a vast forest
that I enter, and I aim to touch but a few branches.
For even if I had an iron voice and shouted with a hundred tongues,
and even if the human breast could breathe forth a hundred sounds,

---

[1] Sedulius 2007, p. 21
[2] For the pointedly antithetical style in Sedulius, as a rule linked to the Christological or trinitarian paradoxes of orthodox faith, see Small 1986, pp. 237–44.

> who could set forth all of his signs, whose number not even
> the stars shining in the sky or the sand in the thirsty deserts can rival?

At the beginning of the second book of the *Georgics*, Virgil had urged Maecenas to accompany him on a voyage (his project of composing the book at hand), promising his patron to keep close to land. This meant that the poet would limit his range of themes. He explicitly refrained from embracing 'everything', *cuncta*, in his verse, regardless of whether he had a hundred tongues, a hundred mouths and a voice of iron at his disposal (2.42–44). The Cumæan cave described in *Aeneid* VI actually has a hundred mouths, that is, a hundred openings for emitting its Pythian messages (6.43, 81), while the Sibyl herself – more or less like the poet of the *Georgics* – makes it clear that she would be unable to retell all the punishments in Tartarus, or the crimes behind them, not even if she had a hundred tongues, a hundred mouths and a voice of iron (6.625–27). Ovid matches his predecessor's wording in the *Metamorphoses*, where he protests his inability to describe the Calydonian hero Meleager's sisters' grief over their treacherously killed brother, not even if a god had given him a hundred mouths (8.533). This topos evidently lent itself to vatic or sibylline announcements; it had a Homeric ring about it (cf. *The Iliad*, 2.488–92), it had already been recycled by Christian poets and now it was being used by the author of the *Paschal Song*.[1] Sedulius could count on it being recognized by his readers, particularly if Michael Mazzega, who has written a separate commentary on the third book of his Bible epic, is right in claiming that the work mainly addressed an educated pagan audience.[2]

All these applications of the cliché of the hundred mouths were designed to combine the topic of affected modesty with that of inexpressibility. Sedulius follows in the footsteps of his famous Golden Age predecessors, but his implementation of the topos can hardly be reduced to a simple instance of *imitatio veterum*. It is, after all, the signs of God's jurisdiction over the ancient world that he is about to retrace, which is something far more awe-inspiring than the tears of Meleager's sisters or the crimes of Tantalus and his likes. By such recycling of his classical models for Christian purposes, Sedulius emphasizes their inferiority in comparison with his own work, as Paul van der Laan points out.[3] This is Biblical epic poetry's preferred form of *aemulatio*, executed in entire series of transpositions and counter-imitations that are anything but reverential. They are certainly not fashioned for aesthetic purposes, quite the reverse. Sedu-

---

[1] For a short survey of the Christian writers' application of the cliché of the hundred mouths from Late Antiquity to the High Middle Ages, see Courcelle 1955a.
[2] Mazzega 1996, the chapter "Die Heiden als Leserschaft", pp. 15–33.
[3] Van der Laan 1993, p. 142.

lius reuses the old devices, relegated in the *Aeneid* to fictitious figures like the Cumæan Sybil, for a completely authenticated message. The way to God we have seen him map out on the basis of Virgil's epic poem ("Show me the way which leads the few to the city of salvation / by the narrow path", 1.79–80) surely has a more authoritative source in the Gospel according to St. John 14.6: "I am the way, and the truth, and the life", in the Vulgate: *sum via et veritas et vita*. Precisely this Biblical resonance is just as evident later in the Easter hymn, where a powerful chiasmus praises the Lord as "the way of light, the path of peace" (2.279), *lucis via, semita pacis*. Sedulius' undaunted reorientation and transmutation of the figurative language of Virgil and the classical past is ultimately based on this fundamental contrast: if the labyrinth (which is "cavernous", "dark" or blind, leading to the Minotaur) could be linked to – or epitomize – the pagan poets' *figmenta*, then the narrow but reliable way (which is illuminated by "the lamp of the word", 1.80, leading to the Good Shepherd) represents unconditional truth.

By and large, for all his innovative energy, Juvencus had been content to retell the Gospels' story rather closely, renouncing hermeneutic speculations. Sedulius, on the other hand, makes the issue of the correct interpretation of the narrated events, and thereby the question of truth, the crucial point of his work.[1] By listing a number of miraculous Old Testament figures and events (1.103–237) and by recapturing the story of Adam's and Eve's fall into sin at the beginning of Book II, he introduced a typological dimension in his Bible epic that inevitably invests its main evangelical story with universal, soteriological significance. In dispensing fish and bread to the starving people, Christ appears as "the true prophet", *verus propheta*, repeating the old miracles of *typicus Moyses* in even greater deeds, *maioribus actis* (3.202–04, recalling Exodus 17.1–6, already recycled in the *Paschal Song* 1.152–59). The new Virgin (Mary) was to atone for the misdeed of the earlier one (Eve, 2.31), while the fraudulent snake in Paradise (2.8), *perfidus ille draco*, appears as a reminder of the original lie (and the betrayal and deceit) that will be invalidated through the Incarnation.[2] Thus the final revelation of truth coincides with the salvific work of Christ. This correlation is ingeniously intimated in the scene from the concluding canto, where Christ is brought before Pilate (5.139–43):

---

[1] Nicole Hecquet-Noti emphasizes the degree of exegesis in Sedulius' and Avitus' Biblical epic works, primarily judging from their numerous authorial intrusions, in contrast to Juvencus' emulation of the narrator's invisible persona in classical epic poetry, 2009, p. 212.

[2] For Sedulius' implementation of typological patterns in his work, see Small 1986, pp. 225–29, and Springer 1988, pp. 83–90.

139 At dominus patiens cum praesidis ante tribunal
140 staret, ut ad iugulum ductus mitissimus agnus,
    nil inimica cohors insontis sanguine dignum
    reperiens, regem quod se rex dixerit esse
    obicit, et verum mendax pro crimine ducit.

But when the Lord stood patiently before the governor's tribunal,
like a lamb most mild that is led to the slaughter,
the hostile throng, finding nothing worthy of death in the innocent one,
threw up the charge that he, a king, said that he was a king,
and in their falseness presented the truth as an accusation.

This extract draws on all the Gospels in the Vulgate version. Matthew describes how Jesus was brought before the *praeses* Pontius Pilate (27.11). All four evangelists have Him answer the question if He was the King of the Jews. Luke makes Pilate affirm: "Look, nothing deserving death has been done by him" (23.15), *ecce nihil dignum morte actum est ei*, and the philosophical John connects the whole interrogation to the issue of veracity. In his version of it, Jesus states that He has come to the world only to bear witness to the truth – "Everyone who is of the truth listens to my voice" – to which Pilate gives his well-known reply: "What is truth?", *quid est veritas?* (18.37–38)

Sedulius in turn links this scene to the battle for epistemic authority that is at the centre of his poem. We have already seen him impress Christological truth on his readers by contrasting it with the classical sources exposed to his counter-imitation. Another strategy he applied for this purpose, reminiscent of Prudentius, was to anchor the message of his *Paschal Song* in the engagement of his own person, treating the poem as vital nutriment for himself and his readers, possibly on the basis of the administration of the Holy Communion. His account of Christ's many miracles would, from this perspective, be conceived as virtual sustenance put at the disposal of the poet's brothers and sisters in faith, in need of edification and hungering for truth.

The poet's personal involvement in the story he is telling is cleverly suggested by the many rhetorical questions, repetitions, and *ut* clauses of indirect command that intersperse his text, implying a strong personal presence behind its words: "Where should the Lord be hallowed, who hallows all things in creating them, / if not in a pious heart, if not in a pure breast? / Let him agree first that it is proper for us to hallow him by our worship" (2.244–47), *Sanctificetur ubi dominus, qui cuncta creando / sanctificat, nisi corde pio, nisi pectore casto? / Ut mereamur eum nos sanctificare colendo, / annuat ipse prior*. Rhythm, syntactical as well as verbal repetition, questions and exhortations cooperate to impress the poet's message. These devices are accumulated to convey his engagement in the story of the betrayal and scourging of Christ, complemented by figures of amplification – expressing particular *pathos*, as in the alignment of invectives directed at Judas Iscariot, "You bloody, savage, impudent, crazy, rebellious, / faithless, cruel, deceitful, venal, evil, / heartless traitor" (5.59–61), *tune cruente, ferox, audax, insane, rebellis, / perfide, crudelis, fallax, venalis, inique, / traditor immitis* – and by exclamations caused by overwhelming emotion: "Ah, how many tears / forestall me as I attempt to tell how the furious crowd / laid their unholy hands on him!" (5.94–96), *heu mihi quantis / impedior lacrimis rabidum memorare tumultum / sacrilegas movisse manus!* The deceit of Judas recalls that of the Edenic serpent, while the narrator sheds his tears over the suffering and sacrifice of Christ, truth (*verum*) personified.

Sedulius gave his work the name *Paschal Song*, he tells Macedonius at the end of his letter, since "Christ our passover has been sacrificed", *quia pascha nostrum immolatus est Christus*.[1] The reader is invited to partake of the poem as a meal, Carl Springer observes in his monograph. Sedulius' poem is presented in terms of food or nutrition, since its subject is Christ, the paschal lamb.[2] This idea has an obvious starting point in the Gospels' stagings of the Last Supper and Paul's exposition of "Christ, our Passover lamb" in 1 Corinthians 5.7. In addition, it recalls Luke's words on the partaking of bread in the kingdom of God (14.15) along with the entire sixth chapter of the Gospel according to St. John, in which Jesus expounds the Old Testament story of the manna in the desert (Exodus 16) as a presage of Himself: "I am the bread that came down from heaven" (6.41), urging the Galileans: "Do not work for the food that perishes, but for the food that endures to eternal life, which the Son of Man will give to you." (6.27)

Altogether, early Christian writers would readily present the Biblical texts as well as their own works in terms of nutrition, of sustenance with the power to appease the hunger for truth and salvation that pagan literature could only leave unsatisfied. This notion was exploited by the letter-writer Jerome in his interpretation of the parable of the prodigal son in the Gospel according to St. Luke (15.11–32). The husks that the starving swineherd longs to be fed with are interpreted by Jerome to signify the inadequate literature, philosophy and rhetoric of the pagans (21.13):[3]

> The food of demons signifies the poets' songs, secular knowledge and the pomp of eloquent words. They all allure us with their charms, and while they capture our ears with their rhythmical, softly modulated verses, they also permeate our souls, fettering our

---

[1] Sedulius 2013, pp. 218f.
[2] Springer 1988, p. 108.
[3] *PL* 22.385 (translation mine).

hearts. Indeed, when people have spent so many efforts and such an amount of work to read through these texts, they get nothing but empty sounds and the noise of words in exchange. They will neither find the satisfaction of truth nor the relief of justice. Those who carry on their studies there are still hungering for truth and are still in want of strength. (VIII)

Jerome captures both true (verbally inspired) and inauthentic (typically metrical, that is, poetic) discursivity in material terms. In the end, while the former is edifying and nourishing, the latter amounts to no more than meaningless noise filling the ears, remotely anticipating the *strepitus* that Augustine was obliged to return to after his and Monnica's shared moment of insight at Ostia. When the Bishop of Hippo argued in favour of the humble style, *sermo humilis*, in a letter from 411 or 412, he similarly conceived of the Bible text as a banquet and highlighted its truth as food for the reader: the Scripture "invites all with its lowly language. And it not only feeds them with the evident truth but also exercises them with the hidden truth" (137.5.18), *invitat omnes humili sermone, quos non solum manifesta pascat, sed etiam secreta exerceat veritate*. A comparable configuration, finally, is to be found in the introductory letter to Gregory the Great's commentary *Moralia, sive Expositio in Job* (*Morals on the Book of Job*), composed at the end of the sixth century; the author seems to be preparing a supper for his readers, serving up "the viands of discourse" appropriately, handling the Biblical announcements of truth in terms of "food for the refreshment of the mind" (3).[1]

Following the path of Jerome and Augustine, Sedulius – setting out to spread the message of the irrefutably true, however miraculous, deeds of Christ – takes as his starting point the only Writ that satisfies our hunger; Books II–V of his *Paschal Song* primarily retell events known from the Gospels, thus linking up with Juvencus. As we have been able to establish, however, it seems insufficient to categorize his Easter hymn as a paraphrase or *amplificatio*. In the prologue, where the author invites the reader to share his "paschal feast", *paschales dapes*, he makes it clear that his guests should not ask for an artistically consummate work: "and do not seek here a literary masterpiece", *nec quaeras opus hic codicis artificis* (PR.1–4). Evidently Sedulius exerted himself to camouflage the poem's inevitable characteristics of being an artefact, a text or literally a 'book', *codex artifex*, emphatically presenting it in terms of a Christological sacrificial meal. He made use of the modes of prayer, praise, curse or lamentation, inviting the reader to take part in an experience that would go far beyond purely

---

[1] "Vel certe quid veritatis dicta, nisi reficiendae mentis alimenta credenda sunt? Quae modis alternantibus multipliciter disserendo, ferculum ori offerimus", *PL* 75.513c. All English quotations from Gregory's *Morals* are from the edition of the Fathers of the Holy Catholic Church 1844.

aesthetic enjoyment or bookish instruction, namely participation in the Christian mystery, based on a consistently typological perspective on the events of the Gospels. As if to be able to accomplish this project successfully, Sedulius explicitly disconnected it from its classical predecessors in Latin epic poetry, firmly linking its message and purpose to the unconditional truth of the Holy Writ (in Book I). Consequently, he was given a rather fair posthumous review by his first editor, Turcius Rufus Asterius, Roman consul in 494, who dedicated an epigram to the *Paschal Song*, the work of a 'truthful poet', detached from 'the vice of fictionality', *veracis dicta poetae, / quae sine figmenti condita sunt vitio*.[1]

Avitus: Non-Fiction

The insistence on truth remains unshaken in the work of Avitus, Bishop of Vienne (a little south of present-day Lyon) in Burgundy, active around the turn of the sixth century, the author of the Biblical epic poem *De spiritalis historiae gestis* (*On the Events of Spiritual History*), composed in classical hexameters, devoted exclusively to a paraphrase of Genesis and Exodus. Avitus provided his work with a short prologue in the form of a dedicatory verse letter addressed to his brother and colleague, Bishop Apollinaris in the nearby town of Valence on the Rhone. In this introductory presentation, he put remarkably tough demands on the poets. Essentially, he exhorted them to completely adapt their discursive mode to their religious vocation, "as much according to the law of faith as that of metre", *non minus fidei quam metri lege*.[2] Avitus made it perfectly clear that the gravity and urgency of the Christian subject must inevitably reject the particular freedom to lie, *licentia mentiendi*, traditionally granted to poets as well as painters:

> For in writing secular verse one is called the more skilled the more "elegantly" one weaves – no, let's be honest, the more "ineptly". I'll say nothing now of those words or names on which we are not allowed to dwell (i.e. read eagerly) even in others' works, let alone write in our own. Because they can signify one thing through another, they provide useful shortcuts for poets. Therefore in the judgement of those who are secular, who will pardon both lack of skill and laziness, <...> we are not using the licence of poets. Once we have begun a work that is more tasking than enjoyable, we drew a firm distinction between divine censure and human opinion. (IX)

---

1 Sedulius 2013, p. 229.
2 Avitus' dedicatory letter is rendered according to D.J. Nodes's edition of *De spiritalis historiae gestis libri I–III*, 1985, p. 16, and, in translation (here with a slight modification), from D. Shanzer's and I. Wood's *Avitus of Vienne. Letters and Selected Prose*, 2002, pp. 260–62.

4 Biblical Epic Poetry: The Orthodoxy of Paraphrase — 571

Obviously there was still an educated aristocracy that considered Christian poetry to be a contradiction in terms, an attitude not unlike the one we have detected in Boethius, Avitus' great contemporary, who maintained a strict distinction between the divine intuition of the intellect and the activities of human imagination. Avitus now sees it as his duty to correct or modify such views, upheld by "those who are secular" cited in his dedication, but for this purpose he has to impose strong restrictions on his Biblical epic project. To start with, it was to be detached from all suggestions of make-believe. Christian faith is in fact compatible with poetic craft, the bishop claims, but it emphatically refutes fictionality, that literary self-indulgence which, by virtue of tradition, produces verbal fabrics on the basis of *falsa*.

In an important article, Michael Roberts has identified the background to this rigorous criticism of fiction, likewise noticeable a few lines further down in the letter to Apollinaris, where the author holds it safer for a clerk composing poetry to be deficient technically – to limp "in his metrical feet", *artis pede* – than to fall short "in tracking truth", that is, following *veritatis vestigium*. The early Christian writers, Roberts remarks, interpreted the classical conception of *licentia poetica* in the light of a neat distinction between matter and style, firmly established in Roman rhetoric. In one of his main theoretical works, the *Orator*, Cicero had analysed the habits of the "sophists" or epideictic speakers (adduced as a contrast to forensic or public orators) to both weave together myths – *intexunt fabulas* – and rely on highly figurated discourse, *verba altius transferunt* (19.65); in the former case, they enjoyed the freedom of matter, in the latter case, the freedom of style. The Christian poets accepted this distinction, Roberts concludes, rejecting the *licentia* of matter on grounds of doctrine – it was associated with pagan mythology – but all the more willingly accepting that of style, which made it possible for them to treat Christological themes with full-blown linguistic ornamentation, including tropes.[1]

Still, as we have seen, not even this technical or discursive licence proved acceptable to Avitus when dealing with Christian literature. His explicit censure of words and terms which "can signify one thing through another", providing "useful shortcuts for poets", *verba illa vel nomina... quae ad conpendia poetarum aliud ex alio significantia plurimum valent*, seems directed at tropes in particular. Roberts assumes that this disapproval specifically concerns mythological terminology: both eponymic metonyms such as Neptune for the sea, Vulcan for fire and so on, and simple periphrases such as the Thunderer for Jupiter, very com-

---

[1] See Roberts 1980, p. 401f.

mon in Prudentius and other early Christian poets.[1] Be that as it may, such criticism of figurative language would indicate a strikingly rigid attitude by the previously accepted standards of Christian Latin poetry, Roberts notes, possibly resulting from a particular sense of responsibility expected of a bishop in sixth-century Gaul. None of the Late Antique Biblical epic poets enjoyed such a high status within the ecclesiastical hierarchy as Avitus. He took great pains to maintain Catholic orthodoxy, hence his remarkably strict attitude towards the use of mythological terminology in Christian poetry. Nonetheless, his attempt to reinvigorate the old argument against *mendacia poetarum* met with little response. On this particular point, Avitus deviated from the general tendency of his time, during the approaching century embodied by poets such as Arator and Venantius Fortunatus (d. ca. 600), which made it increasingly feasible to assimilate the classical inheritance, including mythological language, into their new literature.[2]

Roberts presents a well-substantiated argument, although the integrative or assimilatory efforts of Arator, the next and last of our Late Antique Biblical epic poets, should not be overstated. If anything, Avitus and Arator, each in his own way, with a few decades between them, both demonstrate a rich variety of the anti-fictional proceedings and approaches that I have tried to trace throughout this presentation. If their dismissive attitude in this respect was not altogether characteristic of their transitional age, this is probably, as Roberts suggests with reference to Avitus, due to their positions in the ecclesiastical hierarchy. Any real open-mindedness or susceptibility to pagan culture was hardly to be expected of Catholic clerks or higher officials for a long time. It seems conspicuously absent in the epoch's most powerful pope, Gregory the Great, a learned theologian and an impressive Church leader whose ultimate outlook, in the words of E.K. Rand, was on eternity; he had no time "for comic mirth or Horatian urbanities".[3] This impatience or austerity might at least be inferred from two or three passages interspersed throughout the pope's extensive writings, frequently adduced as indicative of his attitude towards the classics.[4]

---

1 Roberts cleverly demonstrates how the wording *aliud ex alio significantia* occurs in Augustine's *On the Trinity* 15.9.15 and *Against Lying* 10.24, in both cases referring to allegory. The syntagm *aliud ex alio*, however, was also used to cover figures such as metonomy or synecdoche, Roberts adds, and would probably denote a number of tropes in Avitus' dedicatory letter as well, ibid., pp. 403f. This is already the case, on closer inspection, in *Against Lying*, not only in 10.24 but also in 13.28 (cf. above, pp. 236f.).
2 Roberts 1980, pp. 406f.
3 Rand 1929, p. 249.
4 A recent systematic treatment of these utterances is to be found in Moorhead 2013.

In the preface to his voluminous commentary on the Book of Job, *Morals*, designed as a letter to Bishop Leander of Seville, written in 595, Gregory explained the aim and organization of his work. This is an important prefatory piece, not least in view of the allegorical method used throughout the commentary. It will not always be possible for me, the author remarks, to pay close attention to the literal, historical meaning of the Book of Job, since the Holy Writ does not consistently provide us with plain facts; in those cases, the Biblical text is rather liable to engender error, as when the Vulgate tells us how those who carry the world – probably ancient sea monsters – bow beneath God (9.13), *sub quo curvantur qui portant orbem*. Gregory adds: "Now in the case of one so great, who can be ignorant that he never so follows the vain fictions of the poets, as to fancy the weight of the world to be supported by the labour of the giants." (1.3)[1] This comment refers to Leviathan and similar Old Hebrew behemoths but might also recall the antique myth of the Titan giant Atlas, who carried the celestial sphere on his shoulders: poetic nonsense, *vanae poetarum fabulae*, the pope tells us, which the great Biblical author would never approve of. Admittedly, then, the literal level of the Holy Scripture would sometimes be reminiscent of pagan fables, at least where the Biblical writers resorted to figurative discourse. In those cases, the commentator felt entitled to overlook the "superficial form" of the words, their contradictory and misleading *superficies*, being all the more intent on establishing the coherent mystical meaning inherent "within" them, *intus*.[2]

In short, Gregory identified more or less the same problems in the Old Testament texts (self-contradiction, absurdity, ostensibly idolatrous features) that had beset Augustine two centuries earlier, and his way out of this hermeneutic impasse – submitting the supposedly problematic passages to figurative or allegorical interpretation – seems modelled specifically on *On Christian Doctrine*. In addition to this concern with "the vain fictions of the poets", the pope had difficulty with the polish of rhetoric and the regulations of grammar in sacred contexts. This is evident from the same epistolary preface to *Morals*, where Gregory assures Leander that he has tried to circumvent the secular education he was brought up with (1.5):[3]

---

[1] "Et de tanto viro quis nesciat quod nequaquam vanas poetarum fabulas sequitur, ut mundi molem subvehi giganteo sudore suspicetur?" *PL* 75.513d.
[2] *PL* 75.514c.
[3] "Unde et ipsam loquendi artem, quam magisteria disciplinae exterioris insinuant, servare despexi. Nam sicut huius quoque epistolae tenor enuntiat, non metacismi collisionem fugio, non barbarismi confusionem devito, situs motusque et praepositionum casus servare contemno,

> And hence that art of speaking itself, which is conveyed by rules of worldly training, I have despised to observe; for as the tenor of this Epistle also will tell, I do not escape the collisions of metacism, nor do I avoid the confusion of barbarisms, and I slight the observing of situations and arrangements, and the cases of prepositions; for I account it very far from meet to submit the words of the divine Oracle to the rules of Donatus.

Even if such declarations were not unusual among the pious Fathers of Late Antiquity, Gregory's classification of rhetoric and grammar as pedantic or pedestrian arts with no relevance to the higher matters of theology is quite striking.[1] Altogether, Avitus' dismissal of "those words or names" employed by poets "because they can signify one thing through another" seems replicated in the pope's condescending attitude to tropes, *motus*, and other stylistic refinements, on top of everything articulated in one of the Middle Ages' most influential exegetic documents.[2]

Gregory proved just as suspicious of the benefits of grammar when he was informed of the rumour that Desiderius, a successor to Avitus in the episcopal see of Vienne, had taken up grammar teaching in his diocese. This was news that had immediately changed the papal assembly's good temper into distress and depression, the pope reported in an exhortatory letter to the bishop (54, written in June 601). That is because praise of Jupiter and Christ do not belong in the same mouth. To be sure, he had tried to ascertain that the rumour was false, Gregory asseverates in the same letter, but the mere thought of it gave him no rest. That is how distressed he was on hearing such things said about a man of the Church! It now remained for the pope to procure clear proof of the matter. When he had it in black and white that Desiderius was not meddling 'with trifles and secular literature', *nugis et saecularibus litteris*, he would thank God 'who did not allow your heart to be sullied with blasphemous praise of heinous things', *qui cor vestrum maculari blasphemis nefandorum laudibus non permisit*.[3]

---

quia indignum vehementer existimo, ut verba coelestis oraculi restringam sub regulis Donati." PL 75.516b.

1 For similar passages in Ambrose, Jerome, Augustine and Cassiodorus, see Riché 1962, p. 195. Moorhead is inclined to read Gregory's epistolary attack on grammar as an implementation of a topos of humility common in dedicatory letters, 2013, p. 255.

2 The translation of the ambiguous terms *situs* and *motus* is not self-evident, but the latter's meaning of 'trope' can be substantiated with reference to Quintilian 2001, 8.5.35 and 9.1.2. Gregory's disapproval of grammar was regularly re-enacted in early medieval theology, at least down to the twelfth century and works such as Peter Abelard's *Theologia christiana* (3.126, PL 178.1245b) and Alan of Lille's *Distinctiones* (Pr., PL 210.686–87), cf. Evans 1984, pp. 34f., 100.

3 PL 77.1171c–72a.

Gregory did not express himself more circumstantially than this, so his letter is difficult to assess. Some scholars – such as Henri de Lubac or Claude Dagens – have (probably quite rightly) preferred to downplay the pope's aversion to the liberal arts, in itself an instance of Christian rhetorical topics, but there is hardly any doubt of his ingrained distrust of fictional discourse, *vanae poetarum fabulae*. John Moorhead assumes, for good reasons, that it was the study of poetry rather than what we now think of as grammar that Gregory was concerned with.[1] It may be taken as further evidence of the thesis that the problem of fiction, touching on or including the question of mythological tropes, became more and more sensitive to clerks the higher up in the ecclesiastical hierarchy they ascended.[2] Thus when Bishop Desiderius exhibited a personal involvement on behalf of grammar teaching, he had, in view of this discipline's commitment to classical poetry, crossed the line into forbidden territory. Against the background of such papal fulminations, Avitus' dissociation from the poets' lies does not seem to be an isolated phenomenon at this advanced stage of Late Antiquity. As late as 601, the trite label affixed to secular poetry throughout the better part of the period – *nugae*, trifles – could be recycled by the very *pontifex summus* of the Catholic Church.

As in the case with Gregory's forays against grammar, several commentators have found it difficult to understand and evaluate Avitus' letter to Apollinaris. The problem seems partly due to their high appreciation of *On the Events of Spi-*

---

[1] Moorhead 2013, p. 256. Cf. Laistner 1935 and Irvine 1994, pp. 192f. De Lubac stages a virtual apology for Gregory in a learned article from 1960: the pope would have turned against decadent stylistic trends and a lingering paganism in the late sixth century rather than against profane culture or literature in general, pp. 193, 201. Dagens follows a similar line in his monograph from 1977: the *Morals* and the letter to Desiderius were not composed by any pious obscurantist but a deeply religious Church official, "protesting against the exaggerated pretensions of the art of grammar and against the immorality of pagan mythology", p. 34. In fact, both de Lubac and Dagens thus confirm the critical sting against fictional representation in Gregory's statements.
[2] Willy Evenepoel emphasizes that the fifth and sixth centuries' (comparatively) relaxed attitude to profane, and in particular mythological, topics among a number of Christian authors was, in several cases, repudiated by ecclesiastical dignitaries, 1993, pp. 58f. Isabella Gualandri dwells on the Gallic fifth-century poet Sidonius Apollinaris' deprecations of his own literary *nugae* after having been promoted to the bishopric of Clermont: they did not befit the *gravitas* of such an office, 1979, p. 10. Jerome, for his part, in a letter to Pope Damasus, had complained that 'we nowadays see even God's priests set the Prophets and the Gospels aside while reading comedies, singing love songs drawn from bucolic poems, keeping to Virgil, and turning what boys do out of necessity into a voluntarily sin' (21.13), *nunc etiam Sacerdotes Dei, omissis Evangeliis et Prophetis, videmus Comoedias legere, amatoria Bucolicorum versuum verba canere, tenere Virgilium: et id quod in pueris necessitatis est, crimen in se facere voluntatis* [*voluptatis*], PL 22.386.

ritual History, which is, for all practical purposes, the Late Antique Bible epic poem that remains most independent in relation to its source.[1] Obviously, the author's negative opinions on poetic activity do not seem compatible with his work's indisputable quality. After having meticulously registered one remark after another directed against poetic deceit and rhetorical ostentation in the letter to Apollinaris, even a sober-minded commentator such as Dieter Kartschoke benevolently attempts to ascribe "a new level of awareness" to Avitus, as if to play down or mitigate his criticism of fictional discourse.[2]

In my opinion, this effort to save Avitus, as it were, from his own disapproval of poetry seems at least questionable. As a matter of fact, the bishop deliberately aggravated the tension between pagan and pious literature, not only in his critical theory but in his poetic practice as well. The only thing profane and Christian works had in common was a set of rules and regulations: the craft of verse, metrics, and perhaps certain stylistic devices. Already the application of tropes, however, could – as we have seen – constitute a stumbling block for Avitus, and as soon as technical or rhetorical considerations seemed to prevail over the pious message, he deemed it necessary to back out. If, hypothetically, it was possible to account for every idle word that people had uttered, Avitus concludes his dedicatory letter to Apollinaris, we would quickly find that what caused most damage was "a liberty taken with forethought and practice that puts the law of speech before laws of [righteous] living", *quod tractatum adque meditatum, anteposita vivendi legibus loquendi lege*.[3]

That is how elegantly the Bishop from Burgundy expressed the sixth century's orthodox counterpart to the modern watchword "It's all about realism"! Of the five books of *On the Events of Spiritual History* – devoted to the story of the Creation (I – III), Noah and the Flood (IV) and the Exodus from Egypt (V) – it is principally the fourth that echoes this polemic against "the licence of poets". That is because the theme of Book IV, the Flood, naturally recalls the famous tale of Deucalion and his wife Pyrrha, centred on the primeval inundation of the earth, in the introduction to Ovid's *Metamorphoses* (1.253–415). Avitus,

---

1 Lately, Avitus scholarship has highlighted the poet's strikingly original amplifications of – or even deviations from – its Biblical model, most emphatically, perhaps, Ehlers 1985. Daniel J. Nodes takes "the general viewpoint" that, among all poets before Milton, Biblical epic poetry's various elements were brought together most successfully by Avitus, 1993, p. 118. Jacques Fontaine, however, arguably one of the foremost authorities on Late Antique poetry, does not share this positive view, discerning "an aesthetic, or rather anti-aesthetic, rigorism" and an exaggerated "literalism" in Avitus' poem, 1981, pp. 257, 260.
2 Kartschoke 1975, p. 72.
3 Avitus 1985, p. 17.

however, firmly refuses to indulge in any cross-reading of Genesis and Ovid, so as to turn the latter into a confirmation of the former. On the contrary, the Roman poet's mythical story is blatantly rejected as a "false tale" (4.3), *fabula mendax*, in the greatest possible contrast to the faithful version of the Biblical Flood he himself provides, "since I possess the truth" (4.8), *veri compos*.[1]

A little further on in the same book, the bishop becomes even more confrontational when he deals with the giants that, according to the Old Testament, occupied the earth before the Flood (Genesis 6.4, before long a nuisance, as we have seen, to Gregory the Great too): "The Nephilim [giants] were on the earth in those days, and also afterward, when the sons of God came in to the daughters of man and they bore children to them. These were the mighty men who were of old, the men of renown." Avitus reasonably associates this Biblical account with the giants of the Greek myth, whom, however, he categorically discards as being nothing but lies or erroneous vagaries. Owing to such poetical fancies about giants, ancient Greece had been dealing with contrived fictions (4.94), *commenta ficta*, and the old Thracian legend about these giants' war against the gods was quite simply, again, a *mendax fabula* (4.104). Avitus' verdict on his ancient predecessors is harsh, without any conciliatory tones at all: "These are the things the Greek poets in their lying poems tell of the terror bred by primeval giants" (4.108–09), *haec sunt priscorum quae de terrore gigantum / carmine mentito Grai cecinere poetae*.

Specifically, it is Ovid's *Metamorphoses* that appears as the main object of Avitus' polemic, even when he expresses it indirectly, with no mention of particular names or episodes. The Biblical epic poet certainly chose the target of his attacks carefully. Ovid's main subject, the theme of transformation, was designed to bring matters of fictionality to a head. His frequently detailed metamorphoses challenged or nullified reality's customary boundaries between man and nature, between gods and animals, between organic and dead matter, between species and sexes. Plato had already perceived precisely the transformation myths as paradigmatic for literary fiction (above, p. 28). In Avitus, they were to a great extent associated with demonic powers and proceedings. Here, we are in the second part of his work, where the fallen angel is about to ruin the bliss of Paradise. He is, on the whole, depicted as a quick-change artist (2.60–76):

---

[1] For *De spiritalis historiae gestis*, I follow the Latin text in N. Hecquet-Noti's edition 1999–2005. All English extracts from Avitus' poetic works are from G.W. Shea's translation 1997.

60   Et nunc saepe hominum, nunc ille in saeva ferarum
     vertitur ora novos varians fallentia vultus.
     Alitis interdum subito mentita volantis
     fit species habitusque iterum confingit honestos.
     Apparens nec non pulchro ceu corpore virgo
65   protrahit ardentes obscena in gaudia visus.
     Saepe etiam cupidis argentum inmane coruscat
     accenditque animos auri fallentis amore
     delusos fugiens vano phantasmate tactus.
     Nulli certa fides constat vel gratia formae;
70   sed quo quemque modo capiat teneatque nocendo,
     opportuna dolis clausaeque accommoda fraudi
     sumitur exterior simulata fronte figura.
     Maior adhuc etiam saevo permissa potestas,
     ut sanctum fingat. Dudum collata creato
75   sic natura valet, rectam quam condidit Auctor,
     sed post ad pravos subversor transtulit usus.

Often altering his appearance in this way and that, he puts on as a disguise now the face of men, now the savage visage of beasts. At times he will become all at once a counterfeit vision of a winged bird and feign again a virtuous mien. Or, appearing as a girl with a lovely body, he draws men's passionate gazes toward obscene joys. And often, for greedy men he will even shine as heaps of silver and fire their minds with the love of imagined gold. Then, once touched, he flees from the deluded fools, an empty fantasy. For in none of his shapes can one find abiding constancy or grace, but in whatever way he seizes and holds a man to do him harm, masking his real face, he assumes an outward visage fit for guile and suited to secret deceit. And even greater power than this has been granted to this savage creature to make himself appear holy. So it happened that Nature, which the Creator built true and bestowed upon the man he had created, remained sound for a while, but in time this creature bent on ruin turned it to his own depraved uses.

This is a Protean Satan, constantly undergoing transformation. In Avitus' impressing amplification of the scanty Biblical text, the Devil changes his shape (*varians*) as he pleases, easily crossing the boundary between human and animal, appearing as a series of ephemeral phantasms. There are a number of terms that indicate his chimerical nature: *mentita*, *apparens*, the repeated *fallens* and *simulata*, with a climax in the depiction of the souls thirsting for gold, deceived by "an empty fantasy", *vana phantasma*. This whole extract embraces a cluster of phrases – one of the richest I have found in Late Antique literature – virtually charged with implications of fictionality, in which Satan seems capable of simulating everything, including his opposite: a dignified and even holy appearance. Precisely to convey these stratagems, the most deceitful and criminal of all, Avitus resorts to derivations of the Latin verb *fingere*: in the former case *habitus confingit honestos*, "feign again a virtuous mien", in the latter *ut sanctum fingat*, "make himself appear holy". In this context, fictionality suggests (trans)figuration and is certainly not to be to relied on, quite the reverse: it appears as an instrument of cunning, *dolus*, and scheming in the dark, *clausa fraus*.

Avitus returns to the problem in identical terms when shortly afterwards Satan approaches Eve: "when the deceiver with his seductive treachery had put on the serpent's form and had insinuated himself throughout the entire snake, he hastened to the grove" (2.136–38), *ut viperream malesuada fraude figuram / induit et totum fallax processit in anguem, / pervolat ad lucum*. The evil one tempts Eve into perdition by means of dissimulation. Not only does he turn himself into a serpent, but the serpent's hissing is in turn changed into fair speech: "And so with evil intent, his hissing feigned flattering words" (2.161), *haec male blanditam finxerunt sibila vocem*. Thus Eve is exposed to a double illusion. When Satan finally achieves his purpose, he can logically enough end the whole game and let his apparition vanish into thin air: "leaving them trembling in a veil of smoke, his counterfeit body fled through the clouds and vanished" (2.422–23), *in media trepidos caligine linquens / confictum periit fugiens per nubila corpus*, an exit that seems to herald the finale of some mythological opera performance seconds before the curtain falls.

This ill-fated game of make-believe reappears further on in the work when the angel of the Lord gives Noah instructions about the ark. Bring all existing animals on board, the angel admonishes the patriarch, with one exception: beware of the serpent's "deceits" (4.274)! The might of Satanic *figmenta* is indeed tremendous in this Bible epic, a *potestas* that not only represents a remarkable amplification of the serpent in Genesis 3.1–15, but also, from a literary point of view, competes with its classical model, the Protean art of metamorphosis. The constellation is ingenious. Just as Avitus made sure to link his Satan to the ever-changing Proteus of *The Odyssey* and the *Georgics* (and in addition, it has been suggested, to Juno's description of the frightful Fury Alecto in the *Aeneid*, 7.335–40), he associates the whole range of fictional procedures with diabolic witchcraft.[1] Accordingly, his version of the fallen angel can be read as a continuation and an exacerbation of Prudentius' project to demonize fictionality, which here, construed as dissimulation, is held responsible for the ruin of mankind.

Yet even this Biblical epic poet would have felt that as soon as he began to reshape his sacred model in a classical mould, he ventured, at least potentially, into fictional space. Avitus too inevitably recycled phrases, formulas and themes

---

[1] Cf. Nicole Hecquet-Noti's comment in Avitus 1999, p. 195.

from classical poetry, first and foremost Virgil and Ovid, as required.[1] It is true that this paradox – in plain present-day language: to have one's cake and eat it too – was embedded in the genre, but judging by Avitus' letter to Apollinaris it should have been a particularly taxing source of worry for the bishop. Perhaps he also perceived it as a threat to his ecclesiastical dignity, hence his (even in this context) unusually frequent protestations of truth, of the precedence of "faith" and righteous "living" before art. As a matter of fact, it is quite conceivable that the purpose of the sophisticated art of allusion in *On the Events of Spiritual History* was to discredit rather than rehabilitate its classical models. An illuminating example of this literary antagonism is to be found in the first book of the work. There, Avitus allowed himself to counter-imitate Jupiter's famous words to Venus from *Aeneid* I about the "Empire that has no end" which he had granted to the Romans (1.279), *imperium sine fine dedi*, in God's words to Adam and Eve before the Fall: "Progeny I have given you without end" (1.175), *progeniem sine fine dedi*.

God acts curiously ironically here, not only in the obvious sense that the first couple's immediate progeny (after the Fall) were the hapless Cain and Abel. The irony of His words might also hit Avitus' great Golden Age predecessor. After the year 410, people knew all too well the extent to which ill-fated contemporary Roman reality corresponded to Jupiter's grandiose promise to his daughter from *Aeneid* I. In this retrospective light, Virgil's Jupiter and behind him Virgil himself would easily stand out as false prophets.[2] Thus Avitus' advanced anti-classical manoeuvre is as cunning as it is symptomatic. Since he did not have access to any mimetic concept of fiction in the Aristotelian tradition, where *fabulae* or *figmenta* by no means simply translate into *mendacia*, he would cut off rather than secure the possible links between Genesis and Virgil. Precisely where the Biblical and classical narratives cross, and where proponents of intercultural transfer such as Lactantius – and much later the Renaissance humanists – detected evidence of their assumptions about the ancient poets and philosophers as early theologians in pagan disguise, *prisci theologi*, the Burgundian

---

[1] On the reuse of Virgil in *On the Events of Spiritual History*, see Hudson-Williams 1966–67, pp. 15f., Arweiler 1999, where Avitus' literary ancestry is expanded to include Ovid and a series of other ancient and Late Antique poets, and Manfred Hoffman's edition of the work's third book, where the author's project is regarded as a "further development" or a "reaction" to the *Aeneid*, Avitus 2005, p. XLVI (for a critical discussion of earlier views on this topic, see p. XLVII, note 49).

[2] For this ironic treatment of the Virgilian heritage in Avitus, hardly even contemplated by Juvencus a century and a half earlier but already attempted by Prudentius, see Smith 1976, pp. 256–59.

bishop took the opportunity to separate and draw boundaries between the two cultures.

At the beginning of the work's fifth and last book, elaborating on the theme of the flight of the children of Israel from Egypt through the Red Sea, Avitus rejected with much greater emphasis than Juvencus or Sedulius all aspirations to personal renown or artistic brilliance. All he wanted to convey to posterity was authentic events, the historical salvation process as reported by the Bible, the Old Testament *gesta* framed as a series of *signa* or *figurae* (5.9–18). For instance, the water that flooded the earth in the fourth book and turned aside in the fifth book, allowing the Israelites to reach the promised land, presages the New Testament Baptism. Thus the design of *On the Events of Spiritual History* is controlled, like Sedulius' *Paschal Song*, by a typological approach. Here, strictly speaking, Avitus only followed established Christian exegetics, amplifying Paul's application of the notion of Baptism in 1 Corinthians 10.1–2: "our fathers were all under the cloud, and all passed through the sea, and all were baptized into Moses in the cloud and in the sea".[1]

To all intents and purposes, this Bishop of Vienne, the pious eulogizer of the Creation and the Virgin Birth, dealt exclusively with non-fiction. He considered his epic poem to be a kind of hymnal sermon in verse, an *enarratio* (commentary) or *amplificatio* of the Biblical text as well as a typologically framed glorification of Christ, the true hero – heralded by Adam, Noah and Moses – of the implied extension of his Old Testament evidence.[2] In at least two later documents that Karl Forstner has adduced, Avitus even went so far as to completely deny his Biblical poetry any claims to imperative or weighty writing. First, in yet another letter to Apollonaris (51), incidentally our only source for the work's title, he cited "the little book in which, in the midst of having to write serious and more pressing things, I had nonetheless disported myself – the one about the events of biblical history [*de spiritalis historiae gestis*] also in the form of a poem".[3] The choice of the word *lusi* to describe his past involvement with Biblical epic poetry is significant, suggesting mere entertainment and play rather than mature gravity.

Secondly, in the epistolary preface to his later consolatory poem *De virginitate* (*On Virginity*), dedicated to his sister Fuscina who had entered a convent,

---

1 Cf. Kirkconnell 1947 and particularly Ehlers 1985, pp. 355f. The Red Sea typology had already been exploited by Sedulius, 1.143–47, after having been long established within Christian tradition, see Daniélou 1946.
2 Cf. Hecquet-Noti's preface to Avitus 1999, pp. 33–65.
3 "Libellos, quos inter occupationes seria et magis necessaria conscribendi nihilominus tamen de spiritalis historiae gestis etiam lege poematis lusi". Avitus 1883, p. 80, English translation by Shanzer and Wood in Avitus 2002, p. 345. Cf. Forstner 1980, p. 50.

Avitus spoke in a similar way of the more dignified style, *gravior stilus*, demanded of his office and, in addition, of his high age. At this stage, it was time to set aside the kind of "writing that sings in verse to few who understand and measures syllables" in favour of "a more serious style", that is, "what serves many readers and has measured an increase of faith".[1] In his earlier poem, then, Avitus would have addressed a refined minority of readers, probably in possession of a classical education and capable of estimating his metrical skills. As for now, in *On Virginity*, the metre would only serve a functional purpose in order to enhance the cause of faith. Be that as it may, this last declaration does not seem to differ much from Avitus' original intention behind *On the Events of Spiritual History*, where he allegedly had been careful to proceed "as much according to the law of faith as that of metre". In both cases, he renounced emphatically all claims to provide aesthetic pleasure for pleasure's sake.

This somewhat reticent or implicit criticism of classical poetics is expanded into a full-blown attack in the introductory part of *On Virginity*, where the author broadly distinguishes between three kinds of poetry. First, he imagines his sister fulfilling her duties as a nun, including "that responsive and melodious singing of the psalms, which the living harp in your heart adapts to modest harmonies, using its own musical power and the chords within it" (6–8): *alternos recinens dulci modulamine psalmos, / quos vivens in corde chelys virtute canora / interiore sono castis concentibus aptat.*[2] Fuscina's singing virtually fills her entire person. The euphony of her mouth and the music of her heart merge completely, substantiating early psalmody's devout alternative, or rather corrective, to all kinds of artistic dissimulation. This would be the optimal type of poetry. Since Fuscina accomplishes her daily round so thoroughly, her brother, secondly, urges her to 'take delight in some scattered verse of mine, and relieve your tired soul in meditation' (9–10): *excusso libeat tibi ludere versu / atque fatigatam meditando absolvere mentem.* Hence the composition he now intends to present to her, for her consolation: this is poetry at its second best, aimed at meditation and edification. A phrase like 'scattered verse', *excussus versus*, fits in well with the opening lines (3–4), where terms like 'with a light pen', *levi calamo*, and "slight poem", *tenuis cantus*, implement the customary modesty topos.

---

[1] "Decet enim dudum professionem, nunc etiam aetatem nostram, si quid scriptitandum est, graviori potius stilo operam ac tempus insumere nec in eo inmorari, quod paucis intellegentibus mensuram syllabarum servando canat, sed quod legentibus multis mensurata fidei adstructione deserviat." Avitus 1883, p. 275, and, in English, Avitus 2002 (trans. Shanzer and Wood who, incidentally, prefer entitling this poem *De consolatoria castitatis laude*, "About the Praise of Chastity Intended to Console"), p. 264.

[2] *On Virginity* is rendered (in the original) according to Avitus 1883, pp. 285–94.

Thus edifying or meditative poetry, epitomized by this very composition, *On Virginity*, evidently constitutes a humble but still legitimate alternative to liturgical song. However, as the bishop categorically asserts, Fuscina will be spared the third and patently infamous type of poetry, characterized by the mythological tales of pagan literature (11–18):

11	Non hic fallaci tinguetur barbitus unda,
	Pegasus unde leves praevertens motibus auras
	fingitur adsumpto pendens hinnisse volatu,
	dum ferretur equi gravis ungula praepete pinna.
15	Sed nec Pierio ducent hic cantica ludo,
	quas sibi ter ternas mentitur fama sorores.
	Dat tibi germanum sed verax musica plectrum
	et Christum resonans claudetur fistula Phoebo.

This lyre is not tainted by the waters of falsehood, in whose accounts Pegasus is imagined outstripping the swift winds in his movements and then, after taking flight, whinnying in mid-air, as the hooves of a mighty horse are carried along on nimble wings. Nor do the Sisters whom tradition deceives itself by calling three times three inspire my songs in the trivial Pierian fashion, but truthful music presents you with a brother's plectrum true, and this, our pipe, echoing Christ, will be immune to Phoebus' inspiration.

The "waters of falsehood", *fallax unda*, is a fairly transparent allusion to the Castalian Spring, close to Delphi, where the Muses and Apollo were assumed to have refreshed themselves. It was supposed to have sprung forth where the winged horse Pegasus had struck the ground with his hoofs. Avitus sets out to reveal these legendary tales (along with the rumoured powers of inspiration traditionally ascribed to the Castalian Spring) as nothing but deceit. He explicitly repudiates the feigned Pegasus and its 'alleged flight', *adsumptus volatus*, across the skies. The nine Muses are in turn exposed as an invention of mendacious *fama*, and Apollo's panpipe must, more or less as in Paulinus of Nola (above, p. 493), fall silent when tones resounding of Christ are about to rise (by the agency, that is, of Avitus himself). The world of classical fiction is thus evoked by means of one synecdoche after another, only to be refuted and condemned. It proves to be deceitful in all its constituent parts, in its origin, its setting and its participants, while the music the poet's sister Fuscina will now be able to enjoy, her own brother's "plectrum" (a metonym for his poem), is guaranteed to be true, *verax*.

We recognize this anathema on the Muses from quite a few of the authors examined above, even if the poem's dismantling of the antique heritage is carried out with that particular, possibly paradoxical, elegance that characterizes the consummate stylist Avitus. But how are we to understand his unique verdict on his own Biblical poetry, given in *On Virginity*'s epistolary preface, as being nothing but rhythmically sustained diversion? According to Forstner, the explanation is that Avitus was still bound by the classical idea of poetry as light recreation, *otium*. The composition of such poetry seemed both an eloquent and an elitist activity that the ageing bishop had to dismiss.[1] We might just as well draw the conclusion that Avitus by now had given in to the critics he had once rebutted in his epistolary preface to *On the Events of Spiritual History*. In this late letter (51), he seems to understand all metrical activities, the writing (and probably reading) of pagan as well as Biblical epic poetry, as involvement in irresponsible kinds of wordplay. In voicing such anti-literary opinions, as it were, he sounds like a well-behaved, slightly mannered Tertullian. It is significant that already in the dedicatory letter for his Biblical epic poem, quoted above, Avitus had framed the classical notion of poetry's freedom to deviate from generally accepted history or facts, the *licentia poetica*, in terms of the right to lie, *licentia mentiendi*, an utterly disgraceful privilege.

The poetics that emerges from these graceful texts is indeed, in the words of Jacques Fontaine, shockingly reactionary.[2] The fact that it did not prevent the author from creating a substantial Biblical epic poem is, from our point of view, that of fictionality, less important. Since Avitus made revelation rather than mimesis the main concern of verbal art, and since he refused to acknowledge that the freedom of poetry was not reducible to the freedom to lie, he exerted himself to abjure his metrical leisure-time activities. In the eyes of this increasingly stern bishop, not even the doctrine of figuration or allegory's oblique speech could possibly redeem the classics. To all appearances, he completely lacked any operational concept of fictionality.

Arator: *Documenta*

Like his predecessors in the genre, Arator (d. around or shortly after 550), the last of the Late Antique Biblical epic poets, was counted among the minor classics throughout medieval literature. After a civil career as a lawyer and as a functionary at the court of Ravenna, he chose to retire from public administration in the middle of the 530s, a period characterized by increasing political turbulence and strong Byzantine pressure on Italy, during which he was ordained as a subdeacon of the Roman Church by Pope Vigilius. A few years later, in 544, on April 13,

---

[1] Forstner 1980, p. 51.
[2] Fontaine 1981, p. 256.

judging by contemporary accounts, he set out to personally recite the two books – encompassing more than two thousand hexameters – of his work *Historia apostolica* (*History of the Apostles*), a paraphrase of selected parts of the Book of The Acts, in the church of St. Peter in Chains in Rome.¹

The subject was original. As a rule, the earlier Biblical epic poetry had turned to the Pentateuch or the Gospels. Arator devoted, broadly, the first book of his work to Peter and the second to Paul. His recital is said to have gone on for several days and to have invigorated the applauding audience, who were under severe threat from both the north and the east. Totila, the penultimate king of the Ostrogoths, had already put Rome under siege, resulting in starvation and great hardship within the city walls, and Justinian had once again sent his brilliant general Belisarius to Italy. The place for the recital, St. Peter in Chains, was not chosen at random. The chains, *vincula*, that had fettered Peter – Vigilius' first predecessor on the Papal Chair – were preserved within the church as Catholic relics, hopefully warranting the eternal city's survival in times of crisis. This is the core message of the sole passage of the work that is known outside a narrow circle of specialists, the magnificent closing line of the first book, "He who opens the gate in heaven closes the way to wars" (1.1076): *Claudit iter bellis, qui portam pandit in astris.*²

With Arator, not only the mannered style but the allegorical (typological) approach to the Bible as a basis for paraphrase, present in Sedulius as well as Avitus, reached its culmination.³ Whereas the first Biblical epic poet, Juvencus, tried to keep as close to the Gospel text as possible, the genre's last Late Antique representative preferred to expand its elements of explanation and explicit interpretation. To this purpose, he benefitted from the episodic nature of Luke's text, which he emphasized even further in his own work. The occurrences involving Peter and Paul are listed one by one, provided with introductory headings in prose (giving the course of events in brief summary), interspersed with full-blown speeches by the apostles, and usually rounded off with allegorical ex-

---

1 The title of Arator's poem has long been known as *De actibus apostolorum*, given by A.P. McKinlay in his standard edition 1951. Nonetheless, it has been contested by several scholars, among them A.P. Orbán in his edition 2006, used in the present study, entitled *Historia apostolica*.
2 All quotations of Arator in English are from R.J. Schrader's translation volume 1987. For a survey of Arator's life and works, see Orbán's and Schrader's prefaces respectively and, in addition, Hillier 1993, pp. 1–19.
3 Cf. Thraede's informative article "Arator" 1961, p. 188. For Arator's style in general, see the investigation of Johannes Schwind 1995, and for his dependence on Sedulius in particular, see Schwind 1990, pp. 161–79.

planations, some of them polemic, frequently relying on etymology and mystical interpretations of numbers.[1]

In his exhaustive thesis on Arator, Johannes Schwind comes to the conclusion that 975 of the 2,326 lines of verse in *History of the Apostles* – that is, almost half the text – consist of such explanatory matter. A systematizing and exegetic tendency constantly interrupts the poem's narrative flow.[2] It is tempting to relate this episodic and didactic character of the work to the recital that Arator carried out for the pope in the church dedicated to the fettered Peter, although we do not know if he really wrote his poem with a view to any such performance. Altogether, his *History of the Apostles* resembles a series of mini-sermons: an extensive suite of versified pericopes, pedagogically introduced and allegorically annotated for the edification of the congregation, the pope and the city of Rome.[3] If Sedulius had conceived of his poem in sacramental terms – the Easter hymn as an oblation intended for the propagation of faith – Arator pushed his epic beyond the customary outposts of poetry, entering well into the genres of commentary and preaching. A markedly theological, didactic and ideological (or, more precisely, propagandistic, papal and anti-Arian) vein runs throughout his work.

Arator's modern publishers, Arthur P. McKinlay and Arpád P. Orbán, have both printed *History of the Apostles* with three verse dedications, one of which is to Pope Vigilius and another to the author's early friend (and perhaps tutor) from his years in Ravenna, Parthenius. The poem to the pope makes it clear how Arator envisaged the allegory in his work (19–30):

19 Versibus ergo canam quos Lucas rettulit Actus,
20   historiamque sequens carmina vera loquar.
     Alternis reserabo modis, quod littera pandit
         et res si qua mihi mystica corde datur.
     Metrica vis sacris non est incognita libris:
         Psalterium lyrici composuere pedes;

---

[1] The episodic character of *History of the Apostles* remains, even if the prose headings (*argumenta*) were interpolated by some later hand, as McKinlay believes, Arator 1951, p. 155. This assumption has later been confirmed by Hudson-Williams 1953, p. 91, and, most emphatically, by Schwind 1990, pp. 32–36.
[2] Ibid., p. 95. Cf. Kartschoke 1975, p. 93, and McClure 1981, p. 307.
[3] Cf. Fontaine 1981, distinguishing 43 segments in the two books of Arator's poem, each one comprising some fifty lines of verse, p. 262.

25 hexametris constare sonis in origine linguae
     Cantica, Hieremiae, Iob quoque dicta ferunt.
    Hoc tibi, magne pater, cum defero munus amoris,
     respice, quod meritis debita solvo tuis!
    Te duce tiro legor; te dogmata disco magistro;
30 si quid ab ore placet, laus monitoris erit.

> Therefore I shall sing in verses the Acts which Luke related, and following his account I shall speak true poetry. I shall disclose alternately what the letter makes known and whatever mystical sense is revealed in my heart. The power of poetry is not unknown in the Sacred Books; lyric feet formed the Psalter; they say that the Song of Songs, the sayings of Jeremiah, and also Job were composed in hexameters in the original language. Great Father, when I offer this gift of love to you, consider that I am paying the debts I owe to your merits. Under your generalship I am chosen as a new recruit; under your instruction I learn doctrines; if anything from my lips is pleasing, the glory will be the teacher's.

The poet puts himself resolutely at the service of the pope, like a simple foot soldier, taking advantage of the double meaning of the verb *legor:* he is not only drafted ("chosen") but will also, hopefully, be 'read' as Vigilius' recruit. Judging by lines 21–22, his paraphrase takes the form of an allegorical commentary that distinguishes at least two types of meaning in the Acts of the Apostles, one external and the other internal. The poet is about to "disclose" (unlock or open) both the meaning that "the letter makes known", the (external) literal sense, so as to meet the requirement for historical credibility, and the (internal) mystical sense which hopefully will be granted him *corde*, in his heart.[1]

This declaration of intent and these implicit instructions for reading are further specified within the poem itself, most systematically perhaps in the passage that reproduces Paul's farewell speech to the Ephesian Elders. In the Biblical text, the apostle reminds his audience that "for three years I did not cease night or day to admonish every one with tears" (Acts 20.31). Arator follows up these cautioning words with the following comment: "a figure is revealed by this reckoning [of his]: he who utters three doctrines of the Church rather often brings forth the historical and typical Book, proclaiming [also] a moral [sense]" (2.889–91, translation slightly modified), *patet hac ratione figura: / qui canit Ecclesiae tria dogmata saepius edit / historicum, morale sonans, typicumque volumen.* Thus Arator registers three of the four meanings that would be adduced in many medieval commentaries on the Holy Scripture (the so-called *quadriga*, cf. above, p. 246): the historical, the moral and the typological. We

---

[1] Cf. 2 Chronicles 9.23: 'to hear his wisdom, which God had put into his heart', *ut audirent sapientiam quam dederat Deus in corde eius.*

shall soon see him implement figurative representation on various levels more consistently than any of his Biblical epic predecessors, while simultaneously subjecting this particular type of discourse to a critical analysis running throughout his work.

Here, in theory, there is not much room left for any inventive revisions or modulations of the Lucan text. In his monograph on medieval Latin poetics, Paul Klopsch even ventures the hypothesis that Arator's dedication to Vigilius inaugurates an entirely new type of literature, "true poetry", *carmen verum*, a label that earlier would have seemed oxymoronic.[1] That is possibly going too far, but the verbs Arator uses to describe his writerly activities are certainly indicative of his idiosyncratic self-understanding as a poet, halfway between verbal inspiration and critical exegesis. He is going to *follow* the historical layer in the Acts of the Apostles, *disclosing* their meaning, including their mystical sense – provided that it is *revealed* or 'given' to his heart. The poet, or actually the rewriter/decoder, presents himself as a recipient with the passive verb form *datur*, but appears in turn as the supplier of a "gift", a return of favours, to his papal protector.

Arator's linking of his project to classical poetry is subtle but unmistakable, not only in its combination of instruction (*dogmata disco*) and pleasure (*placet*), both generously credited to Vigilius' influence, but, furthermore, in its configuration as a votive offering. Still, whereas Horace, Ovid and the other pagan poets had brought their "gifts" to lavish patrons, it is now the pope who is honoured according to his merits. In addition, Arator presents his Biblical paraphrase as a *munus amoris* – a tribute of (Christian) love – to his pontifical superior, virtually outdoing the equivalent offerings from his predecessors, dictated by the gift economy of imperial Rome. Correspondingly, Charles Witke has pointed out that Arator appealed to Hebrew rather than Latin precedents in order to legitimize his paraphrasing activities: to expound sacred things in verse.[2] Beyond the Romans and beyond the Greeks, there was always the literary example of the Hebrew writers to turn to, those *libri sacri* of the Old Covenant, written in mankind's original language.

The dedication to Pope Vigilius clarifies the author's hermeneutic starting point (the various levels of sense), legitimizes his paraphrase in verse and implements the expected formulas of subservience, modesty and sacrifice. The same range of topics is present in the verse letter to Parthenius, the confidant of Ara-

---

[1] Klopsch 1980, pp. 11f.
[2] Witke 1971, p. 220.

tor's youth. Here, however, it is more intimately framed, first and foremost in the poet's recollections of the lessons and tutorials of bygone days (41–58):

41 Cantabas placido dulcique lepore poetas,
        in quibus ars fallax, pompa superba fuit.
    Sed tamen ad veros remeabas, optime, vates,
        quorum metra fides ad sua iura trahit,
45 qualis in Hyblaeis Ambrosius eminet hymnis,
        quos posito cunis significastis, apes,
    qualis in hac eadem Decentius arte manavit,
        Arvernisque canis, <Sido>niana chelys.
    Cura mihi dudum fuerat puerilibus annis
50   versibus assiduum concelebrare melos,
    scribere quas etiam simulavit fabula partes
        et per inane fretum sub levitate rapi.
    Quae cum nostra tibi fragilis cecinisset arundo
        et mihi, care, tuus saepe faveret amor,
55 "O utinam malles" dixisti "rectius huius
        ad Domini laudes flectere vocis iter,
    ut, quia nomen habes, quo te vocitamus, Arator,
        non abstrusa tibi sit sed aperta seges!"

> You used to recite with a calm and pleasing charm the poets in whom was a deceitful art, a proud display. But nevertheless, o most excellent one, you kept returning to the true bards whose lute draws the meters to its own laws, such as Ambrose, who excels in the Hyblaean hymns which you, o bees, foreshowed to him lying in the cradle; such as Decentius, who abounded in this same art, and you, o Sidonian lyre, [who] sing among the people of Auvergne. It had long been my concern in the youthful years to pursue continual song in my verses, to write of the roles which myth invented, and to be carried off in the power of shallowness through an empty channel. When my fragile reed had sung these things to you, and dear friend, your love was often supporting me, you said, "Oh, would that you had chosen more properly to turn the path of this voice toward praises of the Lord! so that, as you have the name by which we call you, Arator, the crop might not have been hidden, but instead accessible to you."

These dedicatory verses are touched by a polemic note. Arator strategically overlooks the philosophical or didactic aims of pagan poetry in order to emphasize its recreational, hence frivolous aspects. Terms such as *placidus*, *dulcis* and *lepor* (41) are operative in this context, established in Latin literature since the heyday of Catullus and the elegiac lyricists. Here, however, they are explicitly associated with poetry's deceitful and fabulous matters as well as with its pompous style. They are certainly put in sharp contrast to the "true bards", *veri vates*, that the author's cherished friend used to revert to, such as Ambrose, Sidonius Apollinaris (ca. 430–85) and possibly the late fifth-century Biblical epic poet Dracontius, all Christian writers who knew how to adapt their technique to their message rather than the other way round.[1]

Even in this dedicatory address, then, the apologists' old fire at least makes itself felt. Arator, like his predecessors in the genre, highlights the truth of the Biblical episodes at the cost of the poets' proverbial lies: their *ars fallax*. This becomes even more apparent within the work, when the young man Eutychus is wakened from his apparent death (cf. Acts 20.9–12). This event takes place in the seaport of Mysia in Asia Minor, Troas, south of ancient Troy, quite close, that is, to what might be thought of as the very epicentre of classical fiction. Arator takes advantage of this metonymic vicinity, explicitly substituting Troy for Troas (2.753–56):

> 753 Tu quoque signa ferens titulos in carmine nostro,
>   Troia, repone tuos et laudibus adde triumphos,
> 755 qui magis ex vero fulgent tibi clarius actu
>   quam quae pomposo reboant tua bella cothurno!

> You also, o Troy, carrying your standards in our song, put aside your claims to glory and add to your praises triumphs which shine forth for you more brightly from a true action than do those wars of yours which resound in ornate tragic poetry.

The poet addresses the old city with an epic apostrophe, celebrating Paul's "true" miracle while downplaying the old Homeric wars, now fading into legend. Once again, Christian veracity, however miraculous, outshines pagan fiction, however rooted in history. In addition, typically, the cognitive argument 'this is true' is immediately followed by a rhetorical or stylistic corollary: 'that is ornate', *pomposo*, hence suspect from the very start.

The lesson seems crystal clear. In the kind of pagan literature where pleasure (rather than profit) is given pride of place, the extent of ornamentation is in proportion to the degree of fictionality. External pomp and splendour, ostentatious and elegant adornment, correspond to unsubstantial games of make-believe. In order to press home this censure of pagan fiction, Arator adopts a self-critical pose that would be recycled by quite a few self-styled penitents in Western literature (most famously Petrarch): that of the mature poet's sometimes melancholy, sometimes regretful recollections of his youthful missteps. Such a remorseful glance on the author's erroneous past cannot but highlight his present integrity and accuracy. In Arator's dedicatory verse letter to Parthenius (49–52), the poetry of his youth – focused on song and myth, *melos* and *fabula*, that is, blemished by traditional Roman taste, loaded with fabulous tales and anx-

---

[1] Cf. Schrader 1977, p. 66.

ious to please – is metaphorically evoked as an erratic ship, rolling to and fro on an empty sea, *inane fretum*. As is frequently the case in Late Antiquity, critical dissociations from classical literature are framed precisely on the basis of a classical topos, the voyage of writing, here followed by the equally conventional reference to the youthful poet's 'fragile reed pipe' (53), *fragilis arundo*, characteristic of the bucolic genre.

In line 57 of the verse letter to Parthenius, the addressee's alleged allusion to the author's name, Arator, the Latin word for ploughman, is a subtlety typical of the whole work, rich in etymological devices explicitly commented on by the poet himself. When describing Paul's arrival in Corinth, he dwells on the host who received the apostle in his house, the tentmaker Aquila, mainly because his name means 'eagle' in Latin, the bird that, according to an old legend, soars towards the sun at the end of its life, whereupon it is burnt by the heavenly body's overwhelming light and tumbles into the waves, only to rise again, rejuvenated, from the waters: in this context, a figure denoting the regeneration of Christian man by Baptism. Arator comments (2.521–24): "Lest by chance the allegory should lie hidden under ambiguity, I shall sing in what manner is granted [to me]: holy Scriptures often sang that arguments are drawn from a name and the greatest teachings [thence] arise."[1] It is typical of Arator that he refused to be content with the indeterminate suggestiveness that was (and probably still is) associated with fictional discourse. He implemented his figures *sub ambiguo* only to resolve them in an unequivocal sense, *ratio*, ostensibly following the example of the Holy Writ. Thus the rich range of allegories, personifications, mystical numbers and etymologies in *History of the Apostles* conceals certain indispensable "teachings" or doctrines, *documenta*, continually disclosed by the author himself for the benefit of his readers. For that very reason, like few other works examined in this study, Arator's poem stands out as one of the cradles of medieval literature.

*

History of the Apostles, then, seems to represent a turning point between two eras. On the one hand, like practically all Late Antique Biblical epic poetry, it involves a range of adaptations or counter-imitations of classical formulas and *loci*. God is called "the Ruler of Olympus" (1.37), *rector Olympi*, or the "Thunderer" (1.49), *Tonans*, and the two main characters of the work are identified as "the two lights of the world" (2.1219), *duo lumina mundi*, exactly the same epithet attributed to the gods Liber (Bacchus) and Ceres in the *Georgics* (1.5–6): *clarissima*

---

[1] "Tecta sub ambiguo lateat ne forte figura, / qua dabitur ratione canam. De nomine saepe / argumenta trahi documentaque maxima gigni / Scripturae cecinere piae."

mundi / lumina. On the other hand, *History of the Apostles* relies on a whole series of metafictional comments with no parallels in classical epic poetry but with a number of offshoots in later medieval authors such as Alan of Lille or Dante. It is not least for this reason that Richard Hillier chooses to describe the relationship of Arator's work to the Acts of the Apostles as that of a verse commentary rather than as a Bible paraphrase.[1]

We find a clear example of this metareferential, self-registering mode in the final part of *History of the Apostles*, when, during Paul's voyage to Rome, his ship is struck by a storm, depicted principally after the models of Virgil's *Aeneid* (1.81–123) and Lucan's *The Civil War* (5.561–653). The violent winds soon abate, we are told, because the author himself does not want to risk running aground (2.1081–86):

```
1081     Vastas percurrere Syrtes
         historica ratione vocor lacerosque rudentes
         et clavi fragmenta sequi, sed non ego linguam
         tam fragilem committo vadis rapidasque procellas
1085  aufugiam temptare diu, ne forte canenti
         obruat exiguam violentior unda loquelam.
```

> On historical grounds I am called to traverse vast quicksands and pursue mangled halyards and the fragments of the rudder, but I do not commit so frail a tongue to the sea, and I will flee from trying too long the swift gales, lest perhaps a too violent wave drown the meager language for the singer.

This passage nicely illustrates Arator's complex relation to his predecessors. It excels in neat formulas of modesty (the poet's frail tongue and meager language), and in view of the battery of terms drawn from classical epic tradition used to depict the storm, the "too violent wave" in line 1086 might reasonably be read as a reference to the superiority of the author's mighty precursors. Arator does not intend to dwell on the storm, since a long description would only reveal his artistic inadequacy in comparison with overwhelming masters such as Virgil or Lucan: his voice runs the risk of being drowned in theirs. This reading, too, is supported by the old topos of writing as a sea voyage. At the same time, however, it must be emphasized that the most important model text for Arator is (of course) the Acts of the Apostles. Ultimately, his story of the storm is an *amplificatio* of Acts 27.14–44. He modifies, amplifies and expounds an even more authoritative – and, significantly, more "historical" – source than any Latin classic. In his *History of the Apostles*, the modesty topos thus signals a genre with strong

---

[1] Hillier 1993, pp. 153, 155.

ingredients of paraphrase and commentary. It is precisely this metafictional and paraliterary character of the work that, somewhat paradoxically, warrants its innovative force. The fact that earlier generations of scholars sometimes frowned on this kind of textual parasitism need not trouble us. It is mainly Arator's forward-looking project that occupies us here, and for this achievement his fleeting transitions between amplification, allegory and exegesis/commentary play a crucial role.

Notwithstanding such pioneering devices, the poetics emerging from *History of the Apostles* proved incompatible with all concepts of fictionality. In Arator too, any suggestion of *ficta* was cut short by the poet's ideas of inspiration as well as revelation. On several occasions, his comments on his own text are introduced by formulas of modesty such as "if we are rightly inspired" (1.837), *si iure movemur*, that is to say: if we are being guided or literally 'moved' (= inspired) in the right direction, if we (or I) have understood the matter correctly... The author restates and expands one pericope after the other as if to appear as an inspired exegete, a *praedicator* rather than a *narrator*.[1] As a rule, this type of vatic discourse avoids any references to classical sources; it rather seems to have at least one of its starting points in Luke's description of the miracle of the Pentecost (Acts 2.1–13), in *History of the Apostles* designed as a virtual negation of established literary or learned activities: "no letter did its duty, no vein of genius dripped from the ear, nor did wax imprint the notable sayings" (1.123–25), *non littera gessit / officium, non ingenii stillavit ab aure / vena, nec egregias signavit cera loquelas*. Arator thus suggests a new source for the narrative voice of his text, *nova vocis origo*, the origin of another kind of inspiration and another kind of speaking than that of the scholarly rhetor, a matrix which alone will suffice for all the world's orators (1.127–29). In this kind of virtually glowing or blazing discourse, there is (theoretically) no room for any privileged poetic licence or fanciful fabrications whatsoever, since such speech is a divine gift that the poet can only hope to receive from the Spirit of the Lord: "give the gifts of language, You who give languages as a gift" (1.227), *munera da linguae, qui das in munere linguas!*

At his most detailed, Arator returned to such exalted language in his depiction of the Baptism at Ephesus (described in Acts 19.1–6), where Paul sees to it that certain disciples are washed in a "sacred river", *flumen sacrum*. The Holy Spirit immediately fills their mouths, enhancing their usual powers with "a shower of words", *verborum imber* (2.574–76). This episode culminates with the following invocation (2.577–83):

---

[1] Roberts 1985, p. 179.

577 Saepius arma movent ista de parte profani
    et bellare parant: quibus ut contraria possim
    fundere tela loquens, tu nunc mihi largius ora,
580 spiritus alme, riga, sint ut tibi dogmata digna,
    quae dederis! Tu vocis iter, tu semita linguae,
    tu dicture, veni, qui per tua munera semper,
    quod reddamus, agis donique resuscipis usum!

> The profane too often set these weapons [words] in motion and prepare to fight according to their faction; so that I might in speaking pour forth missiles against them, now, o fostering Spirit, moisten my mouth more copiously, that the teachings which You have given might be worthy of You! You road of speech, You path of language, You who are to speak, come, You who, through Your favors, always set in motion what we give back and [who always] recover [our] employment of Your gift!

The cautionary words about "the profane" and their inspired warfare may be interpreted in several ways. They may refer to a general attack on the Catholic faith, an imminent threat during the better part of the turbulent sixth century, possibly with an allusion to Totila's trying siege of Pope Vigilius' Rome at the time of writing. They might just as well appertain to the Pythian or vatic pretensions of the pagan poets, and they most probably contain a reference to those Ephesians who "continued in unbelief, speaking evil of the Way before the congregation" in Luke's Acts (19.9). In any event, it is time for Arator to launch a counterattack, predictably assisted by the Holy Spirit, accomplished by means of a metaphor drawn from the enemy camp, specifically Virgil. Klaus Thraede has aptly characterized the construction "road of speech", *vocis iter*, replicated in the verse letter to Parthenius (56), as a "theological transfer" of the corresponding formula from the *Aeneid* (7.534).[1] While Virgil had merely implemented a periphrase for the throat of a slain warrior, Arator stages an affected and threefold apostrophe of the Holy Spirit, thereby locating its presence to the very organs of speech: "You road of speech, You path of language, You who are to speak"... Even if his chiastic construction *vocis iter, semita linguae* were to allude to Sedulius' corresponding configuration *lucis via, semita pacis* (above, p. 566), it differs from his predecessor's syntagm by precisely this physiological anchorage of the transcendent power.

Thus the idea of inspiration in *History of the Apostles* is exposed to a kind of infinite loop. The Holy Spirit is summoned to shower upon the poet but is also projected onto his speech organs, and as if that were not enough, it finally becomes the recipient of his words, "recovering" the gift it has bestowed on

---

[1] Thraede 1961, p. 192.

him. Consequently, all the key points of the communication process – the sender, the medium and the recipient – are met by the Spirit. Nothing is really left to the author's own initiative. To all intents and purposes, this was a particularly efficient way to keep poetry's propensity for introducing mimetic, not to say fictional configurations at bay.

That is how Arator managed the new authorial concept of Christianity, sketched in terms of divine supervision. The poet's speech actually originates in God or in the Spirit, in accordance with God's continual configuration of His Creation: "You, o God, [are He] who makes all living things in their proper forms by a creative word, and who beholding them on high sees them beforehand, and who begets the shapes of things through their names" (1.338–40), *Tu, qui cuncta, Deus, propriis animata figuris / artifici sermone facis quique edita cernens / ante vides rerumque creas per nomina formas*. This notion of an authorial God transmitted a remarkably powerful impulse to the Christian literature of the High Middle Ages: the topos of the Creator as the first (and highest) Orator, already present in Augustine (above, p. 215). The Creation became God's language, the marvels of Creation became His figures. Such concepts were to exercise a decisive influence on Alan of Lille who, in his epic poem *Anticlaudianus*, would launch a spectacular version of the Godhead as a rhetorically consummate *artifex:* "however he conceives everything by means of a trope and by way of a figure" (5.126–27), *cuncta tamen, mediante tropo, dictante figura / concipit*.[1]

The writerly God of Arator's *History of the Apostles* is a projection of the poet, the epic I, and is in turn reflected in his figure. They are both construed as speakers focused on *elocutio*, dealing with a range of stylistic devices, with the crucial difference that the poet must ultimately fail in his discursive and creative efforts where God paradigmatically succeeds. This is particularly evident when Arator presents his version of the Acts of the Apostles 5.12–16, which narrates how Peter cures sick and possessed people in the streets of Jerusalem (1.459–63):

459   O mihi si cursus facundior ora moveret
460   centenosque daret vox ferrea, lingua diserta
      hac in laude sonos, quantum speciosior esset
      ambitus eloquii, variis aperire figuris
      singula nec modicis includere grandia verbis,
      […].

Oh, if a more eloquent flow of words might move my lips, and an untiring voice and expressive tongue might give a hundredfold sound in this praise [of Peter], how much more splen-

---

[1] I follow J.J. Sheridan's translation 1987 and R. Bossuat's edition 1955 respectively.

did would be the expression of my eloquence, to reveal each detail with diverse figures of speech, and not to confine grand deeds with undistinguished words!

This topic could hardly be more thoroughly tried and tested. The voice of iron reverberating with hundreds of sounds echoes a well-known formula of modesty in ancient literature. Its *locus classicus* is to be found in the *Georgics* as well as in the *Aeneid*, and it had come back into favour with the Biblical epic poets. We have already examined the topos in Sedulius (above, p. 565), and it had been applied with the same skill and to the same effect by Avitus in *On the Events of Spiritual History*.[1] Arator, however, employed the formula to signal, more clearly than his predecessors, his stylistic aims. His elevated subject, the gifts of the Spirit and the acts of the apostles, required a correspondingly dignified and ornate literary treatment. Thus the subdeacon implicitly dismisses the entire *sermo humilis* project. Great events, *grandia*, do not easily lend themselves to plain – "undistinguished" or modest – words.

Even more explicitly than Juvencus, then, Arator aimed at a decorous rather than a humble style in his epic poem. His references to the powerful and captivating forms of expression, the discourse that is *facundus* or *disertus*, suggest primarily the *genus grande*, the high style. It colours the many speeches Arator has included in his poem, a dramatic feature that should have appealed to the audiences at St. Peter in Chains and certainly contributed to the work's popularity in the Middle Ages. But on the whole, this writer's particular eloquence does not depend so much on pathos or elegance as on an abundance of figures, *variae figurae*, characteristic of the intermediate style, a plethora of periphrases, enigmas and all sorts of tropes. In addition, as we have already noted, he is anxious to disclose the meaning of his covert speech, in stark contrast to all kinds of poetics coloured by Ovidian fictionality, where the burden of interpretation is entrusted to the readers or listeners. Arator typically implements his figures while explicitly stressing their mystical – though ultimately inadequate – nature. The poet, as it were, encodes and decodes his work simultaneously, in full view of his audience.

This peculiar method comes to the fore in the passage that amplifies the perhaps most famous lines from the Acts of the Apostles, Paul's speech to the Areopagus in Athens (17.16 – 34), already admired and recycled by Augustine (above, pp. 136, 145f.). Here, by subtle means, Arator contrasts the new Christian faith

---

1 Avitus had reused this topos in order to highlight the impossibility of describing the misery that afflicted the posterity of Adam and Eve. Not even "he whom Mantua gave to the world", *quem Mantua misit*, Virgil (responsible for the conclusive design of the formula!), or 'the Lydian', *Maeonius*, that is Homer, would have been able to manage this tour de force, 3.333 – 37.

with the ancient pagan civilization. The apostle is portrayed in renowned Athens, famous for its masterminds, *ingenii*, and for its eloquence, *linguae*. Consequently, he strategically confronts his opponents with their own weapons: learned as well as profuse and ornate discourse, a "torrent" of eloquence, *eloquium torrens*. In contrast to the Greeks' speech, however, Paul's language expresses the divine will. In the eyes of the Athenians, he stands out as a "sower of words", *verborum sator* (2.443–47).[1] These verbal seeds, *semina*, are soon illustrated by the speech the apostle directs at the Areopagus regarding their altar to an "unknown God" (2.457–73):

457   Vos cernimus aram
         ignoto posuisse Deo, qui condidit astra,
         qui pelagus terrasque dedit, quem vita parentem,
460   ut moveamur, habet, cuius spiramus ab igne,
         cuius imago sumus, de quo cecinere poetae
         hinc hominum constare genus, quem praedico: "Cuncta
         sanxit ab ore suo." Cur haec divina vocatis,
         quae facitis, vacuoque metu caeleste putatis
465   auxilium, quod gignit humus? Natura metalli
         visceribus iacet ima soli, quibus eruta sumit
         ingenii fabricantis opem, seu numina templis
         hinc veniant seu vasa focis; sibi causa timori est,
         ars operata deos; Dominum super omnia fusum
470   claudere nemo potest parvisque artare figuris;
         quod capitur, minus est spatio capientis. In auro
         materia est; opifex rerum non sustinet usum,
         quem simulant, quos ipse creat.

We see that you have set up an altar "to the unknown God," who formed the stars, who gave the sea and the land, whom life has for a parent in order that we may be capable of motion, from whose fire we draw breath, whose image we are, of whom the poets have sung that from Him the human race has its being: [it is He] whom I preach: "He has consecrated all things by his mouth." Why do you call divine these [idols] which you make, and think with empty fear that help which the earth brings forth is heavenly? The essence of metal lies lowest in the bowels of the earth; dug out from there it receives the aid of the talent which fashions it, whether there should come from it gods for the temples or pots for the hearth; the skill which has produced the gods is the cause of your fear; no one can shut in a Lord extended beyond all things and press Him together into small shapes; what is contained is smaller in size than [what] contains [it]. Your material [for cre-

---

1 Arator's amplification of the nickname the Athenians bestow upon Paul in Acts 17.18, the Vulgate's *seminiverbius*, 'sower of words' (a rather misleading translation of the Greek pejorative *spermologos*), is possibly, as Schwind supposes, dependent on Augustine's *sermo* 150.10, 1990, pp. 196f.

ation] is in gold; the Artisan of the universe does not sustain the practice which they simulate, [they] whom He Himself created.

The anonymous divinity proves to be identical with the Christian God, the Creator of heaven and earth. The Athenians, however, had made the mistake of confusing this all-pervading power with the images they had made of Him. Accordingly, they devoted their worship to pictures, sculptures or monuments, to lavishly adorned idols in marble or gold, at the cost of what these effigies represent. But such figures are, after all, only made up of metallic matter extracted from the bowels of the earth. Once again, Arator emphasizes the risk of confounding incidental means of art or artifice with their divine sense. The former can be used for sacred as well as profane purposes, great or small, for an altar or a hearth, whereas the latter is unique. The Lord is not to be found in effigies of metal, figures of rhetoric or in any human imagery whatsoever. If people turn man-made carvings or pictures into cult objects, into idols to fear and to worship, they are embarking on a game of make-believe, *simulatio*, entirely incompatible with the true originator, *opifex*, of the universe.

The Athenians' veneration of their altar to an unknown god seems indicative of the use of fiction in pagan culture, as Arator understood it, a "skill which has produced the gods" (2.469), *ars operata deos*, characterized by a complex figurative language that had become an end in itself. This mode of representation differs greatly from the Biblical style, whose substantial metaphors and allegories basically refer to Christ, the Church and the story of salvation. Arator transferred applicable parts of this Pauline reference system from the Acts of the Apostles to his *History of the Apostles*, complemented as required by his own additions, partly to disclose its unequivocally divine sense and partly to elucidate the fundamental tension between human imagery and sacred doctrine, that is, between what he called *figurae* and *documenta*.

Hence it is his metafictional procedures that so clearly distinguish Arator from his Biblical epic predecessors. The actual narrative of his work is supplied with a running commentary on the narrated events, continually examining their figurative purpose and signification. Considering this intriguing dual discourse, it would be possible to characterize *History of the Apostles* as a piece of "paraliterature", a poetic work in which the author appears as its first reader, a narrative that repeatedly turns into a justification of its representational mode and an interpretation of its figures of speech.[1] That is why medieval readers, Bede and others, could regard it precisely as a regular Bible commentary.[2]

---

[1] It was probably Linda Krauss who, inspired by certain works of Roland Barthes and Jacques

Their judgment is understandable. After all, uncovering figurative meaning had long been one of philology's main responsibilities. Two hundred years earlier, Lactantius had in a similar way set about the task of interpreting the pagan myths in his *Divine Institutes*. To present Saturn as the offspring of heaven and earth was an absurdity, he observes, or rather a literary fiction, *poeticum figmentum*; hence he deemed it expedient to "seek the element of truth which lurks beneath this image" (1.11): *quaeramus ergo quid veritatis sub hac figura lateat.*[1] For Arator, it is a matter of impressing his discursive configurations' 'evidence' or 'teachings', *documenta*, on his audience. An alternative translation of this key term would be 'foundation', since the *documenta* of *History of the Apostles*, exactly as Lactantius' *veritas*, had to be extracted from "beneath" the figures, as if it was a matter of uncovering valuable secrets which, for reasons of security, had been kept under lock and key. "See", the poet urges his audience, echoing Lactantius, after his description of Peter's healing powers on the sick in the streets of Jerusalem, "what teachings lie hidden beneath this [surface] appearance" (1.491): *quaeve sub hac specie lateant documenta, videte!* In this case, the "teachings" ultimately concern anagogic matters: the worldly and the heavenly Church, presaged by the apostle's shadow and body respectively.

Thus Arator adheres to a time-honoured interpretive tradition when he keeps disclosing the actual sense of his tropes and figures, with the crucial difference that he exclusively deals with Biblical figuration for the benefit of a Christian audience. The "teachings" he extracts from "allegory" or, literally, from 'the figure', are intended for those listeners (or readers) "who have deserved to be reborn in the flowing font", that is, in the water of Baptism (1.1027–28): *laeti documenta figurae / discite, qui liquido meruistis fonte renasci*. Specifically, these coveted lessons are primarily of a typological nature. This is evident on many occasions in the work, for example when Arator introduces his allegorical explanation of the episode with Philip and the Ethiopian eunuch (Acts 8.26–40) with the comment that 'the matter of this figure, that shines forth beneath the image of the [eunuch's] obscure region, is not trifling' (1.690–91): *non parva figurae / causa sub obscurae regionis imagine lucet*. The term *obscurus* might be ambiguous in

---

Derrida, introduced the term "paraliterature" in Anglo-Saxon literary criticism, referring to these authors' tendencies "to blur the distinction between literature and criticism", 1980, p. 37. It is exlusively in this very general sense that I, *mutatis mutandis*, apply it to Arator's Biblical epic poem.

2 See Schwind's account of the Arator reception, 1990, p. 13. Incidentally, Schwind also provides a good survey of the terminology of allegory and allegoresis in *History of the Apostles*, pp. 100–05, the subtle distinctions of which I cannot do justice to in my brief sketch.

1 *PL* 6.180b.

this context. Beneath the 'obscure' scenario of *History of the Apostles* or, alternatively, from the dark regions of Ethiopia, emerge Old Testament female figures such as Moses' Cushite wife, the bride of the Song of Songs or the Queen of Sheba, all harbingers of the eunuch's Egyptian queen and, through her, types of the Catholic (universal) Church, *ecclesia ex gentibus*, the main focus of Arator's work (cf. 1.910).

Such, then, are Arator's distinguishing characteristics among the Biblical epic poets of Late Antiquity. As Bruno Bureau has convincingly demonstrated, he implemented a particular kind of "figurative writing" in his work, including but not limited to allegory.[1] Everywhere the subdeacon presented persons, scenes and episodes drawn from the Acts of the Apostles in order to disclose their teachings and, where necessary, to comment on their figurative mode. In the second book of *History of the Apostles*, for instance, he explicitly makes the Apostle to the Gentiles give a lecture on salvation and the imitation of Christ in a figurative manner: *docet hac in parte figuram* (2.327). Shortly afterwards, he chose to summarize the prescriptions of the Pentateuch on the decency and purity of priests thus: 'that figure without which nothing of the old writing abides' (2.361–62), *illa figura, / qua sine nulla vetus subsistit littera*. Here too, it is the term's typological sense that is foregrounded. That is the case for all reminiscences of the Old Testament in Arator's poem: "the teachings of their typical allegory" (2.74), *typicae documenta figurae*, can be summarized in Christ. The paradigmatic example would be the second book's disproof of the necessity of circumcision among the Gentiles. This Jewish custom is, after all, nothing but "the shadow of allegory" (2.247), *umbra figurae*, yet another figure whose "teachings" now, at long last, should be made "more clearly apparent" (2.281), *clarius ut liqueant huius documenta figurae...* In short, it is an *imago* (2.282) that can be done away with after the Incarnation, an old Jewish *figura* (2.303) that has to yield to the new faith which will illumine the hearts of the Gentiles.[2]

Thus the "shadow" ascribed to certain kinds of Biblical figurative discourse, *umbra figurae*, has to be scattered in favour of the (New Covenant's) enduring form, *species mansura* (2.247–48), a typological configuration originating with Paul and culminating with Dante (cf. above, pp. 103f., 257). In *History of the Apostles*, the elucidation of such referential patterns required a rhetorical or hermeneutic competence that, in theory, was as dependent on divine enlightenment as the text production itself. This is apparent when Arator reproduces Acts 9.32–

---

[1] Bureau 1997, p. 87 ("écriture figurée").
[2] See Hillier 1993, pp. 143f., and – on the theme of *umbra futuri* in Arator and his predecessors – pp. 163–69.

35, where Peter cures Aeneas, a man who has been paralyzed, confined to his bed for eight years. Here, the poet is ostensibly not content with a mere paraphrase. The episode has to be interpreted and explained, and to that purpose he sets up a short invocation: "I shall reveal what are the hidden matters of sacred allegory here, if he whose word restores bodies moves my heart within me" (1.771–72), *eloquar hic, sacrae quae sint arcana figurae, / si mihi corda movet, cuius vox corpora reddit*. In Arator's eyes, then, not only the kerygmatic but the exegetic work as well required inspiration from above, acting on the very "heart" of its author. This is in perfect agreement with his dedicatory verses to Pope Vigilius, quoted above, where he promises, in the first place, to carefully follow Luke and "speak true poetry", *carmina vera*, secondly to "disclose" the text's literal meaning "and whatever mystical sense is revealed in my heart", *res si qua mihi mystica corde datur* (20–22).

Still, as we have been able to establish, this poet/exegete, relying on his illumined heart, repeatedly reminds his audience of the insufficiency of human language in general and of figurative discourse in particular. His words cannot do justice to his actual message; in fact, they can barely hint at the divine reality behind the events referred to in the Acts of the Apostles.[1] Such a gap between linguistic reference and divine referent seems inevitable, since Arator on the one hand, as a Biblical epic poet, is as unable as Juvencus, Sedulius or Avitus to refrain from the use of tropes, of which primarily allegory seems crucial to *History of the Apostles*, while on the other hand his singular reliance on paraliterary means as well as mystical thought, possibly related to late Neo-Platonic speculation, results in a persistent disparagement of figurative eloquence. In his work, the criticism which Paul levels against the Gentiles' worship of images or statues of the Godhead, cited above, "no one can shut in a Lord extended beyond all things and press Him together into small shapes" (2.469–70), *Dominum super omnia fusum / claudere nemo potest parvisque artare figuris*, thus seems liable to include figurative language as well.

In conclusion, Arator's work presupposes a consistent subservience of the use of art to the claims of faith. Where the latter were overlooked, especially where figuration was put to the service of idolatry, the former proved not only insufficient but misled, useless, and hence doomed to failure and obsolescence, however proficient and skilful. That is clear from the one single place in *History of the Apostles* where Arator lets the other side – the Gentile non-believers – have their say in a statement of their own. I am referring to the lines based on Acts

---

[1] On the tension between literal narrative and mystical interpretation in Arator, see Roberts 1985, pp. 91–92, 172–80.

19.24–27, where the Ephesian silversmith Demetrius testifies to his desperation at being deprived of his income, since Paul's successful missionary work risks totally discrediting his handmade miniature shrines of the goddess Artemis. Does it not make you ashamed, he asks his colleagues and partners in Arator's amplification of this fairly incidental passage from the Acts of the Apostles, that our great Diana has fallen? If the very gods perish, what hope is there for us mortals? "What statues will [men] now be able to give to shrines, what incense to altar fires? The foreigner Paul terrifies them [the gods] and calls whatever we make in the name of the gods dumb metal; their religion departs from the city, and the rejected Penates have sought flight." (2.696–700)[1]

These lines seem to form a suitable coda to the historical exposé of this book, since they so emphatically contrast the religious and ritual paradigm of the dying Antiquity with the tenets of the new faith, and since the silver that Demetrius hand-hammers and crafts with such expertise could traditionally be associated with eloquent speech.[2] Diana has fallen, the Penates have disappeared from Ephesus, even the gods can die. In Demetrius' eyes, this is the sad outcome of a battle which to a great extent has been fought on the field of language. What the Ephesians call divine, the Apostle calls a metal and nothing else. The land of the losers lies desolate and empty. This is where their gods and their culture, notably based on figurative art, visual or discursive, come to an end. In the eyes of "the foreigner Paul", *advena Paulus*, the Diana shrines do not conceal any mystical *documenta* at all but are dictated purely by the desire for financial profit. Anyone who tries to elicit some sort of message from their crafted figures will only get the dull sound of silver in return.

---

[1] "Quae nunc simulacra sacellis, / quae poterunt dare tura focis? Quos advena Paulus / territat et quicquid gerimus pro nomine divum / muta metalla vocat, quorum discedit ab urbe / religio pulsique fugam petiere Penates."
[2] Schwind 1990, pp. 147f.

V **Epilogue:** *Ecclesia Triumphans*
Fiction and Figuration on the Threshold of the Middle Ages

Preliminary Remarks

> Then Ozymandias said the spouse, the bride
> is never naked. A fictive covering
> weaves always glistening from the heart and mind.
>
> Wallace Stevens, "Notes Toward a Supreme Fiction" (8.19–21)[1]

For our inquiries into Late Antique approaches to fictional representation, we have singled out a few but crucial points of reorientation through the Latin-speaking world. After the apologetic attacks and the breakthrough of Christianity in the Roman Empire during the early fourth century, many leading intellectuals of the Church came to reconsider their standpoint on classical poetry, eloquence and philosophy. A course of assimilation and integration seemed viable, with early harbingers among the apologists themselves, principally Minucius Felix, and with strong theoretical support from Lactantius. Quite a few writers associated with the *ecclesia triumphans* of the fourth and fifth centuries not only perused but also exploited pagan traditions within new genres such as didactic allegorical or Biblical epic poetry. A Christian learned culture and a Christian literature ensued from their combined efforts.

The main features of their pioneering achievement, at times fraught with conflict, have long been known and painstakingly registered among scholars of Late Antiquity. The present work, which is now coming to an end, has attempted to show how this complex acculturation process ultimately required one sacrifice: fictionality, at least as far as this concept – embodied in designations such as *ficta* or *figmenta*, closely linked to the ancient *fabulae* – was associated with Aristotelian *mimēsis* or Ovidian illusionism. The Christian writers themselves did not, of course, apprehend the ongoing cultural change in precisely these terms, but their strategies for establishing a consistent attitude to the pagan literary heritage frequently entailed a critical stance towards its endorsements of pretence or make-believe, particularly when inspired by the ascetic currents marking the decades around the turn of the fifth century. This denunciation comes to the fore in these writers' new amplifications on the cliché of the lies of the poets, their Neo-Platonically inspired criticism of images and imagery, their cautions

---

[1] Stevens 1951, p. 135.

about the faculty of imagination and their rejection of the highflown "pompous" style along with their ingrained misgivings about ancient mythology. The pious spokesmen of the incipient Christian era nurtured a deep distrust of fictionality both in its lingering Peripatetic manifestations, characterized by the *verisimile* ('as if') option, and as pure entertainment. They marked their own literature off – to use the qualification of Hans Robert Jauß – as "antifiction".[1]

On the other hand, those writers who advanced the allegorical discursivity of 'oblique speech' across the confessional boundaries lay the foundations of a new type of literary fiction, mainly relying on recognized principles for the application and analysis of eloquent figuration while conceding a certain (limited) scope for the ancient notion of poetic licence. We have seen how such trends took theoretical shape with the Christian Lactantius in the early 300s as well as with the pagan Servius at the end of that century. This current, too, developed a strong Neo-Platonic bias, quite conspicuous in later writers like Macrobius and Boethius. Jerome could certainly frown at such literary elasticity, and Augustine finally reserved his extreme sensitivity to figuration and subtexts for scriptural exegesis, pushing non-Christian poetry or philosophy aside. Notwithstanding these Fathers' reluctance, the recycling of ancient myths for allegorical purpose was to colour ground-breaking works such as Martianus Capella's *Marriage* and Fulgentius' *Exposition*, thereby constituting a mighty Late Antique heritage to medieval didactic and epic poetry.

In spite of political turbulence and widespread warfare, it was a confident Catholic civilization that rose from the ruins of the ancient Mediterranean world, but its attitude to profane art, literature and scholarship only slowly took more definite forms. Earlier research on this period had a tendency to contrast paganism and Christianity all too sharply, as if it dealt with two well-defined cultures unmistakably marked off from each other, clearly conscious of each other's separate identities. That was not the case; consequently, during the latter half of the twentieth century, a distinctive trend in Late Antique studies has rather emphasized the close links between pagan and Christian poetry and painting, their proponents' common school education, their overlapping repertoires of topics and symbols, their shared cultural heritage. Only against this background has it become possible to give a valid picture of what Antonio Quacquarelli calls "the Christian language under construction [in fabbricazione]".[2]

---

[1] Jauß 1983, p. 425.
[2] Quacquarelli 1972, p. 203. Gemeinhardt consistently highlights this common cultural and educational heritage; a characteristic section heading of his study 2007 reads "Pagan Education as an Introduction to Faith", p. 481.

Drawing that picture would be the subject of another book. The following concluding points are only meant to elucidate a few striking Late Antique approaches to fictional discourse on the threshold of the Middle Ages. To begin with, as we have already been able to determine from our surveys of Avitus' and Arator's works, the Church basically took over the patristic watch against relapses into the old world of *fabulae* and *figmenta*, stubbornly surviving as a kind of subculture interfering with Catholic orthodoxy throughout the Migration Period. The heritage from the apologists was still felt in such attempts at surveillance, which was particularly important for a new institution of Western Christianity: the monasteries. At the same time, a new aristocracy, increasingly a hybrid of Roman nobility and Germanic chieftain families, notably in Gaul, assumed the responsibility of upholding at least a minimum of traditional cultural values. To all appearances, these men and women could take interest in pagan literature as a monument to a lost civilization, as educated divertissements or as illustrative material for teaching grammar and rhetoric. Thus a historic compromise was born that prepared the ground for the Carolingian era's redrawing of the cultural map in Western Europe – and, in addition, for the High Medieval implementations of fictionality in clerical Latin as well as courtly vernacular poetry.

1 The Old Dreams

The Church Fathers' onslaughts on the verbal brilliance of classical literature frequently referred to, or presupposed, the idea of a language that required a correspondence between simple words and crucial deeds, unadorned expression and momentous experience, in explicit opposition to the antique separation of styles.[1] Jerome argued in this direction. Notwithstanding his erudite background, characterized by a solid rhetorical and literary education, he was – increasingly – influenced by contemporary ascetic trends, prevalent from Iberia to Asia Minor. He readily testified to his inclination for the purportedly downright and simple idiom of the Gospels, where style was never allowed to become an end in itself. This approach to linguistic matters colours his commentary on the Epistle to the Galatians (5.6), a virtual manifesto for the apostles' *sermo simplex:* 'Does anyone read Aristotle nowadays? And how many know the books of Plato, or even his name? If you are lucky you might find a few old men with nothing else to do, studying them in a corner. On the other hand, the whole world is talking about our peasants and fishermen, indeed, each and everyone is echoing their words everywhere. And so their simple words should be promulgated in a simple style. For it is the words, I say, that are simple, not their meaning.'[2]

Even considering the polemical circumstances, the depiction of Aristotle and Plato as a couple of half-forgotten has-beens is remarkable. The Bible translator's fulminations seem aimed at their stylistic means, whether the former's elegant syllogisms or the latter's blend of irony and gravity, as well as their philosophical tenets. In the present work I have tried to show how this type of Late Antique anti-rhetorical stance regularly presupposes or interacts with a more or less explicit annulment of the fictional contract drawn up in ancient Greece and Rome. This critical attitude was soon to be transmitted to the incipient monastic culture, which certainly was progressive in the sense that it revolutionized Western techniques of writing and reading. In addition, it was literary in as far as it focused on some instruction in rhetoric and grammar (notably recommended by Cassiodorus in order to further scriptural studies in his Vivarium monastery), on copying ancient manuscripts, on the performance of hymns and on medita-

---

[1] See Auerbach's chapter on "Fortunata" in *Mimesis* 1968, pp. 24–49.
[2] "Quotusquisque nunc Aristotelem legit? quanti Platonis vel libros novere, vel nomen? Vix in angulis otiosi eos senes recolunt. Rusticanos vero et piscatores nostros totus orbis loquitur, universus mundus sonat. Itaque sermone simplici, simplicia eorum verba pandenda sunt. Verba, inquam, non sensus." *PL* 26.401b.

tive studies of the Bible: *lectio divina*.[1] However, at least to begin with, it left little or no room for classical fiction in its curricula.

This omission is evident in the Rule of Saint Benedict, which prescribed collective recitation at the brethren's meals (38) but also attached great importance to their discrete intercourse with books, especially during fasting, perhaps reminiscent of the kind of tacit *lectio* that, as we have seen (p. 108), Augustine was amazed at in Ambrose. However, these early test persons in the history of Western silent reading had to be kept under close observation; they were not allowed to yield to inappropriate distractions. Benedict recommended that one or two senior monks "should be assigned to go around the monastery during the hours the brothers are free for reading and see to it that there is no slothful brother who spends his time in idleness or gossip and neglects his reading; such a one is not only harmful to himself but also a distraction to others" (48.17–18).[2]

The monks were not to be left alone with their books, not even spiritual or sacred books (the only kind of lecture imposed on the brethren of Monte Cassino). Silent reading required supervision and, if necessary, entailed punitive measures. If a monk failed in reading discipline and did not amend, Benedict adds, "he should be subject to the correction of the Rule in such a way that the others are afraid" (48.20), *correptioni regulari subiaceat, taliter ut ceteri timeant*. Such emphasis on studies, manual labour and ritual observance seems typical of Benedict's Rule, which was liable to warn against sloth, *acedia*, as a breeding-ground for idle fantasies and "gossip", *fabulae*, certainly disgraceful for an institution chiefly based on the principle of 'pray and work', to quote the well-known catchphrase of Benedictism: *ora et labora*.

At this early stage of monasticism, as in widespread ascetic currents and ritual settings of the expanding Church, the Christian identity was essentially consolidated by relying on a truth criterion that did not allow for any distance between person and voice. A well-known passage in Benedict's Rule regulates how the monks should comport themselves during prayers and psalm-singing: "So let us consider how we ought to behave in the sight of the divinity and his angels, and stand to sing psalms in such a way that our spirits and voices are in harmony. [...] Let us know that we will be heard not in loquacity but in

---

[1] The modern standard work on monastic *lectio divina* is still Leclercq 1998 (originally published in 1957).
[2] "Ante omnia sane deputentur unus aut duo seniores qui circumeant monasterium horis quibus vacant fratres lectioni et videant ne forte inveniatur frater achediosus qui vacat otio aut fabulis et non est intentus lectioni et non solum sibi inutilis est sed etiam alias distollit."

purity of heart and tearful compunction." (19.6 – 7, 20.3)[1] Evidently, with this Umbrian monastery founder, *multiloquium* should be avoided at all costs when approaching the divine. As Winifrid Cramer has shown, this particular rule is deeply rooted in Stoic philosophy as well as early Christian culture. It is reminiscent of a similar demand for accord between *logos* and *phōnē* in Hellenistic cults influenced by Stoicism. Moreover, it is presaged by equally well-known formulas from the Bible (Psalms 62.5. Matthew 15.8, 1 Corinthians 14.15) and by one of Augustine's later letters: "When you pray to God in psalms and hymns, let what you utter with your voice be weighed in your heart" (211.7), *psalmis et hymnis cum oratis Deum, hoc versetur in corde quod profertur in voce.*[2]

These words reflect the widespread Christian demand for concord in faith and preaching, in meditation and expression, which made Augustine – the proponent of what I have labelled "the speech of the heart" – stage his long and restless farewell to the language of fiction as he was increasingly drawn towards that of prayer and contemplation: "Set me free, O God, from that multitude of speech!", *libera me, Deus meus, a multiloquio* (above, p. 294)! His efforts to make his words faithfully re-echo what he called his "inner teacher's" message resulted at least partly from his dissatisfaction with the role-play or *duplex cogitatio* characteristic of much fictional discourse. The great Western Fathers were inclined to brand the whole of classical culture – against which they and their intellectual fellow believers felt the need to profile themselves with an identity and a language of their own – as rhetorical, grammatical or literary, sometimes in a negative sense. It was considered to be based on suppositions and hypotheses, at best on vaguely proto-Christian intuitions, mostly on unsubstantiated inventions and misguided speculations, at worst on lies and deceit. It was precisely in the third part of his commentary on the Epistle to the Galatians (5.6), compiled in the late 380s and cited above, that Jerome confessed (whether against his better judgment or not) to not having read Tullius, Maro or any other pagan author at all for the last fifteen years, 'and if by chance something from them might sneak into my language, it is because I remember them as old dreams swept in mist', *et si quid forte inde dum loquimur, obrepit, quasi antiqui per nebulam somnii recordamur.*[3] Jerome's simile seems perfectly on target. The persistency of these nebulous dreams, triggering such strong reactions in the

---

[1] "Ergo consideremus qualiter oporteat in conspectu divinitatis et angelorum eius esse et sic stemus ad psallendum ut mens nostra concordet voci nostrae. [...] Et non in multiloquio sed in puritate cordis et conpunctione lacrimarum nos exaudiri sciamus."
[2] Cramer 1980.
[3] *PL* 26.399c–d.

Latin-speaking world around the turn of the fifth century, has been at the core of all the above chapters.

We have been able to conclude, in short, that Jerome's general distrust of the 'old dreams' of fictional representation was shared by quite a few of his brilliant contemporaries such as Augustine, Paulinus and Prudentius. Actually, it was to prove seminal to Late Antiquity's cultural and critical heritage to Christian posterity. Two hundred and fifty years later, it was fully recognizable in yet another learned bishop, the polymath Isidore of Seville, frequently quoted throughout the Middle Ages, blazing behind Boethius in Dante's Heaven of the Sun (Paradiso 10.131). In his moral-theological handbook *Libri sententiarum tres* (*Sentences*), Isidore promulgates an elaborate ban on literary fiction. Just like his famous *Etymologies*, *Sentences* can to a high degree be considered a compilation of earlier sources such as Augustine and Gregory the Great. Consequently, it assembles a list of objections and reservations against literary fiction that we have been able to follow through the present work, hence this quotation *in extenso* (3.13.1–11):[1]

> Christians are thus forbidden to read the fictions of the poets [*figmenta poetarum*], since these incite the mind to indulge in depraved impulses resulting from the enticements of their vain stories [*oblectamenta inanium fabularum*]. For one does not sacrifice to the demons by burning incense only, but by trying to understand their speech as well.
>
> Some people prefer to ponder on pagan writings for their inflated and ornate style rather than on the Holy Writ for its humble eloquence. But what is the use of making progress in worldly learning while depriving ourselves of divine? To follow frail fictions [*caduca figmenta*] while loathing divine mysteries? We must beware of these books and avoid them for love of the Holy Writ.
>
> The pagan writings shine outwards with the eloquence of their words but remain empty of moral wisdom within. The Bible's sacred eloquence, by contrast, seems rude from the exterior, in its words, but shines with mystic wisdom within. That is why the apostle says: *we have this treasure in jars of clay*. For God's speech keeps the light of knowledge concealed and the store of truth in the simplest vessels of words.
>
> Our holy books are therefore written in a simple style so that they will lead people to the faith *not in words of wisdom, but in demonstration of the Spirit*. For if they had been put forth by the tricks of dialectic sophistry or with the eloquence of rhetorical art, faith in Christ would not be believed to consist in God's work but in arguments of human eloquence. And we would not consider it possible for anyone to be called to the faith by divine illumination but rather by seduction through the tricks of words.
>
> Every worldly doctrine resounding with foaming words [*spumantibus verbis*] and praised for its eloquent tumidity is laid bare by the simple and humble Christian doctrine, as it is written: *has not God made foolish the wisdom of the world?*
>
> Condescending and garrulous people find it difficult to appreciate the Holy Writ since its style is simple. In comparison with pagan eloquence, it strikes them as unworthy. But if

---

[1] The Latin text is from P. Cazier's 1998 edition *Isidorus Hispalensis Sententiae*, translation mine.

they try to understand its mysteries with a humble mind, they will immediately notice how elevated everything they disdain in it is.

When reading, we should love not the words but the truth. We often find, however, that simplicity is truthful, and that falseness, ensnaring people in its labyrinth and setting delightful traps with verbal ornaments, is complex.

It is nothing but the pursuit of fame that awakens people's love for secular learning. For the more they study literature, the more their minds are blown up with arrogant pride and the more they swell with boasting. That is why the Psalm duly says: *Since I have not gained any knowledge of literature, I shall enter into the powers of God.*

Simpler texts need not stand back for the cosmetics [*fucus*] of grammatical art. For the best texts are the ordinary ones, precisely because of their simplicity, addressing readers' humility, whereas these others are good for nothing since they blow up people's minds unhealthily.

Grammarians are better than heretics. For after having drained their poisonous drink, the heretics hasten to try persuading people, but the doctrine of grammarians may even be of help in our life, as long as it is put to good use. (I)

Isidore registers moral, religious and aesthetic doubts about the poets' *fabulae*. They encourage lust, emanate from demonic powers and rely on flowery language, in stark contrast to the Bible's simple style. These *Sentences* thus result in a resounding defence of the Holy Scripture's *sermo humilis*, based on the old distinction between texts' *litterae* or *verba* and their *spiritus*, reinforced by allusions to, in turn, 2 Corinthians 4.7, "But we have this treasure in jars of clay", 1 Corinthians 2.4, "my speech and my message were not in plausible words of wisdom, but in demonstration of the Spirit", and 1 Corinthians 1.20, "Has not God made foolish the wisdom of the world?" To these Pauline topics Isidore adds another frequently cited passage from the Old Testament Psalms, where the psalmist thankfully notes that he never studied literature, hence he will gain access to the realm of God (70/71.15–16), *quoniam non cognovi litteraturam / introibo in potentiam Domini*. These verses can be read in several ways and are notoriously difficult to interpret.[1] Isidore, however, makes them substantiate his overall cultural criticism: the prospects of salvation are increased by illiteracy. Such remarks seem directed against secular learning in general, specifically grammar, dialectic and rhetoric, all three identified by name. Even more significant for our approach is the gap between poetry's dubious *ficta* and theology's true *mysteria* that appears to underlie Isidore's text and which Augustine's generation had succeeded in opening two centuries earlier.

In addition to his reuse of the Vulgate, Isidore recycles tropes and figures of speech which are firmly rooted in classical rhetoric and patristic tradition, as

---

[1] Most modern translators refrain entirely from Jerome's reference to 'literature' in Psalms 70/71.15.

when he speaks of "the cosmetics of grammatical art". This is the same *fucus* (red dye, rouge) that Paulinus of Nola had repeatedly associated with the learned philosophers' fictional and/or stylistic pageantry.[1] In his commentary on the Epistle to the Galatians, Jerome had tried rephrasing verse 1.20, "In what I am writing to you, before God, I do not lie!", with the following amplification: 'What I am writing to you is true, and I affirm before God that it is not rouged by means of verbal art or lies', *quae scribo vobis, vera sunt, et Deo teste confirmo, quia nulla arte verborum, nullo sunt fucata mendacio*.[2] Similarly, in the introduction to the third part of his commentary, Jerome had contrasted his own simple language with the beautiful speech that is 'rouged by lying', *fucata mendacio*, like a harlot.[3] Thus Isidore's linking of beautiful or ornate speech with both monetary supplies and prostitution is reminiscent of Jerome as well as Augustine and Ambrose (cf. above, pp. 98, 294f.), but behind these Fathers and all the – fairly standardized – objections to *fucus mendax* or *fucus facundiae*, we can distinguish the doubts about eloquent "rouge" already apparent in classical rhetorical tradition, in Cicero or Quintilian.[4]

Finally, the polymath presents us with an ostensibly minor exception to his overall negative attitude to classical culture. Grammar, accountable for correct linguistic usage, may after all be of some practical benefit, *proficere ad vitam*, presumably if it keeps to its formal area of responsibility, shunning all lecturing on the actual beliefs or key concepts pervading the works in the curricula of its *narratio poetarum*. This might seem to be an insignificant exemption from the categorical ban on fiction in the preceding paragraphs, but such a concession to grammar actually helped to establish the theoretical basis for much medieval poetry, based on the language arts rather than on literary theory proper. The great authority for this development was, of course, Augustine, who had endorsed the sound knowledge of "how to read and write" at the cost of Virgil's *poetica figmenta* (above, p. 124). In conclusion, even if the extract from Isidore's

---

1 See Paulinus' *Letters* 12.4: "the whole technique of philosophers seeks to hide the light of truth by maintaining falsehoods, to wean minds from the truth and enmesh them in the nooses of empty controversies, to deceive them with clever tricks and beguile them with dissimulation [*fucus*] of words", *in hoc omnis ars philosophorum laborat, ut adsertione fictorum lucem veritatis obscuret et inanium contentionum laqueis sollicitatas a vero mentes inplicet et ingenii fraude decipiat et fuco sermonis inducat*, and 16.11 (quoted above, p. 160).
2 PL 26.331b.
3 PL 26.399b.
4 Crassus' warning in Cicero's *On the Orator* against encumbering a speech with ornaments in order to conceal its defects, *vitia*, seems characteristic in this context: such artifice "makes the curls and rouge of the orator or poet jar upon us all the more quickly" (3.25.100), *eo citius in oratoris aut in poetae cincinnis ac fuco offenditur*.

Sentences may appear to form a gloomy epilogue to the Late Antique negotiations of fictionality, the positive consequences of the bishop's allowance for *grammaticorum doctrina* are unmistakable.[1]

Nevertheless, all the Late Antique objections to the alleged lies of the poets, neatly summarized by Isidore, kept popping up throughout the Middle Ages. And, if for a moment we turn our attention away from the specific context, issues and front lines of Late Antiquity, it is easy to see how they would continue to haunt literary criticism up to the present day. From this specific point of view, the era between Lactantius and Isidore appears as a virtual watershed in Western cultural history whose after-effects are still being felt. In premodern Christian Europe, fictionality always attracted loud-voiced enemies, for instance – just to mention a few influential factions – the "Cornificians" of John of Salisbury's twelfth-century Paris, the Dominicans of Dante's, Petrarch's and Boccaccio's fourteenth-century Italy or the Puritans of Early Modern England, against whom Sir Philip Sidney famously launched an updated Aristotelian concept of mimetic fiction.

In a perspective as long as this, the picture has even darkened. While Kantian notions of autonomous or disinterested art have achieved great triumphs over the past two centuries, modern dictatorships have in turn produced a frightening number of new handcuffs for poetry. Dogmatic critics and censors from far and near bear witness to this predicament, with a depressing climax in the *fatwa*, for all practical purposes a sentence of death, pronounced in February 1989 by Ayatollah Khomeini on the Indian-British writer Salman Rushdie for having blasphemed Islam in his novel *The Satanic Verses*. On the other hand, to round off this thumb-nail sketch of the historical vicissitudes of Western fictionality, imaginative literature and drama has to a previously unknown extent been institutionalized and flattened out into a postmodern *otium*, the outcome of dream factories all over the globe, operating day and night. In contrast to such endless ways of killing time, Creusa's demanding shadow might still appear as a provocation long after Augustine apologized for his youthful reading, long after Virgil gave her a voice and long after Troy was left in ashes.

---

[1] Accordingly, in his masterly two-volume doctoral thesis on Isidore and classical culture in Visigothic Spain, Jacques Fontaine prefers to downplay this whole extract's doubts about pagan literature. He reads it first and foremost as a defence of the Bible's simple style against eloquent showiness and as a note of caution against erotic and mythological poetry in the Alexandrian style, 1959, pp. 785–806.

2 The New Library

Despite the sometimes fierce attacks on pagan *figmenta* in the writings of the Fathers and in early Christian poets such as Paulinus of Nola or Prudentius, more forgiving attitudes could infiltrate the Late Antique elite culture of the fifth and sixth centuries, counteracting the persistent hostility of the Church. There are various explanations for these conciliatory approaches. One of them has already been mentioned: the new aristocracy emerging in Gaul and other regions of the dying Empire, assimilating Germanic chieftain families in local cultural settings, appropriating new group identities frequently drawing support from traditional Roman schooling. In major parts of continental Europe, old Germanic cults and creeds did not survive the Migration Period. Consequently, the Catholic Church slowly entered a new victorious phase, assuming religious monopoly in the West. Its opponents were hardly to be seen; their cults and beliefs had, as it were, become memories or phantoms of the past, those 'old dreams swept in mist' reluctantly remembered by Jerome. In short, during the sixth century, when the last strongholds of paganism – mainly the Roman senatorial aristocracy – had been converted to the true faith and even the Germanic conquerors had accepted Christianity, a historic compromise was on its way.

By and large, scholars have been in agreement about this change. Peter Brown, for instance, gives prominence to the year 410, when *Roma aeterna* was revealed as nothing but one of several historical constructs. After that date, Brown remarks, the weakened Imperial court could no longer offer any provocation to the Christians, while the last pagan Roman aristocrats, for their part, at last "adopted the official religion of an Empire which had no power left to hurt".[1] Manfred Fuhrmann has outlined the same historical predicament in slightly different terms: the Christians won the power and the glory at the cost of internal unity. After the vehement conflicts of the late fourth century, it seemed as though the dwindling minority of pagan intellectuals and their Christian counterparts had reached a kind of settlement. On the one hand, the ancient cult of the gods had, with few exceptions, come to an end: the new faith was completely infiltrating most people's old forms of life. On the other hand, farsighted Christians declared that the battle against pagan literature and philosophy was over and done with, or at least suspended, to the effect that the ancient mythology was tolerated within a range of poetic genres.[2] To this should be added victorious Christianity's capacity to reframe and appropriate certain per-

---

[1] Brown 1961, p. 11.
[2] Fuhrmann 1967, pp. 76f. Cf. Staubach 2009, pp. 149f.

sistent pagan ways of thinking, notions or representations. To Augustine, it had been of prime importance to mark off true, monotheistic Christianity from the morass of divination (including astrology), incantations, magical practices and heretical beliefs he detected in his North African environment. Two hundred years later, however, as James J. O'Donnell observes, a host of angels "incorporated the powers of Apollo and Hermes and more besides", while the widespread idea that devils could snatch weak or dying people's souls "made an absolute mockery of everything Augustine, for example, had taught".[1] This could even be said of Pope Gregory the Great's *Dialogi* (*Dialogues*, composed 593–94), replete with signs, miracles and wonders, a rather far cry from Augustine's struggle to ward off all symptoms of pagan superstition from orthodox Christian faith.

For a short time, in the five decades between Julian the Apostate and Alaric's Sack of Rome in 410, Augustine *et consortes* had taken that battle to its extreme, with great energy, with thorough knowledge of their opponents and with supreme rhetorical artifice. As the fifth century went on, however, the debate inevitably subsided. Ancient literature continued to be read while grammar and rhetoric continued to be studied in Roman schools, duly divested of their subversive potential. Jacques Fontaine detects a "relaxation" of the strains between Christian poets and "a poetry, ancient or recent, which from now on was felt as profane rather than pagan". Now, in the wake of the sack of Rome, the gap between uncompromising Christianity and classical pragmatism that had opened up in the late 350s was already, as stated by Robert A. Markus, on the way to being closed.[2]

This truce certainly had consequences for the status of fictionality in Christian culture. There was generally less need than before to repudiate fictional discourse, as appropriated by the poets, for dealing with lies and deceit, false gods and airy nothing. *Ficta* could in fact be acknowledged and exploited by the sometimes hard-pressed literate enclaves of the former Empire, eager to (re)construct a Christian-Roman culture and identity, pretty well the only weapon available – considerably more efficient, as it turned out, than swords and spears – against the barbarian invaders, who were soon naturalized within this budding synthesis of *christianitas* and *romanitas*. The outcome of the heated dispute around the turn of the fifth century may thus seem satisfactory for classical literary culture, but at a price. If its myths, legends and tales were increasingly liable to be redefined from a set of alluring lies to the core of the new provinces'

---

[1] O'Donnell 2009, p. 389. We should remember, though, that the Church Father seems to have assumed the existence of demons as a matter of course. For an overview, see Bailey 2007, pp. 53–59.
[2] Fontaine 1981, p. 284; Markus 1974, p. 13.

cultural heritage, they must, as it were, be pushed back into the dim and distant past, construed as a (commonly misguided) preliminary stage to present-day civilization once and for all in possession of infallible Truth. In other words, the typological pattern of interpretation characteristic of much Biblical exegesis proved capable of incorporating pagan myths and literature as well – not only Adam and Job but figures such as Orpheus and Odysseus were supposed to foreshadow Christ – with the (crucial) difference that in this case the ancient stories, corresponding to the Old Testament events, were considered unhistorical and fabulous, hence fictional.

Such Christian reuse of pagan mythology is already noticeable among the great Fathers of the fourth century (though typically absent in the works of Augustine), apart from its systematic application in Proba's cento. It colours an interesting passage in Ambrose's commentary on the Gospel according to St. Luke (4.2–3), where the Archbishop does not hesitate to use an old Greek *fabula* to reinforce his message. This story is taken from Homer's account of Odysseus' wanderings, previously employed for Christian allegorical use – as we have seen – by the Alexandrian Fathers, and recycled by both Jerome and Paulinus of Nola a few years later.[1] Ambrose, for his part, relies on the dialectic type of argument *a fortiori:* if already on his travels Odysseus had been tempted by the berries of the Lotus-eaters, the herb gardens of the Phaeacians and the songs of the Sirens, 'how much more will not religious men be enchanted by their admiration for heavenly reality', *quanto magis religiosos viros coelestium factorum cedet admiratione mulceri!* The bread of Heaven eclipses the sweet berries of pagan myth, King Alcinous' herbal fruits cannot match the mysteries of Christ, and anyone who listens to His voice will never need to fear shipwreck. Ambrose puts Homer's myth to efficient use, since it colourfully presents an analogy as well as a counter-version to the Biblical message. On the one hand, it promises virtually irresistible pleasures, comparable in intensity to heavenly bliss. On the other hand, it offers a telling contrast to Luke's account of the temptations of Christ (4.1–12); the ancient *fabula* is instructive precisely because of its hedonistic and inferior topics, point by point outdone by the prospect of Christian salvation.

Even this kind of moralizing interpretation of Odysseus' adventures, however, proves to be problematic. Although Ambrose primarily uses the myth as a bleak background scenario, in every sense inferior to its evangelical counterpart, he immediately feels the need to call his juxtaposition of Homer and the Bible into question. Otherwise his readers or listeners might think that he actually be-

---

[1] Cf. above, pp. 70, 500ff., and, in addition, for Boethius and the Sirens, pp. 439f.

lieved in the existence of Sirens, that he was comparing two equally reliable versions of the theme of temptation, only differing in their degree of edification and orthodoxy. Of course this was not the case: there had never been any Lotus-eaters or Sirens. That is why Ambrose, as we shall see, felt obliged to explicitly highlight the difference between the make-believe of the myth and the authenticity of the Gospel. Few passages illustrate so clearly the aporia of fictionality among the great Church Fathers of the West.

The Archbishop takes the opportunity to give us a summary of the Homeric scenario: the monstrous women perform their sweet songs to lure ships onto the rocks for the purpose of devouring their crews. It soon becomes evident that such old wives' tales can only be adduced with great reservations. Ambrose takes pains to demonstrate their ultimate inadequacy: in reality, the human soul shall not be bound to any actual mast by bodily chains, like Odysseus, but fastened to the cross by spiritual ties. The myth is eventually awkward, since it is coloured by poetic fiction: *figmentis enim poeticis fabula coloratur*. The poetic story 'consists of phantoms, and it is adorned with ostentatious similes, feigning the sea, voices, women, and shallow shores', *compositum hoc specie, et ambitiosa comparatione fucatum est; ut mare, vox, feminae, littora vadosa, fingantur*. In other words, the myth is based on pure inventions that nevertheless are supposed to represent real, and dangerous, phenomena. The sea translates into the agitated and treacherous world, billowing with unclean spirits, the Sirens are *figurae* of the temptations of effeminate pleasure, and the shallow shores represent the rocks on which our salvation threatens to run aground.[1] Thus as a matter of precaution, Ambrose feels obliged to strip the myth of all suggestive power and possible ambiguity. It is flattened out to serve as illustrative material: a series of transparent figures, deprived of any original integrity, referring to the Christian drama of salvation.

Critical readers might detect a peculiar duplicity in Ambrose's exegesis: with one hand he takes back what the other hand offers. His manoeuvre, however, only reflects the tensions of this tempestuous era. Probably few readers were taken aback by the introduction of the Homeric episode in a salvational context, since they surely knew it well from their elementary education, notably in grammar. By virtue of its suggestive contrast between steadfast (masculine) virtue, *virtus*, and a (feminine) scenario of art, sex and death, it had long been cited as one of the fundamental and identity-creating narratives of Stoic Greek and Roman

---

1 *PL* 15.1612c–13b.

culture (by Seneca and others).¹ Consequently, it could hardly escape the highly charged patristic strategy of reuse or *chrēsis* that I have repeatedly examined in the present work. Correlation and separation, appropriation and rebuke, application *a fortiori* and disavowal at the same time might seem to constitute a contradiction in terms but were actually part of a consistent Christian allegorical scheme, capable of simultaneously recycling and downplaying pagan fictional discourse, *figmenta poetica*.

This clever pattern appears just as clearly in a Good Friday Sermon by Bishop Maximus of Turin (d. between 408 and 423), cited by Erich Kaiser as well as Hugo Rahner, which was probably indebted to Ambrose (and sometimes attributed to him by copyists in the High Middle Ages).² In this remarkable homily, Odysseus' stratagem when approaching the Sirens is not only a good example for the Christian individual but also a portent of Christ's sacrifice on the cross. On closer inspection, even Bishop Maximus appears to rely on a comparison *a fortiori* rather than a straightforward simile. Admittedly, the Homeric episode with the Sirens is adduced as an instructive moral story of how to overcome the threatening shipwreck of salvation, *naufragium salutis* (the wording reiterates Paulinus' sixteenth epistle, cf. above, p. 499), but Maximus repeatedly emphasizes that it is, all things considered, only an invention. If this *fabula* could show us that Odysseus' fetters to the mast saved him from his imminent danger, how much more powerfully should not the true facts, *quod vere factum est*, be preached? The bishop moves on to develop and explain his reasoning (37.2–3):³

> Today the tree of the cross has snatched the whole human race from the danger of death! For, because Christ the Lord has been bound to the cross, we pass through the world's charming hazards as if our ears were stopped; we are neither detained by the world's destructive sound nor deflected from the course of a better life onto the rocks of wantonness. For the tree of the cross not only hastens the person who is bound to it back to his homeland but also protects those gathered about it by the shadow of its power. That the cross causes us to return to our homeland after many wanderings the Lord says when He speaks to the thief on the cross: *Today you will be with me in paradise*. Indeed, this thief, a wanderer and a shipwrecked man in another way, would have been unable to return to the homeland of paradise that the first man had left had he not been bound to the tree. For a ship's mast is like the cross of the Church which alone, in the midst of the charming and destruc-

---

1 For a generous collection of examples, see Kaiser 1964, pp. 109–36. For an illustration from Plutarch, cf. above, p. 46.
2 Kaiser 1964, pp. 135f.; Rahner 1971, pp. 382f. For a short but well-informed analysis of Maximus' Paschal Sermon against the backdrop of Alexandrian allegoresis and, in particular, Ambrose's Luke commentary, see Merkt 1997, pp. 213–15.
3 I quote Maximus from A. Mutzenbecher's Corpus christianorum edition of *Sermones* 1962, and, in English, from B. Ramsey's translation volume 1989.

tive traps of the whole world, is safe to cling to. On this ship, then, whoever binds himself to the tree of the cross or stops his ears with the divine Scriptures will not fear the sweet tempest of wantonness. For the alluring manner of the Sirens is a kind of enervating desire for pleasures, which weakens the steadfastness of the captive mind with its evil blandishments.

Therefore the Lord Christ hung on the cross so that the whole human race would be freed from the shipwreck of the world. But let us pass over the story of Ulysses, which is fiction and not fact [*quae ficta non facta est*], and see if we can find something similar by way of example in the divine Scriptures, which the Lord, who was later to fulfill everything in Himself, might have intimated beforehand through His prophets. (II)

The same types of argument as in Ambrose are easily detected in Maximus' sermon:

- The comparison *a fortiori*. The well-known story of Odysseus, sometimes considered prototypical for Stoic or even Roman identity, portends in detail the predicament of Christian man or, alternatively, the Holy Passion. The Sirens are expressly introduced as 'a sweet figure', *suavis figura*, for sensual desire; Odysseus corresponds to Christian man in general and to Christ in particular; the mast represents the cross; Odysseus' men represent our fellow human beings or the human race itself, embodied in the crucified criminal at Golgotha; and the homeward-bound Greeks' wanderings across the Mediterranean are a presage of our tortuous journey through life, hopefully in the direction of our paradisiacal homeland. Homer's hero appears virtually as a type for the protagonist in the salvation drama, even though it is not, of course, a matter of typology *sensu stricto* (which can only be based on the Old Testament). The juxtaposition of Odysseus with Christ, unique to Maximus, permeates the whole argument. Thus the Turin Bishop concentrates crucial features of Alexandrian exegesis, already exploited by Ambrose, while carrying the Christological reading of the Odysseus figure to its extreme.
- The separation of Christian *facta* from pagan *ficta*, strategically implemented in both the introduction and the conclusion of this passage, conspicuously reminiscent of Ambrose's similar contrast in his comparison between Christ and Midas quoted at the beginning of this book (p. 69), according to which the mythological king represents *non facta, sed ficta*. Maximus' homily, then, helps to close our circle. The Homeric myth is, after all, only fiction and has to give way to faith, based on the truth of the Bible. Notwithstanding Rahner's enthusiasm for Maximus' energetic exegesis ("For none had previously ventured so bold an interpretation [of Odysseus bound] as this fifth-century preacher's, none did so after him"), it is, ultimately, an orthodox bishop, renowned for his irreproachable commitment to the ecclesi-

astical dogma, who composed this Good Friday sermon.[1] In fact, the outcome of his daring comparison seems fully in line with stern Ambrose's earlier application of the same topos: *omittamus Ulyssis fabulam*. Such, then, is Bishop Maximus' final proposal: let us leave the pagan myth out of consideration, since it had for all practical purposes been made superfluous by the superior typology controlling the Lord's own verbally inspired Holy Writ.

Against this background it would perhaps be possible to speak of a Pyrrhic victory for literary fiction in Late Antique criticism. It won certain acceptance at the cost of its suggestive power and narrative integrity, being diluted into a thin film, as it were, applied with all due circumspection to the core message of a given speech or text. Yet – as we already have been able to establish – the importance of this development should not be underestimated. Both Ambrose's and Maximus' reuse of classical mythology illustrates how the paradigm of 'oblique speech' even began to penetrate Christian genres such as Biblical commentaries and the art of preaching. Admittedly, both bishops were careful to take a final step back, making reservations against the fictitious nature of Homer's writing, but their way of appropriating the classical material for the benefit of pious edification indicates a method for literary recycling that looked to the future. This ongoing integration process, the Christian consolidation of *figmenta poetica* in the particular sense of oblique or covert speech (differing from Aristotelian as well as modern typical versions of fictionality), is a large and entangled area of research, where, however, there are a few preliminary landmarks that should be pointed out before the present investigation is brought to an end.

Benedict warned against the monks' private reading, as we have seen (p. 609), given the risk of distraction from the daily round in the monastery. Nonetheless, the new monastic culture played a decisive role for the study of the classics, in particular as it was developed by Cassiodorus, Boethius' successor at the court of Theoderic (ca. 490–585), after he had retired in his old age to the monastery of Vivarium that he founded in Calabria. There, under the influence of Augustine, he introduced the seven liberal arts – now divided into three *artes* and four *disciplinae*, anticipating the later medieval distinction between the *trivium* and the *quadrivium* – in addition to the study of the Bible, into the curriculum of the monastery school. A basic knowledge of the arts was necessary, he maintains in his *Introduction to Divine and Human Readings*, to be able to understand the Holy Scripture, which benefited from all of them (1.27). In the preface to this treatise, Cassiodorus explained that he would both present "the unbroken line of

---

1 Rahner 1971, p. 383.

the Divine Scriptures", elucidated by means of the commentaries of the Fathers (in Part One), and provide "compendious knowledge of secular letters" (in Part Two), *et scripturarum divinarum series et saecularium litterarum compendiosa notitia*. This seems entirely logical, since the treatise was aimed at furthering "both the salvation of the soul and secular knowledge", *salus animae et saecularis eruditio* (PR.1).[1] Cassiodorus thus cherished an inclusive conception of knowledge (according to which the secular arts are considered instrumental to Biblical exegesis) in strong contrast to the either/or argument we have registered in Gregory the Great one or two generations later. Both these attitudes, the abbot's inclusive as well as the pope's exclusive notions of learning, would influence virtually all later medieval negotiations of fictionality. The Chartrian Platonists and Dante, for example, inherited Cassiodorus' both/and approach, in the Florentine writer coloured by an unprecedented emphasis on the art of poetry, while their mighty opponents, Bernard of Clairvaux and the Italian fourteenth-century Dominicans respectively, essentially relied on Gregory's either/or option.

An even more important "founder" of medieval culture (to borrow E.K. Rand's terminology) was Isidore of Seville. In fact, the eclectic polymath behind *Etymologies* evinced an understanding of poetic inventiveness which for natural reasons seems somewhat suppressed in the moralist who composed the three books of *Sentences* (above, pp. 611ff.). Under the entry *De poetis* (*On the Poets*) in his main work, based on Roman writers such as the imperial secretary and biographer Suetonius (*fl.* ca. 100 CE), Isidore helped to transmit the conception of poets as teachers or theologians in disguise to the Middle Ages. Purportedly, they would have praised the gods by means of a certain kind of lofty speech, replete with brilliant words and pleasing rhythms. Precisely as "makers", *fictores*, of such speech they were called *poetae* (8.7.1–2). To Isidore, this time-honoured idea proves compatible with Lactantius' view of the "poet's business", namely "in transposing reality into something else with metaphor and allusion" (above, pp. 320f.), cited a few paragraphs later. Such segments of Late Antique literary theory, recycled in the Sevillian Bishop's *Etymologies*, are all based on what I have tried to understand as a notion of substitutive (as opposed to mimetic) fictionality. It signals the poet's task to process given circumstances, "things that have actually taken place", *quae vere gesta sunt*, by means of stylistic configurations such as metaphor or allegory (8.7.10). This type of 'oblique speech', analysed or exploited by learned Late Antique authors from Lactantius to Boethius, would substantiate the predominant medieval concept of literary fiction,

---

[1] Cassiodorus is rendered according to R.A.B. Mynors's edition 1937 and L. Jones's translation 1946.

whether transmitted by these two writers' own works – some of which were widely circulated – or through Isidore's powerful agency.

Isidore wrote an inscription for his library in Seville, recorded by the polymath's friend Braulio after his death in 636: 'Here are many sacred works, and many secular ones; if you like any of these poems, pick them up, and read', *sunt hic plura sacra, sunt hic mundalia plura: / ex his si qua placent carmina, tolle, lege.*[1] As Curtius points out, these lines set sacred and secular books side by side without any value judgment, expressing "a somewhat impersonal tolerance".[2] Even if such acceptance was not always maintained during the centuries to come, Isidore's *titulus* appears as a draft for the kind of medieval scholarly culture that did not restrict the exhortation that Augustine heard in the Milanese garden, "Pick it up and read", to the Holy Writ. Indeed, during the last two Late Antique centuries, Christian poets tended to conceive of their activities and tradition in terms of letters, *litterae*, in an unbroken line of descent from (rather than directed against) their classical Greek and Latin predecessors.

This new sense of continuity can already be detected in fifth-century culture, when the anti-pagan polemics of poets such as Paulinus of Nola and Prudentius had waned and Christianity – Catholic or Arian – was steadily gaining dominance across the lacerated Roman Empire. When looking at the volumes of a private library in the neighbourhood of Nîmes, the Gallo-Roman writer Sidonius Apollinaris, Bishop of Clermont, active around the middle of the fifth century, noted in a frequently cited letter the categorical difference between the shelves intended for ladies, replete with devout works, and those arranged for gentlemen, distinguished "by the grandeur of Latin eloquence", *coturno Latiaris eloquii*. In fact, Sidonius observes, these latter writings, however uniform in style, differ considerably from each other in their doctrines. That is, even if they were composed by "writers whose artistry was of a similar kind", *similis scientiae viri*, they included prose works by masters as different as Varro and Augustine, or books of poetry by authors as unlike as Horace and Prudentius. Both these constellations, then, involve writers widely differing in subject matter, *in causis disparibus*, even though they preserved "a similarity of style", *dicendi parilitas* (2.9.4). Admittedly, Church dignitaries would continue to distinguish between secular *nugae* and Christian concerns, but the fact that Sidonius' host gave priority to the writers' technical expertise or way of writing at the cost of their subject matter indicates that the old mythology had slowly begun to be perceived as a literary issue, providing a repository of artistic themes rather than a competing

---

1 *PL* 83.1107c.
2 Curtius 1990, p. 456.

doctrine.¹ Correspondingly, the learned consul Turcius Rufius Asterius, active towards the end of the fifth century, subjected both the *Aeneid* and Sedulius' *Paschal Song* to his editorial care; for all we know, he might have regarded them as basically two complementary contributions to the same literary genre.²

Even if the conflict between Christian faith and classical poetry was still felt, its vital tension was discharged or at least relieved. When, in another letter, Sidonius Apollinaris praised his fellow Bishop, Patiens of Lyon, for giving away his surplus of food in times of hunger, he resorted to the old myth about Triptolemus of Eleusis, known from archaic and classical vase decorations, who taught mankind the art of agriculture. The Homeric Demeter hymn had associated Triptolemus with the Eleusian mysteries (473–82), and Ovid had included him in the *Metamorphoses*, where he mounts Ceres' (Demeter's) chariot of winged snakes, receives seed for sowing from the goddess and travels through the air to scatter the grains across the fields of the inhabited world (5.642–61). As a matter of fact, Sidonius was fully aware of the inappropriate character of such comparisons. He introduces his digression with the admission that "now the inventions of pagan fable must yield pride of place", *fabularum cedant figmenta gentilium*, and he perfectly understands if Patiens, a *religiosus*, would feel offended by being praised "by means of Greek analogies derived from the idolatry of Eleusis, which he regards as inappropriate", *Achaicis Eleusinae superstitionis exemplis tamquam non idoneis* (6.12.6–7). However, all polemic heat and belligerent energy are conspicuously absent from such excuses, ringing somewhat tired and dutiful, actually an unintentional confirmation of ancient mythology's continued attraction and exemplary power in Germanic Gaul. When Sidonius utilized the tale of Triptolemus as an edifying model of Christian charity, he already anticipated the medieval reuse of the classics.

As we have been able to establish, so did Martianus Capella and Fulgentius, both of them probably active in the Vandalic or immediately post-Vandalic North Africa of the fifth and sixth centuries. We have studied their patently easy-going way of presenting (or even, in the case of Fulgentius, fraternizing with) the figures of classical mythology, attenuated to allegorical personifications but at the same time reborn in advanced metafictional machinations and mischiefs. As from the middle of the fifth century, the proverbial talk of the poets' lies had lost much of its polemical bite in the Latin West, albeit surviving as a set of standard clichés ready for new applications in medieval Europe. For all practical purposes, the two cultures were melting into one. Apollo's self-appointed

---

1 Evenepoel 1993, p. 58.
2 Cf. Roberts 1985, pp. 77–79.

vates and God's worn-out vessel had been copied and bound, each in his own codex, for a new and peaceful coexistence in the library of Sidonius Apollinaris' host outside Nîmes in southern Gaul. It testifies to the slow development of a Christian culture based on the incorporation rather than the exclusion of the classics, roughly comparable to those stone blocks from pagan temples that were used to build the new basilicas.

In conclusion: when, towards the end of the Late Antique period, the struggling Church of martyrs had become the triumphant Catholic Church in large regions of Southern and Western Europe (along with North Africa, soon to succumb, however, to the Muslim conquest), when pagan civilization had been reduced to dwindling minority subcultures, when Christianity had, in turn, been Hellenized, Romanized and Germanized with its identity of faith preserved or even strengthened, and, finally, when well-read monks had begun to build a new cultural network across the European continent, increasingly adapting the remnants of the Roman educational system to Christian needs, "the old quarrel" involving *figmenta* seemed to have become obsolete. To quote the apposite observation of Robert A. Markus: "By the time Cassiodorus began work on the *Institutes*, most probably in 562, Augustine's hostility to pagan culture had no relevance. There was no pagan culture now. Christians had made it thoroughly their own. Even the minority culture that classical learning had been was rapidly becoming a thing of the past."[1]

By implication, even if classical learning was disappearing as a "minority culture", it was already beginning to mark the Church's and the monasteries' new civilization, built on the remnants of the former Empire. This resurgence was partly due to the common model of thinking known as *translatio studii:* the idea of historical continuity, of a succession or 'transfer' of cultural values and studies in the liberal arts from Greece and Rome to Christian Europe. With the significant addition of *et imperii*, such a notion proved seminal for the accomplishment of the Carolingian 'reform and renewal' programme, chiefly aimed at the enhancement and unification of handwriting, grammar and liturgy across the new Empire. This *reformatio* and *renovatio* project was principally entrusted to the learned monks and clerics whom Charlemagne (d. 814) had gathered in Aachen, repeatedly acclaimed as the new Athens or the new Rome.[2] The King's establishment of a standardized administration throughout vast areas of Western and Central Europe was thus complemented by an educational reform which would favour the general knowledge of classical literature among the cler-

---

[1] Markus 1990, p. 221.
[2] Jongkees 1967, p. 47; Garrison 1997, p. 130.

gy. One of its great instigators, the Anglo-Saxon deacon Alcuin (d. 804), was a headmaster at the school of York where he had another famous library at his disposal, containing works by the great poets of the Roman Gold and Silver Age.

Alcuin's reform work, the starting point of what has sometimes been labelled the Carolingian Renaissance, supervised by Charlemagne in person (by all accounts hardly able to write), resulted in a true boom for exegesis, commentary literature and Latin poetry, perhaps most conspicuously within the liturgical framework of the Mass. Admittedly, the pious Alcuin himself could adapt Tertullian's or Jerome's objections to pagan fiction to the new cultural context of eighth-century Europe, as in the following letter (124): "Let God's words be read at the episcopal dinner-table. It is right that a reader should be heard, not a harpist, patristic discourse, not pagan song. What has Hinield to do with Christ?"[1] Interestingly, Alcuin substitutes Hinield – possibly identical with Ingeld, a legendary prince of the Germanic Heathobards, included in the Old English epic poem *Beowulf* – for Tertullian's Athens and Jerome's Cicero, thereby providing us with a virtually optimal illustration of the *translatio studii* from Athens via Rome to Aachen.

Nevertheless, we should probably beware of interpreting Alcuin's words as an expression of categorical hostility to fictional representation, whether Latin or Old English, partly because he was a clever poet himself, with a well-documented interest in the *trivium*, and partly because his letter is addressed to a bishop, thus testifying to the same detachment from secular letters expected of high ecclesiastical dignitaries that we have observed in Avitus or Gregory the Great. In the long run, the Carolingian Renaissance would actually establish the theoretical foundation for a viable theory of fiction in medieval Latin literature, basically by virtue of the work of one man, the intellectual giant of the whole period, yet another brilliant mind from the British Isles, the Irish philosopher and poet John Scotus Eriugena (ca. 810–77), engaged at the court of King Charles the Bald and a master of the cathedral school of Laon. In his commentary on Dionysius the Areopagite's exposition of the hierarchy of angels, *De coelesti hierarchia*, translated by himself into Latin, Eriugena was able to legitimize *figmenta* as a side-effect, as it were, of his powerful plea for the presence of symbolic discourse in the great mystic's work. This was possible since he underlined the radical negativity of such discourse. According to Eriugena, it renounces any illusion whatsoever about the possibilities of representing the Godhead in graph-

---

[1] "Verba Dei legantur in sacerdotali convivio: ibi decet lectorem audiri, non citharistam, sermones patrum, non carmina gentilium. Quid Hinieldus cum Christo?" E. Dümmler 1895, p. 183. D.A. Bullough's translation of Alcuin's letter is included as an appendix to his article 1993, see p. 124.

ic or analogical terms, stressing, by contrast, difference, distance or otherness as valid manifestations of divine reality. One of the implications of this Neo-Platonic epistemology or hermenutics, taken to its extreme, was that divine truth, by definition exempt from all fictionality, *non figmentum*, could be represented in its very opposite, in a fictional-symbolic universe (2.1.1–63). Thus theology – at this pre-scholastic stage inseparable from exegetic and contemplative studies of the Bible, *divina pagina* – seemed warranted to make use "of imaginary inventions", *fictis imaginationibus*, and could therefore, in a seminal passage from the second book of Eriugena's commentary, be compared to "a kind of poetics", *quedam poetria* (2.1.124–58).[1]

In such passages, the Irish monk furnished the direct or indirect premises for those poetical works of the High Middle Ages which in important respects would mark the breakthrough of fictionality within the heart of Christian culture, beginning at about 1100. I will have to content myself with citing two of these implementations of poetic licence for devout purposes, one in Latin and one in Italian, both relying on oblique speech – at this stage frequently comprehended in terms of *integumenta* – in a highly self-referential context, and both concerned with the idea of divine inspiration. Their authors have been referred to on several occasions *en passant* in the previous presentation; here, they are only adduced to suggest the High Medieval extension of the theoretical drama that once began with Paul, the apologists and Lactantius.

In the France of the twelfth century, another flourishing cultural era which later times have honoured with the Renaissance label, Alan of Lille composed his epic hexameter poem *Anticlaudianus* (ca. 1180) on the theme of the necessity of a reborn new man, more pious and righteous than the present one. In the prologue, Alan explicitly begs Apollo for inspiration: "Drench your poet, Apollo, with the waters of your fountain" (PR.7), *fonte tuo sic, Phebe, tuum perfunde poetam*. This invocation seems conceived in the ancient pagan style, as Ludwig Gompf remarks in an essay entitled precisely "Figmenta poetarum", while constituting a strong rebuttal of the prevalent scholastic dismantling of poetic authority.[2] Some hundred and thirty years later, an even more artistically consummate albeit idiosyncratic interpreter of the Catholic faith praised Virgil as the epitome of human knowledge, sensibility and intelligence. To Mantua's great son was entrusted the task of escorting the main protagonist of Dante's *Comedy*, the poet's alter ego, through two of the three post-mortal realms of the work. In the intro-

---

1 I follow Barbet's edition, Eriugena 1975. For an extensive analysis of this passage, see Peter Dronke's article "*Theologia veluti quaedam poetria:* Quelques observations sur la fonction des images poétiques chez Jean Scot", 1984, pp. 39–53.
2 Gompf 1973, pp. 57f.

duction to Paradise, which this pagan guide was not allowed to enter, the poet turns to "good Apollo" with a prayer to be blessed by the god's Pythian powers (Paradiso 1.13–15):

13   O buono Appollo, a l'ultimo lavoro
       fammi del tuo valor sì fatto vaso,
15   come dimandi a dar l'amato alloro.

       O good Apollo, for this last labor
       make me into a vessel worthy
       of the gift of your belovèd laurel.

To be a vessel for the god entails a transformation into an instrument, a propensity to put one's own identity at the service of a higher power. This aim was crucial for the great poets of Late Antiquity, a recurrent topos in Paulinus of Nola or Prudentius. At the same time, however, it seems evident that Dante's Delphic invocation differs considerably from that of Paulinus, who, in his best-known verse epistle, had declared that "hearts dedicated to Christ reject the Latin Muses and exclude Apollo" (10.21).[1] It contrasts just as sharply with the stern Prudentius who, in his *Apotheosis*, had relegated the same pagan god to Hell, tormented by "the lightnings of the Word" (403), *fulmina Verbi*.

The Late Antique tension between orthodox religiosity and fictional representation was thus noticeably reconfigured in the grandiose poetic creations of the High Middle Ages. To be sure, even the young Augustine, in Cassiciacum, had envisioned an Apollo compatible with the truth he had newly found in Christ (above, pp. 166ff.), but Alan and Dante would invoke the god for their accounts of an ascension which did not come to a halt until the Trinity itself seemed at hand. Again, it is true that in both *Anticlaudianus* and the *Comedy* imagination and figurative language ultimately had to yield in the vicinity of the Godhead, but they certainly proved instrumental to the layout of these works' way from here to eternity. They shaped and controlled the discursive space which made such bold enterprises possible in the first place. That is quite enough, by all relevant standards, and definitely as far as literary fiction would reach in the European Middle Ages. Consequently, it is time to conclude my attempts to track the shadowy presence of Creusa, rejected or required, through the tumultuous vicissitudes of early Christian culture.

---

[1] Recent Paulinus research considers the poem containing an invocation of 'true Apollo' (51), *salve, o Apollo vere*, numbered II in an appendix to *Carmina* in Hartel's and Kamptner's CSEL volume 30, 1999, p. 349, to be precisely a High Medieval composition. Cf. Walsh's comment in the introduction to his translations 1975, p. 28.

3 The Glory of the Mirror

It has been my intention to stress the ambiguous outcome of the main story running through this book. Despite the development I have indicated, from Late Antiquity's recurrent doubts about the value of art or poetry down to the triumphant cathedrals in words or stone of the twelfth and thirteenth centuries, Christian scepticism of fictional representation remained strong. Even the greatest of poets suffered from a persistent rumour of dealing with vain fabrications. We have seen that if Augustine, in a letter from 411–12, spoke well of Virgil's and other pre-Christian poets' possibilities of heralding the Incarnation, it was because he could agree that they had "mingled many truths with errors" (137.3.12). Such mixed praise was still heard eight centuries later, for instance in Alan of Lille's *Anticlaudianus*. In the first book of this allegorical poem, Virgil, highly esteemed by the author himself and a great name among his contemporary colleagues associated with the school of Chartres, was endowed with a Muse that "shades many a lie and from the appearance of truth weaves a cloak for falsehood" (1.142–43): *Virgilii musa mendacia multa colorat / et facie veri contexit pallia falso.*

When not even intellects as lettered as the divine doctors Augustine and Alan could accept the poet of Creusa without patent reservations, we should perhaps not be surprised at the difficulties orthodox temperaments from all camps up to the present day have experienced with possible worlds and games of make-believe. Yet literary fiction has survived in a rich plethora of avatars, in defiance of both official bans and the kind of theoretical disparagement that has been at the centre of the present work. It would be unfortunate if my focus on the criticism, poetics and aesthetics of Late Antiquity were to conceal the fact that even this period saw a number of fascinating fictional scenarios staged by mythological epic and lyric poetry. To substantiate and amplify this reminder, I would like to end my account with a quick look at the Gallo-Roman fourth-century poet Decimus Magnus Ausonius. He has surfaced in my presentation at several occasions, mostly on account of his correspondence with his recalcitrant pupil Paulinus of Nola. Now it is time for him to step forward in his own right.

If this upholder of classical culture had problems with his former student, who remembered him in his heart but drove his lovingly imparted lessons out of his mind, he was to face an even tougher challenge from posterity's literary historians, who until recently used to accuse him of *Kleinkunst*, flattery and artificial frills. As a matter of fact, Ausonius was the most important poet of his century, the son of a physician from Burdigala (Bordeaux), where he worked as a teacher of grammar and rhetoric for thirty years before he was summoned by the soldier-emperor Valentinian I to be the tutor of his son Gratian in Trier during the 360s. Peter Brown has good reason for labelling him "an *éminence grise* of the western empire".[1] For more than ten years, Ausonius lived as a man of the state, close to the dangerous and turbulent centre of imperial power, in consequence being awarded several distinguished titles, on good terms with Symmachus and other celebrities. He became governor of Gaul and finally a consul (in 379) before he retired, now a wealthy man, to his estates near Bordeaux. He had a long life and was more than eighty years old when he passed away in the 390s.

Ausonius was a Christian, although only on rare occasions did he allow his creed to illumine his poetry. That, after all, was common practice among a number of writers at the time: they adapted themes and style to the audiences of their works, surely a thorn in the flesh of Paulinus and his likes. Accordingly, if Ausonius was (or became, perhaps late in life) a believer by confession, he remained, with one or two exceptions, a pagan by subject, ethos and style. He tried unsuccessfully to persuade Paulinus to continue with his secular writing, or at least to remember his old teacher and to come visit him, and by all accounts he felt sad about his ascetic pupil's polite but negative replies to his entreaties.

The lion's share of his poems are exquisite compositions in the neoteric and elegiac tradition, some of which must have seemed scandalous in the eyes of Christian devotees. Like his contemporary Proba, Ausonius took up cento writing, though in a very different vein: he recycled verses from Virgil in a rather daring montage on the theme of a wedding, focused on the bridal couple's final love-making activities, *Cento nuptialis*. Pious readers were probably not much happier about his epyllion on the tormented love-god Cupid, literally crucified by his angry female victims, *Cupido cruciatus*. Other poems by Ausonius celebrate the memory of his deceased colleagues (rhetors and grammarians) from Bordeaux, or the beauty of Bissula, a slave-girl restored to freedom, whom he got as a reward from the Emperor for his service during a campaign against the Germanic tribes.

Let us bring this selection of Late Antique negotiations of fictionality to an end by accompanying the poet on one of his trips, the journey he made along the Moselle River around 370, from present-day Bingen down towards the imperial city of Trier, on the current frontier between Germany and Luxembourg. He described this expedition in one of his longest poems, the *Mosella*, composed of 483 hexameters. Nowadays his route is frequently recommended for tourist excursions, *der Ausoniusweg*. The *Mosella* depicts a river landscape which in reality

---

[1] Brown 1971, p. 30.

was the site of countless battles between Romans and Germans but which here, in the world of poetry, appears as an undulating *locus amoenus*, possibly a tribute to Ausonius' patron Valentinian and his court at Trier.[1] One scene follows the other in a glistening suite, all united by the writer's enthusiasm and the theme of his journey down the swirling river. The sun is shining, salmon and perch are gliding through the water, the vineyards wave across the slopes on both sides of the river.

However, Ausonius does not content himself with elaborating an idyllic genre picture. It appears that the Moselle scenery does not only please human beings: "I can believe that here the rustic Satyrs and the grey-eyed Nymphs meet together on the border of the stream" (170–71), *hic ego et agrestes Satyros et glauca tuentes / Naidas extremis credam concurrere ripis.*[2] The giddy fauns dance with "the sister-Nymphs of the crystal depths" (179), *vitreas sorores*, protected from inquisitive onlookers by the flickering midday heat. This is the author's particular way of securing the status of mythical wonder in the *Mosella*; the myth is signalled by his clever use of *credo* in the subjunctive mood, a supreme indicator of fictional belief, and its marvels are safeguarded, as it were, in a few *horas / secretas* (180–81), in a special and secluded time, far from the madding crowd and the grim vicissitudes of contemporary reality. No one has actually observed these things, Ausonius stresses. As if to respect their integrity – a gesture that scholars of Late Antique literature are not spoilt with – the poet explains that he would like to leave his fabulous company there, without intruding any further on their festivities. The secrets of fiction, entrusted to the Moselle river banks, should be covered and reverently hidden from prying eyes (186–88): *sed non haec spectata ulli nec cognita visu / fas mihi sit pro parte loqui: secreta tegatur / et commissa suis lateat reverentia rivis.*

Ausonius can thus move on to the physical surroundings of the Moselle valley, only to expose himself to yet another illusory or half-real experience, this time of an optical rather than mythological nature. He observes the impact of light across the running stream and how the dark hills are reflected in the river, so that the vines seem to be growing out of the water. Moreover, this mirror effect is perceived by a group of young oarsmen on their way down the Moselle, replicated in the whirling water: "the wave reflects a watery semblance of sailors to match them. The boys themselves delight in their own counterfeits, wondering at the illusive forms which the river gives back" (227–29), *unda refert alios sim-*

---

[1] Cf. Fontaine 1977, p. 443.
[2] I quote the *Mosella*, in Latin as well as in English translation, from H.G.E. White's Loeb volume 1919.

ulacra umentia nautas. / ipsa suo gaudet simulamine nautica pubes, / fallaces fluvio mirata redire figuras. The key words here are *simulacra* (images, phantoms, semblances), *simulamen* (copy, imitation) and *fallaces figurae* (deceptive figures). They are all highly pertinent to the subject of this book, repeatedly exploited by apologists and ascetics who treat them as terms of abuse. To Ausonius, however, they are perfectly neutral or even delightful, while their literal referents in the poem – the reflections on the waters of the Moselle – arouse nothing but admiration and pleasure among the spectators. By means of a simile, the poet ingeniously links their intriguing impact to another genre picture, that of a young girl who, for the first time, sees herself in a mirror (230–39):

230 Sic, ubi compositos ostentatura capillos
     (candentem late speculi explorantis honorem
     cum primum carae nutrix admovit alumnae)
     laeta ignorato fruitur virguncula ludo
     germanaeque putat formam spectare puellae:
235 oscula fulgenti dat non referenda metallo
     aut fixas praetemptat acus aut frontis ad oram
     vibratos captat digitis extendere crines:
     talis ad umbrarum ludibria nautica pubes
     ambiguis fruitur veri falsique figuris.

> Thus, when hoping soon to display her braided tresses ('tis when the nurse has first placed near her dear charge the wide-gleaming glory of the searching mirror), delighted, the little maid enjoys the uncomprehended game, deeming she gazes on the shape of a real girl: she showers on the shining metal kisses not to be returned, or essays those firm-fixed hairpins, or puts her fingers to that brow, trying to draw out those curled locks; even so, at sight of the reflections which mock them, the lads afloat amuse themselves with shapes which waver between false and true.

Those readers who have had the patience to follow my struggle with Late Antique issues of fictionality up to this point will undoubtedly feel the theoretical charge of this brilliant scene. The girl's mirror seems indicative of the power of fiction, firstly because she confuses it with reality, secondly on account of its suggestive glimmer, *candens*, and thirdly due to its overall scanning of her actual world, *late explorans*. Such is the "wide-gleaming glory of the searching mirror", which in turn, within the rhetorical structure of the poem, emulates the elusive play of shadows on the river, *umbrarum ludibria*, the ambiguous figures dancing on the waters, neither true nor false but a bit of both… In the presence of such splendid instances of fictionality, we can safely terminate our journey here, in the company of Ausonius, somewhere between Bingen and Trier, on the shimmering waves of the Moselle.

Appendix: Original Quotations

I. In the World of Make-Believe

Quintilian, *Institutio oratoria* (6.2.28–30, 34–35)

I. At quo modo fiet ut adficiamur? Neque enim sunt motus in nostra potestate. Temptabo etiam de hoc dicere. Quas *phantasias* Graeci vocant (nos sane visiones appellemus), per quas imagines rerum absentium ita repraesentantur animo ut eas cernere oculis ac praesentes habere videamur, has quisquis bene ceperit is erit in adfectibus potentissimus. Quidam dicunt *euphantasiōton* qui sibi res voces actus secundum verum optime finget: quod quidem nobis volentibus facile continget; nisi vero inter otia animorum et spes inanes et velut somnia quaedam vigilantium ita nos hae de quibus loquor imagines prosecuntur ut peregrinari navigare proeliari, populos adloqui, divitiarum quas non habemus usum videamur disponere, nec cogitare sed facere, hoc animi vitium ad utilitatem non transferemus [...] Ubi vero miseratione opus erit, nobis ea de quibus queremur accidisse credamus, atque id animo nostro persuadeamus. Nos illi simus quos gravia indigna tristia passos queremur, nec agamus rem quasi alienam, sed adsumamus parumper illum dolorem: ita dicemus quae in nostro simili casu dicturi essemus. Vidi ego saepe histriones atque comoedos, cum ex aliquo graviore actu personam deposuissent, flentes adhuc egredi. Quod si in alienis scriptis sola pronuntiatio ita falsis accendit adfectibus, quid nos faciemus, qui illa cogitare debemus ut moveri periclitantium vice possimus?

Jean-Jacques Rousseau, *Confessions*, p. 41

II. Dans cette étrange situation mon inquiete imagination prit un parti qui me sauva de moi-même et calma ma naissante sensualité. Ce fut de se nourrir des situations qui m'avoient intéressé dans mes lectures, de les rappeller, de les varier, de les combiner, de me les approprier tellement que je devinsse un des personnages que j'imaginois, que je me visse toujours dans les positions les plus agréables selon mon gout, enfin que l'état fictif où je venois à bout de me mettre me fît oublier mon état réel dont j'étois si mécontent. Cet amour des objets imaginaires et cette facilité de m'en occuper acheverent de me dégouter de tout ce qui m'entouroit, et déterminerent ce gout pour la solitude, qui m'est toujours resté depuis ce tems-là. On verra plus d'une fois dans la suite les

> bizarres effets de cette disposition si misantrope et si sombre en apparence, mais qui vient en effet d'un coeur trop affectueux, trop aimant, trop tendre, qui, faute d'en trouver d'éxistans qui lui ressemblent est forcé de s'alimenter de fictions. Il me suffit, quant à présent, d'avoir marqué l'origine et la prémiére cause d'un penchant qui a modifié toutes mes passions, et qui, les contenant par elles mêmes, m'a toujours rendu paresseux à faire, par trop d'ardeur à desirer.

Ambrose, *Expositio evangelii secundum Lucam* (6.88)

III. Conferant gentiles, si placet, cum Christi beneficiis deorum suorum non facta, sed ficta. Ferunt certe eorum fabulae fuisse regem quemdam qui quidquid tangebat, aurum fiebat. Sed etiam convivia ipsa feralia; nam et ipsa mantilia digitis apprehensa riguerunt: et cibus in ore crepitabat, ferens non alimenta, sed vulnera: et in gutture potus haerebat, nec penetrare facilis, nec redire. Digna beneficia votis, digna tanto munera precatore, digna liberalitas conferente! Talia sunt idolorum beneficia, ut cum videntur prodesse, plus noceant: at vero Christi munera parva videntur, et maxima sunt. Denique non uni collata, sed populis; nam et cibus edentium in ore crescebat, et videbatur esse corporalis alimoniae, sed sumebatur salutis aeternae.

II. Augustine: A Restless Farewell

Augustine, *Confessiones* (9.10.23–24)

I. Conloquebamur ergo soli valde dulciter et, praeterita obliviscentes in ea quae ante sunt extenti, quaerebamus inter nos apud praesentem veritatem, quod tu es, qualis futura esset vita aeterna sanctorum, quam nec oculus vidit nec auris audivit nec in cor hominis ascendit. sed inhiabamus ore cordis in superna fluenta fontis tui, fontis vitae, qui est apud te, ut inde pro captu nostro aspersi quoquo modo rem tantam cogitaremus.

cumque ad eum finem sermo perduceretur, ut carnalium sensuum delectatio quantalibet, in quantalibet luce corporea, prae illius vitae iucunditate non comparatione sed ne commemoratione quidem digna videretur, erigentes nos ardentiore affectu in idipsum, perambulavimus gradatim cuncta corporalia et ipsum caelum, unde sol et luna et stellae lucent super terram. et adhuc ascendebamus interius cogitando et loquendo et mirando opera tua. et venimus in mentes nostras et transcendimus eas, ut attingeremus regionem ubertatis indeficientis, ubi pascis

Israhel in aeternum veritate pabulo, et ibi vita sapientia est, per quam fiunt omnia ista, et quae fuerunt et quae futura sunt, et ipsa non fit, sed sic est ut fuit, et sic erit semper. quin potius fuisse et futurum esse non est in ea, sed esse solum, quoniam aeterna est: nam fuisse et futurum esse non est aeternum. et dum loquimur et inhiamus illi, attingimus eam modice toto ictu cordis. et suspiravimus et reliquimus ibi religatas primitias spiritus et remeavimus ad strepitum oris nostri, ubi verbum et incipitur et finitur. et quid simile verbo tuo, domino nostro, in se permanenti sine vetustate atque innovanti omnia?

Augustine, *Confessiones* (9.10.25)

II. Dicebamus ergo, "si cui sileat tumultus carnis, sileant phantasiae terrae et aquarum et aeris, sileant et poli, et ipsa sibi anima sileat et transeat se non se cogitando, sileant somnia et imaginariae revelationes, omnis lingua et omne signum, et quidquid transeundo fit si cui sileat omnino (quoniam si quis audiat, dicunt haec omnia, 'non ipsa nos fecimus, sed fecit nos qui manet in aeternum'), his dictis si iam taceant, quoniam erexerunt aurem in eum qui fecit ea, et loquatur ipse solus non per ea sed per se ipsum, ut audiamus verbum eius, non per linguam carnis neque per vocem angeli nec per sonitum nubis nec per aenigma similitudinis, sed ipsum quem in his amamus, ipsum sine his audiamus (sicut nunc extendimus nos et rapida cogitatione attingimus aeternam sapientiam super omnia manentem), si continuetur hoc et subtrahantur aliae visiones longe imparis generis et haec una rapiat et absorbeat et recondat in interiora gaudia spectatorem suum, ut talis sit sempiterna vita quale fuit hoc momentum intellegentiae cui suspiravimus, nonne hoc est: 'intra in gaudium domini tui?' et istud quando? an cum omnes resurgimus, sed non omnes immutabimur?"

Augustine, *De catechizandis rudibus* (2.3)

III. Nam et mihi prope semper sermo meus displicet. Melioris enim avidus sum, quo saepe fruor interius, antequam eum explicare verbis sonantibus coepero: quod ubi minus quam mihi motus est evaluero, contristor linguam meam cordi meo non potuisse sufficere. Totum enim quod intelligo, volo ut qui me audit intelligat; et sentio me non ita loqui, ut hoc efficiam: maxime quia ille intellectus quasi rapida coruscatione perfundit animum, illa autem locutio tarda et longa est, longeque dissimilis, et dum ista volvitur, iam se ille in secreta sua condidit; [...].

Augustine, *Confessiones* (1.13.21–22)

IV. Quid enim miserius misero non miserante se ipsum et flente Didonis mortem, quae fiebat amando Aenean, non flente autem mortem suam, quae fiebat non amando te, deus, lumen cordis mei et panis oris intus animae meae et virtus maritans mentem meam et sinum cogitationis meae? [...]

sed nunc in anima mea clamet deus meus, et veritas tua dicat mihi, "non est ita, non est ita." melior est prorsus doctrina illa prior. nam ecce paratior sum oblivisci errores Aeneae atque omnia eius modi quam scribere et legere. at enim vela pendent liminibus grammaticarum scholarum, sed non illa magis honorem secreti quam tegimentum erroris significant. [...] item si quaeram quid horum maiore vitae huius incommodo quisque obliviscatur, legere et scribere an poetica illa figmenta, quis non videat quid responsurus sit, qui non est penitus oblitus sui? peccabam ergo puer cum illa inania istis utilioribus amore praeponebam, vel potius ista oderam, illa amabam. iam vero unum et unum duo, duo et duo quattuor, odiosa cantio mihi erat, et dulcissimum spectaculum vanitatis, equus ligneus plenus armatis et Troiae incendium atque ipsius umbra Creusae.

Lactantius, *Divinae institutiones* (7.24)

V. Denique tunc fient illa, quae poetae aureis temporibus facta esse iam Saturno regnante dixerunt. Quorum error hinc exortus est, quod prophetae futurorum pleraque sic proferunt et enuntiant, quasi iam peracta. Visiones enim divino spiritu offerebantur oculis eorum, et videbant illa in conspectu suo quasi fieri, ac terminari. Quae vaticinia eorum cum paulatim fama vulgasset, quoniam profani a sacramento ignorabant quatenus dicerentur, completa iam esse veteribus saeculis illa omnia putaverunt, quae utique fieri complerique non poterant homine regnante.

Augustine, *Epistolae ad Romanos inchoata expositio* (3)

VI. Fuerunt enim et prophetae non ipsius, in quibus etiam aliqua inveniuntur, quae de Christo audita cecinerunt, sicut etiam de Sibylla dicitur; quod non facile crederem, nisi quod poetarum quidam in Romana lingua nobilissimus, antequam diceret ea de innovatione saeculi, quae in domini nostri Iesu Christi regnum satis concinere et convenire videantur, praeposuit versum dicens:

Ultima Cumaei iam venit carminis aetas.
Cumaeum autem carmen sybillinum esse nemo dubitaverit. Sciens ergo apostolus ea in libris gentium inveniri testimonia veritatis, quod etiam in Actibus Apostolorum loquens Atheniensibus manifestissime ostendit, non solum ait: *per prophetas suos,* ne quis a pseudoprophetis per quasdam veritatis confessiones in aliquam impietatem seduceretur, sed addidit etiam: *in scripturis sanctis,* volens utique ostendere litteras gentium superstitiosae idolatriae plenissimas non ideo sanctas haberi oportere, quia in eis aliquid, quod ad Christum pertinet, invenitur.

Augustine, *Contra academicos* (3.6.13)

VII. Nam et Proteus ille quanta abs te mentis altitudine commemoratus, quanta intentione in optimum philosophiae genus? Proteus enim ille, ut vos adolescentes non penitus poetas a philosophia contemnendos esse videatis, in imaginem veritatis inducitur. Veritatis, inquam, Proteus in carminibus ostentat sustinetque personam, quam obtinere nemo potest, si falsis imaginibus deceptus comprehensionis nodos vel laxaverit vel dimiserit. Sunt enim istae imagines, quae consuetudine rerum corporalium per istos quibus ad necessaria huius vitae utimur sensus, nos etiam cum veritas tenetur, et quasi habetur in manibus, decipere atque illudere moliuntur.

Augustine, *Sermones* (105.7.10)

VIII. Forte si vellemus hinc exagitare Vergilium, et insultare, quare hoc dixerit; in parte tolleret nos, et diceret nobis: Et ego scio; sed quid facerem qui Romanis verba vendebam, nisi hac adulatione aliquid promitterem quod falsum erat? Et tamen et in hoc cautus fui, quando dixi: *Imperium sine fine dedi,* Iovem ipsorum induxi, qui hoc diceret. Non ex persona mea dixi rem falsam, sed Iovi imposui falsitatis personam: sicut Deus falsus erat, ita mendax vates erat. Nam vultis nosse quia ista noveram? Alio loco, quando non Iovem lapidem induxi loquentem, sed ex persona mea locutus sum, dixi:
Non res Romanae perituraque regna.
Videte quia dixi peritura regna. Dixi peritura regna, non tacui. Peritura, veritate non tacui: semper mansura, adulatione promisit.

Augustine, *De ordine* (1.4.10)

IX. Hic ego multo uberius cernens abundare laetitias meas quam vel optare aliquando ausus sum, versum istum gestiens effudi:
Sic Pater ille deum faciat, sic altus Apollo,
perducet enim ipse, si sequimur quo nos ire iubet atque ubi ponere sedem, qui dat modo augurium nostrisque illabitur animis. Nec enim altus Apollo est, qui in speluncis, in montibus, in nemoribus, nidore thuris pecudumque calamitate concitatus implet insanos, sed alius profecto est, alius ille altus veridicus, atque ipsa (quid enim verbis ambiam?) Veritas: cuius vates sunt quicumque possunt esse sapientes. Ergo aggrediemur, Licenti, freti pietate cultores, vestigiis nostris ignem perniciosum fumosarum cupiditatum opprimamus.

Augustine, *De ordine* (2.14.39)

X. Hinc se illa ratio ad ipsarum rerum divinarum beatissimam contemplationem rapere voluit. Sed ne de alto caderet, quaesivit gradus atque ipsam sibi viam per suas possessiones ordinemque molita est. Desiderabat enim pulchritudinem, quam sola et simplex posset sine istis oculis intueri; impediebatur a sensibus. Itaque in eos ipsos paululum aciem torsit, qui veritatem sese habere clamantes, festinantem ad alia pergere importuno strepitu revocabant. Et primo ab auribus coepit, quia dicebant ipsa verba sua esse, quibus iam et grammaticam et dialecticam et rhetoricam fecerat. At ista potentissima secernendi cito vidit quid inter sonum et id cuius signum esset distaret. Intellexit nihil aliud ad aurium iudicium pertinere, quam sonum eumque esse triplicem: aut in voce animantis, aut in eo quod flatus in organis faceret, aut in eo quod pulsu ederetur. Ad primum pertinere tragoedos vel comoedos, vel choros cuiuscemodi atque omnes omnino qui voce propria canerent, secundum tibiis et similibus instrumentis deputari tertio dari citharas, lyras, cymbala, atque omne quod percutiendo canorum esset.

Augustine, *De ordine* (2.14.41)

XI. Reperiebat divinos et sempiternos, praesertim quod ipsis auxiliantibus omnia superiora contexuerat. Et iam tolerabat aegerrime splendorem illorum atque serenitatem corporea vocum materia decolorari. Et quoniam illud quod mens videt semper est praesens et immortale approbatur, cuius generis numeri apparebant, sonus autem quia sensibilis res est praeterfluit in praeteritum tempus imprimiturque memoriae rationabili mendacio iam poetis favente ratione (quaerendumne quid propagini similiter inesset?), Iovis et Memoriae filias Musas esse confictum est. Unde ista disciplina sensus intellectusque particeps musicae nomen invenit.

Augustine, *Soliloquia* (2.10.18)

XII. R. – Quia scilicet aliud est falsum esse velle, aliud verum esse non posse. Itaque ipsa opera hominum velut comoedias aut tragoedias, aut mimos, et id genus alia possumus operibus pictorum fictorumque coniungere. Tam enim verus esse pictus homo non potest, quamvis in speciem hominis tendat, quam illa quae scripta sunt in libris comicorum. Neque enim falsa esse volunt, aut ullo appetitu sua farsa sunt; sed quadam necessitate, quantum fingentis arbitrium sequi potuerunt. At vero in scena Roscius voluntate falsa Hecuba erat, natura verus homo; sed illa voluntate etiam verus tragoedus, eo videlicet quo implebat, institutum: falsus autem Priamus, eo quod Priamum assimilabat, sed ipse non erat. Ex quo iam nascitur quiddam mirabile, quod tamen ita se habere nemo ambigit.
A.– Quidnam id est?
R. – Quid putas, nisi haec omnia inde esse in quibusdam vera, unde in quibusdam falsa sunt, et ad suum verum hoc solum eis prodesse, quod ad aliud falsa sunt? Unde ad id quod esse aut volunt aut debent, nullo modo perveniunt, si falsa esse fugiunt. Quo pacto enim iste quem commemoravi, verus tragoedus esset, si nollet esse falsus Hector, falsa Andromache, falsus Hercules, et alia innumera? aut unde vera pictura esset, si falsus equus non esset? unde in speculo vera hominis imago, si non falsus homo? Quare, si quibusdam, ut verum aliquid sint, prodest ut sint aliquid falsum; cur tantopere falsitates formidamus, et pro magno bono appetimus veritatem?
A. – Nescio, et multum miror, nisi quia in exemplis istis nihil imitatione dignum video. Non enim tamquam histriones, aut de speculis quaeque relucentia, aut tamquam Myronis buculae ex aere, ita etiam nos ut in nostro quodam habitu veri simus, ad alienum habitum adumbrati atque assimilati, et ob hoc falsi esse debemus; sed illud verum quaerere, quod non quasi bifronte ratione sibique adversanti, ut ex aliqua parte verum sit, ex aliqua falsum sit.
R. – Magna et divina quaedam requiris.

Augustine, *De quantitate animae* (33.72)

XIII. Inventiones tot signorum in litteris, in verbis, in gestu, in cuiuscemodi sono, in picturis atque figmentis; tot gentium linguas, tot instituta, tot nova, tot instaurata; tantum librorum numerum, et cuiuscemodi monumentorum ad custodiendam memoriam, tantamque curam posteritatis; [...] vim ratiocinandi et excogitandi, fluvios eloquentiae, carminum varietates, ludendi ac iocandi causa milleformes simulationes, modulandi peritiam, dimetiendi subtilitatem, numerandi disciplinam, praeteritorum ac futurorum ex praesentibus coniecturam.

Augustine, *Epistolae* (101.2)

XIV. Per eum namque praestatur ut ipse etiam, quae liberales disciplinae ab eis qui in libertatem vocati non sunt appellantur, quid in se habeant liberale noscatur. Neque enim habent congruum libertati, nisi quod habent congruum veritati: unde ille ipse Filius: *Et veritas*, inquit, *liberabit vos*. Non ergo illae innumerabiles et impiae fabulae, quibus vanorum plena sunt carmina poetarum, ullo modo nostrae consonant libertati; non oratorum inflata et expolita mendacia; non denique ipsorum philosophorum garrulae argutiae, qui vel Deum prorsus non cognoverunt vel cum cognovissent Deum, non sicut Deum glorificaverunt, aut gratias egerunt, sed evanuerunt in cogitationibus suis, et obscuratum est insipiens cor eorum, et dicentes se esse sapientes, stulti facti sunt: et immutaverunt gloriam incorrupti Dei in similitudinem imaginis corruptibilis hominis et volucrum atque quadrupedum et serpentium; vel qui istis simulacris non dediti, aut non nimis dediti, coluerunt tamen et servierunt creaturae potius quam Creatori. Absit omnino ut istorum vanitates et insaniae mendaces, ventosae nugae ac superbus error, recte liberales litterae nominentur, hominum scilicet infelicium, qui Dei gratiam per Iesum Christum Dominum nostrum, qua sola liberamur de corpore mortis huius, non cognoverunt, nec in eis ipsis quae vera senserunt.

Augustine, *De trinitate* (8.2.3)

XV. Ecce vide, si potes, o anima praegravata corpore *quod corrumpitur*, et onusta terrenis cogitationibus multis et variis; ecce vide, si potes: Deus veritas est. Hoc enim scriptum est: *Quoniam Deus lux est*; non quomodo isti oculi vident, sed quomodo videt cor, cum audit: Veritas est. Noli quaerere quid sit veritas; statim enim se opponent caligines imaginum corporalium et nubila phantasmatum, et perturbabunt serenitatem, quae primo ictu diluxit tibi, cum dicerem: Veritas. Ecce in ipso primo ictu quo velut coruscatione perstringeris, cum dicitur: Veritas, mane si potes; sed non potes. Relaberis in ista solita atque terrena. Quo tandem pondere, quaeso, relaberis nisi sordium contractarum cupiditatis visco et peregrinationis erroribus?

Augustine, *Epistolae* (7.2.4)

XVI. Alteri generi subiciantur illa quae putamus ita se habuisse vel ita se habere, velut cum disserendi gratia quaedam ipsi fingimus nequaquam impedientia veritatem, vel qualia figuramus cum legimus historias, et cum fabulosa vel audimus vel componimus vel suspicamur. Ego enim mihi ut libet atque ut occurrit animo, Aeneae faciem fingo, ego Medeae cum suis anguibus alitibus iunctis iugo, ego Chremetis et alicuius Parmenonis. In hoc genere sunt etiam illa, quae sive sapientes, aliquid veri talibus involventes figuris, sive stulti, variarum superstitionum conditores, pro vero attulerunt; ut est tartareus Phlegethon, et quinque antra gentis tenebrarum, et stylus septentrionalis continens coelum, et alia poetarum atque haereticorum mille portenta. Dicimus tamen et inter disputandum, puta esse tres super invicem mundos, qualis hic unus est; et, puta quadrata figura terram contineri; et similia. Haec enim omnia ut cogitationis tempestas habuerit, fingimus et putamus.

Augustine, *De vera religione* (50.98)

XVII. Utamur gradibus quos nobis divina providentia fabricare dignata est. Cum enim figmentis ludicris nimium delectati evanesceremus in cogitationibus nostris, et totam vitam in quaedam vana somnia verteremus; rationali creatura serviente legibus suis, per sonos ac litteras, ignem, fumum, nubem, columnam, quasi quaedam verba visibilia, cum infantia nostra parabolis ac similitudinibus quodammodo ludere, et interiores oculos nostros luto huiuscemodi curare non aspernata est ineffabilis misericordia Dei.

Augustine, *Epistolae* (55.7.13)

XVIII. Ad rem sacrate significandam similitudines aptas religiosissima devotione suscipimus, sicut de caetera creatura, de ventis, de mari, de terra, de volatilibus, de piscibus, de pecoribus, de arboribus, de hominibus, ad sermonem quidem multipliciter, ad celebrationem vero Sacramentorum iam christiana libertate parcissime; sicut de aqua, de frumento, de vino, de oleo. [...] Si quae autem figurae similitudinum non tantum de coelo et de sideribus, sed etiam de inferiori creatura ducuntur ad dispensationem sacramentorum, eloquentia quaedam est doctrinae salutaris, movendo affectui discentium accomodata, a visibilibus ad invisibilia, a corporalibus ad spiritalia, a temporalibus ad aeterna.

Augustine, *De vera religione* (51.100 – 52.101)

XIX. Omissis igitur et repudiatis nugis theatricis et poeticis, divinarum Scripturarum consideratione et tractatione pascamus animum atque potemus vasae curiositatis fame ac siti fessum et aestuantem, et inanibus phantasmatibus, tamquam pictis epulis, frustra refici satiarique cupientem: hoc vere liberali, et ingenuo ludo salubriter erudiamur. Si nos miracula spectaculorum, et pulchritudo delectat, illam desideremus videre Sapientiam, quae pertendit usque ad finem fortiter, et disponit omnia suaviter. Quid enim mirabilius, vi incorporea mundum corporeum fabricante et administrante? aut quid pulchrius ordinante et ornante?

Si autem omnes fatentur per corpus ista sentiri, et animum meliorem esse quam corpus, nihilne per se animus ipse conspiciet, aut quod conspiciet potest esse, nisi multo excellentius longeque praestantius? Immo vero commemorati ab iis quae iudicamus, intueri quid sit secundum quod iudicamus, et ab operibus artium conversi ad legem artium, eam speciem mente contuebimur, cuius comparatione foeda sunt quae ipsius benignitate sunt pulchra. *Invisibilia enim Dei, a creatura mundi, per ea quae facta sunt, intellecta conspiciuntur, et sempiterna eius virtus et divinitas.*

Augustine, *De trinitate* (1.1.2)

XX. Ut ergo ab huiusmodi falsitatibus humanus animus purgaretur, sancta Scriptura parvulis congruens nullius generis rerum verba vitavit ex quibus quasi gradatim ad divina atque sublimia noster intellectus velut nutritus assurgeret. Nam et verbis ex rebus corporalibus sumptis usa est cum de Deo loqueretur, velut cum ait: *In tegmine alarum tuarum protege me.* Et de spiritali creatura multa transtulit quibus significaret illud quod ita non esset sed ita dici opus esset, sicuti est: *Ego sum Deus zelans*, et: *Poenitet me hominem fecisse.* De rebus autem quae omnino non sunt non traxit aliqua vocabula quibus vel figuraret locutiones vel spissaret aenigmata. Unde perniciosius et inanius evanescunt qui tertio illo genere erroris a veritate secluduntur hoc suspicando de Deo quod neque in ipso neque in ulla creatura inveniri potest.

Augustine, *De moribus ecclesiae catholicae et de moribus manichaeorum* (1.17.30)

XXI. Quid vultis amplius? Quid imperite atque impie saevitis? Quid indoctas animas noxia suasione pervertitis? Utriusque Testamenti Deus unus est. Nam ut ista sibi congruunt, quae de utroque posuimus, ita etiam cetera, si diligenter et aequo iudicio velitis attendere. Sed quia multa dicuntur submissius et humi repentibus animis accommodatius, ut per humana in divina consurgant, multa etiam figurate, ut studiosa mens et quaesitis exerceatur utilius et uberius laetetur inventis, vos mirifica dispositione Spiritus Sancti ad decipiendos vestros auditores et illaqueandos abutimini. Quod ipsum cur divina providentia vos facere sinat, quamque verissime Apostolus dixerit: *Oportet multas haereses esse, ut probati manifesti fiant inter vos*, longum est disputare, et quod dicendum vobis est, non est vestrum ista intelligere. Non parum mihi cogniti estis. Crassas omnino mentes et corporeorum simulacrorum pestifero pastu morbidas ad divina iudicanda defertis, quae multo altiora sunt quam putatis.

Augustine, *Contra mendacium* (10.24)

XXII. Quae si mendacia dixerimus, omnes etiam parabolae ac figurae significandarum quarumcumque rerum, quae non ad proprietatem accipiendae sunt, sed in eis aliud ex alio est intellegendum, dicentur esse mendacia: quod absit omnino. Nam qui hoc putat, tropicis etiam tam multis locutionibus omnibus potest hanc importare calumniam; ita ut et ipsa quae appellatur metaphora, hoc est de re propria ad rem non propriam verbi alicuius usurpata translatio, possit ista ratione mendacium nuncupari. Cum enim dicimus fluctuare segetes, gemmare vites, floridam iuventutem, niveam canitiem; procul dubio fluctus, gemmas, florem, nivem, quia in his rebus non invenimus, in quas haec verba aliunde transtulimus, ab istis mendacia putabuntur. Et petra Christus, et cor lapideum Iudaeorum: item leo Christus, et leo diabolus, et innumerabilia talia dicentur esse mendacia. Quid quod haec tropica locutio usque ad eam pervenit, quae appellatur antiphrasis, ut dicatur abundare quod non est, dicatur dulce quod acidum est; lucus quod non luceat, Parcae quod non parcant. Unde illud est in Scripturis sanctis: *Si non in faciem benedixerit tibi*; quod diabolus ait Domino de sancto Iob, et intellegitur:

Maledixerit. [...] Hi omnes modi locutionum mendacia putabuntur, si locutio vel actio figurata in mendacio deputabitur. Si autem non est mendacium, quando ad intellegentiam veritatis aliud ex alio significantia referuntur; profecto non solum id quod fecit aut dixit Iacob patri ut benediceretur, sed neque illud quod Ioseph velut illudendis locutus est fratribus, neque quod David simulavit insaniam, nec caetera huiusmodi, mendacia iudicanda sunt, sed locutiones actionesque propheticae ad ea quae vera sunt intellegenda referendae. Quae propterea figuratis velut amictibus obteguntur, ut sensum pie quaerentis exerceant, et ne nuda ac prompta vilescant. Quamvis quae aliis locis aperte ac manifeste dicta didicimus, cum ea ipsa de abditis eruuntur, in nostra quodam modo cognitione renovantur, et renovata dulcescunt. Nec invidentur discentibus, quod his modis obscurantur: sed commendantur magis, ut quasi subtracta desiderentur ardentius, et inveniantur desiderata iucundius. Tamen vera, non falsa dicuntur; quoniam vera, non falsa significantur, seu verbo seu facto: quae significantur enim, utique ipsa dicuntur. Putantur autem mendacia, quoniam non ea quae vera significantur, dicta intelleguntur; sed ea quae falsa sunt, dicta esse creduntur. Hoc ut exemplis fiat planius, idipsum quod Iacob fecit, attende. Haedinis certe pellibus membra contexit: si causam proximam requiramus, mentitum putabimus; hoc enim fecit ut putaretur esse qui non erat: si autem hoc factum ad illud propter quod significandum revera factum est referatur; per haedinas pelles peccata, per eum vero qui eis se operuit, ille significatus est qui non sua sed aliena peccata portavit. Verax ergo significatio nullo modo mendacium recte dici potest. Ut autem in facto, ita et in verbo. Nam cum ei pater dixisset: *Quis es tu, fili?* ille respondit: *Ego sum Esau primogenitus tuus.* Hoc si referatur ad duos illos geminos, mendacium videbitur: si autem ad illud propter quod significandum ista gesta dictaque conscripta sunt, ille est hic intellegendus in corpore suo, quod est eius Ecclesia, qui de hac re loquens ait: *Cum videritis Abraham, et Isaac, et Iacob, et omnes Prophetas in regno Dei, vos autem expelli foras. Et venient ab oriente et occidente et aquilone et austro, et accumbent in regno Dei: et ecce sunt novissimi qui erant primi, et sunt primi qui erant novissimi.* Sic enim quodam modo minor maioris primatum frater abstulit atque in se transtulit fratris. Cum igitur tam vera tamque significentur veraciter, quid hic debet putari factum dictumve mendaciter? Cum enim quae significantur, non utique non sunt in veritate, sed sunt seu praeterita, seu praesentia, seu futura; procul dubio vera significatio est, nullumque mendacium. Sed nimis longum est in hac significatione prophetica enucleate cuncta rimari, in quibus palmam veritas habet, quia ut significando praenuntiata sunt, ita consequendo claruerunt.

Augustine, *Contra mendacium* (13.28)

XXIII. Ubi evangelista dicens: *Ipse autem se finxit longius ire*; etiam ipsum verbum posuit, quo mendaces nimium delectantur, ut impune mentiantur: quasi mendacium sit omne quod fingitur, cum veraciter aliud ex alio significandi causa tam multa fingantur. Si ergo nihil aliud significasset Iesus in eo quod longius ire se finxit, merito iudicaretur esse mendacium: porro autem si bene intellegatur, et ad id quod voluit significare referatur, invenitur esse mysterium. Alioquin erunt cuncta mendacia, quae propter quamdam rerum significandarum similitudinem, cum gesta non sint, tamquam gesta narrantur. Unde est illa de duobus unius hominis filiis, maiore qui mansit apud patrem suum, et minore qui longe peregrinatus est, tam prolixa narratio. In quo genere fingendi humana etiam facta vel dicta irrationalibus animantibus et rebus sensu carentibus homines addiderunt, ut eiusmodi fictis narrationibus, sed veracibus significationibus, quod vellent commendatius intimarent. Nec apud auctores tantum saecularium litterarum, ut apud Horatium, mus loquitur muri, et mustela vulpeculae, ut per narrationem fictam ad id quod agitur, vera significatio referatur; unde et Aesopi tales fabulas ad eum finem relatas, nullus tam ineruditus fuit, qui putaret appellanda mendacia: sed in Litteris quoque sacris, sicut in Libro Iudicum ligna sibi regem requirunt, et loquuntur ad oleam, et ad ficum, et ad vitem, et ad rubum. Quod utique totum fingitur, ut ad rem quae intenditur, ficta quidem narratione, non mendaci tamen, sed veraci significatione veniatur. Haec dixi propter id quod scriptum est de Iesu: *Et ipse se finxit longius ire*; ne quisquam ex hoc verbo, sicut Priscillianistae, licitum volens habere mendacium, insuper etiam Christum contendat fuisse mentitum. Quisquis autem vult intellegere illud fingendo quid praefigurarit, attendat quid agendo perfecerit. Longius namque postea profectus super omnes coelos, non tamen deseruit discipulos suos. Propter hoc significandum futurum divinitus factum, ad praesens illud est humanitus fictum. Et ideo significatio verax in illa est fictione praemissa, quia in hac profectione illius est significationis veritas subsecuta. Ille igitur contendat Christum mentitum esse fingendo, qui negat eum quod significavit implevisse faciendo.

Augustine, *Quaestionum evangeliorum libri duo* (2.51.1):

XXIV. Non enim omne quod fingimus mendacium est; sed quando id fingimus quod nihil significat, tunc est mendacium. Cum autem fictio nostra refertur ad aliquam significationem, non est mendacium sed aliqua figura veritatis. Alioquin omnia quae a sapientibus et sanctis viris, vel etiam ab ipso Domino figurate dicta sunt mendacia deputabuntur, quia secundum usitatum intellectum non subsistit veritas talibus dictis. Non enim homo qui habuit duos filios, quorum minor accepta parte patrimonii sui profectus est in regionem longinquam et cetera quae in illa narratione contexuntur, ita dicuntur tamquam vere fuerit quisquam homo qui hoc in filiis suis duobus aut passus sit aut fecerit. Ficta sunt ergo ista ad rem quandam significandam tam longe alteque maiorem et tam incomparabiliter differentem, ut per illum fictum hominem Deus verus intellegatur. Sicut autem dicta ita etiam facta finguntur sine mendacio ad aliquam rem significandam. Unde est etiam illud eiusdem Domini, quod in fici arbore fructum quaesivit eo tempore quo illa poma nondum essent. Non enim dubium est illam inquisitionem non fuisse veram; quivis enim hominum sciret si non infecunditate vel tempore poma illam arborem non habere. Fictio igitur quae ad aliquam veritatem refertur figura est, quae non refertur mendacium est.

Augustine, *Enarrationes in Psalmos* (103.1.13)

XXV. Videte autem ne putetis nominata allegoria, pantomimi aliquid me dixisse. Nam quaedam verba, quoniam verba sunt, et ex lingua procedunt, communia nobis sunt etiam cum rebus ludicris, et non honestis: tamen locum suum habent verba ista in Ecclesia, et locum suum in scena. Non enim ego dixi quod Apostolus non dixit, cum de duobus filiis Abrahae diceret: *Quae sunt*, inquit, *in allegoria*. Allegoria dicitur, cum aliquid aliud videtur sonare in verbis, et aliud in intellectu significare. Quomodo dicitur agnus Christus: numquid pecus? Leo Christus: numquid bestia? Petra Christus: numquid duritia? Mons Christus: numquid tumor terrae? Et sic multa aliud videntur sonare, aliud significare; et vocatur allegoria. Nam qui putat me de theatro dixisse allegoriam, putet et Dominum de amphitheatro dixisse parabolam. Videtis quid faciat civitas ubi abundant spectacula: in agro securius loquerer; quid sit enim allegoria, non ibi forte didicissent homines, nisi in Scripturis Dei. Ergo quod dicimus allegoriam figuram esse, sacramentum figuratum allegoria est. Et quid hic accipimus: *Ascendit super pennas ventorum?* Diximus, bene accipi figurate ventos animas. Pennae ventorum, pennae animarum quae sunt, nisi a quibus sursum attolluntur? Pennae ergo animarum virtutes, bona opera, recte facta. In duabus alis habent omnes pennas; omnia enim praecepta in duobus praeceptis sunt. Quisquis dilexerit Deum et proximum, animam habet pennatam, liberis alis, sancto amore volantem ad Dominum.

Augustine, *Contra Faustum Manichaeum* (20.9)

XXVI. Hinc vos Paganis dicimus deteriores, eo tantum similes, quod multos deos colitis: eo vero in peiorem partem dissimiles, quod illi pro diis ea colunt quae sunt, sed dii non sunt; vos autem colitis ea quae nec dii, nec aliquid sunt, quoniam prorsus nulla sunt. Habent quidem et illi quaedam fabulosa figmenta, sed esse illas fabulas norunt; et vel a poetis delectandi causa fictas esse asserunt, vel eas ad naturam rerum vel mores hominum interpretari conantur: sicut Vulcanum claudum, quia ignis terreni motus eiusmodi est; et Fortunam caecam, quod ex incerto accidant, quae fortuita dicuntur; [...] et alia permulta in hunc modum. Quocirca hoc in eis irridemus, quod interpretata sic adorant, quae non intellecta, quamvis damnabiliter, tamen excusabilius adorarent. Ipsis quippe interpretationibus convincuntur, non se illum Deum colere, cuius solius participatione mens beata fit, sed ab illo conditam creaturam: nec solas virtutes ipsius creaturae, sicut Minervam, cuius fabulam quod de Iovis capite nata sit, ad prudentiam consiliorum interpretantur, quae rationis est propria, cui sedem capitis etiam Plato dedit; sed etiam vitia, sicut de Cupidine diximus. Unde quidam eorum tragicus ait:

Deum esse amorem, turpis et vitio favens
finxit libido.

Nam et corporalium vitiorum simulacra Romani consecraverunt, sicut Palloris et Febris. Ut ergo omittam quod simulacrorum adoratores circa ipsas corporum figuras habent affectum, ut eas ipsas formas in locis honorabilibus sublimatas, quibus tantum obsequium exhiberi vident, tamquam deos timeant; illae ipsae interpretationes, quibus haec muta, et surda, et caeca, et exanima defenduntur, dignius accusantur: verumtamen et ista quoquo modo sunt, quamvis, ut iam dixi, ad salutem vel aliquam utilitatem nihil sint, et quae ex his interpretantur, in rebus inveniuntur.

Augustine, *Contra Faustum Manichaeum* (22.25)

XXVII. Nihil enim sapiunt, nec intellegunt in magnis animis quasdam virtutes vitiis parvorum esse simillimas, nonnulla specie, sed nulla aequitatis comparatione. Similes autem sunt qui in magnis ista reprehendunt, pueris imperitis in schola, qui cum pro magno didicerint, nomini numeri singularis verbum numeri singularis esse reddendum, reprehendunt latinae linguae doctissimum auctorem, quia dixit: *Pars in frusta secant.* Debuit enim, inquiunt, dicere: Secat. Et quia norunt Religionem dici, culpant eum quia geminata littera dixit: *Relligione patrum.* Unde non absurde fortasse dicatur, in genere suo, quantum distant schemata et metaplasmi doctorum a soloecismis et barbarismis imperitorum, tantum distare figurata facta Prophetarum a libidinosis peccatis iniquorum: ac per hoc, sicut puer in barbarismo reprehensus, si de Virgilii metaplasmo se vellet defendere, ferulis caederetur; ita quisquis cum ancilla suae coniugis volutatus, Abrahae factum, quod de Agar prolem genuerit, in exemplum defensionis assumpserit, utinam non plane ferulis, sed vel fustibus coercitus emendetur, ne cum caeteris adulteris aeterno supplicio puniatur. Minimae quidem illae res, istae autem magnae sunt; nec ad hoc inde ducta similitudo est, ut schema sacramento, et soloecismus adulterio coaequetur: verumtamen proportione sui cuiusque generis, quod in illis locutionum quibusdam virtutibus seu vitiis peritia vel imperitia, hoc in his morum quamvis longe in diverso genere virtutibus seu vitiis sapientia vel insipientia valet.

Augustine, *Confessiones* (3.6.11)

XXVIII. Ubi ergo mihi tunc eras et quam longe? et longe peregrinabar abs te, exclusus et a siliquis porcorum quos de siliquis pascebam. quanto enim meliores grammaticorum et poetarum fabellae quam illa decipula! nam versus et carmen et Medea volans utiliores certe quam quinque elementa varie fucata propter quinque antra tenebrarum, quae omnino nulla sunt et occidunt credentem. nam versum et carmen etiam ad vera pulmenta transfero; volantem autem Medeam etsi cantabam, non adserebam, etsi cantari audiebam, non credebam. illa autem credidi – vae, vae! quibus gradibus deductus in profunda inferi, quippe laborans et aestuans inopia veri, cum te, deus meus (tibi enim confiteor, qui me miseratus es et nondum confitentem), cum te non secundum intellectum mentis, quo me praestare voluisti beluis, sed secundum sensum carnis quaererem. tu autem eras interior intimo meo et superior summo meo.

Augustine, *Epistolae* (44.1.1)

XXIX. Sed nobis in tota illa multitudine perpauci apparebant, qui utiliter ac salubriter agi causam illam, et tantam reique tantae quaestionem prudenter et pie discuti cuperent. Caeteri vero magis ad spectaculum quasi altercationis nostrae prope theatrica consuetudine, quam ad instructionem salutis christiana devotione convenerant. Quapropter nec silentium nobis praebere, nec intente atque nobiscum modeste saltem et ordinate colloqui potuerunt, exceptis, ut dixi, paucis, quorum religiosa et simplex apparebat intentio. Itaque libere pro sui cuiusque animi motu immoderate loquentium omnia strepitu turbabantur, nec evincere sive nos, sive ipse rogando, interdum etiam obiurgando potuimus, ut nobis modestum silentium praeberetur.

III. Oblique Speech

Lactantius, *Divinae institutiones* (1.11)

I. Igitur qui sapere sibi videntur, quia intelligunt vivum terrenumque corpus in coelo esse non posse, totam Ganymedeam fabulam pro falso repudiant; ac sentiunt in terra id esse factum, quia res ac libido ipsa terrena est. Non ergo ipsas res gestas finxerunt poetae; quod si facerent, essent vanissimi: sed rebus gestis addiderunt quemdam colorem. Non enim obtrectantes illa dicebant, sed ornare cupientes. Hinc homines decipiuntur: maxime quod, dum haec omnia ficta esse arbitrantur a poetis, colunt quod ignorant. Nesciunt enim, qui sit poeticae licentiae modus; quousque progredi fingendo liceat: cum officium poetae sit in eo, ut ea, quae gesta sunt vere, in alias species obliquis figurationibus cum decore aliquo conversa traducat. Totum autem, quod referas, fingere, id est ineptum esse, et mendacem potius quam poetam.

Servius, *In Vergilii carmina commentarii* (6.893)

II. Hic umbras veras *per corneam*, per quas *umbras* somnia indicat vera. et poetice apertus est sensus: vult autem intellegi falsa esse omnia quae dixit. physiologia vero hoc habet: per portam corneam oculi significantur, qui et cornei sunt coloris et duriores ceteris membris: nam frigus non sentiunt, sicut et Cicero dicit in libris de deorum natura. per eburneam vero portam os significatur a dentibus. et scimus quia quae loquimur falsa esse possunt, ea vero quae videmus sine dubio vera sunt. ideo Aeneas per eburneam emittitur portam. est et alter sensus: Somnum novimus cum cornu pingi. et qui de somniis scripserunt dicunt ea quae secundum fortunam et personae possibilitatem videntur habere effectum. et haec vicina sunt cornu: unde cornea vera fingitur porta. ea vero quae supra fortunam sunt et habent nimium ornatum vanamque iactantiam dicunt falsa esse: unde eburnea, quasi ornatior porta, fingitur *falsa*.

Macrobius, *Saturnalia* (5.1.18 – 19)

III. Atque adeo non alium secutus ducem quam ipsam rerum omnium matrem naturam, hanc pertexuit velut in musica concordiam dissonorum. quippe si mundum ipsum diligenter inspicias, magnam similitudinem divini illius et huius poetici operis invenies. nam qualiter eloquentia Maronis ad omnium mores integra est, nunc brevis, nunc copiosa, nunc sicca, nunc florida, nunc simul omnia, interdum lenis aut torrens: sic terra ipsa hic laeta segetibus et pratis, ibi silvis et rupibus hispida, hic sicca harenis, hic irrigua fontibus, pars vasto aperitur mari.

Macrobius, *Commentarii in Somnium Scipionis* (1.2.14 – 16)

IV. Cum de his inquam loquuntur summo deo et mente, nihil fabulosum penitus attingunt, sed siquid de his adsignare conantur quae non sermonem tantum modo sed cogitationem quoque humanam superant, ad similitudines et exempla confugiunt. sic Plato cum de *tagathōi* loqui esset animatus, dicere quid sit non ausus est, hoc solum de eo sciens, quod sciri quale sit ab homine non possit, solum vero ei simillimum de visibilibus solem repperit, et per eius similitudinem viam sermoni suo attollendi se ad non comprehendenda patefecit. ideo et nullum ei simulacrum, cum dis aliis constituerentur, finxit antiquitas, quia summus deus nataque ex eo mens sicut ultra animam ita supra naturam sunt, quo nihil fas est de fabulis pervenire.

Macrobius, *Commentarii in Somnium Scipionis* (2.10.11)

V. Et hoc esse volunt quod Homerus, divinarum omnium inventionum fons et origo, sub poetici nube figmenti verum sapientibus intellegi dedit, Iovem cum dis ceteris, id est cum stellis, profectum in Oceanum, Aethiopibus eum ad epulas invitantibus. per quam imaginem fabulosam Homerum significasse volunt hauriri de umore nutrimenta sideribus, qui ob hoc Aethiopas reges epularum caelestium dixit quoniam circa Oceani oram non nisi Aethiopes habitant, quos vicinia solis usque ad speciem nigri coloris exurit.

Fulgentius, *Mitologiae* (2.82–84)
VI. Iuste vel Sol Veneris depalat adulterium, quatenus Luna solet eius celare secretum. Venus cum Marte concubuit, quam Sol inveniens Vulcano prodidit; ille adamante catenas effecit ambosque religans diis turpiter iacentes ostendit. Illa dolens quinque filias Solis amore succendit [id est Pasiphe, Medea, Fedra, Circe, Dirce]. Quid sibi in hoc poetica alludat garrulitas inquiramus. Perstant nunc in nostra vita de hac fabula certe admodum testimonia; nam virtus corrupta libidine sole teste apparet, unde et Ovidius in [quinto] metamorfoseon ait: "Vidit hic deus omnia primus". Quae quidem virtus corrupta libidine turpiter catenata fervoris constrictione tenetur. Haec itaque quinque Solis filias, id est quinque humanos sensus luci ac veritati deditos quasi solis fetus hac corruptela fuscatos [amore succendit]. Ob hac re etiam huiuscemodi nomina quinque ipsis Solis filiabus volverunt: primam Pasiphen ut visum, id est quasi pasinfanon, quod nos Latine omnibus apparentem dicimus – visus enim reliquos quattuor inspicit sensus, quia et eum qui clamat videt et palpanda notat et degustata aspicit et odoranda intendit –, secundam Medeam quasi auditum hoc est medenidean quod nos Latine nullam visionem dicimus – vox enim corpore nuda est –, tertia Circe tactui similis, id est quasi si diceret cironcr<*in*>e Grece, quod nos Latine manuum iudicium dicimus, quarta Fedra quasi odoratus, velut si dicat feronedon quasi adferens suavitatem, quinta Dirce saporis i*u*dex, id est quasi drimoncrine quod nos Latine acrum iudicans dicimus.

Boethius, *De consolatione philosophiae* (1.PR.1)
VII. Quae ubi poeticas Musas vidit nostro adsistentes toro fletibusque meis verba dictantes, commota paulisper ac torvis inflammata luminibus: "Quis," inquit, "has scenicas meretriculas ad hunc aegrum permisit accedere quae dolores eius non modo nullis remediis foverent, verum dulcibus insuper alerent venenis? Hae sunt enim quae infructuosis affectuum spinis uberem fructibus rationis segetem necant hominumque mentes assuefaciunt morbo, non liberant. At si quem profanum, uti vulgo solitum vobis, blanditiae vestrae detraherent, minus moleste ferendum putarem; nihil quippe in eo nostrae operae laederentur. Hunc vero Eleaticis atque Academicis studiis innutritum? Sed abite potius Si-

renes usque in exitium dulces meisque eum Musis curandum sanandumque relinquite."

His ille chorus increpitus deiecit humi maestior vultum confessusque rubore verecundiam limen tristis excessit.

Macrobius, *Commentarii in Somnium Scipionis* (1.2.13–16)

VIII. Sciendum est tamen non in omnem disputationem philosophos admittere fabulosa vel licita; sed his uti solent cum vel de anima vel de aeriis aetheriisve potestatibus vel de ceteris dis loquuntur. ceterum cum ad summum et principem omnium deum, qui apud Graecos *tagathon*, qui *prōton aition* nuncupatur, tractatus se audet attollere, vel ad mentem, quem Graeci *noun* appellant, originales rerum species, quae *ideai* dictae sunt, continentem, ex summo natam et profectam deo: cum de his inquam loquuntur summo deo et mente, nihil fabulosum penitus attingunt, sed siquid de his adsignare conantur quae non sermonem tantum modo sed cogitationem quoque humanam superant, ad similitudines et exempla confugiunt. sic Plato cum de *tagathōi* loqui esset animatus, dicere quid sit non ausus est, hoc solum de eo sciens, quod sciri quale sit ab homine non possit, solum vero ei simillimum de visibilibus solem repperit, et per eius similitudinem viam sermoni suo attollendi se ad non comprehendenda patefecit. ideo et nullum ei simulacrum, cum dis aliis constituerentur, finxit antiquitas, quia summus deus nataque ex eo mens sicut ultra animam ita supra naturam sunt, quo nihil fas est de fabulis pervenire.

IV. Poeta Christianus

Cassian, *Collationes patrum* (14.12)

I. Speciale inpedimentum salutis accedit per illam quam tenuiter videor adtigisse notitiam litterarum, in qua me ita vel instantia paedagogi vel continuae lectionis maceravit intentio, ut nunc mens mea poeticis illis velut infecta carminibus illas fabularum nugas historiasque bellorum, quibus a parvulo primis studiorum inbuta est rudimentis, orationis etiam tempore meditetur, psallentique vel pro peccatorum indulgentia supplicanti aut inpudens poematum memoria suggeratur aut quasi bellantium heroum ante oculos imago versetur, taliumque me phantasmatum imaginatio semper inludens ita mentem meam ad supernos intuitus adspirare non patitur, ut cotidianis fletibus non possit expelli.

Jerome, *Epistulae* (36.14)

II. Scio haec molesta esse lectori, sed de Hebraicis litteris disputantem, non decet Aristotelis argumenta conquirere, nec ex flumine Tulliano eloquentiae ducendus est rivulus: nec aures Quintiliani flosculis et scholari declamatione mulcendae. Pedestris, et quotidianae similis, et nullam lucubrationem redolens oratio necessaria est, quae rem explicet, sensum edisserat, obscura manifestet, non quae verborum compositione frondescat. Sint alii diserti, laudentur, ut volunt, et inflatis buccis, spumantia verba trutinent: mihi sufficit sic loqui, ut intelligar, ut de Scripturis disputans, Scripturarum imiter simplicitatem.

Jerome, *Commentariorum in Isaiam prophetam libri duodeviginti* (10.438–39)

III. Cum autem oculi credentis regem in sua maiestate conspexerint, et cor eius meditatum fuerit timorem, tunc imprudentem populum non videbit, populum Iudaeorum, sive philosophorum et oratorum mundi, qui applaudunt sibi in eruditione et eloquentia saeculari, de quibus nunc ait: *Populum alti sermonis: ita ut non possis intelligere disertitudinem linguae eius*; quorum omnis ornatus in verbis est, qui habent folia tantum umbramque sermonum, et fructum non possident veritatis. Denique sequitur: *In quo nulla est sapientia*, de quibus et alio loco dicitur: *Perdam sapientiam sapientium, et intellectum prudentium reprobabo*. Cur? quia stultam fecit Deus sapientiam huius saeculi.

Paulinus of Nola, *Epistulae* (16.6–7)

IV. Omnium poetarum floribus spiras, omnium oratorum fluminibus exundas, philosophiae quoque fontibus inrigaris, peregrinis etiam dives litteris Romanum os Atticis favis inples. quaeso te, ubi tunc tributa sunt, cum Tullium et Demosthenem perlegis? vel iam usitatiorum de saturitate fastidiens lectionum Xenophontem, Platonem, Catonem Varronemque perlectos revolvis multosque praeterea, quorum nos forte nec nomina, tu etiam volumina tenes? ut istis occuperis, inmunis et liber, ut Christum hoc est sapientiam dei discas, tributarius et occupatus es. vacat tibi ut et philosophus sis, non vacat ut Christianus sis. verte potius sententiam, verte facundiam. nam animi philosophiam non deponas licet, dum eam fide condias et religione; conserta utare sapientius, ut sis dei philosophus et dei vates, non quaerendo sed imitando deum sapiens, ut non lingua quam vita eruditus tam disseras magna quam facias.

Esto Peripateticus deo, Pythagoreus mundo. verae in Christo sapientiae praedicator et tandem tacitus vanitati, perniciosam istam inanium dulcedinem litterarum quasi illos patriae oblitteratores de baccarum suavitate Lotophagos, ut Sirenarum carmina blandimentorum nocentium cantus evita. et quia licet quaedam plerumque de inanibus fabulis ut de vulgaribus aliqua proverbiis in usum veri ac serii sermonis adsumere, dicam non litteras tantum, sed et omnes rerum temporalium species nobis esse Lotophagos vel Sirenas. nam et voluptatum pestifera dulcedo patriae nobis oblivionem facit, cum homini deum, qui est patria omnium communis, oblitterat, et inlecebrae cupiditatum illam Sirenarum fabulam veritate cladis imitantur. nam quod illae Sirenae fuisse finguntur, id vere sunt inlecebrae cupiditatum et blandimenta vitiorum; habent enim in specie lenocinium, in gustu venenum, quorum usus in crimine, pretium in morte numeratur. has oportet ultra Ulixis astutiam cauti non auribus tantum sed et oculis obseratis et animo quasi navigio praetervolante fugiamus, ne sollicitati delectatione letifera in criminum saxa rapiamur et scopulo mortis adfixi naufragium salutis obeamus.

Paulinus of Nola, *Epistulae* (23.30)

V. Et ad auram spiritus sancti sensuum suorum sinus pandunt et cordis sui velum vinculis caritatis ut funibus ad antemnam crucis stringunt. et arbor illis est *virga de radice Iesse,* quae totam corporis nostri quadriremem regit et cui si iuxta illam poeticam fabulam in prophetica veritate nectamur, voluntariis adstricti nexibus et obstructis non cera sed fide neque corporis sed cordis auribus, contra huius mundi varias ad capiendum, pares ad nocendum inlecebras tuti et innocui scopulos voluptatum quasi saxa Sirenum praetervehimur.

Ambrose, *Epistulae* (73.8)

VI. Uno, inquit, itinere non potest perveniri ad tam grande secretum. Quod vos ignoratis id nos dei voce cognovimus, et quod vos suspicionibus quaeritis nos ex ipsa sapientia dei et veritate compertum habemus. Non congruunt igitur vestra nobiscum: vos pacem diis vestris ab imperatoribus obsecratis, nos ipsis imperatoribus a Christo pacem rogamus; vos manuum vestrarum adoratis opera, nos iniuriam ducimus omne quod fieri potest deum putari. Non vult se deus in lapidibus coli; denique etiam ipsi philosophi vestri ista riserunt.

Sedulius, *Epistola ad Macedonium* I

VII. Cur autem metrica voluerim haec ratione componere, non differam breviter expedire. Raro, pater optime, sicut vestra quoque peritia lectionis assiduitate cognoscit, divinae munera potestatis stilo quisquam huius modulationis aptavit, et multi sunt quos studiorum saecularium disciplina per poeticas magis delicias et carminum voluptates oblectat. Hi quicquid rhetoricae facundiae perlegunt, neglegentius assequuntur, quoniam illud haud diligunt, quod autem versuum viderint blandimento mellitum, tanta cordis aviditate suscipiunt, ut in alta memoria saepius haec iterando constituant et reponant. Horum itaque mores non repudiandos aestimo sed pro insita consuetudine vel natura tractandos, ut quisque suo magis ingenio voluntarius adquiratur Deo. Nec differt qua quis occasione imbuatur ad fidem, dum tamen viam libertatis ingressus non repetat iniquae servitutis laqueos, quibus ante fuerat irretitus. Hae sunt, pater egregie, nostri operis causae, non supervacuae, sicut didicisti, sed commodae, quae si probabili ratione non displicent, benignitatis tuae donentur favore, quo paululum ab scripturis celsioribus vacans humilioribus te quoque libenter impertias.

Jerome, *Epistulae* (21.13)

VIII. Daemonum cibus est carmina Poetarum, saecularis sapientia, Rhetoricorum pompa verborum. Haec sua omnes suavitate delectant: et dum aures versibus dulci modulatione currentibus capiunt, animam quoque penetrant, et pectoris interna devinciunt. Verum ubi cum summo studio fuerint ac labore perlecta, nihil aliud, nisi inanem sonum, et sermonum strepitum suis lectoribus tribuunt: NULLA IBI SATURITAS veritatis, nulla refectio justitiae reperitur. Studiosi earum in fame veri, et virtutum penuria perseverant.

Avitus, *Epistola ad Apollinarem [In Dei nomine incipit prologus]* (27–36)

IX. In saeculari namque versuum opere condendo, tanto quis peritior appellatur, quanto elegantius – immo, ut vere dicamus, ineptius – falsa texuerit. Taceo iam verba illa vel nomina quae nobis nec in alienis quidem operibus frequentare, ne dicam in nostris conscribere licet, quae ad conpendia poetarum aliud ex alio significantia plurimum valent. Quocirca saecularium iudicio, qui aut inperitiae aut ignaviae dabunt non uti nos licentia poetarum, plus arduum quam fructuosum opus adgressi, divinam longe discrevimus ab humana existimatione censuram.

V. Epilogue: Ecclesia Triumphans

Isidore of Seville, *Sententiae* (3.13.1–11)

I. Ideo prohibetur christianus figmenta legere poetarum quia per oblectamenta inanium fabularum mentem excitant ad incentiva libidinum. Non enim solum tura offerendo daemonibus immolatur, sed etiam eorum dicta libentius capiendo.

Quidam plus meditare delectantur gentilium dicta propter tumentem et ornatum sermonem, quam scripturam sanctam propter eloquium humile. Sed quid prodest in mundanis doctrinis proficere, et inanescere in divinis; caduca sequi figmenta et caelestia fastidire mysteria? Cavendi sunt igitur tales libri, et propter amorem sanctarum scripturarum vitandi.

Gentilium dicta exterius verborum eloquentia nitent, interius vacua virtutis sapientia manent; eloquia autem sacra exterius incompta verbis apparent, intrinsecus autem mysteriorum sapientia fulgent. Unde et apostolus: *Habemus*, inquit, *thesaurum istud in vasis fictilibus.* – Sermo quippe Dei occultum habet fulgorem sapientiae et veritatis repositum in verborum vilissimis vasculis.

Ideo libri sancti simplici sermone conscripti sunt, *ut non in sapientia verbi, sed in ostensione spiritus*, homines ad fidem perducerentur. Nam si dialectici acuminis versutia, aut rhetoricae artis eloquentia editi essent, nequaquam putaretur fides Christi in Dei virtute, sed in eloquentiae humanae argumentis consistere; nec quemquam crederemus ad fidem divino inspiramine provocari, sed potius verborum calliditate seduci.

Omnis saecularis doctrina spumantibus verbis resonans, ac se per eloquentiae tumorem adtollens, per doctrinam simplicem et humilem christianam evacuata est, sicut scriptum est: *Nonne stultam fecit Deus sapientiam huius mundi?*

Fastidiosis atque loquacibus scripturae sanctae minus propter sermonem simplicem placent; gentili enim eloquentiae conparata videtur illis indigna. Quod si animo humili mysteria eius intendant, confestim advertunt quantum excelsa sunt quae in illis despiciunt.

In lectione non verba sed veritas est amanda. Saepe autem repperitur simplicitas veridica, et conposita falsitas quae hominem suis erroribus inlicit et per linguae ornamenta laqueos dulces adspargit.

Nihil aliud agit amor mundanae scientiae, nisi extollere laudibus hominem. Nam quanto maiora fuerint litteraturae studia, tanto animus arrogantiae fastu inflatus, maiore intumescit iactantia. Unde et bene psalmus ait: *Quia non cognovi litteraturam, introibo in potentias Domini.*

Simplicioribus litteris non est proponendus fucus grammaticae artis. Meliores sunt enim communes litterae, quia simpliciores, et ad solam humilitatem legentium pertinentes; illae vero nequiores quia ingerunt hominibus perniciosam mentis elationem.

Meliores esse grammaticos quam hereticos; heretici enim haustum letiferi sucus hominibus persuadendo propinant; grammaticorum autem doctrina potest etiam proficere ad vitam, dum fuerit in meliores usus adsumpta.

Maximus of Turin, *Sermones* (37.2)

II. Si ergo de Ulixe illo refert fabula quod eum arboris religatio de periculo liberarit, quanto magis praedicandum est quod vere factum est, hoc est quod hodie omne genus hominum de mortis periculo crucis arbor eripuit! Ex quo enim Christus dominus religatus in cruce est, ex eo nos mundi inlecebrosa discrimina velut clausa aure transimus; nec pernicioso enim saeculi detinemur auditu, nec cursu melioris vitae deflectimur in scopulos voluptatis. Crucis enim arbor non solum religatum sibi hominem patriae repraesentat, sed etiam socios circa se positos virtutis suae umbra custodit. Quod autem crux ad patriam post multos errores redire nos faciat, dominus declarat dicens latroni in cruce posito: *Hodie mecum eris in paradyso.* Qui utique latro diu oberrans ac naufragus aliter ad patriam paradysi, de qua primus homo exierat, redire non poterat, nisi fuisset arbori religatus. Arbor enim quaedam in navi est crux in ecclesia, quae inter totius saeculi blanda et perniciosa naufragia incolumis sola servatur. In hac ergo navi quisque aut arbori crucis se religaverit, aut aures suas scripturis divinis clauserit, dulcem procellam luxuriae non timebit. Syrenarum enim quaedam suavis figura est mollis concupiscentia voluptatum, quae noxiis blandimentis constantiam captae mentis effeminat.

Ergo dominus Christus pependit in cruce, ut omne genus hominum de mundi naufragio liberaret. Sed ut omittamus Ulixis fabulam, quae ficta non facta est, videamus si quod in scripturis divinis exemplum simile possumus invenire, quod dominus per semetipsum postea completurus per prophetas suos ante praemiserit!

Bibliography

Primary Sources

Alan of Lille (1955). *Anticlaudianus*. Ed. Robert Bossuat. Textes philosophiques du Moyen âge, 1. Paris: Vrin.

Alan of Lille (1987). *Anticlaudianus or The Good and Perfect Man*. Trans. James J. Sheridan. Medieval Sources in Translation, 14. Toronto: Pontifical Institute of Mediaeval Studies.

Allen, Thomas W., William R. Halliday & Edward E. Sikes, eds. (1963). *The Homeric Hymns*. Amsterdam: Hakkert.

Ambrose (1881). *The Letters of S. Ambrose, Bishop of Milan*. Library of Fathers of the Holy Catholic Church. Oxford: James Parker.

Ambrose (1968–96). *Sancti Ambrosii opera. 10. Epistulae et acta 1–4*. Eds. Otto Faller & Michaela Zelzer. Corpus scriptorum ecclesiasticorum latinorum, 82.1–4. Vindobonae [Vienna]: Hoelder-Pichler-Tempsky.

Ambrose (1999). *Sancti Ambrosii opera. 5. Expositio psalmi CXVIII*. Eds. Michael Petschenig & Michaela Zelzer. Corpus scriptorum ecclesiasticorum latinorum, 62. Vindobonae [Vienna]: Verlag der Österreichischen Akademie der Wissenschaften.

Apuleius (1989). *Metamorphoses*. I–II. Ed. and trans. J. Arthur Hanson. Loeb Classical Library, 44, 453. Cambridge, MA: Harvard U.P.

Arator (1951). *Aratoris subdiaconi De actibus apostolorum*. Ed. Arthur P. McKinlay. Corpus scriptorum ecclesiasticorum latinorum, 72. Vindobonae [Vienna]: Hoelder-Pichler-Tempsky.

Arator (1987). *Arator's On the Acts of the Apostles (De actibus apostolorum)*. Trans. Richard J. Schrader, with Joseph L. Roberts III & John F. Makowski. Classics in Religious Studies, 6. Atlanta, GA: Scholars Press.

Arator (2006). *Aratoris Subdiaconi Historia apostolica*. I–II. Ed. Arpád P. Orbán. Corpus christianorum, Series latina, 130. Turnhout: Brepols.

Aristotle (1957). *On the Soul. Parva Naturalia. On Breath*. Trans. Walter S. Hett. Loeb Classical Library, 288. Cambridge, MA: Harvard U.P.

Aristotle (1962). *The Categories. On Interpretation. Prior Analytics*. Trans. Harold P. Cook & Hugh Tredennick. Loeb Classical Library, 325. London: Heinemann.

Aristotle (1965). *Aristoteles Latinus. 2.1–2. De interpretatione vel Periermenias*. Eds. Gerard Verbeke & Lorenzo Minio-Paluello. Corpus philosophorum Medii Aevi. Leiden: Brill.

Aristotle (1977–80). *Metaphysics*. Trans. Hugh Tredennick. Loeb Classical Library, 271, 287. Cambridge, MA: Harvard U.P.

Aristotle (1995). *Poetics. Longinus: On the Sublime. Demetrius: On Style*. Trans. Stephen Halliwell, William Hamilton Fyfe (rev. Donald A. Russell) & Doreen C. Innes (based on William Rhys Roberts), respectively. Loeb Classical Library, 199. Cambridge, MA: Harvard U.P.

Augustine (1950a). *Against the Academics*. Trans. John J. O'Meara. Ancient Christian Writers, 12. Westminster, MD: Newman.

Augustine (1950b). *The Greatness of the Soul. The Teacher*. Trans. Joseph M. Colleran. Ancient Christian Writers, 9. Westminster, MD: Newman.

Augustine (1965–). *Opera omnia di Sant'Agostino*. I–XLV. Nuova Biblioteca Agostiniana. Rome: Città nuova. From: http://www.augustinus.it/latino/index.htm (1 January 2015).

Augustine (1982). *Augustine on Romans. Propositions from the Epistle to the Romans. Unfinished Commentary on the Epistle to the Romans*. Ed. and trans. Paula Fredriksen Landes. Society of Biblical Literature: Texts and Translations, 23, Early Christian Literature Series, 6. Chico, CA: Scholars Press.
Augustine (1984). *Concerning the City of God against the Pagans*. Trans. Henry Bettenson. Penguin Classics. Harmondsworth, Middlesex: Penguin.
Augustine (1992). *Confessions*. I–III. Ed. James J. O'Donnell. Oxford: Clarendon.
Augustine (1994). *De dialectica*. Trans. James Marchand. From: http://faculty.georgetown.edu/jod/texts/dialecticatrans.html (1 January 2015).
Augustine (1996). *De doctrina Christiana*. Ed. and trans. Roger P.H. Green. Oxford Early Christian Texts. Oxford: Clarendon.
Augustine (1997a). *The Confessions*. Trans. Maria Boulding. The Works of Saint Augustine, a Translation for the 21st Century, 1.1. Hyde Park, NY: New City Press.
Augustine (1997b). *Œuvres de Saint Augustin. Sér. 1, Opuscules. La doctrine chrétienne. De doctrina christiana*. Eds. Isabelle Bochet & Goulven Madec. Trans. Madeleine Moreau. Bibliothèque Augustinienne, 11.2. Paris: Institut d'Études Augustiniennes.
Augustine (2001–05). *Letters*. Eds. John E. Rotelle & Boniface Ramsey. Trans. Roland J. Teske. The Works of Saint Augustine, a Translation for the 21st Century, 2.1–4. Hyde Park, NY: New City Press.
Augustine (2002a). *De musica liber VI. A Critical Edition with a Translation and an Introduction*. Ed. and trans. Martin Jacobsson. Diss. Acta Universitatis Stockholmiensis, Studia Latina Stockholmiensia, 47. Stockholm: Almqvist & Wiksell.
Augustine (2002b). *On Genesis: A Refutation of the Manichees. Unfinished Literal Commentary on Genesis. The Literal Meaning of Genesis*. Trans. Edmund Hill. The Works of Saint Augustine, a Translation for the 21st Century, 1.13. Hyde Park, NY: New City Press.
Augustine (2006). *Earlier Writings*. Trans. John S. Burleigh. Library of Christian Classics. Louisville, KY: Westminster John Knox Press.
Augustine (2007). *On Order [De Ordine]*. Trans. Silvano Borruso. South Bend, IN: St. Augustine's Press.
Augustine (2010). *Revisions*. Ed. Roland J. Teske. Trans. Boniface Ramsey. The Works of Saint Augustine, a Translation for the 21st Century, 1.2. Hyde Park, NY: New City Press.
Ausonius (1919). *Ausonius*. I. Trans. Hugh G. Evelyn White. Loeb Classical Library, 96. London: Heinemann.
Avitus (1883). *Alcimi Ecdicii Aviti, Viennensis episcopi, Opera quae supersunt*. Ed. Rudolph Peiper. Monumenta Germaniae historica, Auctores antiquissimi, 6.2. Berlin: Weidmann.
Avitus (1985). *The Fall of Man. De spiritalis historiae gestis libri I–III*. Ed. Daniel J. Nodes. Toronto Medieval Latin Texts, 16. Toronto: Pontifical Institute of Mediaeval Studies.
Avitus (1997). *The Poems of Alcimius Ecdicius Avitus*. Trans. George W. Shea. Medieval and Renaissance Texts and Studies, 172. Tempe, AZ: Arizona Center for Medieval and Renaissance Studies.
Avitus (1999–2005). *Histoire spirituelle*. I–II. Ed. and trans. Nicole Hecquet-Noti. Sources chrétiennes, 444, 492. Paris: Cerf.
Avitus (2002). *Avitus of Vienne. Letters and Selected Prose*. Trans. Danuta Shanzer & Ian Wood. Translated Texts for Historians, 38. Liverpool: Liverpool U.P.

Avitus (2005). *Alcimus Ecdicius Avitus. De spiritalis historiae gestis, Buch 3. Einleitung, Übersetzung, Kommentar.* Ed. and trans. Manfred Hoffmann. Diss. Beiträge zur Altertumskunde, 217. Munich: Saur.

Beda Venerabilis (1991). *Libri II de arte metrica et De schematibus et tropis. The Art of Poetry and Rhetoric.* Ed. and trans. Calvin B. Kendall. Bibliotheca Germanica, Series Nova, 2. Saarbrücken: AQ-Verlag.

Benedict of Nursia (2011). *The Rule of Saint Benedict.* Ed. and trans. Bruce L. Venarde. Dumbarton Oaks Medieval Library, 6. Cambridge, MA: Harvard U.P.

Bernardus Silvestris (1979). *Commentary on The First Six Books of Virgil's "Aeneid".* Trans. Earl G. Schreiber & Thomas E. Maresca. Lincoln, NE: University of Nebraska Press.

Boethius (1867). *De institutione arithmetica libri duo. De institutione musica libri quinque.* Ed. Gottfried Friedlein. Leipzig: Teubner.

Boethius (1986). *The Consolation of Philosophy.* Trans. Victor E. Watts. Penguin Classics. Harmondsworth, Middlesex: Penguin.

Boethius (1989). *Fundamentals of Music.* Ed. Claude V. Palisca. Trans. Calvin Bower. Music Theory Translation Series. New Haven, CT: Yale U.P.

Boethius (1997). *The Theological Tractates. The Consolation of Philosophy.* Trans. Hugh F. Stewart, Edward K. Rand & S. Jim Tester. Loeb Classical Library, 74. Cambridge, MA: Harvard U.P.

Boethius (2001). *Consolation of Philosophy.* Trans. Joel C. Relihan. Indianapolis, IN: Hackett.

Borges, Jorge Luis (1980). *Ficciones.* Madrid: Alianza.

Broch, Hermann (1932). *Die Schlafwandler. Der dritte Roman. Huguenau oder die Sachlichkeit. 1918.* Munich: Rhein-Verlag.

Caesarius of Arles (1953). *Caesarii Arelatensis opera. I. Sancti Caesarii Arelatensis Sermones. 1: Continens praefationem, sermones de diversis et de scriptura Veteris Testamenti.* 2nd ed. Ed. Germain Morin. Corpus christianorum, Series latina, 103. Turnholti [Turnhout]: Brepols.

Caesarius of Arles (1956). *Sermons. I.* Trans. Mary Magdeleine Mueller. The Fathers of the Church, 31. New York: Fathers of the Church.

Caplan, Harry, trans. (1964). *Ad C. Herennium de ratione dicendi (Rhetorica ad Herennium).* Loeb Classical Library, 403. London: Heinemann.

Cassian, John (1886). *Iohannis Cassiani opera. II. Conlationes XXIV.* Ed. Michael Petschenig. Corpus scriptorum ecclesiasticorum latinorum, 13. Vindobonae [Vienna]: C. Gerold's Sohn.

Cassiodorus (1937). *Cassiodori Senatoris Institutiones.* Ed. Roger A.B. Mynors. Oxford: Clarendon.

Cassiodorus (1946). *An Introduction to Divine and Human Readings.* Trans. Leslie Webber Jones. Records of Civilization, 40. New York: Columbia U.P.

Cicero (1902). *Select Orations and Letters.* Eds. James B. Greenough & George L. Kittredge. Boston: Ginn & Co.

Cicero (1942). *De oratore. I–II.* Trans. Edward W. Sutton & Harris Rackham. Loeb Classical Library, 348–49. Cambridge, MA: Harvard U.P.

Cicero (1943). *De re publica. De legibus.* Trans. Clinton Walker Keyes. Loeb Classical Library, 213. Cambridge, MA: Harvard U.P.

Cicero (1960). *Pro M. Caelio oratio.* Ed. Roland G. Austin. 3rd ed. Oxford: Clarendon.

Cicero (1967). *De natura deorum. Academica.* Trans. Harris Rackham. Loeb Classical Library, 268. Cambridge, MA: Harvard U.P.

Cicero (1988). *Brutus, Orator*. Trans. George L. Hendrickson & Harry M. Hubbell. Loeb Classical Library, 342. Cambridge, MA: Harvard U.P.
Cicero (1993). *De inventione. De optimo genere oratorum. Topica*. Trans. Harry M. Hubbell. Loeb Classical Library, 386. Cambridge, MA: Harvard U.P.
Cicero (2000). *Defence Speeches*. Trans. Dominic H. Berry. Oxford World's Classics. Oxford: Oxford U.P.
Coleridge, Samuel Taylor (1983). *The Collected Works of Samuel Taylor Coleridge. 7. Biographia Literaria or Biographical Sketches of My Literary Life and Opinions*. II. Eds. James Engell & W. Jackson Bate. Bollingen Series, 75. London: Routledge & Kegan Paul.
Copeland, Rita & Ineke Sluiter, eds. (2009). *Medieval Grammar and Rhetoric. Language Arts and Literary Theory, AD 300–1475*. Oxford: Oxford U.P.
Dante Alighieri (1966–67). *La Commedia secondo l'antica vulgata*. I–III. Ed. Giorgio Petrocchi. Milan: Mondadori.
Dante Alighieri (1991). *De vulgari eloquentia*. Ed. and trans. Vittorio Coletti. Milan: Garzanti.
Dante Alighieri (2002–08). *Inferno. Purgatorio. Paradiso*. Trans. Robert & Jean Hollander. New York: Doubleday.
Diels, Hermann & Walther Kranz, eds. (1956). *Die Fragmente der Vorsokratiker, griechisch und deutsch*. II. 8th ed. Berlin: Weidmann.
Donatus (1864). *Probi Donati Servii qui feruntur De arte grammatica libri. Notarum laterculi*. Eds. Heinrich Keil & Theodor Mommsen. Grammatici Latini, 4. Leipzig: Teubner.
Dorsch, T.S., trans. (1974). *Classical Literary Criticism*. Penguin Classics. Harmondsworth, Middlesex: Penguin.
Dümmler, Ernst, ed. (1895). *Epistolae Karolini aevi*. II. Monumenta Germaniae historica, Epistolae, 4. Berlin: Weidmann.
Eliot, T.S. (1963). *Collected Poems 1909–1962*. London: Faber and Faber.
Fischer, Bonifatius, Roger Gryson & Robert Weber, eds. (1994). *Biblia Sacra iuxta vulgatam versionem*. 4th ed. Stuttgart: Deutsche Bibelgesellschaft.
Freeman, Kathleen, trans. (1948). *Ancilla to the Pre-Socratic Philosophers. A Complete Translation of the Fragments in Diels, Fragmente der Vorsokratiker*. Oxford: Blackwell.
Fulgentius (1898). *Fabii Planciadis Fulgentii Opera: Accedunt Fabii Claudii Gordiani Fulgentii De aetatibus mundi et hominis et S. Fulgentii episcopi super Thebaiden*. Ed. Rudolf Helm. Bibliotheca scriptorum Graecorum et Romanorum Teubneriana. Leipzig: Teubner.
Fulgentius (1971). *Fulgentius the Mythographer*. Trans. Leslie G. Whitbread. Columbus, OH: Ohio State U.P.
Fulgentius (1972a). *Expositio Virgilianae continentiae*. Ed. Tullio Agozzino. Trans. Ferruccio Zanlucchi. Accademia patavina di scienze, lettere ed arti, Collana accademica, 4. Padua: Università degli studi di Padova.
Fulgentius (1972b). "Fabius Planciades Fulgentius: Expositio Virgilianae continentiae". Trans. Lynn C. Stokes. *Classical Folia*, 26, pp. 27–63.
Fulgentius (2009). *Virgile dévoilé*. Eds. and trans. Étienne Wolff & Françoise Graziani. Mythographes, 1. Villeneuve d'Ascq: Presses universitaires du Septentrion.
Gregory the Great (1844). *Morals on the Book of Job*. I.1–2. Library of Fathers of the Holy Catholic Church, 18. Oxford: Parker.
Hesiod (2006). *Theogony. Works and Days. Testimonia*. Ed. and trans. Glenn W. Most. Loeb Classical Library, 57. Cambridge, MA: Harvard U.P.
The Holy Bible. English Standard Version (2001). Crossway Bibles. Wheaton, IL: Crossway.

Homer (1919). *The Odyssey*. I–II. Trans. Augustus T. Murray. Loeb Classical Library, 104–05. London: Heinemann.
Homer (1924–25). *The Iliad*. I–II. Trans. Augustus T. Murray. Loeb Classical Library, 170–71. London: Heinemann.
Horace (1989). *Epistles, Book II, and Epistle to the Pisones ("Ars Poetica")*. Ed. Niall Rudd. Cambridge Greek and Latin Classics. Cambridge: Cambridge U.P.
Horace (1997). *The Odes*. Ed. Kenneth Quinn. London: Bristol Classical Press.
Hölderlin, Friedrich (1986). *Selected Verse*. Ed. and trans. Michael Hamburger. Anvil Editions. London: Anvil Press Poetry.
Ibsen, Henrik (1936). *Peer Gynt*. Trans. Robert Farquharson Sharp. Philadelphia, PA: Lippincott.
Ibsen, Henrik (1966). *Peer Gynt*. Ed. Johan Hertzberg. Oslo: Gyldendal.
Isidore of Seville (1911). *Isidori Hispalensis episcopi Etymologiarum sive Originum libri XX*. 1–2. Ed. Wallace Martin Lindsay. Scriptorum classicorum bibliotheca Oxoniensis. Oxonii [Oxford]: Clarendon.
Isidore of Seville (1998). *Isidorus Hispalensis Sententiae*. Ed. Pierre Cazier. Corpus christianorum, Series latina, 111. Turnholti [Turnhout]: Brepols.
Isidore of Seville (2006). *The Etymologies of Isidore of Seville*. Trans. Stephen A. Barney, W.J. Lewis, J.A. Beach *et alii*. Cambridge: Cambridge U.P.
Jerome (1933). *Select Letters of St. Jerome*. Trans. Frederick A. Wright. Loeb Classical Library, 262. London: Heinemann.
John Scotus Eriugena (1975). *Expositiones in ierarchiam coelestem*. Ed. Jeanne Barbet. Corpus christianorum, Continuatio mediaevalis, 31. Turnholti [Turnhout]: Brepols.
John Scotus Eriugena (1993). *Carmina*. Ed. Michael W. Herren. Scriptores Latini Hiberniae, 12. Dublin: Dublin Institute for Advanced Studies.
Juvencus (1891). *Evangeliorum libri quattuor*. Ed. Johann Huemer. Corpus scriptorum ecclesiasticorum latinorum, 24. Vienna: Tempsky.
Juvencus (2012). "*Libri Evangeliorum IIII* of Juvencus (*c.* 330): 1. *Evangelia*, preface (1.1–27)". Trans. Patrick McBrine. From: http://www.pmcbrine.com/juvencus_praef.pdf (1 January 2015).
Keats, John (1977). *Selected Poems and Letters*. Ed. Robert Gittings. Poetry Bookshelf. London: Heinemann Educational.
Kennedy, George A., trans. (2003). *Progymnasmata. Greek Textbooks of Prose Composition and Rhetoric*. Writings from the Greco-Roman World, 10. Atlanta, GA: Society of Biblical Literature.
Lactantius (2003). *Divine institutes*. Trans. Anthony Bowen & Peter Garnsey. Translated Texts for Historians, 40. Liverpool: Liverpool U.P.
Lucan (1928). *The Civil War. Books I–X (Pharsalia)*. Trans. James D. Duff. Loeb Classical Library, 220. London: Heinemann.
Lucretius (1972). *Über die Natur der Dinge*. Ed. and trans. Josef Martin. Schriften und Quellen der alten Welt, 32. Berlin: Akademie-Verlag.
Lucretius (1977). *The Nature of Things*. Trans. Frank O. Copley. New York: Norton.
Macrobius (1990). *Commentary on the Dream of Scipio*. Trans. William H. Stahl. Records of Western Civilization, 48. New York: Columbia U.P.
Macrobius (1994). *Ambrosii Theodosii Macrobii Commentarii in somnium Scipionis*. 2nd ed. Ed. James A. Willis. Bibliotheca scriptorum Graecorum et Romanorum Teubneriana. Stuttgart: Teubner.

Macrobius (2011). *Saturnalia.* I–III. Ed. and trans. Robert A. Kaster. Loeb Classical Library, 510–12. Cambridge, MA: Harvard U.P.
Martial (1993). *Epigrams.* I. Ed. and trans. David R. Shackleton Bailey. Loeb Classical Library, 94. Cambridge, MA: Harvard U.P.
Martianus Capella (1866). *Martianus Capella. Accedunt scholia in Caesaris Germanici Aratea.* Ed. Franz Eyssenhardt. Bibliotheca scriptorum Graecorum et Romanorum Teubneriana. Leipzig: Teubner.
Martianus Capella (1975). *Martiani Capellae De nuptiis Philologiae et Mercurii. Liber secundus.* Ed. and trans. Luciano Lenaz. Biblioteca di cultura. Padua: Liviana.
Martianus Capella (1977). *Martianus Capella and the Seven Liberal Arts. II. The Marriage of Philology and Mercury.* Trans. William H. Stahl, Richard Johnson & Evan L. Burge. Records of Civilization, 84. New York: Columbia U.P.
Martianus Capella (1983). *Martianus Capella.* Ed. James Willis. Bibliotheca scriptorum Graecorum et Romanorum Teubneriana. Leipzig: Teubner.
Martianus Capella (1987). *Martiani Capellae De nuptiis Philologiae et Mercurii. Liber IX.* Ed. Lucio Cristante. Medioevo e umanesimo, 64. Padua: Antenore.
Martianus Capella (2001). *Le nozze di Filologia e Mercurio.* Trans. Ilaria Ramelli. Il pensiero occidentale. Milan: Bompiani.
Marvell, Andrew (1983). *The Complete Poems.* Ed. Elizabeth Story Donno. Penguin English Poets. Harmondsworth, Middlesex: Penguin.
Maximus of Turin (1962). *Maximi episcopi Taurinensis. Collectionem sermonum antiquam nonnullis sermonibus extravagantibus adiectis.* Ed. Almut Mutzenbecher. Corpus christianorum, Series latina, 23. Turnholti [Turnhout]: Brepols.
Maximus of Turin (1989). *The Sermons of St. Maximus of Turin.* Trans. Boniface Ramsey. Ancient Christian Writers, 50. New York: Newman.
Migne, Jacques Paul, ed. (1844–55). *Patrologiae cursus completus, Series latina.* 1–217. Paris: apud J.-P. Migne editorem.
Nestle, Eberhard, Kurt Aland, Barbara Aland *et alii*, eds. (1979). *Novum Testamentum Graece.* 26th ed. Stuttgart: Deutsche Bibelstiftung.
The New American Bible (2010). Revised ed. Harper Catholic Bibles. New York: HarperCollins.
Origen (1920). *Werke. VI. Homilien zum Hexateuch in Rufins Übersetzung. 1. Die Homilien zu Genesis, Exodus und Leviticus.* Ed. Wilhelm A. Baehrens. Die griechischen christlichen Schriftsteller der ersten drei Jahrhunderte, 29. Leipzig: Hinrichs.
Origen (1957). *The Song of Songs. Commentary and Homilies.* Trans. R.P. Lawson. Ancient Christian Writers, 26. Westminster, MD: Newman.
Origen (1978–84). *Traité des principes.* I–V. Eds. and trans. Henri Crouzel & Manlio Simonetti. Sources chrétiennes, 252. Paris: Cerf.
Origen (1980). *Contra Celsum.* Trans. Henry Chadwick. Cambridge: Cambridge U.P.
Origen (1982). *Homilies on Genesis and Exodus.* Trans. Ronald E. Heine. Fathers of the Church, 71. Washington, DC: Catholic University of America Press.
Origen (2001). *Contra Celsum libri VIII.* Ed. Miroslav Marcovich. Supplements to Vigiliae Christianae, 54. Leiden: Brill.
Ovid (1967). *Fasti.* Trans. James G. Frazer. Loeb Classical Library, 253. London: Heinemann.
Ovid (1971). *Metamorphoses.* I–II. Trans. Frank J. Miller. Loeb Classical Library, 42–43. Cambridge, MA: Harvard U.P.

Ovid (1972). *Ovid's Metamorphoses. Books 6–10*. Ed. William S. Anderson. American Philological Association Series of Classical Texts. Norman, OK: University of Oklahoma Press.
Ovid (1985). *The Art of Love, and Other Poems*. Trans. John H. Mozley, rev. by George P. Goold. Loeb Classical Library, 232. Cambridge, MA: Harvard U.P.
Ovid (1996). *Heroides. Amores*. Trans. Grant Showerman, rev. by George P. Goold. Loeb Classical Library, 41. Cambridge, MA: Harvard U.P.
Paulinus of Nola (1966–67). *Letters of St. Paulinus of Nola*. I–II. Ed & trans. Patrick G. Walsh. Ancient Christian Writers, 35–36. Westminster, MD: Newman.
Paulinus of Nola (1975). *The Poems of St. Paulinus of Nola*. Ed. and trans. Patrick G. Walsh. Ancient Christian Writers, 40. New York: Newman.
Paulinus of Nola (1999). *Sancti Pontii Meropii Paulini Nolani opera*. I–II. Eds. Wilhelm von Hartel & Margit Kamptner. Corpus scriptorum ecclesiasticorum latinorum, 29–30. Vindobonae [Vienna]: Österreichische Akademie der Wissenschaften.
Petschenig, Michael *et alii*, eds. (1888). *Poetae christiani minores*. I. Corpus scriptorum ecclesiasticorum latinorum, 16. Vindobonae [Vienna]: Tempsky.
Philostratus (2005). *The Life of Apollonius of Tyana*. I–II. Ed. and trans. Christopher P. Jones. Loeb Classical Library, 16–17. Cambridge, MA: Harvard U.P.
Plato (1925a). *Lysis. Symposium. Gorgias*. Trans. Walter R.M. Lamb. Loeb Classical Library, 166. London: Heinemann.
Plato (1925b). *Statesman. Philebus. Ion*. Trans. Harold N. Fowler & Walter R.M. Lamb. Loeb Classical Library, 164. London: Heinemann.
Plato (1926). *Cratylus. Parmenides. Greater Hippias. Lesser Hippias*. Trans. Harold N. Fowler. Loeb Classical Library, 167. London: Heinemann.
Plato (1937–42). *The Republic*. I–II. Trans. Paul Shorey. Loeb Classical Library, 237, 276. Cambridge, MA: Harvard U.P.
Plato (2005). *Euthyphro. Apology. Crito. Phaedo. Phaedrus*. Trans. Harold N. Fowler. Loeb Classical Library, 36. Cambridge, MA: Harvard U.P.
Plotinus (1966–88). *The Enneads*. I–VI. Trans. Arthur Hillary Armstrong. Loeb Classical Library, 440–45, 468. Cambridge, MA: Harvard U.P.
Plutarch (1927). *Moralia*. I. Trans. Frank C. Babbitt. Loeb Classical Library, 197. London: Heinemann.
Plutarch (1999). *Moralia*. V. Trans. Frank C. Babbitt. Loeb Classical Library, 306. Cambridge, MA: Harvard U.P.
Porphyry (1986). *L'antro delle ninfe*. Ed. and trans. Laura Simonini. Classici Adelphi, 48. Milan: Adelphi.
Porphyry (1991). *On the Cave of the Nymphs*. Trans. Thomas Taylor. Grand Rapids, MI: Phanes Press.
Proba, Faltonia Betitia (1981). *The Golden Bough, the Oaken Cross. The Virgilian Cento of Faltonia Betitia Proba*. Eds. and trans. Elizabeth A. Clark & Diane F. Hatch. American Academy of Religion, Texts and Translations Series, 5. Chico, CA: Scholars Press.
Proclus (1899–1901). *Procli Diadochi in Platonis Rem publicam commentarii*. I–II. Ed. Wilhelm Kroll. Bibliotheca scriptorum Graecorum et Romanorum Teubneriana. Leipzig: Teubner.
Proclus (1970). *Commentaire sur la République*. I–III. Trans. André Jean Festugière. Bibliothèque des textes philosophiques. Paris: Vrin.

Prudentius (1993–95). *Prudentius*. I–II. Trans. Henry J. Thomson. Loeb Classical Library, 387, 398. Cambridge, MA: Harvard U.P.

Quintilian (2001). *The Orator's Education*. I–V. Ed. and trans. Donald A. Russell. Loeb Classical Library, 124–27, 494. Cambridge, MA: Harvard U.P.

Ramelli, Ilaria, ed. and trans. (2006). *Scoto Eriugena, Remigio di Auxerre, Bernardo Silvestre e anonimi. Tutti i commenti a Marziano Capella*. Il pensiero occidentale. Milan: Bompiani.

Rilke, Rainer Maria (1979). *Neue Gedichte. Der Neuen Gedichte anderer Teil*. Frankfurt am Main: Insel.

Roberts, Alexander, James Donaldson, Arthur Cleveland Coxe *et alii*, eds. (1951–57). *The Ante-Nicene Fathers. Translations of the Writings of the Fathers down to A.D. 325*. 1–10. Grand Rapids, MI: Eerdmans. From: http://www.ccel.org/fathers.html (1 January 2015).

Rousseau, Jean-Jacques (1903). *The Confessions of J.J. Rousseau*. Trans. S.W. Orson. London: Privately printed for members of the Aldus Society.

Rousseau, Jean-Jacques (1959). *Œuvres complètes. I. Les confessions. Autres textes autobiographiques*. Eds. Bernard Gagnebin & Marcel Raymond. Bibliothèque de la Pléiade. Paris: Gallimard.

Schaff, Philip *et alii*, eds. (1978–79). *A Select Library of the Nicene and Post-Nicene Fathers of the Christian Church*, 1.1–8. Grand Rapids, MI: Eerdmans. From: http://www.ccel.org/fathers.html (1 January 2015).

Schaff, Philip & Henry Wace, eds. (1978–79). *A Select Library of the Nicene and Post-Nicene Fathers of the Christian Church*. 2.6–11. Grand Rapids, MI: Eerdmans. From: http://www.ccel.org/fathers.html (1 January 2015).

Sedulius (2007). *Opera omnia*. Ed. Johann Huemer, rev. Victoria Panagl. Corpus scriptorum ecclesiasticorum latinorum, 10. Vienna: Verlag der Österreichischen Akademie der Wissenschaften.

Sedulius (2013). *The Paschal Song and Hymns*. Trans. Carl P.E. Springer. Writings from the Greco-Roman World, 35. Atlanta, GA: Society of Biblical Literature.

Servius (2011). *Servii Grammatici qui feruntur in Vergilii carmina commentarii*. I–IV. Eds. Georg C. Thilo & Hermann Hagen. Cambridge Library Collection. Cambridge: Cambridge U.P.

Sextus Empiricus (1998). *Against the Grammarians (Adversus mathematicos I)*. Ed. and trans. David L. Blank. Clarendon Later Ancient Philosophers. Oxford: Clarendon.

Shakespeare, William (1969). *The Tragedy of Hamlet, Prince of Denmark*. Ed. John Dover Wilson. The Works of Shakespeare/The New Shakespeare. Cambridge: Cambridge U.P.

Shakespeare, William (1979). *A Midsummer Night's Dream*. Ed. Harold F. Brooks. The Arden Shakespeare, Second Series. London: Methuen.

Shakespeare, William (2006). *As You Like It*. Ed. Juliet Dusinberre. The Arden Shakespeare, Third Series. London: Thomson Learning.

Sidonius Apollinaris (1936). *Poems. Letters, Books I–II*. Trans. William B. Anderson. Loeb Classical Library, 296. Cambridge, MA: Harvard U.P.

Sidonius Apollinaris (1965). *Letters, Books III–IX*. Trans. William B. Anderson. Loeb Classical Library, 420. London: Heinemann.

Stevens, Wallace (1951). *Transport to Summer*. New York: Knopf.

Söderberg, Hjalmar (1912). *Den allvarsamma leken*. Stockholm: Bonniers.

Tertullian (1954). *Opera*. I–II. Ed. Eligius Dekkers *et alii*. Corpus christianorum, Series latina, 1–2. Turnholti [Turnhout]: Brepols.

Tertullian & Minucius Felix (1977). *Apology. De spectaculis. Octavius*. Trans. Terrot R. Glover, Walter C.A. Kerr & Gerald H. Rendall. Loeb Classical Library, 250. Cambridge, MA: Harvard U.P.
Virgil (1997). *The Eclogues*. Trans. Barbara Hughes Fowler. Chapel Hill: University of North Carolina Press.
Virgil (1998). *Eclogues. Georgics. Aeneid I–VI*. Trans. H. Rushton Fairclough. Loeb Classical Library, 63. Cambridge, MA: Harvard U.P.
Virgil (2000). *Aeneid VII-XII. Appendix Vergiliana*. Trans. H. Rushton Fairclough, rev. George P. Goold. Loeb Classical Library, 64. Cambridge, MA: Harvard U.P.
Virgil (2007). *Aeneid*. Trans. Frederick Ahl. Oxford: Oxford U.P.
Woolf, Virginia (1931). *A Room of One's Own*. London: The Hogarth Press.
Ziolkowski, Jan M. & Michael C.J. Putnam (2008). *The Virgilian Tradition. The First Fifteen Hundred Years*. New Haven, CT: Yale U.P.

Secondary Sources

Adkin, Neil (1984). "The Shadow and the Truth: A Common Antithesis in the Fathers". *Giornale italiano di filologia*, 36, pp. 245–52.
Agozzino, Tullio (1972). "*Secretum quaerere veritatis*. Virgilio, *vates ignarus* nella *Continentia Vergiliana*". In *Studi classici in onore di Quintino Cataudella*, III, Catania: Università di Catania, Facoltà di lettere e filosofia, pp. 615–30.
Akiyama, Manabu (2001). "The Scope of Typology in the Works of Theodore of Mopsuestia: The Keystone of the Liturgy and Exegesis". *Bulletin of the Society for Near Eastern Studies in Japan*, 44.2, pp. 49–66.
Albu, Emily (2011). "Fulgentius the Mythoclast: Cooling Pagan Passions in Christian Late Antiquity". *Electronic Antiquity*, 14.1, pp. 81–94. From: http://scholar.lib.vt.edu/ejournals/ElAnt/V14N1/pdf/albu.pdf (1 January 2015).
Alfonso, Luigi (1966). "Cultura classica e cristianesimo. L'impostazione del problema nel proemio delle *Divinae institutiones* di Lattanzio e nell'*Ep*. XVI di Paolino da Nola". *Le parole e le idee*, no. 8, pp. 1–14.
Allen, Judson Boyce (1982). *The Ethical Poetic of the Later Middle Ages: A Decorum of Convenient Distinction*. Toronto: University of Toronto Press.
Arweiler, Alexander (1999). *Die Imitation antiker und spätantiker Literatur in der Dichtung "De spiritalis historiae gestis" des Alcimus Avitus. Mit einem Kommentar zu Avit. carm. 4,429–540 und 5,526–703*. Diss. Untersuchungen zur antiken Literatur und Geschichte, 52. Berlin: De Gruyter.
Assmann, Aleida (1980). *Die Legitimität der Fiktion. Ein Beitrag zur Geschichte der literarischen Kommunikation*. Theorie und Geschichte der Literatur und der schönen Künste, Texte und Abhandlungen, 55. Munich: Fink.
Astell, Ann W. (1990). *The Song of Songs in the Middle Ages*. Ithaca, NY: Cornell U.P.
Auerbach, Erich (1968). *Mimesis. The Representation of Reality in Western Literature*. Trans. Willard R. Trask. Princeton, NJ: Princeton U.P.
Auerbach, Erich (1984). *Scenes From the Drama of European Literature*. Foreword Paolo Valesio. Theory and History of Literature, 9. Minneapolis, MN: University of Minnesota Press.

Auerbach, Erich (1993). *Literary Language and Its Public in Late Latin Antiquity and in the Middle Ages*. Trans. Ralph Manheim. Bollingen Series, 74. Princeton, NJ: Princeton U.P.
Bailey, Michael D. (2007). *Magic and Superstition in Europe. A Concise History from Antiquity to the Present*. Critical Issues in History. Lanham, MD: Rowman & Littlefield.
Bakhtin, Mikhail (1994). "From the Prehistory of Novelistic Discourse". Trans. Caryl Emerson & Michael Holquist. In David Lodge, ed., *Modern Criticism and Theory. A Reader*, London: Longman, pp. 125–56.
Banniard, Michel (1992). *Viva voce. Communication écrite et communication orale du IVe au IXe siècle en Occident latin*. Collection des Études Augustiniennes, Série Moyen-Âge et temps modernes, 25. Paris: Institut d'Études Augustiniennes.
Barfield, Raymond (2011). *The Ancient Quarrel Between Philosophy and Poetry*. New York: Cambridge U.P.
Bastiaensen, Anton A.R. (1993). "Prudentius in Recent Literary Criticism". In Jan den Boeft & Anton Hilhorst, eds., *Early Christian Poetry. A Collection of Essays* (Supplements to Vigiliae Christianae, 22), Leiden: Brill, pp. 101–34.
Baswell, Christopher (1985). "The Medieval Allegorization of the 'Aeneid': Ms Cambridge, Peterhouse 158". *Traditio*, 41, pp. 181–237.
Bažil, Martin (2009). *Centones Christiani. Métamorphoses d'une forme intertextuelle dans la poésie latine chrétienne de l'Antiquité tardive*. Diss. Collection des Études Augustiniennes, Série Moyen Âge et Temps Modernes, 47. Paris: Institut d'Études Augustiniennes.
Bennett, Camille (1988). "The Conversion of Vergil: The Aeneid in Augustine's Confessions". *Revue des Études Augustiniennes*, 34, pp. 47–69.
Bernard, Wolfgang (1990). *Spätantike Dichtungstheorien. Untersuchungen zu Proklos, Herakleitos und Plutarch*. Beiträge zur Altertumskunde, 3. Stuttgart: Teubner.
Bezner, Frank (2005). *Vela veritatis. Hermeneutik, Wissen und Sprache in der Intellectual History des 12. Jahrhunderts*. Studien und Texte zur Geistesgeschichte des Mittelalters, 85. Leiden: Brill.
Bloch, Herbert (1963). "The Pagan Revival in the West at the End of the Fourth century". In Arnaldo Momigliano, ed., *The Conflict Between Paganism and Christianity in the Fourth Century* (Oxford-Warburg Studies), Oxford: Clarendon, pp. 193–218.
Bloomfield, Morton W. (1958). "Symbolism in Medieval Literature". *Modern Philology*, 56.2, pp. 73–81.
Boer, Willem den (1973). "Allegory and History". In Willem den Boer et alii, eds., *Romanitas et christianitas. Studia Iano Henrico Waszink A.D. VI Kal. Nov. A. MCMLXXIII XIII lustra complenti oblata*, Amsterdam: North-Holland, pp. 15–27.
Bogdanos, Theodore (1977). "'The Shepherd of Hermas' and the Development of Medieval Visionary Allegory". *Viator*, 8, pp. 33–46.
Bonner, Gerald (1970). "Augustine as Biblical Scholar". In Peter R. Ackroyd & Christopher F. Evans, eds., *The Cambridge History of the Bible. 1. From the Beginnings to Jerome*, Cambridge: Cambridge U.P., pp. 541–63.
Bowie, Ewen L. (1993). "Lies, Fiction and Slander in Early Greek Poetry". In Christopher Gill & Timothy P. Wiseman, eds., *Lies and Fiction in the Ancient World*, Exeter: University of Exeter Press, pp. 1–37.
Boys-Stones, George R. (2003). "The Stoics' Two Types of Allegory". In George R. Boys-Stones, ed., *Metaphor, Allegory, and the Classical Tradition. Ancient Thought and Modern Revisions*, Oxford: Oxford U.P., pp. 189–216.

Brann, Eva T.H. (1990). *The World of the Imagination. Sum and Substance.* Lanham, MD: Rowman & Littlefield.
Breyfogle, Todd (1999). "Memory and Imagination in Augustine's *Confessions*". In Todd Breyfogle, ed., *Literary Imagination, Ancient and Modern. Essays in Honor of David Grene*, Chicago: University of Chicago Press, pp. 139–54.
Bright, David F. (1984). "Theory and Practice in the Vergilian Cento". *Illinois Classical Studies*, 9, pp. 79–90.
Bright, Pamela (2003). "Book Ten: The Self Seeking the God Who Creates and Heals". In Kim Paffenroth & Robert P. Kennedy, eds., *A Reader's Companion to Augustine's Confessions*, Louisville, KY: Westminster John Knox Press, pp. 155–66.
Brink, Charles Oscar (1971). *Horace on Poetry. II. The "Ars Poetica".* Cambridge: Cambridge U.P.
Brittan, Simon (2003). *Poetry, Symbol, and Allegory. Interpreting Metaphorical Language from Plato to the Present.* Charlottesville, VA: University of Virginia Press.
Brown, Peter (1961). "Aspects of the Christianization of the Roman Aristocracy". *The Journal of Roman Studies*, 51, pp. 1–11.
Brown, Peter (1971). *The World of Late Antiquity. From Marcus Aurelius to Muhammed.* London: Thames and Hudson.
Brown, Peter (1981). *The Cult of the Saints. Its Rise and Function in Latin Christianity.* The Haskell Lectures on History of Religions, New Series, 2. Chicago: University of Chicago Press.
Brown, Peter (1997). "The World of Late Antiquity Revisited". *Symbolae Osloensis*, 72, pp. 5–30.
Brown, Peter (1999). "Images as a Substitute for Writing". In Evangelos Chrysos & Ian Wood, eds., *East and West: Modes of Communication. Proceedings of the First Plenary Conference at Merida* (The Transformation of the Roman World, 5), Leiden: Brill, pp. 14–34.
Brown, Peter (2000). *Augustine of Hippo. A Biography.* A New Edition with an Epilogue. London: Faber and Faber.
Bullough, Donald A. (1993). "What has Ingeld to do with Lindisfarne?" *Anglo-Saxon England*, 22, pp. 93–125.
Bundy, Murray Wright (1927). *The Theory of Imagination in Classical and Mediaeval Thought.* Illinois Studies in Language and Literature, 12.2–3. Urbana, IL: University of Illinois.
Bureau, Bruno (1997). *Lettre et sens mystique dans l'Historia apostolica d'Arator. Exégèse et épopée.* Collection des Études Augustiniennes, Serie Antiquité, 153. Paris: Institut d'Études Augustiniennes.
Büchner, Karl (1976). *Somnium Scipionis. Quellen, Gestalt, Sinn.* Hermes, Einzelschriften, 36. Wiesbaden: Steiner.
Cain, Andrew (2009). *The Letters of Jerome. Asceticism, Biblical Exegesis, and the Construction of Christian Authority in Late Antiquity.* Oxford Early Christian Studies. Oxford: Oxford U.P.
Calboli Montefusco, Lucia (2003). "*Ductus* and *Color*: The Right Way to Compose a Suitable Speech". *Rhetorica*, 21.2, pp. 113–31.
Cameron, Alan (1966). "The Date and Identity of Macrobius". *Journal of Roman Studies*, 56.1–2, pp. 25–38.

Cameron, Alan (1977). "Paganism and Literature in Late Fourth Century Rome". In Manfred Fuhrmann, ed., *Christianisme et formes littéraires de l'antiquité tardive en Occident* (Entretiens sur l'antiquité classique, 23), Geneva: Fondation Hardt, pp. 1–30.
Cameron, Alan (2004). "Poetry and Literary Culture in Late Antiquity". In Simon Swain & Mark Edwards, eds., *Approaching Late Antiquity. The Transformation from Early to Late Empire*, Oxford: Oxford U.P., pp. 327–54.
Cameron, Alan (2011). *The Last Pagans of Rome*. New York: Oxford U.P.
Cameron, Averil (1993). *The Mediterranean World in Late Antiquity AD 395–600*. Routledge History of the Ancient World. London: Routledge.
Carruthers, Mary (2000). *The Craft of Thought. Meditation, Rhetoric, and the Making of Images, 400–1200*. Cambridge Studies in Medieval Literature, 34. Cambridge: Cambridge U.P.
Cassin, Barbara (1986). "Du faux ou du mensonge à la fiction (de *pseudos* a *plasma*)". In Barbara Cassin, ed., *Le plaisir de parler. Études de sophistique comparée* (Arguments), Paris: Éditions de Minuit, pp. 3–29.
Chadwick, Henry (1966). *Early Christian Thought and the Classical Tradition. Studies in Justin, Clement, and Origen*. Oxford: Clarendon.
Chadwick, Henry (1981). *The Consolations of Music, Logic, Theology, and Philosophy*. Oxford: Clarendon.
Chadwick, Henry (2009). *Augustine of Hippo. A Life*. Oxford: Oxford U.P.
Chaffin, Christopher E. (1972). "Christus imperator. Interpretazioni della IV Egloga di Virgilio nell'ambiente di S. Ambrogio". *Rivista di storia e letteratura religiosa*, 8, pp. 517–27.
Chamberlain, David S. (1984). "Philosophy of Music in the 'Consolatio' of Boethius". In Manfred Fuhrmann & Joachim Gruber, eds., *Boethius* (Wege der Forschung, 483), Darmstadt: Wissenschaftliche Buchgesellschaft, pp. 377–403.
Chance, Jane (1994). *Medieval Mythography. From Roman North Africa to the School of Chartres, A.D. 433–1177*. Gainesville, FL: University Press of Florida.
Charlet, Jean-Louis (1982). *La création poétique dans le Cathemerinon de Prudence*. Collection d'études anciennes. Paris: Société d'Édition "Les Belles Lettres".
Charlet, Jean-Louis (1986). "La poésie de Prudence dans l'esthétique de son temps". *Bulletin de l'Association Guillaume Budé*, 4, pp. 368–86.
Charlet, Jean-Louis (1988). "Aesthetic Trends in Late Latin Poetry (325–410)". *Philologus*, 132.1, pp. 74–85.
Chin, Catherine M. (2008). *Grammar and Christianity in the Late Roman World*. Divinations. Philadelphia: University of Pennsylvania Press.
Cilento, Vincenzo (1960). "Mito e poesia nelle Enneadi di Plotino". In *Les sources de Plotin* (Entretiens sur l'antiquité classique, 5), Geneva: Fondation Hardt, pp. 243–310.
Cizek, Alexandru N. (1994). *Imitatio et tractatio. Die literarisch-rhetorischen Grundlagen der Nachahmung in Antike und Mittelalter*. Rhetorik-Forschungen, 7. Tübingen: Niemeyer.
Colish, Marcia L. (1968). *The Mirror of Language. A Study in the Medieval Theory of Knowledge*. Yale Historical Publications, Miscellany, 88. New Haven: Yale U.P.
Colish, Marcia L. (1983). "The Stoic Theory of Verbal Signification and the Problem of Lies and False Statements from Antiquity to St. Anselm". In Lucie Brind'Amour & Eugene Vance, eds., *Archéologie du signe* (Papers in Mediaeval Studies, 3), Toronto: Pontifical Institute of Mediaeval Studies, pp. 17–43.
Comparetti, Domenico (1997). *Vergil in the Middle Ages*. Trans. Edward F.M. Benecke. Princeton, NJ: Princeton U.P.

Conte, Gian Bagio (1999). *Latin Literature. A History.* Trans. Joseph B. Solodow, rev. by Don Fowler & Glenn W. Most. Baltimore: John Hopkins U.P.

Conybeare, Catherine (2000). *Paulinus Noster. Self and Symbols in the Letters of Paulinus of Nola.* Oxford Early Christian Studies. Oxford: Oxford U.P.

Conybeare, Catherine (2005). "The Duty of a Teacher: Liminality and *disciplina* in the *De Ordine*". In Karla Pollmann & Mark Vessey, eds., *Augustine and the Disciplines. From Cassiciacum to Confessions,* Oxford: Oxford U.P., pp. 49–65.

Copeland, Rita (1991). *Rhetoric, Hermeneutics, and Translation in the Middle Ages. Academic Traditions and Vernacular Texts.* Cambridge Studies in Medieval Literature, 11. Cambridge: Cambridge U.P.

Costanza, Salvatore (1972). "La poetica di Paolino da Nola". In *Studi classici in onore di Quintino Cataudella,* III, Catania: Università di Catania, Facoltà di lettere e filosofia, pp. 593–613.

Costanza, Salvatore (1976). "Le concezioni poetiche di Prudenzio e il carme XVIII di Paolino di Nola". *Siculorum Gymnasium,* 29, pp. 123–49.

Costanza, Salvatore (1985). "Da Giovenco a Sedulio. I proemi degli 'Evangeliorum libri' e del 'Carmen Paschale'". *Civiltà classica e cristiana,* 6, pp. 253–86.

Coulter, James A. (1976). *The Literary Microcosm. Theories of Interpretation of the Later Neoplatonists.* Columbia Studies in the Classical Tradition, 2. Leiden: Brill.

Courcelle, Pierre (1950). *Recherches sur les Confessions de Saint Augustin.* Paris: Boccard.

Courcelle, Pierre (1955a). "Histoire du cliché virgilien des cent bouches (*Georg.* II, 42–44 = *Aen.* VI, 625–627)". *Revue des études latines,* 33, pp. 231–40.

Courcelle, Pierre (1955b). "Les pères de l'église devant les enfers virgiliens". *Archives d'histoire doctrinale et littéraire du Moyen Age,* 30, pp. 5–74.

Courcelle, Pierre (1957). "Les exégèses chrétiennes de la quatrième églogue". *Revue des études anciennes,* 59, pp. 294–319.

Courcelle, Pierre (1963). *Les Confessions de Saint Augustin dans la tradition littéraire. Antécédents et postérité.* Paris: Études Augustiniennes.

Courcelle, Pierre (1967). *La Consolation de philosophie dans la tradition littéraire. Antécédents et postérité de Boèce.* Paris: Études Augustiniennes.

Crabbe, Anna (1981). "Literary Design in the *De Consolatione Philosophiae*". In Margaret Gibson, ed., *Boethius. His Life, Thought and Influence,* Oxford: Basil Blackwell, pp. 237–74.

Cramer, Winfrid (1980). "Mens concordet voci. Zum Fortleben einer stoischen Gebetsmaxime in der Regula Benedicti". In Ernst Dassmann & K. Suso Frank, eds., *Pietas. Festschrift für Bernhard Kötting* (Jahrbuch für Antike und Christentum, Ergänzungsband, 8), Münster: Aschendorff, pp. 447–57.

Curley, Thomas F., III (1986). "How to Read the *Consolation of Philosophy*". *Interpretation,* 14, pp. 211–63.

Curley, Thomas F., III (1987). "The *Consolation of Philosophy* as a Work of Literature". *American Journal of Philology,* 108, pp. 343–67.

Currie, Gregory (1990). *The Nature of Fiction.* Cambridge: Cambridge U.P.

Currie, Gregory (2014). "Afterword: Fiction as a Transcultural Entity". In Anders Cullhed & Lena Rydholm, eds., *True Lies Worldwide. Fictionality in Global Contexts,* Berlin: De Gruyter, pp. 311–24.

Currie, Mark, ed. (1995). *Metafiction.* Longman Critical Readers. London: Longman.

Curtius, Ernst Robert (1990). *European Literature and the Latin Middle Ages*. Trans. Willard R. Trask. Bollingen Series, 36. Princeton, NJ: Princeton U.P.

Dagens, Claude (1977). *Saint Grégoire le Grand. Culture et expérience chrétiennes*. Diss. Paris: Études Augustiniennes.

Daniélou, Jean (1946). "Traversée de la mer Rouge et baptême aux premiers siècles". *Recherches de Science Religieuse*, 33, pp. 402–30.

Dawson, David (1995). "Sign Theory, Allegorical Reading, and the Motions of the Soul in *De doctrina christiana*". In Duane W.H. Arnold & Pamela Bright, eds., *De doctrina christiana. A Classic of Western Culture* (Christianity and Judaism in Antiquity, 9), Notre Dame, IN: University of Notre Dame Press, pp. 123–41.

De Lacy, Phillip (1948). "Stoic Views of Poetry". *American Journal of Philology*, 69, pp. 241–71.

De Vogel, Cornelia (1973). "The Problem of Philosophy and Christian Faith in Boethius' Consolatio". In Willem den Boer *et alii*, eds., *Romanitas et christianitas. Studia Iano Henrico Waszink A.D. VI Kal. Nov. A. MCMLXXIII XIII lustra complenti oblata*, Amsterdam: North-Holland, pp. 357–70.

De Vogel, Cornelia (1985). "Platonism or Christianity: A Mere Antagonism or a Profound Common Ground?" *Vigiliae Christianae*, 39, pp. 1–62.

Demats, Paule (1973). *Fabula. Trois études de mythographie antique et médiévale*. Publications romanes et françaises, 122. Geneva: Droz.

Deproost, Paul-Augustin (1998). "*Ficta et facta*. La condamnation du 'mensonge des poètes' dans la poésie latine chrétienne". *Revue des Études Augustiniennes*, 44, pp. 101–21.

Desbordes, Françoise (1993). "Le texte caché: problèmes figurés dans la déclamation latine". *Revue des études latines*, 71, pp. 73–86.

Dihle, Albrecht (1973). "Zum Streit um den Altar der Viktoria". In Willem den Boer *et alii*, eds., *Romanitas et christianitas. Studia Iano Henrico Waszink A.D. VI Kal. Nov. A. MCMLXXIII XIII lustra complenti oblata*, Amsterdam: North-Holland, pp. 81–97.

Dobell, Brian (2009). *Augustine's Intellectual Conversion. The Journey from Platonism to Christianity*. Cambridge: Cambridge U.P

Doignon, Jean (1972). "Un récit de miracle dans les 'Carmina' de Paulin de Nole. Poétique virgilienne et leçon apologétique". *Revue d'histoire de la spiritualité*, 48, pp. 129–44.

Doignon, Jean (1984–85). "Les 'nobles disciplines' et le 'visage de la verité' dans les premiers dialogues d'Augustin. Un commentaire de *Soliloques* 2,20,35". *Jahrbuch für Antike und Christentum*, 27–28, pp. 116–23.

Doležel, Lubomír (1988). "Mimesis and possible worlds". *Poetics Today*, 9.3, pp. 475–96.

Doležel, Lubomír (1998). "Possible worlds of fiction and history". *New Literary History*, 29.4, pp. 785–809.

Donnini, Mauro (1978). "Alcune osservazioni sul programma poetico di Sedulio". *Rivista di studi classici*, 26, pp. 426–36.

Drake, Harold A. (1985). "Suggestions of Date in Constantine's *Oration to the Saints*". *American Journal of Philology*, 106.3, pp. 335–49.

Dronke, Peter (1974). *Fabula. Explorations into the Uses of Myth in Medieval Platonism*. Mittellateinische Studien und Texte, 9. Leiden: Brill.

Dronke, Peter (1984). *The Medieval Poet and his World*. Storia e letteratura, 164. Rome: Edizioni di storia e letteratura.

Dronke, Peter (1994). *Verse with Prose from Petronius to Dante. The Art and Scope of the Mixed Form*. Cambridge, MA: Harvard U.P.

Duchrow, Ulrich (1965). *Sprachverständnis und biblisches Hören bei Augustin*. Diss. Hermeneutische Untersuchungen zur Theologie, 5. Tübingen: Mohr.
Duval, Yves-Marie (1987). "La poésie latine au IVe siècle de notre ère". *Bulletin de l'Association Guillaume Budé*, no. 2, pp. 165–92.
Dönt, Eugen (1971). "Zur Frage der Einheit von Augustins Konfessionen". *Hermes*, 99, pp. 350–61.
Döpp, Siegmar (1988). "Die Blütezeit lateinischer Literatur in der Spätantike (350–430 n.Chr.): Charakteristika einer Epoche". *Philologus*, 132.1, pp. 19–52.
Döpp, Siegmar (2009). "Narrative Metalepsen und andere Illusionsdurchbrechungen: Das spätantike Beispiel Martianus Capella". In Wolfram Brandes *et alii*, eds., *Millennium. Jahrbuch zu Kultur und Geschichte des ersten Jahrtausends n.Chr.*, 6, Berlin: De Gruyter, pp. 203–21.
Dörrie, Heinrich (1974). "Zur Methodik antiker Exegese". *Zeitschrift für die neutestamentliche Wissenschaft und die Kunde der älteren Kirche*, 65, pp. 121–38.
Eco, Umberto (1976). *A Theory of Semiotics*. Advances in Semiotics. Bloomington, IN: Indiana U.P.
Eco, Umberto (1984). *The Role of the Reader. Explorations in the Semiotics of Texts*. Advances in Semiotics. Bloomington, IN: Indiana U.P.
Eco, Umberto (1986). *Semiotics and the Philosophy of Language*. Advances in Semiotics. Bloomington, IN: Indiana U.P.
Eco, Umberto (1990). *The Limits of Interpretation*. Advances in Semiotics. Bloomington, IN: Indiana U.P.
Eco, Umberto (1994). *Six Walks in the Fictional Woods*. The Charles Eliot Norton Lectures, 1993. Cambridge: Harvard U.P.
Eden, Kathy (1986). *Poetic and Legal Fiction in the Aristotelian Tradition*. Princeton, NJ: Princeton U.P.
Eden, Kathy (1997). *Hermeneutics and the Rhetorical Tradition. Chapters in the Ancient Legacy & Its Humanist Reception*. Yale Studies in Hermeneutics. New Haven, CT: Yale U.P.
Edwards, Mark (2004). "Romanitas and the Church of Rome". In Simon Swain & Mark Edwards, eds., *Approaching Late Antiquity. The Transformation from Early to Late Empire*, Oxford: Oxford U.P., pp. 187–210.
Ehlers, Wilhelm (1985). "Bibelszenen in epischer Gestalt: ein Beitrag zu Alcimus Avitus". *Vigiliae Christianae*, 39, pp. 353–69.
Eigler, Ulrich (2001). "La missione di trasmissione. Girolamo come mediatore di culture differenti". In Gianpaolo Urso, ed., *Integrazione, mescolanza, rifiuto. Incontri di popoli, lingue e culture in Europa dall'Antichità all'Umanesimo*. Atti del convegno internazionale, Cividale del Friuli, 21–23 settembre 2000 (Monografie. Centro ricerche e documentazione sull'antichità classica, 22), Rome: "L'Erma" di Bretschneider, pp. 185–98.
Eiswirth, Rudolf (1955). *Hieronymus' Stellung zur Literatur und Kunst*. Diss. Klassisch-Philologische Studien, 16. Wiesbaden: Harrassowitz.
Ekbom, Moa (2013). *The Sortes Vergilianae. A Philological Study*. Diss. Uppsala: Uppsala University.
Eliot, T.S. (1945). *What is a Classic? An Address Delivered Before the Virgil Society on the 16th of October 1944*. London: Faber and Faber.

Ellspermann, Gerard L. (1949). *The Attitude of the Early Christian Latin Writers Toward Pagan Literature and Learning*. Diss. The Catholic University of America Patristic Studies, 82. Washington, DC.: The Catholic University of America Press.
Erdt, Werner (1976). *Christentum und heidnisch-antike Bildung bei Paulin von Nola mit Kommentar und Übersetzung des 16. Briefes*. Diss. Beiträge zur klassischen Philologie, 82. Meisenheim am Glan: Hain.
Evans, Gillian R. (1984). *The Language and Logic of the Bible. The Earlier Middle Ages*. Cambridge: Cambridge U.P.
Evenepoel, Willy (1993). "The Place of Poetry in Latin Christianity". In Jan den Boeft & Anton Hilhorst, eds., *Early Christian Poetry. A Collection of Essays* (Supplements to Vigiliae Christianae, 22), Leiden: Brill, pp. 35–60.
Feeney, Denis C. (1991). *The Gods in Epic. Poets and Critics of the Classical Tradition*. Oxford: Clarendon.
Feeney, Denis C. (1993). "Towards an Account of the Ancient World's Concept of Fictive Belief". In Christopher Gill & Timothy P. Wiseman, eds., *Lies and Fiction in the Ancient World*, Exeter: University of Exeter Press, pp. 230–44.
Ferrari, Leo (1992). "Beyond Augustine's Conversion Scene". In Joanne McWilliam, ed., *Augustine. From Rhetor to Theologian*, Waterloo, Ontario: Wilfrid Laurier U.P., pp. 97–107.
Finkelberg, Margalit (1998). *The Birth of Literary Fiction in Ancient Greece*. Oxford: Clarendon.
Finkelberg, Margalit (2014). "Diagnosing Fiction: From Plato to Borges". In Anders Cullhed & Lena Rydholm, eds., *True Lies Worldwide. Fictionality in Global Contexts*, Berlin: De Gruyter, pp. 153–65.
Flamant, Jacques (1977). *Macrobe et le néo-platonisme latin, à la fin du IVe siècle*. Études préliminaires aux religions orientales dans l'empire romain, 58. Leiden: Brill.
Fleteren, Frederick van (1994). "Mysticism in the *Confessiones* – A Controversy Revisited". In Frederick van Fleteren, Joseph C. Schnaubelt & Joseph Reino, eds., *Augustine. Mystic and Mystagogue* (Collectanea Augustiniana), New York: Peter Lang, pp. 309–36.
Fleteren, Frederick van (1995). "St. Augustine, Neoplatonism, and the Liberal Arts: The Background to *De doctrina christiana*". In Duane W.H. Arnold & Pamela Bright, eds., *De doctrina christiana. A Classic of Western Culture* (Christianity and Judaism in Antiquity, 9), Notre Dame, IN: University of Notre Dame Press, pp. 14–24.
Fleteren, Frederick van (1999). "Ascent of the Soul". In Allan D. Fitzgerald, John Cavadini & Marianne Djuth, eds., *Augustine Through the Ages. An Encyclopedia*, Grand Rapids, MI: Eerdmans, pp. 63–67.
Flores, Ralph (1975). "Reading and Speech in St. Augustine's Confessions". *Augustinian Studies*, 6, pp. 1–13.
Fontaine, Jacques (1959). *Isidore de Séville et la culture classique dans L'Espagne wisigothique*. I–II. Diss. Paris: Études Augustiniennes.
Fontaine, Jacques (1973). "Les symbolismes de la cithare dans la poésie de Paulin de Nole". In Willem den Boer *et alii*, eds., *Romanitas et christianitas. Studia Iano Henrico Waszink A.D. VI Kal. Nov. A. MCMLXXIII XIII lustra complenti oblata*, Amsterdam: North-Holland, pp. 123–43.
Fontaine, Jacques (1977). "Unité et diversité du mélange des genres et des tons chez quelques écrivains latins de la fin du IVe siècle: Ausone, Ambroise, Ammien". In Manfred Fuhrmann, ed., *Christianisme et formes littéraires de l'antiquité tardive en Occident* (Entretiens sur l'antiquité classique, 23), Geneva: Fondation Hardt, pp. 425–72.

Fontaine, Jacques (1980). *Études sur la poésie latine tardive d'Ausone à Prudence. Recueil de travaux*. Collection d'études anciennes. Paris: Belles Lettres.
Fontaine, Jacques (1981). *Naissance de la poésie dans l'Occident chrétien. Esquisse d'une histoire de la poésie latine chrétienne du IIIe au VIe siècle*. Paris: Études Augustiniennes.
Fontaine, Jacques (1982). "Christentum ist auch Antike. Einige Überlegungen zu Bildung und Literatur in der lateinischen Spätantike". *Jahrbuch für Antike und Christentum*, 25, pp. 5–21.
Fontaine, Jacques (1988). "Comment doit-on appliquer la notion de genre littéraire à la littérature latine chrétienne du IVe siècle?" *Philologus*, 132.1, pp. 53–73.
Fontanier, Jean-Michel (1986). "Christus imago Dei: art et christologie dans l'œuvre de Prudence". *Recherches Augustiniennes*, 21, pp. 117–37.
Ford, Andrew (2002). *The Origins of Criticism. Literary Culture and Poetic Theory in Classical Greece*. Princeton: Princeton U.P.
Forstner, Karl (1980). "Zur Bibeldichtung des Avitus von Vienne". In Joachim Dalfen, Karl Forstner, Maximilian Fussl & Wolfgang Speyer, eds., *Symmicta philologica Salisburgensia. Georgio Pfligersdorffer sexagenario oblata* (Filologia e critica, 33), Rome: Edizioni dell'Ateneo, pp. 43–60.
Foucault, Michel (1973). *The Order of Things. An Archaeology of the Human Sciences*. World of Man. New York: Vintage Books.
Fowden, Garth (1999). "Religious Communities". In Glen W. Bowersock, Peter Brown & Oleg Grabar, eds., *Late Antiquity. A Guide to the Postclassical World*, Cambridge, MA: The Belknap Press of Harvard U.P., pp. 82–106.
Fredriksen, Paula (2000). "Allegory and Reading God's Book: Paul and Augustine on the Destiny of Israel". In Jon Whitman, ed., *Interpretation and Allegory. Antiquity to the Modern Period* (Brill's Studies in Intellectual History, 101), Leiden: Brill, pp. 125–49.
Frend, William H.C. (1974). "The Two Worlds of Paulinus of Nola". In James W. Binns, ed., *Latin Literature of the Fourth Century* (Greek and Latin Studies), London: Routledge & Kegan Paul, pp. 100–33.
Fritz, Kurt von (1962). *Antike und moderne Tragödie. Neun Abhandlungen*. Berlin: De Gruyter.
Fromm, Hans, Wolfgang Harms & Uwe Ruberg, eds. (1975). *Verbum et signum. Beiträge zur mediävistischen Bedeutungsforschung*. I. Munich: Fink.
Fuhrmann, Manfred (1967). "Die lateinische Literatur der Spätantike. Ein literarhistorischer Beitrag zum Kontinuitätsproblem". *Antike und Abendland*, 13, pp. 56–79.
Gallagher, Catherine (2006). "The Rise of Fictionality". In Franco Moretti, ed., *The Novel. 1. History, Geography and Culture*, Princeton, NJ: Princeton U.P., pp. 336–63.
Gamble, Harry Y. (1995). *Books and Readers in the Early Church. A History of Early Christian Texts*. New Haven: Yale U.P.
Garrison, Mary (1997). "The Emergence of Carolingian Latin Literature and the Court of Charlemagne (780–814)". In Rosamond McKitterick, ed., *Carolingian Culture. Emulation and Innovation*, Cambridge: Cambridge U.P., pp. 111–40.
Gemeinhardt, Peter (2007). *Das lateinische Christentum und die antike pagane Bildung*. Studien und Texte zu Antike und Christentum, 41. Tübingen: Mohr Siebeck.
Gersh, Stephen (1986). *Middle Platonism and Neoplatonism. The Latin Tradition*. I–II. Publications in Medieval Studies, 23. Notre Dame, IN: University of Notre Dame Press.
Giannantonio, Pompeo (1969). *Dante e l'allegorismo*. Biblioteca dell'"Archivum Romanicum", Serie I, Storia, letteratura, paleografia, 100. Florence: Olschki.

Giardina, Andrea (1999). "Esplosione di tardoantico". *Studi Storici*, 40.1, pp. 157–80.
Gill, Christopher (1993). "Plato on Falsehood – not Fiction". In Christopher Gill & Timothy P. Wiseman, eds., *Lies and Fiction in the Ancient World*, Exeter: University of Exeter Press, pp. 38–87.
Gnilka, Christian (1979). "Interpretation frühchristlicher Literatur. Dargestellt am Beispiel des Prudentius". In Heinrich Krefeld, ed., *Impulse für die lateinische Lektüre. Von Terenz bis Thomas Morus*, Frankfurt am Main: Hirschgraben, pp. 138–80.
Gnilka, Christian (1980). "Die Natursymbolik in den Tagesliedern des Prudentius". In Ernst Dassmann & K. Suso Frank, eds., *Pietas. Festschrift für Bernhard Kötting* (Jahrbuch für Antike und Christentum, Ergänzungsband, 8), Münster: Aschendorff, pp. 411–46.
Gnilka, Christian (1984). *Der Begriff des "rechten Gebrauchs"*. Chrêsis, Die Methode der Kirchenväter im Umgang mit der antiken Kultur, 1. Basel: Schwabe.
Gnilka, Christian (1993). *Kultur und Conversion*. Chrêsis, Die Methode der Kirchenväter im Umgang mit der antiken Kultur, 2. Basel: Schwabe.
Gnilka, Christian (2000). *Prudentiana I. Critica*. Munich: Saur.
Godel, Robert (1964). "Réminiscences de poètes profanes dans les Lettres de St-Jérôme". *Museum Helveticum*, 21, pp. 65–70.
Gompf, Ludwig (1973). "Figmenta poetarum". In Alf Önnerfors, Johannes Rathofer & Fritz Wagner, eds., *Literatur und Sprache im europäischen Mittelalter. Festschrift für Karl Langosch zum 70. Geburtstag*, Darmstadt: Wissenschaftliche Buchgesellschaft, pp. 53–62.
González Delgado, Ramiro (2003). "Interpretaciones alegóricas del mito de Orfeo y Eurídice por Fulgencio y Boecio y su pervivencia en la *Patrologia Latina*". *Faventia*, 25.2, pp. 7–35.
Grabmann, Martin (1909). *Die Geschichte der scholastischen Methode. 1. Die scholastische Methode von ihren ersten Anfängen in der Väterliteratur bis zum Beginn des 12. Jahrhunderts*. Freiburg im Breisgau: Herder.
Graf, Fritz (2002). "Myth in Ovid". In Philip Hardie, ed., *The Cambridge Companion to Ovid* (Cambridge Companions to Literature), Cambridge: Cambridge U.P., pp. 108–21.
Grebe, Sabine (1999). *Martianus Capella, "De nuptiis Philologiae et Mercurii". Darstellung der sieben freien Künste und ihrer Beziehungen zueinander*. Beiträge zur Altertumskunde, 119. Stuttgart: Teubner.
Green, Dennis H. (2002). *Beginnings of Medieval Romance. Fact & Fiction, 1150–1220*. Cambridge Studies in Medieval Literature, 47. Cambridge: Cambridge U.P
Green, Roger P.H. (1971). *The Poetry of Paulinus of Nola. A Study of his Latinity*. Collection Latomus, 120. Brussels: Latomus.
Green, Roger P.H. (2006). *Latin Epics of the New Testament. Juvencus, Sedulius, Arator*. Oxford: Oxford U.P.
Griffiths, Paul J. (2000). "Seeking Egyptian Gold: A Fundamental Metaphor for the Christian Intellectual Life in a Religiously Diverse Age". *The Cresset*, 63.7, pp. 5–16.
Gruber, Joachim (2006). *Kommentar zu Boethius, De Consolatione Philosophiae*. 2nd rev. and enl. ed. Texte und Kommentare, 9. Berlin: De Gruyter.
Gualandri, Isabella (1979). *Furtiva lectio. Studi su Sidonio Apollinare*. Testi e documenti per lo studio dell'antichità, 62. Milan: Cisalpino-Goliardica.
Gunermann, Hans Heinrich (1973). "Literarische und philosophische Tradition im ersten Tagesgespräch von Augustinus' *De ordine*". *Recherches Augustiniennes*, 9, pp. 183–226.

Haarhoff, Theodore (1920). *Schools of Gaul. A Study of Pagan and Christian Education in the Last Century of the Western Empire*. Oxford: Oxford U.P.
Hagendahl, Harald (1958). *Latin Fathers and the Classics. A Study on the Apologists, Jerome and Other Christian Writers*. Studia Graeca et Latina Gothoburgensia, 6. Stockholm: Almqvist & Wiksell.
Hagendahl, Harald (1967). *Augustine and the Latin Classics*. I–II. Studia Graeca et Latina Gothoburgensia, 20. Stockholm: Almqvist & Wiksell.
Hagendahl, Harald (1983). *Von Tertullian zu Cassiodor. Die profane literarische Tradition in dem lateinischen christlichen Schrifttum*. Studia Graeca et Latina Gothoburgensia, 44. Gothenburg: Acta Universitatis Gothoburgensis.
Haller, Benjamin (2009). "The Gates of Horn and Ivory in Odyssey 19: Penelope's Call for Deeds, Not Words". *Classical Philology*, 104.4, pp. 397–417.
Hanson, Richard P.C. (1959). *Allegory and Event. A Study of the Sources and Significance of Origen's Interpretation of Scripture*. London: SCM Press.
Hardie, Philip (2001). "Coming to Terms with the Empire: Poetry of the Later Augustan and Tiberian Period". In Oliver Taplin, ed., *Literature in the Roman World*, Oxford: Oxford U.P., pp. 119–53.
Hardie, Philip (2002). *Ovid's Poetics of Illusion*. Cambridge: Cambridge U.P.
Hardie, Philip (2012). *Rumour and Renown. Representations of Fama in Western Literature*. Cambridge Classical Studies. Cambridge: Cambridge U.P.
Harrison, Carol (1992). *Beauty and Revelation in the Thought of Saint Augustine*. Oxford Theological Monographs. Oxford: Clarendon.
Harrison, Carol (2000). "The Rhetoric of Scripture and Preaching: Classical Decadence or Christian Aesthetic?" In Robert Dodaro & George Lawless, eds., *Augustine and His Critics. Essays in Honour of Gerald Bonner*, London: Routledge, pp. 213–29.
Havelock, Eric A. (1982). *Preface to Plato*. Cambridge, MA: The Belknap Press of Harvard U.P.
Hays, Gregory (1998). "Varia Fulgentiana". *Illinois Classical Studies*, 23, pp. 127–37.
Hays, Gregory (2003). "The Date and Identity of the Mythographer Fulgentius". *The Journal of Medieval Latin*, 13, pp. 163–252.
Hays, Gregory (2004). "'*Romuleis Libicisque Litteris*': Fulgentius and the 'Vandal Renaissance'". In Andrew H. Merrills, ed., *Vandals, Romans and Berbers. New Perspectives on Late Antique North Africa*, Aldershot: Ashgate, pp. 101–32.
Heck, Eberhard (1988). "Lactanz und die Klassiker. Zu Theorie und Praxis der Verwendung heidnischer Literatur in christlicher Apologetik bei Lactanz". *Philologus*, 132.1, pp. 160–79.
Heck, Eberhard (1990). "*Vestrum est – poeta noster*. Von der Geringschätzung Vergils zu seiner Aneignung in der frühchristlichen lateinischen Apologetik". *Museum Helveticum*, 47, pp. 102–20.
Hecquet-Noti, Nicole (2009). "Entre exégèse et épopée: Presence auctoriale dans Juvencus, Sédulius et Avit de Vienne". In Henriette Harich-Schwarzbauer & Petra Schierl, eds., *Lateinische Poesie der Spätantike*, Internationale Tagung in Castelen bei Augst, 11.–13. Oktober 2007 (Schweizerische Beiträge zur Altertumswissenschaft, 36), Basel: Schwabe, pp. 197–215.
Heidl, György (2009). *The Influence of Origen on the Young Augustine. A Chapter of the History of Origenism*. Gorgias Eastern Christian Studies, 19. Piscataway, NJ: Gorgias Press.

Henry, Paul (1934). *Plotin et l'Occident. Firmicus Maternus, Marius Victorinus, Saint Augustin et Macrobe.* Spicilegium sacrum Lovaniense, Études et documents, 15. Louvain: Université Catholique.
Henry, Paul (1981). *The Path to Transcendence. From Philosophy to Mysticism in Saint Augustine.* Trans. Francis F. Burch. Pittsburgh Theological Monograph Series, 37. Pittsburgh, PA: The Pickwick Press.
Herrera, Robert A. (1994). "Augustine: Spiritual Centaur?" In Frederick van Fleteren, Joseph C. Schnaubelt & Joseph Reino, eds., *Augustine. Mystic and Mystagogue* (Collectanea Augustiniana), New York: Peter Lang, pp. 159–76.
Herzog, Reinhart (1966). *Die allegorische Dichtkunst des Prudentius.* Diss. Zetemata, Monographien zur klassischen Altertumswissenschaft, 42. Munich: Beck.
Herzog, Reinhart (1975). *Die Bibelepik der lateinischen Spätantike. Formgeschichte einer erbaulichen Gattung.* I. Theorie und Geschichte der Literatur und der schönen Künste, 37. Munich: Fink.
Herzog, Reinhart (2002). *Spätantike. Studien zur römischen und lateinisch-christlichen Literatur.* Ed. Peter Habermehl. Hypomnemata, Supplement-Reihe, 3. Göttingen: Vandenhoeck & Ruprecht.
Hillier, Richard (1993). *Arator on the Acts of the Apostles. A Baptismal Commentary.* Oxford Early Christian Studies. Oxford: Clarendon.
Holte, Ragnar (1958). *Beatitudo och sapientia. Augustinus och de antika filosofskolornas diskussion om människans livsmål.* Diss. Stockholm: Svenska Kyrkans Diakonistyrelses Bokförlag.
Holtz, Louis (1981). *Donat et la tradition de l'enseignement grammatical. Étude sur l'Ars Donati et sa diffusion (IVe–IXe siècle) et édition critique.* Documents, études et répertoires. Paris: Éditions du CNRS.
Homeyer, Helene (1970). "Der Dichter zwischen zwei Welten. Beobachtungen zur Theorie und Praxis des Dichtens im frühen Mittelalter". *Antike und Abendland*, 16, pp. 141–52.
Horn, Hans-Jürgen (1979). "Lügt die Kunst? Ein kunsttheoretischer Gedankengang des Augustinus". *Jahrbuch für Antike und Christentum*, 22, pp. 50–60.
Houghton, Hugh (2008). *Augustine's Text of John. Patristic Citations and Latin Gospel Manuscripts.* Oxford Early Christian Studies. Oxford: Oxford U.P.
Hubaux, Jean & Maxime Leroy (1939). *Le mythe du phénix dans les littératures grecque et latine.* Bibliothèque de la Faculté de philosophie et lettres de l'Université de Liége, 82. Paris: Droz.
Hudson-Williams, Alun (1953). "Notes on the Text and Interpretation of Arator". *Vigiliae Christianae*, 7, pp. 89–97.
Hudson-Williams, Alun (1966–67). "Virgil and the Christian Latin Poets. A Lecture Delivered to the Virgil Society 19th November 1966". *Proceedings of the Virgil Society*, 6, pp. 11–21.
Hughes, Kevin L. (2000). "'The Arts Reputed Liberal': Augustine on the Perils of Liberal Education". In Kim Paffenroth & Kevin L. Hughes, eds., *Augustine and Liberal Education*, Aldershot: Ashgate, pp. 95–107.
Hunter, David G. (1995). "The Date and Purpose of Augustine's *De continentia*". *Augustinian Studies*, 26.2, pp. 7–24.
Inwood, Michael J. (1999). *A Heidegger Dictionary.* The Blackwell Philosopher Dictionaries. Malden, MA: Blackwell, 1999.

Irvine, Martin (1994). *The Making of Textual Culture. 'Grammatica' and Literary Theory, 350–1100*. Cambridge Studies in Medieval Literature, 19. Cambridge: Cambridge U.P.

Iser, Wolfgang (1983). "Akte des Fingierens. Oder: Was ist das Fiktive im fiktionalen Text?" In Dieter Heinrich & Wolfgang Iser, eds., *Funktionen des Fiktiven* (Poetik und Hermeneutik, 10), Munich: Fink, pp. 121–51.

Iser, Wolfgang (1990). "Fictionalizing: The Anthropological Dimension of Literary Fictions". *New Literary History*, 21, pp. 939–55.

Jackson, B. Darrell (1972). "The Theory of Signs in St. Augustine's *De Doctrina Christiana*". In Robert A. Markus, ed., *Augustine. A Collection of Critical Essays* (Modern Studies in Philosophy), Garden City, NY: Anchor Books, pp. 92–147.

Jaeger, Werner (1961). *Early Christianity and Greek Paideia*. Carl Newell Jackson Lectures 1960. Cambridge, MA: The Belknap Press of Harvard U.P.

James, Paula (1999). "Prudentius' *Psychomachia*. The Christian Arena and the Politics of Display". In Richard Miles, ed., *Constructing Identities in Late Antiquity*, London: Routledge, pp. 70–94.

Janaway, Christopher (1995). *Images of Excellence. Plato's Critique of the Arts*. Oxford: Clarendon.

Janson, Tore (1964). *Latin Prose Prefaces. Studies in Literary Conventions*. Diss. Acta Universitatis Stockholmiensis, Studia Latina Stockholmiensia, 13. Stockholm: Almqvist & Wiksell.

Jaumann, Herbert (1995). *Critica. Untersuchungen zur Geschichte der Literaturkritik zwischen Quintilian und Thomasius*. Brill's Studies in Intellectual History, 62. Leiden: Brill.

Jauß, Hans Robert (1983). "Zur historischen Genese der Scheidung von Fiktion und Realität". In Dieter Heinrich & Wolfgang Iser, eds., *Funktionen des Fiktiven* (Poetik und Hermeneutik, 10), Munich: Fink, pp. 423–31.

Jeauneau, Édouard (1973). *"Lectio philosophorum". Recherches sur l'École de Chartres*. Amsterdam: Hakkert.

Jones, Julian Ward, Jr. (1961). "Allegorical Interpretation in Servius". *The Classical Journal*, 56.5, pp. 217–26.

Jones, Julian Ward, Jr. (1964). "Vergil as *Magister* in Fulgentius". In Charles Henderson Jr., ed., *Classical Mediaeval and Renaissance Studies in Honor of Berthold Louis Ullman*, I (Storia e letteratura, 93), Rome: Edizioni di storia e letteratura, pp. 273–75.

Jongkees, Adriaan G. (1967). "Translatio Studii: les avatars d'un thème médiéval". In *Miscellanea mediaevalia in memoriam Jan Frederik Niermeyer*, Groningen: Wolters, pp. 41–51.

Jonsson, Inge (1983). *I symbolens hus. Nio kapitel om symbol, allegori och metafor*. Stockholm: Norstedts.

Junod-Ammerbauer, Helena (1975). "Le poète chrétien selon Paulin de Nole. L'adaptation des thèmes classiques dans les *Natalicia*". *Revue des Études Augustiniennes*, 21, pp. 13–54.

Junod-Ammerbauer, Helena (1978). "Les constructions de Nole et l'esthétique de saint Paulin". *Revue des Études Augustiniennes*, 24, pp. 22–57.

Kaiser, Erich (1964). "Odyssee-Szenen als Topoi". *Museum Helveticum*, 21.2, pp. 109–36; 21.4, pp. 197–224.

Kannicht, Richard (1988). *The Ancient Quarrel Between Philosophy and Poetry. Aspects of the Greek Conception of Literature*. University of Canterbury Publications, 40. Christchurch: University of Canterbury.

Kannicht, Richard (1996). *Paradeigmata. Aufsätze zur griechischen Poesie*. Eds. Lutz Käppel & Ernst A. Schmidt. Supplemente zu den Sitzungsberichten der Heidelberger Akademie der Wissenschaften, Philosophisch-historische Klasse, 10. Heidelberg: Winter.

Kartschoke, Dieter (1975). *Bibeldichtung. Studien zur Geschichte der epischen Bibelparaphrase von Juvencus bis Otfrid von Weißenburg*. Diss. Munich: Fink.

Kaster, Robert A. (1980a). "Macrobius and Servius: Verecundia and the Grammarian's Function". *Harvard Studies in Classical Philology*, 84, pp. 219–62.

Kaster, Robert A. (1980b). "The Grammarian's Authority". *Classical Philology*, 75.3, pp. 216–41.

Kaster, Robert A. (1997). *Guardians of Language. The Grammarian and Society in Late Antiquity*. The Transformation of the Classical Heritage, 11. Berkeley, CA: University of California Press.

Kelly, Christopher (1999). "Empire Building". In Glen W. Bowersock, Peter Brown & Oleg Grabar, eds., *Late Antiquity. A Guide to the Postclassical World*, Cambridge, MA: The Belknap Press of Harvard U.P., pp. 170–95.

Kennedy, George A. (1999). *Classical Rhetoric and Its Christian and Secular Tradition from Ancient to Modern Times*. 2nd ed., rev. and enl. Chapel Hill, NC: University of North Carolina Press.

Kenney, John Peter (2005). *The Mysticism of Saint Augustine. Rereading the Confessions*. New York: Routledge.

Kenter, Lucas Petrus (1971). *M. Tullius Cicero, De legibus. A Commentary on Book I*. Diss. Amsterdam: Hakkert.

Kirkconnell, Watson (1947). "Avitus' Epic on the Fall". *Laval théologique et philosophique*, 3.2, pp. 222–42.

Kirsch, Wolfgang (1983). "Die *Natalicia* des Paulinus von Nola als Mittel ideologischer Beeinflussung". *Klio*, 65, pp. 331–36.

Kirsch, Wolfgang (1985). "Zum Verhältnis von Poetologie und Poetik bei Paulinus von Nola". *Mittellateinisches Jahrbuch*, 20, pp. 103–11.

Kirsch, Wolfgang (1988). "Die Umstrukturierung des lateinischen Literatursystems im Zeichen der Krise des 3. Jahrhunderts". *Philologus*, 132.1, pp. 2–18.

Kirsch, Wolfgang (1989a). *Die lateinische Versepik des 4. Jahrhunderts*. Schriften zur Geschichte und Kultur der Antike, 28. Berlin: Akademie-Verlag.

Kirsch, Wolfgang (1989b). "Die spätantike Gesellschaft und die Literatur". *Philologus*, 133.1, pp. 128–46.

Kirwan, Christopher (2001). "Augustine's Philosophy of Language". In Eleonore Stump & Norman Kretzmann, eds., *The Cambridge Companion to Augustine*, Cambridge: Cambridge U.P., pp. 186–204.

Klopsch, Paul (1980). *Einführung in die Dichtungslehren des lateinischen Mittelalters*. Das lateinische Mittelalter. Darmstadt: Wissenschaftliche Buchgesellschaft.

Konstan, David (2004). "'The Birth of the Reader': Plutarch as a Literary Critic". *Scholia*, 13, pp. 3–27.

Krauss, Rosalind (1980). "Poststructuralism and the 'Paraliterary'". *October*, 13, pp. 36–40.

Krämer, Torsten (2007). *Augustinus zwischen Wahrheit und Lüge. Literarische Tätigkeit als Selbstfindung und Selbsterfindung*. Diss. Hypomnemata, 170. Göttingen: Vandenhoeck & Ruprecht.

Kuisma, Oiva (1996). *Proclus' Defence of Homer*. Diss. Commentationes humanarum litterarum, 109. Helsinki: Societas Scientiarum Fennica.

Kupke, Tanja (1992). "Où sont les muses d'antan? Notes for a Study of the Muses in the Middle Ages". In Haijo J. Westra, ed., *From Athens to Chartres. Neoplatonism and Medieval Thought. Studies in Honour of Édouard Jeauneau* (Studien und Texte zur Geistesgeschichte des Mittelalters, 35), Leiden: Brill, pp. 421–36.

Laan, Paul W.A.T. van der (1993). "Imitation créative dans le *Carmen paschale* de Sédulius". In Jan den Boeft & Anton Hilhorst, eds., *Early Christian Poetry. A Collection of Essays* (Supplements to Vigiliae Christianae, 22), Leiden: Brill, pp. 135–66.

Ladner, Gerhart B. (1979). "Medieval and Modern Understanding of Symbolism: A Comparison". *Speculum*, 54.2, pp. 223–56.

Laird, Andrew (1993). "Fiction, Bewitchment and Story Worlds: The Implications of Claims to Truth in Apuleius". In Christopher Gill & Timothy P. Wiseman, eds., *Lies and Fiction in the Ancient World*, Exeter: University of Exeter Press, pp. 147–74.

Laistner, Max L.W. (1935). "The Christian Attitude to Pagan Literature". *History*, 20, pp. 49–54.

Laistner, Max L.W. (1951). *Christianity and Pagan Culture in the Later Roman Empire. Together with an English Translation of John Chrysostom's Address on Vainglory and the Right Way for Parents to Bring Up Their Children*. James W. Richard Lectures in History, 1950–51. Ithaca, NY: Cornell U.P.

Lamberton, Robert (1986). *Homer the Theologian. Neoplatonist Allegorical Reading and the Growth of the Epic Tradition*. The Transformation of the Classical Heritage, 9. Berkeley: University of California Press.

Lamberton, Robert (2001). *Plutarch*. Hermes Books. New Haven, CT: Yale U.P.

Lampe, Geoffrey W.H. (1969). "The Exposition and Exegesis of Scripture. 1. To Gregory the Great". In Geoffrey W.H. Lampe, ed., *The Cambridge History of the Bible. 2. The West from the Fathers to the Reformation*, Cambridge: Cambridge U.P., pp. 155–83.

Lazzarini, Caterina (1984). "Historia/fabula: forme della costruzione poetica virgiliana nel commento di Servio all'Eneide". *Materiali e discussioni per l'analisi dei testi classici*, 12.1, pp. 117–44.

Leclercq, Jean (1998). *The Love of Learning and the Desire for God. A Study of Monastic Culture*. Trans. Catharine Misrahi. New York: Fordham U.P.

LeMoine, Fanny (1972). *Martianus Capella. A Literary Re-Evaluation*. Diss. Münchener Beiträge zur Mediävistik und Renaissance-Forschung, 10. Munich: Arbeo-Gesellschaft.

Lerer, Seth (1985). *Boethius and Dialogue. Literary Method in The Consolation of Philosophy*. Princeton, NJ: Princeton U.P.

Leupin, Alexandre (2003). *Fiction and Incarnation. Rhetoric, Theology, and Literature in the Middle Ages*. Trans. David Laatsch. Minneapolis, MN: University of Minnesota Press.

Lewis, C.S. (1979). *The Allegory of Love. A Study in Medieval Tradition*. Oxford: Oxford U.P.

Lewis, C.S. (1983). *The Discarded Image. An Introduction to Medieval and Renaissance Literature*. Cambridge: Cambridge U.P.

Lieberg, Godo (1982). *Poeta Creator. Studien zu einer Figur der antiken Dichtung*. Amsterdam: Gieben.

Lieberg, Godo (1986). "Poeta Creator: Some 'Religious' Aspects". In Francis Cairns, ed., *Papers of the Liverpool Latin Seminar*. V (Arca, Classical and Medieval Texts, Papers and Monographs, 19), pp. 23–32.

Lim, Richard (1999). "Christian Triumph and Controversy". In Glen W. Bowersock, Peter Brown & Oleg Grabar, eds., *Late Antiquity. A Guide to the Postclassical World*, Cambridge, MA: The Belknap Press of Harvard U.P., pp. 196–218.

Loewe, Raphael (1969). "The Medieval History of the Latin Vulgate". In Geoffrey W.H. Lampe, ed., *The Cambridge History of the Bible. 2. The West from the Fathers to the Reformation*, Cambridge: Cambridge U.P., pp. 102–54.
Louth, Andrew (1989). "Augustine on Language". *Journal of Literature & Theology*, 3.2, pp. 151–58.
Louth, Andrew (2007). *The Origins of the Christian Mystical Tradition. From Plato to Denys.* 2nd ed. Oxford: Oxford U.P.
Lubac, Henri de (1959–64). *Exégèse médiévale: Les quatre sens de l'Écriture*. Théologie. Paris: Aubier.
Lubac, Henri de (1960). "Saint Grégoire et la grammaire". *Recherches de Science Religieuse*, 48, pp. 185–226.
Ludwig, Walther (1977). "Die christliche Dichtung des Prudentius und die Transformation der klassischen Gattungen". In Manfred Fuhrmann, ed., *Christianisme et formes littéraires de l'antiquité tardive en Occident* (Entretiens sur l'antiquité classique, 23), Geneva: Fondation Hardt, pp. 303–63.
MacCormack, Sabine (1998). *The Shadows of Poetry. Vergil in the Mind of Augustine.* The Transformation of the Classical Heritage, 26. Berkeley: University of California Press.
Magee, John (1989). *Boethius on Signification and Mind*. Philosophia antiqua, 52. Leiden: Brill.
Malamud, Martha A. (1989). *A Poetics of Transformation. Prudentius and Classical Mythology*. Cornell Studies in Classical Philology, 49. Ithaca, NY: Cornell U.P.
Mandouze, André (1968). *Saint Augustin. L'aventure de la raison et de la grâce*. Diss. Paris: Études Augustiniennes.
Manieri, Alessandra (1998). *L'immagine poetica nella teoria degli antichi. Phantasia ed enargeia*. Pisa: Istituti editoriali e poligrafici internazionali.
Markus, Robert A. (1972). "St. Augustine on Signs". In Robert A. Markus, ed., *Augustine. A Collection of Critical Essays* (Modern Studies in Philosophy), Garden City, NY: Anchor Books, pp. 61–91.
Markus, Robert A. (1974). "Paganism, Christianity and the Latin Classics in the Fourth Century". In James Wallace Binns, ed., *Latin Literature of the Fourth Century* (Greek and Latin Studies, Classical Literature and Its Influence), London: Routledge & Kegan Paul, pp. 1–21.
Markus, Robert A. (1990). *The End of Ancient Christianity*. Cambridge: Cambridge U.P.
Markus, Robert A. (1994). *Sacred and Secular. Studies on Augustine and Latin Christianity*. Variorum Reprints, Collected Studies Series, 465. Aldershot, Hampshire: Variorum.
Markus, Robert A. (1996). *Signs and Meanings. World and Text in Ancient Christianity*. Liverpool: Liverpool U.P.
Markus, Robert A. (2000). "'Tempora Christiana' Revisited". In Robert Dodaro & George Lawless, eds., *Augustine and His Critics. Essays in Honour of Gerald Bonner*, London: Routledge, pp. 199–211.
Marrou, Henri-Irénée (1938). *Saint Augustin et la fin de la culture antique*. Bibliothèque des Écoles françaises d'Athènes et de Rome, 145. Paris: Boccard.
Marrou, Henri-Irénée (1948). *Histoire de l'éducation dans l'antiquité*. Collections Esprit. Paris: Seuil.
Mastrangelo, Marc (2008). *The Roman Self in Late Antiquity. Prudentius and the Poetics of the Soul*. Baltimore: Johns Hopkins U.P.

Mastrangelo, Marc (2009). "The Decline of Poetry in the Fourth-Century West". *International Journal of the Classical Tradition*, 16.3–4, pp. 311–29.
Matter, E. Ann (1990). *The Voice of My Beloved. The Song of Songs in Western Medieval Christianity*. Middle Ages Series. Philadelphia: University of Pennsylvania Press.
Matthews, Gareth B. (1972). "The Inner Man". In Robert A. Markus, ed., *Augustine. A Collection of Critical Essays* (Modern Studies in Philosophy), Garden City, NY: Anchor Books, pp. 176–90.
Matthews, John (1981). "Anicius Manlius Severinus Boethius". In Margaret Gibson, ed., *Boethius. His Life, Thought and Influence*, Oxford: Basil Blackwell, pp. 15–43.
Mattiacci, Silvia (2002). "'Divertissements' poetici tardoantichi: i versi di Fulgenzio Mitografo". *Paideia* 57, pp. 252–80.
Mayer, Cornelius Petrus (1974). *Die Zeichen in der geistigen Entwicklung und in der Theologie Augustins. II. Die antimanichäische Epoche*. Diss. Cassiciacum, 24.2. Würzburg: Augustinus-Verlag.
Mazzega, Michael (1996). *Sedulius, Carmen paschale, Buch III*. Diss. Chrêsis, Die Methode der Kirchenväter im Umgang mit der antiken Kultur, 5. Basel: Schwabe.
Mazzeo, Joseph Anthony (1962). "St. Augustine's Rhetoric of Silence". *Journal of the History of Ideas*, 23.2, pp. 175–96.
Mazzotta, Giuseppe (1979). *Dante, Poet of the Desert. History and Allegory in the Divine Comedy*. Princeton, NJ: Princeton U.P.
McClure, Judith (1981). "The Biblical Epic and Its Audience in Late Antiquity". In Francis Cairns, ed., *Papers of the Liverpool Latin Seminar. III* (Arca, Classical and Medieval Texts, Papers and Monographs, 7), pp. 305–21.
McMahon, Robert (2006). *Understanding the Medieval Meditative Ascent. Augustine, Anselm, Boethius, & Dante*. Washington, DC: The Catholic University of America Press.
Mehtonen, Päivi (1996). *Old Concepts and New Poetics. Historia, Argumentum, and Fabula in the Twelfth- and Early Thirteenth-century Latin Poetics of Fiction*. Diss. Commentationes humanarum litterarum, 108. Helsinki: Societas Scientiarum Fennica.
Mehtonen, Päivi (2003). *Obscure Language, Unclear Literature. Theory and Practice from Quintilian to the Enlightenment*. Trans. Robert MacGilleon. Annales Academiae Scientiarum Fennicae, 320. Helsinki: Finnish Academy of Science and Letters.
Merdinger, Jane E. (1999). "Councils of North African Bishops". In Allan D. Fitzgerald, John Cavadini & Marianne Djuth, eds., *Augustine Through the Ages. An Encyclopedia*, Grand Rapids, MI: Eerdmans, pp. 248–50.
Merkt, Andreas (1997). *Maximus I. von Turin. Die Verkündigung eines Bischofs der frühen Reichskirche im zeitgeschichtlichen, gesellschaftlichen und liturgischen Kontext*. Diss. Supplements to Vigiliae Christianae, 40. Leiden: Brill.
Messina, Marco Tullio (2002). "Due note su Virgilio in Girolamo". In Isabella Gualandri, ed., *Tra IV e V secolo. Studi sulla cultura latina tardoantica* (Quaderni di Acme, 50), Milan: Cisalpino, pp. 119–39.
Messmer, Ernst (1974). *Laktanz und die Dichtung*. Diss. Munich: Ludwig-Maximilians-Universität.
Milovanović-Barham, Čelica (1993). "Three Levels of Style in Augustine of Hippo and Gregory of Nazianzus". *Rhetorica*, 11, pp. 1–25.
Mohrmann, Christine (1984). "Some Remarks on the Language of Boethius, 'Consolatio Philosophiae'". In Manfred Fuhrmann & Joachim Gruber, eds., *Boethius* (Wege der Forschung, 483), Darmstadt: Wissenschaftliche Buchgesellschaft, pp. 302–10.

Moorhead, John (2013). "Gregory's Literary Inheritance". In Bronwen Neil & Matthew Dal Santo, eds., *A Companion to Gregory the Great* (Brill's Companions to the Christian Tradition, 47), Leiden: Brill, pp. 249–67.

Moos, Peter von (1976). "*Poeta* und *Historicus* im Mittelalter. Zum Mimesis-Problem am Beispiel einiger Urteile über Lucan". *Beiträge zur Geschichte der deutschen Sprache und Literatur*, 98, pp. 93–130.

Most, Glenn W. (2010). "Hellenistic Allegory and Early Imperial Rhetoric". In Rita Copeland and Peter T. Struck, eds., *The Cambridge Companion to Allegory* (Cambridge Companions to Literature), Cambridge: Cambridge U.P.

Mueller-Goldingen, Christian (1989). "Die Stellung der Dichtung in Boethius' Consolatio Philosophiae". *Rheinisches Museum für Philologie*, 132, pp. 369–95.

Müller, Gerhard Anselm (2003). *Formen und Funktionen der Vergilzitate bei Augustin von Hippo. Formen und Funktionen der Zitate und Anspielungen*. Diss. Studien zur Geschichte und Kultur des Altertums, Reihe 1, Monographien, 18. Paderborn: Schöningh.

Murru, Furio (1980). "Analisi semiologica e strutturale della praefatio agli Evangeliorum libri di Giovenco". *Wiener Studien*, 14, pp. 133–51.

Männlein-Robert, Irmgard (2003). "Zum Bild des Phidias in der Antike: Konzepte zur Kreativität des bildenden Künstlers". In Thomas Dewender & Thomas Welt, eds., *Imagination – Fiktion – Kreation. Das kulturschaffende Vermögen der Phantasie*, Munich: Saur, pp. 45–67.

Nat, Pieter G. van der (1973). "Die Praefatio der Evangelienparaphrase des Iuvencus". In Willem den Boer *et alii*, eds., *Romanitas et christianitas. Studia Iano Henrico Waszink A. D. VI Kal. Nov. A. MCMLXXIII XIII lustra complenti oblata*, Amsterdam: North-Holland, pp. 249–57.

Nat, Pieter G. van der (1977). "Zu den Voraussetzungen der christlichen lateinischen Literatur: die Zeugnisse von Minucius Felix und Lactanz". In Manfred Fuhrmann, ed., *Christianisme et formes littéraires de l'antiquité tardive en Occident* (Entretiens sur l'antiquité classique, 23), Geneva: Fondation Hardt, pp. 191–225.

Nodes, Daniel J. (1993). *Doctrine and Exegesis in Biblical Latin Poetry*. Arca, Classical and Medieval Texts, Papers and Monographs, 31. Leeds: Cairns.

Norden, Eduard (1909). *Die antike Kunstprosa vom VI. Jahrhundert v. Chr. bis in die Zeit der Renaissance*. I–II. Leipzig: Teubner.

Norris, Richard A. (2004). "The Apologists". In Frances Young, Lewis Ayres & Andrew Louth, eds., *The Cambridge History of Early Christian Literature*, Cambridge: Cambridge U.P., pp. 36–44.

Nuchelmans, Gabriel (1957). "Philologia et son mariage avec Mercure jusqu'à la fin du XIIe siècle". *Latomus*, 16, pp. 84–107.

Nussbaum, Martha (1999). "Augustine and Dante on the Ascent of Love". In Gareth B. Matthews, ed., *The Augustinian Tradition* (Philosophical Traditions, 8), Berkeley, CA: University of California Press, pp. 61–90.

Nussbaum, Martha (2009). *The Therapy of Desire. Theory and Practice in Hellenistic Ethics*. Martin Classical Lectures, 2. Princeton, NJ: Princeton U.P.

O'Connell, Robert J. (1968). *St. Augustine's Early Theory of Man, A.D. 386–391*. Cambridge, MA: The Belknap Press of Harvard U.P.

O'Connell, Robert J. (1969). *St. Augustine's Confessions. The Odyssey of Soul*. Cambridge, MA: The Belknap Press of Harvard U.P.

O'Connell, Robert J. (1978). *Art and the Christian Intelligence in St. Augustine*. Cambridge, MA: Harvard U.P.
O'Daly, Gerard (1987). *Augustine's Philosophy of Mind*. London: Duckworth.
O'Daly, Gerard (1991). *The Poetry of Boethius*. London: Duckworth.
O'Daly, Gerard (2001). *Platonism Pagan and Christian. Studies in Plotinus and Augustine*. Variorum Reprints, Collected Studies Series, 719. Aldershot, Hampshire: Ashgate.
O'Donnell, James J. (1985). *Augustine*. Twayne's World Authors Series, 759. Boston: Twayne.
O'Donnell, James J. (2005). *Augustine. A New Biography*. New York: HarperCollins.
O'Donnell, James J. (2009). *The Ruin of the Roman Empire*. New York: Ecco.
O'Meara, John J. (1992). "Augustine's *Confessions:* Elements of Fictions". In Joanne McWilliam, ed., *Augustine. From Rhetor to Theologian*, Waterloo, Ontario: Wilfrid Laurier U.P., pp. 77–95.
Ogilvie, Robert M. (1978). *The Library of Lactantius*. Oxford: Clarendon.
Pavel, Thomas G. (1986). *Fictional Worlds*. Cambridge, MA: Harvard U.P.
Pease, Arthur S. (1919). "The Attitude of Jerome towards Pagan Literature". *Transactions and Proceedings of the American Philological Association*, 50, pp. 150–67.
Pépin, Jean (1951). "'Primitiae spiritus'. Remarques sur une citation paulinienne des 'Confessions' de saint Augustin". *Revue de l'histoire des religions*, 140, pp. 155–202.
Pépin, Jean (1976). *Mythe et allégorie. Les origines grecques et les contestations judéo-chrétiennes*. New, rev. and augmented ed. Paris: Études Augustiniennes.
Pépin, Jean (1987). *La tradition de l'allégorie. De Philon d'Alexandrie a Dante. Études historiques*. Paris: Études Augustiniennes.
Pinborg, Jan (1967). *Die Entwicklung der Sprachtheorie im Mittelalter*. Diss. Beiträge zur Geschichte der Philosophie und Theologie des Mittelalters, 42.2. Münster: Aschendorff.
Pollmann, Karla (1996). *Doctrina christiana. Untersuchungen zu den Anfängen der christlichen Hermeneutik unter besonderer Berücksichtigung von Augustinus, De doctrina christiana*. Diss. Paradosis, 41. Freiburg: Universitätsverlag.
Pollmann, Karla (1999). "Zwei Konzepte von Fiktionalität in der Philosophie des Hellenismus und in der Spätantike". In Therese Fuhrer, Michael Erler & Karin Schlapbach, eds., *Zur Rezeption der hellenistischen Philosophie in der Spätantike* (Philosophie der Antike, 9), Stuttgart: Steiner, pp. 261–78.
Pratt, Louise H. (1993). *Lying and Poetry from Homer to Pindar. Falsehood and Deception in Archaic Greek Poetics*. Michigan Monographs in Classical Antiquity. Ann Arbor, MI: University of Michigan Press.
Purcell, William M. (1996). *Ars poetriae. Rhetorical and Grammatical Invention at the Margin of Literacy*. Studies in Rhetoric/Communication. Columbia, SC: University of South Carolina Press.
Quacquarelli, Antonio (1972). "Inventio ed elocutio nella retorica cristiana antica". *Vetera Christianorum*, 9, pp. 191–218.
Quadlbauer, Franz (1974). "Zur 'invocatio' des Iuvencus". *Grazer Beiträge*, 2, pp. 189–212.
Quinn, John M. (1994). "Mysticism in the *Confessiones:* Four Passages Reconsidered". In Frederick van Fleteren, Joseph C. Schnaubelt & Joseph Reino, eds., *Augustine. Mystic and Mystagogue* (Collectanea Augustiniana), New York: Peter Lang, pp. 251–86.
Raby, Frederick J.E. (1957). *A History of Secular Latin Poetry in the Middle Ages*. I–II. 2nd ed. Oxford: Clarendon.
Rahner, Hugo (1971). *Greek Myths and Christian Mystery*. Trans. Brian Battershaw. New York: Biblo and Tannen.

Ralfs, Günter (1984). "Die Erkenntnislehre des Boethius". In Manfred Fuhrmann & Joachim Gruber, eds., *Boethius* (Wege der Forschung, 483), Darmstadt: Wissenschaftliche Buchgesellschaft, pp. 350–74.
Rand, Edward K. (1929). *Founders of the Middle Ages*. Cambridge, MA: Harvard U.P.
Rauner-Hafner, Gabriele (1978). "Die Vergilinterpretation des Fulgentius. Bemerkungen zu Gliederung und Absicht der 'Expositio Virgilianae continentiae'". *Mittellateinisches Jahrbuch*, 13, pp. 7–49.
Reiff, Arno (1959). *Interpretatio, imitatio, aemulatio. Begriff und Vorstellung literarischer Abhängigkeit bei den Römern*. Diss. Würzburg: Triltsch.
Relihan, Joel C. (1984). "Ovid *Metamorphoses* I.1–4 and Fulgentius' *Mitologiae*". *American Journal of Philology*, 105.1, pp. 87–90.
Relihan, Joel C. (1993). *Ancient Menippean Satire*. Baltimore, MD: John Hopkins U.P.
Reutern, Georg von (1933). *Plutarchs Stellung zur Dichtkunst. Interpretation der Schrift "De audiendis poetis"*. Diss. Kiel: Die Hohe Philosophische Fakultät der Christian-Albrechts-Universität zu Kiel.
Reynolds, Suzanne (1996). *Medieval Reading. Grammar, Rhetoric, and the Classical Text*. Cambridge Studies in Medieval Literature, 27. Cambridge: Cambridge U.P.
Riché, Pierre (1962). *Éducation et culture dans l'Occident barbare. VIe – VIIIe siècles*. Diss. Patristica Sorbonensia, 4. Paris: Seuil.
Riggi, Calogero (1977). "Lo scontro della letteratura cristiana antica e della cultura greco-romana". *Salesianum*, 39, pp. 431–52.
Roberts, Michael (1980). "The Prologue to Avitus' 'De spiritalis historiae gestis': Christian Poetry and Poetic License". *Traditio*, 36, pp. 399–407.
Roberts, Michael (1985). *Biblical Epic and Rhetorical Paraphrase in Late Antiquity*. Diss. Arca, Classical and Medieval Texts, Papers and Monographs, 16. Liverpool: Cairns.
Roberts, Michael (1989). *The Jeweled Style. Poetry and Poetics in Late Antiquity*. Ithaca, NY: Cornell U.P.
Robinson, George W. (1918). "Joseph Scaliger's Estimates of Greek and Latin Authors". *Harvard Studies in Classical Philology*, 29, pp. 133–76.
Romano, Domenico (1961). "Licenzio poeta. Sulla posizione di Agostino verso la poesia". *Nuovo Didaskaleion*, 11, pp. 1–22.
Roubekas, Nickolas P. (2012). "Which Euhemerism Will You Use? Celsus on the Divine Nature of Jesus". *Journal of Early Christian History*, 2.2, pp. 80–96.
Ruef, Hans (1995). "Die Sprachtheorie des Augustinus in *De dialectica*". In Sten Ebbesen, ed., *Sprachtheorien in Spätantike und Mittelalter* (Geschichte der Sprachtheorie, 3), Tübingen: Narr, pp. 3–11.
Ryan, Marie-Laure (1991). "Possible Worlds and Accessibility Relations: A Semantic Typology of Fiction". *Poetics Today*, 12.3, pp. 553–76.
Rösler, Wolfgang (1980). "Die Entdeckung der Fiktionalität in der Antike". *Poetica*, 12, pp. 283–319.
Saenger, Paul (1997). *Space Between Words. The Origins of Silent Reading*. Figurae, Reading Medieval Culture. Stanford, CA: Stanford U.P.
Sassen, Ferdinand (1984). "Boethius – Lehrmeister des Mittelalters". In Manfred Fuhrmann & Joachim Gruber, eds., *Boethius* (Wege der Forschung, 483), Darmstadt: Wissenschaftliche Buchgesellschaft, pp. 82–124.
Scarry, Elaine (1980). "The Well-Rounded Sphere: The Metaphysical Structure of the *Consolation of Philosophy*". In Caroline D. Eckhardt, ed., *Essays in the Numerical*

Criticism of Medieval Literature, Lewisburg, PA: Bucknell U.P., and Cranbury, NJ: Associated U.P., pp. 91–140.
Scheible, Helga (1972). *Die Gedichte in der Consolatio Philosophiae des Boethius*. Diss. Bibliothek der klassischen Altertumswissenschaften, Neue Folge, 46. Heidelberg: Winter.
Scheid, John & Jesper Svenbro (2003). *Le métier de Zeus. Mythe du tissage et du tissu dans le monde gréco-romain*. Paris: Errance.
Schelkle, Karl Hermann (1939). *Virgil in der Deutung Augustins*. Diss. Tübinger Beiträge zur Altertumswissenschaft, 32. Stuttgart: Kohlhammer.
Schenkeveld, Dirk M. (1982). "The Structure of Plutarch's *De audiendis poetis*". *Mnemosyne*, 35, pp. 60–71.
Schmidt, Peter L. (1977). "Zur Typologie und Literarisierung des frühchristlichen lateinischen Dialogs". In Manfred Fuhrmann, ed., *Christianisme et formes littéraires de l'antiquité tardive en Occident* (Entretiens sur l'antiquité classique, 23), Geneva: Fondation Hardt, pp. 101–73.
Schottenius Cullhed, Sigrid (2012). *Proba the Prophet. Studies in the Christian Virgilian Cento of Faltonia Betitia Proba*. Diss. Gothenburg: University of Gothenburg.
Schrader, Richard J. (1977). "Arator: Revaluation". *Classical Folia*, 31, pp. 64–77.
Schwind, Johannes (1990). *Arator-Studien*. Diss. Hypomnemata, Untersuchungen zur Antike und zu ihrem Nachleben, 94. Göttingen: Vandenhoeck & Ruprecht.
Schwind, Johannes (1995). *Sprachliche und exegetische Beobachtungen zu Arator*. Abhandlungen der Geistes- und Sozialwissenschaftlichen Klasse, 1995, 5. Mainz: Akademie der Wissenschaften und der Literatur, and Stuttgart: Steiner.
Schäublin, Christoph (1995). "'De doctrina christiana': A Classic of Western Culture?" In Duane W.H. Arnold & Pamela Bright, eds., *De doctrina christiana. A Classic of Western Culture* (Christianity and Judaism in Antiquity, 9), Notre Dame, IN: University of Notre Dame Press, pp. 47–67.
Segal, Charles P. (1962). "Gorgias and the Psychology of the Logos". *Harvard Studies in Classical Philology*, 66, pp. 99–155.
Shanzer, Danuta R. (1986). *A Philosophical and Literary Commentary on Martianus Capella's De Nuptiis Philologiae et Mercurii. Book 1*. University of California Publications, Classical Studies, 32. Berkeley, CA: University of California Press.
Shanzer, Danuta R. (2005). "Augustine's Disciplines: *Silent diutius Musae Varronis?*" In Karla Pollmann & Mark Vessey, eds., *Augustine and the Disciplines. From Cassiciacum to Confessions*, Oxford: Oxford U.P., pp. 69–112.
Shanzer, Danuta R. (2009). "Interpreting the *Consolation*". In John Marenbon, ed., *The Cambridge Companion to Boethius* (Cambridge Companions to Philosophy), Cambridge: Cambridge U.P., pp. 228–54.
Shanzer, Danuta R. (2012). "Augustine and the Latin Classics". In Mark Vessey & Shelley Reid, eds., *A Companion to Augustine* (Blackwell Companions to the Ancient World), Chichester, West Sussex: Wiley-Blackwell, pp. 161–74.
Sheppard, Anne D.R. (1980). *Studies on the 5th and 6th Essays of Proclus' Commentary on the Republic*. Diss. Hypomnemata, Untersuchungen zur Antike und zu ihrem Nachleben, 61. Göttingen: Vandenhoeck & Ruprecht.
Skeat, Theodore C. (1969). "Early Christian Book-Production: Papyri and Manuscripts". In Geoffrey W.H. Lampe, ed., *The Cambridge History of the Bible. 2. The West from the Fathers to the Reformation*, Cambridge: Cambridge U.P., pp. 54–79.

Small, Carolinne D. (1986). "Rhetoric and Exegesis in Sedulius' *Carmen Paschale*". *Classica et mediaevalia*, 37, pp. 223–44.
Smalley, Beryl (1984). *The Study of the Bible in the Middle Ages*. Oxford: Blackwell.
Smith, Macklin (1976). *Prudentius' Psychomachia. A Reexamination*. Princeton, NJ: Princeton U.P.
Smolak, Kurt (1985). "Lecta verba. Aspekte der Sprachästhetik im Latein der Spätantike und des Frühmittelalters". *Wiener humanistische Blätter*, 27, pp. 12–27.
Sparks, Hedley F.D. (1970). "Jerome as Biblical Scholar". In Peter R. Ackroyd & Christopher F. Evans, eds., *The Cambridge History of the Bible. 1. From the Beginnings to Jerome*, Cambridge: Cambridge U.P., pp. 510–41.
Springer, Carl P.E. (1988). *The Gospel as Epic in Late Antiquity. The Paschale Carmen of Sedulius*. Supplements to Vigiliae Christianae, 2. Leiden: Brill.
Stahl, William H., Richard Johnson & Evan L. Burge (1971). *Martianus Capella and the Seven Liberal Arts. I. The Quadrivium of Martianus Capella: Latin Traditions in the Mathematical Sciences, 50 B.C.–A.D. 1250*. Records of Civilization, 84. New York: Columbia U.P.
Starnes, Colin (1992). "Augustine's Conversion and the Ninth Book of the *Confessions*". In Joanne McWilliam, ed., *Augustine. From Rhetor to Theologian*, Waterloo, Ontario: Wilfrid Laurier U.P., pp. 51–65.
Staubach, Nikolaus (2009). "Zwischen Mythenallegorese und Idolatriekritik. Bischof Theodulf von Orléans und die heidnischen Götter". In Christine Schmitz & Anja Bettenworth, eds., *Mensch – Heros – Gott. Weltentwürfe und Lebensmodelle im Mythos der Vormoderne*, Stuttgart: Steiner, pp. 149–65.
Steidle, Wolf (1971). "Die dichterische Konzeption des Prudentius und das Gedicht contra Symmachum". *Vigiliae Christianae*, 25, pp. 241–81.
Stella, Franco (2001). *Poesia e teologia. L'Occidente latino tra IV e VIII secolo*. Eredità medievale, 01/18. Milan: ISTeM/Jaca.
Stierle, Karlheinz (2001). "Fiktion". In Karlheinz Barck, Martin Fontius, Dieter Schlenstedt *et alii*, eds., *Ästhetische Grundbegriffe. Historisches Wörterbuch in sieben Bänden*, 2, Stuttgart: Metzler, pp. 380–428.
Stock, Brian (1998). *Augustine the Reader. Meditation, Self-Knowledge, and the Ethics of Interpretation*. Cambridge, MA: The Belknap Press of Harvard U.P.
Stock, Brian (2001). *After Augustine. The Meditative Reader and the Text*. Material Texts. Philadelphia: University of Pennsylvania Press.
Stock, Brian (2010). *Augustine's Inner Dialogue. The Philosophical Soliloquy in Late Antiquity*. Cambridge: Cambridge U.P.
Stockt, Luc van der (1992). *Twinkling and Twilight. Plutarch's Reflections on Literature*. Diss. Verhandelingen van de Koninklijke Academie voor Wetenschappen, Letteren en schone Kunsten van België, Klasse der Letteren, 145. Brussels: Koninklijke Academie voor Wetenschappen, Letteren en schone Kunsten van België.
Stok, Fabio (2012). "Commenting on Virgil, from Aelius Donatus to Servius". *Dead Sea Discoveries*, 19.3, pp. 464–84.
Stroumsa, Guy G. (2012). "Augustine and Books". In Mark Vessey & Shelley Reid, eds., *A Companion to Augustine* (Blackwell Companions to the Ancient World), Chichester, West Sussex: Wiley-Blackwell, pp. 151–57.
Strubel, Armand (1975). "'Allegoria in factis' et 'Allegoria in verbis'". *Poétique*, 6 (no. 23), pp. 342–57.

Sutcliffe, Edmund F. (1969). "Jerome". In Geoffrey W.H. Lampe, ed., *The Cambridge History of the Bible. 2. The West from the Fathers to the Reformation*, Cambridge: Cambridge U.P., pp. 80–101.
Svenbro, Jesper (1993). *Phrasikleia. An Anthropology of Reading in Ancient Greece*. Trans. Janet Lloyd. Myth and Poetics. Ithaca, NY: Cornell U.P.
Svoboda, Karel (1933). *L'Esthétique de saint Augustin et ses sources*. Diss. Spisy Filosofické fakulty Masarykovy University v Brně, 35. Brno: A. Píša.
Taylor, Charles (1989). *Sources of the Self. The Making of the Modern Identity*. Cambridge: Cambridge U.P.
Teske, Roland J. (1994). "St. Augustine and the Vision of God". In Frederick van Fleteren, Joseph C. Schnaubelt & Joseph Reino, eds., *Augustine. Mystic and Mystagogue* (Collectanea Augustiniana), New York: Peter Lang, pp. 287–308.
Teske, Roland J. (1995). "Criteria for Figurative Interpretation in St. Augustine". In Duane W.H. Arnold & Pamela Bright, eds., *De doctrina christiana. A Classic of Western Culture* (Christianity and Judaism in Antiquity, 9), Notre Dame, IN: University of Notre Dame Press, pp. 109–22.
Teske, Roland J. (2009). *Augustine of Hippo, Philosopher, Exegete, and Theologian. A Second Collection of Essays*. Marquette Studies in Philosophy, 66. Milwaukee, WI: Marquette U.P.
Thor, Andreas (2013). *Studies on Juvencus' Language and Style*. Diss. Uppsala: Uppsala University.
Thraede, Klaus (1961). "Arator". *Jahrbuch für Antike und Christentum*, 4, pp. 187–96.
Thraede, Klaus (1962a). "Epos". In Theodor Klauser *et alii*, eds., *Reallexikon für Antike und Christentum. Sachwörterbuch zur Auseinandersetzung des Christentums mit der antiken Welt*, 5, Stuttgart: Hiersemann, cols. 983–1042.
Thraede, Klaus (1962b). "Untersuchungen zum Ursprung und zur Geschichte der christlichen Poesie". II. *Jahrbuch für Antike und Christentum*, 5, pp. 125–57.
Thraede, Klaus (1963). "Untersuchungen zum Ursprung und zur Geschichte der christlich-lateinischen Poesie". III. *Jahrbuch für Antike und Christentum*, 6, pp. 101–11.
Thraede, Klaus (1965). *Studien zu Sprache und Stil des Prudentius*. Hypomnemata, Untersuchungen zur Antike und zu ihrem Nachleben, 13. Göttingen: Vandenhoeck & Ruprecht.
Tigerstedt, Eugène Napoleon (1968). "The Poet as Creator: Origins of a Metaphor". *Comparative Literature Studies*, 5.4, pp. 455–88.
Todorov, Tzvetan (1992). *Theories of the Symbol*. Trans. Catherine Porter. Ithaca, NY: Cornell U.P.
Trigg, Joseph W. (1998). *Origen*. The Early Church Fathers. London: Routledge.
Trimpi, Wesley (1971). "The Ancient Hypothesis of Fiction: An Essay on the Origins of Literary Theory". *Traditio*, 27, pp. 1–78.
Trimpi, Wesley (1983). *Muses of One Mind. The Literary Analysis of Experience and Its Continuity*. Princeton, NJ: Princeton U.P.
Trout, Dennis E. (1999). *Paulinus of Nola. Life, Letters, and Poems*. The Transformation of the Classical Heritage, 27. Berkeley: University of California Press.
Walla, Marialuise (1969). *Der Vogel Phoenix in der antiken Literatur und der Dichtung des Laktanz*. Dissertationen der Universität Wien, 29. Vienna: Notring.

Vance, Eugene (1982). "Saint Augustine: Language as Temporality". In John D. Lyons & Stephen G. Nichols, eds., *Mimesis. From Mirror to Method, Augustine to Descartes*, Hanover, NH: University Press of New England for Dartmouth College, pp. 20–35.
Vance, Eugene (1989). *Mervelous Signals. Poetics and Sign Theory in the Middle Ages*. Regents Studies in Medieval Culture. Lincoln, NE: University of Nebraska Press.
Warning, Rainer (1983). "Der inszenierte Diskurs: Bemerkungen zur pragmatischen Relation der Fiktion". In Dieter Heinrich & Wolfgang Iser, eds., *Funktionen der Fiktiven* (Poetik und Hermeneutik, 10), Munich: Fink, pp. 183–206.
Watson, Gerard (1986). "Cogitatio". In Karl Heinz Chelius, Cornelius Mayer, Erich Feldmann *et alii*, eds., *Augustinus-Lexikon*, Basel: Schwabe, cols. 1046–1051.
Watson, Gerard (1988). *Phantasia in Classical Thought*. Galway: Galway U.P.
Weismann, Werner (1972). *Kirche und Schauspiele. Die Schauspiele im Urteil der lateinischen Kirchenväter unter besonderer Berücksichtigung von Augustin*. Diss. Cassiciacum, 27. Würzburg: Augustinus-Verlag.
Venuti, Martina (2011). "Allusioni ovidiane nel Prologo delle *Mythologiae* di Fulgenzio". In Lucio Cristante e Simona Ravalico, eds., *Il calamo della memoria. Riuso di testi e mestiere letterario nella tarda antichità*, IV (Polymnia, Studi di filologia classica, 13), Trieste: Edizioni Università di Trieste, pp. 51–64.
Verbaal, Wim (2014). "How the West was Won by Fiction: The Appearance of Fictional Narrative and Leisurely Reading in Western Literature (11th and 12th century)". In Anders Cullhed & Lena Rydholm, eds., *True Lies Worldwide. Fictionality in Global Contexts*, Berlin: De Gruyter, pp. 189–200.
Westra, Haijo Jan (1981). "The Juxtaposition of the Ridiculous and the Sublime in Martianus Capella". *Florilegium*, 3, pp. 198–214.
Westra, Haijo Jan (1998). "Martianus Prae/Postmodernus?" *Dionysius*, 16, pp. 115–22.
Westra, Haijo Jan (2007). "Augustine and Poetic Exegesis". In Willemien Otten & Karla Pollmann, eds., *Poetry and Exegesis in Premodern Latin Christianity. The Encounter Between Classical and Christian Strategies of Interpretation* (Supplements to Vigiliae Christianae, 87), Leiden: Brill, pp. 11–28.
Whitman, Jon (1987). *Allegory. The Dynamics of an Ancient and Medieval Technique*. Cambridge, MA: Harvard U.P.
Whitman, Jon, ed. (2000). *Interpretation and Allegory. Antiquity to the Modern Period*. Brill's Studies in Intellectual History, 101. Leiden: Brill.
Wienbruch, Ulrich (1971). "'Signum', 'significatio' und 'illuminatio' bei Augustin". In Albert Zimmermann, ed., *Der Begriff der Repraesentatio im Mittelalter. Stellvertretung, Symbol, Zeichen, Bild* (Miscellanea mediaevalia, 8), Berlin: De Gruyter, pp. 76–93.
Wiesen, David S. (1971). "Virgil, Minucius Felix and the Bible". *Hermes*, 99.1, pp. 70–91.
Wiles, Maurice F. (1970). "Origen as Biblical Scholar". In Peter R. Ackroyd & Christopher F. Evans, eds., *The Cambridge History of the Bible. 1. From the Beginnings to Jerome*, Cambridge: Cambridge U.P., pp. 454–89.
Williams, Thomas (2005). "Augustine vs Plotinus. The Uniqueness of the Vision at Ostia". In John Inglis, ed., *Medieval Philosophy and the Classical Tradition. In Islam, Judaism and Christianity*, London: Taylor & Francis, pp. 143–51.
Witke, Charles (1971). *Numen litterarum. The Old and the New in Latin Poetry from Constantine to Gregory the Great*. Mittellateinische Studien und Texte, 5. Leiden: Brill.
Wlosok, Antonie (1987). "*Gemina doctrina?* Über Berechtigung und Voraussetzungen allegorischer Aeneisinterpretation". In Sandro Boldrini *et alii*, eds., *Filologia e forme*

letterarie. Studi offerti a Francesco della Corte. II. Letteratura latina dalle origini ad Augusto, Urbino: Università degli studi di Urbino, pp. 517–27.
Vogt, Hermann J. (1999). *Origenes als Exeget.* Ed. Wilhelm Geerlings. Paderborn: Schöningh.
Vogt-Spira, Gregor (2011). *"Prae sensibus.* Das Ideal der Lebensechtheit in römischer Rhetorik und Dichtungstheorie". In Gyburg Radke-Uhlmann & Arbogast Schmitt, eds., *Anschaulichkeit in Kunst und Literatur. Wege bildlicher Visualisierung in der europäischen Geschichte* (Colloquia Raurica, 11), Berlin: De Gruyter, pp. 13–34.
Woleński, Jan (2004). "*Aletheia* in Greek Thought Until Aristotle". *Annals of Pure and Applied Logic*, 127.1–3, pp. 339–60.
Wood, Ian (1999). "Images as a Substitute for Writing: A Reply". In Evangelos Chrysos & Ian Wood, eds., *East and West: Modes of Communication. Proceedings of the First Plenary Conference at Merida* (The Transformation of the Roman World, 5), Leiden: Brill, pp. 35–46.
Wood, Michael (1993). "Prologue". In Christopher Gill & Timothy P. Wiseman, eds., *Lies and Fiction in the Ancient World*, Exeter: University of Exeter Press, pp. xiii–xviii.

Index

Abelard, P.   574
Abraham, Patriarch   223, 245–48, 254, 256, 258, 261, 276
Adeodatus, son of St. Augustine   86, 106
Adimantus, Manichaean apostle   162
Adkin, N.   256
Aeneas, citizen of Lod (Greek: Lydda) west of Jerusalem, paralysed, restored by the agency of Peter   601
Aesop   141, 235–36, 358
Agozzino, T.   402, 404–06
Ahl, F.   21
Akiyama, M.   255
Alan of Lille   209, 383, 436, 451, 467, 574, 592, 595, 627–29
Aland, K.   70
Alaric I, King of the Visigoths   58, 616
Albinus (Caecina Decius Faustus Albinus), Roman senator and consul   434
Albinus (Publius Ceionius Albinus), Roman pontiff   488
Albu, E.   419–20
Alcaeus of Mytilene   485
Alcuin   174, 435, 626
Alexander the Great   41, 402, 537
Alfonso, L.   313, 325
Alfred the Great, King of Wessex   435
Allen, J.B.   547
Allen, T.W.   401
Alypius of Thagaste, friend of St. Augustine, Bishop   142, 177
Ambrose   VII, XIII, 4, 68–69, 71–73, 86, 108, 128, 130, 158, 192, 230, 255, 260, 294–95, 361, 477, 491, 508, 519, 533–35, 574, 589, 609, 613, 617–21
Anacreon of Teos   418
Anderson, W.B.   161
Anderson, W.S.   39
Apelles of Kos   535–37
Aphthonius of Antioch   43, 546
Apollinaris of Valence, Bishop, brother of Avitus   570–71, 575–76, 580–81
Apollonius of Rhodes   351
Apollonius of Tyana   70, 197, 291, 361–62

Apuleius   70, 290–91, 358, 371, 375, 383, 416, 418–19, 428, 525
Aquila, tentmaker, native of Pontus, host of St. Paul at Corinth   591
Arator   136, 174, 486, 572, 584–602, 607
Arcadius, Emperor   535
Archias (Aulus Licinius Archias) of Antioch, poet   547
Archimedes of Syracuse   381
Aristophanes   27
Aristotle   8, 10–11, 16, 19, 23–24, 26, 29–31, 37, 40–41, 43–46, 48–53, 100, 153, 163, 181–82, 184, 197, 204–05, 224, 236, 239, 248, 252, 263, 265, 272–74, 288, 298–99, 311, 321, 331, 340, 354, 357, 361, 381, 390, 404, 413, 421–22, 433, 436, 443–45, 449, 451, 455–56, 458–59, 462, 478, 542, 580, 605, 608, 614, 621
Arius (Areios) of Alexandria, priest and theologian   268
Armstrong, A.H.   88, 94
Arnobius   x, 3–4, 61, 63–67
Arweiler, A.   580
Asclepiades of Myrleia, Hellenistic grammarian   41
Assmann, A.   13
Astell, A.W.   67
Asterius (Turcius Rufius Asterius), Roman aristocrat, consul   570, 624
Atticus, close friend, editor and correspondent of Cicero   42
Auerbach, E.   261–62, 307, 475–76, 482, 608
Augustine   VII–VIII, X–XIII, 4, 9–10, 15, 28, 39, 44, 49, 54, 56, 58, 61, 66, 68, 70–72, 74, 77, 79, 83–94, 96–114, 116–25, 127–33, 135–47, 149, 151, 155, 157–60, 162–81, 183–240, 243–48, 250–51, 253–67, 269–88, 290–99, 305–06, 308, 310, 312–13, 316, 322, 325–28, 332, 340, 345, 349–51, 353, 361–62, 365, 369, 383, 387, 389–90, 394, 399, 402–03, 405, 410, 414, 423,

430–32, 435–36, 438, 444–45, 447, 451, 453, 455, 457–58, 460, 465–66, 471–75, 479, 481–84, 488, 495, 497–98, 500, 508, 519, 522, 525, 529–30, 532–34, 539, 541, 544, 546, 559, 561, 569, 572–74, 595–97, 606, 609–14, 616–17, 621, 623, 625, 628–29
Augustus, Emperor   37–38, 283
Ausonius   56, 75, 155–57, 393, 487–88, 504, 629–32
Avitus of Vienne   144, 483, 486, 566, 570–72, 574–85, 596, 601, 607, 626

Babbitt, F.C.   46, 51
Baehrens, W.   251
Bailey, M.D.   616
Bakhtin, M.   373
Banniard, M.   193
Barbet, J.   627
Barfield, R.   23
Barney, S.A.   44
Barthes, R.   599
Bastiaensen, A.A.R.   518, 522–23
Baswell, C.   412
Bažil, M.   131, 511
Bede (Beda Venerabilis)   174, 261, 599
Belisarius, Byzantine general   585
Benedict of Nursia   59, 472–73, 482, 609, 621
Bennett, C.   131, 165
Bernard of Chartres   412
Bernard of Clairvaux   67, 622
Bernard, W.   51, 241, 527
Bernardus Silvestris   131, 329, 335, 383, 398, 412, 451
Berry, D.H.   547
Bettenson, H.   131
Bezner, F.   367, 407
Bissula, Swabian girl, praised by Ausonius   630
Blank, D.L.   41
Bloch, H.   349
Bloomfield, M.W.   247
Boccaccio, G.   313, 425, 614
Bochet, I.   247
Boer, W.d.   254

Boethius   VII, X, 10, 59, 167, 310, 350, 358, 372, 397, 421, 433–49, 451, 453–67, 500, 571, 606, 611, 617, 621–22
Bogdanos, T.   436
Bonner, G.   92, 257
Borges, J.L.   510
Borruso, S.   165
Bossuat, R.   595
Boulding, M.   VIII, 9
Bowen, A.   134
Bower, C.   439
Bowersock, G.W.   59
Bowie, E.L.   23
Boys-Stones, G.R.   241
Brann, E.   196
Braulio of Zaragoza, Bishop, friend of St. Isidore   623
Breyfogle, T.   113, 196
Bright, D.F.   504
Bright, P.   297
Brink, C.O.   53
Brittan, S.   257
Broch, H.   230
Brown, P.   56, 83–84, 267–70, 278–79, 289, 304, 347–48, 490, 525, 615, 630
Bruno, G.   463
Bryce, H.   63
Büchner, K.   354
Buckhardt, J.   411
Buckley, F.O.   303
Bullough, D.A.   626
Bundy, M.W.   196
Bureau, B.   600
Burge, E.L.   370, 375
Burleigh, J.S.   107, 145, 179, 199, 207

Caecina Albinus, Roman aristocrat and governor   349
Caelius Rufus (Marcus Caelius Rufus), Roman orator and politician   386
Caesar   33, 331, 550
Caesarius of Arles   96
Cain, A.   151
Calboli Montefusco, L.   391
Callimachus of Cyrene   373
Calvino, I.   17

Cameron, Alan   XII, 56, 84, 266, 268, 317, 346–50, 388, 533, 535
Cameron, Averil   266–67
Campbell, H.   63
Caplan, H.   40
Cappuyns, M.   400
Carneades, Greek Sceptic philosopher   421–22
Carruthers, M.   203, 390, 511
Cassian (John Cassian), ascetic, monk and theologian   269, 472–73, 475
Cassin, B.   26
Cassiodorus   160, 164, 574, 608, 621–22, 625
Cato the Elder   152
Cato the Younger   499
Catullus   37, 485, 541, 589
Cazier, P.   611
Celsus (Kelsos)   66, 249–50
Cervantes, M.   9, 510
Chadwick, H.   66, 178, 250, 434, 460
Chaffin, C.E.   137
Chalcidius   365
Chamberlain, D.   439
Chance, J.   425
Charlemagne (Charles the Great), King of the Franks and Langobards, Holy Roman Emperor   625–26
Charles the Bald, King of France and Italy, Holy Roman Emperor   432, 626
Charlet, J.-L.   541, 543, 554
Chaucer, G.   435
Chin, C.M.   307, 309
Chrysippus, Greek Stoic philosopher   423–24
Cicero, Marcus Tullius   31, 39–45, 50, 71, 75, 89, 99, 124, 126, 145, 148–49, 151, 157, 162, 180–81, 183, 197, 211, 219, 224, 242–44, 260, 263, 295, 305, 307, 313–15, 325, 338–39, 341, 346, 354–57, 359, 362, 365, 374–75, 380, 386–88, 390, 392, 409, 416, 438, 447, 455, 478, 481, 483–84, 493, 495, 497, 499, 537, 545–47, 561, 571, 610, 613, 626
Cicero, Quintus Tullius   42
Cilento, V.   60, 295
Cizek, A.N.   546

Clark, E.A.   505
Claudian   XIII, 56, 393
Clement of Alexandria   70, 242, 249–50, 254, 256, 308
Coleridge, S.T.   16, 18–19, 528
Colish, M.L.   83, 178
Colleran, J.M.   186
Commodian   554
Comparetti, D.   130, 308, 329, 411–12, 510–11, 544
Conrad of Hirsau   444
Consentius, lay theologian of the Balearic Islands, correspondent of St. Augustine   221–22, 225, 232, 239
Constantine, Emperor   x, 4, 57, 132–34, 268, 313, 318, 326, 407, 473, 475, 479, 548–49, 554–55
Conte, G.B.   38
Conybeare, C.   35, 96, 157, 165
Cook, H.P.   11
Copeland, R.   309, 547
Costanza, S.   161, 513–14, 551–52, 561–62
Coulter, J.A.   242, 363
Courcelle, P.   90–92, 111, 121, 133–34, 137, 435, 444, 453, 455, 508, 565
Crabbe, A.   436, 454, 458–59
Cramer, W.   610
Crassus (Lucius Licinius Crassus), orator, consul, the chief speaker in Cicero's *On the Orator*   242–43, 387, 613
Crates of Mallus, grammarian, Stoic philosopher   53
Cratylus, Athenian philosopher   413
Cristante, L.   369, 371, 374, 399–400
Crombie, F.   228
Crouzel, H.   228–29
Curley, T.   441–42, 447, 461–62
Currie, G.   10, 12, 16
Currie, M.   370
Curtius, E.R.   XI, 113, 163, 321, 353–54, 420–21, 432, 482, 513–14, 544–45, 547, 558, 623
Cyprian, Bishop of Carthage, orator and martyr   318–19, 495–96

Dagens, C.   575
Damasus I, Pope   58, 478, 485, 575
Daniel, Old Testament Prophet   105
Daniélou, J.   581
Dante Alighieri   62, 76, 120, 126, 188, 198, 208–09, 247, 257, 262, 318, 321, 345, 369, 376, 379, 406–07, 425, 435–36, 439, 454, 467, 592, 600, 611, 614, 622, 627–28
David, King of Israel and Judah   163, 191, 223, 226, 449, 472, 485, 489, 491, 503, 531, 560–61
Dawson, D.   118, 217, 244
De Lacy, P.   273, 413
De Vogel, C.   90, 444
Dekkers, E.   151
Demats, P.   x, 44–45, 60–61, 342, 429–31
Demetrianus, Roman magistrate, possibly proconsul, in Africa   318–19
Demetrius, Ephesian silversmith   602
Democritus of Abdera   336, 381, 413
Demosthenes   499
Deogratias, deacon of Carthage   118
Deproost, P.-A.   xii, 486, 555
Derrida, J.   599
Desbordes, F.   390
Descartes, R. (Cartesius)   18, 95
Desiderius of Vienne, Bishop, martyr, Saint   574–75
Diels, H.   26
Dihle, A.   534
Diocletian, Emperor   63, 269, 313, 316–17, 496
Dionysius (Pseudo-Dionysius) the Areopagite   364, 466, 626
Dobell, B.   90, 111
Doignon, J.   193–94, 491
Doležel, L.   18
Donatus, Aelius   43, 126, 149, 163, 243, 246, 248, 276–77, 308–09, 328, 392, 574
Donatus, Tiberius Claudius   308
Donnini, M.   558
Dönt, E.   109
Döpp, S.   56, 303–04, 398
Dörrie, H.   54

Dorsch, T.S.   7
Dracontius   xiii, 589
Drake, H.A.   133
Dronke, P.   310, 367, 436, 461, 627
Duchrow, U.   98, 107–08, 118
Dümmler, E.   626
Duval, Y.-M.   309

Eco, U.   13–14, 17, 53, 100, 252, 294, 298
Eden, K.   8–9, 145, 257
Edwards, M.   56
Ehlers, W.   576, 581
Eigler, U.   151
Eiswirth, R.   149, 163
Ekbom, M.   308
Eliot, T.S.   3, 378, 555
Ellspermann, G.L.   305
Ennius   40, 61, 153, 310
Epicurus   46, 145, 283, 316, 336, 381
Erdt, W.   161, 204, 497
Esau, son of Rebekah and Isaac, elder twin brother of Jacob   222–25, 253, 256
Euclid of Alexandria   442
Eugenius, rhetorician, Emperor (usurper)   534
Euhemerus   60–61, 306, 310, 320, 423
Euripides   40, 342–43, 449
Eusebius of Caesarea   133, 268
Eutyches, Abbot in Constantinople, Monophysite theologian   466
Eutychus, young man of Troas (Asia Minor), raised from the dead by Paul   590
Evans, G.R.   574
Evenepoel, W.   158, 509, 575, 624
Evodius of Uzalis, friend of St. Augustine, Bishop   186
Eyssenhardt, F.   375, 384, 399
Ezekiel, Old Testament Prophet   78, 109–10, 247

Fairclough, H.R.   21, 79, 132
Faustus of Milevis, Manichaean Bishop   137, 256, 271–72, 275–76
Feeney, D.C.   18, 22–23, 38, 50
Felix of Nola, Saint   74, 488, 491, 494
Ferrari, L.   125
Festugierè, A.J.   144

Finkelberg, M. 22–23, 26, 30
Fischer, B. 70
Flamant, J. 347
Flaubert, G. 18
Flavianus, Roman aristocrat, senator, high priest and praetorian prefect 347
Fletcher, W. 323
Fleteren, F.v. 91–92, 158
Flores, R. 122
Fontaine, J. 55–56, 84, 96, 127, 131, 326, 483, 494, 549, 576, 584, 586, 614, 616, 631
Fontanier, J.-M. 529, 537
Ford, A. 25, 31
Forstner, K. 581, 584
Fortunatianus (Consultus Fortunatianus), Roman rhetorician 390–91
Fortunius, Donatist Bishop 292
Foucault, M. 364
Fowden, G. 59
Fowler, B.H. 132
Fowler, H.N. 140, 293, 450
Frazer, J.G. 35
Fredriksen Landes, P. 135, 261
Freeman, K. 26
Fremantle, W.H. 78
Frend, W.H.C. 157
Friedlein, G. 439
Fritz, K.v. 37, 49
Fromm, H. 413
Fuentes, C. 17
Fuhrmann, M. 55–56, 615
Fulgentius of Ruspe, Bishop and Saint 402
Fulgentius, Fabius Planciades VII, X, 62, 131, 134, 307, 310–11, 329, 335, 349, 372, 394, 402–26, 428–34, 437–39, 441, 459, 465, 508, 606, 624
Fuscina, Gallo-Roman nun, sister of Avitus 581–83

Galen of Pergamon 417
Gallagher, C. 13
Gamble, H.Y. 389
Garnsey, P. 134
Garrison, M. 625
Gelasius I, Pope 509
Gemeinhardt, P. XII, 125, 164, 606

Gersh, S. 346, 426
Giannantonio, P. 243
Giardina, A. 57
Gibbons, E. 56
Gibson, E.C.S. 472
Gildo, Roman general 474
Gill, C. 18
Glover, T.R. 152
Gnilka, C. 71, 136, 159–60, 526, 529, 533, 541
Godel, R. 150
Gompf, L. 627
González Delgado, R. 449
Goold, G.P. 34–36
Gorgias of Leontini 17, 25–27, 30, 288, 290
Grabmann, M. 433
Graf, F. 37, 39
Gratian, Emperor 58, 128, 532, 630
Grebe, S. 381
Green, D.H. 352
Green, R.P.H. 85, 161, 556–57
Greenough, J.B. 547
Gregory of Nyssa 229
Gregory the Great, Pope 55, 289, 474, 486, 518, 569, 572–75, 577, 611, 616, 622, 626
Griffiths, P.J. 159
Grotius, H. 376
Gruber, J. 433, 436
Grubmüller, K. 413
Gualandri, I. 561, 575
Gunermann, H.H. 167
Gutenberg, J. 18

Haarhoff, T. 75, 126, 479
Hagar, servant of Sarah, second wife of Abraham 245, 254, 276
Hagen, H. 328
Hagendahl, H. X, 130–31, 133, 135, 149–51, 156–57, 167, 295–96, 308, 316–17, 485–86, 510–11
Haller, B. 339
Halliday, W.R. 401
Halliwell, S. 29
Hamburger, M. 425
Hannibal 355

Hanson, J.A. 375
Hanson, R.P.C. 208, 241, 250
Hardie, P. 32–33, 39, 50
Harrison, C. 107, 121, 243, 270
Hartel, W.v. 74, 155, 492, 628
Hatch, D.F. 505
Haubrichs, W. 413
Havelock, E.A. 17, 22, 288
Hays, G. 402–03
Heck, E. 158, 305, 313
Hecquet-Noti, N. 566, 577, 579, 581
Heidegger, M. 11, 22
Heidl, G. 255
Heine, R.E. 251
Helm, R. 404
Henry, P. 89–92, 112
Heraclitus of Ephesus 282–83, 336, 381
Hermogenes of Tarsus, Greek rhetorician 546
Hermogenes, Athenian philosopher 293, 413
Herren, M.W. 432
Herrera, R.A. 93
Herzog, R. 57, 254, 313, 508, 510, 528, 548
Hesiod 11, 21–24, 27, 34, 50, 58, 84, 176, 265, 304, 315, 358–59, 416, 515
Hill, E. 102, 217
Hillier, R. 585, 592, 600
Hoffman, M. 580
Hölderlin, F. 425
Hollander, J. 76
Hollander, R. 76
Holte, R. 217
Holtz, L. 277, 308–09
Homer 11, 17, 22–25, 27–28, 30, 32, 45, 47, 49, 53–54, 57, 60–61, 64, 70, 84, 127, 137, 142, 144, 153, 163, 167, 178, 240–41, 249, 265, 273–74, 282, 288, 306, 312, 315, 332, 337, 351–52, 357–58, 362–64, 367–68, 380, 394, 401, 413, 416, 432, 440, 485, 500–03, 506, 520, 522, 535–37, 549, 551, 562, 565, 590, 596, 617–21, 624
Homeyer, H. 173–74, 492
Honorius, Emperor 58, 291, 535

Horace 7, 38, 43, 52–53, 64, 148, 189–90, 235–36, 299, 334, 343, 351–53, 357, 398, 405, 437, 451, 483, 485, 490, 506, 518, 520, 536, 540–41, 546, 553, 557, 572, 588, 623
Horn, H.-J. 178
Hosidius Geta, Roman playwright 504, 561
Houghton, H. 92
Hubaux, J. 326
Hubbell, H.M. 40, 197
Hudson-Williams, A. 128, 580, 586
Huemer, J. 549, 563
Hughes, K.L. 192
Hunter, D.G. 106
Hypatia, Alexandrian Neo-Platonic philosopher 269

Ibsen, H. 13
Ingeld, (legendary) prince and warrior of the Germanic Heathobards 626
Inwood, M.J. 22
Irenaeus 4, 257
Irvine, M. 252, 294, 309, 328, 350, 405, 575
Isaac, son of Sarah and Abraham, Patriarch 223–24, 245
Isaiah, Old Testament Prophet 78, 105, 109, 133–34, 150, 161, 209, 479–81, 501–03
Iser, W. 14, 32
Ishmael, son of Hagar and Abraham 245
Isidore of Seville XI, 44, 55, 59, 61, 164, 227, 237, 309, 321, 331, 334, 413, 611–14, 622–23

Jackson, B.D. 100, 118
Jacob, son of Rebekah and Isaac, Patriarch 222–26, 247, 253, 256
Jacobsson, M. 174
Jaeger, W. 240, 249
James, P. 518
Janaway, C. 11
Janson, T. 373–74, 386, 396
Januarius, Catholic layman, correspondent of St. Augustine 210–11
Jaumann, H. 545
Jauß, H.R. 474, 606

Jeauneau, É.   367
Jeremiah, Old Testament Prophet   133, 159, 587
Jerome   VII, x, 4, 58, 63, 66–68, 70, 72–73, 77–79, 88, 92, 95–96, 100, 126–28, 134–35, 137, 147–51, 155, 157, 160–63, 196, 232–33, 245, 253–55, 269, 306, 313, 317, 319, 361, 471–72, 474, 477–81, 485, 488, 500–01, 509–10, 516, 548–49, 551, 553, 561, 564, 568–69, 574–75, 606, 608, 610–13, 615, 617, 626
Jesse of Bethlehem, father of David   503
Job, Old Testament Prophet   163, 222, 224, 485, 573, 587, 617
John Chrysostom, Archbishop of Constantinople, Saint   405
John of Patmos, author of Revelation, traditionally identified with John the Evangelist   475, 502, 543
John of Salisbury   412, 444, 614
John of the Cross   67
John Scotus Eriugena   364, 398, 432, 626–27
John, Evangelist   19, 75, 110, 113–15, 119, 190, 195, 207, 234, 444, 449, 476, 566–68
Johnson, R.   370, 375, 390
Jonah, Old Testament Prophet   76, 253, 255
Jones, C.P.   362
Jones, J.W., Jr.   330, 332–33, 404–05
Jones, L.   622
Jongkees, A.G.   625
Jonsson, I.   362
Joseph, son of Rachel and Jacob   223, 226
Jovius, Gallo-Roman learned pagan friend, possibly a relative, of Paulinus of Nola   160, 497–501, 511, 513–15
Judah, fourth son of Leah and Jacob, founder of the Israelite tribe of Judah   277, 531
Julian the Apostate, Emperor   57, 59, 268–69, 309, 402, 504, 506, 532, 616
Junod-Ammerbauer, H.   161, 491–93, 514
Justin I, Byzantine Emperor   434
Justin Martyr   3–4
Justinian the Great, Byzantine Emperor   59, 434, 585

Juvenal   405
Juvencus   136, 148, 174, 305, 333, 483, 486, 491, 504, 506, 509, 518, 521, 544, 547–56, 558, 560, 562, 566, 569, 580–81, 585, 596, 601

Kaiser, E.   440–41, 619
Kamptner, M.   74, 155, 628
Kannicht, R.   22–23
Kant, I.   11, 18–19, 291, 614
Kartschoke, D.   545, 576, 586
Kaster, R.A.   XII, 329, 343, 346–48, 352–53
Keats, J.   15–16
Keil, H.   243
Kelly, C.   59
Kendall, C.B.   261
Kennedy, G.A.   43, 145, 388, 390, 546
Kenney, J.P.   90, 122
Kenter, L.P.   42
Kerr, W.C.A.   62
Keyes, C.W.   42, 355
Khomeini, R.   614
Kirkconnell, W.   581
Kirsch, W.   55, 133, 269, 307–08, 326, 483, 487, 504, 517, 549, 554
Kirwan, C.   118
Kittredge, G.L.   547
Klopsch, P.   588
Klopstock, F.G.   544
Konstan, D.   47
Krämer, T.   XII, 158, 165, 233, 296
Kranz, W.   26
Krauss, L.   599
Kroll, W.   144, 198
Kuisma, O.   198, 363–64, 444
Kupke, T.   432

Laan, P.W.A.T.v.d.   150, 525, 556, 565
Lactantius   x, 3, 61, 66, 133–34, 139, 231, 282, 305–06, 308, 310–11, 313–28, 331, 333–34, 343, 352, 359, 407, 426, 433, 481, 483, 486, 504, 506, 508, 518, 521, 525, 553, 555, 559, 580, 599, 605–06, 614, 622, 627
Ladner, G.B.   362

Laeta, daughter of Publius Ceionius Albinus, correspondent of St. Jerome 488
Laird, A. 290
Laistner, M. 186, 406, 472, 575
Lamb, W.R.M. 404
Lamberton, R. 25, 28, 47, 70, 144, 198, 240, 250, 357, 363
Lampe, G.W.H. 252–54
Langland, W. 436
Lawrence (Laurentius) of Rome, Hispano-Roman deacon and martyr, Saint 540–41
Lawson, R.P. 67
Lazzarini, C. 340–41
Leander of Seville, Bishop, Saint, brother of St. Isidore 573
Leclercq, J. 609
Leibniz, G.W. 18
LeMoine, F. 370, 373, 398
Lenaz, L. 375, 379, 382, 393, 421
Lerer, S. 307, 405, 447–49, 461
Leroy, M. 326
Leupin, A. XI–XII, 121, 265, 373, 386
Levi, third son of Leah and Jacob, founder of the Israelite tribe of Levi 531
Lewis, C.S. 356, 369, 400, 443, 527
Lewis, G. 78
Licentius of Thagaste, friend and student of St. Augustine, poet 141, 162, 165–67, 169–71, 458
Licinius, Emperor 4, 57
Lieberg, G. 36, 42, 353–54
Lim, R. 59
Lindsay, W.M. 44
Livy 392
Loewe, R. 58
Longinus 197, 357
Louth, A. 107, 201
Lubac, H.d. 243, 575
Lucan 331, 592
Lucretius 31–32, 37, 145, 303–04, 316–19, 405, 443, 461, 523, 529, 553, 559
Ludwig, W. 151, 519, 521
Luke, Evangelist 68–69, 73, 146, 234, 236, 238–39, 247–48, 275, 531, 567–68, 585–88, 593–94, 601, 617, 619

MacCormack, S. 130, 159, 167, 205, 281, 353
Macedonius, priest, correspondent of Sedulius 556–57, 559, 568
Macrobius X, XII–XIII, 62, 279, 307, 310, 333–34, 339, 346–54, 356–61, 363–68, 372–73, 378, 380, 383, 391, 394–96, 399, 405, 416–17, 431, 433, 441, 447, 449, 455, 459–61, 464–65, 473, 498, 508, 532, 535, 606
Madec, G. 247
Maecenas, Roman statesman, patron of Virgil and Horace 437, 565
Magee, J. 445
Magnus, Roman orator and convert, correspondent of St. Jerome 149, 549
Malamud, M.A. 520, 526–27
Mandouze, A. 92
Mani, prophet, founder of Manichaeism 270
Manieri, A. 32, 52
Männlein-Robert, I. 362
Marbode (Marbodius) of Rennes 19
Marcellinus, Flavius, imperial official, friend and correspondent of St. Augustine 291
Marchand, J. 118
Marcion of Sinope (Pontus), Christian heretic 504
Marcovich, M. 250
Marius Victorinus (Afer) 89, 181, 218
Mark, Evangelist 238
Markus, R.A. X, 66, 102, 108, 118, 248, 261, 268, 270, 616, 625
Marrou, H.-I. 84, 125, 139–40, 221, 227, 482
Martial 396
Martianus Capella VII, XI, 41, 44, 164, 310, 365, 369–78, 380–84, 386–87, 389–405, 409, 412, 415, 417–22, 424, 427, 430, 433–34, 438–39, 441, 454, 465–66, 560, 606, 624
Martin of Tours, Bishop, Saint 74, 502
Martin, J. 303
Martley, W.G. 78
Marvell, A. 543
Mastrangelo, M. 56, 521

Matter, E.A.   67, 255
Matthew, Evangelist   95, 103, 119, 148, 210, 497, 524, 549, 555, 567, 610
Matthews, G.B.   121
Matthews, J.   434, 533
Mattiacci, S.   421
Maximus of Turin, Bishop   502, 619–21
Maximus, Emperor (usurper)   86
Mayer, C.P.   118, 247, 256, 271, 277
Mazzega, M.   565
Mazzeo, J.A.   108
Mazzotta, G.   307
McBrine, P.   549
McClure, J.   586
McKinlay, A.P.   585–86
McMahon, R.   462
Mehtonen, P.   40, 227
Memmius, Gaius, Roman orator and poet, tribune, praetor and governor   405
Memor (Memorius), Bishop of Apulia   190–93
Menander   358
Menzies, A.   152
Merdinger, J.E.   474
Merkt, A.   619
Messina, M.T.   150
Messmer, E.   316, 323
Michelangelo Buonarroti   133
Migne, J.P.   19, 83, 134, 323, 488
Miller, F.J.   33
Milovanović-Barham, Č.   484
Milton, J.   549, 576
Minio-Palluelo, L.   413
Minucius Felix   3, 62, 87, 305–06, 315, 447, 477, 525, 605
Mohrmann, C.   444
Møller Jensen, B.   386
Mommsen, T.   243
Monnica, mother of St. Augustine   58, 86–88, 92, 94, 106–07, 109–12, 116–17, 120–21, 131, 169, 177–78, 186, 194, 218, 285, 295–97, 569
Montaigne, M.d.   212
Moorhead, J.   572, 574–75
Morin, G.   96
Moses   53, 105, 149, 160, 207, 228, 234, 247, 493, 509, 566, 581, 600

Most, G.W.   11, 24, 53
Mozley, J.H.   34
Mueller, M.M.   96
Mueller-Goldingen, C.   443, 461
Müller, G.   130, 138
Murray, A.T.   22–23
Murru, F.   551
Mutzenbecher, A.   619
Mynors, R.A.B.   622
Myron   180

Nat, P.G.v.d.   303, 551
Navigius, brother of St. Augustine   86
Nebridius, from Carthago, friend of St. Augustine   204–05
Nero, Emperor   421, 447
Nesteros, Abbot, Desert Father, interlocutor of John Cassian   472
Nestle, E.   70
Nestorius, Patriarch of Constantinople, Dyophysite theologian   466
Noah   76, 576, 579, 581
Nodes, D.J.   570, 576
Norden, E.   481
Nuchelmans, G.   375
Numa Pompilius, (legendary) King of Rome   535–37
Nussbaum, M.   90, 442

O'Connell, R.J.   90, 125, 170, 199, 221, 273, 296
O'Daly, G.   203, 283, 445, 448, 451, 454, 461
O'Donnell, J.J.   VIII, 9, 87, 92, 100, 116–17, 295, 616
O'Meara, J.J.   84, 89
Octavian, the future Emperor Augustus   283, 516, 532
Odoacer, German warrior, King of Italy   59
Ogilvie, R.M.   316, 320
Orbán, A.P.   585–86
Origen   VIII, 66–68, 70, 150, 159, 161, 208, 228–29, 242, 248–57, 259, 261, 268, 312
Orson, S.W.   14
Ovid   21, 30–39, 50, 73, 139, 166, 168–70, 231, 280, 299, 306, 315, 322, 324,

326, 336, 352–54, 371, 380, 396, 415–16, 419, 425, 428–29, 436–37, 439, 441, 448, 454, 459, 471, 483, 490, 526, 541–42, 553, 565, 576–77, 580, 588, 596, 605, 624

Parmenides of Elea 26, 437–38, 442
Parthenius, Arator's fellow-student in Ravenna, Master of Offices under King Theodebert in Gaul 586, 588, 590–91, 594
Patiens of Lyon, Bishop 624
Paul 73, 76, 86, 88–89, 91–92, 95–97, 101–03, 105–06, 108–09, 111, 116, 120, 125, 135–36, 143, 145–46, 148–49, 152, 156, 162, 191–92, 195, 210, 213, 216–19, 228, 232–33, 237, 245, 247, 251–56, 259, 261, 264, 275–76, 297, 317, 459, 480, 493–94, 522, 524–25, 527, 534, 540–41, 556, 568, 581, 585, 587, 590–93, 596–98, 600–02, 612, 627
Paulinus of Nola 74–76, 96, 134, 151, 155–57, 160–63, 204, 253, 269, 287, 294, 350, 366, 475, 483, 485–95, 497–503, 506, 508–09, 511, 513–15, 520, 524, 531, 544, 551, 583, 611, 613, 615, 617, 619, 623, 628–30
Paulus (Macedonicus), Roman general and consul, father of Scipio Aemilianus 355
Pavel, T.G. 12, 16
Pease, A.S. 135, 149
Peirce, C.S. 294
Pelagius, monk and theologian, probably of Romano-British origin 267
Pépin, J. 53, 111, 229, 241, 243, 326, 358, 360
Perec, G. 402
Pericles 73, 388
Persius 405
Peter (Simon Peter), Apostle 70, 232–33, 523, 585–86, 595, 599, 601
Peter, New Testament writer 70, 251
Petrarch, F. 129, 417, 590, 614
Petrocchi, G. 76
Petronius 358, 412

Petschenig, M. 472, 504
Phidias 361–62, 537
Philip (The Deacon), Evangelist 599
Philo of Alexandria 241–43, 249, 254
Philostratus 52, 197, 361–62
Pico della Mirandola, G. 313, 463
Pilate 10, 71, 202, 314, 566–67
Pinborg, J. 413
Pindar 24, 485, 518
Plato 10, 17–18, 20, 23, 26–31, 34, 39, 46, 50–53, 89–90, 95–96, 101, 129, 140, 144, 158, 163, 169, 175, 181, 186–87, 197–98, 209, 241–42, 249, 265, 272–73, 281, 288–89, 293, 305–06, 315–17, 325, 349, 356–57, 359–60, 362–63, 365–66, 372, 380–81, 401, 404, 413, 421–23, 432, 435–39, 442–44, 447, 449–51, 453–58, 464–65, 498–99, 525, 537, 577, 608
Plautus 148
Pliny the Elder 389
Plotinus 60, 86, 88–95, 100–01, 111, 113, 116, 123, 131, 188, 194, 201, 213, 217–18, 278, 294–95, 310, 361, 413, 444–45, 455, 537
Plutarch VIII, 12, 45–48, 51–52, 141, 241, 318–19, 343, 439, 461, 619
Pollmann, K. XII, 50, 67, 165, 263, 270
Pompey, Roman general and statesman 331, 550
Porphyry 25, 83, 94, 131, 158, 243, 252, 278, 357–59, 361, 456, 459, 498
Possidius, Bishop of Calama, author of a biography of St. Augustine 190
Praetextatus, Roman aristocrat, senator, high priest, urban and praetorian prefect 346–48
Pratt, L.H. 11, 22, 24
Priscian 126
Proba, Anicia Faltonia 503
Proba, Faltonia Betitia 134, 139, 333, 483, 486–87, 503–11, 514–18, 521, 523, 544, 548, 617, 630
Proclus VIII, 52, 62, 144, 197–98, 240, 242, 249, 334, 362–64, 413, 444, 451, 525
Propertius 553

Prudentius   56–57, 99, 127, 134, 136, 144, 161, 254, 269, 287, 371, 383, 471, 486, 495–97, 507–08, 513–14, 518–24, 526–33, 535–44, 551, 553, 562, 567, 572, 579–80, 611, 615, 623, 628
Pseudo-Heraclitus   54, 241, 273
Ptolemy of Alexandria   101, 454, 458, 464, 495
Purcell, W.M.   277
Putnam, M.C.J.   329
Pythagoras of Samos   68, 158, 174, 226, 240, 283, 332, 358–59, 365, 372, 376–77, 381, 404, 458, 494, 499

Quacquarelli, A.   96, 115, 606
Quadlbauer, F.   552
Queen of Sheba, ruler of the Kingdom of Sheba (Saba) in Arabia, contemporary with Solomon   600
Quinn, J.M.   100
Quinn, K.   405
Quintilian   7–9, 21, 40, 44, 50, 124, 126, 185, 197, 211, 215, 219, 224, 242–43, 260, 277, 309, 313, 317, 329, 343, 386, 388, 390, 392, 478, 495, 545–48, 574, 613

Rabanus Maurus   174
Raby, F.J.E.   308
Rackham, H.   45, 126
Rahner, H.   70, 137, 227, 500–01, 619–21
Ralfs, G.   463
Ramelli, I.   371, 376, 398
Ramsey, B.   85, 140, 619
Rand, E.K.   136, 140, 149, 163–64, 188–89, 313, 402, 436, 459, 572, 622
Rauner-Hafner, G.   403, 411–12
Reiff, A.   546
Relihan, J.C.   367, 370, 380, 398–99, 404, 418, 425, 430, 436–37, 461, 465
Remigius of Auxerre   398, 444
Rendall, G.H.   62
Reutern, G.v.   48–49
Reynolds, S.   354
Riché, P.   126, 482, 574
Ricoeur, P.   47
Riggi, C.   482

Rilke, R.M.   559
Roberts, A.   63, 152, 229, 323
Roberts, M.   ix, 481, 520, 545, 571–72, 593, 601, 624
Robinson, G.W.   371
Romanianus, citizen of Thagaste, early patron and friend of St. Augustine   165
Romano, D.   171
Romanus of Antioch (Caesarea), Christian martyr, Saint   496–97, 539
Romestin, H.d.   128
Romulus Augustus, Emperor   59
Roscius, Roman actor   179–80, 278
Rösler, W.   21, 24, 29
Rotelle, J.E.   vii
Roubekas, N.P.   60
Rousseau, J.-J.   14–15
Rudd, N.   7
Ruef, H.   118
Rufinus of Aquileia, Roman priest, theologian and translator   67, 249, 251
Rushdie, S.   614
Russell, D.A.   7
Ryan, M.-L.   18

Saenger, P.   388
Sanders, W.   413
Sarah, wife of Abraham   245, 254, 276
Sassen, F.   434–35
Scaevola, Quintus Mucius, Roman high priest, lawyer and consul   282–83
Scaliger, J.C.   354
Scaliger, J.J.   371
Scarry, E.   461–62
Schaff, P.   78, 83, 128, 472, 485
Schäublin, C.   159
Scheible, H.   453–55, 458
Scheid, J.   12
Schelkle, K.H.   127, 144
Schenkeveld, D.M.   46
Schenkl, K.   504
Schmidt, P.L.   447
Schottenius Cullhed, S.   503–04, 507
Schrader, R.J.   585, 590
Schwind, J.   585–86, 597, 599, 602
Scipio Aemilianus, Roman general and statesman   339, 346, 354–56, 416

Scipio Africanus, Roman general and statesman, adoptive grandfather of Scipio Aemilianus 354–56
Sedulius 134, 161, 174, 486, 509, 525, 544, 551, 555–70, 581, 585–86, 594, 596, 601, 624
Segal, C.P. 26, 290
Seneca the Younger 96, 307, 315, 329, 447–49, 453, 461, 619
Septimus Severus, Emperor 154
Servius x, 281, 307–08, 310, 328–49, 351–54, 359, 367, 391, 412–13, 431, 433, 440, 606
Sextus Empiricus 41, 272
Shackleton Bailey, D.R. 396
Shaftesbury, A.A.C., Earl of 354
Shakespeare, W. 6–7, 9, 13, 495
Shanzer, D. 130, 164–65, 369, 374–75, 378, 393, 444, 465, 570, 581–82
Sharp, R.F. 13
Shea, G.W. 577
Sheppard, A.D.R. 198, 228, 242, 362–63
Sheridan, J.J. 595
Shorey, P. 23
Showerman, G. 35–36
Sidney, Sir P. 614
Sidonius Apollinaris 161, 575, 589, 623–25
Sikes, E.E. 401
Simeon, second son of Leah and Jacob, founder of the Israelite tribe of Simeon 531
Simonetti, M. 228
Simonides of Ceos 485
Simonini, L. 357
Simplicianus, priest, Ambrose's successor as Archbishop of Milan 89, 218
Skeat, T.C. 389
Sluiter, I. 309
Small, C.D. 564, 566
Smalley, B. 255
Smith, M. 56–57, 474, 521, 580
Smolak, K. 99
Socrates 17, 26–28, 34, 274, 401, 413, 435, 442, 450, 525
Söderberg, H. 10
Solomon 115, 149, 188, 294, 458

Solon 24, 36
Sparks, H.F.D. 58, 92
Spenser, E. 552
Springer, C.P.E. 548, 556, 559, 566, 568
Stahl, W.H. 356, 366, 369–71, 375, 384, 390, 399
Starnes, C. 92
Statius 557
Staubach, N. 615
Steidle, W. 514
Stella, F. 555
Stevens, W. 605
Stewart, H.F. 436, 459
Stierle, K. 33
Stock, B. 118, 121–22, 218, 264, 298
Stockt, L.v.d. 46, 51
Stok, F. 328, 343
Stokes, L.C. 403
Stroumsa, G.G. 389
Strubel, A. 261
Suetonius 622
Sulpicius Severus, Aquitanian lawyer, Christian writer, friend of Paulinus of Nola 502
Sutcliffe, E.F. 58
Sutton, E.W. 126
Svenbro, J. 12, 288–89
Svoboda, K. 170, 183–84, 197, 280
Symmachus, Quintus Aurelius Memmius, Roman senator and consul, father-in-law of Boethius 455
Symmachus, Quintus Aurelius, Roman senator, orator, urban prefect and consul 58, 63, 71–72, 87, 279, 299, 347, 524, 532–35, 538–39, 630
Synesius of Cyrene, Neo-Platonic philosopher, Bishop of Ptolemais, Libya 415

Tamar, daughter-in-law of Judah 277
Tasso, T. 354
Tatian 4, 475
Taylor, C. 95
Taylor, T. 357
Terence 40, 561
Tertullian x–xi, 3–4, 39, 62, 127–28, 130, 149, 151–54, 158, 163, 231, 282, 288,

304–06, 318–19, 325–26, 471–72, 475, 484, 504, 525, 538, 584, 626
Teske, R.J.   85, 106, 138, 199, 217, 271
Tester, S.J.   436, 459
Thales of Miletus   274, 315, 336, 381
Theagenes of Rhegium   25, 49, 254
Theoderic the Great, King of the Ostrogoths, King of Italy   59, 433–34, 621
Theodore of Mopsuestia, Bishop, Antiochene theologian and exegete   255
Theodosius, Emperor   4, 58, 128, 266, 269, 326, 347, 503, 519, 524, 534–35, 539
Theophilus of Alexandria, Archbishop and Patriarch   68
Therasia, wife of Paulinus of Nola   74
Thilo, G.   328
Thomas Aquinas   19, 247, 261, 435
Thomson, H.J.   99
Thor, A.   554
Thraede, K.   xi, 113, 150, 482, 496, 514, 552–54, 585, 594
Tigerstedt, E.N.   353
Titus, companion and disciple of Paul   252
Todorov, T.   118
Totila, King of the Ostrogoths   585, 594
Tredennick, H.   11
Trigg, J.W.   250
Trimpi, W.   30, 43, 361–62
Trout, D.E.   157
Trygetius, friend and student of St. Augustine   141

Valentinian I, Emperor   630–31
Valentinian II, Emperor   58, 299, 477, 532–34
Valla, L.   433
Vance, E.   88, 107, 175
Vargas Llosa, M.   17
Varro   71, 164, 265, 282–83, 373, 499, 623
Venantius Fortunatus   174, 572
Venarde, B.L.   473
Venuti, M.   425
Verbaal, W.   19
Verbeke, G.   413
Verecundus, Milanese professor, St. Augustine's host in Cassiciacum   205
Vessey, M.   xii, 165

Vigilius, Pope   584–88, 594, 601
Virgil   21, 38, 50, 73, 75–76, 78–79, 85, 125, 127–48, 150–51, 154, 157–58, 165, 167–68, 170–71, 177–78, 206, 234, 276–81, 284, 286–87, 293, 295, 299, 304–08, 310, 315–16, 322, 324–25, 328–45, 348–54, 366–67, 380, 402–12, 414–17, 432, 448, 471, 481, 483, 485, 491–92, 503–11, 514–16, 521–23, 535, 544, 546, 549, 551–55, 557, 560, 562, 565–66, 575, 580, 592, 594, 596, 610, 613–14, 627, 629–30
Vogt, H.J.   250
Vogt-Spira, G.   32, 341
Volusianus, Roman Senator   137

Wace, H.   78, 128, 472, 485
Walla, M.   326
Walsh, P.G.   74, 155, 492, 511, 628
Warning, R.   37
Watson, G.   196
Watts, V.E.   444, 464
Weismann, W.   180–81, 280
Westra, H.   xii, 138, 279, 292, 397–98
Whitbread, L.   404
White, H.G.E.   631
Whitman, J.   243, 394, 430
Wienbruch, U.   119
Wiesen, D.S.   128, 131, 311
Wiles, M.F.   208, 250
William of Conches   367, 444
Williams, T.   90, 92
Willis, J.A.   356, 370–71, 375, 384, 399
Witke, C.   156, 494, 510–11, 513, 588
Wlosok, A.   367
Woleński, J.   11
Wood, I.   290, 570, 581–82
Wood, M.   18
Woolf, V.   12
Wordsworth, W.   16
Wright, F.A.   163, 488

Xenophanes of Colophon   25, 31, 36–37, 240, 265, 282
Xenophon   499

Ziolkowski, J.M.   329

www.ingramcontent.com/pod-product-compliance
Lightning Source LLC
Chambersburg PA
CBHW052007290426
44112CB00014B/2156